The Routledge Research Companion to Anglo-Italian Renaissance Literature and Culture

The aim of this Companion volume is to provide scholars and advanced graduate students with a comprehensive and authoritative state-of-the-art review of current research work on Anglo-Italian Renaissance studies. Written by a team of international scholars and experts in the field, the chapters are grouped into two large areas of influence and intertextuality, corresponding to the dual way in which early modern England looked upon the Italian world from the English perspective – Part 1: "Italian literature and culture" and Part 2: "Appropriations and ideologies". In the first part, prominent Italian authors, artists, and thinkers are examined as a direct source of inspiration, imitation, and divergence. The variegated English response to the cultural, ideological, and political implications of pervasive Italian intertextuality, in interrelated aspects of artistic and generic production, is dealt with in the second part. Constructed on the basis of a largely interdisciplinary approach, the volume offers an in-depth and wide-ranging treatment of the multifaceted ways in which Italy's material world and its iconologies are represented, appropriated, and exploited in the literary and cultural domain of early modern England. For this reason, contributors were asked to write essays that not only reflect current thinking but also point to directions for future research and scholarship, while a purposefully conceived bibliography of primary and secondary sources and a detailed index round off the volume.

Michele Marrapodi is a Full Professor of English Literature at the University of Palermo, Italy. He is General Editor of the "Anglo-Italian Renaissance Studies" series. His most recent edited volumes include *Shakespeare's Italy* (1993), *The Italian World of English Renaissance Drama* (1998), *Italian Studies in Shakespeare and His Contemporaries* (1999), *Shakespeare, Italy, and Intertextuality* (2004), *Italian Culture in the Drama of Shakespeare and His Contemporaries* (2007), *Shakespeare and Renaissance Literary Theories* (2011), *Shakespeare and the Italian Renaissance* (2014), and *Shakespeare and the Visual Arts: The Italian Influence* (2017).

This wide-ranging collection brings together the best current work in Anglo-Italian studies and forecasts future developments. Theoretically sophisticated and intellectually rigorous, the essays here treat major and minor figures, works, and genres, all the while illuminating hidden movements and cross-currents in literature, history, theology, and other disciplines. The volume, in toto, documents the reciprocal circulation of energies that powered both the Italian and English Renaissances. Prof. Marrapodi's international team of distinguished contributors and bright new voices will inspire and guide scholarly conversations for a long time to come.

— *Robert S. Miola Gerard Manley Hopkins Professor of English / Lecturer in Classics Loyola University Maryland*

Reading this new collection, one is taken aback by how extensive and profound the cultural conversation between early modern Italy and England actually was. Preceded by a deeply researched introduction by Michele Marrapodi, the essays manage to anatomize this dauntingly complex field afresh and rethink familiar figures and configurations while adding a host of unfamiliar ones. What emerges is not just the one-way traffic of "influence" but dynamic and layered exchanges both within and between two separate cultures and cultural moments. It is equally good at recounting the Italian rediscovery of ancient figures, such as Seneca and Lucretius (long prior to their English impact), as it is at exploring original Italian cultural inventions such as courtliness, "civil conversation", and reason of state.

— *John Gillies Professor in Literature, University of Essex*

In this ambitious and extraordinarily useful volume, ably assembled by Michele Marrapodi, distinguished senior and junior scholars from Italy, Great Britain, and North America revisit the crucial questions surrounding the influence of Italy, its literature and its culture on England in the age of Shakespeare. Among the volume's many virtues are its double focus on the original Italian texts and contexts and their appropriation, transformation, and re-visioning in English hands. Equally admirable is its revisitation of the multiple still-valid acquisitions of past scholarship, even while defining the current "state of the field" and its future possibilities. Finally, while the volume's primary inspiration is literary and especially theatrical, it demonstrates a laudable commitment to probing the "mobilities," ambiguities, and political-ideological-religious investments that inform the complex processes of cultural transmission.

— *Albert Russell Ascoli President, Dante Society of America, Terrill Distinguished Professor, Dept. of Italian Studies, University of California, Berkeley*

The Routledge Research Companion to Anglo-Italian Renaissance Literature and Culture

Edited by Michele Marrapodi

LONDON AND NEW YORK

First published 2019 by Routledge
2 Park Square, Milton Park, Abingdon, Oxon OX14 4RN

and by Routledge
605 Third Avenue, New York, NY 10017

First issued in paperback 2021

Routledge is an imprint of the Taylor & Francis Group, an informa business

Library of Congress Cataloging-in-Publication Data
A catalog record for this book has been requested

ISBN 13: 978-1-03-209359-8 (pbk)
ISBN 13: 978-1-4724-1073-3 (hbk)

DOI: 10.4324/9781315612720

To Virginia,

Donna pietosa e di novella etate,
adorna assai di gentilezze umane.

Contents

Contributors

Marco Andreacchio is a specialist of the Italian Renaissance and was awarded a doctorate for his work on Sino-Japanese philosophical literature in dialogue with western philosophical classics (Illinois) and a doctorate for his work on Dante's Platonic interpretation of religious authority (Cambridge, UK). Having published various academic articles, mostly on Dante and Vico, since 2012, Dr Andreacchio has been an editor for *Interpretation: A Journal of Political Philosophy*. Having recently conducted three years of research at the Sorbonne (on Petrarch, Pico and Valla), Dr Andreacchio currently resides in Lyon, France, as a dedicated educator and reviver of Baroque painting.

Richard Andrews is Emeritus Professor of Italian at the University of Leeds, UK, having retired from teaching in 2001. He is the author of *Scripts and Scenarios: The Performance of Comedy in Renaissance Italy* (Cambridge: C.U.P., 1993); and *The Commedia dell'Arte of Flaminio Scala: A Translation and Analysis of 30 Scenarios* (Lanham: Scarecrow Press, 2008). Other essays on early modern Italian theatre have dealt with the rise of the female performer; with relationships between spoken drama and early opera; and with Italian influence on French and English drama. He is currently pursuing a project on "classical European comedy" between 1500 and 1800.

Louise George Clubb is Professor Emerita of Italian Studies and Comparative Literature at the University of California, Berkeley, and founding editor of the University of California Press series "Biblioteca italiana". She has published extensively on early modern Italian and English literature and drama. Her books include *Giambattista Della Porta, Dramatist* (1965), *Italian Plays in the Folger Library* (1968), *Italian Drama in Shakespeare's Time* (1989), *Romance and Aretine Humanism in Sienese Comedy*, with Robert Black (1993), and *Pollastra and the Origins of Twelfth Night* (2010).

Mario Domenichelli is Emeritus Professor of Comparative Literature at the University of Florence, Italy. He taught English, American, and Italian literature in the universities of Bologna, Cagliari, Pisa, all Italy, Middlebury College, USA, and Mogadishu, Somalia. Among his books are *Il limite dell'ombra. Le figure della soglia nel teatro inglese tra Cinque e Seicento* (1994); *Cavaliere e gentiluomo* (2002); *Dizionario dei temi letterari* (co-author, 2007); and *Lo scriba e l'oblio. Letteratura e storia nell'epoca borghese* (2012). He has edited, co-edited, and contributed to, special issues of reviews such as "In forma di parole" (*Petrarchism in England*, 2004) and "Moderna". He has also translated and edited works of Pope, Swift, Galsworthy, Dickens, Conrad, Kipling, and Shakespeare.

Keir Elam is a Professor of English Literature at the University of Bologna, Italy. He is the editor of the Arden Third Series edition of *Twelfth Night* (2008) and author of several articles, chapters, and books on Shakespeare and early modern English drama. His latest monograph is *Shakespeare's Pictures: Visual Objects in the Drama* (2017).

Robert Henke is Professor of Drama and Comparative Literature at Washington University of St. Louis, USA. He is the author of *Pastoral Transformations: Italian Tragicomedy and Shakespeare's Late Plays* (1997); *Performance and Literature in the Commedia dell'Arte* (2002); and *Poverty and Charity in Early Modern Theater and Performance* (2015). He is the editor of *A Cultural History of Theatre in the Early Modern Age* (2017) and a founding member of the international research collective "Theater Without Borders".

Rosalind Kerr is Emeritus Professor in Theatre and Performance, University of Alberta, and currently a fellow at the Centre for Reformation and Renaissance Studies, University of Toronto, both Canada. She specialises in the Golden Age of the *commedia dell'arte* and has published *The Rise of the Diva* (2015). She has several articles and chapters on the actresses including "Sex and the Satyr in the Pastoral Tradition: Isabella Andreini's *La Mirtilla* as Pro-feminist Erotica", and "The Fame Monster: Diva Worship from Isabella Andreini to Lady Gaga". Her current project is an edited translation of Flaminio Scala's *Il finto marito.*

Jason Lawrence is a Senior Lecturer in English at the University of Hull, UK. His research focuses primarily on the literary and cultural relationships between Italy and England in the Early Modern period. His first book, "*Who the Devil Taught Thee So Much Italian?": Italian Language Learning and Literary Imitation in Early Modern England* (2006), explores the parallel relationship between methods of learning Italian and techniques of literary imitation in sixteenth- and seventeenth-century England. His new book *Tasso's Art and Afterlives: The "Gerusalemme liberate" in England* (2017) focuses on the English reception of Tasso, spanning literature, opera, and the visual arts, from the sixteenth to the nineteenth centuries.

Michele Marrapodi is a Full Professor of English Literature at the University of Palermo, Italy. He is General Editor of the "Anglo-Italian Renaissance Studies" series. His most recent edited volumes include *Shakespeare's Italy* (1993); *The Italian World of English Renaissance Drama* (1998); *Italian Studies in Shakespeare and His Contemporaries* (1999); *Shakespeare, Italy, and Intertextuality* (2004); *Italian Culture in the Drama of Shakespeare and His Contemporaries* (2007); *Shakespeare and Renaissance Literary Theories* (2011); *Shakespeare and the Italian Renaissance* (2014); and *Shakespeare and the Visual Arts: The Italian Influence* (2017).

J. R. Mulryne is Emeritus Professor at the University of Warwick, having previously served as Lecturer and Reader in English Literature at the University of Edinburgh, both UK. At Warwick he was Director of the Centre for the Study of the Renaissance and among many offices held was as the University's Pro-Vice-Chancellor. His research interests have been mainly in Renaissance and modern theatre and theatre performance. More recently he has published widely on Early Modern European festivals and is Convenor of the Society for European Festivals Research and General Editor of the Society's *European Festival Studies 1450–1700* series.

Eric Nicholson teaches literature and theatre studies courses at New York University, Florence, and Syracuse University in Florence, both Italy. An active member of Thespis Society, Verona, and of the international research collaborative "Theater Without Borders", with Robert Henke he has co-edited the volumes *Transnational Exchange in Early Modern Theater* (2008) and *Transnational Mobilities in Early Modern Theater* (2014). He has recently contributed the chapter on "Sexuality and Gender" to Volume Three of *A Cultural History of Theatre* (2017). At NYU Florence and elsewhere, he has directed plays by Aristophanes, Shakespeare, Molière, and others.

Mary Partridge studied Modern History at St. Edmund Hall, Oxford, UK. She completed her MA in "Shakespeare and the Cultural History of Renaissance England" at the Shakespeare Institute, University of Birmingham, UK, in 2004. Her doctoral research at the University of

Birmingham explored the cultural impact of Castiglione's *Book of the Courtier* in Elizabethan England. She was awarded the Royal Historical Society's Alexander Prize in 2008. She subsequently completed a Postgraduate Certificate of Education at the University of Cambridge, UK (2011), winning the Charles Fox Prize for the best dissertation and the Simms Prize for the best performance in education from her college, Lucy Cavendish. She currently teaches History at Solihull School, UK.

Alessandra Petrina is Professor of English Literature at the Università di Padova, Italy. Her research focuses primarily on late-medieval and early modern intellectual history, and on Anglo-Italian cultural relations. She has published, among others, *The Kingis Quair* (1997); *Cultural Politics in Fifteenth-century England. The Case of Humphrey, Duke of Gloucester* (2004); and *Machiavelli in the British Isles. Two Early Modern Translations of the Prince* (2009). She is currently working on the early modern English translations of Petrarch's *Triumphi*, and on early modern marginalia.

Chiara Petrolini, post-doc at the University of Vienna, Austria, studied at the Scuola Normale Superiore, University of Pisa, Italy, and wrote her PhD dissertation on Paolo Sarpi and England. She has extensively worked on the topic of conversion and recently published a collection of conversion narratives in Rome and a volume on conversion and violence (along with V. Lavenia, S. Pastore, and S. Pavone). Her main research interest is the interaction between philosophy and religious conflicts in Early Modern Europe. She is currently completing a monograph on Sarpi.

Diego Pirillo is an Associate Professor of Italian Studies at the University of California, USA. Along with several articles and book chapters, he is the author of *The Refugee-Diplomat: Venice, England and the Reformation* (2018); *Filosofia ed eresia nell'Inghilterra del tardo Cinquecento: Bruno, Sidney e i dissidenti religiosi italiani* (2010); and (with O. Catanorchi) *Favole, metafore, storie. Seminario su Giordano Bruno* (2007).

John Roe is a Reader in English and Related Literature, University of York, UK. He is the author of *Shakespeare and Machiavelli* (2002). He has edited *Shakespeare: The Poems* (2006) and *Inspiration and Technique: Ancient to Modern Views on Beauty and Art* (with Michele Stanco, 2007). He contributed to the *Great Shakespeareans* series (Continuum Press).

Gilberto Sacerdoti is a Full Professor of English Literature at Università Roma Tre, Italy. On Giordano Bruno and his relations to English culture (and Shakespeare) he has published *Nuovo cielo, nuova terra. La rivelazione copernicana di Antonio Cleopatra di Shakespeare* (1990 and 2008); and *Sacrificio e sovranità. Teologia e politica nell'Europa di Shakespeare e Bruno* (2002 and 2016).

Duncan Salkeld is Professor of Shakespeare and Renaissance Literature at the University of Chichester, UK. He is author of *Madness and Drama in the Age of Shakespeare* (1993); *Shakespeare Among the Courtesans: Prostitution, Literature and Drama, 1500–1650* (2012); and numerous articles and chapters on Renaissance literature. His latest monograph is *Shakespeare and London* (2018).

Selene Scarsi is a Senior Lecturer at Kingston University London, UK, where she teaches Medieval and Early Modern Literature. In her main area of interest, Anglo-Italian relations in the Renaissance, she has written articles on Tofte, Harington, and Spenser, as well as a monograph, *Translating Women in Early Modern England: Gender in the Elizabethan Versions of Boiardo, Ariosto and Tasso* (2010). She is currently working on a comparative study of English and Italian female sonneteers in the Renaissance.

Cathy Shrank is Professor of Tudor and Renaissance Literature at the University of Sheffield, UK. Publications include *Writing the Nation in Reformation England* (2004); with Mike Pincombe, *The Oxford Handbook of Tudor Literature* (2009); and with Raphael Lyne, *Shakespeare's Poems* (2018). She is currently writing a monograph about early modern English dialogue, as well as editing *Mammon* for the *Independent Works of William Tyndale* (Catholic University of America Press), and *Pierce Penilesse* for the *Collected Works of Thomas Nashe* (Oxford University Press).

Janet Levarie Smarr was for twenty years a Professor of Comparative Literature and Italian at the University of Illinois Urbana-Champaign, USA. Since 2000 she has been a Professor of Theatre History and Dramatic Literature at the University of California San Diego, USA, and a member of the interdepartmental Italian Studies faculty. She has published books and numerous articles on Boccaccio, on the connections of his tales with later theatre, and on women writers of early modern Italy and France.

Jane Tylus is a Professor of Italian and Comparative Literature at Yale, USA. A literary historian who works primarily on late medieval and early modern Europe, Tylus's most recent books are *Siena, City of Secrets* (2015); *Early Modern Cultures of Translation* (co-edited with Karen Newman, 2015); *Poetics of Masculinity in Early Modern Italy and Spain* (co-edited with Gerry Milligan, 2010); and *Reclaiming Catherine of Siena* (2009, winner of the 2010 MLA Howard Marraro Prize for Outstanding Work in Italian Studies). She has translated the complete poetry of Gaspara Stampa and Lucrezia Tornabuoni de' Medici (2010; 2002), and with David Damrosch she edited the early modern volume for the *Longman Anthology of World Literature*. Since 2013 Tylus has served as General Editor of the journal *I Tatti Studies in the Italian Renaissance*.

Melissa Walter is Associate Professor of English at the University of the Fraser Valley, Canada. Her research focuses primarily on early modern drama (including Middleton, Fletcher, Webster, and Shakespeare) and prose fiction, with particular interests in gender and intercultural exchange. She has edited, with Dennis Britton, *Rethinking Shakespearean Source Study: Audiences, Authors, and Digital Technologies* (2018). She is currently completing a book on the Italian novella and Shakespeare's comedies, and editing *The Two Gentlemen of Verona* for Internet Shakespeare Editions.

Michael Wyatt is an independent scholar. He has taught at Northwestern University and Wesleyan University, both USA; the Università degli Studi di Trento, Italy; and Stanford University, USA, where he served as the first Associate Director of the Center for Medieval and Early Modern Studies. He has lectured extensively in the United States, Europe, and Australasia. Among his publications are *The Cambridge Companion to the Italian Renaissance* (2014); *Writing Relations, American Scholars in Italian Archives: Essays for Franca Nardelli Petrucci and Armando Petrucci* (2008); and *The Italian Encounter with Tudor England: A Cultural Politics of Translation* (2005). He is currently working on *Dido's Legacy: Oblivion and Promise in Italy's Past Present*.

Acknowledgements

This companion volume is the result of several years of research and collaboration with a number of colleagues and friends who have proved extremely generous with advice, patient for the long wait, and highly energetic in their critical contributions. I am therefore deeply indebted to all of them for the confidence and perseverance demonstrated throughout the various long stages that led to the book's completion. Over the years, I was fortunate and greatly honoured to have profited from the criticism and expertise of many scholars whose influence I want to acknowledge here. Louise George Clubb inspired much of my activity and expressed faith in the idea of the project from the outset. Keir Elam generously read, guided, and commented on my Introduction. Robert Henke graciously collaborated with me in the direction of international seminars. The late Giorgio Melchiori and Alessandro Serpieri graced me with their friendship and helped me escape from many juvenile errors and conceptual obscurities. Direct and indirect debts to other influencers are enormous and the reader may find their legacy in the lengthy bibliography appended to the volume.

As always, my dearest thoughts of gratitude go to my family and in particular to my youngest daughter, Virginia, who is approaching the study of the classics and to whom this volume is ultimately dedicated.

Introduction

Past, present, and future in Anglo-Italian renaissance studies

Michele Marrapodi

I. Back to the past. Forward to the present

Before moving on to a more systematic account of the volume's two-part structure in the ensuing pages, I wish to begin with a personal recollection, which may serve to introduce the ways I came to approach the field to which this book is dedicated, and to explain the subsequent developments of my critical experience, as summarised below.

When I was a young researcher at the University of Messina and Acting Professor at the University of Palermo in the late 1980s, I invited for a series of lectures Robert S. Miola, whom I had had the pleasure of meeting at Stratford-upon-Avon during one of the biennial International Shakespeare Conferences. This special occasion gave my students and myself the opportunity to look with greater awareness at the relationships between Shakespeare and the classical and Italian world. It also allowed us to explore more closely the involvement of other kinds of sources, borrowings, and the like, as well as the related concern of imitation and adaptation, including the notion of reception in its double aspects of compliance and resistance. In other words, discarding the traditional principles of influence studies of the early 1900s,[1] I began to ponder on the creative circulation of learning in the early modern period, i.e. "social energy" to quote Stephen Greenblatt's inspired terminology,[2] as a complex process of intertextual and interdiscursive appropriation, in which cultural difference and ideological opposition played a fundamental role in accommodating the moral of the original narratives and theatrical practices to domestic dramatic traditions with distinctive social and religious principles. "For the circulation of social energy by and through the stage", concluded Greenblatt's theoretical assumptions of his poetics of culture, "was not part of a single coherent, totalizing system. Rather it was partial, fragmentary, conflictual; elements were crossed, torn apart, recombined, set against each other; particular social practices were magnified by the stage, others diminished, exalted, evacuated".[3] By refusing the limitations of too linear a heritage, and by infringing the monistic concept of source with a wider typology of archetypal patterns within a chain of transmission, the notion of 'deep source' can incorporate the meaning of a multiplicity of possible cultural transactions, connected by common ancestry or legacy, and ranging from direct knowledge to indirect derivation via translations, rewritings, and contaminations with other works, genres, or contexts of the European Renaissance. Thanks to a revisited concept of intertextuality, considered the "'Darwinian' theory of literary heredity by common ancestry",[4] and drawing on Bakhtin's construct of 'dialogism' and Julia Kristeva's term coined in the late 1960s,[5] the romantic idea of the originality of the poet is thus translated into his creative ability to combine, even unconsciously, diverse

DOI: 10.4324/9781315612720-1

established themes, forms, and models, or recurring narremes and theatregrams, in the words of Louise George Clubb,[6] including the iconographical *topoi* of the period's visual culture in an ingenious *ars combinatoria.* Within this ample proposition of a generative source and analogue, also inspired by Robert Miola's 'civil conversations' about the manifold aspects of intertextuality,[7] I began investigating the wider range of influence of the Italian Renaissance through the lens of a number of sundry critical and methodological viewpoints, as opposed to simplistic imitation and deterministic source studies.

Several books by distinguished comparatists, already circulating on this issue within the critical debate, helped me tread some unexplored paths of the Anglo-Italian subject, intercepting and classifying any significant variation of generic intertexuality, manifested in prose narrative, poetry, and drama, hitherto not exhaustively studied. First and foremost, I should mention Leo Salingar's comprehensive inquiry into the converging encounter of classical, medieval, and humanistic traditions foregrounding English drama, which drew closer attention to Shakespeare's power "to bring out parallels and affinities between stories and dramatic devices from separate traditions".[8] Louise George Clubb's original acquisitions from the in-depth exploration of the pristine theatrical forms and structures had the merit of laying the foundations for a renewed confrontation with Italian theatre, signalling the potentially numberless old and new comedic solutions and effective derivations operating on the Elizabethan stage.[9] Clubb's system of theatregrams – a rich repertory of recurring microstructures of dramatic and narrative segments involving character, situation, sexual disguise, apparent death, misplaced love, bed-trick, eavesdropping, recognition, and many other set-pieces – showed the dissemination of Roman New Comedy and its effects on Italian drama, resulting from a strategy of composition based on a *contaminatio* of stock elements and situational variations of seminal theatregrams, interlaced with narremes pertaining to the *novella* tradition. Instead of delving into the kind of positivistic determinism that informed the orthodox view of the Italian legacy, this scholarship led the way towards a reconsideration of the differences and contrasts, rather than towards explicit analogies with the Italian world. This opened up a new trend of analysis that is now moving away from simplistic imitation of a single line of transmission to embrace varying levels of cultural transactions, thereby shifting from the almost passive influence of a retrievable model to a complex and multilayered process of social, religious, and political negotiation, divergence, and subversion.

Other influential sub-genres of Italian drama, departing from their original *commedia* solution (in its threefold expression as *erudita*, *grave*, and *dell'arte*), have been variously investigated by recent theatre historians. Among a number of dedicated scholars, Richard Andrews explored the gradual progression of comedy in Italy, ranging from its learned, scripted formats of Plautine and Terentian derivation to the more popular and experimental acting, based on the fixed repertory of the masks and *scenarios* of improvised theatre.[10] Robert Henke examined the origins of the pastoral mode and its theoretical premises founded on Guarini's and Tasso's mixed drama in relation to Shakespeare's tragicomedies and debated, in a later work, the performance of the *comici* of *commedia dell'arte*, evaluating their pervasive influence as an oral and literary as well as linguistic and stylistic kind of dualistic theatrical communication, often peppered with explicit forms of homoerotic transgression.[11] One of the most pliable and frequently adopted modules, the disguise *topos*, orginating from the primary dramaturgical category of New Comedy's regular structure, produced a social disruption in the play-world by reversing fixed social roles and a more subversive, sexual, disruption when it infringed gender roles. Although both were condemned by the Puritans in the transvestite controversy of the 1580s, the threat of upsetting gender identity and dress differentiation created a greater form of subversion for the all-male cast of the Elizabethan stage than the potential conflicts between social classes.[12] In the general construction and literary legacy of Renaissance dramatic language, sixteenth-century Italy becomes for Keir Elam a great cultural intertext for Shakespeare and his contemporaries. "It was perceived", Elam has argued, "as a sort of generative machine producing powerful models – cultural models, political models, ideological models, iconographic models, behavioural models and so on – which could be freely taken up and transformed by the early modern English".[13] This novel and more comprehensive form of influence may be considered the theoretical platform for the current developments of most recent criticism.

To consolidate this pathway of cultural permeability as a diachronic and transnational process, the absorption in all literary and cultural fields of the conversational strategies of courtesy manuals, namely the influential 'conduct books' by Baldassare Castiglione, Giovanni Della Casa, Giambattista Giraldi Cinthio, and Stefano Guazzo,[14] contributed to the self-fashioning of the courtier, prince, or gentleman for educational purposes within a patriarchal social order. Conversely, it also contributed to their almost total deconstruction or parody with linguistic, social, and political implications concerning both male and female systems and discourses of sex and gender, as accounted for by Harry Berger's precious book on Italian courtesy literature.[15] Thus, the theatrical impact on the Elizabethan and early Stuart stage may also function as an anti-model, rather than a productive imitation, of the coeval courtesy literature, a kind of anti-Petrarchan subversion of the social themes represented in the wake of the Machiavelli-Aretino-Bruno axis of radical theatre, as I will be mentioning later. This further perspective, therefore, does not simply take into account the forms of attention drawn out from the source material as the only target of the critic's interest. This wider approach investigates the 'politics of resistance' or, to put it another way, the 'politics of intertextuality', to adopt Michael Redmond's felicitous formula,[16] inherent in the ideological construction of early modern English drama, in order to debate how and why Italy's multifaceted presence as an alien culture was also subjected to forces of political negotiations imposed by English society and ruled by different and even opposing religious, literary, and political traditions.[17] Neither is this phenomenon univocal and unidirectional. Through a diverse array of compositional strategies – ranging from overt and covert influence, to the mirroring of a single intertext, to a *contaminatio* of narremes and theatregrams taken up from a variety of theatrical modules, sequences, or analogues of one and the same text or within a number of works by the same or different authors – the actual composition of early modern English drama has further proved its transnational and transhistorical genesis in the encounter, confrontation, and exchange of its medieval heritage with the timeless course of appropriation, disruption, subversion, and opposition, rather than solely constructive or generic imitation, of its classical and Italian roots.

Significant evolutions in the gradual progression from cultural exchange to striking transformation are also traceable in the aims of the editors of several collections of essays and gatherings of papers from international seminars. Sergio Rossi's Introduction to *Italy and the English Renaissance*[18] provides a comprehensive survey of the many Italian humanists, writers, and poets whose works penetrated into Renaissance England through a variety of different means, including the period's accommodating practice of translation, in most cases a revised adaptation to the mores of English culture. In one of the most stimulating essays in the collection, Brian Parker identifies in the astonishingly accurate and detailed representation of Venice in Jonson's *Volpone* the very essence of contemporary Venetian decadence, picturing the dark sides of the *Serenissima* drawn from myriad sources and translated on the English stage into "the new urban experience of London, which he, and such fellow dramatists as Dekker and Middleton, had begun to analyse in their new genre of 'city comedy'".[19] In *Theatre of the English and Italian Renaissance*, edited by J. R. Mulryne and Margaret Shewring, a group of specialists from different disciplines deal with the ways the traditions of Italian and English drama intersect, distinguish, and divide in the fruitful encounter with genre models, *topoi*, and set-pieces of Italian theatrical modes and culture, affecting the plot structures, performance practices, and performance spaces of individual playwrights, including Jonson, Lyly, and Shakespeare.[20] In a subsequent volume Mulryne and Shewring extend this research activity to the field of Italian festivals in seventeenth-century Europe, investigating the festival traditions in the theatrical experience of several countries.[21] A broader European outlook on Shakespeare's absorption and rehandling of alien cultures is pursued by Andrew Hadfield and Paul Hammond's edited collection.[22] Among a number of insightful contributions, Richard Andrews highlights Shakespeare's reliance on Italian comedy in its twofold expression of scripted and improvised theatre, the 'regular' *commedia erudita* and the impromptu acting of *commedia dell'arte*, while François Laroque illustrates Shakespeare's geography as a fruitful means to enquire into the dramatic functionality of imaginary and fictional territories alongside historical city states.[23]

The social, philosophical, scientific, and even economic context of the Italian Renaissance, broadly considered as extending from the turn of the fourteenth to the end of the sixteenth century, can be found in Michael Wyatt's edited anthology, *The Cambridge Companion to the Italian Renaissance*.[24] Through a necessarily interdisciplinary approach, the intersecting cultural matrices that make up Italian Humanism are dealt with by experts of various fields in individual essays that nevertheless cohere within a suggestive organic whole, in an attempt to reconstruct the multifaceted aspects of Italian Humanism. Although such topics as literature and the arts are not discussed, the volume offers some valuable chapters on often neglected subjects which explain the editor's deliberate focus on the cultural and scientific world of the Italian 'renaissances', as reflected in the peninsula's fragmented political geography.

The mediation of new propositions in both the linguistic and the theatrical fields, relating to particular aspects of Italian acquisitions that had penetrated into English culture through the works of various Anglo-Italian influencers, including John Florio, have been rediscovered by Jason Lawrence and Michael Wyatt. In Lawrence's *Who the Devil Taught Thee So Much Italian?*,[25] Florio's *Firste Fruites* (1578) and *Second Fruits* (1591) are considered the main cultural vehicles for the Elizabethans' language-learning practices and theatrical appropriations of Italian vernacular, implying a reading knowledge of Italian that was widespread among Shakespeare and his contemporaries. By contrast, Michael Wyatt's *The Italian Encounter with Tudor England* expounds a process of political circulation of ideas imported from Italy through John Florio's versatile activity as teacher, lexicographer, and translator and through other Italian immigrants, refugees, and Protestants, whose timely presence in early modern London provided English culture with an open-ended political doctrine, in comparison with England's traditional isolation, by the absorption of Italian texts in the original as well as in translation.[26] As discussed in a relevant chapter in this volume, Wyatt offers a thorough analysis of Florio's output, discerning his significant role in the diffusion of the written and spoken language of Italy in the late Tudor and early Stuart periods. Furthermore, Wyatt's book assesses the impact of prominent influencers, such as Aretino, Guarini, and Machiavelli, on the constitution of national identity through the appraisal of works printed by Wolfe in Italian or Anglicised by the period's famous translators, hereby becoming the public agency for the introduction of foreign authors and customs into English culture. A reassessment of the circulation of Italian books in the deployment of English printing activity and cultural traditions is the subject of Soko Tomita's richly reconstructed bibliographical catalogue, divided into two separate volumes, which testifies in detail, with the adoption of charts, tables, graphs, and images, to the breadth of Italian publications printed in England under Elizabeth and the early Stuarts, often located in the private libraries of the period's leading intellectuals and aristocrats.[27]

After this short survey, by no means exhaustive but only representative of the most widely shared trends and critical directions in twentieth- and twenty-first century Anglo-Italian approaches, we may now turn to how early modern constructions of Italy actually worked in the drama of Shakespeare and his contemporaries before moving on to the latest contributions and the most indicative prospects for the future.

II. Italy as a stage

Elicited by the lively debate in this engaging area of research, my first collaborative project aimed to reassess the *vexata quaestio* of the Italian setting and 'local colour' theory which was strongly questioned at the time. It may be convenient to recall that the majority of relevant nineteenth- and twentieth-century scholarship insisted on the conviction that the overabundance of Italian-located plays in Shakespeare and early modern drama originated in the Elizabethans' fascination with the peninsula's ambivalent reputation as the cradle of European civilisation, of poetry, and art, as well as, on the other hand, the 'Academie' – in Nashe's words – of political intrigue, poisoners, and sinners.[28] While the idea of the peninsula as the centre of humanistic civilisation was exported through the arts, Italy's notorious fame as a territory of vices, largely exaggerated by defamatory accounts, was also fostered by Protestant England's aversion to Papistry in every religious and political controversy. As a natural home for sin, Italy and Italianate characters of monstrous wickedness were made equal to anti-Christian nationalities, whether Turkish, Moorish, or Jewish. But, as G. K. Hunter's important essay made clear, Italian vices became relevant to English dramatists "only when 'Italy' was revealed as an aspect of England".[29]

The concomitant theory of Shakespeare's supposed voyage to the continent, and to Italy in particular, advanced by some traditional scholars in the past, as an explanation of the plays' presumed topographical accuracy and verisimilitude of location, has never found historical evidence to justify anything more than mere hypothesis or fantasy. Despite a resurgence of interest in this subject among some recent critics, Mario Praz's notable work is still credited as one of the first to have clearly brought the issue of the dramatist's Italian knowledge back to its historical terms.[30] As a consequence, the idea of an alleged 'grand tour' in the countries of classical culture on the part of Shakespeare during his 'lost years' at the turn of the century is losing ground in favour of a newer critical position that takes into consideration the humanistic concept of travelling both as a personal and real experience and as a method of reading, an intellectual journey of the mind, often negatively influenced by biased records that were in turn nourished by libellous pamphlets and fictional voyagers' relations.[31] What John Gillies has called "poetic geography", the Elizabethan imaginative and imaginary vision of the Mediterranean nurtured by the classics, can be extended to construe the theatrical representation of the foreigner and of notorious Italian city states.[32]

In a pioneering paper given at an international conference long ago, Clifford Leech invited further study on "how the idea of locality contributed to the play's structure and effect", implying that the choice, treatment, alternation, or opposition of one stage setting with respect to another were part of the dramatist's ordinary strategy for achieving a 'frame effect', thereby guiding audience response.[33] Although his concluding expectations for a valuable systematic tabulation of the distinct localities used in the plays are still to be fulfilled, the aim of the volume I co-edited in 1993, *Shakespeare's Italy: Functions of Italian Locations in Renaissance Drama*, was to question this much disputed issue by pointing, perhaps more incisively than Leech and others, to dramatic construction and textuality.[34] In this work, the staging of Italianate theatre is set against the framework of the linguistic, thematic, and ideological components of the plays and is regarded as a powerful means to disclose a sub-text of political matters and responses through a variety of rhetorical devices, affecting in the first place individual characterisation, social and political concerns, and audience reaction. In most Tudor and Stuart drama, Italianate scenes are neither occasional nor devoid of stage effects. They are potentially used as an English projection to restrain domestic anxieties of moral punishment and tyrannical oppression, thus offering a cover for political dissent at home, as in the satirical and revenge tragedies of Webster, Marston, Middleton, Tourneur, or Ford. By operating a precise sense of location, as both a conceptual and concrete space signalled by means of deft verbal scenography and coherent metaphoric imagery, period dramatists demonstrate an awareness of ideological implications and control of audience reaction by exploiting old beliefs, commonplaces, and cultural constructs of difference and alterity, thematically intertwined for showcasing Italian vices and topography. Hence, double or multiple localities are often juxtaposed and used metaphorically as a structural indicator to guide us towards the plays' thematic concerns, contributing to character construction and manipulating audience response. Contrastive stage worlds in the double or multiple plots are also used to bring forth the theatrical agency of stereotyped Machiavellian crimes of moral deception and political intrigue. Examples include *Cymbeline* or other Jacobean dramas associated with otherness and foreigness, as opposed to strained self-fashionings of celebrated English virtues embodied in individual characters and public institutions with the intent of carrying out an ideological design of censure and containment in defence of national identity.[35] Other forms of transgression of Italianate romantic and citizen comedies, revenge tragedies, and satiric drama inscribed in late Elizabethan, Jacobean, and Caroline stage – as maintained by some groundbreaking studies of Marxist and materialist criticism like those I will be mentioning later by Jonathan Dollimore, James W. Lever, Margot Heinemann, and Martin Butler, to cite only a few – underscore in different degrees a subterranean opposition to the royal absolutism of the early Stuarts in the guise of varying metaphorical motifs, such as game, lucre, lust, violence, sexual abuse, and moral corruption. These themes are dramatised within a social ambience of Italianate vices and courts, where religious controversy, racial and gender issues, and political dissent could be easily masked, stored, or exorcised through the remote confines of an alien world.[36]

Several scholars have dealt with these same topics variously and differently, attributing primary importance to foreign settings as metaphors for London and England. A case in point is Murray J. Levith's straightforward book,[37] which, in following up G. K. Hunter's seminal essay, basically acknowledges the metaphorical allusions to English habits and customs in his analysis of Shakespeare's Italian plays, mirroring England's own presumed vices; or Jack D'Amico's more sophisticated vision that addresses the dual treatment of Italian urban settings, social environments, and city states in Shakespeare's comedies and tragedies, discovering a common oxymoronic diversity of fascination and repulsion, of popular attraction and danger, and bringing together the worlds of England and Italy by means of some 'spatial analogies' whose recognisable features were accommodated to London urban life by the Elizabethan imagination.[38] Historically, these approaches, however perceptively grounded and coherently focused they may appear, are not altogether new, and some basic principles of their critical assumptions may be found in the classic studies of mid-twentieth-century scholarship, most notably John Lievsay's *The Elizabethan Image of Italy* and R. C. Jones's essay "Italian Setting and the World of Elizabethan Tragedy".[39] Lievsay provided a comprehensive account of the Elizabethan image of Italy, taking into consideration all the possible sources from which early modern dramatists conceived of their Italianate settings, conflating together a variety of historical, literary, and fictional factors that nurtured the Elizabethans' horrified fixation on the Mediterranean nation. Apart from direct knowledge of contemporary political and social events, the influence of the classical and humanistic tradition, and the great bulk of English translations of Italian *novelle*, poetry, and drama, these factors also included the rapid flourishing of treatises, travel books, and travellers' reports, which gave an infamous, if often imaginary, picture of Italy with its tyrannical city states, vicious courts, and vengeful inhabitants. What Jones's view added to this wide-ranging reconstruction was that the so-called 'atmosphere and colour' of Renaissance Italy depended not so much on the locales on which the action was set as on the play's own imagery and figurative system. The world of Italy, he argued, was largely established "through patterns of imagery that do not represent an actual landscape or region".[40] However, the most recurrent metaphorical thread pervading all Italianate drama, from Webster and Marston to Tourner, Middleton, and Ford, was the ingeniously wicked recourse to poisoning, as Jones himself admitted, "an Italian sallet"[41] or method utilised for the advancement of vicious schemers, revengers, and political conspirators. Shakespeare's construction of Italy, however, offers a more innovative, functional connection to the play's overall organisation in both stylistic and thematic terms by means of action pointers, spatial and rhetorical effects, and individual characterisation than the sensational representation staged by his fellow dramatists.

In most of his dramas, Shakespeare's strategic use of Italy exploits an inventive rehandling of theatrical modes and genres, transforming and developing them from the vast repertory of Italian literary and cultural traditions. To illustrate the kind of transformation the dramatist accomplishes out of his Italian models, one possible example of critical analysis among the comedies and tragedies may suffice. In the apparently English opening of *The Taming of the Shrew*, the staging of the *beffa* on Sly, set in an English ambience but derivative of Plautus's and Boccaccio's comedic mode, functions as an interpretive key to the play proper through a series of parallelisms and contrasts, both linguistic and situational, with the changed Italian scene and corresponding mercantile setting in which the characters' shifting roles, disguises, and continuing pretense, including Katherina's final speech, recall the initial improvised playacting of the Lord's proposed jest and related metatheatrical effects, foregrounding the erotic exchanges between Sly and the transvestite page. Thus, the Lord's direction to his stewards' extempore performance, juxtaposed with the arrival of the professional troupe in the second Induction scene, underpins the dramatist's reliance on Italian theatre in the adoption of the impromptu practice of the *commedia dell'arte*.[42] Likewise, the witty word turns and repeated punning between Katherina and Petruchio, fostering the taming process towards a didactic affirmation of new marital bonds based on complicity, irony, and game, are coherently grafted onto the New Comedic theatregrams of supposed and mistaken identities in the Tranio-Bianca-Lucentio sub-plot, as taken up from Ariosto's *I Suppositi*, contributing to the Italianate unity of the play and to a revolutionary reinscription of the old hierarchies of marriage.[43] Like Aretino's *Il Marescalco*, whose *beffa* motif and metatheatrical effects may well be regarded as the most direct intertextual derivations,[44] Shakespeare displays in *The Shrew* a parodic attack on the Petrarchan affectation of courtesy literature implicit in Castiglione's manual, exalting amorous anti-conventionalism over the courtesy tradition of a mannered Petrarchism, so excessively rhetorical and artificial as the 'artful artlessness' paradox raised up to elitist grace in the self-affirmation of Castiglione's *sprezzatura*.[45] *The Courtier*'s aristocratic, male dominated ideology in both the family's and society's patriarchal and misogynistic structure is questioned in the outcome of Shakespeare's play by Petruchio's histrionic characterisation and Katherina's self-ironic lecture:[46]

> I am asham'd that women are so simple
> To offer war where they should kneel for peace,
> Or seek for rule, supremacy, and sway,
> When they are bound to serve, love, and obey.
> Why are our bodies soft, and weak, and smooth,
> Unapt to toil and trouble in the world,
> But that our soft conditions and our hearts
> Should well agree with our external parts?
> (5.2.162–169)[47]

Katherina's overacting parodies Gaspar Pallavicino's antifeminism in *Il Libro del Cortegiano*, echoing the Count's male-chauvinist convictions when the nobleman showcases the natural inferiority of women and states indisputably their proven incapacity to govern:

> [p]erché il mondo non ha utilità dalle donne, se non per lo generare dei figlioli. Ma ciò non intervien degli uomini, i quali governano le città, gli eserciti, e fanno tante altre cose d'importanzia; il che, poi che voi volete così, non voglio disputar come sapessero far le donne; basta che non lo fanno.[48]

> (for the worlde hath no profit by women, but for getting of children. But the like is not of men, which governe Cities, armies, and doe so many other waightie matters, the which (since you will so have it) I will not dispute how women could doe, it sufficeth they doe it not.)[49]

Beneath the rhetoric of the Count's fundamentalistic reasoning lies a case of political gynaephobia, a fear of any social and political power conquered by women. As brilliantly captured by Harry Berger's explanations of Ottaviano's comment at the end of Book 3, the gynaephobia of gender is "specifically centered on the fear of being unmanned in the sense of politically disempowered, whether by men or by women, but a fear that is obviously intensified when the masculine role is performed by strong women".[50] In contrast with Castiglione's concerns and Aretino's misogynist solution, Shakespeare portrays an ironical challenge to the contradictions of contemporary society through the heterosexual couple of Petruchio and Katherina, highlighting in them a rediscovered intimate collaboration. Their final achievement is exalted by the ironical comparison with the other couples, whose marital bonds are founded instead on a conventionally hierarchical and conflictual relationship, which demonstrates immediately, in the wager scene, its deficiency and conceptual failure:

> *Petr.*
> Come, Kate, we'll to bed.
> We three are married, but you two are sped.
> (5.2.185–186)

Observed from the ideological perspective of authorial orientation and public consensus, forms of stage representation and verbal topography, peppered with *commedia* solutions, as in *The Shrew*, are purposefully involved in the double or multiple variations of Shakespeare's Italian-inspired settings, juxtaposed or put into contrast in the self-same drama and often derived from their corresponding Italian intertexts, narratives, or analogues, as in *The Two Gentlemen of Verona, Much Ado About Nothing, All's Well That Ends Well, The Merchant of Venice, Twelfth Night,* and in the more tragicomedic plot organisation of *As You Like It, Measure for Measure,* or *The Winter's Tale,* to mention only the most significant, where the construction of Italy is directly or indirectly evoked, if not explicilty manifest in their most relevant Italian antecedents or models, becoming strategically functional to the play's axiology and a structural constituent of dramatic discourse. As I have written elsewhere, the study of 'topoanalysis' in its broader significance as a concrete and metaphorical medium to the core of the iconic strategy may serve to call attention to:

> [d]ramaturgical space in order to identify diverse ideological procedures of representation of the fictional world of drama. This implies that the use of place and locale is not "neutral", but semantically over-determined: it acts on the playtext, determining the local climate, and colouring the dramatic interactions which take place within its boundaries.[51]

Gillies's concept of "poetic geography" acquires in these contexts a more politically oriented cultural space, alongside conflicting ideas of attraction and repulsion, imitation and subversion, in order to grasp all the potentialities inscribed in the social and political conflicts of the Italianate discourse.

Shakespeare's and his fellow playwrights' adoption of Italy's ambivalent iconology takes on a different route in the tragedies, where the evil sides of the Italian myths are accommodated to tragic ends by relying on the country's notorious reputation for being a site of tyrannical oppression, political cynicism, and sexual violence brought to the fore by the Senecan-Machiavellian tradition. *The Tragedy of Othello* is a significant case in point both in terms of individual characterisation and thematic stucture. Starting from Giraldi Cinthio's *novella*, which he may have read in translation as well as in the original, Shakespeare remakes national stereotyping and a cluster of 'exotic' commonplaces about Italians firmly embedded in the Elizabethans' imagination, in order to give credibility to Iago's character as an Italianate villain: the rise of jealousy and the desire for revenge, the joy for mischief and plotting, Machiavellian astuteness and dissimulation, racist hatred for strangers, Senecan theatricalism, and so forth. These effects of verisimilitude, alongside the spicy local colour and some specific references to Venetian topography, historical buildings, and social customs, enhance the sense of locality as a structural factor, reaching the purpose of accentuating the Italianate colouring of the play.

Although a Venetian urban setting is accurately moulded into the action of Act I through a verbal topography of suggestive sites, streets, and courts, the concrete vices, laws, and customs of Venice are frequently rehearsed by Iago to suit his deceptive strategy of estrangement with the intent of disrupting Othello's self-confidence, displacing his social role as the menacing Other. A general strategy of binary oppositions of antithetical lexical terms ('Heaven/hell', 'angel/devil', 'white/black', 'fair/foul', 'true/false', 'honest/disloyal', etc.), relating to the theme of truth and justice through the imagery of seeing, is sustained by the metaphorical use of the verbs of perception ('to see', 'to look', 'to watch', 'to observe', 'to behold', etc.), engendering the constant Shakespearean dichotomy between appearance and reality, the world of seeming and the world of being, which ultimately underlines the mistaken reliance on man's outward senses and brings to light the two opposing figures of Desdemona and Iago throughout the play's rapid succession from Venice to Cyprus. The double localities thus become an ideal stage for dramatising Italianate passions and vices while distancing them, at the same time, from the protected boundaries of Elizabethan-Jacobean England. The realistic city-setting and evoked urban space of the first Act, containing in itself the racial and patriarchal contradictions of a mythically civilised society, is opposed to the more exotic, utopian island of Cyprus where Iago's improvised performance takes place. Both turn out to be an appropriate arena for the staging of comedy and tragedy, propelling the action from the comedic, if precarious, happy ending of the initial marriage trial to the production of Iago's 'monstrous birth' in the succeeding Acts. As in *The Merchant of Venice*'s courtroom scene, the social contradictions of the *Serenissima* are exemplified in the dramatic characterisation of two disturbing alien figures, Othello and Shylock, whose destabilising roles as foreigners in the stage world represented are simultaneously exploited in military, political, and economic terms, as well as despised and rejected in racial, moral, and religious terms for the benefit of the ruling government of the Venetian state.[52]

Despite some traditional interpretations of Desdemona as a child-like figure, discounting her capacity of discernment of Othello's sexual anxiety, the rhetoric of character construction demonstrates the lady's fundamental role if seen in opposition to that of Iago and for the salvation of the Moor. A comparison between the two antagonistic characterisations of Iago and Desdemona and their opposing rhetorical strategies may throw fresh light on the play's allegorical dimension, allowing Desdemona to be freed from the artificial displacement of the other characters' opinions and making her speak with her own voice to the audience. Observed from this perspective, Desdemona becomes Iago's most natural and direct antagonist, her more active role being necessary for the dynamics of the action and decisively influential for the final recovery of Othello's spiritual knowledge.

In answering Roderigo's warning against robbery, Brabantio's "this is Venice/My house is not a grange" (1.1.105–106)[53] depicts a background of safety and political rigour in line with contemporary accounts of a town administered by strict justice. The feverish mercantile activity of the city, though, the centre of intense trade and banking operations, is embodied as Italian vices in the construction of Iago's characterisation. The Ancient's greed for money and the Machiavellian dissimulation operate, from the outset, as a subversive impact on that moral and social order. His simile of "the fire … spied in populous cities" (1.1.76–77), the obscene visual images of "the black ram" and the "white ewe" (1.1.88–89), of "the beast with two backs" (1.1.116–117), and the recurrent use of economic terms are part of a coherent metaphoric imagery ironically placed in contrast with Brabantio's ideal societal picture. That the evil side of Venice is an inherent aspect of the same society is evident in the abrupt wave of racism and patriarchal authority breaking out against Desdemona's "gross revolt" (1.1.134). In her father's biased opinion, Othello is a negro, a savage, a soldier; so why should Desdemona "fall in love with what she fear'd to look on?" (1.3.98). As I have written elsewhere, despite the traditional view of a passive woman, her role unmasks the contradictions of an apparent stable world and is opposed to that of Iago on both symbolic and linguistic levels.[54] Construed upon the similar characterisation of the 'wondrous woman', the inspired grace-giver heroine of *commedia grave*, Desdemona's rhetoric expresses a positive, didactic function, endowed with spiritual vision, which operates through the 'amplifying' axis of Christian theological doctrine:

> I *saw* Othello's visage in his mind,
> And to his honours, and his valiant parts
> Did I my soul and fortune consecrate.
> (1.3.252–254)

With such words, Desdemona displays a capacity of profound insight that is denied to the other characters and, by stressing the blackness of Othello's face, she implicitly rebuts the sterotyped, racist prejudices propounded by Iago, Roderigo, and Brabantio. Strangely enough, even some traditional feminist readings do not recognise Desdemona's spiritual powers, and certain critical misgivings also appear in more modern interpretations. In Stephen Greenblatt's *Renaissance Self-Fashioning*, Othello's sexual anxiety is seen to be aroused by Desdemona's open nature and by Iago's insinuations about her licentious behaviour and the Venetian women's notorious wantonness. In her frank admission of love to the Moor, Greenblatt finds "the cause of Desdemona's death for it awakens the deep current of sexual anxiety in Othello, anxiety that with Iago's help expresses itself in quite orthodox fashion as the perception of adultery".[55] An attack on Greenblatt's theory of 'cultural poetics' comes from Graham Bradshaw's *Misrepresentations: Shakespeare and the Materialists* which aims at discovering the partiality of the new historicist and cultural materialist approaches, but Bradshaw's search for textual verities misses in the same scene the dramatic function of Desdemona's spiritual perceptivity: "Whatever Desdemona thought she was looking at when 'saw Othello's visage in his mind', she didn't see the mind of the murderer".[56] As the only character endowed with spiritual vision capable of discerning between the true and false game of ambiguity by pleading to God's judgement, Desdemona's role is charged with the redemptive powers of constancy and faith that are necessary for the final salvation of the Moor. Her 'amplifying' linguistic code is put into contrast with the 'attenuative', metalogical axis of Iago's rhetoric, based instead on duplicity and deception, as well as with Othello's spiritual blindness, once his 'tranquil mind' is infected by Iago's 'pestilence'. Unlike Cordelia's propensity for the rhetoric of silence, Desdemona's utterances carry out "an illocutionary force, characterized by a grave and solemn sense of sacrality and devotion which acts in the play with a marked and lasting epideictic and hierophantic action".[57] As opposed to Iago's incessant use of the tropes of negation and suspension, essentially conveyed along the axis of pragmatic communication, Desdemona's language is characterised by a massive presence of apodeictic affirmations, often tending towards a didactic purpose and operating on the level of lexicalised communication.[58] She performs this quality in the great Council scene, protecting Othello from the allegation of witchcraft moved by Brabantio's racial prejudice and patriarchal authority, in defence of Cassio in Act 3, and in the subsequent dramatic confrontation with the Moor. While the Iago-Desdemona dialectic operates from a distant symbolic level, the lady's exchanges with Othello offer concrete instances of moral and spiritual differentiation, through the already mentioned binary opposition of lexical terms, antithetical coupling, and rhetorical tropes. The religious and moral opposition between the two lovers climaxes in chiastic tensions, expressed on both a lexical and rhetorical level, giving evidence of an allegorical design brought forward by the characters' exchanges:

> *Oth.* Why, what art thou?
> *Des.* Your wife, my lord, your *true* and *loyal* wife.
> *Oth.* Come, swear it, damn thyself,
> Lest, being like one of *heaven*, the *devils* themselves
> Should fear to seize thee, therefore be double-damn'd,
> Swear thou art *honest.*
> *Des. Heaven* doth *truly* know it.
> *Oth. Heaven truly* knows, that thou art *false as hell.*
> (4.2.34–40)

The two lovers' rhetoric moves on two different but parallel planes which are necessarily related and therefore interdependent. Desdemona's sacrifice represents a victory over evil inasmuch as it leads to Othello's redemption, to his final recognition, and, consequently, to a re-establishment of a moral and spiritual order. Only from this perspective does her temporary resurrection hold a symbolical connotation, marking the victory of the spirit over the flesh, of the soul over the body, of divine powers over human frailties. The lovers' reunion is marked not only by the reversal of the deceitful world of disrupted and subverted values embodied in Iago and ideologically reproduced onstage by his blasphemous and oppositive language typical of other Machiavellian villains, but also by Othello's gradual process of resolution of the misleading game of antitheses and oxymorons which the Ancient's ambiguous rhetoric has implanted in his mind. For Desdemona's dying words acquire dramatic significance if uttered *for* Othello, for his moral salvation and catharsis; if they can arouse an unexpected, albeit tragic, denouement. That the conative appeal of Desdemona is addressed to the Moor is evident from the emphasis placed on the information and on who is to receive it: "O, falsely, falsely murder'd!" "A guiltless death I die", "Commend me to my kind Lord" (5.2.126, 132, 134). While several commentators have perceived in the lady's calvary an echo of the Christian myth of the Passion of Christ ("Father, forgive them; for they know not what they do", Luke, 23:34), it is surprising that Othello's subsequent reaction has generally passed unnoticed. After a moment of bewilderment following his wife's unexpected forgiveness, the Moor gradually returns to a rediscovery of his past chilvaric values by operating the resolution of the opposites and antitheses transmitted by Iago. The 'just grounds' on which he believes he has proceeded – ironically questioned by Emilia through the iterative use of correct terms on which the Moor had previously equivocated – prove mere calumny; and he takes cognisance of his tragic error, which at first appears to him only 'pitiful' but soon afterwards it becomes the sacrilege that will cast him into hell:

> *Oth.* You heard her say, herself, it was not I.
> *Emil.* She said so, I must needs report a *truth.*
> *Oth.* She's like a liar gone to burning *hell,*
> 'Twas I that killed her.
> *Emil.* O, the more *angel* she, and you the *blacker devil*!
> *Oth.* She turn'd to folly, and she was a whore.
> *Emil.* Thou dost belie her, and thou art a *devil.*
> *Oth.* She was *false* as water.
> *Emil.* Thou as rash as fire
> To say that she was *false*: O, she was *heavenly true*!
> (5.2.128–136)

Like Lear, Othello's anagnorisis leads him to the full awareness of his tragic mistake and coincides with the moral blessing of a discovered spiritual vision. In the attempt to punish the 'honest' Iago for his vicious deception, he gives evidence of having acquired Desdemona's capacity to penetrate into the world of seeming:

> *Oth.* I *look down* towars his feet, but that's a fable,
> If that thou be'st a devil, I cannot kill thee.
> (5.2.287–288)

The play's recurrent use of the verbs of perception has come full circle. The imagery of seeing which only Desdemona's perceptivity has translated from the common mistaken direction into the planes of truth and being passes on now to the Moor, signalling the woman's salvific function and Othello's symbolical reunion with his beloved. In contrast to the rationale of his source, as Marianne S. Adams put it long ago, "Shakespeare incorporated material from the tale for entirely divergent purposes".[59] Significant passages in Cinthio's story are evocative of Shakespeare's parallel variations, as when the ensign hints to the Moor, "I do not wish to come between man and wife, but if you would open your eyes you would see by yourself" and the commander echoes him thus: "If you do not make me see with my own eyes what you have told me, rest assured that I shall give you reason to know that it would have been better for you to have been born dumb".[60] While in Giraldi Cinthio's *Hecatommithi,* inspired by a Counter-Reformation spirit, the imagery of seeing focuses on the theme of a misguiding justice to illustrate the baleful effects of an interracial marriage, implicating a miscegenation prejudice which also informs the Venetian world and the characters in the play, Shakespeare's appropriation of the phrases and linguistic structure of his narrative source marks the rejection of the *novella*'s poetic justice that Cinthio's counter-reformist attitude has inherited from his age.

III. Ideology and politics in Italianate revenge drama

The studied arrangement of the Italian picture for hiding domestic anxiety and political opposition is applied more manifestly in most Jacobean and Caroline theatre. In Middleton's *Women Beware Women*, the Duke of Florence's residence is considered by the jealous-minded Leantio the place where "there is/As much redemption of a soul from hell/ As a fair woman's body from his palace" (3.2.331–333).[61] In a play dominated by female transgression as a refusal to submit to patriarchal norms which differentiate women's vices from men's, revenge is no longer and exclusively gendered male. Strong characterisations of vengeful heroines, exposing their crimes and passions as in Middleton, acquire a steady position as new subjects of tragedy, mirroring in the theatre the period's social change in the construction of female subjectivity.[62] Malevole, in Marston's *The Malcontent*, expresses a similar concept of male anxiety even more directly: "I would sooner leave my lady singled in a bordello than in the Genoa Palace" (3.2.30–31).[63] Disguised as the court malcontent, Malevole manifests his vision of the court world's corruption through a pattern of images of rising and falling which runs throughout the play.[64] Italian mischiefs and plottings are his main targets, and he comments on the freedom gained through his disguise thus:

> Well, this disguise doth yet afford me that
> Which kings do seldom hear, or great men use,–
> Free speech: and though my state's usurp'd,
> Yet this affected strain gives me a tongue,
> As fetterless as is an emperor's.
> (1.3.189–193)

Marston's satiric mode and sententious language, as reflected by the disguised observers of his experiments with Guarini's tragicomedy in *The Malcontent, Antonio and Mellida*, and *Antonio's Revenge*, may have borrowed from *Il pastor fido*, which was available by the so-called 'Dymock' translation since 1602. As Kevin Quarmby has pointed out, "The *Antonio* plays present royal disguise as a theatrical device designed to avert personal threat, as a means to restore ducal power and, ultimately, as an opportunity for bloody revenge".[65] Retaliation in its most violent forms also takes place in the dramas set in Italy, especially when it is carried out as retribution for political intrigue and social corruption. Drawing on the influence of Seneca and Italian Senecan-Boccaccian tradition, as exemplified by Giraldi Cinthio's ideology of horror in *Orbecche* (1541) and in his theory of *tragedia nova*, retaliation assumes on the English scene, even when it is executed by women, the semantic construction of an Italian vice, accomplished under the guise of excessive theatricality and gruesome sensationalism, resulting in what I have called "that kind of sadistic mockery enjoyed by the evil-doers and fashioned with such macabre effects as to appear perversely appealing on the stage".[66] As Giraldi's own tragedy explains to its readers:

> Né mi dèi men pregiar perch'io sia nata
> Da cosa nova e non da istoria antica:
> Che chi con occhio dritto il ver riguarda,
> Vedrà che senza alcun biasimo lece
> Che da nova materia e novi nomi
> Nasca nova Tragedia.
> (3171–3176)[67]

Marco Ariani identifies it as "the poetics of horror", becoming the main distinctive element of Giraldi's contribution to Italian tragedy as well as his most influential trait on the European stage.[68] For the Italian playwright this new approach is felt as a necessity for theorising about a form of tragedy differing from that of Aristotle, whose aesthetics of pathos is regarded as an inherent aspect of a renewed idea of catharsis, as stated in his *Discorso intorno al comporre delle commedie e delle tragedie* (1543):[69]

> Mi son risoluto che la tragedia ha anco il suo diletto, e in quel pianto si scuopre un nascosto piacere che il fa dilettevole a chi l'ascolta e tragge gli animi alla attenzione e gli empie di maraviglia, la quale gli fa bramosi di apparare, col mezzo dell'orrore e della compassione, quello che non sanno, cioè di fuggire il vizio e di seguir la virtù, oltre che la conformità che ha l'essere umano col lagrimevole, gli induce a mirar voluntieri quello spettacolo, che ci dà indizio della natura nostra e fa che l'umanità che è in noi ci dà ampia materia di aver compassione alle miserie degli afflitti.[70]

Interpreting Aristotle's doctrine of tragic catharsis in moral terms, Giraldi uses it – like Castelvetro – as a means to cleanse the passions of the spectator's mind, inducing him to become a better man by the crude exposure of violence (*scelus*).[71] Hence the necessity of exasperated realism, more aggressive and violent than that of Seneca and the parallel rejection of the fabulous, unnaturalistic world of the classical theatre, to reinforce the analogy between stage and life.[72] The horror effect upon the audience comes from the disproportion of the victim's punishment inflicted in a rhetorical game of studied theatricality, melting together the *fictio* of the story with the *actio* itself of *scelus*. The heroine Orbecche, guilty as Desdemona of filial disobedience to patriarchal authority, is given as a wedding present three silver vessels containing the head and hands of her husband and the mutilated bodies of her children. Sulmone's decision to spare his daughter's life but to show the *spettacol crudele* of her kinsmen's mutilated corpses is explained as a kind of didactic form of catharsis intended to promote compassion and expiation through horror in the inner and outer audience alike:

> Se l'uccido, fia fine al suo dolore;
> ché la morte a chi è miser, non è pena,
> ma fine de la pena e de l'angoscia.
> Però se viva ne riman costei
> e co gli occhi ambe due i suoi figli vegga
> morti e 'l marito, tal sarà l'affanno,
> che n'avrà invidia a que', che son sotterra;
> che d'ogni morte è via più grave sempre
> una infelice e miserabil vita.
> (3.3.51–59)

Orbecche's reaction is equally deceitful and spectacular. She pretends to be pleased at the perverse didacticism of his father's mocking jest and asks for capital punishment. Thinking he has obtained filial obedience, Sulmone forgives his daughter. But Orbecche's sudden repentance is only a mockery. She feigns to yield to her father's authority and even offers to punish herself, only to stab him to death. Then she chops off the king's head and hands and, addressing the mortal remains of her kinsmen, commits suicide.

The abundance of morbid outcomes in the performance of revenge dominates the venues in all *Cinquecento* tragedy, portraying onstage lurid stories of deceit, slaughter, mutilation, and cannibalism, often derived from Boccaccio's *Decameron* through the storyline of his most popular *novelle* where the *beffa* motif, after Giraldi's fashion, plays a pivotal role. Neither is all this unique. In Lodovico Dolce's masterpiece *Marianna* (1565), the eponymous heroine receives as a gift from her jealous husband a basin containing the head, heart, and severed hands of her presumed lover.[73] On the other hand, the history itself of contemporary Italy, as recounted by William Thomas's *Historie of Italy* and other historians, offered material for the spectacular treatment of retaliation. In Guicciardini's *Storia d'Italia* several stories of passionate love mixed with political intrigue, provide a suggestive combination of political plotting and transgressive eroticism, making an ideal bridge uniting passionate love and court corruption which the author himself defines "more trivial than the burning ambition to rule".[74]

In Tourneur's *The Revenger's Tragedy*, the representation of court corruption is shown as closely related to excessive sexuality. The court itself becomes "this unsunned lodge/Wherein 'tis night at noon … this luxurious circle" (3.5.18–22),[75] a locale for illicit relations, where Machiavellian plotting and counterplotting as well as all transgressive forms of lust such as adultery, rape, and incest are depicted as inherent aspects of the same process, which, in Dollimore's phrase, "involves an incessant drive for self-fulfillement through domination of others", culminating in dissolution and death.[76] The emblematic hero, Vindice, pursues throughout the play the secret desire to retaliate against the abuse and poisoning of his beloved, Gloriana. The Italianate mark of court corruption is symbolically centred on the idea of transgressive eroticism, depicting a stage world of "strange lust" (1.3.57), masked by Machiavellian dissimulation and from which revenge and counter-revenge originate:

> Oh hour of incest!
> Any kin now next to the rim o' the sister
> Is man's meat in these days, and in the morning,
> When they are up and dressed and their mask on,
> Who can perceive this, save that eternal eye
> That sees through flesh and all?
>
> (1.3.62–67)

The great scene of Vindice's retaliation on the Duke epitomises the revenge themes and is carried out with the same ironic jest as the Italianate revenger, unifying retribution with dramatic mockery. Acting as a pander for the Duke who believes he is being guided to a love meeting, Vindice makes him kiss the poisoned chops of Gloriana's skull. To accentuate the *beffa* on the Duke, he takes off his disguise and reveals the incest between the Duchess and her bastard son, Spurio. Then he forces the poisoned Duke to watch the actual love-making of the incestuous couple:

> Nay to afflict the more,
> Here in this lodge they meet for damned clips:
> Those eyes shall see the incest of their lips.
>
> (3.5.177–179)

The dreadful sight of incest constitutes an important part in Vindice's retaliation, and to be sure the Duke sees the lustful lovers, Vindice and his brother 'tear up' the Duke's eyelids to make him see the actual crime and die in despair:

> Brother,
> If he but wink, not brooking the foul object
> Let our two other hands tear up his lids
> And make his eyes, like comets, shine through blood.
> (3.5.194–197)

In Ford's *'Tis Pity She's a Whore*, Vasques's "Now you begin to turn Italian" (5.4.28) is meant to approve Soranzo's decision to seek vengeance, while Vasques himself triumphantly acknowledges his Italianate attitude at the conclusion: "I rejoice that a Spaniard outwent an Italian in revenge" (5.6.146–147).[77] Retaliation, therefore, in its most gruesome variations is perversely strengthened by acting a grotesque jest as a kind of ironic retribution. The scorn of the victims in John Webster's Italianate tragedies is so ingeniously carried on as to produce bizarre, almost laughable, effects. Revenge and counter-revenge in both *The White Devil* and *The Duchess of Malfi* appear thematically linked to the Italianate colouring of the local court, naturally flowing from it and presented as a common practice for the maintenance and exercise of power in Renaissance Italy. Hence retaliation is depicted in terms of a cynical, sophisticated, and spectacular strategy capable of enhancing the sufferings of the victims with mocking and sadistic gestures, and affecting the audience's imagination with an astonishing sequel of ironic shocks and *coups de théâtre*. Various aspects, elements, and features of typical revenge drama are defined as thoroughly 'Italian', and the relevant foreign setting is purposefully emphasised: "Italian cut-works" (1.1.52), "Italian means" (2.1.161), "Italian coast" (2.1.361), "Italian sallet" (4.2.61), "Italian beggars" (4.3.82), "Italian churchmen" (5.5.138), to refer only to *The White Devil*.[78]

Webster's tragedies in particular mostly radiate their resonance and theatrical strength if we place them against the background of Giraldi Cinthio's theoretical writings and dramatic works (a connection which in the case of *Orbecche* may also have arisen from its narrative version), reassessing the textual significance of his tendency towards intense gnomic verse and visual imagery. In Webster's concern with a grand rhetoric of moral spectacle and dumb-shows is in fact conveyed the idea of learning through scorn and suffering, especially transmitted by theatrical instances of sensational carnage, which the dramatist, notorious for his intertextual activity, may have borrowed from Cinthio's poetics of horror and his didactic tragic form. Guided by Counter-Reformation beliefs, Cinthio's theory of drama depicts a divinely ordered universe that offers the spectator shocking bloodshed with the benign exposure of the cruellest actions (*scelus*). In this philosophy of political dominion man is at the centre of the cosmos, and the individual tyrant appears as a microcosmic reflection of the whole, absorbing and exorcising the evils of the universe. Only in this condition may he act as a model, albeit altogether negative, of humanity, and as such his tragedy of vices and passions serves as a powerfully didactic and moral exemplum.[79] By contrast, Jacobean tragedy centres not on individual faults but on the idea – as the dying Bosola reports – of widespread corruption that characterises a "gloomy world", a "deep pit of darkness", where "Doth womanish and fearful mankind live!" (5.5.100–102).[80] A wave of general misguidance invests the vices of society at all levels, so that in the tragedies of Othello, Coriolanus,

Vittoria, Flamineo, and Bosola – as Jonathan Dollimore has put it – "we 'read' not the working of fate or God, but a contemporary reality which doth creates and destroys them".[81] To Webster, as well as to other Jacobean and Caroline dramatists, Italianate court is thus used as a cover for writing tragical satires exposing contemporary abuses at home, giving this theatrical mode a pervasive distribution among the London audiences of the period's intelligentsia during the growing and long dispute between Court and Parliament. In his *Tragedy of State*, J. W. Lever has suggested that the court of *The Duchess of Malfi* "presents in miniature the court of Whitehall, with its adventurers, its feverish pulling of strings for office and promotion, its heedless and heartless pursuit of privilege".[82] And Martin Butler has also numbered Italian-located Caroline drama among the commonest devices used by a certain type of court theatre which, "without openly bringing political events and issues on stage, alluded to them obliquely".[83] This political consciousness informs what Margot Heinemann has called "opposition drama" in the Puritan society of early Stuart England, implicating forms of social and political dissent which escaped censorship under the metaphorical concealment of the dramas and political satires set in, or associated with, Italy.[84]

The history itself of English language has attested how ideological positions reflect and get social resonance in the broad circulation of learning through sociolinguistic usages brought to light in the art of the theatre. As argued by various cultural and theatre historians, the Elizabethan misinterpretation of Machiavelli's *Il Principe*, mostly derived from the *Contre-Machiavel* by Gentillet as the portrait of an atheistic, deceitful ruler, was responsible for the pejorative meaning that 'policy', 'politic', 'politician', and derivatives, as synonyms for plotting, intrigue, and dissimulation, assumed in the works of Webster, Middleton, Tourneur, and in many other Tudor and Stuart plays.[85] This Italophobic prejudice, alongside the period's largely xenophobic writings and fictional travellers' reports, completes the evil side of the Italian picture, providing a perfect setting for both comedy and tragedy and contributing to the semantic construction of the Italianate court drama as a crossroads of multiple vices.

I would suggest that Webster epitomises, perhaps more eloquently than other dramatists, this period's use of Italy and its related fame as a wicked territory of vices. In *The White Devil*, the *beffa* motif recurs in the episode of the killing of Bracciano. After poisoning his helmet, Lodovico and Gasparo return disguised as Capuchins to bring him "the extreme unction" (5.3.38). Apart from the sharp irony of their feigned religious rite, clearly associated with the poisonous 'unction' sent from the Duke, their intention is to heighten Bracciano's anguish with the shocking revelation of their true identity. The scene provides a crescendo of mocking effects, starting from the sardonic jest of their religious Latin service (5.3.135–146) to the revelation of their real names and the listing of poisonous ingredients, up to the Duke's "true-love knot" (5.3.174) of their final strangulation when Bracciano attempts a desperate reaction. The very process of Bracciano's agony is signalled by a kind of frenzy during which the victim burst into horrid laughter, perceiving the end of his hope of salvation as well as that of Vittoria and her allied brother. Bracciano's inflicted torture is commented on as an Italian vice by Flamineo for the overflow of despair caused by the peculiar way the Duke of Florence commissioned his enemy's death:

> O the rare tricks of a Machivillian!
> He doth not come like a gross plodding slave
> And buffet you to death: no, my quaint knave,

He tickles you to death; makes you die laughing;
As if you had swallow'd down a pound of saffron–
You see the feat, – 'tis practis'd in a trice
To teach court-honesty it jumps on ice.
(5.3.193–199)

A few lines later, Francisco himself praises Lodovico for his cunning scorn towards the dying Bracciano:

Excellent Lodovico!
What! did yoy terrify him at the last gasp?
(5.3.212–213)

This same ironic jest is applied by the hired assassins in the episode of the final retaliation to Flamineo and Vittoria. Again, they enter disguised as Capuchins, announcing that they are bringing a revel which turns out to be a death masque, a sword-dance during which they execute the commissioned murder. But before the killing, they throw off their disguises and reveal that the Moor pensioned by Bracciano was indeed the Duke of Florence himself. Once again the *beffa* motif acts as a fundamental component of the revenge action and is employed to satisfy the perverse sense of moral retribution of the evil-doer. Significantly, Vittoria's last words denounce the duplicity of the court:

O happy they that never saw the court,
Nor ever knew great man but by report.
(5.6.261–262)

The Duchess of Malfi offers the most extraordinary linguistic and thematic affinities with Giraldi Cinthio's *Orbecche*. Ferdinand, the Duchess's tyrant brother, is clearly presented as sexually jealous of his sister, disclosing an incestuous passion similar to that of the tyrant Sulmone for his daughter. Both plays adopt the same rhetoric of animal imagery related to the voracity of the wolf and to the desparate fury of the tiger. Moreover, after the killing of the Duchess, Ferdinand's lycanthropy indicates, in his gradual metamorphosis into a corpse-devouring wolf, the incestuous erotic drive for his own flesh.[86] But it is in the great retaliation scenes of the Duchess's ordeal that we find the most effective linguistic and thematic similarities. The calvary of the Duchess is attentively prepared by Ferdinand. Feigning to be reconciled with his sister, like Sulmone does with his daughter, Ferdinand first gives her in the dark a dead man's hand bearing a ring, which she kisses as a sign of reconciliation. More satirically still, both hand and ring are left as a 'love-token' to the horrified lady. This macabre *beffa* becomes more outrageus when the Duchess is made to see the 'sad spectacle' of the artificial figures of her husband and children, "appearing as if they were dead" (4.1.55). Bosola's comments on the mocking scorn echo the perversely moral effects of Sulmone's *spettacol crudele*:

Look you: here's the piece from which 'twas ta'en:
He doth present you this sad spectacle
That now you know directly they are dead

Hereafter you may wisely cease to grieve
For that which cannot be recovered.
(4.1.56–60)

The systematic torture of the Duchess is completed by the madmen's masque by which Ferdinand aims to cure his sister's faults by bringing her to therapeutic despair:

Your brother hath intended you some sport:
A great physician, when the Pope was sick
Of a deep melancholy, presented him
With several sorts of madmen, which wild object,
Being full of change and sport, forc'd him to laugh,
And so th'imposthume broke: the self-same cure
The duke intends on you.
(4.2.38–44)

At the end of the madmen's dance, a final jest anticipates the actual murder. Bosola, disguised as a bellman, offers the lady the deadly instruments sent from the 'Arragonian brethren': a coffin, some cords, and a bell carried by 'Executioners':

Here is a present from your princely brothers,
And may it arrive welcome, for it brings
Last benefit, last sorrow.
(4.2.166–168)

Like the tyrant Sulmone, Ferdinand rejoices at his sister's suffering. The fact that "she's plagu'd in art" (4.1.111) reveals a secret passion for inflicting perverse punishment intended to scorn his victim's defences through shocking visual effects.

Wider social and political concerns may also be envisaged between Webster's and Giraldi's didactic vision of tragedy. One of the longest scenes in *Orbecche* is the dispute between the tyrant and the counsellor Malecche about the nature of kingship. This enables the Italian playwright to invite thought on the Renaissance debate about the ethics of power as it is portrayed in the dialectic between Sulmone and his counsellor. On the one hand, Sulmone represents the medieval tyrant who believes that he must prove himself to be pitiless and devoid of all compassion in punishing those who have offended him, since his godlike quality is exalted by his absolute power to inflict punishments. As Carla Bella has put it, "to be a *real* king means for him never to forgive".[87] A concept whose widespread diffusion in the early modern Puritan doctrine of royal authority is also proved by Shakespeare's political dialogue between Angelo and Escalus at the beginning of Act 2 in *Measure for Measure.*[88] On the other hand, Malecche – like Escalus – holds the Renaissance, Counter-Reformation view based on mercy and humane understanding of the faults of others. The more capable the king is of forgiving, the more exalted his kingly state, since the quality of mercy pertains to God's prerogatives, as Portia states in *The Merchant of Venice.* This lengthy sequence in *Orbecche* discloses the presence of a political level, which also for its extension in the play has been rightly considered "the centre of gravity of the representation, the very moment in which the court changes from the ideal place for courtly love … to a locale for a debate on power".[89] Despite the cultural differences between Italian and English early modern thinking and the influence of Seneca and the Machiavellian hero,[90] this political perspective bridges the gap between the ideological contents of *Orbecche* and the character of opposition drama of most Stuart plays in which the rubric of power, with its ancillary reflections on the topic of retaliation as an Italian vice, absorbs Italian dramatic tradition and the relevant humanist controversy about the rules of the tragic genre, as reflected in Giraldi's example of *tragedia nova*. For we can find in *Orbecche*, as brilliantly captured by Bruscagli, a subversive potential due to its particular dramaturgical technique, which founds its efficacy on the emotional impact that the horror scenes produce on the audience.[91] In so doing, Giraldi performs an operation of great theatrical awareness and, at the same time, attempts to affect incisively the sociopolitical reality of the age, warning his spectators about the consequences of evil and the abuse of absolute authority. It is certain that the heroine Orbecche, like Webster's Vittoria or the Duchess, is seen with sympathetic participation, which the play's strategy passes on to the audience. Giraldi theorised this successful operation of emotional transfer in his discussion of the didactic character of *tragedia nova*.

IV. Critical approaches to Italian literature and culture

While classical antecedents of both comedy and tragedy have been rediscovered in Robert S. Miola's two important volumes, focusing on Senecan theatricalism in the constitution of revenge drama and Plautus's and Terence's seminal variants of Roman New Comedic models,[92] the creative impact of Italian literature and culture on early modern England is nowadays acknowledged by the majority of scholars, who have charted the varying effects of this widespread influence. The constructive influence of Dante's poetics, from his *Vita Nuova* to *Divina Commedia*, along with the fruitful presence of Petrarca, Boccaccio, Machiavelli, and other Italian humanists, especially in the female embodiment of love and justice from Chaucer to Shakespeare's *The Merchant of Venice* and *Othello*, are examined in detail by Robin Kirkpatrick.[93] However, Dante's and Petrarch's visions of love are alternatively considered homogeneous and interchangeable for each other in contrast in the critics' opinion in relation to the resurgence of Renaissance poetry, ranging from the eve of Elizabethan sonnet sequences to the metaphysical lyrics and elegies of Donne and Milton. A lively critical debate on the issue is reported by Marco Andreacchio in this volume, which testifies to the rich variety of this duel aesthetic vision, whereas Shakespeare's poetic and dramatic works subvert the ideology of Petrarchism on many occasions, humanising the wordly passions and undermining the spiritual *virtù*.

The most comprehensive treatment of Dante's relationship to medieval ideas of authorship and authority throughout his entire oeuvre in the context of the larger European tradition can be found in Albert Russell Ascoli's *Dante and the Making of the Modern Author*.[94] Ascoli traces the evolution of Dante's progressive disruption of the traditional concepts of *auctor* and *auctoritas* in the face of his own quest of identity as a poet of vernacular language, from the early *Vita Nuova* and *canzoni* to the linguistic and political treatises of *De vulgari eloquentia* and *Monarchia*, up to the innovative use and function of *auctoritas* characterising the *Commedia* as a whole. The interlacing connections of literature with history, of individual identity with social order, and their relations to power and politics are also investigated in Albert Ascoli's wide-ranging collection of essays, *A Local Habitation and a Name*.[95] Covering the leading works of the most important humanists of the Italian literary tradition from Petrarca and Boccaccio to Machiavelli, Ariosto, and Tasso, Ascoli provides an in-depth and richly documented analysis of the relationship between literature and history, trenchantly illustrated in the productive encounter of Machiavelli's theatre with Ariosto's *commedia nova* via Boccaccio's *Decameron* and culminating in a final chapter on Tasso's *Gerusalemme Liberata*. While Machiavelli's comedies, as exemplified in *Clizia*, depart from Boccaccio's analogues in a radical way, discarding the normative Western tradition rather than returning to it, Tasso's Counter-Reformation ideals in the *Liberata*, in contrast with the use of madness as the best defence for death in the *Furioso*, transforms death, "and the silence that comes with it", into "the only alternative to an endlessly loquacious madness … freed from the ineluctable servitude of the unkeepable wow … from the horror of the many differences of which world and self alike are composed".[96]

In assessing the breadth of Petrarchan influence on early modern English poetry, though, we have to discern Petrarch's original oeuvre from the vogue of Petrarchism which affected the rise of sonnet writing throughout Europe. A similar phenomenon occurred in the case of Machiavelli, whose major work spread out in English culture through Gentillet's hostile distortion – *Discours Contre Machiavelli* (1576) – as a synonym of atheism, deception, and tyranny, generating the stock figure of the Italianate villain that his name evoked on the Elizabethan stage, as in the prologue of Marlowe's *The Jew of Malta*. Traditional sholarship assigns the discovery of the authentic Machiavelli only after *Il Principe*'s first English translation in 1640, though the Italian original was issued by Wolfe in 1584.[97] More recent studies have revalued the revisionist character of Machiavelli's literary and non-literary works in relation to humanist ideals and advocated the earlier circulation of *The Prince* in manuscript translations, arguing a broad dissemination in early modern England.[98] Alessandra Petrina's well-documented book provides detailed commentary of the annotated editions of two major extant manuscript versions, reassessing the importance of the Machiavellian presence in early modern political thought through the comparison of the texts with the Italian original as well as with French and Latin versions.[99] Machiavelli's literary output as playwright deserves to be treated apart, since his unconventional comedies stand out at the core of what I term "the Machiavelli-Aretino-Bruno axis" of radical drama, determining a significant shift in the parabolic deployment of Italian theatre, starting from the rise of Ariosto's *comedia nova* and ending with the anti-comedy of Bruno's *Candelaio*.

Boccaccio was widely known in seventeenth-century England both for his own *Decameron*, read in the original or in translation by several travellers to Italy, and widely rewritten or readapted in English by his numerous imitators, and for being the forerunner of a long story-telling European tradition. Herbert Wright's rich monograph, tracing the coeval appropriations in both medieval poetry and prose up to the legacy of eighteenth-century literature, is still fundamental for a thorough examination of Boccaccio's widespread influence on the plot construction of Renaissance drama and beyond.[100] Today we are more ready to recognise that early modern theatre developed, and indeed constructed, its dramatic structures by ransacking narrative lines from the novella tradition, and by combining these narremes, as Louise George Clubb has called them, with the theatregrams taken up from the wide repertory of *Cinquecento* drama, originating in turn from the domestic comedies of Plautus, Terence, and his followers.[101] Melissa Walter's chapter in this volume reviews in detail the long Anglo-Italian novella tradition, whose effects on the Renaissance rapidly spread throughout the continent via the adaptations and rewritings of the same stories reproduced in the collection of tales of a number of imitators, examining also the theatrical contributions in terms of gender class, social context, and female characterisation.

As I mentioned earlier, Machiavelli's two major comedies, *La Mandragola* (1518) and *Clizia* (1525), can be considered the first example of 'radical' theatre in the Italian cultural panorama. *La Mandragola* is an inspired blend of elements from Terence and Boccaccio, in which Boccaccio's contribution, as Ezio Raimondi has put it, is also linguistic, being "not so much in the space of the signifier as in that of the signified, as a configuration of events, a set of motifs, or a mixing of situations".[102] The play's subversive nature lies not only in the impudent subject of marital infidelity, already present in Boccaccio, but also in the complicity of the mother – the epitome of Catholic morality – who actively contrives to execute the plan. Ambiguity from the viewpoint of social and religious convention may also be observed when the husband, Nico, and mother-in-law approve of the idea that the man who is to lie with the wife, Lucrezia, must die. The doctrine of a utilitaristic and pragmatic view of life is an essential aspect of Machiavelli's revolutionary philosophy. The play's unconventional ideology is also recognisable in the compliant positions of the other characters: the friar, who complies with the situation to further promise of reward, and Lucrezia, who eventually agrees with hypocritical hesitancy to other assignations. This satirical mode, which invests all levels of society, is amply reflected in the satirical city plays of the Jacobean bourgeois theatre, including the comedies of Marston, Jonson, and Middleton. *Clizia* derives from Plautus's *Casina*, although it differs in its scurrilous and provocative mode flouting contemporary morality. Here the theatregram of the exchanged woman in the dark proves in the end to be a double trick at the expense of the inventor. The first is a failure (that of Nicomaco who hopes to possess, unbeknown to his wife, the young servant Clizia, whom his son loves), while the second is turned against the lewd old man (Nicomaco is compelled to lie with the boy Idrio, believing him to be Clizia). The original comic matrix of inspiration is not so much the Greek and Latin New Comedy as that "species of lay and profane theatre dressed up as a tale",[103] i.e. the *Decameron*, plundered by most playwrights of the day and transformed into that irreverent cynicism characterising the radical axis of Machiavelli, Aretino, and Bruno with its subversive erotic and antimoralising social content. Ariosto's more conformist genre of *commedia nova*, an evocative example of 'integrated' theatre, to use Giulio Ferroni's phrase, "is quite unlike that of Machiavelli's *Mandragola* or Bruno's *Candelaio*, which reveal a surprisingly disruptive critical force that is recognisable in the manner in which the 'public' structure is called into question and overturned".[104]

Aretino's theatre seems to be situated in a midway position, one that is both ambiguous and contradictory, between *commedia erudita*, strictly conforming to classical rules and motifs, and the radical swerve of Machiavelli and Bruno, whose comedic form in both structure and content breaks with tradition, disrupting hierarchical and gender roles with a powerful charge of transgressive sexuality and social satire. In *Cortigiana* (1526), Aretino produces a caricature portrait of court life in Rome and its affectations, with the Boccaccio-like use of the *beffa* against Master Maco, who desires to become a courtier so that he may aspire to a cardinalate, and Signor Parabolano, who is in love with a young woman. Maco is instructed how to pursue vice and to invert every positive attitude of society and the court, since corruption and free language were considered to be the exclusive prerogatives of the courtier. Parabolano goes to an amorous encounter with the strumpet Togna, a baker's wife, organised by the groom Rosso and the procuress Aluigia, but Togna, dressed as a man further to complicate matters, is mistaken for the woman whom Parabolano loves. The *beffa* of the bed-trick is ironically turned by the victim into an invitation to laughter for all the characters involved, including Togna's betrayed husband who in this way saves his reputation. Unconventional humour comes out from Togna's outspoken vindication of her sexual freedom to her husband:

> *Arcolano*. Ahi crudelaccia, perché m'hai tu tradito?
> *Togna*. Che vuoi ch'io faccia di quel che mi avanza, che io lo gitti ai porci?[105]

The play parodies two aspirations of the bourgeoisie of the time: erotic success and admission to court life. A more subversive intent is perhaps to be found in *Il Marescalco* (1533), a work in which the cross-dressing motif is related to the *beffa* at the expense of the misogynistic protagonist, who is obliged by the Duke to take a wife. The whole play develops this design by means of a series of comic episodes that culminate at court in the marriage with the page Carlo dressed as a woman. The transgressive aspect lies in the fact that the revelation of the jest fully satisfies the homosexual and misogynistic tendencies of the Marescalco, who willingly accepts the union with the boy. Aretino's comedy is one of the probable sources of Ben Jonson's *Epicoene, or the Silent Woman* (1609)[106] and a revealing intertext of Shakespeare's *The Taming of the Shrew*.[107]

Giordano Bruno's only theatrical work, *Candelaio* (1582), contains the three main stock types on which *Cinquecento* comedy is constructed in a sort of comical synthesis: the *senex amans* (Bonifacio), the alchemist (Bartolomeo), and the pedant (Manfurio), all of whom are equally duped because of the stupidity of their passions. The figure of the aged dotard is ridiculed by his transformation from a homosexual to heterosexual, inverting his libido from 'candle-maker' to 'ring-maker'; the alchemist is mocked because of his spasmodic search for the magic powder, the '*pulvis Christi*', which will turn everything into gold; while the pedant, as Borsellino has it, is "the most grotescque of all the incarnations of Bruno's polemical antiformalism".[108] Bruno was an opponent of Scholasticism and Aristotelianism and rails against scientific, philosophical, and religious orthodoxy, starting with the prologue, which consists of a series of impudent and caustic darts scattered throughout its various parts, passing from the ironic genre to satire, parody, and linguistic exuberance just for its own sake. Of all Italian prologues, Bruno's contains what can be considered the most innovative example. With its multiple distinction into caudate sonnet, dedication, argument, antiprologue, and propologue, and its exuberant verbal virtuosity, it represents a strong subversive challenge to all accepted conventions in both Italian and European theatrical traditions.

From the satire of *Poetaster* (1601), set in ancient Rome, to the sharp realism of such ironical London plays as *Bartholomew Fair* (1614) and *The Staple of News* (1626), Jonson's inductions and prologues seem to possess a strong Brunian spirit in the way they criticise society on all levels, from orthodox learning to the greed for wealth and power. In Webster's Induction to Marston's *The Malcontent* (1604), a notable case of dialogued prologue in imitation to Shakespeare's use in *The Taming of the Shrew*, the actor William Sly, in the part of a spectator, sits on a stool and talks with a tire-man and other players about the fortunes of the comedy with frequent bawdy puns and topical allusions to the rival Blackfriars company. Echoing the oxymoron of the title, Sly and Condell refer to it as "a bitter play", a tragicomedy, which "'tis neither satire nor moral, but the mean passage of history; yet there are a sort of discontented creatures that bear a stingless envy to great ones" (Induction, 51–54).[109] This kind of comical satire is akin in spirit to

Bruno's *Candelaio* and to the witty game of oppositions that inspires his epigraphic motto "In tristitia hilaris, in hilaritate tristis", resembling the one at the end of the speech "To the Reader", "Sine aliqua dementia nullus Phoebus", and the general use of mottoes in Marston's plays. Indirect allusion to Bruno is evident in Sly's reference to "the art of memory" (Induction, 102), which might recall Bruno's earliest memory work, *De umbris idearum*, published in London in 1582, and his opposition to the Ramist doctrines of memory.[110]

Without doubt, one of the many instances of Bruno's revolutionary ideology clashing with contemporary pinciples, reflecting all the subversive force of his opinions, is to be seen in the monologue pronounced by Vittoria. Here we find a polemical confutation of the dualistic Humanist-Renaissance doctrine of the *corpus mysticum* of the sovereign, as the prince's immortal part (the body politic) is denied in favour of the human or natural component (body natural):

> Non possiamo non far differenza fra il culto divino e quello di mortali. Adoriamo le sculture e le immagini, ed onoriamo il nome divino scritto, drizzando l'intenzione a quel che vive. Adoramo ed onoramo questi altri dei che pisciano e cacano, drizzando la intenzione e supplice devozione alle lor immagini e sculture, perché, mediante queste, premiino i virtuosi, innalzino i degni, defendano gli oppressi, dilatino i loro confini, conservino i suoi, e si faccino temere dall'aversarie forze: il re, dunque, ed imperator di carne ed ossa, si non corre sculpito, non val nulla.[111]

Another feature of Bruno's comedy, interspersed in the dialogue between the characters, is the frequent recourse to irreverent and caustic story-telling, in a more extended and innovative form compared with contemporary uses in Italian drama, a practice which will become a common theatrical expediency on the English stage, especially in the Jacobean satirical tragedies and city comedies of Webster, Jonson, and Middleton. A notorious example is the apologue of the Lion and the Ass recounted by Sanguino to Vittoria in the fifth scene of Act 2 of *Candelaio*:

> Era un tempo che il leone e l'asino erano compagni; ed andando insieme in peregrinaggio, convennero che, al passar de' fiumi, si tranassero a vicenna: com'è dire, che una volta l'asino portasse sopra il leone, ed un'altra volta il leone portasse l'asino. Avendono, dunque, ad andar a Roma, e, non essendo a lor serviggio né scafa né ponte, gionti al fiume Garigliano, l'asino si tolse il leone sopra: il quale natando verso l'altra riva, il leon, per tema di cascare, sempre più e più gli piantava l'unghie ne la pelle, di sorte che a quel povero animale gli penetrorno in sin all'ossa. Ed il miserello, come quello che fa professione di pazienza, passò al meglio che poté, senza far motto. Se non che, gionti a salvamento fuor de l'acqua, si scrollò un poco il dorso, e si svoltò la schena tre o quattro volte per l'arena calda, e passoron oltre. Otto giorni dopo, al ritornare che fecero, era il dovero che il leone portasse l'asino. Il quale, essendogli sopra, per non cascar ne l'acqua co i denti afferrò la cervice del leone: e ciò non bastando per tenerlo su, gli cacciò il suo strumento, – o, come vogliam dire, il …, tu m'intendi, – per parlar onestamente, al vacuo, sotto la coda, dove manca la pelle: di maniera ch'il leone sentì maggior angoscia che sentir possa donna che sia nelle pene del parto, gridando: "Olà, olà, oi, oi, oimé! olà, traditore!" A cui rispose l'asino, in volto severo e grave tuono: "Pazienza, fratel mio: vedi ch'io non ho altr'unghia che questa d'attaccarmi". E cossì fu necessario ch'il leone suffrisse ed indurasse, sin che fusse passato il fiume.[112]

Among many examples in Jacobean theatre, Webster's use of sententious language and mottoes is conspicuous. *The White Devil*'s "Princes give rewards with their own hands/ But death or punishment by the hands of others" (5.6.188–189) and "O happy they that never saw the court/Nor ever knew great man but by report" (5.6.261–262) are perhaps the most significant. In *The Duchess of Malfi*, Ferdinand's tale of reputation to the Duchess recalls Bruno's theatrical appropriation of the function of the art of story-telling in his comedy:

> Upon a time, Reputation, Love, and Death
> Would travel o'er the world; and it was concluded
> That they should part, and take three several ways:
> Death told them, they should find him in great battles,
> Or cities plagu'd with plagues; Love gives them counsel
> To inquire for him 'mongst unambitious shepherds,
> Where dowries were not talk'd of, and sometimes
> 'Mongst quiet kindred that had nothing left
> By their dead parents: "Stay", quoth Reputation,
> Do not forsake me; for it is my nature
> If once I part from any man I meet
> I am never found again.
>
> (3.2.122–133)

Bruno's philosophical and literary output has long produced an intense critical debate among scholars in both the Italian and international forum, which is impossible to synthesise here. The reader will find a rich survey, not limited to reassessing the breadth of Bruno's influence on early modern English culture, in Gilberto Sacerdoti's chapter in the present collection.[113]

V. Prospects of future developments

In the attempt to investigate the dramatic effects of the cultural forces and ideological motivations operating in Anglo-Italian transactions, new critical approaches have questioned the traditional method of the past, often marred by the simplistic debate on slavish imitation and xenophobia, limiting the analysis almost exclusively to a scrutiny of a passive absorption of literary sources. In contrast with the old historical vision of the idea of a borrowed model, albeit artistically rearranged by Elizabethan dramatists, more recent studies are interested in the variegated ways in which the exploitation of Italian culture is deeply rooted in the processes of ideological transformation, implicating questions of political negotiation, antagonism, and opposition.

Following these lines of dissemination, new historicist critic Stephen Greenblatt revisited the subject of Anglo-Italian and European transactions, bringing to light a difficult, formidable, and hard-fought process of trasformation that he termed "cultural" and "theatrical mobility". At the heart of the mobility approach lies the idea that early modern theatre is a transnational phenomenon which, by its very nature, englobes in itself both national and international customs and theatrical practices in a productive antagonism between 'contact zones' and border-crossing exchanges or movements, compounding different social, artistic, and cultural traditions. "Mobility studies", Greenblatt contends, "should be interested, among other things, in the way in which seemingly fixed migration paths are disrupted by the strategic acts of individual agents and unexpected, unplanned, entirely contingent encounter between different cultures".[114] This encounter is never neutral or painless; on the contrary, it is marked by an anxiety of national identity and strong ideological confrontation:

> Mobility often is perceived as a threat – a force by which traditions, rituals, expressions, beliefs are decentered, thinned out, decontextualized, lost. In response to this perceived threat, many groups of individuals have attempted to wall themselves off from the world or, alternatively, they have resorted to violence.[115]

As a consequence, western Renaissance civilisation, through its prominent writers, artists, and thinkers, reacted against medieval and humanist traditions, often inverting the epistemic convictions through a hidden work of transgression and subversion of their reassuring ideologies. Although operating on diverse levels of awareness and different fields and genres, Shakespeare and Bruno, but also Machiavelli, Aretino, and Caravaggio,[116] are all interrelated by the same spirit of innovation and experimentation that produced a decisive swerve towards human thinking, erasing the constraints of literary conventions and making their own way from past to contemporary culture within a broader international context. As Greenblatt has pointed out:

> Shakespeare's imagination worked by restless, open-ended appropriation, adaptation, and transformation. He was certainly capable of making stories up on his own, as in *A Midsummer Night's Dream*, but he clearly preferred picking something up ready-made and moving it into his own sphere, as if the phenomenon of mobility itself gave him pleasure. And he never hinted that the mobility would now have to stop: on the contrary, he seems to have deliberately opened his plays to the possibility of ceaseless change.[117]

To follow up Greenblatt's proposals regarding generic innovations in Shakespeare's poetic and dramatic output, other radical changes in Renaissance culture may be taken productively into account. In most of his plays, the conversion of recurring theatregrams of Plautine and Terentian derivation, rehandled in Boccaccio's narremes and in the plot structures of *comedia* (in its threefold expression as *erudita, grave*, and *all'improvviso*) is evidence of the dramatist's capacity to transform old models into new forms, even through a reversal of their original ideological matrices. Senecan revenge tragedy, so popular in Elizabethan England, achieves its most revolutionary outcome in *Hamlet*, in the tragic hero's overturning of the convention of the avenger tradition.[118] Theology, either Protestant or Catholic, either endowed with Reformist or Counter-Reformist spirit, represented the hard core for any deviant, non-conformist behaviour. In one of his most celebrated sonnets, Shakespeare even subverts the basic Catholic belief in the primacy of the soul, questioning man's spiritual growth as placed against the body's "rebell powres", thereby lamenting earthly suffering and physical decay on behalf of the soul's election. As Rosalie Osmond has argued, the body–soul conflict originates from the ancient confrontation between Platonism, "which saw body and soul as opposed entities, and Aristotelianism, which saw them as differing in function but mutually necessary and complementary".[119] A similar distinction was held by Christian theology between Augustine's dichotomy in which the soul and body war is a consequence of the Fall of Adam, and Aquinas's more composite view, which regarded the prerogatives of both entities as interdependent and complementary. Aquinas's unified vision of man was abandoned in the Reformation in favour of the Augustinian thought, and both Calvin and Luther restored the common tenet that maintained the body–soul dualism as two contrary elements, one physical and mortal, the other immaterial and immortal.[120] In Sonnet 146, Shakespeare disrupts this long-established belief, demonstrating the contrariety to any credence to dogmatic thinking. In the opening octave of the poem, we may read the most disquieting interrogation of seventeenth-century poetry, "a dramatic meditation on the ethics of religion", in Giorgio Melchiori's phrase,[121] about the eschatological mystery of human life and a revolutionary challenging of the reassuring principles of the primacy of the soul – a concept more akin to Bruno's antidogmatic Copernicanism than to the legacy of Christian theology:

> Poore soule the center of my sinfull earth,
> My sinfull earth these rebell powres that thee array,
> Why dost thou pine within and suffer dearth
> Painting thy outward walls so costlie gray?
> Why so large cost hauing so short a lease,
> Dost thou vpon thy fading mansion spend?
> Shall wormes inheritors of this excesse,
> Eate vp thy charge? is this thy bodies end?[122]

As brilliantly captured by Melchiori, the dual meaning of "thy bodies *end*" (i.e. the end and/or the purpose) is the pivotal centre of the entire sonnet, charging the second hemistich's dramatic ambiguity with an unsettling question about the ultimate reason of man's existence, upsetting centuries of undisputed religious doctrine:

> [t]he poem starts from the traditional view of the centrality of the Soul, enclosed in the prison of the Body, only to expose its fallacy by a series of transitions which leave us in the end with poor unaccommodated and sinful man as the centre of a hostile and murderous universe, where the only certainty–the certainty of death–is provided by the Body … The poet knows how unworthy the rebels (men) are, and tries to judge them objectively, to withdraw his sympathy–but the fact remains that they are the one thing he really knows for certain and cares for, since he is one of them.[123]

Shakespeare's natural aversion to any form of fixed, established ideas pinpoints a significant reaction against the conviction of absolute authority in all fields of social, religious, and political life. Greenblatt elsewhere discerns the dramatist's contrariety to absolute values across the multiple genres of his production – the 'anti-Petrarchan' blazon of the *Sonnets*, the unconventional metadramatic form of *Othello, Measure for Measure*, and *The Tempest* – with an unconstrained artistic freedom, by focusing respectively on the four underlying related concerns of Shakespeare's poetic imagination:

> [b]eauty – Shakespeare's growing doubts about the cult of featureless perfection and his interest in indelible marks; negation – his exploration of murderous hatred;

> authority – his simultaneous questioning and acceptance of the exercise of power, including his own; and autonomy – the status of artistic freedom of his work.[124]

In parallel fashion, discarding traditional divisions among the arts, Kristin Phillips-Court, in an important study of the instructive conjunction between Renaissance theatre and pictorial art, speaks of "permeability" and "visual representation", identifying in these concepts and innovative practices "a number of different cultural, social, and psychological interrelationships that derive from painting's lasting cognitive structures and cultural resonances".[125] Phillips-Court indentifies in Bruno's literary works, especially in the *Candelaio*, "an intellectual and artistic culture that focused intently on representation and illusion, on how different points of view revealed different data, and on the role that human perception played in the search for truth".[126] This is a seminal work that has enlarged the critics' perception of the vast influence of the artistic genre on the literary and theatrical world.

Pursuing the same trajectory as Phillips-Court or Stuart Sillars's similar book,[127] searching out the fertile *paragone* of the sister arts in Renaissance drama, Shakespeare's adoptions of visual strategies in the theatrical *actio* of the performance, either explicitly or implicitly inscribed in the texture of his works, are treated with some breadth in the present writer's collection of essays, *Shakespeare and the Visual Arts: The Italian Influence*.[128] Profiting from the freshly mentioned concepts of cultural mobility and permeability between cultures in the early modern period, part of the chapters in this volume deal with the intermediality between Shakespearean theatre and the visual arts, studying drama as a hybrid genre that combines the figurative power of imagery with the plasticity of the performance, reaching an ingenious interchange. Another group of chapters reveal the three-dimensional quality of the dramatic discourse in the verbal-visual interaction and establish the natural legacy of the iconographical *topoi* of painting's cognitive structures, thus extending the theory of theatrical mobility to the field of pictorial arts and their social-cultural resonance. Considering the relationship between Renaissance material art, theatre, and emblems as an integrated and intermedial genre, the volume explores the use and function of Italian visual culture in Shakespeare's oeuvre and questions the appropriation of the arts in the production of the drama of Shakespeare and his contemporaries.

In the same field of the intermedial conjunction among the arts, Keir Elam's recent monograph, *Shakespeare's Pictures*, inquires into the subleties and ambiguities of Shakespeare's various references to visual culture, in the form of physical pictures, miniature portraits, and other materials or images in most of his plays, and explains how, why, and to what extent this regular presence interacts with and integrates the verbal-visual quality of the acting process.[129] The book is a mine of insightful observations about the role of picture tropes and image-making in the ekphrastic language of drama, providing close reading analyses replete with penetrating remarks which illuminate Shakespeare's strategic use of visual objects, whether physically or verbally signalled in the text, in a number of crucial sequences, in the attempt "to place the chosen pictorial moments in the drama at the point of intersection between the competing discourses of visual culture, dramatic and literay poetics and performance".[130] The different modes and materials present in Shakespeare's visual culture encompass paintings, engravings, drawings, miniatures, tapestries, needleworks, emblems, medals, coins, and statues, affecting the materiality and the imaginary level of the performance. While in the text a reference to a visual object is a verbal event, in performance the material picture as a stage prop or allusion "takes on potentially a quite different, non-verbal, dimension, becoming part of the visible stage world of bodies, of objects and of costumes, its material and semantic neighbours",[131] contributing with its ekphrastic description to all the underlying meanings of the dramatic action.

In dealing with the general subject of Shakespeare's appropriation of Italian culture, recent scholarship has also focused on the mutual perspective of a reciprocal confrontation, positing Anglo-Italian relationships alongside the rest of European countries and beyond, and charting their effects with sophisticated analyses starting from the early Renaissance to the media of the contemporary world. In *Shakespeare's Italy and Italy's Shakespeare*,[132] Shaul Bassi addresses the cultural difference of Italy as a social and political encounter of conflicting 'country dispositions', investigating the playwright's Italian plays and Italian afterlife through the categories of place, race, and politics, observed outside the national boundaries of the Anglosphere in a new globalised culture. The confrontation of cultures as a bilateral process of appropriation, exploitation, and divergence helps us to discern the elements of dislocation, opposition, and subversion detectable both in his culture and through ours. This dualistic method allows Bassi to delve into significant examples of ideological appropriations, ranging from such topics as the politics of Italian adaptations under the Fascist regime to the new implications of Machiavelli and Giordano Bruno; from a philosophical approach to *Hamlet* by the neo-Marxist intellectual Massimo Cacciari, to a reconsideration of Venice as a unique place of opposing ideological values, up to a rewarding discussion of the drama film by the Tavani brothers' *Caesar Must Die*, regarding the Rebibbia Prison performance of *Julius Caesar* by Italian convicts. A possible danger of this ideologically minded, post-colonialist research work is that while we learn much about the second term of the chiastic subject – the Italian use and exploitation of Shakespeare's output – probably much less is our understanding of what the playwright made of Italy and the structurally meant, metatheatrical constructions of his Italian-based dramas.

A rewarding attempt to digest the interdisciplinary and transhistorical aspects of the relations between Italian culture and the English world up to contemporary Britain, moving beyond conventional source study to a bilateral process of cultural exchange, and tracing a common thread which combines the early modern perspective with the present age's intermedial appropriations, may be found in Enza De Francisci and Chris Stamatakis's collection of essays, *Shakespeare, Italy, and Transnational Exchange.*[133] The editors have grouped the chapters into three sections of rather broad categories, ranging from the dialogues and networks of the early Anglo-Italian Renaissance, the creative process of translation and rewriting of the eighteenth and nineteenth centuries, up to the cultural transformations and the media adaptations of the present century. This is a line of critical investigation that may open up new interesting horizons of research, bridging the gap between the historical distance of the past and our age's engagement with all forms of media transformations and adaptations of the Shakespeare canon.

Perhaps the most stimulating prospects for future studies in Anglo-Italian scholarship may come from the critical inquiries into the transnational encounter of differing theatrical practices, inside and outside Europe, brought to the fore by two collections of essays, both edited by Robert Henke and Eric Nicholson: *Transnational Exchange in Early Modern Theatre* and *Transnational Mobilities in Early Modern Theatre.*[134] Each volume examines in detail early modern drama as an international phenomenon, considering cultural and theatrical exchanges across national and regional divides, and investigating the forms of contacts that reciprocally communicate beyond the borders through material and performative vehicles. The essays in the first collection explain the transnational openness of the book's title by questioning material, systemic, and historical reasons. These overcome the limited concept of national identity through the different strategies of the travelling acting companies, the (re)generated systems of early modern theatregrams operating by distinct cultures, and the actual historical conditions that favoured the representation of the foreigner within various regional realities. In the attempt to combine different kinds of comparative and transnational methods of analysis, the book aims to construe a unified theory of transnational exchange, demonstrating "that national identity in the early modern period was often porous, hybrid, and dialogically developed in concert with 'foreign' national/regional identities – and that theater was a particularly rich medium for exploring transnational and multiple national identity".[135]

This wider international viewpoint on the productive interchange between diverse theatrical traditions inside and outside the Continent is confirmed and brought forward in the essays of the second collection. By focusing on a major theatre-centred interest that engages in a fruitful confrontation with the material world of live theatre, investigating such items as the actor's body, staging devices, performance practices, clothing, translation theory, and actor–audience relationships, *Transnational Mobilities* provides a substantial platform of rewarding contributions, combining together systemic, material, and theoretical approaches to the subject of early modern theatre, studied comparatively without the limiting confines of national borders and isolated cultural traditions. Drawing on the Greenblattean theory of mobility perspective and distancing Anglo-Italian exclusive approaches, this wide-ranging vision allows the editors to extend "the theatergram concept into the realm of the 'performance text', addressing phenomena such as transportable actors' gags and foreign-produced costume accessories", studying and classifying "how values, properties, and identities are gained, lost, reversed, or transformed as a material or symbolic unit crosses borders".[136] Examining the rich dissemination of Anglo-Italian theatregrams, performance practice, and narrative units in the wider transnational context, the material mobility across cultures encompasses therefore the gestural and other extra-verbal modes of different theatrical modules and genres, including those of the travelling *comici* of the *commedia dell'arte*, the narremes of the novella tradition, and, last but not least, the iconographical *topoi* of painting's cognitive structures. Hence the book's implied suggestion that transnational mobilities incorporate what we may call 'acting-grams', 'novella-grams', 'costumes- and picture-grams' across contact zones of influence, compliance, and resistance, operating among geo-linguistic borders on the material, systemic, and symbolical levels. This totalising, wide-ranging approach to Anglo-Italian Renaissance studies with its open international vision towards European and extra European cultures is probably the best augury for future research.

VI. This volume: Part 1

The aim of this Companion is to provide scholars and advanced graduate students with a comprehensive and authoritative state-of-the-art review of current research work on Anglo-Italian Renaissance studies. Written by a team of international scholars and experts in the field, the chapters are grouped into two large areas of influence and intertextuality, corresponding to the dual way in which early modern England looked upon the Italian world from the English perspective – Part 1: "Italian literature and culture" and Part 2: "Appropriations and ideologies". In the first part, prominent Italian authors, artists, and thinkers are examined as a direct source of inspiration, imitation, and divergence. The variegated English response to the cultural, ideological, and political implications of pervasive Italian intertextuality, in interrelated aspects of artistic and generic production, is dealt with in the second part. Constructed on the basis of a largely interdisciplinary approach, the volume offers an in-depth and wide-ranging treatment of the multifaceted ways in which Italy's material world and its iconologies are represented, appropriated, and exploited in the literary and cultural domain of early modern England. For this reason, contributors were asked to write essays that not only reflect current thinking but also point to directions for future research and scholarship, while a purposefully conceived bibliography of primary and secondary sources and a detailed index round off the volume.

Marco Andreacchio's opening chapter to Part 1 provides a survey of the most representative critical views of Dante and Petrarch by contemporary scholarship, especially with regard to the distinction between ideological and psychological readings of the philosophical concept of love in both authors. To the historicist approach the former pertains to Petrarch's objective particularity, while the latter is ascribed to Dante's subjective universality, opening up a lively debate among scholars centring on the very essence of *Trecento* poetry, and involving Petrarchismo, medieval and contemporary interpretations, and early modern English receptions from Chaucer to Shakespeare. More recent studies tend to highlight a typically Anglican reorientation of lyric poetry, distancing the Italian idealisations of the female object, exposing the emotive, even carnal, dimension of love, and confronting these different dimensions in the search for a historical synthesis. Dante's and Petrarch's different idealisations of love, throughout their work, in relation to the woman's heavenly sublimation and earthly/carnal dimension, remains at the heart of the matter, dividing Dante's more intellectual position from Petrarch's existential vision.

Boccaccio has enjoyed a long fortune in Europe, from the early fifteenth to the late seventeenth century and beyond, both as the forerunner of a multifaceted novella tradition and as a fertile producer of seminal plot-lines for the theatre which he took, arranged, and adapted in his *Decameron* from Plautus's and Terence's exemplars of Roman New Comedy. In her detailed and exhaustive examination of critics' different opinions in regard to Boccaccio's *Decameron* and theatricality, Janet Smarr traces the development of an intense scholarly investigation which has debated and variously explained the theatrical quality of Boccaccio's *novella*, together with his widespread influence on the construction of Renaissance drama in both Italy and early modern England. In the *Decameron*'s *contaminatio* of different theatregrams of Plautine and Terentian derivation lies Boccaccio's extraordinary capacity for imprinting a theatrical mode to his narrative, thus providing early modern dramatists with a pliable combination of tragic and comic, moral and indecent set-pieces, modules, and sequences, to be ingeniously taken from a mixed selection of different tales and adjusted for the main plots and subplots of both comedies and tragedies.

The birth of the *commedia erudita* in Italy, based on the acquisition of classical and Roman antecedents, which Ariosto called *commedia nova*, due to its learned mixture of plots and situations taken up from a *contaminatio* of Plautine and Terentian theatregrams, can be considered the very essence and structure of all subsequent theatrical forms in

Renaissance Italy. All dramatic genres and sub-genres, developing throughout the pre- and post-Counter-Reformation period – *commedia dell'arte, commedia grave*, and pastoral drama – are dependent on the *commedia erudita*, whose established, regular composition of seminal theatregrams is also visible in the reduced three-act format of improvised theatre. Louise George Clubb's masterly exposition of the theatrical origins and generic transformations of *commedia erudita* charts chronologically the various stages of this artistic phenomenon through the social, historical, and religious events which marked the private and public life of Renaissance Italy. Constructed on the ingredients and types of the urban middle-class characters from Roman New Comedy – *senex and adulescens amans, servus correns, servus scaltrus, meretrix, matrona, miles gloriosus, parasitus, leno*, etc., and moved by love, hunger, and avarice, the *commedia erudita* engaged in the "domestic struggle of youth with age, in plots woven by clever servants towards the victory of young lovers over mercenary parents or foolish elderly rivals". Interestingly, the chapter examines the transformations undergone in the period's theatrical practice by the most recurrent theatregrams – misplaced love, sexual disguise, cross-dressing, mistaken identities, presumed death, bed-trick, etc., in the wake of the new spirit and taste arising from the Council of Trent.

Machiavelli's theatre has received much less attention than his philosophical and political works, under the assumption that little or nothing can be grasped from his comedies which might illuminate the total breadth of Machiavelli's output. Duncan Salked's chapter examines the two extant comedies of *Mandragola* and *Clizia*, and the accurate translation of Terence's *Andria*, in light of the prose writings, particularly *The Prince* and *The Discourses*. Salked focuses his analysis on the use of the concepts of *fortuna, necessità*, and *virtù*, which reveal the philosophical centre around which the innovative, and to some extent, radical ideology of Machiavelli's comedies take place. In the general sense, *virtù* is the ability of man to take control of the deceptive course of fortune, an intellectual power acting along with the collaborative assistance of necessity, that in the comedies is assigned to women, demonstrating the author's disruption of fixed gender hierarchies. Evidence of the central role attributed to Machiavelli's experiments with learned comedy comes from many recent scholarly interpretations reviewed in detail in the chapter's conclusions, tracing the legacy of the comedies' ideas into English Renaissance drama, including Shakespeare.

The origin of tragedy in the early Renaissance in Italy and elsewhere in Europe coincides with the discovery of Seneca, whose works were translated, imitated, and compared with the great Greek antecedents. In a detailed and in-depth analysis of the rise of tragedy in both Italy and England, Mario Domenichelli traces the course of a long tradition which has offered manifold examples of tragic structures marked with a strong Senecan character. He also examines the subsequent theoretical debate over the modules of the tragedic style which took place among the humanists and theatre historians of the Renaissance. The translation of *Seneca His Tenne Tragedies* by Thomas Newton in 1581, collected in a quarto volume, published by Thomas Marsch, marks an important date from which a long Senecan tradition began in England, starting with *Gorboduc, or Ferrex and Porrex*, written by Thomas Norton and Thomas Sackville, and followed by Thomas Kyd's *The Spanish Tragedy*, the most popular and influential of Elizabethan revenge tragedies. Domenichelli charts the structural characteristics of Seneca's poetics of horror in both themes and style, along the temporal arc of the revenge play tradition on the Elizabethan, Jacobean, and Caroline stage, while pointing to the stage violence and corrupted evil characters of such dramatists as Chapman,

Webster, Marston, Tourneur, and Middelton. Domenichelli concludes his analysis with John Ford's *'Tis Pity She's a Whore*, whose provocative representation of incest as heroic love is the scandalous triumph of the perfection of body and soul against the world of devilish court corruption in which the story is set.

The rapid dissemination in early modern English culture of the conduct books of the Italian Renaissance, Baldassare Castiglione's *Il Libro del Cortegiano* (1528), Giovanni della Casa's *Galateo* (1558), and Stefano Guazzo's *Civil Conversazione* (1574), respectively translated by Thomas Hoby (1561), Robert Peterson (1576), and George Pettie (1581), and sometimes published alongside the parallel versions of other languages, namely Latin, Spanish, or French, testifies, in Cathy Shrank's richly documented chapter, to the popularity of Italian courtesy literature among the courtiers, poets, and playwrights of Elizabethan England. Some distinctions, however, must be made among the three works with regard to style, local ambience, and different ways of communicating with the reader. While Castiglione's interlocutors are all courtiers and their conversation takes place in a room of a palace, Guazzo and especially della Casa have a more extensive setting. Guazzo's dialogue is also more wide-ranging and his interlocutors belong to a more quotidian ambience of mercantile audience in both the domestic and public spheres, quite unlike the exclusive ambience of Castiglione's court palace in Urbino. Conversely, della Casa's *Galateo* addresses a wider audience, "a worke very necessary & profitable for all Gentlemen, or other", as the title-page of the first English translation states. Also, *Galateo* differs from the other two works in its focus on male readers, in the perspective of an old man addressing a younger, whereas both the *Courtier* and *Civil Conversation* offer extensive discussions of female behaviour. Other crucial differences pertain to form and style. While *Galateo* is monovocal, addressed from an older to a younger man, the *Courtier* and *Civil Conversation* are dialogues in the form of a well-devised conversation, "in which ideas are not merely propounded, but are also debated". The popularity of these works, however, created a sort of anxiety of national identity for the apish tendency of English culture to generate 'Italianate Englishmen'.

The influence of Ariosto on Elizabethan England has produced a long critical tradition which debated how his poetic and theatrical output penetrated into English culture through numerous adaptations and translations. Selene Scarsi traces the fortune of Ariosto's *Orlando Furioso* through the earliest, partial rendition of selected episodes and Harington's first translation of the entire text. The chapter examines the appropriation of the Ginevra and Bradamante episode from the *Furioso*, which is also a remote source for Shakespeare's *Much Ado About Nothing*, in Beverley's, Whetstone's, and Spenser's different adaptations. Unlike the earliest two renditions, Spenser's version is much condensed and focuses on the celebration of temperance. Ariosto's story is reduced to its barest essentials in the direction of a consistent stress on the negative effects and passions of intemperance. In so doing, Spenser displays an intimate knowledge of Ariosto's poem, being "able to interpret, modify, intertwine, and elaborate on episodes, characters, passages as he feels appropriate to what and whom he is writing". The chapter concludes with a skilful synthesis of Harington's misogynistic changes in his complete translation of the *Furioso*.

Richard Andrews's chapter aims to explain how professional Italian *comici* operated, and what they performed, in the seminal period of improvised theatre which dates approximately between 1550 and 1630, and to what extent Italian troupes influenced English drama. Andrews perceptively offers a revised view of what the practice of 'improvisation' actually entailed and argues that the dramas which Italian *comici* were performing included a wide variety of genres and of emotional tones, not just the farcical slapstick comedy which the visual records tend to emphasise. Moreover, in the period under examination, material which was used in improvised scenarios was based on what was also to be found in fully scripted Italian plays – there was no firm distinction between what was offered to audiences by the two performing methodologies. After charting the roles and styles of the major *commedia dell'arte* masks, the chapter stresses how improvised drama and troupes were not separated from plays written by more academic dramatists. Much of the improvised material was recycled, adapted, and rearranged from fully scripted original plays and then transformed in regular five-act forms by current playwrights.

Giordano Bruno's fame was widespread throughout Renaissance Europe. From 1583 to 1585 he lived in England, where he wrote some of his most famous works, including *The Expulsion of the Triumphant Beast*, dedicated to Philip Sidney in 1584. Gilberto Sacerdoti persuasively retraces the stages of Bruno's life in Elizabethan England, reviews the contacts and contrasts he had with London and Oxonian academics, and explains the reciprocal interest that linked Brunian philosophy and Elizabethan policy. Bruno admired Elizabeth's political vision and her natural and civic virtues in governing a nation amid the widespread religious turmoil of the period. He was sympathetic to the inspiration of Elizabeth's religious policy, and he often visited the court. The Queen herself owned a copy of *Lo Spaccio de la Bestia Trionfante*, with *La cena de le ceneri, De la causa principio et uno*, and *De l'infinito universo et mondi*, bound in a black leather volume with her royal arms at the cover, which was to become the source of the first effective divulgation of Bruno's thought in modern Europe. Sacerdoti briefly analyses Bruno's cosmology in the *Supper* and other works, distinguishing the analogies with and differences from Copernico's and Ficino's ideas, and highlights the admiration for Lucretius, whose *De rerum natura* rescued by Poggio Bracciolini in 1417, influenced both Machiavelli and Bruno, thus uniting the two authors together in the cultural swerve investing the entire episteme of the Renaissance.

Robert Henke's chapter shows that the phenomenal success of Tasso's pastoral play, *Aminta*, and Guarini's pastoral tragicomedy, *Il pastor fido*, was not lost on England, although English tragicomedy itself mainly took a non-pastoral turn, if we consider the work of Webster, Middleton, Beaumont, Fletcher, and others. Three English playwrights, however, wrote tragicomedies in the pastoral mode: Samuel Daniel in *The Queene's Arcadia* and *Hymen's Triumph*, John Fletcher in *The Faithful Shepherdess*, and Shakespeare in *The Winter's Tale*, and, if somewhat less obviously, *Cymbeline* and *The Tempest*. Through John Wolfe's clandestine press, the two Italian pastoral plays were made available to Englishmen in print. Fletcher and apparently Daniel were well aware of Guarini's theory of tragicomedy, which explores at length how the pastoral mode can function as a hinge between tragedy and comedy. Both the Italian and English playwrights worked within a similar genre system in the early seventeenth century, consisting primarily of tragedy, comedy, and a 'third', tragicomedic genre, which for the Italians was almost always inflected through the pastoral mode and was so more occasionally for the English. The chapter explores the resonances of Italian pastoral tragicomedy in England, considering the plays of Tasso and Guarini, the dramatic theory of Guarini, other Italian pastoral plays, and the *commedia dell'arte* 'magical pastoral' plays that many have been seen as an intertext of *The Tempest*.

The genre of pastoral – writes Janes Tylus – was one of the most widespread literary forms of the Renaissance, resulting in an unprecedented number of poems, plays, and *novelle* as well as more substantive narratives. From the *Arcadia* of Jacopo Sannazaro through Cervantes' *Don Quixote*, pastoral makes a pervasive appearance throughout Europe, with its most sustained production in England, occurring in the late sixteenth century in the formative works of Sidney (both *Old* and *New Arcadia*), Spenser (*Shepheardes Calendar* and Book VI of *The Faerie Queene*), and Shakespeare (from the haunted woods of *Midsummer Night's Dream* and *As You Like It* through the barren landscape of *The Tempest* and the rustic festivities from Act IV of *The Winter's Tale*). In her chapter, "The pastoral poem and novel", Tylus considers the works in poetry and prose that dominated the Anglo-Italian landscape between the publication of Sannazaro's *Arcadia* in 1504 and that of Mary Wroth's complicated pastoral novel *Urania* in 1621. What is telling about both works (as with Sidney's *Arcadias*), Tylus argues, is the mix of prose and verse, the inclusion of shepherds' spontaneous songs and laments within a narrative that introduces temporality into the supposedly timeless landscape of the bucolic. It is precisely this tension of the temporal that makes Renaissance pastoral more broadly such an intriguing form, as the Theocritan idyll and Virgilian eclogue are both amplified and constrained by what at times can be conceived as the invasive mechanics of plot. The chapter explains the pastoral overtones in works of women lyric poets such as Gaspara Stampa and Laura Battiferri, and the bucolic invocations in the poems of Mary Sidney, particularly in her translation of the Psalms. The pastoral lyric tradition became particularly prominent in England in the 1580s and 1590s with the published poetry of Walter Raleigh, Christopher Marlowe, and Michael Drayton. The translation of the *Quixote* by Thomas Shelton in 1617 marks in some ways the end of an era, as the Spanish model of pastoral begins to become more dominant in England. The natural endpoint to any discussion of English pastoral is Milton's *Lycidas*, but Milton also adheres closely to the tradition of the neo-Latin eclogue, revived by Baptistus Mantuanus in the fifteenth century and followed by Googe and Barclay, as well as Spenser, in England. While the depictions of communities of shepherds on the continent were largely invented ones, often based on mythological details and rarely grounded in the rustic realities of the *Cinquecento*, English poets attempted to treat their landscapes and their pastoral denizens with a modicum of realism, sometimes descending to the realm of satire (as with Sidney's Mopsus), other times taking seriously the rustic festivities that characterised the English countryside (as in *The Winter's Tale* or in Spenser's poems and *The Faerie Queene*).

Jason Lawrence's chapter begins with the earliest English assessment of Tasso's literary achievements, in John Eliot's *Ortho-epia Gallica* (1593), in order to demonstrate the Italian poet's wide-ranging impact in England even before his death in 1595, especially through his pastoral drama *Aminta* (1580) and his epic poem *Gerusalemme liberata* (1581). The most famous, and certainly the most critically examined instance of this almost immediate impact is in Book II of Spenser's *The Faerie Queene* (1590). Lawrence weighs up the voluminous, and differing, critical assessments of Spenser's use of Tasso in his own epic poem. He also charts a significant recent move away from the focus on Spenser as the primary English channel for Tasso's poem in the 1590s, in the context of broader critical considerations of Tasso's influence on contemporary English poets such as Daniel, Southwell, and even Shakespeare. Finally he demonstrates how certain passages in Tasso's poem, from the Rinaldo and Armida episode in particular, had both a wide-ranging and long-lasting impact for at least a century: stanzas imitated by Spenser and Daniel in the 1590s were still being alluded to by Dryden and John Dennis in dramatic operas composed in the 1690s. The influence of Tasso's epic on Milton's *Paradise Lost* (1667) is also reassessed, as well as the significant impact of *Aminta*, which was translated repeatedly between the 1590s and 1690s, and which influenced the development of pastoral drama in England by means of plays performed on the public stage, but also at court and the two universities.

VII. This volume: Part 2

The chapters included in Part 2 deal more specifically, in a roughly chronological and thematic order, with the ideological appropriations of the Italian world in its broadest connotations, considering the elements of transformation, divergence, and opposition that emerge in the works of the most representative authors of the English Renaissance.

In studying the varying presence of Petrarch in English culture from the late fourteenth century onwards, John Roe reports that Petrarch's oeuvre has had a threefold division which produced three separate waves of influence: "the Latin works, peaking in the late fourteenth and early fifteenth centuries, the *Trionfi*, in the fifteenth to sixteenth century, and the *Canzoniere*, in the sixteenth century". He then detects the forms of this influence in Chaucer's *Canterbury Tales* and *Troilus and Criseyde*, in Lord Morley's imperfect translation of the *Trionfi*, and in Tottel's, Wyatt's, and Surrey's different appropriations of the *Canzoniere* in which, especially in the case of Wyatt, Petrarch's adaptations involve questions of style and metre, which the English poet accommodated to his own use, transforming the act of imitation into the creation of his individual voice. With the vogue of the sonnet form in the late sixteenth century, a fresh wave of English Petrarchism can be discerned in the poems of Thomas Watson, Sir Philip Sidney, and Edmund Spenser. Although Sidney, in *Astrophil and Stella*, pursues an unmistakably traditional Petrarchan line in the composition of his sonnet sequence, his poems are "witty, expansive, and confident, while also engendering pathos and reflectiveness", while Spenser's *Amoretti*, the most spiritually engaged of Elizabethan poetic sequences, reveal a religious emphasis coupled with a more voluptuous imagination than Petrarch. In John Donne's Mannerist style, we find the most sophisticated and innovative evolution of the Petrarchan mode, whereas Shakespeare's anti-Petrarchan attitude, with his vituperative treatment of the 'dark lady' and the implicit sexual relationship, manifests the dramatic quality of his sonnets more akin to the passions of his dramas than to the conventions of English Petrarchism.

In Melissa Walter's chapter, Boccaccio's *Decameron* discloses storytelling as an essentially social practice, offering human-centred stories that were both realistic and at times bizarre or unexpected. As part of the Anglo-Italian Renaissance, novellas were a focus for English fears and desires towards an Italian other, but this was by no means their only role. Insofar as novella collections became courtly fictions, representing elite social worlds, they influenced and were influenced by Castiglione's *Book of the Courtier*, which revealed the performance of the courtier's identity and social world. English translations and appropriations of the genre, such as Whetstone's *Heptameron of Civil Discourses*, Edmund Tilney's *Flower of Friendship*, and even *The Cobbler of Caunterburie*, domesticated the Italianate form, while print culture created the illusion of a more broadly shared cultural space accessed through reading. Scholarship on novellas has dealt with developments of genres and with source study. Other works trace sources for plays or iterations of a single story. More recently a focus on the transmission, transformation, and negotiation of ideologies and social issues has been more critically central, questioning women's reading and speaking, their agency and desire. Dramatists were among the important readers of novellas, and their work in turn contributed to the development of the English novel and to the negotiation of social and ideological issues through imaginative forms. The *Palace of Pleasure*, an early Elizabethan anthology of translations from Italian, French, and classical sources, became a model for many plots and sub-plots of the Elizabethan, Jacobean, and Caroline stage. Critical attention has recently turned to the specific cultural contexts of both Italian *novelle* and their English uses. Scholars are now able to arrive at readings that better respect the historical diversity and heterogeneity of cultures, and more accurately portray the historical interventions that each text is making. In England, translations of novellas provided an opportunity to transform, adopt, and react against ideological frameworks and formal constructions that may or may not have remained flagged as Italian in their English iterations. In doing so, the Anglo-Italian novelistic transaction fostered an early modern sensibility in England, while providing key steps in the development of the novel and of the theatre of Shakespeare and his contemporaries.

A second chapter by Duncan Salkeld, this one on Shakespeare and the arts, discusses the dramatist as a multi-media artist, working with language, spectacle, sound, and visual patterns. It traces the rise of theatre as a spectacle in early modern London and covers four main areas: drama, poetry, painting, and music. The argument is inserted in the wider artistic milieu of Elizabethan England, and Salkeld argues that Shakespeare's output suggests a belief in the efficacy of visual language and that his aesthetic understanding was forged in collaboration. The chapter contends that when Shakespeare arrived in London, he had musical knowledge and skills. The chapter also deals with Shakespeare's interest in the relationship between poetry and painting, touching ekphrastic passages in *Lucrece, Cymbeline, Timon of Athens*, and the involvement of music in some sequences of *The Tempest, As You Like It, Two Gentlemen of Verona*, and *A Midsummer Night's Dream*. It further provides some suggestions on Shakespeare's own portraits and familiarity with artists and concludes with insightful observations on the dramatist's use of music in light of recent scholarship, pointing to possibilities for future research work in the four areas of drama, poetry, painting, and music.

The Elizabethan reputation and reception of Baldassarre Castiglione's *Libro del Cortegiano* have engendered a controversial debate among scholars. While *The Courtier*'s pervasive influence on early modern English culture and literature is undisputed, much less certain is the Elizabethans' general adherence to the elitist principles and ideas that Castiglione professed in his dialogues. Mary Partridge's well-grounded chapter reconstructs the fortune of Castiglione's manual in Elizabethan England and points out with historical accuracy the subterranean opposition that gradually arose against the Italian writer, contributing to the formation of an anti-courtier trend of Italophobic prejudice and satirical and parodic attitudes. By the turn of the century, Partridge shows, *Il libro del Cortegiano*'s reputation was suffering from its association with two widely reviled components of Italian culture: popery and Machiavellianism, both charged with hypocrisy and dissimulation. Marston's *Scourge of villanie* and satiric plays are rife with anti-courtier discourse and with parodic attacks against the Castiglionean model of the courtier-lover, while the association with Machiavelli's political vision has hardly improved Castiglione's reputation.

Alessandra Petrina's chapter analyses the development of the concept of *raison d'état* in English literary and political culture, in connection with the circulation of Niccolò

Machiavelli's most controversial political work in the British Isles. After a brief survey of the modalities of this circulation from the reign of Henry VIII to the execution of Charles I, the chapter explores the influence of *The Prince* on a number of key texts of the English Renaissance, such as Reginald Pole's *Apologia ad Carolum Quintum*, anonymous pamphlets such as *Leicester's Commonwealth*, and later discussions on the divine right of kings. These texts show an interesting development in the English reception of Machiavelli's *Prince*, from Pole's horrified rejection to the dialectical acceptance of some of Machiavelli's postulates in seventeenth-century treatises. The traditional representation of Machiavelli in England as a mephitic demon, haunting the Elizabethan stage, displays not only a very partial vision but also the description of a considerably limited phenomenon. Although this view continues throughout the seventeenth century, there is a firm distinction between this popular legend and the political contribution of the Florentine writer that enters the debate on reason of state as early as the second half of the sixteenth century. At the same time, it is worth considering how Machiavelli's political proposals met the renewed interest in Tudor political theory and in the debate to overcome the limits posed by the *speculum principis*, a very popular genre in fifteenth-century England and a mode of writing from which the *Prince* itself took shape.

The emergence of the Italian actresses in the *commedia dell'arte* provides readers with information about where they came from and how their novel presence transformed the Italian professional stage. Rosalind Kerr argues that their appearance was connected with the marketing of a new commercial theatre and reads their success through celebrity theory to show why they were revered across Europe. The chapter shows why they were instrumental to the creation of this new theatrical art form, featuring *prima* and *seconda donnas* as central romantic characters who combined with the established buffoon style theatre of the comic masks. The evidence of how they achieved their fame by using their beauty, classical training, verbal agility, and unsurpassed eloquence helps explain their transnational effect. The lack of actual performances by actresses in England did not limit their deep impact. Direct and indirect referencing of the famous actresses' techniques and the strong portrayal of female characters influenced skilled boy actor performances. Finally, Kerr argues that Shakespeare put himself in the forefront of questioning the nature of sexual differences by having his boy actors reappropriate the transvestite disguises made famous by the actresses, calling attention to the slippage between masculine and feminine sex/gender constructions that the actresses had pioneered.

In asserting the presence of *commedia dell'arte* features in the construction of early modern English drama, Eric Nicholson's chapter argues that Italian improvised theatre vitally shaped and transformed English drama, throughout the period from the 1570s to the 1720s, affecting a vast array of theatrical and para-theatrical expressions, not only limited to the fully scripted plays of Marlowe, Shakespeare, Jonson, Middleton, Fletcher, Wycherley, Behn, Gay, and others but also influencing such theatrical elements and genres as jigs, masques, pageants, clown routines, ballets, operas, pantomimes, and puppet shows. Transregional and transnational mobility fostered the dissemination of *commedia* solutions through the travelling companies which also performed in London, and likewise English travellers to the Continent had opportunities to attend improvised scenarios in the inter-cultural 'contact zone' of the University of Padua and elsewhere in Italy. *Commedia dell'arte* troupes allowed actresses to become star attractions, already called 'divas', for their exceptional bravura in impersonating the fixed roles of *innamorate*, often improvising a variety of roles of *contrasti amorosi*. Numerous gags and routines, especially physical ones, called 'lazzi', were another seminal feature of the *comici* of improvised scenarios, affecting the low comedic parts of clowns and servants of early modern English drama. Crossdressing and cross-gender disguise were particularly frequent, becoming a peculiar comedic variation of extempore acting. Nicholson provides numerous examples of *commedia dell'arte* elements, ranging from established theatregrams to specific improvised motifs in a great variety of English plays of the early Elizabethan and late seventeenth-century period, demonstrating the constructive presence of Italian modes of play-acting and character type techniques belonging to the fixed maschere of Italian *commedia*.

J. R. Mulryne's chapter examines the most significant works of past and present scholarship of Italian and English Renaissance Festivals, surveying the intense critical activity that this particular field of Anglo-Italian studies has enjoyed in recent years. Starting from the indispensable bibliographical collections of material kept in the major European libraries, listing their festival texts and all useful data, together with the relevant artists, architects, and performers, the chapter is a mine of useful information for both students and scholars of festivals and court entertainments in Renaissance Europe. The pervasive Italian influence on English festivity is particularly evident in the flourishing of the court masque, a Jacobean genre of court theatre which is clearly indebted to Florentine practices, specifically for the appearance and management of the masque on stage, as variously and differently reported in the authoritative studies of Stephen Orgel, John Orrell, and Frances Yates. Mulryne himself has launched a series of monographs and collections of essays responding to the growing interest in festival research and criticism – first published by Ashgate and now by Routledge – which offers a Europe-wide group of book-length studies on a great range of festivity theatrical activities, with considerable emphasis on examples from sixteenth- and early seventeenth-century Italy, France, and the rest of Europe. The chapter also surveys the critical contribution of a number of distinguished Italian scholars and concludes by appraising the immediate availability of a variety of electronic resources which provide young scholars with a wealth of varied material, including digitised texts of European festival books, complete or in excerpt, and selective reading lists of scholarly work, intended as a gateway, but certainly not as a substitution of direct inquiry and archive research in this field.

As the principal vehicle of the written and spoken culture of Italy in late Tudor and early Stuart England, John Florio was the first to admit how little prepared he was to play such a significant role in the diffusion of continental Europe's most sophisticated vernacular language. The paradox of an unlearned 'stranger', responsible for 'civilising' the English through the instruments of Italian culture, Michael Wyatt's richly documented chapter explains, was an issue that defined Florio's career in England from beginning to end. The very 'facts' of Florio's life are little documented. What we know of his biography has been reconstructed from the paratextual material Florio provides in his various publications and in fragments of information reported in the writings of his contemporaries. He is known to have spent several years at Oxford as a language teacher around the time of the publication of *Firste Fruites*; by the early 1580s he was living – together with the renegade Domenican friar Giordano Bruno – in the residence of the French ambassador, employed as tutor to his daughter. He was involved later in the 1580s, with his friend Matthew Gwinne, in the editing of Sidney's *Arcadia*. By 1592, Florio was in the service of Henry Wriothesley, the Earl of

Southampton, Shakespeare's patron, and he continued to accrue aristocratic patronage over the ensuing decade. The published work that Florio produced in these years ranged from a translation commisioned by Richard Hakluyt of Jacques Cartier's *A Short and Briefe Narration of the Two Navigations and Discoveries to the Northweast Partes Called Newe France* (1580), to a further volume of language-learning dialogues, *Second Fruits* (1591), the first edition of an ambitious Italian-English dicitionary, *A Worlde of Wordes* (1598), and to the first English translation of Montaigne's *Essais* (1603). Florio's association with Queen Anne is marked by the altered prefatory apparatus of the Montaigne (1613), now almost entirely directed to the queen, and the new title of the greatly expanded dictionary, *Queen Anna's New World of Worlds* (1611). Florio's activities at court are sensitive to the spiritual inclinations of the sovereign he served. Some twenty-odd Counter-Reformational texts found their way into the library of books Florio claims to have consulted for the second edition of his dictionary and the translation of Boccaccio's *Decameron* that he prepared during the final years of Queen Anne's life, which was based in part on the censored Italian text published by Leonardo Salviati in 1582. Florio ended his life in domestic obscurity in Fulham following the premature death of Queen Anne in 1619, leaving as his last project a translation of Traiano Boccalini's satiric *Ragguagli di Parnasso*, subsequently incorporated into William Vaughan's *The New-found Politicke* (1626). This signalled the eclipse of the particular vision of the language arts in cultural advocacy and in the service of political power that Florio's career had always aimed to incarnate. In a 2013 *Guardian* article Saul Frampton argued that Florio was the critical editor of the Shakespeare *First Folio*. An Italo-Canadian professor of French literature, Lamberto Tassinari, has been tirelessly promoting the idea that John Florio was actually William Shakespeare, an effort that has unfortunately attracted a great deal of media attention, diminishing Florio's real and substantive achievements by pegging them to an exaggerated and deeply old-fashioned valorisation of Shakespeare's position in English culture.

In parallel fashion, dealing with Italian reformers and Protestants refugees in Tudor England, Diego Pirillo's chapter discusses the lives and works of such figures as Bernardino Ochino, Peter Martyr Vermigli, Giacomo Aconcio, and Francesco Pucci, who participated in the formation of the Italian Protestant Church in London, guided at first by John Florio's father, Michelangelo, thereby contributing to the dissemination of Italian language and culture in early modern England. As a consequence of religious emigration, the influence of Italian reformers was long and persistent not only as participants in the theological controversies of the Reformation but also in the crucial role they played in the circulation of Renaissance secular culture and in the publication of texts that were prohibited or censored in Italy, such as Niccolò Machiavelli's *Il Principe* and Paolo Sarpi's *Istoria del Concilio*. Working as publishers, editors, and translators within the intercultural circuit that existed between authors and readers, they had a significant impact on the European geography of print by disseminating books and information across linguistic and confessional borders. At the end of Mary's reign, the coronation of Elizabeth nourished new hopes among the Italian reformers. Ochino addressed the English Queen in the *Laberinti del libero arbitrio*, remembering the discussion they had on predestination, while Celio Secondo Curione dedicated to Elizabeth a collection of writings of Olimpia Morata, one of the most sophisticated women reformers of the Italian Renaissance. In Elizabethan London the Italian reformers gathered around print shops, and that of John Wolfe became the most prolific press of Italian texts in sixteenth-century England. The translation of Italian works was also a tireless activity of the Italian refugees who enabled Tudor and Stuart readers, Pirillo's chapter concludes, to access Italian texts while working in various forms in the printing industry as editors, translators, publishers, literary agents, and booksellers.

The growing printing industry and the frequent publication of Italian books in early modern England are also the subject of Mario Domenichelli's second chapter. Regulated by Elizabeth's decree, which changed Mary's papist, Roman-Catholic point of view to an Anglican, reformed standpoint, also controlled by the Stationers' Register, the printing and the publication of Italian books increased, becoming a profitable commercial enterprise. After learning the rudiments of his art during a long stay in Florence, John Wolfe became the most prolific printer of Italian books in early modern London, included in the *index librorum prohibitorum*. He published in rapid succession both Machiavelli's and Aretino's major works with false colophons, with Palermo or other Italian locations given as the place of publication. The colophon forgery was used by another printer for the publication of Giordano Bruno's English works, written during his two-year stay in London and Oxford. Translations of Italian books were also published and became bestsellers, considered tools for self-fashioning, teaching important skills in all aspects of collective life, as Castiglione's *Libro del Cortegiano* and Machiavelli's *Il Principe*. Several handbooks on rhetoric and the art of delivering speeches were also very fashionable and shared their popularity with the copious production of Italian books on sword-fencing and horse-riding. In the literary field, the London book market also witnessed the appearance of several translations from the classics, Cicero, Virgil, Ovid, and Horace, among others, and of Chapman's *Iliad* and *Odyssey*. The collection of Thomas Newton's *Seneca His Tenne Tragedies* in 1581 was of the utmost importance in the development of Elizabethan drama. The most important Tudor collection of poetry, the *Tottel's Miscellany*, was published in 1557, including Wyatt's and Surrey's translations and imitations of Petrarch. Petrarch's most popular work, *I Trionfi*, were translated several times after the first English version by Lord Morley in 1486–1556. Other important Elizabethan translations of Italian authors regarded the influential works of Boccaccio, Ariosto, Tasso, and Guarini, among many others, contributing to a printing industry which marked an indisputable sign in the formation of English literary tastes and own cultural identity.

Chiara Petrolini and Diego Pirillo's chapter focuses on the Servite friar Paolo Sarpi (1552–1623), examining his major works as well as his legacy and situating him at the centre of the 'Seicento anglo-veneto' – the intricate network of contacts that in the early modern period existed between Venice and England. The chapter is divided into five sections. The first introduces readers to the life and thought of Sarpi, discussing his education in Venice and Padua where he interacted with some of the most important scholars of the time, from Galileo Galilei to Tommaso Campanella. In this period Sarpi composed the *Pensieri*, a series of philosophical and scientific annotations, which has been widely discussed by Italian and Anglo-American scholarship in the course of reconstructing the history of early modern atheism. The second section focuses on the most famous episode of Sarpi's life, the Venetian Interdict (1606–1607), when he became the legal and theological adviser of the Republic of Venice by examining the echoes of the controversy in Europe and England. The third explores Sarpi's connections with early modern England, starting with his exchanges with Francis Bacon and James I and moving on to those with the English embassy in Venice. The fourth section is dedicated to Sarpi as historian, focusing especially on the *Istoria del Concilio*

Tridentino, an "historiographical masterpiece" and "the last major literary achievement of the Italian Renaissance". After being published in London in 1619, Sarpi's *Istoria* became essential reading for English Protestants and was celebrated by John Milton in the *Areopagitica*, in which the Servite friar is famously labelled as the "the great unmasker of the Trentine Councel". The fifth and final section provides the reader with an examination of Sarpi's controversial legacy in modern times and of the controversies among scholars who still find it difficult to come to terms with all the masks of the Venetian 'chameleon'.

One of the central themes in this volume is the question of location, regarded as the most popular geographical and geopolitical strategy in early modern drama. Keir Elam's Afterword points out that the function of Italian settings takes a number of different forms. Most evident is the role they assume in reflecting and refracting English perceptions of national identity, as well as English political and commercial ambitions. Another aspect of location is the *locus*, as fictional place but also topos (*locus comunis*). One of the most fruitful lines of research in Anglo-Italian studies has been the far-reaching enquiry into the appropriation, transformation, and dissemination of literary and theatrical *loci* from Greek and Roman New Comedy, via medieval and Renaissance Italian narrative to the Early Modern English stage. Genre-specific *locii*, such as the *locus amoenus* of pastoral, are less places than conventional markers of literary mode. More in general, the distinction between place and literary or dramaturgic tradition is often slight. For the audiences of the Globe, Curtain, or Blackfriars, the Italian settings are narrative spaces, becoming literary constructs prior to their nominal appearance on stage. The Venice of Iago and Volpone, the Verona of Juliet, and the Amalfi of De Bosola – Elam contends – are intertextual rather than geographic places, created or recreated through the descriptive and performative power of the world. 'Venice' and 'Rome' are verbal and scenographic constructs, ontologically posited through allusion and description. This manifold exploitation of *loci* is brought together by Shakespeare in *Cymbeline*. This *sui generis* romance, history play, Roman play, and pastoral tragicomedy is among other things an exercise in the poetics of location. The action moves frenetically from ancient Luds Town (London), to an imperial Rome that actually resembles Renaissance Italy, to 'primitive' pastoral Wales. Each location also becomes a form of narration where the spasmodic shifts in time and place bring with them abrupt changes in genre, while "the veritable feast of intertextual and macrotextual allusions" makes *Cymbeline* a unique case of Shakespearian self-appropriation and generic intertextuality.

Notes

1 See in particular the remarkable work of Lewis Einstein, *The Italian Renaissance in England* (New York: The Columbia University Press, 1903).
2 S. Greenblatt, *Shakespearean Negotiations: The Circulation of Social Energy in Renaissance England* (Oxford: Clarendon Press, 1988) and *Learning to Curse. Essays in Early Modern Culture* (Oxford: Routledge, 1990).
3 Greenblatt, *Shakespearean Negotiations*, p. 19.
4 Michele Marrapodi, "Prologue", in *The Italian World of English Renaissance Drama: Cultural Exchange and Intertextuality*, ed. M. Marrapodi, assoc. ed. A. J. Hoenselaars (Newark: University of Delaware Press, 1998), p. 16.
5 Michael Bakhtin, *The Dialogic Imagination*, ed. M. Holquist, trans. C. Emerson and M. Holquist (Austin: University of Texas Press, 1981); Julia Kristeva, "Word, Dialogue, and Novel", (1967), trans. as "Desire in Language", in *The Kristeva Reader*, ed.

Toril Moi (Oxford: Basil Blackwell, 1986). See also, for a general introduction, *Intertextuality: Theories and Practices*, eds. Michael Worton and Judith Still (Manchester, UK: Manchester University Press, 1990).

6 Louise George Clubb, "Intertextualities: Some Questions", in *The Italian World of English Renaissance Drama: Cultural Exchange and Intertextuality*, pp. 179–89; "Italian Stories on the Stage", in *The Cambridge Companion to Shakespearean Comedy*, ed. Alexander Leggatt (Cambridge: Cambridge University Press, 2002), pp. 32–46; "Pastoral Jazz from the Writ to the Liberty", in *Italian Culture in the Drama of Shakespeare & His Contemporaries: Rewriting, Remaking, Refashioning*, ed. Michele Marrapodi (Farnham, UK: Ashgate, 2007), pp. 15–26.

7 Cf. R. S. Miola's, "Seven Types of Intertextuality", in *Shakespeare, Italy, and Intertextuality*, ed. Michele Marrapodi (Manchester, UK: Manchester University Press, 2004), pp. 13–25, and *Shakespeare's Reading* (Oxford: Oxford University Press, 2000).

8 Leo Salingar, *Shakespeare and the Traditions of Comedy* (Cambridge: Cambridge University Press, 1974), p. 190; see also by Salingar, *Dramatic Form in Shakespeare and the Jacobeans* (Cambridge: Cambridge University Press, 1986).

9 Louise George Clubb, *Italian Drama in Shakespeare's Time* (New Haven, CT: Yale University Press, 1989). See also Clubb's more recent essay, "Looking Back on Shakespeare and Italian Theater", *Renaissance Drama*, n.s. 36/37, "Italy in the Drama of Europe", eds. Albert Russell Ascoli and William N. West (2010), pp. 3–19.

10 R. Andrews, *Scripts and Scenarios: The Performance of Comedy in Renaissance Italy* (Cambridge: Cambridge University Press, 1993).

11 R. Henke, *Pastoral Transformations: Italian Tragicomedy and Shakespeare's Late Plays* (Newark: University of Delaware Press, 1997); *Performance and Literature in the 'Commedia dell'Arte'* (Cambridge: Cambridge University Press, 2002).

12 Cf. Jonathan Dollimore, "Subjectivity, Sexuality, and Transgression: The Jacobean Connection", *Renaissance Drama*, n.s., XVII (1986): 53–81. For an account of the "transvestite controversy" in the social context of Elizabethan and Jacobean England, see in particular Linda Woodbridge, *Women and the English Renaissance. Literature and the Nature of Womankind, 1540–1620* (Brighton, UK: The Harvester Press, 1984), pp. 139–183; Sandra Clark, "*Hic Mulier, Haec Vir* and the Controversy over the Masculine Women", *Studies in Philology*, LXXXII (Spring 1985): 157–83; Jean E. Howard, "Cross-Dressing, the Theatre, and Gender Struggle in Early Modern England", *Shakespeare Quarterly*, 39 (Fall 1988): 418–440; Elizabeth D. Harvey, *Ventriloquized Voices: Feminist Theory and English Renaissance Texts* (Oxford: Routledge, 1992), pp. 15–53; Laura Levine, *Men in Women's Clothing. Anti-Theatricality and Effeminization, 1579–1642* (Cambridge: Cambridge University Press, 1994); Stephen Orgel, *Impersonations: The Performance of Gender in Shakespeare's England* (Cambridge: Cambridge University Press, 1996). A more recent study, oriented towards contemporary trans and genderqueer theory, is Simone Chess's, *Male-to-Female Crossdressing in Early Modern English Literature: Gender, Performance, and Queer Relations* (Oxford: Routledge, 2016).

13 K. Elam, "Italy as Intertext", in *Shakespeare, Italy, and Intertextuality*, p. 255.

14 B. Castiglione, *Il Libro del Cortegiano* (1528), ed. Vittorio Cian (Florence: Sansoni, 1947); G. Della Casa, *Galateo* (1558), ed. Saverio Orlando (Milan: Grzanti, 1988); G. Giraldi Cinzio, *L'uomo di corte. Discorso intorno a quello che si conviene a giovane nobile e ben creato nel servire un gran Principe* (1569), ed. Walter Moretti (Modena: Mucchi Editore, 1989); S. Guazzo, *La civil conversazione* (1575), ed. Amedeo Quondam, 2 vols. (Modena: Franco Cosimo Panini, 1993).

15 H. Berger, Jr., *The Absence of Grace. Sprezzatura and Suspicion in Two Renaissance Courtesy Books* (Stanford, CA: Stanford University Press, 2000).

16 Michael J. Redmond, *Shakespeare, Politics, and Italy: Intertextuality on the Jacobean Stage* (Farnham, UK: Ashgate, 2009).

17 Cf. Michele Marrapodi, "Appropriating Italy: Towards a New Approach to Renaissance Drama", in *Italian Culture in the Drama of Shakespeare & His Contemporaries: Rewriting, Remaking, Refashioning*, pp. 1–12.

18 Sergio Rossi, "Italy and the English Renaissance: An Introduction", in *Italy and the English Renaissance*, eds. Sergio Rossi and Dianella Savoia (Milan: Unicopli, 1989), pp. 9–24.

19 Brian Parker, "An English View of Venice: Ben Jonson's *Volpone*", in *Italy and the English Renaissance*, p. 199.

20 *Theatre of the English and Italian Renaissance*, eds. J. R. Mulryne and Margaret Shewring (Basingstoke, UK: Palgrave Macmillan, 1991).
21 *Italian Renaissance Festivals and Their European Influence*, eds. J. R. Mulryne and Margaret Shewring (Lewiston, MN: Edwin Mellen Press, 1992). The related field of water festivals and pageants in Italy as well as in other European countries is the subject of Margaret Shewring's *Festschrift* for J. R. Mulryne's remakable achievements in the study of Anglo-Italian theatrical traditions and in the editing of several Renaissance plays: *Waterborne Pageants and Festivities in the Renaissance: Essays in Honour of J. R. Mulryne*, ed. M. Shewring (Farnham, UK: Ashgate, 2013).
22 *Shakespeare and Renaissance Europe*, eds. Andrew Hadfield and Paul Hammond (London: Bloomsbury, 2004).
23 Richard Andrews, "Shakespeare and Italian Comedy", in *Shakespeare and Renaissance Europe*, pp. 123–149; François Laroque, "Shakespeare's Imaginary Geography", in *Shakespeare and Renaissance Europe*, pp. 193–219.
24 Michael Wyatt, ed. *The Cambridge Companion to the Italian Renaissance* (Cambridge: Cambridge University Press, 2014).
25 J. Lawrence, *'Who the Devil Taught Thee So Much Italian?' Italian Language Learning and Literary Imitation in Early Modern England* (Manchester, UK: Manchester University Press, 2005).
26 M. Wyatt, *The Italian Encounter with Tudor England. A Cultural Politics of Translation* (Cambridge: Cambridge University Press, 2005).
27 S. Tomita, *A Bibliographical Catalogue of Italian Books Printed in England, 1558–1603* (Farnham, UK: Ashgate, 2009) and S. Tomita and Masahiko Tomita, *A Bibliographical Catalogue of Italian Books Printed in England, 1603–1642* (Farnham, UK: Ashgate, 2014).
28 Thomas Nashe, *Pierce Penilesse His Supplication to the Divell* (1592), in *The Works of Thomas Nashe*, ed. R. B. McKerrow (Oxford: Basil Blackwell, 1958), vol. I, p. 186: "O Italie, the Academie of man-slaughter, the sporting place of murther, the Apothecary-shop of poyson for all Nations: how many kind of weapons hast thou inuented for malice?"
29 G. K. Hunter, "English Folly and Italian Vice: The Moral Landscape of John Marston", in *Jacoben Theatre*, eds. J. R. Brown and Bernard Harris, Stratford-upon-Avon Studies 1 (London: Methuen, 1960). Reprinted with other relevant essays in Hunter's *Dramatic Identities and Cultural Traditions: Studies in Shakespeare and His Contemporaries* (Liverpool: Liverpool University Press, 1978), pp. 103–121.
30 M. Praz, "'The Politic Brain: Machiavelli and the Elizabethans' and 'Shakespeare's Italy'", in *The Flaming Heart: Essays on Crashaw, Machiavelli, and Other Studies in the Relations between Italian and English Literature from Chaucer to T. S. Eliot* (Gloucester, MA: Peter Smith, 1966), pp. 90–145 and 146–167.
31 Cf. Jonathan Bate, "The Elizabethans in Italy", in *Travel and Drama in Shakespeare's Time*, eds. Jean-Pierre Marquelot and Michèle Willems (Cambridge: Cambridge University Press, 1966), pp. 70–71.
32 John Gillies, *Shakespeare and the Geography of Difference* (Cambridge: Cambridge University Press, 1994).
33 Clifford Leech, "The Function of Locality in the Plays of Shakespeare and his Contemporaries", in *The Elizabethan Theatre. Papers Given at the International Conference on Elizabethan Theatre Held at the University of Waterloo, Ontario, in July 1968*, edited and with an introduction by David Galloway (London: Macmillan, 1969), p. 105.
34 Michele Marrapodi et al., eds. *Shakespeare's Italy: Functions of Italian Locations in Renaissance Drama* (Manchester, UK: Manchester University Press, 1993).
35 Cf. A. J. Hoenselaars, *Images of Englishmen and Foreigners in the Drama of Shakespeare and His Contemporaries. A Study of Stage Characters and National Identity in English Renaissance Drama, 1558–1642* (London and Toronto: Associated University Presses, 1992); Lloyd Edward Kermode, *Aliens and Englishness in Elizabethan Drama* (Cambridge: Cambridge University Press, 2009).
36 Cf. Michele Marrapodi, "Introduction: Tradition and Subversion", in *Otherness, Transgression, and Subversion in Early Modern English Culture*, eds. M. Marrapodi and Giuseppe Leone, *InVerbis. Lingue Letterature Culture*, VI, 2 (2016): 11.
37 Murray J. Levith, *Shakespeare's Italian Settings and Plays* (Basingstoke, UK: Macmillan, 1989).

38 Jack D'Amico, *Shakespeare and Italy: The City and the Stage* (Gainesville: University of Florida Press, 2001).
39 John L. Lievsay, *The Elizabethan Image of Italy* (Ithaca, NY: Cornell University Press, 1964); Robert C. Jones, "Italian Settings and the 'World' of Elizabethan Tragedy", *Studies in English Literature 1500–1900*, X (1970): 251–268.
40 Jones, p. 265.
41 John Webster, *The White Devil*, ed. John Russell Brown (Manchester, UK: Manchester University Press, 1977), 4.2.61.
42 On the impact of the masks and scenarios of Italian professional troupes on Shakespeare's improvising strategy of character construction, see Eugene Steele, *Shakespeare and the Italian Professionals* (Taipei: Bookman Books Ltd, 1993).
43 Cf. M. Marrapodi, "Cross-dressing, New Comedy, and the Italianate Unity of *The Taming of the Shrew*", in *Shakespeare Yearbook*, Vol. X, eds. Holger Klein and M. Marrapodi (Lewiston, MN: The Edwin Mellen Press, 1999), pp. 333–358.
44 On the varied influence of Aretino's erotica on the comedy, see Keir Elam's well-documented essay "'Wanton pictures': The Baffling of Christopher Sly and the Visual-Verbal Intercourse of Early Modern Erotic Art", in *Shakespeare and the Italian Renaissance: Appropriation, Transformation, Opposition*, ed. Michele Marrapodi (Farnham, UK: Ashgate, 2014), pp. 123–146.
45 Baldassare Castiglione, *Il Libro del Cortegiano*, ed. Vittorio Cian (Florence: Sansoni, 1947), Libro Primo, XXVI, p. 63: "per dir forse una nova parola, usar in ogni cosa una certa sprezzatura, che nasconda l'arte, e dimostri, ciò che si fa e dice, venir fatto senza fatica e quasi senza pensarvi". On the use of the term *sprezzatura* as a rhetorical device for the self-fashioning of the courtier, see Frank Whigham, *Ambition and Privilege: The Social Tropes of Elizabethan Courtesy Theory* (Berkeley: University of California Press, 1984), pp. 93–95; Catherine Bates, *The Rhetoric of Courtship in Elizabethan Language and Literature* (Cambridge: Cambridge University Press, 1992), pp. 25–44; Susanne Scholz, *Body Narrative: Writing the Nation and Fashioning the Subject in Early Modern England* (London: Macmillan, 2000), pp. 38–56.
46 Cf. Michele Marrapodi, "The Aretinean Intertext and the Heterodoxy of *The Taming of the Shrew*", in *Shakespeare and the Italian Renaissance: Appropriation, Transformation, Opposition*, ed. M. Marrapodi, pp. 235–255.
47 *The Taming of the Shrew*, ed. Brian Morris (London: Methuen, 1981).
48 Baldassare Castiglione, *Il Libro del Cortegiano*, ed. Vittorio Cian, p. 354.
49 *The Book of the Courtier*, trans. Thomas Hoby, intro. J. H. Whitfield (London: J. M. Dent & Sons Ltd, 1974), pp. 220–221.
50 Berger, *The Absence of Grace*, p. 103. In this regard, see my discussion of the representation of female *corteziania* in Shakespeare's comedies, also in relation to Aretino's subversive treatment, "Shakespeare's Romantic Italy: Novelistic, Theatrical, and Cultural Transactions in the Comedies", in *Italian Culture in the Drama of Shakespeare and His Contemporaries*, ed. M. Marrapodi, pp. 51–68.
51 Marrapodi, "Introduction", in *Shakespeare's Italy*, p. 7.
52 Cf. John Drakakis, "Shakespeare and Venice", in *Italian Culture in the Drama of Shakespeare & His Contemporaries*, pp. 169–186. For a more recent reconsideration of Shakespeare's exploitation of the ambivalent myths of Venice, also studied from a presentist perspective, see Graham Holderness, *Shakespeare and Venice* (Farnham, UK: Ashgate, 2010) and the collection of essays, *Visions of Venice in Shakespeare*, eds. Laura Tosi and Shaul Bassi (Farnham, UK: Ashgate, 2011).
53 *Othello*, ed. M. R. Ridley, Arden Edition (London: Methuen, 1958).
54 M. Marrapodi, "'Let Her Witness It': The Rhetoric of Desdemona", in *Italian Studies in Shakespeare and His Contemporaries*, eds. Michele Marrapodi and Giorgio Melchiori (Newark: University of Delaware Press, 1999), pp. 220–244.
55 Greenblatt, *Renaissance Self-Fashioning. From More to Shakespeare* (Chicago, IL: Chicago University Press, 1980), p. 250.
56 G. Bradshaw, *Misrepresentations: Shakespeare and the Materialists* (Ithaca, NY: Cornell University Press, 1993), p. 213.
57 Marrapodi, "'Let Her Witness It': The Rhetoric of Desdemona", p. 237.

58 Cf. Flavia Ravazzoli, "Appunti di nuova retorica, tra semantica e pragmatic", *Strumenti Critici*, 44 (1981): 154–170. "The definition 'amplifying axis' covers the various rhetorical figures based on the analogic-substitutive mechanism: simile, allegory, allegorism, metaphor, menonymy, synecdoche, hyperbole, antonomasia, prosopopoeia, *amplificatio*, etc.: the *metasememes* of the Liège group and also … all tropes in the proper sense. The 'attenuating' axis includes all the figures of negation, reticence, and (pseudo) contradiction: the *metalogisms* of the Belgian group" (p. 158, italics in original, my translation).

59 M. S. Adams, "Ocular Proof' in *Othello* and Its Source", *PMLA*, 79, 3 (1964): 234–241 (p. 234).

60 M. R. Ridley's translation in his Arden edition of the play. A useful survey of Shakespeare's sources and analogues can be found in the monumental work by Geoffrey Bullough, *Narrative and Dramatic Sources of Shakespeare*, 8 vols. (Oxford: Routledge and London: Kegan Paul, 1957–1975), part. vol. 7, "Major Tragedies" (1973). See also Kenneth Muir, *The Sources of Shakespeare's Plays* (Oxford and New York: Routledge, 1977), pp. 182–195. New critical perspectives to source study can be found in the anthology *Rethinking Shakespeare Source Study: Audiences, Authors, and Digital Technologies*, edited by Dennis Austin Britton and Melissa Walter (Oxford and New York: Routledge, 2018).

61 In *Selected Plays by Thomas Middleton*, ed. David L. Frost (Cambridge: Cambridge University Press, 1978).

62 Cf. Catherine Belsey, *The Subject of Tragedy: Identity and Difference in Renaissance Drama* (London: Methuen, 1985).

63 John Marston, "The Malcontent", in *English Drama, 1580–1642*, selected and edited by C. F. Tucker Brooke and Nathaniel Burton Paradise (Boston, MA: D. C. Heath and Company, 1933).

64 Cf. Ejner J. Jensen, "Theme and Imagery in *The Malcontent*", *Studies in English Literature, 1500–1900*, 10 (Spring, 1970): 367–384.

65 Kevin A. Quarmby, *The Disguised Ruler in Shakespeare and His Contemporaries* (Farnham, UK: Ashgate, 2012), p. 77. On the Italianate disguised ruler play as a theatrical sub-genre, see Michael J. Redmond, *Shakespeare, Politics, and Italy*, chap. 4, pp. 121–168.

66 M. Marrapodi, "Retaliation as an Italian Vice in English Renaissance Drama: Narrative and Theatrical Exchanges", in *The Italian World of English Renaissance Drama*, p. 192.

67 G. B. Giraldi, "Orbecche: La tragedia a chi legge", in *Teatro del Cinquecento*, ed. R. Cremante (Milan and Naples: R. Ricciardi Editore, 1988): "Nor must you less esteem me because I am born / Of new material and not of ancient history: / For whosoever looks upon the truth with keen eye / Will see that without any blame from new material / And new names new tragedy may be born". My translation.

68 M. Ariani, "Ragione e furore nella tragedia di G. B. Giraldi Cinthio", in *Tra Classicismo e Manierismo: Il teatro tragico del Cinquecento* (Florence: Olschki, 1974), pp. 115–178.

69 On Renaissance literary theories and the influence of Aristotle's poetics, see Lawrence Danson, *Shakespeare's Dramatic Genres* (Oxford: Oxford University Press, 2000); Michele Marrapodi, "Shakespeare against Genres", in *Shakespeare and Renaissance Literary Theories: Anglo-Italian Transactions*, ed. M. Marrapodi (Farnham, UK: Ashgate, 2010), pp. 1–22; and Sarah Dewar-Watson's recent monograph, *Shakespeare's Poetics: Aristotle and Anglo-Italian Renaissance Genres* (Oxford: Routledge, 2018).

70 G. B. Giraldi Cinzio, *Scritti critici*, ed. C. G. Crocetti (Milan: Marzorati, 1973), pp. 223–224 ("I am convinced that tragedy also has its pleasure, and in that weeping we discover a hidden pleasure that makes it pleasurable to the listener and arouses the attention of the mind and fills it with wonder which makes it desirous of parrying, by means of horror and compassion, that which they do not know, that is to flee vice and to follow virtue, besides which the feeling that men have for the pathetic makes them watch the play willingly. This gives us a sign of our nature and provides the humanity that is within us with ample occasion to have compassion for the misery of the wretched". My translation).

71 See Madeleine Doran, *Endeavors of Art: A Study of Form in Elizabethan Drama* (Madison: University of Wisconsin Press, 1954), pp. 89–90.

72 See Carmelo Musumarra, "La poetica del Rinascimento e la tragedia", in *La poesia tragica italiana nel Rinascimento*, pp. 1–48.

73 See also Girolamo Parabosco's *Progne* (1548), Girolamo Razzi's *Gismonda* (1569), Luigi Groto's *Dalida* (1572), Cesare Della Porta's *Delfa* (1587), and Muzio Manfredi's *Semiramis* (1593), to mention only the most famous. Cf. Marvin T. Herrick, *Italian Tragedy in the Renaissance* (Urbana: University of Illinois Press, 1965).
74 Cf. Francesco Guicciardini, *The History of Italy*, translated, edited with notes, and with an Introduction by S. Alexander (London: Macmillan, 1969), p. 188. Guicciardini's account refers to the Ferrarese story of bloody revenge and passion concerning Ippolito d'Este and his bastard brother Don Giulio.
75 In Cyril Tourneur, *The Revenger's Tragedy*, ed. Brian Gibbons (London: Ernest Benn Limited, 1967).
76 Jonathan Dollimore, *Radical Tragedy: Religion, Ideology and Power in the Drama of Shakespeare and His Contemporaries*, 2nd edn. (New York and London: Harvester Wheatsheaf, 1989), p. 146.
77 John Ford, *'Tis Pity She's a Whore*, ed. Brian Morris (London: The New Mermaids, 1968).
78 John Webster, *The White Devil*, ed. John Russell Brown (Manchester, UK: Manchester University Press, 1977).
79 See Carmelo Musumarra, "La 'riforma' giraldiana e *l'Orbecche*", in *La poesia tragica italiana nel Rinascimento* (Florence: Olschki, 1972), pp. 93–111.
80 J. Webster, *The Duchess of Malfi*, ed. J. Russell Brown (Manchester, UK: Manchester University Press, 1976).
81 Jonathan Dollimore, *Radical Tragedy. Religion, Ideology and Power in the Drama of Shakespeare and His Contemporaries*, p. xxxi.
82 J. W. Lever, *The Tragedy of State. A Study of Jacobean Drama* (London: Methuen, 1971), p. 87.
83 Martin Butler, *Theatre and Crisis, 1632–1642* (Cambridge: Cambridge University Press, 1984), p. 6.
84 Margot Heinemann, *Puritanism and Theatre. Thomas Middleton and Opposition Drama under the Early Stuarts* (Cambridge: Cambridge University Press, 1980).
85 Cf. for instance in *The Duchess of Malfi*: "*Send Antonio to me; I want his head in a business*: – / A politic equivocation! / He doth not want your counsel, but your head" (3.5.28–30).
86 See Robert Ornstein, *The Moral Vision of Jacobean Tragedy* (Westport, CT: Greenwood Press, 1977), p. 140.
87 Carla Bella, "Giovan Battista Giraldi Cinzio", in *Eros e censura nella tragedia dal '500 al '700* (Florence: Vallecchi Ed., 1981), p. 87.
88 Cf. M. Marrapodi, "Beyond the Reformation: Italian Intertexts of the Ransom Plot in *Measure for Measure*", in *Shakespeare, Italy, and Intertextuality*, pp. 73–90.
89 Riccardo Bruscagli, "La corte in scena. Genesi politica della tragedia ferrarese", in *Stagioni della civiltà estense* (Pisa: Nistri-Lischi, 1983), pp. 142–143.
90 Cf. Antonio D'Andrea, "Giraldi Cinthio and the Birth of the Machiavellian Hero on the Elizabethan Stage", in *Il Teatro italiano del Rinascimento*, ed. Maristella de Panizza Lorch (Milan: Edizioni di Comunità, 1980), pp. 605–617.
91 Cf. Riccardo Bruscagli, "La corte in scena. Genesi politica della tragedia ferrarese", pp. 127–159.
92 Robert S. Miola, *Shakespeare and Classical Tragedy: The Influence of Seneca* (Oxford: Clarendon Press, 1992) and *Shakespeare and Classical Comedy: The Influence of Plautus and Terence* (Oxford: Clarendon Press, 1994).
93 Robin Kirkpatrick, *English and Italian Literature from Dante to Shakespeare. A Study of Source, Analogue and Divergence* (London: Longman, 1995).
94 Albert R. Ascoli, *Dante and the Making of a Modern Author* (Cambridge: Cambridge University Press, 2008).
95 Albert R. Ascoli, *A Local Habitation and a Name. Imagining Histories in the Italian Renaissance* (New York: Fordham University Press, 2011).
96 Ascoli, *A Local Habitation and a Name*, p. 333.
97 See, in this regard, Edward Meyer, *Machiavelli and Elizabethan Drama* (Weimar, 1897); Irving Ribner, "The Significance of Gentillet's *Contre-Machiavel*", *Modern Language Quarterly*, 10 (1949): 153–157; Felix Raab, *The English Face of Machiavelli: A Changing Interpretation 1550–1700*, with a foreword by Hugh Trevor-Roper (London: Kegan Paul and

Oxford: Routledge, 1964); Praz, Mario, "The Politic Brain: Machiavelli and the Elizabethans", in *The Flaming Heart*.

98 Cf., among many others, Albert Russell Ascoli and Victoria Kahn, eds. *Machiavelli and the Discourse of Literature* (Ithaca, NY: Cornell University Press, 1993); John Roe, *Shakespeare and Machiavelli* (Cambridge: D. S. Brewer, 2002).

99 A. Petrina, *Machiavelli in the British Isles. Two Early Modern Translations of 'The Prince'* (Farnham, UK: Ashgate, 2009). See also *Machiavellian Encounters in Tudor and Stuart England. Literary and Political Influences from the Reformation to the Restoration*, eds. Alessandro Arienzo and Alessandra Petrina (Farnham, UK: Ashgate, 2013).

100 Herbert G. Wright, *Boccaccio in England: From Chaucer to Tennyson* (London: Athlone Press, 1957).

101 Louise George Clubb, "Italian Stories on the Stage", in *The Cambridge Companion to Shakespearean Comedy*, ed. Alexander Leggatt (Cambridge: Cambridge University Press, 2002), pp. 32–46.

102 N. Machiavelli, *Mandragola, Clizia*, ed. Gian Mario Anselmi, with a presentation by Ezio Raimondi (Milan: Mursia, 1984). The quoted phrase is taken from Raimondi's Presentation, pp. 9–10.

103 The phrase is Nino Borsellino's in Borsellino and R. Mercuri, *Il Teatro del Cinquecento*, p. 12. See also Nino Borsellino, "'*Decameron* come teatro' and 'Aretino e Boccaccio: conclusioni sulla scrittura scenica del Cinquecento'", in *Rozzi e Intronati: Esperienze e forme di teatro dal 'Decameron' al 'Candelaio'* (Rome: Bulzoni Editore, 1976), pp. 13–50 and 213–228 respectively.

104 Giulio Ferroni, *Le voci dell'istrione. Pietro Aretino e la dissoluzione del teatro* (Naples: Liguori, 1977), p. 13. See also by Ferroni, *'Mutazione' e 'riscontro' nel teatro di Machiavelli e altri saggi sulla commedia del Cinquecento* (Rome: Bulzoni Editore, 1972).

105 Pietro Aretino, *Cortigiana*, 5.25, in *La commedia del Cinquecento*, ed. Guido Davico Bonino, vol. 2, p. 313. ("*Arcolano.* Oh cruel woman, why hast thou betrayed me? *Togna.* And what am I to do with what is left to me, throw it to pigs?" My translation). Togna's protofeminist response is almost a literal quotation from Boccaccio's *novella* of Madam Philippa (the seventh tale of the sixth day), whose theme, as governed by Elissa, is the ability of an accused person to use artful language to rebut a charge by providing "a sudden, unexpected and discreet answere, thereby preventing losse, danger, scorne and disgrace, retorting them on the busi-headed Questioners". Cf. *The Decameron*, 1620 English Translation, ed. W. E. Henley, 3 vols (London: David Nutt, 1909), vol. 3, p. 129. See my essay "From Narrative to Drama: The Erotic Tale and the Theater", in *The Italian World of English Renaissance Drama*, ed. M. Marrapodi, pp. 41–70.

106 Cf. Keir Elam, "'Bridegroom uncarnate': Comedy and Castration from *The Eunuch* to *Epicoene*", in *The Italian World of English Renaissance Drama*, pp. 258–281.

107 Marrapodi, "The Aretinean Intertext and the Heterodoxy of the *Taming of the Shrew*", in *Shakespeare and the Italian Renaissance.*

108 Nino Borsellino and Roberto Mercuri, *Il Teatro del Cinquecento*, p. 54.

109 John Marston, *The Malcontent*, ed. George K. Hunter (Manchester, UK: Manchester University Press, 1975).

110 See F. A. Yates, *The Art of Memory* (London: Kegan Paul and Oxford: Routledge, 1966), pp. 260–278. On the lively philosophical debate during Bruno's life in England, see Gabriela Dragnea Horvath, *Theatre, Magic and Philosophy. William Shakespeare, John Dee and Italian Legacy* (Oxford: Routledge, 2017).

111 G. Bruno, *Candelaio*, ed. Giorgio Bàrberi Squarotti (Turin: Einaudi, 1964), 4.1., pp. 78–79. ("We must needs distinguish between the cult of gods and the cult of mortal men. We worship sculptures and images, and honour the written name of the divine, directing our attention to that which lives. We worship and honour these other gods that piss and shit, directing our intentions and suppliant devotion to their images and sculpters, so that through these they may reward the virtuous, elevate the worthy, defend the oppressed, extend their borders, preserve their own, and inspire fear in their enemies: the king therefore, and emperor in flesh and blood, if not sculpted, is worth naught"; my translation).

112 Giordano Bruno, *Candelaio*, ed. Giorgio Bàrberi Squarotti (Turin: Einaudi, 1964), Act 2, Scene 5. ("There was a time when the lion and the ass were friends. As they travelled

together on pilgrimage it became necessary, when they came to rivers, for each to take a turn in carrying the other: that is to say that one time the ass would carry the lion on his back and the next time the lion would carry the ass on his back. Needing to get to Rome, then, they reached the Garigliano and, there being neither boat nor bridge for them to use, the ass took the lion on its back. As they swam to the other shore, the lion, fearful of falling in, dug his claws more and more deeply into the ass's skin so that, in the end, the poor animal was shredded to the bone. And the poor wretch, like one experienced in patience, bore it as well as he could, without uttering a sound, except that when they were safely out of the water, he shook his back a little, rolled over in the hot sand a few times and then continued on. Eight days later, as they were returning, it was the duty of the lion to carry the ass, who, finding himself on top and not wanting to fall into the water, with his teeth gripped the lion by the nape, and this not being enough to steady him, he stuck his instrument – or how can we call it, his ..., well you know, – let's say, to keep it clean, in the hole, under the tail, where there is no fur. The lion felt more pain than a woman in labour and so shouted: 'Hey there, hey there, oh, oh, oh dear me! Hey there, you traitor!' Whereupon the ass replied with a stern face and a serious voice: 'Patience my brother, you see that I have no other claw to grab with but this'. And so the lion had no choice but to suffer and endure until the crossing was over". Translation by Gino Moliterno, in *Renaissance Comedy. The Italian Masters*, Vol. 2, ed. with an Introduction by Donald Beecher (Toronto: University of Toronto Press, 2009), pp. 372–373.

113 On Giordano Bruno's visit to Elizabethan England, see Dorothea Waley Singer, *Giordano Bruno: His Life and Thought* (New York: Greenwood Press, 1968), pp. 26–45; and, especially, by Hilary Gatti, *The Renaissance Drama of Knowledge: Giordano Bruno in England* (New York: Routledge, 1989); *Il teatro della coscienza. Giordano Bruno e Amleto* (Rome: Bulzoni, 1998); and *Essays on Giordano Bruno* (Princeton, NJ: Princeton University Press, 2011).

114 Stephen Greenblatt, "A Mobility Studies Manifesto", in *Cultural Mobility. A Manifesto*, with I. Zupanov, R. Meyer-Kalkus, H. Paul, P. Nyiri, and F. Pannewick (Cambridge: Cambridge University Press, 2010), p. 252.

115 Ibid.

116 For a perceptive comparison between Shakespeare's and Caravaggio's use of the twin concepts of multiplicity and indistinction in the visual representation of waning perspective and mirror imagery, see Rocco Coronato's recent book, *Shakespeare, Caravaggio, and the Indistinct Regard* (Oxford: Routledge, 2018).

117 Greenblatt, "Theatrical Mobility", in *Cultural Mobility. A Manifesto*, pp. 76–77.

118 Cf. Michele Marrapodi, "The Ambivalence of Revenge and the Avenger's Role in *Hamlet*: The Function of Letters and Emblematic Allusions", *Cahiers Elisabethains*, 1, 79 (2011): 19–34.

119 Rosalie Osmond, *Mutual Accusation: Seventeenth-Century Body and Soul Dialogues in Their Literary and Theological Context* (Toronto: University of Toronto Press, 1990), p. 19.

120 Ibid, pp. 13–17.

121 Giorgio Melchiori, *Shakespeare's Dramatic Meditations. An Experiment in Criticism* (Oxford: Clarendon Press, 1976), p. 188.

122 Cited from "The 1609 Text of Shakespeare's Sonnets and *A Lover's Complaint*", in *A Companion to Shakespeare's Sonnets*, ed. Michael Schoenfeldt (Oxford: Blackwell Publishing, 2007), p. 490.

123 Melchiori, p. 194.

124 Stephen Greenblatt, *Shakespeare's Freedom* (Chicago, IL: The University of Chicago Press, 2010), p. 4.

125 Kristin Phillips-Court, *The Perfect Genre. Drama and Painting in Renaissance Italy* (Farnham, UK: Ashgate, 2011), p. 146.

126 Kristin Phillips-Court, pp. 192, 194.

127 Stuart Sillars, *Shakespeare and the Visual Imagination* (Cambridge: Cambridge University Press, 2015).

128 Michele Marrapodi (ed.), *Shakespeare and the Visual Arts: The Italian Influence* (Farnham, UK: Routledge, 2017).

129 Keir Elam, *Shakespeare's Pictures: Visual Objects in the Drama* (London: Bloomsbury Academic, 2017).
130 Ibid., p. 9.
131 Ibid, p. 15.
132 Shaul Bassi, *Shakespeare's Italy and Italy's Shakespeare. Place, 'Race', Politics* (Basingstoke, UK: Palgrave Macmillan, 2016).
133 Enza De Francisci and Chris Stamatakis, eds. *Shakespeare, Italy, and Transnational Exchange. Early Modern to Present* (Oxford: Routledge, 2017).
134 Robert Henke and Eric Nicholson, eds. *Transnational Exchange in Early Modern Theater* (Farnham, UK: Ashgate, 2008) and *Transnational Mobilities in Early Modern Theater* (Farnham, UK: Ashgate, 2014).
135 Henke and Nicholson, eds. *Transnational Exchange*, p. 3.
136 Henke and Nicholson, eds. *Transnational Mobilities*, p. 2.

Part 1

Italian literature and culture

1 Dante's *Vita Nuova* and Petrarchismo

A critical review of contemporary scholarship

Marco Andreacchio

If a philosophical "history of love" were ever to be written or rewritten, it could hardly dispense with Dante's *Vita Nuova* and the early modern European phenomenon of Petrarchismo, whose foremost prototypes are the sonnets (*sonetti* or *soniti*) of Petrarca's *Canzoniere* (hereafter, *Rvf*) and Dante's *dolce stil nuovo*, in turn, arguably a renovation of the seemingly "dead poetics" (*morta poesì*) or rhetorical art of classical antiquity (represented most notably by Vergil and Cicero).[1] Yet, in reading Renaissance "love poetry" along the lines of Renaissance modes of "rediscovery" of classical antiquity, our scholarship speaks not of an unequivocal return to classical conceptions but of an appropriation and transformation of antiquity into modernity. Dante and Petrarca, and even more so Petrarchismo, emerge, if only unwittingly, as catalysts for the coming into being of our own age.[2]

At least on the face of things, modern scholarship offers us two main lines of interpretation of Petrarchismo's "love": the political/economic-ideological (as with Arthur Marotti, Kenneth William, and Zygmunt Baranski)[3] and the psychological (as with Gordon Braden and Dorothy Stephens).[4] This is perhaps unsurprising given the modern-"scientific" and thus prototypically Cartesian roots of our scholarship, for which—again, at least on the face of things—meaning must belong either to a *res cogitans* or to its "objective" transposition into the sensory realm of *res extensa*. Neither are attempts to "sublate" psychology and ideology (whereby subjective/intensive desire comes of age upon returning to itself as objective/extensive creator of all ideologies) surprising if considered in the light of the unfolding of Cartesianism into the inverted-idealism or progressivism (Marxist or otherwise) of our "historical-objective consciousness." The historicist reading of our authors, no less than of Petrarchismo, remains in the immediate background of all psychological and ideological readings.

The present chapter will consider the Yale scholar, Giuseppe Mazzotta, as foremost representative of the historicist reading on account of which, e.g., the subject "Dante" is fully himself only in his ever-evolving audience, his private authorship having been negated in/by his work (e.g., the *Comedy*).[5] Here, what is genuinely meaningful is neither Dante's subjective consciousness/authorship, nor its self-transposition in or as a particular objective work, but the historical reception or appropriation of the work, expressive of "the material forces of history."[6]

The latest scholarly "receptacle" of the historicist approach to Dante and Petrarch is Martin Eisner, *Boccaccio and the Invention of Italian Literature: Dante, Petrarch, Cavalcanti, and the Authority of the Vernacular*, Cambridge Studies in Medieval Literature (Cambridge, UK: Cambridge University Press, 2013). The volume stands on the shoulders of renowned

DOI: 10.4324/9781315612720-3

scholars such as Barolini and Baranski. Throughout Eisner's pages, Boccaccio emerges as the true father of Petrarchismo and—beyond any supposed disjuncture between Petrarca (who, in reconstructing antiquity in a still fragmentary manner, set the stage for the Renaissance) and Dante (whose "universalism inspired the Romantics")—as forerunner of an age, still in the making, defined by the universal construction of communities and traditions through digitalization. Yet, the "logic" depicted by Eisner is very old, if Thucydides' account of Rome's *divide et impera* is not irrelevant to our times. Or, to be more precise, Eisner's work calls to mind Hegel's intuition about History-proper as a tendency to resolve the tension between particular (Petrarca's "empirical fragments"?) and universal (Dante's "idealistic vision"?) into a universal free society. Yet, the "sublating" agency that Hegel names *Geist* appears in Eisner attributed to individual creative personalities (paradigmatically, Boccaccio) affirming their respective wills *ad hoc*, or in a context of historical contingency. In Eisner, history is not to be understood as *self-realization* and, thus, in a crucial sense, as *return*. The "end" of history is necessarily less real, not more real than the beginning. The price—if we are to speak of a loss—for the consummation of historical strife between "subjective" universality (mythical imagination?) and "objective" particularity (empirical rationalism?) appears to be a reification of life in the medium of technology. Petrarca's European literary inheritance (Petrarchismo) would seem to unfold as the working out of an unresolved tension between universal (Dantean love?) and particular (Petrarchean love?)—a tension finally resolved by "idealism" placed on a materialistic or particularistic base, an *inverted* idealism represented by Boccaccio and a European Petrarchismo for which the poet-*sive*-ideologue is supposed to have set the stage through his programmatic reconstruction of Dante and Petrarca.

What remains to be seen is how we are to distinguish the upshot of Eisner's reconstruction from the imposition of a global mask of conformity over a Hobbesian state of nature. Eisner's loose threads invite reconsideration of the distinction between ideological and psychological readings of Renaissance love as pertaining, respectively, to objective particularity (Petrarca's "worlds"?) and subjective universality (Dante's will?). A historicist synthesis of the two would entail (1) the objectification of psychology into a new, universal ideology (whereby, e.g., a particular will affirms itself by adopting a universal mask), and (2) the conversion of particular objects of experience into "subjective" functions of the new ideology (so that experience is now re-grounded constructively in ideology).[7]

Whereas the "ideological" reading of love, articulated in the wake of a "hermeneutics of suspicion," has it that Platonic or "ideal love" is essentially an ideological-objective reification of unfulfilled desire for conventional power (a reification historically expressed, most notably in the institutional control of desires, to speak with Foucault),[8] on a "psychological" (usually neo-Romantic, at times explicitly existentialist)[9] reading, our loftiest desires tend to be understood in terms of private passions and/or fears, if only where these are sublimated into Jungian archetypes.

An extended reading of Petrarca along Jungian lines (with direct bearings on Petrarchism) is found in Ève Duperray, *L'Or des Mots: Une lecture du Pétrarque et du mythe littéraire de Vaucluse des origines à l'orée du XXe siècle*, Histoire du Pétrarquisme en France (Paris: Sorbonne, 1997). Duperray decries a traditional eclipsing of the original allegorical valence of Petrarca's verse beneath the aura of myth that the verse creates around itself in the first place by way of authorizing itself. This problem is taken up *mutatis mutandis* by many other scholars, though usually in an "ideological" key (Duperray's argument brings to mind, e.g., Barolini's call to "de-theologize" Dante).

Now, however, we are invited to recover the "archetypal" sense of Petrarca's myth. Even Laura emerges as a Jungian archetype, namely nature (most notably in Duperray's ch. 1.1: "La Nature, paradigme de Laure"—pp. 40–44):[10] the proper context of Petrarchist love is not poetry, but a psychology encompassing all poetry and unfolding as a historical dialectic (tending, if only asymptotically, to a synthesis) between collective symbols (poetry) and our particular lives "actualized" by appropriating (gathering back into themselves, or recollecting) the symbols into which they normally project themselves.[11]

A narrowly or superficially defined "psychologizing" of poets' mode of allegory, or their "veiled speech," comes to serve as the preliminary stage for the historicizing of poetry: the inscription of Petrarchismo in "History" *singulare tantum* presupposes the uprooting of Petrarchismo from its *own* reasons. Its own reasons are replaced by the Reason of History, if only in anticipation of this latter Reason's explosion into existentialism's Un-Reason. At this point, a reappraisal of Petrarca as prophet of existentialist psychology should not surprise dispassionate, by-standing readers of Nietzsche.

It is perhaps a task for future scholarship to re-investigate "the reason of poetry" in the light of considerations familiar to Renaissance (and medieval) poets, and thus in the light of their "defense of poetry." Such a defense testifies to keen awareness of long-standing debates between Faith/Revelation and Reason—a debate at the center of which stood Averroism as mode of understanding the duplicity of language. The "poetic philosophy" of Dante and Petrarca, but also of a whole tradition of Neo-Latin "poet-theologians" across Europe, not to speak of the Renaissance as a whole, could be understood in terms of thinkers' capacity, not so much to pretend to believe in some article of faith that they would then proceed to unmask as irrational, as to illuminate the conditions or "essential background" of faith.[12] The task would be most daring, considering the Christian distinction between human/civil and divine/canon law—a distinction that had made possible the very rise of Christianity as catholic or trans-political faith. The distinction in question entailed "division of labor" between theologians legislating over properly divine things and political philosophers allowed to deliberate only over *merely* human things. The link between the two "labors" would be delineated most notably by St. Thomas Aquinas, for whom philosophical or "natural" reason leads to a "natural theology," or to *general* conceptions of the divine *from a human standpoint*—truths preparing man to embrace beyond perplexity the catholic revelation of Christianity as coronation of our truly natural aspirations.[13]

Read in the context of an Averroist-like approach to the Christian revelation, Petrarca and Petrarchists could make use of a theological conceptual apparatus, no less than of the authority of Holy Church, to carry out a subtle (*sottile*) critical investigation of the grounds or "inner motives" of faith (and thereby of religious authority). What contemporary scholarship often views as Petrarca's pre-Reformist "psychology" would then entail a poetic posturing or "conceit" (not differing in essence from the one exemplified by Dante in his *Comedy*, or even by Cicero in his "first-person" dialogues) through which the philosophical poet would be disclosing a "hidden" or unconventional arena (a fictitious "wilderness" or *selva/sylva*) for illuminating—in the medium/mirror of a web of judiciously articulated poetic metaphors—the foundations of moral life and order, specifically where morality has come to be viewed *anagogically*, or in Christian terms. Speaking of the divine in human form or "under the veil of vulgar verses" (to cite Boccaccio's *lectura Dantis*), Petrarchists could carry out a covert mission—at once ethical (civilizing/*humanizing*) and intellectual (purely philosophical) —alien to any ideological intent. Classical philosophical prudence, rather than Machiavellian ideological cunning, could make a "heroic" poetry immune to inquisitional condemnation.[14]

By falling short of turning to a serious reconsideration of Averroism, "psychological" approaches to Petrarca's inheritance lend themselves to painting Petrarca as a shadow of our own times. Emblematic, in this respect, is Ève Duperray, *La Postérité Répond à Pétrarque: Sept Siècles de Fortune Pétrarquienne en France* (Paris: Beauchesne, 2006). At least with respect to "unpacking" the psychological (specifically Jungian) approach to Petrarca and his European inheritance, the volume's arguably farthest-reaching, or simply most outspoken contributor is Giuseppe Tognon, whose "Pétrarque est-il encore un humaniste?" (pp. 331–40) carries us through a chain of disenchanted reflections from Petrarch to Paul Ricoeur (behind whom stands, unnamed, Martin Heidegger), or, more generally, post-modernity. Tognon's "exemplary" Petrarca departs from classical and medieval rationalism (including that of Dante; p. 335) to inaugurate an age characterized by the unprecedented discovery that, far from being "a need to satisfy" (Plato), or "a strategy necessary to survive" (Aristotle), love is our very existential condition whose proper home is a *symbolic* language marking the primacy of "comprehension" over "conceptual coherence" (pp. 335, 337–39). Neither reason nor faith, but intimate, anguished acquaintance with our troubled, fractured past—above all, our all-too-worldly fears—is the way to free us from fear (*metus solvere*), the way carrying us into the future (p. 340).[15] At the end of the path stands not Dante's rational love (*intelletto d'amore*) but an awarding of "nobility to the fears of the body" (*noblesse aux peurs du corps*), as well as the "translating into dignity and into virtue all of our inner failings and hardships, the frailty of nature" (p. 337). Echoing Proust's aesthetics (p. 340), Tognon invites a Petrarchism that is entirely cogent with post-modernity's "return to the future."

To summarize the distinction between ideological and psychological readings of Petrarca's inheritance, in one case love is explicated as *object* (ideology) and in another as *subject* (empirically determinate or verifiable carnal impulses). The former reading has been exemplified most programmatically by Baranski, according to whom both Dante and Petrarca were obsessed with using poetry as an ideological tool to establish their respective authority through the dismantling of competing predecessors' reputation.

"Petrarch, Dante, Cavalcanti," Baranski's latest statement on the subject, is found in *Petrarch & Dante: Anti-Dantism, Metaphysics, Tradition*, a volume Baranski co-edited in 2009.[16] The collection of essays includes statements by notable scholars such as Giuseppe Mazzotta ("Petrarch's Dialogue with Dante"—pp. 177–95—confirming the relevance of Mazzotta's earlier work to the editors' leading thesis);[17] Christian Moevs ("Subjectivity and Conversion in Dante and Petrarch"—pp. 226–69—where Petrarch stands as radically modern antithesis to the fideistic, Neo-Platonic Dante that Moevs proposed most notably in 2001);[18] Albert Ascoli ("Blinding the Cyclops: Petrarch after Dante"—pp. 114–73—where, "geographical nuances" reflect Petrarca's departure from and undermining of Dante's poetic theology);[19] and Teodolinda Barolini ("Petrarch as Metaphysical Poet Who Is Not Dante: Metaphysical Markers at the Beginning of the *Rerum vulgarium fragmenta* [*Rvf* 1–21]"—pp. 226–62—where, against attempts to link Petrarca back to the *dolce stil nuovo*[20] (and in tacit dissent with Moevs),[21] the author juxtaposes Dante's "incarnational poetics" to Petrarca's "Neoplatonic" distrust for multiplicity (significantly no mention is made of the Platonic non-monistic doctrines of the plurality/communion of Ideas, and of Emanation)—pp. 200, 216). The volume cites numerous works arguing for a deep, covert, ideological divide between Petrarca and Dante. The volume's contributors join forces to paint Petrarca, if not as viscerally, even cunningly resentful of Dante's authority (Baranski and Chachey), then at least as "metaphysically" at odds with Dante's thought.[22] However, the evidence advanced to support the claim that Petrarca wrote, if only cryptically, within the scope of anti-Dantism, is consistently questionable. Let us succinctly consider three examples from the volume's introduction.

In the wake of Vernani's inquisitorial condemnation of *Monarchia*, why should Petrarca's refrain from publicly naming Dante's Latin works surprise us, or invite us to conclude—as our volume does—that Petrarca was moved by an "anti-Dantean animus" (p. 10)? Secondly, in explaining a passage from Petrarca's letter to Boccaccio (*Fam.* 21.15), in which the former poet openly praises Dante as *fame cupidus* ("desirous of fame"), our volume (esp. Baranski and Moevs, after Gilson) does not give any weight to the poetic or philosophically legitimate valence of fame (cf. Boccaccio's *Amorosa Visione*)[23]—a valence that is entirely compatible with Petrarca's (and Dante's) love of virtue as an end in itself (correcting the *worldly*/empirical pursuit of the Ulysses portrayed in *Inferno* XXVI.94–99, in the light of *Fam.* 21.15). Thirdly, the sonnet "Vergine Bella" (*Rvf* 366)—where, implicitly referring to Christianity's Virgin Mary as "glorious … true beatifying one" (*gloriosa … vera beatrice*), Petrarca is admittedly alluding to Dante's Beatrice (whom, in *Inferno* II.103, Lucia, personification of contemplative light, introduces as "true praise of God" or *loda di Dio vera*)—is now read without question as a vivid, unqualified, expression of Petrarca's supposed anti-Dantism. No effort is made to uncover any alternative authorial intent such that it may be entirely compatible with Dante's own understanding, thus undermining, if not disqualifying, the claim that Petrarca was an anti-Dantist. The assumption that Petrarca's Virgin is incompatible with Dante's Beatrice would seem to presuppose the further assumption that for Petrarca, *against* Boccaccio and the whole Renaissance tradition of *theologia poetica* (not to speak of Petrarca's celebration of Laura), Christian theology is incompatible with philosophical poetry. Furthermore, Dante himself invokes Christianity's Virgin Mary, most notably throughout *Paradiso*, thereby tacitly reminding us that his Lady Beatrice is hardly more than a true poetic invention that has the façade of a lie (*faccia di menzogna*, in *Inferno* XVI.124; compare *Rvf*, 1.12–13). Finally, what forbids us from understanding Petrarca as positing "beautiful" (*bella*) Mary, "lady of the King who loosened our bindings [*lacci*—arguably akin to Dante's *nodi*]/and made the world free and happy," as the muse of all poets? What world could be "free and happy" for Petrarca other than the Parnassus of poets—the Mount that Dante set free (as arguably intimated in *Purgatorio* XXI) for future generations of "compatriots"?[24]

Notwithstanding all possible counter-readings, scholars such as Baranski insist unself-critically upon portraying Petrarch univocally as a covert, if only unself-conscious ideologue. The "ideological thesis" is not always spelled out in an unequivocal manner, but its advocates usually find incisive ways for advancing its cause. Thus, for instance, in McLaughlin et al. (2007),[25] Boitani's "Petrarca and the Barbari Britanni" finds Petrarch devoted to a semiological universe—a labyrinth of words in which the humanist buries himself as cave dweller[26]—standing as mythical mask of ideological, "real," "cultural" conflicting differences that, as covert historical forces, use poetry as fuel.[27] In the "Petrarch and the Self" section of the same volume, we find "Invective against Ignorance," a contribution by Baranski, whose Petrarca again uses the poetic tradition to bolster his own authority/fame. Baranski never addresses a certain difficulty arising from the discrepancy between Petrarca's generally acknowledged disregard for the dominant opinions of his times (even in Boitani's contribution, the humanist comes across as the least flattering of poets) and the allegation that Petrarca uses poetry to acquire worldly fame. Surely Petrarca would have known that appealing to his poetic authorities would not help him gain the graces of his times unless he devoted his energies to bend his "authors" to adorn his audience's self-certainty or vanity.

In general, on an ideological reading, Petrarchismo tends to amplify the political-ideological valence of its literary sources. Thus, for instance, studies of early English receptions of Petrarca (from Chaucer and Spencer to Shakespeare) tend to highlight a typically Anglican reorientation of poetry away from "typically Italian" idealizations of the female object of love (usually, with the tacit understanding that poetry is the mouthpiece of its times).[28] On a psychological reading, Petrarchismo tends to expose the emotive, even carnal, dimension of love (ultimately, not against, but in deep continuity with anti-Petrarchism's parodies).[29] Yet, as Hempfer (*cit.*) confirms, the ideological and the psychological readings can, arguably as they must, mirror each other in pointing conclusively to a *historical* synthesis.

Hempfer's "Per una definizione del Petrarchismo" (*cit.*) remains the most illuminating available general account of contemporary studies of Petrarchismo (outdating Baldacci, *cit.*). Hempfer shows that Petrarch's authority and his "influence" are usually inadequately understood and defined. The scholar proposes to understand Petrarchismo as the interplay of Petrarch's form/"structure") and content/"function" unfolding historically, or in the context of a "global sociocultural system" (*sistema globale socio-culturale;* p. 44). Developing intuitions voiced already by Cian,[30] Forster (*cit.*) and Hoffmeister,[31] among others, Hempfer presents Petrarchismo as a provisional or partial repository of Petrarca's authority (or of the semantic valence of the poet's works), where the definite or real repository is a history in the making. In the context of this history, Petrarchism stands as a step towards a global rhetoric fit for a global society—a society characterized, e.g., by a playful synthesis of all static conceptions of love (pp. 35, 44). The "end" of the history of language commencing, not so much with Petrarch, as with the first appropriations of Petrarch, is given ahead of time only *formally*, or in empty generality, so that the history's *content* is fully disclosed only at the end of the historical process.

Hempfer's argument stands to remind students of Petrarchismo of the importance of concepts ("theoretical hypotheses") in defining our empirical facts (p. 24). Perhaps most importantly, Hempfer's argument testifies to the guiding or metaphysical assumptions underlying contemporary studies of Petrarca's inheritance. Those assumptions are unequivocally Hegelian.

Contemporary studies of Dante and Petrarca tend to remain oriented towards a history to some extent overlapping with the phenomenon of Petrarchismo. Whereas narrowly understood Petrarchismo is inscribed within modernity, broadly understood Petrarchismo comes to coincide with modernity itself in its ongoing unfolding. Dante and Petrarca emerge as keys to an adequate understanding of our times. Yet, historicism teaches us that to understand our authors is to understand their history. The key becomes, so to speak, a function of its lock. The "solution" legitimates the problem. We are thus tempted to conclude that, echoing Pirandellian characters in search of their author, our scholars have sought in Dante and Petrarca their own creators, and in Petrarchismo their own youth, in such a way that the creator is itself created: the Neo-Romantic child begets its own father.

Contemporary scholarly assessments of Petrarchismo justifiably rest on assessments of Dante and Petrarca themselves,[32] if only by considering that it would not be right for us to take our authors for granted. If our times do stand on their gigantic shoulders, then our self-understanding will be nourished as we turn Petrarchismo—conceived as our "youth"—upon its "fathers." Accordingly, recent scholarship turns to our two authors armed with philological exactitude suggesting that our task is not merely to invent our authors but to uncover them from beneath a formerly ill-conceived or unself-conscious history, or to read Petrarchismo in the light of its models.[33] As long as we approach the "history" (viz. Petrarchismo broadly understood) as essentially *listening* to its ostensive models—though perhaps failing to hear them, or hearing them in a distorted, even providentially corrective manner—rather than as merely or blindly *using* them (if only in the unuttered name of a Hegelian *Aufheben*), our scholarly assessment of the valence of love for European Petrarchisti will require a prior reconsideration of love in Dante and Petrarca themselves.[34]

How does contemporary scholarship approach Dante—especially the Dante of the *Vita Nuova*—and Petrarca when it comes to thinking through the problem of love? The simple answer is: by looking at the poets' stance towards their respective beloved Ladies —Beatrice and Laura. Let us begin with Dante. On the subject of love, Teodolinda Barolini's "Dante and the Troubarours: An Overview," *TENSO: Bulletin of the Société Guilhem IX*, 5:1 (Autumn 1989, pp. 3–10), includes a currently standard account of Dante's departure from Provençal predecessors. The account—which tacitly represents *mutandis mutandis* the dilemma confronted by the protagonists of ancient Greek tragedy torn between private, if only ancestral loves (read, *physis*) and public demands (read, *nomos*)—has it that troubadours, tied as they were to pagan or anti-Christian conceptions of love, failed to overcome the private-public impasse, where private interests coincide with love of an earthly woman, whereas public interests coincide with the obligation to love/adore God. Dante's "solution" to the impasse is supposed to have brought to fruition attempts made by the early heralds of the *dolce stil nuovo* school of poetry to resolve the problem of love. Dante's solution calls for a transfiguration, or, in Hegelian terms, a "sublation," of earthly love into divine love. If not within the course of the *Comedy*, at least in the course of Dante's total *œuvre*, Beatrice would emerge from an earthly/carnal state into a heavenly figure that is one with God, so that to love one's woman is *eo ipso* to love God. Earlier attempts to address the problem of love *philosophically* (as in *Convivio*) are abandoned as misguided: when taken seriously and thus as one's way of life, philosophy is ultimately an error to be transcended, if not altogether avoided.[35] Philosophy's attempt to cross the "divided line" between the sensory and the intelligible can be nothing more than a *folle volo*, a "foolish flight" reminiscent of Ulysses' homonymous leap beyond preordained boundaries. Love is consummated by ascending through a spiritual ladder of passion, not a philosophical one of ideas. Or rather, the Platonic ladder of ideas—entailing a passage from the outward/sensory aspect of things to the inner/intelligible core of things—is cast in a new, "Christian" light, whereby it now entails a rehabilitation of the body as pure object of contemplation (akin to a Catholic "cult of Mary").

The reading of Dante exemplified by Barolini presents no small difficulties, which our scholarship has barely or rarely begun to grapple with. To begin, in the text of the *Comedy*, Ulysses invites a flight *within* the realm of sensory experience, not *from* it, so that no abandonment of philosophy can be entailed by his negative example. What is more, the *Comedy* (the locus where Dante is supposed to have given final or highest expression to his insights on love) invites, not literally understood "enthusiasm," but a cryptic "placing-oneself-into-divinity" (*indiarsi*—anticipating *Paradiso* XXXIII.132). Accordingly, in *Paradiso* I.70–72 after 67–69, "self-divinization" is no more than a loss of humanity. Neither is the *finale* of the *Comedy* (*Paradiso* XXIII.131–45) altogether heartening, to the extent that the leap to appropriate the object of love, being a leap to appropriate one's own "self-centered" effigy, is met by a bolt of lightning, if only one through which the poetic will casts *itself* into the Ptolemaic heavens of its own poem (compare XX.1–12 and 22–36). Again, by the end of the poem, Beatrice has long disappeared, a fact suggesting that the poet no longer needs to wait upon his lovely (because beloved?) muse to beatify him: was Beatrice merely a poetic or a-temporal *means* for the apotheosis of poets—a means mediating the human reason of philosophy and the divine reason of theology?[36] Does the disappearance of Beatrice signal a reduction of philosophical reason to a divine counterpart, or does it signal that philosophy hides poetically (i.e., through the use of poetic devices) in theology, as may be deduced from the concluding verses of *Convivio*?

If Barolini's "standard" reading were correct, should we not expect the *Comedy* to spell out an ascent from a *carnal* Beatrice/love to a *spiritual* counterpart? Is any such ascent really taking place in Dante? It is uncontroversial that numerous examples of misguided love populate the *Comedy*, but do these diminish as we exit *Inferno*? If love is consummated in the *background* of all lovable images, is love of an image in the dark any less inherently misguided than love of an image in the light? Can the latter be less misguided than the former independently of a philosophical reflection that, if only in the mirror of divine light, illuminates the difference between images and their constitutive background? Is the carnal/physical love of *Inferno* romantically "sublated" in the remaining two Canticles, or is it replaced by bright counterparts that are no less problematic than their earthly shadows? Does the *Comedy* tend towards the dissolving or the intensifying of the problematicity of love? We might even wonder if the love of *Paradiso* is not *more* problematic than its "underworld" counterpart given that this one remains excruciatingly aware of the contrast between finite objects of love and their background. For the inhabitants of *Paradiso*, the contrast is no longer felt; *Christian* images are sufficiently pleasurable to consign philosophical awareness of their inadequacy to oblivion. Are Christian images ultimately more distracting than pagan ones from the supreme or truest end of human desire?

A further difficulty emerges in consideration of the "Nietzschean" objection to Christianity's supposed "will to power": does Dante's "love" ultimately signal the apotheosis of man's will *as* a divine end in itself?[37] *Or*, is Dante calling into question this apotheosis by casting it in a poetic context guided by an irreducible philosophical doubt? Does the *Comedy* use philosophy to bolster our Will as absolute self-determination, or does it make use of theology to investigate the will's foundations/ground?[38] Is Dante's God ultimately the supreme face-mask or façade (*faccia*) of Will, or is it further or primarily—if only through the very failure of "the lofty imagination" (the *alta fantasia* of *Paradiso* XXXIII.142)—the cradle for a philosophical illumination of volition, i.e., for the clarification of the self-determination of desire and thereby of desire's own nature?[39] Do the concluding verses of *Paradiso* signal the triumph of a will that wills itself, a will turning its back on all questioning, *or* does it confirm the eminence of a philosophical life of questioning that hides at the bottom of every will? Does Dante finally raise the *vita activa* to contemplative heights, or does he point back to a *vita contemplativa*—a silence or stillness—seated at the heart of our *vita* to sustain it as genuinely *activa*, lest our life become subservient to alien powers?

The foregoing questions are not meant to settle, but to rekindle the *problem* of what love means for Dante *even* in the *Comedy*. That problem is not adequately solved without taking into account objections to the neat reduction of philosophy to theology, even if by theology we mean one of its contemporary "Neo-Protestant" guises.

The answer to the problem of love attributed to Dante by our Dante scholars would be typical of medieval Christian theology, if it were not for the fact that in the contemporary Dante profane love is not transfigured into its sacred counterpart *through the Church*, but "subjectively": the transfiguration is not consummated beyond the imagination, in an "objective" otherworld but in one mortal poet's *imagination*. Dante is now *de facto* in tune with a Romantic conception of love on account of which the pure-hearted pursuit of earthly interests leads to, or even coincides with, heaven, so that *pure* philosophy is at best a distraction from "the right way" (*la diritta via*)—a distraction that leads us to mistake the real object of love (being a transfigured or resurrected body) with a mere conceptual abstraction or bodiless soul, an empty shell in which rather than resolving the problem of love, we evade it.

Impatience with philosophical "abstractions," or with Platonism *tout court*, has important antecedents among nineteenth-century Romantics or subjective idealists. Yet, as much as it generally rests upon a Romantic intuition, the contemporary *reception* of Dante's "love poetry" is not entirely Romantic. The Romantic imagination abhors political life; its morality is as cut off from political interests as Kant's Sublime is from the common good. Conversely, the contemporary reading of Dante—from Baranski to Mazzotta—is dominated by awareness of the importance of political interests in the constitution of the pure object of love. The poet's "sublimated" love remains blindly subject to forces blind to it; its purity depends unequivocally upon impurity. Contemporary Dante scholarship is in general geared towards uncovering the political background of Dante's Romantic or proto-Romantic love-flight. Our scholarship does not deny that Dante was and thought of himself as a political man but, if only tacitly, that he possessed an inadequate understanding of political life; otherwise, he would not have been a moral or political *philosopher*, but an intellectual historian. For, then, he would have understood political thought in a *historical* context, or as informed by historical forces impervious to human reason. Dante would not have mistaken *his* authors for *the* authors themselves, but would have realized that his authors were authors only insofar as he *received* and thereby *constructed* them. Not the "objective" study of *originals*, but the *reception* of originals, or rather the reception of receptions, i.e., the reception of terms tied to a *tradition* of discourse, would have been of primary concern to the poet *had he* understood the true nature of political things. When rooting political life and order *directly* in a divine mind (*sanza mezzo spira*), Dante shows to ignore the historical contingency of human thought, or the "historically mediated" manner in which our thoughts arise.

Intellectual historians sympathetic to Dante will at best regard the poet as glimpsing darkly at the truth of History through a glass, without rising to full awareness of the implications History has for human thought and speech.[40] As sympathetic readers, we scholars may approach Dante as forerunner or prehistory of an awareness that we already possess: Dante—and even more so, Petrarca—can at best inspire us to confirm and cherish our own self-awareness as historically determined beings, or—if a circular expression be permitted—as beings historically determined to determine themselves in and *as* History.

Perhaps the most elegant example of the general approach elucidated here is offered by Giuseppe Mazzotta in his *The Worlds of Petrarch* (*cit.*), where the Yale scholar presents Dante as taking a first step towards Petrarca's discovery of the historicity or radical finitude of all thought. Whereas Dante dreams of a grand, unified history "from the desert,"[41] Petrarca explodes the unity of History, discovering a history of fractures or fragments, of discontinuity in things and thought, alike. Petrarca discovers a world that is fundamentally just as post-modernity says it is. Whereas, for Dante love is *still* thought's own form, for Petrarca love opposes thought from without, signaling the existential-historical limits of thought. Dante's love is still intellectual; Petrarca's love is already existential.

Mazzotta is an illustrious example of a scholarship for which our comparison of the thought of Dante and Petrarca is possible and meaningful today strictly within a historical context. The comparison presupposes history as the proper context of all human thought. Contemporary academia does not shake, as might Mount Purgatory, in the face of fundamental objections to the project of reconciling Dante to our intellectual history. Once intellectual history is regarded as the highest standard by which we may judge all thought and discourse, can Dante be anything better today than *our* reception of Dante, i.e., the latest moment of a broadening history of Dante-receptions—a history to which all "Dantes" must belong?[42] The fact that this question resists being exiled to the realm of sheer polemics is brought to light by distinguished scholarly critiques of "reception studies."[43] Following the lead of Gerosa (*cit.*) and Schmidt,[44] Laure Hermand-Schebat's *Pétrarque épistolier et Cicéron: étude d'une filiation* (Paris: PUPS, 2008) rejects talk of "reception" as artificially one-sided—what is at work in our study of sources, no less than in Petrarca's study of classical antiquity, is not mere reception but a cross-fertilizing conversation in the course of which we do not merely appropriate a source but let ourselves be guided by our source as regards the legitimacy of any consequent appropriation. The use we make of Dante and Petrarca is necessarily and actively conditioned by what Dante and Petrarca have to say to us concerning the use we might make of them and thus concerning our *rewriting* of their works in or as our own. The best use presupposes the best "ear"—the best bent upon our source. This way, we do not merely "receive" by way of moving away from our original (Dante's *Vita Nuova* or Petrarca's *Rvf*, as the case may be) but carry the original *qua* original into an ongoing conversation, thereby keeping alive a tradition of interpretation—of writing, reading, and rewriting—that would otherwise remain overshadowed by a wilderness of self-serving appropriations for which the present is necessarily our highest standard of judgment.[45]

Admittedly, contemporary critiques of "reception studies" tend to retain the presupposition that all dialogue takes place within History, so that all dialogues are finally received by the *last* stage of History, namely the age in which "historical consciousness" has fully unfolded. But since such an age is our own, whereas it may not be appropriate to read Petrarca's approach to Cicero in terms of reception, it is nonetheless fair *for us* to receive all of our authors within a historical context that is one with our own sense of certainty as readers. History is a process of cross-fertilization leading to the emergence of the Sense of History itself—a sense that emerges as the pinnacle of all cross-fertilizations and consequently as transcending them. Our sense of History does not enter the process of cross-fertilization; as intellectual historians, we do not bring it into question but retain it as the background or final stage of all dialogues. Does this not mean that intellectual historians necessarily tread in Hegel's shadow (as distasteful as this conclusion would be for Mazzotta), or that dialogue is in some crucial manner over *for us*? To paraphrase Walter Benjamin, we are the Age that looks back and down upon all dialogues from the perspective of their consummation. Consequently, our foremost task will be that of *situating* our sources, rather than of *understanding* them in their own right, i.e., independently of, and even by way of questioning, *any* preconceived context. Our scholarship's *style* (in Dante's sense of the term)—its essential orientation—will be *aesthetic*, rather than philosophical.[46]

The challenge emerges for critical thought to wade the distance between our "aesthetic way" and the "philosophical way" of our sources. How does our scholarship justify its enclosure of the thought of previous ages within our aesthetics? One facile way is by reading the present *into* the past, or by seeing the past as an intimation of *our* "aesthetic" sense of History. Mazzotta is not alone in applying this procedure to Dante and Petrarca (neither is the projection of modern aesthetics into medieval and Renaissance thought a prerogative of Umberto Eco).

Much of our Dante and Petrarca scholarship tends to read either or both authors as anticipating our times—the present. At least ever since Ernest Renan's *Averroès et l'averroisme: essai historique* (Paris: A. Durand, 1852), Petrarca in particular is habitually heralded as "the first modern man" who turns to the ancients by way of transcending the medieval world and ushering into modernity. Bruno Lavillatte's "Petrarca fra il Nulla e l'Essere" (in Secchi Tarugi, *cit.*, pp. 83–93) goes as far as to find in Petrarca the condition of "extreme modernity" (*extreme modernité*) represented by Heidegger's "existential humanism" (*humanisme existentiel*—pp. 84–85). Clues to Petrarca's modernism are sought even in Petrarca's own self-descriptions.[47] For Lionello Sozzi, Petrarca brings Stoicism into Christianity, at the antipodes of the Platonism characteristic of Romantic invocations of Petrarca's name but also in anticipation of later currents of thought.[48]

The move described by Sozzi is reminiscent of a Machiavellianism disclosing the modern world by placing Christian idealism on *a*-political foundations, or by reading Christianity, no longer through Aristotelian-Platonism, but through medieval Christianity's preferred philosophical targets of condemnation: Epicureanism and Stoicism. But is Petrarca's defense of the primacy of contemplation to be understood in terms of Machiavelli's turning political idealism into an instrument of private interests?[49] How do interpreters such as Sozzi[50] account for Petrarca's predilection of Cicero—no Stoic and no Epicurean, but a Platonist at heart? How does the thesis of a Stoic Petrarca square with Petrarca's turn to Plato as a model for a good death—a turn highlighted, e.g., in Fenzi (2003)?[51]

Ursula Rombach's "Francesco Petrarca ed Ercole al Bivio"[52] argues that Petrarca ultimately rejects Cicero's favouring of the *vita activa* over its contemplative counterpart. But is Cicero's defense of *vita activa* anything more than one moment in an argument that ends in the vindication of the primacy of *vita contemplativa*?[53] Would Cicero reject Rombach's Petrarca's conclusion that contemplation is the master key to political life? Rombach proposes this conclusion as Petrarca's *Christian* corrective to Cicero, but one need not be a Christian to swear that purely philosophical reflection is necessary for the salvation of polities. It suffices that one be a Socratic. Yet for Rombach, in privileging contemplation over "occupation," Petrarca is grounding political life in the solitary "decision" of a "free *individual*" (pp. 69–70). Not pure, disinterested contemplation, but a modern *will* sits at the basis of our *vita activa*.[54]

An alternative reading is offered by Hermand-Schebat (*cit.*), whose extensive treatment of the "love" relation between Petrarca and Cicero shows the inadequacy of studies for which Petrarca would be countering Cicero's understanding of solitude. Especially illuminating are the subsections for Hermand-Schebat's volume's ch. VII, "La position de Pétrarque: apologie de l'otium" and "Politien et l'iconographie du Quattrocento: Cicéron défenseur de la libertas." The author argues convincingly that Petrarca's "critique" (in fact an oddly exaggerated offense *ad hominem*) of Cicero's *mores* is to be understood in the light of a subsequent *laude* of the Roman's thought and virtue: Petrarca would be using Cicero as "alter ego" (p. 299), or as mirror in which to highlight the difficulty, not to say the impossibility of resolving the tension between the active and contemplative life—and consequently, between worldly/"immanent" and otherworldly/"transcendent" love—in *this life*.[55] That tension is philosophy itself, understood at once as the art of writing and of living ("un art de vivre"—p. 13); not an individual's solitary decision, but a virtue that, while binding thought and life together, refuses to fuse the two in any decision, no matter how "authentic."[56] The "philosophical tension" stands in the way of any interpretation of "Renaissance love," forcing upon scholars a choice—to either kindle or to smother that love with words.

Notes

1 On the 'Platonic origin' of the sonnet via Dante's precursor, Giacomo da Lentino, see Paul Oppenheimer, "The Origin of the Sonnet," *Comparative Literature*, 34 (Autumn 1982): 289–304. Though necessarily leaving many scholarly resources unnamed, the present review draws upon representatives of contemporary currents of relevant interpretation.

2 Vastly influential, Neo-Kantianism's conception of Renaissance poetry (and consequently its 'love') remains as a stepping stone towards a fully modern conception of nature on account of which sensory phenomena are not masks of metaphysical realities but *termini ad quos* of human creativity and self-discovery. See Ernest Cassirer, *The Individual and the Cosmos in Renaissance Philosophy*, trans. and introd. by Mario Domandi (Chicago, IL: Chicago University Press, 2010 [1927]), p. 143. See further Ugo Dotti, *Petrarca e la scoperta della coscienza moderna* (Milan: Feltrinelli, 1978); and Aldo S. Bernardo, ed., *Francesco Petrarca: Citizen of the World* (Albany, NY: SUNY University Press, 1980).

3 Hardliners within the arena of 'ideological readings' include Arthur F. Marotti, "'Love is Not Love': Elizabethan Sonnet Sequences and the Social Order," *ELH*, 49 (Summer, 1982): 396–428; and Marziano Guglielminetti, *Petrarca e il petrarchismo: un'ideologia della letteratura* (Alessandria, Italy: Edizioni dell'Orso, 1994 [1970]). Within the scope of 'ideological readings,' we also find feminist works (Emma Campbell, "Sexual Poetics and the Politics of Translation in the Tale of Griselda," *Comparative Literature*, 55 [Summer, 2003]: 191–216) and those for which Petrarchismo is an ingenious tool for the propagation of 'theological and ideological' messages. Abigail Brundin, *Vittoria Colonna and the Poetics of the Italian Reformation* (Aldershot, UK: Ashgate, 2008) argues that sixteenth-century Italian Petrarchismo (and by extension, European Petrarchismo in general) served as a means of cover to propagate 'spiritualist' evangelical messages in continuity with proto-Protestant impulses discernable in authors going back at least as far as Dante and his early commentators. On Petrarca as anticipating Reformation purism, see also Michael Wyatt, "Other Petrarchs in Early Modern England," in *Petrarch in Britain: Interpreters, Imitators, and Translators over 700 Years*. Proceedings of the British Academy, eds. Martin Mclaughlin, Letizia Panizza, and Peter Hainsworth (Oxford: Oxford University Press, 2007), pp. 203–16; and W. J. Kennedy, *Authorizing Petrarch* (Ithaca, NY: Cornell University Press, 1994), esp. pp. 67–81. At the fringes of ideological readings stands Leonard Forster, *The Icy Fire: Five Studies in European Petrarchism* (Cambridge: Cambridge University Press, 1969). Forster (esp. ch. II) anticipates Kennedy's argument that what is important for Petrarchismo is the purely *formal* aspect of Petrarch's poetry insofar as it can be imitated; conversely, what is *not* significant for Petrarchismo is the

actual *content* of Petrarch's poetry. Forster's peculiar division between literary form and content—or between syntax and semantics—is arguably retraceable to Cartesianism, presupposing as it does that literary form (as a pure law) can be abstracted to apply successfully to various contents indiscriminately or universally. Indeed, Forster's work seeks general laws of applicability of Petrarch's poetic *form* or 'poetic idiom,' which is intuited as functioning most notably as a way to address various socio-linguistic crises. An alternative, more politically and philosophically promising approach to Petrarca's European influence—beyond Forster's 'supremely imitable' and equally *empty* model for new vernacular languages across Europe—is invited by Federico Cinti, "Per un Atlante del Petrarchismo Neolatino Europeo," in eds. Calitti and Gigliucci, pp. 499–515.

4 On psychological mechanisms (esp. 'flirtation') used self-consciously by Petrarchists in defense against the strife of *Realpolitik*, see Dorothy Stephens, *The Limits of Eroticism in Post-Petrarchan Narrative: Conditional Pleasure from Spencer to Marvell* (Cambridge: Cambridge University Press, 2004). On linking poetic imitation to psychic (usually, gender-relative) frustrations, see further, Gordon Braden, *Petrarchan Love and the Continental Renaissance* (New Haven, CT: Yale University Press, 1999); and Gordon Braden, "Love and Fame: The Petrarchan Career," in *Pragmatism's Freud: The Moral Disposition of Psychoanalysis*, eds. William Kerrigan and J. H. Smith (Baltimore, MD: Johns Hopkins University Press, 1986), pp. 126–58. The present review assumes—against the grain of a Neo-Kantian aesthetics projected to the end of History—that, even within its 'laboratory,' whether it is aware of it or not, philology—even when conceived strictly as *semiotics*—is never an unmoved mover but always presupposes guiding considerations. To read Petrarchism semiotically in terms of a deep maze of seemingly free-floating rhetorical signs is to advance the historicist cause of 'ideological readings' in general. See, for instance, W. T. Rossiter, *Chaucer and Petrarch* (Cambridge: D. S. Brewer, 2010); and W. T. Rossiter, "Petrarchism and Repentance in John Donne's *Holy Sonnets*," in *The Poetry of Religious Sorrow in Early Modern England*, ed. Gary Kuchar (Cambridge: Cambridge University Press, 2008), pp. 151–83.

5 For a recent Foucaultian account of Petrarca's poetry as both constructing and deconstructing the authorial self in a repeated hedonistic failure to transcend time/death, see Gur Zak, *Petrarch's Humanism and the Care of the Self* (Cambridge: Cambridge University Press, 2010). For slightly less sophisticated deconstructions of Petrarca's authority, see Olivia Holmes, *Assembling the Lyric Self: Authorship from the Troubadour Song to the Italian Poetry Book* (Minneapolis: Minnesota University Press, 2000). Developing theses introduced notably in Kennedy (1994), *cit.*, W. J. Kennedy, *The Site of Petrarchism: Early Modern National Sentiment in Italy, France, and England* (Baltimore, MD: Johns Hopkins University Press, 2003) reads modern nationalism back into Renaissance poetry conceived as 'expression' of 'national sentiment,' rather than as fathering national sentiment. We may wonder if Petrarch was 'aware' of being Italian (as Kennedy sustains), or if the poet-theologian did not rather engender awareness of nationality as *civil consciousness* in his readers. In assuming that meaning is produced in the context of a web of commentaries that have no need for an original intent, if not as mask of variable pursuits, Kennedy's historicizing/deconstructing of authorship is questionably collapsing, in a Foucaultian manner, the 'hidden' poet into his poetic-political mask, a form the content of which is now supposed to be supplied by its variable audiences *ex machina*, almost *ex nihilo*.

6 The historicist (usually proto-/philo-Marxist) reading of Dante/Petrarca, and consequently of Petrarchismo, has long dominated the Italian academic scene, at least from Francesco De Sanctis to Cesare Luporini and present day interpreters. On the link between interpretation and 'material history,' see Teodolinda Barolini and H. Wayne Storey (eds.), *Petrarch and the Textual Origins of Interpretation* (New York: Columbia University Press, 2007). Feminist studies of Petrarchismo tend to tread within the historicist scope of Marxist approaches to poetry. See Nancy Vickers, "Diana Described: Scattered Woman and Scattered Rhyme," in *Writing and Sexual Difference*, ed. Elizabeth Abel (Chicago, IL: Chicago University Press), pp. 95–109. For a 'counter-feminist' psychoanalytic approach to Petrarchismo (reading gender-liberating sexual impulses as integral to the making of poetry), see Gordon Braden, "Gaspara Stampa and the Gender of Petrarchism," *Texas Studies in Literature and Language*, 38 "Revising Renaissance Eroticism" (Summer 1996): 115–39. On sexual intrigue as positive subtle undercurrent of Petrarchismo, see Mary Bly, "Bait for the Imagination: Danae and

Consummation in Petrarch and Heywood," *Comparative Literature Studies*, 32, 3 (1995): 343–59.

7 On the project described here, compare Dante, *Inferno* I.91–102 and Giacomo Leopardi, "Proposta di premi fatta dall'Accademia dei Sillografi," in *Operette Morali* (www.leopardi.it /operette_morali.php).

8 On Petrarchismo's love poetry as courtly escape from political problems, see Lauro Martines, *Power and Imagination: City-States in Renaissance Italy* (London: Pimlico, 2002 [1979]), pp. 323–28. According to Stefano Benassi, Petrarca (and by extension, Petrarchismo) transposes unresolved ethical tensions in the sublime's 'vertigo.' See Stefano Benassi, "La vertigine del sublime: Mortalità della poesia e razionalità morale in F. Petrarca," in *Petrarca e la cultura europea*, ed. Secchi Tarugi Luisa (Milan: Editrice Nuovi Orizzonti, 1997), pp. 181–201.

9 On Petrarca as prophet of existentialist psychology, see Silvano Vincenti, "Attualità del Petrarca," in *Attualità del Petrarca*, ed. Silvano Vincenti (Rome: Armando Editore, 2004), pp. 67–89; and Guido Cappelli, "Petrarca (post)moderno: Notelle informali sulla disperazione di parlare di un classico," *Petrarchesca*, 1 (2013): 95–101.

10 The *coincidentia* Laura-Nature allows us to solve, if only beyond Duperray's intent, the longstanding problem of correlating the living and the dead Laura—a problem with which Jo Ann Cavallo wrestles inconclusively in her psychological, at moments 'pop,' interpretation of Petrarca's Laura. See Jo Ann Cavallo, "Croce e delizia: la donna 'sotto' la penna di Petrarca," in ed. Vincenti, *cit.*, pp. 49–66. Taking our cue from Duperray, we might consider the dead Laura in terms of *natura naturans* (or as a poetic muse signalling contemplative love) and the living Laura as *natura naturata*, if not *creata* (in Platonic terms, the physical shadow of a poetic creation).

11 Petrarca's predilection for Cicero would seem to be incompatible with modern readings of universals (as with attempts to overcome the limits of nominalism on a nominalistic basis). Where, in *Tusc. Disp.* V.10, Cicero reads Socrates as having brought Platonic Ideas from the heavens into the *polis*, the attempt to 'realize' the Ideas in the constitution of a collective society succeeds only *poetically*, or 'in words.' The poetic success presupposes a historical failure. The proper context for the fulfillment of (philosophical) *eros* is a perhaps divinely inspired, questionable poetry transcending any history. Modern scholarship has yet to clarify the nexus between Petrarca's return to antiquity and his *theologia poetica*, in the light of Cicero's account of Plato's *Republic*. On Petrarca as *poeta theologus*, see Kristin Phillips-Court, "The Petrarchan Lover in Cinquecento Comedy," in *MLN* (Italian Issue), 125 (January, 2010): 117–40; and Charles E. Trinkaus, *The Poet as Philosopher: Petrarch and the Formation of Renaissance Consciousness* (New Haven, CT: Yale University Press, 1979), pp. 12–13. On Petrarca's 'Dantean Cicero,' see Enrico Santangelo, "Il Cicerone dantesco del Petrarca: 'Familiares' XXIV, 3 e XXIV, 4," *Linguistica e Letteratura*, 1–2 (2002): 81–85.

12 For a 'standard' reading of medieval Averroism, see Étienne Gilson, *Reason and Revelation in the Middle Ages* (New York: Charles Scribner's Sons, 1966 [1938]), pp. 37–84. Gilson's account falls short of considering Averroism as illuminating the conditions of faith. Gilson's shortcoming is arguably bound to his grounding the Christian faith in History, if only as history of the Church (p. 81). While Petrarca may appear alien to Averroism, Marco Baglio shows the poet's 'religiosity' was consistently 'mediated' by Dante. See Marco Baglio, "Presenze dantesche nel Petrarca latino," *Studi Petrarcheschi*, 9 (1992): 77–136. For fideistic readings of Petrarca, see Karlheinz Stierle, *La vita e i tempi di Petrarca: Alle origini della moderna coscienza europea* [*Francesco Petrarca. Ein Intellektueller im Europa des 14. Jahrhunderts*], trans. Gabriella Pelloni (Venice: Marsilio, 2007 [2003]); and Pietro Paolo Gerosa, *Umanesimo cristiano del Petrarca* (Turin: Bottega d'Erasmo, 1966), including a chapter on 'Cicerone. Classicismo e Cristianesimo.'

13 For a more extensive treatment of the delicate subject at hand, see Ralph Lerner and Muhsin Mahdi (eds.), *Medieval Political Philosophy* (Ithaca, NY: Cornell University Press, 1972 [1963]), pp. 12–15.

14 Ernest L. Fortin, *Dissent and Philosophy in the Middle Ages: Dante and His Precursors*, trans. Marc A. LePain (Lanham, MD: Lexington Books, 2001 [1981]).

15 The reading of Petrarch as characteristically anguished is anticipated by Forster (1969), *cit.*, p. 3ff, after Hans Pyritz, *Paul Flemings Liebeslyrik—Zur Geschichte des Petrarkismus* (Göttingen,

Germany: Vandenhoeck & Ruprecht, 1963 [1936]). For both authors, what is most characteristic of Petrarca's poetics is its *acedia* or melancholy born of the poet's incapacity to escape the tension between temporal love and eternal love. No indication is given that classical political philosophy (most notably in the Platonic tradition) thrives in the belly of the aporetic tension between the temporal and the eternal. Since traditionally melancholy is a poetic index of philosophy's proper 'mood,' it is not clear how or why it should be peculiar to Petrarca's poetics.

16 Zygmunt G. Baranski and Theodore J. Cachey (eds.), *Petrarch & Dante: Anti-Dantism, Metaphysics, Tradition* (Notre Dame, IN: Notre Dame University Press, 2009), pp. 50–113.

17 Giuseppe Mazzotta, *The Worlds of Petrarch* (Durham, NC: Duke University Press, 1993).

18 Christian Moevs, *The Metaphysics of Dante's Comedy* (Oxford: Oxford University Press, 2001).

19 Albert R. Ascoli's *Dante and the Making of a Modern Author* (Cambridge: Cambridge University Press, 2008) presents Dante as affected by, "self-centred obsession with 'authority'" (Baranski). On a 'genealogical' continuity (in a Foucaultian sense) between Dante and Petrarca, see Albert R. Ascoli's 'Favola fui': *Petrarch Writes His Reader.* Bernardo Lecture Series No. 17 (Albany, NY: SUNY University Press, 2010), which exposes beneath a Petrarca conceived as representative of 'the modern self' a Petrarca deconstructing the authorial self in terms of its historically evolving audience.

20 On Petrarca's bond to troubadouric poetry (*contra* Maria Picchio Simonelli, *Figure foniche dal Petrarca ai petrarchisti* [Florence: Licosa, 1978]), see Rosanna Bettarini, *Lacrime d'inchiostro nel* Canzoniere *di Petrarca* (Bologna: CLUEB, 1998), pp. 177–85; Maurizio Perugi, "Aux origins de l'*aura* de Pétrarque: la femme blonde chez Chrêtien de Troyes et Arnaut Daniel (avec une note sur Arnaut *c'amas l'aura*)," *Cahiers de Civilisation Mèdiévale X^e^-XIIe siècles*, 52 (2009): 264–75; Benassi, p. 201; and Cassidy Hughes, *Petrarch, Dante and the Troubadours: The Religion of Love and Poetry* (Kidderminster, UK: Crescent Moon Publishing, 1993).

21 Though *formally* appealing to Moevs' account of Dante's metaphysics as 'elegant' (p. 224), with respect to the *content* of her argument, Barolini rejects as entirely erroneous Moevs' cardinal contention that Dante's metaphysics is Neo-Platonic (p. 240). This way, Barolini comes to incarnate the contradiction between form and content that she attributes to Petrarca. For a contrasting account, see Pamela Williams, *Through Human Love to God: Essays on Dante and Petrarch* (Leicester, UK: Troubador, 2007); and, by the same author, "Petrarch and Leopardi," in ed. Martin Mclaughlin, *cit.*: Williams appears favorable to Leopardi's assessment of a fundamental harmony of form and content in Petrarca, against conventionally conceived Platonism. A single brief critical remark must suffice to provide a glimpse into the depths and scope of problems besetting Barolini's text. By way of confirming her thesis that, whereas Dante's Beatrice embraces both otherworldly unity and worldly multiplicity (enabling the poet to emerge as the world's ethical guide), Petrarca's Laura calls the poet to flee monastically from the worldly; Barolini (p. 216) reads *Inferno* II.76–78 against the grain of *Rvf* 17, as pertaining to our merely moral and even collective transcendence of the world. Yet, the cited passage of *Inferno* is tied directly to *Inferno* II.2–3 (*e io sol uno;* in anticipation of XV.85's lesson by Latini) and to II.71–75 and thus to a 'Virgilian' context 'consoling' Beatrice as Muse (compare 67–69 and 75) to show us that only in the vehicle of poetry can man rise 'alone and one' above mortality (*Monarchia* teaches that 'the human species' is eternal only in one *monarch;* but in the *Comedy*, this One is the poet himself, albeit impersonally).

22 Of all contributors, Mazzotta appears the least prone to stressing a divide between Dante and Petrarca, yet only within a historical trajectory leading to postmodern, semiotic aesthetics. Barolini's essay remains silent as regards the extent to which the author's characterization of Petrarca's struggling between time and eternity might apply to most or even all philosophers *qua* philosophers, insofar as they are not *sophoi*, but desirous of wisdom understood as adequate grasp of the (metaphysical) ground of morality, or of the principles of good and evil.

23 On Petrarca's own quest for philosophically legitimate fame, see further, Zak, *cit.*, p. 28. On Petrarca's appreciation of Dante as 'classic,' see Baglio, *cit.*, and Carlo Pulsoni, "Il Dante di Francesco Petrarca: Vaticano Latino 3199," *Studi Petrarcheschi*, 10 (1993): 156–208.

24 On Dante's role as purgatorial liberator, see Marco Andreacchio, "Dante's Statius and Christianity: A Reading of *Purgatorio* XXI and XXII in Their Poetic Context," *Interpretation: A Journal of Political Philosophy*, 39, 1 (Winter 2012): 71–72.

25 Overall, the volume is geared towards establishing a disconnection between the *original* Petrarca (Romanticism's illusion?) and the tradition named after him. Similarly geared, with few/partial exceptions, is Floriana Calitti, L. Chines and R. Gigliucci (eds.), *Il Petrarchismo: Un modello di poesia per l'Europa* (Rome: Bulzoni, 2006)—where, e.g., Ian Fenlon's "Petrarch, Petrarchism and the Origins of the Italian Madrigal" (pp. 129–44) disengages the origins of madrigals from Petrarca's aristocratic verse, tying them instead to a popular social context "encouraged by courtesy books, above all Baldassare Castiglione's *Il cortigiano* which advocates that musical amateurs be … musically literate" (p. 129). To speak in Biblical terms, one might say that on Fenlon's reading the madrigal owes to Aaron as much as the Hebrew Law owes to Moses. For alternative readings of Petrarca's impact on Renaissance and Baroque music, see Valeria Finucci, "In the Footsteps of Petrarch: Poetry, Music, Art, Culture," *The Journal of Medieval and Early Modern Studies*, 35, 3 (2005): 457–66; Pierre Blanc, ed., *Pétrarque en Europe XIVe–Xx^{e} Siècle: Dynamique d'une expansion culturelle*. Acts of the twenty-sixth international congress of the CEFI, Turin and Chambéry, 11–15 December, 1995 (Paris: Honoré Champion, 2001), pp. 467–574; and Gilda P. Mantovani, ed., *Petrarca e il suo tempo* (Milan: Skyra, 2006), pp. 205–46 (Giulio Cattin, "'Vergene bella': da Petrarca a Du Fay," pp. 205–12; Francesco Facchin, "Petrarca e la musica: Padova-Arquà, 1368–1374," pp. 213–24; and Antonio Lovato, "Suoni e ritmi per la lirica del Petrarca. Il madrigale musicale a Padova nel Cinquecento," pp. 225–46).

26 See further, "The Cave and the Labyrinth: Literature and Language," the final chapter of Piero Boitani, *Chaucer and the Imaginary World of Fame* (Cambridge: Cambridge University Press, 1984), pp. 189–216. Boitani's reading of Chaucer is reminiscent of a mode of argumentation that Umberto Eco's *The Name of the Rose* retraces to William of Ockham.

27 See, along identical lines, Warren Ginsberg, "Chaucer and Petrarch: 'S'amor non è' and the *Canticus Troili*," *Humanist Studies & the Digital Age*, 1, 1 (2011), pp. 121–27.

28 See Reed W. Dasenbrock, *Imitating the Italians: Wyatt, Spenser, Synge, Pound, Joyce* (Baltimore, MD: Johns Hopkins University Press, 1991). Dasenbrock's Spenser institutionalizes love in marriage, rather than in death as is supposed to have done Petrarch. Similarly, E. R. Gregory, "Milton's Protestant Sonnet Lady: Revisions in the 'Donna Angelicata' Tradition," *Comparative Literature Studies*, 33, 3 (1996): 258–79, defends Milton's convention-enshrined, chaste, Protestant/Puritan version of Beatrice and Laura as more realistic and thus worthier of admiration, than its 'Italian'/Catholic, ethereal counterparts (on this stereotypical reading see further Campbell (2003), *cit.*, p. 212). Countering postmodern conceptual-relativism (p. 260), Gregory argues that conventional experience (enriched by sexual intercourse within marriage) is a better index of truth than non-empirically verifiable sublimated realities or ideas (p. 277). But are conventional bodies and philosophical ideas mutually exclusive? Is what Milton is *doing* even possible if not on the basis of what Petrarchismo is *doing first*? (For Gregory's Milton, 'conventional Platonism' does not stand on, but replaces philosophical Platonism, which must be misguided—pp. 273–75.) Basing himself on the (fictitious) 'evidence' provided by Boccaccio's *Life of Dante* (pp. 267–70, 274), Gregory swears that Dante's Beatrice was an empirically verifiable woman. As alleged mouthpiece of Thomism, Dante must have leapt from the empirical to the ideal, falsely believing that man's end in this life could/should transcend the carnal (pp. 267, 274, 266, where Gregory seems to reduce man's end in this life to the end of marriage). Poets—even feminist ones—are likely to find Gregory's conventionalist reading of poetry hard to swallow. Decrying English Renaissance comedy's departure from Petrarca's philosophical seriousness, Louise George Clubb notes that, "the conclusion of the *commedia* became increasingly a tour de force of denouement culminating in a revelation, or series of revelations, sweeping all complexities into a neat design of marriages, family reunion, economic recovery, and neighborhood pacification, extending in some late plays even to municipal concord" (Louise George Clubb, *Italian Drama in Shakespeare's Time* [New Haven, CT: Yale University Press, 1989], p. 36). Yet, is it not possible to read the sort of consummation Clubb describes, as highly ironic or dissimulating, even along the lines of Dante's *Comedy*?

29 See Stephen J. Campbell, "Eros in the Flesh: Petrarchan Desire, the Embodied Eros, and Male Beauty in Italian Art, 1500–1540," *The Journal of Medieval and Early Modern Studies*, 35,

3 (2005): 629–62; and Luigi Baldacci, *Il Petrarchismo italiano nel Cinquecento* (Milan: R. Ricciardi, 1974 [1957]). Donald L. Guss, "Wyatt's Petrarchism: An Instance of Creative Imitation in the Renaissance," *Huntington Library Quarterly*, 29, 1 (November 1965): 1–15, invites the possibility of reading instances of long-presumed anti-Petrarchism in terms of 'self-adaptation.' To carry Guss' thesis a step further, or beyond the scope of 'personal adaptations' that are supposed to constitute more fitting a category than that of parody, we might argue that many cases of supposed anti-Petrarchism are in reality cases of genuinely Petrarchan *self-elucidation* (explorations of hidden recesses of Petrarca's own poetic *façade*). Yet, having convincingly critiqued previous accounts of Wyatt's relation to Petrarca, Guss argues that Wyatt injects the problem of justice into a Petrarchist poetry that is otherwise indifferent to it, devoted as it is to entirely otherworldly, Christian pursuits. However, the differences Guss highlights between Wyatt (Stoic lover of virtue) and Petrarca (Christian lover of God) may be accounted for by the fact that Wyatt relies on Petrarca's having already established, through judicious use of theological language, the legitimacy of a poetry that invokes—in its own candid mirror—justice-*qua*-virtue, or that thereupon exposes injustice. Petrarca's *purity*, his Laura (arguably, a 'bait' prompting us to cultivate virtue, thereby echoing Beatrice's function in *Paradiso*), would then consciously invite a successful critique of *impurity* (implicating an *apologia* of virtue), such as the one articulated by Wyatt—and by Petrarca himself in many a context. Though for Guss, Petrarca is a Christian reconciled with the evanescence of the world (seen in the light of Christianity's promised otherworld), whereas Wyatt is a Stoic (notwithstanding invocations of 'the great god' or 'goode lorde') embittered by the world for its indifference to virtue (see, e.g., pp. 11 and 13), might the distinction between the two humanists not be understood as one of *posturing*, or at least of *strategy*, though where both poets aim at the identical end, namely the cultivation of virtue—Petrarca, by *seemingly* raising the virtuous into the heavens, and Wyatt, by retracing the heavenly virtuous into our world? May one not argue further that *poetic* ascent and *philosophical* descent are *both* present in *both* Petrarca and Wyatt? Klaus W. Hempfer, "Per una definizione del Petrarchismo" (in Blanc, ed., *cit.*, pp. 23–52) firmly objects to the integration of anti-Petrarchism within the 'system' of Petrarchism, seemingly because such an integration would point back to Platonic conceptions of identity (pp. 38–41). Strikingly, Hempfer rejects aprioristically the inscription of Petrarchism within the scope of Platonism. Among nominalistic alternatives to Guss' 'personal adaptations' approach to Petrarchism, see Stephen Minta, *Petrarch and Petrarchism, the English and French Traditions*. Literature in Context (Manchester, UK: Manchester University Press, 1980). Minta tends to read Petrarchismo as a phenomenon rooted in Petrarca's name/fame, rather than in the Italian's actual work.

30 Vittorio Cian, "Il maggior petrarchista del Cinquecento, Pietro Bembo," *Annali della cattedra petrarchesca*, 8 (1938): 1–42.

31 Gerhart Hoffmeister, *Petrarkistische Liryk* (Stuttgart, Germany: Metzler, 1973).

32 On the importance of reading Petrarchismo through Petrarca, see Rossiter (2010).

33 Noteworthy in this context is *Petrarchesca: Rivista Internazionale* (Rome: Fabrizio Serra Editore), an international journal inaugurated on January 2013 under the auspices of renowned Renaissance scholars such as Enrico Fenzi and Zygmunt Baranski.

34 For a relatively recent exercise in 'listening' to Petrarca, see Arnaud Tripet, *Pétrarque ou la connaissance de soi* (Paris: Honoré Champion, 2004). For Tripet, Petrarchismo is held together by Petrarca's 'nostalgic' anticipation of Rousseau's love of antiquity—a love that is pre-Romantically torn between antiquity and modernity (an analogous thesis is sustained by Marco Santagata, *I Frammenti dell'anima: Storia e racconto nel* Canzoniere *di Petrarca* [Bologna: Il Mulino, 1992]). On Petrarca as anticipating not only Rousseau but also Stendhal, Mallarmé, and Baudelaire, see Alain Michel, "Pétrarque, rhétorique, sagesse et poésie," in ed. Duperray, *cit.*, pp. 321–29. Though opposing Petrarca to Rousseau, Nicholas Mann presents the former as enigmatically suspended in the ever-thwarted attempt to reduce, beyond aesthetics, the real to an *imaginary* Augustinian/moral universe (Nicholas Mann, *Pétrarque: les voyages de l'esprit* [Grenoble: Millon, 2004], pp. 110–11).

35 See Braden (1999), *cit.* and Williams, *cit.* For a critique of the position represented by Williams, see p. 216 of Marco Andreacchio, "Unmasking Limbo: Reading *Inferno* IV as Key to Dante's *Comedy*," in *Interpretation: A Journal of Political Philosophy*, 40, 2 (Fall, 2013): 199–220.

36 In *Paradiso* XX.37–54 we begin to see that the Trinity apparently alluded to in 1–3 mirrors the work of poets.

37 Donato Sperduto, *Il Divenire dell'Eterno: Su Emanuele Severino (e Dante)* (Rome: Aracne, 2012). Echoes of Nietzsche populate Fenzi's reading of Petrarca in Francesco Petrarca, *Rimedi all'una e all'altra fortuna*, ed. E. Fenzi, trans. G. Fortunato and L. Alfinito (Naples: La Scuola di Pitagora, 2009), pp. 37–38.

38 Meredith J. Gill, *Augustine in the Italian Renaissance: Art and Philosophy from Petrarch to Michelangelo* (Cambridge: Cambridge University Press, 2005) highlights ways in which St. Augustine comes to be used as the conduit for Platonism throughout the Renaissance. Is it possible that Petrarca used the whole linguistic conceptual apparatus of Christian theology to carry out independent research or communicate purely philosophical messages? Petrarca's stance vis-à-vis orthodox Christianity would then be akin to that of painters who took sacred images as occasion, even pretext, for civilizing/humanizing their audience (Stanley Metzoff, *Botticelli, Signorelli and Savonarola: Theologia Poetica and Painting from Boccaccio to Poliziano* [Florence: Leo S. Olschki, 1987]). Many Renaissance paintings may be overtly about Jesus, but we praise each for its own distinctive *interpretation* (whether or not we understand it) of the theme all the paintings share, not for the theme.

39 See Martin Heidegger, *Nietzsche*, ed. and trans. David Farrell Krell (San Francisco: Harper Collins, 1991 [1961]), Vol. I, §10, and Vol. II, §26.

40 I capitalize 'history' by way of emphasizing its existentially overarching valence, according to historicist intuitions.

41 See Giuseppe Mazzotta, *Dante Poet of the Desert: History and Allegory in the* Divine Comedy (Princeton, NJ: Princeton University Press, 1979).

42 In this respect, our foremost duty as Dante scholars would seem to rest in 'leaving no Dante behind.'

43 See esp. the German production of Hans Robert Jauss. A 1978 French collection of Jauss' writings is tellingly titled, *Pour une estétique de la reception*, trans. Claude Maillard (Paris: Gallimard).

44 Peter L. Schmidt, *Traditio Latinitatis Studien zur Rezeption und Überlieferung der Lateinischen Literatur*, eds. J. Fugmann, M. Hose and B. Zimmermann (Stuttgart, Germany: Steiner, 2000).

45 Leo Strauss, *Natural Right and History* (Chicago, IL: Chicago University Press, 1965 [1950]), p. 39.

46 On aesthetics as consummation of philosophy, see Heidegger, cit., Vol. II, §15. Upon tying criticism to self-criticism, 'reception' converts into a two-way conversation between author and reader presenting a further difficulty for intellectual historians: a two-way dialogue between the past and the present entails a coincidence of distinct temporal horizons for interpretation and thus a *static* horizon of thought and discourse that calls to mind the nature of *mythos*, rather than a history as logical unfolding of a mythical prehistory. To read Dante and Petrarca as living protagonists in what Michael Oakeshott called, 'the Conversation of Mankind'; to replace 'History' with our Conversation; this is to orient our interpretations towards a common horizon of permanent problems, rather than a future (end of History) with respect to which we hold a distinct and by no means necessarily deserved advantage over past authors. Anchoring our Conversation onto permanent, even eternal problems—problems in the belly of which we may truly encounter each other—would seem to offer us the only means to remain in genuine dialogue with the past, a dialogue in which we remain at once genuinely receptive and responsive. For an intimation of the dialogue in question, see Petrarca, *Epistolae Seniles*, 17, 3. In her application of Butler's 'gender theory' (arguably, an ideology) to Renaissance poetry, Campbell (2003), *cit.*, identifies Petrarca's reading of Boccaccio's Griselda as index of an exclusivist male humanist ideology that divests women (as *res extensa*) of any virtue to assert deceptively gender-neutral, *abstract* virtue (presumably a mask for the authority of male humanists). Campbell's reading of Petrarca's *virtus* stands at the antipodes of studies pointing to Petrarca's deeply existential and personal understanding of virtue/love. See, e.g., Gianfrancesco Iacono, "La 'Virtus' nelle 'Familiari,'" *Petrarchesca*, 1 (2013): 155–63.

47 Alain Michel, *Pétrarque et la pensée latine: tradition et novation en littérature* (Avignon: Aubanel, 1974). The distinction between Dante and Petrarca is sometimes drawn by appealing to their distinct treatments of pope Celestino (*Inferno* III.59–60 and *De Vita Solitaria*, II.8, which, non-naïvely defending the 'utility' of the contemplative *and* naïve flight from 'the mortal burden' of worldly authority, invites the thought that Dante's veiled reference to Celestino is making a merely provisional concession to pre-established clerical opinions). Dante is usually assumed to reproach Celestino for his privileging contemplation over occupation, whereas Petrarca is read as defending the pope as heralding the primacy of contemplation. In his *lectura dantis*, Boccaccio refers to Celestino as key to the division between orthodoxy and heresy: those who claim that ever since Celestino all popes are false, are 'heretics.' Whether the Church was justified in moving past Celestino, or whether he was justified in turning down his papal mandate, neither Dante nor Petrarca wished to appear heretical (Dante's reference to Celestino is illuminated by *Inferno* I.125, III.38–39, II.45, and III.15).

48 Lionello Sozzi, "Presenza del Petrarca nella Letteratura Francese," in ed. Secchi Tarugi, *cit.*, pp. 243–62.

49 Leo Strauss, *Thoughts on Machiavelli* (Chicago, IL: Chicago University Press, 1978 [1958]).

50 Scholars reading Petrarch as Neo-Stoic include Francesco Rico, Marco Santagata, and Brian Stock.

51 Stressing the importance for Petrarca of Plato as *felix miser* (even against Aristotle), if only in a Christian context, Fenzi concludes that "Petrarca … has never ceased mirroring himself in Plato's death; he recognized himself in it, and through it he suggested to later generations how they would have had to imagine his own" (Enrico Fenzi, *Saggi Petrarcheschi* [Florence: Cadmo, 2003], p. 551; more generally, see "ch. XV: Platone, Agostino, Petrarca," pp. 519–52). Fenzi's argument is strikingly at odds with statements such as one by Kristeller, for whom "Petrarca's thought contains few elements that we could call Platonic" (*il pensiero di Petrarca contiente pochi elementi che potremmo chiamare platonici*—P. O. Kristeller, "Il Petrarca nella Storia degli Studi," in ed. Secchi Tarugi, *cit.*, pp. 7–29, in partic. 25).

52 In Secchi Tarugi, ed., *cit.*, pp. 55–70.

53 Leo Strauss, *Seminar in Political Philosophy: Cicero* (Spring quarter 1959), transcripts at https://archive.org/details/LeoStraussSeminarOnCicerochicago1959 (see esp., pp. 17, 79–80, 87–92, 95, 97, 117, 211–12, 254–55, 263, 280). On Petrarca's allegiance to classical Ciceronian political thought, see Davide Bigalli, "Petrarca: Dal Sentimento alla Dottrina Politica," in *Motivi e Forme delle* Familiari *di Francesco Petrarca*, ed. Claudia Berra, Università degli Studi di Milano: Facoltà di Lettere e Filosofia. Quaderni di Acme 57 (Milan: Cisalpino Istituto Editoriale Universitario, 2003), pp. 99–118. Bigalli argues that for Petrarca the Renaissance/modern tyrant's *liberalitas* serves as guarantor of the *otium* characterizing the philosophical life (pp. 116–18). Bigalli falls short of considering how Ciceronianism might function as staunch critique of tyranny.

54 For Mazzotta, Petrarca's voluntarism is a weak one, characterized by the recognition of the fragmentary, temporal essence of thought: the will underpinning the poet's work is deflated by the sense that all thought is memory and that memory is haplessly divided and governed by forces impervious to it. Any attempt to recollect the order of things remains radically contingent upon the unknowable or unpredictable. Reading Petrarca as following St. Augustine in identifying thought with memory, Mazzotta presents this identification as proof or sufficient evidence of his authors' recognition of the historicity or finiteness of thought. Nothing is said of the Platonic doctrine of *anamnesis*. If thought is recollection of a unity—an absolute beginning—that we fail to appropriate, what prevents us from concluding that thought or mind is its own *telos*—its Alpha and Omega—unfettered by its world (or worlds)? Is the trans-empirical unity of thought to be forsaken as something defined *ad hoc* by an existence beyond all intelligibility, or is it to be understood as a constant *way* or *virtue* anchored in the intelligible boundary of existence? Does thought's incapacity to recollect its beginning depend upon thought's being haplessly lost in a mindless existence, or upon thought's being always active and unfettered, even or especially in its erring? Is the poet's exile from his times a sign of his failure to conquer existence, *or* of his capacity to intervene upon existence without making himself at home in it, and so without seeking the world's recognition?

55 Hermand-Schebat falls short of considering that by subjecting Cicero's *vita activa* to damning disapproval (ironically, what Petrarch is criticizing his 'Cicero' for is *de facto* lack of the prudence Cicero was best known for), Petrarch can raise Cicero's *message* to eternity (*Fam.* XXIV.3 ends with the salutation, *Eternum vale, mi Cicero*). Significantly, *Fam.* XXIV.3–4, highlights the importance of subtracting writing to time or mortal life.

56 Promising, in this respect, is the 'conclusion' reached recently by Luca Marcozzi, "Il Parnaso di Petrarca (Lettura della Canzone 129 dei 'Fragmenta')," *Petrarchesca*, 1 (2013): 55–76.

2 Boccaccio's *Decameron* and theatricality

Janet Levarie Smarr

Although Boccaccio, author of a wide array of genres, never wrote drama (unless one counts eclogues as a dramatic genre), his *Decameron* became strongly associated with theatre in sixteenth-century Italy and later also in England. The *Decameron* was a foundational influence on the development of Italian secular comedy; in England, it was one foreign source among many, and one which required moralizing adaptation.

Boccaccio certainly had an interest in drama, which he viewed as a kind of poetry. He had copied three medieval plays into his notebooks: the *Geta et Birria* (based on Plautus's *Amphitryon*) by Vital de Blois; the *Alda* by Guillaume de Blois; and the *Comedia Lidie* by Matthieu de Vendôme, this last becoming *Decameron* 7.9, and all three mined "as repertoires of rhetorical effects distributed throughout the *Decameron*."[1] He also copied and glossed in his own hand the comedies of Terence,[2] and his early second eclogue quotes from Plautus's *Cistellaria*.[3]

The *Decameron* itself became viewed as a quasi-dramatic work. Petrarch in his letter *Seniles* 17.2 referred to Boccaccio as the "Plautus of our time, with the utmost talent and eloquence."[4] The Aristotelian Giasone De Nores in his *Poetica* (1588) drew from the *Decameron* his examples of both tragedy (4.9) and comedy (5.5); Madeleine Doran notes that the latter is a romantic rather than bawdy comedy and that its "tale of love, intrigue, lost children, mistaken identity, and fortuitous discovery" was probably "suggestive to him of Plautus and Terence";[5] Ronald Martinez calls 5.5 "a pure distillate of Roman comedy."[6] Vittore Branca notes that 5.5 resembles Plautus's *Epidicus*, that 8.4 bears traces of Plautus's *Casina* (the bed-trick arranged by an honest woman to shame the male), and that the name of the father Cremete in the classically set 10.8 may derive from Terence's *Andria*.[7]

Boccaccio's defense of classical poetry in *De Genealogia Deorum Gentilium*, XIV, 9, refers to Plautus and Terence as "the better of the comic poets" who "by their art portray varieties of human nature and conversation, incidentally teaching the reader and putting him on his guard." In this description their work sounds like the *Decameron*. These two "upright men" are writers of useful fiction, distinguished from "so-called comic poets" who "defiled the bright glory of poetry with their filthy creations" (XIV, 19). The reference to "better" Roman comedy is followed directly by the example of Christ's parables, and Boccaccio declares that Jesus himself had spoken a line from Terence.[8] In his commentary on Dante's *Commedia*, for the allegorical explication of the leopard in *Inferno* 1, Boccaccio turns to Plautus, who "wonderfully describes" the mental condition of people with fleshly desires.[9] Similarly in his commentary on *Inferno* 5, he cites Terence for a proverbial line about food and wine as enticements to lust. In short, he saw the writers of comedy as poets with a gift for verbalizing our follies in order to teach us to see and avoid them.

DOI: 10.4324/9781315612720-4

Plautus and Terence are present in the *Decameron* as early as the introduction to Day 1; the names of the narrators' servants come from Roman comedy: Parmeno appears as a servant in three of Terence's plays, Misia in a fourth, and Tindaro in Plautus's *Captivi.*[10] Other servant names come from Juvenal, Martial, or Horace, suggesting an association of Roman comedy with Roman satire. While Roman comedy and satire name the servants, allusions to Vergil, Petrarch, and other literature appear in names of the brigata.

In "The Marriage of Plautus and Boccaccio" I described some of the features that Boccaccio's stories share with Roman comedy, encouraging their association, and some of the divergences.[11] For example, stylistically both share lively dialogue including colloquial speech and a delight in wordplay. Thematically, both deal repeatedly with cleverly devised efforts to possess the beloved; but whereas the Romans offer either girls for sale or marriageable ladies but avoid adultery, the *Decameron* is full of adulterous wives while rejecting women who can be purchased for money. Thus husbands replace slave dealers as a blocking figure along with fathers. Moreover, whereas Roman comedy features the desires of young men while giving little or no stage time to respectable young ladies, Boccaccio includes women as desiring subjects and offers them active leading roles. While Plautus occasionally shows the male in drag, Boccaccio offers women who dress as men in order to avoid being killed or married against their wishes. In Renaissance theatre, male attire enabled female characters from respectable families to leave the windows and doorways of their homes and venture out onto the street to take action among men on stage. While Plautus and Boccaccio share plots based on trickery, the tricks in Plautus have an ulterior aim whereas Boccaccio's tricksters often play a prank for sheer fun. The shared features were enough to link the *Decameron* with Roman comedy, while the divergences enabled the *Decameron* to contribute new elements to Renaissance comedy.

Characters in the *Decameron* are often consciously performing. The very first tale gives us a star performer in ser Cepparello.[12] Whether it is a prostitute pretending to be Andreuccio's half-sister (2.5), or a family fallen on hard times but trying to keep up appearances (2.3), a worker pretending to be a deaf-mute (3.1), or a husband disguised as a priest to hear his wife's confession (7.5), characters frequently put on an act, and sometimes a disguise as well, to fool those around them. Eduardo Saccone points out the physical as well as verbal performances of *Decameron* characters.[13] Angelo and Elizabeth Mazzocco concur: "Indeed, it is the way Boccaccio combines linguistic jests with farcical movements that makes the *Decameron* so humorous and why it lends itself so easily to incorporation into stage comedy."[14] Moments of revelation are often intentionally staged public scenes, especially at dinner gatherings (e.g. 3.9, 5.8, 10.4, 10.10). Of course the tale-telling itself is a performance at a gathering,[15] and the brigata's location for the seventh day is explicitly compared to an amphitheatre:

> Le piagge delle quali montagnette così digradando verso il pian discendevano, come ne'
> teatri veggiamo dalla lor sommità i gradi infino all'infimo venire successivamente ordinati, sempre ristrignendo il cerchio loro.
>
> (6.concl. 21)[16]

The *Decameron* even seems to anticipate *commedia dell'arte.* Masciandaro observes that Isabella, in 7.6, performs as both an improvisor and a director of two "actors," the lovers whom she instructs in their roles.[17] Coincidentally, her name would come to be associated with the *commedia innamorata*. The songs that end each day of narration can even be seen as musical interludes between the "acts."

Asking why the *Decameron* was so often turned into theatre during the sixteenth century, Nino Borsellino called attention to its theatricality and offered a rich array of converging reasons: the satisfying dramatic structure of tales (problems created and resolved, lovers or family members separated and reunited, aims achieved through a clever scheme) divided into scenes or episodes of action; the focus on modern or recent middle-class society; the mix of satiric and romantic tones; the ease with which Boccaccio's stories could be fit into the model of Roman comedy; the treasury of character types, speeches (witty retorts, tirades, internal arguments, reflections on love or Fortune, proverbs, magic spells, etc.), linguistic levels and regional dialects, physical and verbal gags, and dramatic situations; the mimetic and oral qualities of the text, with its attention both to the representation of real life and to audience reactions (within and beyond the tales); the eliciting of audience complicity in the plots of tricksters or in a narrator's sexual innuendos.[18] Angelo and Elizabeth Mazzocco list "witticisms, malapropisms, obscene metaphors … and equivocal terminology" as becoming "an integral part of cinquecento comedy"; the mangling of names or words was especially popular. They point also to physical situations often repeated on stage: beatings, the accidental drinking of a potion, the hiding of a lover in a chest or barrel (which may then be moved), crossdressing, the substitution of one character for another in bed, and the resourceful self-assertion of women in love.[19]

Renzo Bragantini emphasizes dialogic qualities both in and of the *Decameron*: "in" given the many different voices registered; "of" given the relationships among tales. The resultant "mimesi della precarietà valutativa" [mimesis of evaluative precariousness] contributes to the "civiltà dialogica promossa dal *Decameron*" [dialogic civility promoted by the *Decameron*].[20] More recently Tatiana Crivelli and Teresa Nocita have applied an analysis of theatricality to the Hamilton autograph, where colored capital letters break the text in a theatrical manner, highlighting who speaks or acts next. Moreover, this authorial subdivision of the text invites imitators to extract pieces, a fragment of a character's speech or a narrator's general reflection, that can be recomposed into new works.[21]

Not surprisingly, it was Florentine playwrights who first enthusiastically embraced the *Decameron*. Iacopo Nardi, who – like Machiavelli – worked for the government of the Florentine republic and was exiled when the Medici returned, dramatized both 5.5, *I due felici rivali* (1513) and 10.8, *La commedia di amicitia* (1512?), combining Boccaccio's plots with added Plautine characters: scheming slave, braggart soldier, parasite.[22] Bernardo Dovizi da Bibbiena, who had been working hard to bring the Medici back to Florence and into the papacy, was the first to use the *Decameron* not for its plots but for bits and pieces of speech and action. In his *Calandra* Fulvia quotes from the speeches of women in 3.5, 3.6, 5.10, 7.8, and 10.5, while her desperate appeal to a supposed magician may derive from 8.7.[23] Phrases from yet other tales contribute to the creation and mocking of her husband Calandro. Giorgio Padoan calls attention to Act I, scene 2, where the Boccaccian expressions of Lidio and his servant Fessenio are set against the Petrarchism of the tutor Polinico.[24]

Machiavelli's *Mandragola* (1518) similarly drew on several *Decameron* tales and also on the *Calandra*.[25] Callimaco, like Lodovico in 7.7, is a Florentine in Paris who hears the beauty of Italian women praised, and of one woman in particular. Both the trickery to seduce a virtuous wife and the combination of good sex and the threat to her reputation that seal the ongoing affair, resemble events in 3.6.[26] The arguments with which Fra Timoteo persuades Lucrezia that she would be sinning *not* to have sex with another man, draw on 3.4, with its reference to sin that can be washed away with holy water; 3.7, in which Tedaldo, disguised as a pilgrim, convinces the married woman he loves that she has sinned by rejecting her lover; and 3.8, in which a seducing abbot employs the distinction between acts of the body and of the will.[27] Luciano Bottoni argues that Machiavelli confrontationally reused some of the same *Decameron* tales as Bibbiena in order to declare his dramatic rivalry.[28] The *Decameron* thus signified modernized prose comedy. Although on opposing sides politically, these three playwrights celebrated Florence by turning to the *Decameron* for material which they no doubt expected their audiences to recognize.[29]

Besides echoing Boccaccian speeches, Bibbiena reworked the character Calandrino into the wealthier but still stupid and gullible Calandro of his play. The name created an obvious link.[30] Machiavelli turned the same figure into his messer Nicia, who, despite the renaming, evokes Calandrino (8.6) when Ligurio – in a gratuitous gag[31] – gives him bitter aloes to put in his mouth (IV, ix). The vain and stupid husband, who thinks women love him and whose gullibility renders him the perfect butt of jokes, merges the figures of Calandrino and Plautus's *miles gloriosus* into a type that continued to serve the purposes of comedy for a long time. On the other hand, the stage career of the Decameronian fraudulent cleric, wonderfully launched by Machiavelli, was impeded by censorship. The crossdressed female, appearing in the *Calandra* in major roles (one satiric and one romantic), was another oft-repeated theatrical success with Decameronian roots.

Borsellino remarks that the *Mandragola* "spinge all'estremo il valore dissacratorio della beffa decameroniana" [pushes to the extreme the desacralizing power of the decameronian *beffa*], calling into question the institutions of marriage, paternity, and religion.[32] Ronald Martinez notes that just as the *Mandragola*, unlike the *Decameron*, requires a conspiracy rather than an individual to accomplish the *beffa*, so too the effects extend beyond individual loss or gain to the tragedy or rejuvenation of an entire society.[33] Albert Ascoli sees a philosophical influence of *Decameron* 7.9. on Machiavelli's *Clizia*, arguing that Machiavelli saw in it "the very modern notion of domination through ideological manipulations rather than by either rule of law or brute force" as "Boccaccio uncovers the means by which power at once effaces and extends itself."[34]

Ludovico Ariosto, in Ferrara, had also found in the *Decameron* a means to free his plays from too closely following Roman models, shifting his settings to contemporary and local, and creating a cast that, like the novella, emphasized young lovers or students rather than clever slaves.[35] Edmond M. Beame suggests that the plot of the successful *I Suppositi* (1509) with its "rich and noble youth posing as a servant in order to possess his beloved" may draw on *Decameron* 7.7,[36] and the play's pedantic old lawyer on the old judge in 2.10.

The enormous success of these early comedies[37] and their consequent influence on Italian comedy quickly spread their techniques. Later playwrights continued the practice of combining situations from several *Decameron* tales. Aretino's *Filosofo* (1544) combines 2.5 and 7.8, while calling attention to his source by renaming Andreuccio "Boccaccio." Giovan Maria Cecchi's *Assiuolo* (1550) weaves a plot from 3.6, 7.8, and 8.7, while explicitly comparing its amorous impotent old man to Riccardo da Chinzica (2.10), a name the audience was expected to recognize.[38] Michele Marrapodi traces motifs of crossdressing and bed-trick from Roman comedy and the *Decameron* through the plays of Bibbiena and Machiavelli, and on to later comedies.[39] Tale and comedy had thoroughly converged.

Commedia dell'arte, drawing material from both literature and scripted theatre, picked up gags that would serve its purpose. For example, *I Tre Becchi* uses *Decameron* 7.6, in which the wife, whose husband returns while she is being visited by two would-be lovers, sends one lover rushing out with drawn sword and then pretends to her husband that she protected the other from that man's violence.[40] This gag became enormously popular and circulated on its own, into English comedies as we shall see.

The *Decameron* enters Salvatore Di Maria's discussion of Italian Renaissance tragedy in the chapter on women. Just as "the *Decameron* features numerous female characters who denounce the unfairness of the laws and the social customs by which they are required to live" along with an implied audience of more "traditional" females, so too Giraldi's *Orbecche* shows a heroine "of unusual emotional, mental and physical strength" while the prologue suggests that the "gentle disposition" of women in his audience might not endure the violence of events on stage.[41] Boccaccio could serve as a source of both feminist and misogynist attitudes, but his female characters and his attention to the reactions of a female audience had significant influence.

Louise George Clubb sums up the foundational importance of the *Decameron* for Italian theatre:

> In Renaissance drama the *Decameron* enjoyed a unique authority. For the Italian spectator its tales and its language would be evoked continually by innumerable cinquecento comedies and various tragedies of Ghismonda and Tancredi of Salerno. Having plot features from the Decameronian tradition was virtually requisite to the genre *commedia*, from its formative time, even when the Plautine or Terentian models were conspicuously set forth.[42]

Italian influences did not come streaming into English literature until the 1560s, with the translations of Castiglione's *Cortegiano* (1561), Ariosto's *Supposes* (performed at Gray's Inn in 1566), the dramatized *Gismond of Salerne* (1566–67), and the novella in Painter's *Palace of Pleasure* (1566–67). The first translation of the entire *Decameron* came quite late in 1620. Long before then, however, selected tales had appeared in English: Chaucer, with his retelling of tales from Boccaccio, was a source for dramatists who sought, ironically, to celebrate English culture.[43] Painter's *Palace of Pleasure* presented sixteen of the *Decameron* stories, explicitly attributing them to Boccaccio in distinction from other writers in the collection (Bandello, Giraldi Cinthio, Marguerite of Navarre). With tale collections as a popular genre, more *Decameron* tales appeared, though often not acknowledged as such. These appearances have been catalogued and described.[44]

A number of Englishmen – including Shakespeare[45] – could read Italian, and more could read French, where they could find not only the few tales rewritten in Christine de Pizan's *Livre de la Cité des Dames*[46] but also the complete *Cent Nouvelles* translated by Laurent de Premierfait in 1414 (first printed in 1485; but Humphrey Duke of Gloucester owned a manuscript[47]) and, more popularly and more accurately, *Le Decameron* by Antoine le Maçon (first printed in 1545); both French translations were reprinted several times. Ascham's reference to the immoral influence of "Bocace" in *The Scholemaster* (1570) suggests via the form of the name that the *Decameron* was being read in French.[48]

On the one hand, Louise George Clubb and Michele Marrapodi have pointed out that the Renaissance principles of *imitatio* and "creative intertextuality" make a comparative approach natural. Indeed, *imitatio* and *contaminatio* were important features of the Italian influence on English literary and theatrical culture.[49] On the other, precisely because of the continual reworking of materials, these scholars look beyond the traditional comparison of particular texts. Clubb suggests that Italian-English intertextual study needs to take entire genres – the Italian novella or Italian comedy – as one text, comparing, for example, Italian drama and the Shakespearean canon, or Italian and English pastoral theatre.[50] In fact the strongest trend in this kind of intertextual study has focused on Shakespeare's uses of a wide confluence of source materials. Marrapodi advocates that "the traditional idea" of source studies yields to "a larger process of cultural influence."[51] The editors of *Staging Early Modern Romance. Prose Fiction, Dramatic Romance, and Shakespeare* advocate following the suggestion of David Kastan that we shift our gaze from single sources ("a particular verbal root") to "the forests of romance from which these plays were cultivated" and thus to "vernacular culture" as a broad discursive field.[52] Nonetheless, in considering the *Decameron*'s theatricality and its relations with Renaissance theatre, we need to seek specific connections along with a broader contextualization.

Source studies have created lists of sources and analogues, primarily for the plays of Shakespeare.[53] In the other direction, scholars have attempted to catalogue the "fortuna" or influence and imitations of Boccaccio's work.[54] These catalogues are useful but not always accurate. Shakespeareans, if they are interested in sources at all, pursue an ever wider set of analogues; Italianists tend at times to claim an influence that is faint or dubious. Given the impossibility of reading all of European or even English literature for traces of the *Decameron*, later cataloguers sometimes transmit the errors of their predecessors.[55] Moreover, as Keir Elam remarks, it is not always easy or even possible to distinguish between sources and analogues, or to establish whether a particular English playwright knew one textual or theatrical source of a tale, or several sources, or was merely picking up on a widely circulating motif.[56] Changed character names and settings (in Italian plays as well as English ones) make even harder the tracing of direct contact. Piero Rebora claims that the *Decameron* furnished the plots for thirty-three Elizabethan plays, but, frustratingly, does not indicate which ones.[57]

Whereas for Italians the *Decameron* had become a cultural icon, for the English the *Decameron* was simply one among a number of Italian texts, welcomed into England with a mixture of enthusiasm and moral resistance,[58] and also one among an increasing number of tale collections that threw together Italian, French, and Spanish sources. Thus, while it was possible with a knowledge of Italian or French to be aware of the *Decameron* as a whole, English readers were more likely to find the tales taken out of their original context and placed, instead, side by side with stories from Bandello or Giraldi Cinthio. Marrapodi comments that "what the London stage offered in terms of Italian-based drama was an adaptation of heterogeneous Italian materials," dramatic as well as narrative.[59]

The principle of *contaminatio* encouraged reweaving mixed sources. We can see one result of *contaminatio* and the anthologizing of tales in Fletcher and Nathan Field's *Four Playes, or Moral Representations, in One* (1612–15?).[60] The four plays, presenting "The Triumph" of Honor, Love, Death, and Time, dramatize respectively Chaucer's "Franklin's Tale" (indirectly Boccaccio's), *Decameron* 5.7, and Bandello's tale of Didaco and Violante (Part I, novella 42); the final triumph is more spectacle than plot.

Boccaccio's tale had appeared in *Forrest of Fancy* (1579),[61] the Bandello tale in Painter's *Palace of Pleasure*. The use of Italian stories (perhaps even the recognition that Chaucer's tale had an Italian parent) may have seemed appropriate to the Italianate form of a series of triumphs.[62] One might observe, however, that the triumph of Honour presents an English story, while dangerous love and violent vengeance are associated with Italian sources.

As Boccaccio's tales came into England indirectly – at best translated, but often substantially reworded and revised – playwrights were attracted not to his language and phrases but to story lines and dramatic situations. Even Painter, who praises Boccaccio's style, effaces it in his rewritings.[63] Moreover, his praise of style is part of a defence for presenting these tales at all, given their reputation for scandalous immorality. While offering the largest *Decameron* selection of any English tale collection, Painter acknowledges in his preface that many of the stories are better left unread. He presents especially stories from the first, second, and last days: tales of fortune or moral examples; days three and seven through nine, with their tales of trickery and unmarried or adulterous sex, are mostly shunned.[64] The English, wittingly or unwittingly, followed Boccaccio's own suggestion that they select the roses while leaving the thorns untouched;[65] thus they failed to attend to the potential moral quality of the work as a whole. George Turberville's *Tragical Tales, Translated out of Sundrie Italians* (1576, repr. 1587) selected five tales from the tragic fourth day (tales 4, 5, 7, 8, 9) plus 5.8, which ends in marriage, and 10.4, in which lust is curtailed and converted into charitable love. But in 1590 two collections with an express aim of jolly entertainment began to include some merrier tales: *Tarlton's News out of Purgatorie: Onely such a Jest as His Jigge*, retold 6.4 and 7.6, along with 4.2 and 6.10 appreciated for their anticlericalism and ridicule of relics; *The Cobbler of Canterburie* offered a combined 7.1 and 7.8, a combined 5.6 and 5.2, and 3.8, the tale of the husband made to believe that he has died and gone to purgatory.[66] All in all, a fairly wide range of *Decameron* stories, presented in quite different contexts, was available in English well before the 1620 translation of Boccaccio's whole book. Galigani notes that about 40 of the 100 tales had been translated or adapted at least once in England during the 1500s.[67]

Boccaccio has been credited with bringing into England both romantic comedy and romantic tragedy, although the latter claim is disputed. One of the first tales dramatized in England (the text is lost) was a comedy of *Titus and Gisippus* performed at Whitehall by the boys of Paul in 1576–77. Chiefly enacting stories from the classics, the boys' company was drawn to this tale for its classical setting.[68] The story attracted similarly the schoolmaster Ralph Radcliffe, whose *De Titi et Gisippi amicitia* (variously dated 1540–50 or 1569) and *De patienta Griselda* (similarly dated), both now lost, were written for his school boys. Wright notes that Cambridge students at St John's College chose the more comic 4.10, though cleaned up and romanticized, as the basis for a performance in Latin in 1578–79.[69] Explicitly acknowledging their source as "Decamero Bocatius," they justify their changes to the story on the model of Terence's adaptations of Menander, thus associating Boccaccio with classical comedy in a chain of transmission from Greek through Roman theatre and on to their sixteenth-century performance.

Among the earliest romantic tragedies is *Gismond of Salerne*, written by a group of five university men at the Inner Temple for performance before the Queen in 1567–68, and revised for publication in 1591 by Robert Wilmot, one of the five, as

The Tragedie of Tancred and Gismund.[70] Another *Tancredo*, now lost, by Sir Henry Wotton was performed at Queen's College, Oxford around 1586–87. Peter Stallybrass notes the popularity of the Ghismonda story in English theatre. Tracing its transformations through sixteenth- and seventeenth-century English versions, he shows how they:

> [r]eveal new formations of the languages of class and gender. It was these new formations which motivated the rewriting of Ghismunda as weeping widow, of Guiscardo as aristocrat, of Tancredi as sovereign, if tyrannical, ruler. And the transformations in the naming of the tale itself suggest a shift in focus away from the lovers and towards the staging of power.[71]

Its wide circulation and appeal as serious literature were aided by a Latin translation which circulated independently;[72] Stallybrass notes that Bruni's Latinized tale of Ghismonda had seen seventeen editions by 1500.[73] However, the English playwright Wilmot picked up the story from Christine de Pizan and, seeing it perhaps therefore as a woman's story, dedicated it to two of "the Queenes Maidens of Honor."[74] Already we can see the tension between the image of Boccaccio as a humanist writing for scholars and as a romance writer addressing women.[75]

Another tale dramatized early and often was that of Griselda (10.10). Mark Sandona's "Patientia Regina. Patience as a Character from the Morality Play to Jacobean Tragedy," probes the problem for dramatists of creating the "enactment" of a virtue of "significant inaction." He suggests that playwrights' attraction to Griselda can be explained by the solution her story offered for this problem: as a person, not a personification, yet in a situation so extreme as to be almost absurd, "The uncanny quality of her as a character arises from the way she partakes of the allegorical and the mimetic without distinction." Thus John Phillip's *Commody of pacient and meek Grissill* (c.1560) created a "hybrid of morality play and domestic melodrama."[76]

Louise George Clubb observes that tracing English drama to narrative sources leaves out the enormously important middleman of Italian theatre, both scripted and improvised, including not simply the transmission of plots but, more importantly, the disassembly and reassembly of narremes and "theatergrams," "a stage technology that can properly be called the single most generative force in Renaissance dramaturgy."[77] Besides familiarity with *novella*, English writers show a broad awareness of *commedia dell'arte*, where situations and episodes might be transmitted through performance without leaving a textual trace. Some of the many lost Elizabethan plays may have provided similar transmission.

Although the *Decameron* often came into English theatre indirectly, some playwrights were aware of the original. Shakespeare is known to have read in Italian the *Decameron* tales that he used along with their English or French versions. Alastair Fox observes that he therefore would have been paying attention not only to the story but also to how it is told, and to the culturally inflected differences between Italian and English presentations.[78] Reading in Italian would have meant also realizing that the tale belonged to a larger context. Does it make a difference whether playwrights knew the *Decameron* or only extracted stories? For example, although Scragg writes about *All's Well*, "Unlike Boccaccio's story, which is firmly focused on the means by which a resolute young woman achieves a husband, *All's Well* involves the spectator from the outset in the moral health of the social group,"[79] conversely Kay Stanton suggests that Shakespeare was aware of the *Decameron*'s framing when he inserted references to sickness and plague into that play as a metaphor for social ills.[80]

To the extent that playwrights or audiences were aware of the *Decameron*, what did that book mean as a cultural token in England? Michael Redmond comments: "The representation of Italian culture in the London theatre was never an isolated gesture"; we need to consider the "rhetorical implications of using Italian material."[81] A number of studies have recently addressed the complex and contradictory English images of Italy: as the source of progressive ideas in education and the arts, and of commercial dynamism, but also as a site of political disfunction, deceit, and moral decadence.[82] But what about the image of specific books or authors? Might a playwright expect a particular audience response to the recognizable use of *Decameron* material?

Guyda Armstrong, "Boccaccio in English: Translation as Reception" focuses on "the way in which his works in English translation have been understood in the anglophone receiving context" by mustering "simple facts such as the number of translations made, the selection of texts for translation, when and where they were produced, and a consideration of their publication contexts."[83] She warns wisely that "Even within a single linguistic culture ... different reading communities – and even non-reading communities – will make use of the same author," creating a wide range of responses.[84] Her research reveals a shift from the sixteenth century, in which a number of Boccaccio's works were available, to the seventeenth, in which only the *Decameron* continues to be reprinted.

This corresponds temporally with the shifting image of Boccaccio, observed by Galigani and others, from a humanist writer of moralizing narratives about friendship, fortune, and the tragic consequences of illicit love, to his later increasing association with sexual frolics and trickery. Instead of dramatizing a single moral tale, English playwrights began to use an entirely different set of stories predominantly for episodes within plots. But why did this shift occur? Probably there is not one answer. The fact that in 1559, just as the interest in Italian literature was growing intense, the *Decameron* was put on the Index might have recommended it to English Protestants, some of whom identified Boccaccio as a proto-Protestant because of his criticisms of the clergy.[85] On the other hand, as Galigani comments, the emerging reputation of the *Decameron* as a bawdy and immoral work kept potential readers away from it.[86]

Faced with a complex web of cultural exchange, some scholars pursue the reworkings of motifs or character types. One asset of this approach is that it avoids the tendency to see the *Decameron* tales as simple, superficial stories turned into great literature by the English.[87] Rather, it gives equal weight to all versions and (ideally) explores the implications of their differences. Valerie Wayne's "Romancing the Wager: *Cymbeline*'s Intertexts" pursues the wager motif through a wide range of European stories which seem to have contributed to Shakespeare's play along with Boccaccio's text. "Boccaccio initiated this shift to the mercantile context" and apparently introduced the prop of the trunk, but "Most of *Cymbeline* is closer in its setting, character and incidents to these aristocratic romances than to the stories of merchants initiated by Boccaccio."[88] Michele Marrapodi, "Retaliation as an Italian Vice in English Renaissance Drama: Narrative and Theatrical Exchanges," traces the spectacular revenge, especially involving an extracted heart, which starts with *Decameron* 4.1 and 4.9, brings in Senecan tragedy, and becomes a kind of sadistic *beffa* that, in England, "progressively assumed the semantic construction of an 'Italian vice.'"[89]

Kirsten Inglis, seeking to move beyond "a study of direct linear sources and adaptations" to "an entire complex of intertextual relationships between texts and cultures which speak to and through each other," links Machiavelli's use of Boccaccio with Marston's reworking of Machiavelli and shows each playwright using the previous material as a means of reflecting on current political situations. She sees Machiavelli responding to tale 3.6 in the context of the third day's "sense of darkness in Paradise," while "Like Machiavelli, Marston, through the figure of the cuckold, questions the ruler's legitimization of power and exposes … the corruption of the religious institutions inextricably intertwined with the political arena."[90] Later writers appreciated the complexity already in their sources.

The question of use requires historical situation. Alastair Fox intelligently asks why the English developed a sudden intense interest in Italian literature precisely around 1560, and why this interest faded in the early years of King James I. What function was this Italian literature serving at that moment in English history, and how were English writers using it to address their local concerns? His answer springs from the chronological link with the 1559 Acts of Supremacy and of Uniformity, which sought to establish a middle course between Catholicism and radical Protestantism. The ensuing arguments, exacerbated by a series of dangers and crises, over how far reforms should go and thus what the identity of English culture should become, drove writers to seek a way of dealing with these issues vital to the social life of their audiences. Italian texts, embodying the sensual and aesthetic allures opposed by Calvinists and Puritans, and yet attractively tolerant of the realities of human nature, could be combined with other, often English, sources to create dramatic tensions through which these basic issues were engaged.

> Shakespeare was addressing an extremely volatile situation in which primary values, and the regulatory codes – juridical, moral and religious – that were going to be invoked to enforce them, were being vigorously contested … He used Italian sources as a means of constructing a drama that could stimulate his audience into participating through the arousal of their emotional and intellectual energies in a critical appraisal of issues that were of central concern to the society of his day. He did this by using the divergence between the mores and value systems inherent in English and Italian culture to problematize the issues he addressed … All of Shakespeare's plays that make use of Italian material focus upon issues that had been made problematical for Elizabethan Protestants by the Calvinist underpinnings of the religious Settlement of 1559.[91]

Two Shakespeare plays, *All's Well That Ends Well* and *Cymbeline*, draw their main plots from the *Decameron*, 3.9 and 2.9. The complex combination in *Cymbeline* of Boccaccio's story with an anonymous English play and Holinshed's *Chronicles* of ancient British history bear out Fox's notion that Italian tales were being used to help fashion a sense of "England," or in this case – under James I's efforts to unify England, Scotland, and Wales – "Britain." Michael Redmond, *Shakespeare, Politics, and Italy: Intertextuality on the Jacobean Stage*, discusses the relevance of Italian texts – and the expectation that at least some members of the audience would be familiar with them – to *Cymbeline*'s engagement with the debates about English or British identity: "direct allusions to previous books from and about Italy formed part of deliberate rhetorical strategies that exploited audience awareness of intertextuality in order to engage with received ideas about what it meant to be English."[92]

Lienhard Bergel, "Shakespeare's *Cymbeline* and Boccaccio," seeks to compare the two authors with "equal weight."[93] *Frederyke of Jennen*, a German narrative derived from Boccaccio's, had turned the Italian merchants into an international group, so that, with a cynical Italian seducer and a Dutch defender of women, national differences became part of the theme. Shakespeare, familiar with both versions, picked up the idea of combining the wager story with one of national identities to stage "the conflict between a cosmopolitan civilization represented by ancient and Renaissance Rome, and separatist, local-patriotic tendencies." Despite the importance of British history to the play, Bergel suggests that Boccaccio's story allowed Shakespeare "to conduct the action on both the public and private planes … without making one subservient to the other." In a more personal vein, Piero Rebora sees Shakespeare in his later years as suffused with religious melancholy; thus Iachimo's conscience-stricken confession to the husband he had wronged and the husband's charitable pardon, even before learning that his wife was innocent, would both have been impossible for Boccaccio's characters.[94]

Even though Shakespeare took the plot of 2.9 for *Cymbeline*, he broke off a piece of it – the vindictive punishment against the slanderer – to use in a different play, *A Winter's Tale*. Similarly he repeated one piece of 3.9 from *All's Well*, the bed-trick, in *Measure for Measure*. In short, he was not just looking for plots but also for smaller pieces and not thinking simply of matching one tale to one play, but rather making use in various plays of redistributable elements that struck him as theatrically viable.

For *All's Well, Decameron* 3.9 is even more centrally important. Gary Waller observes that the play is "tightly constructed" and "contains two bold theatrical devices, an exchange of sexual partners and a climactic revelatory scene,"[95] without mentioning that both of these "bold theatrical devices" are present in Boccaccio's tale. The added figure of Parolles derives from Plautus's *miles gloriosus*, again linking the *Decameron* to Roman comedy. Herbert Wright long ago suggested that *Decameron* 4.1, the popular story of Ghismonda, may have influenced the play's discussion of the relation between "virtue and gentility";[96] this would imply Shakespeare's attention to Boccaccio beyond the immediate source tale of his plot, and thus to the *Decameron* rather than, or as well as, to the tale separately anthologized. Susan Snyder, pointing to the Frenchified names of the characters, concludes that Shakespeare was reading Boccaccio through the translation of Le Maçon[97] – although that would not have excluded his looking also at the Italian.

Claiming that Boccaccio's story "prompts no deeper questions," Snyder sees *All's Well* as breaking down the story's "neat closure" so as "to generate uneasy questioning." She suggests that the introduction in parallel with Helena of Parolles, "another character without rank" but with "elaborate pretensions" may cast Helena as "another kind of unscrupulous social climber" and that the play has to work hard – through the chorus of Helena's supporters – to stave off that impression. The play reverses genders of the common fairy-tale in which a poor but worthy boy wins the hand of a princess; yet the mix of fairy-tale and realism makes this a "problem" play. For example, like other commentators, she notes that Bertram is morally worse than Beltramo: "there is no counterpoint in Boccaccio for Bertram's repellent lies and cowardly evasions in the play's last scene." Snyder tries to explain some features of her comparison, suggesting, for example, that the theme of love for someone in an unreachably higher class may have resonated with Shakespeare's own experience as expressed in the sonnets.[98]

Waller looks to broader social rather than personal explanations for Shakespeare's changes to Boccaccio's tale:

> In Boccaccio, the King of France is largely a plot device but Shakespeare's king – no doubt in part reflecting the contemporary power of the monarchy and the court, all the more current in the new reign of James I – plays a major role in the play's development.[99]

Thus Bertram's frustration with being "evermore in subjection" (I.i.4) might well reflect the feelings of members of the audience.[100] Yet, although the morality play structure which places Bertram between Parolles and Helena as between his Bad and Good Angels seems to make Bertram rather than Helena the central character, our attention remains on Helena as a rare female character who is the subject rather than object of sexual desire, "an unusual figure of social and gender utopianism."[101] The play, he observes, starkly sets the mutually supportive alliance of women against the mutually betraying group of male companions and sees the final scene as a theatrical performance consciously staged by the women.[102] Might Shakespeare have seen in various tales of the *Decameron* both the "unusual" female and the kind of theatrical performing and directing by women that Masciandaro observes in the tale of Isabella (7.6)?

Shakespearians hesitate to pursue what a sensitive and attentive reader such as Shakespeare might have found in Boccaccio beyond a simple story. Robert Miola, in an essay demonstrating how much *All's Well* draws on Roman New Comedy, remarks that Helena "masterminds the intrigue; like Tranio (both Plautus's and Shakespeare's), she writes the script, casts the characters, directs the play." But although he notes Boccaccio's own interest in Roman comedy, he does not mention that Shakespeare may have obtained from Boccaccio the regendering that permits a woman to take this directorial role.[103] Shakespeare might have considered how Boccaccio was already reworking Plautus.

Rebora observes that Shakespeare chose two of Boccaccio's more serious and romantic tales to dramatize, following the Italian theatrical form of *commedia grave* with a happy ending,[104] and with female characters "di alto e nobile animo" [of lofty and noble spirit]. In fact, he argues, these women were "troppo logiche ed efficienti per Shakespeare" [too logical and efficient for Shakespeare], who weakened their characters despite his attraction to the "donna magnanima, coraggiosa, ingustamente offesa e sospettata" [magnanimous and courageous ladies, unjustly injured and suspected].[105] Kay Stanton similarly notes that Shakespeare picked two of the tales with the most admirable and active females, who compete successfully in the world of men: Giletta first as a medical practitioner, then as an abler administrator of the estate than her husband; and Zinevra, passing as a male, in her role as official overseeing the international market in Alexandria.[106] She argues that Shakespeare shared with Boccaccio a feminist advocacy: just as the *Decameron* ends by inviting readers to make good use of the book, so "'all' will only 'end well' if Shakespeare's audience will 'express content' with Helena's superior ability and her sexual assertiveness."[107] Scragg too sees a feminist message in the reversal of normal gender roles: the female is active in the world, while the male is kept passive as a ward. Bertram's protest at being the prize-object of a successful female quest might make audience members rethink the way traditional quest tales deny the human dignity of the female prize-object.[108]

Martin Butler's introduction to *Cymbeline* first mentions Boccaccio under the rubric "The Woman's Part,"[109] but sees Shakespeare weakening Boccaccio's heroine, "keeping Imogen out of heroic adventures and displacing her from the center of the story." He suggests "that what really interested Shakespeare was the struggle between the two men, and the recurrent anxiety about female chastity that it dramatized." Although Shakespeare veers away from Boccaccio's mercantile couple to the unequal marriage of a princess and a soldier, in the end "her political demotion permits a new balance" in the "marriage reconstructed as a bourgeois partnership of equals." Butler does not draw out the implications of this reconvergence with Boccaccio's model. Roger Warren argues against the notion that Imogen is somehow weakened or decentered; she is the one character who moves among all three plots and "holds them together; she is central to the play in every way."[110] Waller thinks the fact that *All's Well* "centers on an aggressive woman who gets what she wants … may account for much of the play's long-standing 'unfortunate' reputation," noting that Shaw considered it "too modern" for even an early twentieth-century audience.[111] The *Decameron*'s female characters are clearly significant to these Shakespeare studies.

If we move away from the gravitational attraction of Shakespeare to other less studied English playwrights, we can inquire which playwrights were most drawn to the *Decameron* and for what uses. It seems not to have been remarked, for example, that Fletcher, when writing without Beaumont, turned repeatedly to the *Decameron* for episodes. A still unanswered question is why he did this precisely when apart from his usual collaborator? How might this help us define Fletcher as a writer distinct from Beaumont?[112]

Sometimes Boccaccio was, quite reasonably, associated with Chaucer. Fletcher and Field's *Four Plays, or Moral Representations, in One* combined "The Franklin's Tale" and *Decameron* 5.7. *Two Merry Milke-Maids* (1620) by a J.C. (possibly John Cumber), merged the name "Dorigen" from "The Franklin's Tale" with the task of producing fruits and flowers out of season from its analogue *Decameron* 10.5. Fletcher's *Women Pleased*, while deriving its main plot from the "Wife of Bath's Tale," picked up episodes from three *Decameron* stories for its subplot. Do these pairings indicate an understanding of Chaucer's debt to Boccaccio, or only a sense that the writers were similar?

While the main plot of *Women Pleased* (1619–23) involves a conflict between the Duchess of Florence, who seeks to marry her daughter to the Duke of Siena, and her daughter Belvidere, involved in a mutual love with the soldier Silvio, the subplot concerns Isabella, the wife of a miserly usurer. Courted by several men, Isabella nonetheless remains faithful to her husband and even helps him catch one of the more importunate offenders, Bartello, who, as captain of the guard for the prison where Belvidere has been confined, links the two plots.[113] Isabella's tricks derive from a series of *Decameron* tales: 7.6, 7.8, and 8.8. Both the usurer and Bartello end up begging for pardon from their wives, either for their jealous suspicions or for their own infidelities. This supports the main plot's theme, in which Silvio, to save himself from execution, must answer the question of what women want; as in Chaucer's "Wife of Bath's Tale," the answer is mastery, or as Fletcher puts it in the final lines, "Give 'em their sovereign wills."[114] Although Fox has shown that playwrights often set English and Italian sources against each other, Fletcher seems to be suggesting that both Chaucer and Boccaccio – here used, I note, to represent respectively the upper and middle classes – shared a laughing view of male-female relations. Rather than view the earlier writers as "sources," we might view Fletcher's play as offering a reading of their affinity along with a recognition of their differing social contexts.[115]

Act IV of Fletcher's *The Night Walker* (c.1611) reworks *Decameron* 3.8: the Jewish usurer Algripe, who has taken possession of another family's property, is given a sleeping potion and persuaded, on waking, that he is now in hell, where "two Furies with black tapers" pinch and whip him; a boy dressed as an angel tells him that it is not too late to repent and restore the property, which he does, converting also to Christianity.[116] The *Decameron* story in which a husband is persuaded that he has died and gone to Purgatory is relevant to Fletcher's plot, as the usurer has seized the property by marrying the reluctant Maria, who is herself thought to have died before consummating the wedding. Fletcher thus doubles the "putative death" motif while picking up the idea that a *beffa* performance of after-death punishments might be used to reform a man. The original comedy is turned into a dramatic moralizing spectacle, enabling its use in the serious main plot (without the *Decameron* tale's adultery) rather than in a comic subplot. *The Knight of Malta* (1619) again took a *Decameron* tale, 10.4, for a major episode in the main plot while altering the tone. It is the villain who goes to the tomb of his beloved in the hope of finally satisfying his lust. As in the novella, the lady is actually alive; but with a new twist, rivals converge at the tomb site, and the villain finds the tomb already empty. Fletcher was drawn in both plays to dramatic situations of putative death, while changing the mood from comic to lugubrious.

Ben Jonson too made use of the *Decameron*. *The Devil Is an Ass*, like Fletcher's *Women Pleased*, combined several tales in one play, following the technique of *contaminatio*.[117] This might indicate an awareness of the whole *Decameron*.[118] The reference in Jonson's *Volpone* 2.1. to street performers "with their mouldy tales out of Boccaccio" similarly implies a reference to the *Decameron* rather than to anthologies of miscellaneous authors. Nonetheless, like other playwrights, Jonson mixed *Decameron* tales with other materials. Peter Happé observes that Jonson tended to use "a process of combination and juxtaposition," taking pieces from various sources, both narrative and theatrical, and fitting them together into his own design, rather than basing the whole play on one story.[119] Ann Barton remarks that paradoxically it was Jonson's way of trying out a new direction that led him to base this main plot on a pre-existing tale. She does not comment on why Jonson, in seeking for a new path after the "grand fireworks" of *Bartholemew Fair*, might have turned specifically to the *Decameron*.[120] But Michael Redmond observes, "By the time of the first performance of *Volpone*, the *Decameron* had been the inspiration for prominent plays by Dekker, Marston, Middleton, Sharpham, and Shakespeare among others."[121]

The Devil Is an Ass (1616) merges *Decameron* 3.5 and 3.3 with Machiavelli's "Belfagor" and with medieval English vice and devil interludes to satirize Fitzdotterel's foolish vanity, avarice, and ambition,[122] while the wooer's deceit of the husband, rather than leading to adultery with the wife, becomes a means to assure the wife's financial security against Fitzdottrel's gullible vulnerability to con men. Could Jonson's perusal of the *Decameron*, beyond the two tales used in this play, have had an influence on the fact that:

> Frances Fitzdottrel is the first woman in a Jonson comedy who can fairly be described as a heroine. She is young, beautiful, resourceful and intelligent, passionate but chaste – qualities often found united in Shakespeare's women … but previously unheard of in any Jonson play?[123]

The Widdow (1615–16?) was a collaboration of Jonson, Fletcher, and Middleton; all three made use elsewhere of *Decameron* materials. Middleton's *Blurt Master-Constable, or The Spaniard's Night-Walker* (1602) had worked part of *Decameron* 2.5 into the subplot, where a (Spanish) would-be lover is dumped into a sewer. *The Widdow* based its main plot on *Decameron* 2.2, in which a traveler, after being robbed, is let in from the cold and not only dressed and fed but taken to bed by a widow whose lover has suddenly had reason not to arrive as expected. In the usual English manner, the play omits the extra-marital fornication. The plot is made more complicated, as several men are attracted to the widow and several men are robbed. It is the widow's sister, the wife of a judge, who takes in the robbed Ansaldo and gives him some of her husband's clothes, which the husband, still alive, recognizes. This same wife has given her husband a forged letter with a proposed tryst supposedly from a young man named Francisco, a letter which the irate husband shows to Francisco, who understands its intent (*Decameron* 3.3). Francisco, however, is deterred by his conscience from fulfilling its behest, unlike Boccaccio's young lover, and Ansaldo comes at the right moment to take his place. However, Ansaldo too has a reason to leave after dinner and, in a final surprise, turns out to be a female (and marries Francisco). The wife thus remains, somewhat reluctantly, faithful. The Epilogue declares the whole play to have been a Christmas "sport," suggesting that the *Decameron*, properly cleaned up, was seen as merry entertainment. The winter setting of the tale probably suggested it as Christmas holiday fare.

Parra points to Boccaccio's increasing identification with comedy in the seventeenth century.[124] Massinger's *The Great Duke of Florence* (licensed for performance 1627) includes a servant buffoon named Calandrino.[125] Even the Griselda story, dramatized by Dekker, Haughton, and Chettle at the turn of the century, becomes a comedy, its main couple set against an inverse Welsh couple in which the noble wife, Gwenthyan, repeatedly humiliates her socially inferior husband.[126] As Lee Bliss observes, neither Gwenthyan nor the marquis's sister Julia accepts Grissil as a model wife.[127] Rather than a quasi-religious awe for patient suffering, the play mixes moments of pathos with frequently evoked laughter at the problems of marriage, while also satirizing the courtiers who bend with every wind.

As the *Decameron* became a source for gags inserted into English comedies, it is often difficult to tell whether particular scenes come from the *Decameron* directly or indirectly. For example, Edward Sharpham's *Cupid's Whirligig* (1607) is listed by both F.N. Jones and Stych as having made use of *Decameron* 7.6; yet that gag was circulating independently and had already appeared in both Italian and English theatre: in the *commedia dell'arte* scenario *I Tre Becchi* (and no doubt in others), in Will Kemp's jig "Singing Simpkin,"[128] in a subplot of Cyril Tourneur's *Atheist's Tragedie* (1611) where it leads to a violent ending, and in Fletcher's *Women Pleased* (1619–23). Similarly, the clever use of a naïve confessor to become an unwitting go-between, from *Decameron* 3.3, appears repeatedly with variations: in John Marston's *Parasitaster, or the Fawne* (1606) a daughter uses her father in this manner; in Jonson's *The Devil Is an Ass*, Lady Fitzdottrel uses her husband's servant – actually a naïve devil disguised as a human – for the same purpose.[129] In *The Widdow*, with yet another twist, a wife uses her husband, who angrily confronts the surprised but perceptive young man. These gags had become free-floating theatergrams.

Playwrights may often borrow useful dramatic material without expecting, or even wanting, the borrowings to be recognized. But when two or more *Decameron* tales are combined, as in Jonson's *The Devil Is an Ass* or Fletcher's *Women Pleased*, we may more plausibly suspect that at least the playwright knew where these tales came from and that perhaps some members of the audience would recall the *Decameron*.

Scholars of early modern English playwrights are much more likely to discuss debts to Chaucer than to Boccaccio.[130] Even studies on Italian theatre, which regularly acknowledge debts to the *Decameron*, often treat that relationship briefly rather than as a central focus. In studies of English theatre, apart from the scholarship on Shakespeare's two *Decameron*-based plays, Boccaccio is rarely mentioned. Yet the *Decameron* was used by a number of well-known playwrights: Shakespeare, Dekker, Jonson, Fletcher, Massinger, Middleton. Playwrights were looking for material that would work well on stage, and they saw the *Decameron* as offering situations, ironies, and an array of tones – romantic, folkloric, witty, instructive, satiric, or festive – that could enhance the appeal of their plays. The very diversity of the *Decameron* made it a resource for a wide range of theatre, tragic and comic, moral and risqué. Early dramatists took their main plots from serious stories: the trials of patient Griselda, the tragic love of Ghismonda, the mutual generosity of a model pair of friends. By the seventeenth century, Boccaccio's humor was more appreciated, and his tales were providing major episodes for the main plots and subplots of both light and serious comedies. It would be worth inquiring not just how playwrights changed Boccaccio's stories but also what they learned from his own theatricality.

Notes

1 Claude Cazalé Bérard, "Boccaccio's Working Notebooks (*Zibaldone Laurenziano, Miscellanea Laurenziana, Zibaldone Magliabechiano*)," in *Boccaccio: A Critical Guide to the Complete Works*, eds. Victoria Kirkham, Michael Sherberg, and Janet Levarie Smarr (Chicago, IL: University of Chicago Press, 2013), p. 316; Michelangelo Picone, "La *Comedia Lidie* dallo Zibaldone al *Decameron*," in *Gli zibaldoni di Boccaccio: Memoria, scrittura, riscrittura; Atti del Seminario internazionale di Firenze-Certaldo (26–28 aprile 1996)*, eds. Michelangelo Picone and Claude Cazale-Bérard (Florence: Franco Cesati, 1998), pp. 401–23; Jonathan Usher, "Rhetorical and Narrative Strategies in Boccaccio's Translation of the *Comoedia Lydiae*," *Modern Language Review* 84 (1989): 337–44. Vittore Branca, in his notes to the *Decameron, Tutte le Opere* 4 (Milan: Mondadori, 1976), p. 1410 n. 4, suggested that traces of *Birria e Geta* appear in 8.3, i.e. the stoning of Birria by Geta who pretends not to see him. See also Ferruccio Bertini, "Una novella del Boccaccio e l'*Alda* di Guglielmo di Blois," *Maia* 29–30 (1977–78): 135–41, for links between the *Alda* and *Decameron* 3.10. Texts of these medieval plays can be found in *Seven Medieval Latin Comedies*, trans. Alison Goddard Elliott, Garland Library of Medieval Literature vol. 20, ser. B (New York: Garland Publishing, Inc., 1984).

2 Firenze, Biblioteca Medicea Laurenziana, XXXVIII 17; see *Mostra di Manoscritti, Documenti e Edizioni, Firenze-Biblioteca Medicea Laurenziana 22 maggio-31 agosto 1973*, I: *Manoscritti e Documenti*, a cura del Comitato Promotore (Certaldo, 1975), pp. 145–46.

3 See Giuseppe Velli's notes to the *Buccolicum carmen* in *Tutte le opere di Giovanni Boccaccio* (Milan: Mondadori, 1994), vol. 5, part 2, p. 931, n. to line 69 ff.; the line, which is a list of first-person verbs by a distraught lover describing himself, pleased Boccaccio so much that he repeated it in both the *Genealogia* Bk. 3, ch. 23, and the *Esposizioni*, canto 1 alleg. 96. These later works explicitly cite Plautus; Velli notes that the autograph of the *Carmen buccolicum* indicates "Plautus" in the margin.

4 The comparison continues, "but with no less poverty." Francis Petrarch, *Letters of Old Age/ Rerum Senilium libri I–XVIII*, trans. Aldo Bernardo, Saul Levin, and Reta A. Bernardo (Baltimore, MD: Johns Hopkins University Press, 1992), vol. 2, p. 644.

5 Madeleine Doran, *Endeavors of Art: A Study of Form in Elizabethan Drama* (Madison: University of Wisconsin Press, 1954), pp. 133–34 and 176–77.

6 "Also Known As 'Principe Galeotto': (*Decameron*)," in *Boccaccio: A Critical Guide to the Complete Works*, p. 35.
7 *Decameron*, ed. Vittore Branca, *Tutte le opere* 4, p. 1284 n. 1, 1418 n.1, and 1532 n. 6.
8 *Boccaccio On Poetry. Being the Preface and the Fourteenth and Fifteenth Books of Boccaccio's Genealogia Deorum Gentilium*, trans. Charles G. Osgood (Indianapolis, IN: The Bobbs-Merrill Company, 1956), p. 49, 87, and 93. The passage about Paul hearing the words of Terence from the mouth of Christ (*Genealogia* XIV, 18) is repeated almost verbatim in Boccaccio's commentary on Dante's *Commedia*, 1 litt. 103–4. He obviously saw this as a divine sanctioning of the ancient poets.
9 *Boccaccio's Expositions on Dante's Comedy*, trans. Michael Papio (Toronto: University of Toronto Press, 2009), 1 alleg. 95–96.
10 *Decameron*, ed. Vittore Branca, Tutte le opere vol. 4, p. 1000 n. 6.
11 *Heliotropia* 1.1 (2003) www.brown.edu/Departments/Italian_Studies/heliotropia/01-01/smarr.html; reprinted in *Heliotropia 700/10. A Boccaccio Anniversary Volume*, ed. Michael Papio (Milan: LED, 2013), pp. 133–42.
12 Eduardo Saccone, "Azione," in *Lessico critico Decameroniano*, eds. Renzo Bragantini and Pier Massimo Forni (Torino: Bollati Boringhieri, 1995), p. 62, calls the first tale "paradigmatico" as performance that has an effect on reality.
13 Saccone, "Azione," p. 60–72.
14 "The *Decameron* and Italian Renaissance Comedy," in *Approaches to Teaching Boccaccio's Decameron*, ed. James H. McGregor (New York: The Modern Language Association of America, 2000), pp. 142–48.
15 As Saccone reminds us, "Azione," p. 61; Antonio Stauble, "La brigata del *Decameron* come pubblico teatrale," *Studi sul Boccaccio* 9 (1975–1976): 103–17. See also Laura Sanguinetti White, *La scena conviviale e la sua funzione nel mondo del Boccaccio* (Florence: Olschki, 1983).
16 "The sides of these little hills sloped downward toward the plain like tiers in an amphiteater, arranged so that they gradually descended from the summit to the lowest row, continuously diminishing their circles." *Decameron*, trans. Mark Musa and Peter Bondanella (New York: Signet Classic, 2002), p. 481.
17 Franco Masciandaro, "Madonna Isabella's Play and the Play of the Text (*Decameron* VII.6)," *MLN* 118, 1 (January 2003): 245–56. See also G. Pugliese, "Commedia dell'arte Elements in Boccaccio's *Decameron*," in *The Science of Buffoonery: Theory and History of the "commedia dell'arte*," eds. D. Pietropaolo and M. de P. Lorce (Ottowa: Dovehouse, 1989), pp. 69–76, who claims that "the Decameron contains all the distinguishing features of the Italian popular theatre" (p. 69).
18 Nino Borsellino, "'*Decameron* come teatro' and 'Aretino e Boccaccio'," *Rozzi e Intronati. Esperienze e forme di teatro dal Decameron al Candelaio* (Rome: Bulzoni Editore, 1976), pp. 13–50 and 213–28; "Il *Decameron* teatrale nel Rinascimento," in *Boccaccio: Secoli di Vita*, eds. Marga Cottino-Jones and Edward F. Tuttle (Ravenna, Italy: Longo Editore, 1977), pp. 207–23. Although my essay emphasizes studies since 1990, Borsellino's work is too important to ignore.
19 "The *Decameron* and Italian Renaissance Comedy," pp. 145–47.
20 Renzo Bragantini, "Dialogo," in *Lessico critico decameroniano*, pp. 93–115, 110, 112.
21 Tatiana Crivelli and Teresa Nocita, "Teatralità del Dettato, Stratificazioni strutturali, Plurivocità degli esiti: Il *Decameron* fra Testo, Ipertesto e Generi Letterari," in *Autori e Lettori di Boccaccio. Atti del Convegno internazionale di Certaldo (20–22 settembre 2001)*, ed. Michelangelo Picone (Florence: Franco Cesati, 2002), pp. 209–33. Giuseppe Velli, "Memoria," in *Lessico critico decameroniano*, pp. 222–48, demonstrates that Boccaccio himself wrote by taking bits and pieces of remembered readings and recomposing them into his own writings. Thus he made himself part of a chain of citations.
22 Douglas Radcliff-Umstead, *The Birth of Modern Comedy in Renaissance Italy* (Chicago, IL: University of Chicago Press, 1969), pp. 110–12; A. Gareffi, "Il teatro di Jacopo Nardi dalle trame del *Decameron* al comico moralistico del primo '500'," *Biblioteca teatrale* 14 (1976): 38–63; *Tre commedie fiorentine del primo cinquecento*, ed. and introd. Luigina Stefani (Ferrara, Italy: Gabriele Corbo Editore, 1986) includes both of Nardi's plays. *I due felici rivali* was performed, together with Bibbiena's more famous *Calandra* for the 1513 carnival festivities in Urbino.

23 On the *Calandra*'s debts to the *Decameron*, see the excellent introduction by Giorgio Padoan to his edition of *La Calandra, Commedia elegantissima per messer Bernardo Dovizi da Bibbiena* (Padua: Antenore, 1985), pp. 18–32; Angela Guidotti, "Il doppio gioco della *Calandria*," *MLN* 104, 1 (January 1989): 111–14; Smarr, "Marriage," esp. 37ff. Robin Kirkpatrick, *English and Italian Literature from Dante to Shakespeare: A Study of Source, Analogue, and Divergence* (New York: Longman, 1995), pp. 201–7; Carlo Fanelli, *La Calandria, Tematiche e simbologia. Il panorama teatrale del Conquecento e la Calandria di Bernardo Dovizi da Bibbiena* (Florence: Firenze Libri, Atheneum, 1997), pp. 66–72; Giulio Ferroni, "La *Calandra* del Bibbiena tra Plauto e Boccaccio," in *La maschera e il volto: il teatro in Italia*, ed. Francesco Bruni (Venice: Marsilio, 2002), pp. 31–38; Ronald Martinez, "Etruria Triumphant in Rome: Fables of Medici Rule and Bibbiena's *Calandra*," *Renaissance Drama*, 36–37 (2010b): 69–70.

24 *L'avventura della commedia rinascimentale* (Padua: Piccin Nuova Libraria, 1996), p. 30. See further in that book his chapter on "L'alternativa novellistica e la linea toscana," pp. 23–39.

25 Franco Fido, *Le Metamorfosi del Centauro* (Rome: Bulzoni, 1977), pp. 99–101, Padoan, *L'avventura*, pp. 34–35, and Luciano Bottoni, *La Messinscena del Rinascimento II: Il segreto del diavolo e "La Mandragola". Critica letteraria e linguistica* (Milano: Franco Angeli, 2005), pp. 133–35 and 158–66, compare Bibbiena's and Machiavelli's different uses of the *Decameron;* Padoan argues that Machiavelli followed Bibbiena's lead in combining the classical model with the Boccaccian novella, describing Machiavelli's uses of the *Decameron* as sparser but less superficial: "Quel che in Dovizi resta citazione, in Machiavelli è ripensamento e ricreazione." Angela Guidotti, "Il doppio gioco della *Calandria*," pp. 100–104, notes numerous similarities of phrasing between the two plays.

26 Salvatore Di Maria, "From Prose to Stage: Machiavelli's *Mandragola*," *MLN*, 121, 1 (January 2006): 130–55, argues that 3.6 is the primary source for the play but acknowledges the presence of other tales; see also his chapter on the *Mandragola* in his *The Poetics of Imitation in the Italian Theatre of the Renaissance* (Toronto: University of Toronto Press, 2013), pp. 26–44; as a result of his single-source focus, he sees these as alterations to the source features that derive from other tales. Ettore Mazzali, "Introduction," in Niccolò Machiavelli, *Mandragola, Clizia* (Milan: Giangiacomo Feltrinelli, 1995), pp. 36–37, mentions *Decameron* 3.6, 7.7, and 8.9; Gian Maria Anselmi, "Partitura della *Mandragola*," in *Il Teatro di Machiavelli*, eds. Gennaro Barbarisi and Anna Maria Cabrini (Milan: Cisalpino, 2005), p. 260, lists 3.6, 7.7, 8.6; Ronald Martinez, "Comedian, Tragedian: Machiavelli and Traditions of Renaissance Theater," in *The Cambridge Companion to Machiavelli*, ed. John Najemy (Cambridge: Cambridge University Press, 2010a), pp. 206–22, 213, and 215, comments re 3.6, 7.7, and the Calandrino stories. Gay Bardin, "Machiavelli Reads Boccaccio, *Mandragola* Between *Decameron* and *Corbaccio*," *Italian Quarterly* 38, 149–50 (2001): 5–6, indicates the tales mentioned above plus 2.9, 2.10, 3.4, and 4.10. See also Luigi Vanossi, "Situazione e sviluppo nel teatro machiavelliano," in *Lingua e strutture del teatro italiano del Rinascimento* (Padua, 1970), pp. 8–14; Ezio Raimondi, "Presentazione," in Machiavelli, *Mandragola, Clizia*, ed. Gian Maria Anselmi (Milan: Mursia, 1984), pp. 9–12; Giorgio Inglese, "*Mandragola* di Niccolò Machiavelli," in *Letteratura Italiana: Le opere I. Dalle origini al'500*, ed. A. Asor Rosa (Turin: Einaudi, 1992), pp. 1022–23. On *Decameron* 7.9 and Machiavelli's *Clizia*, see Albert Ascoli, "*Clizia*'s Histories," in *A Local Habitation and a Name* (New York: Fordham University Press, 2011), pp. 298–304. Laurie Shepard, "*Decameron* as a Model for Sixteenth-Century Comedy," presented at the International Medieval Conference at Kalamazoo, 2013, suggests that besides offering character types, phrases, and situations, the *Decameron* offered a model for the precise and recent setting of the story and the individualization of characters. Luciano Bottoni, *La Messinscena*, p. 153, asks whether the illustrations accompanying the 1492 edition of the *Decameron* might have influenced the imagination of playwrights.

27 Giuseppe Velli, "Memoria," in *Lessico Critico Decameroniano*, eds. Renzo Bragantini and Pier Massimo Forni (Turin: Bollati Boringhieri, 1995), p. 232, traces this third case from Livy through Boccaccio to Machiavelli.

28 Bottoni, *La Messinscena*, pp. 158–66: "Bibbiena e Machiavelli si confrontino quasi sempre su temi e motivi, battute e tessere, estrapolati dalle stesse novelle, che – a nostro avviso –

può dar senso e rilevanza ad un confronto drammaturgico: a quella sfida dello 'stare a paragone' che Calandro aveva lanciato sulla scena in volgare e che messer Nicia raccoglie" (p. 158).

29 Kirkpatrick, p. 201: "much of the pleasure which the original audience derived from the play must have been due to an understanding … of the skill with which the author had commanded and redirected his literary sources." Doni's *I Marmi* (1553) has a speaker, describing performances of the *Mandragola* and of Cecchi's *L'Assiuolo*, saying, "Mi piace quei passi tratti del Boccaccio si destramente"; *I Marmi*, Parte prima, ragionamento quarto. *Scrittori d'Italia* 106 (Bari, Italy: Laterza, 1928), p. 51. Indeed, humour emerges from the comparison of contexts; for example, the servant Fessenio's description of his *master* Calandro echoes but reverses Fra Cipolla's description of his *servant* Guccio (6.10).

30 Ronald Martinez, "Etruria Triumphant in Rome," 70: "Calandro fits, with anthropological exactitude, into a stereotypical division of Florentine society into the clever and the credulous, into *furbi* and *fessi*."

31 Perhaps inserted for the purpose of evoking the connection to Calandrino.

32 Borsellino, "*Decameron* come teatro," p. 20.

33 Ronald Martinez, "Comedian, tragedian," pp. 214–15.

34 Albert Ascoli, "Pyrrhus' Rules: Playing with Power from Boccaccio to Machiavelli," *MLN* 114, 1 (1999): 14–57, revised into two essays in Ascoli, *A Local Habitation and a Name*, 80–117, pp. 282–305. On the *Mandragola, Clizia*, and *Decameron* 7.9, see also Denis Fachard, "Il teatro machiavelliano e la 'qualità dei tempi'," in *Il Teatro di Machiavelli*, eds. Gennaro Barbarisi and Anna Maria Cabrini (Milan: Cisalpino, 2005), pp. 23–33.

35 Edmond M. Beame, "Introduction," in Ludovico Ariosto, *The Comedies of Ariosto*, trans. and eds. Edmond M. Beame and Leonard G. Sbrocchi (Chicago, IL: University of Chicago Press, 1975), pp. xxiv–xxv.

36 Along with Plautus's *Captivi*, in which a master and servant exchange roles.

37 The *Calandra* was performed again in 1514 and 1515 at Rome, 1522 in Venice, 1520 and 1532 in Mantua, and 1548 in Lyon for King Henri II and his Medici wife; see Fanelli, *La Calandria*, pp. 103–7, for sixteenth-century performances. Giorgio Padoan's edition, *La Calandra. Commedia Elegantissima per Messer Bernardo Dovizi da Bibbiena*. Medioevo e Umanesimo 57 (Padua: Antenore, 1985), pp. 35–39, lists a dozen editions before 1550. The *Mandragola* after its first performance in Florence perhaps in 1518, was staged in Rome in 1520 and 1524, in Venice 1522 and 1526, back in Florence 1526, and later in other parts of Italy; its 1518 publication was followed by an edition in Venice 1522, in Rome 1524, and in Cesena 1526 (Ettore Mazzali, "Introduction," in Niccolò Machiavelli, *Mandragola, Clizia* (Milan: Giangiacomo Feltrinelli, 1995), pp. 30–32). By 1525 it had been anthologized (Martinez, "Comedian, tragedian," p. 206). *I suppositi* was published in an unauthorized edition in 1510, then in Siena 1523, Rome 1524 and 1525, Venice 1525 (Bartolommeo Gamba, *Serie dell'edizioni de' testi di lingua italiana* [Milan: Stamperia Reale, 1812], p. 60). After its original 1509 Ferrara performance, it saw performances in Rome 1519; Venice 1524; back in Ferrara 1525 and 1526; Donald Beecher, "Introduction," Lodovico Ariosto, *Supposes (I suppositi) (1509) translated by George Gascoigne (1566)*, eds. Donald Beecher and John Butler, Carleton Renaissance Plays in Translation 33 (Ottawa: Dovehouse Editions, 1999), p. 19. At Rome in 1524 Minizio Calvo published seven comedies, including the *Suppositi, Calandra*, and *Mandragola;* the *Calandra* and *Mandragola* were still being anthologized in 1554, by Girolamo Ruscelli (Giorgio Padoan, *L'avventura*, 32, p. 156).

38 For an analysis of how Cecchi reworks his sources, see Salvatore Di Maria, *The Poetics of Imitation*, pp. 45–63.

39 Such as Francesco Belo's *Il Pedante*, Anton Francesco Grazzini's *Il Frate*, Giovan Maria Cecchi's *Assiuolo*, Aretino's *Cortegiana*, and Bruno's *Candelaio*, some of which also pick up phrases from the *Decameron*. Michele Marrapodi, "From Narrative to Drama: The Erotic Tale and the Theater," in *The Italian World of English Renaissance Drama. Cultural Exchange and Intertextuality*, ed. Michele Marrapodi (Newark: University of Delaware Press, 1998b), pp. 44–70. An early version of this essay appeared also in Italian as "Da Boccaccio a Shakespeare: Il Racconto dell'Eros e la Trasgressione della Commedia," in *Le forme del teatro 5: Eros e commedia nella scena inglese*, eds. Viola Papetti and Laura Visconti (Rome: Edizioni di Storia e Letteratura, 1997), pp. 133–51.

40 The scenario was published in both Italian and English in K. M. Lea, *Italian Popular Comedy: A Study in the Commedia dell'arte, 1560–1620, with Special Reference to the English Stage* (New York: Russell & Russell, 1962), v. 2, p. 580–84.

41 Salvatore Di Maria, *The Italian Tragedy in the Renaissance: Cultural Realities and Theatrical Innovations* (Lewisburg, PA: Bucknell University Press, 2002), pp. 101–25.

42 Louise George Clubb, "Intertextualities: Some Questions," in *The Italian World of English Renaissance Drama*, ed. M. Marrapodi, pp. 179–89 (p. 180). Richard Andrews, *Scripts and Scenarios: The Performance of Comedy in Renaissance Italy* (Cambridge: Cambridge University Press, 1993), pp. 18–21, similarly stresses that the *Decameron* was "no less important than Plautus and Terence" as a source for Italian comedy and reminds us that, despite their associations with carnival, both the tales and early comedies were aimed at a well-mannered and educated elite.

43 E.g. prologue to *Two Noble Kinsmen*, though for this Chaucer's source is not the *Decameron* but Boccaccio's *Teseida*. Alastair Fox, *The English Renaissance: Identity and Representation in Elizabethan England* (Oxford: Blackwell, 1997), p. 20: "The first writer in England to respond to the influence of the Italian Renaissance was the man whom later generations would regard as 'the father of English poetry,' Geoffrey Chaucer."

44 Herbert Wright, *Boccaccio in England from Chaucer to Tennyson* (London: Athlone Press, 1957); F. S. Stych, *Boccaccio in English: A Bibliography of Editions, Adaptations, and Criticism*, Bibliographies and Indexes in World Literature, 48 (Westport, CT: Greenwood Press, 1995); and Giuseppe Galigani ed., *Il Boccaccio nella cultura inglese e anglo-americana* (Florence: Olschki, 1974) all indicate English tale collections and plays that include *Decameron* stories. Wright and Galigani compare the English versions to the Italian for style, characters, and thematic or moral emphases. Galigani's volume contains two separate essays, one by himself on the sixteenth century and one by Anton Ranieri Parra on the seventeenth. On the one hand, Galigani tries not only to describe English imitations of *Decameron* tales but also to explain the shifting patterns of their selection and adaptation over the course of the century. On the other, the separate and different treatment of sixteenth- and seventeenth-century texts precludes a longer view of how those processes of selection and adaptation continued to change. For the publication history of Boccaccio's works in England and the shift of interest among them over time, see Guyda Armstrong, *The English Boccaccio. A History in Books* (Toronto: University of Toronto Press, 2013). See also Mary Augusta Scott, *Elizabethan Translations from the Italian* (Boston, MA: Houghton Miflin, 1916).

45 For arguments that Shakespeare could read Italian, see Ernesto Grillo, *Shakespeare and Italy* (New York: Haskell House Publishers Ltd, 1973 [1949]), pp. 125–31; Naseeb Shaheen, "Shakespeare's Knowledge of Italian," *Shakespeare Survey* 47 (1994), pp. 161–69; Jason Lawrence, *Who The Devil Taught Thee So Much Italian? Italian Language Learning and Literary Imitation in Early Modern England* (Manchester, UK: Manchester University Press, 2005), p. 118–27, and "'The story is extant, and writ in very choice Italian': Shakespeare's Dramatizations of Cinthio," in *Shakespeare, Italy, and Intertextuality*, ed. Michele Marrapodi, pp. 91–92; Alastair Fox, *The English Renaissance: Identity and Representation in Elizabethan England* (Oxford: Blackwell, 1997), p. 183: "his knowledge of Italian was sufficient for him to refer also to the source stories as they appeared in the original Italian. Several sources, indeed, were available only in Italian."

46 Her book was furthermore translated into English in 1521.

47 Herbert G. Wright, *Boccaccio in England*, p. 114.

48 Roger Ascham, *The Scholemaster*, is available as a searchable text without page numbers, digitized by Judy Boss and copyrighted by the University of Oregon, 1998, at www.luminarium.org/renascence-editions/ascham1.htm. Herbert Wright, *Boccaccio in England*, p. 123, points similarly to Gilbert Banester's fifteenth-century allusion to "Bocas in cent novelys" as an indication of his reading the French.

49 Louise George Clubb, *Italian Drama in Shakespeare's Time* (New Haven, CT: Yale University Press, 1989b), e.g. p. 279: "The contaminatio by which Italian drama was cultivated, and the staple elements that it accumulated into a great repertory, belonged to a theatrical mode of production and a mentality that penetrated European culture"; Michele Marrapodi, "Introduction: Intertextualizing Shakespeare's Text," in *Shakespeare and Intertextuality. The Transition of Cultures between Italy and England in the Early Modern Period*,

ed. M. Marrapodi, Biblioteca di Cultura 610 (Rome: Bulzoni Editore, 2000), p. 11; and in the overlapping volume *Shakespeare, Italy, and Intertextuality, cit.*; p. 1; Di Maria, pp. *The Poetics of Imitation*, 3–25: "Imitation: the Link between Past and Present." For a helpful outline of issues regarding this practice in general, see Robert S. Miola, "Seven Types of Intertextuality," in *Shakespeare, Italy, and Intertextuality*, ed. M. Marrapodi, pp. 13–25.

50 Clubb., esp. pp. 184–86.

51 Michele Marrapodi, Introduction: "Appropriating Italy: Towards a New Approach to Renaissance Drama," in *Italian Culture in the Drama of Shakespeare and His Contemporaries. Rewriting, Remaking, Refashioning*, ed. M. Marrapodi (Aldershot, UK: Ashgate, 2007a), p. 1.

52 Eds. Mary Ellen Lamb and Valerie Wayne (Oxford: Routledge, 2009); the quotation is from their introduction, p. 1. Their reference is to David Kastan, ed., *A Companion to Shakespeare* (Oxford: Blackwell, 1999), p. 220.

53 Geoffrey Bullough's *Narrative and Dramatic Sources of Shakespeare* (Oxford: Routledge, 1957–1975) is an eight-volume classic. Kenneth Muir, *The Sources of Shakespeare's Plays* (London: Methuen, 1977), offers a more modest single volume. Stuart Gillespie, *Shakespeare's Books: A Dictionary of Shakespeare's Sources* (New Brunswick, NJ: Athlone Press, 2001) arranges the sources alphabetically rather than by play; Boccaccio, whom he discusses on pp. 53–60, is one of 23 entries under B alone. Introductions to editions of Shakespeare's and other English dramatists' plays sometimes, but not always, indicate sources.

54 See note 45. Piero Rebora, "Boccaccio e Shakespeare," in *Civiltà Italiana e Civiltà Inglese. Studi e Ricerche* (Florence: Felice Le Monnier, 1936), pp. 109–46, argues, like Hazlitt, that Boccaccio's influence has been under-recognized because of the reluctance of many who used his work to admit to the fact. "Lo si stampava, lo si leggeva, lo si imitava, ma se ne parlava il meno possibile" (p. 113).

55 Florence Nightingale Jones, *Boccaccio and His Imitators in German, English, French, Spanish and Italian literature, "The Decameron"* (Chicago, IL: Chicago University Press, 1910) is enthusiastic but not reliable; she admits that she was not able to check all the texts she mentions. Her suggestion, for example, that Sharpham's *The Fleire* (1608) uses 3.3 is not true. Stych is more careful and more useful; but his claim that Sharpham's *Fleire* uses 2.3 (perhaps merely an erroneous transcription of Jones) is also wrong. Even the *Routledge Guide to William Shakespeare*, ed. Robert Shaughnessy (New York: Routledge, 2011), p. 94, oddly gives the *Decameron* instead of *Il Pecorone* as a source for *The Merchant of Venice*.

56 "Round Table Discussion," in *Shakespeare and Intertextuality*, ed. M. Marrapodi, pp. 298–99.

57 Rebora, "Boccaccio e Shakespeare," p. 116.

58 David Bevington, "Cultural Exchange: Gascoigne and Ariosto at Gray's Inn in 1566," in *The Italian World of English Renaissance Drama*, ed. M. Marrapodi, pp. 25–40, traces a trajectory from "the delights of newness and discovery" to "growing alarm over Italy's supposedly deleterious effect on English values." "In the Jacobean years, these anxieties gain intensity through dismay and cynicism about the perceived decline in morality at James I's court" (p. 26).

59 Michele Marrapodi, "Shakespeare's Romantic Italy: Novelistic, Theatrical, and Cultural Transactions in the Comedies," in *Italian Culture in the Drama of Shakespeare and his Contemporaries*, ed. M. Marrapodi, pp. 51–68 (p. 51). Marrapodi, "Appropriating Italy," p. 3, is right, of course, that "the multifarious ways of exploiting Italianate [or Boccaccian] discourses" is ultimately more interesting than a simplistic concept of source or influence.

60 Ed. Cyrus Hoy, in *The Dramatic Works in the Beaumont and Fletcher Canon* (Cambridge: Cambridge University Press, 1992), vol. 8, pp. 225–344.

61 "Theodore enamoured of Maister Emeries daughter." Two of the *Decameron* tales used by Fletcher in his plays, 3.5. and 5.7, appeared side by side in the *Forrest of Fancy* and not in Painter's *Palace*.

62 The series of triumphs had Italian sources in Petrarch's *Trionfi* and Boccaccio's *Amorosa Visione*, as well as in subsequent representations by visual artists.

63 Galigani, *Il Boccaccio nella cultura inglese*, p. 34.

64 He does include 3.9, in which the aim is marriage rather than adultery, and 8.7, with its harsh revenge for lust.

65 *Decameron*, "Conclusione dell'autore," pp. 18–19.

66 Sergio De Marco's chapter on "La 'beffa' boccaccesca in alcuni 'Jest Books' elisabettiani," in *Il Boccaccio nella cultura inglese*, ed. G. Galigani, pp. 155–84, compares the different uses of Italian materials in English jest books.

67 Galigani, *Il Boccaccio nella cultura inglese*, p. 44. Actually even in the 1620 translation, the story of Alatiel (3.10) was replaced by something less scandalous. Of course, the Italian editions being printed in the late sixteenth century were versions under Church censorship. However, the concerns of the Catholic Church and of Protestant Englishmen were opposite: the church left in tales of sex as long as involvement by the clergy was removed; Protestants liked anticlericalism, but not sexual licence.

68 F. P. Wilson, *The English Drama 1485–1585* (Oxford: Oxford University Press, 1969), pp. 119–20, mentions that during the 1560s the children's companies were performing especially classical tales.

69 Herbert Wright, *Boccaccio in England*, pp. 184–87.

70 See Stych, #318, and the more extensive discussion by Herbert Wright, pp. 178–84. John Cunliffe, "Gismond of Salerne," *PMLA* 21.2 (1906): 436, called it "the earliest extant English tragedy founded upon an Italian novel," noting (pp. 442–44) that it drew as well on Dolce's play *Didone*. "Extant" is the relevant word here; according to F. P. Wilson, *The English Drama 1485–1585*, p. 138, the earliest romantic tragedy based on an Italian novella was a 1562 *Tragical History of Romeus and Juliet* (1562), now lost. Herbert G. Wright has edited *Early English Versions of the Tales of Guiscardo and Ghismonda and Titus and Gisippus* for EETS (Oxford: Oxford University Press, 1937). Many of these versions remained as unpublished manuscripts. See also Louis Sorieri, *Boccaccio's Story of Tito e Gisippo in European Literature*, Institute of French Studies, Comparative Literature Series (New York, 1937).

71 Peter Stallybrass, "Dismemberments and Re-memberments: Rewriting the *Decameron*, 4.1, in the English Renaissance," *Studi sul Boccaccio* 20 (1991), pp. 299–324. Florence Nightingale Jones, 4, observes that across Europe the story of *Tancredi and Ghismonda* (4.1) was one of the most popular and imitated tales, second only to the story of Griselda (10.10). *The Tale of Titus and Gisippus* (10.8) was also among the top few. All three represent the serious Boccaccio.

72 As was the case with the Griselda story (10.10). Petrarch Latinized the tale of Griselda, Leonardo Bruni that of Ghismonda. Chiara Lombardi, "'In principio, mulier est hominis confusio'. Il *Decameron* e la letteratura inglese," in *Il Decameron nella letteratura europea*, ed. Clara Allasia, Storia e Letteratura, Raccolta di Studi e Testi 237 (Rome: Edizioni di Storia e Letteratura, 2006), pp. 167–82, notes (p. 172) Bruni's transmission of this story to several English writers.

73 Stallybrass, "Dismemberments," p. 301, citing Wright.

74 Stallybrass, pp. 310–12.

75 Mary Ellen Lamb and Valerie Wayne, in their introduction to *Staging Early Modern Romance* (p. 9), remark that, on the one hand, "Well before Boccaccio's *Decameron*, the genre of romance was ostensibly directed to woman readers, who had, it was assumed, the requisite leisure and amorous compassion" and that, on the other, "as Juliet Fleming pointed out in 1993, the misogyny of these 'ladies' texts' suggests that the primary audience imagined by their authors was often male."

76 *Comitatus. A Journal of Medieval and Renaissance Studies* 21 (1990): 90–113.

77 Louise George Clubb, "Looking Back on Shakespeare and Italian Drama," *Renaissance Drama*, 36–37 (2010): 3–19.

78 *The English Renaissance*, 184: "This dual approach through the original as well as the translated versions of Italian stories shows that Shakespeare was not simply interested in the stories as stories, but also in the way that they had been culturally inflected during the process of retelling. By going back to the originals, he was able to apprehend the cultural alterity of his sources without the distorting editorial interference that had been introduced by the English translators."

79 Leah Scragg, *Shakespeare's Mouldy Tales. Recurrent Plot Motifs in Shakespearean Drama* (New York: Longman, 1992), p. 105.

80 Kay Stanton, "*All's Well* at the *Decameron*'s Well: Women and Sexual Societal Healing in Boccaccio's *Decameron* III.9 and Shakespeare's *All's Well That Ends Well*," in *The*

Shakespeare Yearbook 10: *Shakespeare and Italy*, eds. Holger Klein and Michele Marrapodi (Lewiston, NY: Edwin Mellen Press, 1999), pp. 225–52, esp. p. 235.

81 Michael J. Redmond, *Shakespeare, Politics, and Italy: Intertextuality on the Jacobean Stage* (Aldershot, UK: Ashgate, 2009), p. 2.

82 Boccaccio, of course, thought of himself not as an Italian but as a Florentine and as such attracted the special attention of Florentine playwrights. For him, Naples, Rome, Venice and Milan were separate countries with quite different governments and cultures. Perhaps as a result of the swallowing up of many of these geographical areas under the power of Spain, the English tended to refer to "Italy" and "Italians," though sometimes acknowledging the still independent nature of Venice.

83 In Pierluigi Barotta and Ana Laura Lepschy eds., *Translation: Transfer, Text and Topic* (Perugia: Guerra Edizioni, 2010), pp. 53–67 – the title at the start of the essay differs from that in the table of contents; and see her book, *The English Boccaccio* (Toronto: University of Toronto Press, 2013), which includes the *Decameron* among other works.

84 So too Michael Redmond, *Shakespeare, Politics, and Italy. Intertextuality on the Jacobean Stage*, urges attention to what playwrights might expect from specific audiences, e.g. of private or public theatres or the Inns of Court. David Bevington, "Cultural Exchange: Gascoigne and Ariosto at Gray's Inn in 1566," in *The Italian World of English Renaissance Drama. Cultural Exchange and Intertextuality, cit.* p. 25, mentions also class and gender differences within theatre audiences as prompting varied responses to Italian texts.

85 Ian Greenless, "Discorso Introduttivo," in *Il Boccaccio nella cultura inglese*, pp. 5–6.

86 Giuseppe Galigani, "Il Boccaccio nel cinquecento inglese," in *Il Boccaccio nella cultura inglese*, pp. 27–57 and 32–33. Parra remarks in the subsequent chapter, "Il Seicento," pp. 60–61, that Restoration England loved the *Decameron*.

87 Howard Cole, *The "All's Well" Story from Boccaccio to Shakespeare* (Urbana: University of Illinois Press, 1981), p. 12, helpfully warns against the tendency "to examine what Boccaccio did mainly in terms of what was done to him, not what he was attempting in his own right" and thus "admiring Shakespeare's complexity and patronizing Boccaccio's simplicity."

88 In *Staging Early Modern Romance*, eds. Lamb and Wayne, pp. 163–87, 172. She observes further that what distinguishes Shakespeare's version is that "This play humbles Imogen more fully than any other story, just as most of its predecessors had humbled Posthumus" (pp. 177–78). Imogen lacks agency even when crossdressed.

89 Michele Marrapodi, "Retaliation as an Italian Vice in English Renaissance Drama: Narrative and Theatrical Exchanges," in *The Italian World of English Renaissance Drama*, pp. 190–207.

90 Kirsten Inglis, *Reading "Circe's Court": Politics and the Bed-trick from Boccaccio to Shakespeare*, MA thesis (Halifax, NS: Dalhousie University, 2007), pp. 5, 15, 52. With regard to 3.9 and *All's Well*, she argues similarly (65) that "within the framework of the third day as a whole, the story exhibits structural complexities and social commentary which critics often ascribe only to Shakespeare's play."

91 Alastair Fox, *The English Renaissance*, p. 215, 217. A possible qualification, but not contradiction, of his thesis might be suggested by the comment of Florence Nightingale Jones, 2, that 1566, which saw the publication of Sansovino's *Cento Novelle Scelte*, Painter's *Palace of Pleasure*, Timoneda's *Petrañuelo* and *Alivio de Caminantes*, and Estienne's *Apologie pour Hérodote*, all containing *Decameron* material, "may be said to mark the culmination of the revival of interest in Boccaccio in the sixteenth century." The international nature of this revival, while not annulling specifically English motives, calls as well for a broader assessment of why the *Decameron* aroused such interest all across Europe at this time.

92 *Cit.*, p. 31. His book provides an excellent introduction to the presence of Italian writings in England even before their English translations were published. His main interest, however, is in Italian writings on history and politics rather than fiction.

93 Galigani, ed., *Il Boccaccio nella cultura inglese*, pp. 203–18.

94 "Boccaccio and Shakespeare," pp. 140–41.

95 Gary Waller, "From 'the Unfortunate Comedy' to 'this Infinitely Fascinating Play': The Critical and Theatrical Emergence of *All's Well, That Ends Well*," in *All's Well, That Ends Well: New Critical Essays*, ed. Gary Waller (New York: Routledge, 2007), pp. 1–56, 1.

96 *Boccaccio in England*, p. 214.

97 *All's Well That Ends Well*, ed. Susan Snyder (Oxford: Clarendon Press, 1993), pp. 1–8, "From Boccaccio to Shakespeare."

98 A complex and fascinating "queering" of Shakespeare's changes to the tale emerges from Nicholas Ray's opening comparative question: why did Shakespeare add a second ring into the story? "Twas Mine, 'twas Helen's': Rings of Desire in *All's Well, That Ends Well*," in Waller ed., *All's Well ... New Critical Essays*, pp. 183–93.

99 Waller, p. 16.

100 So too, in the same volume, Terry Reilly's "*All's Well, That Ends Well* and the 1604 Controversy Concerning the Court of Wards and Liveries," pp. 209–20, looks to specific contemporary issues for an explanation of Shakespeare's relation to his source: "The story of Gilette de Narbona – a story that includes wards and is set in France – provides Shakespeare with ways to compare and to overlay French and English customs and laws as they relate to the contemporary controversy about wardships" (p. 214).

101 Waller, pp. 28–30. For the argument that "in *All's Well* attention remains focused on the husband" see Leah Scragg, *Shakespeare's Mouldy Tales*, pp. 101–2, 108.

102 Waller, pp. 40–41, 50. The idea of "Performing Woman. Female Theatricality in *All's Well, That Ends Well*," is picked up by Kent Lehnhof, in the same volume, pp. 111–24, who intriguingly suggests that Helena's combination of doctoring and performing skills identifies her with the mountebanks.

103 Robert Miola, "New Comedy in *All's Well That Ends Well*," *Renaissance Quarterly* 46, 1 (1993): 23–43, 35.

104 Gary Waller, 4, 6–7, emphasizes this connection to *commedia grave*.

105 Piero Rebora, "Boccaccio e Shakespeare," pp. 118, 120, 128–29, 134. Giam Maria Anselmi, "Tradizione rinascimentale italiana e letteratura inglese," in *Una civile conversazione. Lo scambio letterario e culturale anglo-italiano nel Rinascimento*, eds., Keir Elam and Fernando Cioni (Bologna: CLUEB, 2003), p. 36, similarly remarks on the influence on English theatre of the *Decameron*'s characters, especially "coraggiose, dolci e sfortunate eroine."

106 Kay Stanton, "*All's Well* at the *Decameron*'s Well," esp. p. 229.

107 Stanton, pp. 247–48.

108 Leah Scragg, *Shakespeare's Alternative Tales* (New York: Longman, 1996), pp. 107–30.

109 *Cymbeline*, ed. Martin Butler (Cambridge: Cambridge University Press, 2005), pp. 1–75, esp. pp. 25–36.

110 Warren, ed., *Cymbeline*, p. 36. Boccaccio's influence on the roles of women apparently continues to be felt beyond Italy.

111 Waller, "From 'the Unfortunate Comedy'," pp. 6 and 1; and on p. 30 he cites from Mary Bly, "Imagining Consummation: Women's Erotic Language in Comedies of Dekker and Shakespeare," in *Look Who's Laughing: Gender and Comedy*, ed. Gail Finney (Langhorne, PA: Gordon & Breach, 1994), p. 45: "a radical experiment – a bold effort to place on the comic stage women who show sexual desire, pursue consummation, have intercourse during the five acts, and are celebrated at the end." Radical in England, but typical in the *Decameron*.

112 Mary Cone, *Fletcher without Beaumont: A Study of the Independent Plays of John Fletcher*. Jacobean Drama Studies 60 (Salzburg: Institut für Englische Sprache und Literatur, Universität Salzburg, 1976) looks at Fletcher's techniques, characterizations, and imagery, but not at his selection and reworking of previous materials. Clifford Leech, *The John Fletcher Plays* (Cambridge, MA: Harvard University Press, 1962), similarly makes no reference to Boccaccio. On the other hand, for Fletcher's *Monsieur Thomas*, published in 1639 but perhaps written 1610–13, scholars have proposed various links to the *Decameron*, most of which, however, probably involve other sources. A passing reference (IV,ii,20) to a chambermaid "with a servingman's hose upon her head" evokes *Decameron* 9.2, for no obvious reason other than to contribute to a mood of festive misbehavior. Wright thought there was also a hint of 7.4 in III,iii, but a much closer analogy can be found in the widely popular *Gl'Ingannati*, IV,vi, in which Pasquella, while pretending to have sympathy with Giglio, finds an excuse to enter the house and shut him out. Both Jones and Wright suggested *Decameron* 10.8 as a source for Valentine's giving away his beloved fiancée Cellide to the love-sick Francis; however, a closer analogy is the story of Antiochus, who became physically ill from his repressed love for his stepmother. After a clever physician had

diagnosed the cause of his illness, his loving father King Seleucus gave him his own wife. Fletcher emphasizes the illness, elaborating a satire against foolish doctors who miss the diagnosis. Moreover, anyone recognizing this source would anticipate the play's revelation that Francis is the long-lost son of Valentine. The bed-trick in V,v, in which Thomas, thinking he is with his sweetheart Mary, finds himself with a servant girl, may derive ultimately from *Decameron* 8.4, as Wright suggested, but could just as well come from a number of intervening theatrical versions (e.g. *Calandra*, a major influence on later plays). Nonetheless, the throw-away evocation of *Decameron* 9.2 might sensitize spectators to think (as did Jones and Wright) of Boccaccian analogies.

113 John Fletcher, *Women Pleased*, ed. Hans Walter Gabler, in *The Dramatic Works in the Beaumont and Fletcher Canon*, vol. 5 (Cambridge: Cambridge University Press, 1982), pp. 441–538. Although published in this collection, it is the work of Fletcher alone.

114 The fact that the woman who is a reigning sovereign makes a series of mistakes adds a certain irony to this conclusion, without entirely undermining it. Joyce Boro, "John Fletcher's *Women Pleased* and the Pedagogy of Reading Romance," in *Staging Early Modern Romance*, eds. Lamb and Wayne, pp. 188–202, suggests that Fletcher used a combination of medieval romances "to situate himself within contemporaneous Jacobean debates on women and their reading material." Rather than merely taking plot lines, "The drama plays with the interpretive ambiguities of its sources."

115 Galigani, pp. 35–37, expresses surprise at the failure of the English, who were going through an economic and social transition similar to that of Italy in the thirteenth and fourteenth centuries, to pick up on Boccaccio's themes of mercantile life, even sometimes changing middle-class characters to aristocrats. However, there is an association of *Decameron* tales with middle-class characters in the plays of Fletcher and Jonson, and it is part of the tales' association with Italian comedy. Jean Howard, in her analysis of Dekker's *Honest Whore* Part I as an attempt to work out the new values of an English middle class ("Civic Institutions and Precarious Masculinity in Dekker's *The Honest Whore* (draft version)," http://emc.eserver.org/1-1/howard.html), mentions briefly that the pairing of Candido, the oddly patient shopkeeper, with the abject Bellafront evokes Boccaccio's Griselda. Although she does not pursue this connection, it might be fruitful to consider how English negotiations of class and gender identity made use of Boccaccio after all.

116 *The Night Walker*, ed. Cyrus Hoy, in *The Dramatic Works in the Beaumont and Fletcher Canon*, vol. 7 (Cambridge: Cambridge University Press, 1989), pp. 513–637. The play was revised in 1633 by James Shirley. Lacking the original, scholars have tried to identify Shirley's alterations, as noted by Hoy's introduction.

117 English tale collections occasionally merged two *Decameron* tales; for example George Whetstone's *Heptameron of Civil Discourses* (1582) in which a combination of 4.2. and 8.4 allows the naughty friar to be caught while the wife, enlightened in time, remains chaste, as Galigani observes, pp. 55–56; this combination of tales is discussed by Cesare G. Cecioni, "Un adattamento di due novelle del Boccaccio nello *Heptameron of Civil Discourses* di George Whetstone (1582)," in *Il Boccaccio nella cultura inglese*, pp. 185–91. See also earlier with regard to *The Cobbler of Canterburie*. Of course, Italian drama had been doing this throughout the sixteenth century.

118 Similarly William Percy's *A Forrest Tragaedye in Vacunium* (1602), merging the two extracted-heart tales, 4.1 and 4.9, indicates a knowledge of the *Decameron*. Wright, *Boccaccio in England*, pp. 196–99, describes the play without drawing this conclusion.

119 "Introduction," to Jonson, *The Devil Is an Ass*, The Revels Plays (Manchester, UK: Manchester University Press, 1991), p. 27.

120 Anne Barton, *Ben Jonson, Dramatist* (Cambridge: Cambridge University Press, 1984); see pp. 219–36 for her discussion of *The Devil Is an Ass*.

121 Michael Redmond, *Shakespeare, Politics, and Italy*, p. 58.

122 Jonson's association of Boccaccio and Machiavelli might be worth further thought.

123 Ann Barton, *Ben Jonson*, p. 221.

124 His essay "Il seicento," in *Il Boccaccio nella cultura inglese*, pp. 59–91, lists a number of plays that drew plots or episodes from the *Decameron*. Unlike Galigani's essay on the *cinquecento* in the same volume, Parra simply catalogues chronologically without any attempt to pose questions or draw conclusions.

125 Parra, "Il Seicento," pp. 72–73, misattributes the play to a Massinger-Fletcher collaboration (Fletcher died in 1625) and claims that it draws also from *Decameron* 7.9, but only the name Lidia, used here for a very different sort of woman and situation, can have suggested this.

126 The play was written in 1599, performed in 1600, and published in 1603. The text of *Patient Grissil* is in *The Dramatic Works of Thomas Dekker*, ed. Fredson Bowers, vol. 1 (Cambridge: Cambridge University Press, 1953), pp. 212–90.

127 Lee Bliss, "The Renaissance Griselda: A Woman for All Seasons," *Viator*, 23 (1992): 301–43, 332. See also Dora Faraci, "Il Patto di Griselda. Valori simbolici di una storia fra Chaucer e Dekker," in *La Storia di Griselda in Europa. Atti del Convegno: Modi dell'intertestualità: la storia di Griselda in Europa, L'Aquila, 12–14 maggio 1988*, ed. Raffaele Morabito (L'Aquila, Italy: Japadre Editore, 1990), pp. 103–17, 115–16.

128 Charles Read Baskerville, *The Elizabethan Jig and Related Song Drama*, (Chicago, IL: University of Chicago Press, 1929; repr. New York: Dover, 1965), pp. 444–49. He notes, p. 4: "The jig was also featured by English actors on foreign tours, and in consequence a great deal of Continental material bears on the English form." Will Kemp visited Italy and knew commedia actors.

129 The play's title is part of the devil's self-reproach for allowing himself to be "made an instrument, and could not scent it" (II,vi, 25–26).

130 For example, William W. Appleton's chapter on "Fletcher's Unaided Work," in his *Beaumont and Fletcher: A Critical Study* (London: George Allen & Unwin Ltd., 1956), recognizes the Chaucerian source of the main plot in *Women Pleased*, but not the *Decameron* sources of its subplot episodes. Nonetheless, his observations of Fletcher's "tendency to view the drama as a collection of individual scenes (the spectator's attitude) rather than as a unified tragic or comic action (the reader's attitude)" shows us why it was easy for the playwright to insert several novella into one play. Essays or chapters on Fletcher's sources focus especially on Chaucer, Shakespeare, and Cervantes. An MLA search for Jonson or Fletcher in combination with either Boccaccio or *Decameron* turns up nothing. Neither Rosalind Miles, *Ben Jonson, His Life and Work* (London: Routledge & Kegan Paul, 1986) nor *The Cambridge Companion to Ben Jonson*, eds. Richard Hays and Stanley Stewart (Cambridge: Cambridge University Press, 2000), includes any reference to Boccaccio or the *Decameron*. There is no book-length study parallel to E. Talbot Donaldson's *The Swan at the Well: Shakespeare Reading Chaucer* (New Haven, CT: Yale University Press, 1985).

3 *Commedia erudita*

Birth and transfiguration

Louise George Clubb

The mislabelled *commedia erudita*, more accurately termed *regolare* or *osservata*, written in observation of newly forged rules in the early sixteenth century, was long stereotyped as a laboured Italian imitation of ancient Roman Comedy, the label usually being applied in contrast to the later improvised *commedia dell'arte*, which fed on the "erudite" plots and repertory of theatregrams.[1] The two styles were known in Elizabethan England, characterized by Polonius' praise to Hamlet of a travelling troupe's ability to play both the "writ" and the "liberty". The ideal of *imitation*, which gave birth to the *commedia erudite*, can more properly be understood in the context of the first decades of the century contemporary with the aims and achievements in painting, architecture, linguistics, and literature of the generation of Michelangelo and Raphael, of Sebastiano Serlio, Pietro Bembo, and Baldassare Castiglione.[2]

The Italian peninsula could boast comedy of one sort or another going back to the Atellan farces and rejoiced in the Roman New Comedy of Plautus and Terence, modelled on the Greek comedy of Menander. During the Middle Ages the six plays of Terence were used as Latin school texts, but Plautus was known only in part until the fifteenth century. Comic entertainment was abundant, however, in the activity of buffoons, clowns, and jesters, as well as in the peasant/artisan farce tradition in many regions, exemplified by Cava in Campania, Siena in Tuscany, and Padua in the Veneto. From the late Middle Ages and continuing for centuries there were festivals and religious re-enactments mixing laughter and reverence. Florence was especially known for its municipal confraternity-sponsored *rappresentazioni sacre* dramatizing biblical and hagiographic subjects in rhymed verse, episodic plots without time limits, depicting characters supernatural and human, kings and commoners, serious subjects with comic interpolations.

The fifteenth-century discoveries of lost classical texts and the accompanying interest in philology, followed by experiments in rescuing classical Latin from medieval corruptions and eventually rivalling its achievements, produced in schools and courts a new set of cultural goals. In the Latin schools teaching literacy in preparation for courtly, municipal, or ecclesiastical professions, Terence and Seneca had long been read and played in class, sometimes Christianized by schoolmasters. The awakened attention to the original language of the Greek and Latin texts and genres was spurred by discovery of fourteen unknown comedies of Plautus in 1422 and later intensified by Angelo Poliziano's edition of Terence's *Andria* and his epochal contribution to vernacular drama, *Orfeo, favola mitologica* (ca. 1480). Courtly and academic performances, of Terence in Florence in 1476, of *Oedipus* in Greek and the like in Rome

DOI: 10.4324/9781315612720-5

and elsewhere, declared a new intellectual fashion. For theoretical underpinnings humanists of this generation depended on Horace's *Ars poetica* and the fourth-century commentators Evanthius, author of *De fabula*, and Aelius Donatus, who stated in *De comoedia*, with regard to Terence, that Cicero had declared comedy to be imitation of life, mirror of custom, image of truth.[3]

At the Este court in Ferrara before the turn of the century Plautus was performed both in Latin and then in ponderous Italian translations. Such entertainment was not popular theatre nor was it meant to be; rather, it was an undertaking of high art and ceremony for noble patrons and educated audiences, engaging leading courtiers and literati as writers and actors. As a very young courtier, Ludovico Ariosto participated in the admittedly boring high fashion that was supported by the Estes as a sign of cultural superiority. Rival courts and hubs of power in Milan, Urbino, Florence, and Venice vied and collaborated with them. When Lodovico Sforza, il Moro, asked Ercole I to lend him some of this avant-garde entertainment and a troupe of ducal dependents was accordingly dispatched to perform Plautus in Milan, Ariosto was among them, and they stopped at Reggio Emilia for some additional coaching by Matteo Maria Boiardo.

The Roman academy of Pomponio Leto also performed Plautus, encouraged by the papal court's enthusiasm for every aspect of the ancient Greek and Roman world, beginning with the architectural ruins which lay about them, waiting to be resurrected to the glory of a modern Christian empire. In an Italy torn by internecine wars and foreign invasions, the papacy under Julius II and Leo X aimed not only at consolidating power in the Papal States but also encouraged its humanistically educated adherents towards a cultural unification that would proclaim the new empire, as the famous letter of Raphael and Castiglione to Leo states,[4] by restoring and imitating Roman ruins to recreate past glory and demonstrate the genius of modern Italy. Culture was both a refuge and a defence. In supporting the urban reconstruction of ancient Rome Julius hoped to be a "new Caesar", Leo a "new Augustus", adapting and surpassing the ancients through Bramante's and Raphael's architectural programmes.

For the generation around Leo the classical ruins included all the arts: architecture, painting, literature, and theatre. Pietro Bembo's linguistic analysis of Virgil and Terence likens his project of purifying the literary and diplomatic Latin in use in his time by imitating the best classical models to the restorations and advances in painting and architecture of Michelangelo and Raphael. His proposal to create a worthy Italian literature, shared and disputed with Castiglione and other peers, also defined the force behind creating noble vernacular forms to restore and rival classical literary genres.[5] We see the results in the common enterprise of scholars, writers, artists, and papal advisers, in Bembo's own *Asolani* and *Prose* and in Castiglione's *Libro del Cortegiano*, an ultra-modern neo-classical masterpiece of the dialogue form, incorporating Cicero's *De oratore* and Plato's *Symposium* in a monument of Italian culture.

The *commedia erudita* should be recognized as a major result of this enterprise. Implicit in its structure, sometimes openly declared, was the claim to permanent dignity of a modern comic genre with noble roots, a humanistic display of a new civilization built on and equal to that of the ancients. Just as the linguistic programme presented by Bembo aimed at creating a national language for the literate classes, uniting them in a stratosphere of communication above the Babel of regional dialects, so the *commedia erudita* was intended to establish a national comedy, a deliberately created genre of Italian theatrical culture.

Underlying the development was an almost Linnaean belief fostered by humanism in the existence of prototypical genres in literary nature, as demonstrated by classical models. "Natural" rules were sought in Horace and later in Aristotle, as the *Poetics* was gradually translated and disseminated, resulting in a commitment to the unities of time, place, and plot structure, to verisimilitude and decorum of characters, and to the idea of genre. The quest for genre, belief in literary nature, and the clues to it and its rules in ancient works, arose from the same movement that had moved fifteenth-century humanists to search for classical texts, examine their language, and purify the use and teaching of Latin from corruptions of canon and civil law, thereby laying the foundations of modern philology and making way for the generation of Pietro Bembo to develop a vernacular "lingua aulica" that was Italic rather than regional and dialectal, in order to improve and disseminate the modern idiom so as to rival and surpass the achievement inherited from Greece and Rome.

From the network of the intelligentsia linking Leo's Roman and Florentine power bases with the exemplary Ferrarese theatrical tradition and the other communicating courts, there ultimately emerged the early *commedie erudite* that would be hailed as pre-eminent examples of the new genre. From Leo's immediate circle, which included Bembo, Raphael, and Castiglione, came *La calandria, commedia* (1513) the work of the prime papal adviser Bernardo Dovizi, Cardinal Bibbiena. This had been preceded by *La cassaria* (1508) and *I suppositi* (1509) of the sometimes Ferrarese ambassador to Rome Ariosto and was soon followed by *La mandragola* (ca. 1518) of Niccolò Machiavelli, the erstwhile Florentine secretary now seeking Medici favour.

These heirs of the fifteenth-century humanists produced the model for the new comedy written by educated men, courtiers, schoolmasters, and university wits and printed with their names on title-pages and complimentary dedications to highly placed patrons, noblemen, and popes. When they were performed it was for this kind of audience, in courts, academies, and universities on special occasions, most frequently for Carnival. Depending on the resources available, the single set required by the new rule of unity of place was represented by a city street painted in perspective on a backcloth or by more elaborate wooden constructions with *trompe l'oeil* effects, including Roman ruins. The grandest productions, like that of *Calandria* in Rome in 1514, probably built by Baldassare Peruzzi, made visual the relation of the new comedy to the common endeavour of artists, architects, and writers in their commitment to verisimilitude, temporal specificity, and unity of composition, absorbing the historical past into the present.

The *commedie erudite* of this generation set the standard for the genre which was immediately copied and fully established by 1542, clearly distinguishing what Ariosto called "nova comedia" from earlier theatrical kinds, *farse*, *feste*, or *rappresentazioni* partly or wholly comic. With few exceptions the ingredients were sixteenth-century versions of the urban middle-class stock characters from Roman New Comedy: *senex, senex amans, servus correns, servus scaltrus, meretrix, matrona, miles gloriosus, parasitus, leno, adulescens*. Moved by love, hunger, or avarice, they were engaged in domestic struggles of youth with age, in plots woven by clever servants towards the victory of young lovers over mercenary parents or foolish elderly rivals. The specific design of the intrigue in five acts ordinarily combined situations from Plautus, Terence, and *novelle* from the *Decameron* tradition and was played out in encounters on a single street in some contemporary Italian city within the span of one day, *in medias res*, so that the represented action took place just before the resolution of the crisis. The language was a Boccaccian-inflected modern prose, more or less Tuscan, depending on the playwright's origins, with socially different levels of style and room for slang and some dialect. The mixture of these elements claimed a place for comedy in the programme that engaged the leading writers, painters, and architects of the day to produce Italian forms, incorporating and surpassing those of the ancients. It was a theatrical version of Renaissance neo-classical architecture and paintings of biblical subjects in modern décor and dress with classical ruins in the background. An audience for such productions was prepared, according to Donald Beecher's perceptive analysis, by the general reliance on Donatus' commentary on Terence for a revolution in conceptualizing all subsequent readings and performances of Terence within a body of critical thought that was preoccupied with correctness of form and procedures. The Donatus phenomenon set the model for reception of these plays. "The humanists, in their iconization of this treatise, invented reception theory".[6]

In the decades contemporary with the gestation and debut of *commedia erudita* in the early sixteenth century, other theatrical kinds abounded. Presages had appeared in the late fifteenth century of the use of plays to display social and political power, such as Lorenzo il Magnifico's *Sacra rappresentazione dei SS. Giovanni e Paolo* (1491), ostensibly a saints' play but actually a calculated and self-promoting representation of good government; or *Griselda*, an anonymous secular play based on Boccaccio made to flatter the Este and the Medici courts, a "sacra rappresentazione profana" not published until 1993.[7] Both, however, took the form of the medieval sacred drama without concern for Greek or Roman precedents or the coming wave of neo-classicism. Hybrids also appeared, secular plays using the stanzaic form, meandering episodic procedure, and socially inclusive *dramatis personae* of the sacred dramas: in Siena *Virginia, opera* (1494) on a tale from Roman history, by Bernardo Accolti, known as "l'Unico Aretino", and Giovanni Pollastra's *Parthenio, commedia elegantissima* (1516). The indeterminate use of the term "commedia" illustrates the general awareness of the search for a new genre: Giambattista Dell'Ottonaio said of his *Commedia della Ingratitudine* (1526), "Ella non è commedia, farsa, o festa",[8] distinguishing, as Anton Francesco Grazzini would do twenty years later, between farce and comedy proper in the prologue to his three-act farce *Il frate* (1540): "le farse non son commedie".[9]

The defining difference in the search for form, for keys to construction of the best genres, as if the Greek and Roman past contained scientific criteria of the nature of true art, was the principle of *imitatio*. In its time this was not the "slavish imitation" that would be charged against *commedia erudita* in later centuries, when the skeletal features of the genre seemed sufficient for its characterization by positivistic critics, but was rather a concept of construction that discerned a universal principle in ancient models applicable to a new cultural formation whose features would proclaim its ancestry, history, and continuity while constituting both a sociological innovation and a technological advance. *Imitatio* of course meant using a model but not simply copying or translating Plautus and Terence into Italian. Rather it meant after models were known through translation and performance, constructing a play referential to the model, requiring knowledge of the set of criteria derived from it but departing from it in a spirit of competition.

The principle was invoked as practice and aim, though its interpretation was a matter for argument. But it was agreed that the imitation was not merely of Roman Comedy but that the final result would qualify as *imitatio vitae*, an updating of Donatus' dictum to include modern Italy and demonstrate both continuity and progress. As Adolfo Tura has said, imitation of the ancients was understood as the human search for form, like Bembo's in literature and Machiavelli's in government.[10] Torquato Tasso would later specify in his *Discorsi* that literary creation involved *materia* and *forma* – the first a choice of referential source materials; the second the shaping of them into a new and original structure.[11] The entire procedure constituted the act of *imitatio*.

The trio of regular comedies produced by Ariosto, Bibbiena, and Machiavelli fused situations, characters, encounters, and plot lines from Roman comedy and Boccaccio into building blocks which would become theatregrams of the developing genre. Ariosto announced *La cassaria* (1508) as a "nova comedia … piena di vari giochi, che ne mai latine/ne' greche lingue recitarno in scena",[12] although the plot came from Plautus. It is set in Greece, and the lovers bent on finding money to buy their girls from a pimp are a Greek and a Turk. The girls are slaves, but when later he revised the comedy in 1529 he transferred the action to southern Italy and made the lovers an Italian and a Spaniard. With *I suppositi* (1509) he again used the classical blueprint but departed from Plautine and Terentian hellenizing by bringing the plot home and updating the customs, making the lover a Sicilian student at the university of Ferrara, helped by the tricks and disguises devised by his clever servant to win parental approval of a marriage with the daughter of a prosperous local citizen. It was Ariosto's illustration of proper structure that most aroused admiration in subsequent writers. Giovanmaria Cecchi would proclaim him superior to the Greek and Romans because the form of his comedies demonstrated unity and the logic of successive action, beginning, middle, and end.[13]

La calandria of Cardinal Bibbiena had its debut in 1513 at the court of Urbino before an audience immortalized in Castiglione's *Libro del Cortegiano* and directed by Castiglione himself. Immediately hailed as a paragon of its kind, it was performed again sumptuously in Rome the following year for Leo X and his guest Isabella d'Este, with an elaborate set depicting modern Rome with classical ruins and with *intermezzi* sung and danced between the acts. The intrigue combines a version of Plautus's *Menaechmi* fused with several Boccaccian tales of ill-served young wives and silly old cuckolds in pursuit of courtesans. The struggle towards reunion in Rome of the Greek twins from Methone separated in childhood, one transformed by Bibbiena into a girl, produces transvestite disguises for both with accompanying erroneous identifications, in counterpoint with the deceits and dodges to which Calandro's love-starved wife is driven in her passionate affair with the male twin and the *beffe*, which the husband's lust brings down upon himself. Written in a Tuscan prose modelled on the *Decameron* and rich in linguistic, historical, and political allusions celebrating the glory of the Medicean papacy, the play was a concentration within a unified action, place, and time of theatregrams that would eventually be accumulated into a universal theatrical repertory of comic parts. The finale is an open declaration of the aims of the entire cultural movement which inspired it. The clever servant Fessenio, mastermind of the complex plot and spokesman for Bibbiena, as Bibbiena himself was for Leo's court and other centres of the avant-garde, exults in the conclusion that restores the exiled twins to each other and to better fortune than ever, "As much better as Italy is better than Greece, as Rome is than Methone, as two fortunes are better than one. And we all triumph".[14] Thus modern Italian culture triumphs by assimilating and embellishing its classical past.

The first of Machiavelli's two comedies was part of his bid for employment by the Medici and aimed to attract the attention of Leo's theatrical circle; its date has been disputed, but under the title *Comedia di Callimaco e di Lucretia* it appears to have issued about 1518 from the Sienese press that produced the first editions of *La calandria* (1521) and of *Rosmunda, tragedia* (1525) by Leo's kinsman Giovanni Rucellai.[15] Although *La mandragola* was recognized in its own time as a major achievement in the new genre and today is certainly the best known of all *commedie erudite*, it was criticized for the simplicity of its plot. Based on the adultery *beffe* of the *Decameron*, it represents the seduction of the virtuous wife Lucrezia by young Callimaco through a lethal disguise plot engineered by his hanger-on Ligurio and connived at collectively by Lucrezia's mother, by the friar Timoteo, and by her foolish sterile husband Nicia, who enthusiastically helps to cuckold himself. While Machiavelli eschews the typical Plautine situation, his middle-class Florentine characters are silhouettes of the standard Latin parasite, lover, bawd, and gull, and he employs theatregrams of disguise, bedroom substitution, and rhetorical persuasion. His primary adherence to the innovative regular comedy, however, consists in the compact logical structure of action in a single twenty-four-hour day in Florence, the compression of his witty colloquial Tuscan, and the strong effect of verisimilitude, albeit satirical, political, and possibly allegorical in intent.[16]

The recently rediscovered *Parthenio, commedia elegantissima* of the pro-Medici Aretine schoolmaster in exile, Giovanni Lappoli, known as Pollastra, performed with pomp at the University of Siena in 1516 and published there in 1520 by Giovanni Landi, the beadle who was also responsible for the first editions of *La calandria, Rosmunda*, and, probably, of *Callimaco e Lucrezia*, looks like a hybrid *sacra rappresentazione* trying out the medieval form on a secular subject.[17] But more is going on under the surface; instead of groping indecisively towards a change in form, this play, on the contrary, seems a deliberate compendium of contemporary comic theatre. It is in the tradition of the medieval *festa* but gestures also towards goliardic plays, Latin school recitations, and peasant farces. With an eye on the past, Pollastra aimed at a socially inclusive audience but simultaneously displayed awareness of an avant-garde style of comedy that had only recently become the *sine qua non* of courtly elites in Ferrara, Urbino, and the Vatican. In addition to all the trappings of the old-fashioned stanzaic *rappresentazioni* – exotic settings, a quest through Europe ending in Babylon, magic, royal spectacle, banquets, processions in unlimited time and space – within the principal heroic action Acts IV and V also encapsulate an abbreviated *commedia erudita* seduction plot in tightly unified time and space, tenuously related to the heroic action but showing off Pollastra's knowledge and handling of the latest fashion. It is telling for theatrical history that a poet and pedant bent on impressing the Medicis and on complimenting and thanking Siena for sheltering him in exile would adopt the highly traditional and popular, yet potentially very inclusive and elastic, form of the medieval *rappresentazione* for his acclaimed festival play, but would pointedly embed at the heart of its rambling plot a miniature example of the tightly sculpted structure of the new-wave *commedia erudita.*

This episode, together with the rest of *Parthenio*, lays out a series of theatregrams that would constantly reappear in the *commedia erudita* and its progeny: a heroic cross-dressed *innamorata* seeking her wandering lover, sent in his service to woo another who falls in love with the messenger, her subsequent disguise as a maid-servant, peasant clowns, and lustful lackeys in counterpoint with high-thinking lovers, low slanging matches, innkeepers, a courtesan, a bawd, an old man in love, a letter scene, a substitution in bed, as well as dialogues and monologues on stock *topoi* – country vs. city, justification of love by nature and the gods, and so forth. All is resolved in a multiple recognition scene that reunites long-lost families.

Like the closing claim of Fessenio in *Calandria*, alluding to the grand design shared by the artists and intellectuals of Pope Leo's time, the finale of *Parthenio* goes into detail concerning the achievements of Eastern and Western cultures joined in the match of a noble Roman woman and the Sultan of Babylon's son, creating a new and richer imperial future. For Pollastra Babylon stood for idealized Rome, the world centre redeemed and triumphant through the union of East and West, thereby rising superior to both.

A second generation of literary courtiers and academicians quickly took to the elegant design of the elite *commedia erudita*, which, by the 1540s, was established for the cultured classes as the standard shape of comedy, hospitable to a variety of new contents. But the atmosphere was shattered; the wars intensified, the mood darkened, and the Sack of Rome in 1527 destroyed the grand plan for reviving the glory of the ancient Empire, the dream of Italians expressed over the centuries by Petrarch, Machiavelli, Mazzini, and Mussolini. As the response to Luther's excoriation of the corrupt and paganized Vatican slowly nurtured religious dissent, and the goals of the Counter-Reformation became apparent in all the arts, the major concerns shifted from reviving ancient Roman values to reunifying the Catholic world and reconfirming the power of a reform-minded papacy. The Post-Sack era was a period of general codification, and the *commedie erudite*, multiplying in the changing climate, now testified to a different environment.

Siena remained a theatrical centre, primarily because of the official founding in 1531 by young nobles from the generation taught by Pollastra of the Academy of the Intronati. They jestingly took their name from the reproof of a teacher who dubbed them "Dumbstruck" for their lack of studious engagement, reinterpreting it to indicate their indifference to political upheavals and their decision to concentrate on literary activity. The academicians jointly composed *commedie erudite* and gave them a romantic twist, finding plots in the *Decameron*, not from the bawdy tales of cuckolding and seduction but from those pleasing to the Sienese ladies who formed the audience and occasionally took roles, whose favourite stories were about virtuous enterprising women triumphing over adversity and false accusations. The theatregram of the cross-dressing heroine was especially dear to the Intronati, whose performances courted a feminine public, although their founder Antonio Vignali and others among the author-actors were known privately to prefer men.

The academy's first and most famous play was *Gl'ingannati* (1537–38), in which the transvestite Lelia, her family torn apart by the Sack of Rome, goes in search of her forgetful betrothed who employs her as messenger to his new love who, of course, falls in love with Lelia but is happy in the final family reunion to marry Lelia's twin brother. Fleshed out with comic servants, Spanish swaggerers, and resistant fathers, this regular comedy is a well-wrought urn of theatregrams by then familiar to audiences. Members of the Intronati continued to produce *commedie erudite* of this romantic and increasingly courtly stamp. The independent *innamorate* who, by cross-dressing, escape the ban on decent virgins appearing on the street set had a precedent in Bibbiena's *Calandria*, but in *Ingannati* and subsequent plays, whether in bodices and skirts or doublets and hose, they become protagonists and manifest a sensibility and eloquence hitherto uncommon but destined to change comedy profoundly.

Other themes, social and political, also engaged the Intronati. Alessandro Piccolomini, probably working in committee with his colleagues, used historical events to reflect Sienese politics: the Palermitan revolt in *Alessandro* and the putative Pisan setting in *Ortensio*, shadow forth Sienese hopes of peace and order from the Tuscan ducal policies of Cosimo dei Medici. At the famous celebration of the wedding of Cosimo's son Ferdinando to Christine of Lorraine in 1589, the Intronati comedy of Girolamo Bargagli, *La pellegrina* (written in the 1560s), revised to compliment the French bride, was the featured event in a theatrical festival which also included *commedia dell'arte* performances, splendid scenographic musical *intermezzi* and pageantry. The exception constituted by the Sienese comedies dictated by feminine taste from the 1530s on were prophetic of the more serious, moral, romantic tone of the later sixteenth- and early seventeenth-century comedy which Italian critics of the twentieth century dubbed "commedie lacrimevoli", actually an exaggeration, as very few of them were really any more lachrymose than Shakespeare's romantic comedies.

Elsewhere, scholarly and courtly writers in increasing numbers cultivated and analysed the new form. Donato Giannotti, for example, who conferred with Bembo while writing his *Libro de la republica de vinitiani*, detailed in the prologue to *Il vecchio amoroso, commedia* (1533–36) his Plautine sources and innovative departures from them.[18] By mid-century the regular comedy was no longer just a cutting-edge style of the elite culture but had been established as the primary model for Italian theatrical art, defining anything else as old-fashioned. The number of *commedie erudite* performed and printed multiplied explosively, to the benefit of booksellers.

Without ever dulling his distinctive edge, Pietro Aretino, a former pupil of Pollastra, also eventually adopted the dominant form and used it in all his phases, differently in each. The first version of *Cortigiana* (1525) was all shapeless vitality, barely gesturing at regularity, but the second version and his four other comedies moved mainstream, showing off his technical skill with the *commedia erudita*, while imprinting it with his own self-publicizing, satirical and superabundant verbosity, and making it one of the vehicles for his pen-for-hire. *Il marescalco* (1537?) is a late development of a traditional *beffa* expanded into *commedia erudita* form but unique in that the practical joke is not for the purpose of seduction or marriage but solely for the carrying out of a practical joke in the spirit of court games. The butt of the homophobic joke was very likely a real member of the Gonzaga court in Mantua where Aretino was temporarily employed, but a secondary target was the court itself, satirized in Aretino's signature style. The regular comedy provided him with formal features: a precedent in the boy-bride of Plautus's *Casina*, the use of prose, five acts in crisis structure, such stock characters as a *balia*, a *pedante*, a *ragazzo* etc., but the atmosphere is a fusion of medieval *burla* with the courtly playfulness depicted in Castiglione's *Book of the Courtier*. In contrast, *Talanta* (1540) has a complicated traffic pattern of stock types evolved into Venetians and outsiders, in which Aretino displays his mastery of the rules by pushing them to their limit. The intrigue centres on the figure of Talanta herself, a knowing portrait of the sort of *cortegiana onesta* in whose company he delighted. The play was good publicity for the city and for the Compagnia dei Sempiterni that sponsored its costly production. When his complete works were put on the *Index Librorum Prohibitorum* in 1558, such was the renown of Aretino's *commedie erudite* that they were re-issued in Italy under other names and published in London in 1588 by John Wolfe, the adventurous printer always responsive to English demand for Italian high fashion.

Like Aretino, Ruzante (Angelo Beolco) gradually turned towards the erudite form. Despite his enormous popularity, Ruzante never became part of the mainstream, owing to the Paduan dialect which was the primary, though not the sole, language of his comedies, but as his connections expanded beyond the Veneto he approached Plautus and Terence and, in his own mocking but exploitative way, adopted the "nova comedia" style in his *Piovana* and *Vaccaria* (before 1533) and *L'anconitana* (1536?).

As the formal aspects of the regular comedy were increasingly accepted by audiences and readers, the diversity of the contents grew. The local and political tones sounded early in Ariosto's *Lena* (1528) were heard more often in comedies of the subsequent generation. In Ruzante's *Moscheta*, in Annibale Caro's *Straccioni* (1543), Piccolomini's *Alessandro* (1545), and Benedetto Varchi's *La suocera* (1549), reflections of social reality and the effects of war are seen in varying degrees. In the theatrical climate of Mantua maintained by the Gonzagas, *A Comedy of Betrothal*, written in Hebrew (ca. 1550), was probably a Purim feast play for the Jewish community, but though the subject is Talmudic law and a debate on marriage contracts, it is cast in the mould of the regular comedy, employing familiar theatregrams: a Pantalone type of merchant father in conflict with young *innamorati*, etc. It has been attributed to the theatre director Leone de Sommi, author of a treatise on staging, *Quattro dialoghi in materia di rappresentazioni sceniche* (1556), who also wrote comedies in Italian. He associated as well with professional actors of the *commedia dell'arte*, but his *Tre sorelle* (1588) is a standard *commedia erudita* in five acts, with a unified crisis structure based on a *contaminatio* of *Mandragola* and Publio Filippo's *Formicone*, containing the theatregrams of the braggart and the bawd, feigned madness, and disguises in aid of the usual generational conflict.

Grazzini considered some theatregrams, especially the recognition and reunion of long lost relatives, already old hat by 1555, but neither he nor the next generations stopped using them routinely. His fellow Florentine Giovanmaria Cecchi, most prolific of all *commediografi*, spanned two generations and continued to depend on *commedia erudita* conventions, often in verse, but he tailored his content increasingly to Counter-Reformation taste. *Le maschere* (1585) includes the fashionable comic use of the incest dilemma, resolved by the *cri du sang*.

Illustrations of the *commedia erudita* are rare, but Venetian woodcuts from the 1590s demonstrate the appearance of a variety of typical stages and combinations of characters, theatregrams of groups, and encounters. Intended for use in printed comedies in general, shared by printers, they are indicative of a consensus regarding urban setting, scene divisions, groupings, characters, and of demand by a readership. These appeared late in the century but would have served as well to illustrate any example of the genre, from *Suppositi* and *Calandria* on.[19]

After the middle of the century, when the number of comedies written and printed had multiplied, the effect of a cultural and political climate-change caused by religious dissent and its conflicts appeared in the features of the genre, which by now constituted a repertory of movable parts. The Council of Trent, in session from 1545 to 1563, emphasized the use of the arts for Catholic reform, and many of these theatregrams were modified to support current ideology. The natural and gradual transformation of the regular comedy now appeared as policy. Although the so-called Counter-Reformation has frequently been characterized as repressive, censoring, and hampering, to its sincere adherents it was a reform movement fuelled by faith, aimed at fighting corruption of every kind, and its successes were not without importance for the theatre. In an invigorating attempt to enrich and purge theatre and turn it to serious purposes while using comic situations and traditions to amuse, satirize, and instruct, post-Council policy enlarged the principle of *imitatio vitae* to include abstractions and moral ideals.

The cynical and carnivalesque amorality often evident in plays before mid-century decreased as the number of comedies written and printed multiplied, and the comedic spirit of unruliness receded before the affirmation of social order. The form earlier sometimes described as *commedia grave* by virtue of its studiedly regular construction became graver in content as well, verging on tragicomedy, as witnessed by the emotional and ethically sophisticated comedies of the law professor Sforza Oddi, the scholarly Benedictine prior Vincenzo Borghini, the abbot Bernardino Pino, as by the Neapolitan "mago" Giambattista Della Porta and his learned southern imitators, the Franciscan priest Francesco D'Isa, the duke of Sermoneta, Filippo Caetani, and others.[20]

Political consolidation of power and celebration of rulers hand in hand with the principles of Catholic reform became themes for regular comedy in references to government, not as it was but as it should be. Where Ariosto had represented Ferrarese urban economy in *La Lena*, Machiavelli's *Mandragola* had satirized Florentine institutions, Annibal Caro's *Straccioni* had curried Farnese favour in Rome, and Aretino's *Marescalco* could raise a laugh at the court of Mantua, in the later Cinquecento Pino, Oddi, Bargagli, and Della Porta offered solemn advice to rulers in depictions of situations in which the existence of good rulers offstage guarantees a just resolution of domestic and legal problems in the plot. Often the ordinary characters are socially promoted from merchants to courtiers and nobles, invoking the unseen presence of the ruler.

More infrequently, a figure of authority actually appears and participates in the action, as in Della Porta's *Duoi fratelli rivali* (1601), in which the Viceroy of Salerno has to judge the dispute between his rival nephews and is faced with having to put one of them to death, until divine providence intervenes. This comedy illustrates how the enduringly typical method by which *commedia erudita* had been composed in Ariosto's time was still in use at the end of the century: choosing a tale from Bandello about an event in thirteenth-century Messina (the same that underlies *Much Ado About Nothing*), Della Porta set the action in sixteenth-century Salerno, beginning at the catastrophe, observing the unities of time and place, recasting the characters in Plautine roles, young lovers, parents, servants both clever and stupid, adding a parasite, a nurse, and a braggart captain. In an unusual move, Della Porta used Salernitan history and that of his own family to make the story more relevant to local time and audience but set it not in the time of its writing but in 1504, some twenty years after the Congiura dei Baroni when a viceroy of Naples pardoned the conspirators and appointed a representative to bring good government to Salerno. By means of historical allusion Della Porta gratefully flattered the current Spanish Viceroy of Naples, who had recently signed Salerno into the Royal Demesne and put an end to the buying and selling of the city.[21] As a famous natural historian and suspected magician who had been admonished by the Inquisition to leave off experimenting and stick to writing comedies, Della Porta usually chose themes acceptable to the ruling powers before whom his comedies were often performed, long before he began to print them in 1589. His *Astrologo* (1606), a pitiless satire on astrology set in his own Naples and full of local dialect, was probably his acquiescent self-defence against charges of practising magic and judiciary astrology, both emphatically condemned by the Church. *L'astrologo* was one of the comedies supporting Della Porta's claim to have been the Italian *commediografo* most often adapted in Elizabethan/Jacobean England.[22] As such, his plays represent the *commedia grave* flourishing in Shakespeare's day. They were also favourites with the *commedia dell'arte* players who carried the "liberty" versions of his "writ" everywhere, sowing theatregrams abroad for Shakespeare to harvest.

The shift towards moral orthodoxy and romantic content brought to the fore serious themes, opening the way to psychological probing and rhetorical subtlety. The well-tried theatregrams of *inganno* and *beffa*, and the triumph of wit, continued as staples but were now entwined with motives of dangerous jealousy, murderous hatred, and fear of death. Other grave theatregrams, infused with comic horror, include conversations with hangmen, police bullies, and jailers, as in Della Porta's *La turca* (1606) and *Gli duoi fratelli rivali*, and in Oddi's *Prigion d'amore* (1590), foreshadowing the prison atmosphere of *Measure for Measure*. Moors, Turks, and pirates, exotic figures from chivalric *romanzi*, made plausible by the ever-present Mediterranean conflict with Muslim power to the east and south, appeared onstage more often, offering new possibilities of disguises and encouraging edifying conversions to Christianity, as in Oddi's *Morti vivi* (1576). As Aristotle's *Poetics* became generally available, his esteem for Sophocles' *Oedipus rex*, the tragic theme of incest introduced into tragedies like Sperone Speroni's *Canace* (1546) and Tasso's *Torrismondo* (1587), found its way into comedies like Della Porta's *Sorella* (1604) as incest feared but avoided by invoking the motif of the *cri du sang*.

Some theatregrams disappeared. The figure of the friar was banished from the stage as it was likewise from the expurgated *Decameron*. As early as 1540, before the Council of Trent opened, the prologue to Grazzini's farce *Il frate* admits that it might be improper to depict the clergy behaving badly, but the author did so anyway, with the excuse that a three-act *farsa* is not a genre of high art, that is, a *commedia*. Other theatregrams were modified or reversed, downplaying adultery and fornication, and decrying homosexuality. The pederastic pedants of Bibbiena's *Calandria*, Aretino's *Marescalco*, or the Intronati's *Ingannati*, tacitly become heterosexual in Marc'Antonio Raimondo's *Parto finto* (1618) and paternal in Della Porta's *Tabernaria* (1610), though still caricatured for their absurd Latinate lingo. Homoeroticism, formerly an object of jocose punning in Ariosto's *Suppositi*, or an interpretive key to ambiguous sexual desire in Piccolomini's *Alessandro*, was explicitly condemned as a vice in Oddi's *Prigion d'amore*.

The *innamorati* became more expressively emotional and idealistic, their language in *contrasti amorosi* ever more richly baroque. The dialogue between servants' and lovers' contrasting love of food with the food of love remained a popular theatregram and was joined more frequently by debates between different kinds of lovers on the topic of love versus lust, a subject seriously cultivated in neo-Platonic and courtly dialogue by the generation of Castiglione, Bembo, and Ariosto, which did not find its way into the early *commedia erudita* launched by Bibbiena when they all frequented the courts of Urbino and Rome, but appearing late in the century as an expansion of the theatregram of the *innamorato*.

Even when Counter-Reformation influence is visible in the waning Cinquecento, however, and sex acts of most kinds are comparatively restrained, when chastity in women is more urgently invoked and homosexuality in men castigated, the *commedia erudita* never matched the contemporary Elizabethan reverence for virginity. Unchastity of all sorts remained a common subject and in the lower classes was good-humoredly tolerated, but though Oddi condemned male homosexuality and pederastic pedants disappeared, though Della Porta and Girolamo Bargagli exalted heroically pure *innamorate* as agents of Divine Providence, unchastity in comedy still aroused sympathy or mirth, and reproof was rarely rigorous. Still, the open-ended conclusions that allow for happy continuation of adulterous affairs, a typically Boccaccian outcome in *Calandria,*

La mandragola and Cecchi's *Assiuolo* (1550), were fewer in number in the latter Cinquecento. In their place were sacramental marriages, conversions, and reconciliations buttressed by allegorical *intermezzi*. And though Fortune still aided young love, as it had done in Roman New Comedy, and respectable *innamorate* continued always to get what they wanted, whatever that might be, ultimately Catholic orthodoxy triumphed, and Fortune was displaced by Divine Providence.

Female roles were greatly enlarged in this period, owing partly to the increasingly romantic plots and to the success of the Intronati academy's preference for enterprising heroines, even though men still played women's parts in the courtly and academic venues for which *commedie erudite* were written. But when real women appeared onstage in the *commedia dell'arte* sometime in the 1560s, perhaps earlier, still juicier roles appeared for them in written comedy as well. The most celebrated commercial companies, though best known for their improvised format, "the liberty", were also recruited for scripted plays, "the writ". Isabella Andreini, for example, played the title male character in Tasso's iconic pastoral *Aminta*. We must suppose that she and her rival Vittoria Piissimi played some of the rich female roles in *commedie erudite*, and there is no doubt that they lifted theatregrams from them for mixing in their improvised *commedie a soggetto*. The prominence of such roles in extant *canovacci* was obviously preceded by the players' reading of many *commedie erudite* and more than likely by the performing of them in mixed casts of amateurs and hired professionals. The well-established theatregram of female cross-dressing continued in variations, becoming especially popular in *commedia dell'arte*, and lent itself to more complex characterization and ever-longer rhetorical exercises in self-analysis.

Whores with hearts of gold now became high-minded. Aretino had already elevated the *bona meretrix* of Plautus and Terence, making the eponymous protagonist of *Talanta* intelligent, rich, powerful, and generous, but some later theatrical courtesans surpassed her in moral delicacy, selflessness, and even piety. In Oddi's *Erofilomachia* (1572), Ardelia keeps her lover by being scrupulously honest, unselfish, and psychologically subtle as she contributes to the theme of conflict between eros and friendship. The courtesan Aurelia of Pino's *Ingiusti sdegni* (1553) calms the unjust anger of her lover's father by offering to finance his son's academic and social education, leave him her fortune, and promising to retire to a convent.

The most exemplary behaviour of all was reserved for the theatregram of the *innamorata* who figured as an incarnation of Petrarchan love metaphors, as in Della Porta's *Furiosa* (1609), or as a wonderful manifestation of God's providence, as in Raffaello Borghini's *Donna costante* (1578), Della Porta's *Fratelli rivali*, Bargagli's *Pellegrina*, and Oddi's *Morti vivi*.

Like the baroque language which flowered in the dialogues and interpolated poetry of late *commedie erudite*, the intrigue plots grew in complexity. The double plots learned from Terence had become triple with Caro's *Straccioni* and now reached an extreme in *Gl'intrichi d'amore* (1604), in which Tasso had had a hand, interweaving six love stories. All other competitors in the contest for complexity were outdone by Giordano Bruno, whose *Candelaio* (1582), with every element and theatregram of the *commedia erudita* from prologue to conclusion multiplied by three, is not comparable to others in the mainstream of scripted comedy, however, in that Bruno wrote it far from Italy, probably for non-theatrical reasons of his own without expectation of performance, using the genre as a vehicle for his quirky intellectual exuberance, satire, and homesickness, but thereby illustrating the diverse functionality of its form.

Technical experiments in intrigue structure produced more and more thematized plots like Grazzini's *La gelosia* (1551), in which everyone is jealous, and Pino's *Ingiusti sdegni*, in which everyone is unjustly angry, as well as symbolic plots demonstrating unity achieved through complexity, a motif buttressed by mythical *intermezzi*, which developed into a genre in themselves. The pattern of seemingly unresolvable complexities in plots full of deceit, trickery, disguises, and cross purposes, which are worked out to an unexpectedly simple and satisfying conclusion, the structural ideal of the doubly grave *commedia grave*, was held to be a reflection of the action of divine omniscience. Attempts to adapt the universally admired peripety of *Oedipus rex* to comedy, as was claimed for Flaminio Maleguzzi's *Theodora* (1568), meant transposing sombre dramatic irony into a happy key: unavoidable fate was replaced by unhoped-for providence. The comic peripety, heretofore functional primarily as a mechanism, became itself a content-structure full of orthodox Catholic meaning. The old theatregram of the tangled web, the exclamation of confused and frustrated characters from earlier comedies, "In what a labyrinth do I find myself!" now indicated the signifying form of comedy in the abstract, a sign of the complexity of human life and of a providential pattern which reveals its purposes and resolves all.

The *commedia erudita* of the late sixteenth century, though less known today than its early models, best represents the maturity and fecundity of the genre in all its complexity, technical skill, and innovation, spilling over into other theatrical forms, and it was what contemporary foreign playwrights like Lope, Molière, and Jonson would first have read of Italian theatre. Shakespeare, more than any, employed the methods of the *commedia erudita*, which probably reached him primarily through knowledge of the *commedia dell'arte*, its performances seen or described, demonstrating their evolution from the players' reading of *novelle*, acting in *commedie erudite*, and then adapting the theatregrams to their own specialized format.

In the second half of the century the idea of genre, the dominant theoretical driving force behind the first experiments in creating a modern theatre to rival the ancients, having produced regular comedy and tragedy, fuelled a campaign to rediscover tragicomedy and to dramatize the literary pastoral world of Theocritus, Virgil, and Sannazaro. As the first genre to achieve this aim, the *commedia erudita* served as the foundation for future construction, and its five-act order, intrigue plot, unity of time and place, theatregrams of relationships and dialogues constituted the default form.

In the act of expanding the legacy of theatrical genres from the ancients, playwrights distinguished one genre from the other in critical treatises and theoretical prologues that examined and defended the increasing mixtures and complexities that could be accommodated without losing the name or lineaments of regular comedy or tragedy. While some *commedie gravi*, like Oddi's, Borghini's, and a few of Della Porta's, approached tragicomedy by virtue of the high rank of characters, seriousness of theme, and almost fatal conclusions, the label *tragicommedia* was reserved for verse plays on distant or mythical subjects, like Della Porta's Homeric *Penelope* (1591) and for the most influential result of the mixing: the theatrical pastoral in verse, built from Greek and Latin lyrics, eclogues, and narratives and invoking the mysterious classical satyr play, of which no example was extant. The model of the *commedia erudita* had been proved roomy enough for some subjects and themes not foreseen by strict interpretation of the neoclassical rules, so it provided the foundation for the invention of a third genre, the *tragicommedia pastorale* or *favola boscareccia*, in which country settings, supernatural elements, psychological conversions, and invisible realities could be represented. But all relied on the compact intrigue structure achieved in comedy, with its setting and theatregrams of character reconfigured: the Italian street scene as a woodland pleasance, lovers as nymphs and shepherds, comic servants as goatherds, lustful braggarts as satyrs, courtesans as promiscuous nymphs, nurses and bawds as old nymphs, elders as pagan priests or magicians, and so on.

The essential action represented the forces of love at work rather than the clever tricks by which lovers and servants obtain their goals, but disguises, eavesdropping, and other staples of *commedia erudita* were introduced as needed. The plots turned away from conflicts between money and love, to follow the comic tensions of misplaced affections, misunderstandings, and, above all, change of heart as the lesson of love was learned. Long-lost family reunions occurred, but the resolution of conflicts usually relied finally on dictates from gods or goddesses, always ending in redirected loves, multiple marriages, and reintegration of society, Arcadia by name or implication. When the pastoral play took its structure from *commedia erudita* and the inner world of emotion and the outer world of faith in the supernatural were brought onstage, the signifying plot was made more overt and the labyrinth so often invoked in comedy to express the complexity of plot and eventually extended as a metaphoric recognition of the workings of Providence, was reified in the pastoral by the setting – a clearing on the edge of a dark tangled wood, following Serlio's stage design after Vitruvius.

There were two kinds of pastoral play: the Ovidian kind represented by Alvise Pasqualigo's *Intricati* (1581) and Diomisso Guazzoni's *Andromeda* (1587), on the one hand; and the high tragicomedy of Guarini's *Pastor fido* (1589), Orlando Pescetti's *Regia pastorella* (1589), and Guidobaldo Bonarelli's *Filli di Sciro* (1607), on the other. Both kinds borrowed the essential *commedia erudita* structure, but the Ovidian sort permitted magic, as in *A Midsummer Night's Dream* and *The Tempest*, both of which are pastorals minus pastors, in which shepherds are recostumed as Athenian courtiers and Italian nobles, the magician with his attendant spirit as Oberon and Puck, Prospero and Ariel, comic servants as mechanicals and drunken Neapolitan butlers. In contrast, the Shakespearean reflections of the graver and more verisimilar pastorals appear in *As You Like It*, and the pastoral sections of *Cymbeline* and *The Winter's Tale*, in which noble characters sojourn for a time in Arcadia where they discover truth and the path to redemption. Invariably the pastoral plays end with the recognition that, as Prospero says, a higher power has guided all the humans out of a maze. Inevitably the providential plot invited overtly religious or philosophical content, as in Nicolo Tagliapiero's *Virginia tentata e confirmata, favola rappresentabile* (1625), Barbara Torelli Benedetti's *Partenia, favola boschereccia* (1586), or Cesare Cremonini's *Pompe funebri, over Aminta e Clori* (1590).

Of all the theatrical phenomena to which the *commedia erudita* gave birth, the most famous was the *commedia dell'arte*. A practice rather than a deliberately constructed single genre, this was the professional players' way of presenting plays by improvising on a plot summary. The actors undoubtedly owed much to previous kinds of hired entertainment, but the commercial troupes that began to form in the middle of the sixteenth century established their identity and fame on the actors' appropriation of literary drama, especially the *commedia erudita*. From the scripts they encountered in print and in the private venues where they were summoned to participate in theatrical events, they accumulated the repertories on which they based their *canovacci*, the three-act scenarios which were the basis for innumerable improvisations. In this, their signature format, they presented whatever they acquired from the three established literary genres, but when paid to do so, they also performed five-act regular dramas as written. Thus they played both "the writ and the liberty". Occasionally, the most celebrated *comici* also wrote and published comedies, pastorals, and even tragedies; when they did, significantly, they reverted to the five-act form and features of the literary genres. Some duelled in print with the *commedia erudita*, defending their professional practice of improvising and abbreviating borrowed plots, aspiring to the level of respect enjoyed by their models by demonstrating how well they could imitate them.

The relationship between the *commedia erudita* and its commercial offshoot gradually became symbiotic, as playwrights like Della Porta and Pasqualigo introduced into their comedies figures and modified theatregrams from the *commedia dell'arte. Commedia dell'arte* was born from *commedia erudita*, but ultimately, as Richard Andrews puts it, "script and improvisation were subclasses of a single phenomenon".[23]

If the achievement of the early sixteenth-century exponents of the *commedia erudita* fell short of their goal to create a new Roman Empire of culture, the genre born from their search for form endured. The regular comedy they established remained a standard measure, a norm and form that accommodated variety while admitting, even inviting, plunder. In the last decades of the century the *commedia erudita* in print and in its various modifications in the performances of the *commedia dell'arte* troupes was carried beyond the Alps and across the Channel. Today's scholarship has largely revised earlier opinions of Italian regular comedy and now recognizes the enduring value of the capacious and elastic form which demonstrably left its mark on European dramaturgy.

The direct connection between Molière and the Italian players and playwrights from whom he took his first bearings has always been recognized, as have the many traces of the *commedia dell'arte* in drama and painting throughout northern Europe. In the eighteenth century even Goldoni's comedies, while turning away from *commedia dell'arte* caricatures towards social reality, still held to the compact structure and many basic theatregrams of the *commedia erudita*. The same pattern is visible in the libretti of innumerable comic operas, not only the most obvious, *Il barbiere di Siviglia, Le nozze di Figaro, Così fan tutte*, and the like but also submerged beneath the later trappings of *La rondine, Die Meistersinger*, and *Der Rosenkavalier.*

English cognizance of the *commedia erudita* is less well documented, but Philip Sidney's statement in *The Defense of Poesie* that in Italy even the "common players" constructed their plays better and more according to rule than their English counterparts, attests to the awareness of the principles of playmaking that the professional *comici* had learned from the *commedia erudita.* George Gascoigne's *Supposes* and Ben Jonson's *Volpone* and *The Alchemist* are obviously related to the Italian genre, but more than any, Shakespeare's plays are intimately connected with it. From *A Comedy of Errors* to *The Tempest*, he showed that he could easily construct according to the unities. For the most part, of course, he played fast and loose with the rules but clearly demonstrated that he knew them. He very likely encountered them both through the travelling troupes and accounts of them and through available scripts and performances of *commedie erudite* and pastorals developed from them. All of his comedies betray familiarity with Italian technology and theatregrams.[24]

From the early *Taming of the Shrew* on through other comedies, *Two Gentlemen of Verona, The Merry Wives of Windsor*, and *Twelfth Night*, recognized in its own time as an offshoot of the *Ingannati* family, the Italian form and theatregrams are evident, reshuffled and infused with new English flavours and vigour. The same is true of the darker comedies, *Measure for Measure* and *All's Well That Ends Well*, in which the tone corresponds to that of the gravest of *commedie gravi*. Shakespeare's grasp of the ultra-fashionable Italian *tragicommedia pastorale*, in which noble characters in Arcadia resolve problems of state and discover the truth of their own hearts, is suggested in *Love's Labour's Lost* and *As You Like It*, while the Ovidian magic *pastorale* is unmistakably the generic foundation of *A Midsummer Night's Dream* and *The Tempest*.[25]

Even the tragedies reveal the breadth of content that the form of *commedia erudita* could accommodate. In Italy the tale of Romeo and Juliet had been cast as tragedy in Luigi Groto's *Adriana*, as comedy in Borghini's *Donna costante*, but in both cases the shape of the *commedia erudita* was visible. The latter was a *commedia grave* borrowed more than once by the *commedia dell'arte* players. Shakespeare had a source in Arthur Brooke's narrative, which Brooke said he had lately seen onstage, and Shakespeare dramatized Brooke's poem with theatregrams from the *commedia grave*, minus the happy ending of that genre. More unprecedentedly, in *Othello*, Shakespeare expanded a bare plot from one of Giraldi's *novelle* into the standard shape of a regular comedy about jealousy and deceptions, populating it with familiar theatregrams – jealous husband, boasting warrior, tricky subordinate, courtesan, faithful servant, multiple suitors – and treated it all with a psychological intensity that plunges the shallow farce of supposed cuckoldry and trickery into abysmal tragedy.

The *commedia erudita* has always offered scholars sources for social history as well as rich deposits of material to be excavated for theorizing on attitudes towards political injustice, fiscal usages, crime and punishment, madness, prostitution, class, and family relations. Its intrigue plot has invited interpretation of such structure as a metaphor for the operations of God's providence and has provided a serviceable vehicle for romance and semi-tragedy and for Bruno's pullulating urban impressions of Naples. Only a construction as solid as that of the *commedia erudita* could have allowed him to cram so much into a single comedy without falling into chaos. From the soundness of the form supporting his riotous matter emerged baroque art rather than merely the haemorrhage of an over-stuffed brain.

Earlier studies were focused on language, mining the *commedia erudita* for the history of standard Italian, as of regional dialects and idioms, and on establishing specific sources in Plautus, Terence, Boccaccio, or in local historical happenings. Later, Mario Baratto's Marxist departure pointed to social implications in the genre. Individual figures or theatregrams of character have invited such analyses as Daniel Boughner's of the braggart, Antonio Stäuble's of the pedant, Anthony Ellis' of comic old men, and various others.[26]

Theatregrams and other recycled elements are especially valuable quarries for historical cultural anthropology, under scrutiny along sociological, political, and theoretical lines, with attention to pre-modern sexual identity, gender analysis, domestic hierarchy, power/class conflict, marriage arrangements, and the contrast between law and custom. The frequent appearance onstage of male and female transvestites, more often the latter, especially has generated diverse studies of cross-dressing and homosexuality which illuminate the historical/social context and the audience reception of these phenomena. The *commedia erudita* has yielded to Laura Giannetti's probing some thought-provoking revelations about the age-old subculture of sodomy as it existed in public awareness in the fifteenth and sixteenth centuries, on the whole confirming Foucault's distinction between practice and construction of homosexual identity.[27] Quoting Michael Shapiro, she agrees with the definition of comedy as a privileged space, a "field of play" where these various discourses could be explored.[28] It should be added, however, that the discourses existed only *in potens;* the evidence was not used within the comedies to construct another discourse; the standard structure and plot followed the expected path to a happy ending that was rarely ironic, whether it reaffirmed the social norm or integrated threatening elements into a conclusion that concealed or assimilated aberrations and promised harmonious continuation. The form stood as a stable vehicle for representing a universal domestic reality; destabilizing matters could be introduced but not fully investigated or resolved and were never allowed to subvert the course of the plot towards municipal reconciliation.

With the success of the original quest for genre, the *commedia erudita* became a starting point, a vessel into which a playwright could pour his material, a shape within which he could attempt to assert his originality, a form received by the society and accommodating its changing views. The idea, still popular today, that rules are by definition oppressive and writers admirable for breaking or disregarding them, often obscures the fact that the achievement of rules was one of the most innovative and creative discoveries in theatre history. Emerging from the new vision of culture shared by artists and writers in the early decades of the century, the *commedia erudita* was born of the humanistic belief in the natural existence of norms and forms to which the ancients held a key with which their Italian heirs could unlock future glory. Cecchi prophesied that playwrights to come would imitate the Italians of his time.[29] Clearly, he was right.

Notes

1 Louise George Clubb, *Italian Drama in Shakespeare's Time*, 'Prologue' (New Haven, CT: Yale University Press, 1989). On the influence of Italian comedy on early modern English drama, see also Clubb, "Looking Back on Shakespeare and Italian Theater", in *Renaissance Drama*, n.s. 36/37, ed. Albert Ascoli and William N. West (2010), pp. 3–19. Among the most important works in the field, see part. Marvin T. Herrick, *Italian Comedy in the Renaissance* (Urbana: University of Illinois, 1960), Giulio Ferroni, *'Mutazione' e 'Riscontro' nel teatro di Machiavelli e altri saggi sulla commedia del Cinquecento* (Rome: Bulzoni Editore, 1972), Leo Salingar, *Shakespeare and the Traditions of Comedy* (Cambridge: Cambridge University Press, 1974), Aulo Greco, *L'istituzione del teatro comico nel Rinascimento* (Naples: Liguori, 1976), Guido Davico Bonino, ed. *La commedia del Cinquecento*, 3 vols (Turin: Einaudi, 1977–78), Mario Baratto, *La commedia del Cinquecento: (aspetti e problemi)* (Vicenza: Neri Pozza, 1977), Richard Andrews, *Scripts and Scenarios. The Performance of Comedy in Renaissance Italy* (Cambridge: Cambridge University Press, 1993), Donald Beecher, ed. *Renaissance Comedy. The Italian Masters*. 2 vols. (Toronto: University of Toronto Press, 2008–9), and Ronald L. Martinez, "Etruria Triumphant in Rome: Fable of Medici Rule and Bibbiena's *Calandria*", in *Renaissance Drama*, n.s. 36/37 (2010): 69–98.

2 The cultural and intellectual ambience that nourished regular comedy is splendidly evoked and illustrated in the catalogue to the remarkable exhibition in Padua in 2013, *Pietro Bembo e l'invenzione del Rinascimento*, ed. Guido Beltramini, Davide Gasparotto, and Adolfo Tura (Venice: Marsilio, 2013).

3 "Commediam esse Cicero ait imitationem vitae, speculum consuetudinis, imaginem veritatis", *Aeli Donati quos fertur Commentum Terenti*, ed. P. Wessmer (Leipzig, Germany: Teubner, 1902), I, p. 22.

4 Francesco P. Di Teodoro, "Lettera a Leone X, 1519", exhibit 4.19, in *Pietro Bembo e l'invenzione del Rinascimento*, pp. 262–63.

5 Fabio Finotti makes illuminating observations on the direction of this force in *Retorica della diffrazione. Bembo, Aretino, Giulio Romano e Tasso: letteratura e scena cortigiana*, Parts 1 and 2 (Florence: Leo S. Olschki Editore, 2004).

6 Donald Beecher, ed. *Renaissance Comedy. The Italian Masters*, vol. I, p. 7.

7 Raffaele Morabito, ed. *Una sacra rappresentazione profana: Fortune di Griselda nel Quattrocento italiano* (Tübingen, Germany: Max Niemeyer, 1993).

8 Paola A. Ventrone, *Gli araldi della commedia. Teatro a Firenze nel Rinascimento* (Pisa: Pacini Editore, 1993), p. 127.

9 Nino Borsellino, ed. *Commedie del Cinquecento*, Vol. I (Milan: Feltrinelli Editore, 1967), p. 93.

10 *Pietro Bembo e l'invenzione del Rinascimento*, ed. Guido Beltramini, Davide Gasparotto, and Adolfo Tura, p. 263.

11 *Discorsi del poema eroico*, in Tasso, *Prose*, ed. Ettore Mazzali (Milan and Naples: Ricciardi Editore, 1959), p. 532.

12 Ludovico Ariosto, *Opere minori*, ed. Cesare Segre (Milan and Naples: Ricciardi Editore, 1954), p. 242.

13 Cecchi, *Le pellegrine*, Intermedio 6, in *Commedie inedite di Giovan Maria Cecchi*, ed. Giovanni Tortoli (Florence: Barbèra, Bianchi, 1855).

14 *La calandria*, in Borsellino, *Commedie del Cinquecento*, Vol. II, p. 97.

15 Louise George Clubb, *Pollastra and the Origins of Twelfth Night. Parthenio, commedia (1516) with an English Translation* (Farnham, UK: Ashgate, 2010), p. 16.

16 Like all of Machiavelli's works, this comedy is different from other examples of its genre, and the special status it was accorded in its own century is matched by the continued modern debate over its intentions. Ronald L. Martinez's essay, "Tragic Machiavelli", in *The Comedy and Tragedy of Machiavelli: Essays on the Literary Works*, ed. Vickie B. Sullivan (New Haven, CT: Yale University Press, 2000), pp. 102–19, 214–24, is an illustration, and the unending fertility of *La mandragola* is well represented by other essays in the same volume.

17 For further details on the relationship with the *sacra rappresentazione*, see Clubb, *Pollastra and the Origins of Twelfth Night*, pp. 38–39.

18 Borsellino, *Commedie del Cinquecento*, Vol. I, pp. 8–9.

19 Clubb, "Pictures for the Reader: A Series of Illustrations to Comedy, 1591–1592", *Renaissance Drama*, Old Series 9 (1966): 265–77, with corrigenda in *Renaissance Drama*, New Series I (1968): 340–41.

20 For Della Porta's works and context, see Clubb, *Giambattista Della Porta Dramatist* (Princeton, NJ: Princeton University Press, 1965).

21 Giambattista Della Porta, *Gli duoi fratelli rivali/The Two Rival Brothers*, ed. and trans. Louise George Clubb (Berkeley: University of California Press, 1980), Introduction, pp. 10–16.

22 Mary Augusta Scott, *Elizabethan Translations from the Italian* (Boston, MA: Houghton Miflin, 1916).

23 Richard Andrews, ed. *The Commedia dell'Arte of Flaminio Scala. A Translation and Analysis of 30 Scenarios* (Lanham, MD: The Scarecrow Press, 2008), Introduction, p. xxxiii.

24 Louise George Clubb, "Italian Stories on the Stage", in *The Cambridge Companion to Shakespearean Comedy*, ed. Alexander Leggatt (Cambridge: Cambridge University Press, 2002), pp. 32–46.

25 Further complexities of the Anglo-Italian relationship are penetratingly pursued by Robert Henke, *Pastoral Transformations. Italian Tragicomedy and Shakespeare's Late Plays*, Chapters 1 and 2 (Newark: University of Delaware Press/London: Associated University Presses, 1997).

26 Mario Baratto, *La commedia del Cinquecento*: (*aspetti e problemi*), cit.; Daniel Boughner, *The Braggart in Renaissance Comedy* (Minneapolis: University of Minnesota Press, 1954); Antonio Staüble, *'Parlar per lettera'. Il pedante nella commedia del Cinquecento* (Rome: Bulzoni, 1991); Anthony Ellis, *Old Age, Masculinity, and Early Modern Drama. Comic Elders on the Italian and Shakespearean Stage* (Farnham, UK: Ashgate, 2009).

27 Laura Giannetti, *Lelia's Kiss. Imagining Gender, Sex, and Marriage in Italian Renaissance Comedy* (Toronto: University of Toronto Press, 2009), pp. 191 and 164.

28 Michael Shapiro, "Introduction", *Gender in Play on the Shakespearean Stage: Boy Heroines and Female Pages* (Ann Arbor, MI: University of Michigan Press, 1994), p. 6.

29 *La dote*, Prologo, *Comedie di M. Gianmaria Cecchi*, Vol. I (Venice: B. Giunti, 1585).

4 Machiavelli's comedies of 'virtù'

Duncan Salkeld

Introduction

They say Christ never laughed and one might think the same might be said of Machiavelli, given his reputation. We do not readily think of Machiavelli as a comedian, but he was responsible for two sparkling, sardonic works that reworked the traditions of Roman 'new comedy' into something akin to modern satire. Perhaps the most pertinent point to make about these rarely performed plays is just how seemingly contemporary and boundary-testing they are. Shakespeare is famous for the comic 'bed-trick' involving switched bed-fellows, but Machiavelli used the device in far more radical ways. In *Mandragola*, a young man gulls a dim-wit into requiring a stranger to bed his wife, and then – unsurprisingly – passes himself off as that stranger. In *Clizia*, an old man pretending to be an eager groom finds himself unwittingly in bed with a male servant disguised as the bride. In both, improbable ruses are devised to turn gullible or grasping men into figures of ridicule. These might be called 'sexual comedies' for the risqué bawdiness they exhibit. But they are as much satires as bedroom farces, aimed at the Church and the city-state. The two plays are set, after the manner of Plautus or Terence, mainly in the street outside the main characters' houses. They are relatively easy to cast and perform: *Mandragola* requires eight actors, and *Clizia*, its sequel, ten. The plays' scenes tend to be short and have no more than four players on stage at any one time. *Clizia* requires a space 'aloft' or upstairs where the darkness of a bed-chamber may be imagined. What lends these plays a further apparent modernity is the central role they give to women who conspire in the outwitting of foolish men.[1]

Machiavelli was an extraordinarily varied and productive writer. The range of his work includes advice for princes and rulers, discourses on political theory and strategy, a history of his home city of Florence, familiar letters, and a clutch of literary works, among them these two Renaissance comedies. While his political writings have been of the greatest influence and notoriety, the literary works have tended to be neglected. Machiavelli's comedies seem to have emerged out of the privations of difficult personal circumstances. In 1512, the Florentine state he had so devotedly served turned against him. He was dismissed from his post, wrongly suspected of conspiracy, tortured in prison, and forced into exile at the age of forty-four. By 1513, Machiavelli's world had crumbled, and he had every reason to believe his career a failure. With time on his hands, he took the opportunity not only to reflect upon triumphs and disasters he had witnessed – processions, coronations, battles, and executions – but also to write about them. He produced his famous works on political and military strategy, *The Prince, The*

DOI: 10.4324/9781315612720-6

Discourses, and *The Art of War* in the period between 1513 and 1516. In or around the same time, he penned a very accurate translation of Terence's *Andria* ('The Girl from Andros') and two plays of his own, *Mandragola* and *Clizia*.[2] Turning away from matters of the city and its rulers, Machiavelli's comedies are preoccupied with domestic affairs and their potential for the outrageous, the bizarre, and the utterly ridiculous. A careful reader might trace a bitter, wry humour across both the literary and political writings.

Machiavelli was always a strong realist, yet his literary works prove him a remarkably imaginative writer. He penned tercets on ambition, ingratitude, or envy, on Fortune, a version of *The Golden Ass* (also in tercets), a Dantesque prose story called 'Belfagor', and some carnival songs. He refers to his literary reading in familiar letters, making reference to Ovid, Dante, and Petrarch, and he even composed a handful of sonnets, one to his father, and three to Giuliano, the son of Lorenzo de Medici.[3] The *quatorzaines* betray a sardonic comic talent, touching on his bitter experience of imprisonment and torture. When it came to writing plays, he devised stories in which the over-ambitious strive, with a kind of reckless fixation, to get what they want, even when the consequences are humiliating These narratives were not exactly new, deriving as they did from prototypes in Menander, Plautus, and Terence, but they took the innuendo of those plays to greater extremes.

Machiavelli had an interest in dialects and genres, and he added it into his dramas. His *Dialogue on Language* (c.1515) focused on the provenance of phrases, the origins of idiom, and the significance of proverbial expressions. Written in the form of a letter, the 'dialogue' focuses on differences of nation and language, and the ways in which dialect divides communities even locally. He argued, wryly, that Florentine Italian is superior to all other forms of the language. It is perfectly self-evident, he claims, that Florentines have been "born in a city whose language was such that it was fitter than any other to be used for verse and in prose".[4] As a consequence, his comedies are not just experiments with a pre-existing form but also a test of skill in the flexibilities of his own dialect. He wrote a letter to his friend Guicciardini to explain certain phrases he had used.

This interest in comedy was in part academic. Machiavelli's close translation of Terence's *Andria* – the defining comedy for Renaissance readers and audiences – was made with apparently no thought of performance or publication. But after it, he took much greater risks with comedy. Plautus and Terence stuck to familiar conventions, domestic situations where a young man tries to outwit his father with the help of a wily servant in order to win the girl. Machiavelli's comedies take that domestic conflict to unsettling extremes. In *Mandragola*, Callimaco, a young man, deliberately sets out to sleep with a married woman with the full knowledge and approval of Messer Nicia, her husband. In *Clizia*, a play that follows Plautine conventions, old Nicomaco plots to sleep with the girl he has raised as his daughter. Both plays deploy tricks and ruses after the manner of Plautus and Terence but end up with something far more brutal, hard-edged, and satirical. There is a kind of engineered chaos in these plays, one that ends in toe-curling humiliation for Nicia and Nicomaco. Both plays raise discomfiting ethical questions, only to laugh them off. In comedy, Machiavelli has turned *provocateur*. Does having a husband's approval make bedding his wife morally acceptable? May a man sleep with his adopted daughter as soon as she's old enough? Ought a trusted friar help a girl to have an abortion, or assist an adulterer in achieving his wish? These are uncomfortable notions and Machiavelli knew it. A sixteenth-century modernist, he was making old 'new comedy' new.

Fortune and 'virtù'

Two important concepts feature prominently in Machiavelli's writings: 'Fortune' and 'virtù'.[5] He had spent his career immersed in the affairs of civic administration and international conflict. In *The Prince* and *The Discourses on Livy*, Machiavelli drew on cases of diplomatic and military failure or success he had witnessed first-hand. These he took as exemplars for statecraft and political strategy. In the crises a state will inevitably suffer, Fortune and 'virtù', he argued, can prove decisive. By 'Fortune', Machiavelli means not just fate or chance but a hazardous and unpredictable course of events that can dominate and overwhelm the affairs of men and city-states. 'Fortune' has a certain relentlessness about it: all are subject to it, and every life is shaped by it. By 'virtù', Machiavelli only partly means 'virtùe'. The term also includes prowess, ability, strength, force of character or will. The 'man of virtù', a phrase he favours, is one who has the courage and determination to wrest fortune to his own advantage. This man will not put an end to Fortune's influence, but he can make it work for him, if only for a while. In the end, Machiavelli seems to think that even the strongest man of 'virtù' is likely to fall into Fortune's merciless hands. The contrast between 'Fortune' and 'virtù' travelled, even if it did not always bear Machiavelli's name. It is perhaps unlikely that Shakespeare ever read *The Prince*, but the distinction seems to weigh on Hamlet's mind in his most famous soliloquy:

> *Hamlet*: … Whether 'tis nobler in the mind to suffer
> The slings and arrows of outrageous Fortune,
> Or to take arms against a sea of troubles,
> And by opposing, end them?
>
> (3.1.57–60)

The studious prince, newly returned from university to bury his father, is a youthful idealist. At the most opportune moment for revenge, he holds back, finding Claudius apparently at prayer. Hamlet wants to act in a way that accords with what is 'nobler in the mind'. Yet high-minded thoughts are weighed down with a salt imagination about his mother's indecency. Hamlet may fairly claim to have suffered Fortune's 'slings and arrows' but his attempts at 'virtù' are spectacularly destructive. His is an arc that Machiavelli might easily have predicted.

Machiavelli draws a contrast between 'Fortune' and 'virtù' repeatedly in *The Prince* but also combines it with 'necessity'. This work sets out what he saw as the essential principles by which rulers achieve success or meet with failure. The advice is given with remarkable succinctness and economy. In particular, Machiavelli is concerned to explain how a ruler may hold sway over a city or people. He observes that a hereditary principality is likely to prove safest, for only an 'extraordinary and inordinate force', a seismic twist of fate, is likely to unseat a ruler from it. He cites the example of the unlucky Duke of Ferrara who lost power first to the Venetians in 1484 and then to Pope Julius in 1510.[6] Newer principalities, where the leader has been appointed, are at greater risk since the prince is likely to be compelled by a "common and natural necessity" to "injure those who have made him the new ruler".[7] A ruler who wants to cling onto power will have to suppress the friends and families of those he displaces. Necessity can, therefore, impose its own demands on Fortune or chance. A ruler may find himself simply compelled to kill.[8]

In the penultimate chapter of *The Prince*, Machiavelli famously writes of Fortune as a woman. The chapter carries a title: "How far human affairs are governed by Fortune, and how fortune can be opposed". In it, Machiavelli almost ruefully observes, "I believe that it is probably true that Fortune is the arbiter of half the things we do, leaving the other half or so to be controlled by ourselves".[9] Like an immense flood, it bears down upon its victims and will brook no resistance whatever sea-defences one might erect. As a further example, he cites Julius II whose impetuous attack on Bologna was fortuitously supported by France. Fortune, on that occasion, favoured the 'Warrior Pope' and shaped geo-politics in the region. For this reason, Machiavelli argued, fortune must be dominated. He concludes with another analogy: "Fortune is a woman and if she is to be submissive it is necessary to beat and coerce her. Experience shows that she is more often subdued by men who do this than by those who act coldly". The line has understandably attracted a good deal of criticism and discussion. Elsewhere, Machiavelli writes of 'Fortune' as a dominatrix, describing her as "a cruel goddess" who "sits on high above all and gives commands and rules with fury".[10] But in *Clizia*, it is women of 'virtù' who take control of Fortune and fashion events to their own advantage.

Both *Mandragola* and *Clizia* have as their object the sexual conquest of a woman and the risks a man may take to win her. Because these works are still relatively little known, a short summary of them may prove helpful. *Mandragola* begins with a 'Canzone' designed to be sung by a chorus of nymphs and shepherds. The song touches on life's hardships and struggles, and the fact that without pleasure, we fail to comprehend "what ills and what strange events crush almost all mortals". A subsequent Prologue begs the audience's patience and explains a little of the story to come. Callimaco, a young man, has just arrived from Paris where he'd heard of the celebrated beauty of Lucrezia, the wife of Nicia, a rather credulous Florentine citizen. The Prologue adopts a rather sardonic tone, speaking of the author's "wretched time … There being no reward for his labours".[11] Callimaco's sole objective is to deceive Nicia and sleep with his wife. The satirical point of this play appears to be that only in Florence could such credulity and stupidity be found. At its centre is the notion that "fortune and nature hold the account in balance",[12] and its success depends upon Callimaco's 'virtù' in bringing about the end he desires.

This trickster's farce follows some of the main conventions of Roman new comedy: it keeps to the action of a single day, is set along a city street with doorways to various off-stage 'houses', and opens with Callimaco explaining to his servant Siro a little of his background and his burning desire to win the girl. As Ligurio, a pander or middle-man, explains, Fortune has favoured Nicia despite his stupidity, and it is this turn of fate that Callimaco sets out to overcome. Ironically, it is Nicia who laments that no one in Florence appreciates a man of 'virtù' any more. His misfortune is that he is unable to have children. Setting himself up as a physician especially expert in such matters, Callimaco invents a ruse in which Lucrezia has to drink a potion of mandrake root and then sleep with a man in the dark. The problem is that this man will – Nicia must take his word for it – die just eight days later. Telling Nicia that they should simply find some idle fellow in the street to undertake this task, Callimaco plans to supply the place of the unfortunate fellow. In order to win Lucrezia's assent, Callimaco hires a corrupt yet friendly friar who is able to persuade her mother that this is all a very good idea. Timoteo, the friar, advises Lucrezia to do as instructed because an eventual good will come of it – she will become pregnant. To overcome her doubts, he argues "the will is what sins, not the body".[13] Once Lucrezia has been persuaded, Nicia declares himself "the happiest man in the world". A song at the end of Act 3 dwells on the 'virtù' of a trick that makes "every bitter thing" taste sweet. As might be expected, the dénouement humiliates Nicia. Callimaco is smuggled in disguise into the house. Nicia tells how he forced the unfortunate victim to strip and led him to the bed, where he fumbled in the dark for "how the thing was going".[14] Reassured, Nicia then retires to his mother-in-law's home to let nature take its course. The following morning, Callimaco tells Ligurio about how well he was received. Nicia seems delighted with the outcome – an unwitting agent in his own demise – and together they all celebrate by attending prayers in church.

Clizia is the play's sequel, set in 1494, a year of political humiliation with the French invasion. The work is modelled very clearly on Plautus's comedy *Casina*, the events of which Machiavelli follows fairly closely. At its heart – but never appearing on stage – is the eponymous girl, Clizia, daughter of a French officer. As the story goes, when the French army was forced out by a Milanese, Venetian, and Papal alliance, a French officer left his five-year-old daughter with Nicomaco for safekeeping. Nicomaco and his wife brought the child up as one of their own, but after twelve years, their son Cleandro has now fallen hopelessly in love with her. The great obstacle to this romance is that the father wants her for himself. The play focuses on the ridiculous lengths to which Nicomaco will go in order to achieve his goal. His plan is to marry her off to a pliable servant, Pirro, on condition that he should covertly enjoy her whenever he wishes. Nicomaco's wife, learning of the plot, sets out to frustrate him. Cleandro tries a similar arrangement with a rival servant, Eustachio, though much against his real wishes. In the arguments that follow, Nicomaco suggests they consult Friar Timoteo, a man reputed for his skill in the handling of the pregnancy of Lucrezia in *Mandragola*. Since family members and servants are all at odds with one another, they decide to put the matter to Fortune, drawing lots to see whose plan should be put into effect. When Nicomaco wins, Cleandro laments: "O Fortune! Because you're a woman, you've always had the habit of befriending young men; but this time you've befriended the old men".[15]

Building the play towards its absurd climax, Machiavelli follows his Plautine model, *Casina*. The night to which Nicomaco has so looked forward goes badly. His wife has disguised Siro, a male servant, as Clizia and put him in the marital bed. After the events, Nicomaco tells his friend Damone that he went into the room, got undressed, and in the darkness lay beside the bride. Snuggling up close, he tried to put his hands on her breasts, but got short shrift. He tried a kiss but was again rebuffed. Then, as he went to throw himself all in, a knee hit him so hard it almost cracked one of his ribs. Finding himself rejected, Nicomaco tried using 'sweet, loving words': "come, my sweet soul, why'd you torture me? Come, my dear, why don't you, cede to me willingly what other wives cede willingly to their husbands". When this also failed, he turned to threats. In response, he received a couple of hard kicks. Giving up, Nicomaco turned his back and gradually fell asleep. Before long though, he was awakened by a feeling of being stabbed around the backside area. Half-asleep, he reached round and felt 'something firm and pointy'.[16] Jumping out of bed thinking he was being stabbed with a knife, he woke up Pirro and told him to get a light. They returned to find not Clizia but Siro, completely naked and pulling faces at them. Bruised and rueful, Nicomaco knows that word of the night will get round. Wiping away tears of laughter, Damone promises to try to cover up as much as possible as he goes about the market place.

Ultimately, the story is resolved with the appearance of Ramondo, the long-lost father of Clizia. His approval of the marriage of his daughter to Cleandro puts an end to the dispute, brings Nicomaco to his senses, and lends the play an air of celebration at the end.

In the background to all this domestic hullabaloo is the institution of the church. Ligurio, in *Mandragola*, notes that these 'frati' are cunning fellows sensible not only of their own sins, but those of everyone else too via the confession box. Fra Timoteo's sway over the women shows the power of the church to manipulate family life even so far as in the intimacies of a marriage-bed. His interest in helping Callimaco is governed solely by the jingle of Nicia's pocket. In a test of just how far Timoteo can be led, Ligurio asks him to arrange for a pregnant girl to be given a potion to make her miscarry.[17] However transgressive the move may seem, Timoteo is not hopelessly corrupt. He is well-regarded by Sostrata and Lucrezia but also wise to his neighbours' shenanigans and willing to play them along to his own advantage. He is also resourceful in articulating any kind of theological or homiletic argument that may serve to shape those ends, as his interview with Lucrezia in 3.11 demonstrates. Ironically, Timoteo acts as the play's conscience: he feels himself led astray, but also rues the city's decline in religious devotion. In the church, a light has gone out, and a veil over a Madonna needs changing. Whereas the church used to be so active, he reflects at the start of Act 5, now "none of these things are done", and Timoteo must shift for himself. When *Mandragola* ends with a celebratory church blessing, it is perhaps a sign of Machiavelli's regard for the institution as an essential part of the social fabric. Timoteo's role is very much reduced, but in *Clizia* Nicomaco calls him "a little saint"[18] and (mis)remembers that it was through his prayers that the sterile Lucrezia became pregnant. Sostrata sees right through it: "Some great miracle, a friar making a woman pregnant! It would be a miracle if a nun had made her pregnant!"[19]

Translations and criticism

The most authoritative edition of the two plays in English is the translation provided by Allan H. Gilbert in the second volume of *Machiavelli: The Chief Works and Others* (1958). This lightly annotated volume contains most of Machiavelli's literary writings, including *Mandragola* and *Clizia*, together with various tercets, poems, songs, and letters. Gilbert's translation remains a dependable and valuable resource. It is the only edition to historicise Machiavelli's texts by explaining some of his vocabulary in the wider context of Italian Renaissance literature. Gilbert's notes explicate proverbial forms of Machiavelli's Italian and some of the political or euphemistic implications of particular words or phrases. Hence, when the final song of *Clizia* tells the audience that they have heard "under a flimsy veil … much more besides",[20] it is Gilbert's edition that bears out that impression.

English translations of *Mandragola* and *Clizia* differ in approach, style, and presentation. In 1961, J. R. Hale edited and translated the works in a volume for Oxford University Press, under the title *The Literary Works of Machiavelli*. This small volume also includes translations of the "Dialogue on Language", "Belfagor", and a selection of the letters. A short introduction covers the ways in which the plays break from classical models. Hale transmutes the Italian verse of the songs into English rhyme, but he sanitises the text. In 2.3, Nicia complains Florence is full of careless, ignorant people unappreciative of his personal 'virtù', and he calls them "cacastecchi" ("shitsticks"), a slightly odd expletive to the modern ear, but rendered as "numbskulls" by Hale.[21] In the same speech, Nicia uses the phrase "che ho cacato le curatelle" ("I've shit my guts out") to suggest how hard he's worked to learn a little Latin. Hale politely mutes the obscenity with his translation, "I've worn myself out". In 2.6, Nicia again uses an expletive "potta di san Puccio", which Gilbert renders as "San Puccio's cunt!"[22] and which Hale disappointingly gives as "By the beard of the Baptist".[23]

In 1985, David Sices and James B. Atkinson published their bilingual edition, the Italian text on the left page and English on the right. Sices and Atkinson's declared aim is to follow the pattern of Machiavelli's rhymes and verse forms, but they sometimes elide key political ideas, or allow them to lie unnoticed in the text. Their introduction discusses *Andria, Mandragola*, and *Clizia*, with useful indications of the dating of the plays and some details of early performances. They find an underlying aggression at work in the plays signalled by a tendency towards "raucous, boisterous farce".[24] Noting bathos at the end of *Mandragola*, they argue that a resistance to tidy conclusions distinguished Machiavelli's brand of comedy, a claim not altogether borne out by the endings in Roman 'new comedy'. *Clizia*, they claim, is "the least regarded by audiences and critics".[25] Covering its debts to Roman and Greek precursor plays, they outline the plot but pass rather too politely over events in the final act. Moreover, when Sices and Atkinson suggest that the "defects of *Clizia* result from an imperfect blend of literary traditions",[26] they omit all sense of the rising panic and disorder that comes to a Plautine crescendo in the play's later comic homoerotic moments.

Rather different are the translations of *Mandragola* and *Clizia* published by the Waveland Press. These are slim, handy volumes that provide a close and fairly literal translation of Machiavelli's text. They forego imitation of rhymes, metrical patterns, and stanza forms in the interests of keeping as close as possible to the sentential meaning of the original. *Mandragola* is translated, introduced, and annotated by Mera J. Flaumenhauft. The approach allows for helpful and instructive footnotes that highlight terms bearing a significance for Machiavelli's wider thought. Flaumenhauft attends to the responsibilities of translation, even to the point of considering the significance of word order in distinguishing Callimaco, a younger man, from Nicia, the older man whose wife he seduces.[27] Flaumenhauft's translation is reliable, inexpensive, and portable. The companion work, *Clizia*, also by Waveland and translated by Daniel T. Gallagher with an introduction by Robert K. Faulkner, similarly introduces the play and its context lucidly and adds thought-provoking footnotes to distinctive or problematic features of the text. Both of these editions retain Machiavelli's abrasive and colourful language.

Critical appreciations of the plays are not thick on the ground, but there are signs of a broadening interest in Machiavelli's literary output. A volume of essays on *The Comedy and Tragedy of Machiavelli* (2000) edited by Vickie B. Sullivan takes a fresh look at a wide range of texts and includes essays on both the plays and Machiavelli's awareness of a classical legacy to which his own work was indebted.[28] Harvey C. Mansfield begins the volume with an essay on cuckoldry in *Mandragola*. He argues that the play advocates a regard for the priority of lawfulness or morality over self-interest by an implicit comparison with the famous story of the rape of Lucrece. Mansfield suggests that in the *Discourses*, Machiavelli treated the crime of rape lightly, and later made a joke of it in *Mandragola*. But this ignores the fact that Lucrezia is ultimately complicit in the attempt on her charms and content to cuckold her husband. For Mansfield, respectability is the key element in Machiavelli's social understanding, and the ending requires practical moral adjustment by all the characters: "family values are not enough".[29] In the same volume, Robert Faulkner writes on the illumination of 'private life' in *Clizia*.[30] This essay is a revised version of Faulkner's introduction to the Waveland edition of the play, published in 1996. Faulkner notes that any 'useful lesson' that Machiavelli might have in mind in the play remains unclear. His central thesis is that the play bears out a kind of cynicism that we find elsewhere in Machiavelli's political writings. He notes echoes of Plautine comedy, especially the play *Casina*, but resists seeing Clizia as an attempt is to affirm classical moral virtues.[31] The household, now ruled by Sofronia, is not so much restored as set on a new footing. No longer is each (male) character out for himself, and by the end of the play, it is the women who clearly have the upper hand. Sofronia, Faulkner suggests, has mastered fortune with a 'virtù' that is spirited, cynical, and inventive.

Faulkner's approach to *Clizia* opened the way for a broadly feminist collection of essays on Machiavelli's writing, edited by Maria J. Falco (2004).[32] These essays provide an invaluable assessment of Machiavelli's corpus from the point of view of contemporary critical interests. Machiavelli is especially interesting because he works with such strong notions of gender but also makes powerful and sometimes disturbing comedy out of the vagaries of sexual desire. In her introduction to the collection, Falco notes that throughout the 1980s, feminists took a rather dim view of Machiavelli, one that gradually changed throughout the 1990s. Falco's survey of criticism on Machiavelli is especially helpful, and her guide to the essays in the collection sets Machiavelli up as an interlocutor with feminist criticism, rather than as an opponent. In many ways, Machiavelli becomes an important test case for the project of feminist reading. His unapologetic and sometimes shocking depictions of life in his own era are often not so much a confrontation to contemporary sensibilities, but a challenge. Interested students of Machiavelli will find Falco's bibliography, appended to the end of her introduction, especially useful.[33] In an essay on "Manliness" in *Mandragola*, Mary O'Brien notes that in both *Mandragola* and *Clizia*, the duped husband is "at home", the place with which traditionally the woman is associated. She writes, "At home, the realm of women and their works, must be actively overcome".[34] But if Callimaco engages in an assertion of manliness, in an attempt "to reproduce himself",[35] Fortune remains entirely dependent upon the assent of Lucrezia, the object of his desire and source of his anxieties. Catherine H. Zuckert sees in *Clizia* a complex representation of female 'virtù'.[36] Noting that Nicomaco sounds like a remarkably similar, but shortened version of "Niccolo Machiavelli", Zuckert argues that Machiavelli was willing to sacrifice his good name and indeed would suffer in reputation for his forthcoming work, *The Prince*. As for the Plautine and Terentian influences apparent in both plays, Robert L. Martinez has a well-informed chapter entitled "Comedian, Tragedian: Machiavelli and Traditions of Renaissance Theater" in *The Cambridge Companion to Machiavelli* (2010a). Finally, we may note Yael Manes' book *Motherhood and Patriarchal Masculinities in Sixteenth-Century Italian Comedy* (2011), a relatively short monograph with two chapters devoted to *Mandragola* and *Clizia* respectively. Here the mother figures in the plays are discussed in some detail. Manes argues that, if in *Mandragola* the influence and value of mothers is clearly recognised, so too is the unworthiness of father figures.[37] The play presents the 'virtù' of motherhood in contrast to a fantasy of 'virtù' pursued by the males. In *Clizia*, the role of 'paterfamilias' is entirely subsumed since Sofronia not only wields power but "obtains legitimate *auctoritas* to rule the household".[38]

Critical consensus has noted another of Machiavelli's many surprises, that he should be so self-deprecating in these works; why he should unfashion himself – as both Nicia and Nicomaco – in shame and humiliation, and displace himself so wryly from the ambit of 'virtù'. It is as though Machiavelli felt himself to be no Prince Hamlet but merely an attendant lord, one that will do to "advise the prince" but almost at times a fool, as T. S. Eliot wrote. The irony that so serious a writer should repeatedly turn to comedy, and that this laughter should come at his own expense, is noteworthy. Machiavelli wrote himself into these plays in an act of remarkably brave authorial 'virtù'. Perhaps there was also a kindness somewhere in Machiavelli. He may have castigated himself for his mistakes, as one is prone to do, but he also recognised that if we are to laugh at others, it is best to learn first how to laugh at oneself.

Notes

1 Quotations from *Mandragola* and *Clizia* in this chapter are taken from the Waveland Press editions by Mera J. Flaumenhaft and Daniel T. Gallagher (1981 and 1966).
2 For this chronology, I have followed the introduction to *The Comedies of Machiavelli*, ed. and trans. David Sices and James B. Atkinson (Indianapolis, IN: Hackett, 1985). See also James B. Atkinson, "Machiavelli: A Portrait", in *The Cambridge Companion to Machiavelli*, ed. John M. Najemy (Cambridge: Cambridge University Press, 2010), pp. 14–30.
3 See John Plamenatz, *Machiavelli: The Prince, Selections from The Discourses and Other Writings* (Durham, NC: Duke University Press, 1965), pp. 359–60.
4 See J. R. Hale, ed. and trans. *The Literary Works of Machiavelli: Mandragola, Clizia, A Dialogue on Language, Belfagor, Private Correspondence* (Oxford: Oxford University Press, 1961), p. 189.
5 See, for example, Quentin Skinner, *Machiavelli: A Very Short Introduction* (Oxford: Oxford University Press, 1981), pp. 23–53.
6 George Bull, trans. *Machiavelli: The Prince* (Harmondsworth, UK: Penguin Books, 1961), p. 34.
7 Ibid., p. 35.
8 Ibid., pp. 35–36, 91.
9 Ibid., p. 130.
10 Allan H. Gilbert, ed. and trans. *Machiavelli: The Chief Works and Others* (Durham, NC: Duke University Press, 1958), 3 volumes, vol. II, p. 745.
11 Flaumenhaft, p. 10.
12 Ibid., p. 39.
13 Ibid., p. 36.
14 Ibid., p. 51.
15 Gallagher, p. 40.
16 Ibid., p. 55.
17 Ibid., p. 31.
18 Ibid., p. 21.
19 Ibid., p. 21.
20 Allan H. Gilbert, ed. and trans. *Machiavelli*, p. 864.
21 J. R. Hale, *Literary Works*, p. 21.
22 Gilbert, p. 790.
23 Hale, p. 23.
24 Sices and Atkinson, p. 21.
25 Ibid., 23.
26 Ibid., 27.
27 Flaumenhaft, p. 5.
28 Vickie B. Sullivan, ed. *The Comedy and Tragedy of Machiavelli: Essays on the Literary Works* (New Haven, CT: Yale University Press, 2000).
29 Harvey C. Mansfield, "The Cuckold in Machiavelli's *Mandragola*", in Sullivan, pp. 1–29, p. 28.
30 Robert Faulkener, "*Clizia* and the Enlightenment of Private Life", in Sullivan, pp. 30–56.

31 Ibid., p. 40.
32 Maria J. Falco, ed. *Feminist Interpretations of Niccolo Machiavelli* (University Park, PA: Pennsylvania State University Press, 2004).
33 Falco, *Feminist Interpretations*, pp. 1–37.
34 Mary O'Brien, "The Root of the Mandrake: Machiavelli and Manliness", in *Feminist Interpretations*, ed. Maria J. Falco, pp. 173–96, p. 181.
35 Ibid., 193.
36 Catherine H. Zuckert, "Fortune Is a Woman: But So Is Prudence – Machiavelli's *Clizia*", in *Feminist Interpretations*, ed. Maria J. Falco, pp. 197–212, 208.
37 Yael Manes, *Motherhood and Patriarchal Masculinities in Sixteenth-Century Italian Comedy* (Farnham, UK: Ashgate, 2011), p. 40.
38 Ibid., p. 63.

5 Senecan tragedy in the English Renaissance

Mario Domenichelli

The Italian model: Seneca recalled to life

Because of the *Patres*'s hostility against stage-plays,[1] classical drama was never staged during the Middle Ages, even though the great Greek tragedians such as Euripides, Sophocles, and Aeschylus continued to be read.[2] Seneca's tragedies were not forgotten either in the pre-Gutenberg era. If Boccaccio knew his Seneca by heart, as one can see on reading *The Elegy of Madonna Fiammetta* written in 1343–44, Coluccio Salutati had Seneca's entire *corpus* transcribed around 1370. It was only the beginning of Seneca's European fortune during the Renaissance. Seneca's first works in print were the *Opuscula Philosophica*[3] and the *editio princeps* of the tragedies (Ferrara, André Belfort, 1474–78), re-edited with a commentary by Gellio Bernardino Marmitta and published in Venice by Lazzaro Suardi in 1492. The following year Marmitta and Danilo Gaetani had the tragedies printed again in Venice by Matteo Capcasa; a third Venetian edition by Giovanni Tacuino came forth in 1498. In the first half of the sixteenth century there were six major editions of Seneca's tragedies (Filippo Giunta, Florence 1506 and 1513, edited by Benedetto Riccardini, *philologus;* Josse Bade, Paris 1514; Manunzio, Venice 1517; Gryphius, Lyon 1547 and 1548; Sumptibus Societatis, Amsterdam 1568). Evangelista Fossa was the author of the first Italian translation (in *terza rima*) of a Senecan tragedy, *Agamemnon*, printed by Piero Quarengi in Venice in 1497 (*La nona tragedia de Seneca*, dita *Agamnon*[4]). Another two translations by Pythio Theologo (Francesco Pizio) from Monte Varchi followed that same year: *Hyppolitus* and *Tragedia Prima (Hercules furens)*, both probably printed by Cristoforo Di Pensa in Venice. Seneca, however, had already been discovered, studied, and had become a source of inspiration among the intellectuals gravitating around the university of Padua following Lovato de' Lovati's discovery at Pomposa of the *Codex Etruscus*, containing Seneca's tragedies, at the end of the thirteenth century. Albertino Mussato (1261–1329), a Paduan statesman and a member of the Cenacolo Paduano, a man admired by Petrarch as one of the earliest humanists, wrote *Ecerinis* in 1314 and had it staged in Padua when the town was under the threat of falling back into the hands of Cangrande della Scala, who, in Mussato's tragedy became Ezzelino da Romano, taken as the *exemplum* of the tyrant doomed to fall.[5] It was the first secular tragedy since Roman times and a very popular work staged in Padua for a number of years at every Christmas in order to remind citizens about their patriotic duty. Between 1314 and 1317 came an English contribution to the Senecan revival: Nicholas Trevet – a Dominican Friar who taught at Oxford and was well-known in France and in Italy too as the author of a commentary of Saint Augustin's *De Civitate Dei* – also wrote a commentary of Seneca's tragedies. Clearly

DOI: 10.4324/9781315612720-7

enough, Seneca had become a popular study subject, even though, to our knowledge, Mussato's *Ecerinis* was the only tragedy written and staged in Europe before 1377, when a prose tragedy was written and staged by Ludovico Romano da Fabriano, *De Casu Cesene*, on the fall of Cesena attacked by Giovanni Acuto's (John Hawkwood's) mercenary troops. The next tragedy, *De Captivitate Ducis Jacobi* by Ludovico Zacchia came some ninety years later in 1465. It told the story of the mercenary captain Jacopo Piccinino's assassination ordered by Ferdinando d'Aragona. Only fifty-eight lines remain of another Latin tragedy by Giovanni Manzini della Motta, on the fall of Antonio della Scala, who became the last lord of Verona after slaying his brother Bartolome, after which he had to face the indignation of the people and Gian Galeazzo Visconti's attack on Verona, and had to flee on 19 October 1387. Latin prose works such as *De Rebus Italicis deque triumpho Ludovici XII regis Francorum Tragedia* by Giovanni Armonio Marso (1499); *Historia Baetica* (1492) on the *Reconquista* of Granada by Carlo Verardi; and *Fernandus Servatus* (1493) by Marcellino Verardi, are what may be called chronicle tragedies, if not chronicle plays, mirroring the events of the day and thus explicitly exemplifying the political function of staged tragedy. Yet, that was by no means the only idea of tragedy. Both the classical Aristotelian model and the Senecan tragic model were still active in Antonio Loschi's *Achilles* (1390) and in Gregorio Correr's *Progne* (1429). Other sources were found in the flowering Italian novella tradition. Boccaccio's *Decameron* in particular was a source of inspiration for a number of comedies in the first place, even though the *Decameron* tenth day's third novella inspired Bernardo Accolti's tragedy *Virginia* (1493, published in 1513), while the first novella of the fourth day became the source of Antonio Cammelli's tragedy, *Philostrato e Panfila*, staged in Ferrara in 1499 and published in 1508.

Erasmus' Euripides and the "Orti Oricellari" group

In 1506, Erasmus had his two Latin translations from Euripides – *Hecuba* and *Iphigenia in Aulide* – printed in Paris by Josse Bade and reprinted the following year by Aldo Manuzio (who, by the beginning of the sixteenth century had already published all the tragedies of Sophocles and a two-volumes Euripides minus *Elektra*). Erasmus's choice was of an ideological kind: the subject of both tragedies was the horror of war as the ethical, religious, and political point in Erasmus' undaunted pacifism. *Iphigenia* was introduced by a dedicatory letter in which Erasmus made it clear that in translating Euripides' *Choroi* he had strictly kept to the Senecan metrical model, even though he was proposing a new long-lasting model by mixing and contaminating Senecan and Euripidean plots, characters, as well as metrical structures. By so doing, Erasmus defined the main features of the Italian Renaissance tragedy model later exemplified by Giovan Battista Giraldi Cinzio, Sperone Speroni, and Lodovico Dolce.[6]

Erasmus' versions of *Hecuba* and *Iphigenia in Aulide* were edited by Antonio Francini and republished in 1518 by Filippo Giunta in Florence. Florence, no doubt, was the hub of the Italian tragic production in the Renaissance. At the *Orti Oricellari* (the gardens of Palazzo Rucellai, today Palazzo Venturi-Ginori), not far from Santa Maria Novella, political plans of subversion were being prepared by a group of intellectuals who were to leave Florence and go into exile after their failed plot and attempt on the life of Cardinal Giulio de' Medici in 1522. In the previous years a sort of academy had met at the Orti Oricellari, with a central idea that tragedy might prove an important ideological weapon to be used against tyranny. The result was a sort of flowering of the

Italian genius for tragedy in the ten-year span between 1515 and 1525–26, when Alessandro Pazzi de' Medici translated Aristotle's *Perì Poetiké* and wrote *Dido in Carthagine* (1524, with no sixteenth-century editions); Gian Giorgio Trissino produced his famous model of models for tragedy-writing, *Sophonisba* (published in 1515–24 in Rome by Antonio Blado, and then republished a number of times); and Giovanni Rucellai composed his *Rosmunda* (1515, published in 1525 in Siena by Michelangelo Di Bartolomeo, with a number of reprints before the end of the century). Luigi Alamanni's *Antigone* came after 1522 and was printed in Lyon in 1533 by Sebastian Gryphius, while Lodovico Martelli's *Tullia* (1526–27) was published in 1533 by Antonio Blado in Rome and Melchiorre Sessa in Venice).[7]

Sophonisba, Rosmunda, Dido, Antigone, Tullia: women's names to which we might add Iphigenia, Hecuba, Medea, Phaedra, Elektra, not to mention Giraldi's *Orbecche* (1541, published by Aldo Manunzio in Venice in 1543), and Sperone Speroni's *Canace* (1542): Italian Renaissance tragedy, no doubt, was feminine gendered. This is sometimes explained with Boccaccio and the heroines of *Decameron*, his *De mulieribus claris*, or all the tragic feminine characters in *De Casibus virorum illustrium*, and in *Genealogiae deorum gentilium*. This is, of course, no answer as it rather poses again the same question about Boccaccio: why women as the protagonists of tragic tales? Women of course were acquiring importance in Italian Renaissance court-life. *Donne* from *dominae*, donne di palazzo as the feminine counterpart of the Italian courtier were the governesses of court life: ladies such as Emilia Pio, whose role at the Montefeltro court at Urbino is clearly portrayed in Castiglione's *Book of the Courtier*, or Lucrezia Tornabuoni at the Medici court in Florence, or Beatrice and Isabella d'Este in Milan and Mantua, and Lucrezia Borgia at the Este court in Ferrara. The ladies, this is clear enough, were the most important part of the audience at any Italian court theatrical representations. Women also were the ones who read and for whom most books were written.

According to scholars such as Paola Mastrocola[8] and Corinne Lucas,[9] the Italian classic revival of tragedy at the 'Orti Oricellari' did not follow the Senecan model. It began with the imitation of the Geek model. An imitation of Roman tragedy was out of the question as no Roman tragedy had survived apart from Seneca's works and from the anonymous *Octavia*, also attributed to him. Thus, neither Trissino's *Sophonisba*, nor Rucellai's *Rosmunda* have a five-acts partition which belongs to the Senecan model rather than to the Greek model that had no acts, but *epeisoidia*, divided by choral odes, the *stàsima*, sung by the choir and structured according to the ancient model (*strophé, antistrophé, épodos*). Trissino and Rucellai also established the use of the hendecasyllable as the tragic verse for the Italian Renaissance, while Pazzi de Medici's 1524 Latin translation of Aristotle's *Perì Poetiké* (1514–36) fixed the paradigmatic traits of tragedy (the first Italian translation of that book, by Bernardo Segni, was published in 1549, the most important one, by Alessandro Piccolomini, was printed in 1575). The discovery of Seneca opened a second period in the history of the Italian tragic model, culminating on Lodovico Dolce's translations of Seneca's ten tragedies, published in Venice by Giovan Battista e Melchiorre Sessa in 1560 (Dolce had already produced his Italian translation of Horace's *Ars Poetica* in 1535).[10] The real novelty, one must say, was Giraldi's *Egle*, in which all the potential of a new theatrical genre was discovered in the pastoral, or tragi-comedy, which Giraldi also theorized in his *Discorso sovra il comporre le satire atte alla scena* (1554). The pastoral was no novelty of course. Sannazaro had published *Arcadia*, his pastoral *prosimetrum* (mixing, that is, poetry and prose) in 1502, and Poliziano had already staged his *Favola d'Orfeo*, probably at Mantua in 1480, but it was Giraldi who opened the way to the theatrical pastoral as the tragi-comedy, defining the next two centuries' model perfectly exemplified in Tasso's *Aminta* (1573) and Guarini's *Il pastor fido* (1583–87) as the models of pastoral tragi-comedy, so fashionable in seventeenth- and eighteenth-century drama, as well as in Italian Opera for the two centuries to come. Before the 1550s, Aristotelian rules in tragedy had been definitively affirmed in the commentaries of Robortello (*Librum Aristotelis De Arte Poetica Explicationes*, 1548), Vincenzo Maggi, and Bartolomeo Lombardi (*Explanationes*, 1550). The 1540s were characterized by Giovan Battista Giraldi Cinthio's most influential theoretical and artistic work, and with the famous *polemos* between Giraldi and Speroni on *Canace*,[11] which, according to Giraldi, lacked in tragic intensity due to the fact that no sense of guilt was shown in the two incestuous protagonists, Aeolus's daughter and son, Canace and Macareo.

Seneca into English and the Elizabethan stage

Seneca followed Aristotle's (and Horace's) dicta on tragic style, with complete unity of action, time, place, and, of course, speech-style, and the chorus separating each of the five acts. Also the emphasis on the *horribile visu*, on horror, as the very source of *catharsis* in the audience, came from *Perì Poetické*. All of these elements had great importance in the history of Italian tragedy in early modernity. The theoretical discussion on tragedy, as well as the actual composition and staging of tragedies during the Italian Renaissance powerfully contributed to the growth of the English stage in the last three decades of the sixteenth century.[12] An important English date is 1581 when Thomas Newton collected in a quarto volume, published by Thomas Marsh, *Seneca His Tenne Tragedies*, a collection of English metrical versions of Seneca's *corpus tragicum*.[13] Seven of these had already been published, and all the translators were connected either with the University of Oxford or with Cambridge. Jasper Heywood had published his version of *Troas* in 1559, *Thyestes* in 1560, and *Hercules furens* in 1561. *Oedipus*, translated by Alexander Neville in 1560, had been published in 1563. John Studley had produced his versions of *Agamemnon* and *Medea* in 1566, while his *Hercules Oetaeus* and *Hyppolitus* had been entered in the Stationer's Register in 1566–67. Thomas Nuce's in-quarto version of *Octavia* is undated, but an entry in the Stationers' Register, July 1566 – July 1567, is likely to refer to it. Lastly, Thomas Newton translated what remains of another two Senecan tragedies as if they were one play and collected the two *fragmenta* under the title of *Thebais*, or *Phoenissae*. The importance of Senecan tragedy and of Newton's work has never been undervalued in the history of the growth of Elizabethan tragedy.[14] What is generally either given for granted and/or almost totally obscured is the importance of the Italian intermediation. All the translations collected by Newton were produced in the 1560s, just after Lodovico Dolce's important translation of Seneca's *corpus tragicum*, and some thirty years after the Italian tragedy revival in the *Orti Oricellari* group, and some twenty years after the Giraldi-Speroni debate in the 1540s. The earliest Renaissance Latin translation of Aristotle's *Perì Poetiké*[15] by Bernardo Valla's had been some forty years in print (1498), when Pazzi de Medici's own translation was published with the commentaries of Robortello, of Maggi and Lombardi. Giulio Cesare Scaligero's *Poetices libri Septem* was published in Lyon in 1561, and Ludovico Castelvetro's important new version of Aristotle's book was published with a *Commentary* in 1570.

All told, in the sixteenth century there are some fifteen Greek editions of the *Poetiké*; Pazzi de' Medici's Latin translation had nineteen out of a total of forty Latin editions of Aristotle's book. Of course in Italy there was also a production of personal *poeticae* such as Trissino's *Poetica libri I-IV* published in Vicenza in 1529, and *libri V-VI* written in 1549 and published posthumously in 1562. As far as we know there are no Renaissance English translations of Aristotle's *Perì Poetiké*, even though the terms of the question as far as the English stage was concerned were clear enough in Sidney's *Defense of Poetry* (1580) where the practices of the English players were rejected as ridiculous, and not to the life if compared with 'regular' classical drama. Of course it would be wrong to assume that there was no debate on irregular theatre in England. Regular Aristotelian dramas were staged in universities and schools, yet the fact is that the new English theatre was a commercial enterprise, one might say, almost a pre-industrial phenomenon, whose criterion was the audience's favour and approval. If there was no translation of Aristotle's *Perì Poetiké*, a number of books of rhetoric and poetics were published and read in England. Thomas Wilson's *Rule of Reasons*, for instance, published in 1553, had seven editions until 1593; his *Arte of Rhetorick* had eight between 1553 and 1585; Leonard Cox's *The Art or Craft of Rhetoric* had two editions, in 1524 and in 1532; Richard Sherry wrote two books on specific aspects of the same art or craft: *A Treatyse of Schemes and Tropes* (1550) and *A Treatise of the Figures of Grammar and Rhetoric* (1555). All these books belong to same tradition producing Roger Ascham's *The Schoolmaster*, written in the 1560s and published in 1570. The one most directly connected to play acting is John Hoskins' *Directions for Speech and Style* (manuscript, probably 1599),[16] a book which could be read by players and playwrights alike as 'rhetoric in action'. The same type of *ars rhetorica* or *rhetoriké téchne* we find in Hamlet's instructions to the actors in Act 3, scene 2, which is the most explicit statement about play-acting in Elizabethan Jacobean drama. Cicero's *De oratore*, or Quintilian's *Institutio oratoria*, taught how to move, how to speak, and show, or conceal passions through gestures, looks, expressions, and rhetorical devices. Life itself, in a way, in their works became play-acting. *Ars rhetorica* taught Elizabethan players a kind of technical competence much likelier to produce life-likeness in the eyes of the audience than any strict application of Aristotelian unities. As a matter of fact, in what was shown on the Elizabethan stage, there was a new idea of a true-to-life show breaking all Aristotelian conventions and establishing new and more direct ways of imitation of the 'real' world beyond the invisible fourth wall separating the audience from the show, yet with the consciousness that all the world's a stage (*As You Like It*, 2.7). Seneca's insistence on *horribile visu*, horror, is probably a key-note in order to understand the new English approach, the new mimetic strategy, and, consequently, new realism in the representation of human beings.

A convincing example may be found in the first English tragedy, *Gorboduc, or Ferrex and Porrex*,[17] the fruit of the collaboration between Thomas Norton, who wrote acts 1 to 3, and Thomas Sackville, author of acts 4 and 5. The division into five acts, each of them introduced by a 'dumb show' and closed by the Chorus, characterizes the Senecan model being adopted and also changed by the Elizabethan-Jacobean playwrights who were also influenced by Seneca's Greek antecedents. *Gorboduc* was first performed by 'the Gentlemen of the Inner Temple' during the 1561 Inner Temple Christmas celebration, and then at Queen's Elizabeth's court on 18 January 1562 and printed at least three times in Elizabeth's years (1565, 1570, and 1590). *Gorboduc* is the first verse drama, introducing the use of blank verse in the history of English drama.

The tragedy's subject – the struggle for power between the two sons of Gorboduc, Ferrex and Porrex – is of a Senecan cut. It clearly recalls *Thyestes*, translated by Jasper Heywood in 1560; it recalls even more Seneca's *Thebais*, albeit this was translated by Newton only in 1566. *Gorboduc*, taken from Geoffrey of Monmouth's *Historia Regum Britanniae*, represents, like Seneca's *Thyestes*, the story of the deadly power struggle between the two sons of a King. Gorboduc, King of Britain, intends to divide his realm between his two sons who thus enter a deadly confrontation. The elder son is killed by the younger, who, in his turn, is killed in revenge by his own mother. Both Gorboduc and the Queen are then killed by the people provoked to rebellion by the power struggle. The revolt is quenched in blood by the nobility. The lack of succession[18] to the throne starts a most horrible civil war. Such a subject, no doubt, in Elizabeth's early years, with a still unclear succession to the throne, seemed to conjure up and exorcise at the same time some evil spirits of a near past, while the form of the play, mixing the morality play tradition with the new Senecan model was a first step in the development of the kind of plot, subject, and dramatic form we also find in Shakespeare's *Titus Andronicus* and, of course, *King Lear*, where the deadly struggle between brothers, the two sons of Gloucester, undergoes a mirror effect, as it is the reflexion of the war started by Lear's daughters, Regan and Goneril, crushing Cordelia and wasting Lear's Realm.[19] *Gorboduc* became popular and was imitated by a series of less important Senecan plays such as *Jocasta* (1566), another blank-verse tragedy by George Gascoygne and Francis Kinwelmersh. The complexity of source references may be shown by Lodovico Dolce's own *Giocasta* (1549), which was an adaptation, almost a paraphrase, of Euripides' *Phoinissai*, yet filtered through Seneca's own *Phoenissae*. *Tancred and Gismund* by Robert Wilmot, probably written in the late 1560s and published in 1591. The story was taken from Painter's translation, in *The Palace of Pleasure* (1566), of Boccaccio's fourth day's first *novella* of the *Decameron*. A first version of the play, if not a revision of it by Robert Wilmot, was *Gismund of Salern*, 'acted by some gentlemen of the Inner Temple' before Elizabeth either in 1566 or in 1568. It was the story of Tancred King of Naples and Prince of Salern whose widowed daughter falls in love with one of her father's courtiers. The King kills him and offers his daughter a golden cup containing her lover's heart. Gismund kills herself and so does her father.[20] Another example of early Senecan Elizabethan tragedy is *The Misfortunes of Arthur*, by Thomas Hughes and other gentlemen of the Gray Inn (the writing and staging seems to have been a collective Gray Inn enterprise, staged on 28 February 1587 at Greenwich before Queen Elizabeth). The plot, taken from Geoffrey of Monmouth's *Historia Regum Britanniae*, tells the story of Mordred's betrayal and of the day of the doom when father and son come to a deadly single combat in which both get killed. It is a blank-verse tragedy in which the Senecan model is almost proclaimed by the by now customary five-act Senecan partition. Also the use of dumb-shows and choruses repeats the Senecan model. There is also a number of Senecan *topoi*, the most typical of which appears in the prologue, when the Ghost of Gorlois, killed by Uther Pendragon, father of Arthur, steps on stage asking for revenge, thus defining the return of the past as the fatal perspective in which the whole play is set, and consequently *Ate*'s power as the force of events dead and gone in the past yet shaping the present, and life itself.[21]

In all this story 1592 was an important year. As we read in Philip Henslowe's diary it was the year of the first recorded performance of *The Jew of Malta*, acted by Lord Strange's Men who restaged the play at least seventeen times between 26 February 1592 and 1 February 1593. The success was to last even longer, as the play was performed again a number of times by Sussex's Men and Queen Elizabeth's Men in 1594, and by the *Admiral's Men* between 1594 and 1596. Marlowe's play too follows the Senecan model as we can see from the prologue, with Machiavel represented on stage as the Senecan ghost introducing the tragedy, and thus combining the Senecan model with a more modern and cynical political vision in the age of the French religious war.[22] It is not a question of mere political power, since Barabas, the Machiavellian character of the play, seems to have none; it is rather a question of material power, or of the power of material interests. It is first of all the power exercised by a diabolical intelligence and a deep knowledge of human beings. Barabas has more money than all the Maltese put together. Malta is under the Turkish sway, and Turkish ships and cannons impose a heavy tribute. Barabas as the richest man on the island, and as a Jew, is the one who must pay for it all, so that his money will pay for Malta's freedom. Barabas, thus struck and robbed of all he has, plans revenge. With the help of his servant Ithamore, who hates Christians, and of Abigail, the Jew's beautiful daughter, Barabas succeeds in recovering at least a small part of what he has been robbed. Both Lodowick, the governor's son, and his best friend Mathias, fall in love with Abigail and fight against each other in a deadly duel in which both lose their lives. In consequence of this Abigail repents and becomes a Christian and a nun. Barabas in a sort of murderous cold madness poisons her together with all the other nuns. Barabas also kills two friars and then also Ithamore and Ithamore's prostitute who threatens to disclose Barabas' crimes. This does not avoid him being tried, found guilty, and condemned to death. But he avoids the penalty by feigning to be dead. In the meanwhile the Turks invade Malta with the help of Barabas who therefore becomes the Turkish governor of Malta, in which role he betrays the Turks and helps the Knights of Malta to regain the island. In the end, in the last of his multiple betrayals and mischiefs, the plotter of all plots, the ferocious semi-devil, revenger, and trapper, falls into the trap he has prepared for the Commander of the Turkish fleet, Selym Calymath. The trap is a suspended platform which, once a rope is cut, will let Selym fall into a cauldron. But something goes wrong, or if we are right, it goes exactly as it has to, and Barabas himself becomes the victim of the machine, the trap he has prepared and falls into the cauldron, as if it were the very pit of hell. This sequence is the best and more concrete example of the plotter's destiny. The plotter must become the victim of the machine he has prepared and set in motion; in other words he must become the victim of all those rhetorical and material devices of the *mise en scène* through which he stages the story of his plot, or, better, his own plot as history represented on stage.

From the multiple rewriting of Kyd's *The Spanish Tragedy* to Shakespeare's *Hamlet*

The most popular and the most famous Senecan revenge tragedy before Shakespeare's *Hamlet* is Thomas Kyd's *The Spanish Tragedy*, introducing a most important device in Elizabethan tradition, that is 'the play within the play', in which the play represents itself as the paradoxical fictional mirror and *organon* of truth, and thus its own social, ethical, political function unveiling truth through fiction. *The Spanish Tragedy* was written between 1582 and 1592, most probably in 1587, even though we know from some entries in the diary of the most important theatrical entrepreneur of the age, Philip Henslowe, that *The Spanish Tragedy*, sometimes called simply *Hieronimo* from the name of its protagonist, or *Hieronimo's Mad Again* from a famous line in the tragedy, became popular in the early 1590s when it was staged by the Lord Strange's Men (28 February 1592 at the Rose, or 1594, and again in 1602). We also know that 320 lines were certainly written by a different hand, most probably Ben Jonson's, whom Henslowe paid for the additions, or Shakespeare himself.[23] Be as it may, *The Spanish Tragedy* paved the way for Shakespeare's (1601) *Hamlet* in which all the devices and *topoi* contrived by Kyd were brought to perfection.[24] Thus we have a Senecan ghost, even though in *Hamlet* there's neither induction nor prologue, and the ghost is at first introduced as a vague shadow and then as a sort of objective projection of Hamlet's suspicions and a personification of *Ate*, as it begins to shape the tragedy as the movement of the return of the past. There is a play within the play in which fiction, the dumb-show representing the *Murder of Gonzago*, is the silent unveiling as well as the fictional repetition of the murder of Hamlet's father and thus the Senecan *horribile visu* preparing the *καταστροφή* (*katastrophê*). And, lastly, we have in *Hamlet* another kind of *show* and 'play within the play' in which, as happens in Hyeronimo's plot in *The Spanish Tragedy*, what was given for fictitious becomes true, and what was to be the simulation of a deadly combat, ends with the death of both the duellers, together with the King and the Queen, so that *Ate* can be satisfied and justice be re-established when Fortinbras steps on stage revenging his father's death at the hands of Hamlet's father and conquering Denmark.

In *The Spanish Tragedy* we have the usual ghost, dumb-shows and choruses at the end of each of the five acts. We have, first of all, the play within the play, with the triumph of *Ate*, death, and Revenge. Andrea's ghost, as the personification of *Ate* and of the spirit of Revenge, is always onstage; he is the *chorus* commenting on what is going on; he unveils truth, injustices, and murderous plots. The story develops through Bellimperia, the King's niece and Andreas's former lover, who falls in love again with Horatio, Andreas' best friend. But there is a plan to marry Bellimperia to Balthazar, the son of the King of Portugal, and a consequent plot to murder Horatio. Hieronimo finds the corpse of his son Horatio stabbed and hanged. His wife, Isabella, is driven mad by this and commits suicide; Hieronimo is possessed by *Ate*. He feigns reconciliation and, together with Bellimperia, he plans to stage a play, *Soliman and Perseda*, in which, in front of the king, they will not act, not perform their enemies' death onstage, they will really kill them. Lorenzo and Balthazar are stabbed; Bellimperia after doing the deed kills herself; Hieronimo bites out his own tongue not to speak under torture, after which he kills the Duke and stabs himself to death. In *Hamlet* there is no such a play within the play at the end; however, there is a feigned duel, to be fought with blunt swords by Hamlet and Laertes to celebrate their pacification, were it not that only Hamlet's sword is blunt, while Laertes' is sharp and poisoned. So here, too, what was to be feigned becomes true, and Hamlet in the end, after being wounded to death by Laertes' poisoned sword, first kills his adversary and then King Claudius. Meanwhile Hamlet's mother drinks the poisoned wine offered by Claudius to Hamlet, so that, not only does the dumb-show in 3.2 unveil Claudius's crime and his murder of Hamlet's father, exemplifying the stage's effect on 'guilty creatures' (2.2) but also the duel is a part of the same play within the play, exacting justice and administering death. Thus meta-theatre in Elizabethan Senecan tragedy is the medium through which fiction finds a breech in the fourth wall and what was intended to be the imitation of reality invades reality and gives it its own shape. This is not precisely the case of a Roman tragedy such as Shakespeare's *Julius Caesar* in which, however, words become true and *Ate*,[25] together with 'Mischief' find a way to shape history. Antony, after delivering his speech from the *rostra* in the forum, in Act 3, conjures up *Ate*, as the spirit of revenge and knows that mischief set free is a most powerful instrument shaping history.

Jacobean and Caroline tragedy: the dark world of power – tragedy as Pharmakos

The Revenger's Tragedy was very likely composed in the early years of the seventeenth century, and was staged in 1606 and published as an anonymous work in 1607. For a long time it was attributed to the author of the *Atheist's Tragedy*, Cyril Tourneur, but researchers agree today that *The Revenger* is to be attributed to Middleton.[26] It belongs to what we may call the second Senecan wave in English Tragedy. It does not open with the Senecan ghost's prologue, but with the monologue of the protagonist, Vindice (i.e. Revenger), recalling the past, the reasons of revenge he has, and the court's present corruption, as the fatal forces shaping what is going to happen. The protagonist's name, functional to the role he has to play, is the first Senecan trait, like verbal violence and the use of horror. Vindice completely fulfils his revenger's task, then to be punished for taking revenge which is not what usually happens in Seneca to revengers re-ordering a disordered world. In *The Revenger's Tragedy* stage action is introduced, prepared, indeed projected, in Vindice's *incipit* monologue taking the place of the Senecan ghost's monologue that had already become typical in English tragedy long before the *Spanish Tragedy*. This may suggest that Vindice delivers his monologue from the dead land of the past and that his voice is death's own voice. As a matter of fact, Vindice seems to live among the dead and *in memoriam* of them, brooding over his father's recent death and obsessed by the idea of revenging his beloved who was poisoned by the Duke nine years before. The court is a place of relentless libertinage, where any pleasure can be bought by the ones in power, and nobody's virtue, either mother's or sister's, can be given for granted, so that truth itself must always be kept in disguise, and the play becomes the very *organon* of justice. Vindice, playing the pimp in order to revenge, procures the Duke a meeting with a lady who, as a matter of fact, is an effigy, whose head is the poisoned skull of Vindice's dead beloved. The Duke kisses the skull, before being forced to watch the Duchess betray him with the Duke's son Spurio, then to be stabbed by Vindice. The tragedy then proceeds through other disguises, corpses, and Senecan horrors, with Vindice himself at last accepting death as his reward.

Jacobean and Caroline drama both transformed and intensified the Senecan poetic of horror, stage violence, and deeply corrupted evil characters characterizing Elizabethan tragedy. Indeed, in the seventeenth century, Senecan tragedy seems to define a category including almost any tragedy produced in England before the civil war. Thus George Chapman's *Bussy d'Ambois* (1603–7), which not only inspired Bussy's life and French history but also Seneca's *Agamemnon* and *Hercules Oeataeus*, Plutarch's *Moralia*, and Ovid and Erasmus's *Adagia*, was followed by a sequel, *The Revenge of Bussy* (1612).[27] Shakespeare's Iago is indeed a particular case of revenger, as his actions are not grounded in any objective reasons; he suspects his wife to have been seduced by the Moor; Iago might also have reasons of resentment against the Moor for appointing Cassio as his lieutenant, but the truth is Iago is somehow less, or somehow more, than human. The reasons why he does what he does are never clear, and Iago himself, indirectly questioned by Othello, "demand that demi-devil why he hath thus ensnared my soul and body", simply answers: "Demand me nothing – what you know, you know. From this time forth I never will speak word" (5.2), thus sealing the tragedy with silence, as Hieronimo does in *The Spanish Tragedy* by biting out his own tongue. Quintessential evil is beyond reason and words, and must therefore be kept secret not only to the characters within the play but also to the audience. Indeed this kind of personification of evil was frequently to be seen and heard of on seventeenth-century London stages. In Middleton and Rowley's *The Changeling* (1622),[28] for instance, De Flores, the evil character, certainly has his reasons; he is in love with Beatrice who loves Alsemero and is betrothed to Alonso. Beatrice, indeed, more than De Flores, seems to be the one who sets the tragic nullifying machine in motion by asking De Flores to kill Alonso, so that she can marry Alsemero. However, the fact is that Beatrice seals a terrible pact with De Flores to whose desire she must yield. The world, this is the point, is like the madhouse in the tragedy's subplot, with all the protagonists swayed by their lust and thus driven to death. Bosola, in John Webster's *The Tragedy of the Dutchess of Malfy* (1612–13, published in 1623) is another Iago-like character, with the same nullifying function, in a sort of *tristitia* unveiling in all these characters their melancholy insanity in the contemplation of the dark, dirty world they serve.[29] Webster read the story of the Duchess in William Painter's *The Palace of Pleasure* (1567). Painter's novella is a translation from *Les histoires tragiques* (1570) by Belleforest who, in his turn, had translated it from Matteo Bandello's *Novelle* (1554). Bandello was personally acquainted with Antonio Beccadelli di Bologna and had a personal interest in the series of events that took place between 1508 and 1513. The Duchess of Amalfi, Giovanna d'Aragona, was the daughter of an illegitimate son of Ferdinand I of Naples. After her husband's death, she secretly remarried her butler, Antonio Beccadelli. This provoked the wrath and revenge of her two brothers, Ferdinand and the Cardinal, who murdered the Duchess and her children. Antonio, too, was murdered by Daniele da Bozzolo, a mercenary soldier. Bozzolo, in Webster's tragedy, becomes Bosola and a most important and intriguing, contradictory character, who, intending to murder the Cardinal, by mistake kills Antonio instead. Bosola is in the Duchess's confidence and is perhaps also unknowingly in love with her. Yet Bosola is also Ferdinand's spy, and both the Duchess and her children die at Bosola's executioners' hands. The Cardinal intends to have Bosola murdered as well, but in the end it is Bosola who stabs the Cardinal to death. Ferdinand and Bosola then stab each other, and in the end, the only one to survive is the Duchess's and Antonio's elder son who will become the new Duke of Malfi. Bosola seems to be dispossessed of his will and of his feeling; he is not what he seems, the Cardinal's revenger. He is a revenger both against himself and the ferocious, corrupt world which he desperately inhabits and serves.

We can find the great summa of all the typical traits of a Jacobean drama in Thomas Middleton's *Women Beware Women*,[30] composed at the beginning of the seventeenth century, in which Seneca's tragic vision, the use of horror and *terribilia, Ate*, and Revenge, is considerably lowered in a repulsive cynical landscape of all human baseness. The plot is taken from another sixteenth-century Italian story, exemplifying corruption, in lies, lechery, incest, rape, murder as the effects of power in a society whose only value is money buying life, as life is exactly what is on sale. There are two intertwining plots, referring to two social milieus, the nobility and the middle class. While Bianca, the Venetian heiress married by Leantio, unwilling to live in a comparatively modest condition, leaves her husband to become the Duke's mistress, and Leantio, in his turn, becomes the lover of wealthy Livia. In the second plot Isabella refuses to marry a wealthy man until she understands her arranged marriage can become the cover of her affair with Hyppolito, the man she is in love with. All the main characters get killed in the end in the by now traditional *Spanish-tragedy*-like play within the play. Italy of course is used as a distant mirror, full of corruption, lechery, witchcraft, assassins, and poisons. Webster took the story from an Italian scandal in the years from 1575 and 1585, when Paolo Giordano Orsini, Duke of Bracciano, murdered his wife, Isabella de' Medici, and had Vittoria Accoramboni's husband, Camillo, also murdered in order to marry with his wife thus calling on Vittoria's and his own heads the revenge of Cardinal Montalto, Pope Sistus VI, related to Vittoria's murdered husband. Chronicles tell us that Bracciano and Vittoria left Rome, seeking refuge in the Republic of Venice. Bracciano died in Salò in November 1585. Vittoria was assassinated in Padua shortly after by a Venetian public official, Lodovico Orsini. In Webster's play, instead, Vittoria is indicted in Rome for adultery and murder, and rescued by Bracciano who marries her, only to be shortly after murdered by assassins sent by the Duke of Florence who wants to revenge his sister Isabella's death. Also, Vittoria is murdered a few days after Bracciano's death.

All the stories represented on the Elizabethan-Jacobean-Caroline are characterized by their insistence on moral degradation in a dark, dirty world shaped by power effects and represented in the exotic distance of an Italianated mirror. Power, the struggle for power, the corruption induced by power, political power, material power, power on the body and the mind of others, as a matter of fact, is the great theme often meta-theatrically represented with frequent plays within the plays as the very moment of revelation of some mysterious, obscure, and horrible truth. All the tragedies we have been considering so far focus on the difference between reality and appearance, between the show of power, and what it really entails, what power must cover and unveil at the same time, in a sort of apocalypse of innocence. *Women beware Women* is a most clear example of this, with innocence being first touched and then invaded by the show of corruption, and true, innocent love betrayed by money and power.[31]

An English seventeenth-century outcome of a sixteenth-century Italian controversy

On the seventeenth-century dramatic background we have been describing so far, Ford's *'Tis a Pity She's a Whore* (staged in 1633) with its provocative representation of incest as heroic love, and of the union of two twins, brother and sister as the union of perfect beauty and virtue, shining on a dark background of vice, murder, injustice, is the scandalous triumph of the perfection of body and soul against the world of evil in which the story is set.[32] The twins' incest had already had a long Renaissance tradition. One should not forget that the debate on tragedy and Senecan horrors in sixteenth-century Italy had begun with Giraldi Cinthio's polemical attack on Sperone Speroni's *Canace* (Venice, Vincenzo Valgrisi, 1546), the paradigm of all incest stories and a point of some importance in our discussion.

Giraldi wrote that Speroni's *Canace* lacked in tragic force owing to the absence of any sense of guilt in the two incestuous protagonists. There is no doubt that, from his point of view, Giraldi was right. However, reversing the perspective and considering the general ideological panorama shown by the English theatrical production in the early 1600s, the fact is that the general corruption of the world seemed to call for endogamy as a way of expelling any contamination of the sick, wicked, corrupted world where the two twins in love with each other refuse to live. In Italy, on the other hand, Speroni's incest tragedy had been preceded by Giovanni Falugi's (1529) *Canace* in which the twins' marriage is clearly the marriage of two perfect bodies, two perfect minds. This is true also for Ford's story of Giovanni and Annabella shining in their perfection against the dark background of a wicked world represented at its very worst by Soranzo, to whom Annabella is promised and who wants to take revenge against the two brothers' lovers. At the end of the play, Giovanni steps on stage in front of Soranzo and his guests at a banquet. He holds high over his head a dagger piercing a heart, his sister's heart, ripped off her breast and utters his famous words: "this is a heart, my lords, in which is mine entombed". A heart buried in a heart, a terrible emblem of the union and thus of the perfection in death of the two twins. The date of composition of *'Tis Pity* is unknown; the play may have been staged for the first time in 1623, or 1626, even though the likelier date seems to be 1630. Be that as it may, we may consider Ford's play as a banner of libertine thought pushed to the extreme in the representation of incest, what may be considered the most scandalous among its ideological banners and emblems. This is what we find in Thomas Ellice's epigram dedicated to Ford's *Whore*:

> With admiration I beheld this whore
> Adorned with beauty, such as might restore
> (If ever being as thy Muse hath aimed)
> Her Giovanni, in his love unblamed
> ... and Annabella be
> Gloriously fair, e'en in her infamy.[33]

There are two fundamental traits in Senecan tragedy which may help us understand the entire subversive reach of Ford's tragedy and the link it has with the affirmation of libertine philosophies in seventeenth-century Western Europe. The first Senecan trait is the *nefas*, sacrilege, the impious action of extreme rebellion against all divine and human laws. The second trait is the power theme, with an idea of unchecked, tyrannical, cruel, and blood-thirsty power in what we may define as the hyperbole of horror. Ford's obvious sources include Seneca, as well as Ovid's *Heroides* (II), which were the direct influence on both Speroni's *Canace*, and Gower's *Confessio Amantis* (III), even though there is an edition of Speroni's *Canace* published in 1598, which Ford might have read. Giraldi's major objection to Speroni's tragedy is the lack of any sense of guilt, and even a consciousness of the *nefas*, their crime, which, for the two brothers, or the two twins, is simply the most perfect kind of love of the equals. As a consequence also Power's ruthlessness and cruelty, all the horror of Æolus' father-power, as Æolus, after punishing Canace and Macareus, takes further revenge on their little son by throwing him to the dogs. However, both in Speroni's tragedy and, as a consequence, also in Ford's, there is something Giraldi does not seem to take into consideration. This is the last effect of a long intellectual itinerary and of what was already inscribed in the various tragedy poetics since the 'Orti Oricellari' time. The union of brother and sister, the union of the twins, as it may seem, is the political mark of subversion according to the lines of *le libertinage érudit*. Endogamy, the brother and sister nuptials, is the symbol of the unions of the true *aristoi*, the best ones, mankind's natural aristocracy, the handsomest, the most beautiful, the purest. Their nuptials bring to unity again the two halves of the Platonic androgynous being (*Symposion*), thus subverting both the Gods' and men's power, subverting the father's law. What always and openly seems to be in discussion in Elizabethan-Jacobean-Caroline tragedy, is a bitter reflexion on time, power, violence, and a kind of hyperbole of horror in the contemplation of power. At so many years of distance, this Senecan trait can be seen in continuity with the Florentine tragedians of 'Orti oricellari', and also with both the theory and praxis of tragedy in Giraldi's *Orbecche*, and, of course, all differences told, with Sperone Speroni's vision. Be that as it may, for aught we can see, in spite of all differences in poetics and theory (the English non-compliance with Aristotelian unities, the speech-register's mix, confusing the language of the low and comedy, with the language of the high and tragedy), the Senecan hyperbolic *horribile visu* both in Italian 'regular' drama, and in English irregular theatrical practice shapes, 'performs' the scandal of *adikia* (injustice and wrong-doing) as the very method of tyrannical power and the source of any horror, being as it were, the very source of the law. Thus the violation of the Father's law, the worst *nefas*, incest, neither in Speroni, nor in Ford, cannot be marked by any sense of guilt but only by the sense of interdiction determined by power together with its implicit tragic and nullifying outcomes, even though tragedy must be written, staged, acted in the hope of a renewal of the world.

Notes

1 See St. Augustine's *Confessions*, liber III. The Latin text has been edited by James J. Donnell (Oxford: Oxford University Press, 1992); see also the 1631 English translation by William Watts, *St. Augustine's Confessions* (London: William Heinemann; New York: Macmillan, 1912); Tertullian's *Apology* and *The Spectaculis*, with an English translation by T. R. Glover (London: Heinemann; New York: Putnam, 1931).

2 See Monique Mund-Dopchie, *La survie d'Aeschyle à la Renaissance* (Louvain, Belgium: Peeters, 1985).

3 Napoli, Mattia Moravo, 1475.

4 See Maria Laura Lippi, "Evangelista Fossa: note biografiche e problemi attributivi", *Lettere italiane*, XXXIV (gennaio-marzo 1982): 55–73.

5 Stefano Giazzon, "L'Ecerinis di R. Mussato", in *Quaderni del circolo filologico-linguistico padovano*, n. 22, eds. Gianfelice Peron and Alvise Adreose (Padua: Esedra, 2011), pp. 189–201; See also Giazzon's introduction to his doctoral dissertation, *Lodovico Dolce tragediografo, tra riscrittura dell'antico e traduzione* (doctoral dissertation, University of Padua, 2008).

6 On Italian Renaissance Tragedy, see the first chapter of Giazzon's doctoral dissertation on Dolce (cit.), and also *Venezia in Coturno, Lodovico Dolce tragediografo* (Rome: Aracne, 2011). On Dolce see also Giazzon, "Giocasta di Lodovico Dolce: note su una riscrittura euripidea", *Croniques Italiennes*, XX, 2011. See also Marco Ariani's important book, *Tra Classicismo e manierismo. Il teatro tragico del Cinquecento* (Florence: Holschki, 1974), and, Idem. ed. *Il teatro italiano, parte II. La tragedia del Cinquecento*, Tomo I (Turin: Einaudi, 1977).

7 On the theoretical side of the growth of tragedy in Italian Renaissance, see Ettore Bonora, "La teoria del teatro negli scrittori del '500'", in *Il teatro classico italiano nel '500'* (Rome: Accademia dei Lincei, 1971), pp. 221–51.

8 Paola Mastrocola, *Nimica Fortuna. Edipo e Antigone nella tragedia italiana del Cinquecento* (Rome: Accademia dei Lincei, 1971 and Turin: Tirrenia, 1996) and *L'idea del tragico. Teorie della tragedia nel Cinquecento* (Catanzaro: Rubbettino, 1998).

9 Corinne Lucas, *De l'Horreur au 'lieto fine'. Le contrôle du discours tragique dans le théâtre de Giraldi Cinzio* (Rome: Bonnacci, 1984).

10 On Lodovico Dolce as translator, see Giazzon's doctoral dissertation, cit., p. 211 and fll; see also *Venezia in Coturno*, cit. p. 13 and fll.

11 On Giraldi Cinthio's critical theory and poetics, see Camillo Guerrieri-Crocetti, *G.B. Giraldi e il pensiero critico del XVI sec.* (Milan, Genoa, Naples, Rome: Società anonima editrice Dante Alighieri, 1932); on Giraldi's tragic production, see P. R. Horne, *The Tragedies of Giambattista Giraldi Cinthio* (Oxford: Oxford University Press, 1962); Luigi Donadoni, "L'influence de Sénèque sur les tragédies de Giambattista Giraldi", in *Les Tragédies de Sénèque et le théâtre de la Renaissance*, ed. Jean Jaquot (Paris: Editions du Centre National de la Recherche Scientifique, 1964); Corinne Lucas, *De l'Horreur au 'lieto fine'. Le contrôle du discours tragique*

dans le théâtre de Giraldi Cinzio (Rome: Bonnacci, 1984); Mariangela Tempera, "'Horror … is the sinews of the fable'. Giraldi Cinthio's Works and Elizabethan Tragedy", *Actes des congrès de la Société Française Shakespeare (Shakespeare et l'Europe de la Renaissance)*, 22 (Open edition, 2005); Paolo Cherchi, Micaela Rinaldi and Mariangela Tempera eds. *Giovan Battista Giraldi Cinzio gentiluomo ferrarese* (Florence: Olshki, 2008).

12 See John Cunliffe, *Influence of Seneca on Elizabethan Tragedy* (London: Macmillan, 1893); Madeleine Doran, "History and Tragedy: Italianate Tragedy of Intrigue", in *Endeavours of Art: A Study of Form in Elizabethan Drama* (Madison: The University of Wisconsin Press, 1954); Robert S. Miola, *Shakespeare and Classical Tragedy. The Influence of Seneca* (Oxford: Oxford University Press, 1992); see also Barbara A. Mowat and Paul Werstine's edition of Shakespeare's *Titus Andronicus*, as a sort of paradigm of Senecan revenge tragedies in England.

13 Thomas Newton, *Seneca His Tenne Tragedies* (1581), with an introduction by T. S. Eliot (Bloomington: Indiana University Press, 1964, reprint of the 1927 edition).

14 See Rudolf Fischer, *Zur Kunstentwicklung der englischen Tragödie* (Strassburg: Trübner, 1893); Cunliffe, cit.; Evelyn Mary Spearing, *The Elizabethan Translations of Seneca's Tragedies* (Cambridge: W. Hefner & Sons, 1912); George Williamson, *The Senecan Amble* (Chicago, IL: University of Chicago Press, 1951); Anthony James Boyle, *Tragic Seneca: An Essay in the Theatrical Tradition* (New York: Routledge, 1997).

15 Aristotle's *Perì Poetikê* was known and read in Hermannus Alemannus' 1256 Latin translation from an Arabic version.

16 Princeton, NJ: Hudson, 1935.

17 See Irby B. Cauthen, ed. "Thomas Sackville & Thomas Norton", *Gorboduc, or Ferrex and Porrex* (London: Edward Arnold, 1970); William Tydeman, *Two Tudor Tragedies* (Harmondsworth, UK: Penguin, 1992); on Sackville and Norton's tragedy see Mary Axton, *The Queen's Two Bodies* (London: Royal Historical Society, 1977); Paul Becquet, "L'influence de Sénèque sur *Gorboduc*", *Etudes Anglaises*, 14 (1961) and "L'imitation de Sénèque dans *Gorboduc*", in J. Jaquot and M. Oddon, *Les Tragédies de Shakespeare et le theatre de la Renaissance* (Paris, 1964); M. T. Herrick, "Senecan Influence in *Gorboduc*", in *Studies in Speech and Drama in Honor of A. M. Drummond*, eds. H. A. Wilhelms, C. B. Donalds, Bernard Hewitt and Karl A. Wallace (Ithaca, NY: Cornell University Press, 1944); B. H. C. De Mendonça, "The Influence of Gorboduc in 'King Lear'", *Shakespeare Survey*, 13 (1960).

18 Alice Hunt, "Dumb Politics in *Gorboduc*", in *The Oxford Handbook of Tudor Drama*, eds. Thomas Betteridge and Greg Walker (Oxford: Oxford University Press, 2012), pp. 538–65.

19 B. H. C. De Mendonça, "The Influence of *Gorboduc* in *King Lear*", *Shakespeare Survey*.

20 Michael Winkelman, *Marriage Relationships in Tudor Political Drama* (Farnham, UK: Ashgate, 2005).

21 Thomas Hughes, *The Misfortunes of Arthur: A Critical, Old-Spelling Edition*, ed. Brian Jay Corrigan (New York: Garland, 1992); William Ingram, "The Real Misfortunes of Arthur; or, Not Making It on the Elizabethan Stage", *Medieval and Renaissance Drama in England* 16 (2003): 32–8.

22 Philip Henslowe, *Henslowe's Diary*, edited with supplementary material, introduction, and notes by R. A. Foakes and R. T. Rickert (Cambridge: Cambridge University Press, 1961). On Seneca's influence on Marlowe, see T. S. Eliot, "Senecan Elizabethan Translations", *Selected Essays* (London: Faber & Faber, 1932); F. Kiefer, *Seneca's Influence on Elizabethan Tragedy. An Annotated Bibliography* (Farnham, UK: Ashgate, 2005).

23 See Brian Vickers, "Identifying Shakespeare's Additions in *The Spanish Tragedy* (1602), a Newer Approach", *Shakespeare Survey*, 8 (2012), pp. 13–43; Douglas Bruster, "Shakespearean Spellings and Handwriting in the Additional Passages Printed in the 1602 'Spanish Tragedy'", *Notes and Queries*, 60 (2013): 420–24.

24 Eleanor Prosser, "Revenge on the English Stage 1562–1607", in *Hamlet and Revenge* (Stanford, CA: Stanford University Press, 1967), pp. 36–73; J. R. Mulryne, ed. Thomas Kyd, *The Spanish Tragedy* (London: The New Mermaid Press, 1970); Charles A. Hallet and Elaine S. Hallet, *The Revenger's Madness: A Study of Revenge Tragedy Motifs* (Lincoln: University of Nebraska Press, 1980); Lucas Erne, *Beyond the Spanish Tragedy: A Study of the Works of Thomas Kyd* (Manchester, UK: Manchester University Press, 2009).

25 On *Ate* as the Goddess of discord, see Eric R. Dodds, *The Greeks and the Irrational* (Berkeley: University of California Press, 1951).

26 On the history of the attribution to Middleton, see Gary Taylor and John Lavagnino, eds. *Thomas Middleton and Early Modern Textual Culture* (Oxford: Oxford University Press, 2007).

27 See Katherine Rowe, "Memory and Revision in Chapman's Bussy Plays", in *Renaissance Drama*, 31 (2002): 125–26; John E. Cuman, *Character and the Individual Personality in English Renaissance Drama* (London: Rowman and Littlefield, 2014).

28 David Nicol, *Middleton and Rowley: Forms of Collaboration in the Jacobean Playhouse* (Toronto: University of Toronto Press, 2012); Gordon McMullan, "The Changeling and the Dynamics of Ugliness", in *The Cambridge Companion to English Renaissance Tragedy*, eds. Emma Smith and Garrett A. Sullivan (Cambridge: Cambridge University Press, 2010), pp. 222–35; A. A. Bromham and Z. Bruzzi, *'The Changeling' and the Years of Crisis: 1619–1624: A Hieroglyph of Britain* (London and New York: Pinter, 1990).

29 See Karen Zyck Galbraith, "Tracing a Villain. Typological Intertextuality in the Works of Painter, Webster, Cinthio, and Shakespeare", in *Shakespeare and the Italian Renaissance. Appropriation, Transformation, Opposition*, ed. Michele Marrapodi (Farnham, UK: Ashgate, 2014), pp. 107–19. On Webster's Duchess, see Leah Marcus's introduction to her edition of *The Duchess of Malfi* (London: Macmillan, 2009).

30 See Andrew Hiscock, *Women Beware Women. A Critical Guide* (London: Continuum Publishing Group, 2011); Swapan Chakrawotry, *Society and Politics in the Plays of Thomas Middleton* (Oxford: Clarendon Press, 1996).

31 A. A. Bromham, "The Tragedy of Peace. Political Meaning in *Women Beware Women*", *Studies in English Literature*, 26, 2 (Spring, 1986).

32 On incest in English drama, see Lois E. Bueler, "The Structural Uses of Incest in English Renaissance Drama", *Renaissance Drama*, 15 (1984): 115–45; Richard A. MacCabe, *Incest, Drama, and Nature's Law 1550–1700* (Cambridge: Cambridge University Press, 1993); Luis Martines Zenón, *In Words and Deeds. The Spectacle of Incest in English Renaissance Drama* (Amsterdam and New York: Rodopi, 2002).

33 These lines are imprinted on a certain number of copies of the first edition (London: Nicholas Oakes, 1633) of *'Tis Pity*. More recent editions of Ford's tragedy were edited by Simon Parker (Oxford: Routledge, 1997) and Martin Wiggins (London: A & C. Black, 2003).

6 Masters of civility

Castiglione's *Courtier*, della Casa's *Galateo*, and Guazzo's *Civil Conversation* in early modern England

Cathy Shrank

> *Castilio* primas; *Casa* vendicet ipse secundas;
> Tertia pars *Guatii* est: quarto futura mea est.
>
> (Let Castiglione claim the first place; Casa the second;
> The third place is Guazzo's; the fourth is about to be mine.)[1]

Gabriel Harvey's confident, if erroneous, prediction of the impact of his digest of the qualities required by the courtier and the court lady, made in a volume of Latin poetry prepared for Elizabeth I's visit to Audley End in 1578, speaks to the high profile that Baldassare Castiglione's *Cortegiano* (1528), Giovanni della Casa's *Galateo* (1558), and Stefano Guazzo's *Civil Conversazione* (1574) enjoyed amongst courtly and educated circles in early modern England. These books quickly established an English readership. We know, for example, that within a year of its first publication, Henry VIII's chief minister, Thomas Cromwell, possessed a copy of the Italian text of Castiglione's *Courtier*, as the then diplomat Edmund Bonner requested a loan of it in 1529, along with the "triumphes of petrache", in order that he might live up to Cromwell's desire to "make [him] a good ytalion" in advance of embassies to Bologna and Rome.[2]

Tracing the influence of works is methodologically challenging: to restrict the evidence to moments at which they are alluded to by name risks producing an incomplete and superficial account; conversely, taking a more open view, and looking for echoes and analogies, threatens to distort the picture by constructing direct connections where authors might merely be responding independently to the current concerns and affairs. In the words of Virginia Cox:

> [b]y the time Shakespeare was writing, the ideas of courtesy articulated in *The Courtier* and in subsequent Italian courtesy books like Giovanni della Casa's *Galateo* … and Stefano Guazzo's *Civil Conversation* … had become so profoundly assimilated within English polite society that an attempt to trace their influence would be as complex and ultimately frustrating a process as attempting to trace the influence of Hollywood on modern European manners and culture.[3]

All publications pre-1700 are printed in London, unless otherwise stated. Quotations are in old spelling and punctuation, with u/v and i/j standardised. Since this chapter looks at their reception in early modern England, *the Courtier, Galateo,* and *Civil Conversation* are cited in their sixteenth- and seventeenth-century English translations.

DOI: 10.4324/9781315612720-8

The impact of these books (like Hollywood culture) was far-reaching, even judging – at the most simplistic level – from the amount of times they are cited by subsequent authors.[4] In-depth studies, such as Daniel Javitch's on the *Courtier* or John Lievsay's on Guazzo's *Civil Conversation*, have further uncovered the use and influence of these works in (respectively) Elizabethan court poetry and in texts and genres as diverse as Euphuistic romance and Joseph Swetnam's *Araignment of Lewde, Idle, Froward, and Unconstant Women* (1615).[5] For Anna Bryson, however, "more important than such direct literary influence is the fact that the concept of 'civil conversation' had become well-established within the English phraseology of conduct by the early seventeenth century".[6] The take-up of the phrase in the wake of its first English translation can be sketched through the Early English Books Online-Text Creation Partnership (which currently covers *circa* 34% of that database): prior to the 1581 translation, the phrase had appeared a mere eleven times in six different items, over almost a century of English print; in the subsequent decade (excluding the translation itself), it appeared fifteen times in five records, with momentum increasing in 1590–9 (sixteen hits in thirteen records) and 1600–9 (fifty-five hits in thirty-two records). The significance of the phrase as an expected marker of conduct literature by the mid-seventeenth century is further demonstrated, qualitatively, by a later English translation of della Casa's *Galateo*, which presents itself, on its internal-title page, as "A Correction of several Indecencies crept into Civil Conversation".[7]

The popularity of these works was also sustained, even after new editions had ceased being printed in England. These titles regularly appear, in various languages, in the printed library catalogues of late seventeenth-century dignitaries.[8] A reminder that early modern books had a long shelf-life, well beyond their date of publication, is also provided by the appearance of "Baldestard's *Courtier*" 'in 3. Languages', an edition printed once, in 1588, alongside Guazzo's *Civil Conversation* (last English edition, 1586), in the book-seller Thomas Rookes' list of those works which had survived the fire of London in 1666 and were still available to purchase from his shop in Gresham College.[9]

As those printed book catalogues attest, English readers had access to a variety of editions, and in languages other than the Italian original. Thomas Hoby's 1561 translation of the *Courtier* – with three subsequent editions in 1577, 1588 (the trilingual version), and 1603 – was easily outstripped by Bartholomew Clerke's Latin translation of 1571, which went through at least five further editions, in 1577, 1585, 1593, 1603, and 1612. Guazzo's *Civil Conversation*, Englished by George Pettie, was printed in 1581 and 1586, and Book III (on domestic conduct) was later redacted for, or by, the printer William Barley in 1607 as *The Court of Good Counsel*. Robert Peterson's English 1576 translation of *Galateo* initially seems less than successful: the publisher, Ralph Newberry, was clearly left with excess copies, since the work was repackaged – from the same stock – in 1578, when it was sold, ready bound with Walter Darell's *Short Discourse of the Life of Servingmen*. That Peterson's translation had not been an immediate hit is further suggested by the fact that it is not trumpeted on the title-page of that volume, where its presence – described in the most generic of terms – appears as a supplement, rather than the main attraction: 'Hereunto is also annexed a treatise, concerning manners and behaviours'. Nonetheless, *Galateo* was read avidly, in some form, in sixteenth-century England, as Harvey indicates in the epigraph to this chapter, and in his complaints in 1581 to his friend and collaborator Edmund Spenser that the "*Latine* and *Greeke*" are neglected in favour of Italian books, della Casa's manual amongst them: "But I beseech you, what Newes al this while at Cambridge?" he asks rhetorically:

> *Tully*, and *Demosthenes* nothing so much studied, as they were wonted … *Match-iavell* a great man: *Castilio* of no small reputation: *Petrarch*, and *Boccace* in every mans mouth: *Galateo* and *Guazzo* never so happy: over many acquainted with Unico Aretino.[10]

Moreover, over the course of the seventeenth century, *Galateo* saw more versions printed in England than either the *Courtier* or *Civil Conversation*: in addition to Peterson's translation, a Latin version, *Ethica iuvenilis*, by the German humanist Nathan Chytraeus, was printed in Oxford in 1628; *Galateo Espagnol or the Spanish Gallant*, translated by William Style from Lucas Gracián's Spanish version was issued in 1640; and Nathaniel Walker's translation, "or rather a *Paraphrase*", was printed as *The Refin'd Courtier* in 1663.[11]

The existence in England of multiple versions of these books – in Latin, in Italian and other vernaculars – indicates the polyglot nature of their readership. It is Clerke's translation, for example, not Hoby's, which Richard Burton cites, over twenty-five times, in his *Anatomy of Melancholy* in 1621, as an authority on topics from old age to music to love to women's tears. There is also an odd moment in Samuel Daniel's translation of Paolo Giovio's *Dialogo dell'imprese* (1585), where Daniel seems to elevate Clerke's Latin over Castiglione's original: "I pray you Syr, shal *Castilio* be more reverenced for his courtier, then *D[r] Clarke* admired for investing him with so courtlie robes?" he asks; "shall *Menander* be eternized for his *Comedies*, and *Terence* forgot who gave them credit [?]".[12] Nor was it simply ambitious scholars such as Harvey – described by Peter Burke as being "virtually obsessed by the *Courtier*" – who consumed these works in multiple languages (Harvey owned and annotated English and Italian versions of *Civil Conversation*, and English, Italian, and Latin copies of the *Courtier*).[13] Pettie consulted both Guazzo's Italian and a 1579 French translation by Gabriel Chappuys (who also translated *The Courtier*) when producing his version, and the printed library lists show that multiple copies, in different languages and formats (from large folios to immensely portable duodecimos), habitually graced the shelves of men such as the courtier Kenelm Digby or the clergymen Anthony and Samuel Scattergood.[14]

Besides testifying to the popularity of the *Courtier, Galateo*, and *Civil Conversation*, Harvey's references to these works in his *Gratulationum* and the letter to Spenser (cited above) show the way in which they are recurrently yoked together, then as now. As John Lievsay notes of modern scholarship, "among those English and American writers who have anything to say on the subject of courtesy-books and conduct-literature in England, it has been customary to name [these] three books of especial importance".[15] Yet, in many ways this correlation belies some very real dissimilarities between these works, not least who and what are framed as the over-arching topic and primary addressees. Castiglione's subject is "courtiership": the practice of being a courtier, and a concept for which he – like his translator Hoby – was required to coin a new word ("cortegianía"). His interlocutors are all courtiers, and the conversation takes place in a very constrained setting: in one room of a palace that is presented as a self-sufficient, self-sustaining environment, "so furnished … with everye necessary implement … that it appeared not a palaice, but a Citye in fourme of a palaice".[16] The conversation recorded in the dialogue only begins once they have entered the room, and ceases as they "pass ... out at the great chamber door".[17] As Thomas M. Greene notes, "this sense of enclosure is very strong, and this sense is only heightened by that magical and unexpected moment at the end when a window is opened".[18]

Guazzo and della Casa, in contrast, have a more extensive remit. Like Castiglione's dialogue, Guazzo's is conducted between members of an educated elite (the author's brother and the physician, Annibale Magnocavalli) and takes place in a secluded location: the author's closet, "where I use to have a fewe small books".[19] However, despite a similarly constricted setting to the *Courtier*, Guazzo's dialogue is nonetheless more wide-ranging in terms of the types of interactions and interlocutors that it imagines, in both the domestic and public spheres; as Pettie's title-page (closely modelled on the Italian) announces, the book that follows touches on:

> [t]he manner of conversation, meete for *all* persons, which shall come in *any* companie, out of their owne houses, and then of the particular points which ought to be observed in companie betweene young men and olde, Gentlemen and Yeomen, Princes and private persons, learned and unlearned, Citizens and Strangers, Religious and Secular, men & women ... [and] the orders to be observed in conversation within doores, betweene the husband and the wife, the father and the sonne, brother and brother, the Maister and the servant.
>
> (emphasis added)

In Lievsay's words, "Guazzo envisages civic man in his total relationships".[20] This potentially more quotidian ambience – quite unlike the rarefied atmosphere of Castiglione's palace in Urbino – is reflected in Guazzo's tendency to deploy mercantile imagery, be it the frequent analogy drawn between language and money in the second book, or the use of a human propensity for commerce – "keeping a continuall mercate" – as evidence of their innate love of "conversation" (by which Guazzo means not simply verbal discourse, but interaction more generally).[21] Nor are "buying and selling" framed as manifestations of greed, but are presented positively, as "fit to heale the diseases of povertie, and to get the health of riches". Certainly the book's potential appeal to a mercantile – rather than a courtly – audience is accentuated by the redaction of its third book as *The Court of Good Counsel.* Dedicated to the London alderman, Sir John Jolles, it omits sections from the original which deal with relations between masters and servants where the master is a great gentleman; conversations between princes and courtiers; and gentlemen marrying gentlewomen.[22] It also shows a tendency to tone down Pettie's "learned" words and allusions: "imperfections" are "faults", for example, and the disparity of a "Satyre" appearing among "nymphs" becomes "a Kitchenstuff-wench amongst courtly Ladyes".[23]

Interestingly, the adaptations of della Casa's *Galateo* work in the opposite direction to the "bourgeoisification" of the *Civil Conversation* in *The Court of Good Counsel.* The title-page of its first English translation dubs *Galateo* "a worke very necessary & profitable for all Gentlemen, *or other*" (emphasis added), and this appeal to a potentially less socially elite audience is stronger still in its 1578 repackaging, where – shorn of its dedicatory epistle to Robert Dudley, Earl of Leicester, its learned prefatory poems in Italian, Latin and English, and its address "To the Gentle Reader" (the epithet hinting at the social status of the reader it imagines addressing) –

Peterson's translation is bound up with a manual of advice for, and defence of, servingmen, a class of men "disdained, and had in small regarde amongst a number: yet doth … deserve to be had in high estimation for his worthinesse & calling".[24] Subsequent versions, however, angle for a markedly more elite readership. The title-page of *The Spanish Gallant* targets an audience comprising the "generous youth" and those "exercised in their gentile [i.e. gentle] Education", the primary sense of both adjectives indicating "high-" or "well-born".[25] This shift in prospective audience is further evident in the way that this version expands its scope from della Casa's focus on teaching its reader how to live "in fellowship with men, and in populous Cities" ("nelle città e tra gli uomini"), to advising on how to do so "in Cities *and Courts* amongst much People" (emphasis added).[26] The title of the 1663 translation, *The Refin'd Courtier*, only consolidates this redirection to a more socially elevated readership.

Of course, regardless of which particular social group these various editions are aimed at, all works which position themselves as providing advice on conduct rely on their readers' desire to differentiate themselves from their social inferiors, and propagate and preserve markers of social distinctions to allow them to do so. The authors, and translators, of the *Courtier, Galateo*, and *Civil Conversation* all assume an audience whose "Civilite differeth from the nature and fashions of the vulgar sorte" (as Guazzo's – or Peterson's – Annibal phrases it).[27] So, whilst there is some flexibility around the margins of who might comprise the "vulgar" and the "civil", there is – as Bryson warns us – "nothing in the courtesy literature of the sixteenth and seventeenth centuries" that "supports the notion that 'civility' represents a bourgeois standard of behaviour at odds with the previously established aristocratic ideals of 'courtesy'".[28] Despite the etymological roots of the word "civil", the term was not wedded to a "civic" or urban environment, which was incompatible with the "courtly" one that is semantically related to "courtesy"; rather, the two words and concepts were interchangeable, and Annibal quite unproblematically uses "courteous" as the antithesis of "uncivill".[29]

Galateo does, however, differ from the other two works in its focus on male readers. Written from the perspective of an old man (or – in *Galateo Espagnol* – an elder brother) addressing a younger, it is concerned with male behaviour alone. In contrast, the *Courtier* and *Civil Conversation* include extensive discussions of female behaviour, in their third books (a section enthusiastically underlined, and occasionally annotated, by one anonymous owner of a 1586 edition of the *Civil Conversation*, who was clearly interested in advice about marriage).[30] Once Guazzo's fourth book (strongly influenced by the *Courtier*) is included, both works also feature female interlocutors.[31] Admittedly, men do dominate the conversation in the *Courtier* (the division of speaking parts is more equitable in Guazzo's final book than in Castiglione's dialogue, not least because the company – four women to six men – is more gender-balanced). Nonetheless, significant roles are given to the two women who appear amongst Castiglione's "unusually large" cast of over twenty speakers: Elisabetta Gonzaga ("the Dutchesse") commands the company, whilst Emilia Pia chairs the discussion as her "deputy".[32] As Burke observes, "although neither woman intervenes very often or at great length in the dialogue, when they do so they are presented as effective in changing its course".[33] Guazzo similarly gives authority to a woman, when "Ladie Jane" is "elected Queene" for the evening.[34] However, the women only hold sway in these dialogues because men have relegated those roles: Elisabetta's husband is absent, because he has retired to bed through ill health;

Guazzo's Lord Vespasian – the person of highest social status there present – deliberately sets aside his titles and asks the other guests to "imagine" him "a private man, like anie other".[35] The contingent nature of these women's authority is thus a reminder of the usual patriarchal hierarchies, even as the company temporarily sets those aside.

There are also crucial differences in form between the three texts. As indicated above, *Galateo* is addressed from an older to a younger man. As such, it is monovocal, prescribing a list of things to do, or avoid, if you want to be considered "civil". The *Courtier* and *Civil Conversation* are, in contrast, dialogues: works written in the form of a purported conversation, in which ideas are not merely propounded, but are also debated. These texts thus have an additional complexity: they do not merely tell their readers what constitutes "civil" or "courteous" behaviour (as does *Galateo*); they also demonstrate it, in the polite interactions between interlocutors and the deft management of points of disagreement. Cox also convincingly argues that dialogue is useful way of maintaining "one's reputation for *sprezzatura*", and of avoiding breaching social decorum by "hog[ging] the conversation", since it effaces the "industry and ambition … involved in the production of a literary work".[36] Unlike a treatise, that is, a dialogue does not thrust its author's opinions upon its reader, or present them as inconvertible, but shows ideas being tested and defended, and – almost always – voiced by others, as in the *Courtier* and *Civil Conversation*, where the authors of the texts are depicted as mere rapporteurs, absent from the conversations that they record.

But even here, there are distinctions between Castiglione's and Guazzo's use of the dialogue form. The discussion in Guazzo's dialogue moves in an "ordered" way which is ultimately "incompatible with a plausible representation of informal speech".[37] One of the speakers – Annibal – is also clearly authoritative; the role of his interlocutor – William Guazzo (the author's older brother) – is, in the main, to endorse what Annibal has said, or to show himself persuaded by reasoned argument. As readers, it is always obvious what stance we are expected to approve, and when revising Book III to produce *The Court of Good Counsel*, its adapter accomplishes much of the task by simply removing William Guazzo's interjections, allowing Annibal's contributions to stand as uncontested truth. Castiglione's *Courtier* is, in contrast, "a profoundly equivocal work", which conceals its undoubted order and logic within a text which is constructed to resemble the digressive and free-flowing nature of actual conversation, and in which "multiple viewpoints" are put forward, "without advancing any one as definitive".[38] The one time that Castiglione's own views do seem to come, uncharacteristically, to the fore is in the section on the *questione della lingua*, where the views expressed by Lodovico da Canossa (Hoby's "Count Lewis") – that courtiers should not be constrained to follow the "auntient Tuscane tongue", but ought to choose words "out of every parte of Italye" and "in use also among the people" – can be measured against Castiglione's defence of his own diction in his dedicatory epistle, as well as his actual practice in composing the work.[39] Such a close alignment between Castiglione and his speakers is not always so evident or demonstrable, however.

As we have seen – despite these obvious differences of form, and the more subtle and shifting variations in the nature of the topic and audience addressed – the *Courtier, Civil Conversation*, and *Galateo* were nevertheless perceived by many readers, then and now, as addressing a similar topic: namely, civility/courtesy. Indeed, it is clear that Guazzo at least (as the author of last of the three works) wrote in full awareness of these predecessors and in dialogue with them, and that he assumed that his readers would be *au fait* with them as well. Annibal uses della Casa's book as a convenient shorthand, endorsing and expanding on his opinions, as he wraps up a brief excursus on rules of deportment: "I will not, I say, speake of these things", he insists, "for I should but make a recital of Galatee".[40] Whilst Castiglione is not referenced by name, his discussion of *sprezzatura* is undoubtedly alluded to in Annibal's observation that William Guazzo has:

> [s]warved nothing at all in this discourse from the dutie of a perfect Courtier, whose propertie is to do all things with carefull diligence, and skilfull art: mary yet so the art is hidden, and the whole seemeth to be doone by chance.[41]

Annibal's omission of Castiglione's name at this juncture is, moreover, a manifestation of the very behaviour that he is currently commending in Guazzo, as he praises him for refusing to flaunt his learning by name-dropping at every opportunity, unlike those "having always in their mouth the name, assone of some Philosopher, assone of some Poet, assone of some Orator".

Not only were these three texts yoked together by early readers, they were also regarded as providing practical advice on how "civil" and "courteous" people might set themselves apart from, and above, others ("the vulgar"). Castiglione's work is the most elusive of the three, as critics regularly acknowledge. Castiglione even declares in his opening address to Alfonso Ariosto that he has not produced a handy checklist "the whiche for the moste part is wont to be observed in the teaching of anye thinge": "in 'facion[ing]' his courtier, he insists, he does not "follow any certaine order or rule of appointed precepts".[42] Yet despite the dialogic nature of the book and the ambiguity of the messages that it endorses, Castiglione's work is recurrently depicted as laying out the model of a "perfect" courtier, "as *Tully* [Cicero] faineth his Orator to be, or *Castilio* his Courtier"; as "Tully drawes his Orator, Zenophon his Cyrus, Castilio his Courtier, Galen his just Temperament … Aristotle his *Quadratus*".[43] Holding up the *Courtier* as a template for courtiership – a move which becomes almost commonplace, particularly in tandem with Cicero's orator – is not in itself evidence of a reductive reading of Castiglione's text. Indeed, the conjunction with Cicero could even indicate a thorough appreciation of how Castiglione's dialogue works, as – like Cicero's *Tusculan Disputations* (the influence of which Castiglione acknowledges) – it has its speakers demonstrate the skills that the ideal practitioner requires, rather than enumerating and describing them.[44] Hence we see Castiglione's interlocutors practising their art, moderating their behaviour, preserving the social occasion by tempering serious talk with laughter (and here Greene draws attention to Castiglione's recurrent use of the participle *ridendo* to defuse moments of tension).[45] When encountering a text like the *Courtier*, "abounding in theses and antitheses, but lacking syntheses", any synthesis that is achieved "comes in reading, in the reader's full engagement with the dialectic of the dialogue".[46] The reader learns how to be civil, not by following a check-list, but by observing and experiencing the social interaction.

Nevertheless, there is a distinct tendency amongst both early readers (and twentieth- and twenty-first-century critics) to slip into citing Castiglione as an authority, as if the views that his characters articulate are unproblematically and unambiguously his own:

> Tis an inbred malady in every one of us, there is *seminarium stultitiae*, a seminary of folly, *which if it be stirred up or get an head will run* in infinitum, *and infinitely varies, as wee ourselves are severally addicted*, saith *Balthazar Castilio*,

notes Burton, for example, quoting Cesare Gonzaga's opinions as those of the author himself.[47] Elsewhere we find Canossa's views on courtiership, expressed early in Book I, being propounded as if they were Castiglione's final word on the topic: "the Earle *Balthazar Castilio* in his booke of the Courtier, doth ... specially advise that he should bee skillfull in the knowing of Honor, and causes of quarrel", insists Richard Jones in 1590, appropriating Castiglione as an authority to endorse his own decision to publish a volume about knightly honour and physical combat.[48] Such readiness to equate a character's opinion with Castiglione's own is quite standard in the reception of his work.

The *Courtier*, then, as much as the other two volumes, was read as conveying a series of maxims regarding the type of behaviour which would smooth one's way in society: what della Casa's old man promotes as "a helpe & advancement unto them, that have gotten great perferments", or, in Annibal's words, the means by which "the favour and good will of others [are] obtained".[49] And here the advice conveyed by the speakers of all three texts displays three shared trends. First, the "civil" being is self-contained and self-regulating: they constantly moderate their own behaviour, be it restraining their bodily fluids, overly-exuberant gestures and appetites, or their speech and opinions; as Annibal notes, "no man" should "take al the talke to himself, a thing very unseemely, for al ought to bee partakers aswell of the talke, as they are of the wine".[50] Secondly, the "civil" being should be acutely conscious of how they appear to others: what the historian of manners Anna Bryson (amongst others) calls "representation".[51] Hence the reader of *Galateo*, on returning from relieving himself, is instructed not "so much as [to] washe his hands in sight of honest company: for that the cause of his washing, puts them in minde of some filthy matter that hath bene done aparte".[52] How you portray yourself is paramount. That last piece of advice also highlights the third principle of "civil" behaviour expressed in all three texts: namely, the need for "accommodation" (a term also used by Bryson, amongst others), that is being aware of, and shaping yourself in response to, "the sensitivities and sensibilities of others".[53] The principles of courtly behaviour espoused, and demonstrated, in *The Courtier* – including Castiglione's famous coinage *sprezzatura* ("a certain Reckelesness, to cover art withal") – might be "highly refined and aesthetically loaded", but they are nonetheless "versions of the principles of 'representation' and 'accommodation'" found in the manuals of della Casa and others, and are similarly designed to present a social self that simultaneously displays the courtier's talents and avoids unsettling the company with "affectation" or obvious shows of ambition.[54]

The *Courtier* is a complex and evasive a work; its reduction to the function of a handbook owes much to the role of paratext in shaping its reception. Like Peterson's *Galateo* (deemed "necessary & profitable"), Hoby's translation is sold to its readers on its title-page as being "Very necessary and profitable for yonge Gentilmen and Gentilwomen abiding in Court, Palaice or Place", a statement repeated on all subsequent English editions. Hoby himself presents the work in his dedicatory epistle as a "rule" to be followed in different ways by different degrees of people, and the speed with which readers could extract such profit is further facilitated by the addition of two checklists, rehearsing "The chiefe conditions and qualities in a [male] courtier" and "in a waytyng gentylwoman".[55] The printed marginalia acts as an additional finding aid, allowing the reader to navigate the work more quickly and, if desired, to mine the text for soundbites and instruction without entering into the ebb and flow of argument and counter-argument. The reader of *Galateo* is similarly helped by printed marginalia and by the use of Roman type to distinguish pithy, summative sayings (as well as quotations) from the black letter in which the text is predominantly printed. Its subsequent manifestations – as *The Spanish Gallant* and *The Refin'd Courtier* – maintain this attention to the ease with which readers can locate relevant advice, providing section or chapter headings. *The Spanish Gallant* also enumerates the paragraphs within each chapter (each of which effectively doles out another nugget of counsel), whilst *The Refin'd Courtier* introduces a contents page: again, both are effective navigational aids. Lacking printed marginalia, a contents page (aside from its descriptive title-page, quoted above), and chapter headings, the English editions of the *Civile Conversation* prove less accommodating. In a work of such length (almost 400 pages, even in the three-book edition of 1581), it is thus harder for readers to extract its lessons quite so readily, and it is striking that the redacted version, "set forth as a patterne, for all people to learn wit by", remedies this, by providing both a table of contents and chapter headings.

That these English translations hold up Italy as a "patterne" to follow is indicative of the ways in which Italy was acknowledged as a font of culture during this period: it was the site of the Roman empire that all early modern schoolboys were brought up to admire, and it was seen to have led the way in terms of refining its language and developing a sophisticated vernacular literary culture, commended by William Thomas in 1550 for the "diligence" with which the Italians had tended and improved their native tongue.[56] That the works of Castiglione and Guazzo in particular were felt by contemporaries to represent standards of vernacular language which could and should be emulated is evidenced by the way in which these dialogues seem to have been recurrently used in language teaching. John Florio writes in 1591 of the English learning Italian from "Castilions courtier, or Guazzo his dialogues", and the 1588 edition of the *Courtier*, produced by John Wolfe, prints the work as a trilingual parallel text, in Italian, English (Hoby's translation), and French (Chappuys' translation). We also find Guazzo's *Civil Conversation* set alongside other "good books" (including "classic" authors such as Boccaccio) judged suitable for teaching elegant Italian.[57]

The link between language and manners is a strong one in these texts, and both Hoby's and Pettie's paratextual material pick up on the Italian debates about the direction that the vernacular should take (*la questione della lingua*) which are raised in the works they translated. The English translations consequently reflect self-consciously on matters such as the choice of diction, be it through the letter that Hoby elicits from John Cheke (championing an English tongue "written cleane and pure, unmixt and unmangeled with borrowing of other tunges") or Pettie's prefatory defence of such loan words, particularly the Latinate ones that Cheke sought to purge. As Pettie points out, if Latinate words are "Inkehorne terme[s]", "I know not how we should speake any thing without blacking our mouthes with inke: for what word can be more plaine then this word *plaine*, & yet what can come more near to the Latine?".[58] The act of translation thus provokes thought about the nature of the English language, particularly as the Italian originals are working through, and raising, similar questions.

The translators of all three of the texts discussed in this chapter depict these works as capable of teaching something valuable to their native land. Peterson explains that, since *Galateo* has been "drawn for the profit therof, in to so many languages: I thought his lessons fit for our store".[59] Hoby represents his *Courtier* as part of a wider translation project designed to increase the learning available in English, "that we alone of the worlde maye not be styll counted barbarous in oure tunge, as in time out of minde we have bene in our maners".[60] There is, of course, some irony in the fact that the Italian originals are occupied in debating and (for della Casa at least) codifying civility at a time when contemporary Italians would have regarded their culture as being in decline, as – from the early sixteenth century – the Italian peninsula had become a battlefield for external political forces, its territories fought over by Spain and France in particular. "Lying in the direct route from France to the South", Casale Monferrato – where Annibal and William Guazzo sit, anatomising civil conversation – was situated in one of the areas "which had borne the brunt of constant pillage, occupation, and shuffling of powers".[61] Hints of these conflicts and invasions permeate even the self-contained court of Castiglione's Urbino, glimpsed in Canossa's ("Count Lewis") lament about the "small prowesse in armes" that "the Italians ... have shewed", or Fregosa's ("Sir Fridericke") comment that contemporary Italian fashions "have bene a pronosticate of bondage, the which (me thinke) now is plain ynough fulfilled".[62] That impression of a vanished perfection is also captured by Castiglione's decision to base the dialogue in the past. Even when he first put pen to paper, in 1513, the dialogue (set in 1507) evoked a community that was already fragmented: at least two of its interlocutors (Roberto da Bari, Cesare Gonzaga) were dead; by the time Castiglione finished the final draft (1527), those numbers had swelled still further, as Castiglione acknowledges in his dedicatory epistle to Miguel da Silva, where he alludes to his "grief ... remembringe that the greater part of them that are brought in to reason, are now dead".[63] Some of that nostalgia and regret is perhaps captured in Hoby's volume, both in his reference to an earlier translation being undertaken by an unnamed compatriot (possibly William Thomas) who was "prevented by death" from finishing it, and in the decision to include Cheke's letter about English diction, written "from [his] house in Woodstreete the 16 July, 1557", less than two months before he died and precisely two months to the day of his burial in that very same street.[64] The items with which Hoby surrounds the text thus educe a sense of lost potential as it commemorates other like-minded scholars who had sought to enrich their country's culture.

Despite the tendency to celebrate Italy as a model for both language and manners, English attitudes to Italy were deeply ambivalent, however. On the one hand, as we have seen, it was regarded as the epitome of cultured refinement. On the other hand, it was a land associated with the Church of Rome and all its perceived error and corruption, and its inhabitants were recurrently depicted as lecherous, untrustworthy, and skilled in murderous practices, be it the swift thrust of a thin stiletto, or ingenious methods of poison, stereotypes which were endorsed by the Galenic beliefs that underpinned early modern medical theory and which connected hot climates with the "hot bloodedness" of their inhabitants. The dichotomy between Italophilia and Italophobia is evident in Florio's language manuals, in which – even as he offers up weighty tomes dedicated to teaching the Italian tongue – he feels constrained to acknowledge some potential hostility on the part of his would-be readers. "Thou will urge me with their manners & vices", he notes, "(not remembring that where great vices are there are infinite vertues)".[65] These contradictory attitudes are epitomised by Roger Ascham, who can within the same volume recommend reading Castiglione's *Courtier* (a book to be "diligentilie followed"), commend "Italie and Rome" as having been "to the greate good of us that now live, the best breeders and bringers up of the worthiest men, not onelie for wise speakinge, but also for well doing, in all Civill affaires", and simulataneously condemn that country for its "corrupt maners and licenciousnes of life", likening it to Circe's court for its capacity to "turne men into beastes", and launching into a diatribe against English translations which are (like Hoby's) dedicated to persons of honour.[66] "These be the inchantementes of *Circes*", he writes:

> [b]rought out of *Italie*, to marre mens maners in England: much, by example of ill life, but more by preceptes of fonde bookes, of late translated out of *Italian* into English, sold in every shop in London, commended by honest titles the soner to corrupt honest maners: dedicated over boldlie to vertuous and honorable personages, the easielier to begile simple and innocent wittes.[67]

The types of beasts that Ascham delineates demonstrate the commonly held anxieties about what it might mean to become "an Italianate Englishman", proverbially deemed "the devil incarnate" ("un diabolo incarnate").[68] Of the animals that he lists – asses, foxes, swine, and wolves – it is the first two (representing foolishness and slyness) that pertain most closely to the faults associated with the kind of courtliness, or civility, that readers might find in the works discussed here, for – although Javitch pitches Guazzo's dialogue as an "anti-courtly" volume, critical of "dissimulation, ornamentation, and dilettantism" – as we have seen, the principles of "courtliness" and "civility" ran very close.[69] As Bryson observes, Guazzo's chief interlocutor Annibal "defends a degree of flattery and hypocrisy in 'civil' social intercourse".[70] The practice of accommodation ("when one is at Rome" one is advised "to live as they doe at Rome") and discretion (glossed in a challenging paradox as a "an honest kinde of deceite") threaten to prove incompatible with adhering to strict moral principles, as when Annibal – like Galateo's spokesperson – urges the civil man to hold his peace, even when someone "in companie … chaunce to utter any untrueth":

> [r]ather then to stande in contention with him … we ought modestlye to beare with it: Observing always the rule of Epictere, who sayd: that in companie wee must yeelde humbly too our Superiour, perswade gently with our inferior, and agree quietly with our equall. And by that meanes there shall never bee any falling out.[71]

(Compare the advice of *Galateo*: "*Leave to every man his parte: And bee it right or wronge, consent to the minds of the most, or the most importunate*: and so leave the fielde unto them").[72] Such advice, advocating accommodation, threatens to tip into the vice of hypocrisy, long associated with court living, as can be seen in the characters "Favell" (Flattery), Deceit, and Dissimulation in John Skelton's *Bowge of Courte*, first printed *c.* 1499.

The tendency found in early modern English literature and drama to depict courtiers – particularly Italianate ones – as vapid, effeminate, or dangerously duplicitous – cannot therefore be ascribed to the influence of sixteenth-century courtesy manuals alone. And here it should be noted that, in a political culture, such as that of early modern England, which valorised the idea of counsel and the role of the counsellor as the proper means of deciding policy, a courtier who was distracted by trifles and who was anxious to avoid rocking the boat posed as much risk to the commonweal as a conniving Machiavel. It is not just out-and-out villains who signal the corrupt court culture found in Shakespeare's *King Lear* or *Hamlet*: the vanity of stock characters such as Oswald or Osric play their part too. Moreover, the Italian conduct literature that early modern Europe consumed could stand accused of promoting both deviousness and vain display. Until the later twentieth century, it was customary in the secondary literature to contrast the "idealism" of the *Courtier* with the "realism" of Niccolò Machiavelli's *Prince*, which was circulating in manuscript from 1513, about the very time that Castiglione began drafting his dialogue.[73] However, as Eduardo Saccone and others have pointed out, Castiglione's courtier and Machiavelli's prince have much in common: the aim of both is survival, and both are acutely conscious of the power of self-representation.[74] Further to that, as Javitch notes, "the beautiful tactics necessary in court conduct were all too prone, in actual practice, to lapse into shallowness and fraud", or – in Ascham's terms – the asinine and the vulpine.[75] "A foxe like feate", one reader of Pettie's Guazzo writes in the margin, next to a passage illustrating the instrumentalist principle that "to winne favour, & happily to atchive our purposes, we must always have praysing and pleasing words in our mouth".[76] The following anecdote about della Casa is on one level an entertaining piece of gossip, with a distinctly anti-clerical tinge, well-suited to post-Reformation English humour (della Casa was archbishop of Benevento); on another level, it reveals civility to be nothing more than a mask. "The neglect of their pens hath ruined very many", observes Obadiah Walker:

> [a]nd particularly the great Master of Civility, the Author of *Galateo*. For going to present to the *Pope* a petition, by mistake he delivered a copy of licentious Verses writ by himself: whereby he lost the Popes favour, his own reputation, and all hopes of further advancement.[77]

Civility – like Romish religiosity – is only skin-deep; beneath the archbishop's vestments and polite veneer lurks a bawdy mind.

As the marginalia in the *Civile Conversation* and the tittle-tattle about della Casa show, allegations about hypocrisy were not confined to the *Courtier*, and Harvey (whose simultaneous enthusiasm for, and distrust of, Italian courtesy literature was highlighted earlier) began his satire of the affected courtier by placing the blame for this perceived degeneration of English culture squarely on *Galateo*'s shoulders: "Since *Galateo* came in, and *Tuscanisme* gan usurpe,/Vanitie above all: Villanie next her, Statelynes Empresse".[78] However, as a work which draws together the tenets of "courtiership", it was inevitable that Castiglione's *Courtier* become a lightning rod for anxieties about the potentially dissimulatory nature of manners which were based on principles of representation and accommodation. "Castilio" thus becomes a byword for the "perfum'd" courtier, with all the attendant vices of vanity and sycophancy, as can be seen in the writings of John Marston, where "Castilio" appears as a character in both his *Antonio* plays and as a stock figure in his satirical poetry, where the epitome of the courtier, the "absolute Castilio", shows his skill in "sonneting", "revelling", and "trot[ing] a courser".[79] The subtitle of one of these satires ("quedam videntur, et non sunt"), which serves as a running header across all eleven pages, further highlights the duplicitous performance of court life: things are not what they seem. In the romantic comedy *Antonio and Mellida* (c. 1599), "Castilio" appears as a mere fop (described by his servant as one of a pair "of rapiers, sheathed in one scabberd of folly"), given to "singing fantastically", or "sprinkling" "sweete water" from a "casting bottle".[80] His role in that play is to serve as a comic figure, for the audience and other characters to ridicule. However, *Antonio's Revenge* (1599–600) shows a darker side to the obsequious courtier, more suited to the tragic genre, as he becomes the unwitting, unquestioning instrument of the villainous Duke Piero, helping to strangle the henchman whom Piero has framed for all his crimes.

It was, in other words, potentially problematic to be seen to be imitating "Italian" manners. Even before Hoby's translation of Castiglione and the vogue for Italian courtesy literature (which Harvey lamented in the 1580s), there was something suspect about the Englishman who aped Italian customs, the "Angleso Italiano" mocked by Thomas Wilson, amongst others.[81] How then, do the translators of these books of manners respond to these pressures, and avoid transforming their readers into "the devil incarnate" (as the "English man Italionate" was commonly known).[82] Pettie certainly seems to have been keen to defuse suggestions of Italianate effeminacy in his preface to the reader (in which he stresses the efficacy of such learning for the service of one's prince and country) and in his dedicatory letter, addressed to Margery, Lady Norris, in which he recurrently praises her for her connection to military men, and in particular her six sons, who made names for themselves, fighting in France, Ireland, and the Netherlands. (Their fame is indicated by the fact that they would be remembered in broadside ballads for their martial prowess twenty years or more after the last of them had died.)[83] A nervousness about the Italianate ("Tuscanisme", to use Harvey's derogatory term) might also be evident in attempts to classicise this material (perhaps a reason, too, for the undoubted demand for Latin versions of these texts). Thomas Drant's prefatory poem to Peterson's translation of *Galateo* makes the European dissemination of della Casa's book mirror the expansion of the Roman Empire (which, as noted earlier, Tudor schoolboys were educated to admire), not least through his choice of Latinate names for rivers and peoples, familiar from Roman history:

> This book by Tyber, and by Po hath past,
> ... Iberus, through thy Spanishe coasts as fast
> It after yoade: and Gauls it held in hands,
> Through Rhenus realms it spread in prosperous speede.[84]

The book's passage across Europe is thus depicted not as a contagion (spreading, as might the "Italian" pox), but as akin to the progress of Roman "civilisation". A similar classicising impulse is apparent in Walker's *Refin'd Courtier*, the only one of these translations which attempts to perform more than a "*verbal* Translation", and which therefore risks, in more thoroughly Anglicising the material ("expung[ing], alter[ing], and add[ing]" as he sees fit), producing that dangerous hybrid: the Italianate Englishmen.[85] (Arguably, the other translations, in keeping the Italian context, preserve some distinction between the two cultures, as when Peterson, in his translation, signals in a note to the reader, or in printed marginalia, the untranslatability of the Italian.)[86] Bearing this in mind, it is telling that Walker buttresses his translation with footnotes referencing, not the Italian authors (Boccaccio, Dante) occasionally glossed by his predecessor Peterson, but classical, Biblical, and theological texts, cited in the original Latin and Greek, proof of his scholarship and a potential counterweight to accusations of shallowness. The English reception of Italian courtesy literature thus reflects, in miniature, many of the features of English attitudes to Italy more generally, as a culture which excited English admiration and scorn in almost equal measure, and which could be seen as a bellwether for anxieties about the rise of vernacular literature at the perceived expense of the classical. As Ascham states, he "love[s]" Italian, but only "next the Greeke and Latin tonge".[87]

Notes

1 Gabriel Harvey, *Gratulationum Valdinensium* (1578), sig. K4r; translated George L. Barnett, "Gabriel Harvey's *Castilio sive aulicus* and *de aulica*", *Studies in Philology*, 42 (1945): 146–63 (at 148).
2 National Archives, SP 1/57 f.75. For a list of identified owners of *The Courtier* before 1700, across Europe, see Peter Burke, *The Fortunes of the Courtier: The European Reception of the Courtier* (Cambridge: Polity Press, 1995), pp. 163–78; Lievsay provides a list of English owners of Guazzo's works to 1800 in *Stefano Guazzo and the English Renaissance* (Chapel Hill, NC: University of Carolina Press, 1961), pp. 275–6.
3 Virginia Cox, "Castiglione and His Critics", in Baldassare Castiglione, *The Book of the Courtier*, translated Thomas Hoby, ed. Virginia Cox (London: J. M. Dent, 1994), pp. 409–24 (at 411–12).
4 An EEBO-TCP search of 'Castilio', 1528–700, produces 126 hits in 36 items, excluding false results and references in Thomas Hoby's translation (search conducted 24.9.2104). This, of course, does not pick up references in works which do not have full text keyed in, or which use alternative spellings.
5 Daniel Javitch, *Poetry and Courtliness in Renaissance England* (Princeton, NJ: Princeton University Press, 1978); Lievsay, *Stefano Guazzo*, pp. 78–83, 210–21.
6 Anna Bryson, *From Courtesy to Civility: Changing Codes of Conduct in Early Modern England* (Oxford: Clarendon Press, 1998), p. 56.
7 Giovanni della Casa, *The Refin'd Courtier*, translated Nathaniel Walker (1663), sig. A2r.
8 See, for example, *Bibliotecha Digbeiana* (1680); *A Catalogue of Two Choice and Considerable Libraries of Books* (1680); *A Catalogue of the Library of … Dr. Scattergood* (1697); *Bibliotheca Tillotsoniana* (1695).
9 Thomas Rookes, *The Late Conflagration* (1667), sigs B2v, C1r.
10 Gabriel Harvey, "Master Hs. Short, but Sharpe, and Learned Iudgement of Earthquakes", in Edmund Spenser, *Three Proper, and Wittie, Familiar* letters (1580), sigs D2r-v.
11 Nathaniel Walker, "To the Reader", *The Refin'd Courtier* (1640), sig A8r.
12 Samuel Daniel, *The Worthy Tract of Paulus Jovius, Contayning a Discourse of Rare Inventions* (1585), sig. *4r.
13 Burke, *Fortunes*, 101, 171; Lievsay, *Stefano Guazzo*, p. 275.
14 Digby owned three versions of *Courtier* (Italian, folio and duodecimo; Hoby's English translation in quarto); two duodecimo copies of *Galateo*, in Italian (in della Casa's collected *Rime e Prose*) and Spanish; three versions of *Civil Conversation*: in Latin, as *de Civili Conversatione dissertationes politicae*, duodecimo; Italian, octavo; English, quarto (*Bibliotecha Digbeiana*); the Scattergoods possessed copies of the *Courtier* in Latin (Clerke's translation) and Italian (*Catalogue of the library*).
15 Lievsay, *Stefano Guazzo*, p. 40.
16 Baldassare Castiglione, *The Book of the Courtier*, translated Thomas Hoby, ed. Virgina Cox (London: J. M. Dent, 1994), 23 [1.2]. The number in square brackets refers to the book and chapter of the quotation, which is how *The Courtier* is often referenced in secondary literature.
17 Castiglione, *Courtier*, trans. Hoby, p. 364 [4.73].
18 Thomas M. Greene, "*Il Cortegiano* and the Choice of a Game", in *Castiglione: The Ideal and the Real in Renaissance Culture*, eds. Robert W. Hanning and David Rosand (New Haven, CT: Yale University Press, 1983), pp. 1–15 (at 7).
19 Stefano Guazzo, *The Civile Conversation*, translated George Pettie (1581), sig. A1v.
20 Lievsay, *Stefano Guazzo*, p. 44.
21 Guazzo, *Civile Conversation*, trans. Pettie, sigs G7v, G8r-v, H2r, H7r, I4v; G5v-G6r.
22 Lievsay, *Stefano Guazzo*, p. 186.
23 Lievsay, *Stefano Guazzo*, provides a useful extract, highlighting verbal changes (pp. 188–95).
24 Walter Darell, *A short discourse of the life of servingmen* (1578), sig. A3r.
25 'generous, *adj.*', sense 1a; 'gentle, *adj.*', sense 1a, *Oxford English Dictionary*, www.oed.com (accessed 23.9.2014).
26 Giovanni della Casa, *Galateo*, ed. Giuseppe Bonghi (1996), section I, www.classicitaliani.it/index022.htm; translated Robert Peterson (1576), sig. B2v; *Galateo Espagnol*, trans. William Style, sig. B2r.
27 Guazzo, *Civile Conversation*, trans. Pettie, sigs G8r-v.

28 Bryson, *From Courtesy to Civility*, p. 60.
29 Guazzo, *Civile Conversation*, trans. Pettie, sig. L3v.
30 Huntington Library, San Marino, Callmark 61245.
31 Pettie's 1581 translation omits the fourth book; it was printed, translated by Bartholomew Young, in the 1586 edition of *Civil Conversation*.
32 Burke, *Fortunes*, 25; Castiglione, *Courtier*, trans. Hoby, 28 [1.6]. For differing perspectives on Castiglione's proto-feminism, see Linda Woodbridge, *Women and the English Renaissance: Literature and the Nature of Womankind, 1540–1620* (Chicago, IL: University of Illinois Press, 1984); Valeria Finnuci, *The Lady Vanishes: Subjectivity and Representation in Castiglione and Ariosto* (Stanford: Stanford University Press, 1992).
33 Burke, *Fortunes*, p. 26.
34 Guazzo, *Civile Conversation*, Book 4, translated Bartholomew Young (1586), sig. 2A3v.
35 Guazzo, *Civile Conversation*, Book 4, trans. Young., sig. 2A3r.
36 Virginia Cox, *The Renaissance Dialogue: Literary Dialogue in Its Social and Political Contexts, Castiglione to Galileo* (Cambridge: Cambridge University Press, 1992), pp. 40, 41.
37 Cox, *Renaissance Dialogue*, p. 101.
38 Robert W. Hanning and David Rosand, "Preface", in *Castiglione*, eds. Hanning and Rosand, pp. vii–xvi (at viii).
39 Castiglione, *Courtier*, trans. Hoby, pp. 67, 66, 64 [1.35, 1.34, 1.33].
40 Guazzo, *Civile Conversation*, trans. Pettie, sig. H4r.
41 Guazzo, *Civile Conversation*, trans. Pettie sig. A8r.
42 Castiglione, *Courtier*, trans. Hoby, 22 [1.1].
43 Eleazor Duncan, *The Copy of a Letter Written by E. D. Doctour of Physicke* (1606), sig. D1r; Stephen Jerome, *The Arraignement of the Whole Creature, at the Barre of Religion, Reason, and Experience* (1632), sig. S1r.
44 For a discussion of Castiglione's sophisticated engagement with Cicero, see Jennifer Richards, "Assumed Simplicity and the Critique of Nobility: Or, How Castiglione Read Cicero", *Renaissance Quarterly* 54 (2001): 460–86.
45 Greene, "The Choice of a Game", p. 9.
46 Hanning and Rosand, "Preface", p. viii.
47 Robert Burton, *The Anatomy of Melancholy* (1621), sig. B4v; for the relevant passage in the *Courtier*, see Cox's edition, pp. 30–1 [1.8].
48 Richard Jones, *The Booke of Honor and Armes* (1590), sig. A3r. The relevant passage in Cox's edition is on p. 47 [1.21].
49 Della Casa, *Galateo*, trans. Peterson, sig. B2r; Guazzo, *Civile Conversation*, trans. Pettie, sig. G6r.
50 Guazzo, *Civile Conversation*, trans. Pettie, sig. Q1r.
51 Bryson, *From Courtesy to Civility*, es. pp. 107–10, 179–80.
52 Della Casa, *Galateo*, trans. Peterson, sig. B3v.
53 Bryson, *From Courtesy to Civility*, p. 110.
54 Castiglione, *Courtier*, trans. Hoby, p. 53 [1.26]; Bryson, *From Courtesy to Civility*, p. 122.
55 Castiglione, *Courtier*, trans. Hoby, pp. 4, 367–71, 372–4.
56 William Thomas, *The Principal Rules of Italian Grammer* (1550), sig. π2v.
57 John Florio, *Florios Second Frutes* (1591), sig. A4v; Pietro Paravicino, *The True Idioma of the Italian Tongue* (1660), sigs A3r, A4r.
58 "A Letter of Syr J. Chekes", in *Courtier*, ed. Castiglione, p. 10; Pettie, "To the Reader", in *Civile Conversation*, ed. Guazzo, sig. π2r.
59 Robert Peterson, dedicatory epistle, in della Casa, *Galateo*, sig. A2r.
60 Thomas Hoby, "The Epistle of the Translator", in *Courtier*, ed. Castiglione, p. 7.
61 Lievsay, *Stefano Guazzo*, p. 5.
62 Castiglione, *Courtier*, trans. Hoby, pp. 79 [1.43], 130 [2.26].
63 Castiglione, *Courtier*, trans. Hoby, p. 13.
64 For the argument that William Thomas was this lost translator, see Mary Partridge, "Thomas Hoby's English Translation of Castiglione's *Book of the Courtier*", *Historical Journal*, 50 (2007): 769–86.
65 John Florio, *Second Frutes*, sig. *1v.
66 Roger Ascham, *The Scholemaster* (1570), sigs G4v, H3r, I1r.
67 Ascham, *Scholemaster*, sig. I2r.

68 Ascham, *Scholemaster*, sig. I2r.
69 Javitch, *Poetry and Courtliness*, p. 131.
70 Bryson, *From Courtesy to Civility*, p. 56.
71 Guazzo, *Civile Conversation*, trans. Pettie, sigs D2r, K5v, K6r.
72 Della Casa, *Galateo*, trans. Peterson, sig. I2r.
73 Cox provides a useful summary of this trend in "Castiglione and His Critics", pp. 415–20.
74 Eduardo Saccone, *Le buone e le cattive maniere: letteratura e galateo nel Cinquecento* (Bologna: Il Mulino, 1992), p. 82.
75 Javitch, *Poetry and Courtliness*, p. 131.
76 Guazzo, *Civile Conversation*, trans. Pettie, Huntington Library, San Marino, Callmark 61, 246, sig. E2v.
77 Obadiah Walker, *Of Education, Especially of Young Gentlemen* (Oxford, 1673), pp. 231–2.
78 Gabriel Harvey, "Speculum Tuscanismi", in *Three Proper, and Wittie, Familiar Letters*, ed. Spenser, sig. E2v.
79 John Marston, "In Lectores prorsus indignos", *The Scourge of Villainie* (1598), sigs B1r-B3v (at B1v); "Satyre I", *The Metamorphosis of Pigmalions Image* (1598), sigs C3r–C8r (at C4r, C4v).
80 John Marston, *The History of Antonio and Mellida* (1602), sigs C3r, C3v, E3r.
81 Thomas Wilson, *The Arte of Rhetorique* (1553), sig. P2r.
82 Christopher Bagshaw, *A True Relation of the Faction Begun at Wisbich* (1601), sig. C1v; see also (amongst others) Ascham, *Scholemaster*, sig. I2r; Thomas Beard, *A Retractive from the Romish Religion* (1616), sig. D2v.
83 *Gallants, to Bohemia* (1620); *Lord Willoughby. Or, A True Relation of a Famous and Bloody Battel Fought in Flanders* (1626–80).
84 Thomas Drant, "In Praise of This Book", sig. ¶2r.
85 Walker, "To the Reader", *Refin'd Courtier*, sigs A8r–A10r (at A8v, A8r).
86 See, for example, della Casa, *Galateo*, trans. Peterson, sigs. K3r, L3r.
87 Ascham, *Scholemaster*, sig. H3r.

7 'Did Ariosto write it?'

The *Orlando Furioso* in Elizabethan poetry

Selene Scarsi

Certis this is a braue saying, and learned, did Ariosto write it?
Yea sir, you may reade it in his woorke that is called, Orlando furioso.
(John Florio, *First Fruites*, Chapter 25)

For approximately three decades, all English adaptations of Ludovico Ariosto's *Orlando Furioso* (1532) took the form of versions of single episodes or passages, with the first complete translation, Sir John Harington's, appearing as late as 1591; truly, in Mario Praz's words, "Ariosto at the outset was for the English only a story-teller",[1] read in a way not dissimilar to Bandello or Boccaccio. This chapter aims to survey all the partial versions, imitations, and adaptations which appeared in England between 1566 and the end of Elizabeth's reign, as well as, of course, Harington's complete translation of the poem, particularly significant because of its frequent misogynist and misogamist insertions.

The primary focus of this chapter is on poetry. However, Ariosto's poem penetrated all aspects of Elizabethan culture, starting from Shakespeare, who reveals his knowledge of Ariosto's poem in several plays – from the central scene of *As You Like It*, where a character named Orlando inscribes the name of his beloved on trees in the Ardennes, replicating "one of the most instantly recognisable motifs of the *Orlando Furioso*",[2] to the Claudio/Hero plot (and impersonation allusion) in *Much Ado About Nothing*, as well as verbal parallels in *Othello* so close that they lead scholars such as Jason Lawrence to establish that Shakespeare knew the *Furioso* in the Italian original, following on from Cairncross' 1976 study of the above plays, plus *King Lear*, concluding that the playwright conflated material from early sections of the *Furioso* (cantos IV–VI) into several plays independently of translations.[3] Juliet Dusinberre has recently argued for similarities between Harington's Ariosto (as well as Harington's own poetry, the *Epigrams*) and *Much Ado*, highlighting how "Benedick's role in *Much Ado* as commentator on the action as much as participator in it re-creates Harington's stance in relation to the *Orlando Furioso*", as the translation is peppered with marginal notes which force the poem to "cease to be a master text and … become a partner in a dialogue".[4] We have also a very loose adaptation for the stage of part of canto XXIII in Robert Greene's *The Historie of Orlando Furioso, One of the twelue Pieres of France*, performed in 1592 and printed two years later (and contemptuously referred to by Harington as the "Orlando Foolioso"[5]), and we can find mentions of (and excerpts from) the poem in the bilingual dialogues in language textbooks such as Florio's 1578 *First Fruites*, exemplified in the above epigraph, proving the extent to which the *Furioso* was assimilated into all levels of English Renaissance culture.

DOI: 10.4324/9781315612720-9

Critical interest in the *Furioso*'s influence on Elizabethan literature has always been buoyant, especially in its more creative form: thus, research on Spenser's use of Ariosto, for instance, is both fertile and enduring, with virtually all Spenserian critics recognising the significance of Spenser's borrowings from the *Furioso*. Harington's translation of the epic is also the subject of a wealth of articles and volumes, from Townsend Rich's 1940 monograph onwards. In recent years, increased critical attention to Anglo-Italian relations in the Renaissance has resulted in a number of perceptive readings of Harington's rendition, some of which will be mentioned below, although most have overlooked the widespread misogyny in the English text.

The early partial translations confirm the Elizabethan fashion for the short story of Italian inspiration, already visible in the numerous collections of tales borrowed from Boccaccio, Bandello, and other *novellieri*. This is particularly the case of the first couple of poets mentioned in the chapter, Peter Beverley and George Whetstone, whose works elaborate freely on the same Ariostean episode,[6] a lengthy tale spanning two cantos. Both authors sometimes paraphrase in prose the Italian text, and are, in general, so free as to render it impossible to state with any certainty that they had, at their disposal, Ariosto's original rather than one of the several French translations as an intermediary – a practice that was far from rare in the Renaissance.[7] Let's take a closer look at the versions.

Beverley's Ariodanto and Jenevra

Very little is known about Peter Beverley, the first poet to translate any part of (any) Italian epic poem into English: only one date, that of 1566, when the *Historie of Ariodanto and Jenevra* was entered in the Stationers' Register, is recorded, and Beverley left no other work, with the exception of a commendatory poem on Geoffrey Fenton's *Tragicall Discourses* (1567). The paucity of information on Beverley is mirrored by the scarce critical attention that has been devoted to him; excepting Charles Prouty, his modern editor, only a few critics have concentrated on him beyond the mere mention of his name, and most of this criticism has been negative. Mario Praz's comment is exemplary:

> Beverley was wise in doing so [never mentioning Ariosto's name in his work], because palming off as Ariosto's the ill-conceived embroideries with which the English poem abounds chiefly in the first part, would have been a lie and an insult.[8]

Although it cannot be denied that Beverley's work is a prolix, often excessively ornate poem, his work is historically significant, as it marks the entrance of Ariosto's epic into England. It is a lengthy adaptation, reaching almost 3,000 lines (and therefore becoming thrice as long as the original, which, with 124 octaves, remained below 1,000 lines); it is thus stretched both with the addition of numerous details, not present in the original plot, and with the expansion or the explication of other elements which are briefly mentioned or left implicit in the Italian poem. The two poems differ structurally (Beverley prefers a strict chronological order to Ariosto's *in medias res* start and ensuing flashbacks) and thematically: while Ariosto's focus is on a proto-feminist critique of the gender-specific double-standards of the Scottish law, Beverley concentrates on the relationship between Ariodante and Ginevra, trying to cover all *exempla* of love and frequently creating plot situations independently of Ariosto, which then allow him to explore yet more sides of the sentiment. This is exemplified by the two lovers' unawareness of each other's feelings, which permits some hundred verses of Petrarchist suffering, fitting beautifully in the unrequited love tradition; oneiric interventions spurring Ariodanto away from complaint and into action; archaic passages with Dream, Sleep, Hope, and Slumber allegorised and interacting with one another; a long speech delivered by Ariodanto to a hermit, touching upon the vanity of the world, in accordance with the *vanitas vanitatum* topos of religious literature; and, interestingly, the topos of the *amor de lonh*, which is almost non-existent in Ariosto but is important and extended in Beverley.

In the English poem, issues of guilt or innocence never play a part in Ariodanto's compulsive desire to defend Jenevra: she is "the lampe of light" and as such she must be saved, irrespective of any actual responsibility. In this, Ariodanto resembles Ariosto's Rinaldo, who decides to champion the princess in the original version simply because of the unfair double-standard inherent in Scottish law (IV, LXV). Indeed, "the famous knight Raynaldo" (2569) himself appears towards the end of Beverley's poem. This timely, if awkward, epiphany – Rinaldo had never been mentioned before in the poem and his presence in Scotland is left unexplained – provides the strongest intertextual reference to Ariosto's poem; the paladin seems to have jumped out of the Italian epic as an exemplary *deus-ex-machina*, just in time to rescue the maid Dalinda from an attack in the woods and, as result, provide through his actions the welcome *dénouement* of the long story:

> [U]pon a solome daye, appointed by the king,
> The Princesse and Ariodant, with sacred woords and Ring:
> Receyve the ryght of mariage, as gladde to them as lyfe:
> Who long in blisse did spend their daies and died devoyde of stryfe.
> (2799–802)

Whetstone's Rinaldo and Giletta

Ten years later, the same episode already used by Beverley is adapted – mostly in prose, and with two fresh names for the protagonists: Rinaldo and Giletta – by George Whetstone (1550–87)[9] in the first section of the partially autobiographic *The Rocke of Regard* (1576).

The "Discourse of Rinaldo and Giletta" is an epistolary, prosimetrical text, with the main narrative in prose, interspersed with poems on the part of Rinaldo and letters in prose from Giletta. Rinaldo's poems, always signed, can be divided in two groups, those addressed to Giletta and those that he writes to complain of his love-suffering. At times, Whetstone comments briefly on the poem immediately after Rinaldo's signature, and before proceeding with the rest of the story, in a way rather similar to that used by Dante in another *prosimetrum*, the *Vita Nuova*. Whetstone's narrative is clearly inspired by his friend George Gascoigne's *Adventures of Master F.J.;* indeed, Prouty has commented exhaustively on Whetstone's imitations from his friend, which are to be found especially in the first part of Whetstone's prose narrative and which range from plot parallels (such as the male protagonists' sicknesses) to direct imitations of situations, devices and particularly of poems,[10] as perhaps best exemplified by Whetstone's use, in his "Beautie leaue off to brag" (61–2), of Gascoigne's "Beauty shut up thy shop" (75).

Thematically, the prose narrative does not differ much from Beverley's poem. As Beverley, Whetstone is primarily interested in exploiting as many traditional love *topoi* – from *amor de lonh* to unrequited love – as possible, often in a rather prolix way. Stylistically, Whetstone shares with Beverley the frequent use of praeterition to run through, concisely, the oscillations of the love story, as well as the use of Petrarchist themes, best exemplified by his poem "In bondage free I liue, yet free am fettered faste", which is effectively a paraphrasis of Petrarch's famous sonnet "Pace non trovo e non ó da far Guerra" (*Canzoniere*, CXXXIV). Indeed, the popularity of the lines, which, by the time *The Rocke of Regard* appeared in print, had already been translated into English by Sir Thomas Wyatt, suggests that Whetstone's ensuing gloss is to be intended ironically:

> These verses, although they were in number few, yet the sweetnes of the tune, together with the rareness of the invention, running altogether uppon contraries, made them to be singularly well liked, especially of mistresse Giletta, who could now no longer dissemble her love.
>
> (55)

The use of antitheses is conventional, rather than "rare"; and this is not the only place in the story in which irony can be posited on Whetstone's part. In fact, it could be inferred that his initial profession of the anonymity of the original story is equally ironic. The narrative begins with a brief "argument", which includes the declaration of the anonymity of the original version of the story ("[t]his discourse was first written in Italian by an unknowne authour, the argument of whose woorke insueth", 41–2). It is, of course, possible that Whetstone did not know the *Orlando Furioso*, partly because the first partial translation of the poem, by Beverley, had also made no mention of Ariosto's authorship (Beverley had called his efforts the "unripe fruits of [*his*] barren orchard" ("To The Reader", 2), and partly because the tale itself was already popular in England, both in Bandello's version and through the intermediary of French translations.[11] However, comparable statements elsewhere in the work suggest that Whetstone is here simply playing with his readers, in line with the general tone of his work. Two of the climactic moments of the story, Rinaldo's discovery of Giletta's "unfaithfulness" and his consequent suicidal thoughts, are both described in a playful way. When Rinaldo's rival cunningly hides a letter, written imitating Giletta's hand, inside an apple, Rinaldo discovers it when biting into the fruit, hurting his teeth. His consequent suicide attempt takes the form of a leap into the River Po:

> [A]fter he had a while felt the furie of the floudes, was wearie of dying, so that for life he laboured unto the shoare; which happily recovered, he felt his stomacke at that instant rather ovecharged with water then love.
>
> (75)

The rather poetic mention of the man "wearie of dying" contrasts so heavily with the prosaicity of the author's reflections on his stomach that it could be posited that the whole passage is ironic, and should be read as a parody of the miraculous rescue of Ariodante in the other versions of the tale. The comicality of the episode is heightened when the guilty apple becomes the subject of a poem, in which mythological and biblical references unite in a condemnation of the "needlesse fruit" (76) which ruined

Adam and Eve's prelapsarian happiness, led to the destruction of Troy, and, last but not least, revealed to Rinaldo "Gilettas scorne, that chaung'd her love to yre" (*ibid.*).

Prouty comments that:

> Truly Whetstone has reinterpreted his sources in a most novel manner. As with Beverley, love has been his theme but it has been handled in the latest fashion. The newest refinements and subtleties are all displayed with a liberal dash of melodramatic seasoning.[12]

In this respect, then, Whetstone and Beverley are extremely similar, and both enjoy the addition of details on the theme of love not present in the simple Ariostean story.

In a peculiar, extraordinary way, Whetstone's work is the least novel adaptation of the story, because of the "rhetorical display of fashionable, amorous attitudes and sentiments"[13] already used by Beverley in poetry and inserted within a structure already used by Gascoigne, that of the partially epistolary, prosimetrical text. At the same time, however, its constant, outspoken denial of the imitative quality of the work, its exaggerated exploitation of Petrarchist conventions, and, most importantly, its transformation of pathos into parody render the tale one of the most unique adaptations.

Testament to the tale's immense popularity in the sixteenth century, there is a third English poet who, after Beverley and Whetstone, chose to adapt the story of Ariodante and Ginevra for his own aims: Edmund Spenser.

Spenser's Ariosto

Spenser's ability to mould his sources is pre-eminently visible in his handling, in Book II, canto IV of *The Faerie Queene*, of this tale from the *Furioso* that so inspired Elizabethan readers.

Unlike in all the other versions, in Spenser the tale is narrated by the male protagonist, a squire later named as Phaon, for the valid reason that, by the end of the episode, he is the only extant character: his beloved is dead, and the maid has fled. The version is heavily shortened and simplified: without any introductory material, Phaon's friend Philemon feigns the infidelity of Phaon's betrothed, Claribell, for no specific reason if not "either enuying [Phaon's] toward good,/Or of him selfe to treason ill disposd" (II, IV, 2–3). Ariosto's complex theme of the deception caused by the rival's enamourment and consequent jealousy is here ignored entirely, and, further to hide any direct involvement of the rival, Spenser has a double disguise instead of Ariosto's single one: in *The Faerie Queene*, not only is the maid dressed in her mistress' robes, but Philemon himself is disguised as a "groome of base degree" (XXIV, 3). Similarly, Claribell's maid, Pryene, is persuaded to wear her mistress' clothes simply because she is told that she will look prettier; there is no mention of Ariosto's much more complex scheme, which saw Polinesso declare that his love for Ginevra would be extinguished upon the occasional possession of Dalinda assuming the *persona* of the princess.

However, in those passages that Spenser does maintain, there are evident, direct Ariostean influences. For instance, in the bedroom scene Ariosto's Ariodante feels "trapassato il cor d'estrema ambascia" (V, LV, 6), while Spenser's Phaon laments the "gnawing anguish .../infixed in [his] brest" (XXIII, 1–2) when he discovers his beloved's infidelity; later, Ariosto's authorial comment "[o]r pensa in che ribrezzo, in che dolor"

(L, 5–6) becomes a very similar "[a]h God, what horrour and tormenting griefe" in Spenser (XXVIII, 6), with the stress on the same two feelings on the part of the betrayed lover.

Despite these similarities, what was suicidal desperation in Ariosto becomes a fierce desire for "vengeuance" (XXIX, 2) in Spenser, so that the innocent Claribell is slain by her own Phaon at the first chance. Even when the terrible mistake is revealed through Pryene's quick confession, Phaon's suicidal thoughts are subordinate to a desire for vengeance, this time directed towards the "false faytour *Philemon*" (XXX, 6):

> Thus heaping crime on crime, and griefe on griefe,
> To losse of loue adioyning losse of friend,
> I meant to purge both with a third mischiefe,
> And in my woes beginner it to end.
>
> (IV, XXXI, 1–4)

This is, of course, very far from Ariodante's innocent love, for whom even the discovery of Ginevra's betrayal leads not to vengeful thoughts, but simply to solitary desperation first, and then to isolation. Spenser's story ends with Phaon's encounter with Guyon, who has a role more or less similar to that of the hermit in Beverley, albeit, here, more elaborate. Interrupting Phaon's chase of Pryene, the Palmer reveals that it is temperance that will cure his "fearfully grown affections":

> Wrath, gealosie, griefe, loue do thus expell:
> Wrath is a fire, and gealosie a weede,
> Griefe is a flood, and loue a monster fell;
> The fire of sparkes, the weede of little seede,
> The flood of drops, the Monster filth did breede:
> But sparks, seed, drops, and filth do thus delay;
> The sparks soone quench, the springing seed outweed,
> The drops dry vp, and filth wipe cleane away:
> So shall wrath, gealosy, griefe, loue die and decay.
>
> (IV, XXXV)

Spenser's version is much condensed and constantly concentrated on one purpose, a celebration of temperance; as Alistair Fox notes:

> Spenser has fundamentally relocated the meaning of the story away from Ariosto's focus on the injustice of the sexual double standard that men often invoke in their treatment of women, together with the idea that crimes are ultimately impossible to conceal, to a new emphasis on the interior degeneration that is liable to be set in motion by a failure to bridle intemperate emotions.[14]

Ariosto's story is extremely simplified, reduced to its barest essentials, and only one facet of love analysed, that of unbridled passion. All the superfluous elements are erased, in favour of a consistent stress on the negative effects of intemperance, in the shape of excessive passions – whether they be "wrath, gealosy, griefe", or "loue": this pattern of selective adaptation is seen elsewhere in Spenser's treatment of the *Furioso*, and is entirely justified by the very different aims of the two poems.

Of course, Spenser's use of Ariosto is not limited to the transformation of Ariodante and Ginevra into Phaon and Claribell. On the contrary, it is extensive since Ariosto, perhaps more so than any other poet, is one of the primary influences on the *Faerie Queene*. Spenser's appropriation of Ariosto has been the subject of much critical attention, with almost all Spenserian critics recognising the evidence and the importance of his borrowings from the *Furioso*. It has generally been accepted that, rather than the quantity, it is the quality of these imitations which is fascinating. As Paul Alpers has noted:

> If we start with a single episode in *The Faerie Queene* and seek out its Ariostan sources, we will often get the impression that Spenser's use of Ariosto is capricious and superficial. On the other hand, if we start with an episode in the *Orlando Furioso* and ask what it produces, influences, or suggests in *The Faerie Queene*, we will get a truer sense of Spenser's familiarity with Ariosto's poem and the ease with which he could draw on it for his own … As many Renaissance writers said, imitation is digestion and absorption, not passive copying. When a major poet is profoundly influenced by another major poet, he undoubtedly puts his own stamp on what he borrows … The poet's use of his predecessor involves an unmistakable transmutation, emphasis of some qualities at the expense of others. But at the same time the borrowings of poets like these characteristically reveal a full and intelligent awareness of the poet imitated.[15]

Throughout *The Faerie Queene*, Spenser shows his deep knowledge of Ariosto, a knowledge that seems comparable, for example, to Dante's familiarity with Virgil. And, like Dante, Spenser seems to display two well-defined kinds of acquaintance with Ariosto's poem: sometimes he appears to know the poem so perfectly as to be able to reproduce with great fidelity the passages he needs, sometimes literally translating them; this is especially the case with his numerous terminological borrowings, and it might be supposed that the English poet had a copy of the *Furioso* by his side when writing. The second kind of knowledge is his ability to "digest" Ariosto in the sense used by Alpers: Spenser seems to know the outline of the Italian poem and the development of its episodes in an extraordinarily intimate fashion, and he is thus able to interpret, modify, intertwine, and elaborate on episodes, characters, passages as he feels appropriate for what and whom he is writing. It is also true that Spenser's clear view of what his own poem meant led him to sacrifice certain aspects of the Italian original: sacrifices of tone, exemplified by the omission of the delightful irony which pervades Ariosto's poem and which is much rarer in the English poem, and sacrifices of plot, as exemplified by the story of Phaon and Claribell, in which the original Italian source is so spoiled of ornaments, so rarefied and abstracted, so bare for those who have in mind Ariosto's complex tale, as to recall a tree which, by the time winter comes, has lost all of its fruitful spring-time blossoms.

It is particularly in the third book of *The Faerie Queene* that parallels with the Italian work become especially evident, and are often so striking that, as Neil Dodge has commented:

> To those who read the *Faery Queen* with Ariosto in mind the opening cantos of Book III are almost startling. At the very outset Britomart appears on the scene, and we at once recognise her for a copy of Bradamante.[16]

Indeed, Neil Dodge talks of a "change of world"[17] and believes that, in the third book, the influence of Ariosto on Spenser was so strong that the very method of composition of the latter changed, for the organised, concentrated plots of the initial two books are replaced by:

> Independent knights and ladies, whose paths cross and recross, who come and go much as fate drives them, without definite goal, all dominated by Britomart, but not controlled by her. This is manifestly the world of the *Furioso* ... That [Spenser's] poem should begin in a world peculiarly his own, and then, as if irresistibly, drift into the world of the *Furioso* is perhaps not without significance.[18]

While a thorough analysis of the parallels between Spenser and Ariosto is beyond the scope of this chapter, a mention of a couple of examples will suffice to outline the relevance of the English poet's borrowings. In the first canto of Spenser's Book III, similarities range from the appearance of an enchanted spear, used to gain access to Castle Joyous (both elements modelled on Ariosto), to striking terminological similarities, such as Spenser's choice of the English noun "sell" (III, LX, 6) which clearly recalls, phonetically and graphically, the Italian "sella", (VIII, XVII, 6 and XXIII, XV, 8), and the use of which, in Spenser, is almost unique: the *OED* records it as the second-earliest. Later, Britomart's eleventh-canto discovery of the knight Scudamour by a fountain is inspired by her Italian equivalent Bradamante's finding of the evil Pinabello in the second canto of the *Furioso*. In Ariosto, the heroine is impressed by the sight of the thoughtful, lonely, and melancholic knight in what is described as a typical *locus amoenus*. Spenser describes the discovery of Scudamour in analogous terms, and reproduces the geography of Ariosto's *locus amoenus* very faithfully, retaining most, if not all, of the Ariostean elements.

A further clear parallel is the fifth-canto episode of Belphoebe and Timias, equivalent to that of Angelica and the soldier Medoro in canto XIX of the *Furioso*. Parallels are notable when the reaction of the two women to the view of the wounded men is analysed, showing impressive terminological equality. Ariosto's Angelica

> [I]nsolita pietade in mezzo al petto
> si sentì entrar per disusate porte
> che le fe' il duro cor tenero e molle
>
> (She felt an unusual pity enter into her chest, through some unused doors, and her hard heart was made tender and soft)
>
> (XIX, XX, 5–7)

Spenser's Belphoebe grows

> Full of soft passion and unwonted smart:
> the point of pity pierced through her tender hart.
>
> (V, XXX, 8–9)

Not only are both hearts made "tender" (a perfect translation of the Italian "tenero") by "pity"/"pietade": Belphoebe becomes "full of *soft* passion" (emphasis added) too, which again perfectly translates the rare "molle" in the Italian text. More importantly, the "smart", the stinging pain that Belphoebe suddenly feels, is classified as "unwonted", just like the Italian "pietade" is defined by Ariosto as "insolita", a concept reinforced soon after when the metaphorical doors to her heart are called "disusate", because of the normal coldness of the Asian princess. The terminological similarities are both unusual and imposing and are substantial enough to suggest that Spenser wrote the episode with the exact Ariostean words engraved on his mind, if not with the very text by his side.

The *déroulement* of the episode shows similar analogies: among the various curative herbs that the two girls know, in both cases the "panachæa" occupies a prominent position; even if this herb could have been inspired by the *Aeneid*, the two descriptions of the preparation of the potion bear striking resemblances (including terminological ones) with each other, as both poets devote a full stanza to a very detailed, almost cinematographic visualisation of the procedure used by the women to prepare the medicine. Ariosto writes that Angelica

> Pestò con sassi l'erba, indi la prese,
> e succo ne cavò fra le man bianche;
> ne la piaga n'infuse, e ne distese
> e pel petto e pel ventre e fin a l'anche:
> e fu di tal virtù questo liquore,
> che stagnò il sangue, e gli tornò il vigore.
>
> (Crushed the herb with stones, then took it, and pressed out its juice between her white hands; she put it on the wound, and spread it on his chest, stomach, and even on his hips: and this liquor was so powerful that it clotted the blood, and his vigour returned.)
>
> (XIX, XXIV, 3–8)

Spenser similarly writes:

> The soueraine weede betwixt two marbles plaine
> Shee pownded small, and did in peeces bruze,
> And then atweene her lilly handes twaine,
> Into his wound the iuice thereof did scruze,
> And round about as she could well it vze,
> The flesh therewith shee suppled and did steepe,
> T'abate all spasme, and soke the swelling bruze.
> (V, XXXIII, 1–7)

The herbs are prepared in an identical way, with stones ("marbles" and "sassi"); the hands of the two women are similarly classified as white: "bianche" in Ariosto (and there is plenty of irony in this oxymoronic definition of Angelica as pure and virginal); "lilly" – with metaphor – in Spenser, hinting at the outstanding purity of Belphoebe (who, in fact, will preserve her virginity notwithstanding Timias' love for her). The same implicit irony can be found a few lines later, where Ariosto takes pleasure in highlighting how Angelica's hands spread the dressing on the wound and then progressed lower and lower, around his chest, his stomach and *even* – that "fin", which hides, underneath the fake surprise, a knowing smile and a benevolent tone of *quod placet, licet* – on his flanks. The description in *The Faerie Queene* is, at first sight, not different, because Belphoebe's medicine also expands not only on the wound, but "round about" too; however, there is no malice whatsoever in Spenser, implicit or explicit, as befits a pure maiden like Belphoebe as well as her role as an embodiment of Queen Elizabeth; in fact, the location of the wound is not even mentioned in the English poem. Not surprisingly, Ariosto's characters will celebrate a wedding, unlike their English counterparts, as Belphoebe, embodying virginity, cannot yield to physical passion. The divergence is clearly justified by the two different aims of the poems: if Spenser wanted to represent the Virgin Queen in this character – that side of the Queen which is "a most vertuous and beautifull Lady" and which the poet admits "in some places I doe expresse in Belphœbe"[19] – then obviously no marriage could have been contemplated; Ariosto, on the contrary, needed to wed Angelica in order to justify Orlando's madness, which is after all the *raison d'être* of the poem, and his decision to celebrate the marriage between this most beautiful and royal of princesses and a simple soldier is just yet another example of the Ariostean "smile".

Gascoigne's Ariosto

Book III of the *Faerie Queene* is important for another reason, George Gascoigne's mediating influence on Spenser. This intermediacy is especially evident in Spenser's replication, at the conclusion of the Malbecco story, of some of the descriptions of Sospetto in Ariosto's second of the *Cinque Canti.*[20] Ariosto narrates, with his usual meta-narrative technique, the tale of a suspicious ruler who, having condemned both himself and his wife to a secluded existence in an impenetrable tower, is killed by the woman, for whom such a shielded life has become unbearable. Once in Hell, however, no torment seems to afflict him, because no torment can compare to that state of constant fear and suspicion that he subjected himself to during his lifetime; he is, then, sent back to Earth, condemned to personify, forever, Suspicion itself. Spenser, after describing Hellenore's escape with Paridell, has the jealous Malbecco wander in search of his wife, whom he eventually finds abandoned by Paridell and living among satyrs; when she refuses to return to a secluded life with him, he roams randomly until he becomes the embodiment of Jealousy.

A rather careful paraphrase of Ariosto's tale can be found within George Gascoigne's *The Adventures of Master F.J.* (1573), when F. J., uncertain of Dame Elinor's faithfulness, begins to be devoured by jealousy and suspicion; Spenser's description of Malbecco shares certain similarities with Gascoigne's prose passage, some of which cannot be found in Ariosto's original. For instance, when describing the habits of the long-bearded ruler (who has let his beard grow "least the barbor might do him a good turne sooner than he looked for it", 82), Gascoigne adds a few explanatory details not present in Ariosto: after describing how well-guarded the tower was, due to the presence of a "firce mastiff" (82; "un gran mastin" in Ariosto, XI, 7), Ariosto's character simply double-checks that nobody is in the house, not trusting his wife and his other helpers, while Gascoigne's cannot sleep without difficulty: "betwene fearfull sweate and chyvering cold, with one eye opened & the other closed, he stole somtimes a broken sleepe, devided with many terrible dreames" (82). This detail is shared by Spenser as well, whose Cyclopean Malbecco "dare neuer sleepe, but that one eye/Still ope he keeps" (LVIII, 6–7).

Gascoigne's prose narrative, which started as a literal paraphrase of the Italian text, slowly becomes freer and enriched with details not present in Ariosto, as exemplified by Suspicion's ingenuous means to prevent oversleeping, invented by Gascoigne:

> But to be sure that he shoulde not ouersleepe him selfe, gan stuffe his couch with Porpentines quilles, to the ende that when heauy sleepe ouercame him, and he therby should be constrayned to charge his pallad with more heauie burden, those plumes might then pricke through and so awake him. His garments were steele vpon Iron, and that Iron vppon Iron, and Iron againe, and the more he was armed, the lesse he trusted to be out of daunger.
>
> (84)

This passage well shows Gascoigne's adapting method: while he invents, at times, elaborating freely on the Ariostean text, at other times he provides a faithful, word-by-word prose rendition. This is the case with the final two lines relating Suspicion's dressing: they translate literally Ariosto's "e ferro sopra ferro e ferro veste:/quanto piú s'arma, è tanto men sicuro" ("and he wears iron upon iron upon iron: the more he is armed, the less safe he feels", XX, 3–4).

Gascoigne, however, was inspired by the main body of the *Furioso* too: at the end of his Suspicion tale he inserts a translation of six stanzas relating Bradamante's jealousy, from Ariosto's canto XXXI. Gascoigne's translation is, overall, quite accurate, with the exception of the sixth and concluding octave, an original envoy which acts both as a conclusion and as a contextualisation of the description of Bradamante's jealousy in F. J.'s situation:

> And me even now, thy gall hath so enfect,
> As all the joyes which ever lover found,
> And all good haps, that ever Troylus sect,
> Atchived yet above the luckles ground:
> Can never sweeten one my mouth with mell,
> Nor bring my thoughts, againe in rest to dwell.
> Of thy mad moodes, and of naught elles I thinke,
> In such like seas, fayre Bradamant did sincke.
>
> (85)

Another of Gascoigne's renditions from the main body of the *Furioso* is a translation of Bradamante's XXXIII-canto dream about Ruggiero which, in *A Hundreth Sundrie Flowres*, opens his series of poems with "A translation of Ariosto allegorized" (107); it is a short translation characterised, stylistically, by plenty of repetitions and heavy alliterations, but semantically faithful.

Tofte's tales

Another Elizabethan poet to adapt from Ariosto is Robert Tofte (1562–619), and his "Tales" are particularly interesting as they appear to have been composed as translation exercises. This finds confirmation not only in Tofte's choice of two short, self-contained stories, but also in an extra-literary, but nevertheless significant, element, the printer's note prefacing the *Two Tales*, which qualifies the translation as one made "for his owne priuate exercise":

> Gentlemen, these two Tales translated out of ARIOSTO, and the other Stanzies following, were not done by this Translator, to compare (as it were) with master

> HARRINGTONS verses (for he acknowledgeth himselfe euery way his inferiour) but for his owne priuate exercise, and at the earnest intreatie of some gentlemen his friends, all which he did in the yeere 1592. he [*sic*] being then in Italie.
>
> (Printer's Note)

The note is interesting also for its immediate positing of a comparison between the two English *Furiosi.*[21] The awareness and likely direct knowledge of Harington's translation of the same lines certainly played an important role in Tofte's choice of text and in his attempt to vie with – or, to paraphrase a more famous "contest", to "ouergo" – the first English version of the *Orlando Furioso.*

Both the Ariostean episodes translated by Tofte derive from canto XLIII of the *Orlando Furioso;* both were written in Italy (the first was composed in Siena in July 1592, and the second was compiled in Naples one year after) but published a few years later (1597). The translator not only records the canto and stanza number marking the beginning of his translation, but he even reproduces the first line of the Italian original, thus providing his readers with an exact and unmistakable context for his two versions. The first tale tells of how Rinaldo, travelling through the Pianura Padana, stops along the way at various courts and avails himself of the courts' multicultural environment to conduct a search on the fidelity of women. During his first night near Mantua, the paladin is offered an enchanted cup which, if drunk by a man whose wife is faithful, perfectly holds the wine within, but which spills if drunk by a man who has been betrayed. In this "rewriting of the Fall in modern dress",[22] in Benson's beautiful definition, Rinaldo rejects the temptation to drink, preferring to remain ignorant of his wife's behaviour, and his host, envying his wisdom, tearfully narrates his story. Tofte is engaged with his translation throughout, handling the original fluently and carefully; he also adds an original stanza to the story's bitter conclusion, with a final witty couplet acting as a moral for the whole story. The second episode translated by Tofte, which in Ariosto's poem follows almost immediately the first, is another narrative centred on the theme of the (in)fidelity of women. Rinaldo, still desiring to investigate the subject, moves on towards Ferrara and, during the journey, listens to the tale of Anselmo and his wife Argia, who (successfully) attempts to restore their marriage by getting Anselmo to make the same mistake that she has made – extra-marital intercourse. The story originally presents male faithfulness as equally important as its female counterpart, virtually advocating equality of expectations and conduct in both sexes; it also suggests, as a not too implicit moral of the story, that women might be bad, but men are infinitely worse. Tofte's translation, again, demonstrates the poet's careful reading of the original on several occasions. For instance, the Elizabethan poet is able to pick up and elaborate on Ariosto's irony, often adding remarks of his own, always consonant to the spirit of the original, as exemplified by his additions when Anselmo, overwhelmed by the beauty of a magical palace (which Argia had had built unbeknown to him) and desiring it more than anything else, asks at what price he can buy it; the sodomical Moor's answer will precipitate the end of the story and its happy (for Argia, at least) ending. Whilst Ariosto writes that

> [Anselmo] spesso dice: « Non potria quant'oro
> é sotto il sol pagare il loco egregio ».
> A questo gli risponde il brutto Moro,
> e dice: « E questo ancor trova il suo pregio:

se non d'oro o d'argento, nondimeno
pagar lo puó quel che vi costa meno ».

(Anselmo often said, "Not even all the gold in the world could buy such a glorious place". The ugly Moor replied, "Yet even this has a price: not gold or silver, though – rather, it can be paid with what will cost you the least".)

(CXXXVIII, 3–8)

Tofte has:

And often saith, the Worldes whole Wealth is nought,
In Price to Pallace this so rich and faire:
The lothsome Moore, who long these words had sought
Strait saide, And yet at Worth they valewed are,
Through Gold not Siluer thou for this canst pay,
Yet, what doth cost thee lesse, giue me thou may.

(LXVII, 3–8)

Tofte's unique addition of the line "who long these words had sought" gives a real sense of a plan, revealing that the surreal situation in which Anselmo has incurred is, in fact, all part of the plot cunningly devised by Argia; despite being absent in Ariosto, it suits the context so perfectly that the original seems almost incomplete without it – a clear sign of the effectiveness of Tofte's addition, whose effect on the readers is almost the creation of one of those Ariostean "smiles" which Tofte seems to have fully understood, and truly made his own.

Harington's complete translation

The last version of the *Furioso* analysed here is the only complete translation to appear during Elizabeth's reign: the *Orlando Furioso in English Heroicall Verse*, published by Sir John Harington (1561–612) in 1591. The compositional circumstances of Sir John Harington's translation are as dubious as they are fascinating. The tradition maintains that, in the 1580s, he translated a portion of Ariosto's masterpiece, the tale of Giocondo included in canto XXVIII, and circulated it at court: when it came to the hands of Elizabeth, the Queen proclaimed her disgust at the bawdiness of the story, considered as potentially corrupting for her ladies-in-waiting, and punished the author by confining him to his country estate until the translation of the complete poem was produced. The legend is somewhat backed by the fact that Harington himself wrote, in the *Metamorhosis of Ajax*, that his *Orlando Furioso* was the result of a punishment by the Queen.[23]

The translation, despite being notably shorter than the original in the body of the text, is, however, accompanied by a wealth of extra-textual material: beautiful engravings that render Harington's work one of the richest books of the time, as well as an elaborate critical apparatus, containing, among other sections, an allegory of the poem and a "Preface, or rather a Briefe Apologie of Poetrie, and of the Author and Translator", heavily inspired by the commentaries on the *Furioso* circulating in Italy in the decades after the poem was published, and in particular by the 1549 *Spositione Sopra l'Orlando Furioso* by Simone Fornari.

However, there is one important thematic characteristic that occurs with surprising frequency in Harington's translation of the *Orlando Furioso*: its distinctive misogyny, which can be found throughout the poem to various degrees. Again, a thorough analysis of Harington's misogyny beyond the brief mention of a couple of examples is beyond the scope of this chapter, and has been done elsewhere;[24] suffice it to say that Harington takes, persistently and constantly throughout his work, an unfavourable stance towards the poem's female knights and warriors (Bradamante, Marfisa, and the Amazons). As an example, during the lengthy Amazons episode (cantos XIX and XX) Ariosto pens explicitly proto-feminist passages when he has five visiting knights ask whether the Amazons' island presents, in the ruling of the families and as a mode of living, matriarchy or patriarchy:

> I cavallier domandano a Guidone,
> com'ha sì pochi maschi il tenitoro; (?)
> e s'alle moglie hanno suggezïone,
> come esse l'han negli altri lochi a loro.
>
> (The knights asked Guidone why there were so few men in this land, and whether they were subjected to their wives in the same way that women are subjected to their husbands elsewhere.)
>
> (XX, ix, 1–4)

By wondering whether men are subjected to women on the island as women are subjected to men in the western world, Ariosto effectively acknowledges the intrinsic inequality of the patriarchal system. Harington's version is completely indifferent to Ariosto's feminism and presents instead an assortment of misogynist clichés; for instance, he has the five knights mockingly wonder how on this island a man can satisfy ten women, since in the western world one woman could never be satisfied with just one man:

> [M]uch they wondred at this government,
> They marvell that so great a territorie
> For want of men was not consum'd and spent:
> They thought no lesse the women would be sorie,
> For want of men to live so continent:
> 'Twas strange one man sufficed ten of these,
> Sith one with us can scant one woman please.
>
> (XX, ix, 2–8)

The joke is not to be found anywhere in Ariosto, but is entirely in line with Harington's general attitude; women's sexual insatiability and female wantonness are both widespread *topoi* commonly used in anti-feminist literature.

Apart from Harington's treatment of Ariosto's martial heroines, whose virile activities might have been the source of a specific uneasiness on the translator's part, similar misogynist comments are in fact present in the depiction of virtually every female character of the *Furioso*. Particularly fascinating are a few passages in which Ariosto elaborates on writing and, specifically, women's writing; he devotes much of canto XXXVII to an ample and detailed celebration of women writers. Providing a link with his direct subject matter (Bradamante and Marfisa) through his candid regret that the two knights did not write their own *cantari*, the Italian poet claims that the risk that women be forgotten or ignored has become, nowadays, almost non-existent, as they are now able to render themselves immortal, without having to recur to the help of men, who are so often envious and untrustworthy:

[m]a per invidia di scrittori state
non sète dopo morte conosciute:
il che più non sarà, poi che voi fate
per voi stesse immortal vostra virtute.
Se far le due cognate sapean questo,
si sapria meglio ogni lor degno gesto.

(In conclusion, ladies, every age has been blessed with many a woman worthy of being recorded; but, because of writers' envy, you have been forgotten after your death. This will no longer be the case, because now you can ensure your own immortality yourselves. Had the two sisters-in-law known how to do this (writing their own story), each of their worthy deeds would be better known.)

(XXXVII, XXIII)

Perhaps unsurprisingly, Harington alters the original lines, ascribing the new state of affairs mentioned by Ariosto, i.e. that the risk of women being forgotten has disappeared, not to the fact that women have at last started to write themselves, but to the fact that *he* (Harington) can talk about them and praise them:

But to conclude both these and others prayse,
That I may follow on my present storie,
I say that both in these and former dayes,
Faire dames have merited great fame and glorie;
Which though by writers envie much decayes,
Yet need you not therefore now to be sorie,
Because amongst us all it is intended,
That this foule fault hereafter shall be mended.

(XXXVII, XV)

What is apparently a fairly literal translation introduces in fact a number of deliberate changes. Where Ariosto presents a clear, logical argument exposing how women, by creating their own literature, can "avenge" the unfair treatment they have been subjected to in the past – ignorance and oblivion – Harington admits that men have been envious in the past, but at the same time begs his readers to believe that, from now on, those very same men ("us all") will suddenly change their attitude and sing women's praises.

Ariosto's argument becomes both more persuasive and less theoretical in his enthusiastic celebration of a number of Italian Renaissance women poets, which Harington significantly shortens, including omitting Ariosto's enthusiastic assertion that, since women can now satisfy their thirst at Mount Helicon's spring, they have reached a position in which *they* could write in praise of men, and not *vice versa*. Most significantly, perhaps, the translator is much colder than Ariosto when praising the poetess Vittoria Colonna, a Renaissance Petrarchist who

[h]a non pur sé fatta immortale
col dolce stil di che il meglior non odo;

ma può qualunque di cui parli o scriva,
trar dal sepolcro, e far ch'eterno viva.

(has not only rendered herself immortal with a sweet style which I have never heard bettered; but who can haul out from the grave anybody whom she speaks or writes about, and make them immortal, too.)

(XXXVII, XVI, 5–8)

Harington greatly weakens this panegyric, ignoring the sonneteer's ability to elevate herself to fame and even restricting her capacity to immortalise those she writes about only to her husband:

[w]hose prayse is sounded hyre
By such a wife, so vertuous, chast, and rare,
As ev'n thy soule it selfe could not desire
A louder trumpe thy praises out to sound.
(XXXVII, XIV, 4–7)

Here, women writers seem to be acceptable only when they fulfil the role of virtuous and chaste wives – and limit their poetic ability to the celebration of their husbands. Whether the translator's approach was influenced by the numerous annotated editions of the poem, which were circulating in an attempt to moralise what was considered to be too liberal a work, and which he frequently used, or whether Harington's misogynist treatment of the women in the poem was the result of more personal motives, is virtually impossible to know. However, his wilful terminological additions, his extensive omissions of entire portions of the poem, and his casual insertion of parenthetical sentences are at least partly indicative of a pervasive attitude, certainly consonant with his time, but also surprising in a text that, in its original version, consistently expresses a great degree of esteem towards the female sex.

Notes

1 Mario Praz, *The Flaming Heart: Essays on Crashaw, Machiavelli, and Other Studies in the Relations between Italian and English Literature from Chaucer to T. S. Eliot* (New York: W. W. Norton, 1958), p. 289.
2 Jason Lawrence, "'Non sono io quel che paio in viso': *Othello*, Cinthio and *Orlando Furioso*", in *Shakespeare and Intertextuality. The Transition of Cultures between Italy and England in the Early Modern Period*, ed. Michele Marrapodi (Rome: Bulzoni, 2000), p. 122.
3 Andrew S. Cairncross, "Shakespeare and Ariosto: *Much Ado about Nothing, King Lear*, and *Othello*", *Renaissance Quarterly*, 29, 2 (1976): 178–82.
4 Juliet Dusinberre, "Much Ado about Lying: Shakespeare and Sir John Harington in Dialogue with *Orlando Furioso*", *The Italian World of English Renaissance Drama: Cultural Exchange and Intertextuality*, ed. Michele Marrapodi (Newark, DE: University of Delaware Press, 1998), p. 242.
5 Townsend Rich, *Harington and Ariosto: A Study in Elizabethan Verse Translation* (New Haven, CT: Yale University Press, 1940), p. 178.
6 Ginevra, daughter to the King of Scotland, is condemned to be burnt alive after being accused of having admitted a man into her rooms; the cruel law must be enforced unless a knight champions the princess, defending her honour. Bradamante's brother Rinaldo, walking through the woods in search of the runaway Angelica, decides to protect the princess in accordance with the chivalric code – irrespective of her guilt or innocence – as soon as he hears of the law. On the way, he encounters Ginevra's maid, Dalinda, who reveals that the former is innocent and that it was actually herself, disguised as the princess, who let her own lover into Ginevra's room.

7 It is useful to remember that, in Tudor times, it was not so rare to translate a text through another translation in a third language, different from both the source and the target languages: it is the case, for example, of George Pettie's translation of Guazzo's *Civile conversazione*, the English title of which includes an illuminating "written first in Italian, and nowe translated out of French by George Pettie" (cited in M. Morini, *Tudor Translation in Theory and Practice* (Burlington: Ashgate, 2006), p. 22). Similarly, the only Scottish "translation" of the *Orlando Furioso*, John Stewart of Baldynneis' twelve-canto *Roland Furious*, was based on Desportes' *Roland Furieux*, as well as on Ariosto's original (R.D.S. Jack, *The Italian Influence on Scottish Literature* (Edinburgh: Edinburgh University Press, 1972), pp. 57–71; John Corbett, "Writtin in the Language of Scottis Natioun: Literary Translation into Scots", in *Translating Literature*, ed. Susan Bassnett (Cambridge: D.S. Brewer, 1997), pp. 95–118, pp. 101–2). In the case of Beverley and Whetstone, certain French translations (such as Saint-Gelais and De Baïf's) being very close to the original and the English renditions so liberal, it is impossible to say, even after an accurate linguistic analysis, whether the English writers had, at their disposal, the original or the French translated version.

8 Praz, p. 290.

9 A riend of George Gascoigne (in the praise of whose *A Hundredth Sundrie Flowers* he wrote a commendatory poem), Whetstone is now mostly remembered for *Promos and Cassandra* (1578), a play which inspired the plot of Shakespeare's *Measure for Measure*. He visited Italy in 1580, a trip which resulted in a didactic collection of stories, the *Heptameron of Civill Discourses* (1582).

10 Charles Prouty, "Elizabethan Fiction: Whetstone's *The Discourse of Rinaldo and Giletta* and Grange's *The Golden Aphroditis*", in *Studies in Honour of A. H. R. Fairchild*, ed. Charles Prouty, Vol. 21, no. 1 (Columbia, MO: The University of Missouri Studies, 1946), p. 139.

11 In particular, the literal version begun by Saint-Gelais and completed by De Baïf (1572).

12 Prouty, p. 139.

13 Paul A. Scanlon, "Whetstone's 'Rinaldo and Giletta': The First Elizabethan Prose Romance", *Cahiers Élizabéthains*, 14 (1978): 7.

14 Alistair Fox, *The English Renaissance: Identity and Representation in Elizabethan England* (Oxford: Blackwell, 1997), p. 165.

15 Paul J. Alpers, *The poetry of 'The Faerie Queene'* (Princeton, NJ: Princeton University Press, 1967), pp. 197–8.

16 Neil R. E. Dodge, "Spenser's Imitations from Ariosto", *PMLA*, 12, 2 (1897): 190 (pp. 151–204).

17 *Ibid.*, p. 194.

18 *Ibid.*, p. 193; p. 195.

19 *Letter to Raleigh*, pp. 35–6.

20 The *Cinque Canti* are a development of, mainly, two threads of the *Furioso* (the praise of Ruggiero's deeds, and the betrayal of Gano di Maganza), composed by Ariosto around 1518–19 for inclusion in the poem, precisely after the XLV octave of canto XL. However, Ariosto never brought himself to include the fragment in the *Furioso*, mainly because of the pessimistic tone pervading the cantos, ill-suited to that of the rest of the epic; they were only published posthumously, by his son Virginio, as an appendix to the Aldine edition of 1545. The Sospetto passage is part of the account of Gano di Maganza's treachery.

21 Pursglove, analysing the phrasing of the titlepage of Tofte's Boiardo ("done into English Heroicall Verse"), finds in it an echo of Harington's title, *Orlando Furioso in English Heroical Verse*, thus confirming the possibility of Tofte's knowledge of Harington (Glyn Pursglove, "Robert Tofte, Elizabethan Translator of Boiardo", in *The Renaissance in Ferrara and its European Horizons – Il Rinascimento a Ferrara e i suoi orizzonti europei*, ed. Walter Moretti and June Salmons (Swansea: University of Wales Press, 1984), pp. 111–22 (117). This knowledge is certain by the time of his publication of *Ariosto's Satyres* (in which he quotes from Harington's translation).

22 Pamela J. Benson, *The Invention of the Renaissance Woman* (University Park, PA: Pennsylvania University Press, 1992), p. 113.

23 "The whole work being enjoined me as a penance by that Saint, nay, rather goddess, whose service I am only devoted unto" (cit. in Rich, p. 23).

24 See Selene Scarsi, *Translating Women in Early Modern England: Gender in the Elizabethan Translations of Ariosto, Boiardo, and Tasso* (Aldershot, UK: Ashgate, 2010).

8 The Italian *comici* and *commedia dell'arte*

Richard Andrews

> The best actors in the world, either for tragedy, comedy, history, pastoral, pastoral-comical, historical-pastoral, tragical-historical, tragical-comical-historical-pastoral, scene individable, or poem unlimited. Seneca cannot be too heavy, nor Plautus too light. For the law of writ and the liberty, these are the only men.
>
> (*Hamlet*, Act II, Scene 2)

This much-quoted actors' publicity brochure, delivered orally by Polonius, is applied in *Hamlet* to a fictional group of touring players who are not presented as hailing from Italy. Nevertheless, at least two modern anglophone scholars have already used the phrase 'the law of writ and the liberty' as a peg on which to hang their descriptions of Italian professional companies in the sixteenth and seventeenth centuries. Both Louise George Clubb and Michael Anderson have seen the expression 'the law of writ' as referring to the performance of scripts learned by heart; while 'the liberty' is seen as indicating the famously Italian practice of improvisation on a scenario.[1] (We shall see that the word 'improvisation', granted the baggage of associations which it carries from modern drama schools, may have to be used with some caution.) Clubb and Anderson are making the point that Italian professional troupes were indiscriminately capable of delivering both memorised scripts and devised scenarios, and that it is anachronistic for theatre historians to treat the practice of actors' improvisation as if it were somehow fenced off from other methods of performance, in a world of its own. The mention of a range of tones stretching from Seneca to Plautus also reflects the repertoire of Italian companies. The term *comici* which denotes simply 'actors' – and the much later expression *commedia dell'arte* – should not be translated into an assumption that Italian players interpreted only 'comedy', generically defined. The fictional company whose nationality we do not know, is prepared in its visit to fictional Elsinore to cover a full gamut of dramatic genres, including the bloodthirsty *Murder of Gonzago*, alias *The Mousetrap*. The same flexibility was deployed by groups such as the Gelosi, the Confidenti, the Uniti, and the Fedeli, who built such a reputation touring Italy, France, and Spain. Shakespeare may not have had Italian examples in mind; but whether he did or not, Polonius's speech now provides scholars with an irresistible set of tags which accurately summarise the activities of those internationally famous troupes.

The task of this essay is to explain how professional Italian *comici* operated and what they performed, drawing on accounts offered by the most recent scholarship. The purpose is to enable readers of English Tudor and Stuart plays to make reliable judgements about the extent to which these troupes did, or indeed did not, influence English drama.

DOI: 10.4324/9781315612720-10

For some time, scholars working in English used to gain their picture of Italian improvised theatre from two large-scale (and large-format) publications dating from the early twentieth century: Allardyce Nicoll's *The World of Harlequin*, and *The Italian Comedy* translated from the French of Pierre Louis Duchartre.[2] The material offered there, and its interpretation, are derived from the first wave of '*commedia dell'arte* scholarship' which arose in France in the nineteenth century. In the light of work done since by Italian scholars (most of which has not been translated),[3] those surveys now appear as incomplete or selective: they are also heavily slanted towards a romanticised view, over-influenced by what is known about Italian actors in France in the seventeenth and eighteenth centuries, rather than by their initial period of creative innovation which dates from around 1550–1630. In English, more recently, a much more balanced account has been provided by Kenneth and Laura Richards,[4] and important ground has been broken regarding the methodology of improvisation and the structure of recited texts, by Tim Fitzpatrick and Robert Henke.[5] We have also paid more attention to the choices made by Italian professionals regarding what kind of plots they chose to dramatise, as exemplified by the extensive collections of scenarios which survive from the period.[6] However, the picture painted by Duchartre and Nicoll, and indeed the painted or engraved pictures of actors which they selected for reproduction,[7] have created for anglophone historians and practitioners of theatre a somewhat one-sided view of *commedia dell'arte*, from which it is time to move on.

We could start by pointing out that the term '*commedia dell'arte*' is a late coinage by scholars. In a play of 1750 the Italian dramatist Goldoni referred to '*commedie dell'arte*' in the plural, meaning 'plays mounted by the professionals' of that time.[8] This is the first documented appearance of such an expression. Shifting the plural '*commedie*' to the singular '*commedia*', to designate a whole theatrical genre or practice, was a critical convenience which is now too well entrenched to be easily abandoned, but it has no basis in any usage from the time when this form of theatre was being created. The companies of *comici* who functioned in the period around 1600 are the forerunners of those that Goldoni knew, but they were significantly different in many ways.

The word 'arte' is at least accurate in denoting professionality (the word, among other meanings, denotes an Italian trade 'guild', and also an artisan 'craft'); and there is no doubt that the phenomenon we are discussing, whatever we then call it, was created by professional Italian companies. The first surviving notarial document regarding the constitution of such a group dates from 1545, in Padua.[9] This contract lists no women performers: the first one which does so, and which is still extant, is from 1564. The emergence of the actress in Italy was to have a major seminal effect on the whole of European or 'western' culture: Vincenza Armani and Isabella Andreini paved the way, however distantly, for Sarah Bernhardt, Maria Callas, and Marilyn Monroe. In a historical context, though, it is difficult now to trace how and when female performers first appeared. It is even harder to explain why they were accepted, granted the huge social prejudices which existed against women 'exposing themselves' in public in any performance which claimed cultural or social respectability. Nevertheless, we read from archived correspondence that in 1567 the Duchy of Mantua was visited by two competing theatre companies, both including women: one was directed by an actress whose stage name was 'Flaminia', and the other run jointly by a 'Pantalone' (possibly Giulio Pasquati) and the actress Vincenza Armani. The artistic and commercial rivalry between the groups was made more interesting for the public by the fact that each leading lady was being courted by a different aristocratic patron – it is reported that the whole city was divided between fans of Flaminia and of Vincenza. As well as mounting improvised comic scenarios, each woman is mentioned as starring in a more serious play, one based on the Virgilian story of Dido and the other taken from Ariosto's *Orlando furioso.*[10] By the 1560s, then, professional touring companies were an established fact of life in northern Italy, and women were among their major star attractions. The episode also confirms that *commedia dell'arte* companies did not restrict their repertoire to what Frank Kermode has referred to as 'jocose pantomime':[11] the Dido story could only be treated tragically, and the one derived from Ariosto, however mixed in tone, would involve a serious love story. In fact these dramas seem to linger more in the memory of the Mantuan correspondents of 1567 than do any strictly comic shows.

In fact it is now being argued that the presence of actresses was instrumental in moving the content of Italian improvised theatre up market and away from unbroken scurrility, introducing more demanding levels of rhetoric and emotional display.[12] If English actors preferred to believe the opposite, and to see Italian actresses as mountebank whores, their conservatism was probably professional as well as moral: they wanted to denigrate and exclude what could have been dangerous competition. We know, of course, that they succeeded in keeping actresses off the English stage until the Restoration. In terms of historical origins, though, Tudor and Stuart propaganda may have had a point. The most persuasive theory now offered about who the first Italian actresses were, and how they joined the profession, is that they were recruited from the ranks of high-class courtesans, 'cortegiane oneste', who trained themselves to entertain gentlemanly clients with a sophisticated combination of talents including musical proficiency and the ability to improvise courtly verse.[13] The actress Isabella Andreini (1562–1604) made huge efforts to counter this image, and to establish herself as a cultural and social icon beyond reproach – poetess, member of an Academy, virtuous wife and mother. She was successful in convincing a wide public in France as well as in Italy (to the extent of being granted a civic funeral in Lyon, where she died of a miscarriage while on tour); but her reputation does not seem to have crossed the English Channel.[14]

There were two central features in the methodology of Italian professional *comici*: the use of fixed stereotypical roles (some of which, but not all, were characterised by facial masks); and the technique of constructing a performance which we now refer to as 'improvisation'.[15] Both of these raise questions regarding their possible influence on, or transference into, English theatre.

Most Italian actors specialised in playing one single stereotyped role in the course of a career; and many of them were better known by the name of their stage character than by the name with which they were baptised. Despite our insistence on the broad generic repertoire of Italian professional *comici*, it is clear that the composition of a company was structured around the casting needs of comic plots in particular. A fully constituted troupe would include two male lovers (*Innamorati*); two female lovers (*Innamorate*); at least two specialists in different roles of old comic fathers (*Vecchi*); two comic male servants (*Servi*); and one braggart *Capitano*. A female servant figure eventually also became common, though initially these were often played by a male actor: what the French later called the *soubrette* role for an actress was perhaps slowly becoming established after 1600. Actors playing the Lovers, of both sexes, usually chose a stage name which they hoped would not be re-used: Orazio, Flavio, Lelio, Fulvio, and many others, each tried to present themselves as unique male personalities; as did

Flaminia, Isabella, Lidia, Valeria, and so on, among the women. In non-comic dramas, they then took on whatever name was prescribed by an existing plot; so Isabella Andreini developed her trademark 'mad scenes' using the name Isabella in comedies, but would use the same material under other names (such as, in one case, Alvira[16]) in tragedy. The same was true of braggart Captains: each actor taking such a role would invent for himself a ludicrous name such as Spavento ('Terror'), Matamoros ('Moor-Slayer'), or Coccodrillo ('Crocodile'), and the title 'Capitano' was attached to all of them. It is well known, though, that the names of the most familiar farcical roles – the term *parti ridicole* was expressly attached at the time to the old fathers and the comic servants – began to be passed from one actor to another, over a number of generations. The names and characters which survived for longest among the old patriarchs were the caricature Venetian merchant Pantalone (originally called simply by the Venetian honorific title 'il Magnifico'), and the pseudo-learned Dottor Graziano. Female servants were often called Franceschina: the name Colombina became popular much later. Among the male servants there were variations on the name Zan or Zanni (a northern dialect form for Giovanni), together with the well-defined roles of Pedrolino, Brighella, Scapino, Scaramuccia, and eventually Arlecchino. It is worth noting (though the fact may have limited relevance for studies of Tudor and Stuart theatre) that the name Arlecchino or Harlequin was not especially well known in Italy around the year 1600: at that time the role belonged solely to the single actor who was still developing it, Tristano Martinelli (1557–1630).[17] The days when Italian improvised theatre could rightly be called 'The World of Harlequin' were still in the future: they arose very much from the success of Italian actors playing the role in Paris in the seventeenth and eighteenth centuries. Martinelli had in fact created his stage personality in Paris in the 1580s, adapting a diabolic figure named Hellekin from French and northern European folk legend: the figure is perhaps most familiar now as the Erlkönig, explored in verse by Goethe and in music (among others) by Schubert.[18]

Later in the seventeenth century, the entry into the genre of comic figures such as Coviello, Tartaglia, and especially Pulcinella (Polichinelle in French, Mr Punch in English), signalled a greater participation by actors and stereotyped figures from the southern half of Italy, especially Naples. The regional provenance of the more comic figures was in fact a central part of the Italian 'arte' experience, because each of them used a specific local accent or dialect as one of their most important identifying badges. Before the arrival of Pulcinella, most of the varieties of speech used were from north of the Appenines. Pantalone spoke in Venetian; the Dottore in Bolognese mixed with bad Latin; most of the servants (eventually) in a mocking version of peasant dialect from the valleys round Bergamo; and the earliest Capitani had a heavy Spanish accent. The fact that the Lovers of both sexes spoke academic literary Italian (or 'Tuscan'), and deployed the full force of Petrarchan and Platonic rhetoric, distinguished their roles even more sharply from the *parti ridicole*. All these stylised speech registers remained unchanged in Italian troupes until the eighteenth century and beyond. They were a feature which would have more difficulty in crossing linguistic frontiers. Nevertheless, mockery of strange accents (by both writers and performers) is common to all comic theatre; and one cannot exclude the possibility of some English dramatists noting what the Italians were doing, as well as following their own existing stereotypes. With regard to Shakespeare one could speculate about Dogberry; but most of all about Dr Caius in *The Merry Wives*, with his caricatured French. His personality in other respects is a fusion of two Italian roles: a Dottore and a Capitano.

The more detailed characteristics of Italian fixed 'masks' (whether they were physically masked or not) were inseparable from the roles they were likely to play in a typical comic plot.

The derisive targeting of miserly or lustful old fathers derives ultimately from Plautus – from the sort of intrigue which inspired the earliest fully scripted Humanist comedies in Italian (*commedie erudite*), and then passed seamlessly into scenarios for improvisation. In such stories, the main function of an older man was to be a 'blocking' character against the amorous ambitions of his son, and to be comprehensively tricked and defeated by his scheming slave. In Italian scenarios, Pantalone and Dottor Graziano are very often victims in a similar fashion. Some more moralistic Italian critics disapproved of this tendency to mock the patriarch figure whose authority was the bedrock of social hierarchies. Improvising actors took little notice of this inhibition, because Pantalone and Graziano were popular with audiences; but such sensitivities may partly explain the relative infrequency of such characters on the English stage. Pantalone, in particular, tended to oppose his son in the battle of wits for one of just three reasons: because he was mean with his money; because of a knee-jerk desire to impose his patriarchal will; or because he had conceived an inappropriate lust for one of the young women in the plot, possibly the one whom his son wanted to marry.[19] The emphasis in the last case was on the unquestioning assumption, in this kind of comedy, that old men in love are by definition ridiculous: Pantalone (and also the Capitano) could be characterised by foolishly lovelorn soliloquies. Dottor Graziano too might fall into one of these traps; but his main function was to demonstrate, at great length, the complete failure of his pretensions to scholarly knowledge (which could be in fields literary, legal, or philosophical, more often than medical). The tirades of the greatest Dottori were strictly untranslatable, because they were made up of total nonsense: in stylised Bolognese dialect mixed with macaronic Latin, language and logic were torn apart and almost every word replaced with a similar-sounding one, preferably with sexual or scatological overtones. Other characters on stage were reduced to exasperation – and spectators, by all accounts, to helpless laughter – at the sheer accumulation of gibberish. The Dottore was thus a 'blocking' character in a different sense: his speeches brought dramatic action to a halt, and his interlocutors had to silence him or get him off the stage.[20]

Braggart Capitani were also originally inspired by Plautus (the '*Miles gloriosus*' appears in more comedies than just the one which bears his name); though they then came to express a more topical Italian derision of occupying Spanish soldiers. A Capitano was full of lengthy bombast about his military prowess, but then when actually faced with a fight he either ran away or concocted an elaborate excuse. The bombast itself could be of various types. Extremely banal exploits could be recounted as though they were superhuman – the equivalent of the folk-tale formula of killing 'seven (flies) at one blow'. More often the claims made were in fact superhuman: he has devastated opposing armies single-handed, he has killed people with a frown or a glare. Isabella Andreini's husband Francesco was a Capitano: he published a collection of scenes and speeches from his personal repertoire in which, as often as not, he boasts of consorting with classical gods or abstract personifications in a world of complete fantasy.[21]

In terms of their function in the plot, the clownish servant characters of Italian improvised theatre were derived, via scripted *commedia erudita*, from the Plautine slave. From the start, though, there were some clear divergences. Servants in these comedies were indeed often cunning and tricky, devising elaborate deceptive plots against the patriarchs. However, in many cases their devices failed, or became irrelevant to the real dénouement: in written Humanist comedies, the proportion of successful to unsuccessful conspiracies by servants gives the impression of being about equal. When the professional masks took over, things were not very different. One reads much about a canonical division of roles between the cunning masterful *primo Zani* and the foolish *secondo Zani;* but in practice this distinction was often either blurred or not observed at all.[22]

As regards their character traits, these lower-class masks have tendencies which appear less often in English Renaissance drama. Italian stage servants were usually seen as peasants migrated into town, which explains the choice of country-bumpkin Bergamask as their preferred dialect. Their prevailing comic characteristics were therefore stupidity and verbal confusion; an obsession with food and drink, of which they felt permanently deprived; and a relaxed or predatory attitude to sex, which led them to make immediate advances to female servants. (Harpo Marx, pursuing young women at speed across the cinema screen, can be seen as a direct descendant.) Over the decades there was a shift from verbal confusion to sharp verbal repartee, a move which happened at different speeds in different cases. In fact in all theatrical cultures the pronouncements of a stage clown attain an inconsistent balance between amusing idiocy and equally amusing wit. Female servants, or lower-class female characters in general, tend in Italian comedy to have a low threshold of sexual morality, whether pursued by Zani and Arlecchino or exploited by employers such as Pantalone. There is the clear impression that whereas the higher-class female Lovers have reputations to protect, for themselves and their families, plebeian Franceschina has no 'honour' to lose. Servants of both sexes can be found eavesdropping on the Lovers' conversations and deriding the high-flown language and aspirations which they overhear: another example of the audience laughing in collusion with the clown, rather than at him.

The Lovers themselves played a central role in Italian improvised comedy: the fact that their verbal and emotional style is now so hard to appreciate has sometimes led historians to underestimate their importance and their popularity with the public.[23] Surrounded by masks who expressed scurrility and idiocy in caricatured dialects, these male and female stars developed a repertoire based on the most elaborate and mannered expressions of Baroque literary language. They used this sometimes in order to play what we would characterise as straight 'love scenes'; but most often they performed dialogues of contrast, jealousy and misunderstanding, often involving a kind of stichomythia in which the rhetorical conceit of one interlocutor was developed or twisted by the other in symmetrical patterns. In addition, of course, stage Lovers delivered extended monologues of ecstasy or despair: their long tirades of desperation included the 'mad scenes' for which Isabella Andreini was particularly famous. If we perceive a tendency towards expressing pain rather than delight or affection, this simply depends on the need for their love to encounter obstacles (self-created, or imposed by others) in order to provide drama. We should then note, though, that the range of emotional tone in the stories performed was very wide. The same rhetoric could be applied to misunderstandings which were foolish and farcical, leaving the Lovers themselves as figures of fun; or to serious and painful emotional or moral dilemmas. (Shakespeare, with his perhaps unique complexity, managed to compose a play offering both of these tendencies, in *Much Ado About Nothing*.) Isabella Andreini – whose personal range is unusually well documented in the published scenarios of Flaminio Scala – was clearly capable of covering the whole gamut. She sometimes appears as a commanding moral presence who imposes proper solutions on her wayward fellow-characters. In other plots, though, she can be a daughter pregnant out of wedlock; or a deceiving unfaithful wife; or a betrayed woman adopting male disguise to hunt down her lover. In fact the female lover disguised as a boy was an especially popular plot device: it was launched by scripted Humanist comedies composed in Siena in the 1530s and 1540s, including *Gl'ingannati* of 1532 which is accepted as a source for *Twelfth Night*. Male *Innamorati* in Italian plays could also cover a wide range: fidelity or inconstancy, incompetence or cunning, moral integrity or downright treachery. We can only speculate on how each one of them did this while also retaining the single recognisable stage personality which was crucial for their success with the public. Perhaps a distant clue can be provided by the way in which modern Hollywood stars impose parameters on themselves and their choice of roles.

In fact the retention of an identifiable personality, which could be adapted to a wide range of dramatised stories and functions within a plot, lay at the centre of the artisan technique adopted and developed by Italian professional actors. The servant Pedrolino might sometimes be loyal to his master, sometimes treacherous; he might have the courage to take risks in one story, while at other moments show the comic cowardice usually associated with clowns, and with the lower classes of society. This inconsistency – which might be perceivable even within a single play – did not matter, provided he did everything in a recognisably 'Pedrolino' manner. The stage personality was built on clear-cut external features: Pedrolino's style of bodily gesture, his costume, his mask – and most of all, his accent and his language. Some of these would be modified as the role was passed on from one actor to another; but a degree of consistency and continuity was essential for the mask to be recognised and accepted. The task of an actor playing Pedrolino, or Pantalone, was comparable to that faced in the twentieth century or even later by a 'Professor' who sets himself up on a British holiday beach to voice and manipulate the 'Mr Punch' puppet. He cannot be identical in every way to his rivals and predecessors; he may invent completely new stories with Mr Punch as protagonist; but there are certain key features – most of all, vocal features – which are indispensable. Another analogy can be found in silent film comedies of the early twentieth century. Charlie Chaplin's 'tramp' character was not always a tramp, and he fluctuated wildly between clumsiness and physical skill, between bravery and timidity – but for the viewer he was still always the same person. Then, when sound was introduced to the cinema, the three Marx Brothers characters added clear-cut voices and accents to their unchangeable caricatured faces and costumes, thus representing perhaps the last widely-known incarnation of the professional Italian approach to performed comedy. (Except, of course, that Harpo's 'vocal style' was the absence of any voice at all.) For the Lovers too, as far as we can now judge, it was essential to maintain a particular verbal register, even perhaps a particular level of rhetorical artifice, in order to play their parts acceptably. Here too we might conclude that actors in equivalent roles in Marx Brothers film comedies were doing a similar job: even if the romantic rhetoric was a little more low-key than in the seventeenth century, heroes and heroines made the same determined bid for audience sympathy by constantly saying the right things in the right stereotypical way.

The way in which Italian actors maintained the required consistency for their roles, in all performances, is linked to the most famous element in their methodology – what is now most commonly referred to as 'improvisation'. This technique was so clearly attributed to the Italian professionals as to be designated internationally just as 'Italian comedy', though words corresponding to 'improvised' or 'improvisation' were also used. In Italy itself, the process was most often called *recitare a soggetto* (with the memorisation of a pre-existing script designated as *premeditato*). The 'soggetto' was the plot or story which had been chosen for the performance, the outline of which is sometimes now preserved for us in scenario documents. The 'recitare', the words used to perform the 'soggetto', were supplied by the actors; which means that in the vast majority of cases those words cannot have survived textually. In professional or commercial terms, Italian 'arte' companies simply dispensed with the services of a dramatist. The troupe leader (*capocomico*) would construct a new combination of existing plot relationships, storylines, scenic confrontations, and dénouements, and cobble them into a scenario. Most of the components would be filched from existing printed plays, from other scenarios performed previously, or from a growing stock of narrative units common to the whole profession and passed around by oral dissemination. Some of the individual scenarios created were successful enough to recur over two centuries, with minor adaptations, in a succession of different surviving collections. In all cases, on any given night, the version of the scenario performed had to be tailored to fit the cast available to the company at that moment. It was the job of each actor to come up with words which activated the scenario on stage, and which matched stylistically the characteristics of her or his fixed role.

This, then, was indeed an actors' theatre as opposed to a dramatist's theatre. It was also a theatre of 'improvisation', but it is important to recognise exactly what that term meant at the time, and not to confuse it with techniques and ambitions which are implied by the same word today. For modern students and practitioners of theatre, including those taught by formalised schools such as that of Jacques Lecoq, improvisation is an attempt at constant innovation, a test of an actor's *ad hoc* creativity and inventiveness: the ideal outcome is a performance which will be substantially different every night.[24] From surviving evidence, it would seem that quite different techniques were adopted by Italian professional actors around 1600 – rather than *inventing* their speeches and dialogues afresh for every performance, they *repeated and recycled* suitable material which they had studied in advance, learned in many cases by heart, and incorporated into a personal repertoire. In order to equip themselves, they read extensively, each actor soaking his or her brain in the verbal style and concepts which were suitable to the role they played. The following is an excerpt from an all-purpose seventeenth-century prologue, a virtuosic exercise composed to be attached to any comedy: the serving-maid Ricciolina gives the audience an idea of how her company colleagues have prepared themselves behind the scenes:

> In the morning the Leading Lady summons me: 'Hey, Ricciolina, bring me *Fiammetta* the lover, because I want to study'. Pantalone wants Andrea Calmo's *Letters*. The Captain wants *The Tirades of Capitano Spavento*. Zani wants Bertoldo's *Witty Sayings*, the *Fuggilozio* ['Fleeing Idleness'], and the *Ore di Ricreazione* ['Hours of Recreation']. Doctor Graziano wants the *Sentences* of the Erborenze, and the *Novissima Poliantea*, Franceschina wants the *Celestina*, to learn how to play the bawd. The Lover wants the works of Plato.[25]

The best Italian actors, therefore, based their artisan skills, which on the face of it might seem purely 'oral', firmly on 'literary' or at least printed sources; and a large part of what they delivered on stage was learned and repeated, rather than invented. They *supplied the text* for their performances – they adapted and organised it so that it delivered the events required by the scenario, expressed the required emotions, realised the required comic effects. Whether they *improvised text*, in any modern sense of the word, is a delicate question of semantics. In a treatise explaining his craft, the actor Nicolò Barbieri also underplays spontaneous invention, and highlights second-hand recycling:

> Actors study and fill their memories with a whole load of things – mottoes, conceits, speeches of love, reproaches, despairings and delirium, so as to have them ready for the occasion ... There isn't a single good book that they haven't read, no fine conceit that they haven't taken, no formal description of anything that they haven't imitated, no fine epigram that they haven't gathered, because they're constantly reading and leafing through books. Many of them translate speeches from foreign languages and make them their own, many others invent, imitate, and amplify.[26]

The Italian scholar Siro Ferrone, quoting Ricciolina's prologue, emphasises in particular the complete absence, from this approach to acting and indeed to dramaturgy, of even the most minimal concept of intellectual property.[27] We have to recognise that much of the 'improvisation' of Italian professional actors was built around systematic plagiarism: in so far as each actor possessed an original repertoire, it was largely constructed by a technique analogous to dismantling existing edifices and re-using the bricks. We must also note that the skills involved were verbal, and that the genre was not characterised exclusively by acrobatic slapstick. For as long as these troupes were playing to Italian audiences, they were being listened to at least as much as they were being watched. When they moved abroad and had to conquer a language barrier, the importance of bodily expression was bound to be increased. This is one reason why a scholarly approach based on the French experience has tended to give an impression of a more 'physical' theatre: earlier experience in Italy would have offered a different balance of emphases.[28]

Having said this, though, we must not push the revisionist pendulum too far. Many moments of sheer clownery performed by the *parti ridicole* were no doubt based on genuinely creative invention on the part of an individual actor. Some of the gags were tried and tested, and became the so-called 'lazzi' eventually catalogued with identifying names by some professionals.[29] Others, certainly, arose from *ad hoc* inspiration in the course of an individual performance. If this had not been the case, the very particular admiration which was afforded by international audiences to the 'Italian' method, and to individual star performers, would have had little to base itself on. Moreover, the surviving visual evidence, one-sided as it may perhaps be, has left a vivid impression of grotesque and expressive bodily performance.

The essentially oral nature of the improvisation skill means that it is hard for any text to have survived which could be seen as a '*commedia dell'arte* script': in strict logic, the phrase is a contradiction in terms. Even a direct transcription from a performance would be a little suspect, as regards its accuracy; and there are no extant texts which actually claim such a status. Most of our insights into the style and humour of the various masks come from texts which were published separately, and which in modern terms rank as 'merchandising' material. The techniques or structures which survive in theatrical texts, and which we can identify as possibly relating to improvisation, are both few and speculative. By coincidence, however, one of them is alluded to in a single stage direction in Shakespeare: the moment in *Henry IV, Part 1* (Act II, Scene 4), when Prince Hal and Poins tease the lowly servant Francis in the Eastcheap tavern:

> Here they both call him; the Drawer stands amazed, not knowing which way to go.

No actor can have any difficulty in 'improvising' this short sequence without a written script. The Prince and Poins just have to call out 'Francis!', the Drawer perhaps to repeat 'Anon, anon, sir!', and they can do all this as many or as few times as they choose. The scene is repetitive, and it is also elastic: once the actors grasp its very simple principle, they can just do it. There is a compositional technique involved here which facilitates improvisation, and which elsewhere we have called the 'elastic gag'; and there is enough written material in early modern Italian comedies (and later in French imitators such as Molière) to identify its regular use. Dialogues could fall into modular units which involved repetition, which could therefore be expanded or contracted on each occasion, and for which a punch-line or an interruption would signal the moment to move on. It is a structure which also works perfectly well in written scripts, which explains why it has survived textually.[30] It can be applied to sentimental rhetoric as well as to farce. In the last act of *The Merchant of Venice*, when Lorenzo and Jessica compete with one another in references to classical heroes and heroines who met 'on such a night', they are using the same technique. They could in theory offer more examples, or fewer, than the text includes; and it is very easy to imagine a pair of Italian professionals delivering a similar scene.[31] Alongside this repetitive modular structure, the most obvious other tool for improvisors is the development of monologues or other lengthy set speeches, which can be learned by heart and inserted into any story with appropriate minor modifications. Since such speeches are equally common in scripted theatre of the period, and since they probably possessed largely the same characteristics on both side of the methodological divide, it is difficult for a modern analyst to determine the extent to which one form of performance was borrowing from the other.

The presence, or indeed the absence, of '*commedia dell'arte* influence' on English Tudor and Stuart drama is therefore hard to establish on the level of individual scenes and speeches. However, we do have important material for comparison on a larger scale. We may be deprived of '*commedia dell'arte* scripts', that is of the words actually pronounced on stage by Italian improvising actors. We are not so short of '*commedia dell'arte* texts' of another type – the summaries which tell us what stories the Italian troupes chose to adapt, and how they organised the scene-by-scene deployment of their plots. Surviving scenarios from the seventeenth century amount to more than 350, starting with the fifty actually put into print by Flaminio Scala in 1611. (A similar number survives from the eighteenth century, though these are naturally less relevant to our present purpose.[32]) It is important to understand that although the dates of the surviving collections range forward from 1611 to later in the century, their function was retrospective: they assemble examples of theatre material which had already become canonical in the profession, and which had been used in one variation or another over previous decades. The printed collection of Flaminio Scala, therefore (to take just one example) is a redeployment of numerous established theatregrams – stories, scenes, character confrontations, jokes – many of which had been circulating on professional stages and trestles since well before 1600. This statement is reinforced by the fact, to which we shall shortly return, that much of the material can be traced back to published sixteenth-century Italian plays from as far back as the 1530s. When we discover in Scala's printed volume of 1611 plot elements which are also found in *Romeo and Juliet*, or in *The Tempest*, we cannot of course then start talking about 'sources', using the traditional criteria of textual criticism. Not only can we exclude Scala's text in itself as a 'source' for Shakespeare; it is also highly unlikely that a Shakespeare play was ever read by Scala. What we can deduce, however, is that heroines who drink potions in order to pretend to be dead, and love affairs between children of two feuding families, were ideas which had become familiar over a period of time to theatre practitioners in different cultures. They circulated via casual reading, and via the oral theatrical grapevine, and were perceived as belonging to nobody. They were available to be picked up and recycled, separately or together, in a variety of ways – in this case, often in comedies or tragi-comedies which avoided Shakespeare's tragic dénouement. The fake poison device was used quite often, by Scala in print and by other scenario collectors in manuscript, to contribute to a range of plots which have few other resemblances to *Romeo and Juliet*. The whole story originates, of course, in the non-theatrical *novella* by Bandello; but Italian sources provide enough cumulative evidence to show that its theatrical potential was widely recognised and exploited in a deliberately fragmentary fashion.[33]

Overall, the scenario collections show us the range of stories which Italian professional companies preferred to perform – or perhaps, in the case of private manuscript collections, those which their devotees most enjoyed watching and therefore wanted to preserve as a written reminder. In Scala's published volume of 1611, which is produced in a more considered way with an eye on posterity, they fall into well-defined generic categories. In the more informal assemblages, some of which date from not much later, those distinctions begin to be blurred. Plays categorised as 'comedy' always predominate: this is to be expected, granted that the composition of an acting troupe was dictated by a set of required comic roles. The starting formats for 'comedy' were those which had already been established by written Humanist *commedia erudita* in the sixteenth century: Plautine plots of intrigue involving parents, lovers and servants, rapidly diversified with more romanesque elements derived from medieval narrative. As with scripted comedy, the tone could vary between tales involving relatively demanding moral dilemmas for the lovers and others which were very much more superficial and farcical (though the word 'farce' was as yet rarely used in Italy, and had not yet acquired the meaning which we now apply to it). In fact a template had already been created in many published comedies whereby both tones could appear in the same play, the *Innamorati* playing out serious emotions while the *parti ridicole* pursued intrigues of slapstick humiliation alongside them. The great majority of the tales enacted used marriage between the approved pairs of lovers (approved by the audience, that is, not necessarily by their fathers) to create the happy ending: plays celebrating the triumph of adulterous lovers over a miserable cuckold are also found, but such material is less statistically dominant than some critics suggest. By the time the scenarios were being written down, however, there was a strong tendency to contaminate the comic genre with others, particularly with pastoral. In the manuscript collections, a significant number of plots which end in happy marriages are played out in a rustic setting, sometimes with nymphs and shepherds as protagonists, sometimes even with the participation of magicians, satyrs, or classical deities. A few scenarios classed as tragedies do exist; tragi-comedies are a little more numerous; but there is also a greyer category in which full-scale romance episodes are dramatised, in shows which occasionally even aim at an epic quality. The second volume of the seventeenth-century Locatelli collection, in the Casanatense Library in Rome,[34] opens with a scenario simply entitled *Orlando furioso*, which attempts to get through a number of the central (and most emotionally demanding) episodes of Ariosto's very lengthy poem whose definitive edition dates from 1532. Generically the scenario is categorised as an *opera eroica rappresentativa* (best translated as 'heroic work for the stage'), and it has a cast list of forty-one human characters plus three magical animals. To the modern reader, it raises serious questions of how practicable it was to perform; but its presentation on the page follows exactly the same conventions as are applied to the much more modest comedies of intrigue which appear in the same volume. The message being conveyed is that improvising *arte* troupes were willing to tackle absolutely anything – 'scene individable, or poem unlimited' – provided, one assumes in this case, that they could find a patron rich enough to pay the production costs.

The point which must be insisted on is that all these generic categories – comedies, tragi-comedies, pastorals, tragedies, and various kinds of 'heroic' work – were also published in Italy as fully scripted plays. In fact the narrative and scenic elements which were constantly recycled in different combinations, in order to produce new (but not very new) scenarios, were themselves largely taken from those same published dramas. The technique of 'dismantling and re-using the bricks', which we have suggested above was the basis of small-scale improvisation, was also the basis of large-scale dramaturgy. This turns out to be true for written plays, as well as for improvised scenarios. A leading Humanist dramatist from Siena, Alessandro Piccolomini – a person who would certainly have distanced himself firmly from lower-class professional troupes – has left us a tantalising description of his attempt to construct what we would now call a database of characters, speeches and scenes which could be re-arranged in new dramatic combinations.[35] Sadly his examples have not survived; but the project offers a glimpse of combinatory techniques which may well have been all-pervading in the construction of plays, in Italy and possibly also elsewhere.

Improvised drama, and improvising troupes, were thus an important and even unique feature of the Italian theatrical scene; but they were not in any way separated or fenced off from plays written by more academic dramatists. Professionals were always willing to tackle the '*premeditato*', to learn scripts and recite them, as well as to improvise. Leading actors and actor-managers sometimes re-wrote and published, in 'regular' five-act form, versions of three-act scenarios which had been particularly successful. Much of the improvised material itself was taken, recycled, adapted, kaleidoscopically re-arranged, from fully scripted original plays which are not hard to trace. Seminal scripts by authors such as Pietro Aretino, Machiavelli, 'Ruzante', Sforza Oddi, Giambattista della Porta, and the Sienese Accademia degli Intronati were regularly pillaged by troupe leaders creating scenarios.

In 1623, Giovan Battista Andreini, actor and playwright son of Isabella Andreini, published a complex metatheatrical comedy entitled *Due comedie in comedia.* As the title suggests, it contains two plays within the play, performed in a Venetian street by two different fictional companies (some of whose members, in their true identities, then turn out to be disguised participants in the very complicated main plot). One company is an amateur Academy, the other is a troupe of professional *comici.* The characters in the 'comedia dei comici' include the south Italian mask Tartaglia, and a number of unnamed stereotypes of trades and professions (pastrycook, greengrocer, chimney sweep, etc.); but no other recognisable *commedia dell'arte* masks. The professional actor playing the French pastrycook is actually identified in the end as Flaminio Scala: a fictional role has been given to the actor-manager and compiler of those fifty scenarios printed in 1611, who was also a friend and collaborator of Giovan Battista Andreini. Both of the 'comedie in comedia' include sentimentally characterised lovers, whose marriages are lined up to provide happy endings. But it is the play mounted by the dilettante *Accademici* – not the performance offered by the *comici* – which includes as characters the Magnifico (Pantalone), Dottor Graziano, and a braggart Capitano Medoro. Andreini, whatever his other aims, seems to be depicting a theatrical culture rife with what we would now call 'crossover'.

In the years around 1600, Italian theatre was a single seamless phenomenon, certainly as far as its raw dramaturgical material was concerned. The situation may have become very different a century later. But such influences on Elizabethan and Jacobean theatre which may have come from *commedia dell'arte* also came, in many cases, from a wider body of Italian drama, 'tragical-comical-historical-pastoral', in which the scripted and the improvised are hard to distinguish and may not be worth distinguishing. The important step to take is to recognise in the first place the overall relevance to English drama of Italian material composed for, and performed on, the stage. Anglophone scholars need to accept in principle, against a tradition of rather inexplicable resistance to the notion, that the Italian sources of Shakespeare and his contemporaries are in no way limited to prose *novelle* and verse romances.

Notes

1 See "The Law of Writ and the Liberty: Italian Professional Theatre", the "Epilogue" chapter, pp. 249–80, in Louise George Clubb, *Italian Drama in Shakespeare's Time* (New Haven, CT: Yale University Press, 1989); and Michael Anderson, "The Law of Writ and the Liberty", in *Theatre Research International*, 20, 3 (September 1995): 189–99.

2 Allardyce Nicoll, *The World of Harlequin* (Cambridge, UK: Cambridge University Press, 1963); Pierre Louis Duchartre, *The Italian Comedy* (1929), trans. R.T. Weaver (New York: Dover, 1966).

3 The most ground-breaking studies are listed here, in chronological order. Ferdinando Taviani and Mirella Schino, *Il segreto della commedia dell'arte. La memoria delle compagnie italiane del XVI, XVII e XVIII secolo* (Florence: Usher, 1982); Cesare Molinari, *La commedia dell'arte* (Milan: Mondadori, 1985); Ferruccio Marotti and Giovanna Romei, *La commedia dell'arte e la società barocca: la professione del teatro* (Rome: Bulzoni, 1991); Siro Ferrone, Introduction to the anthology *Commedie dell'Arte* (Milan: Mursia, 1985/6); idem, *Attori Mercanti Corsari. La commedia dell'arte in Europa tra Cinque e Seicento* (Turin: Einaudi, 1993). Also other works by Ferdinando Taviani, Roberto Tessari, and Delia Gambelli. For textual material, see Vito Pandolfi, *La commedia dell'arte, storia e testi*, 6 vols. (Florence: Sansoni, 1957–61).

4 Kenneth and Laura Richards, *The Commedia dell'Arte: A Documentary History* (Oxford: Blackwell, 1990).

5 Tim Fitzpatrick, *The Relationship of Oral and Literate Performance Processes in the Commedia dell'Arte. Beyond the Improvisation/Memorisation Divide* (Lewiston, NY; Queenston, ON; Lampeter, UK: Edwin Mellen Press, 1995); Robert Henke, *Performance and Literature in the Commedia dell'Arte* (Cambridge, UK: Cambridge University Press, 2002). A recent study which also deserves attention is Peter Jordan, *The Venetian Origins of the Commedia dell'Arte* (London: Routledge, 2014).

6 R. Andrews, *The Commedia dell'Arte of Flaminio Scala: A Translation and Analysis of 30 Scenarios* (Lanham, MD: Scarecrow Press, 2008).

7 On the question of visual evidence, see the revisionist views introduced by M.A. Katritzky, in *The Art of Commedia. A Study in the Commedia dell'Arte 1560–1620 with Special Reference to the Visual Records* (Amsterdam & New York: Rodopi B.V., 2006).

8 Carlo Goldoni, *Il teatro comico* (1750), Act I Scene 2. There are numerous modern editions of this play.

9 The text of this document is translated by Richards & Richards, pp. 44–6.

10 This episode is discussed by Cesare Molinari, *La commedia dell'arte*, p. 74, on the basis of archived correspondence. See also Eric Nicholson, "Romance as Role Model: Early Female Performances of Ariosto and Tasso", in *Renassance Transactions: Ariosto and Tasso*, ed. Valeria Finucci (Durham, NC: Duke University Press, 1999).

11 Shakespeare, *The Tempest*, ed. Frank Kermode (London: Methuen, 1975), p. lxvii.

12 Henke, *Performance and Literature*, Chapter 6, pp. 86–106.

13 Taviani and Schino, *Il segreto*, cit., especially pp. 331–4.

14 On Isabella, see R. Andrews, "Isabella Andreini and Others: Women on Stage in the Late Cinquecento", in *Women in Italian Renaissance Culture and Society*, ed. Letizia Panizza (Oxford: Legenda, 2000), pp. 316–33; and "Isabella Andreini's Stage Repertoire: the *Lettere* and *Fragmenti*", in *The Tradition of the Actor-Author in Italian Theatre*, ed. Donatella Fischer (Oxford: Legenda, 2013), pp. 30–40.

15 For a more extended version of what now follows, see the Introduction to R. Andrews, *The Commedia dell'Arte of Flaminio Scala*, pp. xviii–xlv.

16 This clearly established example is the tragic scenario *La forsennata principessa* ('The Demented Princess'), which is no. XLI in Flaminio Scala's printed collection of 1611. See Andrews 2008, pp. 264–73.

17 There is now a full Italian biography of Martinelli in Siro Ferrone, *Arlecchino. Vita e avventure di Tristano Martinelli attore* (Bari: Laterza, 2006).

18 A fourteenth-century French miniature depicts Hellequin pushing a cart full of the souls of dead children – it is reproduced in *Zani mercenario della piazza europea*, ed. Anna Maria Testaverde (Bergamo: Moretti & Vitali, 2003), p. 17. Goethe's Erlkönig steals the soul of a boy from his father's arms.

19 Peter Jordan offers a close study of the Pantalone mask in *The Venetian Origins*, especially Chapters 7–8.

20 'Doctorial' tirades were published in Italy as collections of uncontextualised monologues. Their dramaturgical implications appear most clearly in a French example: the Docteur character in Molière's early farce *La Jalousie du Barbouillé*. The solid influence of Italian comedy on Molière is beyond dispute.

21 Francesco Andreini, *Le bravure del Capitano Spavento*, originally published in 1607; now edited by Roberto Tessari (Pisa: Giardini, 1987).

22 Statements about these sharply delineated roles first appear in the writings of the actor-manager Pier Maria Cecchini (1563–c.1645): these treatises attempt to impose his own practices which were not necessarily accepted by others.

23 An Italian scholar, introducing selected examples of stage lovers' rhetoric, has remarked that their role is the one 'which remains most incomprehensible to us in its artistic significance' (Vito Pandolfi: *La commedia dell'arte*, Vol. II, p. 35).

24 I am indebted here to conversations with the actor Toby Jones, along with observations of his performances; and also to consultation with Peter Jordan. The Wikipedia account of the Lecoq method speaks of 'nurturing the creativity of the performer' and of 'encourag[ing] the student to keep trying new avenues of creative expression'. Other modern teachers of *commedia dell'arte* technique have the same tendency. Simply learning suitable material by rote, and then recycling it with variations, is not as far as I am aware part of any modern acting method.

25 Domenico Bruni, *Prologhi, parte seconda* (Undated seventeenth-cent. ms. in the Brera Library, Milan); my translation. Not all the works alluded to are easily traceable – one of their publication dates puts the prologue's composition later than 1611. *Fiammetta* may be the fourteenth-century work by Boccaccio, full of the laments of an abandoned female lover. Andrea Calmo was the first person to perform a Pantalone-type mask: his published *Lettere* (1547) were a model of humorous invention in Venetian dialect. For Capitano Spavento, see footnote 21. The *Astuzie* of 'Bertoldo' (Giulio Cesare Croce) published in 1611, were a series of witty sayings attributed to an uneducated 'wise fool': the *Fuggilozio* of Tommaso Costa (1601), and the *Ore di ricreazione* (1568) of Ludovico Guicciardini, were similar collections. 'L'Erborenze' was one André de Rezende, who published a collection of Latin

sayings in 1575. *La Novissima Poliantea* is as yet untraced. *La Celestina* was the early sixteenth-century Spanish story about an old bawd bringing two lovers together. The works of Plato would be seen as underwriting the 'Platonic' love relationships regularly celebrated in sixteenth-century literature and philosophy: in Italian translation they would provide both concepts and vocabulary for the more high-flown *Innamorati* parts.

26 Nicolò Barbieri, *La Supplica* (originally published 1634), ed. F. Taviani (Milan: Il Polifilo, 1971), p. 23 and 34; my translation.

27 Siro Ferrone, *Attori Mercanti Corsari*, cit., p. 197.

28 During the 1980s the British Arts Council, in categorising different art forms, included *commedia dell'arte* under the heading of 'Mime/Dance'. We would argue that this is a fundamental misapprehension.

29 The centrality of the *lazzo* (plural: *lazzi*) to improvisation technique is probably exaggerated by modern scholars, on the strength of the jargon which had become common in eighteenth-century France. Some of the earliest collections of scenarios, including the printed one of Flaminio Scala, do not use the term at all; and one of them refers to *azzi* rather than *lazzi*, making arguments about the etymology of the word even more difficult. For a traditional account, see Mel Gordon, *Lazzi: The Comic Routines of the Commedia dell'Arte* (New York: Performing Arts Journal Publications, 1983).

30 This proposal was first made in R. Andrews, "Scripted Theatre and the *Commedia dell'Arte*", in *Theatre of the English and Italian Renaissance*, ed. J.R. Mulryne and Margaret Shewring (Basingstoke, UK and London: Macmillan, 1991), pp. 21–54. I have pursued the concept in other writings, e.g. *Scripts and Scenarios: The Performance of Comedy in Renaissance Italy* (Cambridge: Cambridge University Press, 1993), pp. 175–94; and in relation to Molière in particular in "Molière, Commedia dell'Arte, and the Question of Influence in Early Modern European Theatre", in *Modern Language Review*, 100, 2 (April 2005): 444–63.

31 Cf. R. Andrews, "Shakespeare, Molière, et la Commedia dell'Arte", in *La commedia dell'Arte, le Théâtre Forain, et les spectacles de plein air en Europe: XVIe-XVIIIe siècles*, ed. Irène Mamczarcz (Paris: Klincksieck, 1998), pp. 15–27.

32 For a full bibliographical list of these collections, all but one of which remain in manuscript, see Andrews, *The Commedia dell'Arte of Flaminio Scala*, p. 321.

33 For *Romeo and Juliet*, see Richard Andrews, "Resources in Common: Shakespeare and Flaminio Scala", in *Transnational Mobilities in Early Modern Theater*, ed. Robert Henke and Eric Nicholson (Farnham, UK: Ashgate, 2014). For *The Tempest*, R. Andrews, "*The Tempest* and Italian Improvised Theatre", in *Revisiting "The Tempest": The Capacity to Signify*, ed. Silvia Bigliazzi and Lisanna Calvi (London: Palgrave Macmillan, 2014).

34 Rome, Biblioteca Casanatense, *Manoscritti* 1211 and 1212, datable to the first half of the seventeenth century (its compiler died in 1654), and entitled *Della scena di soggetti comici di B. L.R.* The full text of the *Orlando furioso* scenario is reproduced in Anna Maria Testaverde: *I canovacci della commedia dell'arte* (Turin: Einaudi, 2007), pp. 329–52.

35 For details, see Andrews, *Scripts and Scenarios*, pp. 105–6.

9 Giordano Bruno in England

From London to Rome

Gilberto Sacerdoti

In a despatch dated 25 March 1583, the English ambassador in Paris, Henry Cobham, warned Francis Walsingham, secretary of Elizabeth's Privy Council and head of the secret service, of the impending arrival of an unwelcome foreigner: "Doctor Jordano Bruno Nolano, a professor in philosophy, intends to pass into England, whose religion I cannot commend".[1] "Philosophy", "religion": an occasionally mortal conflict as old as Socrates. In early modern Europe, Bruno's fate will be both its most conspicuous re-enactment and the "logical consequence" of a philosophy whose "ontological monism foreshadows in many respects the philosophy of Spinoza", demonstrating "a profound incompatibility with and radical distancing from Christianity".[2]

Due to the influential interpretation proposed by Frances Yates in 1964,[3] Bruno has been widely, even pre-eminently seen as a "Hermetic magus", but in his works he consistently defined himself "a philosopher, which, if it is true, is the most honoured title a man could have".[4] Though traces of Hermeticism are certainly to be found in his works, they actually appear to be "prevalently imbued with a materialistic naturalism of a kind which, at the last stage of his production … will reveal itself as a kind of universal atomism". Indeed:

> [i]f – mainly by reference to sixteenth-century Italian personalities – we take the term Renaissance to indicate a dynamic period of cultural history which by looking back, through the classical civilization, to the *prisca philosophia*, tries to develop (if only intuitively) the data acquired by the so-called "new science", then a philosopher like Giordano Bruno can legitimately be considered not only as a Renaissance philosopher, but as *the* Renaissance philosopher par excellence.[5]

Bruno arrived in England in 1583, and left in 1585. The explosion of his literary activity during the English period yielded six philosophical dialogues in Italian which mark the zenith of his productive power. He later taught in German universities (Wittenberg and Helmsted), and lived briefly in Prague. Having reached Venice in 1591, in 1592 he was arrested and transferred to the Roman jail of the Holy Office. In 1599 Cardinal Bellarmine confronted him with eight heretical propositions, asking for repudiation. He refused. After eight years of trial, on 20 January 1660, Clement VII ordered that he be condemned as an obstinate heretic. The sentence listed among his errors the infinity of the world, the eternity of the universe, the identification of the Holy Ghost with the soul of the world, the denial of Mary's virginity, plus the allegations that Moses simulated his miracles and invented the Law, that the Holy Scripture was but a dream, that Christ was not God but an impostor and a magician.

DOI: 10.4324/9781315612720-11

After hearing the verdict, he said to his judges: "Perhaps your fears in pronouncing this sentence on me are greater than mine in receiving it".[6] On Thursday 17 February 1600 "his tongue was trapped on the way to the stake erected in Campo de' Fiori, and the most striking philosopher of the European Renaissance, stripped naked and bound to a pole, was burnt alive".[7]

"I do not marvel at his tragedy, but I do marvel at his imprudence", wrote Leibniz in 1710.[8] "The fault of his violent death", wrote Monsignor Mercati in 1942, "was not of the inquisitors but of the accused".[9] Whatever one's opinion, we understand what they mean.

From Naples to London

By the time Bruno reached London, his religion had already caused him trouble. Born in Nola in 1548, he entered the Dominican monastery in Naples in 1565, and left it in 1576: he was accused of having cast away the images of the Saints, and of defending the Arian heresy. He sought refuge in Rome, but when he learned that in Naples his attempt to conceal certain forbidden writings of Erasmus in the convent privy had been unearthed, he decided to shed his habit and flee.[10] In 1578 he reached Geneva. Hoping for a position at the University, he formally adhered to Calvinism, but after a violent attack on a distinguished professor he was threatened with excommunication.

He then fled to France. In Toulouse he taught astronomy and philosophy for two years as an ordinary lecturer. But France was at the time ravaged by "the longest and most dreadful civil war that ever was known in any nation".[11] When in 1581 the bloody strife between the Catholic Holy League and the Calvinist Huguenots advanced toward Toulouse, Bruno sought refuge in Paris, where he published his first works. An *Ars memoriae* dedicated to Henry III was warmly received by the king, who made him *lecteur royal.* He maintained contact with the court for five years, due to close links with the *politique* party, whose major exponent, Jean Bodin, Bruno may have met.[12]

The *politiques* were "the true exponents of modern reason of state in the France of the civil wars", and their aim was "to liberate political interest from ecclesiastical interference and confessional passions".[13] But confessional passions were raging again and a new civil war was looming. In 1592 Bruno told his inquisitors that because of "the tumults" in Paris he had gone to London with royal letters of recommendation to the French Ambassador, Michel de Castelnau (a friend of Bodin),[14] at whose house "he did nothing but being his *gentilhomo*". He stayed there for two and a half years, he "went continuously to Court with the ambassador", and "the Queen knew him".[15]

The French lesson

If the news of his uncommendable religion had preceded him to England, in England Bruno would not forget the lesson of "the turbid Garonne" (Toulouse) and "the bloody Seine" (Paris).[16]

In *The Ash Wednesday Supper*, the first of his dialogues, where he expounds for the first time his new infinite and post- or ultra-Copernican universe, Bruno writes that men, "imbued" since childhood with the "discipline and customs" of their home, hate and despise the "laws" and "rites" of other faiths, so that "it has easily become a tradition that our own people think to offer a sacrifice pleasing the gods when they have oppressed, killed, vanquished and assassinated the enemies of our faith" – and *viceversa*, because "no less is this true of all those others, when they have done the same to us". But besides feeding and sanctifying sectarian violence, Christianity was intellectually dangerous, because "to these convictions in matters of religion and faith are added the convictions about sciences", and it is astonishing "how great is the impact [force] of the habit of believing and of being nourished from childhood with certain persuasions, on blocking the understanding of most evident things".[17]

By "most evident things" he means his new infinite and homogeneous universe which shatters to pieces Aristotle's finite and hierarchical cosmos. "Custom", "faith" and "habit" therefore have pernicious effects on a social and philosophical plane. In Bruno's second dialogue, *On the Infinite Universe and Worlds*, Elpino says that "he who would judge correctly must be able to renounce the habit of belief" and "dismiss all prejudice imbibed since his birth".[18]

Since "Bruno believes he can demonstrate that both Aristotelian philosophy and the Christian religion … have been linked to an erroneous cosmology", his cosmos is both anti-Aristotelian and imbued with a "new concept of divinity" which has "a radically anti-Christian character".[19] When he started preaching his "new gospel of the unity and the infinity of the world",[20] expounding "the doctrine of the decentralized, infinite, and infinitely populous universe" with "the fervor of an evangelist",[21] he was fully aware that his new gospel could not but collide with the old one.

The French disaster, which threatened to spill over into England, had convinced him that Christianity was no longer unquestionable. At the end of the civil wars, 4 million French people – out of a total population of 12–15 million – had lost their lives.[22] The Wars of Religion, writes Voltaire, produced "une èspece de barbarie que les Hérules, les Vandales et les Huns n'avaient jamais connue".[23] On the other hand, in 1587 La Noue writes that the civil wars were "the main cause of the diffusion of atheism", and had engendered "un milion de epicuriens et libertins".[24]

The ghost of this barbarism haunts Bruno's cosmological dialogues, but it comes to the fore in his "moral dialogues". "A right understanding of the historical conditions under which Bruno wrote in England", writes Yates, "is not merely a matter of biographical interest", but "it is of absolutely vital importance for the understanding of his mind".[25] These conditions become most clear in *The Expulsion of the Triumphant Beast*, dedicated to Philip Sidney in 1584.[26]

The blot of the world

In the third part of the work, Bruno makes use of an Hermetic apocalyptic text, the "Lament" of the *Asclepius*, in order to divide history into two cycles, one of light and the other of darkness. In the older one, the "wise" Egyptians knew that "Nature is none other than God in things", that "*natura est deus in rebus*", that "Divinity" is "latent in Nature", and that "all of God is in all things". Aware that "God, as absolute, has nothing to do with us except insofar as he communicates with the effects of Nature", Egyptians did not seek Him outside or beyond or above Nature, but in Nature herself: because, "if he [God] is not Nature herself, he is certainly the nature of Nature". Anticipating Spinoza's *Deus sive natura*, the formula of Bruno's Egyptians seems to be *Deus sive natura Naturae*. But then, as the *Asclepius* prophetized, "strange and barbarous people" will arrive, whose "new justices" and "new laws" will hold it holy "to violate the Law of Nature by another supra- or extra- or contrannatural one". Thus ancient wisdom will be destroyed:

> [s]hadows will be placed before light … capital punishment will still be prescribed for him who will apply himself to the religion of the mind … nothing worthy of heaven or of celestials will be heard. Only pernicious angels will remain, who, mingling with men, will force upon the wretched ones every audacious evil as if it were justice, giving material for wars, rapines, frauds … And this will be the old age and the disorder and the irreligion of the world. But … after these things have occurred, the lord and father God … will doubtlessy then put an end to such a blot, recalling the world to its ancient countenance.[27]

The "Lament" is used as an explanatory key for Europe's crisis. The "old age" of the world is "the Judaeo-Christian cycle".[28] With the "wars" and "disorders" that followed the Reformation this cycle has reached its apex of "darkness", and is therefore nearing exhaustion, for "Fate has ordained the vicissitude of shadows and light".[29] As for the "blot" of the world, it is "Christianity itself", within which a true reformation is "intrinsically impossible", because by dividing an inferior Nature from a transcendent God, the Judaeo-Christian "supra- or extra- or contra-nnatural" religion is the first and ultimate root of the crisis.[30] Such a philosophy of history certainly contributed to the self-fulfilment of the prophecy on "capital punishment". His "religion of the mind" was a threat to Christianity, and was dealt with accordingly.

Bruno's equation of "supernatural" with "contrannatural" ridicules the idea of a God exhibiting his supernatural powers in the violation of natural laws, thus reducing Christ's "miracles" such as "walking over the waves" to "bagatelles, impostures, acts of cunning".[31] The same equation and consequences are to be found, roughly a century later, in the *Theological-Political Treatise* (1670), where Spinoza does not "acknowledge any difference between a phenomenon which is contrary to nature and a phenomenon which is above nature": therefore "a miracle, whether contrary to nature or above nature, is a plain absurdity". If Bruno sets the "contrannatural" Christian religion against the natural religion of the Egyptians, Spinoza does much the same. In Europe "the common people imagine that the power and providence of God are most clearly evident when they see something happen contrary to … their habitual views about nature". This imagination dates back to "the first Jews", who "narrated miraculous stories to convince the pagans of their day, who adored visible gods, like the sun, the moon, water, air, and so on, that those gods were … subordinate to the invisible God". The absurd beliefs of both seventeenth-century common people and the first Jews have a common origin: the imagination "that there are two powers, distinct from each other, the power of God and the power of natural things".[32] Much in the same way that for Bruno "Nature is none other than God in things", for Spinoza "the power of God and the power of natural things" are one and the same.

After the publication of Bayle's *Dictionnaire Historique et Critique* in 1697, "the bombshell" exploded "that Bruno was … a philosophical monist, atheistic naturalist, and denier of miracles … whose 'hypothèse est au fond toute semblable au spinozisme', and that both Bruno and Spinoza 'ne reconnoissent qu'une seule substance'". We can agree with Jonathan Israel that Bayle's interpretation of Bruno was "far closer to the mark than most historians would have been willing to accept until recently. For Bruno *did* indeed believe that substance is eternal and can neither be created nor destroyed but merely changes its manifestations".[33] "All that we see of diversity and difference" writes Bruno in *Cause, Principle and Unity*, "is nothing but diverse aspects of one and the same substance" – "the one infinite substance" which "can be whole in all things".[34]

For Bruno, no true reformation was possible without soldering the imaginary fracture between heaven and earth. "The fundamental error of Christianity, long before the Reformation, was the desire to begin with a divinity conceived in its absoluteness": Bruno, presenting "his vision of an infinite universe in which he sought to re-unify terrestrial physics with celestial physics",[35] was seeking to mend an intellectual error which had produced a bad religion – and what a bad religion could do was proven in France.

The English context

On the other side of the Channel the "afflictions of France" had long been perceived as a "looking glasse" reflecting the dangers that threatened England itself. Identical forces were at work in the two countries, whose monarchies had "common enemies". In 1570 Pius V excommunicated Elizabeth, absolving her subjects from their oath of allegiance. In the decade that followed, Thomas Cartwright, the leader of English Calvinism, would proclaim that a king is "an ordinary member of the church and as such could be excommunicated". In 1593 Richard Bancroft (later archbishop) declared that Cartwright's principles were indistinguishable from the "seditious practices of the Huguenots", and that Geneva was "the birthplace of seditious doctrines that threatened every monarchy in Europe". In fact, "however much Calvinists and Papists might affirm the separation of church and state, they both in reality asserted the supremacy of the church over the state. The Huguenots and Puritans merely substituted many popes for one".[36] Cartwright's views were "as definitely theocratic, as those of the medieval Papacy", and his works were "almost as full as those of Bellarmine of the claim to control the State in the interests of the Church".[37]

In England, the Queen had managed to overpower the Pope and "trample" on him,[38] but by the 1580s the many Puritan popes posed a far more serious threat. "With Elizabeth, the queen often obscures the believer", she had the "independence of a mind which was not possessed by any of the current orthodoxies", and "her conduct of church affairs was above all an act of statesmanship". In July 1583 she decided to act. Archbishop Grindal's death "enabled the Queen to surrender the Church to a disciplinarian who shared her detestation of all faction and disobedience": John Whitgift, the arch-enemy of Cartwright. "The date of Whitgift's election – 23 September 1583 – was a decisive climacteric in the history of the reformed Church of England", for the new archbishop started a ruthlessly anti-Genevan policy which would be pursued by Bancroft, and later the Laudians. So harsh was his treatment of the Puritans that Burghley himself, in 1584, sent Whitgift a letter which has become famous: "the inquisitors of Spain use not so many questions to comprehend and trap their preys". The preys fought back: "1584 saw an intensification of conference and propaganda, culminating at the end of the year in a counter-attack launched through the House of Commons, a political campaign without precedent in parliamentary history … Later, 1584 was remembered as "that fertile year of contentious writings".[39]

A tale of a king and two captains

Bruno landed in England in 1583, and started publishing his vernacular dialogues (all printed by Charlewood with a false place of publication) in 1584.[40] He went frequently to court and lived in the French embassy, and it is "hard to believe" that he might have been unaware of "a struggle between Anglicans and Puritans which at moments seems almost mortal".[41] Bruno was "a political realist, a gentleman attendant to an ambassador, and not a solitary visionary or a recluse".[42] He certainly had his dreams for the future of Europe, but he was also an heir to "one of the most important (and most fruitful) aspects of Italian speculation in the 1500s, namely the unprejudiced and often brutal observation of reality that is to be found in writings from Machiavelli to Cardano".[43] Indeed, the situation he found in London is crucial to the understanding of *The Expulsion*, which in its own (very) peculiar way *is* one the "contentious writings" of "that fertile year" 1584.

In the last section of the work Bruno imagines a "king" who has two "captains". If he "gives so much power and authority to one of his captains ... as to make him superior to himself", that king is "mad" – although one of the two captains is very skilled, and "the realm" might be "as well, and perhaps better governed" by him than by the king. But if the king "should put or leave in the same authority an abject, vile and ignorant man, by whom everything will be ... confused, and turned upside down", then he is not only mad, but "senseless and deserving of a disciplinarian or tutor".[44]

The two captains are Catholicism and Calvinism. The former has such a long experience in that "art of arts and discipline of disciplines, through which men must be governed and repressed",[45] that it can rival the political competence of many a king. The latter is "ignorant" of such delicate arts, and if let free to govern, it would certainly "turn everything upside down". Bruno's words are anything but vaguely general. While the hierarchically descending structure of Catholic episcopacy could be an excellent *instrumentum regni* for a king, if the king took the pope's place at the top of it, the Presbyterian ascending model literally inverted and subverted it. That is why, as James I put it, Presbyterianism "agreeth as well with Monarchy, as *God* and the *Devil*".[46]

Bruno is echoing "the main establishment thesis of Elizabeth's second reign": that "presbyterianism was a conspiracy to overthrow the state" and that "no distinction could be drawn between this threat and that posed by the seminarians and Jesuits". As the Anglican "propaganda litany" kept repeating, puritanism was "subversive, factious and seditious", and it "would precipitate social as well as religious revolution".[47]

What should the Brunonian king do, in order to "govern well" and to be neither mad nor senseless? First he must make sure not to make either of the two captains "superior to himself", so as not to cease being sovereign. Still he should distinguish the better of the two and make good use of his governmental skills – without forgetting to keep him bound in his subordinate role. Had Elizabeth done anything else?

Certainly she was not mad or senseless, nor in need of a tutor to teach her that the conduct of church affairs should be an act of statesmanship, and not of belief. In the first part of her reign she had managed "to exclude the pope and assume supreme powers over the Church".[48] In the second, Whitgift's appointment had made it clear that she had no intention of relinquishing the supreme powers of her crown to the Puritans. If both Cartwright and Bellarmine claimed to control the State in the interests of the Church, she was determined to control the Church in the interests of her State.

Therefore, she did nothing to alter the hierarchical structure inherited from Rome – so much so that at the end of her reign England had "a national, or at least a state faith as well as a state church, to which it is entirely proper to apply the term Anglo-Catholicism".[49]

In its own peculiar way, the *Expulsion* is an anti-Puritan pamphlet, exactly as, ninety years later, the *Theological-Political Treatise* will be an anti-clerical pamphlet, where the analysis of Jewish theocracy is treated as a "symbolical screen" in order to demolish "the Calvinists" claim to dominate Holland spiritually and temporally.[50]

The diva Elizabeth

When the inquisitors asked him why he had praised Elizabeth, Bruno answered:

> I have praised many heretics, and heretical princes among them. But I have never praised them because they were heretics, or in any religious way because of their religion or piety, but only for their moral virtues. In particular, in my book *Of the cause, principle, and one*, I have praised the Queen of England and called her 'diva', not as a religious attribute but as a kind of epithet which the ancients used for their princes, for in England, where I wrote that book, they are in the habit of using such an epithet.[51]

Rightly so. Bruno had celebrated "this celestial Elizabeth, England's ruler" for having such "vision in governing" and "other natural and civic virtues" that despite widespread religious turmoil she had kept her realm in peace. While the Garonne was "turbid", the Seine "bloody" and other rivers of Europe "wrathful" and "furious", the Thames kept "flowing on unchecked and fearless … between its verdant banks".[52]

But these successes were not unrelated to her being the only monarch in Europe who had supreme powers over the Church.[53] Not for nothing had she earned that epithet of "diva" which "the ancients used for their princes", for, as Hobbes will write in the *Leviathan*:

> [i]n all Common-wealths of the Heathen, the Soveraigns have had the name of Pastors of the People … This Right of the Heathen Kings, cannot bee thought taken from them by their conversion to the Faith of Christ; who never ordained, that Kings for beleeving in him, should be deposed, that is, subjected to any but himself, or (which is all one) be deprived of the power necessary for the conservation of Peace amongst their Subjects … therefore Christian Kings are still the Supreme Pastors of their people, and have power to ordain what Pastors they please.[54]

At the very end of *Leviathan* Hobbes warns that it is not "the Romane Clergy onely", that makes use of the "Kingdome of God" in order to secure for itself a "Power distinct from that of the Civill State". If "Qu. Elizabeth", by her "Exorcism", had been able to cast out "the Spirituall Power of the *Pope*" and all his "Kingdome of *Fairies*", the danger was not over. If "the Spirit of Rome" had gone out, "who knows that … an Assembly of Spirits worse than he, enter, and inhabit this clean swept house, and make the End thereof worse than the Beginning?"[55] The last words of the *Leviathan* are then "directed expressly against the possibility of a *Presbyterian* take-over in England".[56]

As Bruno had readily understood, this was the main concern of the Elizabethan establishment in the 1580s. Some unprejudiced analysis of the whole problem, he must have thought, might be welcome.

The Expulsion of the Triumphant Beast: which beast?

In a Protestant country "Beast" could not but recall the pope, commonly associated to the Beast of the *Apocalypse*. But if the title seems to promise an "anti-papist prank", the author is selling a "different merchandise".[57] A cursory reading shows that Protestantism is far more ferociously attacked than Catholicism, and a closer examination reveals that the Beast is Christianity itself – or, as Toland wrote in 1709, "Revealed Religion in whatever form it triumphs in the world".[58] But that is not all.

As "Foolish Faith and Blind Credulity", Christian supernaturalism is first expelled from "the place surrounded by the impregnable wall of true philosophical contemplation ... where truth is revealed, where the necessity of the eternity of all substance is clear".[59] But once separated from philosophical truth, the expelled religion is then recycled in its Catholic variant as a "Fable" for the common people, whose imbibed credulity is not likely to be enlightened by any philosophy, not even Bruno's, anytime soon. Actually, if a monarch could "unify Crown and Tiara", Catholicism offered some "sacrosanct bagatelles" which could be made use of "with very little expense, without any interest and, perhaps, not without gain".[60]

In the extraordinary pages on the "Venation" and the "royal madness" for hunting, the sacrifice of the Mass is first derided with the truculent terms which Calvinism reserved for the Catholic priests who, pretending to "sacrifice" Christ, were "slaughterers" and "butchers" like the ancient priests with their bloody animal sacrifices.[61] But then the same butchery becomes "a heroic virtue" and a "religion" when "a prince pursues a doe" and the "priests of Diana" quarter it "with divine ritual". The first biographer of Bruno thought that "this eulogy of hunting could not displease Elizabeth", the English Diana so fond of pursuing does. But even more fondly she pursued the strengthening of her supreme powers over the Church. The Thirty-Seventh of the Thirty-Nine Articles of the Church of England granted her the "chief government" on matters "Ecclesiastical or Civil", but not the authority of "ministering the Sacraments". Which is what Bruno is farcically hinting at: the Sacrament in itself is a ludicrous "bagatelle", but having or not having the right of ministering it is no laughable matter. Hobbes, who fully understands it, states that a "Christian Soveraign", being "the Supreme Pastor of his own Subjects", has "the Authority to Administer the Sacrament of the Lords Supper", even if "most men deny it".[62]

The *Expulsion* is a purge of the zodiac, whose constellations have become symbols of vices. A General Counsel of the gods, presided by Jove, decides the reformation of an old and discredited religion – Christianity in thin disguise. Worried about what is happening on earth, the gods are ready to confer the "Corona Borealis" on some "heroic prince" who, "with club and fire, will bring back the so-longed-for peace to wretched and unhappy Europe, making impotent the many heads of this monster ... which with multiform heresy spreads its fatal poison".[63]

This poison is the Pauline, Lutheran and Calvinist doctrine that man is not saved by good works, but *sola fide*. This, for Bruno and his gods, wipes out whatever civic usefulness a religious "faith" may have. For "while they [the Calvinists] belittle good works, they extinguish in people all enthusiasm for the construction of new works and the preservation of old".[64] Like Bayle after him, Bruno sees "the principle of salvation by 'faith alone' as ultimately destructive of morality; for good works can then no longer contribute to salvation"[65] – a thoroughly anti-Weberian view of Calvinism.[66]

Separated from a philosophical truth which Christianity is structurally unable to attain, religion, in the *Expulsion*, is treated as *lex* in a thoroughly Averroistic manner.[67] "Natural judgment" teaches that the aim of religious laws is "the convenience of human life", and no matter "whether it descends from heaven or arises from the earth", a religion "which does not bring the utility and convenience" of human life "must be neither approved nor accepted". Religions are to be judged like a tree, "not by its beautiful leaves, but by its good fruit; and those who do not produce fruit should be driven away, and cede their place to those who yeld them"[68] – an ironical application of *Matthew* 12, 33: "The tree is known by his fruit".

Catholicism, for Bruno, may well be a fable, but as fable it can produce some good fruit. Since men "do not see the reward of their virtues in this life", it "presents before their eyes the good and evil of their next life, its rewards and punishments, in accordance with their deeds". This imaginary retribution in another world may belong to the Kingdom of Fairies, but it can encourage real good works in *this* world, thus contributing to the "upholding of society". Not so with the Calvinists. To the utter indignation of the gods, "they say it is not by the good that is done, or by the evil that is not done, that one becomes worthy and pleasing to the gods, but rather it is by hoping and believing, according to their catechism". Since this "mother of all knaveries" cannot but produce "the greatest prejudice of human society", Momus states that "the Southern Crown ... awaits him who is destined by Fate to wipe out this stinking filth of the world".[69]

Minerva agrees, and proposes that the place of Orion (the Calvinists' Christ) be taken by "military art, through which the Peace and authority of the Fatherland may be maintained, barbarians be fought ... and inhuman, porcine, savage and bestial cults, religions, sacrifices, and laws be annihilated".[70] A brutal proposal, but its baroque wording boils down to suggesting that if Calvinism poses a threat to the State, the authority of the Fatherland might have to resort to force – nothing unheard of in 1584.[71]

Justin Champion observes that "there seems to be a Machiavellian element in these statements".[72] There is indeed, but what follows is no less Machiavellian. Force might well chase Orion, but the state will still need cults and sacrifices, for the world "cannot subsist without law and religion".[73] Since no philosophical truth was likely to expel Christianity from one day to another, these cults had to be somehow Christian, and since they must not be Genevan they had to be somehow Roman.

After Minerva's tirade the tone changes. The gods start hinting at a number of occult doctrines and practices of the Catholic cult, which can be provisionally left "in the heaven" – but "only in belief and imagination, so that it may not prevent some other thing from being in that same place, upon which we shall determine on another of these forthcoming days".[74] At the end, the "useless and pernicious Fable" of the "barbarians" is substituted with a "moral Fable", and Orion-Christ is replaced by Chiron-Christ. Half beast and half man, the wisest of the Centaurs is a "demigod" in whom, as in Christ, "two substances concur in one hypostatic union" – an "occult and great mystery" which Jove thinks better not to investigate too closely. But "the altar, the shrine, the oratory, is most necessary": Chiron is deemed "not unworthy of heaven" and left there, "firmly fixed in his sacristy" – provided always that "Fate does not dispose otherwise".[75]

Bruno seems to be envisaging, in the long run, a post-Christian society, where Christianity is substituted with a "civil theology" inspired by the "Egyptian *prisca theologia*".[76] But prudent politics requires compromises, and for the moment Chiron must do.

Machiavellian princes, Freethinkers and Egyptian fables

In the chapter of *The Discourses* entitled "How Important it is to take Account of Religion", Machiavelli states that "those princes" who want "to keep their commonwealth religious, and, in consequence, good and united", should "maintain incorrupt the ceremonies of their religion" and "uphold" its "basic principles ... even though they be convinced that it is quite fallacious" – and "the more should they do this the greater their prudence and the more they know of natural laws".[77]

In the *Expulsion*, the first dialogue dedicated to a member of the English elite, Bruno adumbrates a way of taking account of religion in which the awareness of its "fallaciousness" is the precondition for its civil use. This, writes Aquilecchia, is "one of the typical Renaissance conceptions of religion, namely the Machiavellian one, which – not without an Averroistic inspiration – seemed to advocate religion entirely for pragmatical purposes of a civil and social nature": a notion meant "not for the *vulgus* of the faithful, but for their leaders".[78]

Bruno's prince, writes Badaloni, must be, like the philosopher, "above faith". "Like Spinoza, Bruno recognizes the necessity of Chiron, but only after the purification of the Christian religious myth". Since "the opportunity of maintaining Chiron can be reached only when the wise man has lost any faith in him ... *not* to believe becomes for Bruno a political necessity". A minority of men, liberated from religious faith, must be able to lead the others and impose the order of "reason". Bruno, then, shared "the position of those 'atheists', whose party, in the second half of the sixteenth century, sought to release politics from any subservience to the Church".[79] This way of taking account of religion could be "partly sympathetic with the inspiration of Elizabethan religious policy", but its statement in print was not necessarily helpful for its "practical implementation".[80]

Elizabeth owned *Lo Spaccio de la Bestia Trionfante*, bound with *La cena de le ceneri, De la causa principio et uno*, and *De l'infinito universo et mondi* in a black leather volume with her royal arms on the cover. In 1698 the book was bought by the Freethinker John Toland, who in 1713 published a translation of the work and circulated it among philosophers and aristocratic *libertins*. The Queen's copy is then the source of the first effective divulgation of Bruno's thought in modern Europe.[81] As "a printed work", writes Toland to Leibniz in 1710, "the *Spaccio* ... is I believe the rarest in the world, but on the other hand it is not a secret to be indifferently communicated to everybody".[82]

According to Heinemann, "Enlightenment" – intended as modern man's "coming of age" and "liberation from the authority of the Church" – is first the matter of a few individuals, and then of "select circles, chiefly aristocrats (like Freethinkers, Deists, Pantheists or Freemasons)", who make "distinction of esoteric and exoteric philosophy", and do not try to "transmit the light to the lower classes". Toland is the "inaugurator" of this "second stage". In the third and fourth, the movement becomes "propagandist, public and outspoken", and reaches first the bourgeoisie and then the proletariat.[83]

Bruno's infinite cosmos and animated matter are the direct source of Toland's natural philosophy.[84] But even "more importantly", as Champion insists, he chose to appreciate Bruno as "a civil theologian". Toland shared Bruno's approval of a pre-Judaeo-Christian pattern of religious worship, and he "applauded his scheme for astral reformation because he believed it was a valuable method of inculcating morality in the masses". Besides being "a superb device for exploding the machinery of priestcraft and superstition", the *Spaccio* "was in effect a popular theology".[85]

Toland diffused Bruno's ideas in a group of Freethinkers which included Collins and Shaftesbury, so that in England, "at the beginning of the eighteenth century, there existed a feared minority that attacked all revealed religion", using "the writings of Bruno supplied by Toland".[86] In his *Pantheisticon* (1720), he provides a Socratic Society, strongly reminiscent of the first Lodge of the Freemasons founded in London in 1717, with a philosophical credo which is "a simple literal plagiarism of Brunonian formulas".[87] And then, in a "mixture of serious thought and raillery", he also provides "a ritual which is a persiflage of the Roman Catholic cult".[88] He had not forgotten the *Spaccio*.

In the circles where Toland promoted Bruno's works, it was thought that the Queen herself had allowed its printing, though in very few copies, given its content. In 1717 Thomas Hearne, assistant librarian at the Bodleian, noted that William Stratford, chaplain of the House of Commons and later of George I, had told him "that Iordanus Brunus presented his Books to Q[ueen] Eliz[abeth] and that ... she valued them, and writ E. R. at y^{t} Beginning".[89] On the other hand, from the sentence of the Inquisition we know that in England Bruno was "held to be an atheist", because of a book "di Trionfante bestia".[90] And in 1612 La Galla wrote that "he had deserved ... to be called by Queen Elizabeth of England impious, unbeliever, atheist".[91] An unappealable indictment? Perhaps, but could a prudent prince state otherwise?

Frances Yates held that in the *Expulsion* Bruno was acting as the prophet of a new Hermetic religion in which the warring Protestants and Catholics could resolve their differences by accepting the higher "Egyptian truth, magical truth".[92] On the misconceived presumption that Sidney was a Christian Hermeticist, she holds him to be the natural dedicatee and supporter of Bruno's programme.[93]

Though Sidney "belonged to the puritan party" and "was anything but a Hermetic Magus",[94] magic *is* indeed praised in the *Expulsion*. The Egyptians thought that "just as Divinity descends in a certain manner, to the extent that one communicates with Nature, so one ascends to Divinity through Nature". Those "wise men", then, "with magic and divine rites rose to the height of Divinity by means of the same ladder of Nature by which Divinity descends even to the lowest things". And "here then is why it is that crocodiles, roosters, onions, and turnips were worshipped": because "there is one simple Divinity found in all things".[95]

Is Bruno proposing a magic worship of turnips and onions as a Hermetic way of pacifying Europe? Not necessarily: in the *Expulsion*, Sophia, the personification of Wisdom, informs us that "Egyptian metaphors without any contradiction can be stories to some, fables to others, and figured sentiments to others".[96] Just as the Catholic fable is more useful than the Calvinist one, so Egyptian fables show a higher metaphorical intuition of philosophical truth than either. The ancient worship of "animals and plants", which are "living effects of Nature", was wiser than the "mad rites" of those "senseless and foolish idolaters" who "seek Divinity ... in the excrements of dead and inanimate things"[97] – Catholic relics.

In the fables and metaphors of ancient mythology transpired, as figured sentiment, an intuition of the *deus sive natura* (therefore a metaphysical superiority to Christian supernaturalism) which could and needed to be redeemed. But as fables, they still belong to the exoteric world of myth which is a necessity for the *vulgus* – they do not inhabit the citadel of "true philosophical contemplation" where "truth is revealed" to the few heroic minds able to storm it.[98] In the *Expulsion* "the link between rationalism and esotericism underlies the texture of the whole work", but "the multitude is always exposed to the danger of giving myth a literal meaning".[99] Which is what happens to Yates, whose literal reading of Bruno's Egyptian fables "takes the exoteric for esoteric".[100] She ignores altogether that difference between philosophy and religion which Bruno never forgets: for "faith is required for the rule of the rude populace who must be governed, while demonstration is for the contemplative who know how to govern themselves and others".[101]

Egyptian magic was founded on the idea of rising "to the height of Divinity by means of the same ladder of Nature by which Divinity descends". But when Sophia says this, Bruno had already written *On the Infinite Universe and Worlds*, where "that beautiful order and ladder of nature is but a charming dream, an old wives' tale"[102] – a shaky tool for an ascent to Heaven. In fact, the "first casualty" of Bruno's infinite and homogeneous universe is the Ficinian and Neoplatonic doctrine of the "hierarchy of being".[103] For the "vertical axis" of that ladder, where "the various" below is of an ontologically inferior quality compared with "the One" above, Bruno substitutes "a horizontal axis, abolishing any hierarchical distinction".[104] Let us then turn to his first attempt to preach his new gospel of the unity and infinity of the world.

A juggler in Oxford

Shortly after his arrival, Bruno went to Oxford. The Polish nobleman Albert Laski was also visiting England at the time, and to honour him, at the Queen's request, the University prepared a series of "learned Divertisements" which included academic disputations and lectures. Bruno was invited to take part, and twenty-one years later, in 1604, George Abbot (master of University College, later archbishop of Canterbury, and of "definitely Calvinist and Puritan leanings"[105]) still remembered him:

> Wen that Italian ..., who entitled himself *Philotheus Jordanus Brunus Nolanus* ... had in the train of the Polish duke, seen our University in the year 1583, his heart was on fire to make himself by some worthy exploit to become famous in that celebrious place ... Stripping up his sleeves like some juggler ... he undertook ... to set on foot the opinion of Copernicus that the earth did go round ...; wheras in truth it was his owne head which rather did run round, & his braines did not stand stil.

But lo, a "grave man" of "good place in the University" thought he had read somewhere before something very like what Bruno was saying. After the second lecture, he recalled it. "Repairing to his study, [he] found both the former and later lecture, taken almost verbatim out of the works of Marsilio Ficino", in particular the *De vita caelitus comparanda*. He reported it to the dean of Christ Church, and before taking measures they decided to give Bruno another chance. But "*Jordanus* continuing to be *idem Jordanus*, they caused some to make known to him their former patience ..., and so with great honesty on the little man's part, there was an end of that matter".[106]

"What a marvellous scene!" exclaims Yates "There is the Magus announcing the Copernican theory in the context of the astral magic and sunworship of the *De vita coelitus comparanda*".[107] The scene *is* marvellous. On one side grave Oxonian academics; on the other a gesticulating southern Italian ex-monk, whose career (as Abbott in 1604 must have known) would end at the stake. And this "little man" is not only trying to "set on foot" an opinion which does not stand, but he does not acknowledge his sources. So the dons unmask the cheat and show him discreetly the door.

Bruno never forgot the humiliation and savagely attacked the Oxonian "pedants" in an address "To the most excellent Vice Chancellor of Oxford University", where it is clear that the clash had also been religious. He scurrilously attacks the doctors' *sola fide* doctrine, which treats "our good works" as if they were "dirty with menstrual blood", and systematically insists on the distinction between philosophy and theology, religious law and truth.[108]

But at the centre remains the "opinion" that the earth goes round, and its tacit mingling with Ficino. In the *De revolutionibus* the earth rotates round the sun like the other planets, and is therefore elevated to the status of a star. But the mathematician Copernicus never tried or wanted to confront "the enormous physical problems which derived from his heliocentrism"[109] – the first and foremost being: *why* does the earth (along with all the other stars) go round?

Unlike Copernicus, Bruno's interest, right from the start, lay precisely "in the causes of the motions of which the mathematicians can catch only the measure", and here Neoplatonism came in very handy, because "the primary clue to cosmological understanding for writers like Marsilio Ficino was soul, not geometrical form": "they saw the universe as alive" and thought of "heavenly bodies" in "organismic categories".[110] That is why Bruno, while discarding Ficino's ladder of being, "remained faithful even in his new cosmology to the Platonic world-soul, understanding it as an intrinsic principle of motion for all the celestial bodies".[111]

Back in London he wrote *The Supper*, where "the earth" and "the other stars" move "in virtue of an intrinsic principle, which is their proper soul" – since they "have in themselves life", no "external principle" or "extrinsic movers" are needed.[112] If in Oxford, then, he silently merges together Ficino and Copernicus, his attempt is "surprising only at first sight".[113] Trying to "set on foot" the opinion that the earth goes round, he was already looking for the cause of its motion, and since Copernicus gave no clue, he searched elsewhere – astral magic and sun worship seem beside the point.

With the help of a whole array of ancient sources (Virgil, Orpheus, Empedocles, Plotinus, the Pythagoreans, the Platonists – and "the hermeticists"), in *Cause, Principle and Unity* the world soul, besides being the "principle of movement", becomes an "internal artificer" and "artistic intellect" which "intrinsically contributes to the constitution of things" and "shapes matter, forming it from inside like a seed".[114] When they read these pages, where the Aristotelian dualism of form and matter is abolished, Bayle and Toland "rightly recognized" their author "as a precursor of Spinoza's conception of motion innate in matter", and Diderot commented: "il restera peu de chose à Spinoza".[115]

"The claim that Nature is self-moving, and creates itself, became indeed the very trademark of the *Spinosistes*", and since its immanentism was incompatible with a transcendent God, it was "generally regarded with horror".[116] In the end, all the enormities listed in Bruno's death sentence can be derived from his identification of the Holy Ghost with the world soul. In a "fully animated cosmos" where divinity is *inside* matter "there was no room for revealed religions of any kind".[117] And so "the Holy Scripture was but a dream", "Christ was not God", and so on.

The man who overpassed the margins of the world

Having lost all hope of an academic position, Bruno turned to the aristocratic circles of the capital. Fulke Greville, Sidney's friend, appears as the host of *The Ash Wednesday Supper*, though Bruno told the inquisitors that the Copernican symposium had occurred at the French Embassy. His three cosmological dialogues are anyway dedicated to Castelnau.

If in Oxford he had been humiliated, the *Supper* is a perfect, however belated, vengeance: Theofilo, mouthpiece of Bruno, annihilates two Oxonian arch-pedants. Theofilo reports that "a few days past two emissaries [John Florio and Matthew Gwinne] came to the Nolan on behalf of a royal equerry [Greville] letting him know how much he longed to converse with him so that he could understand his Copernicus".[118] Greville, then, longs to understand "*his*", the Nolan's, Copernicus – who, as he seems to have heard, was not exactly Copernicus' Copernicus. The dialogue satisfies the request.

Yes, says Theofilo-Bruno, as an astronomer Copernicus was "far superior to Ptolemy", but the Nolan "does not see either with the eyes of Copernicus, nor with those of Ptolemy, but with his own". "Being more intent on the study of mathematics than of nature", Copernicus could not "go deep enough" and fathom the meanings of his own discovery. Nonetheless he was a "great mind", who showed "little concern for the foolish multitude". In the ancient world, the movement of the earth had been stated and taught by Nicetas, Philolaus, Ecphantus, Heraclitus of Pontus. Copernicus seized these "rusty fragments" from "the hands of antiquity", and with "his more mathematical than physical discourse" he "repolished" and "cemented them": as a result, a once "ridiculed" argument is now "respected". The Nolan, then, has no intention of being "discourteous" toward a man who was "destined by the gods to be that dawn which was to precede the rising of the sun of the ancient and true philosophy, buried for so many centuries in the dark caverns of blind … ignorance".[119]

This is the first time that the Copernican reform becomes "the metaphor, which was used so much in the subsequent centuries, of the dawning of a new light" – new, of course, "only in comparison to the darkness of the past night of the Middle Ages".[120] Should the reader suspect that dawn will be noon with Bruno, he would be right.

"Now, what shall I say of the Nolan?" – continues Theofilo. The Argonauts were praised for crossing the sea, and "in our times" Columbus is "celebrated" for crossing "the Ocean", disclosing "new realms". But his discovery has only disturbed the "peace" of other nations, "propagating with violence new follies", "planting unheard-of stupidities where none was", and showing "pernicious inventions" and ways to "tyrannize and assassinate one another" which sooner or later, "through the force of the vicissitude of things", will backfire on the inventors – a rare and radical indictment of the evangelization and exploitation of the New World.[121]

By means of another voyage the Nolan has produced "wholly opposite results": he has "set free the human spirit" from a "narrow prison" where men "could contemplate the most distant stars" only "as if through some holes". Convinced that they were living on a lowly earth which the armature of the spheres separated from heaven, men had long been prey to impostors who, born in "caves of the earth", passed themselves off as "Mercuries and Apollinos coming from heaven", spreading "endless folly, beastliness, and vice" under the name of "virtue, piety, and discipline". But here is the one who can "liberate" humanity from these "chimeras".[122]

> Behold now, standing before you, the man who has pierced the air and penetrated the sky, wended his way amongst the stars and overpassed the margins of the world, who has broken down those imaginary divisions between spheres – the first, the eighth, the ninth, the tenth or what you will ... By the fight of sense and reason ... he has thrown wide those doors of truth which it is within our power to open and stripped the veils and coverings from the face of nature. He has given eyes to blind moles ... he has loosened the mute tongues ... he has strengthened the crippled limbs which were too weak to make that journey of the spirit.[123]

"These" writes Yates "are the passages which used to throw the nineteenth-century liberals into ecstasies as the cry of the advanced scientific thinker breaking out of mediaeval shackles". A misunderstanding, for Bruno sees his "ascent through the spheres" as "a breaking of those envelopes by which the Hermetic gnostic ascended and descended through the spheres": he "has made the gnostic ascent, has had the Hermetic experience".[124]

But the "imaginary divisions between spheres" dismantled by Bruno, is in Italian "le fantastiche muraglia de le sfere", which is "literally calqued on Lucretius' *moenia mundi*".[125] And indeed the whole "self-apotheosis" of Bruno as "liberator of the human spirit from the prison walls of the finite universe" is modelled on Lucretius' eulogy of Epicurus.[126] In the first book of *De rerum natura*, the great Greek, "by means of the scientific understanding of the *res naturae* ('the natural world') and the journey through the *omne immensum* ('immeasurable universe')", liberates mankind from "the oppressive weight of *religio*":[127]

> When human life lay prostrate on the ground before our eyes, oppressed by burdensome religion, which showed its face from the regions of heaven, standing over mortals with horrible countenance, a Greek man first dared to raise his mortal eyes against it and to resist it. Stories about the gods, thunderbolts, and heaven with threatening noise did not scare him, but spurred on the eager virtue of his mind even more, so that he wished to be the first to break the tight bolts of the gates of nature. Therefore, the lively force of his mind prevailed, and he progressed far beyond the flaming walls of the world [*flammantia moenia mundi*], and in mind and spirit he wandered the immeasurable universe, whence he brought back to us victorious (report of) what can happen and what is impossible ... Therefore religion is in turn thrown under our feet and trampled down, and his victory has made us equal to heaven.[128]

Though Hermeticism had much to contribute to the intrinsic principle of movement of the celestial bodies, earth included,[129] the most distinctive feature of Bruno's cosmology, his "bold vision of innumerable heliocentered worlds distributed endlessly throughout an infinite homogeneous space", is not to be found in the *Corpus Hermeticum*[130] – nor in Copernicus, whose universe, though heliocentric, is as finite as the Aristotelian cosmos.

Since "the conception of an infinite universe embracing infinitely numerous worlds is familiar in Lucretius",[131] the infinity of Bruno's own cosmology "derives from Epicurus and Lucretius", who, as atomists, "already knew that the universe was homogeneous and infinite".[132] Bruno, whose philosophy "was (no doubt) principally stamped by Epicureanism", realized that "the heliocentric 'paradox' and the unlimited space filled with atoms and worlds built of atoms were connected".[133]

But if "the first man to take Lucretian cosmology seriously was Giordano Bruno",[134] his self-fashioning as a modern Epicurus shows that he is also the first to inherit Lucretius' programme of liberating mankind from the fetters of religion by means of the understanding of the natural world. Since this is not far from an Enlightenment programme, Yates' nineteenth-century liberals may have been less deceived than she thought.

Lucretian philosophy, "so incompatible with the cult of the gods", was "scandalous" even "in the tolerant culture of the classical Mediterranean", but even less could its "subversive theses" be "accomodated by a triumphant Christianity".[135] Rescued by Poggio Bracciolini in 1417, the *De rerum natura* fascinated the young Machiavelli, who "went to the trouble of copying by hand in its entirety the 1495 Venetian edition".[136] "The extent of Lucretius' influence on Machiavelli is still undervalued", though "it is clear that he provides an invaluable key to understanding Machiavelli's view about man's nature, religion and the cosmos".[137]

The same can be said of Bruno. "In Lucretius' view", Epicurus "was nothing less than the saviour" and a "philosophical messiah".[138] Since Bruno "presents himself as what Epicurus was for Lucretius", no wonder he claims to have himself accomplished "the miracles attributed to Christ in the Gospels".[139] If Christ makes "the blind see, the lame walk, … the deaf hear",[140] Bruno "has given eyes to blind moles … loosened the mute tongues … strengthened the crippled limbs". But whereas Christ's pretended violations of the laws of nature are "impostures", the miracles of this philosophical messiah are reached "by the fight of sense and reason", and throw wide "those doors of truth which it is within our power to open".

In the first as in the last Dialogue, *The Heroic Frenzies*, "that effectual cognition of God, which religion promises but does not fulfil", can be reached (insofar as a cognition of God is within our power) only by substituting "the theologians' God" (the *Expulsion*'s "god as absolute", who "has nothing to do with us") with "the pilosophers' *Deus sive natura*".[141] Bruno's works are "a sort of anti-Gospel": if Christ, substituting "the cult of himself" for the ancients' "cult of nature", has "perpetrated a deceit on mankind", Bruno fashions himself as "his legitimate philosophical alternative".[142]

Suppers

The alternative nature of Bruno's gospel is doubly implicit in the very title of its first preaching. In the *Supper* the original elements of the Platonic dialogue are still visible, and "the central reference to a festive meal stands in the tradition of the *Symposium*".[143] Bruno's philosophical meal is then served on a day – Ash Wednesday – when Catholics (and Anglicans) should fast. But "Supper", especially to Protestant ears, cannot but recall the Lord's Supper, i.e. the Eucharist.

That "in the *Cena de le ceneri* the subject of the Supper is as important as the subject of the Copernican theory" has been noted as early as 1940 by Yates, who takes it to be "a mystical Supper which escapes all rational definition". Certainly it is not "a Protestant rite", and since Bruno told the inquisitors that the Supper "really took place at the house of the French ambassador", it would seem that "the Supper of the *Cena* adumbrates a celebration of Mass at the French embassy at which Englishmen are present".[144]

Masses were indeed celebrated at the embassy, but Bruno told the inquisitors that, being "excommunicated", he never attended them.[145] Here, instead, he is the celebrant. But what can possibly be the relation between a Mass and the Copernican theory? According to Yates, "Bruno's insistence that the earth really moves, that the divine breath of life is really in it", is "a 'translation' into philosophical terms of his highly mystical, indeed magical, view of the Sacrament". Bruno, then, was "trying to find a version of Catholic Truth which should do away with the 'troubles in religion'". He was appealing to "a 'politique' group corresponding to the 'politiques' of France", who "wished above all things, in France, to stop the civil wars and, in England, to prevent their outbreak". To this group, including people like Greville and Sidney, Bruno (who "undoubtedly believed that he was a sincere Catholic") proposes his mystical, magical and irenic Sacrament. Therefore, to see "this enthusiast for mystical Catholic union" as "the builder of a purely 'secular' philosophy" is to commit such a "fundamental error" that "it would be difficult to find a more curious example of profound historical misunderstanding".[146]

But the *Supper* is indeed a Lord's Supper in a much deeper, if less magical, philosophical sense. In the Eucharist's "*Hoc est corpus meum*", Christ offers his body as a means of communicating His divinity to men. But for Bruno "only the infinite cosmos itself can be such a thing as the 'embodiment' of the Divinity",[147] and in his *Supper* he offers it to men in a sort of "*Hoc est corpus Suum*". In Bruno the infinite cosmos has literally "taken the place of the Son of God".[148] In *Cause, Principle and Unity* the universe is not only "the great image" of God, but His "sole-begotten nature" ("unigenita natura"), and therefore "the Creation occupies exactly the systematic position that belonged to 'the only-begotten Son' in the theological tradition".[149]

Bruno's Divinity has "fully spent Himself" in nature, "transferring" His infinity to the universe[150] – and he "could not do otherwise".[151] If "divine goodness can indeed be communicated to infinite things", a God withholding something for himself would be a "wealthy owner", but a "miserly, sordid and avaricious donor". A mere "syllogism" is enough to demonstrate that "he who denieth infinite result denieth also infinite power".[152] Therefore "we know for certain" that the universe, "being the effect and product of an infinite cause", must needs be "infinitely infinite according to its bodily capacity".[153]

Since infinite nature is the true and only embodiment of the Divinity, the "basic figure of the Christian self-conception" – God's incarnation in the historical individuality of Christ – becomes, for Bruno, "the fundamental scandal, the offense which could not be supressed by any threat". At the stake, immediately before the pyre burst into flames, he averted his face from the crucifix which was held before him. This refusal of the image of the God who became man, "was not, or was not only, the defiant finale of the escaped monk; it was also, or especially, the gesture that maintains consistency with the vision of a new universe". Therefore he did not die as "one of the heretics whose dogmatic deviations always strike the historical observer as intra-Christian goings-on. Bruno died for a disagreement that was directed at the center and the substance of the Christian system", thus becoming "*the* significant 'heretic' of the beginning of the modern age".[154]

Elizabeth versus Circe

Why was it in England that Bruno chose to preach such a gospel? Though imprudent by nature, nowhere else did he write anything similar to the dialogues published in London. A partial answer is to be found in the masque-like, but clearly autobiographical final pages of his last dialogue, *The Heroic Frenzies.*[155]

Having perilously wandered throughout Europe for ten years (the years of Bruno's wanderings), nine philosophers (the boldest standing for Bruno), in the end reach "the island of Britain", where they are received by the "gracious nymphs of Father Thames" (the most gracious standing for Queen Elizabeth). The philosophers are in a most miserable state, because at the beginning of their peregrination, in a cave of Monte Circeo, between Naples and Rome, they are blinded by an enchantress, the "impious Circe".[156]

As Giovanni Gentile long ago "surely interpreted correctly",[157] this "daughter and mother of darkness", who "for our greater woe, strives to keep us under her eternal control", is the Catholic Roman Church. She owns two vessels: one she is able to open, and with its water she blinds the philosophers. But she is "powerless to open" the second "fatal vessel" – which, writes Gentile, represents "that effectual cognition of God, which religion promises but does not fulfil". On resuming their voyages, the blinded philosophers bring the closed vessel with them, and lo, when in England, the most gracious of the nymphs "clasped it in her hand, and almost spontaneously, opened it herself". The philosophers feel themselves "sprinkled with the longed for water", and "having recovered the light formerly lost", they see "the image of the supreme good on earth".[158]

In the cosmological and operatic finale, the philosophers, disposed in a ring, chant a "Song of the Illuminated", celebrating the vision of "an infinite universe, thought of as the habitat of an immanent divinity", and "absorbing within itself its infinity". Since it is the English Diana who grants the vision, Bruno is paying her "a political as well as philosophical homage". What, then, are the "historical-religious implications of Elizabeth I's presence as the presiding spirit over the ending of Bruno's *Furori*"?[159]

The same that had led him to call her "diva". Bruno must have thought that what was forbidden in Circe's or Calvin's lands, might be permitted under Elizabeth. Maybe a prince able to unify Crown and Tiara could tolerate a greater freedom of thought than both the one Roman and the many Puritan popes. Perhaps in England, where the State controlled the Church, a free enquiry into the *natura rerum* had better chances than where the Church controlled the State.

The Royal Society of London for Improving Natural Knowledge was founded in 1660. In 1665, Spinoza, writing to its Secretary, Henry Oldenburg, first congratulates him on the comfort enjoyed over there by "your philosophers", who are "alive, and mindful of themselves and their republic"; and then announces that he is writing a treatise on his "views regarding Scripture". He feels compelled to do it in order to fight "the prejudices of the theologians", which are "the main obstacles which prevent men from giving their minds to philosophy", and to defend "the freedom to philosophise and to say what we think", which in Holland is "everyway suppressed by the excessive authority of preachers".[160]

In England, the excessive authority of preachers and theologians had been rather successfully checked by Elizabeth. As a result Bruno was able to say, write and publish what he thought. He felt mistreated in Oxford, and he certainly hoped for a warmer reception of his new gospel in London, but in the end, nothing terrible happened to him. In the last page of *The Ash Wednesday Supper* he laments the little attention of his English host, Fulke Greville, who makes him go back home in the dark, without even lending him a "torch" or "a lantern with a candle of animal fat". But then he thinks of the "fifty or a hundred torches which, though he should need walk in midday, would not be lacking to him, were he to die in Roman Catholic soil".[161] A prophecy come true in 1600, a day after Ash Wednesday.

Notes

1 *Calendar of State Papers*, Foreign, January–June 1583, p. 214.

2 Miguel A. Granada, "New Visions of the Cosmos", in *The Cambridge Companion to Renaissance Philosophy*, ed. James Hankins (Cambridge: Cambridge University Press, 2007), p. 281. On Bruno's monism see Hélène Védrine, *La conception de la nature chez Giordano Bruno* (Paris: J. Vrin, 1967), p. 290; Ramon G. Mendoza, "Metempsychosis and monism in Bruno's *nova filosofia*", in *Giordano Bruno: Philosopher of the Renaissance*, ed. Hilary Gatti (Aldershot, UK: Ashgate, 2002), p. 279.

3 Frances Amelia Yates, *Giordano Bruno and the Hermetic Tradition* (London: Routledge & Kegan Paul, 1964).

4 Giordano Bruno, *The Expulsion of the Triumphant Beast*, ed. Arthur D. Imerti (Lincoln, NE and London: University of Nebraska, 1964), p. 247.

5 Giovanni Aquilecchia, "Giordano Bruno as Philosopher of the Renaissance", in Gatti 2002, pp. 6–8. As Aquilecchia remarks, "we have witnessed, particularly during the last decade, a revaluation, certainly in Italy, in France and in Spain, not quite to the same extent in Britain, and only marginally in America, a reaction against the previous predominant interpretation of Bruno's thought as exclusively Hermetic magic". For this reaction: Aquilecchia, *Schede bruniane (1950–1991)* (Manziana: Vecchiarelli, 1993), pp. 41–63, 375–77; Paolo Rossi, "Hermeticism, Rationality and the Scientific Revolution", in *Reason, Experiment and Mysticism in the Scientific Revolution*, eds. Maria Luisa Righini Bonelli and William R. Shea (London: Macmillan, 1975), pp. 247–73; Robert S. Westman, "Magical Reform and Astronomical Reform: The Yates Thesis Reconsidered", in *Hermeticism and the Scientific Revolution*, eds. Westman and J. E. McGuire (Los Angeles: Clark Memorial Library, University of California, 1977); Michele Ciliberto, *La ruota del tempo. Interpretazione di Giordano Bruno* (Roma: Editori Riuniti, 1986), pp. 9–11; Jean Seidengart, *Dieu, l'univers et la sphère infinie. Penser l'infinité cosmique à l'aube de la science classique* (Paris: Albin Michel, 2006), p. 151. For a blunt statement that "the Yates thesis [is] almost wholly unfounded", see Brian Vickers, "Introduction", in *Occult and Scientific Mentalities in the Renaissance*, ed. Vickers (Cambridge: Cambridge University Press, 1984), p. 6.

6 Luigi Firpo, *Il processo di Giordano Bruno* (Roma: Salerno Editrice, 1993), pp. 103–4.

7 Aquilecchia 2002, p. 14.

8 See Saverio Ricci, *La fortuna del pensiero di Giordano Bruno (1600–1750)* (Florence: Le Lettere, 1990), p. 267.

9 Angelo Mercati, *Il sommario del processo di Giordano Bruno* (Vatican City: Biblioteca Apostolica Vaticana, 1942), p. 52. In 1940 Mercati discovered a summary of Bruno's Roman trial held in the Vatican secret archives. For the importance of his discovery see Gatti, *Essays on Giordano Bruno* (Princeton, NJ and Oxford: Princeton University Press, 2011), pp. 312–13.

10 Vittorio Spampanato, *Documenti della vita di Giordano Bruno* (Florence: Olschki, 1933), pp. 125–26.
11 Edmund Burke, *Reflections on the Revolution in France*, ed. Connor Cruise O'Brien (Harmondsworth, UK: Penguin, 1968), p. 137.
12 See Dorothea Waley Singer, *Giordano Bruno. His Life and Thought. With Annotated Translation of His Work On the Infinite Universe and Worlds* (New York: Henry Schuman, 1950), pp. 23–24. See also Yates, "The Mystery of Jean Bodin", *The New York Review of Books*, October 14 (1976).
13 Friedrich Meinecke, *L'idea della ragion di Stato nella storia moderna* (Florence: Sansoni, 1942–44), p. 57.
14 On Castelnau's life, see Gustave Hubault, *Michel de Castelnau, ambassadeur en Angleterre (1575–1585)* (Geneva: Slatkine, 1970). On his relations with Bruno and the *politique* party, Ricci, *Giordano Bruno nell'Europa del Cinquecento* (Rome: Salerno Editrice, 2000), pp. 190–92; Nuccio Ordine, *Contro il Vangelo armato. Giordano Bruno, Ronsard e la religione* (Milan: Cortina, 2007).
15 Firpo, pp. 162, 189.
16 Giordano Bruno, *Cause, Principle and Unity*, ed. Robert De Lucca, with an Introduction by Alfonso Ingegno, (Cambridge, UK: Cambridge University Press, 2004), p. 33.
17 Giordano Bruno, *The Ash Wednesday Supper*, ed. Stanley L. Jaki (The Hague: Mouton, 1975), pp. 69–70.
18 *On the Infinite Universe and Worlds*, in Singer, p. 349.
19 Ingegno 2004, pp. vii, xx.
20 Alexandre Koyré, *From the Closed to the Infinite Universe* (Baltimore, MD: The Johns Hopkins Press, 1957), p. 40.
21 Arthur O. Lovejoy, *The Great Chain of Being* (Cambridge, MA: Harvard University Press, 1933), p. 116.
22 Jean-Hippolyte Mariéjol, *La Réforme et la Ligue. L'Edit de Nantes* (Paris: Hachette, 1908), p. 413.
23 Quoted in Hugh R. Trevor-Roper, *Religion, the Reformation and Social Change* (London: Macmillan, 1967), p. 199. See Gilberto Sacerdoti, "'Self-sovereignty' and Religion in *Love's Labour's Lost: From London to Venice via Navarre*", in *Visions of Venice in Shakespeare*, ed. Laura Tosi and Shaul Bassi (Farnham, UK: Ashgate, 2011), p. 85.
24 René Pintard, *Le Libertinage érudit dans la première moitié du XVIIe siècle* (Geneva: Slatkine, 2000), p. 29.
25 Yates, "The Religious Policy of Giordano Bruno", *Journal of the Warburg and Courtauld Institutes* 3, 3/4 (1940): 192.
26 The following interpretation of the *Expulsion* is more fully treated in Sacerdoti, *Sacrificio e sovranità. Teologia e politica nell'Europa di Shakespeare e Bruno* (Turin: Einaudi, 2002).
27 *The Expulsion of the Triumphant Beast*, pp. 232, 235, 237, 240–42.
28 Michele Ciliberto, *Giordano Bruno* (Bari: Laterza, 1990), p. 154.
29 *The Expulsion of the Triumphant Beast*, p. 236.
30 Michele Ciliberto, "Introduzione", in *Spaccio de la bestia trionfante*, ed. Michele Ciliberto (Milan: Rizzoli, 1985), pp. 36, 44, 45, 47, 271 n.
31 *The Expulsion of the Triumphant Beast*, pp. 255, 257.
32 Benedict De Spinoza, *Theological-Political Treatise*, ed. Jonathan I. Israel (Cambridge: Cambridge University Press, 2007), pp. 81–82, 86–87.
33 Israel, *Enlightenment Contested. Philosophy, Modernity, and the Emancipation of Man 1670–1752* (Oxford: Oxford University Press, 2006), pp. 491–92. See Ricci, "Bruno 'spinozista', Bruno 'martire luterano'. La polemica tra Lacroze e Heumann", *Giornale critico della filosofia italiana* LXV (1986), pp. 42–61; Ricci 1990, pp. 239–42.
34 *Cause, Principle and Unity*, pp. 11, 98.
35 Ingegno 2004, pp. vii, xxi.
36 John Hearsey McMillan Salmon, *The French Religious Wars in English Political Thought* (Oxford: Clarendon Press, 1959), pp. 5, 19, 16, 30, 31 38.
37 John Neville Figgis, *The Divine Right of Kings* (Cambridge: Cambridge University Press, 1914), pp. 189–90.
38 Elizabeth "based the right of the crown to be head of both church and state on the position of the early Christian emperors in the early church". In John Foxe's *Acts and Monuments*

(1563), where she is compared to Constantine, the C of "Constantine" encloses a portrait of the queen: "She sits on the throne" and "the lower part of the letter, beneath Elizabeth's feet, is formed by the body of the Pope, wearing the papal tiara and holding broken keys ... trusting in an 'imperial' authority like that of Constantine, [she] has subdued and overpowered the Pope; the royal crown triumphs over the papal tiara ... The picture of Queen Elizabeth trampling on the Pope in the initial C is thus the climax of the whole book" (Yates, "Queen Elizabeth as Astraea", *Journal of the Warburg and Courtauld Institutes* 10 [1947]: 40–43).

39 Patrick Collinson, *The Elizabethan Puritan Movement* (Oxford: Clarendon Press, 1967), pp. 29, 243, 270, 273.

40 On the ideological choice of not writing in Latin, see "L'adozione del volgare nei dialoghi londinesi di Giordano Bruno", Aquilecchia 1993, pp. 41–63. On the printer, see Tiziana Provvidera, "John Charlewood, Printer of Giordano Bruno's Italian Dialogues, and His Book Production", in Gatti 2002, pp. 167–86.

41 Michele Ciliberto, *Umbra profunda. Studi su Giordano Bruno* (Rome: Edizioni di Storia e Letteratura, 1999), pp. 229–30.

42 Gatti 2011, p. 130.

43 Ingegno, p. xxvii.

44 *Expulsion of the Triumphant Beast*, p. 257. Imerti translates "messo sotto sopra il tutto" with "everything ... thrown into disorder", which misses the crucial idea of a world subverted and "turned upside down". For a fuller analysis of Bruno's "tale" and the whole meaning of the *Spaccio*, see Sacerdoti 2002.

45 *Expulsion of the Triumphant Beast*, p. 145.

46 Charles Howard McIlwain, "Introduction", in *The Political Works of James I* (Cambridge, MA: Harvard University Press, 1919), p. xc.

47 John Guy, "The Establishment and the Ecclesiastical Polity", in *The Reign of Elizabeth I. Court and Culture in the last decade*, ed. John Guy (Cambridge: Cambridge University Press, 1995), pp. 128–29. See *Expulsion of the Triumphant Beast*, p. 150: "[the Calvinists] cause children to rebel against their fathers, servants against their masters, subjects against their superior".

48 Collinson, p. 30.

49 McIlwain, p. xlvii.

50 Geneviève Brykman, *La judéité de Spinoza* (Paris: Vrin, 1972), p. 68.

51 Firpo, pp. 188–89.

52 *Cause, Principle and Unity*, p. 33

53 See Gatti 2011, pp. 136, 139: the "virtues" praised by Bruno are "political rather than religious" and "her way of being a prince as the ancients understood that word ... included the control of the sphere of religion by the Prince in the name of public security and morals". Gatti writes that the conclusion of her chapter ("The sense of an ending in Bruno's *Eroici Furori*") "agrees in many respects with the analysis of the essentially political-religious relationship between Bruno and Queen Elizabeth I put forward in Sacerdoti (2002)".

54 Thomas Hobbes, *Leviathan* (Oxford: Clarendon Press, 1929), p. 421.

55 Hobbes, p. 546.

56 Richard Tuck, *Hobbes's "Christian Atheism"*, in *Atheism from the Reformation to the Enlightenment*, eds. Michael Hunter and David Wootton (Oxford: Clarendon Press, 1992), p. 129.

57 Ricci 2000, p. 307.

58 Ricci 1990, pp. 272, 274, 275.

59 *Expulsion of the Triumphant Beast*, p. 259.

60 *Expulsion of the Triumphant Beast*, pp. 257–59, 270; see Ingegno, *La sommersa nave della religione. Studio sulla polemica anticristiana del Bruno* (Naples: Bibliopolis, 1985), pp. 63, 66, 136, 143–46. On the fusion of Crown and Tiara, see the chapter "La troisième couronne céleste au service des couronnes terrestres?", in Ordine, *Trois couronnes pour un roi* (Paris: Les Belles Lettres, 2011), pp. 201–65. Ordine writes that he reached, by different ways, the "same conclusions" as Sacerdoti 2002, pp. 319–22.

61 See Ingegno, *Regia pazzia. Bruno lettore di Calvino* (Urbino: QuattroVenti, 1987).

62 *Expulsion of the Triumphant Beast*, pp. 260–63; Christian Bartholmess, *Jordano Bruno* (Paris: Ladrange, 1846–47), v. II, p. 104; Hobbes, p. 424. See Sacerdoti 2002, pp. 193–228 and 2011, pp. 95–99.

63 *Expulsion of the Triumphant Beast*, p. 124.
64 *Expulsion of the Triumphant Beast*, p. 151.
65 Israel 2006, pp. 664–65.
66 For a nuanced study of the topic, see "Giordano Bruno and the Protestant Ethic", in Gatti 2002, pp. 145–66.
67 On Bruno's Averroistic conception of religion see Bruno Nardi, *Studi su Pietro Pomponazzi* (Florence: Istituto nazionale di studi sul Rinascimento, 1965), pp. 122–48; Fulvio Papi, *Antropologia e civiltà nel pensiero di Giordano Bruno* (Florence: La Nuova Italia, 1968), pp. 298–303; Rita Sturlese, "'Averroe quantumque arabo et ignorante di lingua greca …' Note sull'averroismo di Giordano Bruno", *Giornale critico della filosofia italiana*, 71 (1992): 248–75; Granada 1999, pp. 305–31; Sacerdoti 2002; Granada, "Introduction", in *De fureurs héroïques* (Paris: Les Belles Lettres, 2008), pp. lxxii–xciv.
68 *Expulsion of the Triumphant Beast*, pp. 126, 145, 147.
69 *Expulsion of the Triumphant Beast*, pp. 124–26; see Andrew D. Weiner, "Expelling the Beast: Bruno's Adventures in England", *Modern Philology*, 78, 1 (1980): 11.
70 *Expulsion of the Triumphant Beast*, pp. 150, 257–58.
71 "1584 was the *annus terribilis* for the Puritans … since their spiritual dissent and anti-hierarchical revolt were regarded as resistance to the queen's authority, the secular arm repeatedly resorted to arrests and executions" (Ricci 2000, pp. 300–301).
72 Justin Champion, *The Pillars of Priestcraft Shaken: The Church of England and its Enemies, 1660–1730* (Cambridge: Cambridge University Press, 1992), p. 153.
73 *Expulsion of the Triumphant Beast*, p. 146.
74 *Expulsion of the Triumphant Beast*, p. 259.
75 *Expulsion of the Triumphant Beast*, pp. 87, 268–70. On this "infamous passage" and its "mocking" of "the union of two natures", see Hans Blumenberg, *The Legitimacy of the Modern Age* (Cambridge, MA: MIT Press, 1983), p. 560.
76 See Champion 1992, pp. 153–54.
77 Niccolò Machiavelli, *The Discourses*, ed. Bernard Crick (Harmondsworth, UK: Penguin, 1974), pp. 142–43.
78 Aquilecchia 2002, p. 10. For Bruno's "rationalistic esotericism", see Ingegno 1985, p. 61.
79 Nicola Badaloni, *Giordano Bruno. Tra cosmologia ed etica* (Bari: De Donato, 1988), pp. 128–30.
80 Ricci 2000, p. 366.
81 Aquilecchia, "Nota su John Toland traduttore di Giordano Bruno", in *English Miscellany. A Symposium of History, Literature and the Arts*, ed. Mario Praz. IX (Rome: Edizioni di Storia e Letteratura, 1958), pp. 83–84, 86; Aquilecchia, "Scheda Bruniana: la traduzione 'Tolandiana' dello *Spaccio*", in *Giornale Storico della Letteratura Italiana*, 152 (1975); Sturlese, "Postille autografe di John Toland allo *Spaccio* del Bruno", *Giornale critico della filosofia italiana*, 65 (1986): 27–28; Champion, *Republican Learning: John Toland and the Crisis of Christian Culture, 1696–1722* (Manchester, UK: Manchester University Press, 2003), pp. 16–18, 31.
82 Ricci 1990, pp. 243, 266; Champion 1992, pp. 130, 150–52.
83 F. H. Heinemann, "John Toland and the Age of Enlightenment", *The Review of English Studies*, 20, 78 (1944): 125–26.
84 Margaret C. Jacob, *The Newtonians and the English Revolution, 1689–1720* (Hassocks, UK: Harvester Press, 1976), pp. 205, 226–29, 232–34, 245–46; Jacob, *The Radical Enlightenment* (London: Allen & Unwin, 1981), pp. 35–40, 41, 47, 61, 87, 202. See Heinemann, p. 141: Toland's God, "indwelling" the infinite universe "as Soul of the World", is "pure Bruno".
85 Champion 1992, pp. 153–54.
86 Jacob, "John Toland and the Newtonian Ideology", *Journal of the Warburg and Courtauld Institutes*, 32 (1969): 326.
87 Seidengart, "L'infinitisme panthéiste de John Toland et ses relations avec la pensée de Giordano Bruno", *Revue de Synthèse*, 2–3 (1995): 340.
88 Heinemann, p. 141. See Jacob 1969, pp. 327–28; Ricci 1990, p. 244.
89 Ricci 1990, pp. 246, 256, 268–71; Ricci 2000, pp. 364–65.
90 Vincenzo Spampanato, *Documenti della vita di Giordano Bruno* (Florence: Olschki, 1933), p. 191.
91 Ciliberto 1999, pp. 276–77. See Ricci 1990, p. 74 n.; Ricci 2000, p. 365; Gatti 2011, pp. 177, 197.

92 Yates 1964, p. 239.
93 For a thorough refutation of Sidney's hermeticism, see Weiner, pp. 2–4, 9. See also Alan Sinfield, "Sidney, Du Plessis-Mornay and the Pagans", *Philological Quarterly*, 58, 1 (1979): 26–39; Robert E. Stillman, *Philip Sidney and the Poetics of Renaissance Cosmopolitanism* (Aldershot, UK: Ashgate, 2008), p. 125.
94 Sinfield, *Faultlines: Cultural Materialism and the Politics of Dissident Reading* (Oxford: Clarendon, 1992), p. 143; Gatti 2011, p. 283.
95 *Expulsion of the Triumphant Beast*, p. 236, 238.
96 *Expulsion of the Triumphant Beast*, p. 267.
97 *Expulsion of the Triumphant Beast*, pp. 235–36.
98 *Expulsion of the Triumphant Beast*, p. 259.
99 Ingegno 1985, pp. 33, 34, 61, 82, 83, 88.
100 Sacerdoti, "Toland e la 'lettura moderna' di Bruno", *Rivista di storia della filosofia*, 3 (2003): 512–13.
101 *On the Infinite Universe and Worlds*, in Singer, pp. 264–65.
102 *On the Infinite Universe and Worlds*, in Singer, p. 239.
103 Ingegno 2004, p. xiii.
104 Aquilecchia 2002, p. 7.
105 Yates 1964, p. 208.
106 Robert McNulty, "Bruno at Oxford", *Renaissance News*, 13 (1960): 300–305; E. McMullin, "Giordano Bruno at Oxford", *Isis*, 77, 1 (1986): 85–87.
107 Yates 1964, p. 209.
108 See Ciliberto 1999, pp. 246–55. The letter to the Vice Chancellor was published in 1583 in a volume dedicated to Castelnau which contained three works on the art of memory. For a still classical analisys see Ludovico Limentani, "La lettera di G. Bruno al Vicecancelliere della Università di Oxford", *Sophia*, 1 (1933): 317–54.
109 Ingegno 2004, p. viii.
110 McMullin 1986, pp. 61–62.
111 Ingegno 2004, p. xiii.
112 *The Ash Wednesday Supper*, pp. 115–16.
113 Gatti 2011, p. 34; the chapter "Between Magic and Magnetism: Bruno's Cosmology at Oxford" explores Ficino's concept of "a spiritus, or elisir, which, by running through all things, joins them to the *anima mundi*, or world soul" (p. 32).
114 *Cause, Principle and Unity*, pp. 37–39.
115 Israel 2006, p. 492, 509; see Jacob 1981, pp. 29–32.
116 Israel 2006, p. 160.
117 Gatti 2011, p. 319.
118 *The Ash Wednesday Supper*, p. 55. Florio and "maestro Guin" are explicitly named in the first redaction of the Dialogue. In 1584 Florio, the translator of Montaigne, was the preceptor of Castelnau's daughter, and lived, like Bruno, at the Embassy. Since the two were close friends, "it seems likely that Florio lent a hand with several aspects of the production" of Bruno's works, "especially regarding dealings with the publisher, given Bruno's lack of English"; Florio's Italian-English dictionary, *A Worlde of Wordes* (1598), extensively draws from Bruno's Dialogues, as well as from Machiavelli's *Mandragola* and Aretino's *Ragionamenti* – "all works printed in Italian in London during the 1580s … and condemned by the Inquisition" (Michael Wyatt, *The Italian Encounter with Tudor England. A Cultural Politics of Translation* [Cambridge: Cambridge University Press, 2005], pp. 196, 231). See also Yates, *The Life of an Italian in Shakespeare's England* (Cambridge: University Press, 1934).
119 *The Ash Wednesday Supper*, pp. 55–58, 98.
120 Blumenberg, *The Genesis of the Copernican World* (Cambridge, MA: MIT Press, 1987), p. 361.
121 *The Ash Wednesday Supper*, pp. 58–60. See Granada, "Giordano Bruno y America: de la crítica de la colonización a la crítica del cristianismo", *Geocrítica*, 90 (1990): 5–63; Ricci, "Infiniti mondi e Mondo Nuovo. Conquista dell'America e critica della civiltà europea in Giordano Bruno", *Giornale critico della filosofia italiana*, 10, (1990): 204–21; Aquilecchia, "Bruno e il 'Nuovo Mondo'", in Id. (1993): 97–99; Elizabeth Tarantino, "*Ultima Thule*:

Contrasting Empires in Bruno's *Ash Wednesday Supper* and Shakespeare's *Tempest*", in Gatti 2002, pp. 225–301.

122 *The Ash Wednesday Supper*, p. 60.

123 Yates 1964, p. 237, her translation (see *The Ash Wednesday Supper*, p. 61).

124 Yates 1964, pp. 237, 239.

125 Ciliberto 1999, p. 53.

126 Blumenberg 1987, pp. 361–62; see Ingegno 1985, p. 122. Even more extensively "Bruno sees himself as Epicurus appeared to Lucretius" in the *De Immenso* (Frankfurt, 1591), a long poem which is an explicit imitation of the *De rerum natura* (Carlo Monti, "Introduzione", in *Opere latine* [Torino: UTET, 1980], p. 44).

127 Vinzenz Buchheit, "Epicurus' Triumph of the Mind (Lucr. 1.62–79)", in *Oxford Readings in Classical Studies. Lucretius*, ed. Monica R. Gale (Oxford: Oxford University Press, 2007), pp. 106, 109.

128 Buchheit's translation, pp. 105–6.

129 In *Corpus Hermeticum* XII "the energy of life" is nothing but "movement", and "in the world" there is "nothing" which is "immobile". The earth itself, though it "seems to be immobile", is "subject to a multitude of movements". For, says Hermes, "would it not be ridiculous to suppose that this nurse of all beings should be immobile, she who causes to be born and gives birth to all things?" The passage is quoted in the chapters on the world soul and universal animation of Agrippa's *De occulta philosophia;* see Yates 1964, pp. 242–43.

130 Westman, *The Copernican Question. Prognostication, Skepticism, and Celestial Order* (Berkeley: University of California Press, 2011), p. 281; McMullin 1986, pp. 66–68.

131 Singer, p. 50.

132 Gatti 2011, pp. 41, 147. For Lucretius' influence on Bruno' cosmology and ethics ("both philosophers sought to free man from superstition and supernatural religion"), see Jacob, "John Toland and the Newtonian Ideology", *Journal of the Warburg and Courtauld Institutes*, 32 (1969): 316–17.

133 Blumenberg 1987, pp. 358–59. See Blumenberg 1983, p. 552: "Bruno takes over from Lucretius the figure of a bringer of salvation, which in Lucretius is the figure of Epicurus … like Epicurus in Lucretius, Bruno also breaks through the walls of the singular cosmos, the limits of a finite world, and gains a homogeneous immeasurability of the cosmic space".

134 Koyré, p. 6.

135 Stephen Greenblatt, *The Swerve. How the World Began Modern* (London: The Bodley Head, 2011), pp. 7, 98.

136 Paul A. Rahe, *Against Throne and Altar: Machiavelli and Political Theory under the English Republic* (Cambridge: Cambridge University Press, 2008), pp. 32–34.

137 Alison Brown, *The Return of Lucretius to Renaissance Florence* (Cambridge, MA: Harvard University Press, 2010), p. xii.

138 Greenblatt, p. 72.

139 Granada, *La reivindicación de la filosofía en Giordano Bruno* (Barcelona: Herder, 2005), pp. 102–3.

140 *Luke* 7, 22 and *Matthew* 11, 5, both based on *Isaiah* 35, 5–6.

141 Giovanni Gentile, in Bruno, *Dialoghi italiani* (Florence: Sansoni, 1985), pp. 1171–72 n.

142 Ingegno 1985, pp. 33, 37, 93, 137; Id. 2004, p. x.

143 Blumenberg 1987, p. 359.

144 Yates 1940, pp. 186–88.

145 Firpo, pp. 161–62.

146 Yates 1940, pp. 190–92, 203–4, 206.

147 Blumenberg 1983, p. 551.

148 Blumenberg 1987, p. 384.

149 *Cause, Principle and Unity*, p. 66; Blumenberg 1983, p. 573.

150 Blumenberg 1983, pp. 551, 562.

151 Koyrè, p. 43.

152 *Of the Infinite Universe and Worlds*, in Singer, pp. 246, 260, 263.

153 *The Ash Wednesday Supper*, p. 112.

154 Blumenberg 1983, pp. 549, 563, 593.

155 On the masque form, see Gatti 2011, pp. 27, 175.
156 Bruno, *The Heroic Frenzies*, ed. Paul Eugene Memmo (Chapel Hill, NC: The University of North Carolina Press, 1964), pp. 258–60. I have in two instances silently revised Memmo's translation.
157 Gatti 2011, p. 130; see Gentile in Bruno 1985, pp. 1171–72 n.
158 *The Heroic Frenzies*, pp. 260–63.
159 Gatti 2011, pp. 119–120, 137; *The Heroic Frenzies*, pp. 265–66.
160 Spinoza, *The Letters* (Indianapolis, IN: Cambridge: Hackett, 1995), pp. 185–86.
161 *The Ash Wednesday Supper*, p. 169.

10 Italian pastoral tragicomedy and English early modern drama

Robert Henke

"Italian pastoral tragicomedy" is, to borrow a phrase from Louise George Clubb, a "phrase to open a debate about genre."[1] This fashionable and controversial form fired the imaginations of Italian playwrights, theorists, designers, actors, and musicians in the academic, courtly, and professional acting spheres of the late Cinquecento and early Seicento. Theatrically successful among *literati* and *comici* alike, touching off a sharp controversy over both the heft of the pastoral form and the possibility of mixing tragedy and comedy, "pastoral tragicomedy" galvanized a lively and usable body of dramatic theory that was integrally linked to practice, whether as post-practice self-justification[2] or as creative prompt. The most famous Italian example of the new kind, Battista Guarini's *Il pastor fido* (begun in 1580, definitively published in 1602) genuinely counts as "world literature," if ephemerally so: it was translated into French, Spanish, English, German, Greek, Swedish, Dutch, and Polish and circulated in print and performance for two centuries. Just as importantly, the prestige and controversy surround Guarini's play made the *idea* of pastoral tragicomedy internationally available. Whereas Shakespeare was completely unknown in Italy—and would remain so for approximately one hundred years—Guarini was as much of a transnational name to conjure with as the famous actress Isabella Andreini. In Ben Jonson's *Volpone*, the consummate English comparatist Lady Politic Would-Be claims that "All of our English writers,/I mean, such as are happy in the Italian,/Will deign to steal out of this author, mainly;/Almost as much as from Montagnié" (3.4.87–92).[3] Those English (of which there were many) who could read Italian could have obtained an Italian imprint of the play published in London by John Wolfe in 1591, only a year after its first publication in Italy; those not "happy in Italian" could have read the play in the so-called "Dymoke" English translation as early as 1602, four years before *Volpone* was first performed.[4]

In 1579, in his *Defense of English Poesie*, Sir Philip Sidney considered tragicomedy (whether pastoral or not) important enough in England to critique it, and the idea of tragicomedy in the pastoral mode or alternatively with the satyr-satirist as representative figure surfaces from John Marston in the *The Malcontent* (1604), Samuel Daniel in the *Queene's Arcadia* (1605) and *Hymen's Triumph* (1612), John Fletcher in *The Faithful Shepherdess* (1608), William Shakespeare in his late tragical-pastoral-comical plays (1608–12), and Ben Jonson in his 1633 *Sad Shepherd*. Although pastoral tragicomedy found its way across Europe, the story of Italian-English transmission carries particular weight and interest because English playwrights, who worked with a large palette of dramatic forms calibrated to audience tastes, were arguably more interested in practical, genre-based dramatic theory than the French and the Spanish. Whereas, in the *Arte nuevo de hacer comedias en este tiempo*, Lope does brandish his awareness of Italian-generated

DOI: 10.4324/9781315612720-12

neo-Aristotelian theory, the "monster of nature" hardly considers generic concepts important for the practicing playwright composing the intrinsically tragicomic, local form of the Spanish *comedia*: "When I have to write a play I lock away the precepts with six keys."[5] Lope here describes a combination of the serious and tragic with the laughable and comic that appears to grow naturally, or at least locally, in response to the tastes of Spanish *corrales* audiences. Certainly the English playwrights, who wrote for as socio-economically diverse an audience as the Spanish, also knew how to "lock away the precepts with six keys," but even the allegedly "natural" playwright Shakespeare found the constituent parts of dramatic genres and modes useable devices in composing plays. A theatrical nation used to Polonius' "tragical-comical-historical-pastoral"—to modular dramaturgy combining genre-coded moving parts[6]—took a keen interest in this belated, constructed Italian form.

To be sure, like the Spanish the English hardly needed Italian theory to write plays that mixed comedy and tragedy. If English early modern drama consistently draws on the native medieval forms of the Corpus Christi play and morality play, tragicomedy, or at least the tragicomic (the adjectival form standing for transportable, modal qualities rather than fleshed-out generic form) would seem as easy as breathing. The grotesque tonal juxtapositions of the York Crucifixion play, with bumbling carpenters torturing the son of man because they cannot measure properly, disturbingly join the high and the low just as sure as Alichino and his band clown it up in Dante's hell.[7] English early modern drama is persistently tragicomic, modally speaking; not only does it mix kings and clowns, but the king or prince can even *play* the clown, as Hamlet does in the guise of his antic disposition. The history play effortlessly slides between the Boar's Head Tavern and the king's court; Webster's tragical satire chops most of its protagonists (with some grand exceptions) down to grotesquely comic size; and even the comedy of the "neo-classical" Jonson attains quasi-tragic purchase, with overreachers such as Mosca and Volpone not content with garden-variety schemes to fleece their victims.

But the idea of Italian tragicomedy, whether explicitly pastoral or not, meant something else, and this something else was of distinct interest to the English. What emerges in late sixteenth-century Italy, after a century of stage experimentation and as distilled in the copious and expansive theoretical corpus of Guarini, is the integral, formally coherent, aesthetically informed genre, or fleshed-out form, of tragicomedy. Spurred by his antagonist Giason Denores, a displaced Cypriot teaching rhetoric at the University of Padua who vociferously argued against the new hybrid form, Guarini contends that components of tragedy and comedy can be carefully mixed together so as to form a satisfying aesthetic whole—not merely combined in the way of medieval drama. In also arguing against Denores that the pastoral form could acquire a certain stature and *gravitas* above the low decorum with which it was most frequently associated, Guarini proposes the pastoral mode as a credible means for integrally combining the genres of tragedy and comedy: not the only means, since frequently Guarini argues for tragicomedy irrespective of pastoral, but clearly the device used in *Il pastor fido* itself. When Sidney, writing in 1579 before Guarini's ideas had made their way to England, decries the mixing of kings and clowns in "mongrel tragicomedy,"[8] he could be seen as implicitly calling for just the kind of tragicomedic poetics that Guarini produced. One suspects that the author of the pastoral romance the *Arcadia*, which mixes social classes and tonal registers in its own right, would have taken Guarini's side of the debate had he not died young as a holy warrior in the Netherlands. Lope, who seems perversely proud that his mixed *comedia* might be called a "minotaur," probably did not have care.

John Fletcher's note "To the Reader," prefacing the 1609 Printing of *The Faithful Shepherdess* after its apparently unsuccessful performance in 1608 at the Blackfriars theater, shows what was at stake, at least for Fletcher, with "pastoral tragicomedy." The remarks suggest some interesting continuities with Sidney's reflections some three decades earlier, and a concern with an integral, coherent poetics of tragicomedy such as had been developed by Guarini, whose work Fletcher knew (the title of his play is an obvious reference to Guarini's masterpiece). Fletcher beseeches the reader to read the note before reading the play "if [he] be not reasonably assurde of [his] knowledge in this kinde of Poeme"[9]—indicating both his anxiety that the new form was not known and his solicitude to educate his public. For Fletcher, his play failed in performance both because the public expected the rustic strains of traditional English pastoral ("whitsun ales, creame, wassel and morris-dances") and "country hired Shepheards, in gray cloakes, with curtaild dogs in strings, sometimes laughing together, and sometimes killing one another." What Fletcher objects to is precisely what the new poetics of tragicomedy would attempt to correct: random juxtapositions of the modally comic ("laughing together") and the modally tragic ("killing one another"). As with Guarini and Daniel (Shakespeare and Jonson are more complicated in this regard), Fletcher's raising of his shepherds to a higher class ("the owners of flockes and not hyerlings") would itself provide aesthetic unity, effectively excising class so that the "beautiful relation between rich and poor"[10] could inhabit the self-same figure. A careful poetics of plot supplants the random juxtapositions of "mirth and killing": "A tragie-comedie is not so called in respect of mirth and killing, but in respect it wants deaths, which is inough to make it no tragedie, yet brings some neere it, which is inough to make it no comedie." Here is the idea, central to tragicomedic poetics, of *calibration*: the playwright carefully adjusts tragedic and comedic features along a spectrum in order to produce a certain effect in the audience.

Since Guarini's theory exemplifies the frequent use of Cinquecento theory to justify practice after the fact, some general idea of pastoral drama in sixteenth-century Italy is instructive. Before the form of pastoral drama was codified in the Ferraran court of the 1550s with Agostino Beccari's pivotal *Il sacrificio*, plays directly or loosely carrying the pastoral label were extremely diverse in respect to style, subject, social register, dramaturgy and where they were performed.[11] Pastoral was mainly introduced to the stage through the dramatization of the literary eclogue, which from Theocritus to Vergil to Renaissance writers featured two or more shepherds (or courtiers disguised as shepherds) engaged in song, or dialogue, or both. Paul Alpers, who discusses the representative figures of shepherds engaged in community, singing and speaking in order to "redress separation, absence, or loss,"[12] emphasizes throughout his magisterial book *What Is Pastoral?* the foundational nature of the dialogic eclogue for the pastoral mode. The "amoebean" exchange between pastoral speakers encodes a humble, but salutary, diminution of the speaker/protagonist's "power relative to world"—not as an idyllic escape but as a felt response to real, altered conditions, such as the dispossession of farmers' lands by Augustus after the civil wars in Vergil's *Eclogues* and the very real economic and theological issues raised in Spenser's *Shepheardes Calendar.* Whereas many pastoral dramas performed in late fifteenth-century and early sixteenth-century Italian courts did stay closely to the diminished, if eloquent eclogue form, many did not. Pastoral could increase in stature simply by taking on mythological strains, as it did in

Poliziano's 1480 *Orfeo* and Niccolò da Correggio's 1487 *Cefalo*. Poliziano's play tilts towards tragedy; *Cefalo* illustrates the possibility of pastoral as generically ambiguous and capacious: neither comedy nor tragedy, but "tale or history, whatever it may be."[13] From the beginning of its introduction onto the Italian stage, a tension of decorum characterizes pastoral. On the one hand, the central function of the shepherd as its representative figure makes it is a "diminished thing" relative to tragedy and epic, with its very poetics deriving from an honest acknowledgment of its limitations in the presence of community. On the other hand, pastoral transplanted to the stage seems inevitably drawn to a higher register. Denores would not have put it this way, but when he objects to Guarini's aggrandizement of pastoral to a tragic or tragicomic register he is arguing that it remain between its conventional modal limitations.

Pre-Ferraran early modern pastoral drama, as Pieri explains, draws from the "double linguistic and social code" that characterizes medieval pastorals such as Adam de la Halle's *Jeu de Robin et de Marion* (1283)—a doubling not really endemic to Theocritus or Vergil.[14] Such socially differentiated drama could explore the relationship between the court or city and the country. If, following Aristotle, the characters of tragedy and comedy are distinguished by social or moral status, such double coding becomes a tragicomedic device. Ruzante's early *La pastoral* (1521) provides the most compelling example of a "doubly-coded" pastoral play. In fact, the double linguistic-social register of the play constitutes its very structure, which is to juxtapose the Sannazaran-inspired pastoral of plangent, Tuscan-speaking courtiers-as-shepherds with the *villanesca* play of real, hungry peasants (*villani*) that Ruzante absorbed from late medieval popular literature and, to some extent, his personal experience growing up in the Paduan countryside.[15] Rather than a "beautiful relation between rich and poor," however, the play stages the sheer *incommensurability* of the new courtly/literary form and the radically materialist world of the peasant. In the first, primarily Tuscan part of the play, the shepherd Milesio commits suicide from love-grief, which causes the younger shepherd Mopso to faint. The shepherd Arpino, who takes Mopso as well as Milesio for dead, forces an encounter between his rarefied world and that of the *villano* because of, in a word, the material body: he needs the peasant "Ruzante's" help in burying the two shepherds. The encounter, however, hardly counts as the "amoebean exchange" of shepherds: Arpino calls out to the desperate and famished Ruzante at the very moment when he is shooting birds in order to feed his impoverished family, and in doing so scares away (to Ruzante's great dismay) the peasant's food source. The Tuscan, literary voice thus does not sing along with, but sharply disrupts his materially fragile world. The subsequent exchange between Arpino, speaking in Tuscan, and Ruzante, speaking in a Paduan dialect, might be compared to the pastoral exchange, also inflected by a double linguistic and social code, between the courtier Touchstone and the real shepherd Corin in Shakespeare's *As You Like It*, except that the worlds of Arpino and Ruzante are so incongruous as to short-circuit real communication. Both the pathos and humor of their encounter turns on the double meaning of Pan(e):

ARPINO: O sacro Pan, pieta dei servi tuoi!
RUZANTE: Tu me vuò dar del pan? Mo su, anagún.
ARPINO: O, sacred Pan, have pity on your servants!
RUZANTE: You want to gimme some bread. Sure man, go ahead.[16]

As with several of Ruzante's early works, before he began to provide more dramatic closure with New Comedic structures in plays in the 1530s such as *L'Anconitana, La pastoral* works more like a dialogue (interspersed with bravado stand-up routines by "Ruzante") than a play. As a dramatic eclogue, an extended exchange between two very different kinds of shepherds, *La pastoral* could be seen either to violate Alpers' notion of pastoral community, insofar as it emphasizes division and incommensurability, or provide an outlying example of it, in that it *convenes* a community of suffering, hungry, materially dispossessed Paduan peasants as they are differentiated from the Petrarchan shepherd. Despite its darkness (the peasants are starving; "Ruzante" essentially has to kill off his father to inherit his goods), *La pastoral* is not a serious candidate for "pastoral tragicomedy," but it does provide an analogue for later English plays, such as *The Winter's Tale* and *The Sad Shepherd*, that restore the popular, festive, and material strains of pastoral after the Ferraran (and, later, Fletcherian) excision of it.

By 1545, when the Ferraran playwright Giraldi Cinthio wrote his pastoral play *Egle* in direct imitation of the ancient Greek satyr play,[17] the neo-Aristotelian theoretical revolution was well under way in humanist Italy. By then, extensive experiments in pastoral drama combined with renewed interest in Aristotle to generate lively inquiry into what might constitute the *third* dramatic genre after tragedy and comedy. The satyr play was the obvious classical exemplar for this *genus incognitus*, all the more provocative and tantalizing because only one example, Euripides' *Cyclops*, survived. Those, like Guarini fifty years later, who wished to theorize the satyr play as an ancient case of tragicomedy, could work from Horace's brief remarks on the form in *Ars poetica*. For Horace, the satyrs were introduced after tragedy had been established on the ancient Greek stage, for spectators who had "observed the rites" and were now "drunken and in lawless mood."[18] And yet despite the fact that tragedy shifts to the festive and mirthful realm of the satyrs, it is not merely tragedy at play. Because, according to Horace, the gods and heroes of tragedy stop short of uttering "vulgar speech in dingy hovels," they accomplish this generic transformation "with no loss of dignity." Tragedy, carefully modulating into the tragicomedic, "satyric" decorum, will shift to the satyr's arena "like a matron bidden to dance on festive days." With such careful attention to the particularly intermediate decorum of the tragicomedic satyr play, Horace appears to advocate just the carefully calibrated, aesthetically coherent form that Guarini would later articulate in more detail.

The idea began to crystalize that the satyr might serve as well as the shepherd as the "representative figure" of the third genre. This notion is most concretely embodied, much later, in the frontispiece to Ben Jonson's 1616 *Works*, which places the figure of "Tragicomoedia" at the top of an arch (the sides of which are supported by "Tragoedia" and "Comoedia"), flanked by a satyr on the left side and a shepherd on the right. By virtue of a productive etymological confusion, "satyr" was conflated with "satire" so that the harshness of the goat-man was joined to the rough strains of the satiric mode. As Northrop Frye has observed, and as we might conclude from the "tragical satire" of John Webster or a Shakespearen "problem play" such as *Troilus and Cressida*, a heavily satiric register tends to diminish the full force of tragedy.[19] If behind the "savage indignation" of satirists such as Jonathan Swift lies a disillusioned idealist, satiric critique might well inhabit the idealistic world of pastoral: the Forest of Arden draws Jacques, and almost all Ferraran pastoral plays include actual satyrs who in their critique of the courtly establishment anticipate Shakespeare's Caliban, whose profit from learning language is to curse. John Marston's 1604 *The Malcontent*, designated in the Stationer's Register as "Tragicomoedia" and according to G.K. Hunter a deliberate attempt to refashion Guarinian tragicomedy into an English form,[20] places the "satyrist" Malevole as a controlling figure shaping the tragicomedic plot and form. Malevole, displaced and dispossessed, stands in a similar position relative to his world to the bereft Vergilian shepherd. Marston, whose vitriolic satires were prohibited under the 1598 Bishops' Ban, turned to the medium of drama where satire could temper tragedic intensity. Both the satyr/satirist and the shepherd—the representative figures of tragicomedy in the Jonson frontispiece—hold "diminished strength relative to their worlds" (Alpers) compared to the protagonists of epic or tragedy. In their lessened stature, they modally temper tragedy to tragicomedy. If we consider Malevole as a kind of "satyr," the *Malcontent* becomes cognate with pastoral tragicomedy.

Giraldi's satyr play was followed by a 1554 theoretical defense of the *satira*—necessary, he says, because of the complete absence of any classical theory on the "third genre" excepting Horace's brief remarks. Giraldi's theorizing, incomplete and relatively neglected, anticipates Guarini in two major respects: 1) it takes a historical approach to genre, rather than the neo-Platonic, hypostatic approach pursued later by Denores; 2) it proposes an aesthetically coherent kind, not merely "tragedy at play" or an inchoate combination of tragedy and comedy, but a carefully calibrated intermediate genre. Stylistically, Giraldi argues that satyric diction strikes "un certo convenevole mezzo tra la comedia e la tragedia" [a certain decorous mean between comedy and tragedy].[21] Emotionally, the satyrs' pathos and the play's surprisingly unhappy ending generates an attenuated, tragicomedic register of "appropriate terror and pity," a calibrated lessening of the affective intensity proper to tragedy. Scenically, Giraldi's *satira*, which was written in the same year when Sebastian Serlio (following Vitruvius) codified the *scena satyrica* as a wholly distinct third type of set design, further articulated the notion of a distinct pastoral place, replete with both the pleasance of woods, fields, and meadow but also with more sublime elements such as dark caverns, mountains, and sheer cliffs (if, as in Tasso's *Aminta*, sometimes evoked by word scenery alone).

Giraldi's experiment with the satyr play was *sui generis* and did not shape the next wave of experiments, also concentrated in Ferrara, in the third kind. A pivotal event, often cited as the Ur-pastoral play of the secondo Cinquecento, was Agostino Beccari's 1555 *Il sacrificio*, whose 1587 staging in a small court near Ferrara was a pivotal event in the production of the pastoral play.[22] But even though a line of filiation can be traced from *Il sacrificio* to *Aminta* to *Il pastor fido*, there were more types of pastoral drama produced during this period than the two canonical examples suggest. Luigi Pasqualigo's 1581 *Gl'intricati* differs from the Tassan-Guarinian model by reprising the "double social and linguistic code" that we observed in Ruzante, if less politically. Anticipating the world of *The Tempest* and the "magical pastoral" plays of the commedia dell'arte,[23] Pasqualigo brings three Arte-type buffoons into an enchanted Arcadia world inhabited by a *maga*, who guards a magic book and terrifies the buffoons with mysterious voices issuing from the woods. Several other pastoral plays, by Pietro Cresci, Gieronomo Vida, Camillo Della Valle, and Giovanni Battista Leoni, and others counter the Tasso-Guarini models by violating, as does Pasqualigo, the principles of verisimilitude by marvelous, magical transformations (in *Aminta* and *Il pastor fido* confined to the *intermedi*).[24] Like Prospero in *The Tempest*, the *maga* or *mago* of the commedia dell'arte pastoral plays wields all manner of fantastic power, even as he also recalls Shakespeare's protagonist by ultimately throwing away his book. The flexible negotiation of verisimilitude and the marvelous, such as characterizes the statue scene at the end of *The Winter's Tale*, is endemic to tragicomedic poetics.

Still, *Aminta* and *Il pastor fido* merit especial consideration in a comparative study because the plays were known by Englishmen from the 1591 Wolfe publication and because they are the most *tragedic* of the Italian pastoral tragicomedies. The character Tirsi, a figure for Tasso himself, describes how *Aminta* will graft the epic and tragedic strains onto a pastoral tree. After having written *Gerusalemme liberata*, Tirsi/Tasso claims that he "returned to these woods … [having] retained something of that [epic] spirit; my pipe does not sing humbly as before, but with a higher and more sonorous voice."[25] Countering the rather low estimation of romantic love that characterizes early *commedia erudita* plays such as Machiavelli's *La mandragola, Aminta* elevates eros to a tragicomic and even tragic register. Potentially tragic love, in fact, is what shifts the play, contra Denores, from a pastoral eclogue to a dramatic action: Aminta's attempted suicide. When announcing the protagonist's apparent death, the tragedic *nuncio* practically quotes from Aristotle's *Poetics*: "Io ho sì pieno il petto di *pietate*/e si pieno d'*orror*" (My heart is so full of pity and terror; 5.2.1624–35, emphasis mine). Before Aminta leaps to what becomes a fortunate fall (he is saved by landing in a bush, and the belief that he has died causes Silvia to fall in love with him), he casts himself as a tragedic actor, uttering "sconguiri orribili" [horrible oaths] in a "pazzo furor" (mad fury).[26] Aminta, if generally an undramatic play, provides a fine example of the tragicomedic modulation of tragedy. The pastoral arena engages the themes, emotions, plots, and characters of tragedy, but replays them into a tragicomedic decorum.

Guarini frames *Il pastor fido* with a tragedic *antefatto*, which will be replayed and refashioned in the *scena satyrica*: the Aminta-Silvia relationship of *Aminta* is converted into an actual suicide (Guarini's Aminta, spurned by Lucrina, actually kills himself). Although Guarini's play has been accused of idyllism, it scarcely counts as soft pastoral: the sweet world fantasized by the female protagonist Amarilli, with its vision of benign, non-violent love, is hardly the Arcadia of *Il pastor fido* itself, which is stricken by a Sophoclean blight caused by goddess Diana, still furious for Lucrina's rejection of Aminta. The tragedic tags of the play go well beyond Tasso's references to the *Poetics* to include a systematic Sophoclean apparatus, including a speech recalling Tiresias' account of terrifying omens from *Antigone* and an extended dialogue effecting the pivotal recognition of the play. In defending *Il pastor fido*'s significant elevation of the pastoral mode against Denores, Guarini defends the tragicity of pastoral. He does this mostly in passages in the two *Verrati* that were not included in the 1602 *Compendio*.[27] For Guarini, "Le pastorali sono capaci della grandezza Tragica, e … d'loro soggetti si possano formare buone Tragedie" [Pastorals are capable of tragedic grandeur, and good tragedies can be made out of pastoral subjects; (I *Verato*, 2: 291)].[28] Guarini's elevation of pastoral to a potentially tragedic register discounts it as a merely "idyllic" and escapist mode. Arcadians, in this higher mode, cannot merely be paragons of virtue but must be capable of tragedic vice or undeserved misfortune. Guarini could never have written *King Lear*, but in arguing that tragic atrocities such as blindness and hanging have stricken shepherds in pastoral literature, he makes theoretical allowance for blind Gloucester on the heath of Shakespeare's "ferocious pastoral."

Guarini, usually considered a literary dramatist par excellence, was actually more of a man of the theater than is genuinely recognized. If extremely hostile to the professional actors, Guarini took an active role in academic-courtly theatrical production on several occasions. With Angelo Ingegneri, he co-directed the famous performance of *Oedipus Rex* at the Teatro Olimpico of Vicenza in 1585; he was probably involved with the pivotal 1587 production of Beccari's *Il sacrificio*, for which he wrote a prologue and *intermedi*; he worked with the Jewish theater impresario Leone de' Sommi on the attempted Mantuan production of *Il pastor fido* from 1591–93; and helped Duke Vincenzo Gonzaga find actors for the pivotal 1598 production. The production history of *Il pastor fido* is a story of fits and starts, with unsuccessful attempts to stage the play in 1584–85 (Ferrara), 1585 (Turin), and 1591–93 in Mantua. Not until 1596 did the first complete staging of the play take place, during Carnival, and the first definitive productions did not occur until the June, September, and November 1598 stagings in Mantua the latter performed in honor of Queen Margeret of Austria just a week after her marriage to Philip III in Ferrara. Guarini's insistence that any production go well beyond the usually humble staging of pastoral plays in the gardens of palaces and villas[29] in order to reach a certain *gravitas* and grandeur, was certainly a major factor in these delays; it can also be observed that the many rehearsals of the play that took place between 1585 and 1596 were not entirely private affairs, and functioned in as experimental a way as did Guarini's "work shopping" of the play script as early as 1584, well before its completion. (The experimental and social nature of Guarini's writing and producing ironically likens him in some respects to his great antagonists, the professional *comici.*)

Certainly the 1598 production had to be a grand affair, and needed a suitable venue. As early as 1591, under continual pressure from Guarini, the Duke began to restore the original ducal theater constructed by Giovan Battista Bertani in 1551, but destroyed by fire in 1588.[30] The November, 1598 production, performed in the restored ducal theater, was a momentous theatrical event, drawing some 1,000 spectators, and despite the aristocratic nature of the audience, the size of the audience vexes any neat distinction between "private" and "public" theater. With many German-speaking audience members in the wake of the Austrian queen's wedding (who needed a German transcription of the play's plot to follow along), as well as Spaniards in the retinue of Philip III, the production was a genuinely international theatrical event.

The *materia* of theatrical production, especially vocal and instrumental music, the marvelous *intermedi*, the construction of the *scena satyrica*, and the general emphasis on performance as pleasure, clarified the *pastorale* as *tragicomedia* rather than *tragedia*. In performance, *Il pastor fido* was "melos-drama," extensively employing both vocal and instrumental music in ways that attenuated the full force of the tragic registers. In a letter to Vincenzo Gonzaga of March 22, 1593, Guarini complains that there were not enough musicians to perform the play (one of the many reasons a full performance was not achieved), which required, both in the dramatic scenes as well as between acts, "concerti molti et vari et pieni, et molti chori et di voci et d'instrumenti" [many, varied, and full musical pieces, and many chorus with both vocal and instrumental music].[31] Italian pastoral tragicomedy and early opera, after all, were developing at the same time in late Cinquecento Italy, both partially based on conjectured reconstructions of ancient Greek drama. For Guarini, committed more or less to verisimilitude within the dramatic scenes, the new sophisticated scenic machines used to change sets, create special effects, and carry divine beings like Hymen through the air were amply employed to marvelous effect in the *intermedi*. Even though Guarini proscribed supernatural interventions in the play itself (except for those narrated in the *antefatto*), surely the effect of the marvelous *intermedi* shaped the overall aesthetic experience of the performance, in a way that also attenuated the rigor of tragedy. The spectacular set was designed by Giambattista Aleotti, and reprised key elements of his landmark design for the 1587 production of Beccari's *Il sacrificio*, which included an octagonal temple consecrated to the pastoral god Pan, and a river running through the stage. The temple alone, anticipatory of the temple of Apollo invoked in *The Winter's Tale*, would have had a tragedic coding in the Renaissance, after Serlio's codification of the tragedic, comedic, and pastoral "scenes."

Soon after Guarini began to share manuscript copies of his incomplete play with literary authorities in the Veneto, Denores attacked him at the end of his 1586 *Discorso*, to which Guarini quickly and angrily replied in his 1588 *Il Verato*. Denores countered in his 1590 *Apologia*, to which Guarini replied in a second treatise, *Il Verato secondo*, completed in 1591 but not published until 1593. Guarini's body of theory, which includes the somewhat calmer, and much shorter 1602 *Compendio della poesia tragicomica*, provides a prime example of "self-justifying theory."[32] That no comparable body of theory exists in the late Cinquecento for comedy and tragedy reflects the relative success of pastoral. Leone de' Sommi actually claimed in 1598 that pastoral drama had single-handedly saved the Italian stage. Guarini is "many people deep": his copious and detailed theory represents the experience and success of many pastoral tragicomedies rehearsed and staged between 1555 and the late 1590s, and he leaves very few elements of drama unconsidered. Aristotelian concepts such as decorum, imitation, verisimilitude, and catharsis might sound conservative to our ears, but Guarini applies them in innovative and experimental ways.

For Guarini, tragicomedy is not Lope's minotaur, but comparable to the mixed government of the Venetian republic, the neither male nor female hermaphrodite, and to hybrid animals such as the mule. Guarini's main responses to Denores can be condensed to three major points: 1) the historicity of genre; 2) the calibration of genre to audience response; and 3) the untethering of the pastoral mode from any fixed, extrinsic form. To Denores' belief that genres do not change in time but are as fixed as Platonic forms, Guarini contends (agreeing with Giraldi, and anticipating the Jonson frontispiece) that genres are historically constructed. If generic codes, structures, attributes and tonalities are not determinative frames but historical conventions, they may be crafted by the playwright: genres become the very materials of dramaturgical creation, capable of being split apart and recombined in almost infinite ways. In a time when tragedy seems (at least to the Italians) to have run its course and when the commedia dell'arte seems to have dealt a fatal blow to courtly/academic comedy, tragicomedy is the genre for our times.

Secondly, and relatedly, Guarini's tragicomedy responds to the attitudes, sensibilities, and emotions of new audiences, carefully considering varieties of cognitive, emotional, and ethical audience response. Following Aristotle's emphasis on the emotions of pity and terror, in a refutation of Plato's critique on the irrational emotions elicited by poems and plays, Guarini attempts to calibrate an intermediate tragicomedic response somewhere between the extremes of pity and terror, on the one hand, and those of raucous laughter on the other. Dramatic genres and styles can be adjusted according to a continuum, much like certain musical instruments:

> Not like bells, but like musical strings that receive greater and lesser tension, the magnificent style can be more and less magnificent, and the low style more and less low, so that the stylistic registers blend into one another like colors.
>
> (*Il Verato*, 3: 226)

Here is the notion, endemic to tragicomedic poetics among the Italians and the English alike, that writing and performing tragicomedy amounts to a kind of *calibration*:

a moving closer to either the tragic or comic poles. Just as Tasso and Guarini pull away from a comic decorum, as does Fletcher in his dismissal of festive mirth, Jonson in turn reinvokes mirth and the popular register, pulling back from what he perceived as the excessively tragic and plangent registers of pastoral tragicomedy as it was being revived in Queen Henrietta Maria's court.

Thirdly, and crucially from an English perspective, Guarini unhitches pastoral from the fixed form of the eclogue or dramatic dialogue, so that can become modally free to take on "forma o tragica or comica o tragicomica" (*Il Verato* 3: 265)—or in the case of pastoral tragicomedy to function as a hinge between tragedy and comedy. As Joseph Loewenstein has argued, "pastoral becomes modal in the Renaissance"[33] and it was in large part due to Guarini, although the English accomplished this on their own terms. The pastoral mode, in Guarini's theory, can modulate or transform tragedy by several mechanisms, of which five may be summarized here. Firstly, as a particularly allusive, capacious, and self-conscious form, pastoral can stage a kind of dialogue between tragedy and comedy, and the points of view they represent. The pastoral arena can call up generic codes as a kind of shorthand, offering varying, alternative perspectives. Secondly (related to the mode's allusiveness), the pastoral space provides a place where tragedy can be replayed, as with the tragedic *antefatto* of *Il pastor fido* restaged with the possibility of an alternative ending. Shakespeare's *The Winter's Tale* replays the Sicilian tragedy of Leontes (and Othello itself) in the Bohemian pastoral of Florizel and Perdita with Polixenes menacingly but not catastrophically lurking in the wings. Thirdly, the *scena satyrica* provides a distinctly alternative place and atmospheric setting to the tragedic court and the comedic city. If not an idyllic escape into the pastoral pleasance, its natural landscapes, temples, huts (sometimes inhabited by representative figures such as the hermit), and rivers can provide a salutary escape from the pressures of the internecine court, while retaining a sense of pathos (and the presence of eros) typical of the pastoral scene. Fourthly, the pastoral mode transforms the emotional extremes of tragedy into something "rich and strange." Its typical notes of pathos, lament, and eros, cast into the musical registers typical of staged Italian pastoral plays, and especially compelling when performed by famous actresses like Isabella Andreini when they performed pastoral plays, provide just that kind of intermediate emotional calibration that theorists from Horace to Giraldi to Guarini advocated. Fifthly, as ambiguous figures in regard to social class the various representatives of pastoral can provide a hinge between the "high" characters of tragedy and the "low" figures of comedy. Either the bridging of social class may be effected by the fiction of the courtier disguised as a shepherd, as is the case in most Ferraran pastoral and in Fletcher's *The Faithful Shepherdess*, or a "double linguistic and social code" may either negotiate or sharpen class difference.

Shakespeare certainly knew about the playwright who, according to Lady Politic Would-be, was the second most quoted foreign writer in England. Rosalind's reference to Silvius as a "faithful shepherd" may be a reference to Guarini's play, and G. K. Hunter has detected echoes of the Dymoke translation in *All's Well that Ends Well*.[34] Marston's *Malcontent*, a conscious if extremely free response to Guarinian tragicomedy, probably influenced Shakespeare's *Measure for Measure*. The controller figures of Malevole and Duke Vincenzo work behind the scenes, more like theater directors than sovereigns, reflecting a diminished power relative to world compared to the tragedic protagonist. These so-called "problem plays," which also include *Troilus and Cressida*, continually and unstably mix tragic and comic registers in ironic juxtapositions.

Still, Marston's Malevole, both behind-the-scenes controller and vitriolic satirist, brings *The Malcontent* closer to the idea of pastoral tragicomedy than these plays of Shakespeare, if the representative figure of the satyr/satirist can be seen to modulate the entire play towards an aesthetically integral third genre in the manner of Guarini. *Troilus and Cressida's* Thersites, of course, easily matches Malevole in vitriolic satire, and harshly ironic registers course through the play, but lacks even the intermediate power relative to world of the pastoral figure.

Although satire, banned as an externally fleshed-out genre, migrated modally to English early modern drama and continued to prosper there well after *The Malcontent*, Marston's model for satyric tragicomedy did not take hold in England. The most dominant and influential model for tragicomedy became plays such as *Philaster* and *A King and No King* by Beaumont and Fletcher. Fletcher, who was bent on constructing a "mixed" and not merely "composite" tragicomedy when he wrote *The Faithful Shepherdess*, successfully achieved an aesthetically coherent hybrid in the new form he created with Beaumont, based an extended use of rhetorical hyperbole, a tightly woven plot that privileged surprise and reversal, the deft management of the "danger not the death," and a persistent musicality. Perhaps reacting to the apparent failure of *The Faithful Shepherdess*, pastoral in Beaumont and Fletcher's tragicomedies plays almost no role as a hinge between tragedy and comedy. The woods in *Philaster* operate merely as a setting for the action, providing no resonant alternative space, like *Cymbeline*'s Wales or *The Winter's Tale*'s Bohemia, that might reframe and transform tragedy.

If Shakespeare already knew about Guarini in the wake of *The Malcontent*, the junior playwright of the King's Men in his late period could have easily told him more when he joined the company around 1610, probably still smarting over *The Faithful Shepherdess*. Fletcher's decision to write a pastoral play, in fact, reflects a revived interest in the pastoral mode in England during the first decade of the seventeenth century. Fletcher's most immediate spur to pastoral would have been through his cousins Giles and Phineas Fletcher, with whom he lived: both of them were steeped in a Spenserian vein of pastoral. Sidney's *New Arcadia* was republished in 1605; Daniel wrote and produced *The Queen's Arcadia* in 1605–6, and the loosely pastoral *Mucedorus* (a possible influence on *The Winter's Tale*) was being revived on the English stage.

Like Ruzante, and unusual among English playwrights, the "upstart crow" Shakespeare had actual experience in the countryside: he descended from a family of farmers and in 1602 purchased 120 acres of arable land in Stratford. Like Ruzante's pastoral protagonists, Shakespearean shepherds like Corin and Perdita's foster-father carry the ring of truth. Shakespeare had a practical interest in the life of farmers and shepherds, and he revives the "double social and linguistic code" of early Cinquecento pastoral that up to that point had been most sharply depicted by Ruzante.

Whether directly inspired by Guarini or not, Shakespeare pursues the idea of pastoral tragicomedy in his late plays; in his case, the harmonies of the hybrid genre are hard-won and precariously sustained. Shakespeare's direct knowledge of Guarini's theory is difficult to ascertain. But because he works with the same tragical-pastoral-comical genre system, and uses the social registers, emotional tonalities, allusive codes, and symbolic resonance of pastoral to bridge tragedy and comedy, Guarini's theory can be instructive in interpreting his late works. As Louise George Clubb has demonstrated, Italian drama and the Shakespearean corpus are instructively comparable not because of one-to-one source influence, but because they worked with remarkably similar genre systems.

Cymbeline, The Winter's Tale, and *The Tempest* each significantly engage the pastoral place and the pastoral mode, in the Wales scenes of *Cymbeline*, the Bohemian segment of the analytically tragical-pastoral-comical *The Winter's Tale*, and the island of *The Tempest*. Each place is conceived, in pastoral fashion, as a "world apart" from the predominantly tragedic places that have dictated the terms of each play: the court from which Imogen is exiled, Leontes' poisonous Sicily, and the Milanese court from which Prospero has been exiled in the tragedic *antefatto* that he narrates to Miranda. Versions of soft, escapist pastoral counter each of these genuinely "hard pastoral" places: Imogen fantasizes about being a "neat-herd's daughter" with Posthumus a "neighbor-shepherd's son" (1.2.80, 81).[35] Polixenes, just before disaster strikes, imagines a pre-sexual idyll of him and Leontes as "twinn'd lambs," and Gonzalo in his "golden age" reverie filched from Montaigne plays escapist idealist to the "satyrists" Antonio and Sebastian. The pastorals staged in these plays, however, are generically and tonally porous, capable of engaging with tragedy and the real world. For one thing, people in these natural habitats actually work, whether forcibly (Caliban) or not; if they don't work, they are chided, as Perdita is by her foster father. The *scena satyrica* of Shakespeare's late plays replay versions of tragedic *antefatto* under providential, transformative time—but in ways that do not efface tragic realities such as Mamillius' death, the years Leontes has lost with Hermione, Prospero's imminent death and the fact that the potential agents of tragedy on the island, Antonio and Sebastian, are left standing and appear unmoved. Pastoral, in Alpers' terms, convenes community in each of these plays in both pastoral dialogue and song: the plangent notes of pastoral that pull it back from tragedic pity and terror are performed and received in community. Guidarius and Arviragus console themselves by singing a funeral lament to the supposedly dead Fidele, using the same strains previously used to lament their dead mother in repeated offices of grief. Songs of mostly bawdy and material strains draw the rough pastoralists of the festive, sheep-shearing community together in *The Winter's Tale*, counterpointing in both social and aesthetic registers the solemn music played by Paulina for Leontes in the statue scene. Ariel sings an invisible song of comfort to Ferdinand—music that creeps by him on the waters to comfort him about a death that, in fact, did not take place. As tragedy is replayed in the pastoral arena; the plangent, healing emotional strains of pastoral tragicomedy supplant the jealous rage of Leontes, and the brooding anger of Prospero. Hate and rage are transformed into the "gentleman-like tears" of the socially elevated shepherds, as they affectively respond to the moving recognitions narrated, not staged, at the end of the play. *The Tempest* finally turns on Prospero's emotional response to Ariel's empathic reaction to Gonzalo's tears before a spectacle staged before the ship-wreck victims in order to change their hearts and minds: a circular community of emotion all the more compelling for the fact that the satyrists Antonio and Sebastian can choose not to join. Socially, Shakespearean pastoral of the late period seems to have it both ways, registering both Ruzante's incommensurability and Guarini's synthesis. The Clown and older Shepherd of *The Winter's Tale* are patently not courtiers disguised as shepherds, and the country wenches who join Autolycus's rough songs need not expect courtly elevation. But as with the boys of Wales in *Cymbeline*, the shepherdess Perdita turns out to be a princess. No better account of the poetics of Shakespeare's pastoral tragicomedy, which in the spirit of the Italians synthesizes generic contraries by transforming plots, emotional registers, and social stations under the aegis of pastoral can be found than in the young shepherd's astonishment, at the end of the play, at the wondrous transformations of kin:

I was a gentleman born before my father; for the king's son took me by the hand, and called me brother; and then the two kings called my father brother; and then the prince, my brother and the princess, my sister, called my father father; and so we wept; and there was the first gentleman-like tears that ever we shed.

(*WT*, 5.2.139–45).[36]

Notes

1 Louise George Clubb, *Italian Drama in Shakespeare's Time* (New Haven, CT: Yale University Press, 1989), p. 29. Clubb's references are to "Italian Renaissance comedy."
2 Daniel Javitch, "Self-Justifying Norms in the Genre Theories of Italian Renaissance Poets," *Philological Quarterly*, 67 (1988): 195–218.
3 Ben Jonson, *Volpone*, ed. Philip Brockbank (New York: Norton, 1968).
4 For a detailed account of these *Pastor fido* publications in England, see Elizabeth Story Donno (ed.), *Three Renaissance Pastorals: Tasso, Guarini, Daniel* (Binghamton, New York: Medieval & Renaissance Texts & Studies, 1993), pp. xi–xiv, xix–xxvii.
5 Citation refers to Allan Gilbert (ed.), *Literary Criticism, Plato to Dryden* (New York: American Book Company, 1940), p. 542.
6 Clubb, *Italian Drama in Shakespeare's Time*, pp. 1–26.
7 Dante, *Inferno* (Cantos 21–23).
8 Citation refers to Gilbert, *Literary Criticism*, p. 451.
9 All *Faithful Shepherdess* citations are from Fredson Bowers (ed.), *The Dramatic Works in the Beaumont and Fletcher Canon*, vol. 3 (Cambridge: Cambridge University Press, 1966), p. 497.
10 This famous phrase is from William Empson, *Some Versions of Pastoral* (New York: New Directions, 1974), p. 11.
11 See Marzia Pieri, *La scena boschereccia nel rinascimento italiano* (Padua: Liviana Editrice, 1983).
12 Paul Alpers, *What is Pastoral?* (Chicago, IL: University of Chicago Press, 1996), p. 81.
13 For a text of *Cefalo*, see Niccolò da Correggio, *Opere*, ed. Antonia Tissoni Benvenuti (Bari: Laterza, 1969), pp. 7–45.
14 Pieri, *La scena boschereccia*, p. 44.
15 For an account of Ruzante's relationship with the *villanesca* and other popular genres, see Ronnie Ferguson, *The Theatre of Angelo Beolco (Ruzante): Text, Context, and Performance* (Ravenna: Longo, 2000), pp. 121–61.
16 Citation is from the definitive edition of Ruzante by Ludovico Zorzi, *Ruzante: Teatro* (Turin: Einaudi, 1967), Scene 11.40–41. All translations from the Italian are my own.
17 For the play, as well as the 1554 treatise mentioned below, see Carla Molinari (ed.), *Egle, Lettera sovra il comporre le satire atte alla scena, favola pastorale* (Bologna: Commissione per i testi di lingua, 1985).
18 All Horace citations refer to *Horace. Satires, Epistles, and Ars Poetica*, trans. H.R. Fairclough, 1929; Loeb Classical Library (Reprint; Cambridge, MA: Harvard University Press, 1978), "Ars Poetica," pp. 468–71.
19 Northrop Frye, *Anatomy of Criticism: Four Essays*, ed. Robert Denham (Toronto: University of Toronto Press, 2006).
20 G. K. Hunter, "Italian Tragicomedy on the English Stage," *Renaissance Drama*, n.s., 6 (1973): 123–48.
21 Molinari (ed.), *Egle*, p. 158.
22 For the production history of *Il pastor fido* and other pastoral plays in the secondo Cinquecento, see Lisa Sampson, "The Mantuan Performance of Guarini's 'Pastor fido' and Representations of Courtly Identity," *Modern Language Review* 98 (2003): 65–83. The reference to the production of *Il sacrificio* is on page 75 of Sampson's article.
23 For studies of the "magical pastoral" scenarios and plays of the commedia dell'arte, with reference to *The Tempest*, see Robert Henke, "Transporting Tragicomedy: Shakespeare and the Magical Pastoral of the Commedia dell'Arte," in *Early Modern Tragicomedy*, ed. Subha Mukherji and Raphael Lyne (Woodbridge, UK: Boydell and Brewer, 2007), pp. 43–58; and Richard Andrews, "The Tempest and Italian Improvised Theatre," in *Revisiting The Tempest:*

The Capacity to Signify, ed. Silvia Bigliazzi and Lisanna Calvi (New York: Palgrave MacMillan, 2014), pp. 45–62.

24 The magisterial treatment of these plays may be found in Clubb, *Italian Drama in Shakespeare's Time*. See especially pp. 153–87.

25 *Aminta* citation is from Torquato Tasso, *Aminta*, ed. Giorgio Bàrberi Squarotti (Padua: R.A. D.A.R., 1968), 1.2.39–43. Line numeration is consecutive, throughout the entire play.

26 *Aminta*, 5.2.1684–85.

27 The issue of pastoral's generic status might have been a particular sticking point with Denores and by 1602, when the Cyprian professor had been dead for twelve years, it might have seemed less pressing.

28 Citations from Guarini's theoretical works refer to *Delle opera del cavalier Battista Guarini*, 4 vols. (Verona: Giovanni Alberto Tumermani, 1738). I refer to the title of the treatise and the volume of the Tumermani edition in which the treatise is found.

29 Sampson, The Mantuan Performance of Guarini's "*Pastor fido*," p. 75.

30 Sampson, The Mantuan Performance of Guarini's "*Pastor fido*," p. 79.

31 Quoted by Alessandro D'Ancona, *Origini del teatro italiano*, vol. 2 (Turin: Ermanno Loescher, 1891), p. 560.

32 Javitch, "Self-Justifying Norms."

33 Joseph Loewenstein, "Guarini and the Presence of Genre," in *Renaissance Tragicomedy: Explorations in Genre and Politics*, ed. Nancy Klein Maguire (New York: AMS Press, 1987), p. 37.

34 Hunter, "Italian Tragicomedy on the English Stage," pp. 123–48.

35 Shakespeare, *Cymbeline*, ed. J. M. Nosworthy, Arden Shakespeare (London: Methuen, 1955).

36 Shakespeare, *The Winter's Tale*, ed. J. H. P. Pafford, Arden Shakespeare (London: Methuen, 1963).

11 The pastoral poem and novel

Jane Tylus

What is Italian about English pastoral? Surprisingly little, especially when one discounts the plays. To be sure, Spenser's *Shepheardes Calendar* is indebted to the eclogues of Baptistus Mantuanus, and the pastoral scenes in *The Faerie Queene* are redolent with echoes of Tasso's *Gerusalemme liberata*. Sidney's *Old Arcadia* follows the prosimetrum schema of Sannazaro's *Arcadia*, and Milton's "Lycidas" recalls the Italian poetry he read and translated as a young man. But Sidney also owes a great deal to Montemayor's popular *Diana*, translated almost immediately into English, unlike Sannazaro's work. And "Lycidas" calls more upon the classical tradition of the idyll and eclogue – and on Spenser – than on the Italians. Spenser's E.K. mentions the French Protestant poet Clément Marot, and the woodblocks in the *Calendar* are modeled on those of the German Sebastian Brant.[1] These works are also, insistently, "English" in their own way, and it is perforce an English language that Spenser's shepherds speak, as E.K. points out. Even though the *novelle* of Bandello or Boccaccio influenced the prose romances of Robert Greene or John Lyly, there is little that can be said to come from Italian pastoral prose traditions, while the country house poem of a Ben Jonson or Marvell would seem to be an entirely new genre divorced from the Italian work altogether. What then, might one say about the Italian pastoral presence in the tradition of early modern English poetry and prose, one that extends from the 1570s and 1580s with Spenser, Sidney, Marlowe, and Raleigh, and into the seventeenth century with Milton and Marvell? Is this a presence best noted for its absence, or at most, its marginalization?

Such will in part be my conjecture in the pages to follow. Even as pastoral is one of the imitative genres par excellence, ever since Virgil framed his *Eclogues* as his first poetic attempts, it has also been seen as a place for fresh beginnings – the "pastures new" into which we, and the shepherd, are propelled at the end of "Lycidas."[2] The fiction of spontaneity and orality that underlies this genre of "simple shepherds" thus encourages a sensibility of immediacy and supposed naturalness: shepherds speak what they think, without disguising their feelings. Thanks to the cultural and religious divisions that tended to mark late-sixteenth-century Europe, this was perceived as a "naturalness" that departed markedly from the wily Italian-ness of the continent. Anti-Catholic and anti-Italian sentiments are especially apparent in English pastoral's origins. Spenser wrote his eclogues, called by Annabel Patterson "the first Elizabethan pastoral of both church and state" just before Sidney went off to fight the Catholics in the Netherlands.[3] Robert Greene, author of the *Pandosto* that was the primary source for Shakespeare's *The Winter's Tale*, wrote a lengthy romance contrasting sneaky Italians with honest, home-grown Englishmen. Or as John Lyly says in *Eupheus and His England*, of 1580, "The morally pure English air mends the wanton courtier's ways."[4]

DOI: 10.4324/9781315612720-13

Needless to say, there were also significant differences in the rural makeup of England and Italy. Throughout the late middle ages and early modern period, the Italian system of *mezzadria* or sharecropping replaced many of the earlier feudal arrangements, especially in the north, while the English policy of enclosure, dating back to the time of Sir Thomas More, closed off grazing privileges to many shepherds and farmers. Additionally, England was engaged in the ambitious new project of colonialism, both overseas and with respect to its Irish "problem" – allowing for a consideration of pastoral worlds in ways that extended beyond either literary antecedents or the direct experience of the English countryside.[5] Spenser's *Views on the Present State of Ireland*, Drayton's *Poly-Olbion*, and Shakespeare's *The Tempest* all participate in telling ways in an extended use of pastoral tropes, many of them critically; Andrew Hadfield argues that Drayton ends up depicting the Renaissance world of pastoral destroyed.[6] Many landowners in Italy saw the rustics tending to their land as barbarous – one might cite Guarini's remarks on the rude *contadini* as he was rewriting his idealizing *Pastor fido*, and the *Alfabeto contro i villani*, from the Veneto, was unrelentingly satiric in its treatment of the peasants.[7] But Italy had no colonies and no overseas engagements, and its references to new worlds modeled on pastoral fictions tend as a result to be far more idealizing than that of British overseers, as in Tasso's description of Armida's garden on the Canary Islands in the *Gerusalemme liberata*.

Finally, we must simply consider the extended temporal lag between the heyday of pastoral poetry and prose in Italy and that in England. The watershed that is Sannazaro's *Arcadia* dates to 1504, although Sannazaro began writing his text twenty years earlier. And indeed, it is to the fifteenth century – as well as to the fourteenth – that one really must look for Italy's greatest contributions in poetry and in that hybrid genre of prose narrative with poetic "inserts" of which Sannazaro was the major, but by no means the first, example. It is a literature that is widely dispersed between various cultural centers, from Florence and Siena to Mantova, Ferrara, Venice, and Naples, with significant variations and often no clear indications as to which poet was influencing whom.[8] In the meantime, as Michelle O'Callaghan points out, the first use of the word pastoral to refer to a literary genre appears only in 1584, five years after the publication of Spenser's *Shepheardes Calendar*, and a century after Sannazaro started working on his *Arcadia*.[9] The situation with pastoral drama, as Robert Henke discusses in another chapter in this volume, is very different: Tasso's *Aminta* was performed in 1572, Guarini's *Pastor fido* a decade later. They thus coincide perfectly with and clearly contributed to the great Elizabethan season of pastoral. But these were almost belated offerings after several hundred years of experiments with pastoral poetry and prose in Italy.

For all of these reasons, and no doubt more, the vast critical literatures that cover both Italian and English pastoral poetry and prose could not be more different. Perhaps one of the key projects in Italian criticism will continue to be, for a long time, trustworthy scholarly editions of pastoral writers both major and minor, along with work that attempts to resolve issues of influence, diffusion, and readership within Italy itself. Carlo Vecce's recent, exemplary edition of the *Arcadia* is one instance of the former, along with earlier editions of the poetry of Filenio Gallo by Maria Antonietta Grignani (1973) and that of Leon Battista Alberti by Guglielmo Gorni (1975). A promised scholarly edition of the writings of Giusto de' Conti still awaits, while the poetry of Lorenzo de' Medici and Angelo Poliziano has also seen major editions in the last few decades.[10] Giuseppe Gerbino's wide-ranging account of the origins of madrigal and opera in pastoral and Jonathan Unglaub's fascinating study of the impact of Tasso's and others' engagement with pastoral on painters, particularly Poussin, are excellent accounts of pastoral poetry's relationship with the other arts.[11] But in fact what defined Italian Renaissance pastoral is still very much an issue in Italian criticism, as three fundamental collections of essays from the late 1990s convey, two of them published in France: *Le genre pastoral en Europe du XVe au XVIIe Siècle, Ville et Campagne dans la Littérature Italienne de la Renaissance*, and *La poesia pastorale nel Rinascimento*.[12] The interface between pastoral and epic in Ariosto's and Tasso's sprawling poems has prompted some of the more innovative work of recent years, as the episode of Erminia and the shepherds and the scene of Orlando's madness in a pastoral setting have inspired scholars to take on issues of authorship, gender, and masculinity.[13]

Scholars of English pastoral have been more theoretically inclined. Some of the finest Italian and American scholars of Renaissance literature of the last fifty years – Harry Berger, Paul Alpers, A. Bartlett Giamatti, Renato Poggioli, Louise George Clubb, and others – wrote extensively on pastoral. Alpers' prize-winning *What Is Pastoral?* is a comparative study of the genre beginning with Virgil, and notable for its elucidation of a dynamics of community in the pastoral poem, novel, and drama. Berger's far-reaching essays collected in *Second World and Green World: Studies in Renaissance Fiction-Making* posited pastoral as the touchstone for early modern explorations of "alternative worlds." Both books are richly comparative, and situate English pastoral in the contexts of its classical, Italian, and Spanish pastoral sources as well as other related works – such as More's *Utopia*. The fact that Alpers's book prompted a recent "sequel" by Ken Hiltner called *What Else is Pastoral?: Renaissance Literature and the Environment* suggests a recent turn in pastoral studies, as Hiltner argues that Alpers failed to consider landscape and rural setting as fundamental to pastoral's definition. It is notable, however, that, unlike Alpers, Hiltner focuses almost exclusively on English pastoral, and indeed, the wide-ranging comparative work of a Berger or Alpers has not been emulated in most recent American and English scholarship. Hiltner's work rather demonstrates a new and focused interest in ecocriticism as he and other critics consider the extent to which pastoral writers may have questioned the deforestation that accompanied enclosure or sympathized with the beasts of burden that are ubiquitous in the pastoral novel or poem.[14] Drayton's *Poly-Olbion* has emerged as particularly compelling for understanding the rural world as less of a backdrop and more of a place with exigencies and problems of its own.[15] Finally, the pastoral romances of Mary Wroth and the works of Mary Sidney have enabled an extensive discourse on the pastoral heroine – a tradition into which Sue Starke places Milton's Eve – while Jeff Dolven considers the Arcadian spaces of *The Faerie Queene* and of Sidney's novels as "scenes of instruction" and education for their inhabitants.[16]

All of this said: there is nonetheless much in this landscape that might prompt us to think about useful comparisons and parallel projects in the "work" that pastoral did in early modernity. I will suggest that we look to some unexpected places in thinking about the future of Italian and English pastoral relations while we might also look backward to Italy from England, especially in regard to some of the more interesting current critical venues regarding ecocriticism.[17] Moreover, there might be ways to consider – or reconsider – questions of influence, even if they are largely in negative terms, with "wholesome" English pastoral spaces presented as escapes from the darkness of an Italian scene often dominated by threats of rape and metamorphosis. Still, Spenser's *The Faerie Queene* is again a notable exception, and a prince's encounters with pastoral beauty in

Sidney's *Arcadia* are reminiscent of the medieval *pastourelle* with its uneven power dynamics. There are, to be sure, continuities that are not simply casual.

In the pages that follow, I sketch out a brief trajectory of Italian pastoral by suggesting that it was inspired by two figures from the distant fourteenth century, Petrarch and Boccaccio, contemporaries of England's first "great" poet and another major influence on Spenser's *Shepheardes Calendar*: Geoffrey Chaucer. Chaucer was fascinated with these two Trecento writers who would be so formative, in ways no doubt unanticipated by either of them, to the revival of ancient pastoral in the Renaissance. Indeed, I would put it even more strongly. The pastoral revival would be unthinkable without them, and not simply because they both wrote Latin eclogues modeled on Virgilian ones. As suggestive as those eclogues are, they do not represent the future of a genre that would flourish in the vernacular. As Charles Dempsey has noted, if

> Latin is the language of the Church, the university, and the chancery ... the vernacular is the language of living experience in the world ... The discovery in Italy of the actuality of lived experience in the natural world arose together with the first flowering of vernacular expression.[18]

Dempsey is writing of the fifteenth century, when pastoral poetry, in its attempts to express the "actuality of lived experience" in a "natural" language, genuinely takes off, spawning novels, plays, operas, and paintings in its wake. By the early seventeenth century, hundreds of plays and poems would litter the libraries, homes, and printing presses of late Renaissance Europe; the exchange between the Curate and Don Quijote's niece early on in Book I of *Don Quijote* is simply one indication of pastoral's predominance.[19] But the vernacular experimentation of Petrarch and Boccaccio was necessary for this "explosion" – their examples leading in at least two different, but not mutually exclusive, directions that would prove fertile for both English and Italian poetry and prose.

Petrarch's version of pastoral is centered on the alienated voice of the frustrated lover, whose distance from and incomprehension of the natural world around him comes to stand for a more existential notion of identity than previously articulated in late medieval literature. Boccaccio's is based on a belief in the "sentimental education" that immersion in a pastoral world might provide, allowing for a collective to form that incorporates the individual within it, but not without tensions. Both of these trajectories had a lasting influence in England from at least the time of the earliest translations of Petrarch's sonnets in the 1530s to the end of the season of the great pastoral prose romances in the first half of the seventeenth century. Indeed, a focus on translation will be central for encouraging more deeply comparative work in the future, both in determining what the English *had* translated from the Italian, and how those translations resonated in – and often against – the English literary experience.[20] This modest intervention will attempt to demonstrate the uses of translation studies by reflecting on Henry Surrey's and Lady Mary Wroth's encounters with the dynamics of Italian pastoral.

But the translation with which one must begin any account of Italian and English pastoral is that of Virgil's *Eclogues*.[21] By the time of the first full translation of the *Eclogues* into Italian in 1482, Renaissance pastoral was already haunted by Petrarch. This work, which deserves to be far better known in the Anglo-American world, was the

Bucoliche elegantissime, printed by the elite Mescomini Press in Florence, and originating as a dedication copy to Lorenzo de' Medici. It consists of the work of five authors – two Sienese, three Florentines – and opens with Bernardo Pulci's translation, into *terze rime*, of Virgil's ten eclogues. Pulci is vigilant in his transformation of poems that every schoolboy would have known; indeed, Lorenzo, no slouch when it came to Latin, had no need for an Italian Virgil. Yet what is telling is that the idiom in which the Italian Virgil is presented to Florence's de facto ruler allows Lorenzo to recognize that the claims he had made for "Tuscan" in the proem to his *Commento* of roughly the same period could, in fact, be substantiated: Pulci's translation of Virgil's incomparable poems into the metrical rhyme scheme invented by Dante was proof of Lorenzo's argument that Italian was capable of holding its own against the great languages of antiquity.

It is not just Dante that one hears in Pulci's poems. Pulci "italianizes" Virgil, introducing him into the poetic traditions of the last two centuries by incorporating what can only be called a Petrarchan voice into the eclogues. Thus one example from the famous first eclogue, the meeting of a contented Tityrus and the exile Meliboeus. Meliboeus opens the poem and thus the "eclogue book," and it is Meliboeus who says, in Pulci's translation, "Tu tytiro nell'ombra e molli prati/Con otio insegni amarilla formosa/Risonare alle silve e monti e lati": "You, Tityrus, beneath the shade, in otium you teach the woods and mountains and verdant fields to resonate with the name of sweet Amaryllis." Virgil had the more restrained "formosam resonare doces Amaryllida silvas": "you teach the woods to resonate with sweet Amaryllis." These additional nouns are standard Petrarchan terms, as we will see. But there is something more too. As he characterizes Tityrus's newly-gained lands, Pulci's Meliboeus dwells lovingly on the habitation itself in language entirely new to the translation: "O fortunato vecchio adunque liete/Harai tue ville e gran pasture ancora." (O lucky old man, here still you will keep your lovely villas and spacious fields). No longer simply fortunate, this *felice* vechio or happy old man has been endowed with "ville," with a "gran pasture," and hence with a place denied to Meliboeus himself, who in another addition by Pulci, observes of himself, "Ecco io col corpo e con la mente affranta" (and here am I, with mind and body broken).

These are, in short, additions that introduce a Petrarchan idiom into the bucolic world: one which can be said to have been anticipated not only by Virgil's mournful Meliboeus, but by the love-stricken Coridon of Eclogue 2, the exiles in Eclogue 9 or the suicidal Gallus in Eclogue 10. Like Pulci, Petrarch places "altri monti" and "selve aspre" together, as in Canz. 129, as places where he might find "qualche riposo." In Canz. 71 he apostrophizes "O poggi, o valli, o fiumi, o selve, o campi," and in 35, we again have a list of "monti et piagge et fiumi et selve" as settings where the speaker goes to flee thoughts of love. Petrarch's subject is different from others who inhabit the same landscape, such as the "avaro zappador" or poor farmer who goes home at the end of the day to burden his table with "rustic food" (povere vivande) or the shepherd who at twilight leaves "l'erba et le fontane e i faggi" (the grass, the fountains, and the beech trees) – nouns that remind us of what Pulci adds to Virgil's Eclogue. Other *canzoni*, such as the paired 125 and 126, are expressive of what Petrarch calls his "rough" mode of writing, to be contrasted with the elegant urban verse forms that will not welcome his own poems. Thus he asks Canz. 125, as though it were an uncultured shepherdess, to stay with him in the wood: "O poverella mia, come se' rozza!/credo che tel conoschi:/rimanti in questi boschi" (O poor little song, how inelegant you are! I think you know it; stay here in these woods).[22] The sestina, which looks back to

Dante and Arnaut Daniel, emerges in Petrarch as a powerful space for lyric complaint in a natural space; as Robin Kirkpatrick usefully notes, "from the first, [the sestina] has also been used to reflect processes – often the cyclical processes of time and nature – and to express the melancholic alienation of the lover from the processes which the poem itself portrays."[23] The repeated endwords in Petrarch's several *sestine* denote the place of pastoral spaces: *boschi, selve, terra.* If on the one hand, then, Petrarch hardly speaks with the voice of the *contadino*, on the other hand, the natural world offers Petrarch the chance to fashion a language that contests the mannered elegance and falsehood of the cities and courts: "le città sono nemici, amici i boschi" he writes in Sestina 237 (Cities are hateful to me, friendly the woods). In this context, the use of the vernacular is both responsive to the naturalness of the setting as well as a means for identifying a new Italia through the presence of its landscape. "Italia mia" (Canz. 128) is one of the collection's most famous *canzoni*, the product of a lone voice crying out in the wilderness as it instructs those "Signori" Petrarch has left behind to "see how time flies and how life flees." His song alone is told to try its fortune as it protests the wars devastating Italy and Europe and cries out "Pace, pace, pace" – the peace that paradoxically eludes the lyric subject as Petrarch wanders, "solo et pensoso," through deserted fields.

If Petrarch's Latin eclogues explicitly took up contemporary affairs such as the revolution of Cola di Rienzo or the corruption of the church – and perhaps tellingly mimicking in their number of twelve the twelve books of Virgil's epic rather than the ten eclogues – the vernacular *Canzoniere* focuses on a solitary lyric voice. At the same time, Petrarch's juxtaposition in both his Latin and vernacular writings of the corrupt city or court with the country as a new locus for personal reflection, as well as dialogue and exchange, sets up a contrast that would be extremely influential for later writers. Pulci's Meliboeus thus takes on the habits of Petrarch's lyric poet, at once accentuating his own solitude and depicting Tityrus's lands as more resplendent than they were in Virgil, precisely because they are not his own. This rift between speaker and natural world in Eclogue 1 is brought about by exile, whereas elsewhere in Virgil love is the cause of alienation, and here too Petrarch functions as a bridge between two kinds of being ill at ease in the world. Indeed, one might think about Petrarch as the "first historian of solitude," in the words of Peter von Moos,[24] as his solitary existence becomes a way of crafting an identity for the new rootless intellectual – one Nancy Struever describes as attempting to write outside of the medieval institutions of the church, university, and commune.[25]

The dynamics between the speaker and the natural world set out in the *Canzoniere* thus illustrated real tensions in the social and intellectual life of Renaissance Europe and would go on to characterize much of fifteenth- and sixteenth-century lyric poetry. That many of these poets identify themselves as "shepherds," taking on the voice of a lamenting denizen of rustic haunts, shows how Petrarchan solitude and the dynamics of Virgilian eclogue were brought together in the period. The itinerant figure Giusto de' Conti includes several explicitly pastoral lyrics in his poetry book *Bella mano* – most notably his "Udite monti alpestri," which looks to Petrarch 35 as well as to Virgil's fifth eclogue – and Lorenzo de' Medici's "Corinto" translates the second eclogue of Virgil with Petrarchan modulations.[26] Such pastoral exercises continue in the sixteenth century with the madrigals and sonnets of figures such as Gaspara Stampa, Laura Battiferri, Torquato Tasso, and Gian Battista Guarini; far from only writing pastoral plays, the latter two poets composed a great deal of pastoral verse both mournful and playful. As noted by Tavoni, Petrarch quickly becomes a way of distancing a voice concerned with difference and elevating itself above a "common language" – so allowing for pastoral to become a double for a new self-consciousness about literary production, an aesthetic space untested and unthreatened by a real world.[27]

At the same time, as Armando Maggi has commented, if Petrarch defined a new meaning of "solitude" for early modernity, this is a solitude that is often "densely populated" insofar as Petrarch sought throughout both his Latin prose writings and poetry such as the *Eclogues* to create an "intimate dialogue with a friend who pursues the same intellectual and spiritual ideals."[28] As Nancy Struever remarks, for Petrarch, "truth is social; consistency with one's friends' point of view is a primary value" (28). If Petrarch's familiar letters place him in dialogue with others in the liminal space where his wanderings take him, those others have the potential for moving beyond the alienating themes of exile and loss to generate the so-called "civil conversations" that will become hallmarks of the Renaissance dialogues of Stefano Guazzo, Bembo, and others. The dialogue in nature would characterize later sixteenth-century English texts as well; Henry Wotton calls the setting in which he brings together conversationalists for his 1579 dialogue on love a "Rurall Colledge."[29] At the same time, if Petrarch leads the way to alienation and dialogue alike, he does so by way of what can only be called imprecise topographies. The real forerunner of the sixteenth-century English debates about *questioni d'amor* found in Lyly, Lodge, and others is Boccaccio, who introduces two innovations to the pastoral inherited from antiquity.[30] One is formal: the development of a continuous prose narrative that contains numerous examples of "song," a form that originates in Boethius's *Consolation of Philosophy*, is revived with Dante's *Convivio* and *Vita nova*, and is then given a new life of its own with Boccaccio's *Ameto* and *Decameron* – to be embraced in turn by Sannazaro, Montemayor, Cervantes, Sidney, Wroth, and others. The second is thematic. Boccaccio gives his new generic formulation a distinct home, a decisive local setting in the hills outside Florence, with local characters, among whom his young women or, in the *Ameto*, his "ninfe" are decisive. Indeed, perhaps the most enduring feature of the Boccaccian model is that it gives speaking roles to female characters, the very figures who are denied a voice in Petrarchan lyric.

For like Petrarch, Boccaccio too is intrigued by pastoral's productivity, even as he had a more dynamic sense of what the place of nature might enable. His best-known work, *Decameron*, is not in any strict sense a pastoral. At the same time, it employs the "escape" and "return" motif that will become a staple of many longer pastoral works, including Sannazaro's *Arcadia* and Shakespeare's *As You Like It*. If Petrarch rejects the city permanently to create a new community in the *campagna*, Boccaccio's Florentines use the space of the villa to perform tale-telling rituals that will allow them to survive the plague that is devastating their city. But tale-telling also prevents them from succumbing to the *otium* to which they might otherwise be prey – an *otium* seen in similarly negative terms in Boccaccio's earlier and more explicitly pastoral work, the *Ameto* or the *Commedia delle ninfe fiorentine* (1342). Indeed, this work was conceived in the sixteenth century by its editor Sansovino not only as a "piccolo Decameron" but as the true model for Sannazaro's *Arcadia*, given its alternation of verse and prose. In this text in which a young man spies a group of lovely nymphs while they are bathing – hence improbably becoming an Actaeon who has seen Diana but lives to tell the tale – tale-telling is indeed put forth as a cure for *otium*. An eclogue sung by two shepherds prior to the nymphs' tales and songs may be the most explicit bit of pastoral in the work, but the *Ameto* as a whole readily partakes in the tranquil, lovely setting that allows for the time of human conversation to align itself with the rise and fall of the sunlight, ensuring that this community of women – and apart from the two shepherds who quickly vanish, a single man, Ameto himself – "fit" within the natural world. The stories told and shared are not simple ones of unrequited love. They rather take part in what I have called elsewhere an education into literacy, as the young hunter Ameto is "civilized" through stories of the nymphs' own growth and recognition of true love. Still, their tales "are not simply autobiographies but at times fanciful mythic accounts of the origins of the cities where [the nymphs] spent their youths: Paris, Athens, Naples, Rome, Florence."[31] As with the future *Decameron*, the tales themselves return the listeners to urban centers, while letting the harmonious, lovely landscape outside Florence act as the lovely place for reflection and, in the case of Ameto, intellectual and moral growth.

The other Boccaccian work of note is the *Ninfale fiesolano*, a lengthy poem that is more etiology than what we might recognize as pastoral. Set again in a precise local context – the little town of "Ponte a Mensola" outside of Florence – it is an origin tale, in which the nymph Mensola loses her virginity to the young, persistant Africo. She gives birth to a son, but is transformed by an angry Diana into a river, while Africo will drown himself in sorrow; his name is given to the body of water that merges, east of Florence, with the Mensola. They thus become the luminous spirits who animate the hills where Boccaccio had his home in the 1340s, while their offspring will become the ruler of Fiesole, the mountain town that looms above the rivers that take the young couple's names.[32] Boccaccio makes ample use of Virgil's *Eclogues*, while going to another suggestive Latin source – Ovid, both his *Metamorphoses* and the *Fasti* – for his myths of transformation and his allusions to the sacred, protected spaces of Diana's nymphs violated by Africo's aggression and, subsequently, Mensola's consent. Like the two Ovidian works, Boccaccio's poem employs both pastoral settings and mythic time, even as Boccaccio emerges from both to move us towards local, political history: he ends the *Ninfale* recounting Fiesole's subsequent destruction by Rome, and the resistance of Africo's people to Totila. Boccaccio's interest in etiological tales is shared by other writers throughout the next few centuries, from Lorenzo de' Medici whose "Ambra" recounts the flight of the nymph Ambra from a river near where Lorenzo had one of his villas, to Spenser, whose unfinished final book of *The Faerie Queene*, the so-called *Mutabilitie Cantos*, explore the mythic past of Ireland. At the same time, it is not easy to argue for the direct influence of a work like the *Ninfale* outside Italy; as Guyda Armstrong has shown, the relatively unknown figure John Golburne translated Boccaccio's poem using a French translation, and in the process turned this work written in *ottave* into prose.[33]

Certainly in Italy, however – and perhaps in England – Boccaccio would prompt a general interest in "localities" with respect to amorous matters and mythological resonances. He also had an ear for the linguistic peculiarities of local Florentine, even as his writing tended to be heavily influenced by the Latinate structure of many of his sources. Such moves towards fidelity to both the language or dialect of the countryside and "appropriate" imagery for rustic characters would fall instead to later fifteenth-century poets, such as Leon Battista Alberti whom contemporaries claimed wrote the first rustic poem in Italian, an "egloga" featuring the two handsome, "richi pastori," both of them "gioveneti amanti," Tyris and Floro. With his insistence on "agrarian" comparisons and occasional attempts to capture the language of the Mugello, Alberti becomes what Calmeta would call "Il primo che in questo stile [bucolico] abbia alcuna perfezione dimostrato."[34] Several decades later, Lorenzo de' Medici would be more serious in depicting the dialect of another rustic lad from the Mugello in his "Nencia da Barberino," a poem that opens with the confession of the young distraught shepherd that he "burns with love and needs to sing/for the lady who destroys [his] heart," a "young girl who leaves her little hut every day with her dog and sheep, and will occasionally meet the young singer at the well."[35]

But Florence would not be the only place for linguistic and thematic experimentation. Matteo Maria Boiardo experimented with the dialect of the Romagnola in his vernacular pastorals, and wrote a series of Latin eclogues as well. In the mid-fifteenth century the Sienese Filleno Gallo wrote two poetic dialogues that would have a formidable success in print, one in which "Lylia" exchanges witticisms with a desperate, Petrarchan-like lover, cautioning him to be temperate in his love. These and other works continue to represent pastoral as a form of education. It is not a big step from some of these dialogues to actual plays with characters fashioned from eclogues. Castiglione's *Tirsi*, for example, his "ecloga" or "stanze pastorali" of 55 *ottave*, was possibly performed at the 1506 carnival in Urbino, while Poliziano's *Orfeo* draws on Virgil, Petrarch, Giusto de' Conti, as well as the Sienese writers with their innovative use of the *sdrucciola* for its "realistic" representation of pastoral life. Finally, while he was primarily a writer – and actor – of rustic plays, Angelo Beolco, better known as Ruzante, wrote in Padovan dialect two "orazioni," or orations, which are essentially lengthy monologues in which he itemizes the food, animals, and women of the "Pavan" countryside, the second of which ends in a rustic *canzoni* sung along with the instruments of the "pivi e zugolari" – the pifferi and zampogna.[36]

Sannazaro's *Arcadia* does not come out of nowhere, while it also represents in its final form a crucial break with the work of Italy's earlier poets. Sannazaro began his work in the 1480s in dialogue – and possibly in competition – with Pulci's recently-published translation of Virgil, with Boiardo's *Pastorali*, with the Sienese legacy that was well-known in Naples. The eclogues of the *Arcadia*, with their echoes of Petrarchan lyric as well as engagements with a newly-discovered Theocritus, are not just exchanges among heartsick shepherds in a beautiful landscape outside Naples, but as critics have shown, poems that emerge out of a politics and a commitment to a particular community. The original text of the *Arcadia*, which had ten chapters and eclogues, was written in the context of the Aragonese court of the late fifteenth century, and shows a Sannazaro adroitly developing different verse forms to characterize his "pastoral" and hence academic affiliations, and thereby redefining intellectual community in ways not unlike what we have seen in Petrarch. Yet the interlocutors of the fictional narrator of the poem, Sincero, are very much with him as they wander in the woods and fields of Arcadia.[37] Evidence of this pastoral collectivity is the fact that, as Matteo Soranzo has pointed out, the Aragonese court showed its dedication to the vernacular through the production of farces, poems in the vernacular, and translations from classical works. As Francesca Bortoletti has recently demonstrated, it is quite probable that the early eclogues – only later inserted into a prose narrative – were performed.[38]

The expanded 1504 *Arcadia* – with twelve rather than ten chapters and eclogues, and with eventually far greater circulation – had a different audience in mind than a local one. In the somber atmosphere that greeted the departure of the Aragonese and Sannazaro himself from Naples in 1501, the new end of the *Arcadia* takes on richly-colored meanings. Whereas the earlier version ends with the narrator still in Arcadia, the revised one has him leaving it for Naples by way of an underground tunnel, and upon his return he finds himself surrounded by images of death – not least those of his unnamed beloved for whose sake he first fled. Both versions of the text, nonetheless, contain the narrator's surprising confession in the seventh chapter that he does not find himself at home in Arcadia, since everything he sees reminds him of his beloved. Unlike Ameto's sojourn among the nymphs, Sincero's pastoral stay is not regenerative, or at least not regenerative in any obvious way – something to bear in mind for Sidney's eventual use of the genre.[39] The sustained narrative in which the narrator only gradually reveals both his identity and his melancholy deepens and complicates earlier habits of thought. The 1504 text will accentuate the author's sense of estrangement, as one small but important alteration notes. Carlo Vecce calls attention to the difference in the course of Sincero's confession of a single word: whereas in reference to watching the wandering "armenti" he had said in the first version that such is "our custom," in 1504 Sannazaro stresses his alienation, writing instead, "this is thus the custom I've taken on in these your woods."[40] But he is also estranged from Naples itself, already apparent in the earlier edition. In the prologue the author suggests that he is writing among "these deserted lands" ("le spiagge deserte") to the listening trees and to the very few shepherds who will hear him – suggesting a rootlessness that returns us vividly to Petrarch and to Virgil's Meliboeus.

What remains is the itinerary of a journey, the transcript of songs sung in consolation and loneliness, a monument to a life, and to death; we end with a "congedo" or good-bye to his "sampogna," the instrument on which he sings his pastoral verse. The *Arcadia* is one of the saddest texts of the sixteenth century. Importantly, it is not simply "about" literature. It is about the political structures that enable cultural ones, and about Sannazaro's decision to follow his monarch and patron King Federico into exile in France. It can also be said to offer a verdict on the serenely confident works of Boccaccio to ground his young shepherds in communities in reassuringly verdant environments. Sannazaro's meditation on social and political sea-changes produces a poet – and perhaps an early modern intellectual – unable to find himself anywhere at home. The pastoral novels that come after the *Arcadia* by and large are unable to take up this dismal formulation, although Sidney's "productive" revisioning of his *Old Arcadia* as the *New* remained unfinished, and the pastoral episode of *Don Quixote*, a book translated almost immediately into English, ends disquietingly with Cardenio's suicide and the disappearance of the boasting Marcela into the woods.[41]

Attending to translation: the poetics of pastoral voice

If these pages have set out a very rough trajectory of Italian pastoral, this final section suggests at least way to think about how that pastoral tradition gets to England. I would suggest starting with the most basic question: the question of translation[42] as involves two works, roughly a century apart: Sir Henry Surrey's translation of Petrarch 310, and the opening of Lady Mary Wroth's encyclopedic pastoral romance, *Urania*. They show us in their different approaches to the pastoral discourses noted above what might have changed between the 1530s, when Henry VIII was on the throne and Italy was all the rage, to the 1620s, when the deeply Protestant Wroth was critical of James's tolerance with respect to Catholic traditions. What is the English response in each of these cases to pastoral and its reception of Petrarchan and Boccaccian sensibilities?

Surrey's sonnet is as follows:

The soote season, that bud and bloom forth brings,
With green hath clad the hill and eke the vale;
The nightingale with feathers new she sings;
The turtle to her make hath told her tale.
Summer is come, for every spray now springs,
The hart hath hung his old head on the pale;
The buck in brake his winter coat he flings;
The fishes flete with new repaired scale;
The adder all her slough away she slings;
The swift swallow pursueth the flyes smale;
The busy bee her honey now she mings
Winter is worn that was the flowers' bale.
And thus I see among these pleasant things
Each care decays, and yet my sorrow springs.

This is indeed a poem about the new season, although a spring mentioned never as a noun but only as a verb, twice: the spray that "now springs" in the wake of summer's coming (line 5), and, in a twist on what has come before, the "sorrow" that springs in the heart of the poem's narrator, even as he surveys the "pleasant things" about him. And those pleasant things are carefully, painstakingly listed as though Surrey was an Adam naming the animals: the nightingale, the turtle, the hart, the buck, and so on, each of which is engaged, for a single line, in some activity that shows that "winter is worn" and that a new life has begun. Indeed, "new" is mentioned twice in the sonnet, each time with reference to an animal's new clothes, whether they be feathers or scales. These are busy animals – like the "busy bee" mixing or "minging" her honey – just as the season itself is framed with an active verb in the opening line, that "soote season, that bud and bloom forth brings," having already "clad the hill and eke the vale" in green. And in contrast to all, in that surprising last line, the narrator can be said to participate in his private spring of grief, the sorrow that bursts forth despite the greening world around him, the world so vividly portrayed, and in such detail, in the three stanzas before.

Petrarch is not the only figure who lies behind this poem; Chaucer does too, as Michael Haldane has recently reminded us, from whom we have the nightingale and the swallow's "pursuit" in *Parlement of Fowles*.[43] But Petrarch alludes to both birds as well – the only animals, in fact, directly mentioned in his own sonnet, which goes like this:

Zephiro torna, e 'l bel tempo rimena,
e i fiori et l'erbe, sua dolce famiglia,
et garrir Progne et pianger Philomena,
et primavera candida et vermiglia.
Ridono i prati, e 'l ciel si rasserena;
Giove s'allegra di mirar sua figlia;
l'aria et l'acqua et la terra è d'amor piena;
ogni animal d'amar si riconsiglia.
Ma per me, lasso, tornano i piú gravi
sospiri, che del cor profondo tragge
quella ch'al ciel se ne portò le chiavi;

et cantar augelletti, et fiorir piagge,
e 'n belle donne honeste atti soavi
sono un deserto, et fere aspre et selvagge.

(Zephyrus returns and leads back the fine weather
and the flowers and the grass, his sweet family,
and chattering Procne and weeping Philomena,
and Spring, all white and vermilion.
The meadows laugh and the sky becomes clear again,
Jupiter is gladdened looking at his daughter,
the air and the waters and the earth are full of love,
every animal takes counsel again to love.
But to me, alas, come back heavier sighs,
which she draws from my deepest heart,
she who carried off to Heaven the keys to it;
And the singing of little birds, and the flowering of meadows,
and virtuous gentle gestures in beautiful ladies
are a wilderness and cruel, savage beasts.) (tr. Durling)

Petrarch's poem offers direct observations not on the animal world but on one inhabited by mythology. Or perhaps these are ghosts of mythology that exist only in the memory of the speaker, whose first word – "Zephiro" – takes us to Ovid and the story of the wind who "rimena" or brings back the "fiori," a word dimly reminiscent of the figure of Flora who is the nymph Cloris transformed. Procne and Philomena are also figures of metamorphosis, while Giove is the king of the gods who delights in gazing at his "figlia," an earth full of love, just as every animal is again, inspired to love. Petrarch's speaker bursts into the poem earlier than does Surrey's, at line 9 – "Ma per me, lasso!" But in effect he has already been present by transcribing onto the landscape the history of myth, especially Ovidian myth, and he is far less specific as to who his animals are. In fact, everything, despite its individual existence – whether the singing of the little birds or the "belle donne" themselves, invoked in line 13 – is reduced to nothing *but* an animal, yet a savage, wild animal, "fere aspre et selvagge," not at all the painstakingly-listed, humanized bird or bee of Surrey's poem. The natural setting, for all its flowering, has become "un deserto" in the wake of the departure of a woman who carried the keys to Petrarch's heart to heaven, as a new violence, comparable to the rape of Chloris or Philomela, is performed on the universe.

For Petrarch's vague generalities about landscape in the first eight lines, Surrey substitutes precision: a list, in fact, that begins in line three when Surrey settles on the nightingale for "Philomena" and then abruptly turns away from his source. Love disappears from the sonnet to be replaced with something else, an attentiveness to the landscape that the narrator passively "sees," and recounts, which the Petrarchan narrator instead gives the effect of reimagining, reinscribing it through a Latin text and then revisioning it completely through his own experience of "gravi sospiri." What Surrey describes stubbornly remains, despite the speaker's sorrow: the animals have their "spring," and he has his, two parallel spaces that do not touch on one another. And perhaps we as readers do not touch on it either. We know nothing of the cause of his sorrow; Surrey's reticent narrator refuses either to project his experience onto the world around him, or to share it with the reader.

Unlike Sannazaro's *Arcadia*, published several decades before Surrey was writing, there are no shepherds, this is not Arcadia, there is little attention to landscape, although a great deal to its inhabitants. And one must not take Surrey, the inventor of blank verse and the figure who imported the Italian sonnet to England, as a model for what would be a century of avid English reception of and experimentation with not only Petrarch, but with Petrarch's own followers in Italy – Sannazaro notably, but also Ariosto, Tasso, and ultimately Marino. With those caveats, however, two things stand out: Surrey's almost complete avoidance of mythological overtones, and his corresponding attentiveness to landscape – an insistence, as it were, on the "thing-ness" of his environment. This is a refusal, perhaps a calculated one, to allow the lyric subject to dominate the poem, even as that subject is identified as a figure out of step with his environment. Surrey lets us imagine that we are allowed to see things on their own terms, to participate in as simple and elemental a process as the shedding of a snake's skin – in itself an event rich with symbolism in the Christian tradition, but Surrey does not allow us to go there, saying nothing – unlike Petrarch – about heaven, or death.

This idea of "seeing things on their own terms" may help to define an early modern, English habit of reticence with respect to Italian pastoral models. Indeed, it helps to define to a large extent what has been one of the predominant critical ways of reading Elizabethan and Jacobean pastoral poetry in the last decade or so, mentioned earlier, ecocriticism, as well as to identify another comparative model that positions Italian poetry in relation to English pastoral as less plot-driven, evincing more a poetics of mood and suspension than one of narrative force. The impact of the georgic on both English and Italian traditions as well may be an outgrowth of this kind of attentiveness to an "ecology" of place. Georgic would dominate descriptions of the English landscape and in ways largely ancillary to the Italian experience, and one might ask why so little attention actually is given to "real" rustics in the Italian context. In 1546 Luigi Alamanni did write his own version of Virgil's *Georgics*, which he called *La Coltivazione*, composed in France for a French sovereign after he left Medicean Florence forever. And Agostino Gallo would write his *Vinte giorni dell'Agricoltura et de' piaceri della villa* in 1569, in the north of Italy, a lengthy dialogue that takes place over "twenty days" on every subject related to managing villas: when to plant trees, how to tend to vines, how to speak to one's peasants.

But it is not clear that a genuine poetic literature ever emerges from these interventions, heavy-handed as they were, or from the interest in and translation of other Roman agricultural works. In contrast, the "nationalism" of the English scene, vexed as it was during the Jacobean and Carolingian reign, comes in striking ways to embrace the detail and attentiveness to land that we see here, from Ben Jonson on. Alistair Fowler has intriguingly suggested that the English fascination with georgic redefined pastoral as early as Spenser, who makes his *persona* in *The Faerie Queene* a farmer; in part, the attraction of didactic poetry, already witnessed in the work of Douglas in 1513, permits this openness to Virgil's didactic poems. But it is also the case that georgic was connected for Virgil's Renaissance readers with the development of an empire, and an empire, to return to earlier remarks in this essay, is what the English felt they had, as Francis Bacon "urged his practical georgic vision of empire as early as 1605, and Raleigh earlier still."[44] It is worth noting that Alamanni dedicates his georgic work to a French king, and Gallo to the Duke of Savoy – whose family would eventually become the ancestors of Italy's first king.

Other English poets would not marginalize so completely the role of the narrating, lyric voice, even as Spenser's calendar forces Colin's lament to be contextualized within a larger series of issues and debates, and Sidney's prose does the same for Mucedorus's sonnets. And the famous short verses of Marlowe – "The Passionate Shepherd to his Love" – is a far cry from either Petrarchan dejection or Surrey's painstaking list of animals. Yet we do hear about the "hills and valleys, dale and field" that might be a generic Petrarchan "listing," while the "coral clasps and amber studs" have a solidness to them that moves from Petrarch's generalities towards Surrey's specificities. Half a century after Petrarch's official entrance into the English poetic tradition, through the partial translations of Surrey and Wyatt, a distinct way of thinking about landscape and individual voice has emerged, along with a critical eye towards taking Petrarchan interiority and solitude too seriously.

Thanks not only to Marlowe but of course to Sidney and Spenser, the pastoral poem enjoyed considerable popularity in the latter part of the sixteenth century and early seventeenth. Like the translation of Virgil's *Eclogues* by Pulci in the Miscomini edition, these poems often appeared in miscellanies, such as *England's Helicon* or collective anthologies like *The Shepheard's Pipe*, edited by William Browne. As Michelle O'Callaghan has demonstrated, there was a "decidedly anti-court turn" in the period following Elizabeth, as well as an ongoing commitment to the ethics of a literary community of poets much influenced by Spenser's work.[45] Tasso's *Aminta* and Guarini's *Pastor fido* (1574; 1587) helped to launch the season of English theatre, from Shakespeare's *As You Like It* to Fletcher's *Faithful Shepherdess* and Jonson's masques – the subject of another chapter in this volume. And with Sidney's *Old Arcadia* the pastoral romance arrives on English soil as princes fall in love with shepherdesses and disguised or displaced children wind up in rustic settings, as in the *Pandosto* of Robert Greene that was to be the basis for *The Winter's Tale* or in Mary Wroth's *The Countess of Montgomery's Urania* of 1621. Such texts significantly complicate the simpler dynamics of Boccaccio's and Sannazaro's less ambitious prose works, influenced as they were by Longus's *Daphnis and Chloe* (translated into French by Jacques Amyot in 1559, on which Angel Day based his 1587 English translation[46]) and Montemayor's *Diana* (completed in the early 1560s and translated into English in 1598).

Indeed, the opening of Wroth's *Urania* can offer a final example of translation from an Italian context into an English one, even as one must be aware of the intervening centuries of experimentation and influence – and even as it takes place on the Italian island of Pantelleria.

> When the Spring began to appeare like the welcome messenger of summer, one sweet (and in that more sweet) morning, after *Aurora* had called all carefull eyes to attend the day, forth came the faire Shepherdesse *Urania* (faire indeed; yet that farre too meane a title for her, who for beautie deserv'd the highest stile could be given by best knowing Iudgments). Into the Meade she came, where usually shee drave her flocks to feede, whose leaping and wantonnesse shewed they were proud of such a Guide: But she, whose sad thoughts led her to another manner of spending her time, made her soone leave them, and follow her late begun custome; which was (while they delighted themselves) to sit under some shade, bewailing her misfortune.

By virtue of Wroth's relations to the famous Sidney family – she was Philip's niece – her work squarely belongs to the second generation of England's great golden age of pastoral literature. It is a novel that partakes of the other Sidneys' literary ambitions, given its length and range; it easily surpasses Philip's *New Arcadia* in terms of both, and the resourcefulness and variety of the many verse kinds found within show Wroth to be a master of the metrical forms in which Mary and Philip excelled. Indeed, the passage cited above shows how good was Wroth's ear and in many ways, how seamless the transition between narrative and poetry: note the lilting rhythm of "Into the Meade she came," the gentle insistence on rhymes such as "spring," "meade," "feede," and "leaping," the sibillance of her frequent "s's." And it also shows Wroth's talent at rendering compactly a fundamental tension not only of her pastoral romance but of pastoral literature more generally, especially its early modern variants. Two sentences into the novel, following an evocative description of a spring moving into summer and a beautiful young woman driving her energetic flock to feed, we get an ominous "But." Rather than rejoice in the tranquility of the "Meade" and tend to her sheep, Urania leaves her charges behind and "bewails" her misfortune, caused not by unrequited love but something far more substantial and telling:

> Alas, Urania, said she … of any miserie that can befall woman, is not this the most and greatest which thou art falne into? Can there be any neare the unhappinesse of being ignorant, and that in the highest kind, not being certaine of mine owne estate or birth? Why was I not stil continued in the beleefe I was, as I appeare, a Shepherdes, and Daughter to a Shepherd? How did I ioy in this poore life being quiet? Blest in the love of those I tooke for parents, but now by them I know the contrary, and by that knowledg, not to know my selfe.

With these lines, Urania introduces disharmony into the idyll, or more specifically, she notes her own "falling out" of pastoral: once she did "joy in this poore life being quiet" and once she was "blest." But now that her parents have fulfilled their duty and told her she's a "changeling," she is cursed by her inability to know her self: she is in, but no longer of, the "Shepherdes" world. The timeless idyll becomes a narrative, even as the lyrical quality of Wroth's prose keeps its reader in a space driven and created by language, the questing mind that creates for itself an alternate, literary language and hence, an alternate world.[47]

Light-years away from Surrey's modest reframing of Petrarch's sonnet, Mary Wroth's lengthy, anti-Catholic, anti-Spanish narrative takes this young noblewoman and plunges her into the midst of travel and adventure.[48] If on the one hand, we see the return of Petrarch isolation, on the other there is the creation of an almost encyclopedic text full of the kind of antique histories, mythological lore, and romance devices already apparent in Boccaccio – not least through the use of frames and double-frames, as well as the patient forging of a community that is inhabited by like-minded souls (and, unbeknownst to our heroine, her long-lost brother). One might thus rightly ask whether pastoral has become a mode that by the 1610s and 1620s has transcended "national" origins – even as *Daphnis and Cloe* and other Hellenistic narratives such as the *Ethiopica* of Heliodorus were models here too. The pastoral romance becomes rather transnational, moving beyond the fixed local contexts where Urania, a so-called "daughter of Italy," was never really at home in any case. The limited, restrained world of Surrey's speaker, precise in its distancing itself linguistically from Petrarch – note all the Anglo-Saxon one-syllabic words – is a world where his speaker will remain, tied to what he knows. Wroth embraces Petrarch to out-Petrarch him, to move him where we would never go: Parthia, Bohemia, India – even as Petrarch may once have dreamt of following in Alexander's footsteps. And as itinerant as Boccaccio's interlocutors may seem to be, their travels are exclusively within Italy, although the stories that the *brigata* tell while sitting in the lovely villa now called Poggio Gherardo take them, in their mind's eye, to India and the Asian steppes as well.

In the course of her adventures, Urania encounters a host of characters who will come to dominate the narrative more than this "changeling" herself, notably Pamphilia who longs for the faithless Amphilanthus, remaining constant to him despite his infidelities. Pamphilia's outpouring of verse in his name constitutes a great many of the *Urania's* poetic interpolations – interpolations that come to no end, as Amphilanthus ultimately marries another woman, and Pamphilia herself ends up with a king. Perhaps with this strong-minded heroine,[49] Wroth overgoes another model here too, already known to Chaucer through Petrarch's Latin translation, and generally almost always overlooked in accounts of Renaissance pastoral, in which "real" shepherds and shepherdesses are almost always absent: Boccaccio's Griselda. Griselda is the rustic figure who represents a beauty and integrity the city or court does not offer, and who yet is not – unbelievably – a lost princess in disguise. She is, in short, the "real thing," and in this kind of inverse *The Winter's Tale* that was the final tale of Boccaccio's *Decameron*, it is the children who come back to life to greet the mother after the hardened husband has supposedly sent them to their graves.

Griselda, that is, might be the pastoral heroine *par excellence*, the toiling shepherdess who received a good moral education despite and because of her impoverishment, who returns to help her widowed father when she has been cast out of her husband's palace. Boccaccio's *novella* might be the most regenerative pastoral text ever written – and yet it is surely the one that is most difficult to fathom, or to recuperate. Is there anything like the story of Griselda in English pastoral, the story with which Boccaccio returns us from his rustic retreat to the city still tainted with plague? Or must we wait for the writings of Thomas Hardy, where there is nonetheless no happy ending to the nightmare that his rustic lasses must suffer?

Notes

1 See Annabel Patterson, *Pastoral and Ideology: Virgil to Valéry* (Berkeley: University of California Press, 1987) for a discussion of Marot, Brant, and Spenser (pp. 92–132). Katherine Little's more recent *Transforming Work: Early Modern Pastoral and Late Medieval Poetry* (Notre Dame, IN: University of Notre Dame Press, 2013) is an attentive reading of Spenser within a discussion of both religious dynamics and the politics of enclosure and agrarian capitalism in England.

2 See, most recently, David Scott Wilson-Okamura, *Virgil in the Renaissance* (Cambridge: Cambridge University Press, 2010). For a work that brings together both Virgil and Theocritus with English Renaissance pastoral, see Judith Haber's excellent *Pastoral and the Poetics of Self-Contradiction: Theocritus through Marvell* (Cambridge: Cambridge University Press, 1994).

3 *Pastoral and Ideology*, p. 126.

4 Quoted on p. 159 of Stephen Mentz, *Romance for Sale in Early Modern England* (Farnham, UK: Ashgate, 2006).

5 For a recent account of different attitudes towards and uses of agricultural lands in the Renaissance, see *Rural Space in the Middle Ages and Early Modern Age: The Spatial Turn in Premodern Studies*, ed. Albrecht Classen (Berlin/Boston, MA: De Gryuter, 2012), especially the introduction by Classen, pp. 1–192. One classic work that places the Italian countryside

into broad historical context is Emlio Sereni, *History of the Italian Agricultural Landscape* (Princeton, NJ: Princeton University Press, 1997).

6 Andrew Hadfield, "Spenser, Drayton, and the Question of Britain," *The Review of English Studies*, 51 (2000): 582–99.

7 See Guarini, *Lettere di G. B. Guarini, Cavalliere* (Venice, 1616) in which he writes his beloved of the "human beasts, whom, to humor myself, I call peasants"; pp. 201–2. The classic work continues on satires against peasants continues to be that of Domenico Merlini, *Saggio di ricerche sulla satira contro il villano* (Milan: Loescher, 1894).

8 For several recent accounts of Italian pastoral (both dramatic and poetry/prose) and its varied local traditions, see Marzia Pieri, *La scena boschereccia nel rinascimento italiano* (Padua: Liviana, 1983), Lisa Sampson, *Pastoral Drama in Early Modern Italy* (London: Legenda, 2006), and *Il mito d'Arcadia: Pastori e amori nelle arti del Rinascimento* (Turin, 2007).

9 For the information about the OED and for one of the best, succinct discussions of English Renaissance pastoral that I know, see Michelle O'Callaghan's essay "Pastoral" for *A New Companion to English Renaissance Literature and Culture*, ed. Michael Hattaway (Chichester, UK: John Wiley & Sons, 2010), II, pp. 225–37.

10 Rosella Bessi compiled exemplary editions of two of Lorenzo's pastoral works: *La Nencia da Berberino* (Rome: Salerno, 1982) and *Ambra* (Florence: Samson, 1986). As for Giusto de' Conti, Italo Pantani is preparing the edition of this fifteenth-century poet's complete works, and in the meantime has written *L'amoroso Messer Giusto da Valmontone* (Rome: Salerno, 2006) and edited an impressive volume of essays, *Giusto de' Conti di Valmontone: Un protagonista della poesia italiana del '400* (Rome: Bulzoni, 2008). One hastens to add that neither Alberti nor Giusto wrote exclusively pastoral poems, but as will become apparent later in this chapter, both of them composed some innovative and influential eclogues as part of their oeuvre in the vernacular.

11 The consideration of musical and especially visual forms of pastoral indeed continues apace in recent articles, such as "La selva e il giardino. Tasso e il paesaggio" by Gianni Venturi in *Archivi dello sguardo: Origini e momenti della pittura di paesaggio in Italia*, ed. Francesca Cappelletti (Ferrara, 2006); and see the collection of essays on Guarini and Tasso *L'arme e gli amori: la poesia di Ariosto, Tasso, e Guarini nell'arte del Seicento* (Livorno: Sillabe, 2001).

12 *Le genre pastoral en Europe du XVe au XVIIe Siècle* (Université de Saint-Etienne, 1980); *Ville et Campagne dans la Littérature Italienne de la Renaissance*, ed. André Rochon (Paris: Université de la Sorbonne Nouvelle, 1976), particularly the essays in Volume I, and *La poesia pastorale nel Rinascimento*, ed. Stefano Carrai (Padua: Antenore, 1998).

13 See in particular the essays by Walter Stephens, Eric Nicholson, and Valeria Finucci in Valeria Finucci, *Renaissance Transactions: Ariosto and Tasso* (Durham, NC: Duke University Press, 1999); Mary-Michelle DeCoste, *Hopeless Love: Boiardo, Ariosto, and Narratives of Queer Desire* (Toronto: University of Toronto Press, 2009); and the current work of Sarah van der Laan, "*Erminia liberata*: Pastoral Transformations and Female Agency in Tasso's *Gerusalemme liberata*," talk for the Renaissance Society of America meeting (Berlin, March 2015).

14 While not exclusively focused on pastoral texts, the following works might be considered useful, particularly in the field of Renaissance pastoral drama of Shakespeare: Karen Raber, *Animal Bodies, Renaissance Culture* (Philadelphia, PA: University of Pennsylvania, 2013), Laurie Shannon, *The Accommodated Animal: Cosmopolity in Shakespearean Locales* (Chicago, IL: University of Chicago Press, 2013).

15 At the same time, this interest in what James Turner called in the late 1970s "a politics of landscape" was already apparent in studies of English pastoral, thanks in no small part to the work of Raymond Williams, as well as for considering seventeenth-century works influenced by the *Georgics;* James Grantham Turner, *The Politics of Landscape: Rural Scenery and Society in English Poetry 1630–60* (Cambridge, MA: Harvard University Press, 1979). See also Hadfield's work on Drayton, mentioned earlier. More recently, see Sukanya Dasgupta, "Silent Spring: Poly-Olbion and the Politics of Landscape," *Cambridge Journal*, 39 (2010): 152–71.

16 Sue Starke, *The Heroines of English Pastoral Romance* (Woodbridge: Derek Brewer, 2007); Jeff Dolven, *Scenes of Instruction in Renaissance Romance* (Chicago, IL: University of Chicago Press, 2007).

17 One recent example is Elizabeth Chesney Zegura's "Uprooted Trees and Slaughtered Peasants: The Saving of Rural Space in Ariosto's *Orlando furioso* (1532)," in *Rural Space in the Middle Ages and Early Modern Age*, ed. Classen, pp. 729–54.

18 Charles Dempsey, *The Early Renaissance and Vernacular Culture* (Cambridge: Harvard University Press, 2012), p. 42.
19 See the discussion with the niece, the curate, and the housekeeper in Chapter 6 of Book I of the *Quixote* – in which Cervantes' own pastoral novel, the *Galatea*, is saved from the fire.
20 Mary Augusta Scott's "Elizabethan Translations from the Italian," *PMLA*, 11 (1896): 377–484 is a fine place to start for assembling a list of the surprising number of Italian texts available to English readers.
21 Theocritus arrives much later as an influence on Italian poetry. Poliziano possessed a manuscript of the Idylls (now in the Laurenziana) and lectured on the poems in Florence in the 1480s. The first modern edition of the poems, the Aldine edition, was printed in 1496 in Venice. Sannazaro clearly draws on the *Idylls* in the *Arcadia.* It is worth noting Leopardi's comment that "I nostri veri idilli teocritei non sono né le egloghe del Sannazaro, né ec. Ec., ma le poesie rusticali come la *Nencia, Cecco da Varlungo* ec., bellissimi e similissimi a quelli di Teocrito nella bella rozzezza e mirabile verità"; cited in Domenico De Robertis, *Editi e rari: Studi sulla tradizione letteraria tra Tre e Cinquecento* (Milan: Feltrinelli, 1978), p. 148. Even though De Robertis goes on to note the idealism inherent in Leopardi's view, he acknowledges the awakening of an interest of the "rustic idyll" in the late fifteenth century as manifest in Lorenzo's *Nencia.*
22 In Robert Durling's edition and translation, *Petrarch's Lyric Poems* (Cambridge, MA: Harvard University Press, 1976), pp. 242–3.
23 Robin Kirkpatrick, *English and Italian Literature from Dante to Shakespeare* (New York: Routledge, 2013), p. 150.
24 Quoted by Armando Maggi in his essay "'You Will be my Solitude': Solitude as Prophecy: *De Vita Solitaria*," in *Petrarch: A Critical Guide to the Complete Works*, eds. Victoria Kirkham and Armando Maggi (Chicago, IL: University of Chicago Press, 2009), p. 179.
25 See Struever's convincing argument for Petrarch's "relocation of inquiry" as an ethical practice in her first chapter of *Theory of Practice: Ethical Inquiry in the Renaissance* (Chicago, IL: University of Chicago Press, 1992).
26 See Italo Pantani, "Il Polimetro Pastorale di Giusto de' Conti," in the volume edited by Stefano Carrai, for the impact of Giusto's pastorals on other Italian poets such as Poliziano and Sannazaro; pp. 1–55.
27 Tavoni, "Italia ed Europa nella linguistica del Rinascimento," p. 43.
28 Maggi, p. 180.
29 *A Courtlie Contrvoersie of Cupids Cautels* (London, 1579), sig. 2H4.
30 See Catherine Bates, "'A Large Occasion of Discourse': John Lyly and the Art of Civil Conversation," *Review of English Studies*, 42 (1991): 469–87.
31 See Jane Tylus, "On the Threshold of Paradise (*Commedia delle ninfe fiorntine*, or *Ameto*)," in *Boccaccio: A Critical Guide to the Complete Works*, ed. Victoria Kirkham, Michael Sherberg, and Janet Levarie Smarr (Chicago, IL: University of Chicago Press, 2013), p. 137.
32 This is a foundation narrative, an origins or etiological tale, and one in which, as Susanna Barsella puts it, "the geographical area delimited by the three rivers that flow from the hils of Fiesole to the Arno in Florence (Mugnone, Africo, and Mensola) is the true protagonist of the story"; "Myth and history: Toward a New Order (*Ninfale fiesolano*)," *Boccaccio: A Critical Guide*, p. 146.
33 See *The English Boccaccio: A History in Books* (Toronto: University of Toronto Press, 2013).
34 For the citation as well as the poem, see Leon Battista Alberti, *Rime e versioni poetiche*, ed. Guglielmo Gorni, pp. 62–9.
35 In the edition of Rossella Bessi, cit., see stanzas 1 and 16 in what Bessi calls Testo V (p. 139, 149).
36 See the Prima and Seconda Oratione in the edition of Ruzante's *Opere*, ed. Ludovico Zorzi (Turin: Einaudi, 1967), pp. 1184–221.
37 See Matteo Soranzo, *Poetry and Identity in Quattrocento Naples* (Farnham, UK: Ashgate, 2014) suggests that the original *libro pastorale intitolato Archadio*, published in the form of a presentation copy, was meant for the famous Ippolita Sforza, a generous patron at the Aragonese court in Naples (p. 75).
38 Soranzo, p. 77; Francesca Bortoletti, "Performances of Pastoral Poetry at the Court of Aragona," talk at the Renaissance Society of America meeting in Berlin, March 2015.

39 This move from Boccaccio's restorative use of narrative is all the more surprising given Sannazaro's obvious stylistic and linguistic reliance on the Boccaccio of the *Ameto;* see Carlo Vecce's comments throughout his edition of the *Arcadia* (Rome: Carocci, 2013) as well as his essay "Boccaccio e Sannazaro (agnioini)," in *Boccaccio angioino. Materiali per la storia culturale di Napoli nel Trecento*, eds. G. Alfano et al. (Brussels: Peter Lang, 2012), pp. 103–18.
40 Carlo Vecce's edition of the *Arcadia*, cit.; p. 163.
41 On Sidney's refashioning of Sannazaro, see the insightful pages of Robin Kirkpatrick in which he suggests that while Sidney's narrative, "like Sannazaro's, is haunted by stasis and allusion it nevertheless sets itself to deliver coherent and well-plotted conclusions"; *English and Italian Literature*, p. 149.
42 See as a recent example, Selena Scarsi, *Translating Women in Early Modern England: Gender in the Elizabethan versions of Boiardo, Ariosto and Tasso* (Farnham, UK: Ashgate, 2010). In reading Spenser along with Tasso and Fairfax's translation, for example, Scarsi shows that the pastoral scene of *The Faerie Queene* Book VI with Calidore is virtually a translation of the episode with Erminia in the *Gerusalemme liberata*, Book 7, when Erminia flees to the banks of the Jordan and a pastoral space. Elsewhere, her attentive reading allows her to capture Tasso's use of the Petrarchan lyric subject in "Chiare, fresche e dolci acque" for representing Erminia's distraught state – and Fairfax's subsequent recognition of the connection as well (pp. 103–4)
43 Michael Haldane, "'The Soote Season': Surrey and the Amatory Elegy," *English Studies*, 87 (2006): 406–14.
44 Alistair Fowler, "The Beginnings of English Georgic," in *Renaissance Genres: Essays on Theory, History, and Interpretation*, ed. Barbara Kiefer Lewalski (Cambridge, MA: Harvard University Press, 1986), p. 106.
45 See *The "Shepheards Nation": Jacobeean Spenserians and Early Stuart Political Culture* (Oxford: Oxford University Press, 2000) as well as her article cited earlier, "Pastoral."
46 Annibal Caro, best known as the translator of the *Aeneid*, translated Longus in the 1530s but never published his work. Enrico Garavelli has recently published the manuscript as *Amori pastorali* (Rome: Vecchiarelli, 2002).
47 See the observation of Mary Ellen Lamb that Wroth demonstrates "an abundant interiority" that renders the romance "in some sense a long, lyric complaint" – not unlike, I might add, Petrarch's *Canzoniere;* "The Biopolitics of Romance in Mary Wroth's *The Countess of Montgomery's Urania*," *English Literary Renaissance*, 31 (2001): 107–30.
48 On Wroth's anti-Catholicism, see, lately, Victor Skretkowicz, *European erotic romance* (Manchester, UK: Manchester University Press, 2010).
49 For a feminist reading of English pastoral fiction and the romance in general, see Helen Heckett, *Women and Romance Fiction in the English Renaissance* (Cambridge: Cambridge University Press, 2000).

12 'Oh that we had such an English Tasso'

Tasso in English poetry and drama to 1700

Jason Lawrence

Even before the poet's untimely death in 1595, the works of Torquato Tasso were being cited by an immigrant language teacher active in England and then Scotland as a primary reason for courtiers to undertake learning the Italian language:

> L'italica favella, non solamente per la sua rara belta, ma anchora per la quantita di rari libri, che in essa & non in altra si leggono, merita d'esser d'ogni nobile spirito saputa; e se non fosse mai per altro, sol per potere intendere i nobili poemi, da pochi anni in qua venuti a luce, del gran poeta Torquato Tasso, di cui parlando il valente suo poeta du Bartas dice. Dernier en age, premieur en honneur.
>
> (The Italian tongue deserves to be known by every noble spirit, not only because of its unique beauty, but also for the number of rare books that can be read in this and no other tongue; and if there were no other reason, only to be able to understand the noble poems that have come to light in the last few years of the great poet Torquato Tasso, about whom the most able poet du Bartas says, "Last in age, but first in honour.")[1]

Iacopo Castelvetro's dedicatory letter, offering his services to King James VI of Scotland and his queen in August 1592, highlights the esteem in which Tasso was already held, not least by prominent European poetic contemporaries. Indeed the recently deceased French poet Du Bartas, one of the Scottish king's own favourites, was indirectly responsible for the earliest printed assessment of the still active Italian poet's achievements in England. Most of the French text in the chapter "Of the dignitie of Orators, and excellencie of tongues" in John Eliot's bilingual French language-learning manual *Ortho-epia Gallica* (1593) is taken almost verbatim from the notes added by the Huguenot scholar Simon Goulart to the "Babilone" section in the posthumous edition of Du Bartas's *La Seconde Sepmaine* (1591), including his commendation, and summary, of Tasso's works, which Eliot merely renders in dialogue form and then in parallel-text English translation:

> Torquato Tasso, *a fine scholer truly, who is yet liuing, the last Italian Poet who is of any great fame in our age, but worthie of the first honour; besides that he is a diuine Poet, he is also a most eloquent Oratour and Rhetoricyan, as his missiue Epistles do shew very well …*
> *What other fine books hath he made?*
> *Many: there are three Toomes of his workes printed at Ferrara, wherein there are diuers sorts of verses of all kinds of fine inuentions: a Commedie, a Tragedie, diuers Dialogues and discourses in Prose, all worthie the reading of the wisest and quickest spirits of Europe.*

DOI: 10.4324/9781315612720-14

> *Is that all that he hath written?*
> *No, for he hath the pen in hand euery day.*
> *You haue forgotten his* Gierusalemme liberata.
> *You say true, this child hath written in Heroicall verses one excellent Poeme amongst all other Italian Poesies, intituled as you say, wherein all the riches of the Greeks and Latines are gathered together and enchaced so cunningly past all others skill, with such grace, breuitie, grauitie, learning, liuelinesse, and uiuacitie that is remarqued to haue bene in* Virgill *the Prince of Latine Poets.*[2]

Although this high praise for Tasso is derived directly from a recent French source, it does accurately reflect the contemporary knowledge and evaluation of his work in England. With the exception of the apparent reference to the *Lettere poetiche* ("*missiue Epistles*"), printed in 1587, there is evidence for the impact in England of *all* of Tasso's other notable achievements in both verse and prose by the time that Eliot's summary was printed in 1593: the pastoral (tragi-) comedy *Aminta* (1580) had already been printed in Italian in London by John Wolfe and Castelvetro in 1591 (along with Guarini's *Il Pastor Fido*), and was translated (into English alliterative verse) in the same year by Abraham Fraunce in *The Countesse of Pembrokes Yvychurch;* the recently printed tragedy *Il Re Torrismondo* (1587) was cited, along with passages from *Aminta* and, more extensively, Tasso's epic, in Fraunce's *The Arcadian Rhetorike* (1588); the prose dialogue *Il padre di famiglia* (1583) was translated by Thomas Kyd as *The Housholders Philosophie* (1588); sonnets and madrigals printed in the first volume of Tasso's collected *Rime* throughout the 1580s provided Samuel Daniel with direct models for sonnets in his *Delia. With the complaint of Rosamond* (1592), which also demonstrated the English poet's sustained engagement with episodes from *Gerusalemme liberata* (1581) in the accompanying female complaint poem, shortly after Spenser's close imitations of passages in the epic poem had been printed in the first edition of *The Faerie Queene* (1590). Like Du Bartas and Goulart in France, these English writers did not hesitate to grant Tasso, and particularly his religious epic, a status comparable to that of the ancients: Fraunce included more than eighty separate illustrations from *Gerusalemme liberata*, alongside quotations from Homer, Virgil and modern European authors, in *The Arcadian Rhetorike;* the Italian poet found himself, alongside Ariosto, in similarly elevated company as an epic model in Spenser's "A Letter of the Authors" addressed to Sir Walter Raleigh at the end of the 1590 *Faerie Queene*, and, a few years after his death, in Daniel's *A Defence of Ryme* (1603), where Tasso's recent epic achievement in *ottava rima* verse is cited as decisive proof of the failure of a mid-sixteenth-century Italian experiment with quantitative measures:

> Nor could it neuer induce *Tasso* the wonder of *Italy*, to write that admirable Poem of *Ierusalem*, comparable to the best of the ancients, in any other forme then the accustomed verse.[3]

Daniel's recently identified familiarity with Tasso's epic poem over a decade before this expression of admiration for it in the early years of the seventeenth century confirms the need for a critical re-evaluation of C. P. Brand's assertion, echoing Mario Praz, that "with the exception of Spenser … the immediate impact of the *Liberata* on English literature is not obvious."[4] Whilst Spenser's extensive imitation of passages from cantos XV and XVI of Tasso's epic in Book II of *The Faerie Queene*, particularly in the Bowre of Blisse episode in the final canto, remains the most discussed and "most famous single borrowing from the *Gerusalemme liberata*,"[5] the critical focus on Spenser's use of Tasso has, until recently, tended to overshadow both the simultaneous (and later) engagement of other English poets and translators, often with the same characters and episodes in the Italian poem, and what Selene Scarsi has described, in her detailed examination of Elizabethan translations of Italian epic poetry, as "the extremely elaborate network of intermediacy and cross-references … with reference to Erminia and Armida in particular, between Fairfax and a number of contemporary poets."[6] Scarsi's study of Edward Fairfax's *Godfrey of Bulloigne* (1600), the first complete English translation of Tasso's poem, highlights effectively the "mediating influence" of both Spenser and Daniel on the translator's later rendering into English, arguing that "these poets, paradoxically, occasionally come closer to the original than Fairfax, Tasso's translator, blurring the borders between creative imitation and translation proper."[7]

Scarsi's study demonstrates the contemporary translator's awareness of, and indebtedness to, *both* of Spenser's principal imitations from the Italian epic, in books II and VI of *The Faerie Queene* respectively, spanning the 1590 and 1596 editions of the poem. The frequent borrowings from the *Erminia fra i pastori* episode in canto VII in Calidore's pastoral interlude in canto ix of Book VI have subsequently been far less noted critically than the imitative passages in Book II, but they were again recognized in the early years of the seventeenth century by William Drummond, who noted in a marginal annotation alongside stanza 20 of the canto in his copy of Spenser's poem that "all this is Tor. Tassos can. 7.1 Gier. of Erminia"[8]; they have recently been considered again by Jason Lawrence in an article, which assesses the borrowings to argue that Spenser's return to imitative engagement with Tasso's poem in the final completed book of *The Faerie Queene* might hint at the Knight of Courtesy's, and indeed the poet's own, increasing ambivalence about the completion of his epic task.[9]

Scarsi's analysis of *Godfrey of Bulloigne* also reveals Daniel's "mediating influence on Fairfax,"[10] focusing particularly on the translator's rendering of Tasso's image of the appearance of a comet to describe the effect the first appearance of the enchantress Armida in canto IV has on the Christian forces, where the added sense of wonder in the English version is closer to Daniel's appropriation of it in *The Complaint of Rosamond* (1592) than the Italian original:

> A l'apparir de la beltà novella
> nasce un bisbiglio e 'l guardo ognun v'intende
> sí come là dove cometa o stella,
> non piú vista di giorno, in ciel resplende. [IV, 28, 3–6]
>
> (At the appearance of this new beauty a murmur arises, and everyone's gaze is averted towards her, as it is towards a comet or a star, which, never before seen by day, shines in the sky.)
>
> Vpon her strange attire, and visage cleare,
> Gazed each soldier, gazed euerie knight,
> As when a comet doth in skies appeare,
> The people stand amazed at the light.
>
> Looke howe a Comet at the first appearing,
> Drawes all mens eyes with wonder to behold it: …
> So did the blasing of my blush appeere,
> T'amaze the world, that holds such sights so deere. [*Rosamond*, 113–19][11]

That Daniel himself was alluding to Tasso directly here in this early poem was recognized by another contemporary English poet, Francis Davison, who on four separate occasions recorded the marginal annotation "Daniels Rosamonde" alongside stanzas in his 1593 edition of *Il Goffredo*.[12] If Davison missed several additional passages of indebtedness to the Italian in the English poem in his reading in the late 1590s, then the association between Daniel's complaint poem and Tasso's epic acknowledged almost immediately by Fairfax and Davison has been almost entirely overlooked by critics for a further 400 years: apart from a brief note highlighting "the reminiscences of the *Liberata* in Sonnet XXXIV [of *Delia*] and in *The Complaint of Rosamond* (the 'garden of pleasure')" in Brand's study of Tasso in the mid-1960s,[13] it is only in the past few years that Daniel's persistent engagement with Tasso in *both* works in his first volume of poetry has been considered again, revealing some significant previously undetected borrowings, such as Tasso's description of Armida's magical palace on the Fortunate Isles at the start of canto XVI as the direct model for Henry II's own secret "Pallace," constructed for his furtive liaisons with Rosamond:

> Tondo è il ricco edificio, e nel piú chiuso
> grembo di lui, ch'è quasi centro al giro,
> un giardin v'ha ch'adorno è sovra l'uso
> di quanti piú famosi unqua fioriro.
> D'intorno inosservabile e confuse
> ordin di loggie i demon fabri ordiro,
> e tra le oblique vie di quell fallace
> ravolgimento impenetrabil giace. [XVI, 1, 1–8]
>
> (The beautiful palace is round; and in its most internal part, which is almost in the exact center of the building, there is a garden, which is more beautiful than any other garden that ever existed. Around it, the demonic workers built a random and intricate series of loggias, and the garden lies, impenetrable, among the tortuous ways of that deceptive maze.)
>
> A stately Pallace he forthwith did buylde,
> Whose intricate innumerable ways,
> With such confused errors so beguil'd
> Th'vnguided entrers with vncertaine strayes,
> And doubtfull turnings kept them in delayes,
> With bootlesse labor leading them about,
> Able to find no way, nor in, nor out.
>
> Within the closed bosome of which frame,
> That seru'd a Center to that goodly round:
> Were lodgings, with a garden to the same,
> With sweetest flowers that eu'r adorn'd the ground. [*Rosamond*, 463–73][14]

The repeated attention to episodes featuring the beguiling Armida in Daniel's borrowings from Tasso in *The Complaint of Rosamond* has been explored further by Lawrence in a recent article, which highlights "the occasionally uncomfortable association of the two figures," the beautiful enchantress and the ghost of a long-dead royal mistress, to conclude that Daniel's poem "marks the earliest sustained engagement in English poetry with one of Tasso's most enduringly alluring creations."[15]

The most conspicuous allusion to Tasso's epic poem in the other work in Daniel's first volume, the sonnets *To Delia*, is his imitation, condensed into fourteen lines, of the celebrated *canto della rosa* [XVI, 14–15], which forms part of a brief *corona* of sonnets emphasizing the devastating effects of time on female beauty. Daniel's version of the song is carefully woven in amongst his close imitations of three Tasso sonnets on the same theme, first printed in the *Rime degli academici eterei* in 1567, and for Scarsi it provides an example of greater fidelity to the original in an imitation than in Fairfax's translation.[16] Despite the compression of the two *ottava rima* stanzas into sonnet form and the enhanced prominence given to the impact of "swift speedy Time" [XXXI, 11], Daniel's renderings of lines 3 and 4 of stanza 15 at the start of his third quatrain ("No Aprill can reuiue thy withred flowers" [9]) and Tasso's final couplet ("But loue whilst that thou maist be lou'd againe" [14]) are strikingly closer to the original than the equivalent lines in either Fairfax's translation, or the better known English intermediary version sung in Spenser's Bowre of Blisse [II, 12, 74–75]. Ann Lake Prescott has suggested that the verbal proximity to Tasso in Spenser's "louely lay" demonstrates a rare moment of "wry self-mockery" in his verse, as "the closeness of the translation suits an episode that comments negatively on imitation" itself.[17] This proximity is perhaps deliberately misleading, though, as the alterations that Spenser makes to the final *carpe florem* invocations, emphasizing the sin of pride and crime respectively, serve to cast the original in a more negative moral light:

> Gather therefore the Rose, whilest yet is prime,
> For soon comes age, that will her pride deflowre:
> Gather the Rose of loue, whilest yet is time,
> Whilest louing thou mayst be loued be with equall crime. [II, 12, 75, 6–9]

> Cogliam la rosa in su 'l mattino adorno
> di questo dí, che tosto il seren perde;
> cogliam d'amor la rosa; amiamo or quando
> esser si puote riamato amando. [XVI, 15, 5–8]

> (Gather the rose in the beautiful morning of this day, which will soon lose its serenity; gather the rose of love: let us love now, when we can still be loved in return while loving.)[18]

The ending of Spenser's version thus subtly undermines the invocation to (sexual) love in the song voiced by a parrot in Armida's garden, but another contemporary manuscript English translation offers a far more radical reworking of the original's conclusion. The poem "Optima Deo," attributed to the Jesuit martyr Robert Southwell in the 1930s, is a generally faithful, though less overtly erotic, translation of Tasso's rose song until its final four lines, where the repeated invocation in the Italian is transformed into a stark warning to pursue a course of virtue over one of vice:

> Then croppe the morening Rose, while it is faire;
> Our day is short, the evening makes it die;
> Yeld God the prime of youth, eare it impaire;
> Least he the dregges of crooked age denie. [13–16][19]

The prominence of these responses to the *canto della rosa* specifically by English poets in the early 1590s suggests a need to take into account the wider poetic context in which these imitations of Tasso were produced. Lawrence has recently considered the authorship and date of "Optima Deo" to argue that Southwell's version, like Fairfax's later translation, demonstrates his awareness of both Spenser and Daniel's earlier renderings, as well as Tasso's original, and that this sacred transformation of the song thus forms part of his avowed poetic mission to encourage contemporary English love poets "to see the error of their works" by means of "some fyner peece wherein it maye be seene, how well Verse and Vertue suite together."[20] In relation to this broader contextual consideration of English reactions to Tasso's increasingly renowned song, it has also been suggested that, shortly afterwards, Shakespeare was alluding discreetly to passages from Armida and Rinaldo's romantic interlude in the arguments proffered by the goddess of love in his Ovidian narrative poem *Venus and Adonis* (1593):

Make use of time, let not advantage slip:
Beauty within itself should not be wasted,
Fair flowers that are not gathered in their prime
Rot, and consume themselves in little time. [129–32][21]

Shakespeare's perceptible engagement with the episode from Tasso's epic here, as the older goddess attempts to seduce a vulnerable young man, also recalls Spenser's reworking of it in the scene discovered by Guyon and the Palmer in the Bowre of Blisse, where the more sinister witch, Acrasia, has entrapped and seduced the unripe boy Verdant. Scarsi's "elaborate network of intermediacy" involving contemporary English poets and translators responding, both directly and indirectly, to Tasso in the 1590s can thus be expanded profitably beyond Spenser, Daniel, and Fairfax to include additionally Davison, Southwell, and Shakespeare.

The *canto della rosa* had emerged, within a dozen years of the poem's first printing in Italy, as the single most popular source for translation and adaptation from Tasso's epic in England, but other passages from the description of Armida's garden were also repeatedly alluded to and imitated. The "closeness of the translation" that Prescott highlights in Spenser's version of the rose song has also been detected by Alistair Fox in relation to the poet's rendering of Tasso's description of the "due donzellette garrule e lascive" [XV, 58, 4], who are discovered playing suggestively in the water of "il fonte del riso" by Carlo and Ubaldo, as they approach Armida's palace to rescue Rinaldo:

Mosser le natatrici ignude e belle
de' duo guerrieri alquanto i duri petti,
sí che fermàrsi a riguardarle; ed elle
seguian pur i lor giochi e i lor diletti.
Una intanto drizzosi, e le mammelle
e tutto ciò che piú la vista alletti
mostrò, dal seno in suso, aperto al cielo;
e 'l lago a l'altre membra era un bel velo. [XV, 59, 1–8]

(The swimming girls were nude and beautiful/and moved the stubborn chests of the two knights/so that they stopped to watch them play awhile,/continuing their games and their delights./One rose so high she showed the men her full/breasts, and all else that could entice the sights/from the hips up, all open to the sky,/while the lake veiled the rest most prettily.)

Two naked Damzelles he therein espyde,
Which therein bathing, seemed to contend,
And wrestle wantonly, ne car'd to hyde,
Their dainty parts from vew of any, which them eyd.

Sometimes the one would lift the other quight
Aboue the waters, and then downe againe
Her plong, as ouer maystered by might,
Where both awhile would couered remaine,
And each the other from to rise restraine;
The whiles their snowy limbes, as through a vele,
So through the christall waues appeared plaine:
Then suddeinly both would themselues vnhele,
And th' amorous sweet spoiles to greedy eyes reuele. [II, xii, 63, 6–64, 8][22]

Fox suggests that "Spenser lifts this sequence practically word for word from his source, but subtly re-orientates the meaning, even when he is following Tasso closely" by making his version "more pornographically titillating,"[23] a feature of Spenser's imitative strategy throughout the Bowre of Blisse episode noted many years earlier by Robert Durling, who also emphasized the more "direct sexual provocation" of the English poet's description of the wrestling bathers, echoed by Fairfax in his translation of the passage, and particularly the "signes of kindled lust" that it provokes in the "greedy eyes" of the observing Guyon (and indeed the reader?), until sternly rebuked by the accompanying Palmer for his intemperate response.[24] The "erotic allure" of Tasso's naked bathers continued to resonate with English readers and imitators for well over a century:[25] almost exactly 100 years after Spenser's rendering, John Dryden recalls the episode in a scene in the fourth act of his dramatic opera (with music composed by Henry Purcell) *King Arthur, or the British Worthy* (1691), where the eponymous king is wandering in an enchanted wood, when he is confronted by the appearance of "*two syrens [who] arise from the Water; they shew themselves to the Waste, and sing*":

Two Daughters of this Aged Stream are we;
And both our Sea-green Locks have comb'd for thee,
Come Bathe with us an Hour or two,
Come Naked in, for we are so;
What Danger from a Naked Foe?
Come Bathe with us, come Bathe, and share,
What Pleasures in the Floods appear.[26]

The rescue of Rinaldo from Armida's palace by Carlo and Ubaldo is itself staged directly in an English dramatic opera, John Dennis's *Rinaldo and Armida: A Tragedy* (with music composed by John Eccles), before the end of the seventeenth century. In the opening act "*Spirits in the Shapes of Shepherds and Nymphs*" appear to the Christian knights to try to distract them from their mission "And with soft Sounds seduce [their] Souls to Pleasure";[27] Kathryn Lowerre has recently suggested that Dennis substituted these disguised spirits for Tasso's alluring bathers exactly because Dryden had already dramatized the episode on the London stage less than a decade earlier.[28] Aaron Hill and Giacomo Rossi, however, had no such compunction about including Tasso's celebrated naked sirens a decade or so after Dennis's dramatic adaptation in their libretto for

Handel's through-sung opera *Rinaldo*, which premiered in London in February 1711. The librettists cleverly combine two of Tasso's most noted scenes of temptation, one visual and one aural, at the beginning of the second act: the two frolicking "*Mermaids [who] Sing and Dance in the Water*" visually recall the "false sirene" who appear to Carlo and Ubaldo in the fountain of laughter, but the song they sing to entice Rinaldo, Goffredo and Eustazio in Handel specifically echoes the earlier song of Tasso's other siren spirit, who rises from the river Oronte to lull Rinaldo to sleep, in order to facilitate Armida's plan to take her revenge on the Christian hero in canto XIV:

> O giovenetti, mentre aprile e maggio
> v'ammantan di fiorite e verdi spoglie,
> di gloria e di virtú fallace raggio
> la tenerella mente ah non v'invoglie! [XIV, 62, 1–4]
>
> (O young men, now, while April vies with May/to deck you in the spoils of leaf and flower,/ah, let not Fame's or Virtue's wisps betray/your tender minds to their delusive power!)
>
> *Il vostro Maggio*
> *De bei verdi Anni*
> *O cori Amanti*
> *Sempre costanti*
> *Sfiorate in Amor;*
> *Nè un falso Raggio*
> *D'Honor v'affanni,*
> *Ch'e sol beato*
> *Chi Amante amato*
> *Possede un bel Cor.* [II, iii][29]

As with Dryden and Purcell's evocation of Tasso's naked bathers in their dramatic opera, from a passage that had already been imitated extensively in Spenser's epic a century before, the celebrated song evoked directly in the second act of Handel and Rossi's *Rinaldo* also had an earlier imitative precedent in English verse of the 1590s, in *The Complaint of Rosamond*, where Daniel had alluded to the siren's specious dismissals of Fame and Virtue as part of the false advice given to Rosamond by the adulterous king's "seeming Matrone": "Fame, whereof the world seemes to make such choyce:/Is but an Eccho, and an idle voice" [258–59].[30]

The sustained engagement with a key episode from Tasso's epic within a decade of its first printing in Book II of *The Faerie Queene* (1590) has led to differing critical interpretations of the depth of the impact of the Italian poem on the development of Spenser's own epic. This is partly related to the uncertainty surrounding the relationship of Tasso's *Allegoria del poema* to the *Gerusalemme liberata* itself: although the allegory, written around 1576, was printed with the first Bonnà edition of the poem in 1581, Brand, with reference to letters printed as part of the poet's *Lettere poetiche* (1587), repeatedly insists that "Tasso admitted that his *Allegory* was an afterthought," composed primarily to appease potential critical objections to the romantic interludes in the epic.[31] More recently, both Treip and Borris, who describes the Italian poet as "a forceful international advocate of allegorical epic,"[32] have argued that Tasso's allegorical exegesis, in which the figures of Tancredi and Rinaldo, in Fairfax's words, respectively "signifie the conflict and rebellion which the *Concupiscent* and *Irefull* powers doe make with the *Reasonable*," epitomized by Goffredo, is fundamental to the formal construction of the poem as printed in the 1580s, and thus to Spenser's immediate and measured response to it.[33] Brand concedes that the references to Tasso's Rinaldo and "Godfredo" as allegorical figures of the "Ethice" or private and "Politice" man respectively in "A Letter of the Authors" to Raleigh suggest that "Spenser must have taken [the allegory] seriously and considered it a correct exposition of the meaning of the poem," though he regards Spenser's as a "rather strained interpretation."[34] The direct impact of the *Allegoria* on Spenser beyond the "Letter of the Authors" is most readily apparent in Book II. Borris argues that "in Tasso's 'Allegoria' for the *Gerusalemme liberata*, the figurative crux of the whole action is the concupiscible danger of sensual love, expressed in Rinaldo's subjection to Armida, and his liberation through Goffredo's supernaturally aided rational intervention";[35] Fox suggests that the English poet's implicit understanding of Tasso's Rinaldo as a "victim of concupiscible intemperance" is a principal factor in his structuring of the Book of Temperance:

> One indication of how important the Rinaldo/Armida episode was to Spenser is his decision to replicate elements from it in five discrete, though closely related episodes.[36]

If the Christian hero Rinaldo's amorous entrapment by Armida symbolically denotes the ireful faculty (temporarily) overcome by the concupiscent in the Italian poem, Spenser's legend of temperance requires a radical reimagining and redistribution of the central roles in Tasso with regard to his own allegorical pattern: the sensual and erotic temptation personified by Armida is divided between Phaedria, who accosts both Cymochles (successfully) and Guyon (unsuccessfully) in the course of the Book, and the more sinister witch Acrasia, who embodies "the solipsistic narcissism and sterility of intemperate lust" in the final canto in Spenser's version.[37] The role of Rinaldo is transferred to the relatively minor (and passive) characters Cymochles and Verdant, while the titular hero Guyon, and the accompanying Palmer, instead assume roles closer to those of Carlo and Ubaldo in the original, who act as the divinely appointed agents of Goffredo's "rational intervention" in their rescue mission to return Rinaldo to the Christian cause. The evident care with which Spenser responded to, reworked, and intensified aspects of Tasso's allegory relating directly to the Rinaldo and Armida episode throughout the Book of Temperance certainly calls into question Brand's conclusion that, ultimately, *The Faerie Queene* "is deficient in that the Italian contribution never quite fits the allegory it serves. The Bower of Blisse stands out as a beautiful but somehow incongruous gem."[38]

Although Brand finally remains unconvinced about the formal benefits of Tasso's influence on Spenser's poem, he could not deny that the English poet frequently "adapted whole stanzas from the Italian poem" in his response to "Tasso's individual treatment of the seduction of the senses" in cantos XV and XVI.[39] In his consideration of the relationship between *Gerusalemme liberata* and a later English epic poem, however, the critic concludes that "the debt to Tasso is not explicit," as in this instance "Milton does not translate sections of Tasso's poetry or rewrite his verse," though he does acknowledge, following F. T. Prince, that Tasso was an important influence on Milton's diction and prosody.[40] This is an assessment which significantly underestimates the influence, both direct and indirect, of Tasso's poem on *Paradise Lost.* While the impact of the Italian epic on Milton's poem may initially be less evident than in the case of Spenser's imitations in Book II, critics since Brand have consistently countered his estimation. The notes to Alistair Fowler's edition of *Paradise Lost* point towards many reminiscences of Tasso's epic in Milton's poem, particularly in the evocation of the Garden of Eden and its inhabitants in Book IV, while Edward Weismiller almost simultaneously explored Milton's indebtedness to Fairfax's translation of Tasso, in relation to his characterization of Satan from elements of the pagan warriors Argante and Solimano, an aspect of the poem expanded on in the most recent Oxford edition of the English translation, whose editors conclude that "it is clear that while Milton nowhere sets out to imitate Fairfax or to allude to him, his poetry is shot through with recollections and echoes, probably quite inadvertent ones of the *Godfrey of Bulloigne*."[41]

In the wake of Fowler's edition, Milton's allusions to the original Italian poem in *Paradise Lost* have tended to be considered as more conscious and overt. Treip has argued that "Milton like Spenser absorbed Tasso," pointing to "an almost incalculable quantity of direct echo of the *Gerusalemme liberata* in *Paradise Lost*, from innumerable verbal details, through extended similes, to much larger descriptive sequences."[42] After claiming to have discovered over sixty examples of "direct echo" from the first four cantos alone in the opening seven books of *Paradise Lost* (sadly without detailing these putative borrowings), Treip focuses instead on the more familiar allusions to canto XVI of Tasso's epic in Milton's description of Eden [IV, 222–68], where "the garden of Armida ... is translated into Eve's blameless bower," and, perhaps more unexpectedly, "so too, not entirely negatively, is Tasso's Armida (a seductress who repents) echoed in Milton's Eve."[43] Fowler had suggested both stanza 12 of canto XVI, and Spenser's imitation of it in the Bowre of Blisse, as direct models for Milton's evocation of "the harmony of bird song, rustling leaves and *murmuring waters*" in paradise, and Judith Kates has concurred that "Milton echoes both Spenser and Tasso in the description of Eden."[44] If the "fruit burnished with golden rind" [IV, 249] in Milton's garden evokes, slightly uncomfortably, the grapes "of burnisht gold/So made by art, to beautifie the rest" [II, xii, 55, 1–2] in Spenser's Bowre, Kates argues that ultimately "Milton insists that we hear Tasso's as the dominant voice" behind the pictorial description:[45]

> lussureggiante serpe alto e germoglia
> la torta vite ov'è piú l'orto aprico:
> qui l'uva ha in fiori acerba, e qui d'or l'have
> e di piropo e già di nèttar grave. [XVI, 11, 5–8]
>
> (The twisted vine luxuriantly winds above and sprouts where the garden is most open: here the unripe grape is blooming, and there they are of gold and red pyrope, and already laden with nectar.)
>
> Another side, umbrageous grots and caves
> Of cool recess, o'er which the mantling vine
> Lays forth her purple grape, and gently creeps
> Luxuriant; [IV, 257–60][46]

By the early 1930s, a hint of the relationship between the dominant enchantress and submissive warrior in her garden had been identified in that of Adam and Eve in Book IV in the Columbia edition of Milton's works, and this same allusion was later to be described by Giamatti, with a very different emphasis on the connection between Eve and Tasso's enchantress than Treip suggests, as "a veiled reminiscence of Tasso," which by negative association "implicates Adam and Eve in the theme of the Italian passage. The figure to suffer most by this allusion is Eve, for the narcissism and sensuality of Armida fleetingly touch Eve":[47]

> L'uno di servitù, l'altra d'impero
> Si gloria; ella in sè stessa, ed egli in lei. [XVI, 21, 1–2]
>
> (For his servitude the one prides himself, the other for her command; she in herself, and he in her.)
>
> For contemplation he and valour formed,
> For softness she and sweet attractive grace,
> He for God only, she for God in him. [IV, 297–99][48]

There are further telling hints of this association between the enchantress and Eve in Milton's depiction of Eden. Kates has detected a similarity between Eve's "unadorned golden tresses," which she wears "as a veil to the slender waist" [IV, 304–5], and Tasso's two naked maidens observed playing in the fountain by Carlo and Ubaldo in canto XV, 59–61, but there are closer parallels with the figure of Armida herself: Antony Esolen cites "the apparent artlessness" of Armida's hair, when she first appears to the Christian forces in the poem ("Fa nove crespe l'aura al crin disciolto,/che natura per sé rincrespa in onde" [IV, 30, 1–2]), as a model for Eve's "dishevelled" hair that "in wanton ringlets waved" [IV, 306], whose innocent appearance at this point is again unnervingly reminiscent of the enchantress's seductive artfulness and control over Rinaldo in canto XVI:

> Ella dinanzi al petto ha il vel diviso,
> e 'l crin sparge incomposto al vento estivo. [XVI, 18, 1–2]
>
> (In front she wears her veil loose to the breast, and her hair spreads wantonly in the summer breeze.)[49]

Although Treip's suggestion from some twenty years ago that "there is still much work to be done on the full scale and nature of Milton's borrowings from Tasso" remains true, there has been a steadily increasing critical acceptance in the past half century that "Tasso's poem served not only as a mine of phrases and motifs, but as a model for Christian epic" for the author of *Paradise Lost.*[50]

The other major work of Tasso to have had an almost immediate, and sustained, influence in England was his pastoral play *Aminta*, originally performed in Ferrara in July 1573 and printed for the first time in late 1580. As with the epic poem, the impact of the pastoral play started to be felt in England within a decade of its appearance in print, and was to continue throughout the seventeenth century. The play was printed in Italian, in an edition also containing Guarini's later pastoral tragicomedy *Il Pastor Fido* (1590), in London by Wolfe and Castelvetro in 1591, with the Italian editor explaining that Tasso's play had been added because the original Italian editions, printed by Aldo Manuzio in Venice throughout the 1580s, and from which his text derived, were so rare:

> Appresso stimai ben fatto di stampare seco l'Aminta del gran TASSO … perche de lei si ritrovano hoggi pocchissimi essempi da vendere.

(Later I considered it worthwhile to print the *Aminta* by the great Tasso along with it, ... because today one finds so few copies of it for sale.)[51]

A copy of the play in Italian had already been perused by Abraham Fraunce, who cited passages from it in *The Arcadian Rhetorike* in 1588, and translated it in its entirety into English alliterative verse in *The Countesse of Pembrokes Yvychurch* in 1591. Initially, though, there seemed to be little sense of Tasso's play as a model for actual theatrical performance in England. A decade after Fraunce's translation, Daniel translated the celebrated first chorus, "O bella età de l'oro," as "*A Pastorall*," which he appended to the *Delia* sonnet sequence in the *Workes* of 1601, as recognized by Sidney Lee more than a century ago.[52] Lee later objected strongly to Daniel's apparent lack of acknowledgement of his direct Italian source,[53] but John Pitcher has recently suggested that the careful placement of the Tasso translation in the folio collection was a conscious acknowledgement of the poet's growing interest in the lyric mode of Italian pastoral drama in the early years of the seventeenth century, confirmed by his further translations and imitations of Tasso's play (and Guarini's *Il Pastor Fido*) in his pastoral tragicomedies *The Queenes Arcadia* (1606) and *Hymens Triumph* (1615).[54] Daniel's skilful and elegant translation of Tasso's chorus resonated with later English translators and playwrights, such as Henry Reynolds and Joseph Rutter, who made use of it, alongside the original, in *Aminta Englisht* (1628) and *The Shepheards Holy-day* (1635) respectively.

Lee also detected traces of the second chorus of *Aminta* ("Amore, in quale scola") in Berowne's speech in defence of love in the fourth act of *Love's Labour's Lost*, a suggestion to which Roger Prior has recently returned in an attempt to uncover further borrowings from Tasso's play in Shakespearean comedies of the 1590s.[55] Prior claims that Lee "does not go far enough" in tracing the specific allusions to the chorus identified in the speech in Shakespeare, suggesting some plausible additional parallels;[56] however, his argument that *Aminta* had a deeper impact on this play and the later pastoral comedy *As You Like It* is far less convincing, as apparent parallels are discovered in Tasso's epilogue, which was not printed in the contemporary Manuzio or Wolfe editions, and the even rarer *Intermedi*, which did not appear in a printed edition until the middle of the seventeenth century. Prior does acknowledge this problem, but offers no evidence for his improbable explanation of Shakespeare's access to an unprinted version of an Italian play, which, according to Castelvetro, was quite hard to find even in print in London:

> He had available, therefore, a text of the *Aminta* which was more "complete" than any that has come down to us from that time. This means that he is likely to have obtained it from an unusually privileged and knowledgeable source. It also suggests that he knew what a complete text was, and took the trouble to get hold of one. There were plenty of incomplete printed editions of the *Aminta* available in England in the 1590s, but Shakespeare seems to have rejected them.[57]

Prior draws attention to these apparent borrowings from Tasso's pastoral drama to suggest that both *Love's Labour's Lost* and *As You Like It* were written initially for an "élite audience" rather than for the popular stage, because "the *Aminta* was much admired in England by the aristocracy and other lovers of Italian culture," unwittingly highlighting a significant factor in the reception of the play in England, its lack of discernible impact on plays written for the public stage. Lois Potter has observed more generally that Italianate pastoral drama in England "was ... more frequently performed in private settings, at court masques and weddings, and in schools and colleges,"[58] and the direct influence of *Aminta*, both structural and linguistic, can be keenly felt in two such examples of plays composed for private performance in the opening decade or so of King James's reign. Daniel's *Arcadia Reformed* was performed by students in front of Queen Anne and Prince Henry during a royal visit to Oxford University in August 1605, and subsequently printed as *The Queenes Arcadia* the following year; this pioneering English pastoral tragicomedy, described dismissively by Joan Rees as merely "a reshuffling of themes and incidents from Italian pastoral drama,"[59] is significantly indebted to both Guarini's *Il Pastor Fido* and Tasso's *Aminta*, from which it borrows characters, incidents, and images, which are occasionally rendered almost verbatim:

> Tu, in guise d'ape che ferendo muore
> e ne le piaghe altrui lascia la vita,
> con la tua morte hai pur trafitto al fine
> quel duro cor che non potesti mai
> punger vivendo. [IV, i, 1615–19]

> And poore *Amyntas*, if thou now be gone,
> Thou hast (like to the Bee that stinging dyes
> And in anothers wound leaft his owne life),
> Transpiercéd by thy death, that marble heart,
> Which, liuing, thou couldst touch by no desert. [IV, iv, 86–90][60]

The eclectic borrowing from various Italian sources is less pronounced in Daniel's second pastoral play, which was performed at Somerset House in London in February 1614 to celebrate the wedding of Queen Anne's chief lady-in-waiting, Jean Drummond. *Hymens Triumph*, which was again printed the year after its performance, rejects the complex structure of Guarinian tragicomedy in favour of the simpler, frustrated love plot of *Aminta*, allowing the playwright to focus more fully in this play on the development of an English pastoral register that Greg described over a century ago as being "instinct with a delicacy and freshness that even Tasso might have envied."[61] Daniel's two experiments with Italianate pastoral tragicomedy helped to prolong the influence of Tasso's play on English private stages: the plot of Rutter's *The Shepheards Holy-day*, which was performed at the Caroline court in the mid-1630s, is clearly indebted to Daniel's *Hymens Triumph*, as well as demonstrating the direct influence of both Tasso and Guarini.

Aminta's continuing popularity in England is also evinced by the periodic appearance in print of new translations throughout the seventeenth century. After Reynolds's *Aminta Englisht* in 1628, a parallel-text edition in Italian with an anonymous English prose translation was printed in Oxford in 1650, in the aftermath of Sir Richard Fanshawe's celebrated translation of *Il Pastor Fido* (1647), to which Tasso's play continued to be inextricably linked in English minds. John Dancer's translation of *Aminta the famous pastoral*, printed in 1660, compared itself unfavourably to Fanshawe's achievement, but stressed the importance of Tasso's play as a model for Guarini's later pastoral. The last English translation of the play in the seventeenth century, printed in 1698, was the only one intended for performance on the public stage, although in the preface John Oldmixon makes it clear that his *Amintas a pastoral acted at the Theatre Royal* had, perhaps unsurprisingly, not been well received by its London audiences. It is noteworthy that the theatrical prologue for this translation was written by John Dennis, whose own stage interpretation of the best-known episode from Tasso's epic was shortly to be performed at the Lincoln's Inn Theatre, in the form of dramatic opera, in *Rinaldo and Armida: A Tragedy* (1699). The final decade of the seventeenth century witnessed a renewed interest in the both the pastoral and epic work of Tasso on the London stage, possibly in the wake of the printing of a third edition of Fairfax's *Godfrey of Bulloigne* in 1687.[62] It is striking, though, that this renewal of interest in Tasso's verse also marked a new direction, in terms of the medium in which the Italian poet's influence was primarily to be felt in England, and indeed throughout Europe, in the eighteenth century: the adaptation of, and allusions to, the celebrated Armida and Rinaldo interlude in dramatic operas by Dryden and Purcell, and Dennis and Eccles, in the last ten years of the seventeenth century paved the way for the regular adoption of the amorous episodes in Tasso's poem as a principal source for opera *libretti*, manifest particularly in England in the triumphant performance of Handel and Rossi's *Rinaldo* on the London stage in early 1711.

The eighteenth century also witnessed a revival of literary curiosity in Tasso's legendary biography throughout Europe, including England, which had already displayed a keen interest in the poet's personal misfortunes even before his death. Almost a century ago Lee described how "Tasso, the youngest of the four supreme masters of Italian poetry, was for Shakespeare's England, a living force in a sense which fails to apply to any other of the great Italian company."[63] This sense of immediacy is apparent in both the sadly lost anonymous play *Tasso's Melancholy*, which was performed at the Rose Theatre on at least ten occasions in 1594 and 1595, the year of its subject's death, before a posthumous revival in 1601, with additions by Thomas Dekker, and also in the one, telling addition that Eliot makes to the assessment of Tasso borrowed from Goulart's notes in Du Bartas in his *Ortho-epia Gallica*: he alludes for the first time in print, almost thirty years before Manso's influential biography, to what was to become the core of the legend of the poet's mournful life until well into the nineteenth century, the suggestion that Tasso's apparent madness and seven-year imprisonment was caused by his inappropriate love for the princess Leonora d'Este, the sister of his patron in Ferrara, Duke Alfonso II:

> This Youth fell mad for the love of an Italian lasse descended of a great house, when I was in Italie.[64]

The almost immediate engagement in England with both the life and work of the last great Italian poet of the sixteenth century lends weight to Lee's observation that "Tasso, as far as chronology goes, might have been the elder brother of Spenser, Shakespeare and their fellow-workers, and they regarded him with something like fraternal sentiment."[65] This English appreciation of his poetic achievements (and sympathy for his personal misfortunes) was to continue posthumously throughout the seventeenth century: it seems, for example, that Milton decided to make the dangerous trip to Naples during his Italian sojourn in the late 1630s expressly to visit Tasso's last benefactor and biographer, Giovan Battista Manso, as recorded in the Latin poem *Mansus*, and Treip has noted parallels in the careers and works of the two poets to suggest that Tasso provided an important model for literary emulation for the later English poet.[66] More recently, however, a third significant English poet has emerged in critical re-evaluations as a potential rival to the more familiar figures of Spenser and Milton as "Tasso's most faithful English disciple":[67] it has become increasingly clear in the past decade or so that it is the poetry of Samuel Daniel which displays the deepest and most sustained engagement in England with Tasso's poetic achievements in the lyric, pastoral, and epic modes, spanning almost a quarter of a century, from the two works in his earliest collection *Delia. With the Complaint of Rosamond* (1592), printed three times before the Italian poet's death in 1595, to the last verse to be printed during the English poet's lifetime, in the pastoral play *Hymens Triumph* (1615).

Notes

1 The dedication to Castelvetro's manuscript translation of the *Ragionamento di Carlo V* is printed in full in John Purves, "Fowler and Scoto-Italian Cultural Relations in the Sixteenth Century," in *The Works of William Fowler*, ed. W. Meikle, 3 (Edinburgh: John Blackwood and Sons, 1940), pp. cxxvii–cxxx. All translations from Italian are mine, unless otherwise stated.

2 John Eliot, *Ortho-epia Gallica. Eliots Fruits for the French* (London, 1593), pp. 30–31.

3 Arthur C. Sprague (ed.), *Samuel Daniel: Poems and a Defence of Ryme* (London: Routledge and Kegan Paul Ltd., 1950), p. 141.

4 C. P. Brand, *Torquato Tasso: A Study of the Poet and of his Contribution to English Literature* (Cambridge: Cambridge University Press, 1965), p. 226. See also Mario Praz, *The Flaming Heart: Essays on Crashaw, Machiavelli and Other Studies of the Relations between Italian and English Literature from Chaucer to T. S. Eliot* (New York: Doubleday Anchor, 1958), p. 309.

5 Donald Cheney, *Spenser's Image of Nature: Wild Man and Shepherd in the Faerie Queene* (New Haven, CT: Yale University Press, 1966), p. 93.

6 Selene Scarsi, *Translating Women in Early Modern England: Gender in the Elizabethan Verse Translations of Boiardo, Ariosto and Tasso* (Farnham, UK: Ashgate, 2010), p. 123.

7 *Ibid.*, p. 109 and p. 123. See particularly pp. 109–20.

8 See Alistair Fowler and Michael Leslie, "Drummond's Copy of *The Faerie Queene*," *TLS* (July 17, 1981): 821–22.

9 Jason Lawrence, "*Calidore fra i pastori*: Spenser's Return to Tasso in *The Faerie Queene* Book VI," *Spenser Studies*, 20 (2005): 265–76; 267–69.

10 Scarsi, *Translating Women*, p. 118.

11 Lanfranco Caretti (ed.), *Torquato Tasso: Gerusalemme liberata* (Turin: Einaudi, 1971), p. 108; Kathleen M. Lea and T. M. Gang (eds.), *Godfrey of Bulloigne* (Oxford: Clarendon Press, 1981), p. 169; Sprague, *Samuel Daniel*, p. 42.

12 See Richard Hatchwell, "A Francis Davison/William Drummond Conundrum," *The Bodleian Library Record*, 15 (1996): 364–67.

13 Brand, *Tasso*, p. 336.

14 Caretti, *Gerusalemme*, p. 473; translation in Scarsi, *Translating Women*, p. 118; Sprague, *Samuel Daniel*, p. 54.

15 Jason Lawrence, "Samuel Daniel's *The Complaint of Rosamond* and the Arrival of Tasso's Armida in England," *Renaissance Studies*, 25 (2010): 648–65; p. 665.

16 Scarsi, *Translating Women*, p. 117.

17 Anne Lake Prescott, "Sources," in *A Critical Companion to Spenser Studies*, ed. Bart Van Es (Basingstoke, UK: Palgrave, 2006), pp. 98–115; p. 112.

18 A. C. Hamilton (ed.), *Spenser: The Faerie Queene* (Harlow, UK: Longmans, 2001), p. 283; Caretti, *Gerusalemme*, p. 478.

19 J. H. McDonald and N. P. Brown (eds.), *The Poems of Robert Southwell, S. J.* (Oxford: Clarendon Press, 1967), p. 110.

20 Jason Lawrence, "'Still Finest Wits are Stilling *Venus* Rose': Robert Southwell's 'Optima Deo'," "*Venus and Adonis*, and Tasso's *canto della rosa*," *Renaissance Studies*, 27 (2013): 389–406.

21 Colin Burrow (ed.), *William Shakespeare: Complete Sonnets and Poems* (Oxford: Oxford University Press, 2002), p. 182.

22 Caretti, *Gerusalemme*, p. 468; translation from *Torquato Tasso: Jerusalem Delivered*, ed. and trans. by Anthony M. Esolen (Baltimore, MD: Johns Hopkins University Press, 2001), p. 297; Hamilton, *Faerie Queene*, p. 281.
23 Alistair Fox, *The English Renaissance: Identity and Representation in Elizabethan England* (Oxford: Blackwell, 1997), pp. 170–71.
24 Robert M. Durling, "The Bower of Bliss and Armida's Palace," *Comparative Literature*, 6 (1954): 335–47; pp. 338–40. See also Arlene N. Okerlund, "Spenser's Wanton Maidens: Reader Psychology and the Bower of Bliss," *PMLA*, 88 (1973): 62–68.
25 Fox, *English Renaissance*, p. 168.
26 John Dryden and Henry Purcell, *King Arthur, or the British Worthy. A Dramatick Opera* (London, 1691), pp. 36–37.
27 John Dennis and John Eccles, *Rinaldo and Armida: A Tragedy* (London, 1699), p. 6.
28 Kathryn Lowerre, *Music and Musicians on the London Stage, 1695–1705* (Farnham, UK: Ashgate, 2009), p. 106.
29 Caretti, *Gerusalemme*, p. 440; translation in Max Wickert, *Torquato Tasso: the Liberation of Jerusalem* (Oxford: Oxford University Press, 2009), p. 268; George Handel and Giacomo Rossi, *Rinaldo* (London, 1711), p. 22.
30 Sprague, *Samuel Daniel*, p. 47. See *Gerusalemme liberata*, XIV, 63, 3–8.
31 Brand, *Tasso*, pp. 100, 230, and 234.
32 Mindele Anne Treip, *Allegorical Poetics and the Epic: the Renaissance Tradition to 'Paradise Lost'* (Lexington: University Press of Kentucky, 1994); Kenneth Borris, *Allegory and Epic in English Renaissance Literature: Heroic Form in Sidney, Spenser and Milton* (Cambridge: Cambridge University Press, 2000), p. 45.
33 Lea and Gang, *Godfrey*, p. 90.
34 Brand, *Tasso*, p. 230.
35 Borris, *Allegory and Epic*, p. 99.
36 Fox, *English Renaissance*, pp. 167 and 165.
37 *Ibid.*, p. 174.
38 Brand, *Tasso*, p. 294.
39 *Ibid.*, p. 233.
40 *Ibid.*, p. 255 and p. 250. See F. T. Prince, *The Italian Element in Milton's Verse* (Oxford: Clarendon Press, 1954).
41 Lea and Gang, *Godfrey*, p. 52; see John Carey and Alistair Fowler (eds.), *The Poems of John Milton* (London: Longmans, 1968), and Edward Weismiller, "Materials Dark and Crude: A Partial Genealogy for Milton's Satan," *Huntington Library Quarterly*, 31 (1967): 75–93.
42 Treip, *Allegorical Poetics*, p. 142.
43 *Ibid.*, pp. 143 and 318.
44 Fowler, *Poems of Milton*, p. 627; Judith A. Kates, *Tasso and Milton: The Problem of Christian Epic* (Lewisburg, PA: Bucknell University Press, 1983), p. 136.
45 Kates, *Tasso and Milton*, p. 145.
46 Caretti, *Gerusalemme*, p. 477; Fowler, *Poems of Milton*, p. 627.
47 Frank Allen Patterson (ed.), *An Index to the Columbia Edition of the Works of John Milton*, 2 (New York: Columbia University Press, 1931), p. 1914; A. Bartlett Giamatti, *The Earthly Paradise and the Renaissance Epic* (Princeton, NJ: Princeton University Press, 1966), pp. 315–16; see also Scarsi, *Translating Women*, p. 119.
48 Caretti, *Gerusalemme*, p. 480; Fowler, *Poems of Milton*, p. 631.
49 Kates, *Tasso and Milton*, p. 146; Esolen, *Jerusalem*, p. 449; Caretti, *Gerusalemme*, pp. 108 and 479.
50 Treip, *Allegorical Poetics*, p. 319; Kates, *Tasso and Milton*, p. 126.
51 Battista Guarini, *Il Pastor Fido* (London, 1591), sig. A2^{v}.
52 Sidney Lee (ed.), *Elizabethan Sonnets* (London: Archibald Constable and Co Ltd, 1904), p. liii.
53 F. S. Boas (ed.), *Sir Sidney Lee: Elizabethan and Other Essays* (Oxford: Clarendon Press, 1929), p. 155.
54 John Pitcher, "Essays, Works and Small Poems: Divulging, Publishing and Augmenting the Elizabethan Poet, Samuel Daniel," in Andrew Murphy (ed.), *The Renaissance Text: Theory, Editing, Textuality* (Manchester, UK: Manchester University Press, 2000), pp. 8–29; p. 16.

55 Sidney Lee, "Tasso and Shakespeare's England," in Boas, *Elizabethan Essays*, pp. 169–83; p. 176. This essay was originally printed in the *Anglo-Italian Review* in September 1918. Roger Prior, "Tasso's *Aminta* in Two Shakespearian Comedies," *Notes and Queries*, 51 (2004): 269–76.
56 Prior, "Tasso's *Aminta*," p. 270.
57 *Ibid.*, p. 275.
58 Lois Potter, "Pastoral Drama in England and Its Political Implications," in *Sviluppi della Drammaturgia Pastorale nell'Europa del Cinque-Seicento*, eds. M. Chiabò and F. Doglio (Rome: Centro studi sul teatro medioevale e rinascimentale, 1992), pp. 159–79; p. 159.
59 Joan Rees, *Samuel Daniel: A Critical and Biographical Study* (Liverpool: Liverpool University Press, 1964), p. 116.
60 B. T. Sozzi (ed.), *Aminta* (Padua: Liviana Editrice, 1957), p. 106; Elizabeth Story Donno (ed.), *Three Renaissance Pastorals* (Binghamton, NY: Medieval and Renaissance Texts and Studies, 1993), p. 230. For Daniel's frequent use of *Aminta* in his pastoral plays see Jason Lawrence, "'The Whole Completion of *Arcadia* Chang'd': Samuel Daniel and Italian Lyric Drama," *Medieval and Renaissance Drama in England*, 11 (1999): 143–71.
61 W. W. Greg, *Pastoral Poetry and Pastoral Drama* (London: A. H. Bullen, 1905), p. 259.
62 Gillespie has also recently dated a complete manuscript translation of Tasso's epic in *ottava rima* to the final quarter of the seventeenth century: Stuart Gillespie, "Gilbert Talbot's Seventeenth-Century Translation of Tasso's *Gerusalemme Liberata*," *Translation and Literature*, 20 (2011): 191–217.
63 Boas, *Elizabethan Essays*, p. 170.
64 Eliot, *Ortho-epia Gallica*, p. 30.
65 Boas, *Elizabethan Essays*, p. 170.
66 Treip, *Allegorical Poetics*, pp. 141–42.
67 Boas, *Elizabethan Essays*, p. 170. This is Lee's description of Spenser in 1918.

Part 2

Appropriations and ideologies

13 Petrarch in England

John Roe

Petrarch was known in England as early as the fourteenth century, shortly following his death. England's foremost medieval poet Geoffrey Chaucer refers to "Fraunceys Petrak" of "Padowe" (Padua) in the "Prologue" to his poem *The Clerk's Tale*, which recounts a story from Boccaccio (*Decameron* 10.10); this Petrarch had famously rendered into Latin as "*De Obedientia ac Fide Uxoria Mythologia*". The story forms the basis of Chaucer's poem on the subject of the patient Griselda from *The Canterbury Tales*. Chaucer's "Clerk" tells us that "Petrak, the lauriat poete" is "now deed and nailed in his chest" (ll. 29–31); Petrarch's death in 1374 would have preceded the first of the compositions of the *Tales* by about thirteen or so years. It used to be imagined that the two poets met each other in 1373, when Chaucer was in Italy and Petrarch had a year to live, but there is no substance to this belief.

Chaucer adapted a poem from the *Canzoniere* (no. 132: "*S'amor non è, che dunque è quell ch'io sento*") as Troilus's love lament, known as the *Cantus Troili*, in his poetic romance *Troilus and Criseyde*. This might suggest an early start in the English sonnet tradition, but things were not so straightforward: Chaucer alters Petrarch's form to fit the seven-line stanza of rhyme royal, in which his romance is written, and correspondingly expands the Italian fourteen lines into three stanzas of twenty-one lines in all. Chaucer wrote no sonnets, and so Petrarch had to wait until the age of Sir Thomas Wyatt to be translated into the form by which is best known in the English-speaking world.

Otherwise Chaucer settles for translating an example of Petrarch's Latin prose, in his rendering of the Griselda story, and in doing so illustrates the point that until the end of the fifteenth century Petrarch's influence abroad lay in his Latin works rather than in his vernacular poetry.[1] Boccaccio's tale of wifely devotion in the face of what appears to be excessive cruelty and maltreatment by her husband receives pride of place as the culminating story of the *Decameron* and Petrarch, viewing it not only as an exemplary story of female virtue but also, and above all, of human constancy, thought it worth retelling in the supreme, universal language of education in the early Renaissance, Latin.[2] Inevitably the story occasioned a good deal of—still-continuing—debate and controversy in the late twentieth century.[3] Boccaccio placed the story at the end of his collection of *novelle* on the final day, following a number of stories that emphasized

I am very happy to acknowledge the help received from Anthony Mortimer and Alessandra Petrina in preparing this chapter.

DOI: 10.4324/9781315612720-16

chastity and abstinence (as much male as female), and in so doing appears to have wished to redeem his book at its close from some of the more licentious tales of the preceding days. Chaucer for his part places the story of Griselda in the so-called marriage group, led memorably by the Wife of Bath and her tale of "wo that is in mariage" ("Prologue", l. 3), and which includes *The Merchant's Tale* of January and May. The ribald nature of the latter tale shows that Chaucer is happy to mingle the various aspects of Boccaccio altogether with no thought of developed moral exemplariness. While Petrarch singles out the tale of Griselda for special attention, Chaucer merely includes it as one of several different ways of regarding the duties or obligations of marriage, and puts these together for literary and dramatic diversity of effect.

In fifteenth-century England Petrarch was known less by translation of his vernacular poetry than by manuscript copies of the Latin works, and these were chiefly the prose works, the *Secretum*, the *De vita solitaria*, and above all the *Remediis utriusque fortunae*. E. H. Wilkins observes that Petrarch's oeuvre has a threefold division: the Latin works (which make up ninety per cent of the whole), the *Trionfi*, and the *Canzoniere*. In turn these create three separate waves of influence: the Latin works, peaking in the late fourteenth and early fifteenth centuries, the *Trionfi*, in the fifteenth to sixteenth century, and the *Canzoniere*, in the sixteenth century.[4]

Alessandra Petrina quotes verses from Lydgate's *Fall of Princes* (1431–38), which shows the range of knowledge of Petrarch's works (all of them Latin) in this period, culminating with the story of Griselda:

> Writing of old, with lettres aureate,
> Labour of poetis, hihli magnefie,
> Record on Petrak, in Rome laureate,
> Which of two Fortunys wrot the remedie
> Certeyn Eclogies and his Cosmographie,
> And a gret conflict, which men may reede & see,
> Of his querellis withyn himself secre.
> (Bk IV, ll. 106–12)

As well as the works listed here, the *De Remediis, Bucolicum Carmen*, the *Itinerarium Syriacum* (as most scholars identify the "Cosmographie"),[5] and *Secretum*, Lydgate goes on to mention other books which have brought Petrarch fame: his translation of the *Penitential Psalms*, the unfinished epic poem the *Africa*, the *De sui ipsius et multorum Ignorantia*, and the *De vita solitaria*. He adds the epistles, in particular the *Liber sine nomine* and concludes with patient Griselda.

As for the availability of manuscript copies of these works, Nicholas Mann in his seminal study, *Petrarch Manuscripts in the British Isles*, observes the dominance of the *De Remediis* but lists also a number of copies of the *Secretum* and the *Africa*.[6] For Mann the prevalence of manuscripts such as the *De Remediis* indicates that Petrarch was valued in the fifteenth-century England as a moral thinker rather than as a poet. Apart from Chaucer's brief stab at adapting *Canzoniere* 132 there are no signs of the vernacular poetry prior to the reign of Henry VIII, and furthermore it is unlikely that contemporary readers would have recognized Petrarch's presence behind the *Cantus Troili*.

George Watson's assertion that in the English Renaissance Petrarch "was a name rather than a book",[7] may seem a little exaggerated, given that forty manuscripts circulated in England in the fifteenth century, but it is true that the first printed English translation of any of the Latin works—and this was the *De Remediis*—appeared as late as 1579. It was produced by Thomas Thynne, with the title, *Phisicke against Fortune as well prosperous as adverse, conteyned in two Bookes*. It was indeed this book that Katherine of Aragon had asked Sir Thomas Wyatt to translate. Wyatt tried to accomplish the task but found the going rather hard and abandoned it with the observation:

> [a]fter I had made a prose of nyne or ten Dialogues, the labour began to seme tedious by superfluous often rehersing of one thyng, which tho parauenture in the latyn shalbe laudable ... yet for lacke of such diuersyte in our tong, it shulde want a great dele of the grace.[8]

Wyatt turned instead to a Latin version of Plutarch, the *De tranquillitate animi*, which he translated as *Quiet of Mind*.[9]

To summarize so far: Wilkins is in no doubt as to the direct influence of Petrarch in the three phases that he describes (see above), whereas Watson speaks of little if any direct influence in England. Yet we know of Wyatt's reading of the *De Remediis*, and of course we know even more of his reading of the vernacular poetry. We will turn to that poetry shortly; meanwhile the question of the impact of Petrarch's writings remains vexed. If anything the Latin works may lay greater claim to an English readership than the Italian ones, at least at an early stage, as Latin was the lingua franca of the fifteenth and sixteenth centuries. It is notwithstanding difficult to assess the degree of English absorption of Petrarch as distinct from followers in the later humanist vein, such as Lorenzo Valla, Filelfo, or Ficino.

As for the question of humanism, Mann observes that translators such as Chaucer in his rendering of the Griselda story stuck to the moral or *sententia* aspect of the story and showed little concern with stylistic effects. He goes on to argue that,

> although evidence has been adduced to show that at the end of the [fifteenth] century and in the first part of the sixteenth, especially in the circle of Thomas More, Petrarch was appreciated in a more enlightened way, notably as a Latin stylist, the manuscripts described here give no clue to this.[10]

Mann is referring to the arguments of Robert Coogan, who is less tentative than Mann in asserting the influence of the Latin manuscripts in the fifteenth century; he also contends that More and John Colet were appreciators of the vernacular poetry, at least the *Trionfi*.[11] As E. H. Wilkins points out, "most fourteenth- and fifteenth-century manuscripts of the Italian poems of Petrarch contain the *Triumphs* and the *Canzoniere*: but among the many that contain only one of the two works, those that contain the *Triumphs* are far more numerous". He says more or less the same thing about fifteenth-century (incunabula) editions, and adds that there are separate editions of the *Trionfi* but none of the *Canzoniere*.[12]

As with the Latin works, it is difficult to assess how far poems such as the *Trionfi* made an impact on the More circle. Coogan argues that More's design of a number of painted cloths with *Trionfi* motifs attests to the importance of Petrarch's poetry to him, but it is hard to say how much. Lydgate's recounting of the titles of a considerable number of Petrarch's Latin works establishes, as we have seen, the prominence of Petrarch's name within English literary circles. If from no other source, Lydgate would have got this list from the library of Duke Humfrey of Gloucester, given to the

University of Oxford in 1439. Does this establish Petrarch as a shaping influence? A number of Continental authors left their mark in various ways on the More-Erasmus group; it is not easy to say that Petrarch played a distinctive or major part. Samuel Daniel—now claimed as the likely translator of *De vita solitaria* for the countess of Clifford[13]—pointed out at the end of the sixteenth century when commenting on the Latin works, "all which notwithstanding wrought him not that glory & fame with his owne Nation, as did his Poems in Italian".[14] This places the Latin works firmly in the secondary category as far as concerns English impact but it leaves the question open as to which has precedence in the primary, the *Canzoniere* or the *Trionfi*.

Henry Parker, Lord Morley

To begin with it would seem that the *Trionfi* carries the day, if only because the first printing of a complete vernacular poem in English of Petrarch's is the translation of the *Trionfi* by Lord Morley in 1553–56. The English title is *The Tryumphes of Fraunces Petrarche* and Morley completed all six of them, Love, Chastity, Death, Fame, Time, and Eternity. As the modern editor, D. D. Carnicelli, observes, the most likely reason for the choice of the *Trionfi* is that it was judged to be more serious than the *Canzoniere*, whether from an older medieval, moral viewpoint or from the perspective of recent scholarly, reflective humanism.[15] Morley, who was always adept at keeping in with whichever monarch was on the throne, had intended to present the poem to King Henry, but the latter's death in 1547 cheated the translator of regal patronage. He then offered it to the young and ascendant Lord Maltravers, as he makes clear in the epistle.[16] Morley apologizes for any inadequacy that his translation may suffer from:

> I have not erred moche from the letter, but in the rhyme, which is not possible for me to folow in the translation, nor touche the least point of the elegancy that this elegant Poete hath set forth in his owne maternall tongue.[17]

He is referring to his inability to do justice to Petrarch's *terza rima* and his decision to make use of rhyming couplets instead. In the general judgment his translation does not rate very highly, and rough or awkward metrics too often register their effect. In defence of Morley, at least in places, Marie Axton points to his "admirable restraint and his preference for the literal sense" and compares him favourably with the Elizabethan Mary Sidney in their respective translations of the *Trionfo della Morte*. (This was the only part of the *Tryumphes* that she attempted.) However, Axton also commends Sidney's "visual clarity" in her more challenging task of rendering the poem in Petrarch's chosen metre.[18] The Scottish poet William Fowler attempted the whole of the *Triumphs* in "plodding four-teeners", and while characteristically disparaging the efforts of others did little to improve matters by his own.[19] Otherwise, a fragment of a translation of *Triumphus Eternitatis*, traditionally attributed to Queen Elizabeth I, was found in Arundel Castle (Petrina); Edward Dyer rendered a bare twenty lines of the *Triumphus Mortis* into English in his *Prayse of Nothing* (1585); John Florio translated part of the *Triumphus Pudicitiae* (1591); and in 1644 Anna Hume translated all of the *Triumphus Amoris, Pudicitiae,* and *Mortis*.

On the subject of the triumphs as visual and iconographic representations, Carnicelli makes the point that only in the *Trionfo dell'amore* does Petrarch speak of a chariot being drawn by beasts, whereas in the various sixteenth-century Flemish tapestries that hang in Hampton Court, for example, every chariot is so conveyed. This suggests that a separate iconographic tradition, such as that of a medieval bestiary, is at work, and involves for good measure such motifs as the Nine Pageants (which certainly influences the painted cloths designed by Thomas More—see above) or even the *Danse Macabre* tradition.[20] Petrarch's influence on the processional triumph tradition as it extends in England, particularly with its later Elizabethan emphasis on unmitigated victory, is somewhat remote.

Morley's translation of the *Trionfi* is not the most reliable thing. He will sometimes misread or misjudge the sense of the original, and will often pad it out in order to complete his rhyme, or settle for a loose approximation. Sometimes he misses out whole chunks of the poem. However, he does make a version of the entire work (more or less) available in print, and its arrival in the middle of the English sixteenth century is nothing if not timely.[21] The *Trionfo della morte* shows us in particular a late encounter between Petrarch and Laura, one that very probably has bearing on Sidney's *Astrophil and Stella.* Laura finally acknowledges her love for Petrarch, a love that she has always felt unable to declare in the *Canzoniere* because of the danger that it would inflame him and cause him to behave recklessly. She confesses that she burnt with an equal flame, although she kept hers secret, whereas he blazed his forth:

Fur quasi eguali in noi fiamme amorose,
almen poi ch'i' m'avidi del tuo foco;
ma l'un le palesò, l'altro l'ascose.
Tu eri di mercé chiamar già roco,
quando tacea, perché vergogna e tema
facean molto desir parer sì poco.
(*Triumphus Mortis*, ll. 139–44)[22]

Morley translates somewhat roughly as follows:

If in this world lyving to my sight
I took in the juste pleasure and delight,
I kept it secret, where thou (I say agayne)
Thy love to all men dydst make it playne.
There was no dyfference in our love at all,
But that my love was joined all
In moost honest wyse so for to be.[23]

Morley omits the line about Petrarch's eagerness to acquire *mercé*, but what concerns us here is the echo of this exchange in Sidney's sonnet sequence. In the "Eighth Song", which comes late in the sequence, among other songs, following the dramatic and climactic breach between the lovers registered in Son. 86, Stella at last gives voice to her feelings for Astrophil in a manner which strongly resembles Laura's address to Petrarch in the second capitol of the *Trionfo della morte*:

"Astrophil" sayd she, "my love
Cease in these effects to prove:
Now be still, yet still beleeve me,
They griefe more then death would grieve me.

If that any thought in me,
Can taste comfort but of thee,
Let me, fed with hellish anguish,
Joylesse, hopelesse, endless languish".
(*Eighth Song*, ll. 73–80)

She explains why she has held out against his pleas:

"Trust me while I thee deny,
In myself the smart I try,
Tyrant honour doth thus use thee,
Stella's selfe might not refuse thee.

Therefore, Deere, this no more move,
Least, though I leave not thy love,
Which too deep in me is framed,
I should blush when thou art named".
(ll. 93–100)[24]

The argument for modesty echoes Petrarch's closely; furthermore the declaration by the addressee of a sonnet sequence that she reciprocated the lover's passion, even as she kept silent about it, draws Sidney very close to Petrarch and in more than the merely routine way of sonnet convention. We shall return to this comparison when we examine the Petrarchan standing of Sidney's sequence below. For now it is enough to say that the *Trionfo della morte*, whether in the original Petrarchan version or in Morley's rendering of it, has a strong, shaping effect on one of the most intimate and moving moments in *Astrophil and Stella*.

Tottel, Wyatt, and Surrey

In the 1550s, then, two print publications of Petrarchan poetry made a significant impact on the reception of Petrarch's vernacular poetry in England: one of these was of course Lord Morley's translation of the *Tryumphes* and the other, published in 1557, was *Tottel's Miscellany* or, to give it its correct, full title, *Songes and Sonettes, Written by the Right Honorable Lorde Henry Haward Late Earle of Surrey, and Other*. Tottel is the publisher Richard Tottel, who in this volume first brought Wyatt's seminal translations of a number of sonnets and *canzoni* by Petrarch to the attention of a wider public. In effect what happened in the 1550s was that poems mostly composed two to three decades earlier, the seminal year being 1527, the time of Wyatt's embassy to Italy and his first encounter with printed editions of the *Canzoniere*, were now visible to an unprecedented degree.[25] Until then the Petrarchan translations (in some cases adaptations) of Wyatt and Surrey existed in handwritten form only, although carefully transcribed in accordance with manuscript tradition. The mid-century marked a kind of coming of age of vernacular poetry in England, with Petrarch as its obvious progenitor, even though the finest fruits of such poetry did not ripen until the later stages of the reign of Elizabeth I.

Although Tottel's heading highlights Surrey rather than Wyatt, the latter makes much more of a foray into Petrarch's poetry, translating no fewer than twenty-seven of them, mainly sonnets with a few *canzoni*. By contrast, Surrey translated or adapted a mere five poems; however, his sonnet output is considerably larger than this and his sonnets, which vary in subject from love lyric to fierce denunciation of tyrannical corruption may all be said to be Petrarchan in temper. A sonnet such as "From Tuscan came my Ladies worthy race", to which Tottel gives the title, "Description and praise of his love Geraldine",[26] enacts in its description of the lady an attempt at a British assimilation of Italian graces and virtues, and stands as an early example of the English responsiveness to Italian renaissance culture. In another poem, "I never sawe my Ladie laye apart",[27] Surrey adapts a *ballata* and makes a sonnet of it, though Petrarch's poem is also in fourteen lines.[28] Again the Surrey example is marked by gracefulness and metrical assurance, and it is easy to see why Tottel chose to put him in the title of his collection to the exclusion of Wyatt, whose metre presents more of a problem, and which indeed Tottel—or his unknown editor—decided needed modifying. On the other hand, Surrey writes with vehement intensity in those thinly veiled attacks on Henry VIII, such as his sonnet praising Wyatt's translation of the *Penitential Psalms*, or that on the tyrant Sardanapalus.[29] These poems may owe something to the ferocity of Petrarch's furious anti-papal sonnets, 136–38. However angry Surrey declares himself, he never puts a foot wrong in metrical terms, and shows a remarkable maturity of versification in an age that was poetically still finding its way.

Wyatt's role in the development and expansion of Petrarchan love poetry in England is a more thoroughgoing one. It is after all thanks to Wyatt's visiting Italy in 1527 that the first translations of Petrarch's vernacular lyrics since Chaucer occurred.[30] Tottel would have taken the poems from various manuscripts, of which the Egerton is the most important.[31] For his inspiration Wyatt drew on a number of Italian poets, to whom several of his lyrics as well as other forms may be traced, but Petrarch is the most important source. Unlike Surrey, he presents a metrical difficulty, as his rendering of sonnets in particular reads awkwardly, not just to the modern reader but also to contemporaries, as the polishing up of various lines by Tottel's editor, to make them more like regular pentameter, proves. This is not true of the many songs, which flow easily, and indeed he occasionally converts an original Petrarchan sonnet into an easy-flowing lyric, as in the case of *Canzoniere* 199, "*O bella man che mi distringi 'l core*", which Wyatt, limiting himself to the octave, turns into a jaunty little song:

O goodly hand
Wherein doth stand
My heart distressed in pain!
Fair hand, alas,
In little space
My life that doth restrain![32]

As for his sonnets, Wyatt often reads powerfully, but with a certain amount of obfuscation, and certainly not as smoothly as Surrey. D. W. Harding has defended Wyatt's handling of metre and sees him as rather closer to an earlier form of English accentuation, which subsequently yielded to iambic scansion.[33] Mortimer, who is sympathetic to Wyatt's efforts, feels that nonetheless experimentally he falls between the two stools of traditional metrics and native stress patterns.[34]

Conveniently for comparative purposes Surrey and Wyatt both translated *Canzoniere* 140, "*Amor, che nel penser mio vive et regna*". Surrey's version, which is indeed the smoother of the two, maintains the tripartite relationship of love, the lover, and the lady, whereas Wyatt brings to his resolution a note of feudal loyalty rather than devotion to the beloved. For the last line, "*Ché bel fin fa chi ben amando more*", Surrey maintains the Petrarchan sense as follows: "Sweet is the death that taketh end by love". Here "love" and "death" find themselves approximately in the relationship that they have in Petrarch's last line, although Surrey sacrifices something of the emphasis on "loving well". Wyatt keeps that, interpreting it as fidelity: "For good is the life ending faithfully". But faithful to whom? If we take the last tercet as a whole, Wyatt reads:

> What may I do when my master feareth,
> But in the field with him to live and die?
> For good is the life ending faithfully.
> (Mortimer, p. 92)

There seems to be slight but palpable shift from the Petrarchan convention of love for the lady to a sense of masculine allegiance according to an ancient code of loyalty. This in turn may indicate an uneasiness about sexual relations that reveals itself in other of Wyatt's love lyrics, the accent falling on the woman's readiness to practice betrayal.

Probably Wyatt's best sonnet translation is his version of *Canzoniere* 189, "*Passa la nave mia colmo d'oblio*", which begins, "My galley charged with forgetfulness". In this poem, which turns famously on a set of navigational metaphors, Petrarch despairs of reaching the port of salvation because his guide, the two sweet stars which are Laura's eyes ("*i duo mei dolci usati segni*") are now hidden from him ("*celansi*"). In the meantime an eternally moistened wind of sighs, hopes, and desire ("*un vento umido eterno/di sospir, di speranze et di desio*") threatens to bring down the sail. Although he keeps the basic design and argument of Petrarch's sonnet, Wyatt virtually dispenses with the love imagery and concentrates on the twin themes of uncertainty and betrayal, which could apply as easily to non-amorous relationships, such as those of courtly intrigue. Sighs, hope, and desire are reduced to "forced sighs and trusty fearfulness", which might denote a situation in which a subject's loyalty is cruelly being put to the test. Petrarch's telling phrase evoking Laura's eyes ("*dolci usati segni*") becomes a reference to the undifferentiated "stars": "the stars be hid that led me to this pain". Wyatt registers a cold, bleak seascape, unalleviated by the gentleness of love, even a love that might be accused of deceptiveness and illusion.

What this means is that Wyatt is something more than a translator. He is, whatever demerits his versification may display, a strong poet who in the act of imitation discovers his own individual voice. For Wyatt Petrarch becomes a facilitator. If he puts others in touch with the Petrarchan original by his own example, he does so with authority. Nine other sixteenth-century poets translated *Canzoniere* 189 after Wyatt, and it is highly likely that some of them at least did so as a result of Wyatt's inspiration.

Following the publication of *Tottel's Miscellany* and Lord Morley's *Tryumphes* in the mid-century, nothing else of Petrarchan note immediately happened. Doubtless the political times, with the oppressive nature of Mary Tudor's persecutory reign, followed by the uncertainties besetting that of the young Elizabeth her successor, put a damper on literary expansiveness. It is certainly true that the flowering of poetic activity came only in the last two full decades of Elizabeth's rule. It should be remembered that Tottel was publishing by and large poetry that had been written two to three decades before. Of the contributors to his collection, only Nicholas Grimald, who may have been the unidentified editor, played any sort of part comparable to that of Wyatt and Surrey; he was a humanist poet of no great distinction, and, more to the point, not a Petrarchan imitator.[35] The impetus to continue translating or even imitating Petrarch did not immediately occur on any kind of scale. The most that could be said is that Petrarch was now irremovably lodged in the English poetic consciousness. Some claim has been made on behalf of a collection of twelve Petrarchan translations, known as the Park-Hill manuscript.[36] However, as Mortimer observes, these translations are derivative rather than original, five of them (the manuscript contains fourteen sonnets translated from the *Canzoniere*) being versions of sonnets which Wyatt had already attempted.[37] They are quite pedestrian in versification and hardly likely to have made waves. In addition they confine themselves to manuscript form, which of course limits wider knowledge. It is indeed remarkable how often English translations of Petrarch throughout the century keep returning to a small group, largely made familiar by Wyatt.

The other major question of the later sixteenth century is why there was no attempt at a complete translation of the *Canzoniere*, following, for example, Arthur Golding's translation of Ovid's *Metamorphoses*, or Morley's version of the *Trionfi*. A complete translation by one Vasquin Philieul appeared in France in 1555,[38] just two years before Tottel, but in England we had to wait till 1859 when Captain Robert Guthrie Macgregor produced the "first complete English version of the *Canzoniere*".[39] Literary culture in France was considerably more advanced than in England, further evidence for which is the existence of the flourishing *Pléiade* group of poets, of whom Ronsard was the supreme member. Some catching up was done at the end of the century when first Sir John Harington translated Ariosto's *Orlando Furioso* and then Edward Fairfax completed an English version of Tasso's *Gerusalemme Liberata*. The cultural commerce between Italy and France was particularly strong, compared with that between Italy and England, as the relative above dates show. Furthermore, Ronsard's successive sequences of sonnets and odes to several Lauraesque mistresses (Cassandre, Marie, Hélène), appearing onwards from the decade of the 1550s, provided an example of native absorption of the Petrarchan manner, which other nations were later to imitate. From this point onwards, direct Petrarchan influence on England is indistinguishable from that of French Petrarchan writing in the sixteenth century, the situation being already complicated, as Wyatt's example shows, by the presence of Italian voices other than Petrarch's at an early stage.[40] By the time a translator might have thought of rendering the entire *Canzoniere* into English, emphasis had quietly shifted to poets creating their own sonnet sequences.

Watson

We come then to the late 1570s and early 1580s, when a fresh stirring of English Petrarchism may be discerned. Three poets in particular stand out: Thomas Watson, Sir Philip Sidney, and Edmund Spenser. The first two of these make a more direct stab at Petrarchan imitation. Although Spenser began by contributing as early as 1569 an English translation of *Canzoniere* 323 to a Dutch publication edited by Jan van der Noot, *The Theatre for Worldlings*, his Petrarchan activity did not effectively show itself until his volume *Complaints* in 1591 (see later), following the successful appearance of the first three books of *The Faerie Queene*. Thomas Watson on the other hand published a collection of 100 strongly Petrarchan poems called the *Hekatompathia*, or

Passionate Century of Love, in 1582. These are not strictly sonnets in form, as they each consist of three stanzas of six lines each, i.e. eighteen lines in all. Nor is Petrarch the major antecedent, if we count the number of poems adapted alone. That distinction belongs to Serafino with ten poems; Petrarch follows with eight, and Ronsard with four. Traces of other Italian poets such as Firenzuola and Parabosco also appear. On the other hand, Petrarch is being relayed equally via the other poets discernible in the volume.

An odd point of interest is that Watson renders four of the Petrarchan sonnets into Latin, including the very last two, nos. 364 and 365, and declares that he has been working on a Latin version of the *Canzoniere*. This he says in a note to his translation of *S'amor non è*, the very choice of which sonnet bespeaks a woeful lack of originality.[41] No other sign of this Latin endeavour has ever appeared, but the enterprise suggests something of the persistence of humanist influence, with its greater valuation of Latin, in the sixteenth century, even as the vernacular was achieving dominance. (We should remind ourselves that for Petrarch—at least officially—the Latin works mattered most, and that his professed ambition was for the success of his epic poem the *Africa*, which he was unable to finish.) Watson's *Passionate Century* cannot be said to have set things alight, and most scholars regard it as a cumbersome curiosity, although recent attempts have been made to interpret it from a fresh perspective.[42]

Sidney

Watson's collection doubtless caused some interest but did not make a stir in any sense that can be registered; that was to come nine years later. Sir Philip Sidney indisputably claims the prize for launching the sonnet vogue in the English renaissance. The Petrarchan sonnet impetus only properly starts—and at long last—with the publication in 1591 of a sequence (interspersed with songs) written roughly a decade earlier, and by a man who emphatically denounces the poetic mode that he so enlivens. This sequence is *Astrophil and Stella*, which for five years after Sidney's death in 1586 existed only in manuscript, until Thomas Newman brought out what we would now call a pirated version, with a colourful introduction by that infamous literary buccaneer, Thomas Nashe. The poems are printed with many flaws and the order does not correspond to what Sidney had written: the eleven Songs, which interrupt the sonnet narrative in a dramatic and stylistically strategic manner, find themselves placed at the end of the volume in 1591. The Countess of Pembroke, Mary Sidney, the sister of the poet, brought out a correct version in 1598, with the Songs properly arranged in sequence.[43]

Despite Astrophil's vigorous reproach of those who persist in singing of "poore Petrarch's long deceased woes" (Son. 15), Sidney pursues an unmistakably Petrarchan line in his composition of the sonnet sequence. The poet-speaker pays court to a lady of unassailable chastity; he pleads with her to alleviate his wretched condition but to no avail. Even as his pursuit of her promises to bear some return, a breach occurs which is never properly healed, and he ends the sequence languishing for love of her. Throughout he practices the art of oxymoron, which Petrarch had made his own, and which had been familiar in England since the translations of "*S'amor non è*" and "*Pace non trovo*". There are of course differences along with the similarities. *Astrophil and Stella* is a more concentrated, dramatic narrative than the *Canzoniere*. Its action can be imagined as being played out over a relatively short space of time, as distinct from Petrarch's sequence, which continues over an entire lifetime, and in addition of course involves the death of Laura. Charles Lamb accurately describes the character of Sidney's poem as being "full, material, and circumstantial" i.e. dramatically well realized.[44] In the foreword to the unauthorized *Astrophil and Stella*, Nashe speaks of a "Theater of pleasure" in which he declares, playing obviously on Stella's name, that "the tragicommody of love is performed by starlight".[45] Nashe catches something of the comic tone, especially of the early part of the sequence, which is markedly different from Petrarch.[46] A principal reason for the comedy is that, again unlike Petrarch, Astrophil finds his love to be reciprocated. Sonnet 66 ("And do I see some cause a hope to feede") makes this clear, and steers the sequence somewhat, though not entirely, in the direction of Shakespeare's *Romeo and Juliet*.[47] Stella, however, is a married woman, which would make the love adulterous were it consummated. In the all-important "Eighth Song", to which I referred previously, Stella retrospectively confesses her love to Astrophil, as Laura does to Petrarch in the *Trionfo della morte*, and the reasons for desisting on the part of the two women are similar.

Astrophil and Stella is witty, expansive, and confident, while also engendering pathos and reflectiveness. Sidney reinvented Petrarch for the Elizabethan age and the result of his efforts was spectacular. The publication of his sequence, even unauthorized, launched the sonnet vogue in England. More sonnets and sonnet sequences were written in the single decade of the 1590s than at any other time in English literary history. The sonnet flourished with an unprecedented fierce intensity, and then burnt out. Sonnet sequences by Anon (*Zepheria*), Barnes, Barnfield, Constable, Daniel, Sir John Davies, Drayton, Giles Fletcher, Griffin, Richard Linche, Lodge, William Smith, Spenser, Robert Tofte, and Thomas Watson (with a second, attributed collection, *The Teares of Fancie*) came out between the years 1592 and 1597. Others delayed publication: William Alexander's sequence was published in 1604, while Greville's *Caelica* appeared only in 1633. Shakespeare's sonnets interestingly did not see print until 1609, and then in a dubious publication, although analysis shows that he was at work on them in the early 1590s; two of them from the so-called "dark lady" section were famously included in yet another text of questionable authority, *The Passionate Pilgrim* (1599).[48] Robert Sidney (Philip's brother) produced a set of sonnets that lay in manuscript until their discovery and publication only in 1973. Other sequences or compilations may similarly be awaiting detection in some obscure corner. A generation later in 1621, Robert Sidney's daughter Lady Mary Wroth published *Pamphilia to Amphilanthus*, a sonnet sequence inspired by that of her uncle Philip.

As well as renewing a sense of Petrarchan possibilities in the writing of sonnets, Sidney taught his peers and successors confidence in the exploration and adaptation of the form. It must be said that interest in the sonnet far outweighed that of the *canzone* or madrigal, although musically the madrigal underwent a separate development.[49] With so many rival sonneteers in the field, the challenge to be constantly versatile and dexterous grew increasingly. This however proved a source of enthusiasm rather than anxiety, as the later Elizabethan phase of sonnet-writing enjoyed demonstrating its relatively sudden and remarkable agility in discovering and applying the resources of the vernacular. English poetry was reaching unprecedented heights of accomplishment and was fulfilling in its own turn the achievements Petrarch had realized when he first began to test out the possibilities of writing himself in the Italian language.

Drayton and Daniel

Of the poets listed above Drayton and Daniel are among the more accomplished, and each of them is interesting in different ways. Drayton adopts a tone which is often accusatory, jocular, and invariably funny, and he resembles Sidney at his wittiest. Sonnet 48 on Cupid, of his collection *Idea*, seems to be reminiscent of Sidney's *AS* 20 ("See there that boy, that murthering boy, I say"):

> Cupid, I hate thee, which I'de have thee know/A naked Starveling ever may'st thou be.[50]

Daniel is more reverent in his addresses, but in his case the question of patronage occupies an interesting position. Although he was dependent on patronage for his various offices of employment, Petrarch shows little if any direct cultivation of a patron in the *Canzoniere*.[51] The passion for Laura is represented as a personal and private affair, and the poetry maintains that posture throughout. For his part, the aristocratic Sidney ignores any interest in patronage in his writing, although like everyone else he found himself in a position of dependency at one point or another. However, once an appeal to a beautiful and noble lady becomes the norm for poetic address, and poetry moves more directly into the social sphere, then it is inevitable that the dedicatee of a collection, especially if she is an accomplished woman herself, should be identified with the subject of the poet's love. Daniel dedicates his sonnet sequence *Delia* to the Countess of Pembroke, Sidney's sister, and addresses her, in the 1594 edition, in a sonnet which is indistinguishable in manner from those of his collection:

> Wonder of these, glory of other times,
> O thou whom Envy ev'n is forst to admyre:
> Great Patroness of these my humble Rymes,
> Which thou from out thy greatness doost inspire.[52]

A subtle shift occurs here from direct poetic expression of anguish to an artful game of flattery, in which reflections or complaints regarding the pain of unrequited love merge with the appeal for preferment.[53] Daniel is also making amends for a moment of indiscretion, for he had allowed, whether willingly or not, several of his sonnets to be printed following those of Sidney in that notorious publication of *Astrophil and Stella* by Thomas Newman of 1591.

Spenser

The sonnet sequences following Sidney tended towards a greater secularization of the treatment of love than Petrarch provides, one notable and compelling exception being Spenser. *Amoretti* together with the poem celebrating his own marriage, *Epithalamion*, appeared in 1595, after several other sequences had already made their way onto the market. However, Spenser's engagement with Petrarch occurs, as we have seen already, much earlier, with his contribution of the English translation of *Canzoniere* 323 to the anti-Catholic *Theatre for Worldlings*. This poem, in a rather complicated history of transmission, was reissued in changed form in *Complaints* (1591), as *Visions of Petrarch*

(Italians know *Canzoniere* 323 as the "*canzone delle visioni*".) Clément Marot had already published Petrarch's *canzone* in French, and Spenser bases his translation on this, just as he shows further evidence of French influence on his early career by adapting Joachim du Bellay's *Antiquitez de Rome* and *Songe* as respectively *The Ruines of Rome* and *Visions of Bellay*, again in the *Complaints* volume.[54] In *Complaints* he alters the earlier derived form of *Visions of Petrarch* to a set of sonnets, i.e. modifying Petrarch's *canzone* form, and making even the *congedo* into a sonnet. What matters most from our perspective is that Spenser chooses to translate a poem of visionary, symbolic nature.[55] Petrarch, either directly or through his French intermediaries, feeds Spenser's taste for allegory, which of course has a determining effect eventually on his great epic *The Faerie Queene*.

In *Amoretti* Spenser shows himself to be the most spiritually concerned of Elizabethan writers of erotic poetic sequences, and for that alone he may be able to claim a place closer to Petrarch than any of his contemporaries. His sonnets reveal a constant attempt to resolve the problem of the conflict of flesh and spirit. A clear religious note is struck by Spenser's introduction of the so-called Lenten section beginning with no. 22, "This holy season fit to fast and pray", and culminating in the famous Easter Day sonnet, no. 68, with its opening address to the "Most glorious Lord of Lyfe that on this day/Didst make thy triumph over death and sin", referring to Christ's Harrowing of Hell (Yale Edition). He closes no. 68 by turning to his beloved: "so let us love, deare love, lyke as we ought,/love is the lesson which the Lord us taught". Whether we can say that Petrarch directly inspires Spenser or whether the latter's religious emphasis is to be identified more properly with the predicament of a puritanical author wrestling with the temptations of the flesh is hard to determine. Certainly he proves to have a more voluptuous imagination than Petrarch, who is discreet in his descriptions of the female body; Spenser by contrast is prey to the delights of the lady's décolleté, seeing her breasts in terms of a banquet (no. 77, for example). Although the two poets run along parallel spiritual lines, they are distinct in temper, and Spenser's sequence, while apparently suffering the sort of breach that besets Sidney's lovers, ultimately resolves itself in an earthly marriage, celebrated in his *canzone Epithalamion*—as opposed to Petrarch's final disavowal of Laura in favour of the Virgin Mary in *Canzoniere* 366.

Spenser's intimate knowledge of the *Canzoniere* may show through in individual sonnets, such as no. 81, which appears to have close echoes of Petrarch's celebrated *Canzoniere* 90, "*Erano i capei d'oro a l'aura sparsi*":

> Fayre is my love, when her fayre golden heares
> with the loose wynd ye waving chance to marke:
> fayre when the red rose in her red cheeks appears,
> or in her eyes the fyre of love does sparke.
>
> (ll. 1–4)

The most obvious point of resemblance is the golden hair moved by the breeze ("*loose wynd*" may be prompted by "*sparsi*"), but also the "fyre of love" creating sparks may echo the "vago lume oltra misura ardea" (line 3 of Petrarch's sonnet) of Laura's eyes. However, Petrarch's poem proceeds with a degree of uncertainty regarding the truth of the vision that the poet is recalling, and even so early in the sequence Laura appears to be marked out for death, whereas Spenser's evocation of his lady's beauties is more confident and far less complex. These differences of treatment do not affect the claim that Spenser has Petrarch's sonnet clearly in mind.[56]

John Donne

Donne is an unusual and interesting case. He does not come to Petrarch's love poetry via the sonnet route, for the simple reason that he didn't write any love sonnet sequences. He did, however, write the *Holy Sonnets* and there is no doubt that the paradoxical manoeuvres by which he expresses his love for and devotion to Christ derive from Petrarchan methodology. In his celebrated *Songs and Sonets*, which stands as one of the greatest achievements of English renaissance lyric poetry, there is nary a sonnet in the conventional fourteen-line form. However, the presence of Petrarch may be felt in many of these poems, and they have in fact been analysed in Petrarchan terms.[57] Donne often depicts a benighted lover suffering at the hands of a cruel lady, whose motive in life seems to be uniquely to inflict misery. In the hands of most contemporary poets this would be conventional enough, but such is the genius and originality of Donne that an idea that would seem to be starved of any capacity for inspiration comes to life with startlingly vivid brilliance in his hands. A sense of humour helps a great deal. Take, for example, one of his most ingenious lyrics, "Twicknam Garden", which opens in a manner reminiscent of Petrarch's famously restless *Canzoniere* 35, "*Solo e pensoso i più deserti campi/vo mesurando*". Donne's opening, whether or not it is a direct imitation, is remarkably similar, and certainly contains familiar Petrarchan effects: "Blasted with sighs and surrounded with tears,/Hither I come to seek the spring". He goes on to develop his theme in a series of moves which have little or nothing in common with orthodox Petrarchan practice, though he ends the poem with a sardonic questioning of the lady's "truth" that might owe something to Petrarch in those moments when he doubts himself for investing so much faith in Laura. What Donne achieves is a Mannerist style, which displays the most sophisticated evolution of the Petrarchan mode. Similarly a poem such as "The Apparition", with its sceptical accusation of the sincerity of the "feigned vestal", owes its extraordinary ingenuity to the success with which it introduces a mischievous Ovidian element into the Petrarchan theme of suffering at the hands of an indomitably chaste lady.

Shakespeare

Like Donne, Shakespeare is difficult to classify along orthodox lines, as his 154 sonnets do not chart a recognizable Petrarchan progress. In his anthology, Mortimer finds only two sonnets that might be said to derive from the *Canzoniere.* One of these is the anti-Petrarchan "My mistress eyes" (no. 130) and no. 106 ("When in the chronicle of wasted time"). These Mortimer links to *Canzoniere* 90 and 186, though with some circumspection. Anti-Petrarchan lyrics (as in 130) belong by this stage to an established tradition; the intercession of other poets needs also to be reckoned with. Sonnets by Samuel Daniel and Henry Constable may have played their part in Sonnet 106;[58] and by now Spenser may be lurking somewhere in the background.[59]

Apart from distinguishing intervening influences, there is the problem of Shakespeare's sonnets as a whole. Uniquely they appear to contain two different addressees: the young man "right fair", and the dark lady. As a result, they divide into two discrete sections, though certain sonnets from each of these may refer to situations evoked by the other, and they are drawn together by the reproaches levelled in nos. 133 and 134. It is unusual, to say the least, to cast a young male friend in the role of the beloved in a sonnet sequence but such an idealization may still be described as Petrarchan. The treatment of the "dark lady" (not in fact a term ever used by Shakespeare) is rather different. Although he may rail at times, Petrarch is never vituperative towards Laura, as Shakespeare is to his "black" mistress, whose "deeds" (which appear to be mainly ones of infidelity) he describes as "hellish" (Sonnets 131 and 147). Most significant of all, it is clear that the poet and his mistress have enjoyed sexual relations, which is utterly out of the question in Petrarch. All English sonnet writers, even Sidney whose character Astrophil's love would be adulterous if consummated, tend to observe the strict convention of keeping the mistress chaste. Unmistakably preoccupations that haunt Shakespeare's dramas find their way into the sonnets, Othello's acute anxiety over the possibility of his wife's unfaithfulness being an obvious instance. We might say, then, that Shakespeare's main source for the themes that occur in his sonnets lies first and foremost in his plays, and that Petrarch appears in the sonnets at a remove.

There is one play that is much more Petrarchan than any of the others, and that is *Romeo and Juliet*. At first this lovers' tragedy would appear to run on familiar enough anti-Petrarchan lines, as the opening scene shows us a Romeo swooning in an exaggerated, deliberately comic fashion over a "Laura" (named in fact as Rosaline) who never appears, and for unrequited love of whom he delivers a series of clichéd sighs: "O heavy lightness, serious vanity,/Misshapen chaos of well-seeming forms" (Weis 2012, I.1.176–77). All this changes dramatically when he meets the real Laura of the play, for whom on his first sight of her he delivers Petrarchan lines which are suddenly no longer funny, but perfectly apt and moving, and of course of striking originality:

> O, she doth teach the torches to burn bright.
> It seems she hangs upon the cheek of night
> As a rich jewel in an Ethiop's ear,
> Beauty too rich for use, for earth too dear.
> (1.5.43–46)

As with Sidney's *Astrophil and Stella*, the key difference from Petrarch is that the love is mutual and earnest on both sides. Like Petrarch, however, it is a love that turns paradoxically on division, as Juliet's lines of foreboding have it: "My only love sprung from my only hate,/Too early seen unknown, and known too late!" (1.5.137–38). The first encounter between the lovers famously consists of a dialogue in sonnet form. Death, which haunts the play from the killing of Mercutio, lies in wait for the lovers, just as in the narrative of the *Canzoniere* the demise of Laura is the single most powerful event, transforming the beauty of the landscape into a form of mourning, and investing hoped-for joy (that is before Laura's illness) with retrospective loss. As one editor puts it, a single word such as the recurrent "yonder", which Romeo delivers first at his initial encounter with Juliet ("What lady's that which doth enrich the hand/Of yonder knight", 1.5.41–42), is placed so as to underline the mournful distance that will always separate them.[60] The *Liebestod* or death-in-love motif is strong in Western medieval literature onwards but in this version of it Shakespeare takes his language unmistakably from that of Petrarch.

Scottish Petrarchism

Space precludes giving more than a very brief examination of the Scottish absorption of Petrarch. A helpful recent analysis is that of R. D. S. Jack, who emphasizes the political character of the response to Petrarch, as it changes throughout the course of the double reign of James VI and I.[61] The earlier Scottish or "Castalian" generation—roughly chronological with the Elizabethan English poets—took their lead as much, if not more, from France than Italy. They include Alexander Montgomerie, King James, John Stewart of Baldynneis, and William Fowler, whom we have already encountered as the translator of the *Trionfi*. Fowler's penchant for Italian authors over French is almost the exception in this group.[62] For example, his sonnet sequence *The Tarantula of Love* is indebted to, if not a direct translation from, the *Canzoniere*. These poets wrote in a markedly Scottish dialect, as approved by the king, who in his *Reules and Cautelis to be observit and eschewed in Scottish Poesie* (1585) reveals the influence of Du Bellay's *La Deffence et Illustration de la Langue Françoyse* (1542).

Following the Union with England, James saw the need for a greater linguistic accommodation and the earlier generation of poets gave way to that of William Drummond of Hawthornden, memorably Ben Jonson's host in 1619. This group, dismissively referred to as the "Scoto-Britanes" by die-hard patriotic Scots, includes Sir William Alexander, Sir David Murray of Gorthy, Alexander Craig, and Sir Robert Ayton.[63] One notices the increased degree of ennoblement in this younger generation. Petrarch is now the dominant inspiration, and English sonneteers exercised a particular influence, Donne on Ayton, and Drayton (who kept writing and re-writing over the first two decades of the seventeenth century) on Alexander and Drummond. The language of these poets, unlike their predecessors', is hardly distinguishable from that of the English. They produced a body of poetry that has its own validity and interest, but it has suffered neglect from the fact that the English got there first, largely because of James's early defensive, nationalistic attitudes.

Conclusion

E. H. Wilkins's proposal that we should consider three different phases of Petrarch's influence (see earlier) works very well in terms of his impact on English literary activity. The Latin prose works were well regarded in England as they were on the Continent, as the number of manuscripts existing in English libraries indicates. Queen Katherine of Aragon's request to Sir Thomas Wyatt for a translation of the popular *De remediis utriusque fortunae* is a clear sign in itself. Chaucer's curious choice to translate—or adapt —just one sonnet from the *Canzoniere* for his romance narrative *Troilus and Criseyde* tells us both that the collection—or parts of it—were known at an early stage in England and that the ground was not yet ready for a poetry of amorous devotion. The tale of Griselda is another isolated case of which not too much can be made, except in so far as it attests to the extraordinary power of Petrarch's name in making the story current beyond its source in Boccaccio.

In the sphere of vernacular poetry, the comparative success of the *Trionfi*, which succeeded in achieving printed translation in their entirety, may have been owing, along with interest in the humanist Petrarch, to the strong religious strain, which remained present in literary life throughout the sixteenth and early seventeenth centuries.

Finally, Wyatt gave a major impetus to the sonnets of Petrarch in England, and his example, further assisted by the development of printing, established vernacular love poetry to an ineradicable degree. The sonnet more than the other forms of the

Canzoniere succeeded in its appeal because it was a ready unit of currency which any number of poets could take up and use. By the time the vogue was at its height in the last decade of the sixteenth century (and in Scotland in the first two decades of the seventeenth), Petrarch's own poetic influence may not only have been indirect but also even eclipsed by intercessors; however, by now his name was inseparable from the writing of sonnets.

Notes

1 Alessandra Petrina, "The Humanist Petrarch in Medieval and Early Modern England", *Journal of Anglo-Italian Studies*, 12. Gen. ed. Peter Vassallo, vol. ed. Gloria Lauri-Lucente (Malta: University of Malta Press, 2013), p. 4.
2 See Herbert G. Wright, *Boccaccio in England from Chaucer to Tennyson* (London: Athlone Press 1957), p. 116: "Though Chaucer's *Clerk's Tale* is ultimately derived from the *Decameron*, it is based on an anonymous French prose translation of the Latin version made by Petrarch and on the revised draft of the text as it left the great humanist's hand shortly before his death in 1374".
3 See the account of David Wallace, "Letters of Old Age: Love Between Men, Griselda, and Farewell to Letters: Rerum senilium libri", in *Petrarch: A Critical Guide to the Complete Works*, ed. Victoria Kirkham and Armando Maggi (Chicago, IL: University of Chicago Press, 2009), pp. 323–29. Also, William T. Rossiter, *Chaucer and Petrarch* (Cambridge: Boydell & Brewer, 2012), pp. 161–90.
4 E. H. Wilkins, "A General Survey of Renaissance Petrarchism", *Comparative Literature*, 2, 4 (1950): 327.
5 See Petrina, p. 10.
6 Nicholas Mann, "Petrarch Manuscripts in the British Isles", *Italia Medioevale e Umanistica*, 18 (1975): 139–509 (passim).
7 George Watson, *The English Petrarchans: A Critical Bibliography of the Canzoniere* (London: Warburg Institute, 1967), p. 3.
8 In Petrina, p. 11.
9 *Tho. wyatis translatyon of Plutarckes boke, of the quyete of mynde* (London: Richard Pynson, 1528), sig. a. II (Petrina 2013, p. 11). Wyatt's apology to the queen for not delivering Petrarch is taken from this translation.
10 Mann, p. 140.
11 Robert Coogan, "Petrarch's Latin Prose and the English Renaissance", *Studies in Philology*, 68, 3 (1971): 271.
12 Wilkins, p. 328.
13 Jessica Stoll, "Petrarch's *De vita solitaria*: Samuel Daniel's translation c. 1610", *The Modern Language Review*, 109, 2 (April 2014): 314.
14 *Samuel Daniel: Poems and a Defence of Rhyme*, ed. Arthur Colby Sprague (Chicago, IL: University of Chicago Press, 1965), p. 141.
15 Lord Morley's *Tryumphes of Petrarch*, ed. D. D. Carnicelli (Cambridge, MA: Harvard University Press, 1971), pp. 18–19.
16 Carnicelli, pp. 77–79. In fact, the epistle makes clear that he had given the translation to the king, who he claims approved of it. He then says that the book has gone missing ("what his highnes dyd with it, is to me unknowen" (p. 78). Is he giving Maltravers a copy? The editor does not offer any interpretation of this curious statement. See further Marie Axton, "Lord Morley's *Tryumphes of Petrarcke*: Reading Spectacles", in '*Triumphs of English*': *Henry Parker, Lord Morley, Translator to the Tudor Court. New Essays in Interpretation*, eds. Marie Axton and James P. Carley (London: The British Library, 2000), p. 174.
17 Carnicelli, p. 78.
18 Axton, pp. 185–86.
19 Carnicelli, p. 37. For Fowler, see *The Triumphs of Petrarcke*, in *The works of William Fowler, Secretary to Queene Anne, wife of James VI.* Vol. I (Verse), ed. Henry W. Meikle (Edinburgh: Blackwood, 1914).

20 Carnicelli, pp. 38–54.
21 Indeed, its popularity at that point irritated Roger Ascham, who complained in *The Scholemaster* that Italianate Englishmen had "in more reverence, the triumphes of Petrarche than the Genesis of Moses" (Carnicelli, p. 54).
22 Francesco Petrarca: *Trionfi, Rime Estravaganti*, etc., ed. Pacca, Vinicio and Laura Paolino (Milan: Mondadori, 1996), p. 136.
23 Carnicelli, p. 128.
24 *The Poems of Sir Philip Sidney*, ed. William A. Ringler, Jr. (Oxford: Clarendon Press, 1962), p. 220.
25 Marie Axton argues that Morley may have completed his translation of the *Trionfi* as early as the 1520s, and even "before Wyatt's and Surrey's experiments with Petrarchan verse forms" (Axton, pp. 174–75).
26 *Tottel's Miscellany*, ed. Amanda Holton and Tom MacFaul (London: Penguin Books, 2011), p. 14.
27 *Tottel's Miscellany*, p. 17.
28 For the *ballata* form, see Marco Santagata (ed.), *Francesco Petrarca: Canzoniere* (Milan: Mondadori, 1996), pp. 52–53.
29 *Tottel's Miscellany*, pp. 44, 47.
30 For biographical details see Susan Brigden, *Thomas Wyatt: The Heart's Forest* (London: Faber, 2012), pp. 103–30.
31 See Kennet Muir (ed.), *Sir Thomas Wyatt: Complete Poems* (London: Routledge & Kegan Paul, 1949), pp. 255–58, and R. A. Rebholz (ed.), *Sir Thomas Wyatt: The Complete Poems* (Harmondsworth, UK: Penguin, 1978), pp. 9–17.
32 Anthony Mortimer, *Petrarch's Canzoniere in the English Renaissance*, Revised Edition (Amsterdam & New York: Rodopi, 2005), p. 117. The poem is not in *Tottel's Miscellany*. Mortimer's anthology is an excellent compilation of mainly sixteenth-century translations and adaptations of Petrarch's lyrics, with a very helpful introduction to the subject.
33 D. W. Harding, "The Rhythmical Intention in Wyatt's Poetry", *English*, 7 (1948): 120–24.
34 Mortimer, p. 13. Rebholz (pp. 44–55) gives a helpful account of Wyatt's metrical practice.
35 See *Tottel's Miscellany*, pp. xx–xxii.
36 Park-Hill MS. Add. 36,529 (British Library).
37 Mortimer, pp. 17–18
38 *Toutes les euvres vulgaires de Franfoys Pe'trarque contenans quatre livres de M. D. Laure d'Avignon* … (Avignon, 1555).
39 Watson, *The English Petrarchans*, p. 11
40 Janet G. Scott's study, *Les Sonnets Elisabéthains: les sources et l'apport personnel* (Paris: Champion, 1929), remains an indispensable source. See also Anne Lake Prescott, *French Poets and the English Renaissance: Studies in Fame and Transformation* (New Haven, CT: Yale University Press, 1978).
41 *Thomas Watson: Poems*, ed. Edward Arber (*English Reprints*, London: A. Constable, 1870), p. 42.
42 Stuart Clukas commends Watson's *centonismo*, the skilful interleaving of poems form different sources. See "Thomas Watson's *Hekatompathia* and European Petrarchism", in *Petrarch in Britain. Interpreters, Imitators, and Translators over 700 Years*, eds. Martin McLaughlin and Letizia Panizza, with Peter Hainsworth (London: British Academy, 2007), pp. 217–28.
43 For Sidney's innovative metrics, see Ringler, pp. liii–lx.
44 Charles Lamb, "Some Sonnets of Sir Philip Sydney" [sic], in his *The Last Essays of Elia* (any edition).
45 *Astrophel and Stella 1591*, Sig, A3.
46 See John Roe, "The Comedy of Astrophil: Petrarchan Motifs in *Astrophil and Stella*", in *Petrarch in Britain*, pp. 229–31 and 238–41.
47 Roe, p. 231.
48 See Jackson P. MacDonald, "Vocabulary and Chronology: The Case of Shakespeare's Sonnets", *Review of English Studies*, 52 (2001): 59–75.
49 Mortimer, pp. 21–22.
50 In *Elizabethan Sonnets*, ed. Maurice Evans, New Edition, revised by Roy Booth (London: Everyman, 1994), p. 99.

51 He makes a reference to his patron Giovanni Della Colonna, following the latter's death, in *Canzoniere* 269, *Rotta è l'alta Colonna e 'l verde lauro'*.
52 *Samuel Daniel: Poems and A Defence of Rhyme*, ed. Arthur Colby Sprague (Chicago, IL: University of Chicago Press, 1965), pp. 170–71.
53 On the topic of the emergence and development of the social nature of such poetry, see Arthur F. Marotti, "'Love is not Love': Elizabethan Sonnet Sequences and the Social Order", *English Literary History*, 49 (1982): 396–428.
54 See *Petrarch and Petrarchism: The English and French Traditions*, ed. Stephen Minta (Manchester, UK: Manchester University Press, 1980), pp. 156–65.
55 For the various versions, see *The Yale Edition of the Shorter Poems of Edmund Spenser*, eds. William Oram and others (New Haven, CT: Yale University Press, 1989).
56 There isn't room here to engage in a detailed comparison between the two poems but I am fairly confident that Spenser's derives from that of Petrarch; the resemblance between the two poems appears not to have been remarked previously.
57 See in particular the study by Donald Guss, *John Donne, Petrarchist: Italianate Conceits and Love Theory in the 'Songs and Sonets'* (Detroit: Wayne State University Press, 1966).
58 Mortimer, pp. 107–8.
59 See Patrick Cheney, "'O Let My Books Be ... Dumb Presages': Poetry and Theater in Shakespeare's Sonnets", *Shakespeare Quarterly*, 52 (2001): 235–36.
60 *Shakespeare: Romeo and Juliet*, ed. René Weis (The Arden Shakespeare; London: Bloomsbury, 2012), p. 169, fn.
61 R. D. S. Jack, "Petrarch and the Scottish Renaissance Sonnet", in *Petrarch in Britain*, pp. 259–73.
62 Baldynneis's adaptation of Desportes's version of the *Orlando Furioso* (noted above) is harder to place.
63 See Jack, p. 266.

14 The novella and the art of story-telling in the Anglo-Italian renaissance

Melissa Walter

Of Italian stories in England, the educator Roger Ascham complained:

> These be the inchantements of Circe, brought out of Italian into English and sold in every shop in London, commended by honest titles the sooner to corrupt honest manners: dedicated over boldlie to vertuous and honorable personages, the easier to beguile simple and innocent wits.[1]

But not everyone saw the stories as a bad influence. Addressing readers of *The Palace of Pleasure*, an early Elizabethan anthology of translations from Italian, French, and classical sources which was dedicated to Ambrose Dudley Earl of Warwick, William Painter suggested that readers could read along with Queen Elizabeth. Painter also characterizes his volume in theatrical terms, introducing a story by declaring, "Heere haue I thought good to summon 2 Gentlewomen of Venice to appeare in Place, and to mount on Stage amongs other Italian Dames to shew cause of their bolde incountrey agaynst the Folly of their two Husbands."[2] Love them or hate them, novella collections portray storytelling as an essentially social practice. They offer human-centered stories that are both realistic and at times bizarre or unexpected. Notable among the readers of novellas were early modern English dramatists. The *Palace of Pleasure* was one source of novella-based plots and sub-plots for the Elizabethan, Jacobean, and Caroline stage. The drama then became an important vector for promulgating narremes or theatregrams from the novella tradition in England. Performed or retold for different audiences, narratives shifted in significance.

Definitions and materials

Though Italian novella collections include many types of stories, typically the stories are short, non-magical, and not designed primarily to convey a moral (though they may illustrate a proverb or a witty remark). They usually appear in a collection and frequently are embedded in a framing narrative. Francesco Bonciani's *Lezioni sopra il comporre delle novelle* (1574) focuses on the novella's tendency to mock human foibles, and theorizes the beneficial effects of laughter in novellas with reference to Aristotle's *Poetics*. Tzevetan Todorov's structural account of Boccaccio's collection, *Le Grammaire du Decameron*, identifies two basic plots in that foundational text, punishment avoided and conversion. Robert J. Clements and Joseph Gibaldi's classic *Anatomy of the Novella* attempts to define a transnational genre (via "Invention, Variety, Verisimilitude, Unity and Harmony, Language and Style, and Brevitas").[3] Clements and Gibaldi also discuss

DOI: 10.4324/9781315612720-17

structural and thematic concerns. Their two appendices of "principal Novella Collections" and "The Novella and the Elizabeth Drama" are useful resources, although due to the problem of generic definition and the question of what constitutes "a source," they may be considered incomplete by some. The translator's introduction to Janet Smarr's Italian *Renaissance Tales* gives another useful overview of the genre and its social context.[4]

The early to mid-twentieth century contributed considerable scholarship in the area of traditional source study. Several compendious works trace early modern translations of Italian *novelle* into English. Herbert Wright's *Boccaccio in England*, an impressive example, traces translations of Boccaccio in England from the fourteenth to the nineteenth century. Flora Ross Amos briefly mentions "the vogue for novellas" that Painter "inaugurates," citing prefaces by Turberville, Pettie, Whetstone, and Painter.[5] These early modern writers translated tales from Boccaccio, Bandello, and other Italian *novelliere*, as well as stories from the novella tradition as it developed and was translated in France by Boiastuau, Belleforest, and Marguerite de Navarre. For overviews of translations of Boccaccio into English, see also F. S. Stych's bibliography of *Boccaccio in English*, and Florence Nightingale Jones, *Boccaccio and his Imitators in German, English, French, Spanish, and Italian Literature.*[6] Less is available on the English adaptations and appropriations of the works of other *novelliere*, but for Bandello, see Rene Pruvost, *Matteo Bandello and Elizabethan Fiction* (1937). More recently, and in Italian, Louis Marfè's 2015 *"In English Clothes," La novella Italiana in Inghilterra: politica e poetica della traduzione* provides a useful overview of the role of French intermediaries Belleforest and Boiastuau in shaping prose translations by Elizabethans. In *English and Italian literature from Dante to Shakespeare: A Study of Sources, Analogue and Divergence*, Robin Kirkpatrick points out differences among various Italian novella collections, such as the emphasis on verisimilitude and interest in the extreme or bizarre in Bandello, or the role of providence and the importance of witnessing in Cinthio, arguing among other points that especially in Cinthio's hands "the novella reveals the tensions that arise when a concern with the fundamentals of Christianity—whether Puritan or Counter-Reformatory—conflict with or seek expression through a highly developed literary imagination."[7] Kirkpatrick also discusses the major English translators and adaptors, noting Geoffrey Fenton's emphasis on Italian depravity and William Painter's relative social conventionality compared to the stories by Matteo Bandello that he translates. Other works of source study trace sources for specific English plays—as in Gunnar Boklund's *The Duchess of Malfi: Sources, Themes, Characters* and Geoffrey Bullough's *Narrative and Dramatic Sources of Shakespeare*—or trace iterations of a single story, as in Howard Cole's *All's Well Story from Boccaccio to Shakespeare* or A. C. Lee's *Decameron: Its Sources and Analogues.*

Janet Smarr's excellent and capacious anthology of *Italian Renaissance Tales*, which includes an introduction tracing the genealogy of the genre, is among several translations that may help English readers approach the novella tradition beyond Boccaccio. These include also Lauro Martines, *An Italian Renaissance Sextet: Six Tales in Historical Context*, which pairs each tale with an interpretive, contextualizing essay, and Valerie and Robert Martone, *Renaissance Comic Tales of Love, Treachery, and Revenge.* Two English editions of Straparola's *Pleasant Nights* now exist, one by Donald Beecher based on W. G. Waters's nineteenth-century translation, and a recent translation and edition by Susanne Magnanini. The latter, published in the "Other Voice in Early Modern Europe" series, investigates the connection to female readership, storytellers, and writers, and intriguingly argues that "the simultaneous presence of male and female and the inability of one gender to fully cancel or displace the other serves as an apt metaphor for the ways in which male and fmale voices intertwine in *The Pleasant Nights*."[8] A contemporary English translation is needed of Bandello's *Novelle* in their entirety, and also of Giraldi's *Hecatommithi* and Ser Giovanni's *Pecorone*.

Several editions of early modern English novella collections and dialogues influenced by Italian novellas have significant contextualizing introductions. These include Donald Beecher's edition of *Riche His Farewell to Militarie Profession* (1581, by Barnabe Riche), Valerie Wayne's edition of *The Flower of Friendship* (1569, by Edmund Tilney), Diana Shklanka's edition of *The Heptameron of Civil Discourses* (1582, by George Whetstone) and Geoffrey Creigh and Jane Belfield's edition of *The Cobler of Caunterburie* and *Tarlton's Newes out of Purgatorie* (1590, both anonymous, the former called by Margaret Schlauch "a minor anonymous masterpiece of the period").[9] In addition, Beecher's recent edition of *A Moral Philosophie of Doni* (1570) includes a thorough introduction with discussion of the *Panchatantra*, Italian Academies and memory games, and emblems relevant to the sixteenth-century English book. *A Moral Philosophie* is a collection of linked animal fables forming a book of advice to princes, translated via Arabic and Italian from the Sanskrit *Panchatantra*. A contemporary edition is needed of the intriguing English *Westward for Smelts* (1620), a seventeenth-century tale collection set on Thames ferry in which the tales are told by fishwives.

History of the novel

The novella forms a part of the history of the English novel, and many authors have rightly acknowledged its significance. Margaret Schlauch's *Antecedents of the English Novel* identifies novellas as a "strong influence,"[10] and Paul Salzman includes discussion of translations from the Italian in a short chapter at the beginning *English Prose Fiction: 1558–1700*. Salzman notes that "Painter and Fenton begin two distinct traditions in the Elizabethan novella: the story which concentrates primarily on plot, on action, and the story which concentrates on rhetoric, on reflection between characters and narrator" and articulates a tension between an avowed moral or instructive purpose, or a "moralizing narrator,"[11] and a sensational or vivid plot. In terms of narrative technique, David Margolies argues that Painter, Fenton, and Pettie all solve problems regarding "forming a relationship with an audience."[12] Other works that situate translations of the novella in a history of the development of the novel are Yvonne Rodax, *The Real and the Ideal in the Novella of Italy, France, and England: Four Centuries of Change in the Boccaccian Tale*, and Walter Davis, *Idea and Act in Elizabethan Fiction*. Sergio de Marco shows how a variety of Elizabethan jestbooks draw on tales from the *Decameron*.[13]

Moving out of strictly literary history towards a New Historicist approach, Constance Relihan has traced how writers of English prose fiction go about "fashioning authority" against and through Italian and French models.[14] Relihan draws on Stephen Greenblatt's concept of self-fashioning and Mikhail Bakhtin's concept of a novelistic discourse in which language is "no longer conceived as a sacrosanct and solitary embodiment of meaning and truth" and "becomes merely one of the many possible ways to hypothesize meaning"[15] to argue that sixteenth-century translators of novellas, such as William Painter, George Whetstone, and Barnabe Riche, construct or fashion their authorship of novelistic discourse using models from the novella tradition, while fashioning themselves against Italian otherness.[16]

Although many of these writers include the novella in their histories of prose fiction or of the early novel, more emphasis could be placed on the fact that the English novel has a transnational base in the Italian novella. The Italian novella not only fed directly into the English novella through translations, but also was translated into other languages such as French, Spanish, German, Dutch, and more, and novellas were translated from many of these languages into English. With its attention to human oddities and passions, realistic narratives, and social contexts, the novella contributed to the development of the novel in Europe.

Readership, orality, and social class

The *Decameron* portrays characters across social classes. Written in Florence, it may be considered "urban" rather than "courtly," although the storytelling space is set apart from regular life and in that sense shares a quality of retreat and leisure with pastoral literature or courtly dialogues such as Baldassare Castiglione's *Courtier*. Sixteenth-century French and Italian novella collections often portrayed a courtly milieu. Participating in print culture, English translations and appropriations of the genre were increasingly aimed at a "middlebrow" readership, a term Steve Mentz uses "to signal the mediated positions of readers and writers of prose fiction on the margins of elite culture."[17] As Valerie Wayne points out in the introduction to her *Flower of Friendship* edition, dialogues such as the *Flower* and Whetstone's *Heptameron of Civil Discourses* portray elite settings, but promote a bourgeois ideology of marriage to some degree. *The Cobler of Caunterburie* represents storytelling in a more popular setting. Print culture created the illusion, and perhaps sometimes the fact, of a more broadly shared cultural space accessed through reading.

There is currently significant interest in salons and other informal discussion spaces, settings which are represented in novella collections. The work of Julie D. Campbell connects salon culture and drama, while Paul Yachnin and Bronwen Wilson's anthology of essays, *Making Publics: People, Things, and Forms of Knowledge*, raises the broader issue of the development of early modern publics.[18] Curtis Perry and Melissa Walter's reading of "secret interiors" in *The Duchess of Malfi* and the early Inns of Court play, *Gismonde of Salerne*, notes the use of novella collections by Inns of Court authors.[19] There is a need for a further consideration of how Italian *novelle* and related texts of civility contributed to a culture of discussion and debate that affected the drama and related senses of a proto-public sphere.

Ladies texts?

An important area of discussion has been the representation of female characters and the interpellation of female readers in the novella in England. Though not all English novella collections explicitly address women, many follow the *Decameron* in addressing women, and all contain some percentage of romance-type tales in which women are among the central characters. What is the significance of the representation in novella collections of women's reading and speaking, and of their agency and desire?

Caroline Lucas's *Writing for Women: The Example of Woman as Reader in Elizabethan Romance* opened up this topic in the 1980s with the central claim that:

> [e]ven though romances written for women by men are, as products of an intensely patriarchal culture, oppressive to women in many ways, these texts can be read in a subversive way which reveals them to be powerful, strongly woman-centered works which give women a scope and freedom denied to them elsewhere.[20]

Lucas draws on the work of Janice Radway and sees parallels between the scope for women's agency and desire in the twentieth-century escapist literature targeting women readers, as analyzed by Radway, and Renaissance prose fiction that draws on novellas.[21]

This early work by Lucas has been criticized, most notably by Lorna Hutson and Juliet Fleming, for a lack of skepticism about the representation of the woman reader.[22] Fleming's short article on "The ladies man in the age of Elizabeth" introduces the concept of the "ladies text," which comes to mean a text ostensibly written for women that actually serves a masculine audience or masculine interests. Fleming offers Boccaccio's *Decameron* as an early instance, and her other examples, William Painter's *Palace of Pleasure* and Barnabe Riche's *Farewell to Militaire Profession*, are also key examples of English storytellers working in and translating from the novella tradition.

Lorna Hutson similarly focuses on a male readership for stories ostensibly addressed to women and featuring developed female characters. She argues that the sixteenth-century humanist men who translated and adapted novellas based their masculine prowess in textual dominance rather than deeds at arms. These male readers and writers expanded the female characters in novellas in ways that served their own needs as male subjects. Female characters were written more elaborately, so that they speak at greater length and display greater independence, in order to demonstrate practices of debate and so that male characters could illustrate textual "husbanding" or rhetorical mastery. According to Hutson, Shakespeare's more elaborated female characters come out of this same tradition and likewise provide opportunities for the demonstration of a certain kind of masculinity rooted in textual prowess. Hutson and Fleming's skepticism about representation of female readers and their emphasis on the power of male readers and interpreters of these texts are valuable. In addition, in the excellent and thorough introduction to *The Flower of Friendship*, a marriage dialogue similar to a *conversazione* and containing one story from the novella tradition (from the *Heptameron* of Marguerite de Navarre), Valerie Wayne discusses the ways in which female readers are interpellated as docile participants in patriarchal marriage:

> Once women are engaged as readers, they are reminded by members of their own sex of the requirements that wives obey their husbands, and of their need to be sexually controlled … Where women themselves offer that advice, it gains a kind of credibility it would not have if presented by men; the women who rule in these dialogues are therefore created as complicitous with the positions of their male authors.[23]

Yet it is important not to lose sight of the possibility, also, that some women did nevertheless read these texts in transgressive ways, or that the representation in these texts of female desire, rhetorical prowess, authority, rebellion, and, for lack of a better word, agency, may not have been useful for women readers as well. The work of Pamela Allen Brown in *Better a Shrew than a Sheep* provides one useful pathway forward. For Brown, novella collections are one of several early modern sites where we can see traces of a "the culture of jest."[24] Along with a reading of *Westward for*

Smelts, a collection of novellas translated and adapted from mostly Italian sources, Brown discusses examples of jokes that could have been told among women with a pro-woman emphasis, and notes the significance of women as audience members in oral storytelling, joking, and theatrical performance. Brown notes:

> I have relied on the work of [Natalie Zemon] Davis and other historians and literary scholars, including Laura Gowing, Margaret Ferguson, Ann Rosalind Jones, Jean Howard, Frances Dolan, Linda Woodbridge, and Margaret Ezell, who have sought to discover how women may have taken part in revising, negotiating, or resisting ideological paradigms rather than assuming that women were tragic victims, passive ciphers, or cultural sponges.[25]

Similarly, women readers of novellas might read them with an emphasis on the significance of female authority and desire. The works of Sasha Roberts (*Reading Shakespeare's Poems in Early Modern England*) and Heidi Brayman Hackel (*Reading Material in Early Modern England*) trace evidence for book ownership and reading practices of English women.[26] Helen Hackett's *Women and Romance Fiction* provides a useful overview and evaluation of the arguments surrounding female readership and the gender politics of these texts, with a full chapter devoted to English novellas of the 1560s and 1570s. Hackett sensibly concludes that:

> [b]oth the pontifications of moralists and the romance authors' invitations to readers assumed that stories of love and courtship had a special appeal for women, and … I suggest that we sustain the idea of some extratextual reference for this. Just as in relation to the question "who read romances?" the rhetorical exaggeration of the female readership need not mean that no female readership existed, so in relation to the question "how were romances read?" an awareness of how courtship narratives served masculine interests need not preclude acknowledgement of the simultaneous use of them to serve female pleasures.[27]

The novella and English drama

In the mid-twentieth century, Madeleine Doran suggested in *Endeavors of Art* that the similarity between tales told as true and those told as fiction in novella collections made way for the development of the expanded fictional drama of Shakespeare and his contemporaries.[28] More recently, Louise George Clubb has argued that Italian stories were one of the ways that theatregrams from the Italian theatre traveled around Europe and to England. Clubb's concept of "a variety of interchangeable structural units or 'theatergrams' (characters, situations, actions, speeches, thematic patterns) which could be combined in dialogue and visual encounters to act out the fiction with verisimilitude" offers one way to register the negotiation of social and ideological issues through imaginative forms.[29] Her classic book on *Italian Drama in Shakespeare's Time* discusses the theatregram of the "woman of wonder" whose presence in the drama and in *novelle* in Europe registers a counter-reformation sensibility.[30]

Among the important recent work on theatregrams or narremes that travel through novella and drama in the early modern period are the collections edited by Michele Marrapodi which contain valuable individual essays about novellas and drama. *The Italian World of English Renaissance Drama*, focused on pathways and forms of cultural exchange, includes several essays focused on the movement from prose to theatre. In "From Narrative to Drama: The Erotic Tale and the Theater," Marrapodi traces two key theatregrams for sixteenth-century comedy (though found in Plautine comedy, their "comic matrix of inspiration" for sixteenth-century theatre is the *Decameron*).[31] First, Marrapodi shows how the motif of twin brothers who impersonate each other in bed and the novellesque theatregram of the bed-trick develop, in English theatre, a concern with the "morality of institutions" and of rulers that may be influenced by Italian theatrical concerns. Second, he suggests that a theatregram of the rhetorically effective "assertive woman" who defends herself in a trial be identified, and traces iterations of this type through Cinquecento, Elizabethan, Jacobean, and Caroline examples.[32] In "Retaliation as an Italian Vice in English Renaissance Drama: Narrative and Theatrical Exchanges," Marrapodi highlights novellas with aesthetically elaborated revenge plots, with attention to the *novelliere* and dramatist, Giambattista Giraldi Cinthio's theorization of the effects of such plots to "cleanse the passions of the spectator's mind."[33] Comparing the representation of revenge in Cinquecento and Jacobean tragedy, Marrapodi finds that the work of a humanist like Cinthio portrays a divinely ordered universe in which passions can be purged and theatregoers cleansed, whereas the more skeptical moral and social dynamics of Jacobean tragedy focus on corruptions and a lack of guidance or order. Though not explicitly using the theatregram vocabulary, A. J. Hoenselaars's essay on the novella of Belfagor in English prose and drama traces dramatic differences in political implications of the same plot deployed in Jacobean and Stuart contexts.[34] In a related essay in a later volume, Michele Marrapodi uses the theatregram of the "lewd magistrate" to elucidate connections between Martin Luther's essay "On Secular Authority," Cinthio's Counter-Reformation novella, and drama by Cinthio and Shakespeare.[35] Melissa Walter's essays in the two "Theater Without Borders" volumes edited by Robert Henke and Eric Nicholson, *Transnational Exchange* and *Transnational Mobilities*, focus on theatregrams of theatrical and readerly enclosed spaces, room and trunk.[36] The work on theatregrams maps out motifs that are taken up in various contexts and forms, including full plays and also dramatic "jigs," supporting the thesis that the *Decameron* and other novella collections provide essential materials through which social and aesthetic issues and conflicts are investigated in Renaissance theatre.[37]

Theatregrams provide one vocabulary, though not the only, to investigate the negotiation of social and ideological issues through prose and drama. Other types of investigations include Susanne Wofford's essay on "Foreign Emotions on the Stage of *Twelfth Night*," which emphasizes less a "gram" of meaning, however transformed, than the transactions between foreign and familiar in emotions of "anger and awe."[38] The essay works between novella and theatre to examine the central importance of foreignness (whether national, ethnic, historical, or other kinds of foreignness) to such emotions. Also worth noting is Charlotte Pressler's examination of "Intertextual transformations: the novella as mediator between Italian and English Renaissance drama," which suggests that the moralizing voice of some English novella narrators becomes increasingly ironized, creating "de-universalized, individuated perspectives"[39] that are then developed on the English stage. The international transaction and traveling of these forms develops a new vision of the self and of its position in societal structures.

Drawing on Alexandra Halasz's *Marketplace of Print*,[40] Steve Mentz makes the important point that "By emphasizing the triumph of the public theater at the expense of printed fiction, early modern studies have long claimed for dramatists like

Shakespeare a cultural independence that they did not have."[41] The expectations of English theatre audiences developed as well through the mediation of English print culture, where readers could encounter Italianate novellas as well as Heliodoran romance.

In England, translations of novellas provided an opportunity to transform, adopt, and react against ideological frameworks and formal constructions that may or may not have remained flagged as Italian in their English iterations. In doing so, the Anglo-Italian novelistic transaction fostered an early modern sensibility in England, while providing key steps in the development of the novel and of the theatre of Shakespeare and his contemporaries.

Visions of Italy

In *Italian Culture in the Drama of Shakespeare and his Contemporaries* Michele Marrapodi rightly characterizes "the otherness of Italy as a powerful storehouse of cultural, political, and ideological models" for English drama.[42] But how did prose fiction in particular contribute? Insofar as novella collections became courtly fictions, representing elite social worlds, they influenced and were influenced by Castiglione's *Book of the Courtier* and other courtly dialogues or *conversazione*. Insofar as they portrayed "ethical ambiguity" they demonstrated affinities with Machiavelli's *Prince*. Italian stories were sometimes taken by Renaissance translators and writers to exemplify a corrupt and corrupting Italy, and scholars sometimes reinforce this view. This view sits well with an assumption that English people engaged in a form of self-fashioning against cultural others, including the disturbingly Catholic Italian other. In this vein, Steve Mentz suggests that in translating, adapting, and appropriating Italian stories in England, English writers sought to "escape Italy," that is to somehow "use Italian models without becoming corrupt and Italianate themselves."[43] Yet works like Michael Wyatt's *Italian and Encounters with Tudor England* remind us of how influential Italian culture was, and of the how often Englishmen and women happily adopted Italian fashions in various registers of culture.[44] Coming from another angle, Marrapodi's collections evince many examples in which foreign materials form part of celebrated and appreciated English comedies. And Susanne Wofford has emphasized how Italian foreignness can function not as a reviled other but as a means of coming to know and recognize "foreign emotions" as a part of one's experience.[45]

Knowledge of language is one axis by which Englishmen could know Italy and read Italian stories, not only in English but also in French or the original Italian. An important point is made by Jason Lawrence, who argues in *Who the Devil taught thee so much Italian?* that Shakespeare likely learned Italian and thus was not confined to reading only translations of novellas.[46] Lawrence provides data to support the thesis that Shakespeare worked with multiple texts and translations, and increasingly commanded the Italian language. It is reasonable to suppose that Shakespeare was not alone in this. This point is key because it provides further context for the images of a corrupt and corrupting Italy. Negative pictures of Italy were partly a response to the fact that a significant number of readers were keen to learn Italian and other continental languages, using side-by-side translations and other learning techniques.

Recently, critical attention has turned to the specific cultural contexts of both Italian *novelle* and their English uses. In addition to essays already mentioned, an excellent example of this type of work is Karina Attar's "Genealogy of a Character,"[47] in which she argues that a full understanding of the context of Cinthio's novella of Disdemona and the Moor (*Hecatommithi* III, 7), long read by Shakespeare's scholars as a source for Shakespeare's *Othello*, shows that Cinthio, like Shakespeare, is engaged in an intervention in a racialized discourse. Whereas Shakespeare scholarship tends to read Cinthio's Moor as more racialized and two-dimensional, less fully drawn as a character. Attar points out that when read in relation to its frame and the context of other novellas about trans-racial relationships, Cinthio's novella emerges as a text that:

> [s]ubverts the trope advertised by [its] dedicatory letter, revealing the wicked underside of outwardly virtuous (white) characters and the noble, albeit weak, nature of outwardly fearsome (black) characters. Read within its immediate historical and literary contexts, Giraldi's tale emerges as one of the most intriguing and original variations on the theme of black-white sexual encounters in the Italian novella.[48]

As will be readily apparent to readers of *Othello*, Shakespeare makes a similar intervention, and understanding the Cinthio novella in context gives a different picture of his authorship. By reading materials in a more contextualized manner, scholars are able to arrive at readings that better respect the historical diversity within and among cultures, and more accurately portray the historical interventions that each text is making.

Notes

1 *The Scholemaster*, 1570, p. 27. Janet Smarr in *Italian Renaissance Tales* (Rochester, MI: Solaris Press, 1983) uses this passage from Ascham as evidence for the novella's popularity in England (Italian Renaissance Tales, xxiv). Also cited in H. G. Wright, *Boccaccio in England from Chaucer to Tennyson* (London: University of London, Athlone Press, 1957), p. 116.

2 W. Painter, *The Palace of Pleasure*, vol. 3, ed. Joseph Jacobs (Mineola, NY: Dover Publications, 1965), p. 125.

3 Robert J. Clements and Joseph Gibaldi, *Anatomy of the Novella: The European Tale Collection from Boccaccio and Chaucer to Cervantes*, vol. vii (New York: New York University Press, 1977), pp. 12–26.

4 Janet Smarr, *Italian Renaissance Tales*, pp. xiii–xxxiv.

5 Flora Ross Amos, *Early Theories of Translation* (New York: Columbia University Press, 1920), pp. 102–3.

6 See also Mary Augusta Scott, *Elizabethan Translations from the Italian* (Boston, MA: Houghton Miffin, 1916).

7 Robin Kirkpatrick, *English and Italian literature from Dante to Shakespeare: A Study of Sources, Analogue and Divergence* (New York: Longman, 1995), p. 226.

8 Suzanne Magnanini (ed., trans. and intro.), *The Pleasant Nights*, by Giovan Francesco Straparola, *The Other Voice in Early Modern Europe* (Toronto: ITER/Center for Reformation and Renaissance Studies, 2015), p. 2.

9 Geoffrey Creigh and Jane Belfield (ed. and intro.), *The Cobler of Caunterburie and Tarltons Newes out of Purgatorie* (Leiden, the Netherlands: Brill, 1987), p. 157.

10 Margaret Schlauch. *Antecedents of the English Novel, 1400–1600, from Chaucer to Deloney* (Oxford: Oxford University Press, 1963), p. 138.

11 Paul Salzman, *English Prose Fiction, 1558–1700* (Oxford: Clarendon Press, 1985), pp. 19, 20.

12 David Margolies, *Novel and Society in Elizabethan England* (London: Croom Helm, 1985), p. 30.

13 Sergio De Marco, "La 'beffa' boccaccesca in alcuni 'Jest Books' elisabettiani," in *Il Boccaccio Nella Cultura Inglese e Anglo-Americana*, ed. Giuseppe Galigani (Florence: Olschki, 1974).

14 Constance Relihan, *Fashioning Authority: The Development of Elizabethan Novelistic Discourse* (Kent, OH: Kent State University Press, 1994).
15 Mikhail Bakhtin, *The Dialogic Imagination. Four Essays*, ed. Michael Holquist (Austin: University of Texas Press, 1981), pp. 369–70, quoted Relihan, *Fashioning Authority*, p. 4.
16 Relihan, *Fashioning Authority*, pp. 1–35.
17 Steve Mentz, *Romance for Sale in Early Modern England: The Rise of Prose Fiction* (Burlington, VT: Ashgate, 2006), p. 18.
18 Julie D. Campbell, "'Merry, Nimble, Stirring Spirit[s}': Academic, Salon, and Commedia dell'arte Influence on the Innamorate of *Love's Labour's Lost*," in *Women Players in England, 1500–1660, Beyond the All Male Stage*, ed. Pamela Allen Brown and Peter Parolin (Aldershot, UK: Ashgate, 2005), pp. 145–70; Bronwen Wilson and Paul Yachnin (rds.), *Making Publics in Early Modern Europe. People, Things, Forms of Knowledge* (New York: Routledge, 2010).
19 Curtis Perry and Melissa Walter, "Staging Secret Interiors: *The Duchess of Malfi* as Inns of Court and Anticourt Drama," in *The Duchess of Malfi: A Critical Guide*, ed. C. Luckyj (London: Continuum, 2011), pp. 87–105.
20 Caroline Lucas, *Writing for Women: The Example of Woman as Reader in Elizabethan Romance* (Milton Keynes, UK: Open University Press, 1989), p. 18.
21 Janice A. Radway, "Women Read the Romance: The Interaction of Text and Context," *Feminist Studies*, 9, 1 (Spring, 1983): 53–78.
22 Lorna Hutson, "Fortunate Travelers: Reading for the Plot in Sixteenth-Century England," *Representations*, 41 (1993): 83–103. Lorna Hutson, *The Usurer's Daughter: Male Friendship and Fictions of Women in Sixteenth-Century England* (London: Routledge, 1994). Juliet Fleming, "The Ladies' Man and the Age of Elizabeth," *Sexuality and Gender in Early Modern Europe: Institutions, Texts, Images*, ed. James Grantham Turner (Cambridge: Cambridge University Press, 1993), pp. 158–81.
23 Wayne, *Flower of Friendship*, pp. 74–75.
24 Pamela Allen Brown, *Better a Shrew than a Sheep: Women, Drama, and the Culture of Jest in Early Modern England* (Ithaca, NY: Cornell University Press, 2003).
25 Brown, *Better a Shrew*, p. 7.
26 Sasha Roberts, *Reading Shakespeare's Poems in Early Modern England* (London: Palgrave Macmillan, 2003); Heidi Brayman Hackel, *Reading Material in Early Modern England. Print, Gender, and Literacy* (Corvallis: Oregon State University, 2009).
27 Helen Hackett, *Women and Romance Fiction in the English Renaissance* (Cambridge: Cambridge University Press, 2000), p. 26.
28 Madeleine Doran, *Endeavors of Arts. A Study of Form in Elizabethan Drama* (Madison: University of Wisconsin Press, 1954).
29 Louise George Clubb, "Italian Stories on the Stage," in *The Cambridge Companion to Shakespearean Comedy*, ed. Alexander Leggatt (Cambridge: Cambridge University Press, 2002), p. 4.
30 Louise George Clubb, *Italian Drama in Shakespeare's Time* (New Haven, CT: Yale University Press, 1989), p. 65 and ff.
31 Michele Marrapodi, "From Narrative to Drama: The Erotic Tale and the Theater," in *The Italian World of English Renaissance Drama: Cultural Exchange and Intertextuality*, ed. M. Marrapodi (Newark: University of Delaware Press, 1998), p. 48.
32 Marrapodi, "From Narrative to Drama," p. 65.
33 Marrapodi, "Retaliation as an Italian Vice in English Renaissance Drama: Narrative and Theatrical Exchanges," in *The Italian World of English Renaissance Drama: Cultural Exchange and Intertextuality*, ed. M. Marrapodi (Newark: University of Delaware Press, 1998), p. 193.
34 A. J. Hoenselaars, "The Politics of Prose and Drama: The Case of Machiavelli's 'Belfagor'," in *The Italian World of English Renaissance Drama: Cultural Exchange and Intertextuality* (Newark: University of Delaware Press, 1998), pp. 106–21.
35 Marrapodi, "Beyond the Reformation: Italian Intertexts of the Ransom Plot in *Measure for Measure*," in *Shakespeare, Italy, and Intertextuality*, ed. M. Marrapodi (Manchester, UK: Manchester University Press, 2004), pp. 73–90.
36 Melissa Walter, "Dramatic Bodies and Novellesque Spaces in Jacobean Tragedy and Tragicomedy," in *Transnational Exchange in Early Modern Theater*, ed. Robert Henke and Eric Nicholson (Farnham, UK: Ashgate, 2008), pp. 63–77; and "'Are You a Comedian?': The Trunk in *Twelfth Night* and the Intertheatrical Construction of Character," in

Transnational Mobilities in Early Modern Theater, ed. Robert Henke and Eric Nicholson (Burlington, VT: Ashgate, 2014), pp. 53–66.

37 For early modern dramatic jigs that draw on the *Decameron*, see *Singing Simpkin and Other Bawdy Jigs: Musical Comedy on the Shakespearean Stage*, ed. Roger Clegg and Lucie Skeaping (Exeter: University of Exeter Press, 2014), pp. 86–118.

38 Suzanne Wofford, "Foreign Emotions on the Stage of Twelfth Night," in *Transnational Exchange in Early Modern Theater*, eds. Robert Henke and Eric Nicholson, pp. 141–57, and p. 156.

39 Charlotte Pressler, "Intertextual Transformations: The Novella as Mediator between Italian and English Renaissance Drama," in *Shakespeare, Italy, and Intertextuality*, ed. M. Marrapodi, pp. 107–17, and p. 116.

40 Alexandra Halasz, *The Marketplace of Print. Pamphlets and the Public Sphere in Early Modern England* (Cambridge: Cambridge University Press, 1997).

41 Steve Mentz, *Romance for Sale in Early Modern England: The Rise of Prose Fiction* (Farnham, UK: Ashgate, 2006), p. 6.

42 Marrapodi, *Italian Culture in the Drama of Shakespeare and His Contemporaries* (Farnham, UK: Ashgate, 2007), p. 4.

43 Steve Mentz, "Escaping Italy: From Novella to Romance in Gascoigne and Lyly," *Studies in Philology* 4, 1 (2004): 153–71, 154.

44 Michael Wyatt, *The Italian Encounter with Tudor England. A Cultural Politics of Translation* (Cambridge: Cambridge University Press, 2005).

45 Wofford, "Foreign Emotions," p. 141.

46 Jason Lawrence, *"Who the Devil taught thee so much Italian?": Italian Language Learning and Literary Imitation in Early Modern England* (Manchester, UK: Manchester University Press, 2005).

47 Karina F. Attar, "Genealogy of the Character: A Reading of Giraldi's Moor," in *Visions of Venice in Shakespeare*, eds. Laura Tosi and Shaul Bassi (Farnham, UK: Ashgate, 2011), pp. 47–66.

48 Attar, p. 62.

15 Shakespeare and the arts of painting and music

Duncan Salkeld

Drama is a multi-media form of entertainment and we should naturally expect Shakespeare to have been immersed in a world of sound and image. But it turns out that we know very little about his specific links with other artists and musicians who helped to bring the words he wrote to life in the playhouse. The roof over the stage seems likely to have shown stars and constellations in "patens of bright gold", as Lorenzo in *The Merchant of Venice* puts it (5.1.59). The pageantry of battle or tournament in the histories and *Pericles* needed heraldic devices. Flourishes, trumpets, drums, and music, like "Sneak's noise" in *2 Henry IV* (2.4.11) or Belarius's "ingenious instrument" in *Cymbeline*, were required at very particular moments, so several others were involved in performing Shakespeare's dramas, in addition to the actors in the company. But little or no information survives to tell us about them. Shakespeare must have interacted, for example, with painters and musicians – but with whom? Will Kemp and Robert Armin, the clowns of Shakespeare's acting companies, could undoubtedly sing, and perhaps play instruments. Kemp seems to have been competent at the lute and virginals and is most famous for his dancing.[1] On leaving Shakespeare's company, he capered from London to Norwich in just over a week, and left a record of the event in his *Nine Days' Wonder* (1600). But the musicians who played at the earliest performances of Shakespeare's plays remain unidentified. Similarly, we know little or nothing about the artists who painted or engraved the surviving portraits we have of early modern players, including Edward Alleyn, Nathan Field and John Lowin. This chapter considers the wider artistic milieu of Shakespeare's work. It argues that his writing suggests a belief in the efficacy of visual language, and that this aesthetic understanding was forged in collaboration. It argues further the simple point that, when he arrived in London around 1590, Shakespeare had musical knowledge and skills.

Poetry and painting

It would be surprising if Shakespeare had not sat for his portrait at some stage in his career. Of all the paintings said to be of him, the "Chandos" work has the longest and best claim to authenticity. Its provenance traces back through Sir William Davenant who claimed to be Shakespeare's illegitimate scion, and ultimately to an actor John Taylor who was also, it seems, its painter.[2] The will of a John Taylor, painter-stainer dwelling in St. Bride's, made on 23 June 1651 sadly makes no mention of any bequest of a painting to anyone but simply leaves all his goods and chattels to his wife Elizabeth.[3] If the "Chandos" painting is indeed an image of Shakespeare from 1600–1610, then it may well have been the second work for which Shakespeare sat.

DOI: 10.4324/9781315612720-18

Mary Edmond was the first to suggest that the Droeshout engraving may have been made from a smaller 1595 work mentioned by George Vertue in 1719, and Peter Holland in his *ODNB* life of Shakespeare, has proposed that it was not initially made for the forthcoming Folio.[4] But beyond these conjectures, we still have very little to go on. We would very much like to know what kinds of ornament adorned the early theatres and who did the work. Arendt van Buchell's famous sketch of the Swan, held in the Library of the University of Utrecht, is the earliest image we have of an early playhouse interior, but gives little decorative detail. Two pillars that support a "shadow" or roof over the stage stand on carved bases. The illustration of the Red Bull playhouse from Francis Kirkman's *The Wits, or Sport upon Sport* shows a candlelit performance circa 1650 in which "drolls" take the stage in front of an ornate tiring-house curtain. The back wall, on either side of the curtain, has drawings or paintings of armies ready for battle. Evidence suggests that these buildings were unusually impressive: John Chamberlain reported the second Globe of 1614 to have been "the fairest that ever was in England", and the same year John Taylor described it as "stately". Similarly, the second Fortune, built in 1622, was said to be "far fairer" than the first.[5] But the detail is lost.

But there have been some significant developments in our understanding of British sixteenth-century painting. In 2006, the National Portrait Gallery published *Searching For Shakespeare*, edited by Tarnya Cooper, a volume that accompanied an exhibition with the same title that year. In her contribution to this volume, Cooper focuses on portraits of men of a roughly equivalent social standing to Shakespeare – merchants, gentlemen and mid-ranking livery men. Cooper points to the ways in which these men sought to highlight their sober dress and religious piety, or their achievement of position and recognition. She shows that musician, composer and dancing-master Thomas Whythorne commissioned his portrait "at least five times". Whythorne clearly had an interest in portraiture but was also a man of relatively modest means. As Cooper explains, an increasing number of the "middling" sort of people had their portraits painted in the latter half of the sixteenth century. Cooper writes, "It is highly probable that Shakespeare had his portrait painted during his lifetime", and she regards it as almost certain that both the Stratford bust and the Folio engraving "derived from earlier sources".[6] The idea that Shakespeare might have sat for his portrait on more than one occasion is by no means implausible.

Cooper's work on Shakespeare has been subsequently extended to a full study of the art of painting in early modern England. In 2015, the British Academy and Oxford University Press published *Painting in Britain, 1500 to 1630: Production, Influences and Patronage*, edited by Tarnya Cooper, Aviva Burnstock, Maurice Howard, and Edward Town. This volume, extensively illustrated and running to over 400 pages, brings together an expert international team of scholars to study the evolution of painting in Tudor and Jacobean England. This necessary work largely supplants the concise and still useful survey volume *Painting in Britain, 1530–1790* by Ellis Waterhouse published in 1953. Divided into four sections: a contextual introduction by Cooper and Howard, material practice, Tudor and Jacobean painters and their workshops, and patronage, markets and audiences, it illustrates the great variety of technique and subject matter in early modern painting in Britain, and highlights the extraordinary intricacy with which many painters worked. It details, for example, the stunning technicalities of hair strands, lace, embroidery and jewellery in the "Phoenix" portrait of Elizabeth I.[7] More unusual perhaps, in terms of subject matter, is the panel painting commissioned by the widow of Sir Henry Unton also discussed in the volume. This narrative work tells in ten episodes the story of his birth, education, grand tour to Padua, service with Leicester in the Low Countries, his diplomatic work and death in France, and the repatriation and interment of his body at Faringdon.[8] As many of the photomicrographs in the book show, paintings from this period very often bear signs of under-drawing revealed by X-ray or infrared techniques.[9] What the volume demonstrates beyond question is the growing sophistication of painting available for view in Britain at the time. Although the book gives no discussion of Shakespeare or contemporaries such as Richard Burbage, it underlines the fact that early modern theatre participated in a culture immersed in visual representations that were not just ornamental but also powerful signifiers of a subject's status, wealth and accomplishment. At the same time, they were often a testament to the painter's skill.

Supplementing this important scholarly work is an essential piece of scholarship by Edward Town, published by the Walpole Society. Town's "Biographical Dictionary of London Painters, 1547–1625" presents 848 biographical entries of painters active in London during this period. Town begins with an introduction that covers the organisation of painters in the metropolis, the role of stranger painters, their working practices and workshops, and their legacies. An impressively full bibliography is then followed by individual entries for the painters Town has uncovered in his meticulous research. An eye-watering 3088 end-notes to the biographical entries gives some indication of the rigour and thoroughness of the work. Beside the fascinating detail that these entries provide, often from scraps or fragments assiduously culled from arcane sources, one of the most interesting features of Town's "Biographical Dictionary" is his identification of London painters according to the parish in which they lived.[10] This grouping shows that the majority of painters belonged to the parish of St Giles without Cripplegate, with the parish of St Botolph without Aldgate its nearest rival. Members of a common trade, it seems, tended to concentrate in particular areas of the city. The significance of Town's contribution to our understanding of painting in the early modern period can hardly be overstated. His "Biographical Dictionary" is likely to remain an indispensable resource for years to come.[11]

For all these developments, it seems we still lack any detailed knowledge of Shakespeare's possible connections with other visual artists. Instead, we find him working towards a more abstract and intellectual understanding of the power of art. There seems to be an evolution in his responsiveness to the painted image. In his early poem *Venus and Adonis*, Shakespeare seems caught up with the red and white of ardent passion (ll. 76–9). Venus chides Adonis not only for his unwillingness to participate in carnal embrace but also for his refusal to answer:

> Fie, lifeless picture, cold, and senseless stone,
> Well-painted idol, image dull, and dead,
> Statue contenting but the eye alone,
> Thing like a man, but of no woman bred
>
> (ll. 211–14)

This notion of a picture as "lifeless" is rare in Shakespeare, and the poem qualifies it with lively images of Adonis's horse ("Look when a painter would surpass the life/In limning out a well-proportioned steed,/His art with nature's workmanship at strife,/As if the dead the living should exceed", ll. 289–92) and the wild boar ("The picture of an angry chafing boar", l.662). The idea of an image as active is more common in Shakespeare and perhaps derives in part from working with images as dramatic artefacts. In *The Rape of Lucrece*, Shakespeare draws again on the standard white and red ("damask") of English poetry. He refers to "Beauty's red" and "this silent war of lilies and of roses,/Which Tarquin viewed in her fair face's field" (ll. 59, 71–2).[12] But Shakespeare also lends images in this poem a certain agency. Tarquin appears with "parling looks" (l. 100) while Lucrece remains "the picture of pure piety" with "pity-pleading eyes" (ll. 542, 561). These are tacit moments that say something. The poem is shot through with allusions to the visual that speak – the most extraordinary example of which occurs in an extended passage when, after the rape and she has resolved to commit suicide, Lucrece falls silent for a while to trace the detail of a tapestry on the wall, a work that depicts a moment of impending disaster, the sack of Troy.

This moment, when Lucrece dwells on the silent narrative of a tapestry, echoes an episode from Book 1 of Virgil's *Aeneid* where Aeneas observed a wall-painting in the Temple of Venus. In his version, Shakespeare mirrors Lucrece's dolour in a series of imagined facial expressions: "O what art/Of physiognomy might one behold" (l. 1395). Greek eyes peer sadly "through loop-holes", "blunt rage" rolls "in Ajax's eye", "the mild glance that sly Ulysses lent showed deep regard and smiling government", grave Nestor's beard "in speech it seemed … wagged up and down" (ll. 1405–6) and in "despairing Hecuba", the "painter had anatomized/Time's ruin, beauty's wrack, and grim care's resign" (ll. 1450–1). The technique of lending words for images is known as *ekphrasis*, and in this example, it is used to demonstrate the efficacy of the image. As Lucrece looks on the images, something happens to her. A kind of exchange takes place: "To pencilled pensiveness, and coloured sorrow;/She lends them words, and she their looks doth borrow" (ll. 1498–9). Moving from image to word, the silent act of looking has a performative effect in restoring flexibility of feeling to the raped woman: "Thus ebbs and flows the current of her sorrow" (l. 1569). These images have an illocutionary force: they *do* something as well as have meaning. Word and image here have re-distributive effects, enabling Lucrece to understand anew and re-think the consequences of her violation. She imagines her legacy for future ages. In this formulation, her "resolution" may be self-destruction but it will also be Collatine's boast. Her suicide may be a tragedy but it will also prove her honour and transfer shame upon Tarquin. Her renown will live among those who "think no shame" of her. Whatever the gender politics of this "resolve" by today's standards, Lucrece cannot have been the only raped woman who contemplates suicide. This moment of ekphrastic meditation – a rare and prolonged piece of art appreciation – is something Shakespeare scarcely repeats, save perhaps for Giacomo's observations of Innogen's bed-chamber in 2.2 of *Cymbeline*. But it seems he held to this idea of the efficacy of the image.

This idea of images as possessing agency did not originate with Shakespeare. A very influential conceit tracing all the way back to Simonides of Ceos (c. 500 BCE) held that painting was a kind of dumb poetry and poetry a form of blind painting. A similar notion lies behind the famous dictum of Horace: "ut pictura poesis" ["a poem is like a painting"]. Leonardo da Vinci picked up on this idea in his manuscript work entitled *Paragone* (c. 1500), in which he argued for the supremacy of painting over poetry: "If you call painting dumb poetry, the painter may call poetry blind painting. Consider, then, which is the more grievous defect, to be blind or dumb?" Leonardo defended the primacy of painting on grounds that it enjoys a greater immediacy, permanence and completeness than any rival art-form. Unlike music, it lasts longer, and the poet can only describe what he has already seen:

> If you, historians, or poets, or mathematicians had not seen the things with your eyes, you could report but imperfectly of them in writing. And if you, O poet, tell a story with your pen, the painter with his brush can tell it more easily, with simpler completeness, and less tedious to follow. If you call painting dumb poetry, the painter may call poetry blind painting. Consider, then, which is the more grievous defect, to be blind or dumb?[13]

These ideas filtered steadily into sixteenth-century English aesthetic theory. Sir Thomas Hoby wrote in *Politique Discourses* (1586), "For as Simonides saide: painting is dumme Poesie, and a Poesie is a speaking Picture".[14] John Davies of Hereford dedicated his collection of "divine meditations" *The Muses Sacrifice* (1612) to three women: Lucy, Countess of Bedford; Mary, Countess-Dowager of Pembroke; and Elizabeth, Lady Cary, wife of Sir Henry Carey. The opening epistle of this work is a long poem in quatrains. Ruminating on language, wit, fortune and time, Davies pauses for a moment to consider the relationship between painting and poetry. For Davies, painting is an earthly pursuit; poetry a divine. Painters come close to poets in presenting images "so lively in dumb Poesie". He adds, "For, Pictures speak, although they still be dumbe" (sig. A3). A funeral elegy appended to this work mourns the demise of Elizabeth Dutton, eldest daughter of Sir Thomas Egerton, who died at the age of sixteen in 1611. Davies writes, "Poets (I grant) have libertie to give/More height to Grace than the Superlative./So hath a Painter licence too, to paint/A saint-like face, till it the Saint out saint".[15] Davies assumes his readers' awareness of Renaissance aesthetics, and in particular the idea that painting and poetry were symbiotic. It is a theme he had already signalled in an earlier work, as we shall see. But perhaps the most famous expression of this idea in the early modern period came in Sir Philip Sidney's formulation of a poem as "a speaking picture", the very heart of his argument in *The Defence of Poesie*.

Throughout the *Defence*, the arts of painting underpin an argument for the superiority of poetry. Although Sidney set out to establish poetry as supreme among the arts, visual metaphors support his argument at key stages. Poets set forth nature as a "rich tapestry" (100/29); "Poetry ever setteth virtue so out in her best colours" (111/27); the poet "doth not only show the way, but giveth so sweet a prospect" (113/20–1); the poet "doth draw the mind" better than any other artist (115/28–9). The poet "pictures what should be" (124/21). Poems name men "but to make their picture more lively" (124/33). Resting on prior metaphors of the visual, Sidney's argument remains locked into Simonides' paradigm. But his interest in painting was not just academic. He sat for his portrait repeatedly, and appears to have discussed perspective with the renowned Elizabethan painter and miniaturist Nicholas Hilliard. His uncle, Robert Dudley, Earl of Leicester, held a fine collection of paintings at Kenilworth, including a miniature portrait of himself by Hilliard. Sidney is also likely to have seen works by Titian hanging in the court of Maximillian II when he visited Vienna in 1573.[16]

We see *ekphrasis* also in the Sonnets, especially poems 1–126 written ostensibly to a young man.[17] The Sonnets are deeply indebted to the language of painting and stage their own contest between word and image. Sonnet 16 reflects upon the inability of the poet's "pencil" or his "pupil pen" to paint either the youth's "inward worth" or his "outward fair" (16: 10–11). In Sonnet 20, the young man's image is by nature's "own hand painted", "a man in hue, all hues in his controlling" (20: 1, 7). Sonnet 24 imagines the poet standing at the windows of a painter's "shop", viewing from a distance a portrait of the beloved which also reflects the poet's heart (24: 1, 14). In these poems, Shakespeare repeatedly deprecates the art of poetry, hinting that it falls too short to paint the beloved's praise. In doing so, he creates an aesthetic of silence: the loveliness and virtue of the young man go beyond words. In Sonnet 83, Shakespeare writes:

> I never saw that you did painting need,
> And therefore to your fair no painting set;
> I found (or thought I found) you did exceed
> The barren tender of a poet's debt.
> (83: 1–4)

The poem observes, "How far a modern quill doth come too short" (83: 7) in setting forth the youth's "worth". The youth is made a sitter for the painter-poet, yet words are insufficient to portray his beauty, and only the sight of this beloved will do. The last two lines of Sonnet 106 press this point home: "For we which now behold these present days,/Have eyes to wonder but lack tongues to praise" (106: 13–14). An act of veneration is performed, and the moment is Catholic in spirit if not in letter. The young man is an icon exalted before the congregation of readers. Now is the beloved incarnate and poetry stills before his silent immanence.

But Shakespeare's interest in art was also practical. In his long and encyclopaedic poetical work *Microcosmos* (1603), John Davies of Hereford devotes a section to consideration of the status of actors and refers directly to William Shakespeare and Richard Burbage as both poet and painter respectively:

> *Players*, I love yee, and your *Qualitie*,
> As ye are Men, that pass-time not abus'd:
> And some I love for *painting, poesie*,
> And say fell *Fortune* cannot be excused,
> That hath for better *vses* you refus'd:
> *Wit, Courage, good-shape, good partes*, and all *good*,
> As long as al these *goods* are no worse vs'd,
> And though the *stage* doth staine pure gentle bloud,
> Yet generous yee are in *minde* and *moode*.

Davies's marginal note to the phrase "some I love" gives the initials of his favourite players, "W.S" and "R.B", William Shakespeare and Richard Burbage. Burbage is known to have been a painter, and thought to have sat for his portrait. The seventeenth-century actor and bookseller William Cartwright, who donated much of his collection to Dulwich College, owned over two hundred paintings, one of which depicted "Mr Burbig his head in a gilt frame a small closet pece".[18] A rather badly damaged and hastily-finished painting survives from the collection which may indeed be this work. It is sometimes said to be a self-portrait, although there is no hard evidence for the claim. But as if to show the connection between Shakespeare, Burbage and sixteenth-century intellectual ideas about art, Davies added another marginal note to this passage, one that touches yet again on the analogical relationship between the arts: "Simonides saith, that painting is a dumb Poesy, & Poesy a speaking painting".[19] Intriguingly, Davies applies the dictum specifically to Shakespeare and Burbage.

It seems that Shakespeare held to a view that images have a certain efficacy or agency throughout his career. Shakespeare's *Timon of Athens* begins with a discussion between a poet and a painter taking gifts for Timon. The poet carries a verse, but it is out-done by an image the painter has made, and the poet admits it:

> Admirable. How this grace speaks in his own standing!/What a mental power this eye shoots forth! How big imagination/Moves in this lip! To th' dumbness of the gesture/One might interpret ... it tutors nature; artificial strife/Lives in these touches, livelier than life.
>
> (1.1.30–4)

The poet admires the image. He agrees that it "speaks in his own standing", it "tutors nature", and imagination may fill in for the "dumbness of the gesture". The painting is, literally, a speaking picture that serves for a theatrical property. Sidney's claim for poetry is one that the poet here makes for painting. The passage also hints that for all Shakespeare's interest in the fabulous and marvellous, he also admired realism: the image is impressive precisely because it is "livelier than life". Portraits at this time were indeed achieving greater verisimilitude, as Caroline Rae has shown in her account of the development of flesh-tone in late sixteenth-century painting. In a comparative discussion of Dutch artists Marcus Gheeraerts the Younger and John de Critz the Elder with the English counterparts, Robert Peake the Elder and William Larkin, she focuses specifically on the artists' handling of light, shade and colour in skin-tone. Rae notes "Gheeraerts's and de Critz's sophisticated skills in painting flesh, and their ability to imbue sitters with a sense of individuality". Peake, by contrast, gave greater attention to the surrounding details that emphasised the sitter's status. Larkin seems to have adopted some of the techniques for painting flesh utilised by Netherlandish painters, but also followed Peake in attending to the intricacies of fabric and lace patterns worn by the subject.[20] The poet's words in *Timon of Athens* suggest that Shakespeare's response to the painted image has grown from the two-tone damask of *Venus and Adonis* and *The Rape of Lucrece*, to an awareness of finer technical effects in early seventeenth-century portrait painting.

We have no reason to doubt that Shakespeare's regard for painting was sincere. Surrounded by pageantry, the performative possibilities of the image were impossible to ignore. A record in 1613 shows Shakespeare collaborating with Burbage on the design of an *impresa*, or heraldic design, for the sixth Earl of Rutland, Francis Manners at the King's Accession day tilt on 24 March. A week after the event, Thomas Screvin, Rutland's steward noted in his *Accounts*:

> Item, 31 Martii to Mr Shakespeare in gold about my Lordes impreso, xliiij^{s}; to Richard Burbage for paynting and making yt, in gold xliiij^{s}. – iiij^{li}. Viij^{s}.[21]

In all likelihood, the kind of impresa Shakespeare and Burbage fashioned for this occasion was modelled on the kind of stage properties used in 2.2 of *Pericles* where a series of combatants, including the Prince of Tyre, display heraldic shields. The creation of such designs for aristocratic tilts could clearly be lucrative work. Sir

Henry Wotton recorded in his *Letters* that some of the emblems at this tilt were "so dark, that their meaning is not yet understood".[22] Davies's reference to the Burbage and Shakespeare in connection with "painting, poesie" might suggest that they had collaborated on similar projects on other occasions. It is striking, in this context, that when Pericles views his future father-in-law, "the good Simonides", he is reminded of his "father's picture" (2.3.36). Moreover, the image "tells" him of the reverence and esteem his father once enjoyed. Not only might these lines conceal a reminiscence of John Shakespeare who led the council at Stratford as justice of the peace and alderman throughout the early 1570s, but they may also hint that he too once sat for his portrait.

Music

This contest of the arts – or *paragone* – is evident also in the field of music. Joseph Barnes's *The Praise of Music*, printed at Oxford in 1586, sets out to defend music against its detractors who regard it as "wayward and troublesome", and useful to cunning men (Barnes does not name these detractors). He argues that men are naturally delighted with music from infancy (p. 42), that just as the rainbow's several colours please the eye, "so musicke being not of one kinde is therefore more welcome to the ear" (p. 7). Music, Barnes holds, suits even the cruellest of tyrants (p. 22), it is becoming to the nobility, and not to be generally decried if some musicians set a bad example, either in licentious behaviour or in playing unskillfully (pp. 28–30). Barnes fourth chapter is concerned with "the effects and operation of music". Here Barnes considers the "force and efficacie" of music, and the ways in which musical sounds "worke in their hearers" (p. 54). Music, he writes, "allayeth anger", "moveth pittie", serves as a "medicine for our sorrowe and remedie for our griefe", and can even restore "madmen to their wittes" (pp. 60–1). In his enthusiasm, Barnes gets a little carried away in his claims that music "cureth diseases", "driveth away spirits", prevents the plague and might even preserve an entire commonwealth. The greater part of his treatise is devoted to defending the use of music in church, but it is clear throughout that Barnes understood music as effectual or performative. As critics have often noted, the performative power of music is especially evident in Shakespeare's later plays, especially as the new genre of the court masque fostered transformative drama.[23]

David Lindley begins his book on *Shakespeare and Music* with just this implication. Lindley starts with *The Tempest*, perhaps Shakespeare's last single-authored play, and in particular the close of the long second scene where Ariel plays and sings, "Come unto these yellow sands". Focusing on the detail of this moment, Lindley highlights the music's agency: it at once draws Ferdinand to Prospero's cell and calms him in order to make his attraction to Miranda all the more plausible. Lindley adds that the music adds a certain "theatrical punctuation" in shifting the mood from hostile exchanges between Prospero and Caliban, to the romantic affection awakening between Miranda and Ferdinand. Lindley conjectures that, since the Folio text of the play was prepared by a scribe, Ralph Crane, it is possible that the actor playing Ariel did not in fact play a musical instrument at this point, but the Folio stage direction at 1.2.378 explicitly states that Ariel is invisible and "playing". Later stage directions similarly have Ariel playing "on a tabor and pipe" and "playing music" (3.2.126 and 150).[24]

The language of music saturates Shakespeare's plays, as several studies have shown, not least Christopher R. Wilson's *Music in Shakespeare: A Dictionary*, an essential resource of impressive breadth and detail. Elsewhere, Wilson devotes a rich, detailed single-chapter discussion to early modern music, especially in relation to Shakespeare's plays. He notes that songs or "airs" were often formed by means of a solo voice accompanied by a lute.[25] In *Much Ado About Nothing*, it seems Shakespeare drew upon a pre-existing lyric by Thomas Ford, available only in manuscript in 1598, and so avoided the need to invent new lines for this moment. A similar feature seems to occur in *As You Like It* where, Wilson argues, the song "It was a lover and his lass" (5.3.14) has been incorporated into the text from Thomas Morley's "First Book of Airs" and then is rather amusingly rubbished. Wilson intriguingly points out musical absences, where a song is announced by a character but subsequently omitted from the printed text.[26] Noting the variety of songs in *The Tempest*, Wilson suggests that Shakespeare's company, the King's Men, may have had additional musical resources available to them at the indoor Blackfriars theatre after 1608. Wilson devotes much of his study to musical cues that signal grand entrances or moments of military or political importance in the plays. Flourishes, alarums, tuckets, and sennets all provided a richly sonorous aura to the plays. Drawing on Lorenzo's famous words to Jessica in *The Merchant of Venice*, where the runaway lovers rest for a while, gaze at the stars and contemplate the "music of the spheres", Wilson suggests that Shakespeare's understanding of music was essentially neo-Platonic and informed in particular by the myth of Orpheus as found in Ovid's *Metamorphoses*. For Wilson, Shakespeare's works absorbed "Renaissance musical philosophy"[27] and showed remarkable flexibility in the use of instruments, including the viol, lute, recorder, tabor, cymbal, trumpet, and drum.

But there remains a simple, practical question that seems not to have been asked directly: was Shakespeare musical? Did he have some training and a knowledge of musical theory? Both Lindley and Wilson discuss Hortensio's absurd music tuition with Bianca in *The Taming of the Shrew* (3.1.62–79). Presenting himself as Licio, a music tutor, to Baptista's second daughter, Hortensio hopes to win her hand in marriage. In the music lesson, he asks Bianca first to read through her "gamut" or scale which proceeds "ut", "re", "mi", "fa", "so", and "la". Encoded into this musical language are Hortensio's overly hopeful protestations of affection. Apart from the fact that this scene is (so far as I'm aware) unique in Renaissance drama, what is especially striking about this language is its technicality. A number of late sixteenth-century printed musical texts give a basic explanation of music theory, and Shakespeare might have derived his knowledge from any one of them. But the important point is that Shakespeare gets the technicalities right: he appears to have had some elementary education in music. William Bathe, in his *A Brief Introduction to the Skill of Song*, laments that he must set out in "tedious" or "prolix" fashion the rules of music. He would far rather, as his "Preface to the Reader" states, concentrate on the essential points of the "long ladder" or "skale" of the "Gam-ut". Just as in painting, skill in song comes by hard work: "But ere the Painter can sure his craft attaine,/Much forward facion transformeth hee in vayne" (sig. Aiii^{r}). Hortensio's line, "D sol re, one clef, two notes have I" in particular shows an acquaintance with music theory. As Bathe explains in a table, the note D does indeed have one clef and two notes. Bathe advises his reader to:

> [b]egin at the lowest word, Gam-ut, and so go upwards to the end still ascending, and learn it perfectly without book, to say it forwards and backwards: to know wherein every key standeth, whether in rule or in space: and how many Clefs, how many Notes is contained in every Key.
>
> (Aiv^{v})

Shakespeare might simply have learned this much from an accompanist in or around the playhouse, but it is also a knowledge he seems to have absorbed.

In a witty exchange between Julia and Lucetta in *The Two Gentlemen of Verona*, Lucetta responds, "Nay, now you are too flat/And mar the concord with too harsh a descant:/There wanteth but a mean to fill your song" (1.2.94–6). Julia replies, "the mean is drowned with your unruly bass" (l. 97). Implicit counterpoint in the word "descant" aptly fits this quick-witted dialogue. In a descant, a melody or plainsong is sung above a lower, bass pattern. Thomas Morley, in his *A plaine and easie introduction to practicall musicke* (1597), explains that "Base descant … Is that kind of descanting, where your sight of taking and using your cordes must be under the plainsong … In base descant the base is the ground" (p. 86). As Wilson notes, references to musicality abound in *A Midsummer Night's Dream*. One particularly well-known example occurs late in the play when Theseus, Egeus and Hippolyta appear on stage to the sound of hunting horns. Hippolyta tells of an occasion when Hercules and Cadmus "bayed the bear" in "a wood of Crete", and the mingled sounds of the hunting dogs seemed "so musical a discord". It's an oxymoron that suits a play of confusions, yet this example similarly shows more than a mere acquaintance with music theory. Bathe explains that a "concord" can be achieved by means of notes such as thirds, fifths, sixths and eighths (octaves), while a "discord" occurs when the second, fourth, or seventh notes are played with their eights. Hippolyta's reference to the groves or depths and skies of Crete lend a kind of mythical geography to the musical contrast that Bathe describes as a "Concord", one that makes "discords betwixt the upper part and the plain song or ground" (Ci^{v}). It is at least worth considering the possibility that, by the time Shakespeare arrived in London in the early 1590s, he had already received some basic instruction and perhaps even acquired some small facility in music. The obvious question that then arises is – where might he have gained such an education?

It is of course possible that Shakespeare may have picked up what rudimentary knowledge of music he had from a tutor at Stratford. In 1586, Henry Flatche of Snitterfield was deemed near illiterate and unsuitable for the ministry but nevertheless "he teacheth to plaie on instruments".[28] Psalms and anthems would have been sung at Holy Trinity Church or the Guild Chapel each week, perhaps to some accompaniment, and drums and trumpets would probably have sounded before festive or devotional processions. Another possibility emerges through the research of E. A. J. Honigmann into Shakespeare's "lost years".[29] In 1985, Honigmann published a study that established connections between Stratford schoolmasters, in particular John Cottam, and the families of Alexander de Hoghton and Sir Thomas Hesketh, both of Lancashire. John Weever, who wrote a sonnet "Ad Gulielmus Shakespeare" also had family connections with these and other Lancashire families.[30] In his will of 1581, Alexander Hoghton left instruction that should his brother be unwilling to keep players, then Sir Thomas Hesketh of nearby Rufford should receive his "instruments belonging to musics & play clothes", and that, in any case, Hesketh should "be friendly unto Fulk Gillom & William Shakeshafte" and "take them unto his service or else to help them to some good master". Honigmann confirmed that Gillom was an actor and argued, following E. K. Chambers, that "Shakeshafte" could easily have passed from Sir Thomas Hesketh's household to that of Henry Stanley, fourth earl of Derby and Baron Strange, as Hoghton's will expressed that he might. Henry Stanley's home stood at Lathom House, Lancashire, about five and a half miles south of Rufford. When, on 30 December 1587, Hesketh visited Lord Strange, the *Derby Household Accounts* record,

"Sir Tho. Hesketh Plaiers went awaie".[31] The title page of the first quarto of *Titus Andronicus* (1594) tells us that it was staged by players including those belonging to "the Earle of Darbie". These connections seem, in the words of Leslie Hotson, "an astonishing coincidence" but for all the intrigue they promise, they remain inconclusive.[32]

The often unreliable antiquary John Aubrey reported the story that Shakespeare had, in his youth, been a schoolmaster in the country. Following a line of enquiry established by E. K. Chambers, Honigmann pursued the possibility that Shakespeare's "lost years" might have been spent as a journeyman schoolmaster at Hoghton Tower near Preston, where he lived under the name "William Shakeshaft". This theory has lately fallen out of favour, but should these conjectures ever be substantiated, their significance could not be over-stated. It is worth bearing in mind that Thomas Savage, trustee and sharer in the original Globe Theatre of 1599, came from Rufford, Lancashire, and left twenty shillings to Hesketh's widow in his will. The will also mentions the fact that his youngest son, John, dwells in the same house as John Heminges in the London parish of St. Mary in Aldermanbury.[33] To this we can add that John Cottam, said to have been Shakespeare's last schoolmaster, came from Tarnacre and Rawcliffe, an area very close by. For the detail of these connections, Honigmann's books of 1985 and 1987 are both essential reading.[34] It is unfortunate that the attempt to demonstrate that Shakespeare was a renegade Catholic has tended to distract from the fascinating web of relationships that Honigmann uncovered. Those connections cannot be lightly dismissed.

There remains one as yet unnoticed fact about several of these Lancashire names that links them with Shakespeare's London circle. They, or their immediate family, were members of Gray's Inn. This institution was the largest of the four London inns of court, a lawyers' college to which young men from the shires might be admitted (sometimes via one of the lesser "inns of chancery") by virtue of their family's local standing. Richard and William Hoghton of Hoghton Tower, Gilbert Gerrard (Richard Hoghton's father-in-law) and his son Radcliffe, Thomas Southworth (witness to Alexander Houghton's will), Thomas Hesketh, and Thomas Butler of Rawcliffe (Weever's cousin) all belonged to Gray's Inn. A Thomas Butler played the role of Vice-Chamberlain in the mock-revels at Gray's in 1594, when Shakespeare's *The Comedy of Errors* was also performed there in 1594. We have already noted that Thomas Savage of Rufford, trustee of the Globe, was a near-neighbour of Sir Thomas Hesketh who styled himself "of Gray's Inn, gent". His fellow Globe trustee, William Leveson, was younger brother of Sir John Leveson who had been admitted to Gray's Inn in 1576. Richard Hoghton was admitted in 1586, the same year as Robert Salusbury, heir to Sir John Salusbury to whom Shakespeare dedicated *The Phoenix and the Turtle.* Henry Stanley and his son William (sixth earl of Derby), who was brother-in-law to Sir John Salusbury, were also members of Gray's Inn. Shakespeare performed *The Comedy of Errors at Gray's Inn* on 28 December 1594. This single London institution unites the interests of all of these individuals and their families, over and above the connections between them established by Honigmann. Yet there remains no persuasive evidence that Shakespeare was "Shakeshafte", and families with that surname lived in the Preston area. Nevertheless, a domestic comedy like *The Taming of the Shrew* seems to exhibit some acquaintance with the kind of larger household in which the arts were, in a limited way perhaps, fostered. Shakespeare may well have had experience similar to that of "Shakeshafte". When Derby's Men played *Titus Andronicus*, Shakespeare plausibly would have been among them. He did not need to have been in Lancashire to have received training in the arts that any young apprentice player might have experienced in a country household.

Shakespeare's relationship with the wider arts of his time raises both theoretical and practical questions. Some of the theoretical problems turn on whether we see him as a fantasy storyteller or a realist. Did he amend life with imagination and transform it, as Ariel sings in *The Tempest*, into something "rich and strange", or did he portray characters with an eye to social observation, as – in Heminges' and Condell's words – "a happie imitator of Nature" ("To the great Variety of Readers", A3^{r})? These kinds of questions are raised by the works themselves, especially in passages that invite comparative judgements about the virtues of drama, poetry, art, and music. Shakespeare worked with a literate and informed awareness of aesthetic practice, and for this he needed two things: a library and practical experience. Life in a large country household could have given him just that. When, in 1594, Shakespeare came to perform *The Comedy of Errors* in the great hall at Gray's Inn, his audience probably included acquaintances, perhaps some from Warwickshire (Thomas, son of Sir Thomas Lucas of Stratford-upon Avon was admitted to Gray's in 1604). In the end, most of these associations remain circumstantial. But we can be certain that by 1592, when Shakespeare was identified as an "upstart crow" in London, he had somewhere acquired skills of poetry, artistry, and musicality that could turn an old tale into something "livelier than life", in the words of Timon's poet.

Notes

1 Edwin Nungezer, *A Dictionary of Actors and of Other Persons Associated with the Public Representation of Plays in England* (New Haven, CT: 1929; Providence, RI: AMS, 1971), pp. 216–22.
2 Tarnya Cooper et al. (eds.), *Searching for Shakespeare* (London: National Portrait Gallery, 2006), p. 54.
3 TNA Prob/11/217.
4 Mary Edmond, "It Was for Gentle Shakespeare Cut", *Shakespeare Quarterly*, 43, 3 (Autumn, 1991): 339–44. Peter Holland, "William Shakespeare", *Oxford Dictionary of National Biography* (Oxford: Oxford University Press, 2004), www.oxforddnb.com/view/article/25200?docPos=8. For a valuable discussion of the Droeshout engraving and the Chandos painting, see Katherine Duncan-Jones, *Portraits of Shakespeare* (Oxford: Bodleian Library, 2015).
5 Glynne Wickham, *English Professional Theatre, 1530 to 1660* (Cambridge: Cambridge University Press, 2000), p. 613, 642.
6 T. Cooper, *Searching For Shakespeare*, p. 52.
7 Tarnya Cooper, Aviva Burnstock, Maurice Howard, and Edward Town, et al., *Painting in Britain, 1500 to 1630: Production, Influences and Patronage* (London: The British Academy/ Oxford University Press, 2015), pp. 66–9.
8 Ibid., pp. 84–7.
9 Ibid., p. 100.
10 Edward Town, "A Biographical Dictionary of London Painters, 1547–1625", *Walpole Society*, 76 (2014): 1–235, Index of Painters by Ward and Parish, pp. 228–35.
11 Other useful accounts of early modern painting are found in Maurice Howard, *The Tudor Image* (London: Tate Gallery, 1995), Robert Tittler, *The Face of the City: Civic Portraiture and Civic Identity in Early Modern England* (Manchester, UK and New York: Manchester University Press, 2007), and Erin C. Blake, "Shakespeare, Portraiture, Painting and Prints", in Mark Thornton Burnett, Adrian Streete and Ramona Wray (eds.) *The Edinburgh Companion to Shakespeare and the Arts* (Edinburgh: Edinburgh University Press, 2011), pp. 409–34.
12 References are from Colin Burrow (ed.), *The Complete Sonnets and Poems* (Oxford: Oxford University Press, 2002).

13 Jean Paul Richter and Irma A. Richter (eds.), *The Literary Works of Leonardo da Vinci, Compiled and Edited from the Original Manuscripts* (Oxford: Oxford University Press, 1939), 2 vols, 1, p. 201.
14 Jean Hagstrum, *The Sister Arts: The Tradition of Literary Pictorialism and English Poetry from Dryden to Gray* (Chicago, IL: University of Chicago Press, 1958), p. 58.
15 John Davies, *The Muses Sacrifice* (London, 1612), p. 113^{v}.
16 See Katherine Duncan-Jones, "Sidney and Titian", in *English Renaissance Studies, Presented to Dame Helen Gardner in Honour of Her Seventieth Birthday* (Oxford: Clarendon Press, 1980), pp. 1–11. Duncan-Jones's *Portraits of Shakespeare* gives important discussion of the Stratford bust, the Droeshout engraving and the Chandos portrait. It argues (pp. 81–91) that the actor Joseph Taylor painted the Chandos portrait between 1610 and 1615, at a time when Shakespeare was still in London.
17 References are from Burrow (ed.), *The Complete Sonnets and Poems* (Oxford: Oxford University Press, 2002).
18 Cooper et al., *Searching for Shakespeare*, p. 133.
19 John Davies of Hereford, *Microcosmos* (London, 1603), p. 215
20 Cooper et al., *Painting in Britain*, 1500–1630, pp. 171–9, 177.
21 E. K. Chambers, *William Shakespeare: A Study of Facts and Problems*, 2 vols. (Oxford: Clarendon Press, 1930), II, p. 153.
22 Ibid., p. 153.
23 For example Janette Dillon, "Shakespeare and English Performance Style: The European Context", *Shakespeare Survey*, 54 (Cambridge: Cambridge University Press, 2001), pp. 191–200, 198.
24 David Lindley, *Shakespeare and Music* (London and New York: Bloomsbury, 2006), pp. 2–3.
25 Christopher R. Wilson, "Shakespeare and Early Modern Music", in Mark Thornton Burnett, Adrian Streete and Ramona Wray (eds.), *The Edinburgh Companion to Shakespeare and the Arts* (Edinburgh: Edinburgh University Press, 2011), pp. 119–41, 120. See also Christopher Marsh, *Music and Society in Early Modern England* (Cambridge: Cambridge University Press, 2010), and Jessie Ann Owens (ed.), *"Noyses, Sounds and Sweet Aires": Music in Early Modern England* (Washington, DC: The Folger Shakespeare Library, 2006).
26 Ibid., p. 121.
27 Ibid., p. 131.
28 Christopher Marsh, p. 207.
29 E. A. J. Honigmann, *Shakespeare. The "Lost Years"* (Manchester, UK: Manchester University Press, 1985).
30 Ibid., xiii.
31 Alan Keen and Roger Lubbock, *The Annotator* (London: Putnam, 1954), p. 47. Keen and Lubbock emphasise the absence of any comma in this line, confirming that the players were Hesketh's. See also E. K. Chambers, *Shakespearean Gleanings* (Oxford: Clarendon Press, 1944), pp. 52–6.
32 Leslie Hotson, *Shakespeare's Sonnets Dated* (London: Rupert Hart-Davis, 1949), p. 129.
33 Honigmann, *Shakespeare. The "Lost Years"*, p. 143.
34 Honigmann, *Shakespeare. The "Lost Years"* and *John Weever: A Biography of a Literary Associate of Shakespeare and Jonson, Together with a Photographic Facsimile of Weever's Epigrammes* (Manchester, UK: Manchester University Press, 1987).

16 'Absolute Castilio'?

The reputation and reception of Castiglione's *Book of the Courtier* in Elizabethan England

Mary Partridge

Woodhouse described Balthazar Castiglione's *Libro del Cortegiano* as the "most widely-known least-read book of the Renaissance".[1] In early modern England it was both widely-known and well-read; the challenge is to explore its reception and influence. First published in Venice in 1528, Castiglione's dialogue purported to record four after-dinner discussions that took place at the brilliant Court of Urbino, where Castiglione served duke Guidobaldo da Montefeltro and his duchess, Elisabetta Gonzago. The discussions were inspired by a challenge that Federico Fregoso devised for the company: "to shape in woordes a good Courtyer".[2] Thomas Hoby published the first complete English translation in 1561, announcing that Castiglione's courtier had "become an Englishman".[3]

In England and elsewhere in Europe, the concept of a "good Courtyer" had traditionally been treated as an oxymoron. Rosemary Horrox notes that criticism of the monarch's *familiares* "remained constant over a surprisingly long period".[4] The consistency of anti-courtier invective is particularly noticeable in descriptions of courtly dress and demeanour. Censorious Anglo-Norman clerics provided a template for such descriptions. William of Malmesbury (c. 1090 – c. 1142) despaired of William II's *familiares*:

> Long flowing hair, luxurious garments, shoes with curved and pointed tips became the fashion. Softness of body rivalling the weaker sex, a mincing gait, effeminate gestures and a liberal display of the person as they went along, such was the ideal fashion of the younger men.[5]

Castiglione acknowledged the pervasive image of the courtier as a wanton fop:

> [t]hey say in these dayes … in Courtes there reigneth nothynge elles but enuye and malyce, yllmaners, and a most wanton lyfe in euery kinde of vice: the women enticefull past shame, and the men womanishe. They disprayse also the apparalle to be dishonest and to softe.[6]

Castiglione's reference to "enuye and malice" also reflects the assumption that courtiers were grasping, sycophantic, back-stabbing individuals, obsessed with their own advancement. This charge was levelled with particular vehemence at successful courtiers

DOI: 10.4324/9781315612720-19

from relatively humble backgrounds. The poet Claudian had warned that "Nothing is so cruel as a man raised from lowly station to prosperity; he strikes everything, for he fears everything".[7] Heinrich Cornelius Agrippa similarly cautioned that "common or meane Courtiers ... alwaiess tande gapinge like Rauins, for giftes of the Courte".[8]

Castiglione's dialogue was novel, because his interlocutors sought to demonstrate that courtiers could make a serious, positive contribution to public affairs. A model courtier would use his wit and accomplishments to win the favour of his prince. He would subsequently encourage the latter to rule justly, wisely and virtuously. "Wherfore", as Ottaviano observes in Book IV of the dialogue, "perhappes a man may say that to beecome the Instructor of a Prince were the ende of a Courtier". Aristotle and Plato had not considered such a task beneath their dignity. Courtiership was a legitimate occupation, with enormous potential.[9] Castiglione therefore provided a comprehensive analysis of the courtier's role and responsibilities.

The claims made by the Urbino interlocutors on behalf of the courtly profession were lofty indeed. Arguably, they reflected the growing political, social, economic and cultural significance of the Court in early modern Europe. The Renaissance Court was a very different entity from its peripatetic medieval predecessor. Elias attributed the enhancement of its status "to the advancing centralisation of state power", which ensured that "the monarch's court and court society formed a powerful and prestigious elite".[10] Other social historians, such as Stone, highlighted "the enormous expansion of the Court and the central administration" in the early modern era. Stone regarded this trend as a crucial component of the "crisis" that he famously imputed to the sixteenth- and seventeenth-century aristocracy: "Everywhere the nobility was sucked into this vortex ... Once-formidable local potentates were transformed into fawning courtiers".[11]

Stone's reference to "fawning courtiers" indicates that the stereotype of the emasculated courtier, politically impotent and personally degenerate, was still alive and well in the twentieth century. It may have encouraged historians to underestimate the significance of courtliness, and courtly conduct literature, whilst acknowledging that the Court itself was a nerve-centre of politics and government. Elton half-jokingly suggested that Court culture was an irritating distraction from the serious business that was transacted at Court. He attempted to differentiate "mere" courtiers, whose expertise was largely confined to entertainment and adornment, from statesmen who happened to be based at Court.[12]

Other factors contributed to the marginalization of *Il Cortegiano* in early modern British historiography. Whiggish historians' preoccupation with the "steadily growing" strength of Parliament in the sixteenth and seventeenth centuries cast the courtier as a doomed anachronism.[13] The march along the high road to civil war left him trailing in its wake. Marxist historians rejected the long-term constitutional emphasis of Whig history, but offered instead their own grand narrative of modernization. They attributed the civil wars and interregnum to the inexorable rise of a politically active "bourgeois" class.[14] This interpretative framework could not easily accommodate *Il Cortegiano* in any capacity, other than that of an obstruction to be flattened by the locomotive of history.

The revisionist emphasis on short-term causality and personal politics (the métier of *Il Cortegiano*) facilitated a reappraisal of the courtier's reputation among historians.[15] This development was reinforced by a more interdisciplinary approach to the study of early modern politics. Investigations into the physical structure of princely households proved particularly fruitful, demonstrating the political significance of these nominally domestic institutions.[16] Starkey highlighted the segregation of royal living quarters from the remainder of the establishment, which occurred (and was enforced with increasing rigidity) during the late medieval and early Tudor period.[17] Access to the Privy Chamber was an invaluable political commodity; it afforded those who enjoyed it the opportunity to cultivate the favour of, and therefore to influence, the prince. *Il Cortegiano* was specifically designed to accomplish these objectives with irresistible grace.

The qualities that distinguished him from the flattering favourites of traditional anti-curial discourse (who also cultivated royal favour assiduously) were his nonchalant grace – *sprezzatura* – and his benevolent agenda. Ottaviano invoked the Ciceronian ethos of public service in his eloquent exposition of the Courtier's ultimate objective:

> The endetherfore of a perfect Courtier … is to purchase him, by the meane of the qualities which these Lordes have given him, in such wise the good will and favour of the Prince he is in service withall, that he may breake his minde to him, and alwaiesenfourme him francklye of the trueth of everie matter meete for him to understande, without fear or perill to displease him. And … to disswade him from euerie ill pourpose, and set him in *th*e waye of vertue.[18]

Starkey describes this passage as "the axis of the *Courtier*", which justifies the dialogue and explains why it was able to counteract deeply embedded assumptions about the depravity of Court culture.[19] In a culture that extolled Cicero's *De officiis*, and wasted few opportunities to quote the injunction that "we be not borne for our selues alone", Castiglione explicitly linked courtly conduct with Ciceronian devotion to the *vita activa* and the commonweal.[20] He rescued the courtier's image from a literary tradition that castigated courtiers as self-serving enemies of the commonwealth.[21] Moreover, as Woolfson observes, "in the dedicatory letter to his translation of the *Cortegiano*, Hoby … presents Castiglione as the new Cicero, the Cicero for Hoby's time".[22] This validated *Il Cortegiano* for an early modern English readership.

Scholars often suggest that, in England, *Il libro del Cortegiano* was assimilated eagerly and (generally) uncritically. Rowse asserts that Castiglione completely defined "the ideal of a courtier", adding that it is "remarkable how closely the profession of courtier, even in England, adhered to his specification".[23] Siegel concurs: "Castiglione's *Courtier*, in Hoby's translation, was the most influential source of [the] ideal of the courtier".[24] Javitch's analysis of Elizabethan courtliness was deliberately based upon *Il libro del Cortegiano*:

> My dependence on the Italian book is not arbitrary … by relying on the Italian code to define model norms of late Tudor courtliness, I actually imitate Elizabethan writers who, instead of formulating anew the requisites of the English courtier, simply deferred to Castiglione's prescriptions.[25]

Woolfson does not suggest that *Il Cortegiano* himself was simply cut and pasted into English cultural consciousness, but uses Hoby's translation – a literary model of Castiglionean *sprezzatura* – to highlight "the imitative origins of the English Renaissance".[26]

Scholars who argue that Castiglione's courtier materialized on the Elizabethan scene fully developed, like Venus from the sea, often cite two contemporary references to

Hoby's translation. Roger Ascham famously commended the work in his *Scholemaster*. Ascham endorsed Castiglione unreservedly, asserting that his teachings should be "diligentlie followed" by young gentlemen. "I meruell", he added, "this booke, is no more read in the Court, than it is, seying it is so well translated into English by a worthie Ientleman Syr Th. Hobbie".[27] The anonymous author of a dialogue *Of Cyuile and Vncyuile Life*, published in 1586, was still more evangelical. During the course of the dialogue, the sophisticated city-dweller Valentine declines to describe a good courtier to his rustic friend, Vincent: "For to take vpon mee to frame a Courtier were presumption, I leaue that to the Earle Baldazar, whose Booke translated by Sir Thomas Hobby, I thinke you haue, or ought to hauereade". Valentine subsequently reiterates that "I will speake no more of Court, but ... wish you to peruse the booke of the Courtier". In the closing exchanges, Vincent summarizes everything he has learned from Valentine. He recounts a few points "Touching the Court and Cittie"; "Concerning the rest, you referre mee to the Booke of the Courtier".[28] Castiglione's work was thus presented as the definitive guide to courtly conduct.

Individual Englishmen were sometimes paid the compliment of being identified with, or as, *Il Cortegiano*. Pietro Bizzari composed a poem in honour of John Astley, the master of Queen Elizabeth's jewel house.[29] Bizzari characterized *Il Cortegiano* as a superhuman paragon – but argued that if anyone could claim to embody him, it was Astley.[30] Gabriel Harvey endorsed this verdict, describing Astley as "a rare gentleman ... I marvel not that Pietro Bizzaro, a learned Italian, proposeth him for a perfect pattern of Castilio's courtier".[31] Writing in praise of Sir Philip Sidney, Thomas Nashe described a discussion that he initiated "with manie extraordinary Gentlemen ... touching the seuerall qualities required in Castalions Courtier". Nashe's companions agreed that *Il Cortegiano* personified an impossible ideal. However, "the vpshot" of the conversation was consensus "that England ... neuer saw any thing more singuler then worthy Sir Phillip Sidney".[32] Nashe and Bizzari both equated *Il Cortegiano* with unobtainable perfection – and then gave him an English face by nominating an Elizabethan courtier as his closest mortal approximation.

The cultural authority of *Il libro del Cortegiano* is indicated by the fact that it was cited to vindicate a range of ideas and activities. The author of the *Booke of Honor and Armes*, for example, used it to justify the controversial practice of duelling:

> [a]lbeit I am not ignorant that publique Combats are in this age either rarely of neuergraunted; yet ... *Balthazer Castilio* in his booke of the Courtier, doth among other qualities require in a gentleman, specially aduise that he should be skilfull in the knowing of Honor, and causes of quarrel.[33]

In his *Autobiography*, the composer Thomas Wythorne tackled the question of whether a gentleman should strive to become a skilled musician, or whether virtuosity was better left to wage-dependent professionals. Wythorne contested the latter argument, noting "*the* book named *Đe Coortier*, doth will [gentlemen] to learne miuzik".[34] Castiglione's approval was thus played like a trump card by apologists for various cultural trends.

Like other early modern texts, *Il libro del Cortegiano* served as a repository of wisdom, from which case studies, phrases and facts were mined and recycled.[35] The plays of Shakespeare have (inevitably) been dusted repeatedly for Castiglione's fingerprints. There is no conclusive proof that Shakespeare read *Il libro del Cortegiano*. Regrettably, the inscription in a 1603 edition – "Thys little Booke I haue reade withe muche pleasure as I do fynde therein manye thinges thate bee righte profitable … Wm Shakespeare" – is a forgery.[36] However, it seems very likely that the playwright was familiar with the work. Whether this likelihood can support some of the theories that have taken it as their foundation is another issue. For example, Mary Augusta Scott's attempt to demonstrate that the "merry war" between Benedick and Beatrice in *Much Ado About Nothing* was a reproduction of the sparring between Pallavicino and Emilia Pia at Urbino is not entirely convincing.[37] As Shrank and Pincombe point out, the advent of New Historicism in the 1980s did not eliminate the assumption that the value of most early modern texts was their capacity to "shed light on familiar, often Shakespearean material".[38] Recently, Anglo-Italian scholars such as Marrapodi have proposed a less restrictive alternative to "the philosophy of the old historical approach [which] insisted on the idea of a borrowed source":

> From the traditional idea of a given source … we have moved on to a larger process of [Italian] cultural influence, mostly operating unconsciously, which has implied the existence of a "deep", ultimate source.[39]

Hence, for example, Cohen analyses Shakespeare's *Henry V* as a "kaleidoscope of courtly character traits", rather than a mere imitation of *Il Cortegiano*.[40] Elam similarly seeks to move away from an interpretative model that demands the one-way, linear transmission of material from an Italian source into the Shakespearean canon: "What takes place between [Renaissance Italian and English] cultures … is a dialogue between dialogues".[41]

As well as facilitating cross-cultural dialogue, *Il libro del Cortegiano* provided guidance on manners and morals. There was a certain tension between representations of the Courtier as an impossible ideal (like More's *Utopia* or Plato's *Republic*), and the idea that his strategies could actually be emulated. In *Greenes Farewell to Folly*, Lady Katherin observes that her mother "séekes not with Baldeslar to figure out a courtier in impossibilities".[42] Oxford's preface to *De Curiali* is slightly ambiguous. Oxford suggests the Courtier represents a perfect – hence purely conceptual – prototype. However, he asserts that men's manners should improve upon nature, and that Castiglione has demonstrated how this can be done.[43]

Burke argues that the process of publication changed the *Courtier* from a complex philosophical text into a straightforward "how-to" guide to court culture. Throughout the sixteenth and seventeenth centuries, the book "acquired an increasingly elaborate 'paratext'". Indexes, notes, tables of contents, even bullet-point summaries of the dialogues, were added.[44] These tools facilitated consultation and cross-referencing, but also, according to Burke "flattened and decontextualized" the work: "the paratext helped transform the *Courtier* from an open dialogue … into a closed treatise, an instruction manual, or one might even say a 'recipe-book'".[45]

Throughout the sixteenth century, demand for manuals that codified and clarified "civil" behaviour became increasingly vociferous. Bryson has explored this phenomenon, addressing elements of ambiguity in the relationship between "specialized literature on prudent and correct behaviour at court" and books directed, more generally, at those who aspired to gentility or social *savoir faire*.[46] She points out that "English conditions" in the early Tudor period were very different to those of the Italian city states in which the most popular courtesy manuals were conceived.[47] The significant distinction was that "England, like France, was a country dominated by a rural aristocracy". In a parochial and paternalistic community, social relations were defined by a linear hierarchy. Italian courtesy literature presupposed an urban(e) environment, in which "friends of equivalent status and culture" were concentrated.[48] Castiglione and Annibale Romei, author of the *Discorsi del conte Annibale Romei* (translated as the *Courtiers academie*), reduced disparity of status among their interlocutors still further by removing the prince from their dialogues. In *Il libro del Cortegiano*, duke Guidobaldo is forced to retire soon after supper "by reason of his infirmytye".[49] In Romei's *Discorsi*, the "gratious conuersation" of the principal interlocutors begins when Alfonso II, duke of Ferrera, disappears to the seaside.[50] In states such as Urbino and Ferrera, the congregation of educated, cultivated equals was characteristic of the city and the Court. Hence, the codes of conduct associated with the two locations were often invoked interchangeably.[51]

Such emphasis on "horizontal" interaction was a relatively novel component of Court culture in Elizabethan England.[52] In medieval chronicles, the chief protagonists at English courts were generally barons or favourites. The former were essentially free agents; their castles, lands and military resources allowed them act independently.[53] The latter, by contrast, were locked in an exclusively bilateral relationship with the prince. They were often accused of manipulating or dominating the monarch. However, they had no other friends or protectors. Once alienated from their masters or mistresses, they were helpless. There is scant precedent in this umbilical relationship for the social virtuosity of *Il Cortegiano. Il Cortegiano* works hard to win his prince's favour, but never ceases to contextualize himself in civil conversation with his peers.[54]

Italian courtesy literature therefore encouraged English readers to identify the values of the Court with those of civil society. "Civil society" encompassed city-dwellers, and the burgeoning number of wealthy or well-born men and women periodically exposed to metropolitan life.[55] Moreover, as the concept of civility was closely intertwined with that of citizenship,[56] it also incorporated provincial gentlemen who devoted themselves to the commonweal.[57] This explains why Castiglione's dialogue was eagerly studied by readers who neither aspired nor expected to attend the royal Court. In an era of social mobility, it facilitated the reinterpretation of notions of courtliness and gentility. Fernie and Wray highlight the recent critical interest in such processes of reinterpretation: "the post-theory twenty-first-century Renaissance has come to be envisaged as an intensely fraught and turbulent period, in which constructions of class, race and gender were negotiated".[58]

English readers' apparent willingness to embrace an Italian model of courtliness might prompt us to ask whether *Il Cortegiano* did, in fact, "become an Englishman", as Hoby claimed. As a translator, Hoby's stated intention was to "folow the very meaning & woordes of the Author" as closely as possible.[59] This attitude can be contrasted with that of Castiglione's Polish translator, Lukasz Górnicki. Górnicki reinvented the Urbino interlocutors as Polish notables, gathered in the villa of Bishop Samuel Maciejowski in the summer of 1549. The title of his translation – *Dworzaninpoliski*, or *The Polish Courtier* – reflects his determination to give *Il Cortegiano* a new context and identity.[60] Hoby had no such ambitions; his *Covrtyer* remained an authentically Italian creature.[61] Yet Waddington argues that English men and women felt a special affinity for Castiglione, who had travelled to England in 1506 to be invested with the Order of the Garter on behalf of duke Guidobaldo. According to Waddington, "members of the

Tudor courts would have seen *The Courtier* as a book written by an honorary Englishman who had participated in the highest ceremony of knighthood".[62] They were consequently willing to overlook the foreignness of the book and its author.

Whether or not Castiglione was regarded as an "honorary Englishman", the Italian origins of *Il libro del Cortegiano* may actually have enhanced its appeal in mid-Tudor England. Hoby translated Book III of the dialogue during Edward VI's reign, dedicating his work to Elizabeth Parr, Marchioness of Northampton.[63] Overell has noted that several Protestant, Edwardian "progressives" were also Italophiles (or at least demonstrated an enthusiastic interest in Italian culture). For instance, the formidably learned Anne Cooke, future wife of Nathaniel Bacon, sister-in-law of Lord Burghley and mother of Francis Bacon, translated the sermons of Bernardino Ochino.[64] The fact that many high-profile Italians in Edwardian England were Protestant refugees may help to explain why reformers like Cooke embraced the language and literature of a predominantly Catholic country.[65] Similarly, as Woolfson observes, Hoby and his fellow Protestant Italophile William Thomas "may well have been drawn to" the mid-sixteenth-century Florentine Academy during their travels in Italy "because of its reformist and anti-clerical tendencies". These tendencies excited them, whilst not entirely eliminating "an already well-established Protestant tradition of negative stereotypes" about Catholic Italy.[66] More generally, as "the centre of humanistic civilization", Italy exuded glamour for progressive intellectuals across the confessional spectrum.[67]

Italian courtliness retained a certain cachet in early-to-mid Elizabethan England. In 1578, Gabriel Harvey could proudly report that Queen Elizabeth had told him he looked just like an Italian when he entertained her with an oration at Audley End.[68] Harvey was ridiculed for this piece of boasting.[69] Yet the glamour of Italian court culture can be gauged from the paratext to Simon Robson's *The Covrte of Ciuill Courtesie* (first published in 1577). The printer, Richard Jones, asserted that the text had been translated "Out of the Italian", "as hee that brought it vnto me made reporte ... by a Gentleman, a freeinde of his, desyringemee that it might bee printed".[70] In fact, it seems probable that Robson was the sole and original author of his entirely English treatise.[71] He clearly regarded Italian conduct manuals as the pinnacle of marketable sophistication.

It is worth noting how seriously many authors and readers took Italian courtesy literature. Traditionally, Court culture had been criticized for its mindless frivolity. However, in 1581, we find the author George Pettie explaining that he has translated an Italian conduct manual because he wishes to be taken seriously as a writer. Pettie had previously published a compendium of stories entitled *A Petite Pallace of Pettie His Pleasure*. In a textbook demonstration of Castiglionean *sprezzatura*, he referred to the *Palace* as "a trifling woorke of mine", which had earned him a reputation for whimsical triviality. Therefore, wrote Pettie, "I thought it stoode mee vppon, to purchase to my selfe some better fame by some better woorke, and to counteruayle my former vanitee, with some formal grauitie".[72] The text with which hoped to build his reputation for *gravitas* was a translation of Stefano Guazzo's *Ciuile conuersation*.

Robert Peterson translated another Italian courtesy manual – Giovanni Della Casa's *Galateo* – as a means of securing preferment. Peterson dedicated his translation, published in 1576, to Robert Dudley, earl of Leicester. Dudley's behaviour conformed very closely to courtesy manual prescriptions. This fact was highlighted by Peterson, who described him as "the patterne to expresse any courtesie ... contained" in the text. Peterson took pains to emphasize that his *Galateo* "presumeth not to be guide" for a courtier as proficient as Dudley. He would merely be grateful "if your honour daine at higheleasure to peruse it". Such a vote of confidence "will so credit the Author, as wil embolden him to presse amongst the thickest throng of Courtiers".[73] Peterson clearly hoped for patronage on the strength of his translation (and Rosenberg suggests that the apparent cessation of his literary activities until 1606 indicates that he was otherwise employed in the interim).[74]

The publication history of a third conduct manual illustrates the momentum of the vogue for Castiglionean courtesy literature during the first two decades of Elizabeth's reign. In 1575, George North produced his English translation of Philibert de Vienne's *Le Philosophe de court.* Vienne's original treatise was in fact a lampoon of Castiglionean courtliness, designed to expose the perversity of the value system advocated by disciples of *Il Cortegiano.*[75] It was first published in Lyons, in 1547. Smith identifies a strong "anti-courtier trend" in mid- to late-sixteenth-century French literature, suggesting that the cult of Castiglione was viewed with growing hostility because of its Italian origins. Italian infiltration of the French court, following the marriage of Catherine de Medici to the Dauphin in 1533, was widely resented by the native population. Catherine's compatriots were cast as self-serving carpet-baggers, whose polished courtly wiles enabled them to cheat honest patriots out of position and influence. Italian conduct literature was savagely satirized.[76] In England, however, North's translation was accepted as a straightforward imitation of *Il libro del Cortegiano.* It is not entirely clear whether North himself was fully aware of the *Philosopher*'s satirical character, or whether he simply failed to register or relay the nuances of Vienne's tongue-in-cheek commentary. Javitch inclines to the latter view. Whilst demonstrating that the translator modified a few of Vienne's more outrageous statements, he argues that this manipulation of the text was not intended to alter its fundamental significance.[77]

Despite this apparently uncritical attitude towards Castiglionean courtesy books, by the mid-1570s, many English authors were becoming increasingly suspicious of Italian literature. It is true that they often treated Castiglione as a honourable exception when Italian manners and morals were criticized. Ascham, for example, juxtaposed praise for *Il libro del Cortegiano* with shuddering censure of Italy and its inhabitants.[78] Nonetheless, as the forces of the Counter-Reformation became more vociferous and militant, Elizabethan attitudes towards Italy became more complex, resulting in what Marrapodi has described as an "ambivalent iconography", whereby Italy was "encoded at the same time as the origin of poetry and art and as the site of intrigue, vice and political corruption".[79] The latter element of this "ambivalent iconography" was highlighted by Lord Burghley, when he castigated the peninsula as a hotbed of vice and irreligion: "suffer not thy Sonnes to pass the Alpes. For they shall learne nothing there, but Pride, Blasphemy, & Atheism".[80] Italian Court culture was also associated with sexual immorality; Elam notes that Thomas Coryate, who visited Venice, claimed that the term courtesan "is derived from the Italian word *cortesia* that signifieth courtesie". Hence, "in Coryate's dubious derivation the courtesan becomes nothing less than an expression of Italian Renaissance *civitas*, with a probably glance at Castiglone's *Il Cortegiano*".[81]

By the 1590s, *Il libro del Cortegiano*'s reputation was suffering from its association with two widely reviled components of Italian culture. The first was "popery" (despite the fact that Castiglione's dialogue had been placed on the Vatican Index of Prohibited Books). As Cohen observes, "Protestant attacks against Cortegiano frequently took issue with what Lionel Trilling has called the 'culture of performance' that is so integral to the dialogue".[82] The second, associated, evil was Machiavellianism. The corrosive effect of these connotations is evident in the satire of Everard Guilpin, who railed against the disingenuous politics practiced by modern, Italianate courtiers. As Marrapodi notes (referring to English drama) "The influence of Machiavelli and Castiglione as source texts ... appears particularly effective ... in parodic and satiric works".[83] Guilpin described "curtesie" as a "mumming device, taught by Signior Machiauell". He then turned his attention to Castiglione: "Come to the Court, and Balthazar affords/ Fountains of holy and rose-water words".[84] The reference to "holy and rose-water words" was confessionally loaded, recalling what Guilpin, and many of his readers, would have regarded as Catholic superstition. It also hints at Balthazar's lack of substance; holy water was a metaphor for something that promised much, but delivered no results. In 1600, for example, John Chamberlain reported that supporters of the disgraced earl of Essex were hopeful that their patron would soon be restored to royal favour. However, until Elizabeth graced Essex with a meaningful boon, Chamberlain resolved to "esteem words as winde and holy water of court".[85] Guilpin's satire thus associated Castiglionean court culture with popery, pretence and *politique* practice:

> [a]ll our actions in a simpathy
> Doe daunce an anticke with hypocrisie,
> And motley fac'd Dissimulation,
> Is crept into our eueryfashion.[86]

Machiavelli and Castiglione stood jointly accused (and convicted) of "hypocrisie" and "dissimulation".

John Marston's treatment of *Il Cortegiano* was equally brutal. Marston's archetypal courtier was "the absolute *Castilio*/He that can all the points of courtship show":

> He that can trot a Courser, break a rush,
> And arm'd in proofe, dare dure a strawes strong push.
> He, who on his glorious scutchion
> Can quaintly show wits *newe* inuention,
> Aduancing forth some, thirstie *Tantalus*,
> Or els the Vulture on Promethius,
> With some short motto of a dozen lines,
> He that can purpose it in dainty rimes.[87]

At the Accession Day tilts, Elizabethan courtiers carried *imprese*, which were presented to the queen and subsequently displayed at Whitehall.[88] Camden defined an *impresa* as "a device with his Motte, or Word, borne by noble and learned personages, to notifie some particular conceit of their owne".[89] It demonstrated that a courtier's martial prowess, to be proved in the lists, was complemented by his learning and mental agility.[90] This seemingly effortless combination of athleticism, erudition and wit was a signature characteristic of *Il Cortegiano*. Hence, Marston's scutcheon-carrying courtier was an "absolute *Castilio*". However, his shield was embellished with images traditionally used to illustrate the depravity and misery of courtiers. Tantalus and the scavenger bird were familiar emblems of anti-courtier discourse. In his *De nugiscurialium* (*Courtier's trifles*), for example, the twelfth-century courtier and cleric Walter Map likened the Court to Hell. "Have you read how Tantalus down there catches at streams which shun his lips?" he inquired conversationally. "Here you may see many a one thirsting for the goods of others which he fails to get, and like a drinker, misses them at the moment of seizure".[91] The images of Tantalus reaching for sustenance that always eludes him, and of the vulture ripping out Prometheus's liver over and over again, suggest voracious appetite and unending torture – both of which were deemed intrinsic to the courtier's condition. Moreover, both Prometheus and Tantalus were arrogant and ambitious, overreaching themselves in attempts to undermine the edicts and authority of the gods.[92] Again, critics of the court had long argued that such tragic flaws were typical of its inhabitants. Through his *impresa*, Castilio therefore revealed his unreconstructed viciousness. Marston subverted the new ideal of a courtier by saddling it, so to speak, with the iconography of medieval anti-curialism.

The satire proceeded with a swipe at the Castiglionean model of the courtier-lover. Castilio, claimed Marston, could only woo with hackney gestures and banal platitudes. He could "dally with his Mistres dangling seake,/And wish that he were it, to kisse her eye/And flare about her beauties deitie".[93] That was about his limit. In the *Scourge of Villanie*, Marston dismissed "perfum'd Castilio" as an idiot:

Who nere read farther then his Mistris lips,
Nerepractiz'd ought, but som spruce capring skips
Nere in his life did other language vse,
But, Sweete Lady, faire Mistres, kind hart, dearecouse.[94]

He was similarly scathing about *Il Cortegiano*'s proficiency as a lover in his Italianate tragedy, *Antonio and Mellida* (c. 1600). The play features a popinjay named Signor Castilio Balthazar, who boasts of the love letters he has received from the besotted ladies of Piero's court. Challenged to produce one such epistle, he shows his companion a "seeming letter", which turns out to be an unpaid tailor's bill (III. 2. 91–106).[95] He thus has the props of a lover; but on closer inspection they prove inauthentic. His financial insolvency, highlighted by the unpaid bill, reflects a general lack of resources.

Returning to the *Scourge of Villanie*, having damned *Il Cortegiano* with sarcastic praise, Marston swung into snarling attack mode:

Tut, he is famous for his reuling,
For fine sette speeches, and for sonnetting,
He scornes the viol and the scraping sticke,
And yet's but Broker of anothers wit.
Certes if all things were well knowne and view'd
He doth but champe that which another chew'd.[96]

The allusion to regurgitation recalls some of the more revolting imagery of the *De curialium miseries* literary tradition.[97] Marston completed his exposé of Castilio's inadequacy with an annihilating exhortation:

Come come Castilion, skim thy posset curd,
Shew thy queere substance, worthlesse, most absurd.
Take ceremonious complement from thee,
Alas, I see Castilio's beggary.[98]

Marston thus claimed to have dispelled the smoke and shattered the mirrors surrounding *Il Cortegiano*, to unmask him for the beggar he was.

Faith in Castiglione's optimistic brand of court politics may also have been undermined by the vigorous revival of anti-courtier discourse during the so-called "nasty nineties". This has often been treated as part of a fin-de-siècle phenomenon. Recently, scholars have evaluated it within the chronological and conceptual framework of Elizabeth's "second reign". They have argued that the distinctive political pressures of the period between 1585 and 1603 provoked a backlash against the royal Court. Fox, for example, attributes the late sixteenth-century proliferation of complaints about the Court and its inhabitants to a breakdown of centralized literary patronage networks. Fox suggests that the deaths of great courtier patrons, such as Sidney and Leicester, in the mid-1580s created a vacuum; hence, "it appears that by the 1590s, very few [writers] were getting the rewards from patronage that they thought they deserved, and once would have had a right to expect".[99] It would hardly be surprising if, under such circumstances, disappointed authors bit the hands that failed to feed them.

Fierce competition for offices, and the queen's unwillingness to reward her courtiers from coffers strained by continental and Irish wars (an unwillingness uncharitably described by Thomas Wilson as an old woman's "Neerness"[100]), also embittered many place-seekers at Court. It was conventional for satirists to liken the courtier's condition to one of perpetual hunger and thirst. Ulpian Fulwell warned of the endless, aching want that awaited prospective courtiers:

> When first I came to Fortunes Court, with hope of happy speede,
> I sawe the fruite like *Tantalus*, but might not thereon feede.
> I smeld the rost, but felt no taste, my hunger to augment:
> I might behold the fragrant Wines, and follow by the sent.[101]

Fulwell's reference to Tantalus evokes the old adage that the court is Hell, and its inhabitants the damned. Images of starvation could also be coupled with zoological metaphors. In a widely transcribed verse by the earl of Essex, the narrator adopts the persona of a "seely bee", who delights in the presence of his queen and is devoted to her service. However, he can obtain no nourishment:

> I suckt the wedes, when moone was in *th*e wane,
> Whilst all the rest in sonne shyne tasted rose,
> On black fear nerootes I seke to suck my bane,
> When on the Eglentyne the rest repose.
> Having to much they still repine for more,
> And cloyed w*i*th swetenes surffitt in their store.[102]

We are surely invited to ask ourselves whether the bee is a fool to continue paying court to the queen, when his only reward is "To see some caterpillars vpstart of late/ Cropping the flowers that should sustain *the* bee".[103] If we conclude that he is a fool, we acknowledge that honest, disinterested service accomplishes nothing at the court of Elizabeth.[104] Such an admission casts a nihilistic question mark over the feasibility of Castiglionean courtiership. The association of attacks upon *Il Cortegiano* with the turbulent politics of the "nasty nineties" reinforces the conceptual framework adopted "by the majority of modern interpreters", which identifies "the morbid fascination for the foreign Other and all matters Italian" as "resonant with manifestations of domestic anxiety".[105]

Throughout the Elizabethan era, anti-courtier literature was written, read and enjoyed by Court veterans and non-courtiers alike. Its prevalence initially did little or nothing to undermine the credibility of *Il libro del Cortegiano*. After all, Castiglione himself acknowledged that virtue and vice flourished side by side in the households of the great. He wrote that critics of the court:

> [w]oulde haue all goodnesse in the worlde withoute any yll, which ys vnpossible. For synceyll is contrarie to good, and good to yll, it is (in a maner) necessarie by contrarietye and a certayne counterpese the one should vnder prompe and strengthen the other, and where the one wanteth or encreaseth, the one to want or encrease also: beecause no contrarye is wythoute hys other contraye.[106]

Castiglione's thesis was simply that a courtier need not be vicious – that he could, in fact, serve the commonwealth as truly and honestly as anyone, and perhaps more effectively than most. In the 1580s and 1590s, however, dramatists and satirists began to interrogate this thesis. They became increasingly critical of the performance based politics advocated by Castiglione and Machiavelli. The association of these two figures was hardly likely to improve Castiglione's reputation. Perhaps Castiglione was also, to a certain extent, a victim of his own success. His dialogue was so widely renowned and respected that authors such as Marston and Guilpin felt the need to address it when censuring courtiers. Conventional complaints about the Court, couched in formulaic language and following ancient or medieval blueprints, were therefore directed at Castiglione. The esteem in which *Il libro del Cortegiano* was held posed a difficult question: why, after its teachings had been read, learned and inwardly digested, was there still so much to criticize at court? John Donne highlighted this problem with characteristic wit and perspicacity in his *Satyres*. Castiglione's rules, he mused, "May make good Courtiers". Regrettably, no-one seemed able to make courtiers good.[107]

Notes

1 J. R. Woodhouse, *Baldesar Castiglione: A Reassessment of the Courtier* (Edinburgh: Edinburgh University Press, 1978), p. ix.
2 Balthazar Castiglione, *The Covrtyer of Count Baldessar Castlio Divided into Foure Bookes*, trans. Thomas Hoby (London: William Seres, 1561), sig. Ci[r].
3 Hoby, *Covrtyer*, sig. *Aiii*[r].
4 Rosemary Horrox, "Caterpillars of the Commonwealth? Courtiers in Late Medieval England", in *Rulers and Ruled in Late Medieval England: Essays Presented to Gerald Harriss*, eds. Rowena E. Archer and Simon Walker (London and Rio Grande, OH: Hambledon Press, 1995), pp. 1–15 (p. 4).
5 William of Malmesbury, *Gestaregvm Anglorvm: The History of the English Kings*, ed. and trans. R. A. B. Mynors, completed by R. M. Thomson and M. Winterbottom, 2 vols (Oxford: Clarendon Press, 1998–99), I (1998), pp. 559–61.
6 Hoby, *Covrtyer*, sig. Li[v]. See also Retha M. Warnicke, "Sexual Heresy at the Court of Henry VIII", *HJ*, 30, 2 (June 1987): 247–68 (251–52).
7 Claudian, "In Eutropium", in *Claudian*, trans. by Maurice Platnauer (Cambridge, MA: Harvard University Press, 1922), p. 153. Walter Map endorsed the wisdom of "the famous poet": "Nothing is harsher than the ennobled clown"; "Nor [is there] any fiercer beast/ Than a slave's vengeance on a freeman's back". Walter Map, *De nugiscurialium: courtiers'*

trifles, ed. and trans. M. R. James, rev. by C. N. L. Brooke and R. A. B. Mynors (Oxford: Clarendon, 1983; repr. 2002), p. 15.

8 Heinrich Cornelius Agrippa, *Of the vanitie and uncertaintie of artes and sciences*, trans. James Sanford (London: Henry Wykes, 1569), sig. 114[v].

9 Hoby, *Covrtyer*, sig. Ssii[v] – Siii[r].

10 Norbert Elias, *The Court Society*, trans. Edmund Jephcott (Oxford: Basil Blackwell, 1983), p. 2.

11 Lawrence Stone, *The Crisis of the Aristocracy: 1558–1641* (Oxford: Clarendon Press, 1965; repr. 1966), p. 385.

12 G. R. Elton, "Tudor Government: The Points of Contact. III. The Court", *THRS*, 5th ser., vol. 26 (1976): 211–28.

13 Winston S. Churchill, *A History of the English Speaking Peoples*, 4 vols (London: Cassell & Company, 1956–58), II (1956), p. 113.

14 R. H. Tawney, "The Rise of the Gentry, 1558–1640", *Economic History Review*, 11, 1 (1941): 1–38; Lawrence Stone, "The Anatomy of the English Aristocracy", *Economic History Review*, 18, 1 and 2 (1948): 1–53 (pp. 1–2). See also Lawrence Stone, *The Causes of the English Revolution: 1529–1642* (London: Routledge and Kegan Paul, 1972; repr. 1973), pp. 26–30.

15 See, for example, Conrad Russell, *The Causes of the English Civil War* (Oxford: Clarendon Press, 1990), pp. 1–25.

16 As Neville Williams remarked, "In an age of personal monarchy, the royal court of England was both the hub of the kingdom's affairs and the setting in which the sovereign lived out his public and private lives". Neville Williams, "The Tudors: Three Contrasts in Personality", in *The Courts of Europe: Politics, Patronage and Royalty 1400–1700*, ed. A. G. Dickens (London: Thames & Hudson, 1977), pp. 147–67 (p. 147).

17 David Starkey, "Court History in Perspective", in *The English Court: From the Wars of the Roses to the Civil War*, eds. Starkey et al. (Harlow: Longman, 1987), pp. 1–24 (pp. 3–4).

18 Hoby, *Covrtyer*, sig. Mm iiii[v] – Nni[r].

19 David Starkey, "The Court: Castiglione's Ideal and Tudor Reality; Being a Discussion of Sir Thomas Wyatt's Satire Addressed to Sir Francis Bryan", *Journal of the Warburg and Courtauld Institutes*, 45 (1982): 232–39 (p. 233).

20 Cicero, *Marcus Tullius Ciceroes thre bokes of duties to Marcus his sonne* (London: Richard Tottel, 1556), fol. 9[v].

21 Sidney Anglo, "The Courtier: The Renaissance and Changing Ideals", in *Courts of Europe*, ed. Dickens, pp. 33–53 (p. 36).

22 Jonathan Woolfson, "Thomas Hoby, William Thomas and Mid-Tudor Travel to Italy", in *The Oxford Handbook of Tudor Literature*, eds. Mike Pincombe and Cathy Shrank (Oxford: Oxford University Press, 2009), pp. 404–17 (p. 414).

23 A. L. Rowse, *The Elizabethan Renaissance: The Life of Society* (London: Macmillan, 1971), pp. 55–56.

24 Paul N. Siegel, "English Humanism and the New Tudor Aristocracy", *Journal of the History of Ideas*, 13, 4 (October 1952): 450–68 (p. 467).

25 Daniel Javitch, *Poetry and Courtliness in Renaissance England* (Princeton, NJ: Princeton University Press, 1978), pp. 4–5.

26 Woolfson, "Mid-Tudor Travel to Italy", p. 416.

27 Roger Ascham, *The Scholemaster* (London: John Daye, 1570), sig. 20[v].

28 Anon, "The English Courtier, and the Cuntry–Gentleman: A Pleasaunt and Learned Disputation, Betweene Them Both", in *Inedited Tracts: Illustrating the Manners, Opinions, and Occupations of Englishmen during the Sixteenth and Seventeenth Centuries*, ed. W. C. Hazlitt (London: Roxburghe Library, 1868; repr. New York: Burt Franklin, [1964?]), pp. 1–93 (pp. 68; 75; 77; 93).

29 See Massimo Firpo, *Pietro Bizzari: esule italiano del Cinquecento* (Turin: G. Giappichelli, 1971), pp. 38–9.

30 Harold S. Wilson, "John Astley, 'Our Inglish Xenophon'", *Huntington Library Quarterly*, 22, 2 (February 1959): 107–18 (p. 112).

31 Gabriel Harvey, *Pierces Supererogation or a New Prayse of the Old Asse* (London: John Wolfe, 1593), p. 51.

32 *The Works of Thomas Nashe*, ed. Ronald B. McKerrow (London: A. H. Bullen, 1904), p. 7.
33 Richard Jones, attrib., *The Booke of Honor and Armes* (London: [Thomas Orwin for] Richard Jones, 1590), sig. A3[r].
34 Whythorne, *Autobiography*, p. 246.
35 Robert Miola, *Shakespeare's Reading* (Oxford: Oxford University Press, 2000), pp. 1–17.
36 BL, Rare Books, 8403 d. 20.
37 Apart from the rhetorical question "Is it possible that the greatest of the Elizabethans, living through the time when translations from the Italian were 'solde in every shop in London,' was ignorant of one of the oldest and best and most popular of them?", Scott summarizes her evidence as follows:

> I would submit, First, that Benedick and Beatrice are plainly of Italian origin; in Italian literature the Lady Emilia is first seen in the Lady Pampinea of the Decamerone. Second, that they do not belong to Hero's story in Bandello, and fit into it loosely in Shakespeare, precisely because they do not belong to any story. Thirdly, that in *Much Ado* they are both detached persons, they have "just growed", precisely as the Lord Gaspare and the Lady Emilia appear in the *Courtyer*. Fifth, that the very vividness of the representation is due to the fact that Benedick and Beatrice were originally real persons, the Lord Gaspare Pallavicino and the Lady Emilia Pia, of *Il Cortigiano*.

Mary Augusta Scott, "The Book of the Courtyer: A Possible Source of Benedick and Beatrice", *PMLA*, 16, 4 (1901): 475–502, 501–2.

38 Mike Pincombe and Cathy Shrank, "Prologue", in *The Oxford Handbook of Tudor Literature*, eds. Pincombe and Shrank, pp. 1–17 (p. 4).
39 Michele Marrapodi, "Appropriating Italy: Towards a New Approach to Renaissance Drama", in *Italian Culture in the Drama of Shakespeare and His Contemporaries*, ed. Michele Marrapodi (Farnham, UK: Ashgate, 2007), pp. 1–12 (pp. 1–3).
40 Adam Max Cohen, "The Mirror of all Christian Courtiers: Castiglione's *Cortegiano* as a Source for Henry V", in *Italian Culture in the Drama of Shakespeare and His Contemporaries*, ed. Marrapodi, pp. 39–50 (p. 40).
41 Keir Elam, "'At the cubiculo': Shakespeare's Problems with Italian Language and Culture", in *Italian Culture in the Drama of Shakespeare and His Contemporaries*, ed. Marrapodi, pp. 99–110 (p. 104).
42 Robert Greene, *Greenes Farewell to Folly* (London: Thomas Scarlet for T. Gubbin and T. Newman, 1591), sig. B3[v].
43 Oxford describes the Courtier as a perfect effigy, to which nothing can be added and in which nothing is redundant. "Edouardus Verus", in *Balthasaris Castilionis Comitis De Curialisiue Aulico*, ed. Balthasar Castiglione, trans. Bartholomew Clerke (London: John Day, 1571/2), sig. *(i)*[r].
44 Hoby's *Covrtyer* supplemented Castiglione's text with a "breef rehersall" of necessary qualifications for a courtier, and a synopsis of the "chief conditions" of a "waytyng gentlylwoman". Hoby, *Covrtyer*, sig. Yyiiii[r] – Zziiii[v].
45 Peter Burke, *The Fortunes of the Courtier: The European Reception of Castiglione's "Cortegiano"* (Cambridge: Polity Press, 1995), pp. 43–44.
46 Anna Bryson, *From Courtesy to Civility: Changing Codes of Conduct in Early Modern England* (Oxford: Clarendon Press, 1998), p. 36.
47 Bryson, *Courtesy to Civility*, p. 61.
48 Bryson, *Courtesy to Civility*, p. 116.
49 Hoby, *Covrtyer*, Aiii[v].
50 Annibale Romei, *The Courtiers Academie*, trans. I. K. (London: Valentine Sims, 1598; facsimile reproduction Amsterdam; New York: Da Capro Press, 1969), p. 4.
51 Bryson, *Courtesy to Civility*, pp. 113–17.
52 Peltonen discusses "vertical" and "horizontal" social relations (those conducted with superiors or inferiors and those conducted with equals respectively) when analysing concepts of honour in early modern England. Markku Peltonen, *The Duel in Early Modern England: Civility, Politeness and Honour* (Cambridge: Cambridge University Press, 2003), pp. 35–39.

See also Mervyn James, *Family, Lineage and Civil Society: A Study of Society, Politics and Mentality in the Durham Region, 1500–1640* (Oxford: Clarendon Press, 1974), pp. 177–98.

53 See, for example, William Baldwin's biography of Richard Neville, Earl of Warwick, "That plaaste and baaste his soveraynes so oft/By enterchaunge". William Baldwin, *A Myrroure for Magistrates* (London: Thomas Marshe, 1559), folslxix^{r} – lxxxi^{v} (lxx^{v}).

54 Morgan observes that the concept of a professional courtier – neither a baron nor a favourite – only really achieved currency in late-fifteenth-century England. D. A. L. Morgan, "The House of Policy: The Political Role of the Late Plantagenet Household, 1422–1485", in *English Court*, ed. Starkey, pp. 25–70 (p. 69).

55 Stone, *Crisis of the Aristocracy*, pp. 385–94.

56 In his Anglo-Italian dictionary, John Florio translated the verb "Inurbare" as "to become or make a citizen or a ciuill man". John Florio, *A Worlde of Wordes, or most copious, and exact dictionarie in Italian and English* (London: Arnold Hatfield for Edward Blount, 1598), p. 191.

57 See Markku Peltonen, *Classical Humanism and Republicanism in English Political Thought: 1570–1640* (Cambridge: Cambridge University Press, 1995), pp. 18–36.

58 Ewan Fernie and Ramona Wray, "Introduction", in *Reconceiving the Renaissance: A Critical Reader* (Oxford: Oxford University Press, 2005), pp. 1–12 (p. 1).

59 Hoby, *Covrtyer*, preface, sig. Bii^{r}.

60 David J. Welsh, "Il Cortigiano Polacco (1566)", *Italica*, 40, 1 (March 1963): 22–27.

61 In 1580, Gabriel Harvey included the *Courtier* in a list of ultra-fashionable Italian texts. He asserted that, in Cambridge, "Matchiauell [was] a great man: Castilio of no small reputation: Petra[r]ch, and Boccace in euerymans mouth: Galateo and Guazzo neuer so happy". Gabriel Harvey and Edmund Spenser, *Three Proper, and Wittie, Familiar Letters* (London: H. Bynneman, 1580), p. 28. In 1591, John Florio suggested that "Castilions Courtier" was frequently consulted by readers who wished to learn "a little Italian". John Florio, *Florios Second Frutes* (London: [T. Orwin] for Thomas Woodcock, 1591), sig. A4^{r}.

62 Raymond B. Waddington, "Elizabeth I and the Order of the Garter", *Sixteenth Century Journal*, 24, 1 (Spring 1993): 97–113 (pp. 104–6).

63 See Mary Partridge, "Hee Is Become an Englishman: Thomas Hoby's Translation of Castiglione's *Book of the Courtier*", *Historical Journal*, 50, 4 (December 2007): 769–86.

64 M. A. Overell, "Edwardian Humanism and *Il Beneficio di Cristo*, 1547–1553", in *Reassessing Tudor Humanism*, ed. Jonathan Woolfson (Basingstoke, UK: Palgrave Macmillan, 2002), pp. 151–73 (pp. 151–60).

65 John L. Lievsay, *The Elizabethan Image of Italy* (Ithaca, NY: Cornell University Press for the Folger Shakespeare Library, 1964), pp. 7–8.

66 Woolfson, "Mid-Tudor Travel to Italy", pp. 408; 411.

67 Marrapodi, "Appropriating Italy", p. 2.

68 Gabriel Harvey, *Gabrielis Harueij Gratulationum Valdinensium* (London: Henry Binneman, 1578), I, 20. The subsequent eulogy to the Italian people was so breathlessly rhapsodic that it seems clear Harvey was writing with his tongue in his cheek (I, 20–1). Nonetheless, there is no reason to doubt that Harvey was genuinely pleased at being likened to an Italian, which he took as a gracious compliment.

69 Thomas Nashe, with whom Harvey became embroiled in an acrimonious pamphlet war, brought up the episode "De vulti Itali" ("of the Italian look") twice. Thomas Nashe, *Strange Newes, of the Intercepting Certaine Letters, and a Conuoy of verses, as They Were Going Priuilie to Victuall the Low Countries* (London: John Danter, 1592), sig. D2^{r}. Nashe referred to the incident again in *Haue with you to Saffron-walden: or, Gabriell Harueys Hunt Is vp* (London: John Danter, 1596), sig. M2^{r-v}.

70 Simon Robson, *The Covrte of Ciuill Courtesie: Fitly Furnished with a Pleasant Porte of Stately Phrases and Pithie Precepts* (London: Richard Jhones, 1577), sig. Aii^{r-v}.

71 Bryson, *Courtesy to Civility*, p. 33.

72 George Pettie, "The Preface to the Readers", in *The Ciuile Conuersation of M. Steeuen Guazzo*, ed. Stefano Guazzo, trans. George Pettie (London: [Richard Watkins], 1581), sig. i^{r}.

73 Giovanni Della Casa, *Galateo: or Rather, a Treatise of the Manners and Behauiours, It Behoueth a Man to vse and Eschewe, in His Familiar Conuersation*, trans. Robert Peterson (London: Raufe Newbery, 1576; facsimile reproduction Amsterdam; New York: Theatrum Orbis Terrarum; Da Capo Press, 1969), sig. Aiii^{r}.

74 Eleanor Rosenberg, *Leicester: Patron of Letters* (New York: Columbia University Press, 1955), pp. 175–79.
75 Daniel Javitch, "The Philosopher of the Court: A French Satire Misunderstood", *Comparative Literature*, 23, 2 (Spring, 1971): 97–124; Sydney Anglo, *The Courtier's Art: Systematic Immorality in the Renaissance* (Swansea: University College of Swansea, 1983), pp. 4–5.
76 Pauline M. Smith, *The Anti-Courtier Trend in Sixteenth Century French Literature* (Geneva: Librairie Droz, 1966), pp. 98–100, 138–47.
77 Javitch, "French Satire Misunderstood", p. 113.
78 Ascham, *Scholemaster*, fols 20^{v}; 23^{r} – 24^{v}.
79 Marrapodi, "Appropriating Italy", p. 3.
80 Burghley gave this much-quoted piece of advice to his son Robert. See Francis Peck, *Desiderata Curiosa* (London: [n. pub.], 1732), I, 65.
81 Keir Elam, "Tis pity she's Italian: Performing the Courtesan on the Early Seventeenth-Century English Stage", in *Shakespeare and Renaissance Literary Theories: Anglo-Italian Transactions*, ed. Michele Marrapodi (Farnham, UK: Ashgate, 2011), p. 239.
82 Cohen, "Mirror of all Christian Courtiers", p. 44.
83 Marrapodi, "Appropriating Italy", p. 9.
84 In Marston's *Antonio and Mellida*, Signor Castilio Balthazar enters "with a casting bottle of sweet water in his hand, sprinkling himself". John Marston, *Antonio and Mellida*, ed. W. Reavley Gair, The Revels Plays (Manchester, UK: Manchester University Press, 1991; repr. 2004), *s.d.*III. 2. 24.
85 *The Letters of John Chamberlain*, ed. N. E. McClure, 2 vols (Philadelphia, PA: American Philosophical Society, 1939), I, p. 107.
86 Everard Guilpin, *Skialetheia: or, a shadowe of truth, in certaine epigrams and satyres*, ed. D. Allen Carroll (Chapel Hill, NC: University of North Carolina Press, 1974), pp. 65–66.
87 John Marston, *The Metamorphosis of Pigmalions Image and Certaine Satyres* (London: [James Robert] for Edmond Matts, 1598), p. 29.
88 Roy Strong, *The Cult of Elizabeth: Elizabethan Portraiture and Pageantry* (London: Thames and Hudson, 1977; repr. 1987), pp. 144–46.
89 William Camden, *Remaines of a Greater Worke, Concerning Britaine* (London: G[eorge] E[ld] for Simon Waterson, 1605), p. [158].
90 See Mary Thomas Crane, *Framing Authority: Sayings, Self and Society in Sixteenth Century England* (Durham, NC: Duke University Press, 1960), pp. 130–33.
91 Map, *De nugiscurialium*, p. 9.
92 Prometheus gave fire to mankind, against the wishes of Zeus. Tantalus "bid the Gods to a ba*n*ket, and he being desyrous to make a triall of their deitie, when they appeared a*t* his house in mennes likenes, did slea his own sonne *Pelops* and set him before the*m* to be eaten". Sebastian Münster, *A briefe collection and compendious extract of the straunge and memorable things, gathered oute of the cosmographye of Sebastian Munster*, trans. [Richard Eden?] (London: Thomas Marshe, 1572), fol. 53^{v}.
93 Marston, *Pigmalions Image*, p. 29.
94 John Marston, *The Scourge of Villanie: Three Bookes of Satyres* (London: J[ames] R[oberts] for Iohn Buzbie, 1598), sig. B^{r}–^{v}.
95 John Marston, *Antonio and Mellida*, ed. W. Reavley Gair, The Revels Plays (Manchester, UK: Manchester University Press, 1991; repr. 2004).
96 Marston, *Pigmalions image*, p. 30.
97 See, for example, Alain Chartier, *Here Foloweth the Copye of a letter Whyche Maistre Alayn Charetier Wrote to Hys Brother*, trans. William Caxton ([Westminster: William Caxton, 1483]), sig. iii^{v}. In a letter ostensibly dissuading his brother from abandoning the rustic life to seek his fortune at Court, Chartier noted:

> Thou mayestete when thou hast hungre / at thyn houre and at thy playsir / And we ete so gredyly & gloutounously that other whyle we caste it vp agayn and make vomytes / Thou passest the nyght in slepyng as longe as it playseth the / And we after ouermoche drynkyng of wynes and grete paynes lye dounofte in beddes ful of vermyne / & somtyme with stryfe & debate.

98 Marston, *Pigmalions image*, p. 30.
99 Alistair Fox, "The Complaint of Poetry for the Death of Liberality: The Decline of Literary Patronage in the 1590s", in *The Reign of Elizabeth I: Court and Culture in the Last Decade*, ed. John Guy (Cambridge: Cambridge University Press, 1995), pp. 229–57 (p. 240).
100 Thomas Wilson, "The State of England anno dom. 1600", in *Camden Miscellany*, XVI (London: Camden Society, 1936), pp. 2–43 (28).
101 Ulpian Fulwell, *The Firste Parte, of the Eygth Liberall Science: Entituled, Ars Adulandi, the Arte of Flatterie with the Confutation Therof* (London: [William How for] Richard Jones, 1579), sig. Fiii^{v}.
102 Bod. MS Rawl. Poet 112, fol. 9^{r}.
103 Bod. MS Rawl. Poet 112, fol. 9^{v}.
104 The Queen Bee is undoubtedly Elizabeth; the poet's reference to the fortunate insects who "on the Eglentyne repose" is unambiguous. Elizabeth was often associated with eglantine: see Roy Strong, *The Cult of Elizabeth: Elizabethan Portraiture and Pageantry* (London: Thames and Hudson, 1977; repr. 1987), pp. 68–73.
105 Marrapodi, "Appropriating Italy", p. 10.
106 Hoby, *Covrtyer*, Li^{v}.
107 John Donne, "Satyre V", in *The Satires, Epigrams and Verse Letters*, ed. W. Milgate, Oxford English Texts (Oxford: Clarendon Press, 1967), lines 2–4.

17 Machiavelli's *Principe* and the new ethics of power

Alessandra Petrina

In *Volpone*, composed and performed between 1605 and 1606, Ben Jonson has one of his characters, Sir Politic Would-Be, exclaim:

> And then, for your religion, profess none,
> But wonder at the diversity of all;
> And, for your part, protest were there no other
> But simply the laws o' th' land, you could content you.
> Nick Machiavel and Monsieur Bodin both
> Were of this mind.
>
> (IV.i.22–27)[1]

As has been noted, in this passage, and especially in lines 24–25, Jonson is alluding to *cuius regio, eius religio*, the statement formulated at the Peace of Augsburg (1555) in order to impose some order on a situation that threatened to become explosive.[2] Interestingly, the statement is associated with Machiavelli (in this instance generically identified with the author of *Il Principe*) and Bodin, though Jonson himself was probably aware that the two writers maintained rather distant positions on the topic; Machiavelli, unlike Bodin, did not advocate religious tolerance, but rather predicated, on the part of the prince, a preservation of the *appearance* of religion, however contrary to the prince's own real beliefs.[3] Modern editors of *Volpone* see this passage as merely a revelation of Sir Politic's ignorance, but Jonson is also playing up to his audience, using a very facile and well-recognized allusion – Machiavelli – together with a reference to Jean Bodin, a thinker much more directly involved, if only for chronological reasons, with the issues of religious tolerance and its role in "reason of state"; an issue that found Ben Jonson, himself a Catholic convert, probably in disagreement. By equating the French and the Italian writers here, Jonson underlines the role Machiavelli played in English imagination by the beginning of the seventeenth century: both spokesmen of agnosticism in politics, Bodin and Machiavelli are represented as grossly distorted images, with the latter simply a recognizable target for moralistic vituperation.

The passage can be usefully compared with a much earlier and more famous apparition of the Florentine writer on the English stage, as the Prologue in Christopher Marlowe's *The Jew of Malta*:

DOI: 10.4324/9781315612720-20

Albeit the world thinke *Machevill* is dead,
Yet was his soule but flowne beyond the *Alpes*,
And, now the *Guize* is dead, is come from *France*,
To view this Land, and frolicke with his friends.
To some perhaps my name is odious,
But such as love me, gard me from their tongues,
And let them know that I am *Machevill*,
And weigh not men, and therefore not mens words:
Admir'd I am of those that hate me most.
Though some speake openly against my bookes,
Yet will they reade me, and thereby attaine
To *Peters* Chayre: And when they cast me off,
Are poyson'd by my climing followers.
I count Religion but a childish Toy,
And hold there is no sinne but Ignorance.
Birds of the Aire will tell of murders past;
I am asham'd to heare such fooleries:
Many will talke of Title to a Crowne.
What right had *Caesar* to the Empery?
Might first made Kings, and Lawes were then most sure
When like the *Dracos*, they were writ in blood.
Hence comes it, that a strong built Citadell
Commands much more then letters can import:
Which maxime had *Phaleris* observ'd,
H'had never bellowed in a brasen Bull
Of great ones envy; o'th poor petty wites,
Let me be envy'd and not pittied![4]

Though there is no certainty about the actual date of the first performance, *The Jew of Malta* was composed between 1588, when the Duke of Guise was assassinated, and 1592, when the theatre financier Philip Henslowe recorded a performance of the play on the part of the Lord Strange's Men.[5] Fifteen years before Jonson's Sir Politic, Marlowe's Prologue appears to be banking on the same awareness, on the spectators' part, of the role of Machiavelli as a spokesman for irreligious, unbounded political ambition, though in this case the anti-Catholic bias is extremely evident, and the reading of the *Principe* possibly closer to the actual text than Jonson's sweeping generalization. Marlowe's was not the first stage appearance of Machiavelli in front of an English audience: in 1578 Gabriel Harvey had presented a caricature of the Florentine writer, in the form of a monologue in Latin, in front of Queen Elizabeth during the latter's visit to Audley End.[6] Yet the popularity of *The Jew of Malta* and its being directed, unlike Harvey's poem, at a general audience, tells us of a spreading awareness of the existence of Machiavelli's works in England, and of a mounting unease at its possible, nefarious effects. Contemporary English writers, from John Case to Simon Patericke, were also evoking images of poison and contagion when referring to Machiavelli,[7] and by the time Jonson staged the musings of Sir Politic, a minor poet, Sir Thomas Andrewe, could attack womanly wiles in a long poem entitled *The Vnmasking of a Feminine Machiauell.*[8] Shakespeare also introduces allusions to Machiavelli in his plays, ranging from topical references to a political villain in his early plays (as in *Henry*

VI, Part 1, V.vii.73–74),[9] to more ironical jokes in later works such as *The Merry Wives of Windsor* (III.i.93). Interestingly, the creation of the Machiavelli myth on stage and page, then as now, was not only divorced from his actual political or philosophical output, but appeared to allude only to the writer of *Il Principe*, irrespective of any other, equally famous work of his.

Jonson's allusion, like Andrewe's title, reduced the name of Machiavelli to a byword for hypocritical immorality, simplifying any reading of his works. On the other hand, Marlowe, probably counting on different levels of knowledge and awareness on the part of his spectators, was asking them to draw a subtler lesson than a simple consideration of Machiavelli's contempt for religion: though counting religion but a childish toy, Marlowe's Machiavel would not simply "profess none", as the literal-minded Sir Politic suggested, but rather use a profession of faith to attain power – in this sense, his reading was actually close to the passage from chapter 18 of *Il Principe* in which the writer exhorted the prince to preserve and enhance the appearance of religiosity. The pointed allusion to the Catholic faith, evident in the allusion to "Peter's chair", is part of an anti-Catholic propaganda that a London audience would readily appreciate; at the same time, the monologue, which gives us a glimpse of Marlowe's very real knowledge of Machiavelli's works,[10] opened up a space for reflection on the nature of power and on the characteristics of a successful ruler. This reflection would become predominant in English discussions on Machiavelli's work in the seventeenth century. The bogey created for the Elizabethan stage began to recede, though it was kept alive in popular imagination thanks to the satire of Thomas Nashe[11] or the allusions contained in anonymous pamphlets; Machiavelli's actual works were being disseminated and translated, and used as one element in the developing discussion on the divine right of kingship, on the nature of power, and on the ideal form of government. Retracing the allusions to the *Principe* involves dealing with a very disparate range of references:[12] given its brevity, its linguistic simplicity and the wealth of examples taken from classical history, the book appears to have been often used as a repository of maxims (as shall be seen in more detail later) but also as a very useful text to undertake the study of the Italian language; the existence of translations in intermediary languages, such as French and Latin, was certainly a determinant factor. In the following pages I will therefore trace the development in the political reading of the treatise by focussing on a number of significant case studies.

As has been seen in the example above, the popular reaction to Machiavelli's writings, or rather the conventional image of Niccolò Machiavelli that we can see in much dramatic and occasional literature, increasingly veered towards the stereotypical. On the other hand, the Florentine writer immediately entered political and ethical discussion at a more sophisticated level. But it should be said that, in this case, some of his political or historical writings other than *Il Principe* played an equally important role. The impact of Machiavelli's writings in sixteenth-century Europe is the object of Sydney Anglo's impressive study *Machiavelli – The First Century*, published in 2005.[13] Given its transnational perspective, this work allows us to gauge the influence of Machiavelli in England within a wider setting; but even a preliminary glance at the fate of Machiavelli's works in print can offer a rough idea of their dissemination, though the influence of scribal circulation cannot be underrated.

During Machiavelli's lifetime, his political works went unpublished; however, they enjoyed manuscript circulation both in Italy and abroad. Only the *Decennale, L'Arte della Guerra* and the comedy *Mandragola* were printed before their author's death – the latter no less than four times;[14] at the same time Agostino Nifo's *De regnandi peritia*, an instance of "creative plagiarism" of the *Principe* on the part of the professor of philosophy at the University of Pisa, appeared in 1523, though its initial impact was limited, and its closeness to the original recognized only centuries later.[15] England was, to a very small extent, among the recipients of the early, scribal circulation: the library of Charlecote Park, Warwickshire, preserves a manuscript of the *Principe*, in Italian, believed to have been composed in the 1520s, in the Roman scriptorium of Ludovico degli Arrighi; and the short note of ownership on the reinforcing vellum guard preceding the text ("This Boke is Nicholas Jonays/With his louing Frindis mareuelus/wity to be hade in Rememberance"), though of doubtful interpretation, points unmistakably to English ownership.[16] More importantly, though the first book by Machiavelli to be translated and printed in England was *L'Arte della Guerra*, published in 1560,[17] and though there would be no other English translations in print until 1636 (when Edward Dacres translated the *Discorsi*, shortly followed by the *Principe* in 1640, as shall be discussed below), early editions of Machiavelli's political works in the Italian original, and soon in Latin or French translations, already circulated in the sixteenth century, along with manuscript translations, some of which appear in multiple copies and suggest a considerable circulation.[18]

The Charlecote manuscript, though implying an early dissemination of the text in England, offers no other information, since the "Nicholas Jonays" mentioned in the guardsheet cannot be traced; but early allusions to the *Principe* in particular offer fascinating glimpses of the kind of reactions the book triggered in England, and among the ruling classes in particular. Cardinal Reginald Pole famously described the treatise as "scriptum ab hoste humani generis, in quo omnia hostis consilia explicantur, & modi, quibus religio, pietas, & omnes virtutis indoles, facilius destrui possent".[19] Like Sir Politic's assessment, this attack was blind to subtler and potentially more dangerous implications, and Pole appeared to ignore the role that could be proposed for a book such as the *Principe*, which proposed itself as a continuator, albeit on radically new terms, of the *speculum principum* tradition.[20] Contemporary politicians opposed to Pole would appear to show greater understanding of the issue: thus Henry Parker, Lord Morley, a great reader and translator of Italian, would recommend this book to Thomas Cromwell, minister to Henry VIII, as "surely a good thing for your Lordship and for our Sovereign Lord in Council".[21] The conventional ambiguity on the purpose and intended readership of the *Principe* – a point that still causes controversy among scholars – is at work here; and other early allusions to the *Principe*, intended not for the theatre audience but for a selected readership, are expressive of the same attempt to draw political lessons and even practical teachings from the text.

A case in point is Sir Philip Sidney, whose staunch Protestantism and personal involvement in the losses deriving from the Massacre of Saint Bartholomew's day (1572) might have made him a blind enemy of Machiavelli and the religious intolerance associated with his name. Sidney mentions Machiavelli in his correspondence to Hubert Languet and in his *Defence of the Earl of Leicester*, and may also have recommended the reading of his works to his brother Robert.[22] Writing to Languet, Sidney uses Machiavelli's name simply to share a joke on Languet's presumed attacks against him:

> Nunquam adduci poteram, ut crederem Machiavellum, bene de nimia clementia fugienda sensisse, donec usu idem mihi venerit, quod ille multis rationibus probare conatus est.[23]

The quotation only shows the familiarity of both with Machiavelli's name. More interesting is what appears in Sidney's *Defence of the Earl of Leicester*, the answer to *Leicester's Commonwealth*, an attack against Sidney's uncle Robert Dudley. *Leicester's Commonwealth*, written in 1584 and published anonymously, possibly in Rouen,[24] was a violent pamphlet that made use of the image of Machiavelli, presented as "Signior Machiavel" and "my Lord's counsellor".[25] It is notable here that though "Machiavel" is frequently only another name for "crafty" or "deceitful" (as in the reference to "subtile and Machiavellian sleight"),[26] the anonymous writer appears to be acquainted with the *Principe*, as when he notes, "it is a settled rule of Machiavel which the Dudleys do observe, that where you have once done a great injury, there must you never forgive".[27] Interestingly, *Leicester's Commonwealth*, first published surreptitiously, circulated in England in different manuscript copies and extracts, among which is London, British Library, Harley 967, a collection which also contains "A short Poem, or Libel, against the last mentioned Tract, by a Papist"[28] and is preceded by a copy of one of the English manuscript translations of the *Principe*.[29] This manuscript is one of the oldest extant copies, written "in a crabbed Elizabethan hand",[30] and one of the few to include also some explicit comments on Machiavelli's work:

> N.M. politia nefaria. To know to abhorr this Politique! maie read Th'ideal ground of his impieties; But not to practise his damned policies! for that, to Auern, doth down the brod waie lead.
>
> (fol. 1r)

and again

> The Prince of Nicholas Machiauel citizen, and secretarie of Florence, dedicated to the noble Prince Laurence, sonn of Peter de Medicis. Whoe telle, and teacheth, what kinges doe in states, But dreames not, Hell is for such potentates. CSM. Translated out of Italien into English.
>
> (fol. 1v)

It might also be added, though this brings us into the realm of hypothesis rather than fact, that Harley 967, in the British Library collection, is adjacent to a small, quarto volume, Harley 968, described in the catalogue as "The Arraignement of Sir Walter Raleigh Kt. at Winchester, on Thursday the 17th of November, A.D. 1603",[31] and, more interestingly, to Harley 966, a small quarto dated 1591–92 and signed by Henry, fourth Lord Mordaunt (1568–609), a minor nobleman of Catholic sympathies. Harley 966 is divided in three sections, the first without title, while the second bears the title "Generalis temporum description" (fol. 13r) and the third is simply headed "Henricus Mordauntius. Octob. 1°. – 1591" (fol. 22r). The three sections are, respectively, a summary account of various forms of government and of the ideal policy of a prince, including a number of axioms taken mostly from the *Principe*, but with some borrowings from the *Discorsi;* a short history of the world, from Adam to Queen Elizabeth; and a series of precepts of rhetoric.

Adjacency is no proof of closeness, but suggests it quite strongly, and the three manuscripts listed here share a number of traits that seem to be due to more than simple coincidence. The contents of Harley 966 and of the two codices sitting next to it appear to corroborate the hypothesis that *Leicester's Commonwealth* was composed and circulated in Catholic circles, the same circles that would show authentic interest in Machiavelli's work, though at the same time regard his alleged political teachings with something akin to horror. Though showing much more awareness of the actual meaning of the *Principe* than is seen in the exclamations and vituperations of earlier writers, these works also indicate quite compellingly that Machiavelli's work was used rather than studied, employed as a target for one or the other political, ideological, or more often religious group in order to attack one's adversaries. As Kevin Sharpe observes, discussing Machiavelli's impact in Tudor and Stuart England, "the man himself, or his reputation, became a text – debated, refuted, yet possessing power".[32] In this, the English reaction to Machiavelli, in the late sixteenth century as in the early seventeenth, found striking analogies with reactions all over Europe.

Sidney's answer to *Leicester's Commonwealth*, probably composed in the same or in the following year, was not published and enjoyed only limited manuscript circulation, as happened with most of his works, generally aimed at a restricted, élite audience.[33] As in a number of his prose writings, we find here a discursive, reasonable tone, far from the virulence of *Leicester's Commonwealth*. Rather than rebutting individual accusations, Sidney appears interested in defending the good name of the Dudleys, and offering general considerations on the nature of calumny. It is in the latter case that the name of Machiavelli crops up, almost casually:

> Who has a father by whose death the Son enherits, but such a nameles historien mai sai his son poisend him. Where mai two talk together but such a spirit of revelation mai surmize thei spake of treason. What neede more or why so much? As though I douted that any woold build beleef uppon such a durty seat, onely when he to borrow a little of his inkhorn, when he plais the Statist wringing veri unlukkili some of Machiavels axiomes to serve his purpos then indeed then he tryumphes.[34]

Sidney seems to have hit on the same point Kevin Sharpe would make four centuries later: Machiavelli's own axiomatic writing was an ideal tool in the hands of writers who would "wring it", make use of his gnomic sentences and bend them to their own purpose. It is therefore unsurprising that among the uses *Il Principe* was put to in early modern England was that of a repository of useful maxims, as is evident in the first section of MS Harley 966, discussed earlier, but also in commonplace books, such as William Drake's collection (now London, University College Library, MS Ogden 7),[35] or in anthologies and collections of maxims that would circulate in printed form, such as *The Quintesence of Wit*, edited by Robert Hitchcock and printed in London in 1590.[36] In this case Machiavelli was set side by side with other political and historical writers, whether classical (Aristotle, Polybius, Sallust, Tacitus) or vernacular (Antonio Guevara, Francesco Guicciardini).[37] It is an interesting anticipation of the company in which the Florentine writer would find himself in the discussion on political theory prevalent in the following century.

The possibility of using Machiavelli's very words to support diametrically opposite causes seems to be a side-effect of the writer's own semantic range. This has been an object of study on the part of historians and linguists: both note in the political works, and in the *Principe* in particular, the use of a limited vocabulary and a simplified syntax, characteristics which at the same time highlight the dramatic impact of what is being said (as happens in a number of especially violent episodes, such as the one involving

Rimirro de Orco, in chapter 7) and draw the reader to focus on selected keywords such as *fortuna* or *virtù*.[38] But these very words undergo a number of denotative and connotative transformations, acquiring different meanings and occasionally pointing to different directions within the space of a few lines. As a recent translator has observed:

> Not only was Machiavelli aware of the past meanings (in both Italian and Latin) of the important words he used – words such as "virtue", "liberty", "state", and "fortune" – he also imbued these words with new meanings that still reverberate in languages that are spoken throughout much of the world.[39]

This sense of diachronic change has ensured a special afterlife to Machiavelli's axioms, used, in the sixteenth century as now, for any purpose that might suit the reader, often misused, transformed or even invented. The attribution to Machiavelli of an ethical or un-ethical stance on politics in the case of English early modern writers is therefore the result of an interesting coincidence: the dissemination of a work like the *Principe*, which, together with the aforementioned characteristics, had brevity and pithiness to recommend it and was therefore ideal not only as a political handbook, and an inverted, if potentially dangerous, *speculum principum*, but also as a book on which to practise one's newly-learned Italian; and the recent attention, on the part of the English, to Italy as a cultural phenomenon. Anti-Catholic polemic could find excellent inspiration in this work, as we have seen in the case of Christopher Marlowe (or, on a European scale, in the case of Innocent Gentillet's *Anti-machiavel*),[40] but the same work could be used in an attack against atheism, or even against Anglicanism. An instance of the latter can be seen in an invective against the Church of England, written by the Catholic controversialist Thomas Harding and printed in Antwerp in 1565:

> What makes so many malepart prentises, pleasant courtiers, discoursing parlement machiavellists, and all other what so ever fleshwormes, Marchantes, idle artificers, to inbrace your gospell, rather than the graver and devouter sort of men which be weaned from the pleasures of this life: but that it was plausible to the world and pleasant to the flesh, from which that kind of man is most hardly drawen?[41]

It is therefore little wonder that, in the hands of political thinkers, the *Principe* appears to lose, at least in part, its topicality and play a less dramatic role, becoming part of a wider discussion on politics and the ideal government. Earlier readings of Machiavelli's thought and of its relation to the theory of the modern state had always been presented within a controversial context, and thus tended to emphasize and simplify his determined separation of religion from politics. Such is the case of John Lesley's pro-Marian *Treatise of Treasons Against Q. Elizabeth*, published in Louvain in 1572 by the Catholic printer John Fowler. John Lesley, Bishop of Ross, had taken an active part in Queen Mary's defence, to the point of being imprisoned for a time in England and being forced to give evidence about the Ridolfi plot, in which he had been involved.[42] His diplomatic skills and historical erudition emerge even in his polemical writings, such as the *Treatise*, which warns its readers in the Prologue against a "Machiavellian State". In spite of its length, the passage is worth quoting in full:

> And that is it, that I cal a Machiauellian State & Regiment: where Religion is put behind in the second & last place: where ye civil Policie, I meane, is preferred

> before it, & not limited by any rules of Religion, but ye Religion framed to serue ye time & policy; wher both by word & example of ye Rulers, ye ruled are taught with euery change of Prince to change also the face of their faith and Religion: where, in apparence and shew only, a Religion is pretended, now one, now an other, they force not greatly which, so that at hart there be none at al: where neither by hope nor feare of ought after this life, men are restrained from any maner vice, nor moued to any vertue what so ever: but where it is free to slaunder, to belie, to forswear, to accuse, to corrupt, to oppresse, to robbe, to inuade, to depose, to imprison, to murther, and to commit euery other outrage, never so barbarous (that promiseth to aduaunce the present Policie in hand) without scruple, feare, or conscience of hel or heauen, of God, or Diuel: and where no restraint, nor allurement is left in the hart of man, to bridle him from euil, nor to inuite him to good: but for vaine fame only & feare of lay lawes, that reache no further then to this body and life: that cal I properly a Machiauellian State and Gouernance.[43]

The word *policy* is here set in opposition to *religion* in order to indicate two different and often conflicting powers: none is negatively connoted, but it is rather the use of religion as a smokescreen for an evil practice of power (used "to aduaunce the present Policie in hand") that is condemned. Elizabethan Machiavellianism often expresses itself in a definition of the Elizabethan government as "Machiavellian", devious and irreligious, and encourages a view of politics as inherently evil; the very words *policy* and *practice*, "in their specialized meaning, became almost the technical terms of Machiavellianism in England, to the extent that whenever they are found with that meaning in an Elizabethan text, a Machiavellian influence may be traced either directly or indirectly",[44] although of course such connotations existed before the circulation of Machiavelli's works in England.[45] But this is an instance in which the writer shows a systematic knowledge of Machiavelli's work, and, though clearly in a polemical context, attempts a simplification of the Florentine's political theory without evoking any Machiavellian spectre, but rather, as Felix Raab has appropriately noted, "the spectre of the secular state".[46]

The traditional representation of Machiavelli in England as a mephitic demon haunting the Elizabethan stage represents not only a very partial view, but also a considerably limited phenomenon: though allusions to the *monster Machivill* continue throughout the seventeenth century, there is an ever sharper distinction between this popular legend and the political contribution of the Florentine writer, that enters the debate on reason of state as early as the second half of the sixteenth century. The turn of the century is characterized by a growing awareness, on the part of England, of its role in European politics;[47]the consciousness of this new role goes hand in hand with James I's determined effort to re-establish the legitimacy of the king's absolute power in the name of his divine investiture. Political discussion thus takes these new themes into account, and Machiavelli is frequently cited in debates on *raison d'état* in conjunction with other, roughly contemporary political writers, such as Justus Lipsius, Giovanni Botero, Hugo Grotius and Thomas Hobbes, as well as the already mentioned Jean Bodin. It was the prelude to Machiavelli's inclusion among the founders of modern politics,[48] and his acknowledgement as the forerunner of the modern concept of republic.[49] On the other hand, as has been justly observed, the gap between Machiavelli and Machiavellianism (the legend and set of symbolic images grown around the use to which Machiavelli had been put in sixteenth-century drama) became wider and more clearly marked: "while Machiavellianism never acquired a fully positive meaning, reason of state could take the shape of good political reason distinguished from a false Machiavellian *practice*".[50] According to some historians, the dichotomy between policy and religion was intensified, during the reigns of James I and Charles I, and Machiavelli's writings even became a testing ground for English political philosophers.[51]

This transformation was probably helped by the appearance in print of English translations of the *Discorsi* and *Il Principe*, respectively in 1636 and 1640.[52] The translation of Machiavelli is no isolated instance: in the 1630s a number of translations of political treatises had appeared, some emphasising or supporting monarchical authority, some exploring the concept of republicanism by making direct reference to the precedent of classical Rome. Indeed, Latin historians were translated and published, as in the case of Polybius, translated (from the French) in 1633 and republished twice over the following two years.[53] The E.D. mentioned in both titles of the Machiavelli translation is Edward Dacres, about whom very little is known, nor are there traces of his literary activity outside these two books; but it is important to note that in both cases Dacres, who had been careful to add in both frontispieces that his translations would contain *animadversions noting and taxing his errours*, also inserted prefaces, in the form of an "Epistle Dedicatory" to James Stuart, Duke of Lennox. The translation of the *Principe* also contained a short "Epistle to the Reader".

As Markku Peltonen has observed, Dacres did not censure Machiavelli's republicanism as it was espoused in the *Discorsi*, but used the text to throw light on the pitfalls of monarchical rule, considering in his comments to the text the precarious balance between the will of the ruler and the needs of the people:

> In his own conception, grounded on the hierarchic view of society, the prince and the people made "onely one politique body" and their aims, in most cases, overlapped. For Dacres, problems arose not because the king had a wholly different set of goals from that of the people, but because of a possible disequilibrium in the balance of the body politic.[54]

Dacres' preface to his translation of *Il Principe* is characteristically prudent. His dedicatee was the grandson of Esmé Stuart, Seigneur d'Aubigny and favourite of King James VI of Scotland; this means that the Duke of Lennox did have some claim to the Scottish crown, but contemporary reports underline his staunch fidelity to the King.[55] It is therefore no surprise that the dedication to Lennox in the *Principe* translation should begin thus:

> Poysons are not all of that malignant and obnoxious quality, that, as destructives of Nature, they are utterly to be abhord; but we find many, nay most of them have their medicinall uses. This book carryes its poison and malice in it; yet mee thinks the judicious peruser may honestly make use of it in the actions of his life, with advantage.[56]

Machiavelli's treatise is thus to be used by rulers as a warning against their own excesses, in order to avoid that disequilibrium of forces that so worried Dacres in the preface to the *Discorsi*. His cautious approach is reiterated in the short epistle to the reader, in which he notes that "he that means well, shall be here warnd, where the deceitfull man learnes to set his snares".[57]

In spite of the extant evidence of readers, translators and annotators of the *Principe* in Stuart England, Dacres' prefatory material, if compared with his far more articulated prefatory material to the *Discorsi*, seems to show that the attention was by this point shifting towards the latter text, as the spectre of the Machiavellian demon was receding from the collective imagination. Machiavelli's writings were now analysed as part of the classical republican heritage, together with the writings of Tacitus, Justus Lipsius, Hugo Grotius: the attention for the Florentine writer was part of the "humanist preoccupation with history in general and antiquity in particular".[58] The Civil Wars would help focus the attention of political thinkers on this aspect, and the contributions of Marchamont Nedham, James Harrington and Algernon Sidney, to name but a few, would underline the role played by the Florentine writer in the development of liberal republicanism.[59] The shadow of the *Machiavel* evoked by Christopher Marlowe seemed to have flown elsewhere.

Notes

1 The edition used is Ben Jonson, *Volpone, or The Fox*, ed. Brian Parker (Manchester, UK: Manchester University Press, 1999). I would like to thank John Roe for discussing this topic with me, and reading this chapter as it was being prepared.

2 Parker, p. 213n.

3 "E [il principe] paia, a udirlo e vederlo, tutto pietà, tutto fede, tutto integrità, tutto umanità, tutto religione; e non è cosa più necessaria, a parere di avere, che questa ultima qualità" (chapter XVIII: "to those who see and hear him, he should seem to be exceptionally merciful, trustworthy, upright, humane and devout. And it is most necessary of all to seem devout"). For the Italian text the edition used is Niccolò Machiavelli, *Il Principe*, ed. Giorgio Inglese (Turin: Einaudi, 2013). For the English translation, see *The Prince*, ed. Quentin Skinner and Russell Price (Cambridge: Cambridge University Press, 1988).

4 *The Jew of Malta*, Prologue, ll. 1–27. *The Complete Works of Christopher Marlowe*, ed. Roma Gill (Oxford: Clarendon Press, 1995).

5 See the Introduction to *The Jew of Malta*, p. xvi.

6 Gabriel Harvey, *Epigramma in effigiem Machiauelli. Machiauellus ipse loquitur, in Kaire, vel, Gratulationis Valdinensis Liber Secundus: Ad Nobilissimum Dominum, & Illustrissimum Heroem, Comitem Leicestrensem, Dominum Suum Optimum, & optatissimum* (London: H. Binneman, 1578), pp. 8–9.

7 See, for some telling instances, John Case, *Sphaera Ciuitatis; Hoc est; Reipublicae recte ac pie secundum leges administrande ratio* (Francofurdi: Apud Ioan. Wechelum, 1589), p. 2; and Simon Patericke's dedicatory epistle prefacing his translation of Gentillet's *Anti-Machiavel* (*A Discovrse Vpon the Meanes of Wel Governing and Maintaining in Good Peace, a Kingdome, or Other Principalitie. Divided into Three Parts, Namely, The Counsell, the Religion, and the Policie, which a Prince Ought to Hold and Follow. Against Nicholas Machiavell the Florentine. Translated into English by Simon Patherícke* (London: Adam Islip, 1602), in which Patericke explicitly refers to "the infectious Machiavelian doctrine".

8 Sir Thomas Andrewe, *The Vnmasking of a Feminine Machiauell* (London: Simon Stafford, 1604).

9 In this case the Earl of Warwick calls the Duke of Alençon a "notorious Machiavel". The audience might have read this as a reference to a more contemporary Duke of Alençon, who had asked for Queen Elizabeth's hand. On this point see John Roe, *Shakespeare and Machiavelli* (Cambridge: D. S. Brewer, 2002), p. 5. For quotations from Shakespeare's plays, the edition used throughout is *The Complete Works*, 2nd edn, ed. Stanley Wells and Gary Taylor (Oxford: Clarendon Press, 2005).

10 The name of Caesar, for instance, is used in a context very similar to that of Machiavelli's *Discorsi*, I.29, in which Caesar is described as a tyrant and usurper.

11 See Nashe's reference to "Nicalao Maleuolo, Great Muster Maister of Hell", in *Pierce Penilesse His Supplication to the Divell*. The edition used is *The Works of Thomas Nashe*, eds. Ronald B. McKerrow and F. P. Wilson (Oxford: Blackwell, 1958); for this quotation, vol. 1, p. 183.

12 As shown in Alessandra Petrina, *Machiavelli in the British Isles. Two Early Modern Translations of the Prince* (Farnham, UK: Ashgate, 2009), pp. 1–45.
13 Sydney Anglo, *Machiavelli – The First Century. Studies in Enthusiasm, Hostility, and Irrelevance* (Oxford: Oxford University Press, 2005).
14 Sergio Bertelli, Piero Innocenti, *Bibliografia Machiavelliana* (Verona: Edizioni Valdonega, 1979), pp. 3–5.
15 For the notion of "creative plagiarism", see Anglo, *Machiavelli – The First Century*, pp. 42–82.
16 Charlecote Park, Warwickshire, MS L. 2. A preliminary study on this manuscript is John Humphreys Whitfield, "The Charlecote Manuscript of Machiavelli's *Prince*", *Italian Studies*, 22 (1967): 6–25 (the dating is discussed on p. 8). A facsimile of the manuscript appears in *Niccolò Machiavelli. Il Principe, with an Essay on The Prince*, ed. J. H. Whitfield (The Hague, the Netherlands: Mouton, 1969).
17 *The Arte of Warre. Certain Waies for the Ordering of Souldiers in Battelray, & Settyng of Battailes, after Diuers Fashions, with Their Maner of Marchyng: And also Fygures of Certaine New Plattes for Fortificacion of Townes: And More ouer, Howe to Make Saltpeter, Gumpoulder, and Diuers Sortes of Fireworkes or Wilde Fyre, with Other Thynges Apertaining to the Warres. Gathered and Set Foorthe by Peter Whitehorne* (London: Ihon Kingston for Nicolas Englande, 1560).
18 As concerns the *Principe* in particular, the first notice of their existence appears in John Wesley Horrocks, "Machiavelli in Tudor Political Opinion and Discussion", DLitt diss. (University of London, 1908). Other pioneer studies of these manuscript translations in England were Napoleone Orsini, "Elizabethan Manuscript Translations of Machiavelli's Prince", *Journal of the Warburg Institute*, 1 (1937): 166–69; *Studii sul Rinascimento Italiano in Inghilterra con alcuni testi inglesi inediti* (Florence: Sansoni, 1937); "Nuove ricerche intorno al machiavellismo nel Rinascimento inglese I: Machiavellismo e polemiche politiche nel manoscritto harleiano 967", *Rinascita*, 1 (1938): 92–101; "Nuove ricerche sul machiavellismo nel Rinascimento inglese II: Appunti inediti dalle 'Storie' del Machiavelli e del Guicciardini", *Rinascita*, 6 (1939): 299–304. Some of Horrocks' discoveries are re-proposed, somewhat uncritically, in Felix Raab, *The English Face of Machiavelli. A Changing Interpretation 1500–1700* (London: Routledge & Kegan Paul, 1964), and in Émile Gasquet, *Le courant machiavelien dans la pensée et la littérature anglaises du XVIe siècle* (Paris: Didier, 1974). A recent, more forceful assessment is proposed in Anglo (*Machiavelli – The First Century*), and more systematically in Petrina, *Machiavelli in the British Isles*, cit. See also Alessandra Petrina, "Translating Machiavelli's *Prince* in Early Modern England: New Manuscript Evidence", *Manuscript Studies*, 3 (2018): 302–33.
19 "I found a book written by the enemy of mankind, giving all the advice of the enemy, and explaining the ways in which religion, pity, and all manners of virtues can be easily destroyed". *Apologia Reginaldi Poli ad Carolum V. Caesarem*, in *Epistularium Reginaldi Poli S. R.E. Cardinalis Et aliorum ad ipsum Collection. Pars I* (Brixiae: Excudebat Joannes-Maria Rizzardi, 1744), pp. 66–171, p. 136.
20 On this point see Allan H. Gilbert, *Machiavelli's Prince and Its Forerunners. The Prince as a Typical Book De Regimine Principum* (Durham, NC: Duke University Press, 1938).
21 Item 285 in *Letters and Papers, Foreign and Domestic, of the Reign of Henry VIII, vol. XIV, part 1*, eds. J. Gairdner and R. H. Brodie (London: Eyre and Spottiswoode, 1864), p. 111. See Anglo, *Machiavelli – The First Century*, p. 97, and K. R. Bartlett, "Morley, Machiavelli, and the Pilgrimage of Grace", in *"Triumphs of English". Henry Parker, Lord Morley, Translator to the Stuart Court*, eds. M. Axton and J. P. Carley (London: The British Library, 2000), pp. 77–85; p. 77.
22 For this last occurrence, see Victoria Kahn, *Machiavellian Rhetoric: From the Counter-Reformation to Milton* (Princeton, NJ: Princeton University Press, 1994), p. 106. I have not, however, been able to find such an allusion in Sidney's extant correspondence to Robert.
23 Sidney's letter to Hubert Languet appears in *The Complete Works of Philip Sidney. The Defence of Poesie, Political Discourses, Correspondence, Translations*, ed. Albert Feuillerat (Cambridge: Cambridge University Press, 1923), pp. 79–98 (this quotation p. 90). English translation: "I never could be induced to believe that Machiavelli was right about avoiding an excess of clemency, until I learned from my own experience what he has endeavoured with many arguments to prove" (*The Correspondence of Philip Sidney and Hubert Languet*, ed. William Aspenwall Bradley [Boston, MA: The Merrimount Press, 1912], p. 60).

24 This is the conjecture of the modern editor. See *Leicester's Commonwealth: The Copy of a Letter Written by a Master of Art of Cambridge (1584) and Related Documents*, ed. D. C. Peck (Athens, OH and London: Ohio University Press, 1985). See also Arthur Kinney's review of this edition in *Renaissance Quarterly* 40 (1987): 565–67.

25 Quotations from *Leicester's Commonwealth* are from the modern spelling edition by Nina Green (2002), available at www.oxford-shakespeare.com/Leicester/Leicesters_Common wealth_1584.pdf (accessed November 2014).

26 *Leicester's Commonwealth*, p. 80.

27 *Leicester's Commonwealth*, p. 93. It should be noted, however, that in this specific instance the sentence might be, as has been noted, "a garbled version of an Italian proverb current in the Renaissance". See Nigel W. Bawcutt, "Some Elizabethan Allusions to Machiavelli", *English Miscellany*, 20 (1969): pp. 53–74, p. 57. As Bawcutt writes, Machiavelli himself echoes similar sentiments in chapter 7 of *Il Principe*.

28 *A Catalogue of the Harleian Manuscripts, in the British Museum. With Indexes of Persons, Places and Matters. In 4 Volumes*, vol. 1 (London: Printed by Command of his Majesty King George III, 1808), p. 486.

29 This manuscript is analysed in Petrina, *Machiavelli in the British Isles*, pp. 56–59, and edited in Ilaria Novati, "Il Principe di Machiavelli in una traduzione rinascimentale inglese (B.L. MS. Harley 967)", *Laurea* diss., Università Cattolica del Sacro Cuore di Milano, 1993–94.

30 Introduction to *Machiavelli's The Prince: An Elizabethan Translation. Edited with an Introduction and Notes from a Manuscript in the Collection of Mr Jules Furthman*, ed. Hardin Craig (Chapel Hill, NC: University of North Carolina Press, 1944), p. xxii.

31 *A Catalogue of the Harleian Manuscripts*, p. 486.

32 Kevin Sharpe, *Remapping Early Modern England: The Culture of Seventeenth-Century Politics* (Cambridge: Cambridge University Press, 2000), p. 67.

33 On this point see Henry Ruxton Woudhuysen, *Sir Philip Sidney and the Circulation of Manuscripts 1558–1640* (Oxford: Clarendon Press, 1996).

34 *The Defence of the Earl of Leicester*, in *The Complete Works of Philip Sidney*, pp. 63–64.

35 This collection of notebooks was first described in Stuart Clark, "Wisdom Literature of the Seventeenth Century: A Guide to the Contents of the 'Bacon-Tottel' Commonplace Books. Part I", *Transactions of the Cambridge Bibliographical Society*, 6 (1976): 291–305, and "Part II", *Transactions of the Cambridge Bibliographical Society*, 7 (1977): 46–73. See also Petrina, *Machiavelli in the British Isles*, pp. 63–67.

36 *The quintesence of wit being a corrant comfort of conceites, maximies, and poleticke deuises, selected and gathered together by Francisco Sansouino* (London: Edward Allde, 1590).

37 Valentina Lepri, "Machiavelli in The Quintesence of Wit and His English Military Readers", in *Machiavellian Encounters in Tudor and Stuart England. Literary and Political Influences from the Reformation to the Restoration*, eds. Alessandro Arienzo and Alessandra Petrina (Farnham, UK: Ashgate, 2013), pp. 45–57.

38 On this point see Fredi Chiappelli, *Studi sul linguaggio del Machiavelli* (Florence: Le Monnier, 1952); Sydney Anglo, *Machiavelli: A Dissection* (London: Gollancz, 1969); Eugene Garver, "Machiavelli's The Prince: A Neglected Rhetorical Classic", *Philosophy and Rhetoric*, 13 (1980): 99–120.

39 William J. Connell, "A Note about the Text and Translation", in *The Prince by Niccolò Machiavelli: With Related Documents* (Boston, MA: Bedford/St Martin's, 2005), p. ix.

40 Innocent Gentillet, *Discours sur les Moyens de bien gouverner et maintenir en bon paix vn Royaume ou autre Principauté. Divisez en trois parties: asauoir, du Conseil, de la Religion & Police que doit tenir un Prince. Contre Nicolas Machiauel, Florentin. A Treshaut & Tres-illustre Prince François Duc d'Alençon, fils & frere de Roy* (Paris, 1576), ed. by C. Edward Rathé (Geneva: Librairie Droz, 1968). It is my contention that Gentillet's influence in early modern English writing has been somewhat overrated, due to a mistaken dating as concerns the first translation of the work into English, and to an underestimation of the circulation of the Principe in early modern England. On these points see Petrina, *Machiavelli in the British Isles*, pp. 19–20, 24–25. See also J. C. Maxwell, "English Anti-Machiavellianism before Gentillet", *Notes and Queries*, 199 (1954): 141, and Nigel W. Bawcutt, "The 'Myth of Gentillet' Reconsidered: An Aspect of Elizabethan Machiavellianism", *Modern Language Review*, 99 (2004): 863–74.

41 Thomas Harding, *A Confutation of a Booke Intituled an Apologie of the Church of England* (Antwerp, 1565), f. 134v, quoted in Anglo, *Machiavelli – The First Century*, p. 329.
42 Rosalind K. Marshall, "Lesley, John (1527–1596)", *Oxford Dictionary of National Biography* (Oxford: Oxford University Press, 2004); online edn, May 2007, www.oxforddnb.com /view/article/16492, accessed November 2014.
43 [J. Lesley], *A Treatise of Treasons Against Q. Elizabeth, and the Croune of England* (Louvain, Belgium: John Fowler), 1572, p. a4.r., a5.r–a5.v. A number of other allusions to Machiavelli in Lesley's writings are discussed in Anglo, *Machiavelli – The First Century*, pp. 333–35. See also L. Arnold Weissberger, "Machiavelli and Tudor England", *Political Science Quarterly*, 42 (1927): 589–607, p. 597.
44 Napoleone Orsini, "'Policy': Or the Language of Elizabethan Machiavellianism", *Journal of the Warburg and Courtauld Institutes*, 9 (1946): 122–34, p. 122.
45 On this point see Nigel W. Bawcutt, "'Policy,' Machiavellianism, and the Earlier Tudor Drama", *English Literary Renaissance*, 1 (1971): 195–209.
46 Raab, p. 61.
47 Jonathan Scott, *England's Troubles: Seventeenth-Century English Political Instability in European Context* (Cambridge: Cambridge University Press, 2000); Michael J. Braddick, *State Formation in Early Modern England, c1550–1700* (Cambridge: Cambridge University Press, 2000).
48 Friedrich Meinecke, *Machiavellism. The Doctrine of Raison d'État and Its Place in Modern History* (New Brunswick, NJ: Transaction, 1997, first ed. 1924).
49 Zera S. Fink, *The Classical Republicans: An Essay in the Recovery of a Pattern of Thought in Seventeenth-Century England* (Evanston, IL: Northwestern University Press, 1945); John G.A. Pocock, *The Machiavellian Moment. Florentine Political Thought and the Atlantic Republican Tradition* (Princeton, NJ: Princeton University Press, 1975; Markku Peltonen, *Classical Humanism and Republicanism in English Political Thought, 1570–1640* (Cambridge: Cambridge University Press, 1995); Quentin Skinner, *Liberty before Liberalism* (Cambridge: Cambridge University Press, 1998).
50 Alessandro Arienzo, "From Machiavellian Policy to Parliamentarian Reason of State", in *Machiavellian Encounters in Tudor and Stuart England*, pp. 141–55, p. 142.
51 Raab, p. 100.
52 *Machiavels discourses. upon the first decade of T. Livius translated out of the Italian; with some marginall animadversions noting and taxing his errours. By E.D.* (London: T. Paine for W. Hills and D. Pakeman, 1636); *Nicholas Machiavel's Prince. Also, The life of Castruccio Castracani of Lucca. And The meanes Duke Valentine us'd to put to death Vitellozzo Vitelli, Oliverotto of Fermo, Paul, and the Duke of Gravina. Translated out of Italian into English; By E.D. With some animadversions noting and taxing his errours* (London: R. Bishop for W. Hils, 1640).
53 *The history of Polybius the Megalopolitan The fiue first bookes entire: with all the parcels of the subsequent bookes vnto the eighteenth, according to the Greeke originall. Also the manner of the Romane encamping, extracted from the discription of Polybius. Translated into English by Edward Grimeston, sergeant at armes* (London: N. Okes for S. Waterson, 1633).
54 Peltonen, p. 303.
55 David L. Smith, "Stuart, James, Fourth Duke of Lennox and First Duke of Richmond (1612–1655)", *Oxford Dictionary of National Biography* (Oxford: Oxford University Press, 2004); online edn, Jan. 2008 [www.oxforddnb.com/view/article/26707, accessed November 2014].
56 *Nicholas Machiavel's Prince*, sig. A2r–v.
57 *Nicholas Machiavel's Prince*, sig. A4v.
58 Jonathan Scott, *Commonwealth Principles: Republican Writing of the English Revolution* (Cambridge: Cambridge University Press, 2004), p. 85.
59 See Vickie B. Sullivan, *Machiavelli, Hobbes, & the Formation of a Liberal Republicanism in England* (Cambridge: Cambridge University Press, 2004).

18 'Boying their greatness'

Transnational effects of the Italian divas on the Shakespearean stage

Rosalind Kerr

When Cleopatra alludes to the "quick comedians" who will stage her "Alexandrian revels" imagining, "some squeaking Cleopatra boy my greatness/I th'posture of a whore" (5.2.216–17), she encapsulates the metatheatrical self-reflexivity frequently displayed by Shakespearean heroines.[1] She knows the limits of the boy actor's ability to portray the full range of the multifaceted accomplishments and infinite charms of a historic female personage such as the Egyptian queen herself. Janet Adelman, noting that these lines only work, "if we simultaneously see the boy actor speaking them and see the 'real' woman who does not want to be played parodically by some squeaking boy actor", suggests that their real effect is to draw attention to Cleopatra's feminine power as surpassing any poor imitation that the underlying boy actor's body might represent.[2] At the same time, this interpretation credits Shakespeare with an awareness that the boy actor impersonating the role was sufficiently skilled to do justice to such a sophisticated metatheatrical commentary as he prophesises how Cleopatra will be immortalised on the English stage in the future.

I am proposing that Shakespeare is drawing attention to the virtuosic acting skills intrinsic to the representation of his many unforgettable female characters and as such paying tribute to the theatrical traditions that had brought them into existence. Since many of these characters were drawn from theatre scripts developed in Italy where a new class of professional actresses were famous for their performances of the female roles, it has been argued that Shakespeare's heroines, despite being played by boys, were heavily influenced by the revolutionary changes that the Italian actresses had brought to the early modern European stage. This chapter will begin by outlining the circumstances that led to the emergence of the Italian actress on the commedia dell'arte stage. Understanding where the actresses came from, and how they transformed the professional stage, and came to be treated as celebrities in the process will provide the framework for examining their transnational impact on the English stage where the boy actor remained supreme. A survey of some of the key findings of scholars who have recently explored the transnational traces linking the two theatres will build the case and speculate on how the early Italian divas affected and effected the boy actors' representations of Shakespeare's female characters. Finally, it will argue that Shakespeare put himself in the forefront of questioning sexual differences by having his boy actors re-appropriate the transvestite disguises made famous by the actresses and, as such, called attention to the slippage between masculine and feminine sex/gender constructions that the actresses had pioneered.

DOI: 10.4324/9781315612720-21

By 1560, professional actresses had become regular members of the commedia dell'arte troupes, appearing in the *prima* and *seconda donna* roles as the refined Petrarchan *innamorata* pursued in marriage as the ultimate object of desire. Since socially respectable women would not have appeared on the public stage, the actresses are generally considered to have come from the same demographic as the "honest courtesan". After the repressive measures of the Council of Trent had curtailed their activities, these classically trained, highly educated, and accomplished salon entertainers turned to the stage. Ferdinando Taviani and Mirella Schino's well-known thesis uses the evidence of their banishment from the major Italian cities to explain the ready-made existence of a significant number of women who brought with them the ability to improvise across a variety of genres in poetry and prose, in song and dance, providing their own musical accompaniment. Such women previously seen only by their aristocratic patrons were now made visible for the first time to the wider public.[3] Much like the great courtesans before them, but on a larger scale, these actresses quickly became known across the Italian cities where they toured widely. Performing in the often revealing sumptuous clothing of the court ladies they impersonated, and known only by their first names, often the names of the characters they played, these unmasked actresses performing on trestle stages or in rented rooms in close proximity to their audiences manifested the "public intimacy" which Joseph Roach has named as the first required characteristic of celebrity.[4] "Public intimacy" – or the illusion of availability – is conveyed by the fact that the actress belongs to everyone with the price of admission to pay to see her and know her by name, even if she exists on the other side of the stage.

Roach's exciting study documenting the rise of celebrity on the long eighteenth-century English stage provides a useful blueprint for looking at the earlier appearance of the first Italian divas on the long sixteenth-century Italian and European stages. His explanation of the conditions which signal that celebrity culture is present are already in evidence a century earlier – perhaps partly owing to the revolutionary effects of putting women on the stage. Once female performers began to appear with the troupes, the crowds were drawn to their novel and, in the opinion of the church, dangerously sinful presence. Seeing "real" women on the stage playing the roles of the idealised court lady proved to be irresistible to audiences seduced by their previously unseen displays of beauty and wit. Soon after their admission, the actresses were attributed with transforming the commedia dell'arte into a new art form by combining its buffoonish roots with the scripted materials from the romantic comedies and pastorals that they excelled in improvising. By the 1560s, except in the Papal States where actresses continued to be banned, most of the troupes included two women to play the *innamorata* roles, and, although not as exclusively, since male actors could still be found in these roles, one to play the *serva* or maidservant. The women who took over the maidservant roles, unlike the *prima donnas*, may have been drawn from the street performers who arrived on the stage via the marketplace.

In trying to determine the circumstances that led to the admission of women onto the professional stage, it is usually argued that economic necessity and changing market conditions made it possible. This seems to have been the case with the migration of the honest courtesan class to the troupes but also is evident in the marketplace origins of the commedia dell'arte. In its earliest beginnings in the 1540s, commedia dell'arte troupes began their precarious existence alongside other mountebanks offering entertainments of various kinds as part of their sales pitch. It became a common practice to use attractive female assistants who displayed their skills as rope-walkers, tumblers, singers, or musicians to help sell the elixirs or whatever magic potions the mountebank was offering. Over time, these female assistants took on acting roles when the travelling companies began to offer longer dramatic presentations. The antitheatricalists made special mention of the presence of female bodies on stage as being the most pernicious because of the lust they excited in the spectators. However none of their attempts to censor scripts, prohibit performances, or to banish the actresses proved sufficient to eliminate this new theatrical art form. The two or three women who joined the troupes of ten players or so were treated as full-fledged members, some even becoming company co-directors or directors. Skilled commedia dell'arte troupes began to flourish, and gained a foothold in the courts as well as the wider public. Supported by court patronage, they made their living touring the cities and courts of northern Italy and continental Europe.

To look at what made the Italian actresses memorable in their performances of the female roles, it is helpful to examine their fame as arising from the celebrity status they achieved by becoming known to the public as individuals. As mentioned, the notoriety of their displaying their female charms on stage led audiences to view them as their intimates, with whom they could share vicariously in a "synthetic experience", as Roach designates this second "star quality".[5] In watching them perform on stage in this new embodied theatrical medium and in following their offstage public appearances, audiences became preoccupied with the intimate details of their lives. Never free from the suggestion of scandal both because of the erotic nature of their performances, and the fact that they travelled with their male counterparts, they were regarded as potentially available for liaisons. Once they started touring with the troupes across Italy and the continent, a mass audience came to know them as *role-icons*, whose images circulated well beyond their actual persons. Even at this early stage of distribution of printed materials, there was sufficient circulation of information across national boundaries to spread preconceived notions of "abnormally interesting personae" whom the public became focused on because of their charismatic appeal.[6] As their reputations began to precede them and stir up audience support even before they arrived in town, they exhibited the "It-Effect (personality-driven mass attraction)" that Roach outlines as the final and most important quality defining multifaceted genius.[7]

The records of the performances that took place in Mantua in the summers of 1567 and 1568 attest to the great acclaim which Flaminia of Rome, and Vincenza Armani received when their companies competed against each other in a series of performances. The excitement they generated swept through the city to the extent that all people could say to each other was, "*I'm for Flaminia: and I'm for Vincenza* and both houses are filled with parties of friends".[8] According to the ducal secretary, Luigi Rogna, while they both attracted large crowds of devoted fans, Flaminia seemed to appeal more to the nobility with her tragicomic improvised adaptation of Dido, outshining Vincenza, in his estimation.[9] Ultimately, Flaminia's superior strength in attracting paying customers during this run may explain why Vincenza's company departed in mid-July whereas Flaminia played on until September.[10]

The kind of celebrity status that Flaminia and Vincenza inspired fits best into the category of what social anthropologist Chris Rojek describes as *achieved* celebrity awarded by the public to individuals, often from humble beginnings, who "possess rare talents or skills".[11] Rojek's important study outlines the connections between the loss of religious faith and the rise of celebrity worship under consumer capitalism where certain figures come to be endowed with magical superhuman powers by their adoring mass audiences.[12] He contrasts the celebrity *ascribed* to royalty by bloodline with the type of *achieved* celebrity based on "the perceived accomplishments of the individual in open competition" that can be earned by outstanding artists and athletes.[13] The unique improvisational style of the commedia dell'arte required all its company members to display the utmost skill in performing their assigned roles in order to carry the action of the scenario forward. For the actresses this meant showing how well they could effortlessly perform the roles of the *innamorate* – attracting lovers to them by their beautiful appearance and skill as singers, musicians, dancers, and rhetoricians specialising in neoplatonic discourse. As improvisors, they expected to be constantly measured against their own performance standards, as well as against their rivals.

The ducal secretary Rogna's commentary applies just such a measurement when, in judging Vincenza's tragic performances to be less successful, he restricts his praise to her musical abilities and beautiful costumes. His discussion of Flaminia's "genius" in adapting Dido into a tragicomedy recognises that she and her troupe were knowledgeable about current erudite versions, and proficient enough to adapt them.[14] In choosing to play Dido as an *innamorata*, Flaminia's reinterpretation would have showcased her powers of invention and enhanced her own erotic appeal.[15] Through the very process of measuring the success of their performances with such adulation, their audiences acknowledged that they were in the presence of unique artists with magical power to transform their materials in ways that defied common understanding. Social anthropologist Alfred Gell, who has labelled this effect "the enchantment of technology", believes that such tour de force displays lead us to endow artists with supernatural powers.[16]

Such recognition of the transformational effects which the Italian actresses worked on the theatre are also found in Tommaso Garzoni's *La piazza universale di tutte le professioni del mondo* (1585). Despite scorning the common troupes, he offered outstanding praise for certain of the divas, among them Vicenza Armani. Crediting her imitation of Ciceronian eloquence with having "put the art of comedy into competition with oratory", he speaks of her as being remembered by audiences "as the most excellent comedienne of our age", although she had died tragically fifteen years earlier. Two other outstanding actresses, Vittoria Piissimi, and Isabella Andreini were also set above the others for their incomparable beauty, grace, and unsurpassed rhetorical skills as improvisers of neoplatonic love poetry. Piissimi was honoured for her "proportioned gestures, smooth and harmonious movements, masterful and pleasing actions, sweet and affable speech, roguish and cunning sighs, sweet and spicy laughter, her tall majestic bearing … a perfect decorum, that looks and belongs to a perfect actress". Andreini "had made her profession so illustrious that while the world lasts, while the centuries unfold, while time and laws endure, every voice, every tongue, every cry will echo the famous name of Isabella".[17]

Of them all, Andreini rose to the greatest heights because of her multi-faceted accomplishments, not only as an actress and company director, but also because she was known as a wife, mother, poet, scholar, playwright, and *literata* who belonged to the prestigious Academy of the Intenti and frequented academic and court circles. If she is accorded the position of the first great international diva, she also models the process of celebrification that produced a class of divas over several generations. Celebrity theorist Richard Dyer argues that the charismatic quality that marks a celebrity can only be accorded to persons known to us as flesh and blood mortals in their offstage existence. In other words, we can only "authenticate" a star's fame if we recognise a living person behind the superhuman qualities.[18] Michael Quinn develops this theory further in "Celebrity and the Semiotics of Acting" when he explains that the transcendent effects occur because of the illusion of "absolute presence" that celebrities are granted by their audiences.[19] What this means is that stars never disappear completely into any role they play, so that when we watch them we are always aware that their private selves are also present at the same time as the characters they are representing. In this way they acquire a larger-than-life existence, appearing to have full knowledge of what is happening on stage, and hence able to satisfy the desires of their fans for a completion they lack.

As the upper echelon of actresses became well known for embodying the female roles with their improvised eloquence, their reputations could not be confined to identifying them solely with the characters they played, but was always extended to refer to the actual actress who had interpreted them. For example, Isabella Andreini was always discernable whether she was playing the *innamorata* Isabella, her nymph role of Filli, or her male persona Fabrizio. The commedia dell'arte's actor-driven theatre based on improvising plotlines through a mixture of physical and gestural actions and partially scripted dialogue demanded self-reflexive performances from all its fixed character types. Actresses, who were unmasked, played their roles by at times identifying with their characters' subjective reactions, and, at others, commenting on how they were performing them. Once they had joined the troupes, they were able to adapt the important new female roles developed in the all-male erudite theatre not only to fit the trademark commedia dell'arte romantic comedy, but across all the genres which were also part of their repertoire. With women taking the parts, "women's roles could enjoy far greater scope than ever realized in erudite comedy".[20] In Flaminio Scala's famous collection covering scenarios from the late 1580s to the early 1600s, the pivotal *prima* and *seconda donna* roles feature a vast range of different female characters from the witty and wise young ingénue, the mad woman, exotic foreigners, learned astrologers, pilgrims in the comedies; Amazonian warriors, tragic queens, and enchantresses in the tragicomic pastorals.[21]

In exploring the transnational impact that the Italian actresses had on the English stage, Louise George Clubb led the way by showing how the commedia dell'arte served as the main vehicle through which the literary, dramatic, and theatrical models of the Italian Renaissance were dispersed across Europe. As key members of the troupes the actresses participated in producing the basic modules called "theatre-grams" (characters, plotlines, actions, *topoi*, dialogic structures, speech-acts, etc.) which were then endlessly recombined to produce new dramatic forms and theatrical practices.[22] Clubb noted how the "actresses enlarged the role of the *innamorata* … with their reserves of memorized material chosen for lyrical, dramatic, and emotional effect".[23] Following Clubb's explorations of several memorable English heroines related to their Italian models, especially Isabella Andreini, Frances K. Barasch suggested that the appearance of unforgettable female characters as Shakespeare's "Juliet, Beatrice, or Rosalind" may have been directly inspired by the central roles taken by actresses like Flaminia and Armani.[24] Pamela Brown traces the new emphasis on "exotically histrionic 'women' who seize the stage to deliver passionate arias of love and despair, scheme with virtuoisic flair, and display elegant wit and rhetorical sophistication" from the late 1570s on, as a follow-up to the news of the great successes of the Italian actresses abroad and the flurry of visits they had made to England.[25]

Likely inspired by glowing reports from Lord Buckhurst and the Earl of Lincoln who had seen performances by the Gelosi in Paris in 1571–72, featuring Vittoria Piissimi, Italian troupes were invited to perform at Queen Elizabeth's court soon after. In 1574, an Italian troupe performed a comedy and a pastoral at Windsor and Reading. Soon after, female acrobats performed in London, earning damning criticism for their "unchaste, shameless and unnatural tomblinge".[26] Later in 1578, Drusiano Martinelli and his company obtained a permit to "play within the Cittie and the Liberties" in 1578, possibly at the newly constructed theatre of James Burbage. Although not mentioned specifically there is strong evidence that the troupe included Drusiano's wife, Angelica Alberghini, and a *seconda donna*, Angela Salamona, and that their performances included a mix of improvised and scripted comedy, as well as music, and tumbling.[27] For whatever reasons, the records of visits of the *comici* dry up after this, and although visits resume later, the Italian theatre never established a foothold in England. Henke and others speculate that the lack of recorded visits may indicate the very strong dislike of the English of the novel presence of women and, especially, of their unseemly acrobatic displays.[28] Certainly Thomas Nashe's wholesale condemnation of the Italian theatre in 1592 on the grounds of its moral inferiority to the English contained the usual defamation of the actress: "Our Players are not as the players beyond sea, a sort of squirting baudie Comedians, that have whores and common Curtizens to play womens partes, and forbeare no immodest speech or unchast action that may procure laughter".[29] Despite the alleged disdain for the Italian stage, the English had built their theatre by borrowing heavily from its repertoire and compositional techniques. Beyond the hostile sentiments expressed against the Italians – to whom they were deeply indebted for their repertoire and compositional techniques – there was also a desire for the competitive London theatre companies to protect their own market.[30]

Since English audiences lacked the opportunity to become familiar with the great Italian actresses by watching them perform, scholars have had to carefully investigate the ways in which their notable influence on the English stage can be discerned. Julie D. Campbell's exciting in-depth exploration of *Love's Labour's Lost* highlights the centrality of the unstoppable main female characters, the charming and dissembling French princess and her ladies who overthrow the composure of the male characters. Behind its fascinating references to the historic French court with its allusions to the risqué behavior of notorious ladies-in-waiting of the *escalon volant* of Marguerite de Valois and Catherine de' Medici, the play also recalls the behaviour of the commedia dell'arte actresses who similarly took towns by storm, as we have seen in the case of Mantua.[31] Campbell suggests that Shakespeare's deliberate conflation of "outlandish yet eloquent Continental female types" would have proved highly entertaining to his English audiences especially as it showed the French court under the influence of the scandalous Italian players. While there is no doubt that the antics of the female characters fed into the English aversion to the Catholic foreigner identified by Nashe and others as whorish, Shakespeare uses the very ambiguity surrounding these characters to underscore their appeal. Having the main female characters appear very much like Italian actresses draws attention to the double-edged nature of the actresses, known as exquisitely refined, eloquent and witty, but also capable of the trickery and deceit befitting their courtesan roots.[32] Shakespeare pays tribute to the acting skills of the actresses famous for their delivery of *contrasti scenici* where pairs of lovers oppose each other in verbal trysts charged with sexual tension. He too tests his audiences by giving the female performers the same kind of control over the action that Italian actresses had in the scenarios, letting them initiate the action, drive the debates, and control the ending – much as they do in Andreini's *contrasti*.[33] Campbell, in raising the larger question about what Shakespeare was trying to convey by portraying learned women engaging in the highest levels of philosophical debate, goes even further to suggest that in leaving the question of the association of love with marriage unresolved, he might have been referencing the ambiguous marital status of most of the actresses whose reputation for touring carried with it the stigma of adultery. All in all, *Love's Labour's Lost* shows Shakespeare paying tribute to the Italian actresses and all they had contributed to bringing women's voices into the theatrical equation as full-fledged provocateurs.

Hamlet is another play where Clubb, and others, including Robert Henke, and Eric Nicholson, have cited the profound influence of the Italian players on Shakespeare, and for our purposes, the portrayal of the *innamorata forsennata* or "frenzied woman in love" by Ophelia whose descent into madness encapsulates the tragic disintegration of the corrupt Danish court. By drawing comparisons with the transformational qualities of mad performances by Italian actresses, Nicholson reclaims Ophelia's vital significance to the meaning of *Hamlet*. He brings new depths to the comparative reading by referencing stage directions found in the "bad" 1603 First Quarto describing her as "playing on a Lute, and her haire downe singing" (scene xiv, line 1690) which signal her conflation with bare-breasted lute-playing Italian actresses who had made the role famous. His richly layered reading turns Ophelia's performance of madness into that of a great actress moving between the heights of tragic grandeur and the depths of bawdy depravity.[34] As she takes over the stage, performing her full descent into the lunatic disposition that Hamlet had only feigned, she recalls the classic performances of the Italian divas driven mad from the heartbreak of disappointed love.[35] The most obvious comparison can be made to Isabella Andreini's virtuosic performance of *La pazzia* at the Medici Wedding Gala of 1589 in which she transformed from a *prima donna* into a frenzied madwoman who ripped off her clothing and tore around the stage "stopping first this person and then another, speaking now in Spanish, now in Greek, now in Italian, and many other languages, but always without making any sense".[36] In her second mad turn, she went further, "imitating the dialects of all her fellow actors – Pantalone, Gratiano, Zanni, Pedrolino, Francatrippa, Burattino, Captain Cardone, and Franceschina", reveling in caricaturing each mask in turn. Then, in keeping with her alchemic powers, she miraculously regains her sanity and brought the comedy to an end with an eloquent discourse on the transcendental powers of love. In the eyewitness account of Giuseppe Pavoni, her performance was so astounding that she "left her audiences murmuring and marvelling" at her unsurpassed "beautiful eloquence and worthiness".[37] Nicholson reveals an Ophelia who comments on the very nature of theatrical imitation itself, leaving us with an unforgettable portrait of a female character powerful enough to turn patriarchal authority upside down – much the way Andreini took over the Medicean court spectacle in 1589.[38]

When Ophelia herself falls out of the decorous "writ" of her script into the "liberty" of improvising as a mad woman, she emblematises the mixing of the two that was the hallmark of the commedia dell'arte.[39] Playing madness allowed actresses to break out of the stylistic and linguistic conventions governing the rules of decorum demarcating the generic boundaries developed in early modern theatre. Shakespeare's recognition of the commedia dell'arte's range in composing and performing "comedies, tragicomedies, tragedies, pastorals, *intermedi*, and other theatrical inventions" as Francesco Andreini boasted, comes through in Polonius's famous description that expands the list even further.[40] By showing Ophelia slipping out of her decorous behaviour as the modest, obedient daughter into the lewd, singing, clownish buffoon, Henke argues that Shakespeare is acknowledging the commedia dell'arte's practice of mixing up "the law of writ and the liberty" that concludes Polonius's speech (*Hamlet*, 2.2.398). As noted earlier, Italian actresses are credited with having transformed the commedia dell'arte when they brought their rhetorical skills in performing written scripts to the buffoon style theatre of the Pantalones and Zannis. Henke labels this form of acting as "mimetic" in contrast to the "virtuosity" of the buffoons, noting evidence for this imitative quality in Adriano Valerini's funeral oration to Armani.[41] Here Valerini references her believability in relation to her playing inside the generic rules:

> If in Comedy she made visible how much ordinary speech is embellished, she then demonstrated differently the gravity of the heroic style in tragedy, using appropriate words, weighty conceits, moral judgments worthy of being pronounced by an oracle; and if it was necessary to deliver a lament over a dead lover or relative, she found words and ways so sad that everyone was forced to experience genuine grief listening to them, and frequently to also be moved to tears, even though they knew for certain that her tears were false.[42]

When he comes to the Pastoral, he goes even further in commenting on her ability to enchant her audiences into experiencing everything she does:

> What shall I say of the pastoral plays that she was the first to introduce on the stage, which she spun out in such charming incidents that she also engulfed her spectators with a superabundance of sweetness and astonishment? And if, on finding some clear fountain she demonstrated a yearning to slake her burning thirst, she induced her audience to have the same desire to drink, and to rest, if she yearned to take a rest under some shady tree, and if, to taste the crystal liquid, she sat in the shade and bent her lips over to drink, the spectators also bent their heads down, accompanying her movements, as if they had been her shadow. Such was the force of the words that she used to describe this or that affect.

Henke's recognition of this "mimetic aesthetic" as the gift of the actresses to early modern theatre explains why their representations of female characters were so memorable.[43] In Armani's case this ability to colour her speech in such a way that her audiences believed in her fictional persona owed a great deal to her training in oratorical persuasion. Valerini reveals as much when he notes that her fans love her performances even more when they know that she is using her great artifice to manipulate them. Such are the attributes of a diva whose fans identify with her, vicariously experiencing everything she does. The effect is theatrically intensified because they are aware of her as both the character she is impersonating and as the celebrity figure, who is always present as Armani herself, and hence able to draw attention to her great technical skills in creating the role.

Shakespeare and his contemporaries were in sufficient awe of the actresses that female parts continued to proliferate on the English stage. By the 1590s when the Italian actresses were reaching the apex of success, English playwrights were writing major female roles demanding similarly great acting skills and rhetorical mastery but without actresses to perform them.[44] For Brown, such an emphasis on female parts indicates that the missing actresses had made a great imprint on the English stage, and that in an effort to compensate for their absence, Shakespeare created them in simulacra for the boy actors to play.[45] One of her striking examples of a counterfeit diva is Portia from *The Merchant of Venice*, who "revels in artifice and theatricality … displays wit, daunting eloquence, a shrewd head for plotting, skill at cross-gender disguise, and obvious pride in her acting and directing … acts suspiciously like the celebrated *innamorata* of the Italian acting troupes".[46] The notion of simulacra is an essential diva quality, proof that the celebrity has acquired an existence in the minds of followers that cannot be extinguished even by death. This supernatural quality meant that even without their actual presence, the divas lived in "effigy" in their transnational representations across the English Channel.[47]

If the "actress gap" remained an issue, the answer as to how the boy actors succeeded in addressing it may be found in their similar combination of starting out by inviting their spectators to accept their artifice and then drawing them in to believe in the emotional truths of the female characters they were performing. The Italian divas, as recognised stars, spoke from strong subject positions, improvising to bring their fictional characters to life, but always drawing attention to their playmaking abilities and virtuosic acting. The boy actors, who were for the most part unknown since their short careers and inferior status as apprentices made it difficult for them to make a name for themselves,[48] had to find ways to capitalise on their youthful androgyny to simulate their diva models, often by drawing the spectators' attention to their obvious gaps in doing so. Boy actors typically drew attention to their physical immaturity, puny stature, changeable voices as a kind of running metatheatrical joke that prepared the spectators to accept their "personations" of the female characters they were playing.[49] This mimetic technique, which we have already seen being practiced by the Italian actresses, was aimed at convincing spectators of the emotional plausibility of what they were witnessing. Michael Goldman has described how Shakespeare responded to address the perceived gap in the boy actor's abilities in the example of the role of Cleopatra by noting how the style of her dialogue and the emotional qualities it reflects change throughout the play. As she moves from one style of self-presentation to a more demanding one, the boy actor who speaks her lines is shown moving beyond the limits of his art.[50] In identifying with his efforts to stretch as far as he could, spectators might actually believe that her greatness had been captured. Since English audiences also knew that Italian divas were performing such roles with the full tragic range they deserved, the simulacra effect may also have helped them to fill in the gaps.

Another transnational actress effect imported to the English stage from the Italian theatre was the widely popular cross-dressed heroine role. Originally developed in the all-male erudite theatre, this role features the exploits of renegade female characters who adopt male disguise in order to circulate freely in public spaces without violating stage decorum.[51] Since respectable female characters were restricted by social conventions from appearing in public places unaccompanied, the device of adopting male dress licensed the cross-dressed heroine to pursue her own desires and enjoy all the prerogatives normally reserved for men. Such transgressive behaviour made her the focus of much of the erotic attention of the play and commonly resulted in her unintentionally attracting the love of another woman, as an ultimate sign of her power. This plot device, which had been passed down from *La Calandra* (*The Comedy of Calandro*), was further developed in *Gl'ingannati* (*The Deceived*) where Lelia disguises herself as the page Fabio, who enters into the service of her master, only to find herself the object of the erotic desire of the woman she is sent to woo on his behalf.[52] Under the protective fiction that Fabio is really Lelia, the all-male players of the Sienese Academy of the Intronati could pretend to appease the female audience members, while at the same time enjoying the underlying references to the homoerotic attraction that Lelia's male costume excites. Fabio, who is described as a young pansy who can trade on his beardless chin, fresh cheeks and rosy lips, fits the stereotype of the younger partner in the male/male relationships that continued to define aristocratic society in Italian urban centres.[53]

When the actresses took over these roles on the professional stage, they also played with their sexual ambiguity by dressing up in the sumptuous clothing of the male courtier, and impersonating the ideal traits and accomplishments associated with members of this new social elite.[54] They also performed the cross-dressed roles self-reflexively, inviting spectators to share with them in breaking the taboos against putting on male disguise. Because they were "real" women making their precarious way in the acting profession, their attempts to negotiate more fluid sexual identities within the dramatic fiction offered spectators the chance to see how they too might break out of the gender conventions that hierarchised male and female sexual differences. The popularity of the transvestite disguise is quantifiable in the Scala scenarios where female characters push at the social boundaries by appearing as Turkish slaves, merchants, male servants, pilgrims, and even, in one case, as a lesbian husband. [55]

The sheer delight in pulling off male imposture is captured by Andreini whose male persona Fabrizio became justly famous.[56] In *Li finti servi* (*The Disguised Servants*, Day 30), she, as Fabrizio, begs her audience for help in resolving the predicament her gentleman page disguise has led her into.[57] Not only has Flaminia, the daughter of the house, fallen madly in love with her, but she also believes that Fabrizio has fathered her child.[58] With all the attention focused on discovering who "he" really is, Fabrizio must continue to keep up his role as her male lover, while at the same time, making every effort to get Orazio, his young master, to see that he is really Isabella under his costume. Her direct appeals to the audience implicate them in seeing her as both the actress and the sexy pageboy whose disguise remains impenetrable until the end. A sustained visual trick, her love scenes with the pregnant Flaminia keep the image of the transgressive lesbian couple in full view for the pleasure of the audience.

Another scenario showing Andreini at the height of her transvestite artistry is *La gelosa Isabella* (*Isabella's Jealousy*, Day 25) which replays the return of the missing identical twin brother in *The Deceived*. The introduction of this plotline allows her to deliver a tour de force performance of her ability to transcend male-female boundaries by having her appear as both "Isabella in male attire", and as her missing brother Fabrizio. All about Isabella's "jealousy", not only of her lover Orazio, but also of her unparalleled acting skills, the scenario turns on the metatheatrical question of whether "Isabella in male disguise" can be distinguished from her Fabrizio impersonation. It begins with Isabella deciding to put on a male disguise in order to challenge her lover Orazio to a duel for having betrayed her and wandering the streets armed with her sword. But then it is complicated by having her also appear as Fabrizio, as that story line is reintroduced by Isabella, but never accepted by the other characters. The joke that no one believes in Fabrizio's existence, but always perceives "him" as Isabella, makes for great comedy and depends upon the spectators buying into Isabella's identity shifts that show her playing masculinity with subtle variations that only they are able to discern. Eventually the scenario comes to its climactic repeat of the ruse where Fabrizio gets taken inside to have sex with the daughter of the neighbouring household, all because he cannot be distinguished from "Isabella in male disguise". When the maid Franceschina exclaims, "Isabella has become a man!" (act 3; 256), and reports on the sexual activity she has seen, echoing the dialogue from *The Deceived*, the ruse is complete, and Andreini could claim that she had outperformed the male actor who presumably also took both Lelia and Fabrizio's parts in the erudite theatre.

Scala's showcasing of Andreini's performances as Fabrizio highlights female transvestite practices as self-reflexive, highly stylised male impersonations that are all about deception. The pleasure that the audience took in watching such performances suggests that wearing the clothing of the opposite sex evoked a strong reaction in the audience that had very little to do with the actual male or female body parts beneath:

> The actor is both boy and woman, and he/she embodies the fact that sexual fixations are not the product of any categorical fixity of gender. Indeed, all attempts to fix gender are necessarily prosthetic: that is, they suggest the attempt to supply an imagined deficiency by the exchange of male clothes for female clothes or of female clothes for male clothes … But all elaborations of the prosthesis which will supply the "deficiency" can secure no essence. On the contrary, they suggest that gender itself is a fetish, the production of an identity through the fixation on specific parts.[59]

Their argument rests on the fact that no female parts could be found under the boy actors' costumes on the English stage, which leads me to suggest that seeing women in male costumes on the Italian and other continental stages worked in a similar prosthetic fashion. If boys could impersonate women by exchanging male for female clothes and women could supply a similar deficiency by putting on male clothes, then spectators who accepted these impersonations were also automatically supplying the lack in both cases.[60]

When the plot of *The Deceived* was refashioned in Shakespeare's *Twelfth Night*, Rachel Poulsen notes the debt to both the cross-dressed heroine who sparks the love of another woman formula, and to the iconic Italian actress for her "desirable beauty, verbal agility, and rhetorical skill".[61] In the opening scene of *Twelfth Night*, both the *prima donna*, Olivia, and the cross-dressed heroine, Viola/Cesario, pay tribute to the Italian actresses' reputation for both gender disguise and rapid improvised repartee. When the dramatically veiled Olivia urges the attractively costumed page to go off his script, and speak extemporaneously to her, the tour de force exchange between them that follows once her veil is removed can only end with her falling madly in love with him. Shakespeare was also capitalising on the erotic attraction of the transvestite disguise, which carried extra significance by referencing the offstage sexual availability and questionable social status of both the actresses and the boy actors.[62] In both cases, in the dramatic fictions where they use their transvestite disguises to insert themselves into the early modern household, the fear of discovery of their actual sex seems to be less a concern then using their renegade sexual appeal to win a place for themselves in the social hierarchy.[63]

As Katherine Kelly describes it:

> [t]he Shakespeare of the comedies … in foregrounding gender as a cultural performance by relating it metaphorically to the actor's art, not only refused to reinforce the prevailing view of women as fixed and stable entities in the Elizabethan social hierarchy but invited a critical reading of gender roles as permanent designations of womanhood and manhood.[64]

Thus, Shakespeare's referencing of Italian stylistic techniques from the actresses' subversively erotic male impersonations suggests that he created his "breeches' parts to similarly expose "gender roles as performed fictions 'put on' by actors for the sake of a viewing public".[65] His other cross-dressed heroines: Julia/Sebastian in *Two Gentlemen of Verona*, Portia/Balthazar in *The Merchant of Venice*, Rosalind/Ganymede in *As You Like It*, and Imogen/Fidele in *Cymbeline* are all crafted so that we see both the skilled boy actor and his female persona superimposed on each other for the maximum theatrical effect. As Brown outlines it:

> [d]iva envy generated pressures that were highly productive for English drama, leading Shakespeare and others to create, for the first time, complex, articulate, and agential female roles that combined the Italianate glamour and methods of the foreign actress with the skills and distinctive identity of the English boy player.

In response he created "a hybrid marvel forged under pressure – neither Italian nor English, neither boy nor woman, but a boy diva".[66]

Shakespeare captured the great artifice of the Italian divas by having his boy actors bring unforgettable female characters to life through similarly enticing "oscillating" layers of disguise.[67] In noting how Shakespeare paid tribute to the actresses, from their courtly sophistication in *Love's Labour's Lost* to the protean madness of Ophelia, the grandeur of Cleopatra, and the subversive comic genius of the cross-dressed heroines, I add my voice to the other scholars who have shown that their impact was far-reaching. Brought to life in fictitious creations, the great female characters acquired an immortality that reflects the transcendent qualities of the famous actresses who had inspired their creation. In this way, Shakespeare went some distance to filling the gap of the missing actresses, showing his awareness of the great contribution they had made to the emergence of the early modern stage. The immortality that Cleopatra longs for echoes the immortality that Italian divas such as Andreini achieved, when after her tragic early death, the shock of her absence led to tributes such as this:

> Cry empty Theatres: still waiting in vain among you for your beautiful Siren She disdains mortal ear and earthly sight and there where she once descended, ascends. Here, LIT with love, with love inflames the eternal Lover; and on the Heavenly Stage filled with angelic lights, she sings sweetly, loves sweetly and shines sweetly.[68]

Notes

1 William Shakespeare, "Anthony and Cleopatra", in *The Complete Works*, eds. Stanley Wells and Gary Taylor (Oxford: Oxford University Press, 1998).
2 Janet Adelman, "Making Defect Perfection: Shakespeare and the One-Sex Model", in *Acting Gender on the English Renaissance Stage*, eds. Viviana Comensoli and Anne Russell (Chicago, IL: University of Chicago Press, 1999), p. 24.
3 Ferdinando Taviani and Mirella Schino, *Il segreto della commedia dell'arte. La memoria delle compagnie italiane del XVI, XVII e XVIII secolo* (Florence: La Casa Usher, 1982), pp. 336–37.
4 Joseph Roach, *It* (Ann Arbor, MI: University of Michigan Press, 2010), p. 3.
5 Ibid., 3.
6 Ibid., 12.
7 Ibid., 3.
8 In Alessandro D'Ancona, *Origini del teatro italiano*. 2 vols. (Turin: Loescher, 1891, repr., Rome: Bardi, 1971), 2, p. 452 (original emphasis). Translations are my own unless otherwise indicated.

9 Ibid., 2:453.
10 Ibid., 2:447. However, Vincenza's departure could also indicate that the market could not support two companies. We know that the rivalry was partly fabricated since the two companies were asked to join together the following year by the Duke of Mantua. Ibid., 2:455.
11 Chris Rojek, *Celebrity* (London: Reaktion Books, 2001), p. 18.
12 Ibid., pp. 52–53.
13 Ibid., pp. 17–18.
14 D'Ancona refers to the two possible sources as *Didone* by Venetian Lodovico Dolce, published in 1547, or by Giambattista Giraldi Cinthio, published in Ferrara in 1583, but probably written much earlier. In *Origini*, 2:449n2.
15 Frances K. Barasch notes that Flaminia's impersonation of Dido as an *innamorata* fell into the tradition of the famous women poets like Gaspara Stampa and Tullia d'Aragona who had "appropriated the classics to redefine heroics within the emotional world of women". "Italian Actresses in Shakespeare's World: Flaminia and Vincenza", *Shakespeare Bulletin*, 18, 4 (2000): 19. Additionally, Robert Henke observes that the "erotic rhetoric of pastoral drama would have well suited Flaminia in performing the role of Dido, especially in composing a pastoral-style *lamento* excoriating her perfidious lover". *Performance and Literature in the Commedia dell'Arte* (Cambridge: Cambridge University Press, 2002), p. 88.
16 Alfred Gell, "The Technology of Enchantment and the Enchantment of Technology", in *Anthropology, Art and Aesthetics*, eds. Jeremy Coote and Anthony Shelton (Oxford: Clarendon Press, 1992), pp. 51–52.
17 Tommaso Garzoni, *La piazza universale*. Excerpted in Ferruccio Marotti and Giovanna Romei, *La Commedia dell'Arte e la Società Barocca: La Professione del Teatro* (Rome: Bulzoni, 1991), pp. 12–13.
18 Richard Dyer defines authenticity as "both a quality necessary to the star phenomenon to make it work, and also the quality that guarantees the authenticity of the other particular values a star embodies. It is the effect of authenticating authenticity that gives the star charisma". "*A Star Is Born* and the Construction of Authenticity", in *Stardom: Industry of Desire*, ed. Christine Gledhill (London and New York: Routledge, 1991), p. 133.
19 Michael L. Quinn, "Celebrity and the Semiotics of Acting", *New Theatre Quarterly*, 6, 22 (1990): 157.
20 Douglas Radcliff-Umstead, "The Erudite Comic Tradition of the *commedia dell'arte*", in *The Science of Buffoonery. Theory and History of the Commedia dell'Arte*, ed. Domenico Pietropoalo (Toronto: Dovehouse, 1989), p. 47.
21 Flaminio Scala, *Il teatro delle favole rappresentative*, 2 vols., ed. Ferruccio Marotti (Milan: Il Polifilo, 1976). Further citations are in the text and indicate act and page number.
22 Louise George Clubb, *Italian Drama in Shakespeare's Time* (New Haven, CT: Yale University Press, 1989), p. 6. See Robert Henke for a discussion of her more recent articles in his "Introduction" and first chapter, "Border-Crossing in the *Commedia dell'Arte*", in *Transnational Exchange in Early Modern Drama*, eds. Robert Henke and Eric Nicholson (Farnham, UK: Ashgate, 2008), pp. 1–15; 19–34. See also, "Back to the Future: A Review of Comparative Studies in Shakespeare and the *Commedia dell'Arte*", *Early Theatre*, 11, 2 (2008): 227–40.
23 Clubb, *Italian Plays (1500–1700) in the Folger Library* (Florence: Leo S. Olschki, 1968), p. xxii.
24 Frances K. Barasch, "Italian Actresses in Shakespeare's World: Vittoria and Isabella", *Shakespeare Bulletin*, 19, 5 (2001): 5.
25 Pamela Allen Brown, "'Cattle of this Colour': Boying the Diva in *As You Like It*", *Early Theatre* 15, 1 (2012): 145.
26 Henke is quoting Thomas Norton (1574), "Border-Crossing", p. 31.
27 Brown, "Cattle of This Colour", p. 147.
28 Henke, "Back to the Future", p. 229.
29 Thomas Nashe, "Pierce Pennilesse His Supplication to the Divill", in *The Works of Thomas Nashe*, ed. Ronald B. McKerrow, 5 vols. (London: Sidgewick and Jackson, 1910), 1, p. 215.

30 Kenneth Richards, "Inigo Jones and the *Commedia dell'arte*", in *The Commedia dell'Arte from the Renaissance to Dario Fo*, ed. Christopher Cairns (Lewiston, ME: Edwin Mellen Press, 1989), pp. 220–21.
31 Julie D. Campbell, "Merry, Nimble, Stirring Spirit[s]: Academic, Salon and Commedia dell'arte Influence on the *Innamorate* of *Love's Labour's Lost*", in *Women Players in England, 1550–1600: Beyond the All-Male Stage*, eds. Pamela Allen Brown and Peter Parolin (Farnham, UK: Ashgate, 2005), pp. 145–46.
32 Ibid., pp. 147–48.
33 Isabella Andreini's *contrasti scenici* featuring several dialogues for opposing lovers that she probably played in herself, show the invincible wit of her female performers. They are collected in *Fragmenti di alcune scritture della signora Isabella Andreini Comica Gelosa, et Academia Intenta. Raccolti da Francesco Andreini Comico Geloso, detto il Capitano Spavento, e dati in luce da Flamminio Scala Comico, e da lui dedicati all'illustrissimo Sig. Filippo Capponi* (Venice: Gio. Battista Combi, 1620).
34 Eric Nicholson, "Ophelia Sings Like a *Prima Donna Innamorata*: Ophelia's Mad Scene and the Italian Female Performer", in *Transnational Exchange*, pp. 81–84.
35 A very popular comic trope, it appears in several Scala scenarios. Three notable ones which resemble the plotline of the missing *La pazzia d'Isabella* are: *Flavio Tradito* (*Flavio Betrayed*, Day 5, 1: 66–74); *La finta pazza* (*The Fake Madwoman*, Day 8, 1: 93–99); and *Il fido amico* (*The Faithful Friend*, Day 29, 2: 293–303).
36 The full script of the scenario that Andreini performed on that occasion is lost, but there are sufficient details to reconstruct the event in the glowing account of Pavoni, Giuseppe, *Diario descritto da Giuseppe Pavoni delle feste celebrate nelle solennissime nozze delli Serenissimi Sposi il Sig. Don Ferdinando Medici e la Sig. Donna Christina di Loreno Gran Duchi di Toscana* (Bologna: Giovanni Rossi, 1589), in Flaminio Scala, *Il teatro*, Appendix 2, 1: lxxiii–lxxv.
37 Ibid., p. lxxv.
38 "Ophelia Sings", p. 96.
39 Henke, "Virtuosity and Mimesis in the *Commedia dell'arte* and *Hamlet*", in *Italian Culture in the Drama of Shakespeare and His Contemporaries: Rewriting, Remaking, Refashioning*, ed. Michele Marrapodi (Farnham, UK: Ashgate, 2005), pp. 70–71.
40 Francesco Andreini, Dedication, from *Le Bravure del Capitano Spavento* (Venice: Somasco, 1607), in Marotti and Romei, p. 218.
41 "Virtuosity and Mimesis", p. 77.
42 Adriano Valerini, *Oratione d'Adriano Valerini Veronese, in morte della divina signora Vincenza Armani, comica excellentissima* (Verona: 1570), in Marotti and Romei, p. 36.
43 "Virtuosity and Mimesis", pp. 77–78.
44 Brown, "Cattle of this Colour", p. 145. For actual line counts to show how much these parts grew, she references the appendix in David Mann, *Shakespeare's Women: Performance and Conception* (Cambridge: Cambridge University Press, 2008).
45 "The Counterfeit *Innamorata*, or, the Diva Vanishes", in *Shakespeare and Italy*, eds. Holger Klein and Michele Marrapodi (*Shakespeare Yearbook*, 10, Lampeter, UK: Edwin Mellen Press, 1999), p. 408.
46 Ibid., p. 411.
47 Roach, *It*, pp. 43–44.
48 However, Roberta Barker names a few and questions the assumption that they were never big names, especially boy-actresses who went on to play men's roles. "'Not One Thing Exactly': Gender, Performance and Critical Debate Over the Early Modern Boy-Actress", *Literature Compass*, 6, 2 (2009): 475.
49 See Andrew Gurr, *The Shakespearean Stage*, 2nd edn. (Cambridge: Cambridge University Press, 1980), p. 98.
50 Michael Goldman, *The Actor's Freedom: Toward a Theory of Drama* (New York: Viking Press, 1975), p. 142.
51 Jane Tylus comments on the prevalent appearance of women in upper-storey windows in the Scala scenarios – evidence that they were not allowed to move freely in public spaces. "Women at the Windows: *Commedia dell'Arte* and Theatrical Practice in Early Modern Italy", *Theatre Journal*, 49, 3 (1997): 325.

52 Robert C. Melzi traces the many variations that the *Gl'ingannati* plot spawned during the seventy years separating it from Shakespeare's *Twelfth Night*, noting that, in addition to being translated into several languages, it also inspired several plays and novellas that may have provided Shakespeare with his models. His particular interest in the transvestite *innamorata* role confirms the enduring dramatic appeal of this transgressive figure. "From Lelia to Viola", *Renaissance Drama*, 9 (1966): 67–81.

53 Fabio is warned about the fleeting nature of his androgynous beauty: "Remember that you are just a young dandy, and you don't really understand how lucky you are. But this fascination with you isn't going to last forever, you know. You're going to grow a beard, your cheeks aren't going to remain so fresh, your lips so red. You won't always be so sought after by everyone – no, sir". *The Deceived*, in *Five Comedies from the Italian Renaissance*, trans. and ed. by Laura Giannetti and Guido Ruggiero (Baltimore, MD: Johns Hopkins University Press, 2003), p. 229.

54 Marjorie Garber sees the practice as reflecting changes in the fabric of society: "Transvestism was located at the juncture of 'class' and 'gender,' and increasingly through its agency gender and class were revealed to be commutable, if not equivalent. To transgress against one set of boundaries was to call into question the inviolability of both, and of the set of social codes – already demonstrably under attack – by which such categories were policed and maintained. The transvestite in this scenario is both terrifying and seductive precisely because s/he incarnates and emblematises the disruptive element that intervenes, signaling not just another category crisis, but – much more disquietingly – a crisis of 'category' itself". *Vested Interests: Cross-Dressing and Cultural Anxiety* (New York and London: Routledge, 1997), p. 32.

55 Scala, *Il teatro*. The fifteen comic examples are: "La fortuna di Flavio" (Day 2), where Alissa appears as Turchetto; "La finta pazza" (Day 8), with Flaminia as Bigolo; "Il marito" (Day 9), with Franceschina as Cornelio; "La sposa" (Day 10), with Isabella as a male servant; "Il pellegrino fido amante" (Day 14), with Isabella as Fabrizio; "Lo specchio" (Day 16), with Isabella as Fabrizio; "Li tragici successi" (Day 18), with Isabella in male disguise; "Li tre fidi amici" (Day 19), with Flaminia in male disguise; "Il finto Tofano" (Day 24), with Isabella as Tofano; "La gelosa Isabella" (Day 25), with Isabella as Fabrizio; "Li tappeti alessandrini" (Day 26), with Isabella as Fabrizio; "La mancata fede" (Day 27), with Isabella in male disguise; "Li finti servi" (Day 30), with Isabella as Fabrizio; "Il ritratto" (Day 39), with Silvia Milanese as Lesbino; "Il giusto castigo" (Day 40), with Isabella in male disguise. Further, the transvestite figure is not restricted to comedy but also assumes tremendous importance in seven of the ten serious mixed genre final scenarios: "Gli avvenimenti, comici, pastorali e tragici" (Day 42), with the nymph Fillide as the shepherd Coridone; "L'Alvida" (Day 43), with the Amazonian warrior Brandino; "L'innocente persiana" (Day 45), with the Amazonian warrior Teodora; "Parte I – Dell'Oreseida" (Day 46), with the princess Eurilla as a shepherd; "III Parte – Dell'Orseida" (Day 48), with the Amazonian warrior Alvida; "L'arbore incantato" (Day 49), with the nymph Fillide as the shepherd Lesio, and "La fortuna di foresta prencipessa di Moscovia" (Day 50), with the princess Lucella in male disguise.

56 She appears as Fabrizio in Days 14, 16, 25, 26, and 30. Richard Andrews noting that the name Fabrizio is borrowed from the transvestite heroine's brother in *Gli ingannati* (*The Deceived*), comments that Scala likely created such scenarios to give Andreini "a chance to display a different dramatic range". *The Commedia dell'Arte Scenarios of Flaminio Scala*, ed. and trans. by Richard Andrews (Lanham, MD: Scarecrow Press, 2008), p. 77.

57 The plot also resembles that of another erudite comedy, Ariosto's *I suppositi* (*The Pretenders*), in which the young lady of the household disgraces herself by becoming pregnant with someone who appears to be a lowly servant. *The Pretenders* in *The Comedies of Ariosto*, trans. and ed. by Edmond M. Beame and Leonard G. Sbrocchi (Chicago, IL: University of Chicago Press, 1975), pp. 52–98. While Ariosto's comedy is eventually resolved by the discovery that the young man in question was impersonating his own servant in order to infiltrate the household, Scala raises the stakes by making the imposter a young woman.

58 It is only later that the mystery is solved by the information that Isabella's brother Cintio has been paying Flaminia nightly visits.

59 Anne Rosalind Jones and Peter Stallybrass, "Transvestism and the 'Body Beneath': Speculating on the Boy Actor", in *Renaissance Clothing and the Materials of Memory* (Cambridge: Cambridge University Press, 2000), p. 217.

60 Laura Giannetti's description of the fluidity of gender categories in early modern Italy supports this argument. She claims "that the different social roles assigned to men and women were based on a patriarchal social order much more than on any natural differences". *Lelia's Kiss: Imagining Gender, Sex, and Marriage in Italian Renaissance Comedy* (Toronto: University of Toronto Press, 2009), p. 15.

61 Rachel Poulsen, "Women Performing Homoerotic Desire in English and Italian Comedy: *La Calandria, Gl'Ingannati* and *Twelfth Night*", in *Women Players in England, 1550–1600: Beyond the All-Male Stage*, eds. Pamela Allen Brown and Peter Parolin (Farnham, UK: Ashgate, 2005), p. 171.

62 Actresses in transvestite disguise suggested their close association with prostitutes and courtesans who wore breeches in public to attract customers. The boy actors were also considered to be sexually vulnerable as apprentices who were the property of the actors who owned them, and could be rented out or sold accordingly.

63 Lisa Jardine argues that the *dependency* governing the practice of transvestism in the marketplace was mirrored in the stage representation of the transvestite who enters into private service in a household. Both dependent youths and dependent women were expected to submit to their masters, unless they could negotiate a more equitable relationship by using their sexual appeal. "Twins and Travesties: Gender, Dependency and Sexual Availability in *Twelfth Night*", in *Erotic Politics: Desire on the Renaissance Stage*, ed. Susan Zimmerman (New York and London: Routledge, 1992), p. 28.

64 Katherine E. Kelly, "The Queen's Two Bodies: Shakespeare's Boy Actress in Breeches", *Theatre Journal*, 42, 1 (1990): 82.

65 Ibid., p. 92.

66 Brown, "Cattle of This Colour", pp. 159–60.

67 Michael Shapiro, *Gender in Play on the Shakespearean Stage: Boy Heroines and Female Pages* (Ann Arbor, MI: University of Michigan Press, 1994), p. 7.

68 Giovanni Battista Marini, in *Lettere della signora Isabella Andreini padovana, comica gelosa e academica Intenta, nominata l'Accesa* (Venice: Marc'Antonio Zaltieri, 1607). In Marotti and Romei, p. 167.

19 *Commedia dell'Arte* in early modern English drama

Eric Nicholson

Preamble: insularity vs. openness

The result of the so-called "Brexit" referendum of June 2016, sanctioning the self-withdrawal of the United Kingdom from the European Union, startled and even shocked millions of observers worldwide. The general expectation was that the "Yes" vote, to remain in the EU, would win out, based on an assumption that the majority of post-World War II British subjects felt themselves to be part of Europe, at least at the economic and basic political levels. Instead, the insular and xenophobic spirit seemed to prevail, in a return to anti-Continental and culturally chauvinist attitudes which have periodically marked English history. Such attitudes, however, are anomalous and by definition reactionary. Overwhelming historical fact confirms that, since the early Middle Ages, English culture, in almost all of its manifestations – and especially artistic ones – has emerged through dynamic mixing, hybridising, and cross-fertilising. To take but two examples, 600 years apart from each other: two of the major literary masterpieces produced in late medieval England, Chaucer's *Troilus and Criseyde* and *The Canterbury Tales*, could not have been written without their author's use of numerous tropes, narratives, and conventions from the Italian and French languages, any more than the innovative popular "rock" music of The Beatles, The Rolling Stones, Led Zeppelin, David Bowie, and their contemporaries could have been produced without the vital influence and assimilation of traditions as diverse as African-American Blues, German cabaret, and Indian raga. In other words, leading English writers, painters, architects, musicians, and performing artists have always tended to look overseas for inspiration. Few pro-"Brexit" votes would be cast by members of such a constituency.

This open-minded, creatively appropriating pattern also applies to early modern English drama, including its usage of the so-called *Commedia dell'Arte*, the innovatively professional and versatile form(s) of performance developed and exported throughout Europe by Italian theatre artists during the late sixteenth and early seventeenth centuries.[1] This assertion is an indisputable one, but it could not have been made with such confidence twenty-five years ago. One of the main objectives of this chapter is to explain and confirm how a wave of international theatre scholarship, among whose eminent leaders is the current volume's editor Michele Marrapodi, has demonstrated that the *Commedia dell'Arte* vitally shaped and transformed English drama, all through the period spanning the 1570s to the 1720s.[2] This transformation was a truly heterogeneous and

DOI: 10.4324/9781315612720-22

global one, in the sense that it affected a vast array of theatrical and para-theatrical expressions: not only the fully scripted plays of Marlowe, Shakespeare, Jonson, Middleton, Fletcher, Wycherley, Behn, Gay, and others, but also jigs, masques, pageants, clown routines, ballets, operas, pantomimes, and puppet shows. I will be citing and assessing examples from these authors and these contexts, with the aim of clarifying the wide range of practices, adaptations, attitudes – including, yes, some hostile and pro-English "protectionist" ones – that pertained to relations and exchanges between the *Commedia dell'Arte* and early modern England. Given that the recognition of these transformative relations and exchanges is still a recent one, numerous opportunities remain for researchers and practitioners in this exciting field.

A new full-time profession for the modern world: theatre

While no exact "launch-date" can be identified for the *Commedia dell'Arte*, there is general agreement that the late 1540s to early 1550s was the decade when, in northern Italy, the first full-time European professional acting companies since late antiquity were formed. Precious evidence comes from the contracts (spanning the years 1545–1553) drawn up in the Veneto region, by the company leaders "Ser Maphio" and Francesco Moschini: this same period, then, saw the formalisation and consolidation of the semi-professional, polyglot troupes led by prominent Veneto playwrights/actors/directors of the preceding generation, like Angelo Beolco ("il Ruzante") and Andrea Calmo.[3] Transregional and transnational mobility, and a reaching out to socially, culturally, and linguistically diverse audiences already distinguish this initial phase of professionalisation. For example, one company petitions for patronage in Rome, while another stages a revival of Bibbiena's *Calandra*, in 1548 at Lyons, France, for the ceremonial entry of King Henri II and his bride Caterina dei Medici, and yet one more receives payment, along with Spanish performers, for having "dawnsed antyck & played dyvers other feats" before the Mayor of Norwich in 1546–1547.[4] Records are sparse and haphazard, but sufficient enough to allow the postulation that early *commedia* troupes also could have performed in London, and likewise that English travellers to the Continent would have had opportunities to attend *commedia* shows. By the mid-sixteenth century, the English "Grand Tour" was beginning to become a fixture for young aristocrats, while the University of Padua, even after the Reformation, continued to host numerous students from the British Isles, among them the physician John Caius and the poet-courtier-soldier Sir Philip Sidney. The latter group found themselves in an inter-cultural "contact zone", also a particularly flourishing area of *commedia* activity, as Shakespeare's *The Taming of the Shrew* seems to acknowledge (more on this play later).

By the 1570s, English familiarity with the *commedia* gains full realisation. With Elizabeth I – herself well-versed in the Italian language – and her court favouring Italianate fashions in literature, music, and design, and negotiations proceeding (if fitfully) for a marriage between the Queen and the French Duc d'Alençon, English ambassadors observed and reported on Italian performances in Paris and Blois. The ambassadors' positive response to such entertainments may have encouraged Italian professional theatrical activity in England in the ensuing years, both at court and in cities. Notable cases include performances of a pastoral play, possibly Tasso's *Aminta*, for the Queen during her formal progress from Windsor to Reading in 1574, and in 1575 the participation of Italian technicians and acrobats – including, possibly, Soldino of

Florence, admired by the Earl of Lincoln two years previously in Paris – in the lavish, three-weeks long festivities presented in Kenilworth by Elizabeth's favourite, Robert Dudley, the Earl of Leicester. In 1578, the prominent company of Drusiano Martinelli, brother of the even more famous Tristano, inventor of the character Arlecchino (Harlequin), was given permission by the Privy Council to "playe within the Cittie [of London] and the Liberties of the same betwene this and the first weeke in Lente".[5] In fact, Martinelli and his colleagues may have played at James Burbage's recently opened Theatre in the Liberties north of the City, where James's young son Richard – destined to become the leading actor in the Lord Chamberlain's and King's Men – could have watched them in action. It is crucial to remember that the Burbages, their colleagues, and their audiences could have seen more than just the improvised "scenarios" for which the Italian *commedianti* were best-known. The troupes' repertoire included scripted comedies, tragedies, and tragicomedies/pastorals, and thus they would have impressed admirers with their versatility. There is no doubt a parodic quality to Polonius's listing of the various genres and hybrid genres – "tragedy, comedy, history, pastoral, pastoral-comical, historical-pastoral, tragical-historical, tragical-comical-historical-pastoral" – which the "best players in the world" can perform, but he is communicating the widespread recognition of the Italian professional companies' range of styles and skills, and their expertise in "the writ and the liberty". Punning on the location of The Theatre and other contemporary venues, Shakespeare also has Polonius praise the professional actors for their mastery of both scripted drama ("the writ") and extempore improvisation ("the liberty").[6]

At the same time, the players who visit the Elsinore of *Hamlet* resemble an English company as much as an Italian one. A true Italian *compagnia* would not have employed a teenaged boy in "chopines" or platform shoes to play female roles, but indeed would have featured at least two highly skilled women playing "innamorate", or young lovers, and often a third as "la serva", the lower-ranking serving-woman or nurse. This facet of the *Commedia dell'Arte*, which allowed actresses to become star attractions already called "divas" ("dive" in Italian), as well as managers and co-managers of their troupes, was duly noted by English observers, and possibly could have contributed to a "protectionist" resistance to the Italian companies. By the 1580s, references to *commedianti* performing in England disappear, a fact that has led scholars to surmise that many English people shared the attitudes expressed by Thomas Norton – who in 1574 had denounced "the unchaste, shameless and unnatural tomblinge of the Italian women" – and by Thomas Nashe, who several years later (1592) published his famous rebuke of the "players beyond sea, a sort of squirting bawdy comedians, that have whores and common courtesans to play women's parts, and forbear no immodest speech or unchaste action that may procure laughter".[7] Still, the impact of the *commedia* "diva" remained, as will be highlighted later in this chapter.

Nashe's scathing description is, after all, a satirical distortion. Even if it did represent a majority opinion, it is qualified by the fact that English theatremakers maintained their receptiveness to Italian plays and players, while less polemical observers appreciated their professional bravura, including that of the actresses. In his travel account entitled *Itinerary* (published 1617), Fynes Moryson mentions his playgoing in Florence, where "the parts of women were played by women, and the chief actors had not their parts fully penned, but spake much extempore or upon agreement among themselves, especially the women, whose speeches were full of wantonness, though not gross bawdry",[8] while the traveller to Venice Thomas Coryate, in his *Crudities* (1611), reveals that in that city he "saw women acte, a thing I had never seen before", confirming that "they performed it with as good a grace, action, and gesture, and whatsoever convenient for a Player, as ever I saw any masculine actor".[9] Such testimonies thus offer an alternate perspective to the insular, anglocentric one, as does the fact that professional English actors regularly toured the Continent, where they would have come into direct contact with Italian modes of performance. This was especially true of their experience in Germany, Austria, and Poland, where performers like Robert Browne, John Green, and George Vincent enjoyed success: along with travelling Italian players, they established the basis for fully developed modern theatrical cultures in these countries. As M. A. Katritzky observes, kinetic and non-verbal elements counted for as much as scripted ones in these transnational performances, especially in the comical vein, for "the succcess of individual troupes was often based to a large extent on the popularity of the chief clowns, notably the Italian-inspired Harlequin, and the Pickelhering of the English actors".[10]

Historical records suggest that artistically fruitful exchange and not mere competition would have marked interactions between the *commedianti* and their English counterparts, the best-documented and best-known case of this phenomenon being that of the famous jigging and jesting Will Kemp (ca. 1560–1603). Along with Shakespeare and Burbage an actor-shareholder of the Lord Chamberlain's Men, and creator of such characters as Peter in *Romeo and Juliet* and Dogberry in *Much Ado About Nothing*, Kemp performed in the service of the Earl of Leicester in the Low Countries in 1585, and the next year travelled to the royal Danish court in Elsinore, to stage a show with Thomas Pope and George Bryan. After leaving the Lord Chamberlain's Men and dancing his celebrated "Nine-Days' Wonder" marathon one-man show from London to Norwich, he encountered the English ambassador Anthony Sherley (possibly his relative) in Rome in 1601, an event commemorated with comical verve in the pseudo-documentary drama *The Travels of the Three English Brothers* (1607), by John Day, William Rowley, and George Wilkins. In a scene of this play, Kemp the character bawdily banters with Sir Anthony about London theatregoers' tastes, before a "Harlequin and his wife" are ushered into their presence. The ensuing sequence is a rich document for assessing contemporary perceptions of the *Commedia dell'Arte*, as it stages Kemp, Harlequin, and the unnamed as well as silent wife improvising a vignette of adulterous intrigue, with the Italian actor offering to play the "jealous coxcomb" husband "Pantaloon", and the English comedian his serving-man who will "keep" or look after his wife. Kemp quickly jests on the sexual double entendre of "keep", kisses the "courtesan" wife in front of Harlequin/Pantaloon, and then, echoing Bottom in *A Midsummer Night's Dream* (a role that he also may have created), cries "O for love sake, let me play that part", trying to cast himself as the "Amorado" ("innamorato") who must make Pantalone a "cornuto". The script therefore expects a certain familiarity with several of the major "maschere" or character-types of the *commedia*, as well as a London audience's knowledge of the Italian "extempore" technique, and their prejudice that female performers and the characters they play will be unchaste and lascivious.[11]

The key point is that Kemp's interaction with the *commedia* is intimate, dynamic, and multivalent, making superfluous any value judgments of a consistently "pro"- or "anti"-Italian "attitude". Professionals in the flourishing, variegated entertainment industry of late sixteenth- to early seventeenth-century London tended to favour what was practically useful to their productions, rather than adhere to a single, coherent set of dramaturgical rules and conventions. In this regard English theatre writers and performers were more like their Spanish than their French contemporaries: the latter were often constrained to conform to neo-classical "decorum", avoiding such representational practises as on-stage violence and loose, non-"verisimilar" treatments of time, place, and action. A striking example of this pragmatic openness to a variety of approaches and techniques is the use of "platts" or plots, concise outlines of stage action which resemble the standard procedure followed by the Italian *commedianti*, in their theatrical "scenarios" or "canovacci" ("rough samples"). These "plots", posted on cards back-stage for actors' quick reference during performance, mainly provided indications of props, entrance points (or "insertion points", as Robert Henke aptly calls them), characters' names, and basic actions. In the surviving sheets for playing *The Dead Man's Fortune*, that most likely belonged to the Lord Admiral's Men and date from the 1590s, precise listing is made of "spectacles" for the Pantalone role, and "flaskets of clothes" for a disguised lover's scene, as well as of details of the sub-plot:

> Enter panteloun whiles he speakes
> validore passeth ore the stage disguised
> then enter passcode to them asspida to
> them the maide with pesscodds apparel.[12]

This formatting of the play's actual performance bears instructive comparison with similar schema from contemporary *commedia* scenarios, as in the following excerpt from "Isabella's Jealousy":

ISABELLA: dressed as a man, having got access to the costume because it was used in a play which she had put on with the other girls. She wants to find Orazio, to prove [in combat] that he is a traitor; she sees her father coming and exits.

PANTALONE: asks Pedrolino what he was getting up to with Orazio and Flavio.[13]

Moreover, the "plots" for *The Dead Man's Fortune* outline the key actions for the romantic tragicomedy that forms the play's main dramatic action, thus also emulating a favourite mixed-genre trend in late Renaissance Italian theatre, seen not only in "The Tragic Events" (a version of the Romeo and Juliet story with a happy ending) and "The Comic, Pastoral and Tragic Events" from Flaminio Scala's printed collection, but in fully scripted plays like Alvise Pasqualigo's *Intricati* (1581).

Thus the Italianate qualities of *The Dead Man's Fortune* are manifold, as demonstrated by Andrew Grewar in his in-depth studies of the play and its "plots". As Grewar also notes, there is another connection with the Burbages, since Richard's name is listed as a player in both *The Dead Man's Fortune* and a similar stage plot of the same period, entitled *The Second Part of the Seven Deadly Sins*.[14] The chronology here is relevant, for direct and indirect references to the *Commedia dell'Arte* appear frequently in English scripted plays of the late 1580s and early 1590s. The Italian companies themselves may have ceased their visits to London, Norwich, Reading, and other English towns, but their influence persisted through the innovative stagecraft and playwriting of the late Elizabethan and early Jacobean era. It is to structural and dramaturgical manifestations of this influence that I now turn attention.

"Lazzi", "theatregrams", and experiments with genre

Numerous gags and routines, especially physical ones, have shown themselves to be eternally and transculturally everlasting in the world of comedy: from the repertoires of ancient Greek to Japanese *Kyogen* to today's international film, television, and internet media, an obvious and exemplary case is that of drunken behaviour, expressed through clumsy and exaggerated movements, boisterous singing, spectacular pratfalls, and ridiculous deformations of speech. Still, some forms of stage business can be associated with specific theatrical contexts, and the early modern *commedia* is one of these. The term commonly applied to the vast array of recognisable routines used by the versatile *commedianti* is "lazzi" (singular "lazzo"), a word that is difficult to translate precisely because of its flexibility and elusive origins. "Lazzi" can be both physical and verbal, and both at once, while the etymology in this case may likewise involve either "lacci" (lasso- or rope-tricks) or "l'atti", "le azioni", short units of various stage actions.[15] They are also marked by their importability, their brevity being crucial to their transnational wit. For instance, the lazzo of tantalising a hungry or gluttonous character with food, and then depriving him of the offered dish, occurs in various Italian scenarii and scripted plays of the sixteenth century. While the routine is one of the oldest in the comic tradition, known in antiquity as "Hercules at table" and appearing in scripts as old as that of Aristophanes's *Frogs*, it took on fresh and altered appeal in the context of recurring real-life famines, and dietary imbalances between overfed aristocrats/wealthy bourgeoisie (like Pantalone) and starving peasant-workers (like Pedrolino and Arlecchino).[16] In act III, scene 2 of *Doctor Faustus*, Marlowe's script, even without stage directions, exploits this same lazzo, and raises the stakes by having Faustus play his food and drink-snatching tricks on the Pope himself. The deprivation jest thus makes the reaction of the high-status Pope – a character-type who could not appear in Italian comedies during the Counter-Reformation – all the more bathetic and self-incriminating, as he childishly and uncharitably rants "My wine gone too? – Ye lubbers, look about/ And find the man that doth this villain,/ Or by our sanctitude, you all shall die" (3.2.76–78). This is a noteworthy example of how the *Commedia dell'Arte*'s abundant repertory of "elastic gags" – a highly useful term coined by Richard Andrews – lent themselves to importation and creative transformation, the elasticity here encompassing anti-Catholic satire.

As noted earlier, the new dramatic form of pastoral tragicomedy was imported into England not only by translations of plays like Tasso's *Aminta* (1573), but also by actual performances of such texts, which included the "sudden reversal lazzo" of refined feminine grace and beauty subduing animalistic male lust, the latter often embodied by a sexually aggressive Satyr. One of the most popular English plays of this period, the anonymous *Mucedorus*, features such a device, when the hungry "wild man" Bremo seizes his prey, the princess Amadine, and with cannibalistic bravado declares "Now glut thy greedy guts with lukewarm blood" (*Mucedorus* scene 11, line 18). After a crescendo of ever more brutal and violent threats, Amadine kneels and prays in expectation of Bremo's murderous blow, but the Satyr-like assailant suddenly finds himself weak and incapable of using his deadly cudgel, and instead confesses "I think her beauty hath bewitched my force/ Or else within me altered nature's course" (*Mucedorus* scene 11, lines 32–33). Beauty tames the beast, Italian pastoral style in action, and English rhyming couplet in words. Returning to comedy and its typically urban scene, a favoured Italian "lazzo" was the male wooer's serenade at his beloved's upper-level window. This potentially romantic set-piece could be given a number of variations, among the funniest being Pantalone's ludicrous attempts to enchant an "Innamorata" with his off-key and garbled singing of Petrarchan love-lyrics.[17] Or a fickle, untrustworthy young "Innamorato" would try to soften a steadfast young maiden's resistance through seductive song, in the process leading to further intrigue. This is the version of the "serenade lazzo" that Shakespeare employs in *The Two Gentlemen of Verona*, act 4, scene 2, when the treacherous Proteus arranges to "give some evening music to her [Silvia's] ear", pretending to do so in order to help his rival Thurio's love-suit, while instead pursuing his own desire for Silvia. While Proteus is untrue to both his best friend Valentine and his lover Julia, he is true to his Italianate characterisation by using Petrarchan lyrical tropes in his elegiac madrigal to Silvia:

> Is she kind as she is fair?
> For beauty lives with kindness.
> Love doth to her eyes repair,
> To help him of his blindness;
> And, being helped, inhabits there
> (4.2.43–47)

At the same time, Shakespeare's script shows its own further trust in Italian theatrical fashions by deploying the "lazzo of overhearing": unbeknownst to Proteus, Julia has disguised herself as a page-boy, and along with her Host becomes an on-stage audience for the serenade. With instrumental music still being played in the background, and the Host admiring "what fine change is in the music", Julia retorts "Ay, that change is the spite. HOST: You would have them always play but one thing? JULIA: I would always have one play but one thing" (4.2.66–68). Her punning words ring oxymoronically false and true, since she is playing something that she is not, but in her cross-gendered disguise she is performing one of the most recurrent and influential "lazzi" of the *commedia*, its own models found in such pre-professional comedies as Bibbiena's *Calandra* (1513) and the Sienese Accademia degli Intronati's *Ingannati* (1532).

The overhearing gag was thus also elastic enough to expand into "play-within-play" episodes, and this fact applies to one of the most ingenious and spectacular importations of *Commedia dell'Arte* in the history of English comedy. The scene of "Scoto the Mountebank" from act 2 of Ben Jonson's *Volpone* (1605) not only cites the *maschere* of "Pantalone dei Bisognosi" and "Franceschina", but elaborately performs a number of specific lazzi associated with Italian stage routines inspired by the contemporary street theatre – or frequently "piazza-theatre" – of early modern "montambanchi", "ciarlatani", and their assistants.[18] The "Innamorata at the window" device again makes a crucial appearance here: in the probable scenario/template for Jonson's scene, the young woman Flaminia "stands at her window to watch the mountebanks", while on to the main stage below enter Burattino, Franceschina, and Pantalone, as they listen to the cross-dressed Turchetto (actually Aliffa, sister of Orazio) play a guitar and sing a song, before Dottore Graziano, "the chief of all the mountebanks", "describes his wares and gives the sales pitch", and his rival the pseudo-mountebank Arlecchino "does the same".[19] The singing and sales pitches offer opportunities for a variety of rhetorical pyrotechnics, but the climactic lazzi arrive with the entrance of the jealous Capitano Spavento, in lust with Flaminia, who pulls Arlecchino down from his temporary stage in front of the Innamorato Orazio's house, causing Orazio to draw his sword on the

Capitano, the Capitano his sword on Orazio, and with Arlecchino running away, "in all the uproar the platform collapses".[20] In his turn, Jonson exploits these gags to the full, and with brilliant variations. Volpone himself masquerades as the mountebank Scoto of Mantua, beneath the window of the beautiful young wife Celia and her insanely jealous husband Corvino, in hopes of impressing the former. As in "La fortuna di Flavio", there is musical accompaniment, provided by Volpone's own dwarf Nano, who in the guise of "Zan Fritada" sings a "verse extempore in honour of" his master's "blessed unguento, this rare extraction". Likewise the young Innamorata appears at her window, as Celia throws down her handkerchief and Volpone/Scoto catches it, prompting him to improvise a lengthy speech in praise of a "powder that made Venus a goddess (given her by Apollo) that kept her perpetually young". And likewise the mountebank's performance is violently interrupted, in this case by Corvino himself, who chases Volpone and Nano off the stage while ranting "is my wife your Franciscina, sir?/ No windows on the whole Piazza, here,/ To make your properties, but mine? But mine?" (Jonson, *Volpone* 2.3.4–6). This particular referencing of the *Commedia dell'Arte* is sometimes attributed to Jonson's diligent research habits, but it also bespeaks awareness of Italian *maschere* and stage practices among Jonson's Globe Theatre and Oxford and Cambridge University audiences, as well as among his King's Men actors: once more Richard Burbage appears, for he could have played either Volpone, or his cunning parasite Mosca.

The world of early modern medicine supplied yet another prominent and enduring comical routine for the *commedia*, which again was imported into seventeenth-century London comedy. Turning dental surgery into grotesque farce, the scenario of "Il Cavadente" ("The Tooth-Puller") flourished with few modifications for 200 years. In Scala's collection, the title character is not a true professional but instead is Arlecchino, again impersonating someone of a higher status trade, and again provoking a violent end-of-act 1 outburst and chase sequence, after he has pulled four good teeth from Pantalone's mouth.[21] Similarly, the tooth-puller in Thomas Middleton's *Widow* (ca. 1616) is an impostor, this time a thief and trickster called Occulto, working as part of a gang led by the aptly named Latrocinio. Occulto proves to be both more dextrous and beneficial than Arlecchino, as he picks his patient Martino's pocket while extracting the latter's truly diseased tooth, enabling him to speak again and declare that he feels "great ease". Indeed, like *The Two Gentlemen of Verona*, which recalls the scenario of "Flavio tradito" ("Flavio Betrayed") in its main plot of a fickle male lover pursuing his sworn best friend's beloved, herself opposed to her father's choice of a foolish braggart for her future spouse, Middleton's comedy relies heavily on *commedia* models, for more than just lazzi. Both of these English plays feature cross-dressing female protagonists, thus adapting one of the major plot devices used by the Italian players. This would be the complete, or "macro-level" framework for specific "micro-level" jests as Isabella's above-cited one from the "Isabella's Jealousy" scenario, recycled with ironic twists in Shakespeare's comedy, when Julia confides to Silvia that

> When all our pageants of delight were played,
> Our youth got me to play the woman's part,
> And I was trimmed in Madam Julia's gown,
> Which servèd me as fit, by all men's judgments,
> As if the garment had been made for me
>
> (4.4.155–59)

The useful term "theatregram" was coined by the distinguished scholar Louise George Clubb to delineate a clearly structured but highly flexible dramatic scheme, well-suited for import and export purposes, and thus one can pertinently identify a range of Italianate theatregrams in early modern English drama.[22] The fact that teenaged boy actors played cross-gendering heroines on English public stages gave added paradoxical and often metatheatrical intrigue to Julia, Portia, Rosalind, Viola, and similar characters in Shakespeare's and his colleagues' plays, but their dramatic patterns remain Italianate. The goal for both the *commedia* practitioners and the English theatre-makers was to devise audience-pleasing variations on the basic, often familiar theatre-gram. Thus Scala's "Marito" ("The Husband"), a scenario he later published as an entire scripted play "Il finto marito", does not have its Prima Donna Innamorata impersonate a male servant in order to pursue her wayward lover, but instead arranges for Isabella's nurse Franceschina to fool almost everyone in the play by posing as "Cornelio", and imitating typically male behaviours like possessive jealousy. In *The Widow*, Middleton goes one step further and surprises the audience as well, only revealing in the play's last scene that the "handsome youth" Ansaldo, perceived and admired as male during the preceding acts, and dressed up in women's clothing and set up for an apparent mock male-male marriage by the would-be adulteress Philippa and her waiting woman Violetta, is the female character Marcia, who had been using cross-gendered disguise all along.

Italianate theatregrams abound in English drama of the early modern era, from the pastoral mingling of gods, nature-sprites, shepherds, and other mortals found in plays like John Lyly's *Woman in the Moone* (ca. 1593) and Shakespeare's *A Midsummer Night's Dream* (ca. 1596) to the tragic sequence of a jealous, tyrannical father killing his daughter's lover and provoking her suicide, as adapted in *The Tragedie of Tancred and Gismund* (published 1591) and at least four other pre-1623 versions,[23] from the miserly and/or impotent old husband being tricked by younger, more vigorous wives and gallants – as in Jonson's *Epicene* (1609), Middleton's *A Chaste Maid in Cheapside* (1613), and Wycherley's *The Country Wife* (1675) – to episodes of feigned or actual madness caused by the pangs of disprized or even hopeful love, with Shakespeare's *Hamlet* (ca. 1601) and Middleton's and Rowley's *Changeling* (1622) being only two of the best-known among many examples. For this latter play, Scala's collection once more includes a close parallel as well as contrasting version. Entitled "La finta pazza" ("The Feigned Madwoman"), this scenario's title character is the Innamorata Isabella, who pretends to be mad in order to avoid marrying the man her father Pantalone prefers for her, and to follow her true love Orazio to another city. After she has performed the antics of her mad routine, she is poisoned by her rival Flaminia, and her apparent death causes the true madness of Orazio. In *The Changeling*, there are truly mad people as well – the patients of Doctor Alibius's asylum – but they do not include the two potential lovers. While the feigned madwoman retains the name of Isabella, as well as the singing and fantastical pseudo-astronomical patter of her Italian role model, crying "About thy head I see a heap of clouds/ Wrapped like a Turkish turban; on thy back,/ A crook'd chameleon-coloured rainbow hung/ Like a tiara down thy hams" (4.3.117–30),[24] she in fact rebukes the advances of Antonio, her would-be seducer who has himself feigned madness to gain access to her. For Middleton and Rowley's Isabella is already married, the unhappy but still faithful wife to Alibius. What deserves emphasis, then, is the way in which – like an accomplished early modern Austrian or German composer working variations on Italian musical themes and motifs – particular

English playwrights and their acting cohorts adhered to while at the same time creatively departed from theatregrams made available by *Commedia dell'Arte* professionals.

In the process, re-combination of theatregrams, and the genres associated with them, was also a key feature of such transnational play-making. The Italians themselves set the terms and examples for this trend in dramatic experimentation. As already noted, the device of a young Innamorata taking a potion to feign death would enable the simultaneous elaboration of comedic intrigue and tragic sentiment, as well as the option for either a sad or happy ending. When mixed with the theatregrams of cross-gendered disguise and love-rivalry/love-madness, as in "The Feigned Madwoman" and "La presunta morta" ("The Woman Presumed Dead"), the combinations can be especially intricate and challenging. In the former, the love-stricken Flaminia pretends to be the male servant Bigolo, and does attempt to murder her supposedly mad rival Isabella; only a fortuitous antidote, repentance, and acts of extreme generosity alter the recipe for tragedy, and provide a comedic resolution. Similar conversions mark one of the most popular of all early seventeenth-century English plays, Thomas Dekker's and Middleton's *The Honest Whore, Part One* (1604), which opens with the presumed death and funeral ceremony of the Innamorata character Infelice (whose name means "the unhappy one"), in this case arranged by her own father, the Duke of Milan. In the play's exceptionally complex and entertaining final scene, Infelice and her beloved Hippolito enter as newlyweds, but in disguise as friars (in order to escape the Duke's detection and eventually change his fury to acceptance), while the title character Bellafront, converted from prostitution to honest living by Hippolito succeeds in getting the Duke to sanction her marriage to her former, first lover Matteo ... and yet another plot, involving the patient, long-suffering Candido and his cruel, tormenting wife, gains resolution! To augment all this *commedia*-style fun and intrigue, the scene takes place in Bethlehem (later known as "Bedlam"), London's hospital for the mentally ill transposed to Milan, where – as in *The Changeling* – a feigned madwoman (Bellafront) appears among real madmen. A fitting site, then, for the dénouement of a mixed romantic-satirical-moral comedy, for as Hippolito pithily comments, "all love is lunatic". Here Bethlehem reclaims its connotations with Christian redemption, in a parallel to how Flaminia's contrition is rewarded at the end of "The Woman Presumed Dead". In this scenario, she repents that she has caused confusion, despair, and multiple conflicts with her "tomb-trick", and her ensuing disguise as Arlecchino, a cross-gendering lazzo which causes farcically repeated reactions of fright from the other characters – including Arlecchino himself – who all believe they are seeing Flaminia's ghost. As proved by the popularity of *The Honest Whore*, and other English plays like *Much Ado About Nothing* and *The Winter's Tale*, the return of a young heroine from "the dead" held a compelling appeal for audiences, and is a transnational theatregram that merits further research and analysis.

Character-types, and the exaltation of play-acting

With its vaunted specialty of bravura improvisation, and its long-lasting, frequently illustrated *maschere* ("character-types") often invented or perfected by famous performers like Tristano Martinelli/Arlecchino, Isabella Andreini/Isabella l'Innamorata, and Silvio Fiorillo/Pulcinella, the *Commedia dell'Arte* has often been called an "actor's theatre", as opposed to the supposed "writer's theatre" of early modern England. This opposition, however, is a distorted and misleading construct. As Ferdinando Taviani, Siro Ferrone, Richard Andrews, Robert Henke, and other Italian, British, and American scholars have convincingly demonstrated, the *commedianti* relied on a coordination of "extempore" or "ad libitum" techniques with memorisation of scripted scenes and speeches, of colloquial prose utterances with extended passages of lyrical poetry, and above all on a versatile mastery of an entire spectrum of genres and dramatic tones.[25] Like their counterparts across the English channel, they performed for large, socially diverse audiences in public, commercial playhouses, and for smaller, more élite ones in private and court theatres, relying like them on collaboration with leading writers of the time. Italian, Spanish, French, and English theatre artists of this era therefore had much in common, and one of their most important shared traits was an overt accentuation, indeed almost an exaltation, of the very business of play-making and play-acting. Hence the frequency and elaboration of plots and routines involving disguise, dissimulation, transformation, multiple and mistaken identities, plays-within-plays, and ambiguous distinctions between illusion and reality, dreams and waking consciousness. A paradigm in this regard is *The Tempest* (1611), traditionally designated as Shakespeare's "play without a source", but actually deriving much from scenarios like Scala's "heroic drama" "Rosalba incantatrice" ("Rosalba the Enchantress") and his "pastoral" "L'arbore incantato" ("The Enchanted Wood"), where an island setting, powerful "magus", a savage "wild man", aristocratic young lovers, and clownish servants all can be found.

To focus on character-types, then, also calls for attention to their vital context of self-aware and dynamic theatricality, a context that enabled them to cross the political, linguistic, and cultural borders of their time. This border-crossing was essential to the specific dramatic adaptations of the players' standard repertoire, so that when the Neapolitan butler Stephano and his friend the professional clown Trinculo encounter Caliban, they are also acting out the meeting between two comical urban "Zanni" and a pastoral "wild man/satyr". This is not to deny but on the contrary to clarify and affirm Shakespeare's innovative artistry as a theatre-poet. Like Jonson, Middleton, and others among his contemporaries, he became skilled in maintaining the essential features and energies of the *maschere*, while inventing particular expressions and interactions for them. Along with their master the Magnifico of Venice and the Veneto region, the Zanni-servants formed the original nucleus of the *commedia* tradition, and their often ridiculous, acrobatic and outlandish routines did eventually lead to the modern English sense of the adjective "zany". There were important distinctions among them, however, and thus the Zane known as Brighella came to stand out from his kindred clowns for his cunning intelligence, his personal ambitions, and deceptive scheming. In *Othello*, seemingly "honest" Iago plays Brighella to Brabantio the Pantalone and Othello the hyperbolic Capitano, but in *The Tempest* Brighella/Stephano finds himself with his Arlecchino/Pulcinella/Trinculo sidekick "alone" on a desert island, ready to live out his dream of power. Ironically, his own weakness for the bottle seems to serve his design to become a king, as the "sack" he has rescued from the shipwreck is first taken for "celestial liquor" by the native islander Caliban, aptly identified by Trinculo as a naïve fool for idolising the drunkard Stephano as if he were a god. Through the very failure of Stephano's pathetically and laughably inept coup attempt, Caliban gains some wisdom, while the two clowns seem stuck in their all-too-familiar roles.

Along the way, the comical triad play lazzi both old and new, such as the changing and re-changing of fancy clothes, and the "giant turtle-monster" with four legs, four arms, and two mouths and voices. When they react apprehensively yet imaginatively to the ongoing tempest – "Yond same black cloud, yond huge one, looks like a foul bombard that would shed his liquor", opines Trinculo – they are also perpetuating the classic gags of hyper-sensitivity to the weather played by stressed and poorly dressed zanni, such as Grumio in *The Taming of the Shrew*. Already the victim of his hot-tempered, "choleric" master Petruchio's blows in an earlier, old-fashioned English verbal spin on the "knock, knock (me) lazzo", the exhausted, begrimed, and shivering Grumio calls himself "a piece of ice", when asked to identify himself by his fellow servant Curtis. When the latter prolongs Grumio's frozen sufferings by his delay in lighting a fire, he in turn receives blows from Grumio, though this does not prevent the two comedians from carrying on their joking verbal patter and storytelling, culminating in Curtis's punch-line "By this reckoning he is more shrew than she", and Grumio's prophetic response "Ay, and that thou and the proudest of you all shall find when he comes home" (3.3.71–73). They may not be called Pedrolino and Arlecchino, but these servant-clowns emulate them in several ways, not least when Grumio plays the tormentor in a food deprivation lazzo ("the mustard without the beef") with Katherina. Their names in fact connect them to several comic traditions and contexts at once, since Grumio (Latin for "dirt-clod") is the ponderous country slave in Plautus's *Mostellaria* ("The Haunted House"), and with his job as Petruchio's horse-minder he could be understood as a pseudo-Italian "groom-io", while Curtis evokes a quintessentially English background. This is yet another of Shakespeare's transnationally hybridising gags, which invite interpretive attention from theatre practitioners as well as scholars.[26]

Such gags are especially salient and indeed integral to this play, because of its two settings – first Warwickshire, and then Padua – and its two sets of characters, one featuring the drunken tinker Christopher Sly and his dismayed Hostess, an unnamed English Lord with a taste for Ovid and practical jokes, and the same Lord's cross-gendering page-boy Bartholomew, the other comprised of a troupe of itinerant players able to perform on command an Italianate comedy, partially based on Ariosto's *Suppositi*. Curtis's clowning with Grumio is thus a part of this English-meets-Italian comedic theatre whole, and appropriately the players offer versions of all the major *maschere* of the *commedia* to their socially mixed audience of Sly, Lord, et alia. The rich, elderly, and gullible suitor Gremio is explicitly identified as a "Pantaloon", and his lengthy monologue, or rather catalogue listing his possessions – "my house within the city/ Is richly furnished with plate and gold,/ Basins and ewers to lave her dainty hands", etc. (2.1.350–80) – is a materialistic showcase faithful to the classic contours of the Venetian Pantalone.[27] With his two daughters, and readiness to employ schoolmasters to instruct Bianca, his favourite, Baptista resembles the other typical father figure, Pantalone's counterpart il Dottore. As for Lucentio, he is a young man from Pisa who enters declaring his intention to study ethical philosophy, but is promptly transformed from a "studioso" to an Innamorato when he falls in love with Bianca at first sight, in a scene with his tricksterish, Brighella-like servant Tranio that itself evokes the gradual arrival of early modern travellers in an Italian city (Henke 2014, 31–36). Hortensio, already in love with Bianca but eventually married to a widow, fits the part of a second Innamorato, while his "good friend" Petruchio, a visitor from Verona, corresponds to the flamboyant and blustering Capitano, the *maschera* who erratically combines the braggart soldier, the lover, the lunatic, and the poet. His speech announcing his intention to woo Katherina is a tour de force of hyperbole, alliteration, anaphora, onomatopeia, and rhetorical crescendo worthy of the best "Bravure" of such illustrious Capitani actors as Francesco Andreini:[28]

> Think you a little din can daunt mine ears?
> Have I not in my time heard lions roar?
> Have I not heard the sea, puffed up with winds,
> Rage like an angry boar chafèd with sweat?
> Have I not heard great ordnance in the field,
> And heaven's artillery thunder in the skies?
> Have I not in a pitchèd battle heard
> Loud "larums, neighing steeds, and trumpets" clang?
> And do you tell me of a woman's tongue,
> That gives not half so great a blow to hear
> As will a chestnut in a farmer's fire?
>
> (1.2.194–204)

The playwright-manager from Stratford would return to providing such Capitano-style set-pieces, both in prose and verse, both in comical and heroic-romantic registers, for characters like the Spanish braggart Don Adriano de Armado in *Love's Labour's Lost*, The Prince of Morocco in *The Merchant of Venice*, the "swaggerer" Pistol in *Henry IV, Parts I* and *II*, Parolles in *All's Well That Ends Well*, and *Othello, the Moor of Venice*. As usual, Shakespeare was not alone in exploiting and elaborating on the resources of both classical comedy and the Italian *commedia*, and thus new stagings and criticism also await characters like Captain Bobadilla in Jonson's *Every Man in His Humour*, Captain Memnon in Fletcher's *The Mad Lover*, and Bessus in *A King and No King*. This last-named play is the immensely popular tragicomedy Fletcher co-wrote with Francis Beaumont, himself the author of *The Knight of the Burning Pestle*, with its Capitano-esque spin-off of Don Quixote, Rafe the apprentice.

Yet the *maschera* which sometimes took precedence over all the others, especially when played by a charismatic and multi-talented "Diva", was that of the Innamorata. As Frances Barasch, Pamela Allen Brown, Rachel Poulsen, and other scholars have been showing in recent studies, the all-male public theatre world of England still made extensive, varied, and often innovative use of the versatile techniques and complex female characterisations developed by such famous Italian performers as Vincenza Armani, Vittoria Piissimi, and Isabella Andreini.[29] Petruchio does meet his match in Katherina, for in the mould of a true Innamorata-Diva she expresses her wit, her passions, her rebelliousness, her determination, and her eloquence. Thanks to the precedents offered by the Italian "Prime Donne", across all the contemporary genres, powerful as well as voluble female protagonists started to appear on Elizabethan stages, among them Bel-Imperia of Kyd's *Spanish Tragedy*, Marlowe's *Dido, Queen of Carthage*, Alice Arden of *Arden of Faversham*, and Shakespeare's Queen Margaret of his first Henriad. The much-admired and internationally extolled capacity of Italian actresses to render depths and subtleties of emotion thus gave impetus to the creation of characters like Juliet, Cleopatra, Webster's *Duchess of Malfi* (1614), Middleton's Livia in *Women Beware Women* (1623), and Ford's Annabella in *'Tis Pity She's a Whore* (1630). As noted above, the theatregram of love-madness was a particular favourite, holding urgent interest for audiences across early modern Europe during a time when reason, sanity, and their opposites were at the center of social consciousness and cultural debate. The best-known of all of Isabella Andreini's many achievements as an actor, poet, playwright, and producer was in fact "La Pazzia di Isabella" ("The Madness of Isabella"), which she performed in various versions, including not only improvised "antics" and "nonsense patter" but also bawdy singing, dishevelled hair, violent gestures, and wearing of disordered clothes. Thus while Middleton and Rowley's Isabella translates and extends this pattern, so too do Ophelia of *Hamlet* and The Gaoler's Daughter of Shakespeare's and Fletcher's *Two Noble Kinsmen*, in even more complex and provocative ways. The revealing stage direction printed in the First Quarto of *Hamlet*, "Enter Ophelia, playing on a Lute, and her haire downe singing", combined with the often suggestive, bawdily erotic lyrics of her songs, and above all her spectacular upstaging of the other characters in her mad scene, make her closely akin to the charismatic, enthusiastically admired "innamorate forsennate" (or "demented female lovers") played by the leading actresses of the contemporary Italian *commedia*. For her part, the Gaoler's Daughter makes her Italianate qualities all the more evident by her readiness to dance with the guidance of a dancing-master named Giraldo, whom she identifies as a conjurer, requesting him to "raise me a devil now and let him play/ *Chi passa* o'th' bells and bones" (3.5.86–87). She thus alludes to "Chi passa per 'sta strada", one of the most popular Italian street and theatre ballads of the era, while her "bells and bones" reference can be a double entendre for "belle e buone", an Italian slang term for prostitutes.[30]

In scenes of madness, then, the Innamorata/young woman in love could take on a theatrical power that invited and even insisted upon heightened audience engagement with the performance. If the character-type did not exactly play to the audience, she did play *for* and *with* the audience. One more specialty of the Innamorata actress deserves emphasis. This was the verbal duel or debate, performed with a male interlocutor, which she almost always won with a "touché" flourish, called the "stoccata" in Italian (a term derived in fact from fencing). Again, a leading practitioner of these duel-like dialogues was Isabella Andreini, who received attribution as the author of a series of "*Amorosi contrasti*" ("Lovers' Debates") in a posthumous publication edited by her spouse and co-star Francesco Andreini.[31] Covering a spectrum of topics including not only such amorous questions as "true love" and "is it better to pursue or flee love", but also aesthetic and sociological ones like "tragedy", "comedy", and "arms vs. letters", the *Contrasti* allow the female speaker to display her quick wit, her impressive erudition, and her skill at both flirting with and outshining her male partner. They also juggle with and sometimes challenge contemporary notions of passive femininity and active masculinity, in a way that provided yet another model for Shakespeare's skirmishes of wit scripted for Katherina and Petruchio, Beatrice and Benedick, and even Helen and Parolles. In most of these comedic cases, the intellectual and verbally adept Innamorata holds her own with ther male sparring partner, and often she puts him down, in various senses: "she speaks poniards [daggers], and every word stabs", says Benedick of his former lover, and future wife. Such scenarios also call for further research and interpretation, as part of the ongoing critical exploration of how early modern English drama staged sexuality and gender in ambiguous, provocative, unconventional and multivalent ways.

Finale: from masques to Punch and Judy shows, but not only

This all too brief survey has concentrated on full-length plays of the late sixteenth to early seventeenth centuries, in good measure because these productions are the best-known to students, and the ones most readily grouped with literature of the period. For this same reason, however, it is appropriate to widen the perspective, and conclude with some rich examples of both the extensive para-theatrical impact of the *Commedia dell'Arte* in England, and of its lasting vitality through the late seventeenth and early eighteenth centuries.

In terms of budget, political objectives, and avant-garde technical artistry, the court masques sponsored by the courts of King James I and his son Charles I were the most lavish and ambitious of all English entertainments of this period. In keeping with the Italianate set and costume designs created by Inigo Jones, who had travelled and studied in Italy himself, Ben Jonson's scripts made explicit and pertinent use of various *maschere*. In *The Vision of Delight*, presented at court for the Christmas celebrations of 1617, the first grotesque and comical "antimasque" consists of "a she-monster delivered of six burratines that dance with six pantaloons".[32] While this association of the young "zanni" burratino and the old "pantalone" mask with monstrous births may enact King James's diatribe against Italian fashions as seductive corrupters of London and its women,[33] it nevertheless confirms the well-established presence of these theatrical figures in the English cultural landscape. "Pantaloon", the label used almost twenty years previously by Jaques in *As You Like It* to designate the sixth and most elderly "age"/"act" of a man's life, had entered English vocabulary, there to remain as the word for long male leggings, eventually shorted in American usage to "pants". Even in English culture, the *Commedia dell'Arte* spilled out beyond the confines of theatrical playing spaces. In fairgrounds, the Neapolitan *maschera* Pulcinella evolved – and miniaturised – into the immensely popular, still thriving puppet of Punch. During the eighteenth century, this more irate, hot-tempered version of the original Italian character joined up with his equally belligerent spouse Judy to form the most successful puppet comedy team in the history of the English-speaking world.

At the same time, *Commedia dell'Arte* characters and movements were adapted and codified into English dance and eventually pantomime, aimed primarily to satisfy bourgeois and upper-class taste. Between 1712 and 1728, London's leading dance-master and dance theorist John Weaver published a series of books explaining how the new art of scenic dance ought to follow the example of Italian performers, unrivalled for their "grimaces, posture, motions, agility, suppleness of limbs, and distortion of their faces".[34] In analysing and delineating the major new types of narrative dance as the "serious" and the "grotesque", Weaver – whose own successful performing career depended on his partnership with the brilliantly talented Esther Booth alias "Arlec-china" – made deliberate up-datings of the Italian *commedia* tradition that reflected the influence of recent scientific work in physics, anatomy, and geometry. He also counted on his English readers' and spectators' knowledge of the tradition. As Domenico Pietropaolo observes, "the performance literacy of the audience of theatrical dance *includes* sufficient familiarity with the physical style of Commedia dell'Arte characters to be able to recognize it on stage".[35] Like the distinguished artist and art theorist William Hogarth, whose *Analysis of Beauty* (published 1753) includes a section on the physical-visual language and choreographic stylisation of danced *commedia* characters, Weaver devotes special attention to Harlequin and Scaramouch, who by then had emerged as the dynamic duo of English pantomime. Their rise to pantomimic fame and fortune undoubtedly owed much to one of the most imaginative and satirically trenchant English farces of the late seventeenth century, itself a triumph of transnational play-writing. Adapted from the anonymous French play *Arlequin, Empereur dans la lune*,

Aphra Behn's *The Emperor of the Moon* (first performed 1687) makes Scaramouch more of a resourceful, quick-witted, and stage-managing servant-trickster than the flamboyant Capitano-esque figure adapted from the earlier Scaramuzza *maschera* and perfected by Tiberio Fiorilli (1604–94) in contemporary Paris.[36] He and his less agile and less brilliant, but equally funny rival-sidekick Harlequin are the key players in the scheme of the play's young lovers to ridicule and overcome the obstacles posed by the play's quixotically foolish Dottore character, Baliardo, obsessed with the moon and its magically, indeed divinely powerful supposed inhabitants.

Despite or maybe even because of his "microscope, his horoscope, his telescope, and all his scopes", the learnèd Baliardo is blind to the realities in his own house and family, and in classic *Commedia dell'Arte* fashion he is outwitted by his own daughter, his niece, their female servant (these three characters now played by distinguished English actresses), their lovers, and their servant-accomplices. While he does have an Italian name, and lives in the Naples of the play's setting, the Doctor might also represent the myopic, self-absorbed, and xenophobically prejudiced Englishman, who may need a telescope at least twenty feet long to perceive the truth of his country's heterogeneous, internationally vibrant theatrical tradition. As Scaramouch advises him, with the help of such an outward-looking instrument "you may discover all". Indeed, there remains much for future researchers, commentators, actors, and directors to discover in the world of *Commedia dell'Arte* and early modern English theatre.

Notes

1 The current author trusts that most readers will know that the term "Commedia dell'Arte" does not mean an exclusively improvising form of comic theatre played outdoors by travelling companies, but rather the "professional theatre practice" favoured by most Italian companies during the two centuries preceding the term's coinage by the "reforming" Venetian playwright Carlo Goldoni.

2 Among an entire series of important articles and volumes, see Michele Marrapodi, "Prologue", in *The Italian World of English Renaissance Drama: Cultural Exchange and Intertextuality* (Newark, DE: University of Delaware Press, 1998), "Introduction: Appropriating Italy: Towards a New Approach to Renaissance Drama", in *Italian Culture in the Drama of Shakespeare and His Contemporaries: Rewriting, Remaking, Refashioning* (Farnham, UK: Ashgate, 2007), pp. 1–12, and "Shakespearean Subversions", in *Shakespeare and the Italian Renaissance: Appropriation, Transformation, Opposition* (Farnham, UK: Ashgate, 2014), pp. 1–17. Professor Marrapodi is the editor of all three of these cited volumes.

3 See Richard Andrews, *Scripts and Scenarios: The Performance of Comedy in Renaissance Italy* (Cambridge: Cambridge University Press, 1993), and Robert Henke, "Border-Crossing in the *Commedia dell'Arte*", in *Transnational Exchange in Early Modern Theater*, eds. Robert Henke and Eric Nicholson (Burlington, VT: Ashgate Press, 2008), pp. 19–21.

4 The Lyons performance is cited by Henke, p. 26, while the Norwich record is quoted by Andy Grewar, in his chapter "The Old Man's Spectacles: Commedia and Shakespeare", in *The Routledge Companion to Commedia dell'Arte*, eds. Judith Chaffee and Olly Crick (New York: Routledge, 2016), p. 300.

5 See E. K. Chambers, *The Elizabethan Stage*, 4 vols. (Oxford: The Clarendon Press, 1923), p. 277.

6 See Louise George Clubb, "Pastoral Jazz from the Writ to the Liberty", in *Italian Culture in the Drama of Shakespeare*, ed. Michele Marrapodi, pp. 15–26. On the crucial, shaping effects of Italian literature and drama on the writings and intellectual culture of Elizabethan and Jacobean England, see Michael Wyatt, *The Italian Encounter with Tudor England: A Cultural Politics of Translation* (Cambridge: Cambridge University Press, 2005), and Jason Lawrence, *Who the Devil Taught Thee So Much Italian?: Italian Language Instruction and Literary Imitation in Early Modern England* (Manchester, UK: Manchester University Press, 2005). Also by Jason

Lawrence, see *Tasso's Art and Afterlives: The "Gerusalemme Liberata" in England* (Manchester, UK: Manchester University Press, 2017).

7 The first quotation appears in Lea, Kathleen M., *Italian Popular Comedy: A Study in the Commedia dell'Arte, 1560–1620 with Special Reference to the English Stage*, 2 vols. (Oxford: Clarendon Press, 1934), vol. 2, p. 354, and the second in Thomas Nashe, *The Unfortunate Traveler and Other Works*, ed. J. B. Steane (Harmondsworth, UK: Penguin, 1971), p. 115.

8 Lea, p. 343.

9 Thomas Coryate, *Coryate's Crudities* (London, 1611), p. 247.

10 M. A. Katritzky, "English Troupes in Early Modern Germany: The Women", in *Transnational Exchange*, eds. Robert Henke and Eric Nicholson, p. 36.

11 As Anthony Parr, editor of the play in the anthology *Three Renaissance Travel Plays* (Manchester, UK: Manchester University Press, 1995), notes, "Harlequin acts as straight-man to Kemp's bawdy clown, and the scene could be played either as co-operative comedy or as Kemp's outwitting of his foreign rival" (p. 106). On Kemp, see also the important study by David Wiles, *Shakespeare's Clown: Actor and Text in the Elizabethan Playhouse* (Cambridge: Cambridge University Press, 2005), chap. 3.

12 See Grewar, p. 304.

13 Flaminio Scala, "La gelosia di Isabella", translated as "Isabella's Jealousy" by Richard Andrews, in his volume *The Commedia dell'Arte of Flaminio Scala: a Translation and Analysis of Thirty Scenarios* (Baltimore, MD: Scarecrow Press, 2008).

14 Grewar, p. 305.

15 See Mel Gordon, *Lazzi* (New York: PAJ Publications, 1983), pp. 10–12.

16 See Robert Henke, *Poverty and Charity in Early Modern Theatre and Performance* (Iowa City: University of Iowa Press, 2015).

17 Illustrations of this routine were extremely popular, appearing in both prints and paintings: see M. A. Katritzky, *The Art of Commedia. A Study in the Commedia dell'Arte 1560–1620 with Special Reference to the Visual Records* (Amsterdam and New York: Rodopi, 2006).

18 On early modern Italian *montambanchi*, see especially Eamon 1996, chap. 7, and Katritzky 2007.

19 This scenario was published as part of "La fortuna di Flavio", in Scala's 1611 anthology. Also see Jane Tylus, "Women at the Windows: Commedia dell'Arte and Theatrical Practice in Early Modern Italy", *Theatre Journal*, 49 (1997): 323–42.

20 Scala/Andrews, pp. 22–23.

21 Scala/Andrews, pp. 64–65.

22 See Louise George Clubb, *Italian Drama in Shakespeare's Time* (New Haven, CT: Yale University Press, 1989).

23 The popularity of the tragic Tancredi and Ghismonda tale attests to the importance of Giovanni Boccaccio's *Decameron* as a recurring source of dramatic plots and characters in early modern English drama.

24 These lines recall the "purgative"-giving "rainbow" and "Jupiter wants to sneeze and Saturn wants to fart" gags of "The Madness of Isabella", also included by Scala; more commentary on this particular scenario, and its connections with Ophelia, the Gaoler's Daughter, and other English female characters later.

25 See Ferdinando Taviani and Mirella Schino, *Il segreto della Commedia dell'Arte* (Florence: Casa Usher, 1986); Siro Ferrone, *Attori mercanti corsari: La Commedia dell'Arte in Europa tra Cinque e Seicento* (Turin: Einaudi, 1993); Richard Andrews, *Scripts and Scenarios*, cit.; and Robert Henke, *Performance and Literature in the Commedia dell'Arte* (Cambridge: Cambridge University Press, 2002).

26 See for example the chapter by Romersberger, Sara, "Shakespeare's Clown Connection: Hybridizing Commedia's Zanni", in Chaffee and Crick, pp. 312–20.

27 On Gremio as a fully articulated Pantalone figure, see Perlman, Mace, "Reading Shakespeare, Reading the Masks of the Italian Commedia: Fixed Forms and the Breath of Life", in eds. Robert Henke and Eric Nicholson, pp. 225–38.

28 See Francesco Andreini, *Le bravure di Capitano Spavento* (1607), ed. Roberto Tessari (Pisa: Giardini, 1987).

29 See Frances Barasch, "Italian Actresses in Shakespeare's World: Vittoria and Isabella", *Shakespeare Bulletin*, 19, 3 (2001): 5–9; Pamela Allen Brown, "The Counterfeit Innamorata,

or the Diva Vanishes", in *Shakespeare Yearbook*, Vol. 10, eds. Holger Klein and Michele Marrapodi (1999), pp. 402–26, "Dido, Boy Diva of Carthage: Marlowe's Dido Tragedy and the Renaissance Actress", in *Transnational Mobilities in Early Modern Theater*, eds. Robert Henke and Eric Nicholson (Burlington, VT: Ashgate, 2014), pp. 113–30; Campbell, Julie D., "Merry, Nimble, Stirring Spirit(s)': Academic, Salon and Commedia dell'arte Influence on the *Innamorate* of *Love's Labour's Lost*", in *Women Players in England: Beyond the All-Male Stage*, eds. Pamela Allen Brown and Peter Parolin (Burlington, VT: Ashgate Prees, 2005), pp. 154–70; and Eric Nicholson, "Ophelia Sings Like a *Prima Donna Innamorata*: Ophelia's Mad Scene and the Italian Female Performer", in *Transnational Exchange*, eds. Robert Henke and Eric Nicholson, pp. 81–98.

30 See Robert Nicholson, "Ophelia Sings …", pp. 91–98.

31 Isabella Andreini (and Francesco), *Fragmenti di alcune scritture* (includes the "Amorosi contrasti") (Venice: Combi, 1622).

32 Ben Jonson, *The Complete Masques*, ed. Stephen Orgel (New Haven, CT: Yale University Press, 1969), p. 245.

33 See Leah Marcus, *The Politics of Mirth: Jonson, Herrick, Milton, Marvell and the Defense of Old Holiday Pastimes* (Chicago, IL: University of Chicago Press, 1989), p. 71.

34 John Weaver, *An Essay towards an History of Dancing* (London, 1712), p. 168, cited by Domenico Pietropaolo, in "Commedia dell'Arte as Grotesque Dance: Decline or Evolution?", in Chaffee and Crick, p. 339.

35 Pietropaolo, p. 343.

36 See Aphra Behn, "The Emperor of the Moon", in *The Rover and Other Plays*, ed. Jane Spencer (Oxford: Oxford University Press, 2008); on Fiorilli and Scaramouche, see Stephen P. J. Knapper, "Carnival, Comedy, and the Commedia: A Case Study of the Mask of Scaramouche", in Chaffee and Crick, pp. 96–107.

20 The scholarship of Italian and English renaissance festivals

J. R. Mulryne

In recent years, research sources and interpretive studies focusing on Italian and English Renaissance festivals have become a great deal more plentiful, in both printed and electronic forms. This chapter offers a guide to the more accessible and wide-ranging of these sources and studies, with particular but not exclusive reference to English-language publications, and a relatively narrow chronological focus on the sixteenth and seventeenth centuries. It owes a considerable debt to bibliographies already in print, the editors and titles of which are mentioned later, but in addition attempts to supplement these and to bring them more fully up to date.

The chapter is arranged first under available bibliographies and then under recent printed and electronic sources. An underlying aim is to encourage a wider interpretation of festival study than is currently the case. My approach to the topic has perhaps diluted the emphasis shared by chapters in this book on Italo-British cultural relations, but there are I believe compensations in this approach, since the study of festivals has rightly proceeded heretofore on a pan-European basis. I am under no illusion that the account that follows is comprehensive.

Finding lists and bibliographies

An indispensable research tool for the study of festival in Europe, including Italy, is the bibliographical collection of material in *Festivals and Ceremonies. A Bibliography of Works relating to Court, Civic and Religious Festivals in Europe, 1500–1800* brought together by Helen Watanabe-O'Kelly with Anne Simon (London: Mansell, 2000). The bibliography draws on the holdings of major libraries, listing their collections of festival texts in chronological order, and further organising the included material under types of festival, the names of participants and commissioning individuals, together with artists, architects and performers.

The bi-lingual (French and English) *Spectaculum Europaeum* (Harrassowitz Verlag: Wiesbaden, 1999) edited by Pierre Béhar and Helen Watanabe-O'Kelly takes in, as the volume's sub-title indicates, "Theatre and Spectacle in Europe (1580–1750)". The volume covers a wide range of theatre forms including drama, opera, ballet and tournament originating in European countries from Spain, France and Italy to England, the Low Countries, Scandinavia, Poland and Hungary. As a multi-faceted performative kind, festival is embedded in the religious, political and social life of contemporary Europe, with the result that much that is noted under other forms and places will be

DOI: 10.4324/9781315612720-23

relevant to the study of Renaissance festivals in Italy and England. Of particular interest to students of Italian festival is the book's final section, under the title "Entries and Festivals", and in particular Paulette Choné's "Entrées, feux d'artifice, et fêtes religieuses en Italie". Choné introduces a long perspective from ancient Triumphs to sixteenth- and seventeenth-century court and civic festivals, noting the mimicry of ancient forms and a new interest in humanism and allegory. Choné's "Appendice" offers particular assistance to research scholars, opening with a general survey of existing research, noting its achievements and limits and indicating where further work is needed. The chapter then turns to "Feux d'Artifice" and "Fêtes Religieuses" before, in a very helpful arrangement of material, dealing separately with individual cities and city states, including detailed discussion of Florence and Rome, but summarising also existing work on smaller locations such as Parma, Pavia and Verona.

Of a similarly wide geographical scope, but focused, as the sub-title declares, on "Court and Civic Festivals in Early Modern Europe", is the two-volume *Europa Triumphans* (MHRA in conjunction with Ashgate: Aldershot, UK and Burlington, VT, 2004) edited by J. R. Mulryne, Helen Watanabe O'Kelly, and Margaret Shewring, with Elizabeth Goldring and Sarah Knight as Associate General Editors. Drawing on a wide range of scholarly expertise, the volumes present excerpts from, or full texts of, a wide range of Festivals drawn from, and in the languages of, eight European countries. Unusually, a section of volume II discusses festivals originally presented in colonial America. A particular feature of the collection is the translation of the chosen texts into unshowy modern English. A series of General Introductions addresses themes common to festivals across the board, covering such topics as "The Early Modern Festival Book: Function and Form" (Helen Watanabe-O'Kelly), "Court Festivals as Political Spectacle: The Example of Sixteenth-Century France" (R. J. Knecht), "The Baroque Court Festival: The Example of German Courts around 1700" (Ute Daniel), "Music and Festival" (Iain Fenlon), "The Staging of Courtly Theatre: 1560s to 1640s" (Roger Savage), and "Looking for the Unknowable: The Visual Experience of Renaissance Festivals" (Henri Zerner). Not all of these writers specialise in festival studies, with the result that at several points they introduce wider perspectives than is often the case with specialist works. Characteristically for this collection, an early chapter by R. J. Knecht, with Mark Greengrass, Nicolas Le Roux and Margaret M. McGowan, traces the route taken by Henri III from Cracow and Venice to Orléans and Rouen, discussing the festivals he encountered along the way and thus weaving his Italian experience into a pan-European political framework. Each of the book's sections attempts as a central tactic to diversify its account of a festival or group of festivals by situating it or them within a series of related perspectives, from social and dynastic politics to performance on the streets or indoors in the relevant court. In the case of the chapter, "Festivals in Genoa in the Sixteenth and Seventeenth Centuries", five scholars support principal researcher Maria Ines Aliverti's account of the printed sources by exploring topics such as the city's search for legitimation (Carlo Bitossi), its image (Lucia Nuti), temporary architecture and public decoration (Lauro Magnani), official dress (Bruna Niccoli), and orations for the election of the Doge (Franco Vazzoler). Readers will notice that major cities such as Rome and Florence are not given a chapter or section, on the grounds that these places have received a great deal of scholarly attention elsewhere in comparison with other festival locations in Italy. Generally speaking, the two volumes provide a basis and perhaps a template for working scholarship, rather than an attempt to offer comprehensive "coverage" of their chosen topic.

Other printed publications

The founding publications from which modern study of festival may be said to take its origin appeared in four volumes between 1956 and 1976 under the direction of Jean Jacquot (Paris: CNRS). Each volume derived from a conference exploring a unitary theme, a tactic that permitted specialist exploration of specific topics while preserving an overall scholarly coherence. It also permitted the inclusion of reflective pieces, including wide-ranging summaries, principally by Jacquot himself. The coverage of festival occasions by an international range of scholars is wide, and presented with exemplary attention to existing primary and secondary sources. Volume 2 of the series, *Fêtes et Cérémonies au Temps de Charles Quint* (Paris: CNRS, 1960) will be of particular interest to readers of this book. Among notable chapters are André Chastel's "Les Entrées de Charles Quint en Italie", Sydney Anglo's "Le Camp du Drap d'Or et les entrevues d'Henri VIII et de Charles Quint", and Frances A. Yates's "Charles Quint et l'idée d'empire". Forty-seven black-and-white plates illustrate the volume's topic, often from sources not otherwise easily accessible.

Roy Strong's *Art and Power* (Woodbridge, UK: The Boydell Press, 1984), a revised version of his 1974 *Splendour at Court. Renaissance Spectacle and the Theatre of Power*, offers in his own words "a point of departure and a basic work of reference for anyone who needs to study renaissance festivals". Though superseded in various respects by subsequent publications, this remains the single readily-available study of festival across the most part of Europe. Strong offers an account of the classical and medieval origins of festival and in addition devotes individual chapters to "Charles V and the Imperial Progress", "Catherine de' Medici and Valois Court Festivals", "The Grand Duke Ferdinand and the Florentine 'intermezzi'", and "Charles I and the Stuart Court Masques". These last two chapters benefit in particular from Strong's wide knowledge as an art historian of the visual character of festival, and bring to bear his awareness of the interplay between Italian, especially Florentine, art and culture and the festivals of seventeenth-century England. Similar perceptions also vividly inform *Henry, Prince of Wales and England's Lost Renaissance* (London: Thames and Hudson, 1986), Strong's study of the life and cultural interests of Henry, James I's eldest son, with one chapter dealing specifically with "The Prince's Festivals". Strong's awareness of the wider cultural context of festival and ceremony, in particular its Italian connections, may be thought to have set a paradigm observed by art-historical studies such as the National Gallery's richly-informative *The Lost Prince: The Life and Death of Henry Stuart* (London, 2012), with its referencing of European politics and Italian art as essential context for interpreting the centrally-significant if all-too-short life of this royal figure.

A particularly useful source for the study of Anglo-Italian cultural interchange is *Writing Royal Entries in Early Modern Europe*, edited by Marie-Claude Canova-Green and Jean Andrews, with Marie-France Wagner (Turnhout, Belgium: Brepols, 2013). This volume, which addresses entries across Europe, features lengthy bibliographies as well as seventeen figures, one plate, one table and one map. Chapters with particular relevance to the topic of Anglo-Italian festival and theatre include Maria Ines Aliverti, "Travelling with a Queen: The Journey of Margaret of Austria (1598–1599). Between Evidence and Reconstruction", which discusses Queen Margaret's travels in Italy during her journey to marry Philip III. Aliverti cites Bonner Mitchell's two books (1986 and 1990: see later), the second of which focuses especially on Ferrara. She also cites Elisa Battilla's on-line discussion of "Le fonti a stampa italiane" (http://mdaustria.arte.unipi.it/margheritaprogramma.html) as well as her own contribution to *Europa Triumphans*, focused on Genoa, and her "Il viaggio in Italia di Margherita d'Austria … ingressi, feste e ceremonie" (delivered at a conference in Pisa, 2006, with publication to follow). Of special interest to students of Anglo-Italian cultural relations, Aliverti discusses in some detail *A Briefe Discovrse of the Voyage and Entrance of the Queene of Spaine into Italy*, the most complete and informative of the published primary sources, printed by John Wolfe in 1599 with a particular eye on the educated group of Catholic reformers then living in London. Equally concerned with dual cultural sources, in this case Spanish-English, is Alexander Samson's "Images of Co-Monarchy in the London Entry of Philip and Mary (1554)", referring to an entry conceived as a means (at best no more than partially successful) of assuaging public and religious hostility to an unprecedented royal marriage. The chapter by Sara Mamone and Caterina Pagnini entitled "Florentine Festivals for the Entry of Archduke Leopold V of Austria in 1618" emphasises "the cult of Medici tradition", with festival called on to foreground Medici policies and affirm alliances at the critical moment of the outbreak of the Thirty Years War. My own chapter, "Entries and Festivals in Late Sixteenth- and Early Seventeenth-Century Florence as Precedents for Court and Theatre in England (1600–1620)", traces connections between Florentine festivals, especially the 1608 pageant on the Arno, and the court culture of Jacobean England, paying attention to the cultural life of Prince Henry's Florentine-absorbed court and to Thomas Middleton's *Women Beware Women* with its account of the life and death of Francesco de' Medici's second duchess, Bianca Cappello.

Court Festivals of the European Renaissance, edited by Mulryne and Goldring (Ashgate: Aldershot, UK and Burlington, VT, 2002) casts its net wide, reflecting the interconnectedness of festival events and topics across the continent, visual, aural and architectural. Of particular interest to students of Italian festival are the chapters grouped under the heading "Recovering the Past", including an extensive survey by Helen Watanabe-O'Kelly of "Early Modern European Festivals – Politics and Performance, Event and Record", offering among much else a valuable working distinction between "Ceremonies" and "Spectacles". Also included is Margaret M. McGowan's "The Renaissance Triumph and its Classical Heritage", to be read alongside her major study, *The Vision of Rome in Late Renaissance France* (New Haven, CT: Yale University Press, 2000). The section of the book headed "Festivals for Charles V" includes Bernard Schimmelpfennig's study of "The Two Coronations of Charles V at Bologna, 1530", while the section on "Festival and Architecture" offers a study of "The First Temporary Triumphal Arch in Venice (1557)" by Maximilian L. S. Tondro, and Peter Davidson's particularly innovative and intriguing "The *Theatrum* for the Entry of Claudia de' Medici and Federigo Ubaldo della Rovere into Urbino, 1621". This last focuses on "seventeen canvases painted at Urbino in the Marche in the year 1621 by the Veronese painter Claudio Ridolfi (1570–1644) assisted by the Urbinese Girolamo Cialdieri (1593–1646)"; these make up "the most extensive survival from any one festival to have come hitherto to [the author's] notice". Perhaps the volume's major contribution comes in the section "The Performance of Festival: Music, Theatre and Event". Here Iain Fenlon studies "Rites of Passsage: Cosimo I de' Medici and the Theatre of Death", noting how "music of all kinds, from the pealing of church bells … to specially composed polyphony, was a fundamental element in the many varieties of Italian early modern spectacle and display", ranging from Florentine *intermedi* to obsequies for Medici rulers. In the same section, Nicoletta Guidobaldi offers a discussion of music and especially dance in Italian Festivals more generally, Dinko Fabris studies "Musical Festivals at a Capital without a Court: Spanish Naples from Charles V (1535) to Philip V (1702)", Flora Dennis deals with "Music in Ferrarese Festivals: Harmony and Chaos", with special reference to music for "the tournaments known as the *spettacoli cavallereschi*", while Roger Savage contributes a witty discussion of the staging of Renaissance theatre, drawing together under the title "Checklists for Philostrate" Shakespeare's *A Midsummer Night's Dream* and, among other contemporary prefaces and treatises, the anonymous Florentine survey *Il Corago*.

An earlier collection of studies can be found in *Italian Renaissance Festivals and Their European Influence* edited by Mulryne and Shewring (Lewiston, NY, Queenston, ON, and Lampeter, UK: Edwin Mellen Press, 1992). The contents include chapters on specific festivals, including Alessandro Marcigliano, "Cavallerie a Ferrara, 1561–1570", Lina Urban, "Feste Veneziane Cinquecentesche", Christopher Cairns, "Theatre as Festival: The Staging of Aretino's *Talanta* (1542)", and Jessica Gordon, "Entertainments for the Marriages of the Princesses of Savoy in 1608". Also included are more genre-wide readings contributed by Günter Berghaus "Theatre Performances at Italian Renaissance Festivals: Multi-Media Spectacles or *Gesamtkunstwerke*?" and Roger Savage, "Staging an *Intermedio*: Practical Advice from Florence *circa* 1630". Further sections consider the Italian influence on festivals in German-speaking lands, in France and in both Denmark and England. An unusual feature of the seminar from which the collection derived was the showing of Channel 4's *Una Stravanganza dei Medici*, a television recreation, using modern technology, of an *intermedio* from the 1589 Florentine festival. This (albeit with music only) was subsequently issued in the Virgin Classics series as a commercial CD. Glimpses of the television performance are available as backing to a YouTube video under the *Una Stravaganza* title.

Theatre of the English and Italian Renaissance, edited by Mulryne and Shewring (Basingstoke, UK: Macmillan, 1991) directs its attention, as its title suggests, to the more general theatrical scene in Italy and to English theatrical performance paralleling the theatre of the Italian courts. Several chapters specifically address courtly plays in performance, providing a context (including lists of further reading) in relation to which those interested in researching festivals as performance can develop their work. A section of Mulryne's contribution to the Canova-Green and Andrews volume directs attention to the traceable influence of a *naumachia* staged on the Arno in 1608 for the Grand Duke Ferdinando and his bride Maria Magdalena, and on a river pageant on the Thames in 1613 celebrating the wedding of the English Princess Elizabeth to the Elector Palatine Frederick V. The status of such English river pageants as versions of a widely-developed trans-European theatre form is patent not only on this occasion but on multiple occasions throughout the sixteenth and seventeenth centuries, as readers of Margaret Shewring (ed.) *Waterborne Pageants and Festivities in the Renaissance* (Farnham, UK and Burlington, VT: Ashgate, 2013) will be fully aware.

A more pervasive Italian influence on English festivity is evident in the flourishing English *genre* of the Court Masque, even if masques might more plausibly be categorised as court theatre rather than festivals. A study such as John Peacock's *The Stage Designs of Inigo Jones: The European Context* (Cambridge: Cambridge University Press, 1995) demonstrates how widespread Italian and especially Florentine influence was on the entire apparatus of the masque, and specifically on the appearance and management of the masque on stage. This is a topic which receives authoritative attention in the magnificent two-volume illustrated study by Stephen Orgel and Roy Strong, *Inigo*

Jones: The Theatre of the Stuart Court (Berkeley, Los Angeles and London: Sotheby Parke Bernet, University of California Press, 1973), and in studies by Stephen Orgel, *The Jonsonian Masque* (Cambridge, MA: Harvard University Press, 1965), and by John Orrell, *The Theatres of Inigo Jones and John Webb* (Cambridge: Cambridge University Press, 1985) as well as in numerous volumes making up the wide-ranging cultural scholarship of Frances A. Yates.

Responding to advances in festival scholarship made possible by collections of essays by specialist research scholars, Ashgate Publishing Ltd. have initiated a series of studies under the title "European Festival Studies 1450–1700" (general editors: Mulryne, McGowan, and Shewring). The first collection of essays in the series, edited by Margaret M. McGowan, addresses *Dynastic Marriages 1612/1615: A Celebration of the Hapsburg and Bourbon Unions* (Farnham, UK and Burlington, VT: Ashgate, 2013). Of more direct interest to students of Italian festivals, the second publication, edited by Margaret Shewring, considers *Waterborne Pageants and Festivities in the Renaissance* (Farnham, UK and Burlington, VT: Ashgate, 2013). Italy-centred chapters include Evelyn Korsch, "Renaissance Venice and the Sacred-Political Connotations of Waterborne Pageants", a study which addresses "Venetian political self-understanding during the sixteenth century and after" as represented by waterborne festivals, paying attention among others to the ceremony invoking the marriage of the Doge with the Sea. Iain Fenlon's "*Rex Christianissimus Francorum*: Themes and Contexts of Henry III's Entry to Venice, 1574" situates a specific festival within its historical moment, while Maria Ines Aliverti researches both printed and archival sources in her "Water Policy and Water Festivals: The Case of Pisa under Ferdinando de Medici (1588–1609)". My own chapter questions both the political significance and the practicalities of a well-known festival occasion under the title "Arbitrary Reality: Fact and Fantasy in the Florentine *Naumachia*, 1589". A wider context for festival is provided by Marie-Claude Canova-Green in her consideration of "Lepanto Revisited: Water-fights and the Turkish Threat in Early Modern Europe (1571–1656)", while Mary M. Young describes and assesses a more unusual festival type in "The Ice Festival in Florence, 1604". Melanie Zefferino meanwhile considers a less-publicised festival location in her study from primary sources of "The Savoy Naumachia on the Lake Mont Cenis: A Site-specific Spectacle in the 'Amphitheatre' of the Alps", while Helen Watanabe O'Kelly links a distinguished German-speaking visitor with his Italian travels in "Sailing Towards a Kingdom: Ernst August von Braunschweig-Lüneburg (1629–1698) in Venice in 1685 and 1686". An entertaining and erudite chapter by Eric Nicholson is entitled "Sing Again, Sirena: Translating the Theatrical Virtuosa from Venice to London".

The third collection in the Ashgate series (2015), edited by Mulryne with Maria Ines Aliverti and Anna Maria Testaverde, entitled *Ceremonial Entries in Early Modern Europe: The Iconography of Power* (Farnham, UK and Burlington, VT: Ashgate, 2015), offers a Europe-wide group of studies, with considerable emphasis on examples from sixteenth- and early seventeenth-century France, but with important chapters on Italy by Testaverde (on the *Book of Ceremonies* by Francesco Tongiarini), Fenlon (on festival music), and Lucia Nuti (on Roman *Possessi*). Nuti also contributes a valuable Appendix transcribing the Register of Leonardo di Zanobi Bartolini for the coronation of Leo X in 1513. A welcome extension of the geographical and chronological scope of topics previously covered by the series comes in three chapters dealing with English and then Scottish festival events: Margaret Shewring's "The Iconography of Populism" finds intriguing parallels between waterborne entries to London by Anne Boleyn, Catherine of Braganza and Elizabeth II;

Sara Trevisan's study linking politics, legend and iconography in early modern Lord Mayor's shows; and Lucinda H.S. Dean's wide-ranging study of the entries of foreign consorts to Scottish cities from the mid-fifteenth century to the end of the sixteenth.

Two further collections in the series, edited by Krista De Jonge, Pieter Martens, Richard Morris, and J. R. Mulryne have just announced by Routledge, in association with PALATIUM, a European Science Foundation research network. These deal with *Architectures of Festival in Early Modern Europe: Fashioning and Re-fashioning Urban and Courtly Space* (2018) and with *Occasions of State: Early Modern European Festivals and the Negotiation of Power*, edited by J. R. Mulryne and Krista De Jonge (forthcoming). All volumes include full bibliographies, in the case of the second and subsequent volumes arranged to follow each chapter in order to permit specific reference to the chapter's topic, and in the case of the more obviously delimited first volume at the end of the book. A collection of essays on *Princely Funerals in Europe, 1400–1700* edited by Monique Chatenet, Murielle Gaude-Ferragu, and Gérard Sabatier is expected to be published in 2019. The essay collections will be joined by monographs, several of which are in active preparation, including a study by Felicia M. Else of *The Politics of Water in the Art and Festivals of Medici Florence: From Neptune Fountain to Naumachia* (publication scheduled for 2019).

A series of facsimile festival texts with detailed scholarly introductions by H. M. C. Purkis, D. MacFarlane, Richard Cooper, Ronald Knowles and Sydney Anglo among others, initiated by and under the general editorship of Margaret M. McGowan, has appeared under the title *Renaissance Triumphs and Magnificences*. The series, published initially by Theatrum Orbis Terrarum (Amsterdam) from 1974, and subsequently by the Arizona Center for Medieval and Renaissance Studies, has included entries into major cities in France within an interest in the varying forms of festival across Europe from dance to triumphal entries.

The leading scholar of festivals in England remains Sydney Anglo, whose pioneering study of *Spectacle, Pageantry and Early Tudor Policy* (Oxford: Oxford University Press, 1969) led the way in recognising the close interrelationship of English court politics with festival from the accession of Henry VII to the coronation of Elizabeth I. A second edition, with new prefatory material summarising relevant scholarship on English festival, together with a full bibliography, appeared in 1997 (Oxford: Clarendon Press). Anglo's numerous other publications on festival include *The Court Festivals of Henry V* (Manchester, UK: John Rylands Library, 1960) and *The London Pageants for the Reception of Katharine of Aragon, November 1501* (London: The Institutes, 1963). Written with a light touch and skeptical wit, these studies, in common with Anglo's other work, combine a bracingly common-sense approach with wide-ranging scholarship.

A study with what seems at first sight a limited focus, Helen Watanabe-O'Kelly's *Triumphal Shews: Tournaments at German-Speaking Courts in Their European Context 1560–1730* in fact keeps faith with its reference to European context by offering a detailed discussion of tournaments as widely-significant political events. Watanabe allows us to glimpse the international perspective in which such shows may be most fruitfully understood, relating the book's central concern with German-speaking lands to French and Italian parallels.

Scholarship of the Italian festival

Among those who have written with particular insight and scholarship on Italian festivals, Bonner Mitchell occupies a special place. His work with Andrew C. Minor on *Festivities for the Marriage of Cosimo I, Duke of Florence, in 1539* (Columbia: University of Missouri Press, 1968) features, unusually, an extended presentation of the occasion's music; his *The Majesty of the State* (Florence: Olschki, 1986) interprets the triumphal progresses of foreign sovereigns in Italy between 1494 and 1600 by offering a descriptive bibliography of their entries; and his fascinatingly detailed *1598, a Year of Pageantry in Late Renaissance Ferrara* (Binghamton, NY: Medieval & Renaissance Texts and Studies, 1990) evokes the political tensions between an accomplished but relatively small city state and the mighty Papacy, in which festival played a mind-influencing part. In a somewhat similar vein another American scholar, James M. Saslow, combines a study of art and social history with a fully-documented discussion of the month-long celebrations, from *intermezzi* to animal baiting, that marked *The Medici Wedding of 1589* (New Haven, CT: Yale University Press, 1996). A lengthy 583-page, painstakingly-researched, investigation by Edmund A. Bowles of *Musical Ensembles in Festival Books, 1500–1800* (Ann Arbor, MI: UMI Research Press, 1989) offers, as its subtitle declares, "an iconographical and documentary survey" of an extraordinarily wide if selective range of festival events, including Italian and English, with a focus on their musical accompaniments. The result is informative for the study of festivals, including those which fall within the limited range of years which is the concern of this chapter. A. M. Nagler's much-cited, authoritative *Theatre Festivals of the Medici, 1539–1637* (New Haven, CT: Yale University Press, 1964) offers 136 black-and-white illustrations to complement its discussion of festivals stretching from those for the wedding of Cosimo I to those saluting the wedding of Vittoria della Rovere to Ferdinando II, the latter taking in, among other events, a memorable performance of the opera *Le Nozze degli dèi* featuring the nuptials of four pairs of Olympian gods. Nagler's focus on performance, musical as well as visual, ensures that his book remains a continuing source of stimulus as well as information for today's students and scholars.

An absorbing study with a wide cultural focus may be found in Iain Fenlon's *The Ceremonial City* (New Haven, CT: Yale University Press, 2007), an account, to cite the book's sub-title, of "History, Memory and Myth in Renaissance Venice". Fenlon interprets festival as one element in a cultural matrix expressing the self-identification of Venice through architecture (the Piazza di San Marco) ritual, society and politics during the brilliant but conflict-ridden years that followed Lepanto (1571) – a very welcome corrective to the sometimes myopic focus of otherwise scholarly festival studies.

Italian scholars have been far from inactive in their discussion of festival. *Teatro e Spettacolo nella Firenze dei Medici* (Florence: Leo S. Olschki, 2001), edited by Elvira Garbero Zorzi and Mario Sperenzi, takes as its origin an exhibition of the same title at the Palazzo Medici Riccardi, and partly as a result moves decisively away from book-centred study of festival to a study of its realisation in civic and theatrical space. Chapters such as Elvira Garbero Zorzi's "I modelli dei luoghi teatrali a Firenze", Cesare Molinari's masterly and wide-ranging "La scena vuota" and Sara Mamone's "Il sistema dei teatri e le accademie" focus on the staging of spectacle, an emphasis extended to illuminating effect both in the numerous and by no means always familiar photographic illustrations of theatre space, drawn both from historic sources and from current models of early theatres, and by the "Catalogo" chapters dealing with, among other venues, the *Cortile* of the Palazzo Medici, the Palazzo degli Uffizi and the Palazzo Pitti, the two former chapters by Elvira Garbero Zorzi and the last by Luigi Zangheri. A multi-lingual bibliography, centring on studies by Italian scholars, but taking in also a very wide range of work from other sources, occupies fifteen closely-printed pages and could in itself serve as a guide to the recently-current state of festival research, especially as it concerns performance.

It would be impossible in the space available, and were it possible it would be invidious, to pick out the most informative and influential studies of festival by Italian writers and scholars. A useful summary, *Teatro e spettacolo nel Rinascimento* by Giovanni Attolini (Rome: Editori Laterza, 1988), deals in a chapter entitled "La festa e gli spettacoli" with "la festa spettacolo", "l'entrata trionfale", "il banchetto", "il trionfo", and "gli spettacoli agonistici". While Attolini maintains a considerable emphasis on Florence, his examples bring in other Italian cities and city states, within a broad understanding of the European exploration of theatre forms in the Renaissance period. A book-length work such as Ludovico Zorzi's *Il teatro e la citta: Saggi sulla scena italiana* (Turin: Giulio Einaudi Editore, 1977), with its intensively-researched and helpfully-illustrated chapters entitled "Ferrara: il sipario ducale", "Firenze: il teatro e la città", and "Venezia: la Repubblica a teatro", has exercised a strong influence on subsequent research and publication. Very numerous journal articles have also moved research forward. Names such as Garbero Zorzi, Mamone, Molinari and Ludovico Zorzi would recur in any overview, but a newer name such as Anna Maria Testaverde, with her excitingly innovative article "L'officina delle nuvole. Il Teatro Mediceo del 1589 e gli Intermedi del Buontalenti" (*Musica e Teatro* 11/12, 1991), would also need to be entered. It is however noticeable how typically – and understandably – Italian scholars tend to confine their most extended research to Italian festivals and their societies, curtailing to this extent the pertinence of much of their work for the topic of this chapter.

Electronic resources

Perhaps unsurprisingly, research sources relating, at least in part, to Italian and other European festivals, including English, are increasingly available online to supplement those in print. These electronic sources vary in content and in the research opportunities they offer. Some include a range of metadata, others present no more than plain text. Some carry illustrations and explanatory and contextualising scholarly essays, others do not. Some are searchable under a series of headings, others are not. The data collections mentioned later offer a wealth of material, but it should not be supposed that this replaces direct enquiry in the catalogues of the great European libraries and archives such as, in London, the British Library, the British Museum, the Warburg Institute (University of London) and the Victoria and Albert Museum (National Art Library); in Paris, the Bibliothèque de l'Arsenal and the Bibliothèque nationale de France; in German cities, the Herzog August Bibliothek, Wolfenbüttel, the Bayerische Staatsbibliothek, Munich, and the Staatliche Kunstsammlungen, Dresden. These should be consulted together with the great collections in Italy including the Biblioteca Apostolica Vaticana, Rome, the Biblioteca Nazionale Centrale, Florence, and the Biblioteca Nazionale Marciana, Venice. This is not to mention the wealth of material in United States libraries and archives, including the Getty Research Institute, Los Angeles, and the New York Public Library. Increasingly, Eastern European collections, in Poland, for example, and Russia, are becoming available in digitised form. More and more access is now possible via the catalogues of these institutions and their digitised links, as a route to locating and (with permission) downloading text and illustrations.

Finding the required texts can, it is true, be an arduous if richly rewarding process, requiring as it does an advance knowledge of what is there to be found.

Electronic resources have made research material more immediately available and provided a stimulus to enquiry by students and scholars. An early online resource emerged from a research project supported by the UK's Arts and Humanities Research Board (now Research Council) and the University of Warwick. This resource is accessible via the British Library website/Search our Catalogue, under the heading Treasures in Full/Renaissance Festival Books. The site includes 253 digitised texts of European Festival books from 1475 to 1700, complete or in excerpt. These are supplemented by introductory essays, one of which deals with Festivals in Italy (Mulryne), introducing festival culture in Italian city states, in particular Rome, Florence, Venice, and Genoa. The essay also offers a selective reading list of scholarly studies, intended as a gateway to initial exploration of the field. Three short essays by Watanabe-O'Kelly deal with wider aspects of festival, asking the question "Who were festival books aimed at?" and discussing these books as history and panegyric. A short essay by Roger Savage focuses on the performance and staging of courtly theatre. The digitised texts are fully searchable by keywords including location, dynasty, date, and personal name. Each text carries a selection of metadata. The project was undertaken by a team working with principal investigators J. R. Mulryne and Margaret Shewring, and included leading scholars Helen Watanabe-O'Kelly, Margaret M. McGowan, Robert Knecht and Karin Friedrich. The project was made possible as a result of co-operation with a number of senior British Library staff, including Kristian Jensen and Chris Wootton. Detailed research, involving the selection, cataloguing and XML coding of festival volumes was carried out by Sarah Cusk and Alexander Samson, at the time Research Fellows of the Centre for the Study of the Renaissance, University of Warwick.

The transition from print to electronic finding aids is best represented by *Festivals and Ceremonies* (http://festivals.mml.ox.ac.uk), a revised and enlarged electronic version of the invaluable bibliographical guide of the same name mentioned above. Under principal investigator Helen Watanabe-O'Kelly the electronic version has been checked and appropriately extended and amplified by Madeleine Brook, and made available as the result of a grant from Oxford University Press. It now references more than 3000 festival books published between 1500 and 1800. These are drawn from five major libraries, the British Library (London), the Bibliothèque de l'Arsenal (Paris), the Herzog August Bibliothek (Wolfenbüttel), the Piot Collection of the British National Art Library at the Victoria and Albert Museum (London) and, as an addition to the available printed version, the Bayerische Staatsbibliothek (Munich). The editors hope to add further libraries in the United States and Europe. Searching this enhanced database is facilitated by an easily navigable series of headings, including Books, Festivals, Artists, Events, Participants and Places. Under these headings a wealth of information leads the researcher to the full title of the festival book, the author(s), the year and type of the event, a brief description and notes, together with illustrations and the names of associated ruler(s) and artists. A very helpful feature is the inclusion of the URL of books known to have been digitised elsewhere, so that a link can be followed to the "external" electronic version. The shelf marks of printed volumes in the collections of libraries holding the books in question, including a good selection of Italian festival books, are also usefully given.

The Herzog August library at Wolfenbüttel (www.hab.de) offers a collection of materials of international importance in the fields of Medieval and Early Modern literature, history and visual art. A collection known as the Wolfenbüttel Digital Library "presents in digital facsimile selected items from its collections which are rare, outstanding, frequently used, or currently most relevant for research". This collection is of especial value for situating individual festivals, including Italian, within the wider European context. Many of the completed and current projects are collaborative, in keeping with the Herzog August Library's ethos of joint research, taking in institutions within the academic and independent sectors. Information on and access to the projects – for example "Festkultur Online" or "Emblematica Online" – can be obtained under the designations "completed projects" and "current projects", with the material arranged chronologically.

Two further collections in German archives complement the collection at Wolfenbüttel. These are at the Bayerische Staatsbibliothek, Munich (www.bsb-muenchen.com) and the Staatliche Kunstsammlungen, Dresden (www.skd.museum), the second of which houses a rich historic collection reaching back to the sixteenth century. Both libraries offer targeted digital access. As a printed companion, Watanabe-O'Kelly's *Court Culture in Dresden: From Renaissance to Baroque* includes a chapter investigating "The Italian Ideal: The Sixteenth-Century Reception of Italian Culture", with an emphasis on architecture, equestrian practice, tournaments, and princely education; these serve as an illuminating parallel to cultural developments in England.

The Warburg Institute, now part of the School of Advanced Study, University of London (www.warburg.sas.ac.uk), is a long-established research institution with a particular emphasis on the history of the classical tradition. Its 350,000 volumes make it the world's largest specialist collection focusing on Renaissance studies and the inheritance of classical literature and art. Many of its holdings are digitised, including a set of more than 100 festival texts, principally from the sixteenth to the eighteenth centuries. These are clearly reproduced and freely available for consultation, downloading and non-commercial use. Metadata is limited to cataloguing and bibliographical information. Researchers will find the associated iconographic database of particular interest. Arranged under such headings as "Gods and Myths", "Portraits", and "Religious Iconography" this collection of digitised images, drawn from sources including woodcuts, engravings, paintings and sculpture, offers the student unparalleled access to the visual lexicon familiar to and employed by creators of festival events.

The Herla project is based at the Fondazione Mantova, Capitale Europea dello Spettacolo (www.capitalespettacolo.it/eng/ric_gen.asp), a research institute dedicated to the gathering and recording of documentary materials relating to festivals and other "spectacular activities", including plays which were staged under the patronage of the Gonzaga, from 1480 until 1630. This apparently tight focus does not prevent the inclusion of a wide range of materials from Italy and, through the multiple connections of the Gonzaga court, across Europe. The website includes a very useful annotated list of sources, surveying archives in major Italian cities from Mantua itself to Rome, Turin, and Venice, together with a series of locations in other European countries including Paris, Madrid, and Vienna. The project is ongoing. Completed work includes "Isabella d'Este e le arti dello spettacolo tra Ferrara e Mantova (1493–1540)" and "Commedia dell'Arte" including a wide survey of the activities and personnel of the Commedia troupes. Work under development includes "Festeggiamenti per le nozze di Ferdinando d'Austria con Caterina Gonzaga (1582)" and "Rapporti tra i Gonzaga e i territori della

Serenissima". The archive, holding at present in excess of 11,800 documents, can be accessed by the title of the document (usually the *incipit* and the author) together with its archival description, citing e.g. place and date. Alternatively, entering a category search leads to a document that is fully referenced and tagged to the archive in which it is held. Fourteen publications are listed as already entered in the public domain by scholars such as Simona Brunetti and Cristina Grazioli.

The rich collection of festival books housed at the Bibliothèque de l'Arsenal, part of the Bibliothèque nationale de France (BnF), Paris (www.bnf.fr), is particularly notable for the Rondel collection, which comprises printed books and other relevant documents at the BnF's Richelieu site, dealing with festivals and ceremonies both public and private in France and abroad from the sixteenth century to 1930. The collection is accessed via the general catalogue of the BnF under the designation "département des Arts du spectacle" and then "collection Auguste Rondel". A detailed manuscript catalogue of the collection in seventy-five volumes is in the course of being incorporated into the BnF General Catalogue, and will then be available online. Among collections in England, the specialised Piot collection at the Victoria and Albert Museum (mentioned earlier; http://catalogue.nal.vam.ac.uk) features 650–700 festival books which can be located online by genre, while the rich collections at the British Library can be partially accessed in digital form in the research collection mentioned above. In Italy, the Biblioteca Nazionale Firenze (www.bncf.firenze.sbn.it) holds a vast collection which can be searched online under the usual categories of author, title, topic (useful if the precise title of the work is unknown). The online website of the Biblioteca Nazionale Marciana in Venice offers a section devoted to the "Biblioteca digitale" which, while it does not feature a festival heading, nevertheless leads to numerous relevant materials when the searcher knows the book's or document's title. The comprehensive website www.archivi.beniculturali.it faces the enquirer with an often complex search that can be rewarding in leading to such materials as the Archivio di Stato di Reggio nell'Emilia and the Padovan archives, which might otherwise be overlooked as potential sources of interest. On the farther side of the Atlantic, the Getty Research Institute's festival collections (www.getty.edu/research) range from Renaissance prints and illustrated books to a collection of 280 Italian festivals online, while the New York Public Library collection (www.nypl.org) rewards a search under the designation "festivals", displaying extensive digitised materials arranged under individual Italian cities and city states.

Conclusion

The range of both printed and electronic sources for the investigation of festival culture grows ever wider. This increasing richness has brought with it advances in the understanding of festival within the political, social, architectural and theatrical life of countries across Europe. If it is true that most studies tend to be confined, understandably, within a single national or academic-specialist context, there are notable exceptions to this generalisation, a number of which were cited earlier. The study of festival must rank among the most demanding of academic disciplines, requiring for its satisfactory pursuit a range of interests and competencies that include a command of, or at the least a reasonable acquaintance with, a set of skills normally sheltered within traditional boundaries. Thus a working knowledge of, or preferably a fluency in several European languages, modern and classical, is desirable, while acquaintance with current if not cutting-age research in say cultural and political history, economics, architecture and the theory and practice of indoor and outdoor theatre – territories often jealously guarded by accredited practitioners – is almost obligatory. Advances in printed and electronic finding aids will not make these boundaries more porous, but they may well assist the student-scholar in navigating what must seem otherwise a thoroughly intimidating landscape. It is in pursuit of this hope that the present chapter has been researched and written.

21 John Florio and the circulation of Italian culture

Michael Wyatt

The principal conduit of the written and spoken culture of Italy in late Tudor and early Stuart England, John Florio was the first to admit how little prepared he was to play such a significant role in the diffusion there of continental Europe's most advanced vernacular language. In the dedicatory epistle of his language-learning dialogue book *Firste Fruites*, published in London in 1578, Florio asks Robert Dudley, the Earl of Leicester – "the onely furtherer, maintayner, and supporter of al well disposed mindes toward any kinde of studie" – to overlook the potential disqualifier "that little, or (to say truth), none at all is the learning I have, and smal is the seede, plant and grase whence these, altogether wilde, and unsaverie fruites doo spring."[1] What might be mistaken here as the false modesty typical of writers of the period toward their patrons – almost always praised in such over-the-top paeans – is in Florio's case a sincere declaration of his curious pedigree: having been born in England, probably in 1553, to a mother of uncertain nationality (likely English) and an Italian Protestant father but soon thereafter forced to flee with his family to the continent following the death of King Edward VI and the restoration of Catholic polity that accompanied the accession of Queen Mary. The young John Florio was raised in a remote Alpine village, Soglio, in the Protestant but Italian-speaking Swiss region of the Grigioni, and there his father, Michelangelo, would have served as his principal tutor. Efforts at situating John in Tübingen in the circle of the humanist Catholic-bishop-turned-Lutheran Pier Paolo Vergerio in what would have been the younger Florio's secondary school years have proven to be inconclusive (a signature, Johannus Florentius, on a document in a Tübingen archive sometimes cited as proof, could be that of almost anyone, and the young Florio's potential Florentine identity rests only on his father's earlier claim: Michelangelo describes himself as 'Fiorentino' on the title-page of his 1563 Italian translation of Agricola's *De re metallica*). John Florio's silence on the matter is at any rate telling given both Vergerio's good press in Elizabethan England and Florio's tendency in other circumstances to play up his network of connections and patrons. The paradox of an unlearned 'stranger' – the legal term for the foreigner in early modern England (though it may not have strictly applied to Florio, he was considered as such by his many detractors) – responsible for 'civilizing' the English through the instruments of Italian, and later French, culture was an issue that defined Florio's career in England from beginning to end.

Life and work

The facts of Florio's life are little documented.[2] In spite of the graceful secretarial script evident in the only manuscripts that survive in Florio's own hand – a collection of proverbs, *Il giardino di ricreatione;* a draft of the Italian grammar that accompanies *Firste*

DOI: 10.4324/9781315612720-24

Fruites; and the only translation Florio ever made into Italian, of James VI/I's treatise on kingship, *Basilikon Doron*[3] – as well as his last will and testament, there are few extant letters of his own[4] (it can safely be assumed that most of the Italian letters of Queen Anne addressed to her wide circle of correspondents were written in Florio's hand, but no work has yet been done to systematically analyze this correspondence), and much of what we know of his life has been reconstructed from the paratextual material Florio provides in his various publications and in fragments of information reported in the writings of his contemporaries and in documents pertaining to his acquaintances. Florio had likely returned to England by the mid-1570s; he is known to have spent several years at Oxford as a language teacher around the time of the publication of *Firste Fruites* (he never matriculated at the university although he may have attended lectures thanks to his status as factotum of an aristocratic student, Emmanuel Barnes); by the early 1580s he was working in the residence of the French ambassador, Michel de Castelnau, employed as tutor to his daughter in the same period in which the renegade Domenican friar Giordano Bruno was living there; he was involved later in the 1580s, together with his friend Matthew Gwinne, in the posthumous editing of Sir Philip Sidney's *Arcadia*; by 1592, Florio was in the service of Henry Wriothesley, the Earl of Southampton, Shakespeare's early patron, and he continued to accrue aristocratic patrons over the ensuing decade. Many of these figures were marginalized following the attempt of their effective leader Robert Devereux, the Earl of Essex, to depose Queen Elizabeth in 1601, but their fortunes were restored with the coming of the Stuarts to England, and through their graces Florio found a place in the new court as Queen Anne of Denmark's Italian Secretary and Groom of her Privy Chamber.

The published work that Florio produced in these years ranged from a translation commisioned by Richard Hakluyt of Jacques Cartier's *A Short and Briefe Narration of the Two Navigations and Discoveries to the Northweast Partes Called Newe France* (1580);[5] a further volume of language-learning dialogues, *Second Fruits* (1591), the first edition of an ambitious Italian-English dictionary, *A Worlde of Wordes* (1598); and the first English translation – indeed the first complete translation into any other language – of Michel de Montaigne's *Essais, The Essayes, or Morall, Politike and Millitarie Discourses* (1603). Both the dictionary and the translation of Montaigne were republished in second editions well into Florio's tenure in the Stuart court, and his association with Queen Anne is marked by the completely altered prefatory apparatus of the 1613 Montaigne, now almost entirely directed to the queen, and by the 1611 title of the greatly expanded dictionary, *Queen Anna's New World of Worlds.*

Traces of Florio's activities at court are registered in letters addressed to him and in other material in which he is passingly mentioned, but one significant aspect of the more than fifteen years Florio spent in the queen's circle has gone largely unnoted: while many of the English ladies connected to the queen sported impeccable Protestant credentials, there is suggestive evidence that Florio – himself the product, if not obviously the heir, of a radical Protestant tradition – was sensitive to the Catholic confession of the sovereign he served.[6] Some twenty-odd Counter-Reformational texts found their way into the library of books Florio claims to have consulted for the second edition of his dictionary – among them a life of Pius V, the pope who had excommunicated Queen Elizabeth in 1570 – and the translation of Boccaccio's *Decameron* that Florio prepared during what would be the final years of Queen Anne's life was based in part on the heavily censored Italian text published in Florence by Leonardo Salviati in 1582, an edition organized to satisfy the censorial demands of the

Roman Inquisition, when earlier, more accurate, sixteenth-century editions would have been easily available to the translator (Florio's translation was issued anonymously in 1620).

While Florio's name figures in diplomatic negotiations with several Italian princes regarding potential husbands for the young Princess Elizabeth Stuart, Florio was apparently excluded from James I's re-opening of formal relations with Venice that involved key political and religious figures from both sides of the equation, and he ended his life in domestic obscurity in Fulham following the premature death of Queen Anne in 1619 (she was only 45 at the time). One last project occupied him, however, in the period just prior to his death in late summer 1625, a translation of selections from Traiano Boccalini's fiercely satiric *Ragguagli di Parnasso*, whose anti-Spanish agenda would have found considerable resonance in an England only recently liberated from the prospect of Prince Charles's marriage to the Infanta Maria of Spain, and still reeling from the Hapsburg victory in Bohemia over James' son-in-law Frederick V that initiated the Thirty Years' War. Florio's translation of Boccalini forms the first part of William Vaughan's *The New-found Politicke* (1626), in which Vaughan and a third translator contributed further selections from the *Ragguagli* in English.

Language learning

The two language-learning dialogue books, *Firste Fruites* (1578) and *Second Fruits* (1591), demarcate the early phase of Florio's career in Elizabethan England. These are challenging contributions to foreign-language pedagogy in England that cover a wide range of contemporary Italian vernacular usage (perhaps indeed too much so, given that neither book saw a second edition, unlike the considerably less demanding manuals issued by Claudius Hollyband and other London-based language teachers that were reissued repeatedly for decades).[7] Florio's approach sought to associate the mastery of another language with the acquisition of the culture refracted through it, and the language learner in Florio's hands is meant to be engaged in a performance: to speak Italian in England is perform another identity in a way similar to the actor taking on another's *persona* on stage. The first public theater in England was opened in London by James Burbage in 1576 while Florio would have been at work on *Firste Fruites*, and in the years immediately following its publication the first hostile anti-theatrical tracts began to appear in England. *Second Fruits* is even more self-consciously theatrical in its structure, a reflection of the rapid maturation of the English theater in the intervening years, but many of the issues taken up in the later book are already present in a less polished guise in its predecessor.[8]

Firste Fruites is arranged in forty-two chapters of varying lengths that address a wide array of topics: typical social situations; "*parlar familiare*/familiare speache"; proverbs; the problematic position of foreigners in England, and the willful provincialism of the English; exempla drawn from classical literature (or, possibly, from compendia of such in translation); moralizing '*detti*/sayings,' many of them translated from Antonio Guevara, the Spanish bishop and confidant of Charles V; and, in the most ambitious chapter in the volume, a consideration of the relationship between learning, writing and philosophy.

The Italian gentleman in Bk. 27 surprises his English interlocutor first with his rapidly acquired mastery of the English language, and then by explaining how he had come by it:

> *Quanto tempo siete stato qui in questo regno?*
> *Io sono stato qui circa un anno.*
> *Come havete fatto a imparare a parlar Inglese così presto?*
> *Io ho imparato Inglese, leggendo.*
> *Si può imparare una lingua leggendo così presto?*
> *Signor sì, che si può imparare.*
>
> Howe long have you beene here in this Realme?
> I have been here about a yeare.
> How have you done to learne to speake English so soone?
> I have learned English by reading.
> May a man learn a language so soone, by reading?
> Yea sir, a may may learne it.[9]

There may well be the hint of an autobiographical element in this exchange, for whatever English John Florio may have acquired growing up in Switzerland there is a bookish quality to the English on display in *Firste Fruites* that betrays its frequently awkward foreign-ness, and the English books that Florio might have read in his early adult years in England are reflected in the highly moralizing texts utilized in his own volume. Bk. 27 goes on to develop a justification for learning foreign languages by arguing for their civilizing effects when acquired with seriousness, and not – as the Italian gentleman here believes of the typical Englishman – as fodder for superficially posh repartee.

The volume concludes with a brief vocabulary, prayers, and directions for Italian merchants to follow in pronouncing English. This latter is of particular interest for the history of the English language, offering one of the earliest testimonies to the actual sound of contemporary English by way of examples that would be familiar to Italians, and noting stumbling blocks for them such as this:

> ["h"] is the most difficult letter for Italians to pronounce due to its great force, particularly in words such as these: Thou (*tu*), that (*quello*), this (*questo*). In order to pronounce such words as they should be, one must as it were to hold the teeth almost clenched while supporting the tip of the tongue between them, then in speaking immediately pull it back so as to rest it on the palate of the mouth. To pronounce what (*che cosa*), which (*quale*), who (*qui*), where (*dove*), one must make as if to sip, holding the tongue steady in the middle of the mouth without touching anything, starting to speak slowly. But in words beginning with "h" such as hay (*fieno*), hat (*capello*), how (*come*), hen (*una gallina*), and other such innumerable, one must use a certain tremendous might in pronunciation, particularly when the "h" is pronounced fully and heavily.[10]

Florio begins his presentation here with a disparaging account of English, calling it "the most confused of all languages … derived as it is from many others, and every day borrowing anew from them."[11] But *Firste Fruites* was written early in Florio's career in England, and he was to discover in the years following that far from being a shortcoming, the mongrel character of English is one of the keys to its genius. While there is no evident rhyme or reason to the organization of the heterogeneous material in *Firste Fruites*, the more fully articulated *Second Fruits* shares with the earlier book an extensive lexical range and employs the full gamut of Italian grammatical structures (*Firste Fruites* also provides an Italian grammar). Both dialogue books would have posed a formidable challenge to their users and must have been intended for a readership already well along in acquiring the language.

The most characteristic feature of *Second Fruits* is its extensive employment of proverbs (Florio also published in 1591 a repertory of some 6000 proverbs entitled *Il giardino di ricreatione*, the first such collection in the Italian language),[12] distillations of popular orally transmitted culture whose effects depend on subtleties easily lost on non-native speakers and that occasionally lose their punch in translation. The curt symmetries of "*Da chi mi fido guardami Dio/che da chi non mi fido guarderò io*" are, for instance, flattened out in "From those which I doo trust good Lord deliver me/From such as I mistrust, ile harmeles care to be";[13] and "*Sapete bene, che chi si contenta gode*" trips up as "You know well that content is pleased."[14] There is, nevertheless, a conversational flow in the dialogues of *Second Fruits* missing in the earlier volume that convey a palpable sense of the 'staged' nature of speaking a foreign language in Elizabethan England (the facing-page Italian/English format of both *Fruit(e)s* might also be seen as contributing to this dynamic in laying bare the 'stage props' of the language lesson).

The topics in *Second Fruits* are addressed in a more sustained form within each chapter than they were in *Firste Fruites*, and more than one commentator has noted that these dialogues provide a kind of period-specific snapshot of upwardly mobile English social life inflected by the elite Italian culture of courtesy.[15] But Florio's interlocutors are often as unmeasured as the world that they represent, and in this they share something with the unruly fictions of Thomas Nashe that appeared in just these years.[16] In a virtuosic though somewhat over-determined cascade of proverbs that runs on for fifteen pages in Bk. 6, Stefano proffers solicited advice to Pietro, who is about to embark on an extensive trip abroad:

> E se vuoi esser viandate & andar salvo per il mondo, habbi sempre & in ogni luoco, Occhio di falcone, per veder lontano; Orecchie d'asino, per udir bene; Viso di cimia, per esser pronto al riso; Bocca di porcello, per mangiar tutto; Spalle del camelo, per portar ogni cosa con patientia; e Gambe di cervo, per poter fuggire i pericoli. E non voler mai haver diffetto di duo sacchi ben pieno, cio è uno di patientia, perché con essa si vince il tutto; & l'altro di denari, perché
> Quegli che hanno ducati,
> Signori sono chimati
>
> (And if you will be a traveller, and wander safely through the world, wheresoever you come, have alwayes the eies of a Faulcon, that ye may see farre, the ears of an Asse, that ye may heare wel, the face of an Ape that ye may be ready to laugh, the mouth of a Hog, to eate all things, the shoulder of a Camell, that you may beare any thing with pateience, the legges of a Stagg, to flie from dangers. And see that you never want two bagges very full, that is one of patience, for with it a man overcomes all things, and another of money, for
> They that have good store of crownes
> Are called Lords though they be clownes)[17]

Evident in the English column is the tendency, much lamented by Florio's contemporary detractors, to fill out in English what might otherwise be expressed with greater economy, a likely consequence of the non-native speaker's zeal. But there is also something here of the knowing cross-cultural swagger of Nashe's Jack Wilton in *The*

Unfortunate Traveler (1594), a text that reflects its author's aim "to make an inflated discourse out of [what appear to be] the thinnest materials"[18] and that refracts in multiple ways the London marketplace of the foreign in which Florio operated and to which his *Fruits* were addressed.

The presence of one recent Italian visitor to England is clearly registered in the topics of several of the dialogues of *Second Fruits*, and generally in its proverbial strategies and linguistic choices. 'Il Nolano' – the nickname of Giordano Bruno, born in Nola, ouside of Naples – is the first interlocutor of the first dialogue, in which he comes to stir a lazy, supercilious acquaintance, Torquato, who not coincidentally shares the name with one of the two pedants who arrogantly but unsuccessfully challenge the new cosmological ideas in Bruno's *La cena de le ceneri*, published in London in 1584 (a first redaction of which had Florio and his friend Matthew Gwinne accompanying Bruno through a dark and menacing city en route to the dinner party at which the debate took place). Here, Torquato has a very hard time getting himself out of bed and after a series of testy, foppish exchanges between him and his stubborn servant Ruspa an exasperated Nolano, speaking entirely in proverbs, aims to shame his friend straight:

> N *Voi mi fate sentire una delle doglie da morire col tanto aspettarvi.*
> T *Quali son le doglie da morire.*
> N *Aspettar e non venire. Star' in letto e non dormire. Ben servir' e non gridare. Haver cavallo che non vuol' ire. E servitor che non vuol' ubidire. Esser' in prigione e non poter fuggire. Et ammalato e non poter guarire. Smarrar la strada, quando un vuol' gire. Star alla porta quand' un non vuol aprire. Et haver un amico che ti vuol tradire. Sono dieci doglie da morire.*
> T *Queste sono doglie ch'io ho patito & patisco sovvente volte.*
> N *La prima di esse io patisco adesso.*
>
> (*N* You make me feele one of the deadly griefs, staying so long for you.
> *T* Which be those deadly griefes.
> *N* To long for that which coms not. To lye a bed and sleepe not. To serve well and please not. To have a horse that goes not. To keepe a man obeyes not. To lye in jayle and hope not. To bee sick and recover not. To loose ones waye and knowe not. To waite at doore and enter not, and to have a friend we trust not. Are ten such spites as hell hath not.
> *T* They be such spites as I have felt, and oftentimes doo feele.
> *N* The first of them I feele now.)[19]

Unlike the problematic figure he had cut with many of those he encountered in his several years in England, 'il Nolano' was for Florio a sober model of personal and intellectual integrity, and the starring role he plays here at the outset of *Second Fruits* is the first signal of the huge impact Bruno had had on the development of Florio's cultural sensibility. He is recalled as Giordano in Bk. 7, where in an exchange with his English interlocutor, Edward, the Italian sword-master Vincenzo Saviolo – widely considered to be the finest such instructor in Elizabethan England – is described in these terms:

> Esso colpirà ogniuno o di punta, o di stoccata, o di stramazzone, o d'imbroccata, o di mandritto, o di riverso, o di taglio, o di costa, o di piatto, o come gli piace.

(Hee will hit any man, bee it with a thrust or a stoccada, with an imbroccada or a charging blow, with a right or reverse blowe, be it with the edge, with the back, or with the flat, even as it liketh him.)[20]

Throughout this scene, Giordano's praise of Saviolo as an examplary Italian in England can also be read as an auto-referential evocation of the daring linguistic and conceptual innovations that Bruno introduced through his one comedy *Il candelaio* (The Candle-bearer) published in Paris in 1582, and in the six Italian dialogues he published in London in 1584–1585, all texts woven deeply into the texture of *Second Fruits.*[21] Bruno's daring 'reformation' of language provided Florio with an entirely new way of thinking about the questions that would shape his subsequent work as a lexicographer and translator.[22]

Second Fruits is almost entirely free of the sometimes heavy-handed moralizing of the earlier volume, another consequence of the opening up of horizons that Florio's encounter with the unorthodox and idiosyncratic 'Nolano' had made possible, and a sign of the growing confidence Florio was developing in these years with respect to his promotion of a novel cultural program in which the vernacular aimed to achieve at least an equal footing with the authority of classical culture (an issue, as we shall see, of central importance for Florio's translation of Montaigne), a rewriting of the rules of humanist engagement in conspicuous contrast to established models of school and university education in England and on the Continent.

Lexicography

Florio's vernacular advocacy extended next in presenting through the two editions of his Italian-English dictionary an authoritative alternative to the conservative linguistic politics of sixteenth-century Italy. There had been one earlier Italian-English lexical aid, the *Dictionarie for the Better Understanding of Boccace, Petrarcha, and Dante* appended to William Thomas's *Principal Rules of the Italian Grammer* (1550), but as its title makes clear the scope of this dictionary was limited to the vocabulary found in the vernacular works of the *tre corone* or 'three crowns' of the Italian literary canon. Florio's *A Worlde of Wordes*, first published in 1598 and then in a greatly expanded second edition in 1611 as *Queen Anna's New World of Words*, cast a decisively wider net.[23]

Thomas – having fled to Italy following a legal brush-up with an aristocratic patron, he would later become a member of King Edward VI's inner circle – originally wrote his book in 1548 for an English gentleman in Italy in need of quickly learning Italian, and two years later it was published for "all suche of our nation."[24] But in basing his own work upon earlier efforts of Alberto Accarisio da Cento and Francesco Alunno, who had compiled concise dictionaries to help with reading the *tre corone* in line with Pietro Bembo's judgment that Petrarch, Boccaccio, and (to a lesser extent) Dante should be considered the chief arbiters of Italian linguistic style, Thomas does not stray in his dictionary from this restricted and already archaic standard (these model writers having been active two centuries earlier). But in his introductory epistle he argues for a more expansive sense of the Italian vernacular, that with regard to the depth and breadth of ancient Greek and Latin:

[r]emaigning yet (as they dooe) in great estimacion, so seemeth this [Italian] nowe to growe as a third towardes them. For besides the auctours of this tyme (whereof

> there bee manie woorthie) you shall almoste finde no parte of the sciences, no part of any woorthie historie, no parte of eloquence, nor any parte of fine poesie, that ye have not in the Italian tongue.[25]

Other Italians were to develop lexicons later in the period that challenged Bembist orthodoxy – Alessandro Citolini's *Tipocosmia* (1561), and Tommaso Garzoni's *La piazza universale di tutte le professioni del mondo* (1585) the most important of these – and Florio drew extensively on them and on a number of other sixteenth-century dictionaries of French, Spanish, and Latin as he compiled what would become the most wide-ranging index of the Italian language published anywhere until well into the eighteenth century.

A World of Words encompasses some 46,000 entries drawn from a heterogeneous library of 72 books; while *Quenn Anna's New World of Words*, published thirteen years later, grew to roughly 74,000 lemmas gathered from 252 books.[26] The scope of Florio's dictionary was to move well beyond the canonical language of the *tre corone*, though by no means ignoring it, in order to encompass the fullest possible range of the Italian language gleaned from the books Florio would have had at his disposition in England and in his interactions there with Italians visiting the country in living commerce with the language in a way that he could not have been. The scope of the first edition of the *Vocabolario* of the Florentine Accademia della Crusca, published in 1612 and containing about 28,000 entries, by contrast sought to provide an idealized survey of the Italian language completely in keeping with the language of the *tre corone* and subsequent writers who had carefully, even slavishly, imitated them.

It would be difficult to overestimate the importance of the library in Florio's dictionaries, given the impression that it offers of both the variety and depth that the Italian language had achieved by the end of the sixteenth century, demonstrating a wide range of linguistic registers from the popular to the erudite. Florio's library also demonstrates the sort of literary and historiographical canon that would only be more fully identified as such by the nineteenth-century theoreticians of the Renaissance Michelet, Burckhardt, and Symonds.[27] In addition to four commented editions of Dante's *Commedia*, there is the complete Italian poetry of Petrarch, and Boccaccio's vernacular works ranging from the *Elegia di Madonna Fiammetta, Il filocolo*, the *Decameron*, and *Il corbaccio;* pastoral poetry is represented by the *Arcadia* of Sannazaro, and Bembo's *Asolani;* courtesy literature by *Il cortegiano* of Baldassare Castliglione, *Galateo* by Giovanni della Casa, and Stefano Guazzo's *La civile conversazione;* the chivalric tradition is there in Luigi Pulci's *Morgante, Orlando innamorato* of Boiardo, Ariosto's *Orlando furioso*, and *Gerusalemme liberata* by Tasso; shorter-form prose narrative is represented by Carlo Gualteruzzi's edition of the *Novellino* [here *Cento novelle antiche*], three volumes of the *Novelle* of Bandello, and Giraldi Cinzio's *Hecatommiti*. Theatrical texts are the most typical literary element in the library, some thirty-seven plays largely by authors unknown today: Parabosco, Razzi, Sorboli, Pini, Grazzini, Groto, Secchi, Bracciolini, Bargagli, Salviani, Domenichi, Oddi, Gelli, in addition to the more widely recognized dramatists Machiavelli, Ariosto, Aretino, the Accademia degli Intronati, Tasso, and Giovanni Battista Guarini; and there are other books dealing with spectacle: the *Bravure del Capitano Spavento*, dialogues about the *commedia dell'arte;* the *Feste di Milano del 1605* celebrating the birth of the Spanish Prince Philip Dominic Victor, the future Philip IV; and the *Descrittione delle feste fatte a Firenze del 1608*, recounting the festivities for the wedding of Cosimo [later II] de' Medici and Mary Magdalen of Austria. Cooking and entertainings are represented in *Dell'arte della cucina* and *Libro nuovo d'ordinar banchetti, et conciar vivande* by Cristoforo Messisbugo. Books dedicated to history (of Italy, Florence, Venice, Naples, Scandinavia, Hungary, Persia, China, and the wider then known world), politics (the complete works of Machiavelli, Guicciardini, Botero's *Ragion di*

Stato and its *Aggiunte*), and geography (the *Relazioni universali* of Botero), account for some twenty-six titles. But given the considerable British interest in Italian architecture at this time it is surprising that none of the principal treatises – of Vitruvio or Alberti in Italian translation, Serlio, or Palladio – should be listed; there is only the *Nuovo Theatro* of Zonca that, like several other texts in Florio's library, deal primarily with mechanics and engineering, and there are nine volumes dedicated to arms, artillery, and military matters. Science and medicine are represented by ten entries, including translations of Pliny and Conrad Gessner as well as Tommaso Garzoni's *La sinagoga degl'ignoranti*. Much of Florio's professional time in the circle of Queen Anne was spent writing correspondence on her behalf, and we find fifteen titles of letter collections, encompassing many more volumes, in the dictionary's library in addition to treatises on the role of the secretary by Bartolomeo Zucchi and Guarini. A handful of authors recur in the library with the frequency to suggest something of Florio's *forma mentis*: Boccaccio, Aretino, Doni, and Bruno; but at the same time we find entirely heterogeneous religious texts of the radical reformers, Aretino's controversial religious biographies, and both polemical and devotional post-Tridentine Catholic writings that appear to register the shifting nature of Florio's own religious coordinates.

The language culled from these books in the lemmas of Florio's dictionary provides a broad index of Italian as it was represented in printed writing through the early seventeenth century, and in addition to the standard Tuscan form of the language codified from fourteenth-century literary models there are a number of regional variants represented, Neapolitan first among them, this again a direct consequence of Florio's friendship with Bruno.[28] But as was the case with a number of other books that Florio had clearly drawn on but are not cited in his dictionary's library, Bruno's *Candelaio* furnished him with a rich vein of non-standard usage, of which here a few examples:[29]

> [c]he par che, co' crocchi, rampini ed arpagoni, sii stato per forza tirato dal profondo abisso
>
> (it seems that with hooks, clasps, and harping irons, you have been raised up from the deepest abyss)[30]

as Arpàgo, *a harping iron, a great hooke, dragging hooke, flesh hooke, weeding hooke, or pot-hooke. Also a grubber.*[31]

Di fave cocchiaron, gran maccarone/Ch'a l'oglio fusti posto a infusion.

> (Great eater of favas, huge dimwit/you have been left to marinate in oil)[32]

Cocchiarone *a great eater of spoone meates.*

Maccaróne *a gull, a lubby, a loggerhead that can doe nothing but eat Maccaróni.*[33]

Ad altare scarrupato non s'accende candela; a scrigno sgangherato non si scrolla sacco

> (On a ruined altar no candle is lit; to an open treasure chest no sack is shaken)[34]

Scarupare *to ruine or breake downe any wall or building pieces.*[35]

Entirely unlike the academicians of the Crusca – Italy's contemporary arbiters of linguistic propriety – Florio's lexicographic imagination embodied all of the forms of Italian that he would have known through both his lived and studied experience of the language, thus articulating a fundamental principle of much more recent linguistic theory: that 'low' elements are as constituent of the polyvalent vitality of language as are its more 'sophisticated' features, that they confound conventional hierarchies of linguistic practice and value.

Translation

It is a striking paradox of Florio's career that he was to find his most distinctive voice in translating the words of others. Following earlier occasional efforts – translations into English of Jacques Cartier, *A Short and Briefe Narration of the Two Navigations and Discoveries to the Northweast Partes Called Newe France* (1580) as well as two anonymous 'news' pamphlets, a *Letter Lately Written from Rome* (1585) and the *Perpetuall and Naturall Prognostications of the Change of Weather* (1591) – Florio's most significant translation was the first complete English version of the *Essais* of Michel de Montaigne, *The Essayes, or Morall, Politike and Millitarie Discourses* (1603).[36] Appearing in print just as Queen Elizabeth was dying, this text marked a liminal moment between her reign, characterized by an intense but concurrent insularity in England's relations with European cultures, and the very different engagement with the continent which would develop under the Stuarts. The timing of the publication of Florio's translation might appear to be remarkably serendipitous, but there seems to have been a plan behind the appearances: the accession of James VI to the English throne had been more or less assured by default since the death of his mother, Mary Queen of Scots, in 1587 and by Elizabeth's failure to marry and produce an heir, and the patrons honored in the 1603 edition of the *Essayes* were among those who helped to prepare the way for the Stuarts in England.

Edward Wotton, whom Florio names as the instigator of his translation in his prefatory address "To the Curteous Reader," had been made Elizabeth's ambassador to the Scottish court in 1585 and would thus have been in a position to understand the potentially strategic utility of a weighty translation into English of an already famous contemporary text written in the only continental vernacular language James was completely at home in. Among a range of salient issues, Wotton would have grasped the lessons to be gleaned from Montaigne's dismay in the *Essais* regarding the French wars of religion, a situation that had never reached in England the sustained catastrophic form that it had in France, a disaster which the theologically informed Scots king had followed closely and which James was intent on not seeing develop in the volatile English realm he would imminently be ruling.

The *Essayes* is prefaced in its first edition with the most elaborate encomiastic apparatus of any of Florio's work, and its three pairs of aristocratic lady-dedicatees – a pair for each of the three books of the collection – read as an index to the success Florio enjoyed with a particular segment of the Elizabethan elite and his consequently rising prospects with the dawning Stuart era. Book I of the *Essayes* is dedicated to Lady Ann Harington and her daughter, Lucy Harington Russell, Countess of Bedford (whom as we have seen Florio had already singled out for praise in his preface to *A Worlde of Wordes*). Lucy was married to Edward Russell, who had been involved in the Essex rebellion against Elizabeth in 1601, and through her father's mother, Lucy Sidney Harington, she was a second-cousin of Philip Sidney. The Harington ladies were among an unofficial embassy to Queen Anne in Edinburgh immediately following the death of Elizabeth, and Lady Ann and her husband John (cousin of the translator of Ariosto) entertained the queen on her progress to England, subsequently assuming responsibility for the upbringing and later arrangements for the marriage of Princess Elizabeth. Though Wotton had provided the initial spur for the *Essayes*, Florio names Lucy as both its guiding inspiration and his tough-minded taskmistress throughout what he describes as an arduous, even epic, ordeal. A great deal of the work for this translation was done at the Harington estate, Combe Abbey, near Coventry, and Florio describes Lucy's role during its genesis in these terms:

> I say not you tooke pleasure at shore … to see me sea-tosst, wether-beaten, shippe-wrackt, almost drowned. Nor say I, like this mans [Montaigne's] Indian King, you checkt with a sower-sterne countenance the yerneful complaint of your drooping, neere-dying subject … you enduced, yea commaunded, yea delighted to see me strive for life, yea fall out of breath. Unmercifull you were, but not so cruell … like the Spartan imperious Mother, a shield you gave me, but with this word: *Aut cum hoc, aut in hoc.*[37]

The final allusion here refers to the admonition of Spartan mothers to their battle-bound sons to either "come home with your shield, or on it."[38] Situating his work of translation under the aegis of such a determined feminine control, the *Essayes* in English are clearly addressed to a learned feminine readership, but the rhetoric of conquest and colonization evident at the end of this passage underscores an unresolved tension at the heart of Florio's language practice, an ambivalence which mirrors on the one hand the public rehearsal of gendered roles on the contemporary Elizabethan stage, in print, and in the persona of the English queen still on the throne during the gestation of this translation.

Even if Elizabeth is nowhere named in the *Essayes*, her dominating presence over the world in which Florio moved is registered in a number of other respects, not least of which negatively, and the ghosts of both Philip Sidney and Robert Devereux, the Earl of Essex, preside as tutelary spirits over the dedications of the 1603 edition, presaging Florio's good fortune under the Stuarts in having been associated with the dissident wing of the late Elizabethan aristocracy. Book II of the *Essayes* is dedicated to Elizabeth Sidney Manners, the Countess of Rutland, and to Lady Penelope Rich. Elizabeth was Philip Sidney's only child, and she was married to another of the Essex conspirators, Roger Manners; while Penelope was Essex's sister, pleaded to save her brother's life before a resolute Elizabeth, and had been Sidney's lover, as Florio slyly emphasizes by appropriating a passage from Giordano Bruno's *Eroici furori* (a text dedicated to Sidney), "Et siete in terra quel' ch' in ciel le stelle" [You are on earth that which the stars are in heaven].[39] Though the citation is directed to the attention of both dedicatees and more generally aimed at those whom Bruno had characterized (in Florio's words) as "you ladies of England … not women … but in … likenesse Nymphs, Goddesses, and of Celestiall substance," the association of Penelope Rich with the female protagonist of Sidney's sonnet sequence *Astrophil and Stella* was an open secret among the Elizabethan elite. It is surely a sign of Florio's intimacy with his dedicatees that he felt free to play with such language, and particularly in Lady Penelope's case given her contemporary libertarian fame. But that he should immediately follow this allusion with another passage from Bruno's treatise, "Qual è tra voi quel che tra gl' astri il sole?" [Who among you is as the sun among the stars?] which in its original context refers to Elizabeth as the Diana expected to usher in a radically new era in human engagement with the cosmos, hints in Florio's dedication at a calculated strategy in so closely re-aligning women disgraced through the Essex conspiracy with the monarch it meant to displace. When the *Furori* was conceived in England in the mid-1580s Elizabeth was still vigorous and at the height of her power, but with the queen close to death as the *Essayes* went to press in 1603, the citation of Bruno's text evokes a very new era indeed in the expectation that these 'stelle' might ensure that their Italian tutor not be neglected in the shower of preferments which would soon accompany the arrival of the Stuarts in England.

Each of the three dedications to the *Essayes* functions as a sort of abbreviated 'essay' in itself, but unlike Montaigne's practice of *bricolage* Florio develops two themes consistently in these prefaces: praising his dedicatees, he applauds himself as the teacher of such accomplished students; and in praising Montaigne's singularity, he implies that here, finally, is a subject worthy of both himself and his pupils. Bk. III of the *Essayes* is dedicated to Lady Elizabeth Grey, soon to be one of Queen Anne's favored attendants, and Lady Mary Nevill, the daughter of Thomas Sackville, Lord Treasurer from 1599–1608 and, earlier, collaborator on both the tragedy *Gorboduc*, and the collection of Tudor poetry, the *Mirror of Magistrates*; and Florio acknowledges Sackville's hospitality during the period of his work on the Montaigne translation, "no small parte," he writes, having been done "under his roofe." This third preface develops an argument in favor of modern language learning, registering again the extraordinary talents of his patronesses in this direction with regard to French, such:

> [d]oth it grace your tongues, so does your tongue grace it. As if written by men it may have a good garbe, spoken by you it hath a double grace: for so have I heard some of you speake it, as no man, few women, would come-neare their sweete-relisht ayre of it ... that as Tullie averred of his Roman Ladies for Latine.[40]

Though Florio makes a strong case in this dedication for the multi-faceted utility of knowing modern languages, he does so by way of introducing a translation; and while he acknowledges here that his livelihood depends on a public eager to acquire such knowledge, he nowhere seems to understand that the act of translation into English that his version of Montaigne represents would potentially render his services as a language teacher obsolete. Nevertheless, Florio's ladies are the harbingers of a new phase of erudition through which the authoritative voice of classical culture, as refracted through the lens of Latin and Greek oriented Renaissance humanism, gives way to the valorization of contemporary languages and their emerging cultures, a genealogy of learning that in his preface to the reader Florio acknowledges having acquired from Bruno:

> [m]y old Fellow Nolano tolde me, and taught publikely, that from translation all Science hadst's of-spring. Likely, since even Philosophie, Grammar, Rhetoricke, Logicke, Arithmetike, Geometrie, Astronomy, Musicke, and all the Mathematikes yea hold their name of the Greek's and the Greekes drew their baptizing water from the conduit-pipes of the Egiptians, and they from the well-springs of the Hebrews or Chaldees.[41]

Arguing here for the interconnectedness of all learning through its successive translation from one culture to another, Florio yet again confirms the critical role that Bruno had played in his own intellectual formation. Yates faulted Florio for making "such a bad translation that it is nearly an original work,"[42] but she failed to grasp that the practice of translation in the early modern period often aspired to just this end. 'Literal' or 'authentic' were categories that may have had some currency among theorists of translation in the period, but translators came to their work with a considerably more pragmatic approach to the task at hand. Florio's work subsequent to the *Essayes* – a translation into Italian of James VI's treatise on kingship, *Basilikon Doron* (exact date unknown) as well as translations into English of Boccaccio's *Decameron* (1620) and selections of Traiano Boccalini's *Ragguagli di Parnasso* (1626) – reveals a malleable *modus operandi* adapted to the exigencies of specific texts translated for particular situations.[43]

Afterlife

The translation of Montaigne was published posthumously in a third corrected edition in 1632 in which the translator's name does not appear on the title page, and Florio was after that largely forgotten until Victorian scholars recognized in his work and that of other 'monumental' translators of the late sixteenth and seventeenth centuries paradigms for the 'national' English culture that had extended itself throughout the world by the late nineteenth century. Frances Yates published the first complete appraisal of Florio's career based upon documentary evidence in 1934, and others working in the middle decades of the twentieth century – most notably Arundel del Re – helped to fill in details she had missed. Further studies from the 1990s onward – by Warren Boutcher, Michael Wyatt, Jason Lawrence, William Hamlin, Guyda Armstrong, and Carla Rossi – have built upon this pioneering work by situating Florio within a wider matrix of recent developments in cultural and intellectual history.[44] Still others have attempted to read into Florio's life and career more than can be reasonably ascertained about them.

The most ambitious of these latter efforts is a 2011 novel by the Swiss author and journalist, Anne Cuneo, *Un monde de mots*, grounded in serious archival research and often quite insightful: having visited Fulham (where Florio lived after the death of Queen Anne) and attentively re-read the same documents Yates had consulted regarding Florio's final years, for example, Cuneo convincingly challenges the scenario Yates had developed of a pathetic Florio dying forgotten and in penury; but the novel frequently stretches verifiable facts to fill in the considerable gaps in Florio's biography, and extensive wholly invented dialogue further weakens its integrity.[45]

In a 2013 *Guardian* article, Saul Frampton argued that Florio was the crucial textual editor for the publishers of the 1623 Shakespeare *First Folio*.[46] Apart from the inadequacy of Frampton's parameters – a shaky grasp of both bibliographical studies and the history of publishing, and a reliance on digital analysis of word recurrences (a practice still in its infancy and prone to questionable conclusions) – a further argument against such an intriguing hypothesis is that Florio had his own considerable work to do in this period: on the third editions of both his dictionary (later published by Giovanni Torriano in 1659) and translation of Montaigne as well as his new translation of Boccalini; Florio would have had little time or energy at this stage in his life for a huge project such as editing Shakespeare's collected plays for the first time.

And finally, Lamberto Tassinari, an Italo-Canadian professor of Italian language and literature, has together with a group of English, Italian, and Swiss enthusiasts been tirelessly promoting the idea – entirely untethered from any sense of how to read either literary texts or historical documents, and completely ignorant of historical editorial practices – that John Florio was actually William Shakespeare.[47] This is an effort that has unfortunately attracted some media attention, particularly in Italy, in the process diminishing Florio's real and substantive achievements by pegging them to an exaggerated and anachronistic sense of Shakespeare's position in his own contemporary world and in subsequent global culture.[48]

Notes

1 Florio, *Firste Fruites* (London: Thomas Woodcocke, 1598), p. *iv.

2 The first thorough treatment of John Florio's life and career was Frances Yates, *John Florio: The Life of an Italian in Shakespeare's England* (Cambridge: Cambridge University Press, 1934; reprinted High Wycombe, UK: Octagon Books, 1968), though Arundel del Re's edition of *First Fruit* (Taipei: Taihoku Imperial University, 1936) provides significant further

information and analysis, a good deal of it corrective to Yates. Carla Rossi will soon be publishing two volumes dedicated to the full range of Florio's life and work based on extensive research in European libraries and archives.

3 All in the British Library, respectively: Add MS 15,214; Harley MS 847, fols. 67–95 (where the Italian is in Florio's hand, but the English is written in another; cf. Del Re, *op. cit.*, vol. 2, xxi, n. 70); and Royal MS 14 A V.

4 See https://celm2.dighum.kcl.ac.uk/authors/floriojohn.html#british-library-royal_id683357 for the extant letters and other Florio manuscripts in British archives and libraries.

5 About which, see, Diego Pirillo, "Voyagers and Translators in Elizabethan England: Richard Hakluyt, John Florio and Renaissance Travel," in *Travels and Translations: Anglo-Italian Cultural Transactions*, eds. A. Yarrington et al. (Amsterdam: Rodopi, 2013), pp. 27–47.

6 Del Re is the only earlier scholar of Florio to have understood the significance of his ambiguous religious identity for the not always smooth sailing he encountered in both his life and work; see vol. 2, xxxiv, n. 111.

7 There was a French/Italian version of *Second Fruits* published by Gomes de Trier in Amsterdam in 1623 that nowhere acknowledges Florio's authorhip of the text; cf. Yates, p. 346.

8 On Florio's language teaching, see Michael Wyatt, *The Italian Encounter with Tudor England: A Cultural Politics of Translation* (Cambridge: Cambridge University Press, 2005), pp. 157–202; and Jason Lawrence, *Who the Devil Taught Thee so Much Italian? Italian Language Learning and Literary Imitation in Early Modern England* (Manchester, UK: Manchester University Press, 2005).

9 Florio, *Firste Fruites*, 50^{r}.

10 *ibid.*, p. 162^{r-v}, translation my own.

11 *ibid.*, p. 160^{r}.

12 See Vincenzo Spampanato, "Giovanni Florio, un amico del Bruno in Inghilterra," *La critica. Rivista di Letteratura, Storia, e Filosofia*, 21 (1923): 189–91, on the significance of the proverbs Florio collected in *Il giardino*.

13 Florio, *Second Fruits*, pp. 18–19.

14 *ibid*, pp. 29–30.

15 Del Re notes in *The Secret of the Renaissance and Other Essays and Studies* (Tokyo: Kaitakusha, 1930), p. 160, that both *First* and *Second Fruits* are important Elizabethan registers of London social customs.

16 On Florio's relations with Nashe, see Yates, cit., pp. 128–29 and 174–87; and Del Re, cit., vol. 2, xxxvii.

17 Florio, *Second Fruits*, pp. 92–93.

18 Jason Scott-Warren, "Thomas Nashe," in *The Oxford Handbook of English Prose, 1500–1640*, ed. Andrew Hadfield (Oxford: Oxford University Press), p. 214 [bracketed phrase my own].

19 Florio, *Second Fruits*, 12–13.

20 *ibid.*, 118–19.

21 See Spampanato *La critica* 21 (1923): 56–60, 113–25, 189–92, 313–17; and *La critica* 22 (1924): 56–61, 116–24, 246–53.

22 See Michele Ciliberto, *Lessico di Giordano Bruno*, Vol. 1 (Rome: Edizioni dell'Ateneo & Bizzarri, 1979), pp. xxvi–xxxi, for an excellent discussion of the revolutionary character of Bruno's understanding of language, and its fundamental role in the articulation of his philosophical program.

23 On Florio's dictionary, see Wyatt, *The Italian Encounter*, pp. 203–54.

24 Thomas, *Principal Rules of the Italian Grammer* (London: Thomas Berthelet, 1550), 1. unpaginated].

25 *ibid.*, pp. 2–3.

26 Spampanato (1924), p. 60, points out that while the total number of lemmas is somewhat deceptive as it does not take into account various forms of repetition (such as conjugated forms of verbs or alternate spellings) Florio's dictionary represents an unparalleled contribution to Italian lexicography in the period.

27 Here I cite titles from the expanded library in the unpaginated prefatory material in *Queen Anna's New World of Words* (London: Edward Blount and William Barret, 1611).

28 For a thorough account of Bruno's language in Florio's dictionary, see Spampanato, *op. cit.*, from which the following examples are drawn.
29 For several extended examples of the range of lemmas in Florio's dictionary, see Wyatt, *The Italian Encounter*, pp. 231–44.
30 Giordano Bruno, *Il candelaio*, "Antiprologo," in *Il teatro italiano II.3: La commedia del Cinquecento* (Turin: Einaudi, 1978), p. 150; translation assistance here and with following passages by Gerardo Pisacane.
31 Florio, *Queen Anna's New World of Words*, 39. 'Gruber' here is as in 'money grubber,' relevant to the context of the passage but unnoted by any of the comedy's commentators from Spampanato to Acquilecchia.
32 Bruno, *Candelaio*, III.6, 201.
33 Florio, *Queen Anna*, pp. 106, 292.
34 Bruno, *Candelaio*, IV.8, 228.
35 Florio, *Queen Anna*, p. 473.
36 See William Hamlin, *Montaigne's English Journey: Reading the Essays in Shakespeare's Day* (Oxford: Oxford University Press, 2014) on the diffusion and impact of Florio's translation in seventeenth-century England; Boutcher, Warren, *The School of Montaigne in Early Modern Europe* (Oxford: Oxford University Press, 2017) offers a comprehensive study of the reception of Montaigne's *Essais* throughout Europe in the seventeenth century with a significant chapter dedicated to Florio (vol. 2, pp. 189–271).
37 Florio, "The Epistle Dedicatorie," *Essayes*, $A2^{v}$-3^{r}.
38 See Timothy Murray, "Translating Montaigne's Crypts: Melancholic Relations and the Sites of Altarbiography," *Bucknell Review*, 35, 2 (1992): 143–45.
39 Bruno, "De gli eroci furori," in *Dialoghi filosofici italiani*, ed. Michele Ciliberto, p. 777.
40 Florio, "The Epistle Dedicatorie" to Bk. III, *Essayes*, $Rr1^{r}$.
41 Florio, "To the Curteous Reader," *Essayes*, $A5^{r}$.
42 Yates, *John Florio*, p. 228; Mack, Peter, "Montaigne and Florio," in *The Oxford Handbook of English Prose, 1500–1640*, provides a much needed corrective to Yates narrow view of Florio's translation.
43 On each of these translations, see Wyatt, "John Florio's Translation of Kingship: An Italian Baptism for James VI/I's *Basilikon Doron*," in *Exiles, Emigrés, and Intermediaries: Anglo-Italian Cultural Transactions*, ed. Barbara Schaff (Amsterdam: Rodopi, 2010), pp. 71–84; "Translating for Queen Anne: John Florio's Decameron," in *The Forms of Renaissance Thought, New Essays in Literature and Culture*, eds. Leonard Barkin, Bradin Cormack, and Sean Keilen (New York: Palgrave Macmillan) pp. 75–85; and "Fictions of Fact: Antonio Pérez in Traiano Boccalini's *Ragguagli di Parnasso* and William Vaughan's *New-found Politicke*," *Journeys through Changing Landscapes* (Pisa: Pisa University Press, forthcoming). In addition, Guyda Armstrong is currently preparing a critical edition of the Florio *Decameron* to be published in the MHRA Tudor and Stuart Translations series.
44 See notes above for Boutcher, Wyatt, Lawrence, Hamlin, Armstrong, and Rossi.
45 Anne Cuneo, *Un monde de mots* (Orbe, Switzerland: Bernard Campiche, 2011).
46 See Saul Frampton, "Who Edited Shakespeare?" www.theguardian.com/books/2013/jul/12/who-edited-shakespeare-john-florio.
47 See www.johnflorio-is-shakespeare.com/.
48 See Catherine Belsey, "Iago the Essayist: Between Montaigne and Shakespeare," in *Renaissance Go-Betweens: Cultural Exchange in Early Modern Europe* (Berlin: Walter de Gruyter, 2005), pp. 262–78, for a richly nuanced reading of Shakespeare's deep textual reliance on Florio's Montaigne in *Othello* that demonstrates the efficacy of serious scholarship with respect to facile biographical musings.

22 Heretics, translators, intelligencers

Italian reformers in Tudor England

Diego Pirillo

Was there an Italian reformation?

Why didn't Renaissance Italy accomplish a religious reformation like that which occurred in sixteenth-century Germany?[1] Raised by Jacob Burckhardt in *The Civilization of the Renaissance in Italy*, this question nourished intense debates in Italy between the Risorgimento and Fascism, becoming a recurrent point of contention in the controversies between Church and State that followed unification. Generations of scholars and intellectuals saw the consequences of the failed Italian Reformation extending into the nineteenth century to inform the precarious national consciousness. According to the Italian historian Giorgio Spini, however, modern scholarship on the Italian Reformation was born only in the 1930s, when opposition to the Lateran Pacts between Mussolini and the Vatican instigated the rediscovery of the history of religious dissent in Italy.[2] It was in this context that in 1933 Benedetto Croce published his famous study of Galeazzo Caracciolo, the sixteenth-century Neapolitan marquis who moved to Geneva to openly profess his Calvinism.[3] In the wake of Max Weber, Croce situated the Calvinist ethic at the origins of modern liberalism and rebutted the Fascist appropriation of the Counter-Reformation. Moreover, by focusing on the lives of Italians who in the sixteenth century emigrated to Protestant Europe, Croce intertwined history and autobiography, projecting onto the past his own dilemma over remaining in Fascist Italy or going into exile.[4] The opposition to dictatorship also explains why Croce's scholarly interest in the Italian Reformation was so strong and persistent, as indicated by his edition of Juan de Valdés's *Alfabeto cristiano* and by his attention for the *Beneficio di Cristo*.[5]

While Protestant historiography had long been interested in the history of the Italian reformers and of the martyrs of the Roman Inquisition, it is true that the 1930s marked an historiographical revolution and enabled a new generation of scholars to "overcome the antiquated formulas derived from confessional apologetics," and to consider "the religious life of the sixteenth century for its own specific historical characteristics, and not for martyrs of free thought or for acts of heroism in resisting oppression."[6] A crucial role in this shift was played by Delio Cantimori's *Eretici italiani del Cinquecento*, published in 1939 after an intense discussion with Croce.[7] The *Eretici italiani* established a fundamental framework, a true "paradigm," that shaped all successive research on the Italian Protestant diaspora.[8] Abandoning the controversies that arose during the Risorgimento over the absence of a religious reform in Italy, "Cantimori's studies accomplished a sort of reversal of perspective, so that the question of the failed Protestant Reformation in Italy became to a certain extent that of the Italian Reformation in the Protestant world."[9] Indeed, at the center of the *Eretici italiani* there

DOI: 10.4324/9781315612720-25

was the attempt to reconstruct the legacy of the Italian Reformation in Northern Europe, from Poland to Switzerland and England, to shed light on the long history of religious toleration and on the hidden connections between the Italian heretics and the Enlightenment. For this reason, the main focus was not directed toward the Italian followers of the magisterial Reformation but rather toward the Anabaptists and Antitrinitarians, "rebels against every form of ecclesiastical organization," often at odds with the new no less than with the old orthodoxies.[10]

Recovering the lives and ideas of figures such as Bernardino Ochino, Giacomo Aconcio, and Francesco Pucci, Cantimori also touched upon the history of the Italian Protestant Church in London, later reconstructed in greater detail by Luigi Firpo.[11] Created in 1550 and guided at first by John Florio's father Michelangelo, a former Franciscan born into a Tuscan family of converted Jews, the Italian Church functioned as a cultural no less than a religious hub, contributing to the dissemination of Italian language and culture in England.[12] Indeed, in the *Schoolmaster*, thinking of those Italianate Englishmen who attended the service not for religious piety but rather to practice the language, Roger Ascham famously warned against those who "have in more reverence the *Triumphs* of Petrarch than the Genesis of Moses … a tale in Boccaccio than a story of the Bible."[13] Despite Ascham's harsh criticism, the Italian influence in early modern England was long and persistent and was to a large extent the result of the Italian religious emigration. As John Tedeschi has pointed out, the Italian reformers not only participated in the theological controversies of the Reformation but also played a crucial role in the European circulation of Renaissance secular culture, often publishing texts that were prohibited or censored in Italy, such as Niccolò Machiavelli's *Il Principe* and Paolo Sarpi's *Istoria del concilio*.[14] Working as publishers, editors and translators within the "communication circuit" that existed between authors and readers, they had a significant impact on the European geography of print by disseminating books and information across linguistic and confessional borders.[15]

The Italian reformation and its English afterlife

Following the death of Henry VIII, the Archbishop of Canterbury Thomas Cranmer invited several Continental reformers to come to England to participate in a Protestant council intended to oppose the one recently opened in Trent.[16] Even though the projected council never took place, in December 1547 Bernardino Ochino and Peter Martyr Vermigli did cross the channel, bringing into England the religious restlessness of sixteenth-century Italy. Suppressed at home, the Italian Reformation seemed to gain new life under the Tudors. While Vermigli was appointed Regius Professor of Divinity at Oxford and contributed to the revision of the Book of Common Prayer, Ochino was soon introduced at court, where the young princess Elizabeth translated into Latin his sermon *Che cosa è Christo*, presenting the author as someone "who, expelled from his homeland on account of religion and Christ, is driven to lead his life in foreign places and among unknown men."[17] The following year Edward Courtenay, nephew of Cardinal Reginald Pole, dedicated to Edward VI his English translation of the *Beneficio di Cristo*, the "manifesto" of the Italian Reformation, in the attempt to be released from the Tower of London.[18] To be sure, these were not episodic examples. Despite the fact that the reign of Edward VI was destined to end soon with the Catholic restoration of Mary, the attention that English Protestantism dedicated to the ideas of their fellow reformers in Italy was long, persistent and not limited to courtly circles. Indeed, while crossing the Atlantic, Puritans brought with them several texts by Italian reformers, starting with Vermigli, whose epistle *De fuga in persecutione* was used by English dissidents like Thomas Shepard to justify the decision to move to New England.[19] The American circulation of the life of the Italian Calvinist Galeazzo Caracciolo, often republished in Boston in the eighteenth century in William Crashaw's English translation, is perhaps the best evidence of the impact that the Italian Reformation had in the Atlantic world.[20]

Along with Vermigli, Caracciolo, and Ochino, English Protestants looked at the Italian Reformation through the story of Francesco Spiera.[21] A lawyer and a prominent figure in the evangelical community of Cittadella, near Vicenza, Spiera was denounced to the Inquisition in November 1548. Having recanted and renounced Protestantism publicly, he was convinced of having committed a sin against the Holy Ghost, fell into despair and died shortly after. Included in John Foxe's *Acts and Monuments*, appropriated by several Elizabethan playwrights and probably a source of Christopher Marlowe's *Doctor Faustus*, Spiera became the most famous figure of the Italian Reformation, nourishing for centuries controversies on nicodemism and predestination. Accounts of his death circulated widely and were reprinted in Britain well into the nineteenth century. Indeed, "a purely mechanical count of editions would assign Petrarch a place in English literature a rung or two below that held by Francesco Spiera."[22] For generations of English Protestants Spiera became the archetype of the apostate, serving as a "terrible warning against the temptation to abandon the rigors of religious dissent and sectarianism and conform to an oppressive orthodoxy."[23] Knowledge of the case arrived immediately in England. In 1550 Edward Aglionby translated the account given by the Italian reformer Matteo Gribaldi who had visited Spiera in Padua. The text was introduced with a preface by Calvin, who considered Spiera's despair the state of damnation that God inflicted on those who committed apostasy.[24] The relevance of the case soon became clear with Mary's succession in 1553. According to Foxe, when Lady Jane Gray found out that her father's chaplain Thomas Harding intended to return to Catholicism, she invited him to remember "the lamentable case of Spira, whose case (me thynke) should be yet so green in your remembrance, that being a thing of our time, you should fear the like inconvenience seeing you are fallen into the like offence."[25]

After the end of Mary's reign, the coronation of Elizabeth nourished new hopes among the Italian reformers on the Continent. While in 1561 Ochino addressed the English Queen in the *Laberinti del libero arbitrio*, remembering the discussions that they once had on predestination, in the following year Celio Secondo Curione dedicated to Elizabeth a collection of the writings of Olimpia Morata, a fellow reformer and one of the most sophisticated women writers of the Italian Renaissance.[26] On the frontispiece, the device of the Italian Protestant printer Pietro Perna – a woman with a lantern surrounded by a citation from the Psalms (119: 105) – contained another homage to Morata, who in her letters cited the same passage, as she suggested to her friend Cherubina Orsini to "let the word of the Lord be a lamp unto your feet" and to consider not "what the vast majority does, but what the saints have done and continue to do."[27] Addressing Elizabeth, Curione clarified the reasons for his dedication explaining that there was no better reader of Morata's works than a learned and pious queen[28]

> these memorials of Olympia Morata, a woman most famous for piety and letters … I publish under your most fortunate name, and entrust them to your faith and protection. For to whom could the writings of a woman so learned and pious be better entrusted than to Elizabeth the Queen, the most learned and religious of all?

Curione also commented prudently on the role of women in politics, an issue that was still controversial in England after the publication of John Knox's *The First Blast of the Trumpet Against the Monstrous Regiment of Women* in 1558. According to the Italian humanist, women like Elizabeth confirmed what Plato argued in the fifth book of the *Republic*:

> [t]hat there should be the same training for women and for men, both in arts and letters as well as in gymnastics and military science … And while he concedes that they are weaker in body than men, he makes them equals in soul. Since that is so, what can be more admirable than those heroic women?[29]

Despite the fact that Curione never set foot in England, his works enjoyed a significant circulation, starting with the *Pasquino in estasi*, published in an English translation in 1566 and again in 1584.[30]

In 1565, after Ochino's *Laberinti* and Morata's *Opera*, Perna's printing press published in Basel another work dedicated to the English Queen, the *Satanae stratagemata* by the Italian heretic Giacomo Aconcio, a keystone in the history of religious toleration that circulated widely in the seventeenth century not only in Latin but also in English translations.[31] Unlike Curione, who never set foot in England, Aconcio crossed the channel in 1559 when he was granted a royal pension thanks to his expertise in military engineering.[32] With the dedication of the *Satanae stratagemata*, however, Aconcio intended not only to express his gratitude to Elizabeth but also to place his radical views on religious toleration under the protection of a powerful patron. Indeed, in 1560 he had been at the centre of an harsh controversy that erupted in the Strangers' Church in London, in which he had supported the Dutch minister Adrian Haemstede against the French Calvinist Nicolas des Gallars and defended the Anabaptist members of the Church, who were ultimately forced to leave England. The echo of this dispute is clear in the *Satanae stratagemata*, in which he attacked the intolerance of both old and new orthodoxies and considered persecution nothing but a "stratagem" used by the devil to divide Christianity. To put an end to confessional strife, Aconcio suggested a reduction of religion to morality, narrowing its dogmatic apparatus while extending the number of adiaphora, the doctrines indifferent to and regarded as not essential for reaching salvation. Even a small theological dispute could produce wider unexpected controversies and for this reason Paul suggested avoiding them altogether[33]

> For concerning vain questions we have a command of *Paul*, not to refute whatever shal be falsly asserted, but to avoyd the questions themselves … But here you wil say is the great difficulty, the great labor to distinguish between questions unprofitable and questions that contain matter of damnable *Error*. For whatever a man shal pitch his mind upon, presently *Satan* endeavors to perswade him that it is a weighty point.

Under no circumstances, argued Aconcio, could religious disputes be solved by killing heretics. Echoing the Italian reformers' protests against Calvin after the execution of

Miguel Servet, Aconcio argued that persecution, instead of establishing the truth, would only lead magistrates to abuse their power and to execute anyone with different religious ideas:

> But who is there bearing the sword, that will not be accounted godly, and that will not account for an Heretique whosoever thwarts him in matters of Religion? So that this will unavoydably follow, that, look what authority you allow a pious Magistrate against true Heretiques, that will every Magistrate usurpe against every one that shal dissent from him.[34]

Translating the renaissance

As Elizabeth Eisenstein famously argued, wandering scholars in the age of confessions often gathered around print shops, which served as "miniature international houses." Acting as "a meeting place, message center, sanctuary and cultural center all in one," print shops favored the emergence of "an ethos which was specifically associated with the Commonwealth of Learning ... often combining outward conformity to diverse established churches with inner fidelity to heterodox creeds."[35] In Elizabethan London the Italian reformers found such a space in the print shop of John Wolfe, who thanks to his foreign collaborators became the most prolific printer of Italian texts in sixteenth-century England.[36] Along with Pietro Aretino and Torquato Tasso, Wolfe also published several texts by Italian reformers including Aconcio's *Essortatione al timor di Dio*.[37] The text was dedicated to Philip Sidney and edited by Giovanni Battista Castiglione, another Italian reformer who made his career as Elizabeth's Italian tutor.[38] Wolfe's most remarkable achievement, however, was his publication of almost all of Machiavelli's *opera*, including *Il Principe, I Discorsi*, the *Arte della guerra*, the *Istorie fiorentine*, and several literary works.[39] All these reprints were published surreptitiously and presented as the work of Italian presses in Palermo, Roma, and Piacenza. Wolfe intended to profit not only from the English but also from the Continental book market, presumably smuggling his editions into Italy as well, where Machiavelli had been placed on the Index of prohibited books. The anonymous preface to Wolfe's edition of *I Discorsi*, which appeared in London in 1584, invited the reader to disregard contemporary anti-Machiavellianism and to consult Machiavelli's works with a more discerning eye, as in this way the author himself had discovered "how great a difference there was between a just Prince and a Tyrant, between the government of many good men and a few wicked, between a well-regulated republic and a confused licentious multitude."[40] At the same time *I Discorsi* was presented as an authoritative work on *ars historica*, a guide to the reading of ancient history for useful political counsel for the present. In Machiavelli it was possible to find "new doctrine, new acuteness of intellect, and new ways to learn how to draw out useful lessons from the pleasant reading of history. And in short" – continues the anonymous preface – "I found that I learned more about the governments of the world in one day than I had in my life until that point through the reading of history."[41] While there is no definitive evidence to prove who the author of this preface was, it is worth noting that the following year the same words were used by Alberico Gentili, the prominent Italian lawyer, appointed Regius Professor of civil law at Oxford in 1587. In his *De legationibus*, appeared in 1585 and dedicated to Philip Sidney, Gentili argued that Machiavelli's real aim was not to serve princes but to unmask the "arcana imperii" and to reveal the very logic of politics itself. Thus Gentili invited his readers to unearth the republican message hidden in Machiavelli's lines, arguing that the Florentine thinker was not the counselor of tyrants but rather

> [a] eulogist of democracy, and its most spirited champion ... And so, naturally, he did not favor the tyrant. It was not his purpose to instruct the tyrant, but by revealing his secret counsels to strip him bare, and expose him to the suffering nations ... The purpose of this shrewdest of men was to instruct the nations under the pretext of instructing the prince.[42]

The republican reading of Machiavelli was common among the Italian reformers, who often used *Il Principe* and *I Discorsi* as guidebooks against tyranny and as tools to shed light on the political and religious crisis of sixteenth-century Italy. Indeed, in 1580, the Italian Protestant printer Pietro Perna published in Basel the Latin translation of *Il Principe* by Silvestro Tegli, rebutting in the preface the growing wave of Protestant anti-Machiavellainism that followed in the wake of the Saint Bartholomew's massacre and arguing that Machiavelli "established not tyranny but rather the true prince."[43]

As suggested by the case of Machiavelli, Italian literature circulated on the Continent as well as in the British Isles not only through vernacular but also through Latin translations, which have not yet been thoroughly studied.[44] Castiglione's *Courtier*, for example, was read frequently in England not only in Thomas Hoby's version but also in Bartholomew Clerke's Latin translation published in 1571 and frequently reprinted well into the eighteenth century.[45] Similarly, in 1584, a partial Latin translation of Tasso's *Liberata* appeared in London at Wolfe's press, long before the first English translations by Richard Carew and Edward Fairfax, published only in 1594 and 1600.[46] The Latin version of canto I was dedicated to Queen Elizabeth while the partial translation of canto IV – containing the description of the Infernal council that strongly influenced John Milton – was dedicated to Philip Sidney.[47] The translator was Alberico Gentili's brother Scipione, also destined to an important career as a professor of law in Germany. The classicist inspiration of his translation, his intention to rewrite Tasso's vernacular octaves closely imitating Vergil's Latin hexameters, was clearly announced in the first verses. As it has been noted, *Solymeidos* appears to be more a rewriting of the *Aeneid* than of the *Liberata*, whose *incipit*, "Canto l'arme pietose e 'l capitano/che 'l gran sepolcro liberò di Cristo" ("I sing of war, of holy war and him, Captain who freed the Sepulchre of Christ") was translated by Gentili with an unequivocally Virgilian intonation: "Arma ducemque cano, Solymae qui primus in oris/Aeterni tumulum regis monimentaque fecit/Libera."[48] Attentively read in Italy in the midst of the debate between Tassisti and Ariostisti, Gentili's *Solymedios* was republished in 1585 in Venice with a new preface by Aldo Manuzio the younger. In 1587 Tasso himself praised Gentili's verses defining them "truly elegant and refined" ("leggiadrissimi invero e politissimi").[49]

"Pragmatic readers"

In the last decades of Elizabeth's reign, along with Machiavelli, Aretino, and Tasso, the Italian reformers also brought to early modern England several travel narratives and recent accounts of geographical discoveries. Circulating new information on the expanding world, they progressively enabled scholars such as John Dee and Richard

Hakluyt to question the Iberian monopoly on the new commercial routes and to invent a new image of England as a colonial power. Because of their capacity to provide their English patrons with both "learning" and "intelligence," it may be argued that in the late sixteenth century the Italian reformers served as "pragmatic readers," a term used by Lisa Jardine and William Sherman to describe the knowledge transactions between professional readers and their employers in Elizabethan England.[50] Indeed, while seeking updated information on new geographical horizons, Hakluyt often relied on Italian religious exiles as translators and "facilitators," able to turn foreign geographical texts into tools for Elizabethan expansionism.[51] In reading Ramusio, for example, the author of the *Principal Navigations* asked for the assistance of the Italian lexicographer John Florio, who translated into English *Le navigazioni di Iacques Carthier*, printed in Italian in the *Navigationi e viaggi* but originally published in Paris in 1545 following Cartier's expedition to Canada.[52] Well known today for his Anglo-Italian dictionaries and especially for his translation of Montaigne's *Essais*, Florio had met Hakluyt in Oxford, while working as a language teacher at Magdalen College. Their close connection is further confirmed by the verses that Hakluyt inserted in Florio's *Firste Fruites*, a dialogical textbook for the study of Italian published in 1578.[53] Translating Cartier's *Brief récit* from the Italian version included in Ramusio, Hakluyt and Florio hoped that a full English translation of *Navigationi* would have followed soon after. Despite the fact that the project did not come to pass, Cartier's *A shorte and briefe narration* nonetheless had an important role in supporting the idea of an English America. Indeed, Florio's translation coincided with the opening of a wide debate over the New World that erupted in England a few years later following the Roanoke expedition. Like Thomas Harriot's *A Briefe and True Report of the New Found Land of Virginia*, Florio's preface advanced an idealized description of the American Indians, as innocent and gentle, which Elizabethans could envision through John White famous watercolours. Signed by Florio but strongly influenced by Hakluyt, it describes the New World as "a Countrey no lesse fruitful and pleasant in al respects than is *England, Fraunce, or Germany* … whiche aboundeth with Golde and other Mettalles."[54] The simple and innocent nature of its inhabitants foretold their easy submission, since the American Indians "though simple and rude in manners, and destitute of the knowledge of God or any good lawes, yet of nature gentle and tractable" are considered "most apt to receive the Christian Religion, and to subject themselves to some good government."[55] These observations owe much to Cartier's first account, in which the marvel before the New World and the incapacity to understand the language of the natives "allowed a certain agreeable latitude in construing the signs of the other."[56]

At times, interest in the discoveries led the Italian reformers to financially support the English expansion overseas, as in the case of Horatio Palavicino, the powerful Genoese merchant, who in 1584 confessed to Hakluyt his interest in becoming "an adventurer in those westerne voyages."[57] Italian mapmakers also played an important role in disseminating knowledge of the English transoceanic ventures, nourishing discussions about the world outside of Europe and England's imperial ambitions. In 1588 Baptista Boazio drew the maps for Walter Bigges' account of Francis Drake's voyages to the West Indies, later republished by Hakluyt in the *Principal Navigations*.[58] Baptista had an important career in England and in the late sixteenth century he became the cartographer of Robert Devereux, second Earl of Essex, as is suggested by his maps of Cadiz, the Azores, and Ireland.[59] It is not hard to understand why the New World had such an important impact on the Italian reformers. Indeed, the new ethnographic information constituted a formidable ideological weapon against the Catholic colonial empires and was often used to denounce the interplay between spiritual and political conquest. In 1566, the *Mappe-monde nouvelle papistique* by the Italian exile Giovanni Battista Trento, which appeared in Geneva with a dedication to Queen Elizabeth, made clear how the encounters with the American Indians could be employed in religious controversies. Bringing American cannibalism into European confessional strife, Trento attacked the doctrine of transubstantiation, comparing Brazilian anthropophagy with Catholic theophagy. As the *Mappe-monde* argued, in the provinces under the rule of the Pope, they "eat almost nothing but meat, like some peoples of Brasil, that are called Cannibals, who eat human flesh."[60]

Along with the first navigations across the Atlantic, the last decades of Elizabeth's reign were marked by new contacts with the Muslim Mediterranean. As has been argued, "it was during Elizabeth's reign that, encouraged by crown policy and an aggressive community of entrepreneurial merchants, English relations with Muslim states put religion aside and flourished in unprecedented ways."[61] While in May 1580 Murad III conceded a new set of trade Capitulations to English merchants, in 1589 Hakluyt included in the *Principal Navigations* the correspondence between Elizabeth and the Sultan, editing the original letters in order to emphasize a common religious ground and ultimately to undermine the traditional stereotypes of the cruel Turks.[62] In the attempt to update English knowledge of the Ottomans, Hakluyt turned again to the Italian reformers, promoting the publication of the *Itinerario da Vienna a Costantinopoli* by the Italian traveller Marco Antonio Pigafetta.[63] Raised in the same family of the far more famous Antonio, Marco Antonio Pigafetta began to question his Catholic faith in Vicenza, one of the Italian centers of diffusion of Protestant doctrines.[64] In November 1580 he registered at the Italian Protestant Church in London, soon after which he met Hakluyt.[65] In the first edition of the *Principal Navigations* Pigafetta inserted some laudatory verses in Italian celebrating the work as the ideal continuation of Ramusio's *Navigationi*.[66]

Published in London in 1585, though written between 1568 and 1569, when the author travelled to Constantinople, Pigafetta's *Itinerario* described Constantinople as a cosmopolitan and multilingual city where different confessions were allowed. Pigafetta underlined that the Ottomans tolerated several religious minorities, such as Catholics, Orthodox Christians and Jews, who fled to Constantinople once expelled from Spain but nonetheless kept their own language.[67] As the *Itinerario* observed, several areas in Constantinople, such as Pera, had been traditionally occupied by foreigners, ambassadors, merchants and various non-Muslim confessional groups. The degree of tolerance was high also with regard to Christians, as suggested by the presence in Pera of two Christian monasteries, one Franciscan and the other Dominican, that were free to celebrate their own rites.[68] This view of Constantinople as a cosmopolitan and tolerant city was common among early modern travel writers.[69] It also circulated among the circles of Italian radical reformers, who at times, in the wake of Sebastian Castellio, contrasted the intolerance of both Rome and Geneva with the example of the Ottoman capital, where the three religions of the book were able to coexist.[70] Writing about distant lands was often a disguised way to address controversial topics at home, and it is perhaps not just a coincidence that the *Itinerario*, and its praise of the tolerant Ottoman empire, found its way to the press following Pigafetta's harsh disputes with the Italian Protestant Church in London, increasingly divided between its Calvinist and radical wing.[71]

Conclusion

Repressed at home by the Counter-Reformation, the religious restlessness of sixteenth-century Italy found new expression in early modern England and influenced Protestants on both sides of the Atlantic. As a substantial amount of evidence suggests, English interest in the protagonists of the texts of the Italian Reformation was long and persistent. While the young princess Elizabeth translated Ochino for her brother Edward VI, the Puritans in New England used Vermigli's epistle *De fuga in persecutione* to justify their decision to flee. Ballads and plays appropriated the death of Spiera to warn against apostasy and religious dissimulation, while the English translation of Balbani's *Vita di Galeazzo Caracciolo* continued to be published in London and Boston well into the eighteenth century. Along with the moderate wing, who ended up conforming to the new Protestant orthodoxies, the radical wing discovered by Cantimori, composed by those reformers who rebelled "against every form of ecclesiastical organization," also had a significant impact in early modern England. This is confirmed by the circulation of Aconcio's *Satanae stratagemata*, which originally appeared in Basel in 1565 with a dedication to Queen Elizabeth and was later republished and translated in seventeenth-century England, where it continued to nourish controversies over religious toleration in the years of the Revolution.

The Italian Protestant diaspora of the sixteenth century also shaped the ways in which the Italian Renaissance arrived in early modern England. Indeed, the Italian reformers brought across the channel not only the religious turmoil of sixteenth-century Italy but also the secular culture and learning of their homeland, as they circulated such authors as Machiavelli, Aretino, Tasso, Ramusio, and Sarpi.[72] For this reason, the study of the English reception of the Italian Renaissance cannot ignore these "forgotten middlemen of literature" who enabled Tudor and Stuart readers to access Italian texts while working in the printing industry as editors, translators, publishers, literary agents, and booksellers.[73] Moving across geographical and confessional borders the Italian reformers also mediated among different languages and cultures, translating the Italian Renaissance and refashioning it for an English Protestant audience. Finally, the Italian reformers also served as "pragmatic readers," contributing to the circulation of both learning and information between Catholic and Protestant Europe. Gathering intelligence not only about Italy and the Continent but also about the expanding world, from America to the Muslim Mediterranean, they facilitated the first English colonial ventures and contributed to shaping a new image of England as imperial and global power.

Notes

1 Jakob Burckhardt, *The Civilization of the Renaissance in Italy*, trans. Samuel G. C. Middlemore, intr. P. Gay (New York: Modern Library, 2002), p. 320.

2 Giorgio Spini, "Qualche riflessione su *Per una storia religiosa dello stato di Milano* di Federico Chabod," in *Federico Chabod e la nuova storiografia italiana 1919–1950*, ed. Brunello Vigezzi (Milan: Jaca, 1984), pp. 233–41. On the historiography of the Italian Reformation see Adriano Prosperi, "Riforma in Italia, Riforma italiana?" in *Breve storia della Riforma in Italia*, ed. Manfred Welti (Casale Monferrato: Marietti, 1985), pp. VI–XVI, and Massimo Firpo, "Historiographical Introduction," in *The Italian Reformation of the Sixteenth-Century and the Diffusion of Renaissance Culture: A Bibliography of the Secondary Literature*, ed. John Tedeschi (with the assistance of James M. Lattis) *(Ca. 1750–1997)* (Modena: Panini, 2000), pp. XVIII–XLIX.

3 Benedetto Croce, *Vite di avventure di fede e di passione*, ed. Giuseppe Galasso (Milan: Adelphi, 1989), pp. 197–297.

4 See Gennaro Sasso, *Per invigilare me stesso: i Taccuini di lavoro di Benedetto Croce* (Bologna: Il Mulino, 1989), pp. 118–26. On Croce's conception of autobiography see Michele Ciliberto, "Filosofia e autobiografia in Croce," *Studi storici*, 4 (1992): 693–712, republished in Id., *Figure in chiaroscuro. Filosofia e storiografia nel Novecento* (Rome: Edizioni storia e letteratura, 2001), pp. 219–42.

5 Juan de Valdés, *Alfabeto cristiano, dialogo con Giulia Gonzaga*, intro., notes, and appendix Benedetto Croce (Bari: Laterza, 1938), Benedetto Croce, "*Il Beneficio di Cristo*," *Critica*, 38 (1940): 115–25, Benedetto Croce, "Su l'autore del *Beneficio di Cristo*. Lettera a S. Caponnetto," *Appello*, 7 (1942): 69.

6 Delio Cantimori, "Studi di storia della Riforma e dell'eresia in Italia e studi sulla storia della vita religiosa nella prima metà del '500 (Rapporto fra i due tipi di ricerca)," *Bollettino della Società di Studi Valdesi*, 76/102 (1957): 29–38, English translation in *The Late Italian Renaissance*, ed. Eric Cochrane (New York: Harper & Row, 1970), pp. 211–25 (220). In this passage Cantimori is discussing the Italian echoes of Lucien Febvre's "Une question mal posée: les origines de la Réforme française et le problème des causes de la Réforme," *Revue historique*, CLXI (1929): 1–73.

7 Delio Cantimori, *Eretici italiani del Cinquecento: ricerche storiche* (Florence: Sansoni, 1939). On Cantimori's discussion with Croce and on his passage from philosophy to history see Adriano Prosperi, "Introduzione," in *Eretici italiani del Cinquecento*, ed. Delio Cantimori (Turin: Einaudi, 1992), pp. XI–LXII.

8 See the remarks by Anne Jacobson Schutte, "Periodization of Sixteenth-Century Italian Religious History: The Post-Cantimori Paradigm Shift," *Journal of Modern History*, 61 (1989): 269–84.

9 Firpo, "Historiographical Introduction," p. XLVI.

10 Cantimori, *Eretici italiani*, "Avvertenza."

11 On the history of the Italian Protestant Church in London see Firpo, Luigi, "La Chiesa italiana di Londra nel Cinquecento e i suoi rapporti con Ginevra," in *Ginevra e l'Italia*, eds. Delio Cantimori, Giorgio Spini, Franco Venturi, and Valdo Vinay (Florence: Sansoni 1959), later republished in Luigi Firpo, *Scritti sulla Riforma in Italia* (Naples: Prismi, 1996), pp. 117–94, and more recently Owe Boersma and Auke J. Jelsma, *Unity in Multiformity. The Minutes and Coetus of London, 1575 and the Concistory Minutes of the Italian Church in London, 1570–1591* (London: Huguenot Society of Great Britain and Ireland, 1997), and Stefano Villani, "The Italian Protestant Church of London in the Seventeenth Century," in *Exiles, Emigrés and Intermediaries*, ed. Barbara Schaff (Amsterdam: Rodopi, 2010), pp. 217–36.

12 On Michelangelo Florio see Frances A. Yates, *John Florio. The Life of an Italian in Shakespeare's England* (Cambridge: Cambridge University Press, 1934), pp. 1–26, and more recently Michael Wyatt, *The Italian Encounter with Tudor England. A Cultural Politics of Translation* (Cambridge: Cambridge University Press, 2005), pp. 98–101.

13 Roger Ascham, *The Schoolmaster*, ed. Lawrence V. Ryan (Ithaca, NY: Cornell University Press, 1967), p. 70.

14 John Tedeschi, "The Cultural Contributions of Italian Protestant Reformers in the late Renaissance," in *Libri, idee e sentimenti religiosi nel Cinquecento italiano*, eds. Adriano Prosperi and Albano Biondi (Modena: Panini, 1987), pp. 81–108.

15 On the notion of "communication circuit" see Robert Darnton, *The Kiss of Lamourette. Reflections in Cultural History* (New York: Norton, 1990), pp. 107–35.

16 Diarmaid MacCulloch, *Thomas Cranmer. A Life* (New Haven, CT: Yale University Press, 1996), pp. 394–96.

17 Elizabeth I, *Translations, 1544–1589*, eds. Janel M. Mueller and Joshua Scodel (Chicago, IL: Chicago University Press, 2009), pp. 302–3.

18 See M. Anne Overell, *Italian Reform and English Reformations, c. 1535 – c. 1585* (Farnham, UK: Ashgate, 2008), pp. 61–80.

19 Giorgio Spini, "Riforma italiana e mediazioni ginevrine nella Nuova Inghilterra puritan," in *Ginevra e l'Italia*, pp. 451–89, later republished in Giorgio Spini, *Barocco e puritani. Studi sulla storia del Seicento in Italia, Spagna e New England* (Florence: Vallecchi, 1991), pp. 239–69.

20 Niccolò Balbani, *The Italian Convert: News from Italy of a Second Moses. Or the Life of Galeacius Caracciolus, the Noble Marquis of Vico* (Boston, MA: Thomas Fleet, 1751). It was republished in Boston by S. Hall in 1794.
21 On the English circulation of the story of Francesco Spiera see Lily B. Campbell, "Doctor Faustus: A Case of Conscience," *Publications of the Modern Language Association of America*, 67 (1952): 219–39, Brian Opie, "Nathaniel Bacon and Francis Spiera: The Presbyterian and The Apostate," *The Turnbull Library Record*, 18 (1985): 33–50, Michael MacDonald, "The Fearefull Estate of Francis Spiera: Narrative, Identity, and Emotion in Early Modern England," *Journal of British Studies*, 31 (1992): 32–61, M. Anne Overell, "The Exploitation of Francesco Spiera," *Sixteenth Century Journal*, 26 (1995): 619–37. On its Italian and European echoes see Adriano Prosperi, *L'eresia del Libro Grande. Storia di Giorgio Siculo e della sua setta* (Milan: Feltrinelli, 2000), pp. 102–30, and Silvano Cavazza, "Una vicenda europea: Vergerio e il caso Spiera, 1548–49," in *La fede degli italiani. Per Adriano Prosperi*, eds. Guido Dall'Olio, Adelisa Malena, and Pieroberto Scaramella (Pisa: Edizioni della Normale, 2011), pp. 41–51.
22 Tedeschi, *The Cultural Contributions*, p. 93.
23 MacDonald, "The Fearefull Estate of Francis Spiera," p. 35.
24 Matteo Gribaldi, *A notable and marveilous epistle … concernyng the terrible iudgement of God, upon hym that for feare of men, denyeth Christ and the knowen veritie: with a preface of Doctor Calvine. Translated out of Latin into English by E.A.* (Worchester, UK: John Oswen, 1550). English translation after Gribaldi's *Historia de quodam quem hostes Evangelii in Italia coegerunt abiicere agnitam veritatem*, 1549.
25 John Foxe, *The Ecclesiasticall History, Contayning the Actes & Monuments of thinges Passed in Every Kinges Time, in This Realme, Especially in the Churches of England*, 2 vols. (London: John Day 1576), I: 1351.
26 Olimpia F. Morata, *Orationes, Dialogi, Epistolae, Carmina* (Basel: Pietro Perna, 1562). Curione published Morata's work for the first time in 1558 with a different dedication to Isabella Bresegna. I am citing from the expanded edition of Morata's *Opera* published by Perna in 1580. On Morata see Ruth Chavasse, "Humanism in Exile: Caelio Secondo Curione's Learned Women Friends and Exempla for Elizabeth I," *Parergon*, 14/1 (1996): 165–86 and Janet Smarr, "Olimpia Morata: from Classicist to Reformer," in *Phaeton's Children: The Este Court and Its Culture in Early Modern Ferrara*, eds. Dennis Looney and Deanna Shemek (Tempe, AZ: Center for Medieval and Renaissance Studies, 2005), pp. 321–43. See in addition, also for further bibliography Lisa Saracco, "Morato (Morata), Olimpia Fulvia," in *Dizionario Biografico degli Italiani*, 76 (Rome: Istituto della Enciclopedia Italiana, 2012), pp. 540–42.
27 *Opera* Morata, p. 220, English trans. by Holt N. Parker, *Olympia Morata. The Complete Writings of an Italian Heretic* (Chicago, IL: Chicago University Press, 2003), p. 152.
28 Morata, *Opera*, p. *5v, English trans, p. 72.
29 Morata, *Opera*, p. *4v, English trans, p. 72.
30 Celio Secondo Curione, *Pasquine in a Traunce. A Christian and Learned Dialogue … Whereunto Are Added Certaine Questions Then Put Foorth by Pasquine to Have Been Disputed in the Councell of Trent* (London: Thomas Este, 1584). On the English circulation of the work see Letizia Panizza, "Pasquino among Anglican Reformers: the two editions in English (1566 and 1584) of Celio Secondo Curione's *Pasquino in estasi*," in *Ex marmore: pasquini, pasquinisti, pasquinate nell'Europa moderna*, eds. Chrysa Damianaki, Paolo Procaccioli, and Adriano Romano (Rome: Vecchiarelli, 2006), pp. 407–28.
31 Giacomo Aconcio, *Satanae stratagemata* (Basel: Pietro Perna, 1564). On its English reception see Giorgio Caravale, *Storia di una doppia censura: gli Stratagemmi di Satana di Giacomo Aconcio nell'Europa del Seicento* (Pisa: Edizioni della Normale, 2013).
32 On Aconcio see Paolo Rossi, *Giacomo Aconcio* (Milan: Bocca, 1952), Charles David O'Malley, *Jacopo Aconcio* (Rome: Edizioni di storia e letteratura, 1955), Paola Giacomoni and Luigi Dappiano, *Jacopo Aconcio. Il pensiero scientifico e l'idea di tolleranza* (Trento: Dipartimento di scienze filologiche e storiche, 2005). For further bibliography see A. Gordon Kinder, "*Jacobus Acontius*," in *Bibliotheca dissidentium: répertoire des non-conformistes religieux des seizième et dix-septième siècles* (Baden-Baden, Germany: Koener, 1994), pp. 55–117.

33 Giacomo Aconcio, *Darkness Discovered or the Devils Secret Stratagems laid open* (London: John Macock, 1651), p. 26. See the original Latin text in Giacomo Aconcio, *Stratagematum Satanae libri VIII* (Florence: Valecchi, 1946), pp. 70–72.

34 Aconcio, *Darkness Discovered*, p. 100; Aconcio, *Stratagematum Satanae*, p. 236.

35 Elizabeth L. Eisenstein, *The Printing Press as an Agent of Change. Communications and Cultural Transformations in Early Modern Europe* (Cambridge: Cambridge University Press, 1979), pp. 139–40.

36 On Wolfe see Clifford Chalmers Huffman, *Elizabethan Impressions: John Wolfe and his Press* (New York: AMS Press, 1998), Fabio Massimo Bertolo, "John Wolfe, un editore inglese tra Aretino e Machiavelli," in *Il Rinascimento italiano di fronte alla Riforma: letteratura e arte*, eds. Chrysa Damianaki, Paolo Procaccioli, and Adriano Romano (Rome: Vecchiarelli, 2005), pp. 199–208, Jason Lawrence, *"Who the Devil Taught Thee so Much Italian?" Italian Language Learning and Literary Imitation in Early Modern England* (Manchester, UK: Manchester University Press, 2005), pp. 187–201, and Wyatt, *The Italian Encounter with Tudor England*, pp. 185–98.

37 Giacomo Aconcio, *Una essortatione al timor di Dio con alcune rime italiane nuovamente messe in luce* (London: John Wolfe, 1579).

38 See Massimo Firpo, "Castiglione, Giovanni Battista," *Dizionario Biografico degli Italiani*, 22 (1979): 82–84.

39 See Adolph Gerber, "All of the Five Fictitious Editions of Writings of Machiavelli and Three of Those of Pietro Aretino Printed by John Wolfe of London (1584–1588)," *Modern Language Notes*, 22 (1907): 2–6, 129–35, 201–6, Peter S. Donaldson, *Machiavelli and Mystery of State* (Cambridge: Cambridge University Press, 1988), pp. 86–110, Diego Pirillo, "Republicanism and Religious Dissent: Machiavelli and the Italian Protestant Reformers," in *Machiavellian Encounters in Tudor and Stuart England. Literary and Political Influences from the Reformation to the Restoration*, eds. Alessandro Arienzo and Alessandra Petrina (Farnham, UK: Ashgate, 2013), pp. 121–40.

40 *Lo stampatore al benigno lettore*, in *I discorsi sopra la prima deca di Tito Livio*, cit., *2v.

41 Ibidem.

42 Alberico Gentili, *De legationibus libri tres* (London: Thomas Vautrollier, 1585), p. 109, English trans. Laing, Gordon J., *De legationibus libri tres* (New York: Oceana, 1924), p. 156.

43 Perna's epistle inserted in the 1580's reprint of Tegli's translation of *Il Principe* has been republished by Leandro Perini, "Gli eretici italiani del Cinquecento e Machiavelli," *Studi storici*, 10, 4 (1969): 916–18. On the republican reading of Machiavelli see also Diego Pirillo, "Republicanism and Religious Dissent," pp. 121–40.

44 On Latin culture in early modern England see especially James Binns, *Intellectual Culture in Elizabethan and Jacobean England: the Latin Writings of the Age* (Leeds, UK: Cairns, 1990). On the persistence of Latin in early modern Europe see also Ann Blair, "La persistance du latin comme langue de science à la fin de la Renaissance," in *Sciences et langues en Europe*, eds. Roger Chartier and Pietro Corsi (Paris: Centre Alexandre Koyré, Ecole des Hautes Etudes en Sciences Sociales, 1996), pp. 21–42, and Peter Burke, *Languages and Communities in Early Modern Europe* (Cambridge: Cambridge University Press, 2004), pp. 43–60.

45 Baldassarre Castiglione, *De curiali sive aulico libri quatuor* (London: John Day, 1571).

46 Scipione Gentili, *Solymeidos libri duo priores de Torquati Tassi Italicis expressi* (London: John Wolfe, 1584). On the first English translations of the *Liberata* see Charles Peter Brand, *Torquato Tasso: A Study of the Poet and of His Contribution to English Literature* (Cambridge: Cambridge University Press, 1965), pp. 238–46, where Gentili is, however, mentioned only briefly. A more detailed analysis can be found in Clifford Chalmers Huffman, "The Earliest Reception of Tasso in Elizabethan England," *Rivista di Letterature Moderne e Comparate*, 32 (1979): 245–61, Guido Baldassarri, "Poema eroico o 'romanzo'? Riscrittue della Liberata dal Camilli al Gentili," in *Scritture di scritture: testi, generi, modelli nel Rinascimento*, eds. Giancarlo Mazzacurati and Michel Plaisance (Rome: Bulzojni, 1987), pp. 439–59, and Diego Pirillo, "Tasso at the French Embassy: Epic, Diplomacy and the Law of Nations," in *Authority and Diplomacy from Dante to Shakespeare*, eds. Jason E. Powell and William T. Rossiter (Farnham, UK: Ashgate, 2013), pp. 135–53.

47 Torquato Tasso, *Plutonis concilium: ex initio quarti libri Solymeidos* (London: John Wolfe, 1584). On Tasso's influence on Sidney see Barbara Brumbaugh, "*Jerusalem Delivered* and the allegory of Sidney's Revised Arcadia," *Modern Philology*, 101 (2004): 337–70.

48 Gentili, *Solymeidos*, I.v.1–3, 1r, alluding to the incipit of Virgil's *Aeneid*. I am quoting Tasso from *Gerusalemme Liberata*, ed. Lanfranco Caretti (Bari: Laterza, 1981), I.3 (English translation by Max Wickert, *The Liberation of Jerusalem*, with intro. and notes by Mark Davie (Oxford: Oxford University Press, 2009), p. 3.

49 *Le lettere di Torquato Tasso*, ed. Cesare Guasti, 5 vols. (Florence: Le Monnier, 1853), III.785 (letter to Alberto Parma, March 29, 1587).

50 Lisa Jardine and William Sherman, "Pragmatic readers: knowledge transactions and scholarly services in late Elizabethan England," in *Religion, Culture and Society in Early Modern Britain. Essays in Honour of Patrick Collinson*, eds. Anthony Fletcher and Peter Roberts (Cambridge: Cambridge University Press, 2006), pp. 102–24.

51 I borrow the term "facilitator" from Jardine, Lisa and Anthony Grafton, "*Studied for Action*: How Gabriel Harvey Read His Livy," *Past & Present*, 129 (1990): 30–78.

52 Jacques Cartier, *Brief récit, & succinte narration, de la navigation faicte es ysles de Canada, Hochelage & Saguenay & autres, avec particulières meurs, langaige & ceremonies des habitans d'icelles* (Paris: Roffet & Le Clerc, 1545); J. Cartier, *A Shorte and Briefe Narration of the Two Navigations and Discoveries to the Northweast Partes Called Newe Fraunce: First Translated Out of French into Italian, by that Famous Learned Man Gio: Bapt: Ramusius, and Now Turned into English by Iohn Florio: Worthy the Reading of All Venturers, Travellers, and Discoverers* (London: H. Bynneman, 1580).

53 John Florio, *His Firste Fruites: Which Yeelde Familiar Speech, Merie Proverbes, Wittie Sentences, and Golden Sayings* (London: Thomas Dawson, for Thomas Woodcocke, 1578), pp. **iiiv–**iiiir. Florio's *Firste Fruites* circulated widely in England. In his copy of the work Gabriel Harvey noted in the margins that not only Elizabeth but also Dudley and Sidney "could speak fluently Italian": see Virginia F. Stern, *Gabriel Harvey. A Study of His Life, Marginalia, and Library* (Oxford: Clarendon, 1979), p. 156.

54 Cartier, *A Shorte and Briefe Narration*, B1r–B2r. See Yates, *John Florio*, p. 58: "it seems, therefore, that it was really the voice of Hakluyt which had been heard in 1580 speaking through Florio before he had as yet published anything in his own name." The same view was expressed a few years earlier by George Bruner Parks in his classical study, *Richard Hakluyt and the English Voyages* (New York: F. Unger, 1928), p. 64, though Yates does not refer to it.

55 Cartier, *A Shorte and Briefe Narration*, B1r.

56 Stephen Greenblatt, *Marvelous Possessions: The Wonder of the New World* (Chicago, IL: University of Chicago Press, 1991), p. 104. Cf. Cartier, *A shorte and briefe narration*, p. 18: the Americans:

> [c]ame verye friendlye to us, rubbing oure armes with their owne handes, then woulde they lifte them uppe toward heaven, shewing manye signe of gladnesse: and in such wise were we assured one of another, that we very familiarly beganne to trafficke of whatsoever they had, till they had nothing but their naked bodies, for they gave us al what soever they had, and that was but of small value. We perceived that this people might verie easily be converted to our religion.

57 Letter from Richard Hakluyt to Sir F. Walsingham, 1584, in *The Original Writing & Correspondence of the Two Richard Hakluyts*, with intr. and notes by E. G. R. Taylor, 2 vols. (London: The Hakluyt Society, 1935), I, pp. 208–10, 209. On other occasions, Italian exiles financed translations of travel accounts, like the civil lawyer sir Julius Cesar Adelmare, the eldest son of the Italian physician Cesare, who in 1598 supported the author of the *Principal Navigations* for the translation of Jan Huygen van Linschoten's *Discours of Voyages into the Easte and West Indies* (London: John Wolfe, 1598). On Adelmare see Delio Cantimori, *Adelmare Cesare*, in *Dizionario Biografico degli Italiani*, 1 (Roma: Istituto della Enciclopedia Italiana, 1960), p. 265.

58 Walter Bigges, *A Summarie and True Discourse of Sir Frances Drakes West Indian Voyage* (London: Richard Field, 1589). The text was republished in Richard Hakluyt, *The Principal Navigations, Voyages, Traffiques and Discoveries of the English Nation* (London: Bishop,

Newberry & Barker, 1600), III, pp. 534–48. On Boazio see *Sir Francis Drake. An Exhibition to Commemorate Francis Drake's Voyage around the World 1577–1580* (London: British Museum Publications, 1977), pp. 107–8, and Mary Frear Keeler (ed.), *Sir Francis Drake's West Indian Voyage 1585–86* (London: The Hakluyt Society, 1981), pp. 317–19.

59 On Baptsta Boazio's later career as Essex's cartographer see Edward Lynam, "English Maps and Map-Makers of the Sixteenth Century," *The Geographical Journal*, 116, 1/3 (1950): 7–25 (esp. pp. 23–25), and John Harwood Andrews, *Shapes of Ireland. Maps and Their Makers 1564–1839* (Dublin: Geography Publications, 1997), pp. 57–88.

60 Jean Battiste Trento et Pierre Eskrich, *Mappe-Monde nouvelle papistique*, eds. Frank Lestringant and A. Preda, (Geneva: Droz, 2009), p. 267. On the *Mappe-Monde* see Dror Wahrman, "From Imaginary Drama to Dramatized Imagery: The Mappe-Monde Nouvelle Papistique, 1566–67," *Journal of the Warburg and Courtauld Institutes*, 54 (1991): 186–205, Luca Ragazzini, "Pedagogia delle parole e pedagogia delle immagini: l'Histoire de la Mappe-Monde Papistique di Giovan Battista Trento e Pierre Eskrich (1566)," *Rivista di Storia e Letteratura Religiosa*, 38, 3 (2003): 427–73. On the history of Protestant association between Eucharist and cannibalism see especially Frank Lestringant, *Une sainte horreur, ou le voyage en Eucharistie (XVIe-XVIIIe siècles)* (Paris: Presses universitaires de France, 1996).

61 Gerald M. Maclean and Nabil Matar, *Britain and the Islamic World, 1558–1713* (Oxford: Oxford University Press, 2011), p. 45.

62 Richard Hakluyt, *The Principall Navigations Voiages and Discoveries of the English Nation* (Cambridge: Cambridge University Press, 1965), I, pp. 163–71. On the 1580 Capitulations as a turning point in the history of Anglo-Muslim relationships see Matthew Dimmock, "*Captive to the Turke*: Responses to the Anglo-Ottoman Capitulations of 1580," in *Cultural Encounters Between East and West* 1453–1699, eds. Matthew Birchwood and Matthew Dimmock (Newcastle-upon-Tyne: Cambridge Scholars, 2005), pp. 43–63. See also Matthew Dimmock, *New Turkes: Dramatizing Islam and the Ottomans in Early Modern England* (Farnham, UK: Ashgate, 2005). On Renaissance stereotypes on the Turks see Timothy Hampton, "*Turkish Dogs*: Rabelais, Erasmus and the Rhetoric of Alterity," *Representations*, 41 (1993): 58–82.

63 Marco Antonio Pigafetta, *Itinerario da Vienna a Costantinopoli* (London: John Wolfe, 1585).

64 On Pigafetta's biography see Daria Perocco, "Introduzione," in *Itinerario da Vienna a Costantinopoli*, ed. Marco Antonio Pigafetta (Padua: Il poligrafo, 2008), pp. 9–60.

65 See Boersma and Jelsma, *Unity in Multiformity*, cit., pp. 176–82.

66 R. Hakluyt, *The Principal Navigations, Voyages, Traffiques Ad Discoveries of the English Nation*, 3 vols. (London: George Bishop, Ralph Newberie, and Robert Barker, 1599), I: **3v.

67 Pigafetta, *Itinerario*, p. 47: "moltissimi Giudei, di quelli massime che con grandissima utilità de Turchi furono scacciati di Spagna da i Re Catolici Ferdinando e Isabella. Questi Giudei tengono ancora la lingua Spagnuola."

68 Pigafetta, *Itinerario*, p. 47.

69 Eric R. Dursteler, *Venetians in Constantinople. Nation, Identity and Coexistence in the Early Modern Mediterranean* (Baltimore, MD: Johns Hopkins University Press, 2006).

70 Sébastien Castellio, *De haereticis an sint persequendi* (1554), (Geneva: Droz, 1954), p. 137: "Sunt Constantinopoli Turcae, sunt Christiani, sunt et Iudaei, tres nationes inter se de religione maxime dissentientes, quae tamen inter se pacate vivunt."

71 Firpo, *La chiesa italiana di Londra*, pp. 388–91, Boersma and Jelsma, *Unity in Multiformity*, pp. 176–82.

72 Tedeschi, "The Cultural Contributions."

73 Darnton, *The Kiss of Lamourette*, pp. 136–53.

23 Italy, printing industry, and the cultural market in Elizabethan England

Mario Domenichelli

During the Elizabethan age the two English universities, Oxford and Cambridge, had a constant and substantial increase in the number of students. Many of them were "commoners"[1] coming from the families of merchants and craftsmen who could afford a university education which might give their sons a chance to climb the social ladder. However, only a few could expect to find some intellectual job as a secretary in some aristocratic mansion, or enter either an ecclesiastic or an academic career. The majority had no such perspective and could only invest their university-educated talents in the impressive growth of the English cultural market in the second half of the sixteenth century in concomitance with the growth of the printing industry. They became authors, playwrights, players, or translators, novelists, poets, pamphleteers; in short, professional writers.

In 1557, the year before Elizabeth's crowning, the activities of the ancient guild of bookbinders and booksellers (created in 1403), with the new addition of printers, were regulated by a decree of Queen Mary and Philip of Spain. "Considered the amount of seditious, heretical, schismatic publications printed by a number of scandalous, malign, schismatic and heretical persons,"[2] the new decree entrusted the Stationers' Company, under the supervision of the Star Chamber – the Tudor political Tribunal – with the control of all printing and publishing activities. Two years later, in 1559, Elizabeth confirmed Mary's decree from a different viewpoint and a different doctrinal position, not Mary's "papist," Roman Catholic point of view, but an Anglican, Protestant, reformed standpoint. For all differences, the former Catholic decree and its Anglican reinforcement were in the same logic and affirmed the same necessity of the Crown's strict control of the cultural market in the new age of print after Gutenberg's invention in the early 1450s. The Royal decree on printing activities established a new liveried company, the "Stationers' Company," a new "guild" of arts and crafts to which all the booksellers, the printers, publishers, binders must belong by law. A new control tool was established as well, the Stationers' Register, in which, after the payment of a four to six pence tax, all works printed and published were to be registered.[3] The Stationers' Register had a double function: it was the warranty of a sort of *copyright* (granted to printers and theatrical companies who often registered their texts in order to affirm their copyright against literary and theatrical piracy). However, the register's real function was of a political kind, as it granted the Stationers' Company the monopoly of control, and thus the hegemony on the kingdom's book and culture market. The Stationers' Company was given the power of sending to the stake forbidden books and of pursuing their printers. The Stationers' Register was no *index librorum prohibitorum*, of course, even though the Company had the power to burn all non-approved printing and prosecute

DOI: 10.4324/9781315612720-26

any infraction of the law, in synergy with the royal censor, the Master of the Revels, controlling theatrical activities. The question involved the political-religious opposition of the Puritan dissenters against the Crown and the Anglican Church. The Stationers' Company was by no means in real total control of the printing market, neither was the Master of the Revels in control of theatrical shows throughout the country. Nonetheless the institution of official political censorial apparatuses makes us understand what was at stake in the ideological war fought for control of the cultural market.

Booksellers were also publishers responsible for the material printing of books. Any book's colophon included both the seller's and the printer's name. In the colophon of most Elizabethan books we also read where the books were sold, usually at St Paul's Churchyard. Books could also be bought at fairs such as Saint Bartholomew fair on August 24 at West Smithfield, outside Aldersgate of the City of London, or at Stourbridge commons fair at Cambridge on September 14, the feast of the Holy Cross. Book printing and selling had become a profitable commercial enterprise, as is shown by the growth of the publishing industry in the second half of the sixteenth century, when England became the main competitor of Spain both in the eighty-year war in the United Provinces, the Netherlands, and in the other war fought on the Atlantic Ocean for the control of routes to America. As England grew in political and financial importance, the English book trade and theaters became very profitable activities in the early industrial cultural business, with an increasing amount of investments. The Stationers' Guild, in such a situation, obviously needed a guild's politically conditioned deontology, such as the one often transgressed and later formalized by the poet George Wither (1588–1667) in *The Schollers' Purgatory, discovered in the Stationers Commonwealth* (1625). An honest stationer, printer, binder, or book seller, wrote Wither, "exercizeth his mystery" (profession, office, or calling) "with more respect to the glory of God and the publicke advantage, than to his owne commodity,"[4] even though what the glory of God and the "publicke advantage" might be, according to the different doctrinal and political positions, was a highly discretional matter.

The printing trade was business, but it was also the new weapon of the truly Christian soldier, either a fervent Anglican, or an English Puritan ranging on a more radical Protestant side, both willing to sacrifice their lives as martyrs of God's Word. As a matter of fact pamphleteering, the writing war, could even be a profitable, though a dangerous activity. In April 1588, for instance, Robert Waldegrave was imprisoned for printing the Puritan pamphlets by John Udall (1560–92) the author of *The State of the Church of England.* The anonymous pamphlet starting the famous Martin Marprelate controversy, *Oh, Read Over Dr. Bridges, for It Is a Worthy Work,* was printed by the secret press of John Penry and Robert Waldegrave in the house of Mrs Crane in London and was signed Martin Marprelate. The publication of that first pamphlet started a long doctrinal *polemos* between partisans of the Anglican Church on the one side and Puritan spiritual warriors on the other. The polemical battle involved all the "biting" pens of those years, and Waldegrave did not surrender, continuing to print the Martin Marprelate Puritan anti-Anglican pamphlets careless of the danger he was facing. His associate in a very risky printing adventure, John Penry (1559–93), also one of the Marprelate pens, perhaps Martin Marprelate in person, was tried and hanged for sedition. The last of the Marprelate pamphlets, *The Protestation of Martin Marprelate,* was printed by Waldegrave on August 14, 1589 when his secret workshop was discovered and destroyed by the Queen's police.

A printer's luck changed according to the times and political situations. John Day, for instance, who had been indicted and imprisoned for publishing seditious (Puritan) books under the reign of Mary, the Catholic Queen, under the reign of Elizabeth became a successful and wealthy man. His workshop at Aldersgate produced a number of bestsellers such as *ABC with Little Catechism* (1559), or *Cosmographical Glasse* (1559) by William Cunningham. But John Day's bestseller with a number of reprints was *The Whole Booke of Psalms*, in Thomas Sternhold e John Hopkins's translation, published in 1562.[5] John Day had another bestseller, maybe the most important book of the entire Puritan production, John Foxe's *Actes and Monuments* (or *The Book of Martyrs*), published in 1563.[6]

An apprentice in John Day's printer's workshop, John Wolfe, the son of another printer in London, Reyner Wolfe, after learning the rudiments of his art with his father first, and then with Day, went to Italy and worked in a Florentine book-printing workshop (probably the one belonging to the Giunta family), also perhaps establishing in Florence a workshop of his own. Back in London in the late 1580s, Wolfe published in London, and in Italian, both Machiavelli's and Aretino's major works, all of them included in the *index librorum prohibitorum*. Wolfe's Machiavelli books were published with false colophons and with anonymous introductions probably written by some Italian exile, either Jacopo Castelvetro or, more probably, Petruccio Ubaldini. In 1584 *I discorsi sulla prima Deca di Tito Livio*, were given as published by the "eredi di Antoniello degli Antonielli" in Palermo; in 1584, again with the same colophon, Wolfe published *Il Principe*, and in 1587 another two books *Historie fiorentine* and il *Libro dell'arte della guerra* (*The Arte of Warre*, translated by Peter Whitehorn had already been printed in London in 1560–62 by John Kingston, to be sold at Nicholas England's bookshop). In 1588 Wolfe published *L'asino d'oro di Niccolò Machiavelli con tutte l'altre sue operette* (*Dell'Occasione, Di Fortuna, Dell'Ingratitudine, Dell'ambizione, Belfagor, Compendio, Mandragola, Clitia*) and, that same year, *Quattro commedie del divino Pietro Aretino* (*La Cortigiana, La Talanta, L'Hipocrito*, Il Marescalco). The publisher's name in the colophon forgery of these two books was again Antoniello degli Antonelli, with Palermo given as the place of publication. In 1589 Wolfe also published *I Ragionamenti* di Pietro Aretino, this book too published in London, yet given as published in Rome by Gio. Andrea del Melograno.[7]

Wolfe was not the only one printing Italian texts in London. Giordano Bruno, while in England and far from the Inquisition, in London and Oxford – between 1583 and 1586, published in London a series of books for which, under the suspicion of heresy as he was, he could find no printer in Italy. *Degli eroici furori*, in whose colophon we read "Parigi, appresso Antonio Baio," was printed in London by John Charlewood in 1585; *Lo spaccio della bestia trionfante*, dedicated to Sir Philip Sidney, with no publisher's name in colophon and given as printed in Paris, was published in London in 1584. Also *De la causa, principio, et uno* (1584), *De l'infinito universo et mondi* (1584), and *Cabala del cauallo Pegaseo* (1585),[8] given as printed in Paris, or in Venice, with no printer's name, were published in London by Charlewood.

Some of these English printed Italian books, *all'indice* (on the Inquisition's register), perhaps almost all of them, were smuggled to Italy.[9] But it would be unlikely to think that those books did not also have an English market. The Italian language was widely read and spoken in Renaissance England and not only by scholars, philosophers, translators, and "letterati." As a matter of fact, Italian was a "must" for politicians, merchants, and almost all persons of some "quality." Machiavelli's, Aretino's, and Bruno's books printed in Italian in London were a printing bargain. Those books *all'indice* could not be printed in Italy but could be printed and smuggled to Italy. Wolfe and Charlewood certainly knew they did not really endanger themselves by publishing those Italian books in London with a fake colophon. Had all these books an English audience, as we tend to think? Or were all the printed copies of them immediately sent to Italy? This is difficult to ascertain; we only know that a certain number of copies of *Il Principe* in Wolfe's print were once sequestered by the Venetian customs. Italian books were fashionable for the very simple reason they were considered tools for self-fashioning, teaching that science of the self Shakespeare at least once in *Love's Labour's Lost* (1.1) had called "living art," *ars vivendi*, the ancient Greek *téchne tou biou*. This is an expression which needs some explanation, as it is a general label under which all *tékhnai*, all *artes*, all arts and crafts could be listed. The Italian courtly cultural milieu had discovered the importance of writing handbooks in order to teach important skills in all aspects of collective life; all these skills were called arts, or crafts, translating the Latin *artes* (from the Greek *téchnai*, crafts, techniques, know-hows) concerning all aspects of common social life. The two main books which, in different ways, were meant to teach the living art, *ars vivendi*, as a general art including all the different life-crafts, the *tékhnai* any gentleman and gentlewoman was supposed to know, were Baldassar Castiglione's *Libro del Cortegiano* and Machiavelli's *Il Pincipe*.

Interpretations of *Il Cortegiano* (1513) must be seen in the light of the enormous *longue-durée* fortune and European diffusion of the model shaped by Castiglione's book. Boscán's Spanish translation in 1534, Colin's first French translation in 1537, Hoby's *The Courtyer of Count Baldessar Castilo* in 1561,[10] Chappuys's second French version in 1580: these four famous translations – Johann Engelbert Noyse von Capenhouten's Augsburg German version, *Der Hofmann*, came later in 1593 – made *The Courtier* a transnational bestseller and indispensable self-fashioning tool à *l'âge classique*. This is also the reason why that book is often taken for what it is not. *The Courtier* was (and still is) read in some Epicurean, even libertine key, on the one side, as the very book of vanities, and, on the other, as a (if not *the*) Machiavellian handbook for actors on the aristocratic social scene, the court, *le grand théâtre*, as it was called. In order to act on the "great" worldly stage, one must be expert in the twin arts of dissimulation and simulation. This also conceals three important aspects of Castiglione's book and, even more so, its declared "buon fine" and very constitutive reason.

In the 1528 first printed Venice edition of *Il libro del cortegiano*, in the dedicatory letter to don Michele da Silva, we find something which is frequently neglected by the book's interpreters:

> Other say, because it is so hard a matter and (in a maner) unpossible to finde out a man of such perfection, as I would have the Courtier to be, it is but superfluous to write it: for it is a vaine thing to teach that can not be learned. To these men I answere, I am content to err with Plato, Xenophon, and M. Tullius, leaving a part the disputing of the intelligible world and of the Ideas or imagined fourmes: in which number, as (according to that opinioun) the idea or figure conceived in imagination of a perfect commune weale, and of a perfect king, and of a perfect Oratour are conteined: so is it also of a perfect Courtier.
>
> (Hoby's translation, London, Dent 1928, p. 13)

Thus Castiglione through those names, Plato, Xenophon, Marcus Tullius, expresses his intention to write a handbook teaching how to achieve self-knowledge and mastery on oneself (*Enkrateia,* or *continentia, temperantia*), i.e. self-control, which is the very condition for the government of others. One must immediately remember that passage in *The Book of the Courtier* where the general strategy of the book is covertly proclaimed through the metaphor of the bitter medicine in a cup anointed "about the brimme with some sweet licour" (p. 265; Castiglione IV, x). Thus Castiglione's insistence on the "living art," on the various aspects of life-craft, must be there in order to make another message pass regarding an extremely hard to obtain and hard to practice mastery over oneself and one's own desires and passions. *Dolce vita, savoir vivre,* the *ars vivendi,* the *grazia* and *leggiadria,* as the binary warranty of social harmony, of *harmonia mundi* are there for the very same strategical reasons. Mastery of oneself, self-control, and the stoic mask of impassibility, all refer to a kind of every-day life-training, shaping the very "fourm" of life. "Fourm" is the very basic condition of harmony, the utopian principle inspiring the whole architecture of the self, of society, the State, and the *ars regia* with which the political subject, the politician, the one who aspires to become the *kybernetes,* the gubernator, the statesman, must totally coincide. Harmony, being the principle, and the end of it all, is the very "fourm" so hard to obtain and only at the price of a rigorous self-discipline.

The second important point generally neglected on reading and interpreting *The Book of the Courtier,* is that sort of cover illustration, the representation of the *exemplum* of the perfect gentleman, the paradigm the reader is referred to, the bitter medicine to be swallowed, represented by the unforgettable portrait of Duke Guidubaldo in contrast with the portrait of Duke Federigo, his father, the very aristocratic emblem of success and of greatness, both in military and civil life, with great battles won, and the castle of Laurana built in Urbino as the great *memento* of Federigo's passage in life. Guidubaldo, instead, was born under an ill star: a noble and promising nature tried in such an unlucky life:

> Before Duke Guidubaldo was xx. yeares of age, he fell sicke of the goute, the which increasing upon him with most bitter paines, in a short time so nummed him of all his members, that he coulde neither stand on foote, nor move himself. And in this manner was one of the best favoured, and towardliest personages in the world, deformed and marred in his greene age.

And everything Guidubaldo "took in hande," "came always to ill successe" in spite of Guidubaldo's "most wise counsaile" and "invincible courage." However, "never virtue yielded to fortune" and Guidubaldo, "despising her stormes," had "great dignitie and estimation among all men; in sicknesse, as one that was sounde, and in adversitie, as one that was most fortunate." Of course Castiglione's "sprezzando" – translated in Hoby's as "despising!" (rightly enough here, while "sprezzatura," Castiglione's *virtus virtutum,* elsewhere in Hoby's is "a certain recklessness" which only partially translates the Italian word) – "sprezzando fortuna," scorning luck, anyhow is Castiglione's first *stigma* characterizing both the courtier and the *donna di palazzo,* the lady, as people of quality. And Guidubaldo is the example of a heroic "sprezzatura" taken as life's golden rule, and self-fashioning discipline.

What is being discussed in Guidubaldo's "cover" portrait is the very principle of any self-fashioning and *epimeleia heauton (cura sui),* that is *fortitudo animi contra fortunam,* impassibility in mishap, as the very ethic principle of "sprezzatura." Castglione's word is translated in Hoby's as "a certain recklessness" which is the very source of all grace,

grace being the very "fourm" of aristocratic life and the condition of harmony. But the key of all this is to be found in IX, xi, when Castiglione says that no expertise in any of the life-arts can be an end in itself: such a hard life-discipline with so much study required and such pain would make no sense unless turned to some superior end, and "in a man of estimation rather to be dispraised than commended" (p. 261, IX, xi):

> The ende therefore of a perfect Courtier ... is to purchase him, by the meane of the qualities which the Lordes have given him in such wise the good will and favour of the Prince ... that he may breake his minde to him, and always enforme him franckly of the truth of every matter meete for him to understand, without feare of perill to displease him ... to disswade him from every ill purpose, and to set him in the way of virtue.
>
> (p. 261, IX, xi?)

Thus the "good end" of all the assembling of all traits of the model of the superior man, that *speculum principis* through the *encheiridion militis*, becomes the definition of the perfect state and of the perfect "prince," and "sprezzatura" is not only dissimulation, a *facies*, a mask, a *persona* with more than the suspicion of hypocrisy used as a political tool for success in life; "sprezzatura" is a *habitus* of indifference to oneself in the light of some superior end to be looked for in the architecture of the state.

Other discipline books on life *tékhnai* were produced in England, frequently as translations from Italian. Monsignor della Casa's *Galateo of Manners and Behaviours* was translated by Robert Peterson and published in 1576. In 1581 George Pettie (1548–89) translated into English the first part of Stefano Guazzo's *The Civile Conversation*, probably through Gabriel Chappuy's French version, published that same year, with corrections and addenda suggesting Pettie's reading of the 1580 Venetian edition of Guazzo's book. The second part was translated in 1586 by Bartholomew Young 1560–1612).[11]

No Renaissance printed English translation of Machiavelli's *Il principe* is known to exist; however, semi-clandestine manuscript translations of the book were circulating in England long before Edward Dacres's 1640 version.[12] If Castiglione's *The Book of the Courtier* is a posthumous book, in its own way Machiavelli's *The Prince* too must be "posthumous" and a kind of *Trauerarbeit*, of "grief work" for some vanished world. It was written, as it were, in some empty space left by the disappearing of that world, with the end of the Republic of Florence and Machiavelli's farewell to his political career as the State Secretary of the Florentine Republic. On reading Machiavelli this must be kept in mind together with the late Quattrocento Italian politically fragmented situation of mercenary troops and consequent endless war. Machiavelli's book must not be read as a handbook of perennial political philosophy but as a product of a given historical situation. Machiavelli's outspokenness must not be taken as the very truth of things. On the contrary, reality and truth were a much more complicated matter than the usual Machiavellian (not Machiavelli's) utilitarian formula reducing all questions *in primam figuram*. This, of course, is not what Machiavelli meant. In 1513 the former State Secretary of the Florentine Republic had been imprisoned, tortured, and heavily fined – a thousand florins – under the charge of plotting with Agostino Capponi against the Medici family who were in power again. In 1513 he was released, and exiled at San Casciano, where he had some lands. He started writing *I discorsi sulla prima Deca di Tito Livio*, but the projected book was interrupted; another idea became more urgent, *Il Principe*, the "opuscolo," *De Principatibus*, was announced as finished in Machiavelli's famous letter to Vettori (December 10, 1513). Be that as it may – composition dates cover a period from 1510 to 1520 – Machiavelli's book began to circulate, and by 1532 it had already acquired a fame, as is shown by Agostino Nifo's 1523 plagiaristic Latin translation *De Regnandi Peritia* (the first Latin translation is dated 1560, by Silvestre Teglio or Silvestro Tegli, an Italian Protestant, and was published in Basel). However, the circulation of the "opuscolo" found obvious difficulties. In Catholic countries it became an entry in the 1559 first *index librorum prohibitorum* on account of its devilish atheism and obvious lack of any ethical feeling; in reformed countries it was considered the *instrumentum diabolicum* of popery and was generally known through Gentillet's *Contre-Machiavel* (*Discours sur les moyens de bien gouverner*, 1576), even though it is true that it could be found not only in the Latin translation but also in Italian, published by John Wolfe in London, with an anonymous introduction (either by Ubaldini, or Jacopo Castelvetro); the first French translation (Jacques Gohory) was published in 1571; no edition of *The Prince* was published in Spain before the nineteenth century; the first German translation is dated 1692 (by Christian Albrecht von Lenz). The book was scandalous, no doubt, to all sects and confessions in Reformation-Counter-reformation Europe. And yet, one must say, what we seem to imagine as completely and astoundingly new in Machiavelli's *Prince*, as a matter of fact was no novelty at all. In the Italian fifteenth century we find the same kind of perspective in Alberti's *Theogenius*, as well as in his *Momus, sive de Principe*; Poggio Bracciolini in *De Infelicitate Principum*, had somehow already reversed a commonplace perspective.[13]

Both *The Courtier* and *The Prince* clearly belong to what we might also call Renaissance self-fashioning poetics inherited from the classic tradition. In Machiavelli too there is some superior end to be achieved through a strict life-discipline aimed at either the acquisition or the preservation of power, with the commonwealth stability considered as the ultimate good. Of course Machiavelli's book was read, or was also read in a strictly individual key in the early modernity he so powerfully contributed to shape. All such readings follow the logic of Shakespeare's "universal wolf" in *Troilus and Cressida* (Ulysses' speech in I.iii), as the *figura* of endless, insatiable greed in the world of ceaseless war *omnium contra omnes* (Hobbes' *Leviathan*). Thus *The Prince* could be read as a cynical breviary to personal success. Gabriel Harvey, for instance, a roper's son, who studied at Oxford and became professor of rhetoric there, is the example of the Elizabethan Italianate intellectual. In the 1590s he wrote a number of notes, comments, and *glossae*, as *Marginalia* to the books he read. In a comment to Erasmus' *Parabolae sive similia* we find the briefly and nervously drawn traits of a new-model man taken from Aretino and Machiavelli:

> A right fellow to practice in ye world: one that knowith fashions: & prettily spiced with the ye powder of experience & meetly well temperid with ye powder of Experience. So Machiauel, & Aretine knew fashions, and were acquainted with ye cunning of ye world. Mach. & Aretine were hot to lerne how to playe their partes, but were prettily beaten to ye doings of ye world- Mach & Aretine knew theyr lessons by hart & were hot so to seke how to vse ye wicked world, ye flesh, & ye Diuel. They had lernid cunning enowgh: and had seen fashions enowgh; and cowld and woold vse both, with aduantage enowgh. Two curtisans politiques … Vita, militia: vel togata vel armata. First cast to shoot right; then be suer to shoot

home ... Aime straight, draw home. Risoluto per tutto .... Angelus in sermonibus et consiliis. Furius in actionibus et negotiis.[14]

Harvey is commenting here on Machiavelli's idea of readiness, and quickness as the quintessence of political virtue in dealing with time, and Fortune. His model is twofold: Angelus and Furius. The latter is only part of the new model: quick decision, quick actions, since readiness is all, but the other face, or head of this two-headed man, is the Angelus who does word-work and is therefore the contemplative analytical part, while the Furius is the active part. This change in the use of the Christian common-place definition of the complementarity of contemplative and active life not only turns upside down the usual idea of what a *kybernetes* should be and become (I am referring of course to Elyot's *Boke Called the Governour*). It also moves the perspective from the collective to the individual point of view in the cynical key of self-knowledge as key to *la connaissance du monde*, not as an *instrumentum regni*, but as the key to personal success. Thus Machiavelli's strenuous self-discipline turn to the good end, i.e. the formation and preservation of a unitary State, can be read, in its utilitarianism, as a handbook of personal acquisitive interests and personal success in the thievish, violent, murderous business that is life. But the fact is the Machiavellian *ars regia*, the *techne politiké* aims not at the triumph of individualism. On the contrary, it seems to entail self-abnegation as life-discipline: not the triumph but, as it were, the annihilation of subjectivity, according to that form of stoic indifference to oneself we also find, surprisingly enough, in Castiglione's *Book of the Courtier*.

There was also an English production of books teaching some know-how, some *tékhné*. The most common books on the *thékhnai* were handbooks on rhetoric, the art of delivering speeches, or persuading through words, according to Cicero's *De Oratore*, not simply a book on Rhetoric, but a book on the *paideia*, the education of the *vir bonus* and of his models of thought, the way one was to think and then decide according to justice in the common perspective of many a Renaissance English rhetorician. Here is a list: Thomas Wilson (1524–81), *Rule of Reason* – seven editions between 1553 and 1593, *Arte of Rhetoric* (eight editions between 1553 and 1585), to Leonard Cox (1495–c.1549) *The Art or Craft of Rhetoric*, 1524, 1532); Richard Sherry (c.1506–c.1555), *A Treatise of Schemes and Tropes* (1550) and *A Treatise of the Figures of Grammar and Rhetoric*, 1555). All these books belong to the same pedagogic tradition also producing Roger Ascham's *The Schoolmaster*[15] (1515–68), written in the 1560s and posthumously published in 1570. These books exercised a long-lasting influence. We can mention also Richard Mulcaster's *The First Part of the Elementary, Which Entreateth Chefly of the Right Writing of our English Tongue* (1582); George Gascoigne's *Certain Notes of Instruction concerning the Making of Verse or Rime in English* (1575), Willam Webbe's *Discourse of Englishe Poetry* (1586); Thomas Campion's *Observations in the Art of English Poesy* (1602), Samuel Daniel's *Defense of Rime* (1603), George Puttenham's *Art of English Poesy* (1589), and John Harington's (1591) *Brief Apology of Poetry;* almost all of these books are indebted to Sidney's *Apology for Poetry* (1579–80).

Roger Ascham was educated at St. John's College, Cambridge, one of the centers of English humanism. A preceptor of Elizabeth, Ascham also became the Queen's Latin Secretary. *The Scholemaster* is much more than a Latin handbook; as a matter of fact through *exempla* that book is a life-craft manual teaching how to become a gentleman. *Toxophilus*, being an archery handbook, teaching a traditional English *téchne*, is also somehow an Italianate book, written in the same perspective of a discipline and "living art" handbook in the ancient stoic and platonic tradition. *Toxophilus* not only reminds one of Plato and Xenophon, it also chimes in with Castiglione's *Cortegiano*, as the life-discipline it means to teach is also the very source of grace, that *leggiadria* and *armonia* taught by Castiglione's, and by Elyot in *The Book called the Governour.*

Book III of Ascham's *Toxophilus* is dedicated to *comeliness*, according to the following principle: "For this I am sure, in learning all other matters, nothing is brought to the most profitable use, which is not handled after the most comely fashion." This principle – writes Ascham – belongs to the archer, as to the sword-fencer, to the cook, the artisan, the architect and the construction of any building. Archery is one and the same thing with life-discipline to be learnt from early childhood: "To shoote streyght is the leaste maysterie of all, yf a man order hym selfe thereafter in hys youthe," thus:

> I am sure the rules which I gaue you will neuer disceyve you, so that there shal lacke nothynge, eyther of hitting the marke alwayes, or elles verye nere shootynge, excepte the faulte be onely i youre owne selfe, which maye come II ways, eyther in hauing a faynt harte or courage, or elles in sufferynge your selfe ouer muche to be led with affections: if a mans mynde fayle hym, the bodye which is ruled by the mynd, can neuer do his duetie, yf lacke of courage were not, men myght do more mastries than they do.[16]

Thus we must remember the *Apology for Poetry* (1579? publ. 1595) where Sidney jokingly remembers Gian Pietro Pugliano, the Emperor's horse master at Vienna, to make the reader understand that tools and hands must never be confused. To Pugliano the horse was – says Sidney – the perfect exemplum of what a knight and a gentleman ought to be, while to Sidney discipline must not be an end in itself; it must be a tool for self-fashioning. Even poetry, writing, artistic *operari* as end in themselves, and as any other discipline, horse-riding included, would be mere vanity, while they ought to be life-shaping tools on the background of Sidney's religiosity. Fulke Greville (1554–1628), Sidney's good friend, in his *The Life of the Renowned Sir Philip Sidney*, writes for his friend a sort of epitaph explaining much of Sidney's idea of what writing, prose, or poetry, stand for:

> The truth is his ende was not writinge, even while he wrott; nor his knowledge moulded for tables or schooles, but both his witt, and understandinge bent upon his heart, to make himselfe, and others, not in words, or opinioun; but in life and action good, and great, in which Architectonical Art he was a master, with so commaunding and yet equall wayes amongst men; that wheresoever he went, he was believed and obeyed; yea into what action soever he came last at the first, he became first at the last; the whole manageing of busines, not by usurpation of voyolence, but (as it were) by right and aknowledgement fallinge into his hands, as into an naturall center.[17]

Of course not all *tékhnai* books show the kind of perspective we find in Ascham and in Sidney. There was a copious production of Italian books on sword-fencing, and horse-riding with no transcendental ambitions. Italians were masters in the arts of arms – they taught rapier and sword-fencing also in London, and wrote manuals, such as Vincentio Saviolo (*Vincentio Saviolo His Practice*, London, John Wolf, 1595; the second part of the book is a translation of Girolamo Muzio's *Il duello*, Venezia, Giolito, 1551), and Giacomo Di Grassi (*Di Grassi, His True Art of Defence*, 1594, London, at the Sign of Hand and Starr, 1594). Of course there was also an English fencing school represented by George Silver who wrote *Paradoxes of Defense*, published by Edward Blunt in 1599. Skill in sword, dagger, and rapier fencing was not only an art any man of quality was supposed to know and practice; it was first of all a necessity for any gentleman in everyday life and a question of honor, if not of mere survival.

Another traditionally very relevant manly *téchne* was horsemanship. Horse-riding, of course, was also symbolically a relevant aspect of social life as it referred to what any man of quality was supposed to be, a knight, which does not translate the Italian *cavaliere*, or the French *chevalier*, but which implies the same symbolical relevance as any man of quality was also a warrior, a *cavaliere*, a horse-soldier, a *bellator, miles* in Latin. The most famous Renaissance English book on horsemanship is Thomas Blundeville's translation of Federico Grisone's famous book on *Gli ordini di cavalcare*, Napoli, Giovanni Paolo Suganappo, 1551, translated as *The Arte of Riding and Breaking greate Horses*, London, William Seres, 1560. Blundeville is also the author of his own book on horsemanship, *The Four Chiefest Offices Belonging to Horsemanship*, London, William Seres, 1580. Grisone was the first yet not the only expert in horsemanship; other important Italian manuals on *ars equitandi* were Claudio Corte's *Il cavallarizzo*, Venezia, Giordano Zilletti, 1562, and Pasquale Caracciolo, *La Gloria del cavallo*, Venezia, Gabriel Giolito de' Ferrari, 1566. No doubt Italian horse masters were generally considered the best. People of Quality throughout Europe knew the names of Cesare Fiaschi (*Trattato dell'imbrigliare, atteggiare e ferrare cavalla, 1556*); of Claudio Corte, who was the Horse Master at Queen Elizabeth's court; of Giovanni Pietro Pugliano, the Emperor's Horse Master in Vienna, mentioned by Sidney in his *Defence of Poesie;* and last but not least Giovan Battista Pignatelli who kept a famous horse-riding school in Naples and had the universal renown of the master of masters,

The "living art," however, was much more than archery, sword/rapier fencing, and horsemanship; it was even more than court life, or politics, if one considers the religious version of it as the *imitatio Christi* tradition, in all the different versions of it we find in Renaissance Literature, such as Erasmus' books dedicated to court life (*Enkeiridion militis christiani*) and to the education of the Prince (*Institutio Principis Christiani*). What may appear today to be the most important of all *artes*, the *tékhne politiké* divergently treated in Castiglione's *Libro del Cortigiano*, and in Machiavelli's *Il Principe*, in the English version became Sir Thomas Elyot's *The Book called the Governour* (1531), not a book on politics, really, but a book on ethics, addressed to those entrusted with the practical, local government of the country at the King's service, with a particular insistence on truth, loyalty, kindness, and, of course, harmony seen as the ideal form of social life allegorized in the movements of a country dance. Elyot names Castiglione (whose *Cortegiano* had been printed for the first time two years before in 1528) and Erasmus as his antecedents, and, of course, other books might be mentioned such as, for instance, Cicero's *De Oratore*, or Quintillian's *Institutio oratoria*. As a matter of fact, his sources seem to be looked for in Francesco Patrizzi's *De regno et regis institutione*, printed in Paris the same year as Erasmus' *De Institutio Principis Christiani* in 1519. Patrizzi's *De Regno* had been abridged in English by Richard Robinson and printed in London by Thomas Marshe in 1576.

Queen Elizabeth was a cosmopolitan polyglot. She spoke and wrote French, Italian, Spanish, Flemish, German, Greek, and Latin. She translated from Latin Horace's *De*

Arte poetica, Boethius' *De Consolatione philosophiae*, and, from Italian, Petrarch's *Il trionfo dell'Eternità*.[18] Elizabethan London too spoke and read languages – not only Latin and Italian fashionable authors but also a quantity of French and Spanish books were translated.[19] London was a somewhat cosmopolitan cultural crossroads whose growing book market daily needed new entries – the classics, of course.[20] In 1558 Richard Tottel also published Grimaldi's translation of Cicero's *Three Bookes of Dueties, to Marcus His Sonne*; Henry Billingsley translated Euclides in 1570;[21] Thomas Phaer (1510–60) published his translation of nine cantos of Virgil's *Eneyde* between 1554 and 1562. The translation of Virgil's poem was completed by Thomas Twyne (1543–1616) in 1573; Twyne is also the translator of a very important book by Petrarch, *De remediis utriusque fortunae, Phisique against Fortune* (1579); Arthur Golding (1536–1605) published his translation of Ovid's *Metamorphoses* between 1565 and 1567; Thomas Drant (1540–78) translated *Horace's Satires, Epistles and Art of Poetry* between 1566 and 1567; George Chapman (1559–1634) translated Homer's *Iliad* (1598–1611) and *Odyssey* (1614). All of Seneca's tragedies that had so strongly influenced the Italian revival of political Tragedy in Italian early Renaissance and had been translated by Lodovico Dolce and published in 1560 by Sessa in Venice, were metrically translated also in English between the late 1550s and 1560s by Jasper Heywood (1535–98), John Studley (1545?–90?), Thomas Newton (1542–1607), Thomas Nuce (†1617). All these translations were collected by Thomas Newton in *Seneca His Tenne Tragedies* in 1581. This book was of the utmost importance in the development of English drama in the Elizabethan Age.[22] Plutarch's *Bioi paralleloi* were translated by Thomas North (1535–1604) from Amyot's French version in 1579, with a number of reprints and re-editions until 1603; William Warner (1558–1609) translated all of Plautus in the 1590s, even though his only surviving translation is *Maenechmi* (1595); Richard Bernard (1548–1641) published *Flowres of Terence* in 1598; Philemon Holland (1552–1637) published his version of Plutarch's *Moralia* in 1603; in 1601 he had already published Plinius' *Natural History* in 1601, Svetonius's *Lives of the Twelve Caesars* in 1606, and Xenophon's *Cyropaedia* in 1632.

The most important Tudor collection of poetry, the *Tottel's Miscellany*, was published in 1557. It included Wyatt's and Surrey's translations and imitations of Petrarch. Much of the Elizabethan Petrarch is inscribed in that book, a bestseller of the age, also containing the poems of the early Tudor period, Wyatt, Surrey, Nicolas Grimaldi, Thomas Norton, Thomas Vaux, and also anonymous verse, all of them exercising a powerful impulse on the renewal of English letters. However, the English Petrarch owes much to France and is often translated from French as happens in John Sowthern's *Pandora* (1584), in Spenser's Du Bellay, and in all the "minor lutenists" mentioned by Jusserand a long time ago.[23]

Be it as it may, Petrarch's *Canzoniere* was fully translated into English only in the nineteenth century. However, Petrarch was popular in England not only through Wyatt's and Surrey's translations and imitations. Thomas Watson's (1555–92) *Hekatompathia* (1582), printed by John Wolfe, also contains a number of both English and Latin translations, and of imitations from Petrarch,[24] together with *canzoni* and *strambotti* from Serafino Aquilano, Ariosto, Ronsard, Teocrito, Orazio, Spenser, and Du Bellay. However, Petrarch's most frequently translated work in the English Renaissance is *I Triumphi*, translated into English for the first time in 1550 by Henry Parker Lord Morley (1486–1556) – *The Triumphes of Francis Petrarcke* (we have only the second 1554 edition). *I Triumphi* were also translated by William Fowler (1560–1612) in 1587;[25] *Il Trionfo della morte* was beautifully translated into *The*

Triumph of Death by Mary Sidney[26] in the late 1590s. The popularity of *I Triumphi* is also important when one comes to a consideration of the spiritualization process of the Sequence sonnet. The very paradigm of this is represented by the twenty-six sonnets of Anne Locke's *A Meditation of a Penitent Sinner*, published in 1560 and bound in one volume with the translations of a number of Puritan-cut sermons. Each of the sonnets in the sequence is an illustration of one verse in King David's *Psalm 51.*[27] In 1595 Henry Locke, probably Anne's son, published two sonnet sequences (some 200 sonnets), reprinted in 1597 together with his translations of the *Psalms* and of the *Quehlet* (*Ecclesiastes … Whereunto are Annexed Sundrie Sonets of Christian Passion*).

Of course not only religious texts were translated. Boccaccio's *Boke which is entitled Philocopo* was translated by an anonymous H.G in 1566; *Amorous Fiammetta* was translated in 1587 by R. Young; Ariosto's *Orlando furioso* was memorably translated by John Harington (1561–1612) "in English Heroical Verse" in 1591;[28] in 1594 Richard Carew (1555–1620) published five cantos of Tasso's *La Gerusalemme Liberata* under a new title: *Godfrey of Bulloigne or the Recoverie of Hierusalem;* under the same title all of Tasso's great poem was translated in 1600 by Edward Fairfax (1575–1635).[29] Among Robert Tofte's (1562–1619) translations from French and Italian, there are three satires by Ariosto (1597) and the following year three cantos from Book the first of Boiardo's *L'Orlando innamorato*. Tasso's *Aminta* (1573, published 1580) and Guarino's *Il pastor Fido* (1590), instead, were published directly in Italian by John Wolfe in 1591 and contributed to the Arcadian fashion both in prose writing (Sidney's *Old* and *New Arcadia*) and in drama.

If the classic and Italian models were important for English culture, London's book trade was also open to cosmopolitan, fashionable, mainly French, yet also Spanish influences.[30] Thomas Danett's (1608) translation of the *Mémoires de Philippe de Commines* (1565, published 1596) and John Florio's[31] (1553–1625) memorable translations of Montaigne's *Essays* (1603) are important dates in English cultural history. However, the print industry acquired a tremendous importance in the context of the Reformation/Counter-reformation doctrinal and theological polemos, and also of armed wars opposing Catholic against Protestant forces (the wars of Religion in France, the eighty years' war in the Netherlands, both with the English intervention on the Protestant side). On the Protestant side particular importance must be given to *Les discours politiques et militaires* (1587) by François de la Noue – an important name in Protestant culture and a great captain during the French wars. De la Noue's book was registered by *Stationers' Company* in 1587 as *Politic and Martial Discourses*, yet it was published only in 1594 in Joshua Sylvester's translation as *The Profit of Imprisonment* (the book had been written by de la Noue in the years of prison in Spain). Arthur Golding, the great translator of Ovid's *Metamorphoses*,[32] in 1587 published his translation of *La vérité de la Religion* by Philippe Du Plessis Mornay. Philip Sidney had translated a first part of that book before being killed in the Netherlands in 1586. His sister, Mary Sidney (1561–1621), in 1592 went on with her brother's project and translated Philippe Du Plessis Mornay's other book, *Discours de la vie et de la mort* (1576) under the title of A *Discourse of Life and Death.* Also *La Semaine ou la création du Monde*, Guillaume Du Bartas's poem (1578) was translated into English by Joshuah Sylvester (1563–1618) and published in 1607.

However, French culture was important not only from the point of view of the religious debate. There was also a French influence on literary taste and also on social life. English Petrarchanism in the Elizabethan period, in the second half of the sixteenth century, is often filtered by French culture. Edmund Spenser translates Joachim Du Bellay's *Regretz* into his English *Complaints* (1591) also containing *Visions of Petrarcke* (a translation of canzone CCCXXIII from Petrarch's *Canzoniere* which Spenser probably took from Marot), and the English translations of Du Bellay's *Les antiquitez de Rome* (1558, *The Ruins of Rome*), also including *Visions of Du Bellay* – the translation of fifteen sonnets and of *Le Songe* already printed and published by John Van der Noodt in 1569 (*a Theatre wherein be represented as wel the miseries and calamities that folow the voluptuos wordlings and also the greate joyes and pleasures which the faithful do enjoy … devised by S. John Vander Noodt*).

Spain in Elizabethan eyes was of course the Spain of the *Leyenda negra* of those years, the Spain England was at war with, and not only for religious questions but also for more substantial reasons, i.e. the control of the Atlantic routes to America in the decisive fight not for European but for what was to become world hegemony. Yet Spain was not only the Spain of *la Invencible armada* and of the terror-spreading cruelness of the *tercios*, the long peaks of the imperial fanterie. It was also the literary Spain of moral philosophers, of *picaros*, and knights. *El reloj de principes* (1529) by Antonio de Guevara (a sort of compendium of Marcus Aurelius's *Ta eis eauton* (*To himself*) was translated in 1534 and published in 1546 by John Bourchier Lord Berners, and in Thomas North's new translation (1535–1604), *The Diall of Princes* in 1557. *La vida de Lazarillo de Tormes* (1554), the beginning of the picaresque tradition, was translated into English by David Rowland of Anglesey (*The Pleasant History of Lazarillo de Tormes*, published in 1576); the first edition is lost and we have only the 1596 edition and, of course, the series of seventeenth-century editions). Bartholomew Young (1577–1621?) translated Montemayor's *Diana* in 1598. Anthony Munday[33] (1560?–1633), a very eclectic writer, playwright, and poet, translated a number of Spanish chivalry books from the French version, the very Don Quixote's library one might say (*Amadis de Gaula*: 1589 books 1 and 2 printed by Edward Allde, and 3 to 5 by John Wolfe, complete edition in 1618–19; *Palmerin* in 1588, *Primaleon of Greece* in 1596; *Don Belianis of Greece* di Antonio Fernandez (1547) in 1598). The first part of Cervantes's *Don Quijote* was translated by Thomas Shelton in 1605 and the second part in 1615; the first part was printed in 1612 and the second in 1620 by Blount & Barrett.[34]

Whatever might be the importance of French books, whatever the fascination of the powerful enemy, Spain, the Italian cultural model was as culturally hegemonic in Elizabethan England as *le modèle italien* was in contemporary France.[35] William Painter (1540–94) in *The Palace of Pleasure* published in 1566, with a second edition by T. Marsh in 1575, translated and adapted stories from ancient and contemporary authors (Bandello, Boccaccio, Ser Giovanni Fiorentino, Giovanni Francesco Straparola, Margherita di Navarra, Giovan Battista Giraldi Cinthio, Erodotus, Plutarch, Aulus Gellius, Elianus, Livius, Tacitus, Quintus Curtius). Painter was a sort of reference book for Shakespeare who found there plots for *Romeo and Juliet, Timone d'Atene, All's Well that Ends Well*), for Beaumont and Fletcher (*The Triumph of Death*), and John Webster (*The Duchess of Malfi*). One year after the publication of Painter's book, another collection of thirteen stories translated from Boisteau and Belleforest's French translation of eighteen of Bandello's *Novelle* was published by Geoffrey Fenton (c.1539–1608) in *Tragical Discourses*. As to Boccaccio, the first English translation of the whole *Decameron*, attributed to John Florio, was published only in 1620 and was based not on the Florentine text but on Antoine de Maçon's (1545) French translation, which the English translator expurgated of all "obsceneness." Yet, indeed, Boccaccio's major work had already been ransacked and many of the novellas translated and collected in works such as Painter's and Fenton's.[36] The Italianate model was not only shaped by Innocent Gentillet's reading of *The Prince* in his *Contre Machiavel* (1576), soon translated into Latin probably by Lambert Deneau.[37] That kind of character, the evil plotter, using words and working in the hiatus between what is and what seems to be was even more sinister, dark, and deadly when out of a political context, as happens for instance in Giovan Battista Giraldi Cinzio's *L'Alfiere* (in *Hecatommiti*, 1565), as a model for Shakespeare's Iago in Othello, or in other Italian tales, novellas, and stories mixing love, sex, power, and political plots, revenge, and extreme violence where the image of Italy combined horror and fascination in a series of apocalyptical emblems of the corruption of innocence, with a devilish power principle of all-devouring greed.

Notes

1 Christopher Brooke and Roger Highfield, *Oxford and Cambridge* (Cambridge: Cambridge University Press, 1988); Victor Morgan, *A History of the University of Cambridge, 1546–1750* (Cambridge: Cambridge University Press, 2004).

2 See the online decree text: cam.ac.ok/cam/pdf/uk_1557_1.pdf. On the entire question see *Censorship and the Press*, eds. Cyndia Susan Clegg, Mark Goldie, Geoff Kemp, and Jason McEllyot (London: Pickering and Chatto, 1984), vol. I.

3 Edward Arber, *A Transcript of the Register of the Company of Stationers of London 1554–1640*, 5 vols. (London: prv. Pr., 1875–1894); W. W. Greg and E. Boswell, eds. *Records of the Court of the Stationers' Company 1576 to 1602* (London: The Bibliographical Society, 1930); William A. Jackson, ed. *Records of the Court of the Stationers' Company 1602–1640* (London: the Bibliographical Society, 1957). See *The Cambridge History of English and American Literature* (Cambridge: Cambridge University Press, 1907–21) eds. E. A. Ward et al., 1 vol. IV, and Chapter XVIII, *The Book Trade*, by H. G. Aldy (online ed. Bartleby.com); E. K. Chambers, *The Elizabethan Stage*, 4 vols. (Oxford: Clarendon Press), vol. 3, pp. 160–77, 186–89; Henry S. Bennett, *English Books and Readers* I: *1475–1557* (1952); 1558–1603 (1965) (Cambridge: Cambridge University Press); L. Ray Patterson, *Copyright in Historical perspective* (New York: Vanderbilt University Press, 1968); Cyprian Blagden, *The Stationers' Company 1403–1959* (Stanford, CA: Stanford University Press 1977); Elizabeth L. Eisenstein, *The Printing Press as an Agent of Change in Early Modern England*, 2 vols. (Cambridge: Cambridge University Press, 1979); Annabel Patterson, *Censorship and Interpretation. The Conditions of Writing and Reading in Early Modern England* (Madison: University of Wisconsin Press, 1984, repr. 1991).

4 Cit. by J. J. Jusserand, *A Literary History of the English People*, II (London: C. Fisher Unwin, 1906, 1926), p. 316.

5 On John Day see *The Cambridge History of English and American Literature*, IV, xviii, para. 15.

6 On J. F. John Foxe Mozley, *John Foxe and His* Book (London: SPCK, 1940); William Freeman, *Foxe's First Book of Martyrs and the Elect Nation* (London: Jonathan Cape, 1963).

7 Adolf Gerber, "All of the Five Fictitious Italian Editions of Writings of Machiavelli," *Modern Language Notes*, XXII (1907): 2–6, 129–35, 187–206; H. Sellers, "Italian Books printed in England before 1640," *The Library*, V (1924): 105–28; T. F. Crane, *Italian Social Customs of the Sixteenth Century and Their Influence on The Literatures of Europe* (New Haven, CT: Yale University Press, 1920); G. S. Gargano, *Scapigliatura Italiana* (Florence: La Nuova Italia, 1923). See, of course, Gordon Braden, Robert Cummings, and Stuart Gillespie, *The Oxford History of Literary Translations in English, vol 2, 1550–1660* (Oxford: Oxford University Press, 2010).

8 On Italian books printed in England see Harry Sellers, "Italian Books Printed in England before 1640," *The Library*, 4th series, 122–28.

9 See S. Bertelli and P. Innocenti, *Bibliografia machiavelliana* (Verona: Valdonega, 1979), p. LXII.

10 The second English edition was published in 1577 (in 1576 *Il Cortegiano* had been inscribed in the *Index librorum prohibitorum* by the Spanish Inquisition). Hoby is also the author of an autobiography, *The Travail and Life of Me*, ed. E. Powell (London: Camden Society, 1902), now online). On Hoby's famous translation and on the English fortune of the gentlemanly model proposed by Castiglione's book, see J. William Hebel, Hoyt H. Hudson and Francis R. Johnson, *Prose of the English Renaissance* (New York: Appleton-Century-Crofts, 1952), pp. 146–83; on Castiglione and Hoby see Edward Chaney, *The Evolution of the Grand Tour: Anglo-Italian Cultural Relations Since the Renaissance* (Oxford: Routledge, 2000); John Hale, *England and the Italian Renaissance*, ed. Edward Chaney (Oxford: Blackwell, 2005); Peter Burke, *Fortunes of the Courtier: The European Reception of Castiglione's Cortegiano* (London: Polity Press, 1995).

11 See *The Civile Conversation of M. Steeven Guazzo*, the first three books translated by George Pettie, 1581, and the Fourth by Barth. Young, 1586, with an introduction by Sir Edward Sullivan, 2 vols. (New York: AMS Press, 1967).

12 See Alessandra Petrina, *A Florentine Prince in Queen Elizabeth's Court*, in *The First English Translations of Machiavelli's Prince*, ed. Roberto De Pol (Amsterdam: Rodopi, 2010), pp. 83–115; and, by the same, *Machiavelli in the British Isles. Two Early Modern Translations of The Prince* (Farnham, UK: Ashgate, 2009).

13 See D. Quaglioni, *Il modello del principe Cristiano. Gli 'Specula Principum', fra Medioevo e prima età moderna*, in *Modelli nella storia del pensiero politico*, vol. I, saggi a cura di V. I. Comparato (Florence: Olschki, 1987), pp. 103–22.

14 G. Harvey, *Marginalia*, collected and ed. G. C. Moore Smith (Stratford-upon-Avon, UK: Shakespeare Head Press, 1913), p. 147. See also Napoleone Orsini, *Studi sul Rinascimento italiano in Inghilterra* (Florence: Sansoni, 1937), cap. IV; T. H. Jameson, *The Machiavellianism of Gabriel Harvey, PMLA*, 56 (1941): 645–56; H. Haydn, *The Counter-Renaissance* (New York: Scribner, 1950): (*Il Contro-Rinascimento* (Bologna: il Mulino, 1970) and *The Portable Elizabethan Reader* (New York: Viking, 1946), pp. 235–40.

15 Roger Ascham, *Whole Works, Life and Letters*, eds. J. A. Giles and E. Grant (London: Smith, 1865); L. V. Ryan, *Roger Ascham* (Stanford, CA: Stanford University Press, 1963); on Tudor treatises of rhetoric see *The Cambridge History of English and American Literature*, III (*Renaissance and Reformation*), xiv (Elizabethan Criticism, by George Saintsbury, xix, *English Universities, Schools and Scholarship in the XVI Century*, by W. H. Woodward (see para. 9–12: Wilson, Ascham, Mulcaster).

16 *Toxophilus*, online in archive.org, p. 164; see E. Peter, *Medine's Critical Edition* (Tempe, AZ: Arizona Center for Medieval Studies, 2002); J. K. Wilson, "*Toxophilus* and the Rules of Art," *Renaissance Quarterly*, 29, 9 (Spring 1976).

17 Mark Caldewell, ed. *The Prose of Fulke Greville* (New York: Garland, 1987), p. 13.

18 Janel Mueller and Joshua Scodel, *Elizabeth I: Translations 1544–1589*, 2 vols. (Chicago, IL: Chicago University Press, 2009).

19 See Gordon Braden, Stuart G. Gillespie and Robert Cummings, eds. *The Oxford History of Literary Translation*, 4 vol. (Oxford: Oxford University Press, 2010), vol. 2, 1550–1660.

20 See Stuart G. Gillespie, *English Translation and Classical Reception* (Oxford: Wiley & Blackwell, 2011), cap. 3; John Denton, "The Significance and Impact of Translations in the English Renaissance," in *Übersetzung, Translation, Traduction*, eds. H. Kittel, J. House and B. Schultze (Berlin: De Gruyter, 2007), vol 2. pp. 1389–96; James Winny, ed. and intro. *Elizabethan Prose Translation* (Cambridge: Cambridge University Press, 1960). (Hoby, *The Courtier*, 1561; Newton, Thomas, *The Touchstone of Complexions*, 1555, from Lemnius; William Aldington, *The Golden Ass* from Apuleius, 1566; Thomas Underdowne, *An Aethiopian History* from Eliodorus, 1569; North's Plutarch was established in 1579; *Lazarillo de Tormes* was translated by David Rowland in 1586.

21 See F. O. Matthiessen, *Translation, an Elizabethan art* (Cambridge, MA: Harvard University Press, 1931).

22 Evelyn Mary Spearing Simpson, *The Elizabethan Translations of Seneca's Tragedies* (Cambridge: Heffer, 1912); T. S. Eliot, "Seneca in Elizabethan Translations," "Shakespeare and the Stoicism of Seneca" (both published in 1927), gathered in *Essays on Elizabethan Drama* (New York: Harcourt Brace, 1956).

23 Jusserand, *A Literary History*, cit., II, p. 375; on Petrarch in England see Jackson Campbell Boswell and Gordon Braden, *Petrarch's English Laurels* 1475–1700 (Farnham, UK: Ashgate,

2012). This important reference lists and describes all translations and quotations from and of Petrarch in the period taken into consideration.

24 A. E. B. Coldiron, "Watson's *Hekatompathia* and Renaissance Lyric Translation," in *Translation and Literature*, 5, 1 (1996): 3–25. On Petrarch in England see Martin McLaghilin, Letizia Panizza and Peter Hainsworth, *Petrarch in Britain* (Oxford: Oxford University Press, 2007) (British Academy Publications online 2012).

25 On the Elizabethan fortune of *I Triumphi*, see Alastair Fowler, *Triumphal Forms: Structural Patterns in Elizabethan Poetry* (Cambridge: Cambridge University Press, 1970).

26 Frances Berkeley Young, ed. *Mary Sidney* (London: Nutt, 1912); Waller, G.F. ed. *The Triumph of Death and Other Unpublished Poems* (Salzburg: Salzburg Institute für Englische Sprache und Literatur, 1977); Margaret P. Hannay, Noel J. Kinnamon and Michael G. Brennan, *The Collected Works of Mary Sidney Herbert* (Oxford: Clarendon, 1998).

27 On Ann Locke's sequence, see Donatella Pallotti, *Tra sacro e profano*, in M. Domenichelli e D. Pallotti, eds. *Petrarca in Europa 1/2*, in *In forma di parole*, XXIV, IV, 3, tomo secondo, luglio-settembre 2004, pp. 465–66.

28 Townsend Rich, *Harington and Ariosto. A Study of Elizabethan Verse Translation* (Hew Haven, CT: Yale University Press, 1940); Selene Scarsi, *Translating Women in Early Modern England. Gender in the Elizabethan Versions of Boiardo, Ariosto and Tasso* (Farnham, UK: Ashgate, 2010).

29 See Kathleen M. Lea and T. M. Gang, '*Godfrey of Bulloigne*': *A Critical Edition of Edward Fairfax's Translation of Tasso's 'Gerusalemme Liberata', Together with Fairfax's Original Poems* (Oxford: Clarendon, 1981).

30 Charles Whibley, "The Book Trade," in *The Cambridge History of English and American Literature*, cit, IV, xviii, para 1. "The Translators"; F. O. Matthiessen, *Translation, an Elizabethan Art*; Julia S. Ebel, "A Numerical Survey of Elizabethan Translations," *The Library*, s5–xxii, 2 (1967): 93–103; C. B. Wright, "Translations for the Elizabethan Middle Class," *The Library*, sc–xiii, 3 (1932): 312–31; Helen Smith and Louise Wilson, *Renaissance Paratexts* (Cambridge: Cambridge University Press, 2011); Fred Schurink, *Tudor Translation* (London: Macmillan, 2011).

31 Frances Yates, *John Florio: The Life of an Italian in Shakespeare's England* (Cambridge: Cambridge University Press, 1934; repr. 1968); si veda anche Giovanni Saverio Gargano, *Scapigliatura italiana a Londra sotto Elisabetta e Giacomo* (Florence: Battistelli, 1923).

32 Louis Thorn Golding, *An Elizabethan Puritan: Arthur Golding, the Translator of Ovid's Metamorphoses ab, And also of John Calvin's Sermons* (1937) (Freeport, NY: Books for Library Press, 1971).

33 Tracey Hill, *Anthony Munday and Civic Culture* (Manchester, UK: Manchester University Press, 2004).

34 J. A. G. Ardila, "Traducción y receptión del Quijote en Gran Bretagna – 1612–1774," *Annales cervantinos*, XXXVII (2005): 253–65; on Elizabethan translation from Spanish see John Garrett Underhill, *Spanish Literature in the England of the Tudors* (New York: Macmillan, 1899).

35 Fernand Braudel, *Le modèle italien* (Paris: Arthaud, 1989); See the accurate catalogue edited by Soko Tomita, *A Bibliographcal Catalogue of Italian Books 1558–1603* (Farnham, UK: Ashgate, 2009), listing and describing 451 Italian books published in England during the Elizabethan age.

36 See, on this, Boccaccio, and *Decameron* in the title and names index of Soko Tomita's *A Bibliographical Catalogue of Italian Books Printed in England 1558–1603*, cit.

37 *Commentarium de Regno … adversus Nicolaum Machiavellum Florentinum* (Geneva, J. Stoer, 1577); the first printed translation is by Simon Patericke (1602). See Sidney Anglo, *Machiavelli, the First Century* (Oxford: Oxford University Press, 2005); A. Petrina, cit.; Michael Redmond, *Shakespeare, Politics, Italy* (Farnham, UK: Ashgate, 2009).

24 Anglo-Venetian networks

Paolo Sarpi in early modern England

Chiara Petrolini and Diego Pirillo

Introduction

In December 1607 the English Ambassador to Venice, Henry Wotton, managed to smuggle a portrait of Paolo Sarpi to London.[1] The portrait had been specially commissioned as a gift for King James I, who admired the Venetian friar and hoped to entice him to his court.[2] A scientist who numbered Galileo among his friends, and a prominent historian, philosopher, and politician, Sarpi became famous throughout Europe for his fierce defence of the independence of Venice against the pope's interference. His fame even crossed the Atlantic, given that a copy of the English translation of his *Historia dell'interdetto* was part of the library of John Brewster, one of the Mayflower pilgrim fathers who founded the colony of Plymouth, Massachusetts.[3] Sarpi enjoyed even more notable success in England, where in the seventeenth century he was the most widely translated Italian author,[4] and where his works continued to be read, pondered, and praised in subsequent centuries: Francis Bacon, Thomas Hobbes, Thomas Browne, John Selden, John Milton, David Hume, Samuel Johnson, Bertrand Russell, Edward Gibbon, and Alfred North Whitehead were just some of his British admirers. It took very little time for copies of the painting depicting Sarpi, pen in hand, at work, to become collectors' items in the Republic of Letters. They could be seen on display in eminent places frequented by English society, from the king's palace to the libraries of Oxford and Cambridge to the sacristy of St. Paul's Cathedral, where John Donne was dean.

In Italy, however, the situation was very different, at least outside Venice. Just a few months before the portrait sent by Wotton arrived in England, on 5 January 1607 Pope Paul V excommunicated Sarpi and planned to have him burnt in effigy, in response to Sarpi's refusal to appear in Rome to explain himself and be subjected to an inquisitorial trial for alleged heterodoxy. In October of that same year, Sarpi was stabbed in the face on the bridge of Santa Fosca, by hired assassins said to have been encouraged by Rome. He recovered, but the scars remained, and Wotton was quick to have them added to the portrait being delivered to the English king. Indeed, James referred to the attack in his official speech marking the anniversary of the Gunpowder Plot, drawing a parallel between himself and the Venetian, both potential martyrs of the over-reaching power of the papacy.[5] The divergence between Sarpi's destiny inside and outside his homeland is reflected in the diffusion of his works. It is adequate to note that of the 186 editions of his writings published between 1619 and 1799, only 11 were printed in Venice.[6] The manuscript sheets of the most famous of these, the *Istoria del concilio tridentino*, were

DOI: 10.4324/9781315612720-27

transported from Venice to London divided into 14 folders disguised as collections of madrigals.[7] This risky underground trade involved merchants, booksellers, archbishops, and ambassadors and continued for months until, in spring 1619, the *Istoria* was published in Italian by the King's printer, John Bill. The precious velvet-bound volume appeared in folio format and was part of the most prestigious publishing series in the kingdom, which included nine texts deemed to be the cornerstones of James I's cultural policy. Shortly afterwards, the *Istoria* was translated into Latin, English, and French, and was to become a key work of modern historiography.[8]

The reasons for Sarpi's changeable fortunes in Italy are many and complex. The first and greatest obstacle to the dissemination of his thinking was the censorship imposed by the Congregation of the Index, which banned people from reading his works, on pain of excommunication. All writings by and about Sarpi were still included in the list of banned publications in the last edition of the *Index Librorum Prohibitorum* (1945). Along with censorship, Sarpi's controversial legacy is well described by the dissensions around his burial. On Sarpi's death in 1623, the Roman Curia let it be known that it would not tolerate the erection of even a stone bearing his name. Moreover, finding it intolerable that Fra Paolo, a man who had been excommunicated, had been buried in a church, they demanded on more than one occasion to have the coffin removed and dumped in a common grave. When Sarpi's body was found, by chance, during restoration work on the Servite church in 1722, Pope Innocent XIII expressed his wish that the body be buried along with others without distinguishing the spot or marking it with his name, so that, over time, his memory would fade and be lost forever. A letter from one of the pope's informers in Venice says that it was necessary to "bury that memory", "incinerate it", but to do so "without clamour".[9] Even as late as 1942, the Holy Office in Rome took provisions against three Servite Friars who had written on Sarpi's ideas of the relations between Church and State. In spite of the anathema, the memory of the Servite friar survived, but was – and still is – the subject of controversy and dispute, and not just in terms of the problem of religious orthodoxy in the post-Tridentine church.

Another obstacle to Sarpi's reception was the more general difficulty, first for the Venetian leading class and then for Italian culture as a whole, of describing such a complex individual who devoted his life to what had always been a thorny problem for Italy: the relationship between Church and State. Indeed, the Venetian friar has never been a "neutral" subject for study. Like Niccolò Machiavelli or Giordano Bruno, he has become a symbol to be manipulated, to be made into a martyr or a hypocrite, as the case may be, while at the same time losing sight of his true features. Only in recent years has a more balanced and less partisan critical analysis emerged, though Sarpi remains a historiographic problem that has yet to be resolved. But how to explain the extraordinary success he enjoyed in England? And how to explain Sarpi's own interest in that country, perhaps more than in any other? Although he was in some respects a unique figure, an anomaly in the Italian context and impossible to pigeonhole, to answer these questions we need to set the author within the political, religious, and cultural reality of his times, at the centre of the international tensions and radical theological and political crisis that was sweeping Europe and during which a mutual interest was sparked between Venice and London.

New science and religious scepticism

Born in Venice in 1552, Sarpi entered the monastic order of the Servites when he was still only a boy. Having distinguished himself by his intelligence and prodigious memory, he gained his doctorate in theology from Padua and rapidly became the procurator general of his Order. Sarpi spent three years in Rome but, disgusted by the lifestyle of the Curia, he decided to return to Venice for good to devote his time entirely to scientific study. Sarpi's interests and skills were incredibly broad in scope – indeed, encyclopaedic. His studies encompassed anatomy, optics, mathematics, philosophy, chemistry, mechanics, and astronomy, in each of which he reached the highest level. An active figure in the scientific revolution, he earned the admiration of his contemporaries, who viewed him as "the miracle of our times" or, in the words of Henry Wotton, "the most deep and general scholar of the world". Galileo believed that no one in Europe could surpass the friar in mathematical studies. And in fact it was with Galileo, from the roof of his monastery, that in 1609 Sarpi looked to the skies through the telescope that he himself had helped to build.[10] Sarpi's interest in the English world can be traced back to those years of febrile scientific research, when he read and admired the British scientist William Gilbert's work on magnetism, *De Magnete.* His insatiable desire for knowledge led him to frequent not just learned circles, like those of Morosini on the Grand Canal and Vincenzo Pinelli in Padua, but also the workshops of foreign merchants, where he had them recount the stories and customs of distant lands and caught up with the political news.[11]

Sarpi's *Pensieri*, his private booknotes, bear witness to this intense intellectual life and to the radical originality of Sarpi's meditations. In his notes on the subjects of morality, religion, and knowledge, which combine a reading of ancient and modern writers, we can discern a sceptical wisdom, a way to find an intact space of internal freedom through systematic and solitary work on the self.[12] In an openly relativistic, materialistic, and mechanistic framework in which there is no substantial difference between human beings and animals, Sarpi examines the historic religions as though he were dealing with natural phenomena, describing them as human constructs born of physiological necessity without any providentialist vision. The exercise of doubt is placed at the centre of the cognitive process, and in one of his more extreme observations Sarpi even claims that if men were not intrinsically ill, they would live happily without laws and without God, because both the State and religion are "medicines", not "food".[13] But only the wise man may aspire to such independence; for the others, a "supreme power" is indispensable. It would be fruitless to seek confirmation of these opinions in the works published by Paolo Sarpi: indeed, many of them openly contradict the thinking that runs through his public discourse, even though a subterranean and non-linear continuity exists. The *Pensieri*, which were the focus of the twentieth-century historiographic debate on Sarpi, were not just a proof of his multi-faceted nature and the profundity of his thinking but also provided a theoretical horizon against which to set his enigmatic figure in sharp relief, the better to understand it. It is in these notes, for example, which remained unpublished for centuries, that we can seek a key to Sarpi's enthusiasm for the work of Francis Bacon, whose work he promoted in the Italian translations.

The Venetian interdict

Everything changed in the spring of 1607, when the solitary intellectual who theorised in his notes on abstention from all forms of public action became a leading actor in Venetian public life. The man who pointed to Socrates and his simplicity as the model of the wise man, now wore the garments of the political counsellor in his day-to-day civil commitment. What had happened that caused Sarpi, at 54 years of age, to change his way of life so visibly? He himself explained the change using the concept of "opportunity", without which, he wrote, "man can do nothing". A special juncture in history – the clash between the Republic of Venice and Pope Paul V – convinced him to enter the fray and show his hand publicly. The international diplomatic situation, and the internal political situation in Venice, which saw a group of his friends – combative patricians known as the party of "young men" – in power, made the possibility of a profound change a credible possibility, in a great political and religious reform; a change to which Sarpi devoted the rest of his life.[14] It is in this period of change that the mutual interest between Sarpi and the English world must be set.

The history of relations between Venice and Rome had not been without friction and tension, but when Camillo Borghese became pope, taking the name Paul V, and Leonardo Donà became Doge, conditions deteriorated. A request arrived from Rome, to release two clergymen found guilty of murder and rape and imprisoned by the Venetian court, and to hand them over to the Church's own court. Rome also asked Venice to repeal a law prohibiting the construction of churches in the Venetian state without first seeking and obtaining the authorisation of the Senate. The Venetian government refused to give way on any point and to defend its position on 28 January 1606 appointed Paolo Sarpi as *consultore in iure* (that is, a juridical and theological adviser). The pope excommunicated the Doge and laid an Interdict on the entire Veneto region. The Interdict remained in force for a year, but its consequences were much longer lasting. It was a powerful weapon that hit the entire population, because it suspended all religious functions and prevented not just the Mass but also marriages and funerals, and burials on consecrated ground from being celebrated. In other words, it struck at the very heart and the rhythm of the community's daily life.[15] It was Sarpi who provided the Republic with the legal and theological justifications for resistance against Rome, with the result that the Venetian clergy were forced to ignore the pope's order and continue with their normal liturgical functions. The Company of Jesus, which refused to follow the Senate's dictates, was expelled from Venetian territory and was to return only after 50 years had passed.

And so began the Interdict crisis, an event of extraordinary resonance which, as Sarpi wrote to the French jurist Jacques-Auguste De Thou, "kept the entire world suspended" and introduced a "principle of freedom"[16] to Italy. The clash between Rome and Venice was sensational from a publishing perspective too. In just a few months a flood of writings was produced: over 150 pamphlets in 300 editions, to which should be added countless lampoons, graffiti, hand-written pamphlets, and sermons that circulated on both sides. This "war of writings" marked an important chapter in the history of political-religious relations in Europe. It was Sarpi's view that state and church should proceed on two parallel roads that would never meet; they should be kept clearly distinct to avoid generating a monstrous confusion that would weaken politics and distort religion. Sarpi immediately realised the possible theoretical implications of the battle against Rome and sought to transform the Interdict from a local judicial dispute into a pan-European discussion over the nature of temporal and spiritual authority.

Diplomatic relations between Venice and England dated from 1300 but had been interrupted during the reign of Elizabeth I as a result of the schism. It was James I who restored the relationship by appointing the aforementioned Henry Wotton, a cultivated art-lover and polyglot, as resident ambassador.[17] Wotton, who had studied at Oxford with the Italian jurist Alberico Gentili, arrived in Venice in September 1604 and was joined there by the chaplain, William Bedell, a theologian and moderate Calvinist. Bedell formed a close relationship with Sarpi and provided decisive input on his knowledge of the English world and the dissemination of his works in that country.[18] When we speak of Venice, it is vital to bear in mind the city's unique urban layout. The building housing the English embassy was located in the Cannaregio district, just steps away from the Servite monastery (which was destroyed during the French domination to create a vineyard and stables). Sarpi and Fulgenzio Micanzio entered and left that building twice a week, judging by the intelligence gleaned by the pope's informants and the report by the English traveller Thomas Coryat, who was Wotton's guest in 1608. The two friars were taking English lessons at the Embassy and practised translating along with Bedell, who had written a short grammar for them. Their interest was anything but anodyne and the texts selected for study anything but random. They included the *Book of Common Prayer*, *A Relation of the State of Religion* (to which Sarpi made some important additions), and the book by James I, *Triplex nodo, triplex cuneus. Or an Apology for the Oath of Allegiance.*[19] Years later, Micanzio drew on the knowledge acquired at this time to attempt a translation of an essay on superstition by Francis Bacon, omitted from the Italian edition.

Venice was, as we know, a cosmopolitan city *par excellence*. It was the setting purposefully chosen by Bodin as the place where the dialogue between seven wise men of different philosophical and religious backgrounds should take place in his *Colloquium heptaplomeres*. Coryat provides a good description of the variety to be found in the crowd thronging St Mark's Square, where "you may see many Polonians, Slavonians, Persians, Grecians, Turks, Jewes, Christians of all the famousest regions of Christendome, and each nations distinguished from another by their proper and peculiar habits".[20] But relations between the Venetian ruling class and the English community (relations that were in theory prohibited by a law banning the patricians from conversing with foreign ministers) were seen as cause for alarm in Rome, where fear was growing that Venice might become "another England". A fear, in other words, that the diplomatic dispute between the Serene Republic and the papacy might lead to a separation from the Church of Rome – a schism on Italian soil. Was there a real risk of that occurring?

There can be no doubt that James I was observing the situation closely as it developed and, viewing Venice as the "weakest link in the chain of Roman Catholicism",[21] encouraged the attempts to make a Protestant outpost of the city. An incessant stream of news flowed between Venice and London and, in his speeches to the Senate, Ambassador Wotton assured the Venetian government of his country's total support, including from the military point of view in the event of armed conflict. Sarpi recognised that during the years of the Interdict, and afterwards, the English had shown much greater solidarity towards Venice than had the French. He gave them credit for this in the *Istoria dell'Interdetto*, a book which William Bedell transcribed and brought with him to England, where he edited the Latin edition in 1626.[22] The English Embassy in Venice had become a clandestine workshop for dissident texts and ideas. The individuals who gravitated towards it, both English and Italian, did everything they could to encourage a definitive break with Pope Paul V. Probably at their impetus, sheets were published in London describing the strongly anti-Roman sermons that could be heard in the churches of the Italian city, and an overlap between the Venice of Donà and Sarpi and the England of James I was suggested with growing insistence. Here is Wotton again, in the letter accompanying the portrait of Sarpi mentioned earlier, describing the Venetian clergyman as "a sound Protestant, as yet in the habit of a friar", more similar "to Melanchthon than to Luther".[23]

To get to the roots of the special bond between Venice and London at the start of the seventeenth century, it is important to consider the chronological and ideological proximity between the Interdict and another event of historic import, the Gunpowder Plot: the thwarted attempt to blow up the English Parliament on 5 November 1605. In January 1606, the king issued an Oath of Allegiance obliging his Catholic subjects to swear loyalty to the Crown and deny the doctrine that legitimised the pope's excommunication of the king. This gave rise to a theological and political dispute with Pope Paul V that was crucial to the elaboration of the sovereignty theory of modern nation states. Like the Interdict, this debate too generated a multi-layered, many-voiced and international controversy, with an outburst of writing, a true "war of words and books" that was, however, no less "toilsome than a war of steel", as Sarpi wrote.[24] He followed each stage of the dispute closely, with the same attention with which the developments of the Interdict had been followed from London. Practically contemporaneous, the two episodes – the resistance to the Interdict and the Oath of Allegiance – were perceived by key protagonists as analogous and closely connected and marked the beginning of a close relationship between Venice and London. In this "Anglo-Veneto century" as it has been described,[25] England was a beacon for all those seeking a model of sovereignty that could emancipate them from what Sarpi called the *Totatus*, meaning the political, religious, and cultural hegemony of the post-Tridentine Roman Church. Sarpi was not alone in his interest in the English world. It was shared by many members of his circle, some of whom chose James I's England as their permanent or temporary homeland, without ever cutting their links with Venice. Instead, they created a true network in which books, men, and ideas circulated.

Unlike those associates, Sarpi never left Italy. He distrusted the unspecified religious disquiet and spiritual yearnings that drove his fellows to change church and country without taking into account the "effective reality" of things.[26] James I invited him three times to move to his court but three times received a firm but polite refusal in return. Although he had openly disputed the legitimacy of the Roman Church, which he deeply distrusted, for Sarpi leaving Venice was unthinkable. He did not openly embrace any reformed church, perhaps because the abstract and intellectual – almost Spinosian – religiosity that can be deduced from his thinking went beyond the very idea of "church". There can be no doubt that he studied the Church of England as a possible model for a national church emancipated from Rome, to be established in Venice.[27] He appreciated that church's attempt to keep its distance from the bitterest theological disputes, and its pragmatic approach to questions of doctrine and its simplification of worship. Above all, he saw the appeal of subordinating religious authority to the temporal power of the king and was fully convinced that a renunciation of coercive power by the church was a vital condition to halt the distortion of Catholicism that had been under way since the age of Constantine.

According to Sarpi, "papal tyranny" was the principal cause of the religious and political crisis in Europe. On this, all of his writings agree, from the private letters to the *consulti* officially read to the Senate. The "immense power" of the pope, for which no foundation could be found in Scripture, was the "Gorgon's head to be severed".[28] The Servite friar maintained that all of Christianity had the right and the duty to oppose what appeared to him to be, to all effects, a degeneration. For this reason, in one of his first official *consulti*, he submitted a proposal for a free and general council. The proposal was too provocative and radical to be espoused by the other councillors or by the Venetian government but received an enthusiastic welcome from James I, given that the conciliarist tradition was one of the key elements of the Stuart sovereign's kingdom.

Defending the Prince

In the end, a reconciliation with Rome prevailed and, thanks to the mediation of French diplomats, the crisis of the Interdict came to an end on 21 April 1607. This marked the end, too, of an experiment in liberty, a collective awakening of conscience, as Sarpi had defined it, often evoking an image of a state of sleep into which his fellow citizens risked falling as though by effect of powerful opiates. The pacification, however, was more apparent than real: "the fire had been covered, but not extinguished", wrote a disappointed – but certainly not resigned – Sarpi. Although excommunicated, not only did he remain in his position as councillor of the Republic for 17 years, but he actually stepped up his work and drafted over 1000 *consulti*. Neither did the international scope of his work lessen. Indeed, his contacts with the countries of Northern Europe increased and, together with his alter ego, Fulgenzio Micanzio, Sarpi found himself at the centre of a close network of international and interfaith relations in years when Europe was steeped in a climate of expectation and tension, the prelude to the Thirty Years War. As Gaetano Cozzi wrote, it is truly impossible to understand Sarpi's political and religious experience unless it is understood in a European context and not simply Italian or Venetian.[29]

The link with England remained strong even after the departure of Ambassador Wotton and his circle in 1610. When Sarpi died in 1623, the Senate issued an order to transcribe all of his public writings in parchment tomes and to seal the papers kept in his monastic cell. Many of the papers left on Sarpi's desk concerned England, its history, its trade, and the hierarchical structure of its society, as testimony to his continuing interest in the country.[30] The acme of that association was the publication, in London, of the *Istoria del concilio tridentino*, but the connection went further than that initiative, sensational as it was. Confirmation of Sarpi's deep interest in the model of power represented by England came in 2006, when Nina Cannizzaro found the unfinished manuscript of *Della potestà de' prencipi*, a tract long thought to be lost.[31] Probably written in the autumn of 1610, *Della potestà de' prencipi* is an amalgam of archaisms and modernity that seems to have been conceived to support the theory of the divine right of kings as defended by James I against Robert Bellarmine. It seems, that is, to be framed by the "Anglican Dispute".

It is impossible to reconstruct here all the stages of the clash between Cardinal Bellarmine (acting as spokesman for Rome) and James I. Sarpi followed each step of the affair, read James's *Apologie for the Oath of Allegiance* as soon as it came out – he had the English version translated without waiting for the Latin edition – and praised it, albeit with some reservations. Most notably, he criticised the English king for having inopportunely mingled politics and theology and thus lost sight of the crux of the problem, i.e. the threat that the excessive power of the popes posed for all sovereigns, regardless of the faiths practised in the territories they governed. It was in reaction to a book written by Bellarmine against the English king that Sarpi decided to write *Della potestà de' prencipi*. The international situation had changed, because the death of the French king, Henry IV, killed on 10 May 1610, had changed the political landscape of early seventeenth-century Europe. Sarpi viewed with alarm the extension of the "yoke of Rome" by the Company of Jesus to a country like France, which had been a bulwark of freedom and independence, to adopt it as a model.[32]

It is in this web of theoretical reasoning and concrete concerns that the genesis of the treatise, which, had it been completed, would in Micanzio's view have been "the finest and most important composition ever to appear to the world", should be sought. *Della potestà de' prencipi* focused on the need to re-establish authority and obedience. In so doing, it theorised a secular power that would fully regulate subjects' religious lives and delineated an absolutism that would further reduce the already few limits imposed on the sovereign by Bodin. A power that was fairly close to that formulated by Thomas Hobbes was described thus by Sarpi:

> The king who is sovereign does not command according to the laws but the laws themselves and remains obliged only to God and to his conscience.[33]

The bond between subject and sovereign is presented as sacred and indivisible, almost a form of worship because "the Prince [is] second after God and does not have anyone greater, other than God".[34] The defence of sovereignty underpinned Sarpi's entire public career, as a reading of the *consulti* – still partly unpublished – by Corrado Pin has shown.[35] However, while Sarpi was always careful to cautiously balance his own ideological claims with the interests of his interlocutors, the patricians, when acting as a councillor, in *Della potestà dei principi* he displays an extreme and disruptive radicality. Parts of the manuscript were circulated after the friar's death. For instance, Hugo Grotius notes the table of contents in the manuscript of *De Imperio summarum potestatum circa sacra*, because it seemed to him that Sarpi had addressed the same topic that he was tackling in *De imperio*, i.e. the supremacy of magistrate over minister, state over church.[36]

However, we need to remember that Sarpi never completed, nor thought of publishing, *Della potestà*. Why did he stop working on the tract? Perhaps he realised that the text was weak and somewhat confused. Another possibility is that he had stopped believing both in the medium he had chosen – a systematic treatise – and in the framework in which the work was to be set. The dispute between Bellarmine and James I was becoming ever-more entrenched and sterile, while Europe stood on the precipice of the Thirty Years War. The esteem and hope felt for James I were fading away. England had not kept its promise of being a bulwark of a single international Protestant front that could stand against the predominance of the Hapsburg block. We can follow this gradual disillusionment in Micanzio and Sarpi's correspondence with Ambassador Dudley Carleton and with William Cavendish, count of Devonshire.[37] The letters are increasingly angry and sombre in tone. The Venetian writers give up trying to analyse the events; they confine themselves to merely observing and recording facts that were becoming more and more impenetrable. Their once enthusiastic view of James I takes on first a perplexed and then a detached tone. The writers were disappointed by the imbalance between James's expressed intentions and his actions, by the deep gulf between words and facts. These letters should not be seen merely as private "venting"; in fact their content was often divulged. The most striking case concerned the correspondence between Micanzio (but Sarpi read and often contributed to these letters) and Cavendish, translated into English by Thomas Hobbes, at that time secretary to Cavendish. They had met Sarpi and Micanzio in 1615, during the Venice stage of the count's European tour. Their correspondence continued until the death of Cavendish in 1628.[38]

This was a correspondence of action, replete with information on the military and political situation in Europe. But there were plenty of references to other matters too. One notable example is the high praise they contain for Francis Bacon, considered by the two Venetian friars to be the most perfect product of the age. They managed to acquire nearly all of the philosopher's works and went to great lengths to promote their dissemination in Italy. Micanzio wrote that the works of Bacon had met with enormous success in Venice, among the nobility and even among the friars of his monastery. This prompted him to try his hand at translating the essay "Of Religion", which had been censored from the Italian edition because it states that "all men ought to unite their forces and wits for the destruction of that doctrine which under the pretence of piety teaches massacres".[39]

Unmasking the Council

In the *Pensieri medico-morali*, Sarpi argued that:

> [i]f you can remain masked with all, then do not be concerned if someone sees your face; and if you cannot stand the itch and must let your face be seen, then choose wisely … saying, with Epicurus: each of us is enough of an audience for the other.[40]

On the necessity for the scholar to dissimulate and to hide his real thoughts, Sarpi commented more than once also in his correspondence, starting with the famous letter to Jacques Gillot in which he wrote that he was "compelled to wear a mask", as "nobody could survive in Italy without one".[41] In the last few decades scholars have written extensively on these passages in an attempt to unmask Sarpi, while considering him at various points a crypto-Calvinist, a Nicodemite, a sceptic, or an atheist who believed that the state could exist without a religious foundation.[42] Whether any of these interpretations is able to fully explain the multi-faceted personality of the Servite friar, the insistence on dissimulation could also suggest a new reading of Sarpi's masterpiece, the *Historia del Concilio Tridentino*, published for the first time in London in 1619 and soon translated into English, Latin, French, and German.[43] While traditionally the *Historia* has been seen as "the last major literary achievement of the Italian Renaissance", almost as an ideal continuation of Francesco Guicciardini's *Storia d'Italia*, Sarpi's decision to dismiss orations and speeches in favour of official documents points out his distance from humanist historiography and the necessity to situate his work within the genre that the age of Tacitism and reasons of State called "secret history".[44] In other words, for Sarpi, history was not simply a branch of rhetoric, intended to provide readers with moral examples to imitate. It was, rather, a form of unmasking, aimed at unveiling the hidden truths of the *arcana imperii*, as John Milton also famously argued, considering the Servite friar "the great unmasker of the Trentine Councel".[45] The historian's task for Sarpi consisted of moving beyond appearances and penetrating the secret causes of past events, while history was conceived of as the reign of hypocrisy and simulation, in which actors never revealed their real intentions. The controversies between Empire and Papacy that preceded the opening of the Council offered a powerful validation of this conviction. Indeed, while Charles V's high regard of the Pope was nothing but "an Arte of government covered with the cloacke of religion", Paul III also never disclosed his authentic views.[46] Drawing on Tacitus's famous portrait of Tiberius, Sarpi described Paul III as "a prelate endowed with good qualities, and among all his vertues, made more esteem of none then of dissimulation", who never showed his fears and "saw very well that this colour of a Councell might serve to cover many matters, and to excuse him in not doing those things which were contrary to his will".[47] Unmasking the Council meant, therefore, revealing its real consequences and demonstrating that, while it was "desired and procured by godly men, to reunite the Church … hath so established the Schisme, and made the parties so obstinate, that the discords are become irreconciliable".[48] Along with exacerbating the confessional strife, the Council was accused of having transformed the Roman Church into a papal monarchy, weakening the authority of the bishops and reinforcing the "exorbitant power" of the Roman court "unto an unlimited excesse".[49] Trent, "the Iliade of our age", was therefore situated at the origin of the Venetian Interdict and of the jurisdictional conflicts caused by the Papacy's attempt to expand its authority beyond spiritual affairs into the secular domain, which Sarpi sarcastically labelled a "totato" rather than a "primato".[50]

Not surprisingly, Sarpi's *Historia* sparked intense controversies in Rome and was repeatedly rebutted by Catholic historiography. While in 1656 the Italian Jesuit Pietro Sforza Pallavicino began to publish his refutation of Sarpi's *Historia*, a trace of anti-Sarpian controversy can still be detected in the fundamental *History of the Council of Trent* by Hubert Jedin, who recognised that Sarpi had "political talent" and that he was "a gifted writer and a master of the Italian language" but concluded that "as a historian he cannot be relied upon".[51] Despite the fact that Sarpi's reconstruction was long questioned by Catholic historians, who pointed out the partiality and unreliability of the sources that he used, it was ultimately possible to ascertain that the *Historia* relied on the papers of Cardinal Marcello Cervini, later pope Marcellus II, containing the correspondence between the papal legates at the Council and Rome.[52]

More recently, the new interest in the history of "early modern Catholicism" has reopened the discussion on the "Sarpian paradigm" and its influence on modern historians, from Benedetto Croce to Paolo Prodi and beyond.[53] According to Simon Ditchfield, the long shadow of Sarpi is still visible in Prodi's interpretation of the Tridentine period, which focused on the new relationship between spirituality and temporality established by the "two souls" of the "papal prince", at the same time prince and pastor, ruler of a secular state and universal head of Christendom.[54] It is true that liberal historiography traditionally appropriated Sarpi and considered the Counter-Reformation in negative terms, as a period of decadence and repression that compromised the creation of a modern national state in Italy. But it should also be stressed that this view has been seriously challenged in the last few decades, starting with the "confessionalisation thesis" and its attempt to compare the Protestant and Catholic Reformations, considering Trent not as the beginning of Italy's decline but as a crucial turning point in the history of social discipline and in the making of modern Europe.[55]

The controversies that Sarpi's *Historia* raised in Catholic Europe have often concealed the impact of the work among Protestants. Indeed, it should not be forgotten that along with defending Venice against the Roman *totato*, Sarpi intended to intervene in the dispute between Gomarists and Arminians that animated the Synod of Dordrecht. In this respect, the publication of the *Historia* in London by the royal printer John Bill clarifies that the work was promoted directly by James I and used by the Archbishop of Canterbury, George Abbott, to attack the Arminian party, which counted Hugo Grotius among its intellectual leaders.[56] Sarpi's antipathy towards the Protestant groups who looked for an irenic solution to the religious question is further confirmed by his harsh reactions to the preface and title that the Italian heretic Marco Antonio de Dominis added to the *editio princeps* of the *Historia*. As has been pointed out, the point of disagreement derived from the fact that while de Dominis intended to use the *Historia* for his ecumenical plan of church unity, Sarpi considered it a cautionary tale for Protestants, warning them not to compromise with Rome when considering the transformation of the Catholic Church after Trent.[57]

Finally, the multiple audiences and polemical targets of the *Historia* both within and outside of Italy suggest the need to reconsider the work beyond the jurisdictional controversies that accompanied its reception and read it as further evidence of Sarpi's use of information. As new research has suggested, in contrast with the insistence on secrecy common to literature on reason of State, Sarpi understood that spreading information was a more effective tool of government than censorship.[58] Remarkably, this was a lesson that the Servite friar learned during the Interdict from his opponents, by carefully watching the behaviour of the Jesuits. They, being well aware of the relationship between power and persuasion, knew that communications were the nerves of government and that the best defence against slanderous books was pre-emptive attack, so that "they defend themselves by changing the subject and heaping up such slanders against others and with such petulance that everything said against them is forgotten".[59]

Conclusion

John Selden, one of the several distinguished English readers of Sarpi, wrote in his *Table Talk* that "in troubled water you can scarce see your face; or see it very little, till the water be quiet and stand still. So in troubled times you can see little truth; when times are quiet and settled, then truth appears" (p. 168).[60] And yet, even today, when the waters of the past seem calm, it is difficult to compose an unequivocal and agreed picture of Sarpi. In spite of the most recent painstaking and innovative research, Fra Paolo's face remains indecipherable, his personality an enigma, as it was for many of his contemporaries. Thanks not least to the discovery in the twentieth century of a number of his unpublished texts, we have, rather, a gallery of different portraits, each of which is valid but incomplete.[61] And how to reconcile the Epicurean tones of the *lathe biosas, live in obscurity*, of the *Pensieri medico-morali* with the day-to-day civil commitment during the Interdict and then with Sarpi's work as Councillor? How to combine his "vivisection" of religion, whose origin he discerned more in the fear and proud mind of a man who is unable to accept his mortal spirit, with his painful account of the hopes of reform of a Christianity betrayed in the Council of Trent? And how, lastly, to reconcile the boldness of the *Pensieri* regarding the hope for an atheist, anarchic, and happy civilisation with the sad doctrine of blind obedience to the sovereign and the theorisation of the divine right of the prince contained in *Della Potestà dei Prencipi*?

After discovering the *Pensieri*, even Gaetano Cozzi, who initially presented Sarpi as essentially Calvinist, acknowledged the need to "tone down" that view and to underscore that Sarpi's religious stance was "extremely complex".[62] It moved between faith and scepticism, idealism and concreteness. Drawing also on the *Pensieri*, David Wootton considered Sarpi to be a man deeply divided between a visible exterior and a hidden interior, in open contradiction with his own self and undoubtedly an atheist: a "moral atheist" who appropriated or anticipated some of the free thinkers' criticism of religion.[63] While Vittorio Frajese followed and expanded upon the line suggested by Wootton, highlighting the French sources (above all Charron) of Sarpian scepticism, Boris Ulianich focused on Sarpi's more strictly religious element, as shown for example in his interest in the thinking of Saint Paul and the organisation of the Church.[64] More recently, by making available the enormous amount of still unpublished *Consulti*, Corrado Pin has shown us a Sarpi without his mask who revealed himself in his 17 years of day-to-day work renewing the baselines and structures of Venetian culture. This Sarpi deliberately chooses the step-by-small-step approach, concentrating on the little details and apparently insignificant questions but without ever losing sight of the broader picture in which his work was set: the idea of a different and, essentially, more free civilisation. This public Sarpi took great care to adapt his discourse to the interlocutor and the occasion. But he did not spare Venetian society – drowsy and stagnant – or its ruling class, with which he collaborated for years and towards which he exercised an extraordinary authoritativeness, from criticism and the accusation of seeking to defend anachronistic privileges and values. He did not believe in, or contribute to, the "Venetian myth". The isolation and neutrality boasted by the Republic no longer seemed feasible to Sarpi. Venice had to take a stand, choose which side it was on, and act accordingly, on pain of being consigned to irrelevance and decadence.[65]

The English dimension both enriches and complicates these multi-form reflections of Sarpi's personality. His *Della potestà de' Prencipi* and *Consulti* and his correspondence enable us to examine more closely the insights of Richard Tuck, who had already pointed out the affinities between Sarpi, Hobbes, and Bacon.[66] These affinities are profound and amount to more than just a similar diagnosis of the crisis of the period in which they lived and the quest for solutions, political first and foremost. We can only mention some possible lines of research here, but with Bacon, for example, Sarpi shared an impatience with all forms of abstract intellectualism for its own end: "knowledge" must "serve", must always respond to a "need". Otherwise, it becomes a cause of "servitude and harm". But he also agreed with the idea of matter in perpetual motion, driven by incessant "appetites", and with the analysis of the human mind's irresistible tendency to error and self-deception, and the need for a wholesale renewal of the system of knowledge. With Hobbes, Sarpi not only shared ideas about political-theology and the civic function of religion but also about natural philosophy, starting with the common intention to move away from Aristotelianism and to understand the world as a simply mechanical system.[67]

To conclude, while the paradigm of "civic humanism" has faded away, Sarpi no longer appears today as the last tardy representative of the Florentine humanist tradition, as in the popular interpretation by William Bouswma,[68] but as a vigilant observer of the new attainments of modernity in the scientific, political, and social fields. This also prompts us to review the myth of Sarpi as a champion of freedom of speech and of the printed word first disseminated by John Milton, who cites the Venetian historian 30 times in his Commonplace Book. In reality, on the problem of censorship, Sarpi again shows a pragmatic attitude anchored in historic reality. He does not deny the legitimacy of some forms of censorship; on the contrary, in some cases, he does not hesitate to invoke the ban on selling and distributing certain books he judges to be dangerous for the equilibrium of society and of the Venetian government.[69] That said, his condemnation of censorship as a form of political aggression by the Church of Rome, its exploitation of ignorance, and the destruction of culture to which the practice of expurgating and revising even those texts not directly linked to doctrinal questions, is most definite. Above all, the absolute importance of the printed word and of information is utterly clear to Sarpi, as a famous passage from the *History of the Inquisition* shows:

> The matter of bookes seemes to be a thing of small moment, because it treats of words, but through these words comes opinions into the world, which cause partialities, seditions, and finally warres. They are words, it is true, but such as in consequence draw after them Hosts of armed men.[70]

Notes

1 This chapter is the result of collaborative work between the authors. Chiara Petrolini is primarily responsible for the first four sections and Diego Pirillo for the fifth. The conclusion was written together. Many thanks to Filippo De Vivo for his helpful comments on an earlier version of the chapter.

2 Frances A. Yates, "Paolo Sarpi's History of the Council of Trent", *Journal of the Warburg and Courtauld Institutes*, 7 (1944): 123–44, 137. See also Fulgenzio Micanzio, *Vita del padre Paolo*, in Paolo Sarpi, *Istoria del Concilio Tridentino*, ed. Corrado Vivanti, 2 vols. (Turin: Einaudi, 2011), II, p. 1392.

3 Giorgio Spini, "Riforma italiana e mediazioni ginevrine nella nuova Inghilterra puritana", in *Ginevra e l'Italia. Raccolta di studi promossa dalla Facoltà Valdese di Teologia di Roma*, ed. Delio Cantimori (Florence: Sansoni, 1959), pp. 454–55.

4 M. A. Scott, "Elizabethan Translations from the Italian", *PMLA*, X, 2 (1895): 249–93. On Sarpi's popularity in England, see John Lievsay, *Venetian Phoenix: Sarpi and Some of His English Friends (1606–1700)* (Lawrence, KS: University Press of Kansas, 1973).

5 *Calendar of State Papers and Manuscripts Relating to English Affairs Existing in the Archives and Collections of Venice and in Other Libraries of Northern Italy*, ed. Rawdon Brown, 38 vols. (London: Longman, Roberts and Green, 1864–1947), XI, p. 64.

6 Mario Infelise, "Ricerche sulla fortuna editoriale di Paolo Sarpi", in *Ripensando Paolo Sarpi. Atti del Convegno Internazionale di Studi nel 450° anniversario della nascita di Paolo Sarpi*, ed. Corrado Pin (Venice: Ateneo veneto, 2006), p. 521.

7 Dorit Raines, "Dopo Sarpi: il patriziato veneziano e l'eredità del Servita", in *Ripensando Paolo Sarpi*, ed. Corrado Pin, p. 114

8 Maria Wakely and Graham Rees, "Folios Fit for a King: James I, John Bill, and the King's Printers, 1616–20", *Huntington Library Quarterly*, 68, 3 (2005): 467–95.

9 Ugo Balzani, "Di alcuni documenti dell'archivio del Santo Uffizio di Roma relativi al ritrovamento del cadavere di Paolo Sarpi", *Rendiconti della reale Accademia dei Lincei*, 5, 4 (1895), pp. 595–617.

10 The best account of Sarpi's involvement in the origins of the telescope is Massimo Bucciantini, Michele Camerota, and Franco Giudice, *Il Telescopio di Galileo: Una storia europea* (Turin: Einaudi, 2012). See also Mario Biagioli, "Did Galileo copy the telescope? A 'new' letter by Paolo Sarpi", in *The Origins of the Telescope*, eds. A. Van Helden, S. Dupré, R. Van Gent, and H. Zuidervaart (Amsterdam: KNAW Press, 2010), pp. 203–30. On Sarpi's scientific interests see Libero Sosio, "Fra Paolo Sarpi e la cosmologia", in Paolo Sarpi, *Pensieri naturali, metafisici e matematici*, eds. Luisa Cozzi and Libero Sosio (Milan: Ricciardi, 1996), pp. LXXXVIII–CXCIV.

11 On Venice as a point of news exchange, see Filippo De Vivo, *Information and Communication in Venice: Rethinking Early Modern Politics* (Oxford: Oxford University Press, 2007).

12 Paolo Sarpi, *Pensieri naturali, metafisici e matematici*. See David Wootton, *Paolo Sarpi between Renaissance and Enlightenment* (Cambridge: Cambridge University Press, 1983).

13 Sarpi, *Pensieri naturali, metafisici e matematici*, pp. 306–7.

14 See Corrado Pin, "Capo, maestro e consultore d'un infamissimo scisma: Paolo Sarpi e l'Interdetto di Venezia del 1606–1607", in *Lo Stato Marciano durante l'Interdetto: atti del*

XXIX convegno di studi storici, Rovigo, 3–4 novembre 2006, organizzato dall'Associazione culturale Minelliana, ed. Gino Benzoni (Rovigo, Italy: Minelliana, 2008), pp. 189–220.

15 See Anthony David Wright, "Why the Venetian Interdict?" *English Historical Review*, lxxxix (1974): 534–50; Paul F. Grendler, "Books for Sarpi: The Smuggling of Prohibited Books in Venice during the Interdict of 1606–1607", in *Essays Presented to Myron P. Gilmore*, eds. Sergio Bertelli and Gloria Ramakus, 2 vols. (Florence: La Nuova Italia, 1978), I, pp. 105–14; Francis Oakley, "Complexities of Context: Gerson, Bellarmine, Sarpi, Richer, and the Venetian Interdict of 1606–1607", *Catholic Historical Review*, lxxxvi (1996): 369–96.

16 Paolo Sarpi, *Lettere ai gallicani*, ed. Boris Ulianich (Wiesbaden, Germany: Steiner, 1961), p. 168; Sarpi, Paolo, *Lettere ai protestanti* (Bari: Laterza, 1931), p. 19.

17 See Logan Pearsall Smith, *The Life and Letters of Sir Henry Wotton* (Oxford: Clarendon Press, 1907). On the role played by Wotton during the Interdict, see Filippo De Vivo, "Francia e Inghilterra di fronte all'interdetto di Venezia", in *Paolo Sarpi. Politique et religion en Europe*, ed. Marie Viallon (Paris: Édition Classiques Garnier, 2010), pp. 163–88.

18 Evelyn S. Shuckburgh, *Two Biographies of William Bedell, Bishop of Kilmore, with a Selection of His Letters and an Unpublished Treatise* (Cambridge: Cambridge University Press, 1902).

19 Cf. Gaetano Cozzi, "Sir Edwin Sandys e la 'Relazione dello stato della religione'", *Rivista storica italiana*, lxxix (1967): 1096–121; Stefano Villani, "La prima edizione in italiano del Book of Common Prayer (1685), tra propaganda protestante e memoria sarpiana", *Rivista di storia e letteratura religiosa*, xliv (2008): 24–45.

20 Thomas Coryat, *Coryat's Crudities* (1611), 2 vols. (Glasgow: J. MacLehose, 1905), I, p. 318.

21 Noel Malcolm, *De Dominis: Venetian, Anglican, Ecumenist and Relapsed Heretic* (London: Strickland & Scott Academic Publications, 1984), p. 37.

22 Paolo Sarpi, *Istoria dell'interdetto*, in Paolo Sarpi, *Scritti scelti*, ed. Giovanni Da Pozzo (Turin: Unione tipografico-editrice torinese, 1968), pp. 165–391. The English version edited by Cristopher Potter, rector of Queen's College Oxford, was published in the same year by J. Bill.

23 Smith, *The Life and Letters of Sir Henry Wotton*, II, p. 260.

24 Sarpi, *Lettere ai protestanti*, II, pp. 50–52. On the controversies over the Oath of Allegiance and the Interdict, see Stefania Tutino, *The Empire of Souls: Robert Bellarmine and the Christian Commonwealth* (Oxford: Oxford University Press, 2010), pp. 81–158; J. H. M. Salmon, "James I, the Oath of Allegiance, the Venetian Interdict, and the Reappearance of French Ultramontanism", in *The Cambridge History of Political Thought, 1450–1700*, eds. James H. Burns and Mark Goldie (Cambridge: Cambridge University Press, 1991), pp. 247–53; W. B. Patterson, *King James VI and I and the Reunion of Christendom* (Cambridge: Cambridge University Press, 1998).

25 Enrico De Mas, *Sovranità politica e unità cristiana nel Seicento anglo-veneto* (Ravenna: Longo, 1975).

26 Gaetano Cozzi, "Paolo Sarpi tra il cattolico Philippe Canaye de Fresnes e il calvinista Isaac Casaubon", *Bollettino dell'Istituto di storia della società e dello stato veneziano*, I (1959): 27–154.

27 Gaetano Cozzi, "Fra Paolo Sarpi, l'anglicanesimo e la 'Historia del Concilio Tridentino'", *Rivista storica italiana*, lxviii, 6 (1956): 559–619.

28 Sarpi, *Lettere ai gallicani*, p. 148.

29 Gaetano Cozzi, *Paolo Sarpi tra Venezia e l'Europa* (Turin: Einaudi, 1979).

30 Corrado Pin, "Le scritture pubbliche trovate alla morte di Fra Paolo Sarpi nel convento dei Servi", *Memorie dell'Accademia delle Scienze di Torino*, V, II (1978): 311–79; and "Tra religione e politica: un codice di memorie di Paolo Sarpi", in *Studi politici in onore di Luigi Firpo*, eds. Silvia Rota Ghibaudi and Franco Barcia (Milan: Franco Angeli, 1990), pp. 145–85.

31 Paolo Sarpi, *Della potestà de' prencipi*, ed. Nina Cannizzaro, with an essay by Corrado Pin (Venice: Marsilio, 2006).

32 Sarpi, *Lettere ai Gallicani*, p. 131.

33 Sarpi, *Della potestà de' prencipi*, p. 52.

34 Sarpi, *Della potestà de' prencipi*, pp. 35 and 63.

35 Paolo Sarpi, *I Consulti*, ed. Corrado Pin, 2 vols. (Pisa: Istituti editoriali e poligrafici internazionali, 2001).

36 H. J. Van Dam, "Italian Friends. Grotius, De Dominis, Sarpi and the Church", *Netherlands archief voor Kerkgeschiedenis*, 75 (1995): 210–14.

37 Paolo Sarpi, *Il carteggio con l'ambasciatore inglese Sir Dudley Carleton*, in Sarpi, *Opere*, pp. 635–720; Micanzio, Fulgenzio, *Lettere a William Cavendish (1615–1628) nella versione di T. Hobbes*, ed. Roberto Ferrini (Rome: Istituto storico O.S.M., 1987); Thomas Hobbes, *Translations of the Letters of Fulgenzio Micanzio and Other Cavenbdish-related Writings*, ed. Filippo De Vivo, in *The Clarendon Edition of the Works of Thomas Hobbes* (in press). Cf. Vittorio Gabrieli, "Bacone, la riforma e Roma nella versione hobbesiana d'un carteggio di Fulgenzio Micanzio", *The English Miscellany*, 8 (1957): 195–250. On Sarpi's opinion of King James, see Eugenia Levi, "King James I and Fra Paolo Sarpi in 1612", *The Athenaeum*, 3689 (1898): 66–67.

38 Noel Malcolm, "Hobbes, Sandys, and the Virginia Company", *The Historical Journal*, 24, 2 (1981): 297–321 (also in Noel Malcolm, *Aspect of Hobbes* [Oxford: Oxford University Press, 2007], pp. 53–80); Gregorio Baldin, "Hobbes and Sarpi: Method, Matter, and Natural Philosophy", *Galilaeana*, X (2013): 85–118.

39 Micanzio, *Lettere a Cavendish*, p. 73.

40 Sarpi, *Pensieri*, p. 626, quoting Seneca, *Epistles*, VII, 11.

41 Sarpi, *Lettere ai gallicani*, p. 133.

42 Corrado Vivanti, "Introduzione", in *Istoria del Concilio Tridentino*, ed. Paolo Sarpi, pp. xxix–xcii; David Wootton, *Paolo Sarpi. Between Renaissance and Enlightenment*; Pasquale Guaragnella, *La prosa e il mondo: "avvisi" del moderno in Sarpi, Galilei e la nuova scienza* (Bari: Adriatica, 1986); Boris Ulianich, "Paolo Sarpi 'riformatore' 'irenico'? Note sulla sua ecclesiologia, sulla sua teologia, sulla sua religione", in *Fra Paolo Sarpi dei Servi di Maria*, eds. Pacifico Branchesi and Corrado Pin (Venice: Comune di Venezia, 1986), pp. 44–100; Vittorio Frajese, *Sarpi scettico. Stato e chiesa a Venezia tra Cinque e Seicento* (Bologna: Il Mulino, 1994); Michele Ciliberto, "Alcune ipotesi su Paolo Sarpi", in ed. M. Ciliberto, *Pensare per contrari. Disincanto e utopia nel Rinascimento* (Roma: Edizioni di Storia e Letteratura, 2005), pp. 441–76. See more recently Corrado Pin, "Paolo Sarpi senza maschera: l'avvio della lotta politica dopo l'interdetto del 1606", in *Paolo Sarpi. Politique et religione en Europe*, ed. Marie Viallon, pp. 55–103, and Jaska Kainulainen, *Paolo Sarpi: A Servant of God and State* (Leiden, the Netherlands: Brill, 2014).

43 *Historia del Concilio Tridentino* (London: John Bill, 1619).

44 Peter Burke, "Sarpi storico", in *Ripensando Paolo Sarpi*, pp. 103–9. William J. Bouwsma, *Venice and the Defense of Republican Values in the Age of the Counter Reformation* (Berkeley: University of California Press, 1968), p. 623. On Sarpi as historian see also Corrado Vivanti, "Introduzione"; Alberto Asor Rosa, "*Istoria del concilio tridentino* di Paolo Sarpi", in *Genus italicum. Saggi sulla identità letteraria italiana nel corso del tempo*, ed. A. Asor Rosa (Turin: Einaudi, 1997), pp. 343–407.

45 *Areopagitica*, in *Selected Poetry and Prose*, ed. John Milton (New York: Norton, 2011), p. 344. On Sarpi and Milton, see Nigel Smith, "Milton and the Index", in *Of Paradise and Light: Essays for Alan Rudrum*, eds. Holly F. Nelson and Donald R. Dickson (Cranbury, NJ: Rosemont, 2004), pp. 101–22.

46 Paolo Sarpi, *The Historie of the Councel of Trent* (London: Robert Barker and John Bill, 1620), p. 41.

47 Sarpi, *The Historie of the Councel*, pp. 71–72. Sarpi is echoing Tacitus, *Annals*, IV, 71.

48 Sarpi, *The Historie of the Councel*, p. 2.

49 Sarpi, *The Historie of the Councel*, p. 2.

50 Letter to Jacques Gillot (September 15, 1609), in Sarpi, *Opere*, p. 275.

51 Pietro Sforza Pallavicino, *Istoria del Concilio di Trento ... ove insieme rifiutasi con autorevoli testimonianze un'Istoria falsa divolgata nello stesso argomento sotto nome di Pietro Soave Polano* (Rome: Angelo Bernabò for Giovanni Casoni, 1656–1657), Hubert Jedin, *A History of the Council of Trent*, 2 vols. (London: T. Nelson, 1957–61), II, p. 520. Only the first two volumes of the *Geschichte des Konzils von Trient* (Freiburg i/Br, Germany: Herder, 1949–75) have been translated into English.

52 Corrado Vivanti, *Quattro lezioni su Paolo Sarpi* (Naples: Bibliopolis, 2005), pp. 121–57.

53 Simon Ditchfield, *In Sarpi's Shadow: Coping with Trent the Italian Way*, in *Studi in memoria di Cesare Mozzarelli*, 2 vols. (Milan: Vita e Pensiero, 2008), I, pp. 585–606.

54 Ditchfield, *In Sarpi's Shadow*. See also Ditchfield, "Tridentine Catholicism", in *The Ashgate Research Companion to the Counter-Reformation*, eds. Alexandra Bamji, Geert H. Janssen, and Mary Laven, (Farnham, UK: Ashgate, 2013), pp. 24–28; Paolo Prodi, *The Papal Prince: One Body and Two Souls. The Papal Monarchy in Early Modern Europe* (Cambridge: Cambridge University Press, 1987).
55 Useful surveys on this wide debate include Paolo Prodi and Wolfgang Reinhard (eds.), *Il concilio di Trento e il moderno* (Bologna: Il Mulino, 1996); Ronnie Po-Chia Hsia, *The World of Catholic Renewal 1540–1770* (Cambridge: Cambridge University Press, 1998); Adriano Prosperi, *Il concilio di Trento: una introduzione storica* (Turin: Einaudi, 2001); Alain Tallon, *Le concile de Trente* (Paris: Édition du Cerf, 2000) John O'Malley, *Trent and All That: Renaming Catholicism in the Early Modern Era* (Cambridge, MA: Harvard University Press, 2000).
56 See Frances A. Yates, "Paolo Sarpi's *History of the Council of Trent*", *Journal of the Warburg and Courtauld Institutes*, VII (1944): 123–43; Gaetano Cozzi, "Fra Paolo Sarpi, l'anglicanesimo e la *Historia del Concilio Tridentino*", *Rivista storica italiana*, LXIII (1956): 559–619.
57 Malcolm, *De Dominis 1560–1624*, pp. 56–60. See also Eleonora Belligni, *Auctoritas e potestats. Marcantonio de Dominis fra l'Inquisizione e Giacomo I* (Milan: Franco Angeli, 2003).
58 Filippo De Vivo, "Paolo Sarpi and the Uses of Information in Seventeenth-Century Venice", *Media History*, 11, 1/2 (2005): 37–51.
59 "Del confutar scritture malediche", in *Opere*, ed. Sarpi, pp. 1170–180 (1173), partial English trans. in Dooley, Brendan (ed. and trans.), *Italy in the Baroque. Selected Readings* (New York: Garland Publishing, 1995), pp. 332–36. On the relationship between power and persuasion in early modern Italy see Adriano Prosperi, *Tribunali della coscienza. Inquisitori, confessori, missionari* (Turin: Einaudi, 1996), p. XV.
60 John Selden, *The Table Talk* (Chiswick, UK: Press of C. Wittingham, 1818), p. 168.
61 Michele Ciliberto, "Alcune ipotesi su Paolo Sarpi", in *Pensando per contrari*, pp. 441–76 (447).
62 Gaetano Cozzi, "Rinascimento Riforma Controriforma", in *La storiografia italiana negli ultimi vent'anni*, 2 vols. (Milan: Marzorati, 1970), II, p. 1210.
63 Wootton, *Paolo Sarpi between Renaissance and Enlightenment*.
64 Frajese, *Sarpi scettico. Stato e chiesa a Venezia tra Cinque e Seicento* (Bologna: Il Mulino 1994); B. Ulianich, "Teologia paolina in Sarpi?", in *Ripensando Paolo Sarpi*, ed. C. Pin, pp. 73–101.
65 Corrado Pin, "'Qui si vive con esempi, non con ragione': Paolo Sarpi e la committenza di Stato nel dopo-Interdetto", in *Ripensando Paolo Sarpi*, ed. C. Pin, pp. 843–94; C. Pin, "Paolo Sarpi", in *Enciclopedia italiana di scienze, lettere ed arti. Ottava appendice: Il contributo italiano alla storia del pensiero. Filosofia*, pp. 258–67 (www.treccani.it/enciclopedia/paolo-sarpi_%28Il-Contributo-italiano-alla-storia-del-Pensiero:-Filosofia%29/); C. Pin, "Paolo Sarpi senza maschera: l'avvio della lotta politica dopo l'Interdetto del 1606", in *Paolo Sarpi. Politique et religion en Europe*, ed. Marie Viallon, pp. 55–103.
66 Richard Tuck, *Philosophy and Government, 1572–1651* (Cambridge: Cambridge University Press, 1993).
67 Gregorio Baldin, "Hobbes and Sarpi". On the relationship between Sarpi and Hobbes see also Micanzio, *Lettere a William Cavendish and Hobbes, Translation of the Letters of Fulgenzio Micanzio and other Cavendish-Related Writings*.
68 Bouwsma, *Venice and the Defense of Republican Liberty*.
69 On the ambiguities of censorship in Sarpi, see Federico Barbierato, "Paolo Sarpi, the Papal Index and Censorship", in *Censorship Moments*, ed. Geoff Kemp (London: Bloomsbury, 2014), pp. 63–70.
70 Paolo Sarpi, *The History of the Inquisition*, trans. Robert Gentilis (London: Humphrey Mosley, 1639), p. 69.

Afterword

Location and narration

Keir Elam

One of the recurring themes in this volume, and one that I wish to take up briefly in this Afterword, is the question of location. This topic takes a number of different forms and meanings in the chapters in this volume. The most evident meaning is the choice of geographical setting, and specifically of Italian settings: a choice that in turn mirrors what is certainly the most popular dramaturgical and geopolitical strategy in early modern plays. This book devotes considerable attention to the ideological implications of Italian locales, especially their role in reflecting and refracting English perceptions of national identity, as well as English political and commercial ambitions: see especially Michele Marrapodi's Introduction. In the following pages I would like to discuss other possible meanings and implications of 'location' in Elizabethan and Jacobean plays. My closing argument is that many of these implications come together in one of Shakespeare's late romances, namely *Cymbeline*.

The second kind of location in play here is the *locus*: fictional place but also literary and dramatic *topos* (*locus comunis*). As this volume shows, one of the most fruitful lines of research in Anglo-Italian studies has been the far-reaching enquiry into the appropriation, transformation, and dissemination of literary and theatrical *loci* from Greek and Roman New Comedy, via medieval and Renaissance Italian narrative to the early modern English stage. Louise George Clubb's felicitous and highly generative notion of the theatregram is the most conspicuous case in point. It is the theatregram – bringing together as it does narrative plots and situations, verbal and corporeal *lazzi*, and dramatic themes – that becomes the main unit of meaning and of contamination in the extraordinary ringing of combinatorial changes that make up the history of erudite and popular comedy alike, as Clubb's chapter in this volume on the historical transformations of *commedia erudita* goes to confirm. Eric Nicholson's chapter, instead, discusses the impact of *topoi* from *commedia dell'arte* on English drama. One might also mention the chapters by Duncan Salked on Machiavellian comedy and by Mario Domenichelli on Senecan tragedy as further examples of the transmission of dramatic conventions and *loci*. On a more strictly theatrical front, the English inheritance of Italian actorial and stage theatregrams is explored in Richard Andrews's chapter on professional Italian *comici* and in Rosalind Kerr's chapter on the influence of Italian actresses.

On the relationship between dramatic and theatrical *loci*, in *Shakespeare and the Popular Tradition in the Theater* Robert Weimann famously develops and extends Richard Southern's distinction between *locus* as fictional space, and *platea* as stage space, in the late medieval and early modern theatre:

DOI: 10.4324/9781315612720-28

> What the Shakespearean text seems to project are two different (and potentially divisive) locations of authority: the represented locus of authority, and the process of authorization on the platform stage … The locus was associated with the localizing capacities of the fictional role and tended to privilege the authority of what and who was represented in the dramatic world; the other, the platea, being associated instead with the actor and the neutral materiality of the platform stage, tended to privilege the authority of what and who was representing that world.[1]

The locations of early modern drama are both fictional and theatrical, since it is the 'authority' of the material stage performance that gives body to the imaginary Italian locales of the play.

The *locus* is powerfully associated with literary and dramatic genre. Genre-specific *loci*, such as the *locus amoenus* of pastoral, are not so much dramatic places or settings as conventional markers of literary mode. The chapters by Robert Henke and Jane Tylus on the appropriation and reworking of pastoral conventions in English drama show, among other things, how the idealised *locus* as space and as *topos* survived, with cultural modifications, in English plays, including Shakespeare's late romances. As Jason Lawrence's chapter on the English fortunes of Tasso, John Roe's on the inestimable impact of Petrarch, and Melissa Walter's on Boccaccio in England – among others – suggest, early modern English drama is often located, first and foremost, in the great virtual space of the Italian intertext. For this reason, the distinction between place and literary or dramaturgic tradition is often slight. The London of early modern city comedy, for example, not only recalls but virtually recreates the *urbs* of Latin comedy. Location is a vehicle of cultural history and prestige: the Florence of Ben Jonson's *Every Man in His Humour*, with its geopolitical kudos, becomes London in the revised Folio version (1616). Jonson's change of locale is made possible not only by the fact that both derive from the cities of Plautine comedy but also by the implicit specular relationship between the two cities and indeed the two nations (London is the new Florence).[2]

Locations are above all narrative spaces. For the audiences of the Globe, Curtain, or Blackfriars, Italian settings are always and already literary constructs, prior to their nominal appearance on stage. The Venice of Iago and Volpone, the Verona of Juliet, and the Amalfi of De Bosola are intertextual rather than geographic places, accessible through travel literature from Moryson to Coryat, through Florio's didactic 'tours' of Italy, or through translations of Boccaccio and Bandello. They are ink and paper cities, created or recreated through the descriptive and performative power of the word. This is true of the plays themselves, in which 'Venice' and 'Rome' are verbal – and sometimes scenographic – constructs, ontologically posited through allusion and description. It is for this reason that the distance between 'England' and 'Italy' can be covered by a line of prose or by an exit and entrance, as Philip Sidney observes in his neoclassical critique of English "mongrel tragi-comedy" in the *Apology* (1595):

> But they [English dramatists] will say, How then shall we set forth a story, which containeth both many places and many times? And do they not know that a tragedy is tied to the laws of Poesy, and not of History … many things may be told which cannot be showed, if they know the difference betwixt reporting and representing. As, for example, I may speak (though I am here) of Peru, and in speech digress from that to the description of Calicut; but in action I cannot represent it without Pacolet's horse.[3]

More caustic still is Ben Jonson's satire on excessive crossing of seas and borders in the Induction to *Every Man Out of His Humour*:

MITIS: Well, we will not dispute of this now. But what's his scene?
CORDATUS: Marry, *Insula Fortunata*, sir.
MITIS: Oh, the Fortunate Island? Mass, he has bound himself to a strict law there.
CORDATUS: Why so?
MITIS: He cannot lightly alter the scene without crossing the seas.
CORDATUS: He needs not, having a whole island to run through, I think.
MITIS: No! how comes it, then, that in some one play we see so many seas, countries, and kingdoms, passed over with such admirable dexterity?
CORDATUS: O, that but shews how well the authors can travail in their vocation, and outrun the apprehension of their auditory.

(256–65)[4]

Be that as it may, the narrative multiplication of locations is an English dramaturgic vice that not even Jonson's formidable scorn could eradicate.

Many of the themes discussed in this volume - intertextuality, genres, loci, *topoi*, theatregrams, Anglo-Italian settings – are brought together by Shakespeare in that extraordinary compendium of plots and genres that is *Cymbeline*. This *sui generis* romance, history play, Roman play, cross-dressing comedy, and pastoral tragicomedy is among other things an exercise in the poetics of location. The action moves frenetically from ancient Luds town (London), to an imperial Rome that actually resembles Renaissance Italy, to 'primitive' pastoral Wales. It is thus a play about border-crossing: in the first instance, geographical and geopolitical border-crossing, namely the traversing of national and regional confines within ancient Britain and between Britain, Gaul, and Rome, which is one of the play's most intense and politically resonant activities, involving nearly all its *dramatis personae*. These spasmodic shifts in place are accompanied by journeys through time, and the two are sometimes superimposed through processes of polychronicity (multiple time schemes) and polytopicity (multiple simultaneous places): a conspicuous case in point is the Machiavellian Iachimo, who sets out from an ancient Rome that resembles nothing so closely as the Venice of Iago, and then crosses ancient Gaul in order to seduce and slander Innogen in a geographically and historically distant Britain that patently reflects contemporary England.

The movements in place and time in *Cymbeline* bring with them abrupt changes in genre. Each location is also a mode of narration and of dramatic representation. The play seems knowingly to fulfil Polonius's prophetic vision of a 'complete poem' comprising a mix of all known, and some unknown, genres ("tragedy, comedy, history, pastoral, pastoral-comical, historical-pastoral, tragical-historical, tragical-comical-historical-pastoral, scene individable, or poem unlimited", *Hamlet*, 2.2). The veritable feast of intertextual and macrotextual allusion, moreover, makes of the play a unique case of Shakespearian self-appropriation, since no other work borrows so overtly the plots, the theatrical devices, and the language of the dramatist's own earlier texts,[5] from *Romeo and Juliet* and its poisons, to the cross-dressing comedies, to *Othello* with its deadly mixture of jealousy and Machiavellian machinations, to the Roman plays, of which it is in some ways the last exemplum.[6] The dramatist writes his own critical commentary on the dramatisation of Anglo-Italian cultural relations across multiple forms of dramatic expression.

In order to reach Posthumus, the play's female protagonist has to journey not to Rome but to Wales. Here we have Innogen as Juliet again, since her "why may not I/Glide thither in a day?" discourse in 3.2 reworks Juliet's famous "Gallop apace, you fiery-footed steeds" speech (3.2) while waiting for Romeo and the night, with the difference that Innogen is tricked into her journey by a false letter from her husband. Her eulogy to the Welsh locale of Milford Haven, a toponym on which she puns ("such a haven", i.e. refuge but also heaven, although it turns out to be somewhat hellish) raises the question of the choice of this relatively small port in Pembrokeshire as the geopolitical hub of the romance. Milton Haven is the most overdetermined little town in Shakespeare. Everybody comes and goes there, and crosses different borders to get there: Posthumus and Iachimo to and from Italy, likewise the Roman army, joined from Lud's town by Innogen, Cloten, and, in the end, Cymbeline, whose sons turn out to be Welsh citizens. In geographical or maritime terms, Milford Haven as fictional *locus* makes little sense. Situated in southern Pembrokeshire, it is impossibly distant from Lud's town, but above all it is on the opposite coast with respect to Gaul or France and Italy, and is thus a highly improbable port of call for continental traffic, which came and went from the southeast coast.

There are various possible explanations for Shakespeare's choice. The first is that of collective historical memory, since the Romans probably used Milford Haven as a base for their patrolling fleets from what is now the Cardiff area. The second is Jacobean nationalist policy. Milford Haven in the early seventeenth century was celebrated as 'the happy Port of Union', symbol of Stuart peace policy. As a peaceful Anglo-Welsh colony outside the domain of the Roman empire, it was the perfect expression of King James's continuing desire for the unification of Great Britain under his kingship, despite Parliament's rejection of the Union in 1607. Anglo-Celtic Wales, with its tragicomic-pastoral-historical traffic, its apparently savage but at the same time highly civilised 'Britons' Bellarius and family, and its military victory against the Romans, is the idealised locus for the birth of British national identity. The unified Britain of Milford Haven is an imagined community, in Benedict Anderson's terms,[7] a virtual British nation that in 1610 did not exist and had no immediate prospect of existing, but that is nonetheless celebrated as a political ambition projected onto a legendary past that justifies and historicises it.

To this possible staging of an imagined Great Britain, however, I would like to add a final consideration, and a final border to cross. Milford Haven was not the point of departure and arrival for Italy, but it was so for another kind of colonial expedition, namely to and from Ireland. It is thus redolent with English and Shakespearian history: Richard II left for Ireland from Milford Haven, as later did Oliver Cromwell. Coming the other way, Henry Tudor, born in Pembroke Castle just off the waterway, also landed in Milford Haven when he came to challenge and defeat Richard III in 1485. Equally significantly the Earl of Essex went to and from Milford Haven in his disastrous attempt to vanquish Ireland and tame the Irish, prior to his rebellion against Elizabeth, a sequence of events that was very much part of English cultural memory. Milford Haven may thus also be a metonymy for Ireland as the last outpost of an imagined British nation, destined, like Cymbeline's Britain itself, to thwart, or cross, colonial aspirations.

In *Cymbeline*, border- and genre-crossing also come to involve gender-crossing. When Innogen wanders across wild and rocky Wales – introducing into the play its most distinctly pastoral scenes – she does so cross-dressed as a boy wearing "doublet, hat, hose, all" (3.4.169).[8] Above all she wears a sword, since she is exposed to the physical dangers of the Roman-British wars: "This attempt/I am soldier to" (3.4.182–83). She literalises Rosaline's reverie in *As You Like It*, 2.1, about becoming a soldier, and her male role is necessarily more virile than that of her predecessors in the comedies. Indeed, in some ways, she herself becomes the missing object of her quest, namely her lost husband Posthumus, who in turn crosses borders and armies, while there is even a suggestion that the two estranged spouses temporarily exchange gender roles. Such is the power of Anglo-Italian location: namely, to bring into play and into question multiple forms of spatial, temporal, literary, and identity hybridism.

Notes

1 Robert Weimann, *Shakespeare and the Popular Tradition in the Theater: Studies in the Social Dimension of Dramatic Form and Function*, ed. Robert Schwartz (Baltimore, MD: Johns Hopkins University Press, 1978), p. 184. Weimann's original edition was published in Germany in 1967. The reference to Richard Southern regards the seminal work, *Medieval Theatre in the Round: A Study of the Staging of the "Castle of Perseverance" and Related Matters*, revised and expanded edition (New York: Theatre Arts Books, 1975; first ed. 1958). On location in early modern English drama, see also *Shakespeare's Italy: Functions of Italian Locations in Renaissance Drama*, eds. M. Marrapodi, A. J. Hoenselaars, Marcello Cappuzzo, and Lino Falzon Santucci (Manchester, UK: Manchester University Press, 1997).

2 See James W. Lever's parallel-text edition, *Every Man in His Humour* (Lincoln: University of Nebraska Press, 1971). Cf. Robert S. Miola, "The Italian *Every Man in His Humour,*" in *The Italian World of English Renaissance Drama: Cultural Exchange and Intertextuality*, ed. Michele Marrapodi; assoc. ed. A. J. Hoenselaars (Newark: University of Delaware Press, 1998), pp. 208–24.

3 Philip Sidney, *An Apology for Poetry*, ed. Geoffrey Shepherd (London: Nelson, 1965), pp. 134–35.

4 Ben Jonson, *Every Man Out of His Humour*, in *The Cambridge Edition of the Works of Ben Jonson*, eds. David Bevington, Martin Butler, and Ian Donaldson, 7 vols. (Cambridge: Cambridge University Press, 2012), vol. 1, pp. 272–73.

5 On self-quotation in Shakespeare, see Robert S. Miola, "Seven Types of Intertextuality," in *Shakespeare, Italy, and Intertextuality*, ed. Michele Marrapodi (Manchester, UK: Manchester University Press, 2004), pp. 13–25.

6 See David M. Bergeron, "*Cymbeline*: Shakespeare's Last Roman Play," *Shakespeare Quarterly*, 31, 1 (Spring, 1980): 31–41.

7 Benedict Anderson, *Imagined Communities: Reflections on the Origin and Spread of Nationalism* (London: Verso, 1983).

8 References are to *Cymbeline*, ed. Valerie Wayne (London: The Arden Shakespeare, third series, 2017).

Bibliography

A Catalogue of the Harleian Manuscripts, in the British Museum. With Indexes of Persons, Places and Matters, Vol. 4 (London: Printed by Command of his Majesty King George III, 1808).

Aconcio, Giacomo, *Satanae stratagemata* (Basel: Pietro Perna, 1564).

Aconcio, Giacomo, *Una essortatione al timor di Dio con alcune rime italiane nuovamente messe in luce* (London: John Wolfe, 1579).

Aconcio, Giacomo, *Darkness Discovered or the Devils Secret Stratagems Laid Open* (London: John Macock, 1651).

Aconcio, Giacomo, *Stratagematum Satanae libri VIII* (Florence: Valecchi, 1946).

Adams, Marianne S., "'Ocular proof' in *Othello* and Its Source," *PMLA*, 79, 3 (1964): 234–41.

Adelman, Janet, "Making Defect Perfection: Shakespeare and the One-Sex Model," in *Acting Gender on the English Renaissance Stage*, eds. Viviana Comensoli and Anne Russell (Chicago: University of Chicago Press, 1999).

Alpers, Paul, *What Is Pastoral?* (Chicago: University of Chicago Press, 1996).

Alpers, Paul J., *The Poetry of 'The Faerie Queene'* (Princeton: Princeton University Press, 1967).

Amos, Flora Ross, *Early Theories of Translation* (New York: Columbia University Press, 1920).

Anderson, Benedict, *Imagined Communities: Reflections on the Origin and Spread of Nationalism* (London: Verso, 1983).

Anderson, Michael, "The Law of Writ and the Liberty," *Theatre Research International*, 20, 3 (September 1995): 189–99.

Andreacchio, Marco, "Dante's Statius and Christianity: A Reading of *Purgatorio* XXI and XXII in Their Poetic Context," *Interpretation: A Journal of Political Philosophy*, 39, 1 (Winter 2012): 71–72.

Andreacchio, Marco, "Unmasking Limbo: Reading *Inferno* IV as Key to Dante's *Comedy*," *Interpretation: A Journal of Political Philosophy*, 40, 2 (Fall 2013): 199–220.

Andreini, Francesco, *Le Bravure del Capitano Spavento* (Venice: Somasco, 1607).

Andreini, Francesco, *Le bravure di Capitano Spavento* (1607), ed. Roberto Tessari (Pisa: Giardini, 1987).

Andreini, Isabella, *Contrasti scenici*, in *Fragmenti di alcune scritture della signora Isabella Andreini Comica Gelosa, et Academia Intenta. Raccolti da Francesco Andreini Comico Geloso, detto il Capitano Spavento, e dati in luce da Flamminio Scala* Comico, *e da lui dedicati all'illustrissimo Sig. Filippo Capponi* (Venice: Gio. Battista Combi, 1620).

Andreini, Isabella (and Francesco), *Fragmenti di alcune scritture* (includes the "Amorosi contrasti") (Venice: Combi, 1622).

Andrewe, Sir Thomas, *The Vnmasking of a Feminine Machiauell* (London: Simon Stafford, 1604).

Andrews, John Harwood, *Shapes of Ireland. Maps and Their Makers 1564–1839* (Dublin: Geography Publications, 1997).

Andrews, Richard, "Scripted Theatre and the *Commedia dell'Arte*," in *Theatre of the English and Italian Renaissance*, eds. J. R. Mulryne and Margaret Shewring (Basingstoke: Macmillan, 1991).

Andrews, Richard, *Scripts and Scenarios: The Performance of Comedy in Renaissance Italy* (Cambridge: Cambridge University Press, 1993).

Andrews, Richard, "Shakespeare, Molière, et la Commedia dell'Arte," in *La commedia dell'Arte, le Théâtre Forain, et les spectacles de plein air en Europe: XVIe–XVIIIe siècles*, ed. Irène Mamczarcz (Paris: Klincksieck, 1998).

Andrews, Richard, "Isabella Andreini and Others: Women on Stage in the Late Cinquecento," in *Women in Italian Renaissance Culture and Society*, ed. Letizia Panizza (Oxford: Legenda, 2000).

Andrews, Richard, "Molière, Commedia dell'Arte, and the Question of Influence in Early Modern European Theatre," *Modern Language Review*, 100, 2 (April 2005): 444–63.

Andrews, Richard (ed.), *The Commedia dell'Arte of Flaminio Scala. A Translation and Analysis of 30 Scenarios* (Lanham: The Scarecrow Press, 2008).

Andrews, Richard, "Resources in Common: Shakespeare and Flaminio Scala," in *Transnational Mobilities in Early Modern Theater*, eds. Robert Henke and Eric Nicholson (Farnham: Ashgate, 2014).

Andrews, Richard, "*The Tempest* and Italian Improvised Theatre," in *Revisiting 'The Tempest': The Capacity to Signify*, eds. Silvia Bigliazzi and Lisanna Calvi (Basingstoke, UK: Palgrave Macmillan, 2014).

Anglo, Sydney, *Machiavelli: A Dissection* (London: Gollancz, 1969).

Anglo, Sydney, *The Courtier's Art: Systematic Immorality in the Renaissance* (Swansea: University College of Swansea, 1983).

Anglo, Sydney, *Machiavelli – The First Century. Studies in Enthusiasm, Hostility, and Irrelevance* (Oxford: Oxford University Press, 2005).

Anon, "The English Courtier, and the Cuntry–Gentleman: A Pleasaunt and Learned Disputation, Betweene Them Both," in *Inedited Tracts: Illustrating the Manners, Opinions, and Occupations of Englishmen during the Sixteenth and Seventeenth Centuries*, ed. William Carew Hazlitt (London: Roxburghe Library, 1868; repr. New York: Burt Franklin, [1964?]).

Anselmi, Giam Maria, "Tradizione rinascimentale italiana e letteratura inglese," in *Una civile conversazione. Lo scambio letterario e culturale anglo-italiano nel Rinascimento*, eds. Keir Elam and Fernando Cioni (Bologna: CLUEB, 2003).

Anselmi, Gian Maria, "Partitura della *Mandragola*," in *Il Teatro di Machiavelli*, eds. Gennaro Barbarisi and Anna Maria Cabrini (Milan: Cisalpino, 2005).

Appleton, William W., *Beaumont and Fletcher: A Critical Study* (London: George Allen & Unwin Ltd., 1956).

Aquilecchia, Giovanni, "Nota su John Toland traduttore di Giordano Bruno," in *English Miscellany. A Symposium of History, Literature and the Arts*, Vol. IX, ed. Mario Praz (Rome: Edizioni di Storia e Letteratura, 1958).

Aquilecchia, Giovanni, "Scheda Bruniana: la traduzione "Tolandiana" dello *Spaccio*," *Giornale Storico della Letteratura Italiana*, 152 (1975).

Aquilecchia, Giovanni, *Schede bruniane (1950–1991)* (Manziana: Vecchiarelli, 1993).

Aquilecchia, Giovanni, "Giordano Bruno as Philosopher of the Renaissance," in ed. Hilary Gatti (Farnham: Ashgate, 2002).

Arber, Edward, *A Transcript of the Register of the Company of Stationers of London 1554–1640*, 5 vols. (London: prv. Pr., 1875–1894).

Ardila, J. A. G., "Traducción y receptión del Quijote en Gran Bretagna – 1612–1774," *Annales cervantinos*, XXXVII (2005): 253–65.

Ariani, Marco, "Ragione e furore nella tragedia di G. B. Giraldi Cinthio," in *Tra Classicismo e Manierismo: Il teatro tragico del Cinquecento*, ed. M. Ariani (Florence: Olschki, 1974).

Ariani, Marco, *Tra Classicismo e manierismo. Il teatro tragico del Cinquecento* (Florence: Holschki, 1974).

Ariani, Marco (ed.), *Il teatro italiano, parte II. La tragedia del Cinquecento*, Tomo I (Turin: Einaudi, 1977).

Arienzo, Alessandro, "From Machiavellian Policy to Parliamentarian Reason of State," in *Machiavellian Encounters in Tudor and Stuart England*, eds. Alessandro Arienzo and Alessandra Petrina (Farnham: Ashgate, 2010).

Arienzo, Alessandro and Alessandra Petrina (eds.), *Machiavellian Encounters in Tudor and Stuart England. Literary and Political Influences from the Reformation to the Restoration* (Farnham: Ashgate, 2013).

Ariosto, Ludovico, *Opere minori*, ed. Cesare Segre (Milan and Naples: Ricciardi Editore, 1954).

Ariosto, Ludovico, *The Comedies of Ariosto*, trans. and ed. by Edmond M. Beame and Leonard G. Sbrocchi (Chicago: University of Chicago Press, 1975).

Armstrong, Guyda, *The English Boccaccio: A History in Books* (Toronto: University of Toronto Press, 2013).

Ascham, Roger, *The Scholemaster* (London: John Daye, 1570).

Ascham, Roger, *Whole Works, Life and Letters*, ed. J. A. Giles and E. Grant (London: Smith, 1865).

Ascham, Roger, *The Schoolmaster*, ed. Lawrence V. Ryan (Ithaca: Cornell University Press, 1967).

Ascoli, Albert, "Pyrrhus' Rules: Playing with Power from Boccaccio to Machiavelli," *MLN*, 114, 1 (1999): 14–57.

Ascoli, Albert R., *Dante and the Making of a Modern Author* (Cambridge: Cambridge University Press, 2008).

Ascoli, Albert R., "Favola fui": *Petrarch Writes His Reader* Bernardo Lecture Series No. 17 (Albany: SUNY University Press, 2010).

Ascoli, Albert R., *A Local Habitation and a Name. Imagining Histories in the Italian Renaissance* (New York: Fordham University Press, 2011).

Ascoli, Albert R. and Victoria Kahn (eds.), *Machiavelli and the Discourse of Literature* (Ithaca: Cornell University Press, 1993).

Asor Rosa, Alberto, "*Istoria del concilio tridentino* di Paolo Sarpi," in *Genus italicum. Saggi sulla identità letteraria italiana nel corso del tempo*, ed. Alberto Asor Rosa (Turin: Einaudi, 1997).

Atkinson, James B., "Machiavelli: A Portrait," in *The Cambridge Companion to Machiavelli*, ed. John M. Najemy (Cambridge and New York: Cambridge University Press, 2010).

Attar, Karina F., "Genealogy of the Character: A Reading of Giraldi's Moor," in *Visions of Venice in Shakespeare*, eds. Laura Tosi and Shaul Bassi (Farnham: Ashgate, 2011).

Axton, Marie, "Lord Morley's *Tryumphes of Petrarcke*: Reading Spectacles," in *'Triumphs of English': Henry Parker, Lord Morley, Translator to the Tudor Court. New Essays in Interpretation*, eds. Marie Axton and James P. Carley (London: The British Library, 2000).

Axton, Mary, *The Queen's Two Bodies* (London: Royal Historical Society, 1977).

Badaloni, Nicola, *Giordano Bruno. Tra cosmologia ed etica* (Bari: De Donato, 1988).

Baglio, Marco, "Presenze dantesche nel Petrarca latino," *Studi Petrarcheschi*, 9 (1992): 77–136.

Bagshaw, Christopher, *A True Relation of the Faction Begun at Wisbich* (1601), sig. C1v.

Bakhtin, Michael, *The Dialogic Imagination*, ed. Mikhali Holquist, trans. by C. Emerson and M. Holquist (Austin: University of Texas Press, 1981).

Balbani, Niccolò, *The Italian Convert: News from Italy of a Second Moses. Or the Life of Galeacius Caracciolus, the noble Marquis of Vico* (Boston: Thomas Fleet, 1751).

Baldacci, Luigi, *Il Petrarchismo italiano nel Cinquecento* (Milan and Naples: R. Ricciardi, 1974 [1957]).

Baldassarri, Guido, "Poema eroico o 'romanzo'? Riscritture della Liberata dal Camilli al Gentili," in *Scritture di scritture: testi, generi, modelli nel Rinascimento*, eds. Giancarlo Mazzacurati and Michel Plaisance (Rome: Bulzoni, 1987).

Baldin, Gregorio, "Hobbes and Sarpi: Method, Matter, and Natural Philosophy," *Galilaeana*, X (2013): 85–118.

Baldwin, William, *A Myrroure for Magistrates* (London: Thomas Marshe, 1559).

Balzani, Ugo, "Di alcuni documenti dell'archivio del Santo Uffizio di Roma relativi al ritrovamento del cadavere di Paolo Sarpi," *Rendiconti della reale Accademia dei Lincei*, 5, 4 (1895): 595–617.

Baranski, Zygmunt G. and Theodore J. Cachey (eds.), *Petrarch & Dante: Anti-Dantism, Metaphysics, Tradition* (Notre Dame: Notre Dame University Press, 2009).

Barasch, Frances K., "Italian Actresses in Shakespeare's World: Flaminia and Vincenza," *Shakespeare Bulletin*, 18, 4 (2000).

Barasch, Frances K., "Italian Actresses in Shakespeare's World: Vittoria and Isabella," *Shakespeare Bulletin*, 19, 3 (2001).

Baratto, Mario, *La commedia del Cinquecento: (aspetti e problemi)* (Vicenza: Neri Pozza, 1977).

Barbierato, Federico, "Paolo Sarpi, the Papal Index and Censorship," in *Censorship Moments*, ed. Geoff Kemp (London: Bloomsbury, 2014).

Barbieri, Nicolò, *La Supplica* (originally published 1634), ed. F. Taviani (Milan: Il Polifilo, 1971).

Bardin, Gay, "Machiavelli Reads Boccaccio, *Mandragola* Between *Decameron* and *Corbaccio*," *Italian Quarterly*, 38 (2001): 149–50.

Barker, Roberta, "'Not One Thing Exactly': Gender, Performance and Critical Debate over the Early Modern Boy-Actress," *Literature Compass*, 6, 2 (2009).

Barolini, Teodolinda and H. Wayne Storey (eds.), *Petrarch and the Textual Origins of Interpretation* (New York: Columbia University Press, 2007).

Bartholmess, Christian, *Jordano Bruno* (Paris: Ladrange, 1846–1847).

Bartlett, K. R., "Morley, Machiavelli, and the Pilgrimage of Grace," in *'Triumphs of English'. Henry Parker, Lord Morley, Translator to the Stuart Court*, eds. M. Axton and J. P. Carley (London: The British Library, 2000).

Barton, Anne, *Ben Jonson, Dramatist* (Cambridge: Cambridge University Press, 1984).

Baskerville, Charles Read, *The Elizabethan Jig and Related Song Drama* (Chicago: University of Chicago Press, 1929; repr. New York: Dover, 1965).

Bassi, Shaul, *Shakespeare's Italy and Italy's Shakespeare. Place, "Race", Politics* (Basingstoke: Palgrave Macmillan, 2016).

Bate, Jonathan, "The Elizabethans in Italy," in *Travel and Drama in Shakespeare's Time*, eds. Jean-Pierre Marquelot and Michèle Willems (Cambridge: Cambridge University Press, 1966).

Bates, Catherine, "'A Large Occasion of Discourse': John Lyly and the Art of Civil Conversation," *Review of English Studies*, 42 (1991): 469–87.

Bates, Catherine, *The Rhetoric of Courtship in Elizabethan Language and Literature* (Cambridge: Cambridge University Press, 1992).

Bawcutt, Nigel W., "Some Elizabethan Allusions to Machiavelli," *English Miscellany*, 20 (1969): 53–74.

Bawcutt, Nigel W., "'Policy,' Machiavellianism, and the Earlier Tudor Drama," *English Literary Renaissance*, 1 (1971): 195–209.

Bawcutt, Nigel W., "The 'Myth of Gentillet' Reconsidered: An Aspect of Elizabethan Machiavellianism," *Modern Language Review*, 99 (2004): 863–74.

Beame, Edmond, "Introduction," in Ludovico Ariosto, *The Comedies of Ariosto*, trans. and ed. by Edmond M. Beame and Leonard G. Sbrocchi (Chicago: University of Chicago Press, 1975).

Beard, Thomas, *A Retractive from the Romish Religion* (1616), sig. D2v.

Becquet, Paul, "L'influence de Sénèque sur *Gorboduc*," *Etudes Anglaises*, 14 (1961).

Becquet, Paul, "L'imitation de Sénèque dans *Gorboduc*," in *Les Tragédies de Shakespeare et le theatre de la Renaissance*, eds. J. Jaquot et M. Oddon (Paris, 1964).

Beecher, Donald, "Introduction," to Lodovico Ariosto, *Supposes (I suppositi) (1509) translated by George* Gascoigne *(1566)*, ed. Donald Beecher and John Butler (Carleton Renaissance Plays in Translation 33, Ottawa: Dovehouse Editions, 1999).

Beecher, Donald (ed.), *Renaissance Comedy. The Italian Masters*, 2 vols. (Toronto: University of Toronto Press, 2008–2009).

Behn, Aphra, *The Emperor of the Moon*, in *The Rover and Other Plays*, ed. Jane Spencer (Oxford: Oxford University Press, 2008).

Bella, Carla, "Giovan Battista Giraldi Cinzio," in *Eros e censura nella tragedia dal '500 al '700* (Florence: Vallecchi Ed., 1981).

Belligni, Eleonora, *Auctoritas e potestats. Marcantonio de Dominis fra l'Inquisizione e Giacomo I* (Milan: Franco Angeli, 2003).

Belsey, Catherine, *The Subject of Tragedy: Identity and Difference in Renaissance Drama* (London: Methuen, 1985).

Belsey, Catherine, "Iago the Essayist: Between Montaigne and Shakespeare," in *Renaissance Go-Betweens: Cultural Exchange in Early Modern Europe* (Berlin: Walter de Gruyter, 2005).

Beltramini, Guido, Davide Gasparotto, and Adolfo Tura (eds.), *Pietro Bembo e l'invenzione del Rinascimento* (Venice: Marsilio, 2013).

Benassi, Stefano, "La vertigine del sublime: Mortalità della poesia e razionalità morale in F. Petrarca," in *Petrarca e la cultura europea*, ed. Secchi Tarugi Luisa (Milan: Editrice Nuovi Orizzonti, 1997).

Bennett, Henry S., *English Books and Readers vol. I, 1475–1557 and vol. II, 1558–1603* (Cambridge: Cambridge University Press, 1952 and 1965).

Benson, Pamela J., *The Invention of the Renaissance Woman* (University Park: Pennsylvania University Press, 1992).

Berger, Harry Jr., *The Absence of Grace. Sprezzatura and Suspicion in Two Renaissance Courtesy Books* (Stanford: Stanford University Press, 2000).

Bergeron, David M., "*Cymbeline*: Shakespeare's Last Roman Play," *Shakespeare Quarterly*, 31, 1 (Spring 1980): 31–41.

Bernardo, Aldo S. (ed.), *Francesco Petrarca: Citizen of the world* (Albany: SUNY University Press, 1980).

Bertelli, Sergio and Piero Innocenti, *Bibliografia Machiavelliana* (Verona: Edizioni Valdonega, 1979).

Bertini, Ferruccio, "Una novella del Boccaccio e l'*Alda* di Guglielmo di Blois," *Maia*, 29–30 (1977–78): 135–41.

Bertolo, Fabio Massimo, "John Wolfe, un editore inglese tra Aretino e Machiavelli," in *Il Rinascimento italiano di fronte alla Riforma: letteratura e arte*, eds. Chrysa Damianaki, Paolo Procaccioli, and Adriano Romano (Rome: Vecchiarelli, 2005).

Bessi, Rossella, *L'amoroso Messer Giusto da Valmontone* (Rome: Salerno, 2006).

Bessi, Rossella (ed.), *Giusto de' Conti di Valmontone: Un protagonista della poesia italiana del '400* (Rome: Bulzoni, 2008).

Bettarini, Rosanna, *Lacrime d'inchiostro nel* Canzoniere *di Petrarca* (Bologna: CLUEB, 1998).

Bevington, David, "Cultural Exchange: Gascoigne and Ariosto at Gray's Inn in 1566," in *The Italian World of English Renaissance Drama*, ed. M. Marrapodi (Newark: University of Delaware Press, 1998).

Biagioli, Mario, "Did Galileo copy the telescope? A 'new' letter by Paolo Sarpi," in *The Origins of the Telescope*, eds. Albert Van Helden, Sven Dupré, Rob van Gent, and Huib Zuidervaart (Amsterdam: KNAW Press, 2010).

Bigalli, Davide, "Petrarca: Dal Sentimento alla Dottrina Politica," in *Motivi e Forme delle* Familiari *di Francesco Petrarca*, ed. Claudia Berra, Università degli Studi di Milano: Facoltà di Lettere e Filosofia. Quaderni di Acme 57 (Milan: Cisalpino Istituto Editoriale Universitario, 2003).

Bigges, Walter, *A Summarie and True Discourse of Sir Frances Drakes West Indian Voyage* (London: Richard Field, 1589).

Binns, James, *Intellectual Culture in Elizabethan and Jacobean England: The Latin Writings of the Age* (Leeds: Cairns, 1990).

Blagden, Cyprian, *The Stationers' Company 1403–1959* (Stanford: Stanford University Press, 1977).

Blair, Ann, "La persistance du latin comme langue de science à la fin de la Renaissance," in *Sciences et langues en Europe*, eds. Roger Chartier and Pietro Corsi (Paris: Centre Alexandre Koyré, Ecole des Hautes Etudes en Sciences Sociales, 1996).

Blake, Erin C., "Shakespeare, Portraiture, Painting and Prints," in *The Edinburgh Companion to Shakespeare and the Arts*, eds. Mark Thornton Burnett, Adrian Sreete, and Ramona Wray (Edinburgh: Edinburgh University Press, 2011).

Blanc, Pierre (ed.), *Pétrarque en Europe XIV*e*-Xx*e *Siècle: Dynamique d'une expansion culturelle.* Acts of the twenty-sixth international congress of the CEFI, Turin and Chambéry, 11–15 December, 1995 (Paris: Honoré Champion, 2001).

Bliss, Lee, "The Renaissance Griselda: A Woman for All Seasons," *Viator*, 23 (1992): 301–43.

Blumenberg, Hans, *The Legitimacy of the Modern Age* (Cambridge, MA: MIT Press, 1983).

Blumenberg, Hans, *The Genesis of the Copernican World* (Cambridge, MA: MIT Press, 1987).

Bly, Mary, "Bait for the Imagination: Danae and Consummation in Petrarch and Heywood," *Comparative Literature Studies*, 32, 3 (1995): 343–59.

Boas, F. S. (ed.), *Sir Sidney Lee: Elizabethan and Other Essays* (Oxford: Clarendon Press, 1929).

Boccaccio, Giovanni, *Decameron, Tutte le Opere* 4, ed. Vittore Branca (Milan: Mondadori, 1976).

Boccaccio, Giovanni, *Buccolicum carmen* in *Tutte le opere di Giovanni Boccaccio*, ed. Giuseppe Velli, Vol. 5 (Milan: Mondadori, 1994).

Boccaccio, Giovanni, *Decameron*, trans. by Mark Musa and Peter Bondanella (New York: Signet Classic, 2002).

Boccaccio, Giovanni, *Boccaccio's Expositions on Dante's Comedy*, trans. by Michael Papio (Toronto: University of Toronto Press, 2009).

Boersma, Owe and Auke J. Jelsma, *Unity in Multiformity. The Minutes and Coetus of London, 1575 and the Concistory Minutes of the Italian Church in London, 1570–1591* (London: Huguenot Society of Great Britain and Ireland, 1997).

Boillet, Danielle and A. Pontremoli (eds.), *Il mito d'Arcadia: Pastori e amori nelle arti del Rinascimento* (Florence: Olschki, 2007).

Boitani, Piero, *Chaucer and the Imaginary World of Fame* (Cambridge: Cambridge University Press, 1984).

Bonora, Ettore, "La teoria del teatro negli scrittori del '500," in *Il teatro classico italiano nel '500* (Rome: Accademia dei Lincei, 1971).

Boro, Joyce, "John Fletcher's *Women Pleased* and the Pedagogy of Reading Romance," in *Staging Early Modern Romance*, ed. Lamb and Wayne (New York: Routledge, 2009).

Borris, Kenneth, *Allegory and Epic in English Renaissance Literature: Heroic Form in Sidney, Spenser and Milton* (Cambridge: Cambridge University Press, 2000).

Borsellino, Nino (ed.), *Commedie del Cinquecento* Vol. I (Milan: Feltrinelli Editore, 1967).

Borsellino, Nino, "*Decameron* come teatro" and "Aretino e Boccaccio," in *Rozzi e Intronati. Esperienze e forme di teatro dal Decameron al Candelaio* (Rome: Bulzoni Editore, 1976).

Boswell, Jackson Campbell and Gordon Braden (eds.), *Petrarch's English Laurels 1475–1700* (Farnham: Ashgate, 2012).

Bottoni, Luciano, *La Messinscena del Rinascimento II: Il segreto del diavolo e "La Mandragola". Critica letteraria e linguistica* (Milan: Franco Angeli, 2005).

Boughner, Daniel, *The Braggart in Renaissance Comedy* (Minneapolis: University of Minnesota Press, 1954).

Boutcher, W., *The School of Montaigne in Early Modern Europe* (Oxford: Oxford University Press, 2017).

Bouwsma, William J., *Venice and the Defense of Republican Values in the Age of the Counter Reformation* (Berkeley: University of California Press, 1968).

Bowers, Fredson (ed.), *The Dramatic Works of Thomas Dekker*, Vol. 1. (Cambridge: Cambridge University Press, 1953).

Bowers, Fredson (ed.), *The Dramatic Works in the Beaumont and Fletcher Canon*, Vol. 3 (Cambridge: Cambridge University Press, 1966).

Boyle, Anthony James, *Tragic Seneca: An Essay in the Theatrical Tradition* (New York: Routledge, 1997).

Braddick, Michael J., *State Formation in Early Modern England, 1550–1700* (Cambridge: Cambridge University Press, 2000).

Braden, Gordon, "Love and Fame: The Petrarchan Career," in *Pragmatism's Freud: The Moral Disposition of Psychoanalysis*, eds. William Kerrigan and J. H. Smith (Baltimore: Johns Hopkins University Press, 1986).

Braden, Gordon, "Gaspara Stampa and the Gender of Petrarchism," *Texas Studies in Literature and Language*, 38 "Revising Renaissance Eroticism" (Summer, 1996): 115–39.

Braden, Gordon, *Petrarchan Love and the Continental Renaissance* (New Haven: Yale University Press, 1999).

Braden, Gordon, Robert Cummings, and Stuart Gillespie, *The Oxford History of Literary Translations in English, 1550–1660* (Oxford: Oxford University Press, 2010).

Bradley, William Aspenwall (ed.), *The Correspondence of Philip Sidney and Hubert Languet* (Boston: The Merrimount Press, 1912).

Bradshaw, Graham, *Misrepresentations: Shakespeare and the Materialists* (Ithaca: Cornell University Press, 1993).

Bragantini, Renzo, "Dialogo," in *Lessico critico decameroniano*, eds. R. Bragantini and P. M. Forni (Turin: Bollati Boringhieri, 1995), pp. 93–115.

Brand, Charles Peter, *Torquato Tasso: A Study of the Poet and of His Contribution to English Literature* (Cambridge: Cambridge University Press, 1965).

Braudel, Fernand, *Le modèle italien* (Paris: Arthaud, 1989).

Brigden, Susan, *Thomas Wyatt: The Heart's Forest* (London: Faber, 2012).

Britton, Dennis Austin and Melissa Walter (eds.), *Rethinking Shakespeare Source Study: Audiences, Authors, and Digital Technologies* (Oxford and New York: Routledge, 2018).

Bromham, A. A., "The Tragedy of Peace. Political Meaning in *Women Beware Women*," *Studies in English Literature*, 26, 2 (Spring 1986).

Bromham, A. A. and Zara Bruzzi, *'The Changeling' and the Years of Crisis: 1619–1624: A Hieroglyph of Britain* (London and New York: Pinter, 1990).

Brooke, Christopher and Roger Highfield, *Oxford and Cambridge* (Cambridge: Cambridge University Press, 1988).

Brown, Alison, *The Return of Lucretius to Renaissance Florence* (Cambridge, MA: Harvard University Press, 2010).

Brown, Pamela Allen, "The Counterfeit Innamorata, or the Diva Vanishes," in *Shakespeare Yearbook*, Vol. 10, eds. Holger Klein and Michele Marrapodi (1999).

Brown, Pamela Allen, *Better a Shrew than a Sheep: Women, Drama, and the Culture of Jest in Early Modern England* (Ithaca: Cornell University Press, 2003).

Brown, Pamela Allen, "'Cattle of this Colour': Boying the Diva in *As You Like It*," *Early Theatre*, 15, 1 (2012).

Brown, Pamela Allen, "Dido, Boy Diva of Carthage: Marlowe's Dido Tragedy and the Renaissance Actress," in *Transnational Mobilities in Early Modern Theater*, eds. Robert Henke and Eric Nicholson (Burlington: Ashgate, 2014).

Brown, Rawdon (ed.), *Calendar of State Papers and Manuscripts Relating to English Affairs Existing in the Archives and Collections of Venice and in Other Libraries of Northern Italy*, 38 vols. (London: Longman, Roberts and Green, 1864–1947).

Brumbaugh, Barbara, "Jerusalem Delivered and the allegory of Sidney's Revised Arcadia," *Modern Philology*, 101 (2004): 337–70.

Brundin, Abigail, *Vittoria Colonna and the Poetics of the Italian Reformation* (Farnham: Ashgate, 2008).

Bruni, Domenico, *Prologhi, parte seconda* (Undated seventeenth-cent. ms. in the Brera Library, Milan).

Bruno, Giordano, *Candelaio*, ed. Giorgio Bàrberi Squarotti (Turin: Einaudi, 1964a).

Bruno, Giordano, *The Expulsion of the Triumphant Beast*, ed. Arthur D. Imerti (Lincoln: University of Nebraska, 1964b).

Bruno, Giordano, *The Heroic Frenzies*, ed. Paul Eugene Memmo (Chapel Hill: The University of North Carolina Press, 1964c).

Bruno, Giordano, *The Ash Wednesday Supper*, ed. Stanley L. Jaki (The Hague: Mouton, 1975).

Bruno, Giordano, *Il candelaio*, in *Il teatro italiano II.3: La commedia del Cinquecento* (Turin: Einaudi, 1978).

Bruno, Giordano, *Dialoghi italiani* (Florence: Sansoni, 1985).

Bruno, Giordano, *Cause, Principle and Unity*, ed. Robert De Lucca, with an Introduction by Alfonso Ingegno (Cambridge: Cambridge University Press, 2004).

Bruno, Giordano, *The Candlemaker*, trans. by Gino Moliterno, in *Renaissance Comedy. The Italian Masters*, Vol. 2, ed. with an Introduction by Donald Beecher (Toronto: University of Toronto Press, 2009).

Bruscagli, Riccardo, "La corte in scena. Genesi politica della tragedia ferrarese," in *Stagioni della civiltà estense* (Pisa: Nistri-Lischi, 1983).

Bruster, Douglas, "Shakespearean Spellings and Handwriting in the Additional Passages Printed in the 1602 'Spanish Tragedy'," *Notes and Queries*, 60 (2013): 420–24.

Brykman, Geneviève, La judéité de Spinoza (Paris: Vrin, 1972).

Bryson, Anna, *From Courtesy to Civility: Changing Codes of Conduct in Early Modern England* (Oxford: Clarendon Press, 1998).

Bucciantini, Massimo, Michele Camerota, and Franco Giudice, *Il Telescopio di Galileo: Una storia europea* (Turin: Einaudi, 2012).

Buchheit, Vinzenz, "'Epicurus' Triumph of the Mind (Lucr. 1.62–79)," in *Oxford Readings in Classical* Studies. *Lucretius*, ed. Monica R. Gale (Oxford: Oxford University Press, 2007).

Bueler, Lois E., "The Structural Uses of Incest in English Renaissance Drama," *Renaissance Drama*, 15 (1984): 115–45.

Bull, George (trans.), *Machiavelli: The Prince* (Harmondsworth: Penguin Books, 1961).

Bullough, Geoffrey, *Narrative and Dramatic Sources of Shakespeare*, 8 vols. (Oxford: Routledge and London: Kegan Paul, 1957–1975), vol. 7, "Major Tragedies" (1973).

Burckhardt, Jakob, *The Civilization of the Renaissance in Italy*, trans. by Samuel G. C. Middlemore, intr. P. Gay (New York: Modern Library, 2002).

Burke, Edmund, *Reflections on the Revolution in France*, ed. Connor Cruise O'Brien (Harmondsworth: Penguin, 1968).

Burke, Peter, *Fortunes of the Courtier: The European Reception of Castiglione's 'Cortegiano'* (Oxford: Polity Press, 1995).

Burke, Peter, *Languages and Communities in Early Modern Europe* (Cambridge: Cambridge University Press, 2004).

Burrow, Colin (ed.), *William Shakespeare: Complete Sonnets and Poems* (Oxford: Oxford University Press, 2002).

Burton, Robert, *The Anatomy of Melancholy* (1621), sig. B4v.

Butler, Martin, *Theatre and Crisis, 1632–1642* (Cambridge: Cambridge University Press, 1984).

Cairncross, Andrew S., "Shakespeare and Ariosto: *Much Ado About Nothing, King Lear*, and *Othello*," *Renaissance Quarterly*, 29, 2 (1976): 178–82.

Caldwell, Mark (ed.), *The Prose of Fulke Greville* (New York: Garland, 1987).

Calendar of State Papers, Foreign, January-June 1583.

Calitti, Floriana, L. Chines, and R. Gigliucci (eds.), *Il Petrarchismo: Un modello di poesia per l'Europa* (Rome: Bulzoni, 2006).

Camden, William, *Remaines of a Greater Worke, Concerning Britaine* (London: G[eorge] E[ld] for Simon Waterson, 1605).

Campbell, Emma, "Sexual Poetics and the Politics of Translation in the Tale of Griselda," *Comparative Literature*, 55, Summer (2003): 191–216.

Campbell, Julie D., "'Merry, Nimble, Stirring Spirit[s}': Academic, Salon, and Commedia dell'arte Influence on the Innamorate of Love's Labour's Lost," in *Women Players in England, 1500–1660, Beyond the All Male Stage*, eds. Pamela Allen Brown and Peter Parolin (Farnham: Ashgate, 2005).

Campbell, Lily B., "Doctor Faustus: A Case of Conscience," *Publications of the Modern Language Association of America*, 67 (1952): 219–39.

Campbell, Stephen J., "Eros in the Flesh: Petrarchan Desire, the Embodied Eros, and Male Beauty in Italian Art, 1500–1540," *The Journal of Medieval and Early Modern Studies*, 35, 3 (2005): 629–62.

Cantimori, Delio, *Eretici italiani del Cinquecento: ricerche storiche* (Florence: Sansoni, 1939).

Cantimori, Delio, "Studi di storia della Riforma e dell'eresia in Italia e studi sulla storia della vita religiosa nella prima metà del '500 (Rapporto fra i due tipi di ricerca)," *Bollettino della Società di Studi Valdesi*, 76/102 (1957): 29–38.

Cantimori, Delio, *Adelmare Cesare*, in *Dizionario Biografico degli Italiani*, Vol. 1 (Roma: Istituto della Enciclopedia Italiana, 1960).

Cappelli, Guido, "Petrarca (post)moderno: Notelle informali sulla disperazione di parlare di un classico," *Petrarchesca*, 1 (2013).

Caravale, Giorgio, *Storia di una doppia censura: gli Stratagemmi di Satana di Giacomo Aconcio nell'Europa del Seicento* (Pisa: Edizioni della Normale, 2013).

Caretti, Lanfranco (ed.), *Torquato Tasso: Gerusalemme liberata* (Turin: Einaudi, 1971).

Carey, John and Alistair Fowler (eds.), *The Poems of John Milton* (London: Longmans, 1968).

Carlo, Vecce, "Boccaccio e Sannazaro (angioini)," in *Boccaccio angioino. Materiali per la storia culturale di Napoli nel Trecento*, eds. G. Alfano et al. (Brussels: Peter Lang, 2012).

Carnicelli, D. D. (ed.), Lord Morley's *Tryumphes of Petrarch* (Cambridge, MA: Harvard University Press, 1971).

Carrai, Stefano (ed.), *La poesia pastorale nel Rinascimento* (Padua: Antenore, 1998).

Cartier, Jacques, *Brief récit, & succinte narration, de la navigation faicte es ysles de Canada, Hochelage & Saguenay & autres, avec particulières meurs, langaige & ceremonies des habitans d'icelles* (Paris: Roffet & Le Clerc, 1545).

Cartier, Jacques, *A Shorte and Briefe Narration of the Two Navigations and Discoveries to the Northweast Partes Called Newe Fraunce: First Translated Out of French into Italian, by that Famous Learned Man Gio: Bapt:*

Ramusius, and now Turned into English by Iohn Florio: Worthy the Reading of All Venturers, Travellers, and Discoverers (London: H. Bynneman, 1580).

Case, John, *Sphaera Ciuitatis; Hoc est; Reipublicae recte ac pie secundum leges administrande ratio* (Francofurdi: Apud Ioan. Wechelum, 1589).

Cassirer, Ernest, *The Individual and the Cosmos in Renaissance Philosophy*, trans. and introd. by Mario Domandi (Chicago: Chicago University Press, 2010 [1927]).

Castellio, Sébastien, *De haereticis an sint persequendi* (1554) (Geneva: Droz, 1954).

Castiglione, Baldassare, *De curiali sive aulico libri quatuor* (London: John Day, 1571).

Castiglione, Baldassare, *Il Libro del Cortegiano* (1528), ed. Vittorio Cian (Florence: Sansoni, 1947).

Castiglione, Baldassare, *The Book of the Courtier*, trans. by Thomas Hoby, intro. J. H. Whitfield (London: J. M. Dent & Sons Ltd., 1974).

Castiglione, Baldassare, *The Book of the Courtier*, trans. by Thomas Hoby, ed. Virgina Cox (London: J. M. Dent, 1994).

Castiglione, Balthasar, *Balthasaris Castilionis Comitis De Curialisiue Aulico* trans. by Bartholomew Clerke (London: John Day, 1571/2).

Castiglione, Balthazar, *The Covrtyer of Count Baldessar Castlio Divided into Foure Bookes*, trans. by Thomas Hoby (London: William Seres, 1561).

Cauthen, Irby B. (ed.), Thomas Sackville & Thomas Norton, *Gorboduc, or Ferrex and Porrex* (London: Edward Arnold, 1970).

Cavazza, Silvano, "Una vicenda europea: Vergerio e il caso Spiera, 1548–49," in *La fede degli italiani. Per Adriano Prosperi*, eds. Guido Dall'Olio, Adelisa Malena, and Pieroberto Scaramella (Pisa: Edizioni della Normale, 2011).

Cazalé Bérard, Claude, "Boccaccio's Working Notebooks *(Zibaldone Laurenziano, Miscellanea Laurenziana, Zibaldone Magliabechiano)*," in *Boccaccio: A Critical Guide to the Complete Works*, eds. Victoria Kirkham, Michael Sherberg, and Janet Levarie Smarr (Chicago: University of Chicago Press, 2013).

Cecchi, Gianmaria M., *Comedie di M. Gianmaria Cecchi, La dote*, Vol. I (Venice: B. Giunti, 1585).

Cecchi, Giovan Maria, "*Le pellegrine*, Intermedio 6," in *Commedie inedite di Giovan Maria Cecchi*, ed. Giovanni Tortoli (Florence: Barbèra, Bianchi, 1855).

Cecioni, Cesare G., "Un adattamento di due novelle del Boccaccio nello *Heptameron of Civil Discourses* di George Whetstone (1582)," in *Il Boccaccio nella cultura inglese*, ed. G. Galigani (Florence: Olschki, 1974).

Chakrawotry, Swapan, *Society and Politics in the Plays of Thomas Middleton* (Oxford: Clarendon Press, 1996).

Chambers, E. K., *The Elizabethan Stage*, 4 vols. (Oxford: The Clarendon Press, 1923).

Chambers, E. K., *William Shakespeare: A Study of Facts and Problems*, 2 vols. (Oxford: Clarendon Press, 1930).

Chambers, E. K., *Shakespearean Gleanings* (Oxford: Clarendon Press, 1944).

Champion, Justin, *The Pillars of Priestcraft Shaken: The Church of England and Its Enemies, 1660–1730* (Cambridge: Cambridge University Press, 1992).

Champion, Justin, *Republican Learning: John Toland and the Crisis of Christian Culture, 1696–1722* (Manchester: Manchester University Press, 2003).

Chaney, Edward, *The Evolution of the Grand Tour: Anglo-Italian Cultural Relations Since the Renaissance* (Oxford: Routledge, 2000).

Chartier, Alain, *Here foloweth the copye of a letter whyche Maistre Alayn Charetier wrote to hys Brother*, trans. by William Caxton (Westminster: William Caxton, 1483).

Chavasse, Ruth, "Humanism in Exile: Caelio Secondo Curione's Learned Women Friends and Exempla for Elizabeth I," *Parergon*, 14, 1 (1996): 165–86.

Cheney, Donald, *Spenser's Image of Nature: Wild Man and Shepherd in the Faerie Queene* (New Haven: Yale University Press, 1966).

Cheney, Patrick, "'O Let My Books Be...Dumb Presages': Poetry and Theater in Shakespeare's Sonnets," *Shakespeare Quarterly*, 52 (2001): 235–36.

Cherchi, Paolo, Micaela Rinaldi, and Mariangela Tempera (eds.), *Giovan Battista Giraldi Cinzio gentiluomo ferrarese* (Florence: Olshki, 2008).

Chess, Simone, *Male-to-Female Crossdressing in Early Modern English Literature: Gender, Performance, and Queer Relations* (New York and Oxford: Routledge, 2016).

Chiappelli, Fredi, *Studi sul linguaggio del Machiavelli* (Florence: Le Monnier, 1952).

Churchill, Winston S., *A History of the English Speaking Peoples*, 4 vols. (London: Cassell & Company, 1956–58). II (1956).

Cian, Vittorio, "Il maggior petrarchista del Cinquecento, Pietro Bembo," *Annali della cattedra petrarchesca*, 8 (1938): 1–42.

Cicero, Marcus Tullius, *Marcus Tullius Ciceroes thre Bokes of Duties to Marcus His Sonne* (London: Richard Tottel, 1556).

Ciliberto, Michele, *Lessico di Giordano Bruno*, Vol. 1 (Rome: Edizioni dell'Ateneo & Bizzarri, 1979).

Ciliberto, Michele, "Introduzione," in *Spaccio de la bestia trionfante*, ed. Giordano Bruno (Milan: Rizzoli, 1985).

Ciliberto, Michele, *La ruota del tempo. Interpretazione di Giordano Bruno* (Rome: Editori Riuniti, 1986).

Ciliberto, Michele, *Umbra profunda. Studi su Giordano Bruno* (Rome: Edizioni di Storia e Letteratura, 1999).

Ciliberto, Michele, "Filosofia e autobiografia in Croce," *Studi storici*, 4 (1992): 693–712, republished in Ciliberto, *Figure in chiaroscuro. Filosofia e storiografia nel Novecento* (Rome: Edizioni storia e letteratura, 2001).

Ciliberto, Michele, "Alcune ipotesi su Paolo Sarpi," in *Pensare per contrari. Disincanto e utopia nel Rinascimento*, ed. M. Ciliberto (Rome: Edizioni di Storia e Letteratura, 2005).

Clark, Sandra, "*Hic Mulier, Haec Vir* and the Controversy over the Masculine Women," *Studies in Philology*, LXXXII, Spring (1985): 157–83.

Clark, Stuart, "Wisdom Literature of the Seventeenth Century: A Guide to the Contents of the 'Bacon-Tottel' Commonplace Books. Part I," *Transactions of the Cambridge Bibliographical Society*, 6 (1976): 291–305.

Classen, Albrecht (ed.), *Rural Space in the Middle Ages and Early Modern Age: The Spatial Turn in Premodern* Studies (Berlin and Boston: De Gryuter, 2012).

Claudian, "In Eutropium," in *Claudian*, trans. by Maurice Platnauer (Cambridge, MA: Harvard University Press, 1922).

Clegg, Cyndia Susan, Mark Goldie, Geoff Kemp, and Jason Mcellyot, *Censorship and the Press*, Vol. 1 (London: Pickering and Chatto, 1984).

Clegg, Roger and Lucie Skeaping (eds.), *Singing Simpkin and Other Bawdy Jigs: Musical Comedy on the Shakespearean Stage* (Exeter: University of Exeter Press, 2014).

Clements, Robert J. and Joseph Gibaldi, *Anatomy of the Novella: The European Tale Collection from Boccaccio and Chaucer to Cervantes* (New York: New York University Press, 1977).

Clubb, Louise George, *Giambattista Della Porta Dramatist* (Princeton: Princeton University Press, 1965).

Clubb, Louise George, "Pictures for the Reader: A Series of Illustrations to Comedy, 1591–1592," *Renaissance Drama*, Old Series 9 (1966): 265–77, with corrigenda in *Renaissance Drama*, New Series I (1968): 340–41.

Clubb, Louise George, *Italian Plays (1500–1700) in the Folger Library* (Florence: Leo S. Olschki, 1968).

Clubb, Louise George, "The Law of Writ and the Liberty: Italian Professional Theatre," in *Italian Drama in Shakespeare's Time*, ed. Louise George Clubb (New Haven: Yale University Press, 1989a).

Clubb, Louise George, *Italian Drama in Shakespeare's Time* (New Haven: Yale University Press, 1989b).

Clubb, Louise George, "Intertextualities: Some Questions," in *The Italian World of English Renaissance Drama: Cultural Exchange and Intertextuality*, ed. M. Marrapodi (Newark: The University of Delaware Press, 1998).

Clubb, Louise George, "Italian Stories on the Stage," in *The Cambridge Companion to Shakespearean Comedy*, ed. Alexander Leggatt (Cambridge: Cambridge University Press, 2002).

Clubb, Louise George, "Pastoral Jazz from the Writ to the Liberty," in *Italian Culture in the Drama of Shakespeare & His Contemporaries: Rewriting, Remaking, Refashioning*, ed. Michele Marrapodi (Farnham: Ashgate, 2007).

Clubb, Louise George, *Pollastra and the Origins of Twelfth Night. Parthenio, commedia (1516) with an English Translation* (Farnham: Ashgate, 2010).

Clubb, Louise George, "Looking Back on Shakespeare and Italian Theater," *Renaissance Drama*, 36/37, ed. Albert Ascoli and William N. West (2010): 3–19.

Clukas, Stuart, "Thomas Watson's *Hekatompathia* and European Petrarchism," in *Petrarch in Britain. Interpreters, Imitators, and Translators over 700 Years*, eds. Martin McLaughlin and Letizia Panizza, with Peter Hainsworth (London: British Academy, 2007).

Cochrane, Eric (ed.), *The Late Italian Renaissance* (New York: Harper & Row, 1970).

Cohen, Adam Max, "The Mirror of all Christian Courtiers: Castiglione's *Cortegiano* as a Source for *Henry V*," in *Italian Culture in the Drama of Shakespeare and his Contemporaries. Rewriting, Remaking, Refashioning*, ed. M. Marrapodi (Farnham: Ashgate, 2007).

Coldiron, A. E. B., "Watson's *Hekatompathia* and Renaissance Lyric Translation," *Translation and Literature*, 5, 1 (1996): 3–25.

Cole, Howard, *The "All's Well" Story from Boccaccio to Shakespeare* (Urbana: University of Illinois Press, 1981).

Collinson, Patrick, *The Elizabethan Puritan Movement* (Oxford: Clarendon Press, 1967).

Commentarium de Regno... adversus Nicolaum Machiavellum Florentinum (Geneva: J. Stoer, 1577).

Cone, Mary, *Fletcher without Beaumont: A Study of the Independent Plays of John Fletcher*, Jacobean Drama Studies 60 (Salzburg: Institut für Englische Sprache und Literatur, Universität Salzburg, 1976).

Connell, William J., "A Note about the Text and Translation," in *The Prince by Niccolò Machiavelli: With Related Documents* (Boston: Bedford/St Martin's, 2005).

Coogan, Robert, "Petrarch's Latin Prose and the English Renaissance," *Studies in Philology*, 68, 3 (1971): 271.

Cooper, Tarnya et al. (eds.), *Searching for Shakespeare* (National Portrait Gallery, 2006).

Cooper, Tarnya, Aviva Burnstock, Maurice Howard, Edward Town et al. *Painting in Britain, 1500 to 1630: Production, Influences and Patronage* (The British Academy/Oxford University Press, 2015).

Corbett, John, "Writtin in the Language of Scottis Nation: Literary Translation into Scots," in *Translating Literature*, ed. Susan Bassnett (Cambridge: D.S. Brewer, 1997).

Cornelius Agrippa, Heinrich, *Of the Vanitie and Uncertaintie of Artes and Sciences*, trans. by James Sanford (London: Henry Wykes, 1569).

Coronato, Rocco, *Shakespeare, Caravaggio, and the Indistinct Regard* (Oxford: Routledge, 2018).

Coryat, Thomas, *Coryat's Crudities* (1611), 2 vols. (Glasgow: J. MacLehose, 1905).

Cottino-Jones, Marga and Edward F. Tuttle (ed.), "Il *Decameron* teatrale nel Rinascimento," in *Boccaccio: Secoli di Vita* (Ravenna: Longo Editore, 1977).

Cox, Virginia, *The Renaissance Dialogue: Literary Dialogue in Its Social and Political Contexts, Castiglione to Galileo* (Cambridge: Cambridge University Press, 1992).

Cox, Virginia, "Castiglione and His Critics," in Baldassare Castiglione, *The Book of the Courtier*, trans. by Thomas Hoby, ed. Virginia Cox (London: J. M. Dent, 1994).

Cozzi, Gaetano, "Fra Paolo Sarpi, l'anglicanesimo e la *Historia del Concilio Tridentino*," *Rivista storica italiana*, LXIII (1956): 559–619.

Cozzi, Gaetano, "Paolo Sarpi tra il cattolico Philippe Canaye de Fresnes e il calvinista Isaac Casaubon," *Bollettino dell'Istituto di storia della società e dello stato veneziano*, i (1959): 27–154.

Cozzi, Gaetano, "Sir Edwin Sandys e la 'Relazione dello stato della religione'," *Rivista storica italiana*, lxxix (1967): 1096–121.

Cozzi, Gaetano, "Rinascimento Riforma Controriforma," in *La storiografia italiana negli ultimi vent'anni*, 2 vols. (Milan: Marzorati, 1970).

Cozzi, Gaetano, *Paolo Sarpi tra Venezia e l'Europa* (Turin: Einaudi, 1979).

Craig, Hardin (ed.), *Machiavelli's The Prince: An Elizabethan Translation. Edited with an Introduction and Notes from a Manuscript in the Collection of Mr Jules Furthman* (Chapel Hill: University of North Carolina Press, 1944).

Crane, Mary Thomas, *Framing Authority: Sayings, Self and Society in Sixteenth Century England* (Durham, NC: Duke University Press, 1960).

Crane, T. F., *Italian Social Customs of the Sixteenth Century and Their Influence on the Literatures of Europe* (New Haven: Yale University Press, 1920).

Creigh, Geoffrey and Jane Belfield (ed. and intro.), *The Cobler of Caunterburie and Tarltons Newes out of Purgatorie* (Leiden: Brill, 1987).

Crivelli, Tatiana and Teresa Nocita, "Teatralità del Dettato, Stratificazioni strutturali, Plurivocità degli esiti: Il *Decameron* fra Testo, Ipertesto e Generi Letterari," in *Autori e Lettori di Boccaccio. Atti del Convegno internazionale di Certaldo (20–22 settembre 2001)*, ed. Michelangelo Picone (Florence: Franco Cesati, 2002).

Croce, Benedetto, "Il Beneficio di Cristo," *Critica*, 38 (1940): 115–25.

Croce, Benedetto, "Su l'autore del *Beneficio di Cristo*. Lettera a S. Caponnetto," *Appello*, 7 (1942): 69.

Croce, Benedetto, *Vite di avventure di fede e di passione*, ed. Giuseppe Galasso (Milan: Adelphi, 1989).

Cuman, John E., *Character and the Individual Personality in English Renaissance Drama* (London: Rowman and Littlefield, 2014).

Cuneo, Anne, *Un monde de mots* (Orbe: Bernard Campiche, 2011).

Cunliffe, John, "Gismond of Salerne," *PMLA*, 21, 2 (1906): 436.

Cunliffe, John, *Influence of Seneca on Elizabethan Tragedy* (Basingstok: Macmillan, 1893).

Curione, Celio, *Secondo, Pasquine in a Traunce. A Christian and Learned Dialogue … Whereunto Are Added Certaine Questions Then Put Foorth by Pasquine to Have Been Disputed in the Councell of Trent* (London: Thomas Este, 1584).

Da Correggio, Niccolò, *Opere*, ed. Antonia Tissoni Benvenuti (Bari: Laterza, 1969).

D'Amico, Jack, *Shakespeare and Italy: The City and the Stage* (Gainesville: University of Florida Press, 2001).

D'Ancona, Alessandro, *Origini del teatro italiano*, 2 vols. (Turin: Loescher, 1891, repr., Rome: Bardi, 1971).

D'Andrea, Antonio, "Giraldi Cinthio and the Birth of the Machiavellian Hero on the Elizabethan Stage," in *Il Teatro italiano del Rinascimento*, ed. Maristella de Panizza Lorch (Milan: Edizioni di Comunità, 1980).

Daniel, Samuel, *The Worthy Tract of Paulus Jovius, Contayning a Discourse of Rare Inventions* (1585), sig. ⋆4r.

Daniel, Samuel, *Samuel Daniel: Poems and A Defence of Rhyme*, ed. Arthur Colby Sprague (Chicago: University of Chicago Press, 1965).

Danson, Lawrence, *Shakespeare's Dramatic Genres* (Oxford: Oxford University Press, 2000).

Darell, Walter, *A Short Discourse of the Life of Servingmen* (1578), sig. A3r.

Darnton, Robert, *The Kiss of Lamourette. Reflections in Cultural History* (New York: Norton, 1990).

Dasenbrock, Reed W., *Imitating the Italians: Wyatt, Spenser, Synge, Pound, Joyce* (Baltimore: Johns Hopkins University Press, 1991).

Dasgupta, Sukanya, "Silent Spring: Poly-Olbion and the Politics of Landscape," *Cambridge Journal*, 39 (2010): 152–71.

Davico Bonino, Guido (ed.), *La commedia del Cinquecento*, 3 vols. (Turin: Einaudi, 1977–1978).

Davies, John, *The Muses Sacrifice* (London, 1612).

Davies of Hereford, John, *Microcosmos* (London, 1603).

DeCoste, Mary-Michelle, *Hopeless Love: Boiardo, Ariosto, and Narratives of Queer Desire* (Toronto: University of Toronto Press, 2009).

De Francisci, Enza and Chris Stamatakis (eds.), *Shakespeare, Italy, and Transnational Exchange. Early Modern to Present* (Oxford: Routledge, 2017).

Della Casa, Giovanni, *Galateo: Or Rather, a Treatise of the Manners and Behauiours, It Behoueth a Man to vse and Eschewe, in His Familiar Conuersation*, trans. by Robert Peterson (London: Raufe Newbery, 1576; facsimile reproduction Amsterdam; New York: Theatrum Orbis Terrarum; Da Capo Press, 1969).

Della Casa, Giovanni, *The Refin'd Courtier*, trans. by Nathaniel Walker (1663), sig. A2r.

Della Casa, Giovanni, *Galateo* (1558), ed. Saverio Orlando (Milan: Garzanti, 1988).

Della Porta, Giambattista, *Gli duoi fratelli rivali/The Two Rival Brothers*, ed. and trans. by Louise George Clubb (Berkeley: University of California Press, 1980).

Del Re, Arundel, *The Secret of the Renaissance and Other Essays and Studies* (Tokyo: Kaitakusha, 1930).

De Marco, Sergio, "La "beffa" boccaccesca in alcuni "Jest Books" elisabettiani," in *Il Boccaccio Nella Cultura Inglese e Anglo-Americana*, ed. Giuseppe Galigani (Florence: Olschki Editore, 1974).

De Mas, Enrico, *Sovranità politica e unità cristiana nel Seicento anglo-veneto* (Ravenna: Longo, 1975).

De Mendonça, Barbara Heliodora Carneiro, "The Influence of Gorboduc in 'King Lear'," *Shakespeare Survey*, 13 (1960).

De Robertis, Domenico, *Editi e rari: Studi sulla tradizione letteraria tra Tre e Cinquecento* (Milan: Feltrinelli, 1978).

De Spinoza, Benedict, *The Letters* (Indianapolis: Hackett, 1995).

De Spinoza, Benedict, *Theological-Political Treatise*, ed. Jonathan I. Israel (Cambridge: Cambridge University Press, 2007).

de Valdés, Juan, *Alfabeto cristiano, dialogo con Giulia Gonzaga*, intro., notes, and appendix by Benedetto Croce (Bari: Laterza, 1938).

De Vivo, Filippo, "Paolo Sarpi and the Uses of Information in Seventeenth-Century Venice," *Media History*, 11, 1/2 (2005): 37–51.

De Vivo, Filippo, *Information and Communication in Venice: Rethinking Early Modern Politics* (Oxford: Oxford University Press, 2007).

De Vivo, Filippo, "Francia e Inghilterra di fronte all'interdetto di Venezia," in *Paolo Sarpi. Politique et religion en Europe*, ed. Marie Viallon (Paris: Édition Classiques Garnier, 2010).

Dempsey, Charles, *The Early Renaissance and Vernacular culture* (Cambridge, MA: Harvard University Press, 2012).

Dennis, John and John Eccles, *Rinaldo and Armida: A Tragedy* (London, 1699).

Denton, John, "The Significance and Impact of Translations in the English Renaissance," in *Übersetzung, Translation, Traduction*, eds. H. Kittel, J. House, and B. Schultze (De Gruyter, 2007).

Dewar-Watson, Sarah, *Shakespeare's Poetics: Aristotle and Anglo-Italian Renaissance Genres* (Oxford: Routledge, 2018).

Di Maria, Salvatore, *The Italian Tragedy in the Renaissance: Cultural Realities and Theatrical Innovations* (Lewisburg: Bucknell University Press, 2002).

Di Maria, Salvatore, "From Prose to Stage: Machiavelli's *Mandragola*," *MLN*, 121, 1 (January 2006): 130–55.

Di Maria, Salvatore, *The Poetics of Imitation in the Italian Theatre of the Renaissance* (Toronto: University of Toronto Press, 2013).

Dillon, Janette, "Shakespeare and English Performance Style: The European Context," in *Shakespeare Survey*, Vol. 54 (Cambridge: Cambridge University Press, 2001).

Dimmock, Matthew, "*Captive to the Turke*: Responses to the Anglo-Ottoman Capitulations of 1580," in *Cultural Encounters Between East and West 1453–1699*, eds. Matthew Birchwood and Matthew Dimmock (Newcastle-upon-Tyne: Cambridge Scholars, 2005).

Dimmock, Matthew, *New Turkes: Dramatizing Islam and the Ottomans in Early Modern England* (Farnham: Ashgate, 2005).

Ditchfield, Simon, "In Sarpi's Shadow: Coping with Trent the Italian Way," in *Studi in memoria di Cesare Mozzarelli*, 2 vols. (Milan: Vita e Pensiero, 2008).

Ditchfield, Simon, "Tridentine Catholicism," in *The Ashgate Research Companion to the Counter-Reformation*, eds. Alexandra Bamji, Geert H. Janssen, and Mary Laven (Farnham: Ashgate, 2013).

Dodds, Eric R., *The Greeks and the Irrational* (Berkeley: University of California Press, 1951).

Dodge, Neil R. E., "Spenser's Imitations from Ariosto," *PMLA*, 12, 2 (1897): 151–204.

Dollimore, Jonathan, "Subjectivity, Sexuality, and Transgression: The Jacobean Connection," *Renaissance Drama*, XVII (1986): 53–81.

Dollimore, Jonathan, *Radical Tragedy: Religion, Ideology and Power in the Drama of Shakespeare and His Contemporaries*, 2nd ed. (New York and London: Harvester Wheatsheaf, 1989).

Dolven, Jeff, *Scenes of Instruction in Renaissance Romance* (Chicago: University of Chicago Press, 2007).

Donadoni, Luigi, "L'influence de Sénèque sur les tragédies de Giambattista Giraldi," in *Les Tragédies de Sénèque et le théâtre de la Renaissance*, ed. Jean Jaquot (Paris: Editions du Centre National de la Recherche Scientifique, 1964).

Donaldson, E. Talbot, *The Swan at the Well: Shakespeare Reading Chaucer* (New Haven: Yale, 1985).

Donaldson, Peter S., *Machiavelli and Mystery of State* (Cambridge: Cambridge University Press, 1988).

Donne, John, *The Satires, Epigrams and Verse Letters*, ed. W. Milgate, Oxford English Texts (Oxford: Clarendon Press, 1967).

Donnell, James J. (ed.), *Augustine's Confessions*, Liber III, The Latin Text (Oxford: Oxford University Press, 1992).

Donno, Elizabeth Story (ed.), *Three Renaissance Pastorals* (Binghamton: Medieval and Renaissance Texts and Studies, 1993).

Dooley, Brendan (ed. and trans.), *Italy in the Baroque. Selected Readings* (New York: Garland Publishing, 1995).

Doran, Madeleine, "History and Tragedy: Italianate Tragedy of intrigue," in *Endeavours of Art: A Study of Form in Elizabethan Drama* (Madison: The University of Wisconsin Press, 1954).

Dotti, Ugo, *Petrarca e la scoperta della coscienza moderna* (Milan: Feltrinelli, 1978).

Drakakis, John, "Shakespeare and Venice," in *Italian Culture in the Drama of Shakespeare & His Contemporaries. Rewriting, Remaking, Refashioning*, ed. Michele Marrapodi (Farnham: Ashgate, 2007).

Drant, Thomas, "In praise of This Book," sig. ¶2r.

Dryden, John and Henry Purcell, *King Arthur, or the British Worthy. A Dramatick Opera* (London, 1691).

Duchartre, Pierre Louis, *The Italian Comedy* (1929), trans. by R. T. Weaver (New York: Dover, 1966).

Duncan, Eleazor, *The Copy of a Letter Written by E. D. Doctour of Physicke* (1606), sig. D1r.

Duncan-Jones, Katherine, "Sidney and Titian," in *English Renaissance Studies, Presented to Dame Helen Gardner in Honour of her Seventieth Birthday* (Oxford: Clarendon Press, 1980).

Duncan-Jones, Katherine, *Portraits of Shakespeare* (Oxford: Bodleian Library, 2015).

Duperray, Ève, ed. *La Postérité Répond à Pétrarque: Sept Siècles de Fortune Pétrarquienne en France* (Paris: Beauchesne, 2006).

Durling, Robert M., "The Bower of Bliss and Armida's Palace," *Comparative Literature*, 6 (1954): 335–47.

Dursteler, Eric R., *Venetians in Constantinople. Nation, Identity and Coexistence in the Early Modern Mediterranean* (Baltimore: Johns Hopkins University Press, 2006).

Dusinberre, Juliet, "Much Ado about Lying: Shakespeare and Sir John Harington in Dialogue with *Orlando Furioso*," in *The Italian World of English Renaissance Drama: Cultural Exchange and Intertextuality*, ed. Michele Marrapodi (Newark: University of Delaware Press, 1998).

Dyer, Richard, "*A Star Is Born* and the Construction of Authenticity," in *Stardom: Industry of Desire*, ed. Christine Gledhill (Oxford and New York: Routledge, 1991).

Ebel, Julia S., "A Numerical Survey of Elizabethan Translations," *The Library*, s5-xxii, 2 (1967): 93–103.

Edmond, Mary, "It Was for Gentle Shakespeare Cut," *Shakespeare Quarterly*, 43, 3 (Autumn 1991): 339–44.

Einstein, Lewis, *The Italian Renaissance in England* (New York: The Columbia University Press, 1903).

Eisenstein, Elizabeth L., *The Printing Press as an Agent of Change in Early Modern England*, 2 vols. (Cambridge: Cambridge University Press, 1979).

Elam, Keir, "'Bridegroom uncarnate': Comedy and Castration from *The Eunuch* to *Epicoene*," in *The Italian World of English Renaissance Drama. Cultural Exchange and Intertextuality*, ed. Michele Marrapodi (Newark: University of Delaware Press, 1998).

Elam, Keir, "'At the cubiculo': Shakespeare's Problems with Italian Language and Culture," in *Italian Culture in the Drama of Shakespeare and His Contemporaries. Rewriting, Remaking, Refashioning*, ed. M. Marrapodi (Farnham: Ashgate, 2007).

Elam, Keir, "'Tis Pity She's Italian: Performing the Courtesan on the Early Seventeenth-Century English Stage," in *Shakespeare and Renaissance Literary Theories: Anglo-Italian Transactions*, ed. Michele Marrapodi (Farnham: Ashgate, 2011).

Elam, Keir, "Italy as Intertext," in *Shakespeare, Italy, and Intertextuality*, ed. Michele Marrapodi (Manchester: Manchester University Press, 2014).

Elam, Keir, *Shakespeare's Pictures: Visual Objects in the Drama* (London: Bloomsbury Academic, 2017).

Elias, Norbert, *The Court Society*, trans. by Edmund Jephcott (Oxford: Basil Blackwell, 1983).

Eliot, John, *Ortho-epia Gallica. Eliots Fruits for the French* (London, 1593).

Eliot, T. S., "Senecan in Elizabethan Translations," in *Selected Essays* (London: Faber & Faber, 1932).

Eliot, T. S., "'Seneca in Elizabethan Translations' and 'Shakespeare and the Stoicism of Seneca'," in *Essays on Elizabethan Drama* (New York: Harcourt Brace, 1956).

Elizabeth, I., *Translations, 1544–1589*, eds. Janel M. Mueller and Joshua Scodel (Chicago: Chicago University Press, 2009).

Ellis, Anthony, *Old Age, Masculinity, and Early Modern Drama. Comic Elders on the Italian and Shakespearean Stage* (Farnham: Ashgate, 2009).

Elton, G. R., "Tudor Government: The Points of Contact. III. The Court," *THRS*, 5th ser., 26 (1976): 211–28.

Empson, William, *Some Versions of Pastoral* (New York: New Directions, 1974).

Erne, Lucas, *Beyond the Spanish Tragedy: A Study of the Works of Thomas Kyd* (Manchester: Manchester University Press, 2009).

Esolen, Anthony M. (ed and transl.), *Torquato Tasso: Jerusalem Delivered* (Baltimore: Johns Hopkins University Press, 2001).

Evans, Maurice (ed.), *Elizabethan Sonnets*, New Edition revised by Roy Booth (London: Everyman, 1994).

Fachard, Denis, "Il teatro machiavelliano e la 'qualità dei tempi'," in *Il Teatro di Machiavelli*, eds. Gennaro Barbarisi and Anna Maria Cabrini (Milan: Cisalpino, 2005).

Falco, Maria J. (ed.), *Feminist Interpretations of Niccolo Machiavelli* (University Park: Pennsylvania State University Press, 2004).

Fanelli, Carlo, *La Calandria, Tematiche e simbologia. Il panorama teatrale del Conquecento e la Calandria di Bernardo Dovizi da Bibbiena* (Florence: Firenze Libri, Atheneum, 1997).

Faraci, Dora, "Il Patto di Griselda. Valori simbolici di una storia fra Chaucer e Dekker," in *La Storia di Griselda in Europa. Atti del Convegno: Modi dell'intertestualità: la storia di Griselda in Europa, L'Aquila, 12–14 maggio 1988*, ed. Raffaele Morabito (L'Aquila: Japadre Editore, 1990).

Faulkener, Robert, "*Clizia* and the Enlightenment of Private Life," in *The Comedy and Tragedy of Machiavelli: Essays on the Literary Works*, ed. Vickie B. Sullivan (New Haven: Yale University Press, 2000).

Fenzi, Enrico, *Saggi Petrarcheschi* (Florence: Cadmo, 2003).

Ferdinando, Taviani and Mirella Schino, *Il segreto della commedia dell'arte. La memoria delle compagnie italiane del XVI, XVII e XVIII secolo* (Florence: La Casa Usher, 1982).

Ferguson, Ronnie, *The Theatre of Angelo Beolco (Ruzante): Text, Context, and Performance* (Ravenna: Longo, 2000).

Fernie, Ewan and Ramona Wray, "Introduction," in *Reconceiving the Renaissance: A Critical Reader* (Oxford: Oxford University Press, 2005).

Ferrone, Siro, "Introduction" to the *Commedie dell'Arte* (Milan: Mursia, 1985/6).

Ferrone, Siro, *Attori mercanti corsari: La Commedia dell'Arte in Europa tra Cinque e Seicento* (Turin: Einaudi, 1993).

Ferrone, Siro, *Arlecchino. Vita e avventure di Tristano Martinelli attore* (Bari: Laterza, 2006).

Ferroni, Giulio, *"Mutazione" e "Riscontro" nel teatro di Machiavelli e altri saggi sulla commedia del Cinquecento* (Rome: Bulzoni Editore, 1972).

Ferroni, Giulio, *Le voci dell'istrione. Pietro Aretino e la dissoluzione del teatro* (Naples: Liguori, 1977).

Ferroni, Giulio, "La *Calandra* del Bibbiena tra Plauto e Boccaccio," in *La maschera e il volto: il teatro in Italia*, ed. Francesco Bruni (Venice: Marsilio, 2002).

Fido, Franco, *Le Metamorfosi del Centauro* (Rome: Bulzoni, 1977).

Figgis, John Neville, *The Divine Right of Kings* (Cambridge: Cambridge University Press, 1914).

Fink, Zera S., *The Classical Republicans: An Essay in the Recovery of a Pattern of Thought in Seventeenth-Century England* (Evanston: Northwestern University Press, 1945).

Finney, Gail (ed.), *Look Who's Laughing: Gender and Comedy* (Langhorne: Gordon & Breach, 1994).

Finotti, Fabio, *Retorica della diffrazione. Bembo, Aretino, Giulio Romano e Tasso: letteratura e scena cortigiana* (Florence: Leo S. Olschki Editore, 2004).

Finucci, Valeria, *The Lady Vanishes: Subjectivity and Representation in Castiglione and Ariosto* (Stanford: Stanford University Press, 1992).

Finucci, Valeria (ed.), *Renaissance Transactions: Ariosto and Tasso* (Durham: Duke University Press, 1999).

Finucci, Valeria, "In the Footsteps of Petrarch: Poetry, Music, Art, Culture," *The Journal of Medieval and Early Modern Studies*, 35, 3 (2005): 457–66.

Firpo, Luigi, "La Chiesa italiana di Londra nel Cinquecento e i suoi rapporti con Ginevra," in *Ginevra e l'Italia*, eds. Delio Cantimori, Giorgio Spini, Franco Venturi, and Valdo Vinay (Florence: Sansoni, 1959).

Firpo, Luigi, *Il processo di Giordano Bruno* (Rome: Salerno Editrice, 1993).

Firpo, Luigi, *Scritti sulla Riforma in Italia* (Naples: Prismi, 1996).

Firpo, Massimo, *Pietro Bizzari: esule italiano del Cinquecento* (Turin: G. Giappichelli, 1971).

Firpo, Massimo, "Castiglione, Giovanni Battista," *Dizionario Biografico degli Italiani*, Vol. 22 (1979).

Firpo, Massimo, "Historiographical Introduction," in *The Italian Reformation of the Sixteenth-Century and the Diffusion of Renaissance Culture: A Bibliography of the Secondary Literature*, ed. John Tedeschi (with the assistance of James M. Lattis) *(Ca. 1750–1997)* (Modena: Panini, 2000).

Fischer, Donatella, *The Tradition of the Actor-Author in Italian Theatre* (Oxford: Legenda, 2013).

Fischer, Rudolf, *Zur Kunstentwicklung der englischen Tragödie* (Strassburg: Trübner, 1893).

Fitzpatrick, Tim, *The Relationship of Oral and Literate Performance Processes in the Commedia dell'Arte. Beyond the Improvisation/Memorisation Divide* (Lewiston: Edwin Mellen Press, 1995).

Flaumenhaft, Mera J. and Daniel T. Gallagher (eds.), *Clizia* (Waveland Press Editions, 1966).

Flaumenhaft, Mera J. and Daniel T. Gallagher (eds.), *Mandragola* (Waveland Press Editions, 1981).

Fleming, Juliet, "The Ladies' Man and the Age of Elizabeth," in *Sexuality and Gender in Early Modern Europe: Institutions, Texts, Images*, ed. James Grantham Turner (Cambridge: Cambridge University Press, 1993).

Fletcher, John, "*Women Pleased*," in *The Dramatic Works in the Beaumont and Fletcher Canon*, Vol. 5, ed. Hans Walter Gabler (Cambridge: Cambridge University Press, 1982).

Florio, John, *His Firste Fruites: Which Yeelde Familiar Speech, Merie Proverbes, Wittie Sentences, and Golden Sayings* [...] (London: Thomas Dawson, for Thomas Woodcocke, 1578).

Florio, John, *Florios Second Frutes* (London: [T. Orwin] for Thomas Woodcock, 1591).

Florio, John, *A Worlde of Wordes, or most copious, and exact dictionarie in Italian and English* (London: Arnold Hatfield for Edward Blount, 1598).

Florio, John, *Firste Fruites* (London: Thomas Woodcocke, 1598).

Florio, John, *Queen Anna's New World of Words* (London: Edward Blount and William Barret, 1611).

Ford, John, *'Tis Pity She's a Whore*, ed. Brian Morris (London: The New Mermaids, 1968).

Forster, Leonard, *The Icy Fire: Five Studies in European Petrarchism* (Cambridge: Cambridge University Press, 1969).

Fortin, Ernest L., *Dissent and Philosophy in the Middle Ages: Dante and His Precursors*, trans. by Marc A. LePain (Lanham: Lexington Books, 2001 [1981]).

Fowler, Alastair, *Triumphal Forms: Structural Patterns in Elizabethan Poetry* (Cambridge: Cambridge University Press, 1970).

Fowler, Alistair, "The Beginnings of English Georgic," in *Renaissance Genres: Essays on Theory, History, and Interpretation*, ed. Barbara Kiefer Lewalski (Cambridge, MA: Harvard University Press, 1986).

Fowler, Alistair and Michael Leslie, "Drummond's Copy of *The Faerie Queene*," *TLS* (July 17, 1981): 821–22.

Fowler, William, *The Triumphs of Petrarcke*, in The *Works of William Fowler, Secretary to Queen Anne, wife of James VI. Vol. I. (Verse)*, ed. by Henry W. Meikle (Edinburgh: Blackwood, 1914).

Fox, Alistair, "The Complaint of Poetry for the Death of Liberality: The Decline of Literary Patronage in the 1590s," in *The Reign of Elizabeth I: Court and Culture in the Last Decade*, ed. John Guy (Cambridge: Cambridge University Press, 1995).

Fox, Alastair, *The English Renaissance: Identity and Representation in Elizabethan England* (Oxford: Blackwell, 1997).

Foxe, John, *The Ecclesiasticall History, Contayning the Actes & Monuments of Thinges Passed in Every Kinges Time, in this Realme, Especially in the Churches of England* [...], 2 vols. (London: John Day, 1576).

Frajese, Vittorio, *Sarpi scettico. Stato e chiesa a Venezia tra Cinque e Seicento* (Bologna: Il Mulino, 1994).

Freeman, William, *Foxe's First Book of Martyrs and the Elect Nation* (London: Jonathan Cape, 1963).

Frye, Northrop, *Anatomy of Criticism: Four Essays*, ed.. Robert Denham (Toronto: University of Toronto Press, 2006).

Fulwell, Ulpian, *The The Firste Parte, of the Eygth Liberall Science: Entituled, Ars Adulandi, the Arte of Flatterie with the Confutation Therof* (London: [William How for] Richard Jones, 1579).

Fumagalli, E., M. Rossi, and R. Spinelli (eds.), *L'arme e gli amori: la poesia di Ariosto, Tasso, e Guarini nell'arte del Seicento* (Livorno: Sillabe, 2001).

Gabrieli, Vittorio, "Bacone, la riforma e Roma nella versione hobbesiana d'un carteggio di Fulgenzio Micanzio," *The English Miscellany*, 8 (1957): 195–250.

Galbraith, Karen Zyck, "Tracing a Villain. Typological Intertextuality in the Works of Painter, Webster, Cinthio, and Shakespeare," in *Shakespeare and the Italian Renaissance: Appropriation, Transformation, Opposition*, ed. Michele Marrapodi (Farnham: Ashgate, 2014).

Galigani, Giuseppe (ed.), *Il Boccaccio nella cultura inglese e anglo-americana* (Florence: Olschki, 1974).

Gamba, Bartolommeo, *Serie dell'edizioni de' testi di lingua italiana* (Milan: Stamperia Reale, 1812).

Garavelli, Enrico, *Amori pastorali* (Rome: Vecchiarelli, 2002).

Garber, Marjorie, *Vested Interests: Cross-Dressing and Cultural Anxiety* (New York and Oxford: Routledge, 1997).

Gareffi, A., "Il teatro di Jacopo Nardi dalle trame del *Decameron* al comico moralistico del primo '500," *Biblioteca teatrale*, 14 (1976): 38–63.

Gargano, Giovanni Saverio, *Scapigliatura italiana a Londra sotto Elisabetta e Giacomo* (Florence: Battistelli, 1923a).

Gargano, Giovanni Saverio, *Scapigliatura Italiana* (Florence: La Nuova Italia, 1923b).

Garver, Eugene, "Machiavelli's *The Prince*: A Neglected Rhetorical Classic," *Philosophy and Rhetoric*, 13 (1980): 99–120.

Gary, Taylor and John Lavagnino (eds.), *Thomas Middleton and Early Modern Textual Culture* (Oxford: Oxford University Press, 2007).

Garzoni, Tommaso, "*La piazza universale*," in *La Commedia dell'Arte e la Società Barocca: La Professione del Teatro*, Excerpted in Ferruccio Marotti and Giovanna Romei (Rome: Bulzoni, 1991).

Gasquet, Émile, *Le courant machiavelien dans la pensée et la littérature anglaises du XVIe siècle* (Paris: Didier, 1974).

Gatti, Hilary, *The Renaissance Drama of Knowledge: Giordano Bruno in England* (New York: Routledge, 1989).

Gatti, Hilary, *Il teatro della coscienza. Giordano Bruno e Amleto* (Rome: Bulzoni, 1998).

Gatti, Hilary, *Essays on Giordano Bruno* (Princeton: Princeton University Press, 2011).

Gell, Alfred, "The Technology of Enchantment and the Enchantment of Technology," in *Anthropology, Art and Aesthetics*, eds. Jeremy Coote and Anthony Shelton (Oxford: Clarendon Press, 1992).

Gentili, Alberico, *De legationibus libri tres* (London: Thomas Vautrollier, 1585).

Gentili, Alberico, *De legationibus libri tres*, English trans. by Gordon J. Laing (New York: Oceana, 1924).

Gentili, Scipione, *Solymeidos libri duo priores de Torquati Tassi Italicis expressi* (London: John Wolfe, 1584).

Gentillet, Innocent, *Discours sur les Moyens de bien gouverner et maintenir en bon paix vn Royaume ou autre Principauté. Divisez en trois parties: asauoir, du Conseil, de la Religion & Police que doit tenir un Prince. Contre Nicolas Machiauel, Florentin. A Treshaut & Tres-illustre Prince François Duc d'Alençon, fils & frere de Roy* (Paris, 1576), ed. by C. Edward Rathé (Geneva: Librairie Droz, 1968).

Gerber, Adolph, "All of the Five Fictitious Editions of Writings of Machiavelli and Three of Those of Pietro Aretino Printed by John Wolfe of London (1584–1588)," *Modern Language Notes*, 22 (1907).

Gerosa, Pietro Paolo, *Umanesimo cristiano del Petrarca* (Turin: Bottega d'Erasmo, 1966).

Giacomoni, Paola and Luigi Dappiano, *Jacopo Aconcio. Il pensiero scientifico e l'idea di tolleranza* (Trentino: Dipartimento di scienze filologiche e storiche, 2005).

Giamatti, A. Bartlett, *The Earthly Paradise and the Renaissance Epic* (Princeton: Princeton University Press, 1966).

Giannetti, Laura, *Lelia's Kiss: Imagining Gender, Sex, and Marriage in Italian Renaissance Comedy* (Toronto: University of Toronto Press, 2009).

Giannetti, Laura and Guido Ruggiero (eds.), *Five Comedies from the Italian Renaissance* (Baltimore: Johns Hopkins University Press, 2003).

Giazzon, Stefano, *Lodovico Dolce tragediografo, tra riscrittura dell'antico e traduzione* (Doctoral Dissertation, Università di Padova, Italy, 2008).

Giazzon, Stefano, *Venezia in Coturno, Lodovico Dolce tragediografo* (Rome: Aracne, 2011).

Giazzon, Stefano, "Giocasta di Lodovico Dolce: note su una riscrittura euripidea," *Croniques Italiennes*, website, XX (2011).

Giazzon, Stefano, "L'Ecerinis di R. Mussato," in *Quaderni del circolo filologico-linguistico padovano*, n. 22 eds. Gianfelice Peron and Alvise Adreose (Padua: Esedra, 2011).

Gilbert, Allan (ed.), *Literary Criticism, Plato to Dryden* (New York: American Book Company, 1940).

Gilbert, Allan H., *Machiavelli's Prince and Its Forerunners. The Prince as a Typical Book De Regimine Principum* (Durham: Duke University Press, 1938).

Gilbert, Allan H. (ed. and trans.), *Machiavelli: The Chief Works and Others*, 3 vols. (Durham: Duke University Press, 1958).

Gill, Meredith J., *Augustine in the Italian Renaissance: Art and Philosophy from Petrarch to Michelangelo* (Cambridge: Cambridge University Press, 2005).

Gillespie, Stuart, *Shakespeare's Books: A Dictionary of Shakespeare's Sources* (New Brunswick: Athlone Press, 2001).

Gillespie, Stuart, "Gilbert Talbot's Seventeenth-Century Translation of Tasso's *Gerusalemme Liberata*," *Translation and Literature*, 20 (2011): 191–217.

Gillespie, Stuart G., *English Translation and Classical Reception* (Oxford: Wiley and Blackwell, 2011).

Gillies, John, *Shakespeare and the Geography of Difference* (Cambridge: Cambridge University Press, 1994).

Gilson, Étienne, *Reason and Revelation in the Middle Ages* (New York: Charles Scribner's Sons, 1966 [1938]).

Ginsberg, Warren, "Chaucer and Petrarch: 'S'amor non è' and the *Canticus Troili*," *Humanist Studies & the Digital Age*, 1, 1 (2011): 121–27.

Giraldi Cinzio, G. B., *Scritti critici*, ed. C. G. Crocetti (Milan: Marzorati, 1973).

Giraldi Cinzio, G. B., "*Orbecche – La tragedia a chi legge*," in *Teatro del Cinquecento*, ed. R. Cremante (Milan and Naples: R. Ricciardi Editore, 1988).

Giraldi Cinzio, G. B., *L'uomo di corte. Discorso intorno a quello che si conviene a giovane nobile e ben creato nel servire un gran Principe* (1569), ed. Walter Moretti (Modena: Mucchi Editore, 1989).

Golding, Louis Thorn, *An Elizabethan Puritan: Arthur Golding, the Translator of Ovid's Metamorphoses ab, And also of John Calvin's Sermons*, 1937 (Freeport: Books for Library Press, 1971).

Goldman, Michael, *The Actor's Freedom: Toward a Theory of Drama* (New York: Viking Press, 1975).

Goldoni, Carlo, *Il teatro comico* (1750).

Gordon, Mel, *Lazzi* (New York: PAJ Publications, 1983).

Granada, Miguel A., "Giordano Bruno y America: de la crítica de la colonización a la crítica del cristianismo," *Geocrítica*, 90 (1990): 5–63.

Granada, Miguel A., *La reivindicación de la filosofía en Giordano Bruno* (Barcelona: Herder, 2005).

Granada, Miguel A., "Introduction," in *De fureurs héroïques*, ed. Giordano Bruno (Paris: Les Belles Lettres, 2008).

Granada, Miguel A., "New Visions of the Cosmos," in *The Cambridge Companion to Renaissance Philosophy*, ed. James Hankins (Cambridge: Cambridge University Press, 2007).

Greco, Aulo, *L'istituzione del teatro comico nel Rinascimento* (Naples: Liguori, 1976).

Green, Nina, ed., *Leicester's Commonwealth* (2002), available at www.oxford-shakespeare.com/Leicester/Leicesters_Commonwealth_1584.pdf (accessed November 2014).

Greenblatt, Stephen, *Renaissance Self-Fashioning. From More to Shakespeare* (Chicago: Chicago University Press, 1980).

Greenblatt, Stephen, *Shakespearean Negotiations. The Circulation of Social Energy in Renaissance England* (Oxford: Clarendon Press, 1988).

Greenblatt, Stephen, *Learning to Curse. Essays in Early Modern Culture* (Oxford: Routledge, 1990).

Greenblatt, Stephen, *Marvelous Possessions: The Wonder of the New World* (Chicago: University of Chicago Press, 1991).

Greenblatt, Stephen, "A Mobility Studies Manifesto," in *Cultural Mobility. A Manifesto*, with I. Zupanov, R. Meyer-Kalkus, H. Paul, P. Nyiri, and F. Pannewick (Cambridge: Cambridge University Press, 2010a).

Greenblatt, Stephen, "Theatrical Mobility," in *Cultural Mobility. A Manifesto*, with I. Zupanov, R. Meyer-Kalkus, H. Paul, P. Nyiri, and F. Pannewick (Cambridge: Cambridge University Press, 2010b).

Greenblatt, Stephen, *Shakespeare's Freedom* (Chicago: University of Chicago Press, 2010c).

Greenblatt, Stephen, *The Swerve. How the World Began Modern* (London: The Bodley Head, 2011).

Greene, Robert, *Greenes Farewell to Folly* (London: Thomas Scarlet for T. Gubbin and T. Newman, 1591).

Greene, Thomas M., "*Il Cortegiano* and the Choice of a Game," in *Castiglione: The Ideal and the Real in Renaissance Culture*, eds. Robert W. Hanning and David Rosand (New Haven: Yale University Press, 1983).

Greg, W. W., *Pastoral Poetry and Pastoral Drama* (London: A. H. Bullen, 1905).

Greg, W. W. and E. Boswell (eds.), *Records of the Court of the Stationers' Company 1576 to 1602* (London: The Bibliographcal Society, 1930).

Gregory, E. R., "Milton's Protestant Sonnet Lady: Revisions in the 'Donna Angelicata' Tradition," *Comparative Literature Studies*, 33, 3 (1996): 258–79.

Grendler, Paul F., "Books for Sarpi: The Smuggling of Prohibited Books in Venice during the Interdict of 1606–1607," in *Essays Presented to Myron P. Gilmore* ed. Sergio Bertelli and Gloria Ramakus, 2 vols. (Florence: La Nuova Italia, 1978).

Grewar, Andy, "The Old Man's Spectacles: Commedia and Shakespeare," in *The Routledge Companion to Commedia dell'Arte*, ed. Judith Chaffee and Olly Crick (New York: Routledge, 2016).

Gribaldi, Matteo, *A Notable and Marveilous Epistle… Concernyng the Terrible Iudgement of God, upon Hym that for Feare of Men, Denyeth Christ and the Knowen Veritie: With a Preface of Doctor Calvine. Translated out of Latin intoo English by E.A.* (Worchester: John Oswen, 1550). English translation after Gribaldi's *Historia de quodam quem hostes Evangelii in Italia coegerunt abiicere agnitam veritatem*, 1549.

Grillo, Ernesto, *Shakespeare and Italy* [1949] (New York: Haskell House Publishers Ltd., 1973).

Guarini, Battista, *Il Pastor Fido* (London, 1591), sig. A2^{v}.

Guasti, Cesare (ed.), *Le lettere di Torquato Tasso*, 5 vols. (Florence: Le Monnier, 1853).

Guazzo, Stefano, *The Civile Conversation*, trans. by George Pettie (1581), sig. A1v.

Guazzo, Stefano, *The Civile Conversation of M. Steeven Guazzo* the first three books translated by George Pettie, anno 1581, and the Fourth by Barth. Young, Anno 1586, with an introduction by sir Edward Sullivan, 2 vols. (New York: AMS Press, 1967).

Guazzo, Stefano, *La civil conversazione* (1575), ed. Amedeo Quondam, 2 vols. (Modena: Franco Cosimo Panini, 1993).

Guazzo, Stefano, *Civile Conversation*, trans. by George Pettie, Huntington Library, San Marino, Callmark 61246, sig. E2v.

Guerrieri-Crocetti, Camillo, *G. B. Giraldi e il pensiero critico del XVI sec* (Milano-Genova-Napoli-Roma: Società anonima editrice Dante Alighieri, 1932).

Guglielminetti, Marziano, *Petrarca e il petrarchismo: un'ideologia della letteratura* (Alessandria: Edizioni dell'Orso, 1994 [1970]).

Guicciardini, Francesco, *The History of Italy*, trans., ed. with notes, and with an Introduction by S. Alexander (Basingstoke: Macmillan, 1969).

Guidotti, Angela, "Il doppio gioco della *Calandria*," *MLN*, 104, 1 (January 1989): 111–14.

Guilpin, Everard, *Skialetheia: Or, a Shadowe of Truth, in Certaine Epigrams and Satyres*, ed. D. Allen Carroll (Chapel Hill: University of North Carolina Press, 1974).

Gurr, Andrew, *The Shakespearean Stage*, 2nd ed. (Cambridge: Cambridge University Press, 1980).

Guss, Donald L., "Wyatt's Petrarchism: An Instance of Creative Imitation in the Renaissance," *Huntington Library Quarterly*, 29, 1 (November 1965): 1–15.

Guss, Donald L., *John Donne, Petrarchist: Italianate Conceits and Love Theory in the 'Songs and Sonnets'* (Detroit: Wayne State University Press, 1966).

Guy, John, "The Establishment and the Ecclesiastical Polity," in *The Reign of Elizabeth I. Court and Culture in the last decade*, ed. John Guy (Cambridge: Cambridge University Press, 1995).

Haber, Judith, *Pastoral and the Poetics of Self-Contradiction: Theocritus through Marvell* (Cambridge: Cambridge University Press, 1994).

Hackel, Heidi Brayman, *Reading Material in Early Modern England. Print, Gender, and Literacy* (Corvallis: Oregon State University Press, 2009).

Hackett, Helen, *Women and Romance Fiction in the English Renaissance* (Cambridge: Cambridge University Press, 2000).

Hadfield, Andrew, "Spenser, Drayton, and the Question of Britain," *The Review of English Studies*, 51 (2000): 582–99.

Hadfield, Andrew and Paul Hammond (eds.), *Shakespeare and Renaissance Europe* (London: Bloomsbury, 2004).

Hagstrum, Jean, *The Sister Arts: The Tradition of Literary Pictorialism and English Poetry from Dryden to Gray* (Chicago: University of Chicago Press, 1958).

Hakluyt, R., *The Principal Navigations, Voyages, Traffiques Ad Discoveries of the English Nation* [...], 3 vols. (London: George Bishop, Ralph Newberie, and Robert Barker, 1599).

Hakluyt, Richard, *The Principal Navigations, Voyages, Traffiques and Discoveries of the English Nation* (London: Bishop, Newberry & Barker, 1600).

Hakluyt, Richard, *The Original Writing & Correspondence of the Two Richard Hakluyts*, with intr. and notes by E. G. R. Taylor, 2 vols. (London: The Hakluyt Society, 1935).

Halasz, Alexandra, *The Marketplace of Print. Pamphlets and the Public Sphere in Early Modern England* (Cambridge: Cambridge University Press, 1997).

Haldane, Michael, "'The Soote Season': Surrey and the Amatory Elegy," *English Studies*, 87 (2006): 406–14.

Hale, John, *England and the Italian Renaissance*, ed. by Edward Cheney (Oxford: Blackwell, 2005).

Hale, J. R. (ed. and trans.), *The Literary Works of Machiavelli: Mandragola, Clizia, A Dialogue on Language, Belfagor, Private Correspondence* (Oxford: Oxford University Press, 1961).

Hallet, Charles A. and Elaine S. Hallet, *The Revenger's Madness: A Study of Revenge Tragedy Motifs* (Lincoln: University of Nebraska Press, 1980).

Hamilton, A. C. (ed.), *Spenser: The Faerie Queene* (Harlow: Longmans, 2001).

Hamlin, William, *Montaigne's English Journey: Reading the Essays in Shakespeare's Day* (Oxford: Oxford University Press, 2014).

Hampton, Timothy, "*Turkish Dogs*: Rabelais, Erasmus and the Rhetoric of Alterity," *Representations*, 41 (1993): 58–82.

Handel, George and Giacomo Rossi, *Rinaldo* (London, 1711).

Hannay, Margaret P., Noel J. Kinnamon, and Michael G. Brennan (eds.), *The Collected Works of Mary Sidney Herbert* (Oxford: Clarendon Press, 1998).

Harding, D. W., "The Rhythmical Intention in Wyatt's Poetry," *English*, 7 (1948): 120–24.

Harding, Thomas, *A Confutation of a Booke Intituled an Apologie of the Church of England* (Antwerp, 1565).

Harvey, Elizabeth D., *Ventriloquized Voices: Feminist Theory and English Renaissance Texts* (Oxford and New York: Routledge, 1992).

Harvey, G., *Marginalia*, collected and edited by G. C. Moore Smith (Stratford-upon-Avon: Shakespeare Head Press, 1913).

Harvey, Gabriel, *Epigramma in effigiem Machiauelli. Machiauellus ipse loquitur, in Kaire, vel, Gratulationis Valdinensis Liber Secundus: Ad Nobilissimum Dominum, & Illustrissimum Heroem, Comitem Leicestrensem, Dominum Suum Optimum, & optatissimum* (London: H. Binneman, 1578).

Harvey, Gabriel, *Gabrielis Harueij Gratulationum Valdinensium* (London: Henry Binneman, 1578).

Harvey, Gabriel, "Master Hs. Short, but Sharpe, and Learned Iudgement of Earthquakes," in *Three Proper, and Wittie, Familiar Letters*, Edmund Spenser (1580), sigs D2r-v.

Harvey, Gabriel, *Pierces Supererogation or a New Prayse of the Old Asse* (London: John Wolfe, 1593).

Harvey, Gabriel, *Gratulationum Valdinensium* (1578), sig. K4r; translated George L. Barnett, "Gabriel Harvey's *Castilio sive aulicus* and *de aulica*," *Studies in Philology*, 42 (1945): 146–63.

Harvey, Gabriel and Edmund Spenser, *Three Proper, and Wittie, Familiar Letters* (London: H. Bynneman, 1580).

Hatchwell, Richard, "A Francis Davison/William Drummond Conundrum," *The Bodleian Library Record*, 15 (1996): 364–67.

Haydn, H., *The Portable Elizabethan Reader* (New York: Viking, 1946).

Haydn, H., *The Counter-Renaissance* (New York: Scribner, 1950; *Il Contro-Rinascimento*, Bologna: il Mulino, 1970).

Hays, Richard and Stanley Stewart (eds.), *The Cambridge Companion to Ben Jonson* (Cambridge: Cambridge University Press, 2000).

Hebel, William T., Hoyt H. Hudson, and Francis R. Johnson, *Prose of the English Renaissance* (New York: Appleton-Century-Crofts, 1952).

Heckett, Helen, *Women and Romance Fiction in the English Renaissance* (Cambridge: Cambridge University Press, 2000).

Heidegger, Martin, *Nietzsche*, ed. and trans. by David Farrell Krell (San Francisco: HarperCollins, 1991 [1961]). Vol. I, §10, and Vol. II, §26.

Heinemann, F. H., "John Toland and the Age of Enlightenment," *The Review of English Studies*, 20, 78 (1944): 125–26.

Heinemann, Margot, *Puritanism and Theatre. Thomas Middleton and Opposition Drama under the Early Stuarts* (Cambridge: Cambridge University Press, 1980).

Henke, Robert, *Pastoral Transformations: Italian Tragicomedy and Shakespeare's Late Plays* (Newark: University of Delaware Press, 1997).

Henke, Robert, *Performance and Literature in the 'Commedia dell'Arte'* (Cambridge: Cambridge University Press, 2002).

Henke, Robert, "Virtuosity and Mimesis in the *Commedia dell'arte* and *Hamlet*," in *Italian Culture in the Drama of Shakespeare and His Contemporaries: Rewriting, Remaking, Refashioning*, ed. Michele Marrapodi (Farnham: Ashgate, 2005).

Henke, Robert, "Transporting Tragicomedy: Shakespeare and the Magical Pastoral of the Commedia dell'Arte," in *Early Modern Tragicomedy*, eds Subha Mukherji and Raphael Lyne (Woodbridge: Boydell and Brewer, 2007).

Henke, Robert, "Back to the Future: A Review of Comparative Studies in Shakespeare and the *Commedia dell'Arte*," *Early Theatre*, 11, 2 (2008a): 227–40.

Henke, Robert, "Border-Crossing in the *Commedia dell'Arte*," in *Transnational Exchange in Early Modern Drama*, ed. Robert Henke and Eric Nicholson (Farnham: Ashgate, 2008b).

Henke, Robert, *Poverty and Charity in Early Modern Theatre and Performance* (Iowa City: University of Iowa Press, 2015).

Henke, Robert and Eric Nicholson (eds.), *Transnational Exchange in Early Modern Theater* (Farnham: Ashgate, 2008).

Henke, Robert and Eric Nicholson (eds), *Transnational Mobilities in Early Modern Theater* (Farnham: Ashgate, 2014).

Henslowe, Philip, *Henslowe's Diary*, ed. with intro. and notes by R. A. Foakes and R. T. Rickert (Cambridge: Cambridge University Press, 1961).

Herrick, Marvin T., "Senecan Influence in *Gorboduc*," in *Studies in Speech and Drama in Honor of A. M. Drummond*, eds. H. A. Wilhelms, C. B. Donalds, Bernard Hewitt, and Karl A. Wallace (Ithaca: Cornell University Press, 1944).

Herrick, Marvin T., *Italian Tragedy in the Renaissance* (Urbana: University of Illinois Press, 1965).

Herrick, Marvin T., *Italian Comedy in the Renaissance* (Urbana: University of Illinois, 1960).

Hill, Tracey, *Anthony Munday and Civic Culture* (Manchester: Manchester University Press, 2004).

Hiscock, Andrew, *Women beware Women. A Critical Guide* (London: Continuum Publishing Group, 2011).

Historia del Concilio Tridentino (London: John Bill, 1619).

Hobbes, Thomas, *Translations of the Letters of Fulgenzio Micanzio and Other Cavendish-related Writings*, ed. Filippo De Vivo, *The Clarendon Edition of the Works of Thomas Hobbes* (in press).

Hobbes, Thomas, *Leviathan* (Oxford: Clarendon Press, 1929).

Hoenselaars, A. J., *Images of Englishmen and Foreigners in the Drama of Shakespeare and His Contemporaries. A Study of Stage Characters and National Identity in English Renaissance Drama, 1558–1642* (London and Toronto: Associated University Presses, 1992).

Hoenselaars, A. J., "The Politics of Prose and Drama: The Case of Machiavelli's 'Belfagor," in *The Italian World of English Renaissance Drama: Cultural Exchange and Intertextuality*, ed. Michele Marrapodi, associate editor A. J. Hoenselaars (Newark: University of Delaware Press, 1998).

Hoffmeister, Gerhart, *Petrarkistische Liryk* (Stuttgart: Metzler, 1973).

Holderness, Graham, *Shakespeare and Venice* (Farnham: Ashgate, 2010).

Holland, Peter, "William Shakespeare," in *Oxford Dictionary of National Biography* (Oxford: Oxford University Press, 2004).

Holmes, Olivia, *Assembling the Lyric Self: Authorship from the Troubadour Song to the Italian Poetry Book* (Minneapolis: Minnesota University Press, 2000).

Holton, Amanda and Tom MacFaul (ed.), *Tottel's Miscellany* (London: Penguin Books, 2011).

Honigmann, E. A. J., *Shakespeare, the 'Lost Years'* (Manchester: Manchester University Press, 1985).

Honigmann, E. A. J., *John Weever: A Biography* (Manchester: Manchester University Press, 1987).

Horace. Satires, Epistles, and Ars Poetica, trans. H.R. Fairclough, 1929; Loeb Classical Library (Reprint; Cambridge: Harvard University Press, 1978).

Horne, P. R., *The Tragedies of Giambattista Giraldi Cinthio* (Oxford: Oxford University Press, 1962).

Horrocks, John Wesley, "Machiavelli in Tudor Political Opinion and Discussion," DLitt. diss. (University of London, 1908).

Horrox, Rosemary, "Caterpillars of the Commonwealth? Courtiers in Late Medieval England," in *Rulers and Ruled in Late Medieval England: Essays Presented to Gerald Harriss*, ed. Rowena E. Archer and Simon Walker (London: Hambledon Press, 1995).

Horvath, Gabriela Dragnea, *Theatre, Magic and Philosophy. William Shakespeare, John Dee and Italian Legacy* (Oxford: Routledge, 2017).

Hotson, Leslie, *Shakespeare's Sonnets Dated* (London: Rupert Hart-Davis, 1949).

Howard, Jean E., "Cross-Dressing, the Theatre, and Gender Struggle in Early Modern England," *Shakespeare Quarterly*, 39 (Fall 1988): 418–40.

Howard, Maurice, *The Tudor Image* (London: Tate Gallery, 1995).

Hoy, Cyrus (ed.), *The Dramatic Works in the Beaumont and Fletcher Canon* Vol. 7 (Cambridge: Cambridge University Press, 1989).

Hoy, Cyrus, *The Dramatic Works in the Beaumont and Fletcher Canon*, 8 vols. (Cambridge: Cambridge University Press, 1992).

Hubault, Gustave, *Michel de Castelnau, ambassadeur en Angleterre (1575–1585)* (Geneva: Slatkine, 1970).

Huffman, Clifford Chalmers, "The Earliest Reception of Tasso in Elizabethan England," *Rivista di Letterature Moderne e Comparate*, 32 (1979): 245–61.

Huffman, Clifford Chalmers, *Elizabethan Impressions: John Wolfe and His Press* (New York: AMS Press, 1998).

Hughes, Cassidy, *Petrarch, Dante and the Troubadours: The Religion of Love and Poetry* (Kidderminster: Crescent Moon Publishing, 1993).

Hughes, Thomas, *The Misfortunes of Arthur: A Critical, Old-Spelling Edition*, ed. Brian Jay Corrigan (New York: Garland, 1992).

Hunt, Alice, "Dumb Politics in *Gorboduc*," in *The Oxford Handbook of Tudor Drama*, Thomas Betteridge and Greg Walker (Oxford: Oxford University Press, 2012).

Hunter, G. K., "English Folly and Italian Vice: The Moral Landscape of John Marston," in *Jacoben Theatre*, eds. J. R. Brown and Bernard Harris, Stratford-upon-Avon Studies 1 (London: Methuen, 1960).

Hunter, G. K., "Italian Tragicomedy on the English Stage," *Renaissance Drama*, n.s., 6 (1973): 123–48.

Hunter, G. K., *Dramatic Identities and Cultural Traditions: Studies in Shakespeare and His Contemporaries* (Liverpool: Liverpool University Press, 1978).

Hutson, Lorna, "Fortunate Travelers: Reading for the Plot in Sixteenth-Century England," *Representations*, 41 (1993): 83–103.

Hutson, Lorna, *The Usurer's Daughter: Male Friendship and Fictions of Women in Sixteenth-Century England* (Oxford: Routledge, 1994).

Iacono, Gianfrancesco, "La 'Virtus' nelle 'Familiari'," Petrarchesca, 1 (2013): 155–63.

Infelise, Mario, "Ricerche sulla fortuna editoriale di Paolo Sarpi," in *Ripensando Paolo Sarpi. Atti del Convegno Internazionale di Studi nel 450° anniversario della nascita di Paolo Sarpi*, ed. Corrado Pin (Venice: Ateneo Veneto, 2006).

Ingegno, Alfonso, *La sommersa nave della religione. Studio sulla polemica anticristiana del Bruno* (Naples: Bibliopolis, 1985).

Ingegno, Alfonso, *Regia pazzia. Bruno lettore di Calvino* (Urbino: QuattroVenti, 1987).

Inglese, Giorgio, "*Mandragola* di Niccolò Machiavelli," in *Letteratura Italiana: Le opere I. Dalle origini al' 500*, ed. Alberto Asor Rosa (Turin: Einaudi, 1992).

Inglis, Kirsten, *Reading "Circe's Court": Politics and the Bed-trick from Boccaccio to Shakespeare*, MA thesis (Halifax: Dalhousie University, 2007).

Ingram, William, "The Real Misfortunes of Arthur; or, Not Making It on the Elizabethan Stage," *Medieval and Renaissance Drama in England*, 16 (2003): 32–38.

Israel, Jonathan, *Enlightenment Contested. Philosophy, Modernity, and the Emancipation of Man 1670–1752* (Oxford: Oxford University Press, 2006).

Jack, R. D. S., *The Italian Influence on Scottish Literature* (Edinburgh: Edinburgh University Press, 1972).

Jack, R. D. S., "Petrarch and the Scottish Renaissance Sonnet," in *Petrarch in Britain. Interpreters, Imitators, and Translators over 700 Years*, ed. Martin McLaughlin and Letizia Panizza, with Peter Hainsworth (London: British Academy, 2007).

Jackson, MacDonald P., "Vocabulary and Chronology: The Case of Shakespeare's Sonnets," *Review of English Studies*, 52 (2001): 59–75.

Jackson, William A. (ed.), *Records of the Court of the Stationers' Company 1602–1640* (London: The Bibliographical Society, 1957).

Jacob, M. C., "John Toland and the Newtonian Ideology," *Journal of the Warburg and Courtauld Institutes*, 32 (1969): 316–17.

Jacob, M. C., *The Newtonians and the English Revolution, 1689–1720* (Brighton: Harvester Press, 1976).

Jacob, M. C., *The Radical Enlightment* (London: Allen & Unwin, 1981).

James, Mervyn, *Family, Lineage and Civil Society: A Study of Society, Politics and Mentality in the Durham Region, 1500–1640* (Oxford: Clarendon Press, 1974).

Jameson, T. H., "The Machiavellianism of Gabriel Harvey," *PMLA*, 56 (1941): 645–56.

Jardine, Lisa, "Twins and Travesties: Gender, Dependency and Sexual Availability in *Twelfth Night*," in *Erotic Politics: Desire on the Renaissance Stage*, ed. Susan Zimmerman (New York and Oxford: Routledge, 1992).

Jardine, Lisa and Anthony Grafton, "*Studied for Action*: How Gabriel Harvey Read His Livy," *Past & Present*, 129 (1990): 30–78.

Jardine, Lisa and William Sherman, "Pragmatic Readers: Knowledge Transactions and Scholarly Services in Late Elizabethan England," in *Religion, Culture and Society in Early Modern Britain. Essays in Honour of Patrick Collinson*, ed. Anthony Fletcher and Peter Roberts (Cambridge: Cambridge University Press, 2006).

Javitch, Daniel, "The Philosopher of the Court: A French Satire Misunderstood," *Comparative Literature*, 23, 2 (Spring 1971): 97–124.

Javitch, Daniel, *Poetry and Courtliness in Renaissance England* (Princeton: Princeton University Press, 1978).

Javitch, Daniel, "Self-Justifying Norms in the Genre Theories of Italian Renaissance Poets," *Philological Quarterly*, 67 (1988): 195–218.

Jedin, Hubert, *A History of the Council of Trent*, 2 vols. (London: T. Nelson, 1957–61).

Jensen, Ejner J., "Theme and Imagery in *The Malcontent*," *Studies in English Literature, 1500–1900*, 10 (Spring, 1970): 367–84.

Jerome, Stephen, *The Arraignement of the Whole Creature, at the Barre of Religion, Reason, and Experience* (1632), sig. S1r.

Jones, Anne Rosalind and Peter Stallybrass, "Transvestism and the 'Body Beneath': Speculating on the Boy Actor," in *Renaissance Clothing and the Materials of Memory* (Cambridge: Cambridge University Press, 2000).

Jones, Florence Nightingale, *Boccaccio and His Imitators in German, English, French, Spanish and Italian literature, "The Decameron"* (Chicago: Chicago University Press, 1910).

Jones, Richard, *The Booke of Honor and Armes* (London: [Thomas Orwin for] Richard Jones, 1590).

Jones, Robert C., "Italian Settings and the 'World' of Elizabethan Tragedy," *Studies in English Literature 1500–1900*, X (1970): 251–68.

Jonson, Ben (ed.), *Philip Brockbank* (New York: Norton, 1968).

Jonson, Ben, *The Complete Masques*, ed. Stephen Orgel (New Haven: Yale University Press, 1969).

Jonson, Ben, *Volpone, or The Fox*, ed. Brian Parker (Manchester: Manchester University Press, 1999).

Jonson, Ben, "*Every Man Out of His Humour*," in *The Cambridge Edition of the Works of Ben Jonson*, 7 vols. eds. David Bevington, Martin Butler, and Ian Donaldson, vol. 1 (Cambridge: Cambridge University Press, 2012).

Jordan, Peter, *The Venetian Origins of the Commedia dell'Arte* (Oxford: Routledge, 2014).

Jusserand, J. J., *A Literary History of the English People*, II (London: C. Fisher Unwin, 1906).

Kahn, Victoria, *Machiavellian Rhetoric: From the Counter-Reformation to Milton* (Princeton: Princeton University Press, 1994).

Kainulainen, Jaska, *Paolo Sarpi: A Servant of God and State* (Leiden: Brill, 2014).

Kastan, David (ed.), *A Companion to Shakespeare* (Oxford: Blackwell, 1999).

Kates, Judith A., *Tasso and Milton: The Problem of Christian Epic* (Lewisburg: Bucknell University Press, 1983).

Katritzky, M. A., *The Art of Commedia. A Study in the Commedia dell'Arte 1560–1620 with Special Reference to the Visual Records* (Amsterdam and New York: Rodopi B.V., 2006).

Katritzky, M. A., "English Troupes in Early Modern Germany: The Women," in *Transnational Exchange in Early Modern Theater*, eds. Rob Henke and Eric Nicholson (Farnham: Ashgate, 2008).

Keeler, Mary Frear (ed.), *Sir Francis Drake's West Indian Voyage 1585–86* (London: The Hakluyt Society, 1981).

Keen, Alan and Roger Lubbock, *The Annotator* (London: Putnam, 1954).

Kelly, Katherine E., "The Queen's Two Bodies: Shakespeare's Boy Actress in Breeches," *Theatre Journal*, 42, 1 (1990).

Kennedy, W. J., *Authorizing Petrarch* (Ithaca: Cornell University Press, 1994).

Kennedy, W. J., *The Site of Petrarchism: Early Modern National Sentiment in Italy, France, and England* (Baltimore: Johns Hopkins University Press, 2003).

Kermode, Lloyd Edward, *Aliens and Englishness in Elizabethan Drama* (Cambridge: Cambridge University Press, 2009).

Kerr, Rosalind, "The Counterfeit *Innamorata*, or, the Diva Vanishes," in *Shakespeare and Italy*, ed. Holger Klein and Michele Marrapodi, *Shakespeare Yearbook*, Vol. 10 (Lampeter: Edwin Mellen Press, 1999).

Kiefer, F., *Seneca's Influence on Eliozabethan Tragedy. An Annotated Bibliography* (Farnham: Ashgate, 2005).

Kinder, A. Gordon, *Jacobus Acontius*, in *Bibliotheca dissidentium: répertoire des non-conformistes religieux des seizième et dix-septième siècles* (Baden-Baden: Koener, 1994).

Kinney, Arthur. Review of *Leicester's Commonwealth*, in *Renaissance Quarterly* 40, (1987): 565–67.

Kirkpatrick, Robin, *English and Italian Literature from Dante to Shakespeare. A Study of Source, Analogue and Divergence* (London: Longman, 1995).

Koyré, Alexandre, *From the Closed to the Infinite Universe* (Baltimore: Johns Hopkins Press, 1957).

Kristeva, Julia, "Word, Dialogue, and Novel" (1967), trans. as "Desire in Language," in *The Kristeva Reader*, ed. Toril Moi (Oxford: Basil Blackwell, 1986).

Lamb, Charles, "Some Sonnets of Sir Philip Sydney," in *Elia and the Last Essays of Elia*, ed. E. V. Lucas (Adelaide: The University of Adelaide Library, 2014).

Lamb, Mary Ellen, "The Biopolitics of Romance in Mary Wroth's *The Countess of Montgomery's Urania*," *English Literary Renaissance*, 31 (2001): 107–30.

Laroque, François, "Shakespeare's Imaginary Geography," in *Shakespeare and Renaissance Europe*, ed. Andrew Hadfield and Paul Hammond (London: Bloomsbury, 2004).

Lawrence, Jason, "'The Whole Completion of *Arcadia* Chang'd': Samuel Daniel and Italian Lyric Drama," *Medieval and Renaissance Drama in England*, 11 (1999): 143–71.

Lawrence, Jason, "'Non sono io quel che paio in viso': *Othello*, Cinthio and *Orlando Furioso*," in *Shakespeare and Intertextuality. The Transition of Cultures between Italy and England in the Early Modern Period*, ed. Michele Marrapodi (Rome: Bulzoni, 2000).

Lawrence, Jason, "'The story is extant, and writ in very choice Italian': Shakespeare's Dramatizations of Cinthio," in *Shakespeare, Italy, and Intertextuality*, ed. Michele Marrapodi (Manchester: Manchester University Press, 2004).

Lawrence, Jason, *'Who the devil taught thee so much Italian?' Italian Language Learning and Literary Imitation in Early Modern England* (Manchester: Manchester University Press, 2005).

Lawrence, Jason, "*Calidore fra i pastori*: Spenser's Return to Tasso in *The Faerie Queene* Book VI," *Spenser Studies*, 20 (2005): 265–76.

Lawrence, Jason, "Samuel Daniel's *The Complaint of Rosamond* and the Arrival of Tasso's Armida in England," *Renaissance Studies*, 25 (2010): 648–65.

Lawrence, Jason, "'Still finest wits are stilling *Venus* Rose': Robert Southwell's 'Optima Deo', *Venus and Adonis*, and Tasso's *canto della rosa*," *Renaissance Studies*, 27 (2013): 389–406.

Lawrence, Jason, *Tasso's Art and Afterlives: The Gerusalemme Liberata in England* (Manchester: Manchester University Press, 2017).

Lea, Kathleen M., *Italian Popular Comedy: A Study in the Commedia dell'Arte, 1560–1620 with Special Reference to the English Stage*, 2 vols. (Oxford: Clarendon Press, 1934).

Lea, Kathleen M. and T. M. Gang, *'Godfrey of Bulloigne': A Critical Edition of Edward Fairfax's Translation of Tasso's 'Gerusalemme Liberata', Together with Fairfax's Original Poems* (Oxford: Clarendon Press, 1981).

Lee, Sidney (ed.), *Elizabethan Sonnets* (London: Archibald Constable and Co Ltd, 1904).

Leech, Clifford, *The John Fletcher Plays* (Cambridge, MA: Harvard University Press, 1962).

Leech, Clifford, "The Function of Locality in the Plays of Shakespeare and His Contemporaries," in *The Elizabethan Theatre. Papers Given at the International Conference on Elizabethan Theatre Held at the University of Waterloo, Ontario, in July 1968*, ed. and with an introduction by David Galloway (London: Macmillan, 1969).

Lepri, Valentina, "Machiavelli in The Quintesence of Wit and His English Military Readers," in *Machiavellian Encounters in Tudor and Stuart England. Literary and Political Influences from the Reformation to the Restoration*, eds. Alessandro Arienzo and Alessandra Petrina (Farnham: Ashgate, 2013).

Lerner, Ralph and Muhsin Mahdi (eds.), *Medieval Political Philosophy* (Ithaca: Cornell University Press, 1972 [1963]).

Leslie, J., *A Treatise of Treasons Against Q. Elizabeth, and the Croune of England* (Louvain: John Fowler, 1572).

Lestringant, Frank, *Une sainte horreur, ou le voyage en Eucharistie (XVIe-XVIIIe siècles)* (Paris: Presses Universitaires de France, 1996).

Lever, James W. (ed.), *Every Man in His Humour* (Lincoln: University of Nebraska Press, 1971).

Lever, James W., *The Tragedy of State. A Study of Jacobean Drama* (London: Methuen, 1971).

Levi, Eugenia, "King James I and Fra Paolo Sarpi in 1612," *The Athenaeum*, 3689 (1898): 66–67.

Levine, Laura, *Men in Women's Clothing. Anti-Theatricality and Effeminization, 1579–1642* (Cambridge: Cambridge University Press, 1994).

Levith, Murrey J., *Shakespeare's Italian Settings and Plays* (Basingstoke: Macmillan, 1989).

Lievsay, John, *Stefano Guazzo and the English Renaissance* (Chapel Hill: University of Carolina Press, 1961).

Lievsay, John, *The Elizabethan Image of Italy* (Ithaca: Cornell University Press, 1964).

Lievsay, John, *Venetian Phoenix: Sarpi and Some of His English Friends, 1606–1700* (Lawrence: University Press of Kansas, 1973).

Limentani, Ludovico, "La lettera di G. Bruno al Vicecancelliere della Università di Oxford," *Sophia*, 1 (1933): 317–54.

Lindley, David, *Shakespeare and Music* (Basingstoke: Bloomsbury, 2006).

Lippi, Maria Laura, "Evangelista Fossa: note biografiche e problemi attributivi," Lettere italiane, XXXIV (Gennaio-Marzo 1982): 55–73.

Little, Katherine, *Transforming Work: Early Modern Pastoral and Late Medieval Poetry* (Notre Dame: University of Notre Dame Press, 2013).

Loewenstein, Joseph, "Guarini and the Presence of Genre," in *Renaissance Tragicomedy: Explorations in Genre and Politics*, ed Nancy Klein Maguire (New York: AMS Press, 1987).

Lombardi, Chiara, "'In principio, mulier est hominis confusio.' Il *Decameron* e la letteratura inglese," in *Il Decameron nella letteratura europea*, ed. Clara Allasia, Storia e Letteratura, Raccolta di Studi e Testi 237 (Rome: Edizioni di Storia e Letteratura, 2006).

Lovejoy, Arthur O., *The Great Chain of Being* (Cambridge, MA: Harvard University Press, 1933).

Lowerre, Kathryn, *Music and Musicians on the London Stage, 1695–1705* (Farnham: Ashgate, 2009).

Lucas, Caroline, *Writing for Women: The Example of Woman as Reader in Elizabethan Romance* (Milton Keynes: Open University Press, 1989).

Lucas, Corinne, *De l'Horreur au 'lieto fine'. Le contrôle du discours tragique dans le théâtre de Giraldi Cinzio* (Rome: Bonnacci, 1984).

Lynam, Edward, "English Maps and Map-Makers of the Sixteenth Century," *The Geographical Journal*, 116, 1/3 (1950): 7–25.

MacCabe, Richard, *Incest, Drama, and Nature's Law 1550–1700* (Cambridge: Cambridge University Press, 1993).

MacCulloch, Diarmaid, *Thomas Cranmer. A Life* (New Haven: Yale University Press, 1996).

MacDonald, Michael, "The Fearefull Estate of Francis Spiera: Narrative, Identity, and Emotion in Early Modern England," *Journal of British Studies*, 31 (1992): 32–61.

Machiavelli, Niccolò, *The Arte of Warre. Certain Waies for the Ordering of Souldiers in Battelray, & Settyng of Battailes, after Diuers Fashions, with Their Maner of Marchyng: And also Fygures of Certaine New Plattes for Fortificacion of Townes: And More ouer, Howe to Make Saltpeter, Gumpoulder, and Diuers Sortes of Fireworkes or Wilde Fyre, with Other Thynges Apertaining to the Warres. Gathered and Set Foorthe by Peter Whitehorne* (London: Ihon Kingston for Nicolas Englande, 1560).

Machiavelli, Niccolò, *Il Principe, with an Essay on The Prince*, ed. J. H. Whitfield (Paris-La Haye: Mouton, 1969).

Machiavelli, Niccolò, *The Discourses*, ed. Bernard Crick (Harmondsworth: Penguin, 1974).

Machiavelli, Niccolò, *Mandragola, Clizia*, ed. Gian Mario Anselmi, with a Presentation by Ezio Raimondi, (Milan: Mursia, 1984).

Machiavelli, Niccolò, *The Prince*, ed. Quentin Skinner and Russell Price (Cambridge: Cambridge University Press, 1988).

Machiavelli, Niccolò, *Il Principe*, ed. Giorgio Inglese (Turin: Einaudi, 2013).

Mack, Peter, "Montaigne and Florio," in *The Oxford Handbook of English Prose, 1500–1640*, ed. Andrew Hadfield (Oxford: Oxford University Press, 2013).

Maclean, Gerald M. and Nabil Matar, *Britain and the Islamic World, 1558–1713* (Oxford: Oxford University Press, 2011).

Maggi, Armando, "'You Will be my Solitude': Solitude as Prophecy: *De Vita Solitaria*," in *Petrarch: A Critical Guide to the Complete Works*, eds. Victoria Kirkham and Armando Maggi (Chicago: University of Chicago Press, 2009).

Magnanini, Suzanne (ed., trans., and intro), *The Pleasant Nights*, by Giovan Francesco Straparola, *The Other Voice in Early Modern Europe* (Toronto: ITER/Center for Reformation and Renaissance Studies, 2015).

Malcolm, Noel, "Hobbes, Sandys, and the Virginia Company," *The Historical Journal*, 24, 2 (1981): 297–321.

Malcolm, Noel, *De Dominis: Venetian, Anglican, Ecumenist and Relapsed Heretic* (London: Strickland & Scott Academic Publications, 1984).

Malcolm, Noel, *Aspect of Hobbes* (Oxford: Oxford University Press, 2007).

Malmesbury, William, *Gestaregvm Anglorvm: The History of the English Kings*, ed. and trans. by R. A. B. Mynors, completed by R. M. Thomson and M. Winterbottom, 2 vols. (Oxford: Clarendon Press, 1998–9).

Manes, Yael, *Motherhood and Patriarchal Masculinities in Sixteenth-Century Italian Comedy* (Farnham and Burlington: Ashgate, 2011).

Mann, David, *Shakespeare's Women: Performance and Conception* (Cambridge: Cambridge University Press, 2008).

Mann, Nicholas, "Petrarch Manuscripts in the British Isles," *Italia Medioevale e Umanistica*, 18 (1975): 139–509.

Mann, Nicholas, *Pétrarque: les voyages de l'esprit* (Grenoble: Millon, 2004).

Mansfield, Harvey C., "The Cuckold in Machiavelli's *Mandragola*," in Sullivan (ed.), *The Comedy and Tragedy of Machiavelli: Essays on the Literary Works*, ed. Vickie B. Sullivan (New Haven: Yale University Press, 2000).

Mantovani, Gilda P. (ed.), *Petrarca e il suo tempo* (Milan: Skyra, 2006).

Map, Walter, *De nugiscurialium: courtiers' trifles*, ed. and trans. by M. R. James, rev. by C. N. L. Brooke and R. A. B. Mynors (Oxford: Clarendon, 1983; repr. 2002).

Marcozzi, Luca, "Il Parnaso di Petrarca (Lettura della Canzone 129 dei 'Fragmenta')," Petrarchesca, 1 (2013): 55–76.

Marcus, Leah, *The Politics of Mirth: Jonson, Herrick, Milton, Marvell and the Defense of Old Holiday Pastimes* (Chicago: University of Chicago Press, 1989).

Marcus, Leah (ed.), *The Duchess of Malfi* (London: Macmillan, 2009).

Margolies, David, *Novel and Society in Elizabethan England* (London: Croom Helm, 1985).

Mariéjol, Jean-Hippolyte, *La Réforme et la Ligue. L'Edit de Nantes* (Paris: Hachette, 1908).

Marini, Giovanni Battista, *Lettere della signora Isabella Andreini padovana, comica gelosa e academica Intenta, nominata l'Accesa* (Venice: Marc'Antonio Zaltieri, 1607).

Marlowe, Christopher, "The Jew of Malta," in *The Complete Works of Christopher Marlowe*, ed. Roma Gill (Oxford: Clarendon Press, 1995).

Marotti, Arthur F., "'Love is not Love': Elizabethan Sonnet Sequences and the Social Order," *English Literary History*, 49 (1982): 396–428.

Marotti, Ferruccio and Giovanna Romei, *La commedia dell'arte e la società barocca: la professione del teatro* (Rome: Bulzoni, 1991).

Marrapodi, Michele, "Da Boccaccio a Shakespeare: Il Racconto dell'Eros e la Trasgressione della Commedia," in *Le forme del teatro 5: Eros e commedia nella scena inglese*, ed. Viola Papetti and Laura Visconti (Rome: Edizioni di Storia e Letteratura, 1997).

Marrapodi, Michele (ed.), *The Italian World of English Renaissance Drama: Cultural Exchange and Intertextuality* (Newark: University of Delaware Press, 1998a).

Marrapodi, Michele, "From Narrative to Drama: The Erotic Tale and the Theater," in *The Italian World of English Renaissance Drama. Cultural Exchange and Intertextuality*, ed. Michele Marrapodi (Newark: University of Delaware Press, 1998b).

Marrapodi, Michele, "Prologue," in *The Italian World of English Renaissance Drama: Cultural Exchange and Intertextuality*, ed. M. Marrapodi (Newark: University of Delaware Press, 1998c).

Marrapodi, Michele, "Retaliation as an Italian Vice in English Renaissance Drama: Narrative and Theatrical Exchanges," in *The Italian World of English Renaissance Drama. Cultural Exchange and Intertextuality*, ed. M. Marrapodi (Newark: University of Delaware Press, 1998d).

Marrapodi, Michele, "'Let her witness it': The Rhetoric of Desdemona," in *Italian Studies in Shakespeare and His Contemporaries*, eds. M. Marrapodi and Giorgio Melchiori (Newark: University of Delaware Press, 1999a).

Marrapodi, Michele, "Cross-dressing, New Comedy, and the Italianate Unity of *The Taming of the Shrew*," in *Shakespeare Yearbook*, Vol. X, eds. Holger Klein and M. Marrapodi (Lewiston: The Edwin Mellen Press, 1999b).

Marrapodi, Michele, "Introduction: Intertextualizing Shakespeare's Text," in *Shakespeare and Intertextuality. The Transition of Cultures between Italy and England in the Early Modern Period*, ed. M. Marrapodi, Biblioteca di Cultura 610 (Rome: Bulzoni Editore, 2000).

Marrapodi, Michele, "Beyond the Reformation: Italian Intertexts of the Ransom Plot in *Measure for Measure*," in *Shakespeare, Italy, and Intertextuality*, ed. M. Marrapodi (Manchester: Manchester University Press, 2004).

Marrapodi, Michele, "Appropriating Italy: Towards a New Approach to Renaissance Drama," in *Italian Culture in the Drama of Shakespeare & His Contemporaries: Rewriting, Remaking, Refashioning*, ed. M. Marrapodi (Farnham: Ashgate, 2007a).

Marrapodi, Michele, "Shakespeare's Romantic Italy: Novelistic, Theatrical, and Cultural Transactions in the Comedies," in *Italian Culture in the Drama of Shakespeare and His Contemporaries: Rewriting, Remaking, Refashioning*, ed. M. Marrapodi (Farnham: Ashgate, 2007b).

Marrapodi, Michele, *Italian Culture in the Drama of Shakespeare and His Contemporaries* (Farnham: Ashgate, 2007c).

Marrapodi, Michele, "Shakespeare against Genres," in *Shakespeare and Renaissance Literary Theories: Anglo-Italian Transactions*, ed. M. Marrapodi (Farnham: Ashgate, 2010).

Marrapodi, Michele, "The Ambivalence of Revenge and the Avenger's Role in *Hamlet*: The Function of Letters and Emblematic Allusions," *Cahiers Elisabethains*, 1, 79 (2011): 19–34.

Marrapodi, Michele, "Shakespearean Subversions," in *Shakespeare and the Italian Renaissance: Appropriation, Transformation, Opposition*, ed. M. Marrapodi (Farnham and Burlington: Ashgate, 2014a).

Marrapodi, Michele, "The Aretinean Intertext and the Heterodoxy of *The Taming of the Shrew*," in *Shakespeare and the Italian Renaissance: Appropriation, Transformation, Opposition*, ed. M. Marrapodi (Farnham: Ashgate, 2014b).

Marrapodi, Michele, "Introduction: Tradition and Subversion," in *Otherness, Transgression, and Subversion in Early Modern English Culture*, ed. M. Marrapodi and Giuseppe Leone, *InVerbis. Lingue Letterature Culture*, VI, 2 (2016): 1–11.

Marrapodi, Michele (ed.), *Shakespeare and the Visual Arts: The Italian Influence* (Oxford: Routledge, 2017).

Marrapodi, Michele et al. (eds), *Shakespeare's Italy: Functions of Italian Locations in Renaissance Drama* (Manchester: Manchester University Press, 1993).

Marrapodi, Michele, A. J. Hoenselaars, Marcello Cappuzzo, and Lino Falzon Santucci (eds.), *Shakespeare's Italy: Functions of Italian Locations in Renaissance Drama*, rvd., pb. ed. (Manchester: Manchester University Press, 1997).

Marsh, Christopher, *Music and Society in Early Modern England* (Cambridge: Cambridge University Press, 2010).

Marshall, Rosalind K., "Lesley, John (1527–1596)," in *Oxford Dictionary of National Biography* (Oxford: Oxford University Press, 2004).

Marston, John, "In Lectores prorsus indignos," *The Scourge of Villainie* (1598), sigs B1r-B3v. Marston, John, "Satyre I2, *The Metamorphosis of Pigmalions Image* (1598), sigs C3r-C8r.

Marston, John, *The Metamorphosis of Pigmalions Image and Certaine Satyres* (London: [Iames Robert] for Edmond Matts, 1598).

Marston, John, *The Scourge of Villanie: Three Bookes of Satyres* (London: J[ames] R[oberts] for Iohn Buzbie, 1598).

Marston, John, *The History of Antonio and Mellida* (1602), sigs C3r, C3v, E3r.

Marston, John, *The Malcontent*, in English Drama, 1580–1642, selected and edited by C. F. Tucker Brooke and Nathaniel Burton Paradise (Boston: D. C. Heath and Company, 1933).

Marston, John, *The Malcontent*, ed. George K. Hunter (Manchester: Manchester University Press, 1975).

Marston, John, *Antonio and Mellida*, ed W. Reavley Gair, The Revels Plays (Manchester: Manchester University Press, 1991; repr. 2004).

Martines, Lauro, *Power and Imagination: City-States in Renaissance Italy* (London: Pimlico, 2002 [1979]).

Martinez, Ronald L., "Tragic Machiavelli," in *The Comedy and Tragedy of Machiavelli: Essays on the Literary Works*, ed. Vickie B. Sullivan (New Haven: Yale University Press, 2000).

Martinez, Ronald L., "Comedian, Tragedian: Machiavelli and Traditions of Renaissance Theater," in *The Cambridge Companion to Machiavelli*, ed. John Najemy (Cambridge: Cambridge University Press, 2010a).

Martinez, Ronald L., "Etruria Triumphant in Rome: Fable of Medici Rule and Bibbiena's *Calandria*," *Renaissance Drama*, 36–37, ed. Albert Russell Ascoli and William N. West (2010b): 69–98.

Masciandaro, Franco, "Madonna Isabella's Play and the Play of the Text (*Decameron* VII.6)," *MLN*, 118, 1 (January 2003): 245–56.

Mastrocola, Paola, *Nimica Fortuna. Edipo e Antigone nella tragedia italiana del Cinquecento* (Torino: Tirrenia, 1996).

Mastrocola, Paola, *L'idea del tragico. Teorie della tragedia nel Cinquecento* (Catanzaro: Rubbettino, 1998).

Matthiessen, F. O., *Translation, an Elizabethan Art* (Cambridge, MA: Harvard University Press, 1931).

Maxwell, J. C., "English Anti-Machiavellianism before Gentillet," *Notes and Queries*, 199 (1954): 141.

Mazzali, Ettore, "Introduction," in *Mandragola, Clizia*, ed. Niccolò Machiavelli (Milan: Giangiacomo Feltrinelli, 1995).

Mazzotta, Giuseppe, *Dante Poet of the Desert: History and Allegory in the* Divine Comedy (Princeton: Princeton University Press, 1979).

Mazzotta, Giuseppe, *The Worlds of Petrarch* (Durham: Duke University Press, 1993).

McClure, N. E. (ed.), *The Letters of John Chamberlain*, 2 vols. (Philadelphia: American Philosophical Society, 1939).

McDonald, J. H. and N. P. Brown (eds.), *The Poems of Robert Southwell, S. J* (Oxford: Clarendon Press, 1967).

McGregor, James H. (ed.), *Approaches to Teaching Boccaccio's Decameron* (New York: The Modern Language Association of America, 2000).

McIlwain, Charles Howard, "Introduction," in *The Political Works of James I* (Cambridge, MA: Harvard University Press, 1919).

McKerrow, Ronald B. (ed.), *The Works of Thomas Nashe* (London: A. H. Bullen, 1904).

McLaughlin, Martin, Letizia Panizza, and Peter Hainsworth (eds.), *Petrarch in Britain* (Oxford: Oxford University Press, 2007).

McMillan Salmon, John Hearsey, *The French Religious Wars in English Political Thought* (Oxford: Clarendon Press, 1959).

McMullan, Gordon, "The Changeling and the Dynamics of Ugliness," in *The Cambridge Companion to English Renaissance Tragedy*, eds. Emma Smith and Garrett A. Sullivan (Cambridge: Cambridge University Press, 2010).

McMullin, Ernan, "Giordano Bruno at Oxford," *Isis*, 77, 1 (1986): 85–87.

McNulty, Robert, "Bruno at Oxford," *Renaissance News*, 13 (1960): 300–305.

Meinecke, Friederich, *L'idea della ragion di Stato nella storia moderna* (Florence: Sansoni, 1942–44).

Meinecke, Friedrich, *Machiavellism. The Doctrine of Raison d'État and Its Place in Modern History* (New Brunswick: Transaction, 1997, first ed. 1924).

Melchiori, Giorgio, *Shakespeare's Dramatic Meditations. An Experiment in Criticism* (Oxford: Clarendon Press, 1976).

Melzi, Robert C., "From Lelia to Viola," *Renaissance Drama*, 9 (1966): 67–81.

Mendoza, Ramon G., "Metempsychosis and Monism in Bruno"s *nova filosofia*," in *Giordano Bruno: Philosopher of the Renaissance*, ed. Hilary Gatti (Farnham: Ashgate, 2002).

Mentz, Steve, "Escaping Italy: From Novella to Romance in Gascoigne and Lyly," *Studies in Philology*, 4, 1 (2004): 153–71.

Mentz, Steve, *Romance for Sale in Early Modern England: The Rise of Prose Fiction* (Burlington: Ashgate, 2006).

Mercati, Angelo, *Il sommario del processo di Giordano Bruno* (Città del Vaticano: Biblioteca Apostolica Vaticana, 1942).

Merlini, Domenico, *Saggio di ricerche sulla satira contro il villano* (Milan: Loescher, 1894).

Metzoff, Stanley, *Botticelli, Signorelli and Savonarola: Theologia Poetica and Painting from Boccaccio to Poliziano* (Florence: Leo S. Olschki, 1987).

Meyer, Edward, *Machiavelli and Elizabethan Drama* (Weimar, 1897).

Micanzio, Fulgenzio, *Lettere a William Cavendish (1615–1628) nella versione di T. Hobbes*, ed. Roberto Ferrini (Rome: Istituto storico O.S.M., 1987).

Micanzio, Fulgenzio, "*Vita del padre Paolo*, in Paolo Sarpi," in *Istoria del Concilio Tridentino* ed. Corrado Vivanti, 2 vols. (Turin: Einaudi, 2011).

Michel, Alain, *Pétrarque et la pensée latine: tradition et novation en littérature* (Avignon: Aubanel, 1974).

Middleton, Thomas, *Selected Plays by Thomas Middleton*, ed. David L. Frost (Cambridge: Cambridge University Press, 1978).

Miles, Rosalind, *Ben Jonson, His Life and Work* (Oxford: Routledge and London: Kegan Paul, 1986).

Milton, John, *Areopagitica*, in *Selected Poetry and Prose* (New York: Norton, 2011).

Minta, Stephen, *Petrarch and Petrarchism, the English and French Traditions*. Literature in Context (Manchester: Manchester University Press, 1980).

Miola, Robert S., *Shakespeare and Classical Tragedy: The Influence of Seneca* (Oxford: Clarendon Press, 1992).

Miola, Robert S., "New Comedy in *All's Well That Ends Well*," *Renaissance Quarterly*, 46, 1 (1993): 23–43.

Miola, Robert S., *Shakespeare and Classical Comedy: The Influence of Plautus and Terence* (Oxford: Clarendon Press, 1994).

Miola, Robert S., "The Italian Every Man in His Humour," in *The Italian World of English Renaissance Drama: Cultural Exchange and Intertextuality*, ed. Michele Marrapodi; assoc. ed. A. J. Hoenselaars (Newark: University of Delaware Press, 1998).

Miola, Robert S., *Shakespeare's Reading* (Oxford: Oxford University Press, 2000).

Miola, Robert S., "Seven Types of Intertextuality," in *Shakespeare, Italy, and Intertextuality*, ed. Michele Marrapodi (Manchester: Manchester University Press, 2004).

Moevs, Christian, *The Metaphysics of Dante's Comedy* (Oxford: Oxford University Press, 2001).

Molinari, Cesare, *La commedia dell'arte* (Milan: Mondadori, 1985).

Monti, Carlo, "Introduzione," in *Opere latine*, ed. Giordano Bruno (Turin: UTET, 1980).

Molinari, Carla (ed.), *Egle, Lettera sovra il comporre le satire atte alla scena, favola pastorale* (Bologna: Commissione per i testi di lingua, 1985).

Morabito, Raffaele (ed.), *Una sacra rappresentazione profana: Fortune di Griselda nel Quattrocento italiano* (Tübingen: Max Niemeyer, 1993).

Morata, Olimpia F., *Orationes, Dialogi, Epistolae, Carmina* (Basel: Pietro Perna, 1562).

Morgan, D. A. L., "The House of Policy: The Political Role of the Late Plantagenet Household, 1422–1485," in *The English Court: From the Wars of the Roses to the Civil War*, ed. David Starkey (London: Longman Group, 1987).

Morgan, Victor, *A History of the University of Cambridge, 1546–1750* (Cambridge: Cambridge University Press, 2004).

Mortimer, Anthony, *Petrarch's Canzoniere in the English Renaissance*, Revised Edition (Amsterdam and New York: Rodopi, 2005).

Mozley, J. F., *John Foxe and His* Book (London: SPCK, 1940).
Mueller, Janel and Joshua Scodel, *Elizabeth I: Translations 1544–1589*, 2 vols. (Chicago: Chicago University Press, 2009).
Muir, Kenneth, *The Sources of Shakespeare's Plays* (Oxford and New York: Routledge, 1977).
Mulryne, J. R. (ed.), Thomas Kyd, *The Spanish Tragedy* (London: The New Mermaid Press, 1970).
Mulryne, J. R. and Margaret Shewring (eds.), *Theatre of the English and Italian Renaissance* (Basingstoke: Palgrave Macmillan, 1991).
Mulryne, J. R. and Margaret Shewring (eds.), *Italian Renaissance Festivals and Their European Influence* (Lewiston: Edwin Mellen Press, 1992).
Mund-Dopchie, Monique, *La survie d'Aeschyle à la Renaissance* (Louvain: Peeters, 1985).
Münster, Sebastian, *A Briefe Collection and Compendious Extract of the Straunge and Memorable Things, Gathered Oute of the Cosmographye of Sebastian Munster*, trans. by Richard Eden (London: Thomas Marshe, 1572).
Murray, Timothy, "Translating Montaigne's Crypts: Melancholic Relations and the Sites of Altarbiography," *Bucknell Review*, 35, 2 (1992): 143–45.
Musumarra, Carmelo, "La poetica del Rinascimento e la tragedia," in *La poesia tragica italiana nel Rinascimento* (Florence: Olschki, 1972).
Nardi, Bruno, *Studi su Pietro Pomponazzi* (Florence: Istituto nazionale di studi sul Rinascimento, 1965).
Nashe, Thomas, *Strange Newes, of the Intercepting Certaine Letters, and a Conuoy of Verses, as They Were Going Priuilie to Victuall the Low Countries* (London: John Danter, 1592).
Nashe, Thomas, *Haue with You to Saffron-walden: or, Gabriell Harueys Hunt Is vp* (London: John Danter, 1596).
Nashe, Thomas, "Pierce Pennilesse His Supplication to the Divill," in *The Works of Thomas Nashe*, ed. Ronald B. McKerrow. 5 vols. (London: Sidgewick and Jackson, 1910).
Nashe, Thomas, "Pierce Penilesse His Supplication to the Divell (1592)," in *The Works of Thomas Nashe*, Vol. 1 eds. Ronald B. McKerrow and F. P. Wilson (Oxford: Basil Blackwell, 1958).
Nashe, Thomas, *The Unfortunate Traveler and Other Works*, ed. J. B. Steane (Harmondsworth: Penguin, 1971).
Newton, Thomas, *Seneca His Tenne Tragedies (1581)*, with an introduction by T. S. Eliot (Bloomington: Indiana University Press, 1964 [1927]).
Nicholson, Eric, "Romance as Role Model: Early Female Performances of Ariosto and Tasso," in *Renassance Transactions: Ariosto and Tasso*, ed. Valeria Finucci (Durham, NC: Duke University Press, 1999).
Nicholson, Eric, "Ophelia Sings Like a *Prima Donna Innamorata*: Ophelia's Mad Scene and the Italian Female Performer," in *Transnational Exchange in Early Modern Theater*, eds. R. Henke and E. Nicholson (Farnham: Ashgate, 2008).
Nicol, David, *Middleton and Rowley: Forms of Collaboration in the Jacobean Playhouse* (Toronto: University of Toronto Press, 2012).
Nicoll, Allardyce, *The World of Harlequin* (Cambridge: Cambridge University Press, 1963).
Novati, Ilari, "*Il Principe* di Machiavelli in una traduzione rinascimentale inglese (B.L. MS. Harley 967)," *Laurea* diss., Università Cattolica del Sacro Cuore di Milano, 1993–94.
Nungezer, Edwin, *A Dictionary of Actors and of Other Persons Associated with the Public Representation of Plays in England* (New Haven, 1929; AMS, 1971).
Oakley, Francis, "Complexities of Context: Gerson, Bellarmine, Sarpi, Richer, and the Venetian Interdict of 1606–1607," *Catholic Historical Review*, lxxxvi (1996): 369–96.
O'Brien, Mary, "The Root of the Mandrake: Machiavelli and Manliness," in *Feminist Interpretations of Niccolò Machiavelli*, ed. M. J. Falco (University Park: The Pennsylvania State University Press, 2004).
O'Callaghan, Michelle, "Pastoral," in *A New Companion to English Renaissance Literature and Culture*, ed. Michael Hattaway, 2 vols. (Chichester: John Wiley & Sons, 2010).
O'Callaghan, Michelle, *The 'Shepheards Nation': Jacobean Spenserians and Early Stuart Political Culture 1612–25* (Oxford: Oxford University Press, 2011).
Okerlund, Arlene N., "Spenser's Wanton Maidens: Reader Psychology and the Bower of Bliss," *PMLA*, 88 (1973): 62–68.

O'Malley, Charles David, *Jacopo Aconcio* (Rome: Edizioni di storia e letteratura, 1955).

O'Malley, John, *Trent and All That: Renaming Catholicism in the Early Modern Era* (Cambridge, MA: Harvard University Press, 2000).

Opie, Brian, "Nathaniel Bacon and Francis Spiera: The Presbyterian and the Apostate," *The Turnbull Library Record*, 18 (1985): 33–50.

Oppenheimer, Paul, "The Origin of the Sonnet," *Comparative Literature*, 34 (Autumn 1982): 289–304.

Ordine, Nuccio, *Contro il Vangelo armato. Giordano Bruno, Ronsard e la religione* (Milan: Cortina, 2007).

Ordine, Nuccio, *Trois couronnes pour un roi* (Paris: Les Belles Lettres, 2011).

Orgel, Stephen, *Impersonations: The Performance of Gender in Shakespeare's England* (Cambridge: Cambridge University Press, 1996).

Ornstein, Robert, *The Moral Vision of Jacobean Tragedy* (Westport: Greenwood Press, 1977).

Orsini, Napoleone, "Elizabethan Manuscript Translations of Machiavelli's *Prince*," *Journal of the Warburg Institute*, 1 (1937): 166–69.

Orsini, Napoleone, *Studii sul Rinascimento Italiano in Inghilterra con alcuni testi inglesi inediti* (Florence: Sansoni, 1937).

Orsini, Napoleone, "Nuove ricerche intorno al machiavellismo nel Rinascimento inglese I: Machiavellismo e polemiche politiche nel manoscritto harleiano 967," *Rinascita*, 1 (1938): 92–101.

Orsini, Napoleone, "Nuove ricerche sul machiavellismo nel Rinascimento inglese II: Appunti inediti dalle "Storie" del Machiavelli e del Guicciardini," *Rinascita*, 6 (1939): 299–304.

Orsini, Napoleone, "'Policy': Or the Language of Elizabethan Machiavellianism," *Journal of the Warburg and Courtauld Institutes*, 9 (1946): 122–34.

Osmond, Rosalie, *Mutual Accusation: Seventeenth-Century Body and Soul Dialogues in Their Literary and Theological Context* (Toronto: University of Toronto Press, 1990).

Overell, M. Anne, "Edwardian Humanism and *Il Beneficio di Cristo*, 1547–1553," in *Reassessing Tudor Humanism*, ed. Jonathan Woolfson (Basingstoke: Palgrave Macmillan, 2002).

Overell, M. Anne, "The Exploitation of Francesco Spiera," *Sixteenth Century Journal*, 26 (1995): 619–37.

Overell, M. Anne, *Italian Reform and English Reformations, c. 1535- c. 1585* (Farnham: Ashgate, 2008).

Owens, Jressie Ann (ed.), *"Noyses, Sounds and Sweet Aires": Music in Early Modern England* (Washington, DC: The Folger Shakespeare Library, 2006).

Padoan, Carlo, *L'avventura della commedia rinascimentale* (Padua: Piccin Nuova Libraria, 1996).

Padoan, Giorgio (ed.), *La Calandra, Commedia elegantissima per messer Bernardo Dovizi da Bibbiena* (Padua: Antenore, 1985).

Painter, W., *The Palace of Pleasure*, vol. 3, ed. Joseph Jacobs (Dover Publications, 1965).

Pallavicino, Pietro Sforza, *Istoria del Concilio di Trento... ove insieme rifiutasi con autorevoli testimonianze un'Istoria falsa divolgata nello stesso argomento sotto nome di Pietro Soave Polano* (Rome: Angelo Bernabò for Giovanni Casoni, 1656–1657).

Pallotti, Donatella, "Tra sacro e profano," in *Petrarca in Europa*, ed. M. Domenichelli and D. Pallotti, *In forma di parole*, XXIV, IV, 3, tomo secondo (luglio-settembre 2004): 465–66.

Pandolfi, Vito, *La commedia dell'arte, storia e testi*, 6 vols. (Florence: Sansoni, 1957–61).

Panizza, Letizia, "Pasquino among Anglican Reformers: The Two Editions in English (1566 and 1584) of Celio Secondo Curione's *Pasquino in estasi*," in *Ex marmore: pasquini, pasquinisti, pasquinate nell'Europa moderna*, eds. Chrysa Damianaki, Paolo Procaccioli, and Adriano Romano (Rome: Vecchiarelli, 2006).

Papi, Fulvio, *Antropologia e civiltà nel pensiero di Giordano Bruno* (Florence: La Nuova Italia, 1968).

Papio, Michael (ed.), *Heliotropia 700/10. A Boccaccio Anniversary Volume* (Milan: LED, 2013).

Paravicino, Pietro, *The True Idioma of the Italian Tongue* (1660), sigs A3r, A4r.

Parker, Brian, "An English View of Venice: Ben Jonson's *Volpone*," in *Italy and the English Renaissance*, eds. Sergio Rossi and Dianella Savoia (Milan: Unicopli, 1989).

Parker, Holt N., *Olympia Morata. The Complete Writings of an Italian Heretic* (Chicago: Chicago University Press, 2003).

Parks, George Bruner, *Richard Hakluyt and the English Voyages* (New York: F. Unger, 1928).

Parr, Anthony (ed.), *Three Renaissance Travel Plays* (Manchester: Manchester University Press, 1995).

Partridge, Mary, "Hee Is Become an Englishman: Thomas Hoby's Translation of Castiglione's *Book of the Courtier*," *Historical Journal*, 4, 50 (December 2007): 769–86.

Patericke, Simon, "Dedicatory epistle" Prefacing his Translation of Gentillet's *Anti-Machiavel* (*A Discovrse Vpon the Meanes of Wel Governing and Maintaining in Good Peace, a Kingdome, or Other Principalitie. Divided into Three Parts, Namely, The Counsell, The Religion, and The Policie, which a Prince Ought to Hold and Follow. Against Nicholas Machiavell the Florentine. Translated into English by Simon Pathericke* (London: Adam Islip, 1602).

Patterson, Annabel, *Censorship and Interpretation. The Conditions of Writing and Reading in Early Modern England* (Madison: University of Wisconsin Press, 1984).

Patterson, Annabel, *Pastoral and Ideology: Virgil to Valéry* (Berkeley: University of California Press, 1987).

Patterson, Frank Allen (ed.), *An Index to the Columbia Edition of the Works of John Milton* Vol. 2 (New York: Columbia University Press, 1931).

Patterson, Ray L., *Copyright in Historical perspective* (New York: Vanderbilt University Press, 1968).

Patterson, W. B., *King James VI and I and the Reunion of Christendom* (Cambridge: Cambridge University Press, 1998).

Pavoni, Giuseppe, *Diario descritto da Giuseppe Pavoni delle feste celebrate nelle solennissime nozze delli Serenissimi Sposi il Sig. Don Ferdinando Medici e la Sig. Donna Christina di Loreno Gran Duchi di Toscana* (Bologna: Giovanni Rossi, 1589), in Flaminio Scala, *Il teatro*, Appendix 2, 1: lxxiii–lxxv.

Peck, D. C. (ed.), *Leicester's Commonwealth: The Copy of a Letter Written by a Master of Art of Cambridge (1584) and Related Documents* (Athens, OH: Ohio University Press, 1985).

Peck, Francis, *Desiderata Curiosa* (London: [n. pub.], 1732).

Peltonen, Markku, *Classical Humanism and Republicanism in English Political Thought, 1570–1640* (Cambridge: Cambridge University Press, 1995).

Peltonen, Markku, *The Duel in Early Modern England: Civility, Politeness and Honour* (Cambridge: Cambridge University Press, 2003).

Perini, Leandro, "Gli eretici italiani del Cinquecento e Machiavelli," *Studi storici*, 10, 4 (1969): 916–18.

Perlman, Mace, "Epilogue: Reading Shakespeare, Reading the Masks of the Italian Commedia: Fixed Forms and the Breath of Life," in *Transnational Exchange in Early Modern Theater*, eds. R. Henke and E. Nicholson (Farnham: Ashgate, 2008).

Perocco, Daria, "Introduzione," in *Itinerario da Vienna a Costantinopoli*, ed. Marco Antonio Pigafetta (Padua: Il poligrafo, 2008).

Perry, Curtis and Melissa Walter, "Staging Secret Interiors: *The Duchess of Malfi* as Inns of Court and Anticourt Drama," in *The Duchess of Malfi: A Critical Guide*, ed C. Luckyj (London: Continuum, 2011).

Perugi, Maurizio, "Aux origins de l'*aura* de Pétrarque: la femme blond chez Chrêtien de Troyes et Arnaut Daniel (avec une note sur Arnaut *c'amas l'aura*)," *Cahiers de Civilisation Mèdiévale X^e-XIIe siècles*, 52 (2009): 264–75.

Peter, E., *Medine's Critical Edition* (Tempe: Arizona Center for Medieval Studies, 2002).

Petrarca, Francesco, *Petrarch's Lyric Poems*, ed. Robert Durling (Cambridge, MA: Harvard University Press, 1976).

Petrarca, Francesco, *Canzoniere*, ed. Marco Santagata (Milan: Mondadori, 1996).

Petrarca, Francesco, *Trionfi, Rime Estravaganti*, etc., ed. Vinicio Pacca and Laura Paolino (Milan: Mondadori, 1996).

Petrarca, Francesco, *Rimedi all'una e all'altra fortuna*, ed. E. Fenzi, transl. G. Fortunato and L. Alfinito (Naples: La Scuola di Pitagora, 2009).

Petrarch, Francis, *Letters of Old Age/Rerum Senilium libri I-XVIII*, trans. by Aldo Bernardo, Saul Levin, and Reta A. Bernardo, Vol. 2 (Baltimore: Johns Hopkins University Press, 1992).

Petrina, Alessandra, *Machiavelli in the British Isles. Two Early Modern Translations of 'The Prince'* (Farnham: Ashgate, 2009).

Petrina, Alessandra, "A Florentine Prince in Queen Elizabeth's Court," in *The First English Translations of Machiavelli's Prince*, ed. Roberto De Pol (Amsterdam: Rodopi, 2010).

Petrina, Alessandra, "The Humanist Petrarch in Medieval and Early Modern England," *Journal of Anglo-Italian Studies*, 12 ed. Gloria Lauri-Lucente (Malta: University of Malta Press, 2013).

Pettie, George, "The Preface to the Readers," in Stefano Guazzo, *The Ciuile Conuersation of M. Steeuen Guazzo*, trans. by George Pettie (London: [Richard Watkins], 1581).

Phillips-Court, Kristin, "The Petrarchan Lover in Cinquecento Comedy," *MLN*, 125 (January 2010): 117–40.

Phillips-Court, Kristin, *The Perfect Genre. Drama and Painting in Renaissance Italy* (Farnham: Ashgate, 2011).

Picchio Simonelli, Maria, *Figure foniche dal Petrarca ai petrarchisti* (Florence: Licosa, 1978).

Picone, Michelangelo, "La *Comedia Lidie* dallo Zibaldone al *Decameron*," in *Gli zibaldoni di Boccaccio: Memoria, scrittura, riscrittura. Atti del Seminario internazionale di Firenze-Certaldo (26–28 aprile 1996)*, eds. Michelangelo Picone and Claude Cazalé-Bérard (Florence: Franco Cesati, 1998).

Pieri, Marzia, *La scena boschereccia nel rinascimento italiano* (Padua: Liviana, 1983).

Pierluigi, Barotta and Ana Laura Lepschy (eds.), *Translation: Transfer, Text and Topic* (Perugia: Guerra Edizioni, 2010).

Pietropaolo, Domenico, "Commedia dell'Arte as Grotesque Dance: Decline or Evolution?", in *The Routledge Companion to Commedia dell'Arte*, eds. Judith Chaffee and Oliver Crick (Oxford: Routledge, 2014).

Pigafetta, Marco, Antonio, *Itinerario da Vienna a Costantinopoli* (London: John Wolfe, 1585).

Pin, Corrado, "Le scritture pubbliche trovate alla morte di Fra Paolo Sarpi nel convento dei Servi," *Memorie dell'Accademia delle Scienze di Torino*, V, II (1978): 311–79.

Pin, Corrado, "Tra religione e politica: un codice di memorie di Paolo Sarpi," in *Studi politici in onore di Luigi Firpo*, eds. Silvia Rota Ghibaudi and Franco Barcia (Milan: Franco Angeli, 1990).

Pin, Corrado, "'Qui si vive con esempi, non con ragione': Paolo Sarpi e la committenza di Stato nel dopo-Interdetto," in *Ripensando Paolo Sarpi. Atti del Convegno internazionale di studi nel 450° anniversario della nascita*, ed. Corrado Pin (Venice: Ateneo Veneto, 2006).

Pin, Corrado, "Capo, maestro e consultore d'un infamissimo scisma: Paolo Sarpi e l'Interdetto di Venezia del 1606–1607," in *Lo Stato Marciano durante l'Interdetto: atti del XXIX convegno di studi storici, Rovigo, 3–4 novembre 2006, organizzato dall'Associazione culturale Minelliana*, ed. Gino Benzoni (Rovigo: Minelliana, 2008).

Pin, Corrado, "Paolo Sarpi senza maschera: l'avvio della lotta politica dopo l'interdetto del 1606," in *Paolo Sarpi. Politique et Religion en Europe*, ed. Marie Viallon (Paris: Garnier, 2010).

Pincombe, Mike and Cathy Shrank, "Prologue," in *The Oxford Handbook of Tudor Literature: 1485–1603*, eds. Mike Pincombe and Cathy Shrank (Oxford: Oxford University Press, 2009).

Pintard, René, *Le Libertinage érudit dans la première moitié du XVIIe siècle* (Geneva: Slatkine, 2000).

Pirillo, Diego, "Republicanism and Religious Dissent: Machiavelli and the Italian Protestant Reformers," in *Machiavellian Encounters in Tudor and Stuart England. Literary and Political Influences from the Reformation to the Restoration*, eds. Alessandro Arienzo and Alessandra Petrina (Farnham: Ashgate, 2013).

Pirillo, Diego, "Tasso at the French Embassy: Epic, Diplomacy and the Law of Nations," in *Authority and Diplomacy from Dante to Shakespeare*, eds. Jason E. Powell and William T. Rossiter (Farnham: Ashgate, 2013).

Pirillo, Diego, "Voyagers and Translators in Elizabethan England: Richard Hakluyt, John Florio and Renaissance Travel," in *Travels and Translations: Anglo-Italian Cultural Transactions*, eds. A. Yarrington et al. (Amsterdam: Rodopi, 2013).

Pitcher, John, "Essays, Works and Small Poems: Divulging, Publishing and Augmenting the Elizabethan Poet, Samuel Daniel," in *The Renaissance Text: Theory, Editing, Textuality*, ed. Andrew Murphy (Manchester: Manchester University Press, 2000).

Plamenatz, John, *Machiavelli: The Prince, Selections from The Discourses and Other Writings* (Durham, NC: Duke University Press, 1965).

Po-Chia Hsia, Ronnie, *The World of Catholic Renewal 1540–1770* (Cambridge: Cambridge University Press, 1998).

Pocock, John G. A., *The Machiavellian Moment. Florentine Political Thought and the Atlantic Republican Tradition* (Princeton: Princeton University Press, 1975).

Potter, Lois, "Pastoral Drama in England and Its Political Implications," in *Sviluppi della Drammaturgia Pastorale nell' Europa del Cinque-Seicento*, eds. M. Chiabò and F. Doglio (Rome: Centro studi sul teatro medioevale e rinascimentale, 1992).

Poulsen, Rachel, "Women Performing Homoerotic Desire in English and Italian Comedy: *La Calandria, Gl'Ingannati* and *Twelfth Night*," in *Women Players in England, 1550–1600: Beyond the All-Male Stage*, eds. Pamela Allen Brown and Peter Parolin (Farnham: Ashgate, 2005).

Praz, Mario, *The Flaming Heart: Essays on Crashaw, Machiavelli, and Other Studies in the Relations between Italian and English Literature from Chaucer to T. S. Eliot* (Gloucester, MA: Peter Smith, 1958).

Prescott, Anne Lake, *French Poets and the English Renaissance: Studies in Fame and Transformation* (New Haven: Yale University Press, 1978).

Prescott, Anne Lake, "Sources," in *A Critical Companion to Spenser Studies*, ed. Bart Van Es (Basingstoke: Palgrave, 2006).

Pressler, Charlotte., "Intertextual Transformations: The Novella as Mediator Between Italian and English Renaissance Drama," in *Shakespeare and Intertextuality: The Transition of Cultures between Italy and England in the Early Modern Period*, ed. Michele Marrapodi (Rome: Bulzoni, 2000; Manchester: Manchester University Press, 2004).

Prince, F. T., *The Italian Element in Milton's Verse* (Oxford: Clarendon Press, 1954).

Prior, Roger, "Tasso's *Aminta* in Two Shakespearian Comedies," *Notes and Queries*, 51 (2004): 269–76.

Prodi, Paolo, *The Papal Prince: One Body and Two Souls: The Papal Monarchy in Early Modern Europe* (Cambridge: Cambridge University Press, 1987).

Prodi, Paolo and Wolfgang Reinhard (eds.), *Il concilio di Trento e il moderno* (Bologna: Il Mulino, 1996).

Prosperi, Adriano, "Riforma in Italia, Riforma italiana?", in *Breve storia della Riforma in Italia*, ed. Manfred Welti (Casale Monferrato: Marietti, 1985).

Prosperi, Adriano, "Introduzione," in *Eretici italiani del Cinquecento*, ed. Delio Cantimori (Turin: Einaudi, 1992).

Prosperi, Adriano, *Tribunali della coscienza. Inquisitori, confessori, missionari* (Turin: Einaudi, 1996).

Prosperi, Adriano, *L'eresia del Libro Grande. Storia di Giorgio Siculo e della sua setta* (Milan: Feltrinelli, 2000).

Prosperi, Adriano, *Il concilio di Trento: una introduzione storica* (Turin: Einaudi, 2001).

Prosser, Eleonor, "Revenge on the English Stage 1562–1607," in *Hamlet and Revenge* (Stanford: Stanford University Press, 1967).

Prouty, Charles, "Elizabethan Fiction: Whetstone's *The Discourse of Rinaldo and Giletta* and Grange's *The Golden Aphroditis*," in *Studies in Honour of A. H. R. Fairchild*, ed. Charles Prouty, Vol. 21, no. 1 (The University of Missouri Studies, 1946).

Provvidera, Tiziana, "John Charlewood, Printer of Giordano Bruno's Italian Dialogues, and His Book Production," in *Giordano Bruno Philosopher of the Renaissance*, ed. H. Gatti (Farnham: Ashgate, 2002).

Pugliese, G., "Commedia dell'arte Elements in Boccaccio's *Decameron*," in *The Science of Buffoonery: Theory and History of the "commedia dell'arte,"* eds. D. Pietropaolo and M. de P. Lorce (Ottowa: Dovehouse, 1989).

Pulsoni, Carlo, "Il Dante di Francesco Petrarca: Vaticano Latino 3199," *Studi Petrarcheschi*, 10 (1993): 156–208.

Pursglove, Glyn, "Robert Tofte, Elizabethan Translator of Boiardo," in *The Renaissance in Ferrara and Its European Horizons – Il Rinascimento a Ferrara e i suoi orizzonti europei*, eds. Walter Moretti and June Salmons (Swansea: University of Wales Press, 1984).

Purves, John, "Fowler and Scoto-Italian Cultural Relations in the Sixteenth Century," in *The Works of William Fowler*, ed. W. Meikle. Vol. 3 (Edinburgh: John Blackwood and Sons, 1940).

Pyritz, Hans, *Paul Flemings Liebeslyrik – Zur Geschichte des Petrarkismus* (Göttingen: Vandenhoeck & Ruprecht, 1963 [1936]).

Quaglioni, D., "Il modello del principe Cristiano. Gli 'Specula Principum', fra Medioevo e prima età moderna," in *Modelli nella storia del pensiero politico*, Vol. I, ed. V. I. Comparato (Florence: Olschki, 1987).

Quarmby, Kevin A., *The Disguised Ruler in Shakespeare and His Contemporaries* (Farnham: Ashgate, 2012).
Quinn, Michael L., "Celebrity and the Semiotics of Acting," *New Theatre Quarterly*, 6, 22 (1990): 157.
Raab, Felix, *The English Face of Machiavelli: A Changing Interpretation 1550–1700*, with a foreword by Hugh Trevor-Roper (Oxford: Routledge and London: Kegan Paul, 1964).
Raber, Karen, *Animal Bodies, Renaissance Culture* (Philadelphia: University of Pennsylvania, 2013).
Radcliff-Umstead, Douglas, *The Birth of Modern Comedy in Renaissance Italy* (Chicago: University of Chicago Press, 1969).
Radway, Janice A., "Women Read the Romance: The Interaction of Text and Context," *Feminist Studies*, 9, 1 (Spring, 1983): 53–78.
Radcliff-Umstead, Douglas, "The Erudite Comic Tradition of the *commedia dell'arte*," in *The Science of Buffoonery. Theory and History of the Commedia dell'Arte*, ed. Domenico Pietropoalo (Toronto: Dovehouse, 1989).
Ragazzini, Luca, "Pedagogia delle parole e pedagogia delle immagini: l'Histoire de la Mappe-Monde Papistique di Giovan Battista Trento e Pierre Eskrich (1566)," *Rivista di Storia e Letteratura Religiosa*, 38, 3 (2003): 427–73.
Rahe, Paul A., *Against Throne and Altar: Machiavelli and Political Theory under the English Republic* (Cambridge: Cambridge University Press, 2008).
Raimondi, Ezio, "Presentazione," in *Machiavelli, Mandragola, Clizia*, ed. Gian Maria Anselmi (Milan: Mursia, 1984).
Raines, Dorit, "Dopo Sarpi: il patriziato veneziano e l'eredità del Servita," in *Ripensando Paolo Sarpi. Atti del Convegno Internazionale di Studi nel 450° anniversario della nascita di Paolo Sarpi*, ed. Corrado Pin (Venice: Ateneo Veneto, 2006).
Ravazzoli, Flavia, "Appunti di nuova retorica, tra semantica e pragmatica," *Strumenti Critici*, 44 (1981): 154–70.
Rebora, Piero, "Boccaccio e Shakespeare," in *Civiltà Italiana e Civiltà Inglese. Studi e Ricerche* (Florence: Felice Le Monnier, 1936).
Redmond, Michael J., *Shakespeare, Politics, and Italy: Intertextuality on the Jacobean Stage* (Farnham: Ashgate, 2009).
Rees, Joan, *Samuel Daniel: A Critical and Biographical Study* (Liverpool: Liverpool University Press, 1964).
Relihan, Constance, *Fashioning Authority: The Development of Elizabethan Novelistic Discourse* (Kent, OH: Kent State University Press, 1994).
Ribner, Irving, "The Significance of Gentillet's *Contre-Machiavel*," *Modern Language Quarterly*, 10 (1949): 153–57.
Ricci, Saverio, "Bruno 'spinozista', Bruno 'martire luterano'. La polemica tra Lacroze e Heumann," *Giornale critico della filosofia italiana*, LXV (1986): 42–61.
Ricci, Saverio, "Infiniti mondi e Mondo Nuovo. Conquista dell"America e critica della civiltà europea in Giordano Bruno," *Giornale critico della filosofia italiana*, 10 (1990a): 204–21.
Ricci, Saverio, *La fortuna del pensiero di Giordano Bruno, 1600–1750* (Florence: Le Lettere, 1990b).
Ricci, Saverio, *Giordano Bruno nell"Europa del Cinquecento* (Rome: Salerno Editrice, 2000).
Richards, Jennifer, "Assumed Simplicity and the Critique of Nobility: Or, How Castiglione Read Cicero," *Renaissance Quarterly*, 54 (2001): 460–86.
Richards, Kenneth, "Inigo Jones and the *Commedia dell'arte*," in *The Commedia dell'Arte from the Renaissance to Dario Fo*, ed. Christopher Cairns (Lewiston: Edwin Mellen Press, 1989).
Richards, Kenneth and Laura Richards, *The Commedia dell'Arte: A Documentary History* (Oxford: Blackwell, 1990).
Richter, Jean Paul and Irma A. Richter (eds.), *The Literary Works of Leonardo da Vinci, Compiled and Edited from the Original Manuscripts*, 2 vols. (Oxford: Oxford University Press, 1939).
Roach, Joseph, *It* (Ann Arbor: University of Michigan Press, 2010).
Roberts, Sasha, *Reading Shakespeare's Poems in Early Modern England* (Basingstoke: Palgrave Macmillan, 2003).
Robson, Simon, *The Covrte of Ciuill courtesie: Fitly Furnished with a Pleasant Porte of Stately Phrases and Pithie Precepts* (London: Richard Jones, 1577).

Rochon, André (ed.), *Ville et Campagne dans la Littérature Italienne de la Renaissance* (Paris: Université de la Sorbonne Nouvelle, 1976).

Roe, John, *Shakespeare and Machiavelli* (Cambridge: D. S. Brewer, 2002).

Roe, John, "The Comedy of Astrophil: Petrarchan Motifs in *Astrophil and Stella*," in *Petrarch in Britain, Interpreters, Imitators, and Translators over 700 Years*, eds. Martin McLaughlin and Letizia Panizza, with Peter Hainsworth (London: British Academy, 2007).

Rojek, Chris, *Celebrity* (London: Reaktion Books, 2001).

Romei, Annibale, *The Courtiers Academie*, trans. by I. K. (London: Valentine Sims, 1598; facsimile reproduction Amsterdam; New York: Da Capro Press, 1969).

Romersberger, Sara, "Shakespeare's Clown Connection: Hybridizing Commedia's Zanni," in *The Routledge Companion to Commedia dell'Arte*, eds. Judith Chaffee and Olly Crick (New York: Routledge, 2016).

Rookes, Thomas, *The Late Conflagration* (1667), sigs B2v, C1r.

Rosenberg, Eleanor, *Leicester: Patron of Letters* (New York: Columbia University Press, 1955).

Rossi, Paolo, *Giacomo Aconcio* (Milan: Bocca, 1952).

Rossi, Paolo, "Hermeticism, Rationality and the Scientific Revolution," in *Reason, Experiment and Mysticism in the Scientific Revolution*, eds. Maria Luisa Righini Bonelli and William R. Shea (London: Macmillan, 1975).

Rossi, Sergio, "Italy and the English Renaissance: An Introduction," in *Italy and the English Renaissance*, eds. Sergio Rossi and Dianella Savoia (Milan: Unicopli, 1989).

Rossi, Sergio and Dianella Savoia (eds.), *Italy and the English Renaissance* (Milan: Unicopli, 1989).

Rossiter, William T., "Petrarchism and Repentance in John Donne's *Holy Sonnets*," in *The Poetry of Religious Sorrow in Early Modern England*, ed. Gary Kuchar (Cambridge: Cambridge University Press, 2008).

Rossiter, William T., *Chaucer and Petrarch* (Cambridge: D. S. Brewer, 2010).

Rowe, Katherine, "Memory and Revision in Chapman's Bussy Plays," *Renaissance Drama*, 31 (2002): 125–26.

Rowse, A. L., *The Elizabethan Renaissance: The Life of Society* (Basingstoke: Macmillan, 1971).

Russell, Conrad, *The Causes of the English Civil War* (Oxford: Clarendon Press, 1990).

Ruzante, *Opere*, ed. Ludovico Zorzi (Turin: Einaudi, 1967).

Ryan, L. V., *Roger Ascham* (Stanford: Stanford University Press, 1963).

Saccone, Eduardo, *Le buone e le cattive maniere: letteratura e galateo nel Cinquecento* (Bologna: Il Mulino, 1992).

Saccone, Eduardo, "Azione," in *Lessico critico Decameroniano*, eds. Renzo Bragantini and Pier Massimo Forni (Turin: Bollati Boringhieri, 1995).

Sacerdoti, Gilberto, *Sacrificio e sovranità. Teologia e politica nell"Europa di Shakespeare e Bruno* (Turin: Einaudi, 2002).

Sacerdoti, Gilberto, "Toland e la "lettura moderna" di Bruno," *Rivista di storia della filosofia*, 3 (2003): 512–13.

Sacerdoti, Gilberto, "'Self-sovereignty' and Religion in *Love's Labour's Lost: From London to Venice via Navarre*," in *Visions of Venice in Shakespeare*, eds. Laura Tosi and Shaul Bassi (Farnham: Ashgate, 2011).

Salingar, Leo, *Shakespeare and the Traditions of Comedy* (Cambridge: Cambridge University Press, 1974).

Salingar, Leo, *Dramatic Form in Shakespeare and the Jacobeans* (Cambridge: Cambridge University Press, 1986).

Salmon, J. H. M., "James I, the Oath of Allegiance, the Venetian Interdict, and the Reappearance of French Ultramontanism," in *The Cambridge History of Political Thought, 1450–1700*, eds. James H. Burns and Mark Goldie (Cambridge: Cambridge University Press, 1991).

Salzman, Paul, *English Prose Fiction, 1558–1700* (Oxford: Clarendon Press, 1985).

Sampson, Lisa, "The Mantuan Performance of Guarini's 'Pastor fido' and Representations of Courtly Identity," *Modern Language Review*, 98 (2003): 65–83.

Sampson, Lisa, *Pastoral Drama in Early Modern Italy* (London: Legenda, 2006).

Sanguinetti White, Laura, *La scena conviviale e la sua funzione nel mondo del Boccaccio* (Florence: Olschki, 1983).

Santagata, Marco, *I Frammenti dell'anima: Storia e racconto nel* Canzoniere *di Petrarca* (Bologna: Il Mulino, 1992).

Santangelo, Enrico, "Il Cicerone dantesco del Petrarca: 'Familiares' XXIV, 3 e XXIV, 4," *Linguistica e Letteratura*, 1–2 (2002): 81–85.

Saracco, Lisa, "Morato (Morata), Olimpia Fulvia," in *Dizionario Biografico degli Italiani*, Vol. 76 (Rome: Istituto della Enciclopedia Italiana, 2012).

Sarpi, Paolo, *The Historie of the Councel of Trent* (London: Robert Barker and John Bill, 1620).

Sarpi, Paolo, *The History of the Inquisition* (trans. Robert Gentilis; London: Humphrey Mosley, 1639).

Sarpi, Paolo, *Il carteggio con l'ambasciatore inglese Sir Dudley Carleton*, in Sarpi, *Opere* (J. Mulleri, 1768).

Sarpi, Paolo, *Lettere ai protestanti* (Bari: Laterza, 1931).

Sarpi, Paolo, *Lettere ai gallicani*, ed. Boris Ulianich (Wiesbaden: Steiner, 1961).

Sarpi, Paolo, Istoria dell'interdetto, in Paolo Sarpi, *Scritti scelti*, ed. Giovanni Da Pozzo (Turin: Unione tipografico-editrice torinese, 1968).

Sarpi, Paolo, *I Consulti*, ed. Corrado Pin, 2 vols. (Pisa: Istituti editoriali e poligrafici internazionali, 2001).

Sarpi, Paolo, *Della potestà de' prencipi*, ed. Nina Cannizzaro, with an essay by Corrado Pin (Venice: Marsilio, 2006).

Sasso, Gennaro, *Per invigilare me stesso: i Taccuini di lavoro di Benedetto Croce* (Bologna: Il Mulino, 1989).

Scala, Flaminio, *Il teatro delle favole rappresentative*, 2 vols., ed. Ferruccio Marotti (Milan: Il Polifilo, 1976).

Scala, Flaminio, "'La gelosia di Isabella,' translated as 'Isabella's Jealousy,'" in *The Commedia dell'Arte of Flaminio Scala: A Translation and Analysis of Thirty Scenarios*, ed. Richard Andrews (Lanham: Scarecrow Press, 2008).

Scala, Flaminio, *The Commedia dell'Arte Scenarios of Flaminio Scala*, ed. and trans. by Richard Andrews (Lanham: Scarecrow Press, 2008).

Scanlon, Paul A., "Whetstone's 'Rinaldo and Giletta': The First Elizabethan Prose Romance," *Cahiers Élizabéthains*, 14 (1978): 7.

Scarsi, Selena, *Translating Women in Early Modern England: Gender in the Elizabethan versions of Boiardo, Ariosto and Tasso* (Farnham: Ashgate, 2010).

Schlauch, Margaret, *Antecedents of the English Novel, 1400–1600, from Chaucer to Deloney* (Oxford: Oxford University Press, 1963).

Schmidt, Peter L., *Traditio Latinitatis Studien zur Rezeption und Überlieferung der Lateinischen Literatur*, eds. J. Fugmann, M. Hose, and B. Zimmermann (Stuttgart: Steiner, 2000).

Scholz, Susanne, *Body Narrative: Writing the Nation and Fashioning the Subject in Early Modern England* (Basingstoke, UK: Macmillan, 2000).

Schurink, Fred, *Tudor Translation* (Basingstoke: Macmillan, 2011).

Schutte, Anne Jacobson, "Periodization of Sixteenth-Century Italian Religious History: The Post-Cantimori Paradigm Shift," *Journal of Modern History*, 61 (1989): 269–84.

Scott, Janet G., *Les Sonnets Elisabéthains: les sources et l'apport personnel* (Paris: Champion, 1929).

Scott, Jonathan, *England's Troubles: Seventeenth-Century English Political Instability in European Context* (Cambridge: Cambridge University Press, 2000).

Scott, Jonathan, *Commonwealth Principles: Republican Writing of the English Revolution* (Cambridge: Cambridge University Press, 2004).

Scott, Mary Augusta, "Elizabethan Translations from the Italian," *PMLA*, X, 2 (1895): 249–93.

Scott, Mary Augusta, "Elizabethan Translations from the Italian," *PMLA*, 11 (1896): 377–484.

Scott, Mary Augusta, "The Book of the Courtyer: A Possible Source of Benedick and Beatrice," *PMLA*, 16, 4 (1901): 475–502.

Scott, Mary Augusta, *Elizabethan Translations from the Italian* (Boston: Houghton Miflin, 1916).

Scott-Warren, Jason, "Thomas Nashe," in *The Oxford Handbook of English Prose, 1500–1640*, ed. Andrew Hadfield (Oxford: Oxford Univeristy Press).

Scragg, Leah, *Shakespeare's Mouldy Tales. Recurrent Plot Motifs in Shakespearean Drama* (New York: Longman, 1992).

Scragg, Leah, *Shakespeare's Alternative Tales* (New York: Longman, 1996).
Seidengart, Jean, "L'infinitisme panthéiste de John Toland et ses relations avec la pensée de Giordano Bruno," *Revue de Synthèse*, 116, 2–3 (1995): 315–43.
Seidengart, Jean, *Dieu, l'univers et la sphère infinie. Penser l'infinité cosmique à l'aube de la science classique* (Paris: Albin Michel, 2006).
Selden, John, *The Table Talk* (Chiswick: Press of C. Wittingham, 1818).
Sellers, Harry, "Italian Books Printed in England before 1640," *The Library*, 4th series, V (September 1924): 105–28.
Sereni, Emilio, *History of the Italian Agricultural Landscape* (Princeton: Princeton University Press, 1997).
Shaheen, Naseeb, "Shakespeare's Knowledge of Italian," *Shakespeare Survey*, 47 (1994): 161–70.
Shakespeare, *Cymbeline*, ed. J. M. Nosworthy and Arden Shakespeare (London: Methuen, 1955).
Shakespeare, *The Winter's Tale*, ed. J. H. P. Pafford and Arden Shakespeare (London: Methuen, 1963).
Shakespeare, W., *The Tempest*, ed. Frank Kermode (London: Methuen, 1975).
Shakespeare, W., *Anthony and Cleopatra*, in *The Complete Works*, eds. Stanley Wells and Gary Taylor (Oxford: Oxford University Press, 1998).
Shakespeare, W., *The Complete Works*, 2nd ed., eds. Stanley Wells and Gary Taylor (Oxford: Clarendon Press, 2005).
Shakespeare, W., *Romeo and Juliet*, ed. René Weis (The Arden Shakespeare; London: Bloomsbury, 2012).
Shakespeare, William, *Othello*, ed. M. R. Ridley, Arden Edition (London: Methuen, 1958).
Shakespeare, William, *The Taming of the Shrew*, ed. Brian Morris (London: Methuen, 1981).
Shakespeare, William, *All's Well That Ends Well*, ed. Susan Snyder (Oxford: The Clarendon Press, 1993).
Shakespeare, William, *Cymbeline*, ed. Martin Butler (Cambridge: Cambridge University Press, 2005).
Shakespeare, William, "The 1609 Text of Shakespeare's Sonnets and *A Lover's Complaint*," in *A Companion to Shakespeare's Sonnets*, ed. Michael Schoenfeldt (Oxford: Blackwell Publishing, 2007).
Shakespeare, William, *Cymbeline*, ed. Valerie Wayne (London: The Arden Shakespeare, third series, 2017).
Shannon, Laurie, *The Accommodated Animal: Cosmopolity in Shakespearean Locales* (Chicago: University of Chicago Press, 2013).
Shapiro, Michael, *Gender in Play on the Shakespearean Stage: Boy Heroines and Female Pages* (Ann Arbor: University of Michigan Press, 1994).
Sharpe, Kevin, *Remapping Early Modern England: The Culture of Seventeenth-Century Politics* (Cambridge: Cambridge University Press, 2000).
Shaughnessy, Robert (ed.), *Routledge Guide to William Shakespeare* (New York: Routledge, 2011).
Shepard, Laurie, "*Decameron* as a Model for Sixteenth-Century Comedy," presented at the International Medieval Conference at Kalamazoo (2013).
Shewring, Margaret (ed.), *Waterborne Pageants and Festivities in the Renaissance: Essays in Honour of J. R. Mulryne* (Farnham: Ashgate, 2013).
Shuckburgh, Wvelyn S., *Two Biographies of William Bedell, Bishop of Kilmore, with a Selection of his Letters and an Unpublished Treatise* (Cambridge: Cambridge University Press, 1902).
Sices, David and James B. Atkinson (eds. and transl.), *The Comedies of Machiavelli* (Indianapolis: Hackett, 1985).
Sidney, Philip, *The Complete Works of Philip Sidney. The Defence of Poesie, Political Discourses, Correspondence, Translations*, ed. Albert Feuillerat (Cambridge: Cambridge University Press, 1923).
Sidney, Philip, *The Poems of Sir Philip Sidney*, ed. William A. Ringler, Jr. (Oxford: Clarendon, 1962).
Sidney, Philip, *An Apology for Poetry*, ed. Geoffrey Shepherd (London: Nelson, 1965).
Siegel, Paul N., "English Humanism and the New Tudor Aristocracy," *Journal of the History of Ideas*, 13, 4 (October 1952): 450–68.
Sillars, Stuart, *Shakespeare and the Visual Imagination* (Cambridge: Cambridge University Press, 2015).
Simpson, Evelyn Mary, *The Elizabethan Translations of Seneca's Tragedies* (Cambridge: Heffer, 1912).
Sinfield, Alan, "Sidney, Du Plessis-Mornay and the Pagans," *Philological Quarterly*, 58, 1 (1979): 26–39.

Sinfield, Alan, *Faultlines: Cultural Materialism and the Politics of Dissident Reading* (Oxford: Clarendon, 1992).
Singer, Dorothea Waley, *Giordano Bruno. His Life and Thought. With Annotated Translation of His Work On the Infinite Universe and Worlds* (New York: Henry Schuman, 1950).
Singer, Dorothea Waley, *Giordano Bruno: His Life and Thought* (New York: Greenwood Press, 1968).
Sir Francis Drake. An Exhibition to Commemorate Francis Drake's Voyage around the World 1577–1580 (London: British Museum Publications, 1977).
Skinner, Quentin, *Machiavelli: A Very Short Introduction* (Oxford: Oxford University Press, 1981).
Skinner, Quentin, *Liberty Before Liberalism* (Cambridge: Cambridge University Press, 1998).
Skretkowicz, Victor, *European Erotic Romance* (Manchester: Manchester University Press, 2010).
Smarr, Janet, *Italian Renaissance Tales* (Rochester: Solaris Press, 1983).
Smarr, Janet, "Olimpia Morata: From Classicist to Reformer," in *Phaeton's Children: The Este Court and Its Culture in Early Modern Ferrara*, eds. Dennis Looney and Deanna Shemek (Tempe: Center for Medieval and Renaissance Studies, 2005).
Smith, David L., "Stuart, James, Fourth Duke of Lennox and First Duke of Richmond (1612–1655)," in *Oxford Dictionary of National Biography* (Oxford: Oxford University Press, 2004).
Smith, Helen and Louise Wilson, *Renaissance Paratexts* (Cambridge: Cambridge University Press, 2011).
Smith, Logan Pearsall, *The Life and Letters of Sir Henry Wotton* (Oxford: Clarendon Press, 1907).
Smith, Nigel, "Milton and the Index," in *Of Paradise and Light: Essays for Alan Rudrum*, eds. Holly F. Nelson and Donald R. Dickson (Cranbury: Rosemont, 2004).
Smith, Pauline M., *The Anti-Courtier Trend in Sixteenth Century French Literature* (Geneva: Librairie Droz, 1966).
Soranzo, Matteo, *Poetry and Identity in Quattrocento Naples* (Farnham: Ashgate, 2014).
Sorieri, Louis, *Boccaccio's Story of Tito e Gisippo in European Literature*, Institute of French Studies, Comparative Literature Series (New York, 1937).
Sosio, Libero, "Fra Paolo Sarpi e la cosmologia," in Paolo Sarpi, *Pensieri naturali, metafisici e matematici*, eds. Luisa Cozzi and Libero Sosio (Milan: Ricciardi, 1996).
Southern, Richard, *Medieval Theatre in the Round: A Study of the Staging of the 'Castle of Perseverance' and Related Matters*, revised and expanded edition (New York: Theatre Arts Books, 1975; first ed. 1958).
Sozzi, B. T. (ed.), *Aminta* (Padua: Liviana Editrice, 1957).
Spampanato, Vincenzo, "Giovanni Florio, un amico del Bruno in Inghilterra," *La critica. Rivista di Letteratura, Storia, e Filosofia*, 21 (1923): 189–91.
Spampanato, Vincenzo, *Documenti della vita di Giordano Bruno* (Florence: Olschki, 1933).
Spearing, Evelyn Mary, *The Elizabethan Translations of Seneca's Tragedies* (Cambridge: W. Hefner & Sons, 1912).
Spenser, Edmund, *The Yale Edition of the Shorter Poems of Edmund Spenser*, eds. William Oram et al. (New Haven: Yale University Press, 1989).
Sperduto, Donato, *Il Divenire dell'Eterno: Su Emanuele Severino (e Dante)* (Rome: Aracne, 2012).
Spini, Giorgio, "Riforma italiana e mediazioni ginevrine nella nuova Inghilterra puritana," in *Ginevra e l'Italia. Raccolta di studi promossa dalla Facoltà Valdese di Teologia di Roma*, ed. Delio Cantimori (Florence: Sansoni, 1959).
Spini, Giorgio, "Qualche riflessione su *Per una storia religiosa dello stato di Milano* di Federico Chabod," in *Federico Chabod e la nuova storiografia italiana 1919–1950*, ed. Brunello Vigezzi (Milan: Jaca, 1984).
Spini, Giorgio, *Barocco e puritani. Studi sulla storia del Seicento in Italia, Spagna e New England* (Florence: Vallecchi, 1991).
Sprague, Arthur C. (ed.), *Samuel Daniel: Poems and a Defence of Ryme* (Oxford: Routledge and London: Kegan Paul Ltd, 1950).
Stallybrass, Peter, "Dismemberments and Re-memberments: Rewriting the *Decameron*, 4.1, in the English Renaissance," *Studi sul Boccaccio*, 20 (1991): 299–324.
Stanton, Kay, "*All's Well* at the *Decameron*'s Well: Women and Sexual Societal Healing in Boccaccio's *Decameron* III.9 and Shakespeare's *All's Well That Ends Well*," in *The Shakespeare Yearbook* 10: *Shakespeare and Italy*, eds. Holger Klein and Michele Marrapodi (Lewiston: The Edwin Mellen Press, 1999).

Starke, Sue, *The Heroines of English Pastoral Romance* (Woodbridge: Derek Brewer, 2007).
Starkey, David, "The Court: Castiglione's Ideal and Tudor Reality; Being a Discussion of Sir Thomas Wyatt's Satire Addressed to Sir Francis Bryan," *Journal of the Warburg and Courtauld Institutes*, 45 (1982): 232–39.
Starkey, David, "Court History in Perspective," in *The English Court: From the Wars of the Roses to the Civil War*, eds. Starkey et al. (Harlow: Longman, 1987).
Staüble, Antonio, "La brigata del *Decameron* come pubblico teatrale," *Studi sul Boccaccio*, 9 (1975–1976): 103–17.
Staüble, Antonio, *"Parlar per lettera". Il pedante nella commedia del Cinquecento* (Rome: Bulzoni, 1991).
Steele, Eugene, *Shakespeare and the Italian Professionals* (Taipei: Bookman Books Ltd, 1993).
Stefani, Luigina (ed.), *Tre commedie fiorentine del primo cinquecento* (Ferrara: Gabriele Corbo Editore, 1986).
Stephens, Dorothy, *The Limits of Eroticism in Post-Petrarchan Narrative: Conditional Pleasure from Spencer to Marvell* (Cambridge: Cambridge University Press, 2004).
Stern, Virginia F., *Gabriel Harvey. A Study of His Life, Marginalia, and Library* (Oxford: Clarendon Press, 1979).
Stierle, Karlheinz, *La vita e i tempi di Petrarca: Alle origini della moderna coscienza europea* [*Francesco Petrarca. Ein Intellektueller im Europa des 14. Jahrhunderts*], transl. By Gabriella Pelloni (Venice: Marsilio, 2007 [2003]).
Stillman, Robert E., *Philip Sidney and the Poetics of Renaissance Cosmopolitanism* (Farnham: Ashgate, 2008).
Stoll, Jessica, "Petrarch's *De vita solitaria*: Samuel Daniel's translation c. 1610," *The Modern Language Review*, 109, 2 (April 2014): 314.
Stone, Lawrence, "The Anatomy of the English Aristocracy," *Economic History Review*, 18, 1 & 2 (1948): 1–53.
Stone, Lawrence, *The Crisis of the Aristocracy: 1558–1641* (Oxford: Clarendon Press, 1965; repr. 1966).
Stone, Lawrence, *The Causes of the English Revolution: 1529–1642* (Oxford: Routledge and London: Kegan Paul, 1972; repr. 1973).
Strauss, Leo, *Natural Right and History* (Chicago: Chicago University Press, 1965 [1950]).
Strauss, Leo, *Thoughts on Machiavelli* (Chicago: Chicago University Press, 1978 [1958]).
Strong, Roy, *The Cult of Elizabeth: Elizabethan Portraiture and Pageantry* (London: Thames and Hudson, 1977; repr. 1987).
Struever, Nancy S., *Theory of Practice: Ethical Inquiry in the Renaissance* (Chicago: University of Chicago Press, 1992).
Sturlese, Rita, "Postille autografe di John Toland allo *Spaccio* del Bruno," *Giornale critico della filosofia italiana*, 65 (1986): 27–28.
Sturlese, Rita, "'Averroe quantumque arabo et ignorante di lingua greca…' Note sull'averroismo di Giordano Bruno," *Giornale critico della filosofia italiana*, 71 (1992): 248–75.
Stych, F. S., *Boccaccio in English: A Bibliography of Editions, Adaptations, and Criticism*, Bibliographies and Indexes in World Literature, Vol. 48 (Westport: Greenwood Press, 1995).
Sullivan, Vickie B. (ed.), *The Comedy and Tragedy of Machiavelli: Essays on the Literary Works* (New Haven: Yale University Press, 2000).
Sullivan, Vickie B., *Machiavelli, Hobbes, & the Formation of a Liberal Republicanism in England* (Cambridge: Cambridge University Press, 2004).
Tallon, Alain, *Le concile de Trente* (Paris: Édition du Cerf, 2000).
Tarantino, Elizabeth, "*Ultima Thule*: Contrasting Empires in Bruno's *Ash Wednesday Supper* and Shakespeare's *Tempest*," in *Giordano Bruno. Philosopher of the Renaissance*, ed. Hilary Gatti (Farnham: Ashgate, 2002).
Tasso, Torquato, *Plutonis concilium: ex initio quarti libri Solymeidos* (London: John Wolfe, 1584).
Tasso, Torquato, *Prose*, ed. Ettore Mazzali (Milan and Naples: Ricciardi Editore, 1959).
Tasso, Torquato, *Aminta*, ed.. Giorgio Bàrberi Squarotti (Padua: R.A.D.A.R., 1968).
Tasso, Torquato, *Gerusalemme Liberata*, ed. Lanfranco Caretti (Bari: Laterza, 1981).
Tasso, Torquato, *The Liberation of Jerusalem*, English trans. by Max Wickert, with intro. and notes by Mark Davie (Oxford: Oxford University Press, 2009).

Taviani, Ferdinando and Mirella Schino, *Il segreto della Commedia dell'Arte* (Florence: Casa Usher, 1986).

Tawney, R. H., "The Rise of the Gentry, 1558–1640," *Economic History Review*, 11, 1 (1941): 1–38.

Tedeschi, John, "The Cultural Contributions of Italian Protestant Reformers in the late Renaissance," in *Libri, idee e sentimenti religiosi nel Cinquecento italiano*, eds. Adriano Prosperi and Albano Biondi (Modena: Panini, 1987).

Tempera, Mariangela, "'Horror … is the sinews of the fable.' Giraldi Cinthio's Works and Elizabethan-Tragedy," *Actes des congrès de la Société Française Shakespeare (Shakespeare et l'Europe de la Renaissance)*, 22 (2005).

Tertullian, A., *Apology* and *The Spectaculis* with an English translation by T. R. Glover (London: Heinemann and New York: Putnam, 1931).

Tessari, Roberto, *Le bravure del Capitano Spavento di Francesco Andreini*, originally published in 1607 (Pisa: Giardini, 1987).

Testaverde, Anna Maria, *Zani mercenario della piazza europea* (Bergamo: Moretti & Vitali, 2003).

Testaverde, Anna Maria, *I canovacci della commedia dell'arte* (Turin: Einaudi, 2007).

The Travail and Life of Me, ed. E. Powell (London: Camden Society, 1902)

Thomas, William, *Principal Rules of Italian Grammar* (London: Thomas Berthelet, 1550, sig. π2v).

Tittler, Robert, *The Face of the City: Civic Portraiture and Civic Identity in Early Modern England* (Manchester: Manchester University Press, 2007).

Tomita, Soko, *A Bibliographical Catalogue of Italian Books Printed in England, 1558–1603* (Farnham: Ashgate, 2009).

Tomita, Soko and Masahiko Tomita, *A Bibliographical Catalogue of Italian Books Printed in England, 1603–1642* (Farnham: Ashgate, 2014).

Tosi, Laura and Shaul Bassi (eds.), *Visions of Venice in Shakespeare* (Farnham: Ashgate, 2011).

Tourneur, Cyril, *The Revenger's Tragedy*, ed. Brian Gibbons (London: Ernest Benn Limited, 1967).

Town, Edward, "A Biographical Dictionary of London Painters, 1547–1625," *Walpole Society*, 76 (2014): 1–235.

Townsend, Rich, *Harington and Ariosto. A Study of Elizabethan Verse Translation* (New Haven: Yale University Press, 1940).

Treip, Mindele Anne, *Allegorical Poetics and the Epic: The Renaissance Tradition to 'Paradise Lost'* (Lexington: University Press of Kentucky, 1994).

Trento, Jean, Battiste et Pierre Eskrich, *Mappe-Monde nouvelle papistique*, eds. Frank Lestringant and A. Preda (Geneva: Droz, 2009).

Trevor-Roper, Hugh R., *Religion, the Reformation and Social Change* (Basingstoke: Macmillan, 1967).

Trinkaus, Charles E., *The Poet as Philosopher: Petrarch and the Formation of Renaissance Consciousness* (New Haven: Yale University Press, 1979).

Tripet, Arnaud, *Pétrarque ou la connaissance de soi* (Paris: Honoré Champion, 2004).

Tuck, Richard, *Hobbes's "Christian Atheism," in Atheism from the Reformation to the Enlightenment*, eds. Michael Hunter and David Wootton (Oxford: Clarendon Press, 1992).

Tuck, Richard, *Philosophy and Government, 1572–1651* (Cambridge: Cambridge University Press, 1993).

Turner, James Grantham, *The Politics of Landscape: Rural Scenery and Society in English Poetry 1630–60* (Cambridge: Harvard University Press, 1979).

Tutino, Stefania, *The Empire of Souls: Robert Bellarmine and the Christian Commonwealth* (Oxford: Oxford University Press, 2010).

Tydeman, William, *Two Tudor Tragedies* (Harmondsworth: Penguin, 1992).

Tylus, Jane, "Women at the Windows: Commedia dell'Arte and Theatrical Practice in Early Modern Italy," *Theatre Journal*, 49 (1997): 323–42.

Tylus, Jane, "On the Threshold of Paradise (*Commedia delle ninfe fiorentine*, or *Ameto*)," in *Boccaccio: A Critical Guide to the Complete Works*, eds. Victoria Kirkham, Michael Sherberg, and Janet Levarie Smarr (Chicago: University of Chicago Press, 2013).

Ulianich, Boris, "Paolo Sarpi 'riformatore' 'irenico'? Note sulla sua ecclesiologia, sulla sua teologia, sulla sua religione," in *Fra Paolo Sarpi dei Servi di Maria*, eds. Pacifico Branchesi and Corrado Pin (Venice: Comune di Venezia, 1986).

Ulianich, Boris, "Teologia paolina in Sarpi?," in *Ripensando Paolo Sarpi. Atti del Convegno Internazionale di Studi nel 450° anniversario della nascita di Paolo Sarpi*, ed. Corrado Pin (Venice: Ateneo Veneto, 2006).

Underhill, John Garrett, *Spanish Literature in the England of the Tudors* (New York: Macmillan, 1899).

Usher, Jonathan, "Rhetorical and Narrative Strategies in Boccaccio's Translation of the *Comoedia Lydiae*," *Modern Language Review*, 84 (1989): 337–44.

Valerini, Adriano, "*Oratione d'Adriano Valerini Veronese, in morte della divina signora Vincenza Armani, comica excellentissima* (Verona: 1570)," in *La Commedia dell'Arte e la Società Barocca: La Professione del Teatro*, eds. Ferruccio Marotti and Giovanna Romei (Rome: Bulzoni, 1991).

Van Dam, H. J., "Italian Friends. Grotius, De Dominis, Sarpi and the Church," *Netherlands archief voor Kerkgeschiedenis*, 75 (1995): 210–14.

Van der Laan, Sarah, "*Erminia liberata*: Pastoral Transformations and Female Agency in Tasso's *Gerusalemme liberata*," talk for the Renaissance Society of America Meeting, Berlin, March 2015.

Van Linschoten, Jan Huygen, *Discours of Voyages into the Easte and West Indies* (London: John Wolfe, 1598).

Vanossi, Luigi, "Situazione e sviluppo nel teatro machiavelliano," in *Lingua e strutture del teatro italiano del Rinascimento* (Padua, 1970).

Vecce, Carlo (ed.), *Arcadia* (Rome: Carocci, 2013).

Védrine, Hélène, *La conception de la nature chez Giordano Bruno* (Paris: J. Vrin, 1967).

Velli, Giuseppe, "Memoria," in *Lessico Critico Decameroniano*, eds. Renzo Bragantini and Pier Massimo Forni (Turin: Bollati Boringhieri, 1995).

Ventrone, Paola A., *Gli araldi della commedia. Teatro a Firenze nel Rinascimento* (Pisa: Pacini Editore, 1993).

Venturi, Gianni, "La selva e il giardino. Tasso e il paesaggio," in *Archivi dello sguardo: Origini e momenti della pittura di paesaggio in Italia*, ed. Francesca Cappelletti (Ferrara, 2006).

Vickers, Brian, "Introduction," in *Occult and Scientific Mentalities in the Renaissance*, ed. Brian Vickers (Cambridge: Cambridge University Press, 1984).

Vickers, Brian, "Identifying Shakespeare's Additions in *The Spanish Tragedy* (1602), a Newer Approach," *Shakespeare Survey*, 8 (2012): 13–43.

Vickers, Nancy, "Diana Described: Scattered Woman and Scattered Rhyme," in *Writing and Sexual Difference*, ed. Elizabeth Abel (Chicago: Chicago University Press, 1982).

Villani, Stefano, "La prima edizione in italiano del *Book of Common Prayer* (1685), tra propaganda protestante e memoria sarpiana," *Rivista di storia e letteratura religiosa*, xliv (2008): 24–45.

Villani, Stefano, "The Italian Protestant Church of London in the Seventeenth Century," in *Exiles, Emigrés and Intermediaries*, ed. Barbara Schaff (Amsterdam: Rodopi, 2010).

Vincenti, Silvano, "Attualità del Petrarca," in *Attualità del Petrarca*, ed. Silvano Vincenti (Rome: Armando Editore, 2004).

Vivanti, Corrado, *Quattro lezioni su Paolo Sarpi* (Naples: Bibliopolis, 2005).

Waddington, Raymond B., "Elizabeth I and the Order of the Garter," *Sixteenth Century Journal*, 24, 1 (Spring 1993): 97–113.

Wahrman, Dror, "From Imaginary Drama to Dramatized Imagery: The Mappe-Monde Nouvelle Papistique, 1566–67," *Journal of the Warburg and Courtauld Institutes*, 54 (1991): 186–205.

Wakely, Maria and Graham Rees, "Folios Fit for a King: James I, John Bill, and the King's Printers, 1616–20," *Huntington Library Quarterly*, 68, 3 (2005): 467–95.

Walker, Nathaniel, "To the Reader," *The Refin'd Courtier* (1640), sig A8r.

Walker, Obadiah, *Of Education, Especially of Young Gentlemen* (Oxford, 1673).

Wallace, David, "Letters of Old Age: Love Between Men, Griselda, and Farewell to Letters: Rerum senilium libri," in *Petrarch: A Critical Guide to the Complete Works*, eds. Victoria Kirkham and Armando Maggi (Chicago: University of Chicago Press, 2009).

Waller, Gary, "From 'the Unfortunate Comedy' to 'this Infinitely Fascinating Play': The Critical and Theatrical Emergence of *All's Well, That Ends Well*," in *All's Well, That Ends Well: New Critical Essays*, ed. Gary Waller (New York: Routledge, 2007).

Waller, G. F. (ed.), *The Triumph of Death and Other Unpublished Poems* (Salzburg Institute für Englische Sprache und Literatur, 1977).

Walter, Melissa, "Dramatic Bodies and Novellesque Spaces in Jacobean Tragedy and Tragicomedy," in *Transnational Exchange in Early Modern Theater*, eds. Robert Henke and Eric Nicholson (Farnham: Ashgate, 2008).

Walter, Melissa, "'Are you a Comedian?' The Trunk in *Twelfth Night* and the Intertheatrical Construction of Character," in *Transnational Mobilities in Early Modern Theater*, eds. Robert Henke and Eric Nicholson (Burlington: Ashgate, 2014).

Ward, E. A., A. R. Waller et al. (eds.), *The Cambridge History of English and American Literature* (Cambridge: Cambridge University Press, 1907–21).

Warnicke, Retha M., "Sexual Heresy at the Court of Henry VIII," *HJ*, 30, 2 (June 1987): 247–68.

Watson, George, *The English Petrarchans: A Critical Bibliography of the Canzoniere* (London: Warburg Institute, 1967).

Watson, Thomas, *Thomas Watson: Poems*, ed. Edward Arber (*English Reprints*, London: A. Constable, 1870).

Watts, William, *St Augustine's Confessions*, 1631 English translation (London: William Heinemann and New York: Macmillan, 1912).

Wayne, Valerie (ed.), *Cymbeline* (London: The Arden Shakespeare, third series, 2017).

Weaver, John, *An Essay Towards an History of Dancing* (London, 1712).

Webster, John, *The Duchess of Malfi*, ed. John Russell Brown (Manchester: Manchester University Press, 1976).

Webster, John, *The White Devil*, ed. John Russell Brown (Manchester: Manchester University Press, 1977).

Weimann, Robert, *Shakespeare and the Popular Tradition in the Theater: Studies in the Social Dimension of Dramatic Form and Function*, ed. Robert Schwartz (Baltimore: Johns Hopkins University Press, 1978).

Weiner, Andrew D., "Expelling the Beast: Bruno's Adventures in England," *Modern Philology*, 78, 1 (1980): 11.

Weismiller, Edward, "Materials Dark and Crude: A Partial Genealogy for Milton's Satan," *Huntington Library Quarterly*, 31 (1967): 75–93.

Weissberger, L. Arnold, "Machiavelli and Tudor England," *Political Science Quarterly*, 42 (1927): 589–607.

Welsh, David J., "Il Cortigiano Polacco (1566)," *Italica*, 40, 1 (March 1963): 22–27.

Wessmer, P. (ed.), *Aeli Donati quos fertur Commentum Terenti* Vol. 1 (Leipzig: Teubner, 1902).

Westman, R. S., *The Copernican Question. Prognostication, Skepticism, and Celestial Order* (Berkeley: University of California Press, 2011).

Westman, Robert S., "Magical Reform and Astronomical Reform: The Yates Thesis Reconsidered," in *Hermeticism and the Scientific Revolution*, eds. R. S. Westman and J. E. McGuire (Los Angeles: Clark Memorial Library, University of California, 1977).

Whigham, Frank, *Ambition and Privilege: The Social Tropes of Elizabethan Courtesy Theory* (Berkeley: University of California Press, 1984).

Whitfield, John Humphreys, "The Charlecote Manuscript of Machiavelli's *Prince*," *Italian Studies*, 22 (1967): 6–25.

Wickert, Max, *Torquato Tasso: The Liberation of Jerusalem* (Oxford: Oxford University Press, 2009).

Wickham, Glynne, *English Professional Theatre, 1530 to 1660* (Cambridge: Cambridge University Press, 2000).

Wiles, David, *Shakespeare's Clown: Actor and Text in the Elizabethan Playhouse* (Cambridge: Cambridge University Press, 2005).

Wilkins, E. H., "A General Survey of Renaissance Petrarchism," *Comparative Literature*, 2, 4 (1950): 327.

Williams, Neville, "The Tudors: Three Contrasts in Personality," in *The Courts of Europe: Politics, Patronage and Royalty 1400–1700*, ed. A. G. Dickens (London: Thames & Hudson, 1977).

Williams, Pamela, *Through Human Love to God: Essays on Dante and Petrarch* (Leicester: Troubador, 2007).

Williamson, George, *The Senecan Amble* (Chicago: University of Chicago Press, 1951).

Wilson, Bronwen and Paul Yachnin (eds.), *Making Publics in Early Modern Europe. People, Things, Forms of Knowledge* (New York: Routledge, 2010).

Wilson, Christopher R., "Shakespeare and Early Modern Music," in *The Edinburgh Companion to Shakespeare and the Arts*, eds. Mark Thornton Burnett, Adrian Streete, and Ramona Wray (Edinburgh: Edinburgh University Press, 2011).

Wilson, F. P., *The English Drama 1485–1585* (Oxford: Oxford University Press, 1969).

Wilson, Harold S., "John Astley, 'Our Inglish Xenophon," *Huntington Library Quarterly*, 22, 2 (February 1959): 107–18.

Wilson, J. K., "*Toxophilus* and the Rules of Art," *Renaissance Quarterly*, 29, 9 (Spring 1976).

Wilson, Thomas, *The Arte of Rhetorique* (1553), sig. P2r.

Wilson, Thomas, "The State of England anno dom. 1600," in *Camden Miscellany*, Vol. XVI (London: Camden Society, 1936).

Wilson-Okamura, David Scott, *Virgil in the Renaissance* (Cambridge: Cambridge University Press, 2010).

Winkelman, Michael, *Marriage Relationships in Tudor Political Drama* (Farnham: Ashgate, 2005).

Winny, James (ed.), *Elizabethan Prose Translation* (Cambridge: Cambridge University Press, 1960).

Wofford, Suzanne, "Foreign Emotions on the Stage of *Twelfth Night*," in *Transnational Exchange in Early Modern Theater*, eds. Robert Henke and Eric Nicholson (Burlington: Ashgate, 2008).

Woodbridge, Linda, *Women and the English Renaissance. Literature and the Nature of Womankind, 1540–1620* (Brighton: The Harvester Press, 1984).

Woodhouse, J. R., *Baldesar Castiglione: A Reassessment of the Courtier* (Edinburgh: Edinburgh University Press, 1978).

Woolfson, Jonathan, "Thomas Hoby, William Thomas and Mid-Tudor Travel to Italy," in *The Oxford Handbook of Tudor Literature*, eds. Mike Pincombe and Cathy Shrank (Oxford: Oxford University Press, 2009).

Wootton, David, *Paolo Sarpi between Renaissance and Enlightenment* (Cambridge: Cambridge University Press, 1983).

Wootton, David, "Paolo Sarpi. Between Renaissance and Enlightenment," in *La prosa e il mondo: "avvisi" del moderno in Sarpi*, Galilei *e la nuova scienza*, ed. Pasquale Guaragnella (Bari: Adriatica, 1986).

Worton, Michael and Judith Still, *Intertextuality: Theories and Practices* (Manchester: Manchester University Press, 1990).

Woudhuysen, Henry Ruxton, "Wisdom Literature of the Seventeenth Century: A Guide to the Contents of the 'Bacon-Tottel' Commonplace Books. Part II," *Transactions of the Cambridge Bibliographical Society*, 7 (1977): 46–73.

Woudhuysen, Henry Ruxton, *Sir Philip Sidney and the Circulation of Manuscripts 1558–1640* (Oxford: Clarendon Press, 1996).

Wright, Anthony David, "Why the Venetian Interdict?" *English Historical Review*, lxxxix (1974): 534–50.

Wright, C. B., "Translations for the Elizabethan Middle Class," *The Library*, sc-xiii, 3 (1932): 312–31.

Wright, Herbert G. (ed.), *Early English Versions of the Tales of Guiscardo and Ghismonda and Titus and Gisippus* (Oxford: Oxford University Press, 1937).

Wright, Herbert G., *Boccaccio in England: From Chaucer to Tennyson* (London: Athlone Press, 1957).

Wyatt, Michael, *The Italian Encounter with Tudor England. A Cultural Politics of Translation* (Cambridge: Cambridge University Press, 2005).

Wyatt, Michael, "Other Petrarchs in Early Modern England," in *Petrarch in Britain: Interpreters, Imitators, and Translators over 700 Years*. Proceedings of the British Academy, eds. Martin Mclaughlin, Letizia Panizza, and Peter Hainsworth (Oxford: Oxford University Press, 2007).

Wyatt, Michael, "John Florio's Translation of Kingship: An Italian Baptism for James VI/I's *Basilikon Doron*," in *Exiles, Emigrés, and Intermediaries: Anglo-Italian Cultural Transactions*, ed. Barbara Schaff (Amsterdam: Rodopi, 2010).

Wyatt, Michael (ed.), *The Cambridge Companion to the Italian Renaissance* (Cambridge: Cambridge University Press, 2014).

Wyatt, Michael, "Fictions of Fact: Antonio Pérez in Traiano Boccalini's *Ragguagli di Parnasso* and William Vaughan's *New-found Politicke*," in *Journeys through Changing Landscapes*, eds. Carla Dente and Francesca Fedi (Pisa: Pisa University Press, 2017).

Wyatt, Michael, "Translating for Queen Anne: John Florio's *Decameron*," in *The Forms of Renaissance Thought, New Essays in Literature and Culture*, eds. Leonard Barkin, Bradin Cormack, and Sean Keilen (New York: Palgrave Macmillan, 2009).

Wyatt, Thomas, *Sir Thomas Wyatt: Complete Poems*, ed. Kenneth Muir (Oxford: Routledge and London: Kegan Paul, 1949).

Wyatt, Thomas, *Sir Thomas Wyatt: The Complete Poems*, ed. R. A. Rebholz (Harmondsworth: Penguin, 1978).

Yates, Frances A., *John Florio: The Life of an Italian in Shakespeare's England* (Cambridge: Cambridge University Press, 1934).

Yates, Frances A., "The Religious Policy of Giordano Bruno," *Journal of the Warburg and Courtauld Institutes*, 3, 3/4 (1940): 192.

Yates, Frances A., "Paolo Sarpi's *History of the Council of Trent*," *Journal of the Warburg and Courtauld Institutes*, VII (1944): 123–43.

Yates, Frances A., "Queen Elizabeth as Astraea," *Journal of the Warburg and Courtauld Institutes*, 10 (1947): 40–43.

Yates, Frances A., *Giordano Bruno and the Hermetic Tradition* (Oxford: Routledge and London: Kegan Paul, 1964).

Yates, Frances A., *The Art of Memory* (Oxford: Routledge and London: Kegan Paul, 1966).

Yates, Frances A., "The Mystery of Jean Bodin," *The New York Review of Books*, October 14 (1976).

Young, Frances Berkeley (ed.), *Mary Sidney* (London: Nutt, 1912).

Zak, Gur, *Petrarch's Humanism and the Care of the Self* (Cambridge: Cambridge University Press, 2010).

Zegura, Elizabeth Chesney, "Uprooted Trees and Slaughtered Peasants: The Saving of Rural Space in Ariosto's *Orlando furioso* (1532)," in *Rural Space in the Middle Ages and Early Modern Age*, ed. Albrecht Classen (Fundamentals of Medieval and Early Modern Culture 9: 2012).

Zenón, Luis Martines, *In Words and Deeds. The Spectacle of Incest in English Renaissance Drama* (Amsterdam-New York: Rodopi, 2002).

Zuckert, Catherine H., "Fortune Is a Woman: But So Is Prudence: Machiavelli's *Clizia*," in *Feminist Interpretations of Niccolò Machiavelli*, ed. M. J. Falco (University Park: The Pennsylvania State University Press, 2004).

Index

For Product Safety Concerns and Information please contact our EU
representative GPSR@taylorandfrancis.com
Taylor & Francis Verlag GmbH, Kaufingerstraße 24, 80331 München, Germany

www.ingramcontent.com/pod-product-compliance
Lightning Source LLC
Chambersburg PA
CBHW081353090726
47908CB00011B/2662

* 9 7 8 1 0 3 2 0 9 3 5 9 8 *